W9-ARX-463

Antique Trader
Antiques&
Collectibles
2007 Price Guide

Edited by
Kyle Husfloen

©2006 by Krause Publications

Published by

krause publications
An Imprint of F+W Publications

700 East State Street • Iola, WI 54990-0001
715-445-2214 • 888-457-2873

Our toll-free number to place an order or obtain
a free catalog is (800) 258-0929.

All rights reserved. No portion of this publication may be reproduced or
transmitted in any form or by any means, electronic or mechanical, including
photocopy, recording, or any information storage and retrieval system,
without permission in writing from the publisher, except by a reviewer who
may quote brief passages in a critical article or review to be printed in a
magazine or newspaper, or electronically transmitted on radio, television, or
the Internet.

Library of Congress Catalog Number: ISSN 1536-2884

ISBN 13-digit: 978-0-89689-332-0
ISBN 10-digit: 0-89689-332-4

Designed by Wendy Wendt
Edited by Kyle Husfloen

Printed in the United States of America

Something for every collecting taste

A bigger, better and more colorful Annual Price Guide for 2007

Every year as mid-summer approaches I find myself in quite a frenzy of activity with the deadline for our new *Antique Trader Antiques & Collectibles Price Guide* nearing. For months I have worked hard to gather thousands of new listings and color photos for this tome and now the fruits of my labor are about to come to fruition. Although many hurdles have popped up during the preparation the final result is always worth the labor and I'm very pleased to now present our new guide for 2007. Since we began producing our guides in all-color back in 2005 we're very proud that the *Antique Trader Antiques & Collectibles Price Guide* has become one of the largest selling guides in the field. Today you hold in your hands a reference with over 11,500 individual price listings and over 5,800 full-color pictures.

This is quite a remarkable growth from our fairly humble beginning as a quarterly paperback magazine back in 1970. Within a few years that guide became a bi-monthly publication to be followed in 1984 but our first large annual compilation. It has been my honor to be a part of this growth and evolution for nearly 20 years.

Because it is important to remain a leader in this specialty-publishing field, I am always seeking to expand and update our many categories. Each year ALL of our listings are original to that book, but in addition, I like to add some new "hot" collecting fields. Over the past half-century many collecting trends have developed and evolved and today quite a few traditional collecting specialties are undergoing changes. The dynamics of collecting today are quite different from those of the 1950s and 1960s, so it is very important for me to keep abreast of these changes and make sure our flagship price guide offers the most up-to-date information possible. With the help of a myriad of sources, including auction houses, knowledgeable collectors and dealers, collecting clubs and more, I keep myself apprised of what's what in the fascinating world of antiques and collectibles. Gathering, organizing and entering into a database this huge volume of information is my goal, and I hope you will find the results a valuable tool. However, it is always important to keep in mind that this book is just a guide to collecting and that the values listed here reflect a cross-section of what is bought and sold each year. Many factors, including quality, rarity, condition and regional market demand, will all influence what a specific piece may bring in the current marketplace.

In order to make this guide as easy to use as possible, we have arranged our hundreds of categories and sub-categories in alphabetical order according to the popular category name. Since there are so many separate categories in the fields of Ceramics, Glass and Furniture, we have separated these fields into their own large sections. Within each of these sections the categories are listed in alphabetical order. A great many of our categories will begin with a brief introduction to that field and in the Ceramics and Glass sections, the introduction may also include a copy or copies of factory or maker's marks or logos, an added bonus for those researching their pieces. Our brief introductions may also include cross-references to other listings included in this guide or mention specialty reference books.

To make things even easier for our readers, we also include an extensive Index of categories at the end of our listings. This Index includes many more cross-references to special collecting niches, a bonus for collectors searching for items that may not have their own separate category. For example, Pop Culture Collectibles may include a variety of Beatles or Elvis Presley collectibles, as well as other interesting items.

As I mentioned above, each year I include some new and different collecting categories and this edition offers quite a few including: Eyewear; Foxy Grandpa Collectibles; Lipstick Tubes; Snowman Collectibles; Syrocowood and Toy Booklets & Catalogs. You'll also find some new sub-categories under "Lighting Devices," "Perfume Bottles" and "Purses and Bags." In the Ceramics section, I have also added listings of Harris Strong Designs and Lotus Ware.

Of course this book is not the result of one person's efforts and I have received tremendous assistance from a large number of experts, and I offer them my special thanks here. Their hard work and dedication is evident throughout this guide and further details on these people can be found in the SPECIAL CONTRIBUTORS listings that follow. This year I have also had the pleasure of working with a new contract assistant, Torsten Kerr. Tor, an antiques enthusiast, has learned quickly the mechanics of price guide compilation and has been a real pleasure to work with.

There are many other individuals and firms who have aided me this year and I must thank them also. Among the photographers who have contributed to this edition are: Stanley L. Baker, Minneapolis, Minn.; Charles Casad, Monticello, Ill.; Susan N. Cox, El Cajon, Calif.; Susan Eberman, Bedford, Ind.; Joe Fex, Littleton, Colo.; Mary Ann Johnston, New Cumberland, W. Va.; Vivian Kromer, Bakersfield, Calif.; Pat McPherson, Ramona, Calif.; Pat Moore, San Francisco, Calif.; Margaret Payne, Columbus, Ind.; and John Petzold and Dr. Leslie Pina.

For other photographs, artwork, data or permission to photograph pieces from their collections we sincerely express appreciation to the following auctioneers, galleries, individuals and shops: Alderfers, Hatfield, Pa.; Brunk Auction Services, Asheville, N.C.; Charlton Hall Galleries, Columbia, South Carolina; Christie's, New York, New York; Cincinnati Art Galleries, Cincinnati, Ohio; Early Auction Company, Milford, Ohio; Fontaines Auction Gallery, Pittsfield, Mass.; Garth's Auctions, Delaware, Ohio; Glass-Works Auctions, East Greenville, Pa.; Green Valley Auctions, Mt. Crawford, Va.; and Guyette and Schmidt, West Farmington, Maine.

Also to Norman Heckler & Company, Woodstock Valley, Conn.; Jackson's International Auctioneers, Cedar Falls, Iowa; James D. Julia, Fairfield, Maine; McMasters Harris Auctions, Cambridge, Ohio; Metz Superlative Auction, Roanoke, Va.; Neal Auction Company, New Orleans, La.; New Orleans Auction Galleries, New Orleans, La.; Richard Opfer Auctioneering, Inc., Timonium, Md.; Pacific Glass Auctions, Sacramento, Calif.; Past Tyme Pleasures, Los Altos, Calif.; Rich Penn, Waterloo, Iowa; Dave Rago Arts & Crafts, Lambertville, N.J.; Skinner, Inc., Bolton, Mass.; Slater's Americana, Inc., Indianapolis, Ind.; Sotheby's, New York, N.Y.; R. and K. Townsend, Rochester, Minn.; Tradewinds Antiques, Manchester-by-the-Sea, Mass.; and Treadway Gallery, Cincinnati, Ohio.

I hope everyone who uses the new *Antique Trader Antiques & Collectibles Price Guide 2007* will find it interesting, exciting and colorful - a volume that will become a cornerstone of your collecting reference library. As always, I welcome all letters from readers, especially those of constructive critique and I will make every effort to respond. Now, with guide in hand, go out and enjoy the amazing antiquing adventures that await you.

Kyle Husfloen, Editor

SPECIAL CONTRIBUTORS
Index by Subject

ABC Plates: Joan M. George
Black Americana: Leonard Davis and Caroline Torem-Craig
Bottle Openers: Charles Reynolds
Character Collectibles: Dana Cain
Chase Brass & Copper Company: Donald-Brian Johnson
Children's Books: Jim Trautman
Christmas Seals (Christmas Collectibles): Jim Trautman
Cigarette Lighters (Tobacciana): Jim Trautman
Clocks: R.O. Schmitt and The Clocksmith
Coca-Cola Items: Metz Superlatives Auction
Compacts & Vanity Cases; Lipstick Tubes & Solid Perfumes (Perfume Bottles) - Roselyn Gerson
Eyewear: Donald-Brian Johnson
Foxy Grandpa Collectibles: Kerra Davis
Jewelry (Costume): Marion Cohen
Kitchenwares:
    Coffee Mills: Mike White
    Cow Creamers: LuAnn Riggs
    Egg Cups: Joan M. George
    Egg Timers: Ellen Bercovici
    Napkin Dolls: Bobbie Zucker Bryson
    Pie Birds: Ellen Bercovici
    Reamers: Bobbie Zucker Bryson
    String Holders: Ellen Bercovici
Lighting: Carl Heck
Lighting Devices:
    Miniature Lamps: Robert Culver
    Mid-Century Modern Lighting: Dana Cain
    Moss Lamps: Donald-Brian Johnson
Plant Waterers: Bobbie Zucker Bryson
Pop Culture Collectibles: Dana Cain
Purses: Whiting & Davis and Novelty Purses - Donald-Brian Johnson
Ribbon Dolls: Bobbie Zucker Bryson
Soda Fountain Collectibles: Jim Trautman
Snowman Collectibles: Kerra Davis

Steins: Andre Ammelounx and Gary Kirsner
Syrocowood: Donald-Brian Johnson
Toy Booklets & Catalogs: Kerra Davis

CERAMICS

Abingdon: Elaine Westover
American Painted Porcelain: Dorothy Kamm
Amphora-Teplitz: Les and Irene Cohen
Banko Ware: Arlene Rabin
Belleek (American): Peggy Sebek
Belleek (Irish): Del Domke
Blue & White Pottery: Steve Stone
Blue Ridge Dinnerwares: Marie Compton
Blue Willow: Jeff Siptak
Ceramic Arts Studio of Madison: Tim Holthaus and Donald-Brian Johnson
Clarice Cliff Designs: Laurie Williams
Doulton/Royal Doulton: Reg Morris and Louise Irvine
Fiesta: Mick and Lorna Chase
Flow Blue: K. Robert and Bonne L. Hohl
Geisha Girl Wares: Elyce Litts
Hall China: Marty Kennedy
Harker: William A. and Donna J. Gray
Harris Strong Designs: Donald-Brian Johnson
Haviland: Nora Travis
Hull: Joan Hull
Ironstone: General - Bev Dieringer; Tea Leaf - Dale Abrams and the Tea Leaf Club International
Jewel Tea - Autumn Leaf: Jo Cunningham
Limoges: Debby DuBay
Lotus Ware: William A. and Donna J. Gray
Majolica: Michael Strawser
McCoy: Craig Nissen
Mettlach: Andre Ammelounx

Morton Potteries: Burdell Hall
Mullberry: Ellen R. Hill
Noritake: Tim Trapani
Old Ivory: Alma Hillman
Phoenix Bird & Flying Turkey: Joan
  Collett Oates
Quimper: Sandra Bondhus
Red Wing: Gail Peck
Royal Bayreuth: Mary McCaslin
Royal Copenhagen: Ellen Bercovici
Royal Copley: Donald-Brian Johnson
R.S. Prussia: Mary McCaslin
Russel Wright Designs: Kathryn Wiese
Sascha Brastoff: Donald-Brian Johnson
Schafer & Vater: Gary Kirsner
Shawnee: Linda Guffey
Shelley China: Mannie Banner; David
  Chartier; Bryand Goodlad; Edwin E.
  Kellogg; Gene Loveland and Curt
  Leiser
Stoneware and Spongeware: Bruce
  and Vicki Waasdorp
Torquay Pottery: Lee and Marlene
  Graham
Uhl Pottery: Lloyd Martin
Vernon Kilns: Pam Green
Warwick China: John Rader, Sr.
Watt Pottery: Jim and Jan Seeck

Zeisel (Eva) Designs: Kathryn Wiese
Zsolnay: Federico Santi/ John Gacher

GLASS

Animals: Helen and Bob Jones
Cambridge: Helen and Bob Jones
Carnival Glass: Jim and Jan Seeck
Central Glass Works: Helen and Bob
  Jones
Depression Glass: Debbie and Randy
  Coe
Duncan & Miller: Helen and Bob Jones
Fenton: Helen and Bob Jones
Fostoria: Helen and Bob Jones
Fry: Helen and Bob Jones
Heisey: Helen and Bob Jones
Higgins Glass: Donald-Brian Johnson
Imperial: Helen and Bob Jones
McKee: Helen and Bob Jones
Morgantown: Helen and Bob Jones
New Martinsville: Helen and Bob Jones
Paden City: Helen and Bob Jones
Pattern Glass: Green Valley Auctions
Wall Pocket Vases: Bobbie Zucker
  Bryson
Westmoreland: Helen and Bob Jones

Contributor Directory

Dale Abrams
960 Bryden Rd.
Columbus, OH 43205
(614) 258-5258

Andre Ammelounx
P.O. Box 136
Palatine, IL 60078
(847) 991-5927

Mannie Banner
126 S.W. 15th St.
Pembroke Pines, FL 33027

Ellen Bercovici
360 -11th Ave. So.
Naples, FL 34102

Sandra Bondhus
P.O. Box 100
Unionville, CT 06085
e-mail: nbondhus@pol.net

Bobbie Zucker Bryson
1 St. Eleanoras Lane
Tuckahoe, NY 10707
(914) 779-1405
Napkindoll@aol.com

Dana Cain
5061 S.Stuart Ct.
Littleton CO 80123
e-mail: dana.cain@att.net

David Chartier
1171 Waterside
Brighton, MI 48114

Mick and Lorna Chase
Fiesta Plus
380 Hawkins Crawford Rd.
Cookeville, TN 38750
(931) 372-8333
e-mail: fiestaplus@yahoo.com
Web: www.fiestaplus.com

The Clocksmith
806 El Camino Real
San Carlos, CA 94070
Web: www.theclocksmith.com

Debbie and Randy Coe
1240 S/E/ 40th Ave.
Hillsboro, OR 97123
e-mail: coeran@aol.com

Les and Irene Cohen
Pittsburgh, PA
    or
Amphora Collectors International
21 Brooke Dr.
Elizabethtown, PA 17022
e-mail: tombeaz@comcast.net

Marion Cohen
14 Croyden Ct.
Albertson, NY 11507
(516) 294-0055

Neva Colbert
69565 Crescent Rd.
St. Clairsvville, OH 43950
(740) 695-2355
e-mail: georgestreet@1st.net

Marie Compton
M&M Collectibles
1770 So. Randall Rd., #236
Geneva, IL 60134-4646
eBay: brdoll

Caroline Torem-Craig
New York, New York

Robert N. Culver
3081 Sand Pebble Cove
Pinckney, MI 48169
e-mail: rculver107@aol.com

Kerra Davis
925 Bud St.
Blackshear, GA 31516
e-mail: kbb@gate.net

Leonard Davis
New York, New York

Bev Dieringer
P.O. Box 536
Redding Ridge, CT 06876
e-mail: dieringer1@aol.com

Del E. Domke
16142 N.E. 15h St.
Bellevue, WA 98008-2711
(425) 746-6363
e-mail: delyicious@comcast.net

Debby DuBay
Limoges Antiques Shop
20 Post Office Ave.
Andover, MA 01810
(978) 470-8773

Joan M. George
67 Stevens Ave.
Oldbridge, NJ 08856
e-mail: drjgeorge@nac.net

Roselyn Gerson
12 Alnwick Rd.
Malverne, NY 11565
(516) 593-8746
e-mail: compactlady@aol.com

Lee and Marlene Graham
North American Torquay Society
214 N. Rondu Rd.
McHenry, IL 60050
(815) 385-2040

William A. and Donna J. Gray
2 Highland Colony
East Liverpool, OH 43920
e-mail: harkermate@comcast.net

Pam Green
You Must Remember This
P.O. Box 822

Hollis, NH 03049
e-mail: ymrt@aol.com
Web: www.ymrt.com

Green Valley Auctions
2259 Green Valley Lane
Mt. Crawford, VA 22841
(540) 434-4260
Web: www.greenvalleyauctions.com

Linda Guffey
2004 Fiat Court
El Cajon, CA 92019-4234
e-mail: Gufantique@aol.com

Burdell Hall
201 W. Sassafras Dr.
Morton, IL 61550
(309) 263-2988
e-mail: bnbhall@mtco.com

Carl Heck
Box 8516
Aspen, CO 81612
(970) 925-8011
Web: www.carlheck.com

Ellen R. Hill
P.O. Box 56
Bennington, NH 03442
(603) 588-4099
MSMULB@aol.com

Alma Hillman
197 Coles Corner Rd.
Winterport, ME 04496
e-mail: oldivory@adelphia.net

K. Robert and Bonne L. Hohl
47 Fawn Dr.
Reading, PA 19607

Tim Holthaus
P.O. Box 46
Madison, WI 53701-0046
    or
CAS Collectors
206 Grove St.
Rockton, IL 61072
Web: www.cascollectors.com

Joan Hull
1376 Nevada S.W.
Huron, SD 57350

Hull Pottery Association
11023 Tunnel Hill N.E.
New Lexington, OH 43764

Louise Irvine
England: (020) 8876-7739
e-mail: louiseirvine@blueyonder.co.uk

Helen and Bob Jones
Berkeley Springs, WV
e-mail: Bglances@ aol.com

Donald-Brian Johnson
3329 South 56th St., #611
Omaha, NE 68106
e-mail: donaldbrian@webtv.net

Dorothy Kamm
10786 Grey Heron Ct.
Port St. Lucie, FL 34986
e-mail: dorothykamm@adelphia.net

Edwin E. Kellogg
4951 N.W. 65th Ave.
Lauderhill, FL 33319

Gary Kirsner
Glentiques, Ltd.
1940 Augusta Terrace
P.O. Box 8807
Coral Springs, FL 33071
e-mail: gkirsner@myacc.net

Curt Leiser
National Shelley China Club
12010 - 38th Ave. NE
Seattle, WA 98125
(206) 362-7135
e-mail: curtispleiser@cs.com

Elyce Litts
P.O. Box 394
Morris Plains, NJ 07950
(908) 964-5055
e-mail:
happymemories@worldnet.att.net

Gene Loveland
11303 S. Alley Jackson Rd.
Grain Valley, MO 64029

Lloyd Martin
1582 Gregory Lane
Jasper, IN 47546
e-mail: nlmartin@insightbb.com

Mary McCaslin
6887 Black Oak Ct. E.
Avon, IN 46123
(317) 272-7776
e-mail: Maryjack@indy.rr.com

Susan N. Cox and Pat McPherson
Country Town Antiques
738 Main St.
Ramona, CA 92065

Metz Superlatives Auction
P.O. Box 18185
Roanoke, VA 24014
(540) 985-3185
Web: www.metzauction.com

Reg G. Morris
2050 Welcome Way
The Villages, FL 32162
e-mail: modexmin@comcast.net

Craig Nissen
P.O. Box 223
Grafton, WI 53024-0223

Joan C. Oates
1107 Deerfield Lane
Marshall, MI 49068
e-mail: koates120@earthlink.net

Gail Peck
Country Crock Antiques
2121 Pearl St.
Fremont, NE 68025
(420) 721-5721
Arlene Rabin
P.O. Box 243
Fogelsville, PA 18051
e-mail: jwhelden@enter.net

John Rader, Sr.
Vice President, National Assn. of
Warwick China & Pottery Collectors
780 S. Village Dr., Apt. 203
St. Petersburg, FL 33716
(727) 570-9906
Author of "Warwick China" (Schiffer
Publishing, 2000)
                    or
Betty June Wymer, 28 Bachmann Dr.,
Wheeling, WV 26003, (304)
232-3031) Editor, "The IOGA" Club
Quarterly, newsletter

Charles Reynolds
2836 Monroe St.
Falls Church, VA 22042
(703) 533-1322

LuAnn Riggs
1781 Lindberg Dr.
Columbia, MO 65201
e-mail: artichokeannies@bessi.net

Tim and Jamie Saloff
P.O. Box 339
Edinboro, PA 16412
e-mail: tim.salofff@verizon.net

Federico Santi
The Drawing Room Antiques
152 Spring St.
Newport, RI 02840
(401) 841-5060
Web: www.drawrm.com

R.O. Schmitt Fine Arts
P.O. Box 1941
Salem, NH 03079
(603) 893-5915

Peggy Sebek
3255 Glencairn Rd.
Shaker Heights, OH 44122
e-mail: pegsebek@earthlink.net
Jim and Jan Seeck
Seeck Auctions
P.O. Box 377
Mason City, IA 50402
(641) 424-1116

e-mail: jimjan@seeckauction.com

Jeff Siptak
4013 Russellwood Dr.
Nashville, TN 37204

Steve Stone
12795 W. Alameda Pkwy.
Lakewood, CO 80225
e-mail: Sylvanlvr@aol.com

Michael G. Strawser Auctions
P.O. Box 332
Wolcottville, IN 46795
(260) 854-2859
Web: www.majolicaauctions.com

Mark and Ellen Supnick
7725 NW 78th Ct.
Tamarac, FL 33321
e-mail: saturdaycook@aol.com

Tea Leaf Club International
P.O. Box 377
Belton, MO 64012
Webb: www.tealeafclub.com

Tim Trapani
7543 Northport Dr.
Boynton Beach, FL 33437

Jim Trautman
R.R. 1
Orton, Ontario CANADA L0N 7N0
e-mail: trautman@sentex.net

Nora Travis
13337 E. South St.
Cerritos, CA 90701
(714) 521-9283
e-mail: Travishrs@aol.com

Bruce and Vicki Waasdorp
P.O. Box 434
Clarence, NY 14031
(716) 759-2361
Web: www.antiques-stoneware.com

Elaine Westover
210 Knox Hwy. 5
Abingdon, IL 61410-9332

Kathryn Wiese
Retrospective Modern Design
P.O. Box 305
Manning, IA 51455
e-mail: retrodesign@earthlink.net

Laurie Williams
Rabbitt Antiques and Collectibles
(408) 248-1260
e-mail: rabbitt3339@yahoo.com

ABC PLATES
Ceramic

These children's plates were popular in the late 19th and early 20th centuries. An alphabet border was incorporated with nursery rhymes, maxims, scenes or figures in an apparent attempt to "spoon feed" a bit of knowledge at mealtime. An important reference book in this field is A Collector's Guide to ABC Plates, Mugs and Things *by Mildred L. and Joseph P. Chalala (Pridemark Press, Lancaster, Pennsylvania, 1980).*

"Base Ball Caught on the Fly" Plate

"Base Ball Caught on the Fly," 6 3/16" d., from the "American Sports" series, black transfer of a baseball game in action showing a fielder catching the ball (ILLUS.) **$650**
Cricket game, 7 1/4" d., brown transfer of cricket game in progress **$175**

Letter "A" ABC Plate

"A, Apple, Ape, Air," 6" d., black transfer w/color added to an apple and ape w/large "A" in center & words "Apple, Ape, Air" above picture, red line on rim, probably part of a series (ILLUS.) **$225**

"Crusoe Finding the Foot Prints"

"Crusoe Finding the Foot Prints," 8" d., from "Robinson Crusoe" series, Brownhills Pottery Company, sepia transfer w/color added of Robinson Crusoe discovering Friday's footprints, letters printed in sepia around edge of plate (ILLUS.)..... **$175**

"Band of Hope" ABC Plate

"Band of Hope - The Sabbath Keepers," 6" d., center illustration of congregation filing into church over "Rise early and thankfully put up your prayer - Be at school in good time and be diligent there," color has been added (ILLUS.).... **$225**

"England's Hope" ABC Plate

"England's Hope. Prince of Wales," 7" d., black transfer of image of young prince astride pony, black lines around edge (ILLUS., previous page) **$500**

"The Favourite Rabbits" ABC Plate

"Favourite Rabbits (The)," 5" d., one of a series, black & white, "How joyous at each sunshine hour - I haunted ev'ry green retreat - of forest, garden, heath & bower - Their cell to store with clover sweet" surrounds center illustration of girl in period dress feeding pet rabbits, older plate (ILLUS.) **$300**

"Franklin's Proverbs," 5" d., "Keep thy shop and thy shop will keep thee" over center illustration of merchant **$175**

George Washington ABC Plate

George Washington, 7 1/2" d., black portrait of George Washington, same as picture used on one-dollar bill (ILLUS.) **$600**

Hens & rooster, 6 1/2" d., colorful transfer of rooster & hens, pale blue embossed alphabet border, probably Germany **$85**

"John Gilpin Pursued as a Highwayman," 6 1/4" d., black print w/slightly painted details, one of a series showing the humorous anniversary adventures of

"John Gilpin" ABC Plate

a 19th c. draper, illustrations based on Cruikshank's published in 1828 (ILLUS.). **$250**

"Leopard and the Fox" ABC Plate

"Leopard and the Fox," 6 1/2" d., part of early "Aesop Fables" series, black & white, center w/illustration of leopard & fox in wooded setting, large letters around rim (ILLUS.) **$275**

"The Lion" ABC Plate

"Lion (The)," 7 5/16" d., from the "Wild Animals" series, Brownhills Pottery Company, sepia transfer w/color added (ILLUS., previous page) **$325**

"Little Red Riding Hood," 8 3/16" d., from the "Nursery Tales" series, multicolor transfer in reserve of Little Red Riding Hood & the wolf, scattered alphabet to the side, Staffordshire **$325**

"Little strokes fell great Oaks," 8 1/4" d., black transfer w/red, yellow & green illustration of man w/ax standing by felled tree, Staffordshire..................................... **$150**

Boys Playing Marbles ABC Plate

Marbles, 6 3/16" d., blue transfer of three boys in period clothes playing marbles, red lines around rim (ILLUS.) **$250**

"Marine Railway Station, Manhatton [sic] Beach Hotel," 7" d., illustration of station in center, Staffordshire **$135**

"The Milk Girl" ABC Plate

"Milk Girl (The)," 5 1/2" d., black transfer of girl carrying bowl, another woman milking a cow in a field (ILLUS.) **$350**

Musicians, 6" d., mulberry transfer of two children playing stringed instruments, made for H.C. Edmeston, England **$175**

"Soldier Tired" ABC Plate

"Soldier Tired," 7 1/4" d., black transfer of sleeping boy in dress w/a sword & hat nearby guarded by a dog (ILLUS.).......... **$300**

"Thames Tunnel" ABC Plate

"Thames Tunnel," 5 1/4" d., black transfer picture illustrating the opening of the Tunnel in London, 1843, w/people in period dress (ILLUS.) **$225**

"Victoria Regina" ABC Plate

"Victoria Regina," 5 1/16" d., black transfer of portrait of Queen Victoria as a young woman over words "Born 25 of May 1818. Proclaimed 20 of June 1837" (ILLUS.) **$1,000**

ADVERTISING ITEMS

Thousands of objects made in various materials, some intended as gifts with purchases, others used for display or given away for publicity, are now being collected. Also see various other categories and Antique Trader Advertising Price Guide.

Backbar bottle, label-under-glass type, clear cylindrical body w/cut fluted base & shoulder, w/a shield-shaped lable in red, gold, blue & black enclosing the color bust portrait of a lovely Victorian lady, tooled flared mouth, smooth based embossed "W.N. Walton Pat. Sept. 23/62," some crazing in label border, ca. 1860-80, 10" h. **$224**

Backbar bottle, "Paul Jones" in white enamel script, bulbous tapering clear glass w/pinched-in sides, painted in colored enamels w/the half-length figure of an elderly man pouring a glass of whiskey above the wording, smooth base, tooled mouth, period facet-cut glass stopper, ca. 1885-1910, 8 1/4" h. **$112**

Calendar, 1916, "DeLaval Cream Separators," full-color illustration of overalled young boy holding bouquet of buttercups & teasing young fair-haired girl seated on packing crate, below "De Laval Cream Separators" & above box with informational paragraph starting "Do You Like Butter?," 12 x 24" (cover sheet partially separated from full date pad) **$345**

1925 U.S. Cartridge Calendar

Calendar, 1925, "US Shot-Shells Cartridges," long rectangular print w/a large color image of a duck hunter shooting from his boat, artwork by H.G. Edwards, top metal hanger & one date sheet for November, several edge tears at bottom & top corner, 16 1/4 x 34" (ILLUS.) **$2,760**

1920 Winchester Calendar

Calendar, 1920, "Winchester," long rectangular print w/a large color image of a duck hunter carrying his game & stepping out of a small boat where his son sits, water in the background, full pad at the bottom, 19 3/4 x 38 1/2" (ILLUS.) **$805**

Rare 1934 Winchester Calendar

Calendar, 1934, "Winchester," long rectangular print w/a large color image of a young boy seated on a rail fence w/his hunting dog seated below, artwork by Eugene Ward, calendar pad at bottom, excellent condition, framed, image 16 x 27 1/4" (ILLUS.) **$2,185**

1946 Dr. Pepper Color Calendar

Calendar, 1946, "Dr. Pepper," rectangular, cardboard w/original hanging strip, color images of a pretty young lady hugging a snowman, complete, small area of insect damage at extreme upper margin, 13 1/2 x 22" (ILLUS.)................................. **$210**

Dog n Suds Electric Wall Clock

Clock, "Dog n Suds," electric wall light-up bubble-type, diamond-shaped w/the round logo in orange, yellow, black & white above the orange & black wording "Dog n Suds - world's creamiest root beer," sweep seconds hand, ca. 1950s-60s, some minor losses, 15" w. (ILLUS.) . **$201**

Dr. Pepper Electric Wall Clock

Clock, "Dr. Pepper," electric wall type, round black metal frame enclosing a white dial w/Arabic numerals, the 10, 2 & 4 in red, Dr. Pepper rectangular logo in

the lower center, w/sweep seconds hand, by General Electric, 1940s, only medium case wear, 15" d. (ILLUS.) **$204**

Early Milkmaid Milk Wall Clock

Clock, "Milkmaid Milk," Baird-style wall-mounted round embossed metal frame in brown w/raised white wording "Milkmaid Milk - Now's The Time to Buy It," stained paper dial w/Roman numerals, hinged glass dial cover w/brass trim, includes the pendulum, 17 1/2" d. (ILLUS.)........... **$460**

Sauer's Extracts Advertising Clock

Clock, "Sauer's Extracts," regulator, wood case w/reverse glass decorated door front advertising "Sauer's Flavoring Extracts - Best By Every Test," tin dial w/Arabic numerals, w/key & pendulum, New Haven Clock Co., New Haven, Connecticut, 5 3/4 x 17", 41" h. (ILLUS.)............. **$1,323**
Clock, "Squirt Soda," square, light-up variety, white face w/black Arabic numerals on the hour, half hour & quarter hours, black dots for other numbers, w/center square of brightly colored orange w/yellow Squirt logo in center reading "Enjoy Squirt," "The drink with the Happy Taste"

in lower left, image of smiling Squirt mascot standing next to bottle of Squirt at right **$143**

Counter display, "Pirika Dollar a Pound Chocolates," wood grain litho on tin, rectangular w/transparent slant lid, the lid w/panel at top reading "Pirika - Dollar a Pound - Chocolates - in - 5¢ - Bar Form - 5¢" in white **$330**

Unusual Poll Parrot Counter Display

Counter display, "Poll Parrot Shoes," animated, h.p. molded composition figure of Poll Parrot in a bent wire cage on a drum-type base, head would nod back & forth w/continuous voice mechanism playing, ca. 1962, w/photocopy of letter from International Shoe Company dated 1989 stating this was one of 25 made, w/original packing crate, overall 41" h. (ILLUS.) **$1,380**

Purity Pretzel Counter Display

Counter display, "Purity Butter Pretzels," cardboard, die-cut easel-back type w/color illustration of fair-haired boy in white shirt w/sleeves rolled up & red tie holding giant pretzel, red rectangular panel at bottom reads "Purity Butter Pretzels - Purity Pretzel Co." in white lettering along w/location & proprietor, 12 1/2 x 22" (ILLUS.) **$121**

Sego Milk Counter Display

Counter display, "Sego Milk," die-cut color-printed cardboard, tri-fold, arched w/the center panel in black w/white lettering above a can of the product, the smaller side panels printed in muted colors w/a scene of a lady or gentleman eating, ca. 1930s, only light wear, 47" l., 27" h. (ILLUS.) **$193**

Counter display box, "Briggs Bros. & Co. Seeds," wooden w/applied paper labels, a long low rectangular box w/a string-hinged flat lid, the interior w/a large color-printed label showing various vegetables, front of box w/long advertising label centered by a small spread-winged eagle, contains about 190 original full seed packets, late 19th - early 20th c., 10 1/4 x 24", 5 1/4" h. (ILLUS. open, top next page) **$1,380**

Rare Belding Spool Cabinet

Rare Early Seed Display Box with Original Labels

Counter display cabinet, "Belding Silk," walnut, wording on ornate crestrail centered by a clock dial, thirty drawers w/curved glass fronts on upper drawers, mirrors center door at top, ca. 1890, 17 x 34", 45" h. (ILLUS., previous page) **$3,500-4,500**

Diamond Dyes "Court Jester" Cabinet

Counter display cabinet, "Diamond Dyes," birch w/tin lithographed front panel showing "Court Jester" scene, ca. 1890, 10 1/4 x 21", 27 1/4" h. (ILLUS.)
.... **$2,800-3,600**

Counter display cabinet, "Humphreys' Specifics," molded wooden case w/front & back tin panels, the front door w/lithographed blue tin panel reading "Humphreys' Specifics" & listing 35 specific ailments that could be treated w/contents of cabinet, the interior w/all but one of the 34 original numbered drawer compartments, 7 x 21 1/2", 28" h. (back panel has been painted, some wood loss to cabinet) **$575**

Rare Humphreys' Specifics Cabinet

Counter display cabinet, "Humphreys' Veterinary Specifics," walnut, front-opening, w/heavily embossed composition panel w/a profile of a horse, scarce version reading "Humphreys' Veterinary Homeopathic Specifics," dated 12/14/87, 10 x 21", 34" h. (ILLUS.) **$5,500-7,000**

Coats Boilfast Thread Counter Case

Counter display case, "J. & P. Coats Boilfast Thread," low rectangular woodgrained metal three-drawer case, black printing on top & front of top drawer, early 20th c., 17 x 19", 6 1/2" h. (ILLUS.).......... **$288**

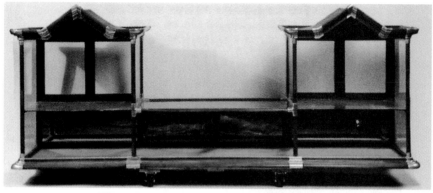

Rare Double Cathedral Countertop Showcase

Counter display case, walnut case reinforced w/German silver, rare double cathedral style, front tag reads "Quincy Show Caseworks, Quincy, Ill.," one glass panel cracked, 38" h., 96" l. (ILLUS., top of page) **$5,750**

Counter display case, "Zeno Gum," oak case w/marquee embossed "ZENO," slant front, mirrored rear door, three glass shelves, ca. 1910, 8 x 10", 17 1/2" h. **$949**

Rare G.E. Radio Display Figure

Counter display figure, "G.E. Radio," tall jointed wood standing figure of a drum major wearing a tall red & yellow hat & red & yellow jacket, design attributed to Maxfield Parrish, decal on foot reads "Art Quality by Cameo Products, Penn. USA," overall excellent condition, early 20th c., 18" h. (ILLUS.) **$920**

Chicos Spanish Peanuts Display Jar

Counter display jar, "Curtiss Chicos Spanish Peanuts 5¢," upright squared clear glass w/rounded corners, colorful fitted metal id & embossed yellow band base w/advertising & dispensing flap, early 20th c., 8" w., 11" h. (ILLUS.).................. **$403**

Ex-Lax Door Push

Pinkerton's Detective Agency Door Push

Door push, "Ex-Lax," rectangular, porcelain on metal, blue, white, yellow & red, product package in center marked "For Relief of Constipation - Ex-Lax - the Chocolated Laxative," top marked "Pull" & bottom w/"Get Your Box Now!," ca. 1920s, 4 x 8" (ILLUS., previous page) **$200-250**

Door push, "Pinkerton's National Detective Agency," rectangular, porcelain on metal, black w/white letters reading "Member of The Jewelers' Security Alliance - For Protection Against Burglary - Sneak Theft - Holdup - Pinkerton's Nat. Detective Agency - Detective Agents for the Alliance" w/red & white oval image of reclining dog, ca. 1920, 3 3/8 x 7 1/4" (ILLUS., top of page) **$500-750**

Colorful Poll Parrot Target Game

Game, "Poll Parrot 'Big Game Hunt'," battery-operated, lithographed Masonite w/a large image of Poll Parrot & round targets w/other animals, printed in green, yellow, black, white & red, together w/original placard, target pistol missing, ca. 1960, overall 24" l. (ILLUS.) **$144**

B.P.O.E. Match Safe

Match safe, "B.P.O.E." (Benevolent & Protective Order of Elks), brass w/silver plate, rectangular, embossed fraternal symbols & marked "Cervus Alles," ca. 1910, 1 1/2 x 2 3/4" (ILLUS.)............ **$150-200**

Match safe, "Beach Wickham Grain," metal & celluloid, rectangular, lithograph of horse head above "At Your Service," reverse marked "Compliments of Beach Wickham Grain Co. - Board of Trade - Chicago," three match heads shown in upper right corner, litho by Whitehead & Hoag, ca. 1900, 1 3/8 x 2 1/4" (ILLUS. of both sides, top next page)................. **$200-250**

Blatz Beer Match Safe

Match safe, "Blatz Beer," brass, rectangular, embossed floral decoration at corners, center marked "Blatz Brewing Co. - Milwaukee - U.S.A.," ca. 1910, 1 1/2 x 2 3/4" (ILLUS.) **$175-250**

Rare Early Hires Root Beer Mug

Mug, "Drink Hires Rootbeer," pottery footed barrel-shape w/D-form handle, color transfer-print of the little Hires boy, late 19th - early 20th c., 4 1/4" h. (ILLUS.)....... **$532**

Pair of Hires Root Beer Mugs

Mugs, "Hires Root Beer," pottery, footed barrel-shaped w/ringed rim & arched loop handle, cream ground printed in color w/the bust portrait of the Hires boy below "Drink Hires Rootbeer," late 19th - early 20th c., one w/minor stains, 4 1/4" h., pr. (ILLUS.)..................................... **$476**

Paperweight, bronzed metal, advertising-type, model of a small electric motor, rectangular black & gold label reading "Carl Schaeffer Electric Co.," early 20th c., 2 3/4" l. **$57**

Paperweight, cast bronzed metal, figural, a round disk base centered by the standing figure of a chubby man wearing a tam & long apron, embossed wording down his front, embossed wording around the base "Thatcher Furnaces," early 20th c., 3 1/2" h............................. **$115**

Paperweight, cast iron, a round dished base centered by a large knob, embossed around inside "Samuel Noyes Tailors & Trimmings, Boston," late 19th c., 3 1/2" d. **$80**

Unusual Shoe Advertising Penknife

Penknife, "Men's Patriot Shoes - $3.50 - Star Brand Shoes Are Better," yellow celluloid case shaped like a man's shoe, one-blade, early 20th c., 2 3/4" l. (ILLUS.)......... **$587**

Deering Harvester Pinback Button

Pinback button, "Deering Harvester Co.," celluloid, round, w/color illustration of field w/man driving horse-drawn harvesting machine, "Deering Harvester Co. - Chicago" printed around edge, 1896, made by Whitehead & Hoag of Newark, New Jersey, 1 1/4" d. (ILLUS.)................... **$44**

Ducks Unlimited Celluloid Pin

Pinback button, "Ducks Unlimited," celluloid, round, w/color illustration of duck flying over marsh, above "Ducks Unlimited - 1949," by Western Badge & Novelty Co. of St. Paul, Minnesota, 1 1/4" d. (ILLUS.) ... **$77**

Cracker Jack Pocket Mirror

Pocket mirror, "Cracker Jack," round, celluloid, dark blue w/white, red & blue package in center below "The More You Eat - The More You Want." w/"Look At The Cracker Jack On The Other Side - Rueckheim Bros. & Eckstein, Chicago" at the bottom, ca. 1897, 2" d. (ILLUS.)... **$200-275**

Old Reliable Coffee Pocket Mirror

Pocket mirror, "Old Reliable Coffee," round, celluloid, colorful lithograph of man wearing red jacket & brown hat, one elbow resting on can, marked "Old Reliable Coffee - Always Good," litho by Bastian Bros., ca. 1910, 2" d. (ILLUS.) **$100-150**

Remington Typewriter Pocket Mirror

Pocket mirror, "Remington Typewriters," round, celluloid, red w/white sawtooth border, lithographed image of typewriter in center w/white lettering above reading "To Save Time is to Lengthen Life - Standard" & "Remington Typewriter," below, litho by Parisian Novelty Company, ca. 1915, 3 1/2" d. (ILLUS.) **$175-225**

Scott-Wilkerson Pocket Mirror

Pocket mirror, "Scott-Wilkerson Ambulance Service," round, celluloid, scene of antique vehicle w/trees in background, marked at bottom "Scott-Wilkerson Superior Ambulance Service - Memphis, Tenn.," ca. 1915, 3 1/2" d. (ILLUS.) ... **$125-175**

Studebaker Pocket Mirror

Pocket mirror, "Studebaker," oval, celluloid, lithograph scene of automobile production plant by Bastian Bros., marked "Studebaker Vehicle Works - Largest in the World - South Bend, Ind. U.S.A.," ca. 1900, 1 3/4 x 2 3/4" (ILLUS.)............. **$200-250**

Travelers Insurance Pocket Mirror

Pocket mirror, "Travelers Insurance Company," oval, celluloid, depicts approaching train engine w/skyline in background, "The Travelers Insurance Company - Hartford, Conn." in red letters above & "The Railroad Men's Reliance" in red lettering below, ca. 1900, 1 5/8 x 2 3/8" (ILLUS.)...................... **$125-175**

Victor Victrola Pocket Mirror

Pocket mirror, "Victor Victrola," rectangular w/rounded corners, celluloid, lithograph by Parisian Novelty shows logo in upper left corner opposite "Have You A Victrola In Your Home," image of phonograph center right opposite "This is a Victrola XI

Early Friends Rolled Oats Shipping Crate

- \$100 - Mahogany or Oak - Other Styles \$15 to \$200 - We Will Demonstrate It and Play Any Music You Wish to Hear," dealer information at bottom, ca. 1910, 1 5/8 x 2 3/4" (ILLUS., previous page) **\$175-225**

Stoneware Advertising Preserve Jar

Preserve jar, cov., salt-glazed stoneware, swelled cylindrical base w/a fitted domed cover, molded & trimmed in cobalt blue w/"Nosegay - Trade-Mark - Club Cheese," glued hairline & chips on cover, ca. 1900, 3 3/4" h. (ILLUS.) **\$55**

Black Diamond Matches Crate

Shipping crate, "Black Diamond Matches," low rectangular pine box w/hinged lid, printed black advertising on ends & paper label on side, early 20th c., 13 1/4 x 24 3/4", 9" h. (ILLUS.) **\$58**

Shipping crate, "Friends Rolled Oats," low rectangular pine box w/hinged lid, printed w/large black wording & a bust portrait of a Quaker woman on the front, Muscatine, Iowa, early 20th c., 20 x 27", 12" h. (ILLUS., top of page) **\$201**

Early Heinz 57 Varieties Crate

Shipping crate, "Heinz 57 Varieties," deep rectangular pine box w/lid, black advertising on each end & a large "57" on the wide side, early 20th c., 16 1/2 x 20 1/2", 15 1/2" h. (ILLUS.) **\$58**

Clark Bar Thermometer

Thermometer, "Clark Bar," rectangular, wood w/glass bulb & metal fasteners, image of Clark bar over a clock w/"4PM - 'Clark Bar O'Clock'" & "Clark Bar - Join The Millions In This Mid-Afternoon Candy Delight," dated Dec. 7, 1920, 5 1/2 x 19" (ILLUS.) **\$450-650**

Three Soda Thermometers

Thermometer, "Dr. Pepper," arch-topped rectangle, metal, red on ambered white ground, top ring in red w/"Dr. Pepper" & 10 - 2 - 4 symbol above a small thermometer beside red & black blocks reading "frosty cold," red bottom panel w/"Dr. Pepper," ca. 1940s-50s, light scratches, 7" w., 16" h. (ILLUS. left with Dr. Pepper & Squirt thermometers, top of page) **$193**

Thermometer, "Dr. Pepper," arch-topped rectangle, metal, red on white ground, red top panel w/"Hot or Cold" above a white panel w/ "Enjoy" above a small thermometer beside red wording reading "the friendly 'Pepper Upper,'" red bottom oval w/"Dr. Pepper," ca. 1950s, lightly ambered at edges, light scratches, 16" h. (ILLUS. center with Dr. Pepper & Squirt thermometers, top of page) **$187**

Thermometer, "Squirt," round metal, white ground w/yellow panel above a green & yellow bottle beside the thermometer, red wording reading "Drink Squirt - it's in the public eye," ca. 1940s-50s, few minor spots & marks, tiny chips around mounting holes, 9" d. (ILLUS. right with Dr. Pepper thermometers) **$231**

ARCHITECTURAL ITEMS

In recent years the growing interest in and support for historic preservation has spawned a greater appreciation of the fine architectural elements that were an integral part of early building, both public and private. Where, in decades past, structures might be razed and doors, fireplace mantels, windows, etc., hauled to the dump, today all interior and exterior details from unrestorable buildings are salvaged to be offered to home restorers, museums and even builders who want to include a bit of history in a new construction project.

EX-LAX Thermometer

Thermometer, "EX-LAX," porcelain on metal, blue, black w/red & white bands at top & bottom, reads "EX-LAX - the chocolated laxative - keep 'regular' with EX-LAX - Prescriptions - Drugs - Toilet Articles," ca. 1920s, 8 x 36" (ILLUS.)....................... **$225-300**

Gothic-style 19th Century Bronze Door

Door, bronze, decorated w/three tall narrow pierced Gothic-style upper panels above three smaller square panels & three vertical molded panels, the frame mounted w/large diamond-shaped bolt heads, the inside fitted w/a hinged glazed panel & lock, some denting to lock are, loose back panel top left, glass missing from one panel, 19th c., 33 5/8" w., 76 1/8" h. (ILLUS., previous page) **$1,610**

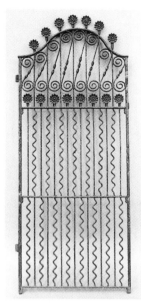

Victorian Aesthetic Iron Gate

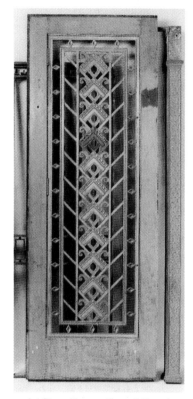

Art Deco Bronze Door & Panels

Frontispiece, bronze & brass, Art Deco style, probably from the interior of a bank, a tall single door w/an openwork vertical design of diamonds & small scrolls, along w/two high fence panels & four uprights w/cast fish scale designs, apparently complete except for glass insert & possibly some missing pieces from the door, 1930s, fence sections 60" w., 74" h., door 30 1/2" w., 85" h., the group (ILLUS.) **$460**

Gate, cast- and wrought-iron, Victorian Aesthetic Movement style, the arched top w/a pair of cast sunflowers on twisting wrought stems, the row of flowers repeating in the body of the gate, last quarter 19th c., American-made, 35 1/2" w., 82 1/2" h. (ILLUS., top next column) **$1,038**

Half a Gate from a Set of Two Gates

Gates, cast iron, each section composed of vertical bars separated by pairs of opposing quarter-arches filled w/scrolls beside the figure of a standing crowned lion, tight scroll panels along the bottom & side, 19th c., each pair 60" w., one pair 104" h., the other 72" h., two pairs (ILLUS. of one panel) **$7,763**

Elegant Victorian Renaissance Revival Window Cornice

Grate, wrought iron, demilune shape composed of iron scrolls painted green, America, 19th c., 52 3/4" l., 27" h. (paint loss, rusty surface) **$705**

English Mahogany Library Steps

Library steps, mahogany, in the form of a staircase w/newels & newel posts, railings & turned spindles leading to a platform w/gallery, on molded legs joined by stretchers w/brass casters, George III-Style, England, 23 1/2 x 39", 5' 9" h. (ILLUS.) **$1,840**

Wall panels, painted & parcel-gilt wood, tall narrow rectangular form, in the Napoleon III "Pompeian" taste w/banded narrow panels surrounding a tall central armorial panel in gold, red, black & green, France, late 19th c., 24" w., 5' 2" h., pr. (ILLUS. of one, top next column)............................ **$3,680**

Window cornice, giltwood & burl walnut & walnut, Victorian Renaissance Revival style, the long molded top centered by a carved upright acanthus leaf on a raised

medallion & w/carved palmette finials at each end above the dentil-carved frieze band. shaped & blocked end bracket supports w/turned finial drops, American-made, ca. 1870s, 63" l., 30" h. (ILLUS., top of page)... **$748**

One of Two Ornate Wall Panels

ART DECO

Interest in Art Deco, a name given an art movement stemming from the Paris International Exhibition of 1925, continues to grow today. This style flowered in the 1930s and actually continued into the 1940s. A mood of flippancy is found in its varied characteristics - zigzag lines resembling the lightning bolt, sometimes steps, often the use of sharply contrasting colors such as black and white and others. Look for prices for the best examples of Art Deco design to continue to rise. Also see JEWELRY, MODERN.

Rare Edgar Brandt Art Deco Wrougt-Iron Cobra Bookends

Bookends, wrought iron, modeled as a large stylized coiled cobra ready to strike, designed & signed by Edgar Brandt, ca. 1930, 7 1/2" h., pr. (ILLUS., top of page) **$23,900**

Art Deco Nephirte Bowl in Box

Bowl, carved nephrite, shallow oblong shape, w/14k gold & cabochon sapphire fitting, unsigned, in a Cartier fitted red morocco box inscribed & dated 1921 (ILLUS., previous column) **$2,350**

Bowl, porcelain, low footring supporting the deep rounded sides w/a wide flat rim, h.p. w/a colorful design w/wide pink & white stripes around the exterior & interior, the exterior further decorated w/a colorful stylized landscape w/a church on a hill w/small hills below & a sailing ship at sea below blue & yellow clouds, designed by Gio Ponti, executed by Richard Ginori, Italy, ca. 1925, signed, 5 3/4" d., 2 7/8" h. (ILLUS., bottom of page) **$13,145**

Small Colorful Art Deco Painted Porcelain Bowl

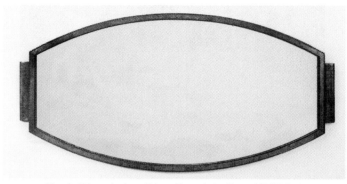

Simple Wrought-iron Edgar Brandt Art Deco Wall Mirror

Art Deco Opalescent Glass Table Lamps

Lamps, table, art glass, the body formed from a glass vase w/opalescent pulled flowers on a tapered form w/a wide rim, chrome top & base, ca. 1930s, base 12" h., overall 30" h., pr. (ILLUS.).............. **$300**

Unusual Straw Marqueterie Mirror

Mirror, inlaid straw marqueterie, wide flat rectangular frame w/diamond-shaped corner panels & an inlaid compass star at the center top, in the style of Jean-Michel Prank, France, ca. 1940, 16 3/4 x 20 5/8" (ILLUS.).. **$2,629**

Mirror, wall-type, wrought-iron long frame gently arched at the top & bottom & w/flat ends w/flat bars, designed & signed by Edgar Brandt, ca. 1930, 27 5/8 x 55" (ILLUS., top of page) **$14,340**

Rare Puiforcat Art Deco Silver Covered Tureen & Undertray

Tureen, cover & mirrored undertray, silver, a long low round dish w/tapering cylinrical sides incised w/panels, the low domed cover w/further radiating lines centered w/a vertical pink onyx ring handle, the undertray w/a stepped edge, designed & signed by Jean E. Puiforcat, Paris, France, ca. 1926, tureen 10" d., undertray 13" d., the set (ILLUS.) **$31,070**

ART NOUVEAU

Art Nouveau's primary thrust was between 1890 and 1905, but commercial Art Nouveau productions continued until about World War I. This style was a rebellion against historic tradition in art. Using natural forms as inspiration, it is primarily characterized by undulating or wavelike lines and whiplashes. Many objects were made in materials ranging from glass to metals. Figural pieces with seductive maidens with long, flowing hair are especially popular in this style. Interest in Art Nouveau remains high, with the best pieces by well known designers bringing strong prices. Also see JEWELRY, ANTIQUE.

German Art Nouveau Silver Plate Card Tray

Card tray, silver plate, figural, a large oblong flattened shape forming a pond
w/water lilies & pads & an Art Nouveau
maiden rising from the water at one end,
leaf & vine-formed feet, by WMF, Germany, late 19th - early 20th c.,
7 3/4 x 10 1/2" (ILLUS., top of page)......... **$210**

Early Art Nouveau-style Covered Pitcher

Pitcher, cov., silver-mounted cut glass, the
swelled slightly tapering cylindrical glass
body rock crystal-cut w/large rounded stylized blossoms among swirling bands,
thick applied handle w/futher leaves, the
low domed sterling silver hinged cover
w/thumbrest & a small chased shell & floral design, cover marked inside by Tiffany
& Co., New York, 1886, 9" h. (ILLUS.) **$4,541**

Punch bowl & ladle, sterling silver, the
rounded lobed & ruffled foot supporting
the wide rounded bowl w/a deeply ruffled
flaring rim, the sides chased w/pears,
fuschia & leaves, two loop side handles,
matching ladle, Martelé silver by Gorham
Mfg. Co., Providence, Rhode island,
1918, bowl 21" l., 2 pcs. (ILLUS., top next
page).. **$50,190**

Unique Ivory & Martelé Silver Ewer

Ewer, silver-mounted ivory, tall cylindrical
ivory body mounted around the base
w/an undulating sterling silver flaring
band chased w/design of morning glories
& wavy vines, the rim w/a matching wide
band w/a high arched spout, rim & base
joined by a long serpentine chased handle, Martelé silver by Gorham Mfg. Co.,
Providence, Rhode Island, 1897,
14 1/4" h. (ILLUS.) **$31,070**

Extremely Rare Gorham Martelé Sterling Punch Bowl & Ladle

Unusual Art Nouveau Chalkware Vase

Vase, chalkware, creamy white, a bulbous squatty gently swirled base tapering to a tall cylindrial neck molded up the side w/an Art Nouveau maiden wearing a long flowing gown clinging to the flowering vines drooping around the two-lobed mouth, late 19th - early 20th c., 22 1/4" h. (ILLUS.) **$144**

AUDUBON PRINTS

John James Audubon, American ornithologist and artist, is considered the finest nature artist in history. In about 1820 he conceived the idea of publishing a full color book portraying every known species of American bird in its natural habitat. He spent years in the wilderness capturing their beauty in vivid color only to have great difficulty finding a publisher. In 1826 he visited England, received immediate acclaim, and selected Robert Havell as his engraver. "Birds of America," when completed, consisted of four volumes of 435 individual plates, double-elephant folio size, a combination of aquatint, etching and line engraving. W.H. Lizars of Edinburgh engraved the first ten plates of this four-volume series. These were later retouched by Havell, who produced the complete

set between 1827 and early 1839. In the 1840s, another definitive work, "Viviparous Quadrupeds of North America," containing 150 plates, was published in America. Prices for Audubon's original double-elephant folio size prints are very high and beyond the means of the average collector. Subsequent editions of "Birds of America," especially the chromolithographs done by Julius Bien in New York (1859-60) and the smaller octavo (7 x 10 1/2") edition of prints done by J.T. Bowen of Philadelphia in the 1840s, are those that are most frequently offered for sale.

Anyone interested in Audubon prints needs to be aware that many photographically produced copies of the prints have been issued during this century for use on calendars or as decorative accessories, so it is best to check with a print expert before spending a large sum on an Audubon purported to be from an early edition.

Audubon Red Headed Woodpecker

Red headed Woodpecker - Plate XXVII, hand-colored etching, engraving & aquatint by Robert Havell, Jr., London, 1823-38, pale uneven staining & some foxing, small tear in upper margin edge, 24 1/8 x 28 1/8" (ILLUS.) **$3,585**

Fine White Heron Audubon Print

reattached & backed, 25 5/8 x 38 1/4"
(ILLUS., top of page)............................ **$17,925**

Texas Lynx by Audubon

Audubon Rough-legged Falcon

Rough-legged Falcon - Plate CCCCXXII,
hand-colored etching, engraving & aquatint by Robert Havell, Jr., London, 1823-
38, losses & tears along margin edges,
time staining & foxing at edges,
26 x 39 1/4" (ILLUS.)............................... **$3,107**

Savannah Finch - Plate CIX, hand-colored
etching, engraving & aquatint by Robert
Havell, Jr., London, 1836, framed,
25 3/4 x 38 3/8" (occasional foxing, binding holes along left, few soft handling
creases, taped to the overmat) **$2,151**

Texas Lynx - Plate 92 - hand-colored lithograph by J.T. Bowen, Philadelphia, ca.
1846, framed, 19 x 25" (ILLUS., top next
column) **$2,588**

White Heron - Plate CCCLXXXVI, hand-
colored etching, engraving & aquatint by
Robert Havell, Jr., London, 1827-38,
framed, small tears in heron's body, three
repaired tears in background, several
tears along margin, title text information

AUTOGRAPHS

Signed Photo of Charles Atlas

Atlas, Charles (1893-1972), famous body
builder, SP, pose of Atlas flexing his mus-
cles, 8 x 10" (ILLUS.) **$93**

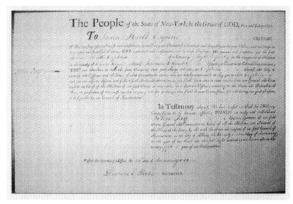

Early Document Signed by John Jay

Gerald Ford-signed Caricature

Ford, Gerald (1913-), 38th President of the United States, signed caricature, also signed by the artist, (Oscar) Berger, minor crease at top, 11 x 14" (ILLUS.).......... **$411**

Scarce Dashiell Hammett Signed Photo

Hammett, Dashiell (1894-1961), mystery writer & author of "The Maltese Falcon" & "The Thin Man" series, SP, inscribed & dated 1928, mounted, 5 x 7" (ILLUS.)....... **$974**

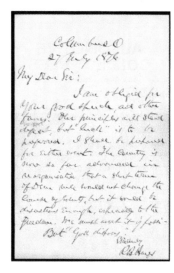

Hayes Letter with Rare Content

Hayes, Rutherford B. (1822-93), 19th President of the United States, ALS, written by Hayes during his 1876 campaign for the presidency, rare content, dated July 27, 1876 (ILLUS.) **$1,837**

Jay, John (1745-1829), first Chief Justice of the Supreme Court, SD, printed document signed while he was New York Governor appointing Isaac Hall a captain in the State Militia, dated January 21, 1801, signature in left margin (ILLUS., top of page).. **$1,072**

Lincoln, Robert Todd (1843-1926), eldest son of Abraham Lincoln, carte-de-visite photo of Lincoln standing, signed on the back, photo by Brady (some soiling on reverse & toning on card) **$4,675**

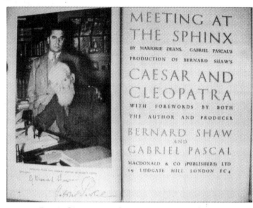

Book Signed by George Bernard Shaw

Shaw, George Bernard (1856-1950), British playwright, critic & essayist, signed book, "Meeting at the Sphinx" by Shaw & Gabriel Pascal, signed by Shaw & Pascal on the frontispiece below their photo, w/original dust jacket (ILLUS., top of page) **$658**

AUTOMOTIVE COLLECTIBLES

Also see Antique Trader Advertising Price Guide.

1950s Phillips 66 Advertising Clock

Clock, "Phillips 66 - Tires - Batteries," round electric back-lit wall-type w/double-bubble dome over the logo & working in black & red, white border band printed w/black Arabic numerals, black hands & red sweep seconds hand, working, ca. 1950s, 15" d. (ILLUS.)............................... **$546**

Clock, "Quaker State Oils & Greases," round electric wall-type w/silver composition frame around the white dial w/black Arabic numerals around the green advertising panel reading "Time to Change to Quaker State Oils & Greases," black hands & sweep seconds hand, designed to be inserted into a tire store display, ca.

1930-1950, some loss to frame, missing cord, 20" d. (ILLUS., below) **$650-750**

Quaker State Electric Wall Clock

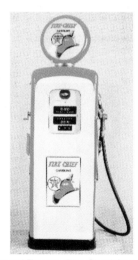

Restored Texaco Fire Chief Gas Pump

Gas pump, "Texaco Fire Chief," Wayne Pump Co. Model 80 series, patent dated 1951, w/reproduction glass globe & Ande

Rare Eastman's Yellow Dock Bitters

Eastman's (Dr. E.P.) Yellow Dock Bitters - Lynn, Mass., rectangular w/wide beveled corner panels, short neck w/applied mouth, iron pontil scar, ca. 1840-60, aqua, 8" h. (ILLUS.) **$2,240**

Yellow The Fish Bitters Bottle

Fish (The) Bitters - W.H. Ware, Patented 1866, figural fish, "W.H. Ware Patent 1866" on bottom, applied small round collared mouth, smooth base, ca. 1866-1875, yellow w/faint amber & olive tones, 11 5/8" h. (ILLUS.) **$1,456**

Sample Size Ferro Quina Stomach Bitters

Ferra Quina Stomach Bitters Mnfg. by Rossi - S.F. Cal., square w/paneled sides & lady's leg neck, tooled lip, smooth base, 95% original paper labels on the sides, original contents, ca. 1890-1900, amber, sample size, 3 3/4" h. (ILLUS.).................. **$672**

Extremely Rare Green The Fish Bitters

Fish (The) Bitters - W.H. Ware, Patented 1866, figural fish, "W.H. Ware Patent 1866" on bottom, applied small round collared mouth, smooth base, ca. 1866-1875, yellowish green, 11 7/8" h. (ILLUS.)...... **$14,560**

Gilbert's Sarsaparilla - Bitters - N.A. Gilbert & Co. - Enosburgh Falls, VT., octagonal, applied square collared mouth, golden amber, some light interior haze, 8 5/8" h. **$672**

Semi-cabin Shaped Golden Bitters

Golden Bitters, semi-cabin shape w/peaked side panels, applied collar mouth, smooth base, ca. 1865-75, bluish aqua, thin open bubble on neck, 10 3/8" h. (ILLUS.) **$420**

The Great Tonic Triangular Bottle

Great Tonic (The) - Caldwell's - Herb Bitters, triangular w/tall neck & applied sloping collar mouth, iron pontil, ca. 1870-80, medium amber shading to deeper amber at neck & base, 12 3/4" h. (ILLUS.)......... **$392**

Gordon's Kidney & Liver Bitters

Gordon's Kidney and Liver Bitters - A Most Effectic Cathartic and Blood Purifier, square w/thin beveled corners, tooled lip, smooth abse, ca. 1890-1910, yellowish amber, 9 1/4" h. (ILLUS.)......... **$504**

Greeley's Bourbon Bitters Bottle

Greeley's Bourbon Bitters, barrel-shaped, ten rings above & below center band, applied mouth, smooth base, ca. 1860-75, deep strawberry puce, some minor highpoint wear, 9 1/4" h. (ILLUS.).................. **$784**

Bluish Green Hartwig - Kantorowicz

Hartwig - Kantorowicz - (Star of David enclosing fish) - Posen - Berlin - Hamburg -Germany, tall lobed form w/tall slender neck & applied mouth, smooth base w/a "K," 98% original paper label on reverse, Germany, ca. 1890-1910, rich bluish green, 10 1/4" h. (ILLUS.) **$364**

Yellowish Green Hartwig - Kantorowicz

Hartwig - Kantorowicz - (Star of David enclosing fish) - Posen - Berlin - Hamburg -Germany, tall lobed form w/tall slender neck & applied mouth, smooth base w/a "S," Germany, ca. 1890-1910, bright yellowish green, 10 1/4" h. (ILLUS.) **$420**
Harvey's Prairie Bitters - Patented (on shoulder), square w/indented panels &

roped corners & lattice shoulder panels, applied sloping collared mouth, shaded golden yellow w/an olive tone, two tiny pinpoint flakes on rings at one corner, ca. 1860-70, 9 1/2" h. **$22,400**

German Hertrichs Bitter Bottle

Hertrichs Bitter, Einziger Fabrikant, Hans Hertrich Hof Gesetzlich Geschutzt, footed ball-shaped w/tall ringed neck, applied double collar mouth, smooth base, Germany, ca. 1880-1900, yellowish olive green, 9 1/4" h. (ILLUS.) **$336**

Amber Holtzermann's Patent Bitters

Holtzermann's Patent Stomach Bitters (on roof), cabin-shaped, two-roof, smooth logs, applied sloping collar mouth, smooth base, ca. 1865-75, amber, smoothed out chip on one log, tiny faint iridescent bruise on one roof, 9 3/8" h. (ILLUS.) **$784**

Rare Dr. A.S. Hopkins Bitters Bottle

Hopkins (Dr. A.S.) - Bitters - Hartford, Conn., cylindrical w/lady's leg neck, applied sloping collared mouth w/ringsmooth base, yellowish amber, one of three known examples, 1860-70, 12 1/4" h. (ILLUS.) **$6,160**

Aqua Jewitt's Celebrated Health Bitters

Jewitt's (Dr. Stephen) - Celebrated Health Restoring Bitters - Rindge, N.H., rectangular w/wide beveled corners, rounded shoulder, applied mouth, pontil scar, bluish aqua, ca. 1840-60, 7 1/4" h. (ILLUS.) .. **$784**

Kimball's Jaundice Bitters Bottle

Kimball's - Jaundice - Bitters - Troy, NH, rectangular, iron pontil, applied sloping collar mouth, yellow amber w/olive tone, ca. 1840-60, 6 3/4" h. (ILLUS.) **$1,344**
Kimball's - Jaundice - Bitters - Troy, NH, rectangular w/beveled corners, applied sloping collared mouth, iron pontil, yellowish amber w/olive tone, probably Stoddard, New Hampshire, ca. 1845-60, 6 7/8" h. **$1,904**

Hutchings Dyspepsia Bitters

Hutchings Dyspepsia Bitters - New York, rectangular w/applied mouth, iron pontil scar, aqua, ca. 1840-60, 8 1/2" h. (ILLUS.) **$960**

Moulton's Oloroso Bitters in Aqua

Moulton's Oloroso Bitters Trade Mark (design of pineapple), round w/tall neck & applied sloping double collar mouth, smooth base, ca. 1865-75, bluish aqua, shallow flake off one panel at base, 11 3/8" h. (ILLUS.) **$280**

National Bitters Bottle in Yellowish Amber

National Bitters, figural ear of corn, "Patent 1867" on base, applied sloping collared mouth w/ring, smooth base, medium golden yellowish amber, ca. 1867-75, 12 1/2" h. (ILLUS.) **$840**

Shaded Amber National Bitters Bottle

National Bitters, figural ear of corn, "Patent 1867" on base, applied sloping collared mouth w/ring, smooth base, medium to deep amber, ca. 1867-75, 12 1/2" h. (ILLUS.) **$476**

Topaz National Bitters Bottle

National Bitters, figural ear of corn, "Patent 1867" on base, applied sloping collared mouth w/ring, smooth base, yellowish topaz, ca. 1867-75, 12 1/2" h. (ILLUS.) **$2,352**

Figural Pineapple Bitters Bottle

Pineapple figural, embossed diamond-shaped panel, applied top, smooth base, ca. 1865-75, medium amber, 9" h. (ILLUS.) **$308**

Yellowish Amber Roback's Bitters

Roback's (Dr. C.W.) - Stomach Bitters - Cincinnati, O., barrel-shaped, applied sloping collar mouth, smooth base, ca. 1865-75, medium yellowish amber, 9 3/4" h. (ILLUS.) **$308**

Rare Marked Pineapple Bitters Bottle

Pineapple figural - W. & Co. N.Y. (in small diamond), embossed diamond-shaped panel, applied double collar mouth, iron pontil, ca. 1865-75, yellowish olive green, 8 3/4" h. **$6,160**

Roback's Stomach Bitters in Amber

Roback's (Dr. C.W.) - Stomach Bitters - Cincinnati, O., barrel-shaped w/rings above & below center band, applied sloping collar mouth, smooth base, ca. 1860-70, yellowish amber, 9 1/4" h. (ILLUS.).... **$364**

Romaine's Crimean Bitters - W. Chilton & Co., square modified cabin form w/paneled sides, columnar corners & angled paneled shoulder, "Romaine's Crimean Bitters - Patent 1863" around base band, applied sloping collared mouth, smooth base, light olive yellow, ca. 1860-80, 10 1/4" h. **$7,280**

Extremely Rare Seely's Stomach Bitters

Seely's (C.C.) Strengthning Stomach Bitters - Pittsburgh, PA., rectangular w/indented chamfered-corner panels on three sides, short neck w/applied sloping mouth, red iron pontil scar, ca. 1845-60, medium shading to deep amber, very rare, 9 3/8" h. (ILLUS.) **$15,680**

Rare Figural Simon's Centennial Bitters

Simon's Centennial Bitters - Trade Mark, bust of George Washington on pedestal,

applied mouth, smooth base, ca. 1876-78, medium red shading to yellowish amber, 10 1/8" h. (ILLUS.) **$4,760**

Soule's (Dr.) Hop Bitterine - 1872, semi-cabin form w/indented panels, applied sloping collared mouth w/ring, smooth base, brilliant topaz, ca. 1860-80, minor interior haze, minor pinpoint flake at mouth, 9 3/8" h. **$616**

Steele's (John W.) - Niagara Star Bitters, semi-cabin shaped w/paneled sides, wording in two panels, molded eagle holding three arrows in another panel, applied mouth w/ring, smooth base, dark root beer amber, ca. 1860-80, 10 1/4" h. **$1,120**

Amber-Yellow Figural Suffolk Bitters

Suffolk Bitters - Philbrook & Tucker Boston, figural pig, applied double collar mouth, smooth base, golden amber shading to yellow, ca. 1863-1870, 10 " l. (ILLUS.).. **$1,232**

Tippecanoe - H.H.Warner Bitters Bottle

Tippecanoe (birch bark & canoe design), H.H. Warner & Co., cylindrical, "Patent Nov. 20. 83 - Rochester - N.Y." on smooth base, applied disc mouth, ca. 1880-95, medium amber shading to yellowish amber, 9" h. (ILLUS.) **$112**

Ulmer's Mountain Ash Bitters

Ulmer's Mountain Ash Bitters - New German Remedy, slightly oval w/narrow side panels, short neck w/applied mouth, open pontil, aqua, ca. 1840-60, lightly cleaned, 7" h. (ILLUS.).......................... **$1,120**

Whitwell's Temperance Bitters

Whitwell's Temperance Bitters, Boston, rectangular w/beveled corners, rounded shoulder & short neck w/applied mouth, open pontil, greenish aqua, ca. 1840-60, 7 1/4" h. (ILLUS.) **$448**

Figurals

Rare Walton's Bitters Bottle

Walton's Bitters - Saml. W. Walton & Co. - Cincinnati, Ohio, square w/paneled sides & rounded shoulders, applied mouth, smooth base, ca. 1875-85, amber, 9 1/2" h. (ILLUS.) **$784**

West India Stomach Bitters - St. Louis Mo., square w/beveled corners & applied sloping collared mouth, smooth base marked "WIMCO," four original paper labels, golden amber, ca. 1860-80, 8 1/2" h. **$1,344**

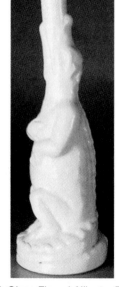

Milk Glass Figural Alligator Bottle

Alligator, seated upright animal on a round base, a tall cylindrical neck issuing from the mouth, pontil scar on base, sheared & tooled mouth, milk glass, chip off tail filled in w/white plaster-of-Paris, probably French, ca. 1880-1910, 10" h. (ILLUS.) ... **$168**

Bear, seated on haunches, applied face on head, cylindrical neck w/sheared mouth at top of head, thick shaped base, front clear w/artificial amethyst tint glass, probably European, 1890-1910, 10" h. (ILLUS.)...... **$179**

French Lady Bather Figural Bottle

Dark Peacock Blue Bear Bottle

Bather, standing lady bather clinging to a tall rockwork formation ending in a tooled mouth, pontil scar, w/original swirled rib stopper, base marked "Deposé," clear, French, ca. 1880-1915, 11 3/4" h. (ILLUS.)..................................... **$56**

Bear, seated on haunches, applied face on head, cylindrical neck w/sheared mouth at top of head, thick shaped base, deep peacock blue glass, American or European, 1870-90, 10 5/8" h. (ILLUS.) **$616**

Milk Glass Billiken Figural Bottle

Billiken, seated chubby comical figure on a rectangular base titled "Billiken" at the front, "Patent Design" on the smooth base, ground lip, original metal screw-on lid, opalescent milk glass, ca. 1910-15, 4 1/4" h. (ILLUS.) **$246**

Birdcage, a wide disk foot supporting a barrel-shaped birdcage w/pagoda-shaped lid, smooth base marked "Pat. Apl'd For," light teal blue w/original gold paint trim, probably American, ca. 1920-34, 4 3/4" h. **$56**

Bear Bottle with Artificial Tint

Figural Black Amethyst Cockatoo Bottle

Child with Butterfly Figural Bottle

Child with butterfly, standing chubby figure on a round base, an embossed butterfly on the chest & back, sheared & ground lip, smooth base, clear, probably American, ca. 1890-1915, 5 3/4" h. (ILLUS.) **$78**

Cockatoo, large bird on a round foot, smooth base, sheared & ground lip, black amethyst, Europe, ca. 1890-1910, 13 1/2" h. (ILLUS.) **$213**

Figural Dressing Case Bottle

Dressing case, upright case w/arched top & short neck w/sheared & ground lip, smooth base, side embossed "Patent - T&C (monogram) - Dressing Case," an applied mirror in one indented side panel, clear, American, ca. 1890-1915, 5 3/8" h. (ILLUS.).. **$146**

Early Mold-blown Blue Clam Bottle

Clam, mold-blown w/pontil scarred base & tooled lip, deep cobalt blue, probably American, ca. 1850-65, 4" h. (ILLUS.) **$280**

Duck, upright position w/neck extending from bird's beak, Atterbury Glass Co., ca. 1870-80, milk glass ground decorated w/raspberry red looping, 11 1/2" h. **$1,344**

Bearded Man with Bag & Broom Bottle

Man holding bag & broom, a short beaded man wearing a cap extended up to form the tall neck w/sheared lip, smooth base, clear, American, ca. 1890-1915, 7 1/2" h. (ILLUS.).. **$56**

Octopus on Silver Dollar Figural Flask

Octopus on silver dollar, relief-molded design w/short cylindrical neck & ground lip w/original screw-on metal cap, dollar dated "1901," milk glass, 4 1/2" h. (ILLUS.)
.... **$504**

Pistol, hand revolver type, ground mouth w/screw threads & metal closure, smooth base, bright sapphire blue, America, ca. 1880-90, 7 3/4" l. **$672**

Flasks

Flasks are listed according to the numbers provided in American Bottles & Flasks and Their Ancestry *by Helen McKearin and Kenneth M. Wilson.*

Washington-Taylor Flask in Copper/Amber

GI-37 - Washington bust below "The Father of His Country" - Taylor bust below "Gen Taylor Never Surrenders" below upper band w/"Dyottville Glass Works Philada," smooth edges, sheared lip, pontil, light to medium copper amber, some light exterior high point wear, qt. (ILLUS.) **$2,800**

Rare Dark Washington - Taylor Flask

GI-37 - Washington bust below "The Father of His Country" - Taylor bust below "Gen Taylor Never Surrenders" below upper band w/"Dyottville Glass Works Philada," smooth edges, sheared mouth, smooth base, dense burgundy-black, highpoint wear, qt. (ILLUS.) **$2,800**

Washington - Taylor Sapphire Blue Flask

GI-37 - Washington bust below "The Father of His Country" - Taylor bust below "Gen Taylor Never Surrenders" below upper band w/"Dyottville Glass Works Philada," smooth edges, sheared mouth, pontil scar, bright sapphire blue, qt. (ILLUS., previous page) **$6,160**

Washington-Taylor Portrait Flask

GI-38 - Washington bust below "The Father of His Country" - Taylor bust, "Gen. Taylor Never Surrenders, Dyottville Glass Works, Philad.a.," sheared mouth, smooth edges, pontil scar, yellowish olive, pt. (ILLUS.) **$1,792**

GI-38 - Washington bust below "The Father of His Country" - Taylor bust, "Gen. Taylor Never Surrenders, Dyottville Glass Works, Philad.a.," sheared mouth, smooth edges, smooth base, deep plum amethyst, pt. **$3,080**

GI-40a - Washington bust below "The Father of His Country" - Taylor bust below "Gen Taylor Never Surrenders," smooth edges, sheared mouth, pontil scar, cobalt blue, some light interior haze, pt. **$2,128**

Lafayette - Liberty Cap Yellow Olive Flask

GI-86 - "Lafayette" above bust & "Coventry - C-T" below - French liberty cap on pole & semicircle of eleven five-pointed stars above, "S & S" below, fine vertical ribbing, two horizontal ribs at base, sheared

mouth, pontil scar, yellowish olive, "S & S" weak near base on Liberty cap side, 1/2 pt. (ILLUS.) **$1,456**

Wheeling Glassworks Franklin Flask

GI-98 - Franklin bust below "Benjamin Franklin," "Wheeling Glassworks" in semicircle above bust of Thomas Dyott, vertically ribbed edges, plain neck, pontil scarred base, sheared & tooled lip, one of only a few w/Wheeling Glassworks embossing, deeper than normal color, deep bluish aqua w/hint of green, pt. (ILLUS.) **$6,440**

GII-61 - American eagle below "Liberty" - inscribed in four lines "Willington - Glass Co - West Willington - Conn," smooth edges, applied sloping collar mouth, smooth base, yellowish green w/an olive tone, qt. **$1,344**

Rare American Eagle/Willington Flask

GII-64 - "Liberty" above American eagle w/shield facing left on leafy branch - "Willington - Glass - Co - West Willington - Conn," smooth sides, applied mouth, smooth base, brilliant blue green, pt. (ILLUS.) **$2,688**

Rare Eagle & Anchor Flask

GII-66 - American eagle w/head turned left below seven five-point stars - anchor below ribbon w/"New London" & above a ribbon w/"Glass Works," applied double collared mouth, smooth base, citron, quart, some light interior stain, tiny bruise on one wreath leaf (ILLUS.) **$6,160**

Flying Eagle - Anchor Flask in Apricot

GII-68 - American eagle in flight in downward position - large anchor w/"New London" in banner above & "Glass Works" in banner below, iron pontil on base, applied double collar mouth, smooth sides, apricot, tiny flake on base, pt. (ILLUS.) **$2,016**

Rare Flying Eagle - Anchor Flask

GII-68 - American eagle in flight in downward position - large anchor w/"New London" in banner above & "Glass Works" in banner below, iron pontil on base, applied double collar mouth, smooth sides, yellow olive, pt. (ILLUS.) **$5,600**

GIII-14 - Cornucopia with Produce & curled to right - Urn with Produce, vertically ribbed edges, sheared mouth, tubular pontil, bluish green, 1/2 pt. **$672**

GIII-17 - Cornucopia w/Produce - Urn, sheared mouth, tubular pontil scar, Lancaster, New York Glassworks, deep bluish green, pt. **$672**

Masonic - American Eagle Olive Flask

GIV-2 - Masonic emblems - American eagle w/ribbon reading "E Pluribus Unum" above & "HS" below in oval frame, applied double collared mouth, pontil scar, yellowish olive, some interior residue, pt. (ILLUS.).. **$5,040**

Pint Railroad Flask in Yellow Amber

GV-7 - Embossed horse pulling cart, reverse identically embossed, smooth base, applied collar mouth, thought to have been blown at Mt. Vernon, New York, Glassworks, one of the rarer flasks in the railroad group, light yellow amber w/olive tone, pt. (ILLUS.) **$2,016**

GVIII-5 - Sunburst w/twenty-four rounded rays obverse & reverse, horizontal corrugated edges, sheared mouth, pontil scar, deep forest green, some minor high point wear, pt. **$2,128**

GVIII-5a - Sunburst w/twenty-four rounded rays obverse & reverse, horizontal corrugated edges, pontil scarred base, sheared mouth, light olive yellow, pt. **$4,760**

Sunburst "KEEN" Flask in Olive

GVIII-9 - Sunburst w/twenty-nine triangular sectioned rays, obverse & reverse, center raised oval w/"KEEN" in reverse on obverse & w/"P & W" on reverse w/twenty-nine rays, sheared mouth, pontil scar, yellowish olive, 1/2 pt. (ILLUS.)................. **$840**

Sunburst Flask in Light Yellow Olive

GVIII-16 - Sunburst w/twenty-one triangular sectioned rays obverse & reverse, sheared & tooled lip, pontil, brilliant light yellow olive, small shallow burst bubble on one ray, faint small spider crack on shoulder, 1/2 pt. (ILLUS.)........................ **$728**

Rare Moonstone Colored Scroll Flask

GIX-2 - Scroll w/large inverted heart-shaped frame formed by medial & inferior scrolls & containing a large six-point star w/a similar star above frame, sheared mouth, pontil scar, moonstone w/lavender tint, qt. (ILLUS.).. **$2,128**

Scroll Flask in Rare Sapphire Blue

GIX-2 - Scroll w/two six-point stars obverse & reverse, vertical medial rib, long neck, pontil scarred base, sheared & tooled lip, brilliant sapphire blue, tiny flat chip on top of mouth slightly buffed, other minor mouth roughness, qt. (ILLUS., previous page) **$5,320**

GIX-4 - Scroll w/two six-point stars, lower star larger than upper, obverse & reverse, vertical medial rib, applied mouth w/ring, iron pontil scar, medium yellowish green, some very minor high point wear, tiny flake at side of mouth, qt. **$1,568**

GIX-11 - Scroll w/six-point stars, a small one in upper space & medium sized one in lower space obverse & reverse, vertical medial rib, sheared mouth, pontil scar, medium yellowish green, pt. **$3,080**

Rare Sapphire Blue Scroll Flask

GIX-14 - Scroll w/six-point star above seven-point star obverse & reverse, vertical medial rib on edge, tooled lip, pontil, brilliant medium sapphire blue, tiny flat flake on top of mouth, pt. (ILLUS.) **$3,920**

Rare Citron-colored Scroll Flask

GIX-15 - Scroll w/medium-sized eight point star at top & in medial space above lower

space w/"Louisville" - similar obverse w/"Glass Works" in lower space & upper six-point star & small lower five-point star, sheared mouth, pontil scar, citron, pt. (ILLUS.) **$2,576**

GIX-37 - Scroll w/eight-point star & small pearl above a fleur-de-lis obverse & reverse, vertical medial rib, sheared mouth, iron pontil scar, light to medium bluish green, 1/2 pt. **$1,456**

Nice Aqua Fancy Scroll Flask

GIX-45 - Scroll, corset-waist style, elaborate scroll decoration forming acanthus leaves w/four-petal flower at top & diamond at center obverse & reverse, vertical medial ribs, pontil scar, sheared mouth, deep aqua almost a pale bluish green, pt. (ILLUS.) **$1,792**

General Taylor & Grapevine Flask

GX-5 - Cannon framed by "Genl Taylor Never Surrenders" - Grapevine frame around "A Little More Grape Capt Bragg," smooth sides, aqua, weak impression, pt. (ILLUS.) **$308**

GX-6 - Cannon framed by "Genl Taylor Never Surrenders" in oval - Grapevine frame around "A Little More Grape Capt Bragg," vertically ribbed sides, sheared mouth on especially long neck, pontil scar, brilliant apricot, pinpoint chip at top of crude mouth, weak embossing, 1/2 pt. **$504**

GX-18 - Spring Tree (leaves & buds) - Summer Tree, smooth edges, applied sloping double collar mouth, pontil scar, light bluish green, qt. **$364**

GXIII-4 - Hunter facing left wearing flat-top stovepipe hat, short coat & full trousers, game bag hanging at left side, firing gun at two birds flying upward at left, large puff of smoke from muzzle, two dogs running to left toward section of rail fence - Fisherman standing on shore near large rock, wearing round-top stovepipe hat, V-neck jacket, full trousers, fishing rod held in left hand w/end resting on ground, right hand holding large fish, creel below left arm, mill w/bushes & tree in left background, calabash, edged w/wide flutes, open pontil, medium bluish green, qt. **$392**

GXIII-17 - Horseman wearing cap & short tight coat on a racing horse w/flying tail - Hound walking to the right, applied sloping collared mouth w/ring, smooth base, bright golden yellow, unusual double bubble in shoulder, pt. **$364**

Anchor - Sheaf of Grain Flask

GXIII-48 - Anchor between fork-ended pennants inscribed "Baltimore" & "Glass Works" - Sheaf of grain w/crossed rake & pitchfork, yellowish orange, qt. (ILLUS.) **$1,904**

"Baltimore Glassworks" Flask in Olive

GXIII-49 - Anchor w/fork-ended pennants inscribed "Baltimore" & "Glassworks" - Sheaf of grain w/rake & pitchfork crossed behind sheaf, smooth edges, smooth base, applied mouth, light yellow olive, 1/2 pt. (ILLUS.) **$3,360**

Drink & Duck Historical Flask

GXIII-29 - "Will You Take A Drink?" (w/small floral design) & "Will A [picture of duck] Swim?" - plain reverse, applied sloping collared mouth w/ring, smooth base, deep aqua, 1/2 pt. (ILLUS.) **$616**

Vertically Ribbed Flask in Sapphire Blue

Anchor & Phoenix Flask in Unusual Color

GXIII-53 - Anchor w/fork-ended pennants inscribed "Baltimore" & "Glass Works" on obverse - Phoenix rising from flames on rectangular panel inscribed "Resurgam" on reverse, applied square collared mouth, smooth base, unusual yellow olive, tiny flat chip to top of mouth, slight interior residue, pt. (ILLUS.) **$1,904**

western U.S., ca. 1820-40, shallow chip on side of mouth, 6 7/8" h. (ILLUS.) **$1,120**

Midwestern Ten-Diamond Flask

Pattern molded, flattened ovoid shape w/sheared mouth, pontil scar, ten-diamond patt., Midwest U.S.A., probably Zanesville, OH, 1815-30, aqua w/numerous threads of amber in the neck, 5" h. (ILLUS.) **$616**

Anchor-Phoenix Baltimore Flask

GXIII-54 - Anchor w/fork-ended pennants inscribed "Baltimore" & "Glass Works" on obverse - Phoenix without crest rising from flames on rectangular panel inscribed "Resurgam" on reverse, applied collared mouth, smooth base, smooth edges, yellowish orange, some exterior high point wear, some light interior stain spots, pt. (ILLUS.) **$420**

GXIV-7 - "Traveler's Companion" arched above & below stylized duck - eight-pointed star, smooth sides, sheared mouth, iron pontil, golden amber, 1/2 pt. **$420**

Pattern molded, flattened ovoid shape tapering to a sheared mouth, pontil scar, twenty-four vertical ribs, bright sapphire blue w/two faint darker blue striations, Mid-

Midwestern Ten-Diamond Amber Flask

Pattern molded, flattened ovoid shape w/sheared mouth, pontil scar, ten-diamond patt., Midwest U.S.A., probably Zanesville, OH, 1815-30, brilliant golden amber, exterior wear & scratches, 5" h. (ILLUS., previous page) $616

Pattern molded, flattened ovoid shape w/sheared mouth, pontil scar, ten-diamond patt., Midwest U.S.A., probably Zanesville, OH, 1815-30, light golden amber, 4 7/8" h. $840

Early New England Pitkin Flask

Pitkin, thirty-six ribs swirled to the right, sheared mouth, tubular pontil scar, probably New England, 1780-1830, light olive yellow, 6 1/8" h. (ILLUS.) $1,064

Inks

Fine Forest Green Pitkin Flask

Pitkin, thirty ribs swirled to the left, brilliant forest green, sheared mouth, pontil scar, Midwestern U.S., ca. 1820-40, 6 1/2" h. (ILLUS.) $952

Forest Green Pitkin Flask

Pitkin, thirty-six ribs swirled to the right, sheared mouth, pontil scar, possibly Pitkin Glass Works, East Hartford, Connecticut, 1783-1830, brilliant forest green, 5" h. (ILLUS.) $1,064

Rare Large Harrison's Master Ink

Cylindrical, master size, cobalt blue, "Harrison's Columbian Ink," applied mouth, open pontil, ca. 1840-60, pinhead size flake off base edge, 9 5/8" h. (ILLUS.) ... $3,360

Cylindrical, yellowish green, embossed "S. Fine - Blk. Ink," inward rolled neck, pontil scar, 1840-1860, 2 7/8" h. $784

Cylindrical w/octagonal base, master-size, paneled sloping shoulder embossed "Wilber's Ink," applied sloping collared mouth, smooth base, dense black amber, small hard-to-see potstone bruise in base, ca. 1860-80, 7 5/8" h. $420

Short Cylindrical Lyons Ink

Cylindrical w/thick shoulder & base ring, medium cobalt blue, short center neck w/tooled lip, smooth base, embossed around sides "Lyons Ink," ca. 1880-95, 2 7/8" h. (ILLUS.) **$235**

Eight-sided w/central neck, deep yellow olive, paneled base embossed "Farleys - Ink," sheared mouth, pontil scar, probably Stoddard glasshouse, Stoddard, New Hampshire, 1845-1860, 1 7/8" w., 1 3/4" h. **$1,344**

Igloo-form w/side neck, bright yellow topaz, paneled base embossed "J - & - I - EM," tooled mouth, smooth base, pinpoint burst bubble at base corner, 1860-1880, 1 1/8" w., 1 3/4" h. **$1,008**

Low Octagonal Aqua Ink Bottle

Octagonal, bluish aqua, short squatty shape w/central neck w/sheared & rolled lip, pontil scar, some very light inside haze, ca. 1840-60, 1 3/4" h. (ILLUS.)........ **$202**

Very Rare A.B. Laird's Ink in Green

Octagonal w/angled shoulder to short wide cylindrical neck, medium bluish green, open pontil, inward rolled lip, embossed around paneled lower sides "A.B. Laird's - Ink," ca. 1840-60, very rare, 2 1/8" h. (ILLUS.) **$4,480**

Marked & Labeled Harrison's Ink

Octagonal, aqua, short neck w/cupped applied mouth, open pontil scar, paneled embossed "Harrison's - Columbian - Ink - Patent," 98% original paper label reading "Harrison's Columbian Ink - Black...," ca. 1840-60, small chip on underside of lip (ILLUS. of front & back)............................ **$560**

Cobalt Blue Cut Glass Ink

Teakettle-type fountain inkwell w/neck extending up at angle from base, cobalt blue cut glass, sheared & ground lip, polished pontil, original metal neck ring & hinged cap, some tiny flakes on paneled edges, ca. 1875-95, 2 1/4" h. (ILLUS.)...... **$224**

Cobalt Blue Teakettle Ink

Teakettle-type fountain inkwell w/neck extending up at angle from base, cobalt blue, sheared & ground lip, smooth base, ca. 1875-95, 1 5/8" h. (ILLUS.)........ **$392**

Fine Cobalt Blue Umbrella Ink

Umbrella-type (8-panel cone shape), deep cobalt blue shading almost to violet, smooth base, inward rolled lip, ca. 1855-70, 2 1/2" h. (ILLUS.) **$840**

Rare Amethyst Umbrella Ink

Umbrella-type (8-panel cone shape), medium amethyst, smooth base, inward rolled lip, ca. 1855-65, 2 1/2" h. (ILLUS.)............ **$1,680**

Medium Bluish Green Umbrella Ink

Umbrella-type (8-panel cone shape), medium bluish green, open pontil, inward rolled lip, ca. 1840-60, very shallow flake on base edge, 2 5/8" h. (ILLUS.).............. **$364**

Fine Yellowish Olive Green Ink

Umbrella-type (8-panel cone shape), medium yellowish olive green, open pontil scar, inward rolled lip, ca. 1840-60, 2 1/2" h. (ILLUS.) **$672**
Umbrella-type (8-panel cone shape), midnight blue, inward rolled mouth, tubular pontil scar, 1830-1860, 2 1/4" w., 2 3/8" h. **$1,792**

Medicines

Barrell's Indian Liniment Bottle

Barrell's Indian Liniment - H.C.O. Cary, rectangular w/paneled sides, rolled lip, open pontil scar, ca. 1840-60, aqua, 4 3/4" h. (ILLUS., previous page) **$112**

Brant's Indian Pulmonary Balsam Bottle

Brant's Indian - Pulmonary Balsam - M.T. Wallace - Proprietor, slender eight-sided body w/applied sloping collar mouth, pontil scar, pale bluish aqua, some light milky interior stain, 7" h. (ILLUS.) **$101**

Buckhout's Dutch Liniment Bottle

Buckhout's (E.A.) Dutch Liniment (design of standing man) - Prepared at Mechanicville Saratoga Co. N.Y., flattened rectangle w/rounded shoulders & rolled lip, open pontil scar, ca. 1840-60, bluish aqua, 4 3/4" h. (ILLUS.) **$560**

Carter's Extract of Smart Weed Bottle

Carter's Extract of Smart Weed - Erie, rectangular w/paneled sides, tall neck w/applied sloping mouth, open pontil scar, ca. 1840-60, aqua, 5 1/2" h. (ILLUS.).. **$258**

Celery Compound - Compound (superimposed on bunch of celery), square semi-cabin w/paneled sides, tooled sloping collared mouth, smooth base, original color paper label in one panel, ca. 1890, yellowish amber, short hairline fissure in one corner post, 9 1/2" h. **$336**

Small Cerisiaux Rheumatic Antidote Bottle

Cerisiaux Rheumatic Antidote or Electric Liniment - New York, rectangular w/paneled sides, applied sloping mouth, open pontil scar, ca. 1840-60, aqua, 5 1/4" h. (ILLUS.) **$269**

Front & Back of Clemen's Indian Tonic

Clemen's Indian Tonic - Prepared by Geo. W. House (w/standing Indian), oval w/tall neck w/wide rolled lip, open pontil scar, ca. 1840-60, reverse w/99% original paper label reading "Clemen's Indian Tonic, Infallible Cure for Ague & Fever, G.W. House, Nashville, Tenn.," aqua, 5 3/8" h. (ILLUS. of front & back) **$672**

Dr. Davis's Compound Syrup Bottle

Davis's (Dr.) - Compound - Syrup of - Wild Cherry - and Tar, eight-sided w/embossing on five consecutive indented panels, applied sloping mouth, open pontil scar, ca. 1840-60, bluish aqua, cleaned, 7" h. (ILLUS.) **$101**

Blue Dr. Ellel's Liver Regulator Bottle

Ellel's (Dr.) Liver Regulator - South Bend, Ind., rectangular w/arched panels & rounded shoulders, tall neck w/tooled lip, smooth base, ca. 1885-1910, cobalt blue, cleaned, 5 3/4" h. (ILLUS.) **$269**

Rare Fairchild's Sure Remedy Bottle

Fairchild's - Sure - Remedy, cylindrical w/alternating wide & narrow panels, rounded shoulder, applied sloping mouth, open pontil scar, ca. 1840-60, aqua, very rare, 7 7/8" h. (ILLUS.) **$1,239**

Emerald Green Gargling Oil Bottle

Gargling Oil, Lockport, N.Y., rectangular w/arched side panels & arched shoulder, short neck w/applied sloping collared neck, smooth base, ca. 1865-75, medium emerald green, larger size, 7 3/8" h. (ILLUS.) **$202**

Ivans & Hart (Drs.) - New York, eight-sided w/each side separated by a small additional panel, applied sloping mouth, open pontil scar, ca. 1840-60, aqua, some inside stain in one panel, 7 3/8" h. (ILLUS., previous page) **$1,008**

Small Merchant Bottle with Labels

Merchant (G.W.) - Lockport, N.Y., rectangular w/tall neck & applied sloping mouth, pontil scar, 80% back & 95% front paper labels reading "Merchant's Celebrated Gargling Oil - Adapted to Family Use" above a scene of a lady purchasing a bottle in a shop, ca. 1840-60, emerald green, 5" h. (ILLUS.) **$672**

Small Merchant Variant Bottle

Merchant (G.W.) - Lockport, N.Y., rectangular w/tall neck & applied sloping mouth, pontil scar, ca. 1840-60, variant lacking the + on back panel, medium bluish green, 4 7/8" h. (ILLUS.) **$336**

Large Dr. Myer's Vegetable Extract

Myer's (Dr.) Vegetable Extract - Sarsaparilla Wild Cherry Dandelion - Buffalo, N.Y., rectangular w/paneled sides, applied sloping mouth, iron pontil, ca. 1840-60, bluish aqua, bold impression, 9 5/8" h. (ILLUS.) **$1,680**

No. 1 Shaker Syrup Bottle

No. 1 Shaker Syrup - Canterbury, N.H., rectangular w/paneled sides, applied sloping mouth, open pontil scar, ca. 1840-60, aqua, rarer larger variant, 7 3/4" h. (ILLUS.) **$168**

Old Dr. - J. Townsend's - Sarsaparilla - New York, square w/beveled corners, applied sloping collar mouth, iron pontil, light sapphire blue, ca. 1845-60, some minor highpoint wear, 9 1/4" h. **$2,128**

Yellowish Amber Rohrer's Tonic Bottle

Rohrer's - Expectoral Wild Cherry Tonic - Lancaster, PA, tapering square w/rope corners, applied sloping double collar mouth, smooth base, ca. 1860-75, medium yellowish amber, 10 5/8" h. (ILLUS.)... **$392**

Sanderson's Blood Renovator - Minto, VT, oval w/applied collared mouth, pontil scar, aqua, ca. 1880, 8" h. **$1,344**

Sanford's Extract of Hamamelis or Witch Hazel, round w/indented embossed panels & beveled corners, applied square collared mouth, smooth base, cobalt blue, ca. 1860-80, 11 1/4" h. **$672**

Blue Sandford's Radical Cure Bottle

Sanford's Radical Cure, rectangular w/paneled sides, tooled mouth & smooth base w/"Potter Drug & Chem. Corporation - Boston, Mass USA," ca. 1870-80, cobalt blue, 7 1/2" h. (ILLUS.) **$67**

Shaker Cherry Pectoral Syrup - Canterbury, NY, No. 1, rectangular w/paneled sides, applied mouth, open pontil scar, ca. 1840-60, aqua, some very faint inside haze, 5 3/8" h. (ILLUS., top next column) **$101**

Shaker Cherry Pectoral Syrup Bottle

Sparks Perfect Health (below Trade Mark) - bust of man - for Kidney & Liver Diseases, Camden, N.J., rectangular w/cabin-type roof shoulder & beveled corners, tooled mouth, smooth base, ca. 1880-95, cleaned, yellowish amber, 9 1/2" h. **$616**

Cobalt Blue Stearns Medicine Bottle

Stearns, cylindrical w/applied double collar mouth, smooth base, ca. 1865-75, medium cobalt blue, contained Citrate of Magnesia, cleaned, 7 1/8" h. (ILLUS.) **$123**

Swaim's Panacea - Genuine - Philadelphia, rectangular w/beveled corners & applied sloping collared mouth, pontil scar, ca. 1840-60, aqua, 7 3/4" h. **$960**

Swaim's - Panacea - Philada, cylindrical w/rounded shoulder & paneled sides, applied sloping collar mouth, smooth base, medium bluish green, ca. 1840-60, 7 1/2" h. **$392**

Mineral Waters, Sodas & Sarsaparillas

medium bluish green, very thin small open bubble on one edge, 7 5/8" h. (ILLUS.) **$960**

Rare Central Spring Quart Bottle

Central Springs - Green & Co. - Sheldon, VT., wide cylindrical body w/a tall neck & applied double collar mouth, smooth base, ca. 1865-75, deep bluish green, qt. (ILLUS.)... **$8,400**

Champlain Spring - Alkaline Chalybeate - Highgate, VT, cylindrical w/tall neck & sloping collared mouth w/ring, smooth base, emerald green, ca. 1860-70, quart
.... **$532**

Large Bear Lithia Water Bottle

Bear Lithia Water - Bear Lithia Water (embossed on walking bear) - Trade Mark - Near Elkton, VA. - E.H.E. Co., wide cylindrical body w/a wide rounded shoulder & short neck w/tooled mouth, smooth base, ca. 1880-1900, greenish aqua, 10" h. (ILLUS.) **$280**

Campbell Mineral Spring Co. - C - Burlington, VT, cylindrical w/tall neck & applied sloping collared mouth w/ring, smooth base, deep aqua, some minor highpoint wear, ca. 1860-70, quart **$1,232**

Carpenter & Cobb Soda Water Bottle

Carpenter - & Cobb - Knickerbocker - Soda - Water - Saratoga - Springs, tensided cylindrical form tapering to an applied blob mouth, iron pontil, ca. 1840-60,

J. & W. Coles Soda Water Bottle

Coles (J. & W.) - Superior Soda & Mineral Water - Staten Island, cylindrical tapering to a tall neck w/applied blob mouth, iron pontil, ca. 1840-60, medium cobalt blue, cleaned, 7 3/8" h. (ILLUS.) **$420**

M.T. Crawford Blue Mineral Water

Crawford (M.T.) - Springfield. - Union Glass Works Philad. - Superior Mineral Water, cylindrical w/paneled base, slender neck w/heavy applied collared mouth, iron pontil, ca. 1840-60, deep cobalt blue shading to violet at base, 7 5/8" h. (ILLUS.) **$840**

Rapp - Dyottville Blue Mineral Water

Dyottville Glass Works - Philada - A.W. Rapp - New York - Mineral Water - R - This Bottle Is Never Sold, cylindrical tapering to a tall neck w/applied sloping mouth, iron pontil, ca. 1840-60, medium cobalt blue, some scratching, minor flake on side of lip, lip bubble w/tiny opening, uncleaned, 7 3/4" h. (ILLUS.) **$280**

Highrock Congress Spring (design of a rock), C. & W. Saratoga N.Y., cylindrical w/applied sloping collared mouth, smooth base, teal blue, ca. 1865-75, tiny pick mark below the mountain, pint **$532**

Hyatt & Co. Patent Jan. 1869 New York - Cod Liver Oil - Soda Water, cylindrical w/heavy sloping collared mouth, smooth base, dark golden amber, some heavy exterior wear, 1860-70, 5 7/8" h. **$616**

Amber Iodine Spring Water Bottle

Iodine Spring Water - L - South Hero. VT, cylindrical w/tall cylindrical neck w/applied double collar mouth, smooth base, ca. 1875-75, deep old amber, qt. (ILLUS.) **$1,568**

Iodine Spring Water - L - South Hero. VT, cylindrical w/tall cylindrical neck w/applied sloping collared mouth w/ring, smooth base, golden amber, ca. 1860-80, qt. **$1,680**

S.S. Knicker Bocker Cobalt Blue Bottle

Knicker (S.S.) Bocker - Soda Water - 164. 18th St. N.Y. 1848, ten-sided cylinder tapering to an applied mouth, iron pontil, ca. 1845-60, cobalt blue, 7" h. (ILLUS.) **$1,120**

Rare Wortendyke Mineral Water Bottle

Wortendyke (R.C.) - Agent - Superior - Mineral Water - XX, ten-sided cylinder tapering to an applied blob mouth, iron pontil, ca. 1840-60, 7 3/8" h. (ILLUS.).... **$1,344**

Rare C.M. Walter Soda Water Bottle

Walter (C.M.) M. Holly N.J., wide flat bottom & cylindrical sides to rounded shoulders, tall neck w/an applied double collar mouth, iron pontil, ca. 1840-60, light to medium bluish green, 7" h. (ILLUS.) **$1,344**

Pickle Bottles & Jars

Aqua, four-sided cathedral-type, four fancy Gothic arches, ringed wide outward rolled neck, iron pontil, Willington, Connecticut, ca. 1845-60, 11 1/2" h. **$1,120**

Aqua, four-sided cathedral-type, four Gothic arches, ringed wide outward rolled neck, large tubular pontil, Willington, Connecticut, ca. 1840-60, 7 1/2" h. **$2,128**

Rare Early Yellowish Green Pickle Jar

Light yellowish green, squared upright cloverleaf-form, outward rolled mouth, pontil scar, probably a Stoddard, New Hampshire glasshouse, ca. 1840-60, 7 3/4" h. (ILLUS.)... **$1,008**

W. Wood, Pittsburgh Soda Water

Wood (A.) - Pittsg PA, wide flat bottom & cylindrical sides to a rounded shoulder, tall neck w/applied sloping collar mouth, tubular open pontil, ca. 1840-60, medium bluish green, professionally cleaned, 7 3/8" h. (ILLUS.) **$1,344**

Bright Green Cathedral Pickle Jar

Medium green, four-sided cathedral-type w/fancy Gothic windows, outward rolled mouth, smooth base, ca. 1860-80, 11 3/8" h. (ILLUS.) **$1,120**

Rare Cathedral Pickle Jar

Medium green, six-sided cathedral-type w/ornate Gothic windows, cylindrical ringed neck w/outward rolled mouth, smooth base, ca. 1860-70, 13" h. (ILLUS.) **$2,464**

Rare Amber Cathedral Pickle Bottle

Olive amber, four-sided cathedral-type w/fancy Gothic arch windows on three sides, ringed cylindrical neck w/outward rolled mouth, pontil scar, severely cracked in shoulder & one panel, probably Willington Glass Works, West Willington, Connecticut, 1840-60, 8 1/8" h. (ILLUS.) **$2,464**

Amber Lobed Pickle Bottle

Reddish amber, octofoil upright lobed design w/a tapering shoulder & flaring neck w/flattened rim, smooth base, Stoddard, New Hampshire, 1860-70, 8 1/8" h. (ILLUS.) **$1,008**
Yellowish amber w/a topaz tone, cylindrical blown in a three-piece mold, outward rolled mouth, smooth base, Stoddard, New Hampshire, 1860-70, 3 1/2" d., 8 1/4" h. **$784**

Amber Cloverleaf-form Early Pickle Jar

Yellowish amber with reddish tone, squared upright cloverleaf-form, outward rolled mouth, smooth base, from Stoddard, New Hampshire, ca. 1860-70, 7 3/4" h. (ILLUS.) **$1,568**

Poisons

Small Blue Diamond Lattice Poison

Cobalt blue, cylindrical w/overall embossed diamond lattice design, tooled lip, smooth base marked "W.T. Co.," ca. 1890-1910, 3 7/8" h. (ILLUS.) **$101**

Diamond Lattice Poison with Marked Base

Cobalt blue, cylindrical w/overall embossed diamond lattice design, tooled lip, smooth base marked "H.B. Co.," ca. 1890-1910, 7" h. (ILLUS.) **$112**

Scarce Skull-shaped Poison Bottle

Cobalt blue, model of a skull w/a cylindrical neck at the top, cross bone base marked "Poison," back of neck marked "Pat. Appl'd For," lip w/several small & one large chip, 4 1/4" h. (ILLUS.).............................. **$776**

Golden amber, coffin-shaped w/overall hobnails, tooled round collared mouth, smooth base marked "Norwich 16A," American, 1890-1900, extremely rare, 7 1/2" h. **$13,440**

Moss Green Six-sided Poison Bottle

Moss green, six-sided oblong form w/horizontal ribbing & four panels w/"Poison," tooled mouth, smooth base marked "C.L.G. Co. - Patent Applied For," ca. 1890-1910, 5 1/2" h. (ILLUS.) **$168**

Smoky Green Diamond Lattice Poison

Smoky bluish green, cylindrical w/overall embossed diamond lattice design, tooled lip, smooth base,ca. 1890-1910, some very faint inside haze, 4 5/8" h. (ILLUS.)... **$308**

Whiskey & Other Spirits

Very Rare D. Davis Cobalt Blue Beer

Beer, "D. Davis," cylindrical 12-paneled sides w/sloping shoulder to an applied mouth, smooth base, ca. 1845-60, deep cobalt blue, tiny flake on lip edge, 10 1/8" h. (ILLUS.) **$2,352**

Rare Dr. Cronk - R.McCoun Beer

Beer, "Dr. Cronk - R.McCoun," cylindrical 10-paneled sides w/sloping shoulder to an applied mouth, iron pontil, ca. 1845-60, deep cobalt blue, 8 1/4" h. (ILLUS.) **$2,464**

Rare Dr. Cronk Cobalt Blue Beer Bottle

Beer, "Dr. Cronk - R.Mc C.," cylindrical 12-paneled sides w/sloping shoulder to an applied mouth, iron pontil, ca. 1845-60, deep cobalt blue, minor high point wear, one internal bubble, 10 1/4" h. (ILLUS.).............. **$1,680**

Rare H.H.P. & Co. Cobalt Blue Beer

Beer, "H.H.P. & Co.," cylindrical 12-paneled sides w/sloping shoulder to an applied mouth, iron pontil, ca. 1845-60, deep cobalt blue, 9 3/4" h. (ILLUS.).................... **$1,344**

Cobalt Blue H.H.P. Early Beer Bottle

Beer, "H.H.P.," cylindrical 12-paneled sides w/sloping shoulder to an applied mouth, smooth base, ca. 1845-60, deep cobalt blue, 9 3/4" h. (ILLUS.).......................... **$1,456**

Very Rare S. Smith Cobalt Blue Beer

Beer, "S. Smith - Auburn, N.Y.," cylindrical 12-sided w/sloping shoulder to an applied mouth, smooth base, ca. 1845-60, deep cobalt blue, very rare, 9 3/4" h. (ILLUS.) **$5,040**

Rare Green M. Richardson Beer Bottle

Beer, "M. Richardson," cylindrical w/sloping shoulder to an applied mouth, smooth base, ca. 1845-60, yellowish emerald green, shallow sliver chip off underside of neck collar, 9 3/4" h. (ILLUS.) **$1,680**

Udolpho Wolfe's Schnapps Bottle

Schnapps, "Udolpho Wolfe's Aromatic Schnapps, Schiedam," rectangular w/beveled corners, applied sloping collar mouth, iron pontil, ca. 1855-65, yellowish olive green, 7 7/8" h. (ILLUS.).................. **$200**

Spirits, mold-blown club form w/tall neck & applied round collared mouth, pontil scar, twenty-four ribs swirled to the right, Midwest, early 19th c., medium yellowish green, two small spider cracks at the shoulder, 4 1/2" h. **$672**

Spirits, pattern-molded w/24 ribs swirled to the right, globular w/tall neck & outward rolled mouth, pontil scar, probably Zanesville, Oh, 1820-40, bright yellowish amber, 7 3/4" h. **$1,568**

Barrel-shaped Bennett & Carrol Whiskey

Whiskey, "Bennett & Carroll - 120 Wood St. - Pittsburgh," barrel-shaped w/rings above & below center band, applied mouth, smooth base, ca. 1860-75, medium to deep amber, pinhead flake on base edge, 9 1/2" h. (ILLUS.) **$840**

Bininger's Old Dominion Wheat Tonic

Whiskey, "Bininger's Old Dominion Wheat Tonic - A.M. Bininger & C0., No. 338 Broadway, N.Y.," square w/beveled corners, applied sloping mouth, smooth base, ca. 1855-70, yellowish olive, pinhead flake on base edge, 9 3/4" h. (ILLUS.)......... **$616**

Variation of Booz's Old Cabin Whiskey

Whiskey, "Booz's (E.G.) Old Cabin Whiskey - 120 Walnut St. Philadelphia" on roof, "1840 - E.G. Booz's Old Cabin Whiskey" on sides, cabin-shaped w/beveled roof ends, applied sloping collar mouth, smooth base, ca. 1865-75, deep root beer amber, 7 7/8" h. (ILLUS.)........ **$3,920**

Chestnut Grove Whiskey Handled Flask

Whiskey, "Chestnut Grove Whiskey, C.W. (on applied seal)," chestnut flask-shaped w/applied neck handle, applied mouth, ca. 1855-75, tobacco amber, 9" h. (ILLUS.) **$280**

Whiskey, "Cutter's (R.B.) Pure Bourbon," ovoid body w/applied collared mouth & handle, pontil scar, apricot, ca. 1855-65, 8 1/8" h. **$1,680**

Whiskey, "Duffy Crescent - Saloon - 214 Jefferson Street - Louisville, KY" w/crescent moon & rooster, figural pig, ground lip, smooth base, clear, ca. 1870-80, 7 1/2" l. **$2,350**

Whiskey, "Good Old Rye - In A Hogs," figural pig, ground mouth, smooth base, rare fiery opalescent milk glass w/blue, green & red splotches along the top, ca. 1880-1900, some mouth roughness & chips in the making, 8 1/2" l. **$2,128**

Flask-shaped Wharton's Whisky

Whiskey, "Wharton's Whisky (sic) 1850 Chestnut Grove (all inside a linked chain)," flask-shaped w/short neck w/applied mouth, smooth base, ca. 1855-75, cobalt blue, 5 1/8" h. (ILLUS.) **$728**

"Good Night" Whiskey Pocket Flask

Whiskey nip, "Good (impressed bust of man in nightcap) Night," pocket flask w/screw-on metal cap, smooth base, ca. 1885-1910, fiery opalescent milk glass, 4 1/8" h. (ILLUS.) **$112**

"Night Cap" Whiskey Pocket Flask

Whiskey nip, "Night (impressed bust of man in nightcap) Cap," pocket flask w/screw-on metal cap, smooth base, ca. 1885-1910, fiery opalescent milk glass w/99% of original colorful paint, 4 1/8" h. (ILLUS.)..................................... **$216**

Wine, "I. Hubbard" in applied shoulder seal, tall neck w/applied sloping collared mouth w/ring, pontil scar, yellowish olive, England, ca. 1820-40, 10 1/2" h. ... **$1,064**

Wine, "Imperial Levee - J. Noyes Hollywood Miss.," in the form of a large cluster of grapes & grape leaves on a stump, tall neck w/applied mouth w/ring, iron pontil, shaded yellowish amber, tiny flake on top of mouth, 1845-60, 9 1/4" h. **$3,640**

Wine, "Pickering - Dodge" in applied seal on shoulder, embossed "Ricketts Glassworks" on the base, cylindrical w/slender neck & applied sloping collared mouth, pontil scar, medium yellowish green, England, ca. 1820-40, faint small star crack on shoulder, 10" h. **$728**

BOXES

Desk box, banded & inlaid mahogany, rosewood, holly, ebony & fruitwood, the rectangular box w/a hinged cover w/sloped edges & flat top elaborately banded & inlaid w/various woods & a large floral panel on top, opening to an interior fitted w/a framed mirror & solid mahogany, the box sides also banded & centering large floral-inlaid panels, mounted on a wide conforming platform base w/a scroll-carved apron, Europe, second quarter 19th c., 9 1/4 x 14 1/2", 7 1/2" h. **$1,093**

Fine Early Paint-decorated Document Box

Document box, cov., painted & decorated pine, nailed construction, long rectangular form w/a hinged flat cover, the top decorated w/a large colorful basket of flowers in a framed & double pinstripe border w/fanciful finish, the front base decorated w/a similar fanciful basket of flowers falnked by deep red scroll designs,each end w/a colorful bold large spray of flowers, the back decorated w/a series of sponged dots, the interior painted white, cover attached w/old wire hinges, originally w/a simple leather heart attached to front now missing, couple of small splits on the front, found in Massachusetts, 19th c., 6 1/4 x 12 1/2" (ILLUS.)......................... **$2,070**

Colorful Old Scandinavian Box

Storage box, cov., painted & decorated, rectangular w/a hinged low-domed top w/scalloped ends painted on the exterior w/a red background w/multiple colorful fleur-de-lis berries & flowers in white, blue, yellow, green & black, the wire handle opens top w/reveal a white-painted interior decorated w/a long leafy sunflower-like blossom on a leaf stem in shades of blue, green, pink & yellow, interior lidded compartment, the exterior w/an overall dark red painted background, the ends painted w/large rounded stylized flowerheads, the front w/an ornate leafy scroll & berry design in shades of blue, white, black, brown & green, low serpentine front & side aprons, Scandinavia, 19th c., couple of old age splits, 6 x 10 1/4", 6 1/2" h. (ILLUS.) **$805**

Small Wallpaper-covered Box

Storage box, wallpaper-covered, square w/a fitted flat lid, the base wrapped in a paper w/a lattice & florette & dot design, the top paper w/flowerheads & undulating bands, some fading, first half 19th c., 3 1/4" w., 2" h. (ILLUS.)............................. **$259**

Storage box, rectangular w/slide-out cover, painted & decorated poplar, dovetailed sides & wooden pegged bottom, original decoration w/a dark brown stained ground decorated on the sides & flat top w/stylized large tulips & petaled blossoms w/crosshatched center in thick yellow, orange & black, molded rim band decorated w/small white bands, thin base molding, attributed to Berks County, Pennsylvania, small flaked areas, cover w/corner damage, early 19th c., 8 x 12", 4 1/2" h. (ILLUS., top next page)......... **$29,900**

Very Rare Early Pennsylvania Slide-Lid Box with Floral Decoration

BUTTER MOLDS & STAMPS

Acorn stamp, round w/one-piece handle, lightly scrubbed surface, 19th c., 4" d. **$403**

American eagle stamp, round, carved w/a stylized eagle w/a shield on its breast, stained, minor edge flakes, 4 5/8" d. **$316**

American eagle stamp, round, shallow carved bird w/a shield in its talons, enclosed by leafy branches, one-piece handle, old refinishing, 2 5/8" d. **$230**

Compass star & hearts stamp, round, large one-piece handle also w/a faintly carved compass star, scrubbed surface, 4 1/4" d. **$489**

Unusual Scoop & Lollipop Butter Stamp

Lollipop stamp & scoop, carved wood w/natural brown patina, a wide shallow rounded scoop blade w/a projecting top handle ending in a small flat round print carved w/a small cow, edge wear on scoop, 19th c., 6 3/4" w., 12" l. (ILLUS.) ... **$575**

Swan stamp, miniature cased stamp of swan w/extended wings, 1 3/4" d. **$330**

CANDLESTICKS & CANDLEHOLDERS

Also see Antique Trader Books Lamps & Lighting Price Guide.

Unusual Cottage-form Butter Mold

Cottage mold, carved wood, four-part, the interior sides carved w/cottage windows, a pitched roof & door, 5 3/4" w., 7" h. (ILLUS.) **$58**

Lollipop stamp, carved w/a stylized eagle & leaf design, refinished, 4" d., 9" l. **$385**

Lollipop stamp, round, carved wood, border w/star center, metal-covered handle w/metal insert, stamped patent mark on back, edge wear, worm holes, 9" l. **$275**

Candelabra with Oriental Figures

Early 20th Century American Sterling Silver Candelabra

Candelabra, gilt-bronze, three-light, Oriental taste, a square foot supporting a heavy dark patinated reeded column below the figure of an Oriental man on one & an Oriental woman on the other, each of them w/leafy scrolls w/tiny bells issuing from their heads below a leaf-cast blossom supporting three leaf-trimmed upturned & outswept candlearms ending in bird heads topped by leaf-cast inverted bell sockets, objects missing from hand of one figure, France, late 19th c., 20 1/2" h., pr. (ILLUS., previous page) **$1,610**

Napoleon III-style Candelabra

Candelabra, patinated bronze, four-light, in the "Pompeian" taste, a tripod base w/three paw feet on disks w/scrolled leaves surrounding the tall slender reeded shaft w/a ring-turned urn-form top supporting the three upturned candlesocket arms in the form of an Ancient Roman lamp surrounding a central taller socket, Napoleon III-style, France, third quarter 19th c., 23 1/4" h., pr. (ILLUS.) **$1,840**

Candelabra, sterling silver, five-light, a large waisted & ogee-domed base w/four scroll feet, supporting a baluster-form standard set w/a detachable set of four reeded serpentine branches around a central short column, all topped by a candlesocket, decorated overall w/elaborate chased gadroons & acanthus leaves, America, ca. 1920, 20" h., pr. (ILLUS., top of page) **$2,070**

Candelabra, sterling silver, three-light, a shaped round base w/a scroll & gadroon border, rising to a knopped baluster-form stem, topped by a pair of detachable branches w/reeded arms & three spool-form sockets, each w/a removable nozzle, mark of Tiffany & Co., New York, New York, ca. 1920, 15" h., pr. **$10,458**

Unusual Late Wrought-Iron Candelabra

Candelabra, wrought iron, an arched tripod base w/penny feet supporting a slender tall rod fitted w/a spring-adjustable cross bridge w/the top bar fitted at each end w/a small cylindrical candle socket, 20th c., 12" w., 21 3/4" h. (ILLUS., previous page) **$360**

Adjustable Trammel-style Candleholder

Candleholder, wrought iron trammel-type, a slender bar ending in a U-shape fitted w/a small cylindrical candle socket, the bar adjusting in a sawtooth trammel bar w/a long hooked top, some rust & pitting, early, adjusts for 14" to 22 1/2" (ILLUS.).................. **$173**

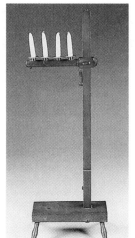

Old Wooden Adjustable Candlestand

Candlestand, wooden, adjustable, a cricket-style Windsor base fitted w/a tall square wood shaft w/a turn-key adjustable bridge arm fitted w/four brass candle cups, early, 14 1/2" w., 44" h. (ILLUS.)
.... **$201**

Candlestick, brass, high ringed cone-shaped base below the four-knob slender standard supporting the tall ringed cylindrical socket w/side hole for removing candle stub, probably Europe, possible Dutch, 18th c., 6 1/4" d., 10 1/2" h. (ILLUS., top next column) **$230**

Tall Early European Brass Candlestick

Fine Early Federal Brass Candlesticks

Candlesticks, brass, Federal style, a square stepped base tapering sides to the tall plain square & slightly flaring standard w/a flared, ringed top supporting a tall ringed bell-form socket w/a wide rolled rim, American, ca. 1790-1815, 10" h., pr. (ILLUS.) **$690**

Brass "King of Diamonds" Candlesticks

Candlesticks, brass, "King of Diamonds" patt., square foot w/beveled corners below the stepped base & ring-turned shaft w/a large diamond-cast center knob, tall socket w/flaring rim, bases marked, push-ups present, England, late 19th - early 20th c., 12 1/4" h. pr. (ILLUS.).......... **$460**

French Victorian Figural Candlesticks

Candlesticks, gilt-brass, slate & wood, Napoleon III style, each modeled as the figure of a seated putto holding aloft a candle socket, on black wood pedestal base wrapped w/a wide brass band embossed w/frolicking putti above the cylindrical black slate base, France, third quarter 19th c., 32" h., pr. (ILLUS.) **$1,265**

Bronze & Enamel Altar-type Candlesticks

Candlesticks, gilt-bronze & enamel, pricket altar-type, the domed & scroll-pierced base raised on three outswept paw feet, the sides of the dome fitted w/round medallions w/a red enamel ground, one w/the initials "S.J.," one with building tools & the third w/flowers, each separated by a small jeweled cabochon, the tall ringed standard trimmed w/cast leaves & swags, a wide low scallop-topped bobeche around the pricket candleholder, probably from St. Joseph's Altar, France, late 19th c., 25" h., pr. (ILLUS.) **$978**

Rare 17th Century Pewter Candlesticks

Candlesticks, pewter, round tapering ringed foot below a wide squatty bulbous base centered by the ring- and knob-turned shaft w/a cylindrical socket, Europe, 17th c., one shaft slightly bent, unmarked, base 5" d., 7 1/2" h., pr. (ILLUS.) **$1,200**

Early Hog Scrapper-style Candlesticks

Candlesticks, steel, hog scrapper-style, a wide round & slightly domed base & cylindrical shaft w/a push-up ejector, flattened rim w/thin curved finger grip, possibly Shaker-made, 19th c., 5 1/2" h., pr. (ILLUS.)... **$345**

Candlesticks, sterling silver, Art Nouveau style, in the Athenic patt., a round ringed base applied w/leaves & openwork arched undulating bud supports continuing to the base of the tapering cylindrical stem chased w/swirling leaves, the vase-form sockets similarly decorated, w/removable circular nozzle, mark of Gorham Mfg. Co., Providence, Rhode Island, ca. 1905, 10 1/4" h., pr. (ILLUS., top next page)... **$10,158**

Candlesticks, sterling silver, George II-style w/a square gadrooned base rising to a knopped stem, topped by a spool-form socket, removable round nozzle, mark of Ensko, New York, New York, 20th c., 10 1/2" h., set of 4 .... **$6,573**

Rare Gorham Art Nouveau Candlesticks

Unusual Tall Iron Pricket Candlesticks

Candlesticks, wrought iron, a wide round dished base raised on three scroll feet, centering a very tall slender center shaft topped by a pricket-style candleholder fitted w/an open ring candle support, a flattened angled small candle arm about halfway down the shaft w/a small ringed candleholder, a small angled hanging hook further up the shaft, overall 23 1/2" h., pr. (ILLUS.) **$780**

Old Brass Chamberstick

Chamberstick, brass, a shallow round dished base w/a rim loop handle w/finger grip, the central cylindrical shaft w/a flattened rim, w/ejector knob on the shaft, 6" d., 4" h. (ILLUS.) **$143**

Two Pairs of Swiss Silver Chambersticks

Chambersticks, silver, an oval dished base w/reeded rim, the cylindrical stem w/a pierced slot for sliding knob to raise the candle & a long loop handle, detachable round socket nozzle, marked by Ludwig Friedrich Brugger, Bern, Switzerland, ca. 1810, 8" h., pr. (ILLUS. left with other Swiss chambersticks, bottom previous page) **$1,912**

Chambersticks, silver, oval dished base w/a shaped reeded rim, the cylindrical stem w/a pierced slot for a sliding knob w/scroll handle to raise the candle & a long open loop handle, detachable circular socket nozzle, stem engraved w/a crest & motto beneath a coronet, marked by Ludwig Friedrich Brugger, Bern, Switzerland, ca. 1810, 8 1/4" h., pr. (ILLUS. right with other pair of Swiss chambersticks, bottom previous page) **$1,912**

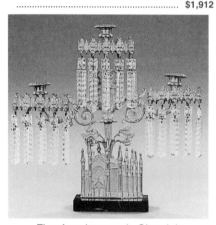

Fine American-made Girandole

Girandole, gilt-brass & marble, three-light, Bigelow Chapel design, a rectangular black marble base supporting the silhouetted gilt model of a cathedral w/a reeded back upright mounted w/leafy scrolls & continuing up to a tall central scrolled shaft topped by a socket & a grapevine-cast ring suspending long facet-cut prisms, two scrolls arms at the sides, each ending in a matching socket & prism-hung ring, signed by W.F. Shaw, Boston, Massachusetts, ca. 1850, 17" w., 16 1/2" h. (ILLUS.) **$633**

Rush light holder, iron & wood, heavy, roughly turned large wood block base supporting a tightly spiral-twisted wrought-iron upright w/a pliers-style top for gripping a rush light, the other arm of the hinged pliers also tightly twisted & angled to support a round candle pan, late 18th c., overall 10 3/4" h. (ILLUS., top next column) **$575**

Early Wood & Iron Rush Light Holder

CANES & WALKING STICKS

Walking Stick with Carved Man's Head

Burl wood & stick walking stick, the burl knot handle carved w/a realistic head of a bearded man w/open mouth, inset glass eyes & turban-type head cover, a thin bone ferrule to the knotty stick shaft w/a nice dark patina, age cracks, late 19th - early 20th c., overall 39 1/2" l. (ILLUS.) **$201**

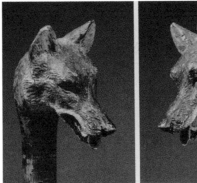

Two Views of a Finely Carved Fox Head Cane Handle

Carved & painted wood cane, the arched handle realistically carved as a fox head w/an open mouth & tongue & small glass eyes h.p. w/a naturalistic painted finish, the neck continues into the varnished wood shaft w/a metal tip, late 19th c., age crack, handle 3 x 3", overall 36" l. (ILLUS. of two views of the handle).... **$1,208**

Two Views of a Carved Foxhound Head Cane Handle

Carved & painted wood cane, the arched handle realistically carved w/a foxhound head w/natural painted coloring in tans, browns, black & white & inset eyes, neck continues into the mottled wood shaft w/a peeling varnish finish, iron tip, late 19th c., handle 1 1/4 x 2 1/2", overall 37 3/4" l. (ILLUS. of two views of the handle) **$1,150**

Two Views of a Carved Boar Head Cane

Carved & stained wood cane, the angled short wood handle carved as a realistic boar head w/a dark-stained head, inset glass eyes & ivory tusks, a narrow sterling silver ferrule w/English hallmarks, on a malacca shaft ending in a worn horn tip, one glass eye chips, late 19th - early 20th c., handle, 1 1/2 x 2 3/4", overall 35" l. (ILLUS. of two views) **$633**

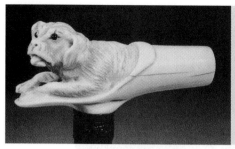

Two Views of a Dog in Shoe Carved Ivory Cane Handle

Ivory & mahogany or walnut cane, the T-shaped ivory handle carved as a Spaniel-like dog emerging from a large stylized shoe, head up w/open mouth & jet bead eyes, narrow embossed silver collar, light mahogany or walnut shaft w/a worn horn tip, late 19th c., handle 1 3/4 x 4", overall 33 3/4" l. (ILLUS. of two views of the handle) **$920**

mouth, pierce-carved horns & nice patina, a thin silver collar & worn brass & iron ferrule attached to the wooden shaft, late 19th c., handle 1 3/4 x 1 3/4", overall 34 1/2" l. (ILLUS. of two views of the handle, bottom of page) **$920**

Sterling & Ivory Elephant Head Cane

Walking Stick with Ivory Bulldog Head

Ivory & sterling silver & bamboo cane, the T-shaped handle in ivory w/one end carved w/a realistic elephant headd w/jet bead eyes, the rest of the ivory handle decorated w/sterling silver overaly in an engraved floral vine design, silver ferrule above the bamboo-type shaft ending in a white metal tip, restoration where head meets shaft, late 19th - early 20th c., handle 1 1/2 x 4 1/4", overall 34 3/4" l. (ILLUS.) **$575**

Ivory & malacca walking stick, the ivory handle carved as a realistic Bulldog head w/inset glass eyes, a gold-plated collar & malacca shaft, late 19th c., handle 2 x 2", overall 34 1/4" l. (ILLUS.) **$805**

Ivory & rosewood walking stick, the ivory handle carved as a buffalo head w/open

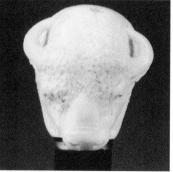

Two Views of Buffalo Head Walking Stick Handle

Two Views of a Carved Soldier Head with Helmet Walking Stick

Silver Snake Head Cane Handle

Silver & exotic wood cane, the silver figural handle in the form of a realistic cobra snake head w/detailed scales & red cabochon eyes, silver marked "900," on an exotic wood shaft w/a worn horn tip, late 19th c., handle, 2 3/4 x 3 1/4", overall 35 1/2" l. (ILLUS.)..................................... **$518**

Naughty French Victorian Cane

Partridgewood & ivory cane, brothel-type, a smooth partridgewood shaft w/a white metal & iron ferrule & rope-turned silver collar joining it to the figural carved walrus ivory handle, the handle carved as a French lady of pleasure wearing a fancy hat & a high-collared fashionable dress w/a flimsy blouse revealing her breasts, the reverse inscribed "Madame Plaisir, Orleans" (Lady Pleasure), France, ca. 1880, overall 36" l. (ILLUS. of handle) **$4,480**

Sterling Silver Swan Head Cane Handle

Sterling silver & exotic wood cane, the
sterling silver L-shaped handle in the form
of a realistic swan head w/a long bill, detailed feathers & inset glass eyes, English
hallmarks & the name "Brigg," the exotic
wood shaft ending in a worn white metal &
iron tip, late 19th c., handle 2 1/4 x 3 1/2",
overall 34 1/2" l. (ILLUS.) **$1,035**

**White metal, ivory & mahogany walking
stick,** the handle w/the carved ivory
head of a bearded soldier wearing a ornately chased white metal helmet
w/cheek guards & collar, on a tapering
mahogany shaft w/a white metal tip, late
19th - early 20th c., handle 3 1/2" h.,
overall 34" l. (ILLUS.of two views, top of
previous page) **$920**

CANS & CONTAINERS

Pennzoil Aviation Oil 5 Quart Can

Aviation oil, "Pennzoil Safe Lubrication,"
cylindrical 5 qt. can, printed in yellow,
black & red w/a large image of a United
Airplines propellor-driven airplane over
the company logo, ca. 1940s-50s, a few
dents & scratches, light rust (ILLUS.)........ **$121**

Early BB Special Coffee 5 lb. Pail

Coffee, "BB Special High Grade Coffee,"
cylindrical 5 lb. pail, red & black sides,
domed unpainted shoulder & short cylindrical neck w/a fitted cover & wire bail
handle w/turned wood grip, a few random
chips, light wear, early 20th c. (ILLUS.) **$191**

Ten-Pound Betteryet Peanut Can

Peanuts, "Betteryet Whole Salted Peanuts," round 10-pound tin w/a gold
ground printed w/thin red stripes, the
front w/a large black & gold oval band enclosing more advertising & facing figures
of black men each holding a large peanut, Old Dominion Peanut Corp. early
20th c., overall very good, 9 1/2" d.,
7 1/2" h. (ILLUS.) **$270**

English Mazawattee Tea Tin

Tea, "Mazawattee Tea," rectangular three-
pound tin w/a fitted cover & rounded corners, printed on the top & sides w/a colored scene of three young black boys
drinking tea, England, early 20th c., good
w/scattered scrapes & scratches,
5 1/2 x 8 1/2", 5 3/4" h. (ILLUS.) **$115**

Large Sweet Cuba Tobacco Can

Tobacco, "Sweet Cuba Tobacco," large cylindrical can w/a thin squared hinged lid, printed in dark blue & gold w/a finely striped background centered by a large rectangular brown panel w/gold lettering, held 48 packages of tobacco, early 20th c., 8 1/2" d., 11 1/2" h. (ILLUS., previous page) **$115**

Large Sweet Mist Chewing Tobacco Bin

Tobacco, "Sweet Mist Chewing Tobacco," large cylindrical store bin w/squared hinged lid, bright yellow background w/red lettering around a large round scene of small children playing in a fountain, held 48 packages, late 19th c., overall very good condition, 8 1/4" d., 11 1/2" h. (ILLUS.) **$288**

Rectangular Sweet Mist Tobacco Bin

Tobacco, "Sweet Mist Chewing Tobacco," large upright rectangular store bin, cardboard w/tin base & rectangular top w/hinged lid, bright yellow background w/red lettering around a large round scene of small children playing in a foun-

tain, held 48 packages, late 19th c., some rust & stains, 8 1/2" d., 11" h. (ILLUS.) **$288**

Early World's Navy Tobacco Tin

Tobacco, "World's Navy Tobacco," nearly square tin, the top in red w/yellow wording around a gold circle printed w/two views of the world globe above navy ships, yellow sides w/black wording, overall wear & light rust, ca. 1930s, 6 x 7" (ILLUS.) **$25**

CASTORS & CASTOR SETS

Castor bottles were made to hold condiments for table use. Some were produced in sets of several bottles housed in silver plated frames. The word also is sometimes spelled "Caster."

Six-bottle Castor Set in Footed Frame

Castor set, a silver plated frame w/central fancy arched & pierced tall handle & pedestal base, a stamped band of geometric design around the top of the domed base & the bottle holder frame, holds six clear pressed & etched glass bottles, late 19th c., overall 19" h. (ILLUS.) **$138**

Five-bottle Castor Set in Pairpoint Frame

Castor set, a silver plated frame w/central fancy pierced tall handle & pedestal base, two clear engraved tall cruets, two tall clear engraved shaker bottles & one short clear engraved shaker, frame marked by Pairpoint, late 19th c., overall 16 1/2" h., the set (ILLUS.)........................ **$201**

Rare French Liqueur Castor Set

Castor set, "cave à liqueurs," a large rectangular gilt-bronze framework w/beveled glass sides & tops folding up to display the interior fitted w/a tiered gilt-brass rack containing four parcel-gilt etched glass liqueur decanters w/cut glass stoppers & ten matching liqueur goblets, the interior base lined w/a mirror, cut starbursts centered on each glass side, w/original gilt-

brass key, France, late 19th c., case 14 1/2" l., 12" h., the set (ILLUS.)........... **$4,140**

Pickle Castor with Clear Pressed Glass Insert

Pickle castor, clear pressed glass cylindrical arched loop design insert, in ornate silver plate frame w/high domed cover, tongs, & a pickle fork, the frame w/a Meriden mark, 19th c., 10 1/2" h. (ILLUS.)....... **$288**

Decorated Cobalt Blue Pickle Castor

Pickle castor, cobalt blue blown glass insert, ovoid shape ornately enameled w/gold scrolls & tiny dotted blossoms, in a footed silver plate holder w/high arched handle & tongs at the side, late 19th c., overall 12" h. (ILLUS.)............................... **$500**

Pickle Castor with Cranberry Glass Insert

Cranberry Glass Pickle Castor with Fork

Pickle castor, cranberry mold-blown insert in the Inverted Thumbprint patt., cylindrical body enameled w/white & yellow daisies & green leaves w/gilt trim, domed & stepped silver plate cover w/pierced flat round finial, ornate silver plate stand & tongs, silver marked by the Brooklyn Silver Co., late 19th c., overall 11" h. (ILLUS.).............................. **$403**

Pickle castor, cranberry mold-blown insert in the Inverted Thumbprint patt., squatty bulbous base w/a wide cylindrical body, ornate silver plate stand & fork, late 19th c., resilvered, overall 10" h. (ILLUS., next column) **$475**

CERAMICS

Also see Antique Trader Pottery & Porcelain Ceramics Price Guide, *5th Edition.*

Abingdon

From about 1934 until 1950, Abingdon Pottery Company, Abingdon, Illinois, manufactured decorative pottery, mainly cookie jars, flowerpots and vases. Decorated with various glazes, these items are becoming popular with collectors who are especially attracted to Abingdon's novelty cookie jars.

Abingdon Mark

Abingdon Leaf Ashtray

Ashtray, Leaf, in the shape of a maple leaf, white interior, black exterior, No. 660, 1948-50, 5 1/2" d. (ILLUS.)
.... **$35**

Abingdon Donkey & Elephant Ashtrays

Ashtray, round, black w/black donkey standing on top, No. 510, 1940-41, 5 1/2" d. (ILLUS. left, w/elephant ashtray, top of page) **$150**

Ashtray, round, white w/black elephant standing on top w/trunk raised, No. 509, 1940-41, 5 1/2" d. (ILLUS. right, w/donkey ashtray, top of page) **$150**

Bookends, figures of Russian dancers w/arms crossed at chest, fez-type hats, rectangular bases, white, No. 321, 1934-40, 6 1/2" h. (ILLUS., bottom of page) **$250-300**

Bookends, model of sea gull, spread wings, No. 305, ivory glaze, 1934-1942, 6" h., pr. (ILLUS. left w/model of sea gull, top of page 114) **$150-165**

Bookends/planters, model of dolphin, No. 444D, blue glaze, 5 3/4" h., pr. **$80**

Abingdon Chinese Bowl

Bowl, 9 x 11" oval, Chinese, gently flaring body on short rectangular feet, white floral decoration on white ground, No. 345, 1935-37 (ILLUS.) **$200**

Abingdon Russian Dancer Bookends

Abingdon Salad Bowl & Candleholders

Bowl, salad, 10" d., 5" h., Rope patt., scalloped rim, ropetwist foot, turquoise, No. 313, 1934-36 (ILLUS. center w/Quatrain candleholders, top of page)......................... **$75**

Candleholder, double, No. 479, Scroll patt., 4 1/2" h. **$15**

Candleholders, Quatrain patt., quatrefoil shapes w/center hole for candle, turquoise, No. 360, 1935-36, pr. (ILLUS. w/Rope salad bowl, top of page)................. **$75**

Console bowl, No. 532, Scroll patt., 14 1/2" l. **$20**

Cookie jar, Baby, No. 561, 11" h. **$750-1,000**

Cookie jar, Bo Peep, No. 694D, 1950, 12" h. **$375**

Cookie jar, Clock, No. 563, 9" h. **$130**

Cookie jar, Daisy, No. 677, 1949-50, 8" h. (ILLUS., next column) **$95**

Cookie jar, Floral/Plaid, No. 697, 8 1/2" h. **$150-250**

Cookie jar, Humpty Dumpty, No. 663, 10 1/2" h. **$275**

Abingdon Daisy Cookie Jar

Cookie jar, Little Ol' Lady, No. 471, 9" h., various decorations, each (ILLUS. of three, bottom of page)....................... **$200-300**

Little Ol' Lady Cookie Jars

Abingdon Gull Figurine & Bookends

Model of heron, No. 574, tan glaze,
5 1/4" h. **$68**

Model of peacock, No. 416, turquoise
glaze, 7" h. **$96**

Model of sea gull, w/spread wings, No.
562, 1942, 5" h. (ILLUS. right w/book
ends, top of page) **$50-75**

Pitcher, 15" h., Grecian patt., No. 613 (ILLUS.
right w/vase) **$150**

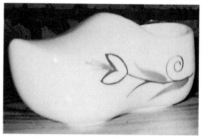

Abingdon Dutch Shoe Planter

Planter, Dutch shoe, stylized tulip decoration on white ground, No. 655D, 1948,
5" l. (ILLUS.)... **$125**

Planter, model of a puppy, No. 652D,
6 3/4" l. **$75**

Planter, short foot, flared sides rising to
scroll ends, white, No. 476, 10" w., 3" h.
(ILLUS., bottom of page)............................ **$30**

String holder, Chinese head, No. 702,
5 1/2" h. **$500**

Vase, 3 1/2" h., No. A1, whatnot type............ **$100**

Grecian Pitcher & Vase

Abingdon Planter

Vase, 10 1/4" h., Fern Leaf, tall ribbed leaf-shape sides taper out to top opening, blue, No. 422, 1937-39 (ILLUS. left w/smaller Fern Leaf vase, top of previous page) $95

Vase, 15" h., floor-type, Grecian patt., No. 603 (ILLUS. left w/pitcher, page 114)........ $150

Wall pocket, figural butterfly, No. 601, 8 1/2" h.. $150

Wall pocket, figural Dutch boy, No. 489, 10" h. $150

Abingdon Wall Pockets

Wall pocket, Leaf, overlapping pink veined leaves, No. 724, 1950, scarce, 10 x 5 1/2" (ILLUS. top w/Triad wall pocket) $75

Morning Glory Wall Pocket

Wall pocket, Morning Glory, trumpet form, pink, No. 377, 1936-50, 7 1/2" h. (ILLUS.).... $35

Wall pocket, Triad, in the form of three pink connected flowerpots, No. 640, 1940, 5 1/2 x 8" (ILLUS. bottom w/Leaf wall pocket) $40-50

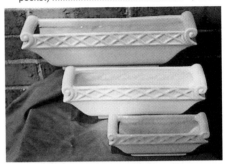

Various Sized Window Boxes

Window boxes, No. 477, 13 1/2" l., No. 476, 10 1/2" l., No. 475, 7" l., each (ILLUS.).... $25-35

American Painted Porcelain

During the late Victorian era, American artisans produced thousands of hand-painted porcelain items including tableware, dresser sets, desk sets, and bric-a-brac. These pieces of porcelain were imported and usually bear the marks of foreign factories and countries. To learn more about identification, evaluation, history and appraisal, the following books and newsletter by Dorothy Kamm are recommended: American Painted Porcelain: Collector's Identification & Value Guide, Comprehensive Guide to American Painted Porcelain, *and* Dorothy Kamm's Porcelain Collector's Companion.

Berry spoon holder, pierced handles, decorated w/two clusters of blackberries, light blue border, burnished gold rim & handles, marked "Bavaria," ca. 1894-1914, 4 5/8 x 10" $65

Bonbon Box with Peacock Decor

Bonbon box, cov., round, low domed cover decorated w/a conventional design of three intertwined peacocks, baby blue base, burnished gold rims & feet, opal luster interior, marked "T&V Limoges - France," 1892-1907 (ILLUS.) $125

Bonbon dish, round w/gold upright ring handles, decorated w/clusters of currants on a multicolored ground, an inner border band w/gilded outlines of spider webs & currant clusters, burnished gold rim, signed "I.A. Johnson, 1915" & marked "UNO-IT - Favorite - Bavaria," 6 3/8" d. **$55**

Bouillon cup & saucer, decorated w/a curvilinear geometric design in burnished gold outlined in dark blue, burnished gold rims & handles, marked "T & V - Limoges - France," ca. 1892-1907........................... **$30**

Small Footed Bowl

Bowl, 5 1/2" d., 2 3/4" h., pedestal foot, decorated w/a conventional border in moss, yellow, orange & burnished gold on an ivory ground, dark green base, burnished bold rim & band, marked w/"La Seynie - P and P - Limoges - France," 1903-17 (ILLUS.)........................... **$50**

Butter tub, round, decorated w/forget-me-nots on an ivory ground, burnished gold rim & handles, signed "Tossy," marked "T & V - Limoges - France," ca. 1892-1917 (no pierced insert) **$50**

Cake plate, pierced rim handles, scalloped edge, decorated w/a four-panel design w/conventional-style flowers in each panel, burnished gold border outlines, dotted grounds & rim, signed w/illegible cipher & marked "HR - Charlotte - Bavaria," ca. 1887+, 9 1/8" d........................... **$95**

Individual Cake Plate with Wild Roses

Cake plate or cookie tray, individual size, paneled sides, open handles, decorated w/a cluster of pink wild roses on a multicolored pastel ground, signed "R.J. '30" (ILLUS.)...................................... **$35**

Celery dish, long narrow shallow boat-form w/squared ends, decorated w/a border design of daisies & leaves on a pastel polychrome ground, ivory center, signed "Weiler," 1900-20, 5 3/4 x 12 3/4" (ILLUS., bottom of page)........................... **$67**

Chocolate cup & saucer, decorated w/yellow primrose on a shaded yellow brown ground, burnished gold rims, cup base & handle, signed "A. Brown," marked "Haviland - Limoges - France," ca. 1894-1931 .... **$35**

Chocolate pot, cov., decorated w/cluster of pink roses on a pastel polychrome ground, burnished gold knob & handle, signed "M.H. Dorothy," marked "GDA - France," ca. 1900-41.................................. **$225**

Cracker jar, cov., decorated w/white wild roses on a pastel polychrome ground w/burnished gold handles, signed "A.S.S.," marked "Royal" & wreath w/"O. & E.G.," 1898-1918 .... **$70**

Celery Dish with Daisy Border

Hair receiver, cov., squatty round form on three gold curved legs, decorated w/a conventional rose design in burnished gold, burnished gold rim & feet, signed "Ferver," ca. 1900-10, 3 7/8" d., 3 1/4" h. (ILLUS., previous page) **$50**

Decorated Hairpin Box

Hairpin box, cov., oval, decorated w/a conventional-style rose, leaf & stem border on a burnished gold ground, ivory top, light blue base, marked "Favorite - Bavaria," ca. 1908-1915, 1 1/2 x 4 1/2", 1 3/4" h. (ILLUS.) **$30**

Mayonnaise bowl & underplate, decorated w/clusters of forget-me-nots on a pale blue border, ivory ground, burnished gold rims & feet, signed "AG," marked "Stouffer," 1906-1914, bowl 4 1/2" d., underplate 5 7/16" d., 2 pcs. **$40**

Muffin dish, cov., round, decorated w/pink wild roses & greenery on a pastel polychrome ground, burnished gold rim & handles, signed "E. Starer," marked "J & C - 'Louise' - Bavaria," ca. 1902, 9 1/4" d., 4" h. **$325**

Mug, decorated w/colorful yellow & yellowish red gooseberries on a polychrome ground, marked w/a crown & two shields w/"Vienna - Austria," ca. 1900-15, 4 3/4" h. **$65**

Mustard jar w/attached underplate & cover, decorated w/conventional-style water lilies on a light blue & burnished gold ground, burnished gold handle & rims, marked "D. & Co. - France," ca. 1879-1900, 3" h. **$45**

Napkin ring, decorated w/forget-me-nots, white enamel trim & burnished gold rims, signed "Luken," ca. 1895-1926, 2" d. **$20**

Nut bowl, decorated in polychrome colors w/a squirrel, acorns & oak leaves on a branch, opal lustre interior, burnished gold feet & fluted rim, signed "Mrs. O.C. Oakes," 1900-20 .... **$100**

Olive dish, ring-handled, decorated w/heliotrope, w/etched & burnished gold border & burnished gold handle, marked "T & V - Limoges - France," ca. 1892-1907, 7 3/8" d. **$50**

Decorated Orange Cups

Orange cups, footed, decorated w/designs of orange blossoms on light blue & yellow grounds, embellished w/white & yellow enamel, burnished gold rim, base band, foot & prongs, signed "CKI," marked "T & V - France - Deposé," ca. 1900-15, 3 1/4" d., 2 3/4" h., pr. (ILLUS.) **$130**

Perfume Bottle with Daisy Decoration

Perfume bottle w/original gold stopper, squatty bulbous base tapering to a tall slender cylindrical neck, decorated around the lower body w/daisies & leaves on an ivory ground, burnished gold rim & stopper, marked w/a wreath & "O. & E.G. - Royal - Austria," 1898-1918, 4 3/4" h. (ILLUS.).. **$75**

Pin Tray with Moth Decoration

Pin tray, oval, decorated w/a border design of four blue & burnished gold moths, connected by a burnished gold & black band, ivory ground, burnished gold rim, signed "E. Arrindell - 1-2/18," marked w/a crown & double-headed eagle & "MZ - Austria," 1918 (ILLUS.)... **$50**

Pitcher, 9 3/4" h., claret-type, decorated w/a conventional Art Nouveau-style floral design outlined in gold, burnished gold handle & edges, signed "V.B. Chase," ca. 1890-1914 .... **$70**

American Painted Willets Belleek Tea Set

Salt & Peppers with Blue Insects

Salt & pepper shakers, tapering square form w/domed gold top, white ground decorated w/a conventional design of blue-winged insects, burnished gold tops, 1905-20, 3" h., pr. (ILLUS.) **$50**

Sandwich tray, double pierced handles, decorated w/a polychrome conventional design, burnished gold rim & handles, marked w/a crown & crossed scepters w/"Rosenthal - Bavaria," 1908-25, 10" l. .. **$110**

Sherbet, decorated w/daisies on an ivory ground, mother-of-pearl lustre interior, burnished gold border, rim & foot, signed "M. Paddock," marked "Epiag - Czechoslovakia," ca. 1920-39, 3 1/8" h....... **$50**

Soup plates, flanged rim decorated w/three clusters of seashells & seaweed on a very pale polychrome ground, burnished gold rims, signed "ALB," marked "H. & Co. - Haviland - Limoges - France," 1876-1879, 9" d., pr... **$55**

Sugar shaker, decorated w/Art Nouveau-style florals & squiggling border band in burnished gold, burnished gold pierced top, signed "E.C.R.," ca. 1905-15, 2 3/4" d., 4 1/2" h..................................... **$120**

Syrup jug, cov. decorated w/pink & ruby roses on a polychrome ground, burnished gold handle, knob & rims, opal lustre spout interior, marked "ADK - France," ca. 1891-1910, 4" h. (missing underplate) **$35**

Table top centerpiece, decorated w/a cluster of daisies on a pastel polychrome ground, burnished gold rim, signed "E. Miller," marked "T & V - Limoges - France," ca. 1892-1907, 11 5/8" d. **$90**

Tea set: cov. teapot, cov. sugar bowl & creamer; footed wide flattened cylindrical bodies, flat covers w/gold peg finials, angular gold handles, each decorated w/bur-

nished gold designs of stylized floral roundels alternating w/gold panels, artist-signed "MSF," Willets Belleek blanks, ca. 1880-1909, the set (ILLUS., top of page) **$300-400**

Toast set: plate & cup; 9 3/16 w. plate decorated w/conventional-style strawberries on an ivory ground, opal lustre cup interior, burnished gold borders, rims & handle, ca. 1925-30, 2 pcs........................ **$75**

Toothpick holder, decorated w/double violets on a pastel ivory & green ground, burnished gold rim, signed "Wats" & "Pitkin & Brooks Studio," marked "T & V - Limoges - France," 1903-10, 2 3/4" h. **$55**

Art Deco Design Painted Vase

Vase, 7 7/8" h., bulbous baluster-form w/wide flared neck, decorated w/two Art Deco-style floral panels in lustre & burnished gold, gold center band & base & neck bands, signed "M.D.P. 1920," marked w/a shield & "Thomas" (ILLUS.) ... **$125**

Vase, 7" h., bulbous base tapering to a tall slender neck, two-handled, decorated w/pink & yellow roses on a pastel polychrome ground, burnished gold rim, accents & handle, ca. 1900-20 .... **$65**

Jewelry

American painted porcelain jewelry comprises a unique category. While the metallic settings and porcelain medallions were inexpensive, the painted decoration was a work of fine art. The finished piece possessed greater intrinsic value than cos-

tume jewelry of the same period because it was a one-of-a-kind creation, but one that was not as expensive as real gold and sterling silver settings and precious and semiprecious jewels. Note that signatures are rare, backstamps lacking.

Dorothy Kamm

Bar pin, decorated w/pink roses & greenery, brass-plated bezel, ca. 1880s, 7/16 x 1 1/2" **$30**
Bar pin, decorated w/pink roses on a pale green ground, burnished gold tips & brass-plated bezel, ca. 1900-1915, 2 5/8" w. **$50**

Belt Buckle Brooch with Portrait

Belt buckle brooch, oval, decorated w/a profile of a woman wearing a pink top & white shawl, pink roses in her curly brown hair, black choker at her neck, burnished gold rim, gold-plated bezel, signed "M.e.M.," 1900-17, 1 7/8 x 2 3/8" (ILLUS.) **$175**

Belt Buckle Brooch with Pansy

Belt buckle brooch, oval, decorated w/a white pansy, accented w/white enamel, on a burnished gold ground, gold-plated bezel, 1900-17, 1 11/16 x 2 1/4" (ILLUS.) **$75**

Art Nouveau Florals on Belt Brooch

Belt buckle brooch, oval, decorated w/an Art Nouveau-style water lily design outlined w/raised paste, petals filled in w/lavender enamel, burnished green & gold background, gold-plated bezel, 1900-17, 1 7/8 x 2 5/8" (ILLUS.) **$150**

Bachelor Buttons on Belt Brooch

Belt buckle brooch, oval, decorated w/blue bachelor buttons & greenery on a polychrome ground, irregular burnished gold border outlined in black, gold-plate bezel, 1900-17, 1 7/8 x 2 5/8" (ILLUS.) **$115**
Belt buckle brooch, oval, decorated w/roses & greenery on a polychrome ground, burnished gold scalloped border outlined in black, gold-plated bezel, 1900-17, 1 15/16 x 2 11/16" **$125**
Brooch, decorated w/violets on a light yellow brown ground w/raised paste scrolled border covered w/burnished gold & burnished gold rims, gold-plated bezel, ca. 1890-1920, 1 1/2" d **$65**
Brooch, oval, decorated w/a conventional-style Colonial dame in light blue & yellow w/opal lustre background & burnished gold rim, brass-plated bezel, ca. 1915-25, 1 5/8 x 2 1/8" **$60**
Brooch, oval, decorated w/a conventional-style lavender iris & green leaves outlined in black on a yellow lustre ground w/white enamel highlights on petal edges & yellow enamel highlights on flower centers, burnished gold rim, gold-plated bezel, ca. 1900-20, 1 5/8 x 2 1/8" **$80**

Hatpin Head with Wild Roses

Hatpin, circular head, decorated w/pink wild roses & greenery on a yellow ground, burnished gold rim, gold-plated filigree setting, head 1 1/16" d., shaft 9" l. (ILLUS. of head) **$125**

Pendant, decorated w/a purple pansy w/white enamel center accents & burnished gold border, gold-plated bezel, ca. 1880s-1914, 1" d. **$60**

Pendant, oval, decorated w/forget-me-nots on a pastel polychrome ground w/white enamel highlights & burnished gold rim, gold-plated bezel, ca. 1900-25, 1 1/4 x 1 3/4" **$65**

Scarf pin, medallion-shaped, decorated w/violets, brass-plated bezel & shank, ca. 1880-1920, medallion 1 1/4" d., shank 3" l. **$75**

Shirtwaist Button with Clover Leaf

Shirtwaist button, oval w/shank, decorated w/a three-leaf clover in green on a yellow & brown ground, burnished gold rim, 7/8 x 1 1/16" (ILLUS.) **$25**

Shirtwaist Button with Flower

Shirtwaist button, round w/eye, decorated w/a conventional stylized long blossom flanked by pointed oval leaves in pale yellow, dark blue & black on a burnished gold ground, 1 1/16" d. (ILLUS.) **$35**

Shirtwaist set: oval brooch & pr. of oval cuff links; decorated w/blue forget-me-nots on an ivory background w/white enamel highlights, brass-plated mounts, ca. 1900-10, brooch w/burnished gold free-form border & rim, 1 3/8 x 1 3/4", cuff links w/burnished gold rims, 13/16 x 1 1/16", the set **$250**

Brooch from Shirtwaist Set

Shirtwaist set: oval brooch & two round buttons w/shank; each decorated w/forget-me-nots & greenery on a pastel polychrome ground, burnished gold rim, gold-plated bezel, brooch 1 1/4 x 1 3/4", buttons 15/16" d., the set (ILLUS. of brooch) ... **$90**

Watch chatelaine, oval, decorated w/a woman wearing a rose-colored bodice, light shading to dark warm green ground, set in gold-plated rim w/twisted gold edge, ca. 1880s, 1 1/8 x 1 3/8" **$175**

Amphora - Teplitz

In the late 19th and early 20th centuries numerous potteries operated in the vicinity of Teplitz in the Bohemian region of what was Austria but is now the Czech Republic. They included Amphora, RStK, Stellmacher, Ernst Wahliss, Paul Dachsel, Imperial and lesser-known potteries such as Johanne Maresh, Julius Dressler, Bernard Bloch and Heliosine.

The number of collectors in this category is growing while availability of pieces is shrinking. Prices for better, rarer pieces, including those with restoration, are continuing to appreciate.

The price ranges presented here are retail. They presume mint or near mint condition or, in the case of very rare damaged pieces, proper restoration. They reflect such variables as rarity, design, quality of glaze, size and the intangible "in-vogue factor." They are the prices that knowledgeable sellers will charge and knowledgeable collectors will pay.

Various Amphora-Teplitz Factory Marks

Bowl, 14 1/2" w., 4 3/8" h., an exotic Paul Dachsel design of calla lilies growing out of stems which originate at the bottom & gracefully extend around the sides to fully developed calla lilies at each end, in the center on each side are several "jewels" w/abstract leaves of high-glazed green w/gold overtones, mottled texture w/"jeweled" greenish gold embellishments, stamped over glaze w/intertwined "PD - Turn-Teplitz," handwritten over glaze "0/45" (ILLUS., bottom of page) .... **$10,500 - 11,000**

Bust of Richard Wagner

Bust of Richard Wagner, the somber looking composer mounted on a pedestal emblazoned "Wagner" on the front, the head w/a beautiful soft flesh-toned Amphora glaze, the pedestal w/a shriveled tan & white glaze w/shades of olive green highlights, one of a rare series of composers, impressed "Amphora" & "Austria" in ovals w/a crown, a circle w/"Imperial Amphora" & "250 -1," 19 3/4" h. (ILLUS.)...................... **$5,000-5,500**

Rare Amphora Candlestick

Candlestick, rare Amphora piece w/many of its special characteristics including jewels, spider webs, butterflies & wonderful soft muted Amphora glazes w/reds, blues & gold, a large handle extends from near the top of the socket, four smaller handles extend up & outward from the base, eleven jewels of various sizes & colors, impressed "Amphora" in an oval & a crown & "28," 14" h. (ILLUS.).. **$7,000-7,500**

Exotic Paul Dachsel Bowl

Amphora Russian Folk Art Teapot

Teapot, cov., Russian Folk Art Series, tall ovoid form w/flared foot & flat rim, arched C-form handle from rim to shoulder, short angled shoulder spout w/an arched brace to the rim, decorated on center front w/a large stylized bust portrait of a Russian cleric w/black beard & brown & blue hat, the portrait enclosed by a ring of blue stars & blue dots w/other bands of dots & teardrops about the top & base, all against a tan ground, the reverse w/a design of multiple triangles enclosed w/a ring of stars, impressed "Austria - Amphora" in ovals & "11892,47 - G" plus a crown, ca. 1907-08, 8 1/4" h. (ILLUS.) **$295**

Blue & Cream Amphora Teapot

Teapot, cov., wide squatty bulbous body tapering sharply to a small cylindrical neck bulbed at the top w/an arched handle from the back of the neck to the shoulder & a double-arch bracket from the neck to the tip of the long angled straight spout, the center of the side w/a large almond-shaped reserve w/a dark blue ground

decorated w/three stylized Macintosh Roses & flanked by a dark blue band continuing up the spout that is decorated w/a dark blue band decorated w/small yellow flower clusters, neck in blue w/matching florals, blue handle & brackets, the background of the body in creamy mottled white ground decorated w/scattered small yellow blossoms, similar to designs by Paul Dachsel, ca. 1906-07, impressed "Austria" & "Amphora" in ovals & a crown, impressed numbers "3974," overall 8" h. (ILLUS.) **$695**

Fine Amphora Portrait Vase

Vase, 5 3/8" h., bulbous base tapering to a cylindrical body w/a flattened shoulder centered by a tiny neck w/a flattened gold rim, the sides decorated in gold & white w/the bust profile portrait of a lovely Art Nouveau woman w/large white flowers in her swirling hair, base marked "Amphora - 477," missing two tiny pinhead size gold dots on shoulder (ILLUS.) **$2,300**

Small Dachsel Mushroom Vase

Vase, 5 1/2" h., cylindrical form w/a narrow angled shoulder to the cylindrical reticulated neck trimmed in gold, the sides decorated w/a birch forest landscape in white, blue, pinks & green w/a band of relief-molded brown & white mushrooms around the base, a Paul Dachsel design, marked "Paul Dachsel - Turn Teplitz - Made in Austria" (ILLUS.)...................... **$1,265**

Rare Amphora Cat Head Vase

Vase, 9" h., wide bulbous tapering form, rare form suggesting an inverted Tiffany lamp shade, four large Persian cat heads molded in full relief & projecting from the sides w/a forest of abstract trees w/160-170 opal-like translucent "jewels" symbolizing fruits, the jewels in various sizes & shades of opal blue mounted in gold surrounds, heavy gold rim, the tree branches extending to the jewels on a background of Klimt-like subtle gold circles, holes behind the jewels permit candlelight or an electric bulb to illuminate the jewels, cat heads finished in a soft pinkish gold w/traces of green & gold highlights on the ears, impressed "Amphora - Austria" in a lozenge, a crown & "8183 - 28" (ILLUS.) .... **$25,000+**

Vase, 10 5/8" h., figural, in the form of a prancing male lion, snarling open mouth, standing on a broad base narrowing at the top, numerous concentric circles form bands around the top & bottom, lion reflects an iridescent gold, green & rose combination of color, body of base in metallic green w/undertones of blues & splotches of reds, impressed "Amphora" & "Austria" in oval, a crown & "500-52," handwritten in black ink over glaze "CB - 613417," estimated value without jewels, $1,500-2,000, value w/jewels **$3,500-4,500**

Vase, 11" h., four gold Persian cat heads adorn a center-pillared body w/four surrounding gold "jeweled" arms extending from each cat head to the base, metallic blue w/a gold wash, cobalt blue "jewels," rare design, more common versions have cabochons instead of animal heads, marked "Amphora" & "Austria" in ovals, a crown & impressed "Imperial" circle mark & "11677 - 51" (ILLUS., next column) **$6,500-7,000**

Vase, 12 3/4" h., elegant form consisting of four beautifully veined tall leaves forming the funnel of the vase w/the stem of each leaf forming a handle extending into the

bottom, each stem issues an additional flat leaf extending across the bottom, leaves finished in a mottled orange w/touches of greens & yellows w/gold overtones (although marked by Ernst Wahliss the design indicates the work of Paul Dachsel who worked at various Amphora factories), rare, stamped over glaze "EW" red mark, impressed "9491," "9786a - 10" in ink over the glaze **$8,000-8,500**

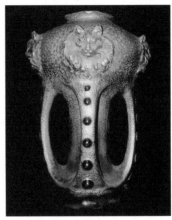

Vase with Persian Cat Heads

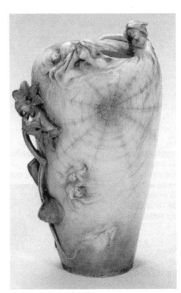

Teplitz Vase with Spider Web & Maidens

Vase, 12 3/4" h., tall ovoid body in creamy white decorated around the sides w/a gold spider web & molded around the closed rim w/emerging heads of Art Nouveau maidens w/other maiden heads around the sides, a large gold flower vine up one side, Teplitz mark, base drilled, ca. 1900 (ILLUS.) **$863**

Arequipa

Dr. Philip King Brown established The Arequipa Sanitorium in Fairfax, California, in the early years of the 20th century. In 1911 he set up a pottery at the facility as therapy for his female tuberculosis patients since he had been impressed with the success of the similar Marblehead pottery in Massachusetts.

The first art director was the noted ceramics designer Frederick H. Rhead who had earlier been art director at the Roseville Pottery.

In 1913 the pottery was separated from the medical facility and incorporated as The Arequipa Potteries. Later that year Rhead and his wife, Agnes, one of the pottery instructors, left Arequipa and Albert L. Solon took over as the pottery director. The corporation was dissolved in 1915 and the pottery closed in 1918 although the sanitorium remained in operation until 1957.

Arequipa Marks

Bowl, 6 1/2" d., 2 1/4" h., wide flat bottomed form w/squatty bulbous incurved sides w/a wide flat mouth, embossed w/eucalyptus branches under a dark matte green & blue glaze, stamped mark, incised "KH - 11" **$880**

Vase, 3 1/2" h., 2 1/2" d., miniature, simple ovoid body w/closed rim, decorated in squeeze-bag w/a rim band of holly leaves & red berries against a matte, mottled greenish blue ground, by Frederick Rhead, white & brown glaze mark **$6,325**

Vase, 4 1/4" h., 7" d., footed wide squatty bulbous form w/the wide shoulder tapering to a short flared neck, enamel-decorated w/a plant w/white berries against a semi-matte greyish blue ground, rare early mark, incised "AP - 1911" **$660**

Banko Ware

These collectible Japanese pottery wares were produced for domestic use and also exported in the late 19th and early 20th century. Pieces are finely detailed and composed of very thin clays in various colors including white, marbleized, grey, brown and tapestry. Traditional as well as whimsical pieces were produced, especially teapots. Banko Ware pieces generally have impressed markings on the base or handle. Decorative details could be painted, incised or applied in low or high relief.

Bowl, 6" w., green lotus-form w/attached frog at rim, heavily enameled **$150**

Creamer, bulbous paneled body w/a wide rim & small spout, applied handle, swirled green & tan clays, signed, 2" h. (ILLUS. left with marquetry creamer, bottom of page) **$20**

Creamer, Grayware, painted flowers & marked "Souvenir of Asbury Park" **$20**

Creamer, marquetry-style, bulbous sides tapering to a low ruffled rim & rim spout, slender applied handle, in shades of brown, green, cream & tan w/a gold rim band, signed, 2" h. (ILLUS. right with green & tan swirled creamer, bottom of page) **$45**

Creamer, marquetry-style, checkerboard design in brown & tan **$38**

Banko Swirled Clay & Marquetry Creamers

Banko Brown Creamer with Flowers

Creamer, ovoid body w/a wide arched spout, applied handle, dark brown clay enameled w/white & pink blossoms & green leaves, signed (ILLUS.).................... $30

Banko Marquetry Demitasse Cup & Saucer

Cup & saucer, demitasse-size, marquetry-style, round quilted-body cup in greens, brown & tans on a matching gently scalloped saucer, signed (ILLUS.).................... $45

Banko Leaf-shaped Dish with Owl

Dish, figural, molded of a green leaf w/a small owl perched on a branch at the rim, applied nut in the dish, impressed rectangular panel reads "Souvenir of Syracuse, N.Y.," marked "Made in Japan," 5" l. (ILLUS.)..................................... $55
Figure group, hand-formed row of three monkeys marked "Speak, Hear, See No Evil," late 19th c., 3" h. $135
Figure of an Oriental man, nodder-type w/long bald head, 5" h............................... $225
Planter, hanging-type, Grayware, enameled w/cranes, w/matching hanging chain $45
Planter, hanging-type, molded w/morning glories, w/matching hanging chain $75
Salt & pepper shakers, figural, model of a monkey holding a peach, inscribed fur, 2 1/2" h., pr... $100

Banko Grayware Enameled Tea Jar

Tea jar, cover & insert, Grayware, bulbous ovoid body w/a short cylindrical neck w/a fitted cover, enameled w/red & red leaves on a white-dotted ground, 3" h. (ILLUS.)..... $75
Teapot, cov., figural, model of a duck painted in natural colors & applied w/iris blossoms & leaves, 8" l. (ILLUS., top next page).. $300
Teapot, cov., figural, model of a peacock, tan clay w/colored enamels, marked "Made in Japan," 1920s $110
Teapot, cov., figural, model of a quail w/enameled floral decoration, 5" h........... $350
Teapot, cov., figural, model of a rectangular hut w/thatched roof, applied flowers & birds in colored enamels, small size, 5" l. (ILLUS. right with large hut teapot, middle next page) $295
Teapot, cov., figural, model of a rectangular hut w/thatched roof, applied flowers & a scene of people in a house in colored enamels, large size, 8" l. (ILLUS. left with small hut teapot, middle next page) $395
Teapot, cov., figural, model of an elephant w/mahout, marked "Made in Japan," 1930, 6 1/2" h... $125
Teapot, cov., figural, model of cat sitting up, enameled floral decoration........................ $400

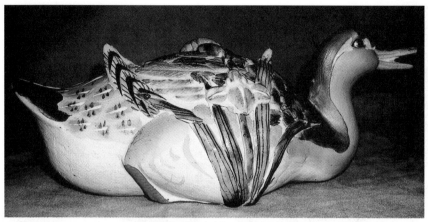

Banko Figural Duck Teapot

Large & Small Thatched Roof Hut Teapots

Teapot, cov., figural, shows the seven household Gods of Good Luck.................. **$325**

Teapot, cov., figural, the body molded w/six faces, face of a man forms the cover, 6" h. **$275**

Teapot, cov., gray clay decorated w/applied "Treasures," applied brown & gray rope tied in bows, impressed signature, 4" l...... **$100**

Teapot, cov., Grayware, applied grapes & leaves, heavily enameled, w/tea infuser insert, artist-signed.................................... **$120**

Teapot, cov., Grayware, squatty bulbous body w/short spout, low domed cover w/twisted applied handle w/further handles flanking the wide mouth, decorated overall w/hand-applied grapes & leaves & brightly enameled w/birds & flowers, impressed artist's signature, Japan, ca. 1900, 5" l., 3 1/2" h. (ILLUS., next column) **$150**

Banko Teapot with Grapes & Birds

Teapot, cov., marquetry & tapestry-style, cover w/spinning finial, impressed signature, 4" h.. **$70**

Banko Grayware Vase with Flowers

Vase, 4 1/2" h., Grayware, a tall trumpet-form base supporting a wide cylindrical body w/a wide tapering shoulder & flaring neck, enameled up the sides w/large white & yellow daisy-like flowers on green leafy stems, signed (ILLUS.)............. $50

Vase, 5" h., bulbous base w/long neck, flowing glaze enameled w/cranes...................... $75

Vase, 8" h., marbleized brown & tan clays enameled w/flying cranes, signed, late 19th c. $250

Wall pocket, figural, molded colorful bird........ $85

Wall pocket, figural, molded God of Good Fortune, 1916.. $85

Wall pocket, figural, molded woman carrying a basket... $75

Bauer

The Bauer Pottery was moved to Los Angeles, California, from Paducah, Kentucky, in 1909 in the hope that the climate would prove beneficial to the principal organizer, John Andrew Bauer, who suffered from severe asthma. Flowerpots

made of California adobe clay were the first production at the new location, but soon they were able to resume production of stoneware crocks and jugs, the mainstay of the Kentucky operation. In the early 1930s, Bauer's colorfully glazed earthen dinnerwares, especially the popular Ring-Ware pattern, became an immediate success. Sometimes confused with its imitator, Fiesta Ware (first registered by Homer Laughlin in 1937), Bauer pottery is collectible in its own right and is especially popular with West Coast collectors. Bauer Pottery ceased operation in 1962.

Bauer Mark

Bowl, batter, Ring-Ware, large................. $75-100

Casserole, w/holder, Ring-Ware, 5 1/2" h.
.... $60-75

Cookie jar, pastel Kitchenware.............. $100-150

Cup & saucer, Monterey Moderne patt. $20-30

Custard cup, Ring-Ware............................ $15-25

Gravy boat, Monterey patt........................ $30-40

Jug, ball-shape, La Linda patt. $40-50

Mixing bowl, speckled, 1950s, 6" h. $15-20

Oil jar, #122, 20" h. $750-1,000

Plate, chop-type, Ring-Ware, 15" d. $75-100

Plate, luncheon-type, Ring-Ware $20-25

Refrigerator set, stacking, Ring-Ware, 4 pcs. $250-350

Shakers, La Linda patt., old style.............. $20-25

Sugar bowl, Monterey patt. $20-25

Teapot, cov., Aladdin Lamp-shape, tan glaze (ILLUS., bottom of page) $80-120

Teapot, cov., Ring-Ware patt., yellow, 2-cup size... $125

Teapot, cov., Ring-Ware patt., yellow, 6-cup size.. $100-150

Teapot, Ring-Ware, 6 cup capacity........ $100-150

Teapot, cov., Ring-Ware patt., orangish red, 2-cup size.. $125

Vase, 8" h., Billy-type $50-75

Bauer "Aladdin Lamp" Teapot

Belleek

American Belleek
Marks:

American Art China Works - R&E, 1891-95

AAC (superimposed), 1891-95

American Belleek Company - Company name, banner & globe

Ceramic Art Company - CAC palette, 1889-1906

Colombian Art Pottery - CAP, 1893-1902

Cook Pottery - Three feathers w/"CHC," 1894-1904

Coxon Belleek Pottery - "Coxon Belleek" in a shield, 1926-1930

Gordon Belleek - "Gordon Belleek," 1920-28

Knowles, Taylor & Knowles - "Lotusware" in a circle w/a crown, 1891-96

Lenox China - Palette mark, 1906-1924

Ott & Brewer - crown & shield, 1883-1893

Perlee - "P" in a wreath, 1925-1930

Willets Manufacturing Company - Serpent mark, 1880-1909

Cook Pottery - Three feathers w/"CHC"

Baskets and Bowls
Lenox, bowl, 10 1/2" d., 3" h., h.p. Art Deco cameos of tulips accented w/heavy gold, artist-signed "Clara May," dated "22," palette mark **$325**

Ott and Brewer, basket, applied floral & leaf decoration, crown & sword mark, 6 x 8", 3" h.. **$600**

Ott and Brewer, bowl, h.p. flowers on a cream ground w/gilded thistle handles, crown & sword mark................................. **$500**

Handpainted Bowl with Gilt Trim

Willets, bowl, ovoid form w/small h.p. sprays of flowers over entire outside, gilding on ruffled rim, foot & handles, serpent mark (ILLUS.).................................... **$600**

Willets, bowl, 6 1/2" d., 3" h., handled, h.p. delicate floral sprays, ruffled top trimmed w/gold, gilt shaped handles, serpent mark **$425**

Willets, bowl, fruit, 10" d., 4" h., deep scalloped rim, h.p. inside & out w/images of grapes & foliage, highlighted w/heavy gold **$700**

Candlesticks and Lamps
Lenox, candlestick lamps, hexagonal inverted tulip shaped shades, h.p. roses joined by green swags & gilding, artist-signed "Trezisc," palette mark, shades 6" d., overall 18" h., pr............................. **$560**

Cups and Saucers
Ceramic Art Company, cabinet cup, on square footed base, enameled pink & gold saucer, 3 3/4" h. **$125**

Ceramic Art Company, cup & saucer, "Tridacna" body shape, cream-colored exterior, blue lustre interior w/gold handle & trim, CAC palette mark, saucer 5 1/4" d.... **$225**

Coxon Belleek, demitasse cup & saucer, h.p. "Boulevard" patt. gold around the rim of the cup & saucer, saucer 5" d. **$125**

Cup with Sterling Holder & Saucer

Lenox, demitasse cup & saucer, colored porcelain w/double gold rim & pink border w/enameled flowers, hammered sterling holder & saucer, palette mark, 2 1/2" d. saucer (ILLUS.).. **$95**

Demitasse Cup & Saucer with Holder

Lenox, demitasse cup & saucer, cream-colored porcelain w/double gold bands, flared rim, sterling saucer & reticulated holder w/angled handle, palette mark, 2" h. cup, 2 3/4" d. saucer (ILLUS.)............. **$75**

Morgan, cup & saucer, h.p. in the "Orient" patt., urn mark, saucer 5 1/4" d................ **$200**

Ott and Brewer, cup & saucer, "Tridacna" body shape, cream-colored exterior, blue lustre interior w/gold handle & rim, crown & sword mark, saucer 5 1/4" d. $225

Willets, bouillon cup & saucer, "Tridacna" body patt., pearlized pale blue exterior & white interior, serpent mark, 6 1/2" d. saucer $200

Willets, cup & saucer, coffee-size, cream-colored fluted body w/gold handle & trim, serpent mark, saucer 5 1/2" d. $175

Jars and Boxes

Ceramic Art Company, box, cov., lid w/ruffled edge, h.p. w/violets & foliage, accented w/gold, CAC palette mark, 1 3/4" h., 3 7/8" w. $295

Lidded Dresser Jar

Ceramic Art Company, dresser jar, cov., hand-decorated w/gold paste roses & stripes, CAC palette mark, 3 1/2" d., 5" h. (ILLUS.)... $195

Knowles, Taylor & Knowles Lotus Ware, rose jar, cov., "Orleans," body & lid w/ornately patterned & pierced overall design $3,200

Morgan Covered Mustard

Morgan, mustard, cov., h.p. cobalt band w/Deco-style enameled basket of fruit on front, gold-colored finial on lid w/opening for spoon, 5" h., 4" d. (ILLUS.) $150

Ott and Brewer, cracker jar & cover, hand-decorated w/gold paste flowers & gold handles, sword & crown mark, 5" d., 7" h. $475

Willets, humidor, cov., h.p. college crest on one side & painting of cigarettes & matches on other, serpent mark, 5 1/2" h., 4 1/4" w. $375

Mugs

Ceramic Art Company, Art Deco design w/heavy gold accents, CAC palette mark, 7" h.. $200

Baluster-form Mug

Ceramic Art Company, baluster-form, h.p. overall w/flowers & foliage on green ground, artist signed, CAC palette mark, 6" h. (ILLUS.) $175

Ceramic Art Company, h.p. peasant women in the Delft style of monochromatic blue on white, CAC palette mark, 5 1/2" h.. $175

Ceramic Art Company, h.p. scene of children flying kites, artist-signed "CHT," CAC palette mark, 4 3/4" h., 5 1/4" d. $225

Ceramic Art Company, portrait-type, h.p. portrait of a Native American Chief, CAC palette mark, 6" h. $1,100

Stein-type Mug with Grape Design

Ceramic Art Company, stein-type, h.p. all over w/images of grapes & foliage on blue & purple ground, CAC palette mark, 7 1/2" h. (ILLUS.) $225

Willets, tapering cylindrical form w/gilt handle, h.p. w/grape foliage on lilac band on paler ground, artist signed "M. Schaffer '10," serpent mark, 6" h. **$125**

Pitchers, Creamers and Ewers

Ceramic Art Company, cider pitcher, h.p. all around w/large pink roses & leaves, accented w/gold, beaded gold handle, CAC palette mark, 8" h., 6" d. **$400**

Cider Pitcher with Currants

Ceramic Art Company, cider pitcher, h.p. orange & currants & pale green leaves, 8" h., 6" d., CAC palette mark (ILLUS.) **$400**

Ceramic Art Company, pitcher, 6 1/2" h., tankard-type, h.p. grapes, leaves & vines on rust ground, heavy gold accents, CAC palette mark **$800**

Lenox Silver Overlay Creamer

Lenox, creamer, cream-colored body w/swags of silver overlay, 5 1/4" h., palette mark (ILLUS.) **$75**

Lenox, lemonade pitcher, w/h.p. lemons & foliage over entire body, artist-signed, 10 1/2" h., palette mark **$450**

Lenox, pitcher, 9" h., jug-type, handled, h.p. w/an overall floral design, trimmed in gold, palette mark **$500**

Ott and Brewer, creamer, cream-colored, hand-decorated w/gold paste foliage & an applied gilded thistle handle, crown & sword mark, 3 1/2" h. **$400**

Willets, apple cider pitcher, decorated w/h.p. apples & foliage on purple to pale ground, 6" h. **$550**

Willets Jug with Cavalier

Willets, pitcher, 8" h., jug-type, handled wide ovoid form w/short neck, h.p. scene of a bearded cavalier seated at a table w/a wine jug & goblet, serpent mark, (ILLUS.) **$500**

Willets, pitcher, 11 1/4" h., tankard-type, dragon-handled, h.p. w/wisteria, artist-signed **$900**

Willets, pitcher, 15" h., tankard-type, h.p. blackberries, leaves & vines on light green matte ground, artist-signed "Fisher," serpent mark..................................... **$825**

Plates and Platters

Gordon Belleek, plate, 8" d., decorated w/birds, heavy enameling & gold trim **$75**

Lenox, plate, 7 1/2" d., h.p. medallions surrounded & connected by heavy silver overlay by the Rockwell Silver Company, palette mark **$65**

Lenox, platter, 16 1/2" l., Art Deco design w/h.p. border & solid handles w/gold trim, palette mark **$130**

Morgan, plate, 10 1/2" d., decorated w/intricate enameled design of fruit, flowers & birds **$175**

Salt Dips

Scalloped-rim Salt Dip

Ceramic Art Pottery, h.p. violets & leaves, scalloped gold rim, CAC palette mark, 1 1/2" d. (ILLUS.) **$50**

Lenox, h.p. w/a soft pink ground & small purple blossoms & green leaves w/gold trim, palette mark, 1 1/4" d., set of 12 .... **$250**

Lenox Creamer & Sugar Bowl

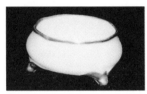

Footed Lenox Salt Dip

Lenox, three-footed, lustre body, gold-trimmed feet & scalloped rim, palette mark, 1 1/4" d. (ILLUS.) **$35**

Footed Willets Salt Dip

Willets, three-footed, lustre exterior w/gold rim & feet, serpent mark, 3" d. (ILLUS.) **$25**

Sets

Lenox, cider set: pitcher & six cups; h.p. red apples, leaves & stems in an overall design, palette mark, cups 5" h., pitcher 6" h., the set **$750**

Lenox, creamer & cov. sugar bowl, pedestal base, urn-form bodies, cream ground w/hand-decorated Art Deco design of enameled beading & gold paste, palette mark, 7" h., pr. (ILLUS., top of page) **$400**

Lenox, creamer & open sugar, cream color w/silver overlay of flying geese, trees & foliage, palette mark, 3" h., pr. (ILLUS., bottom of page) **$225**

Silver Overlay Creamer & Sugar

Vases

Lenox Vase with Landscape Band

Lenox, 13" h., cylindrical w/slightly incurved rim, a wide rim band h.p. w/a
stylized country landscape & gold border, the lower body w/a pale ground h.p.
overall w/diamond devices, palette mark
(ILLUS.) **$525**
Lenox, 18 1/2" h., decorated w/h.p. roses
accented w/gold, heavily gilded shaped
handles, palette mark **$2,500**

Willets Gourd-style Vase

Willets, 7" h., gourd-type, w/h.p. flowers &
foliage on white ground, serpent mark
(ILLUS.) **$325**

Miscellaneous
Willets, chalice, decorated overall w/white
dogwood blossoms & foliage ona darker
green ground, serpent mark, 11" h. **$575**
Willets, jardiniere, overall h.p. forest scene,
serpent mark, 8" d., 6 1/2" h **$600**

Irish Belleek
*Belleek china has been made in Ireland's
County Fermanagh for many years. It is exceed-
ingly thin porcelain. Several marks were used,*

*including a hound and harp (1865-1880), and a
hound, harp and castle (1863-1891). A printed
hound, harp and castle with the words "Co. Fermanagh Ireland" constitutes the mark from 1891.
The earliest marks were printed in black followed
by those printed in green. In recent years the
marks appear in gold.*

*The item identification for the following listing
follows that used in Richard K. Degenhardt's reference "Belleek - The Complete Collector's Guide and
Illustrated Reference," first and second editions.
The Degenhardt illustration number (D...) appears
at the end of each listing. This number will be followed in most cases by a Roman numeral "I" to
indicate a first period black mark while the Roman
numeral "II" will indicate a second period black
mark. In the "Baskets" section an Arabic number
"1" indicates an impressed ribbon mark with "Belleek" while the numeral "2" indicates the impressed
ribbon with the words "Belleek - Co. Fermanagh."
Both these marks were used in the first period,
1865-1891. Unless otherwise noted, all pieces here
will carry the black mark. A thorough discussion
of the early Belleek marks is found in this book as
well as at the Web site: http://mem-
bers.aol.com/delyicious/index.html.*

*Prices for items currently in production may
also be located at this site, especially via the 1983
Suggested Retail Price List. Prices given here are
for pieces in excellent or mint condition with no
chips, cracks, crazing or repairs, although, on
flowered items, minimal chips to the flowers is
acceptable to the extent of the purchaser's toler-
ance. Earthenware pieces often exhibit varying
degrees of crazing due to the primitive bottle kilns
originally used at the pottery.*

Basket Ware
Basket, cov., oval, small size (D114-I) **$6,000**

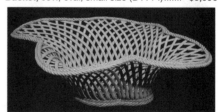

Four-lobed Belleek Basket

Basket, four-lobed form w/widely flared
rims, D1693-1 (ILLUS.) **$3,000**

Belleek Melvin Basket

Basket, Melvin Basket, painted blossoms,
D1690-5 (ILLUS.) **$800**

Two Belleek Shamrock Baskets

Basket, Shamrock basket, three different flowers around the rim, small size, D109-1, each (ILLUS. of two, top of page) **$520**

Box, cov., Forget-Me-Not trinket box, flower blossoms on the cover (D111-III) **$600**

Flower bouquet, hand-formed in green ware, features samples of all flower styles used on Belleek wares, mounted in a shadowbox frame, marked with two ribbons & "Belleek (R) Co. Fermanagh," ca. 1955-79 .... **$2,200**

Cherub Candelabra

Unique Belleek Woven Mirror Frame

Frame, woven mirror frame, oval, unique, Second Period Mark II (ILLUS.) **$5,000**

Menu holder, decorated w/applied flowers, various designs, D275-II, each.................. **$600**

Comports & Centerpieces

Candelabra, Cherub Candelabra, w/drip cups, D341-II (ILLUS.,top next column) **$6,000**

Comport, Bittern Comport, figural tall birds form pedestal, gilt trim, D6-II (ILLUS., next column)....................................... **$10,000**

Rare Belleek Bittern Comport

Earthenware

Earthenware Bowl with Inscription

Bowl, deep sides, Celtic inscription that translates "Friendship is Better than Gold," D857-II (ILLUS.) **$400**

Jelly mold, deep slightly flaring rounded sides, design on the interior (D880-I) **$460**

Transfer-printed Belleek Plate

Plate, 10" d., black transfer-printed pottery scene in the center, a crest on the flanged rim, D887-I (ILLUS.) **$400**

Toothbrush tray, cov., found w/various transfer-printed designs (D932-I) **$440**

Floral-decorated Earthenware Tray

Tray, oval, brown transfer-printed floral design, D900-I (ILLUS.) **$400**

Figurines

Belgian Hawkers Figurines

Belgian Hawker, female, fully-decorated, D15-II (ILLUS. right) **$3,000**

Belgian Hawker, male, fully-decorated, D21-II (ILLUS. left) **$3,000**

Bust & Figure of Lesbie

Bust of Lesbie, trimmed w/flowers & highlighted w/colors, D1651-I (ILLUS. right)... **$3,600**

Boy & Girl Figural Candlesticks

Candlestick, boy w/basket on shoulder, fully decorated & pierced, D1126-I (ILLUS. left) **$3,200**

Candlestick, girl w/basket on her shoulder, fully-decorated & pierced, D1137-I (ILLUS. right with Boy candlestick, previous page) **$3,200**

Belleek Figure of a Cavalier

Figure of Cavalier, standing, D22-II (ILLUS.) **$3,400**

Rare Belleek Crouching Venus Figure

Figure of Crouching Venus, gilt highlights, D16-I (ILLUS.) **$10,000**
Figure of Lesbie, standing, highlighted w/colors, D1656-I (ILLUS. left with bust of Lesbie) **$3,600**
Model of Horse & Snake, D1139-II **$12,000**

Religious Items & Lithophanes
Figure of the Blessed Virgin Mary, large size (D1106-II)....................................... **$1,800**

Sacred Heart Holy Water Font #4

Holy water font, Sacred Heart font, #4, D1115-III (ILLUS.).................................... **$260**
Lithophane, Madonna, Child & Angel (D1544-III) **$3,200**

Child Looking in Mirror Lithophane

Lithophane, round, child looking in mirror, D1539-VII (ILLUS.) **$480**

Tea Ware - Common Patterns (Harp Shamrock, Limpet, Hexagon, Neptune, Shamrock & Tridacna)

Harp Shamrock Plate for Butter

Harp Shamrock butter plate, D1356-VI (ILLUS.).. **$100**

Shamrock Marmalades & Mustard

Hexagon Pattern Belleek Teapot

Belleek Harp Shamrock Teakettle

Harp Shamrock teakettle, overhead handle, large size, gilt trim, D1359-III (ILLUS.) $660

Hexagon teapot, cov., large size, D407-II (ILLUS., next column) $600

Neptune biscuit jar, cov. (D531-II) $460

Neptune teapot, cov., medium size, green tint (D415-II) $480

Shamrock bread plate, round w/loop handles (D379-III) $180

Shamrock marmalade jar, cov., barrrel-shaped, D1561-IV (ILLUS. right with marmalde & mustard, top of page) $100

Shamrock marmalade jar, cov., cup marmalade, D1323-III (ILLUS. center with mustard & marmalade, top of page) $100

Shamrock mug, large size, D216-II (ILLUS. right, bottom of page) $120

Shamrock mug, Name Mug, impressed reserve for name, small size, D216-II (ILLUS. left, bottom of page) $140

Shamrock mustard jar, cov., footed spherical form, D298-III (ILLUS. left with marmalades, top of page) $100

Shamrock Large & Name Mugs

Shamrock Low-Shape Cup & Saucer

Shamrock teacup & saucer, low shape,
D366-III (ILLUS.)...................................... **$160**

Tridacna Boat-shaped Creamer

Tridacna creamer, boat-shaped, D247-VI
(ILLUS.)... **$60**

Tea Ware - Desirable Patterns (Echinus, Limpet (footed), Grass, Hexagon, Holly, Mask, New Shell & Shell)

Echinus creamer & open sugar bowl,
decorated (D647-I & D648-I), pr.............. **$1,000**
Echinus egg cup, footed (D666-I)................ **$400**
Grass coffeepot, cov., large size (D1402-I)
.... **$1,600**

Grass Egg Cup with Crest

Grass egg cup, footed, crested decoration,
D754-I (ILLUS.)... **$600**
Grass honey pot, cover & stand, model of
a beehive on a low table-form base, the
set (D755-I)... **$1,000**
Mask powder bowl, small size, D1548-III **$160**

Tea Ware - Museum Display Patterns (Artichoke, Chinese, Finner, Five O'Clock, Lace, Ring Handle Ivory, Set #36 & Victoria)

**Chinese creamer w/dragon head spout &
open sugar bowl,** decorated (D485-I &
D486-I), pr... **$1,400**

Chinese Pattern Teacup & Saucer

Chinese teacup & saucer, decorated,
D483-I (ILLUS.)... **$800**
Chinese teapot, cov., small size, decorated
(D484-I).. **$2,000**

Tea Ware - Museum Display Patterns (Artichoke, Chinese, Finner, Five O'Clock, Lace, Ring Handle Ivory, Set #36 & Victoria)

Lace Pattern Belleek Teapot

Lace teapot, cov., medium size, D800-II
(ILLUS.).. **$1,000**
Lace tray, round, decorated (D803-I)......... **$6,000**

Belleek Aberdeen Pattern Breakfast Tea Set

Tea Ware - Rare Patterns (Aberdeen, Blarney, Celtic (low & tall), Cone, Erne, Fan, Institute, Ivy, Lily (high & low), Scroll, Sydney, Thistle & Thorn)
Aberdeen breakfast set: cov. teapot, creamer, open sugar & cups & saucers; no tray, D494-II (ILLUS., top of page).... **$2,200**
Cone teacup & saucer, pink tint (D432-II)
.... **$440**

Fern Pattern Teacup & Saucer

Fan teacup & saucer, decorated, D694-II (ILLUS.).. **$600**

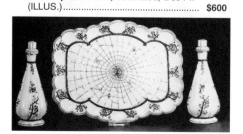

Thorn Brush Tray & Scent Bottles

Thorn brush tray & scent bottles, turquoise & gilt decoration, D333-I & D335-I (ILLUS.)... **$2,200**

Thorn teapot, cov., small size, decorated (D759-I)... **$800**

Teawares
Tea set: cov. teapot, open sugar & creamer & two cups & saucers; Low Lily patt., green tint w/gold trim, 2nd period, creamer & open sugar, $400-500; cup & saucer, $260-320; teapot only (ILLUS. of set, top next page) **$700-800**

Another Version of the Rare Chinese Tea Urn

Tea urn, Chinese (Dragon) patt., fancy dark pink, black & heavy gold trim, 17" h., 1st period (ILLUS.)......................... **$18,000-25,000**

Low Lily Tea Set with Green Tint & Gold Trim

Extremely Rare Decorated Chinese Pattern Tall Tea Urn

Tea urn, Chinese (Dragon) patt., fancy pale pink, black & heavy gold trim, 17" h., 1st period (ILLUS.) **$18,000-25,000**

Grass Pattern Teakettle with Multicolored Decoration

Teakettle, Grass patt., multicolored decoration w/gold, 1st period (ILLUS.) **$600-1,000**

Gold-trimmed Ringhandle Teakettle

Teakettle, Ringhandle patt., undecorated except gold trim, 3rd period (ILLUS.) **$1,000-1,400**

Sydney Pattern Teapot with Pink Tint

Teapot, Sydney patt., pink tint, 2nd period
(ILLUS.)... **$600-800**

Early Undecorated Thistle Pattern Teapot

Teapot, Thistle patt., undecorated, 1st peri-
od (ILLUS.).. **$600-800**

Gold-trimmed Thorn Pattern Teapot

Teapot, Thorn patt., gold trim, 1st period
(ILLUS.)... **$600-1,000**

Early Tridacna Teapot with Gold Trim

Teapot, Tridacna patt., gold trim, 1st period
(ILLUS.)... **$400-600**

Vases & Spills

Belleek Coral and Shell Vase

Coral and Shell Vase, D133-II (ILLUS.)....... **$880**

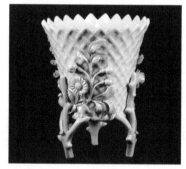

Belleek Flowered Spill

Flowered Spill, raised on twig feet, large
size, D45-III (ILLUS.) **$380**

Belleek Marine Jug Vase

Marine Jug Vase, coral designs, ruffled foot, D134-II (ILLUS, previous page.) **$800**

Belleek Ram's Head Flower Holder

Ram's Head Flower Holder, figural, D1180-I (ILLUS.)................................... **$1,400**

Belleek Ribbon Vase

Ribbon Vase, flowered, D1220-III (ILLUS.)
.... **$340**
Triple Fish Vase, painted (D1231-I) **$4,600**

Belleek Typha Jug Spill

Typha Jug Spill, decorated w/shamrocks, D1790-VI (ILLUS.) **$120**

Tea Wares - Miscellaneous
Items produced, but with NO matching tea set pieces.

Cardium on Shell dish, Size 2, pink tint, D261-I (ILLUS. center with Sycamore & Worcester plates, top of next page) **$180**

Greek Dessert Plate with Scene

Greek dessert plate, tinted & gilt-trimmed, h.p. center scene titled "Eel Fishery on the Erne," by E. Sheerin, D29-I (ILLUS.).. **$3,600**

Armorial Souvenir Loving Cup

Loving cup, three-handled, armorial souvenir, D1503-I (ILLUS.)............................... **$400**

Shell-shaped Nautilus Creamer

Cadmium on Shell Dish & Sycamore and Worcester Plates

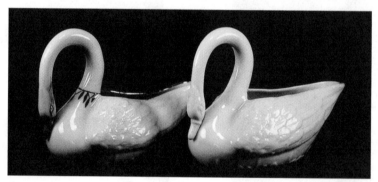

Two Large Swan Creamers

Nautilus creamer, shell-shaped, pink tint, D279-I (ILLUS., previous page) **$600**

Shell creamer, large size (D601-I)............... **$720**

Swan creamer, figural, large size, D254-III (ILLUS. left, second from top) **$320**

Swan creamer, figural, large size, D254-VI (ILLUS. right, second from top) **$120**

Sycamore plate, leaf-shaped, Size 2, pink tint, D642-II (ILLUS. right with Cardium on Shell dish, top of page) **$120**

Toy creamer & open sugar bowl, Ivy patt., small size (D241-I), pr. **$240**

Worcester plate, Size 2, D682-II (ILLUS. left with Cardium on Shell dish, top of page) **$120**

Bisque

Bisque is biscuit china, fired a single time but not glazed. Some bisque is decorated with colors. Most abundant from the Victorian era are figures and groups, but other pieces, from busts to vases, were made by numerous potteries in the United States and abroad. Reproductions have been produced for many years, so care must be taken when seeking antique originals.

Charming Bisque Group of Girl & Puppy

Figure group, a young Victorian girl seated in her feeding chair & holding a puppy in her lap & tying a napkin around its neck, decorated w/naturalistic coloring, late 19th c., 12 1/2" h. (ILLUS.)....................... **$230**

Pair of Bisque Little Girls with Pets

Figures of little girls, each standing wearing short-sleeved light blue smocks w/tiny red flowers & lace trim, one holding a wriggling brown & white puppy & the other holding a white & grey kitten, standing on small rounded rockwork bases, late 19th c., 12" h., pr. (ILLUS.) **$230**

Man & Lady in 18th Century Costume

Figures of man & woman, each dressed in colorful 18th c. costume, she wearing a draped windswept dress painted w/tiny flowers & a pink lace-trimmed bodice, a blue bonnet behind her blonde-haired head, he wearing flower-painted knee breeches & vest & ruffled shirt under a pink jacket, holding his black tricorn hat as it blows off his head, each on a round molded base w/gilt scroll trim, Victorian-style, each 18" h., pr. (ILLUS.) **$489**

Figures of man & woman, each dressed in pale green outfit w/peach-colored bows & decorations, the man w/knee breeches & jacket, holding flowers in one hand, a staff in the other, the woman in dress w/laced bodice & elbow-length sleeves, each standing on ornate scroll base that holds trellis-like backdrop w/molded flowers, h.p. features, unmarked, late 19th c., Germany, 16" h., pr. (ILLUS., top next column).. **$288**

Figures of Man & Woman with Molded Flowers

Bisque Figures of Young Woman & Man

Figures of young woman & man, each dressed in Renaissance-style costumes in pale pink & cream shades trimmed in white & decorated w/darker peach flowers, each wearing brimmed hat, the woman holding one hand to forehead, the other holding skirt, h.p. features & florals on tinted ground, unmarked, Germany, ca. 1900, 16 1/2" h., pr. (ILLUS.) **$316**

Figures of Woman & Man in Rose Outfits

Figures of young woman & man, the woman wearing rose-colored dress w/gold bodice trimmed in white lace & pale aqua short sleeves, the narrow skirt w/pale aqua bows down front & matching wide sash at waist, white long gloves, pink shoes, elaborately styled powdered hair, the fair-haired man w/long curls, wearing rose-colored short lace-trimmed pants & matching jacket w/gold trim & pale aqua cloak, rose boots, h.p. features, gilt accents, unmarked, Germany, ca. 1900, 16" h., pr. (ILLUS.) **$173**

Blue Ridge Dinnerwares

The small town of Erwin, Tennessee, was the home of the Southern Potteries, Inc., originally founded by E.J. Owen in 1917 and first called the Clinchfield Pottery.

In the early 1920s Charles W. Foreman purchased the plant and revolutionized the com-

pany's output, developing the popular line of handpainted wares sold as "Blue Ridge" dinnerwares. Freehand painted by women from the surrounding hills, these colorful dishes in many patterns continued in production until the plant's closing in 1957.

Blue Ridge Dinnerwares Mark

Ashtray, individual, Tralee Rose patt............. **$15**

Shell-shaped Blue Ridge Bowl

Bowl, 9" d., Belvedere patt., deep shell shape, in shades of blue & red (ILLUS.) **$75**
Butter pat/coaster, Lyonnaise patt., 4" d. **$100**
Cake lifter, Pomona patt., 9" l. (ILLUS., bottom of page).. **$32**
Cake tray, maple leaf shape, French Peasant patt. **$125**

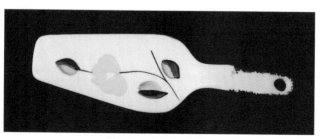

Blue Ridge Cake Lifter

Colonial Shape Creamer & Sugar

Fruit Fantasy Leaf-Shaped

Celery, leaf-shaped, Fruit Fantasy patt., 10 1/2" l. (ILLUS.) $75
Coffeepot, cov., ovoid, various floral patterns, 10 1/2" h., each $150
Creamer, Mardi Gras patt. $15
Creamer & cov. sugar bowl, Colonial shape, Garden Lane patt., the set (ILLUS., top of page) $45
Pie plate, Cassandra patt., wine-colored border.. $30
Pitcher, 5" h., china, Annett's Wild Rose patt., Antique shape $85
Pitcher, china, decorated w/grapes, Helen shape $95
Plate, 6" d., Bluebell Bouquet patt..................... $8
Plate, 6" sq., "Milkmaid," Provincial Farm Scene, Candlewick shape.......................... $65
Salt & pepper shakers, Dogtooth Violet patt., pr. $75

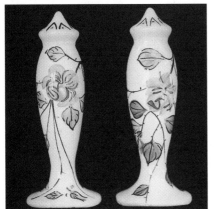

Ruff Rose Salt & Pepper Shaker

Salt & pepper shakers, tall, footed, Ruff Rose patt., brown & green leaves & various floral decorations, 5 1/2" h. pr. (ILLUS.)......... **$75**

Blue Ridge Adoration Pattern Teapot

Teapot, cov., Ball shape, Adoration patt., 6 3/4" h. (ILLUS.) **$150**
Teapot, cov., Ball shape, Bluebelle Bouquet patt. **$225**

Blue Ridge Cherry Pattern Teapot

Teapot, cov., Colonial shape, Cherry patt., 8 3/4" h. (ILLUS.) **$175**
Vase, 5 1/2" h., china, Hampton patt., Hibiscus shape **$80**
Vegetable bowl, open, round, Ridge Daisy patt. **$20**

Blue & White Pottery

The category of blue and white or blue and grey pottery includes a wide variety of pottery, earthenware and stoneware items widely produced in this country in the late 19th century right through the 1930s. Originally marketed as inexpensive wares, most pieces featured a white or grey body molded with a fruit, flower or geometric design and then trimmed with bands or splashes of blue to highlight the molded pattern. Pitchers, butter crocks and salt boxes are among the numerous items produced, but other kitchenwares and chamber sets are also found. Values vary depending on the rarity of the embossed pattern and the depth of color of the blue trim; the darker the blue, the better. Some entries refer to several different books on Blue and White Pottery. These books are: Blue & White Stoneware, Pottery & Crockery *by Edith Harbin (1977, Collector Books, Paducah, KY);* Stoneware in the Blue and White *by M.H. Alexander (1993 reprint, Image Graphics, Inc., Paducah, KY); and* Blue & White Stoneware *by Kathryn McNerney (1995, Collector Books, Paducah, KY).*

Basin, embossed Bow Tie patt. w/rose decal, Brush-McCoy Pottery Co., basin 15" d. **$150**

Lovebird Butter Crock

Butter crock, cov., embossed Lovebird patt., A.E. Hull Pottery Co., 6" d., 4 34" h. (ILLUS.) **$650**

Stenciled Dutch Boy Creamer

Creamer, ovoid form, stenciled Dutch Boy patt., 4 1/4" h. (ILLUS.) **$225**

Rare Anchovies Storage Crock

Crock, anchovies storage-type, swelled cylindrical form, three blue bands around top & bottom, stenciled on the side "A. Rensch & Co. - Anchois (sic) Mustard [over a fish] - Toledo, O.," impressed on the bottom "Burley, Winter & Co. - Crooksville, O.," 10 1/2" h. (ILLUS.) **$575**
Cuspidor, embossed Poinsettia and Basketweave patt., 9 3/4" d., 9" h. **$180**

Small-mouthed Apple Blossom Ewer

Ewer, embossed Apple Blossom patt., small mouth, Burley-Winter Pottery Co., 8" h. (ILLUS.) **$400**
Ewer & basin set, embossed Apple Blossom patt., Burley-Winter Pottery Co., pr. (ILLUS. right with small Apple Blossom ewer) **$700**

Decorated Bow Tie Ewer & Basin Set

Ewer & basin set, embossed Bow Tie patt. w/Flying Bird decal, Brush-McCoy Pottery Co., basin 15" d., ewer 11" h., pr. (ILLUS.) **$625**

Avenue of Trees Pitcher

Pitcher, 8" h., embossed Avenue of Trees patt. (ILLUS.) **$325**

Beaded Swirl Pattern Pitcher

Pitcher, 6 1/2" h., embossed Beaded Swirl patt., A.E. Hull Pottery Co. (ILLUS.).......... **$950**

Embossed Cherry Band Pitcher

Pitcher, 9 1/2" h., embossed Cherry Band patt., Red Wing Pottery Co., 8 pt., available in numerous sizes, the smallest being the most valuable, often seen w/printed advertising, which adds $300 minimum to the value, without advertising (ILLUS.)... **$225-400**

Large-sized Cow Pitcher

Graduated Lincoln Head with Log Cabin Pitchers

Pitcher, embossed Cow patt., A.E. Hull Pottery Co., five sizes, rarest 5 3/4" h. to 9" h. (ILLUS. of 9" size, previous page) **$250-600**

Pitcher, 7 1/2" h., 6 1/4" d., embossed Dainty Fruit patt., A.E. Hull Pottery Co. **$550**

Dutch Boy and Girl Kissing Pitcher

Pitcher, 9" h., embossed Dutch Boy and Girl Kissing patt., Brush-McCoy Pottery Co. or J.W. McCoy Pottery Co. (ILLUS.) **$250**

Embossed Eagle Pattern Pitcher

Pitcher, 8" h., embossed Eagle patt., A.E. Hull Pottery Co. (ILLUS.) **$650**

Grape Cluster & Trellis Pattern Pitcher

Pitcher, embossed Grape Cluster on Trellis patt., four sizes, 5" to 9 1/2" h., depending on size, each (ILLUS. of....) **$165-245**

Pitcher, embossed Lincoln Head with Log Cabin patt., Uhl Pottery Co., five sizes, one gallon size largest & most valuable, depending on size (ILLUS., top of page) **$575-1,500**

Pitcher, 7" h., 7" d., embossed Paul Revere patt., Whites Pottery Co. **$450**

Pine Cone Pattern Pitcher

Pitcher, 9 1/2" h., 5 3/4" d., embossed Pine Cone patt., Burley-Winter Pottery Co. (ILLUS., previous page) **$1,500**

Pitcher, 8 3/4" h., embossed Rose on Trellis patt., also comes in smaller size **$375**

Embossed Windy City Pitcher

Pitcher, 8 1/2" h., embossed Windy City patt., Robinson Clay Products Pottery Co. (ILLUS.) **$325**

Pitcher, 7" h., embossed Windmill & Bush patt., J.W. McCoy Pottery Co. & Brush-McCoy Pottery Co. **$250**

Printed Nautilus Pattern Pitcher

Pitcher, 8 1/2" h., stenciled Nautilus patt., A.E. Hull Pottery Co. (ILLUS.) **$300**

Salt box, cov., embossed Daisy patt., 6" d., 6 1/2" h. **$250**

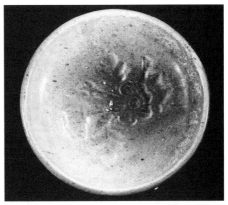

Embossed Flower Cluster Soap Dish

Soap dish, embossed Flower Cluster w/Fishscale patt., small round form, 4 1/2" d., 3/4" h. (ILLUS.) **$135**

Wildflower/Arches & Columns Soap Dish

Soap dish, cover & drainer, stenciled Wildflower patt. on embossed Arches & Columns shape, Brush-McCoy Pottery Co., 5 1/4" d., 2" h. (ILLUS.) **$600**

Spice jar, cov., stenciled Snowflake patt., various spices, A.E. Hull Pottery Co., each **$150-225**

Windy City Pattern Stein

Stein, embossed Windy City patt., 5 1/2" h. (ILLUS., previous page) **$165**

Stewer, cov., embossed Willow (Basketweave & Morning Glory) patt., Brush-McCoy Pottery Co., 4 qt. **$275**

Blue & White Pottery Teapot

Teapot, cov., Swirl patt., spherical body w/row of relief-molded knobs around the shoulder, inset cover w/knob finial, swan's-neck spout, shoulder loop brackets for wire bail handle w/turned wood grip, blue 6" d., 6" h. (ILLUS.) .... **$800+**

Tumbler, stenciled Wildflower patt., tapering cylindrical form, no printed designs inside, 5" h. **$300**

Umbrella stand, embossed Two Stags patt., solid blue, Logan Pottery Co., 21" h. **$1,500**

Vase, Diffused Blue, wide ovoid body w/short flared neck & pointed shoulder handles .... **$300+**

Canton

This ware has been decorated for nearly two centuries in factories near Canton, China. Intended for export sale, much of it was originally inexpensive blue-and-white hand-decorated ware. Late-18th- and early-19th-century pieces are superior to later ones and fetch higher prices.

Fine Canton Lobe-edged Bowl

Bowl, 9" d., 4 1/2" h., serpentine four-lobed rim, 19th c. (ILLUS.) **$1,035**

Nice Large Scalloped Canton Bowl

Bowl, 10" d., 2 1/4" h., wide shallow shape w/a flaring scalloped rim, orange peel glaze bottom, 19th c. (ILLUS.) **$460**

Set of Seven Old Canton Plates

Plates, 7 1/4" d., shallow dished shape, 19th c., one w/a repaired edge, set of 7 (ILLUS.) **$316**

Set of Ten Old Canton Plates

Plates, 8 1/2" d., shallow dished shape, 19th c., two w/small chips, one w/spider cracks, one w/very old tight hairline, set of 10 (ILLUS.) **$575**

Canton Covered Warming Dish

Large Canton Covered Tureen

Tureen, cov., footed deep oblong base w/boar's head end handles, low domed cover w/large center handle & a butterfly design edge band, 19th c., 9 1/2 x 11 1/2", 9" h. (ILLUS.) **$550**

Warming dish, cov., shallow oblong base w/angled corners & filling hole at one end, domed cover w/nut-like finial, 19th c., 9 3/4 x 15" (ILLUS., top of page) **$1,265**

Capo-di-Monte

Production of porcelain and faience began in 1736 at the Capo-di-Monte factory in Naples. In 1743 King Charles of Naples established a factory there that made wares with relief decoration. In 1759 the factory was moved to Buen Retiro near Madrid, operating until 1808. Another Naples pottery was opened in 1771 and operated until 1806 when its molds were acquired by the Doccia factory of Florence, which has since made reproductions of original Capo-di-Monte pieces with the "N" mark beneath a crown. Some very early pieces are valued in the thousands of dollars but the subsequent productions are considerably lower.

Dessert service: twelve 7 3/4" d. dessert plates, eight teacups & seven saucers; each plate painted w/a crested coat-of-arms trimmed in gilt, the border molded in low relief w/mythological figures at leisure pursuits, the bases marked w/blue crowned "N" mark & museum accession numbers & two w/gilt inscription "A Madame la Comtesse de Spilinbergo," late 19th - early 20th c., the set **$1,410**

Ornate Molded Capo-di-Monte Ewer

Ewer, Baroque-style, the pedestal base composed of brightly colored molded scrolls & mounted with two figures of child mermaids blowing horns & w/a dolphin, the tall cylindrical body ornately molded w/ nude figures w/leafy trim & oval blue reserves all in bold colors, the wide shoulder w/fancy molded details includingt a seated bearded mermain w/his arms wrapped around the arched spout & grasping the horns of a grostesque seat creature, the ornate S-scroll handle down his back, blue mark on base, late 19th - early 20th c., 16 3/4" h. (ILLUS.) **$920**

Capo-di-Monte Teapot with Scenes

Teapot, cov., three gold paw feet supporting the spherical body decorated w/two large round reserves w/colorful landscapes w/naked frolicking figures, a cobalt blue background & inset cover w/ball finial, pink ribbed serpentine spout & ornate pink-trimmed C-scroll handle, late 19th - early 20th c., 9 1/2" w., 6 1/4" h. (ILLUS.)...................... **$374**

![Capo-di-Monte Campana-form Urns]

Capo-di-Monte Campana-form Urns

Urns, campana-form, a gilded square foot supporting a bell-shaped base w/a red & white band below a green & yellow leaf band, the large urn w/large green & yellow leaves around the swelled base w/double mask head gold handles below the tall cylindrical sides & wide rolled rim w/red trim, the sides molded in bold relief w/semi-nude classical figures decorated in bright colors, blue mark on base, late 19th - early 20th c., 6" w., 8" h., pr. (ILLUS.)..................................... **$489**

Urns, cov., a stepped square base supporting a short pedestal below the tall slightly flaring cylindrical body w/molded lion mask side handles & a high stepped cover w/pineapple finial, decorated w/molded low-relief Bacchic putti riding a goat & a donkey decorated in color, gold trim, 20th c., 12" h., pr. **$353**

Pair of Ornate Capo-di-Monte Urns

Urns, cov., a tripartite plinth base supporting three incurved legs & a rounded dish all in white w/gold trim, the base supporting a large bublous urn-form body molded in bold relief w/a continuous scene of knights in battle & decorated w/poly-

chrome, the incurved shoulder w/reticulated panels below the gilt rim supporting a high domed matching reticulated cover topped w/a crown-form finial in gold & dark blue, late 19th - early 20th c., crown finials restored, 12" h., pr. (ILLUS.)........... **$489**

Ceramic Arts Studio of Madison

During its 15 years of operation, Ceramic Arts Studio of Madison, Wisconsin, was one of the nation's most prolific producers of figurines, shakers, and other decorative ceramics. The Studio began in 1940 as the joint venture of potter Lawrence Rabbitt and entrepreneur Reuben Sand. Early products included hand-thrown bowls, pots, and vases, exploring the potential of Wisconsin clay. However, the arrival of Betty Harrington in 1941 took CAS in a new direction, leading to the type of work it is best known for. Under Mrs. Harrington's artistic leadership, the focus was changed to the production of finely sculpted decorative figurines. Among the many subjects covered were adults in varied costumes and poses, charming depictions of children, fantasy and theatrical figures, and animals. The inventory soon expanded to include figural wall plaques, head vases, salt-and-pepper shakers, self-sitters, and "snuggle pairs".

Metal display accessories complementing the ceramics were produced by another Reuben Sand firm, Jon-San Creations, under the direction of Zona Liberace (stepmother of the famed pianist). Mrs. Liberace also served as the Studio's decorating director.

During World War II, Ceramic Arts Studio flourished, since the import of decorative items from overseas was suspended. In its prime during the late 1940s, CAS produced over 500,000 pieces annually, and employed nearly 100 workers.

As primary designer, the talented Betty Harrington is credited with creating the vast majority of the 800-plus designs in the Studio inventory--a remarkable achievement for a self-taught artist. The only other CAS designer of note was Ulle Cohen ("Rebus"), who contributed a series of modernistic animal figurines in the early 1950s.

The popularity of Ceramic Arts Studio pieces eventually resulted in many imitations of lesser quality. After World War II, lower-priced imports began to flood the market, forcing the Studio to close its doors in 1955. An attempt to continue the enterprise in Japan, using some of the Madison master molds as well as new designs, did not prove successful. An additional number of molds and copyrights were sold to Mahana Imports, which released a series of figures based on the CAS originals. Both the Ceramic Arts Studio-Japan and Mahana pieces utilized a clay both whiter and more lightweight than that of Madison pieces. Additionally, their markings differ from the "Ceramic Arts Studio, Madison Wis." logo, which appears in black on the base of many Studio pieces. However, not all authentic Studio pieces were marked (particularly in pairs); a more reliable indicator of authenticity is the "decorator tick mark". This series of colored dots, which appears

Group of Child Musician Figures

at the drain hole on the bottom of every Ceramic Arts Studio piece, served as an in-house identifier for the decorator who worked on a specific piece. The tick mark is a sure sign that a figurine is the work of the Studio.

Ceramic Arts Studio is one of the few figural ceramics firms of the 1940s and '50s which operated successfully outside of the West Coast. Today, CAS pieces remain in high demand, thanks to their skillful design and decoration, warm use of color, distinctively glossy glaze, and highly imaginative and exquisitely realized themes.

Many pieces in the Ceramic Arts Studio inventory were released both as figurines and as salt-and-peper shakers. For items not specifically noted as shakers in this listing, add 50 percent for the shaker price estimate.

Complete reference information on the Studio can be found in Ceramic Arts Studio: The Legacy of Betty Harrington by Donald-Brian Johnson, Timothy J. Holthaus, and James E. Petzold (Schiffer Publishing Ltd., 2003). The official Ceramic Arts Studio collectors group, "CAS Collectors", publishes a quarterly newsletter, hosts an annual convention, and can be contacted at www.cascollectors.com The Studio also has an official historical site, www.ceramicartsstudio.com. Photos for this category are by John Petzold.

Ceramic Arts Studio Marks

Al the Hunter & Kirby the English Setter,
7 1/2" h. & 2" l., pr. (ILLUS., top next column) **$275-375**
Angel Trio (Praying, Star & Singing),
4 1/2" h., 6 1/2" h. & 3 1/2" h.., the set **$300-360**
Angel with Candle, 5" h. **$65-75**
Bali-Hai & Bali-Lao, 7 3/4" h. & 8 1/2" h.,
pr. **$180-220**
Bass Viol Boy, 5" h. (ILLUS. second from right with other child musicians, top of page) **$120-140**

Al the Hunter & Kirby the Setter Figures

Bedtime Girl

Bedtime Girl, 4 3/4" h. (ILLUS.)................ **$75-95**
Berty, w/ball, 4 1/2" h. **$240-270**
Betty, sleeping, 5 1/2" l. **$240-270**
Betty & Benny, running bunnies, 3" h.,
2 1/4" h., pr.. **$260-300**
Big Dutch Boy & Girl, 4" h., pr................. **$30-40**
Birch bark canoe, Indian group, 7 1/2" l.
.... **$100-125**

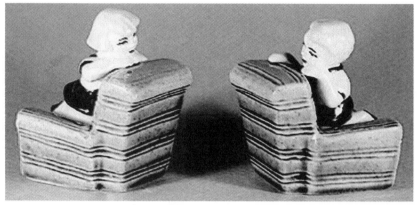

Children in Chairs

Blythe, 6 1/2" h....................................... **$150-175**
Bobby, sitting, 3 1/4" h............................ **$240-270**
Boy Doll, 12" h................................. **$1,200-1,400**
Boy with Puppy, shelf-sitter, 4 1/4" h...... **$75-100**
Boy with Towel, 5" h............................ **$300-350**
Bride & Groom, 4 3/4" h. & 5" h., pr. **$250-300**
Bruce & Beth, 6 1/2" h. & 5" h., pr......... **$80-100**
Budgie & Pidgie, parakeets, shelf-sitters,
     6" h... **$100-120**
Bunny, Indian group, 1 3/4" h. **$35-45**
Burmese Chinthe, 5" h.......................... **$175-200**
Burmese Man & Woman, 4 3/4" h., pr.
     .... **$250-400**
Burmese Man, Woman & Chinthe,
     4 3/4" h. & 5" h., the set **$425-620**
Butch & Billy Boxer, 3" l., 2" l., pr. **$120-160**
Carmen & Carmelita, 7 1/4" h. & 4 1/4" h.,
     pr. **$300-350**
Cellist Man, 6 1/2" h.............................. **$500-600**
Children in Chairs, boy looking over back
     of one armchair, girl looking over
     matching chair, 1" to 1 1/2" h., each
     piece (ILLUS., top of page).................. **$60-80**
Chinese Boy & Girl, 4 1/4" h. & 4" h., pr. ... **$30-40**
Chinese Boy & Girl on Bamboo Planters,
     5" h.. **$60-70**
Chinese Emperor & Empress, 7" h., pr.
     .... **$1,600-2,000**

Chinese Lantern Man & Woman wall
     plaques, 8" h., pr. **$120-140**
Chipmunk, Indian group, 2" h. **$35-45**
Chubby St. Francis, 9" h...................... **$180-200**
Cinderella & Prince, 6 1/2" h., pr. **$60-80**
Circus Clown & Dog snugglers, 3 3/4" h.
     & 2 1/2" h., pr. **$150-190**
Cocker Spaniel, shelf-sitter, paws over the
     edge, 5" l. **$80-100**
Collie mother, shelf-sitter, 5" h............... **$75-100**
Collie pup sleeping, 2 1/4" l.................... **$50-60**
Colonel Jackson, 7 1/4" h........................ **$40-50**
Colonial Boy & Girl, 5 1/2" & 5" h., pr... **$200-250**
Colonial Boy & Girl, shelf-sitters, 5" h.,
     5 1/4" h., pr.. **$250-300**
Colonial Man & Woman, 6 1/2" h., pr. .. **$130-170**
Comedy & Tragedy, dark green, 10" h., pr.
     .... **$160-200**
Cowboy, shelf-sitter, 4 1/2" h.................. **$125-150**
Cowgirl, shelf-sitter, 4 1/2" h.................. **$125-150**
Crocodile & Boy salt & pepper shakers,
     4 1/2" l., 3" h., pr............................... **$200-240**
Cupid, 5" h. **$275-500**
Daisy, Ballet Group, standing, 6" h. **$260-280**
Daisy Donkey, 4 3/4" h. (ILLUS. left with
     Elsie Elephant, bottom of page).......... **$85-100**
Dance Moderne Man & Woman, 9 1/2" h.,
     pr... **$140-220**

Daisy Donkey & Elsie Elephant

Dawn, 6 1/2" h. **$175-200**
**Dem (donkey) & Rep (elephant) salt &
pepper shakers,** 3 3/4" h., pr. **$200-250**
Drum Girl, 4 1/2" h. (ILLUS. far left with oth-
er child musicians, top of page 153) .. **$160-180**
Drum Girl bank, 4 1/2" h. **$220-250**
Duck Vase, two-sided, 4" h. **$225-250**
Dutch Dance Boy, 7 1/2" h. **$200-250**
Dutch Dance Girl, 7 1/2" h. **$200-250**
Dutch Love Boy & Dutch Love Girl, 5" h.,
pr. **$120-140**
Egyptian Man, 9 1/2" h. **$700-750**
Elsie Elephant, 5" h. (ILLUS. right with
Donkey, previous page) **$85-110**
En Pose & En Repose shelf-sitters,
4 3/4" h., pr. **$100-140**
Encore Man & Woman, 8 1/2" & 9" h., pr.
.... **$200-250**

Dark Red Fire Man & Fire Woman

Fire Man & Fire Woman, dark red,
11 1/4" h., pr. (ILLUS.) **$400-450**
Flute Girl, 4 1/2" h. (ILLUS. second from left
with other child musicians, top of page
153) **$140-160**
Hansel & Gretel, one-piece, 3" h. **$125-150**
Jim & June, 4 3/4" h. & 4 1/2" h., pr. **$80-100**
**Manchu & Lotus Standing Lantern Man &
Woman,** 9" h., pr. **$80-120**
Masquerade Man & Woman plaques,
8" h., pr. **$1,600-2,000**

Purple Mother & Calf Snugglers

Mother Cow & Calf snugglers, in purple,
5 1/4" h. & 2 1/2" h., pr. **$100-300**

Peek-A-Boo Pixie Tray, 4 1/2" **$125-150**

Peter Pan & Wendy

Peter Pan & Wendy, 5 /4" h., pr. (ILLUS.)
.... **$220-270**
Peter Rabbit, 3 1/2" h. **$100-125**
Pied Piper, Nursery Rhyme Group,
6 1/4" h. **$200-225**
Pioneer Sam & Pioneer Susie, 5 1/2" h. &
5" h., pr. **$80-100**
Pitcher, 3" h., miniature, relief-molded
Adam & Eve decoration, branch handle
.... **$40-50**
Polish Boy & Girl, 6 3/4" & 6" h., pr. **$60-80**
**Praise Angel (hand up) & Blessing Angel
(hand down),** 6 1/4" h. & 5 3/4" h., pr.
.... **$180-240**
Praying Girl, Nursery Rhyme Group, 3" h.
.... **$60-80**

Promenade Man & Woman

Promenade Man, 7 3/4" h. (ILLUS. right)
.... **$100-150**
Promenade Woman, 7 3/4" h. (ILLUS. left
with Promenade Man) **$100-150**
Ralph the goat, 4" h. **$75-100**

Rhumba Man & Woman

Rhumba Dancers, man & woman, 7 1/4" h.
& 7" h., pr. (ILLUS.) **$80-120**

Rose, Ballet Group, stooping, 5" h. **$260-280**
Running Boy, Nursery Rhyme Group,
3 1/2" h. **$60-80**
Running Girl, Nursery Rhyme Group,
3 1/4" h. **$60-80**
Sad Imp with Spear, 5" h. **$500-550**
Saint George, on charger, 8 1/2" h. **$145-175**
Sambo & Tiger, tiger 5" l., Sambo 3 1/2" h.,
pr. **$500-575**
**Santa Claus & evergreen tree salt & pep-
per shakers,** figural, 2 1/4" h. & 2 1/2" h.,
pr. **$325-375**
Saucy Squirrel, 2 1/4" h. **$175-350**
Saxophone Boy, 5" h. (ILLUS. far right with
other child musicians, top of page 153)
.... **$140-160**
Scottie, Sooty, black, 3" h. **$45-65**
Scottie, Taffy, brown, 3" h. **$45-65**
Sea gull, Indian group, hooks onto side of
canoe, 4" w. wing span **$800-850**
Sea horse & Coral salt & pepper shakers,
3 1/2" h. & 3" h., pr. **$100-140**
Seal Mother, 6" l. **$400-450**
Seal Pup, 3" l. **$350-400**
Seal Pup on rock, 5" l. **$450-500**
See No Evil candleholder, 5" h. **$80-100**
Shadow Dancer A & B plaques, 8" h. &
7 3/4" h., pr. **$60-80**

Shepherd & Shepherdess

Shepherd & Shepherdess, 8 1/2" h. &
8" h., pr. (ILLUS.) **$180-220**

Skunky Bank

Skunky bank, 4" h. (ILLUS.) **$260-280**
Space bowl, 5 1/4" h. **$100-125**
Speak No Evil candleholder, 5" h. **$80-100**
Spring Sue, Four Seasons group, 5" h.
.... **$140-170**

Square Dance Boy & Girl

Square Dance Boy, 6 1/2" h. (ILLUS. left
w/girl) **$100-125**
Square Dance Girl, 6 1/2" h. (ILLUS. right
w/boy) **$100-125**
Squeaky Squirrel, 3 1/4" h. **$50-70**
St. Agnes with Lamb, 6" h. **$260-285**
Straight Tail Fish salt & pepper shakers,
pr. **$160-200**
Sultan on Pillow, 4 1/2" h. **$120-145**
Sultan only, 4" h. **$130-155**
Summer Sally, Four Seasons group,
3 1/2" h. **$100-130**
Sun-Li & Su-Lin, shelf-sitters, 5 1/2" h., pr.
.... **$50-80**

Suzette Poodle & Pillow Shaker Set

**Suzette Poodle & Pillow salt & pepper
shakers,** 3 1/4" h. & 1" sq., pr. (ILLUS.)
.... **$130-160**
Swan Lake Man, 7" h. **$900-950**
Swan Lake Woman, 7" h. **$900-950**

Swedish Dance Couple

Swedish Dance Couple, 6 1/2 & 7" h., pr.
(ILLUS.) **$180-240**

Tembo & Tembino Elephants

Swish & Swirl Fish (straight tail/twist tail), 3 1/2", 3" **$130-170**
Tembo & Tembino Elephant, w/trunk up, 6 3/4" h., w/trunk down, & 2 1/2" h., pr. (ILLUS., top of page) **$345-415**
Temple Dance Man, 7" h. **$450-500**
Temple Dance Woman, 6 3/4" h. **$450-500**
Thai & Thai-Thai salt & pepper shakers, Siamese cats, reclining, 4 1/2" l., 5 1/2" l. **$70-90**
Thunder Stallion, 5 3/4" h. **$150-175**
Ting-A-Ling & Sung-Tu, 5 1/2" h., 4" h., pr. **$50-80**
"Toadstool Pixie," elf on mushroom, 4" h. **$40-50**
Tom Cat, standing, 5" h............................ **$75-95**
Tony the Barber bank, bust of man, 4 3/4" h... **$75-100**
Tortoise with Cane, 2 1/4" h. **$120-140**
Wee Eskimo Boy & Girl salt & pepper shakers, 3 1/4" h. & 3" h., pr. **$50-70**
Wee French Boy & Girl salt & pepper shakers, 3" h., pr. **$80-90**

Chinese Export

Large quantities of porcelain have been made in China for export to America from the 1780s, much of it shipped from the ports of Canton and Nanking. A major source of this porcelain was Ching-te-Chen in the Kiangsi province, but the wares were also made elsewhere. The largest quantities were blue and white. Prices fluctuate considerably depending on age, condition, decoration, etc.

ROSE MEDALLION and CANTON export wares are listed separately.

Unusual Famille Rose Export Pitcher

Pitcher, 6 1/2" h., Famille Rose palette, slightly swelled cylindrical shape w/a deeply scalloped rim & pointed rim spout, jagged arched handle, the sides decorated w/large colorful panels of flowers, minor rim chips, 19th c. (ILLUS.) **$863**

Early Fitzhugh Pattern Export Plates

Plates, 9 3/4" d., blue Fitzhugh patt., early 19th c., pr. (ILLUS.).................................. **$575**

Chinese Export Tea Set for the American Market

Rose Mandarin Export Sauce Tureen

Sauce tureen, cov., Rose Mandarin design, a deep flaring foot supporting the squatty bulbous oblong body w/double loop end handles, the high domed & stepped cover w/a largber large gold flower finial, 19th c., 8" l., 6" h. (ILLUS.)..................... **$1,265**

Large Chinese Export Soup Tureen

Soup tureen, cov., footed squatty bulbous oval body w/twisted branch end handles, domed cover w/large flower blossom finial, cobalt blue & gilt trim, orange peel glaze, 19th c., 8 x 13 1/2", 11" h. (ILLUS.) **$1,870**

Tea set: cov. teapot, cov. tea caddy, helmet-shaped creamer, cov. cream pot & handleless cup; the oval teapot w/upright sides & a tapering shoulder to the inset cover w/berry finial, the bulbous tapering cream pot w/domed cover, upright flat-sided rectangular tea caddy w/arched shoulder, short neck & domed cap, each piece h.p. on the side in sepia, orange & gold w/a spread-winged American eagle w/shield, made for the American market, late 18th c., teapot 8 1/2" l., the set (ILLUS., top of page) .. **$5,175**

Fine Tall Export Umbrella Stand

Umbrella stand, Famille Rose palette in a Mandarin design, the tall cylindrical ribbed body decoratged up the sides w/three bands containing alternating figural & floral panels, 19th c., 24 3/4" h. (ILLUS.) **$4,025**

Clarice Cliff Designs

Clarice Cliff was a designer for A.J. Wilkinson, Ltd., Royal Staffordshire Pottery, Burslem, England when it acquired the adjoining New-

port Pottery Company, whose warehouses were filled with undecorated bowls and vases. In about 1925 her flair with the Art Deco style was incorporated into designs appropriately named "Bizarre" and "Fantasque" and the warehouse stockpile was decorated in vivid colors. These hand-painted earthenwares, all bearing the printed signature of designer Clarice Cliff, were produced until World War II and are now finding enormous favor with collectors.

Note: Reproductions of the Clarice Cliff "Bizarre" marking have been appearing on the market recently.

Two Pairs of Clarice Cliff Candlesticks

Clarice Cliff Mark

Bowl, 5" d., 3" h., footed flared cylindrical form, Autumn Crocus patt., a yellow band on the inside rim, the exterior w/blue, orange & purple flowers, ca. 1930s (minor glaze scratches)..................................... **$345**

Bowl, 6 1/4" d., octagonal flanged rim on the rounded body, Woodland patt., stylized landscape w/trees in orange, green, black, blue, purple & yellow, marked **$550**

Bowl, 8 3/8" d., 3 1/2" h., round w/deep upright sides, Keyhole patt., a geometric design in yellow, black & green, stamped marks, ca. 1929 (glaze wear)................... **$374**

Bowl, 9" d., deep rounded sides, the upper half w/a wide band in polychrome featuring large stylized cottages w/pointed orange roofs beneath arching trees, lime green banding, marked........................... **$900**

Bowl, 9 1/2" d., 4 1/2" h., orange, green & blue h.p. poppies...................................... **$600**

Butter dish, cov., "Bizarre" ware, short wide cylindrical body w/an inset cover w/large button finial, Secrets patt., decorated w/a stylized landscape in shades of green, yellow & brown w/red-roofed houses on a cream ground, marked, 4" d., 2 5/8" h. **$550**

Candleholders, figural, modeled as a kneeling woman w/her arms raised high holding the candle socket modeled as a basket of flowers, My Garden patt., orange dress & polychrome trim, marked, 7 1/4" h., facing pr. **$1,200**

Candleholders, Fantasque line, cylindrical form w/flared base & rim, Melon patt., decorated w/a band of overlapping fruit in predominantly orange glaze w/yellow, bluish green & brown outline, stamped on base "Hand Painted Fantasque by Clarice Cliff Wilkinson Ltd. England," ca. 1930, minor glaze nicks, two small firing cracks to inside rim of one, 3 1/4" h., pr. **$1,000**

Candlestick, loop-handled, Tonquin patt., red **$30**

Candlesticks, slender baluster-form shaft above a disk foot & w/a wide flattened rim, painted w/bold geometric designs in blue, orange & green, Delicia Citrus patt., brightly painted fruits on a cream ground pr. (ILLUS. left & right) **$2,500**

Candlesticks, squared pedestal foot supporting a tall square tapering shaft & cylindrical socket w/flared rim, decorated in bold geometric designs in orange, cream, green, blue & yellow, pr. (ILLUS. center).. **$2,900**

Condiment set: two jars w/silver-plated lids & a small open bowl fitted in a silver-plated frame w/a looped center handle; each piece h.p. w/stylized red & blue flowers on an ivory ground, marked, tray 4 1/2 x 5", the set (small chip on one piece) **$523**

Cracker jar, cov., "Bizarre" ware, Blue Chintz patt., stylized blue, green & pink blossom forms w/blue border band **$1,200**

Delicia Citrus Cracker Jar & Vases

Cracker jar, cov., "Bizarre" ware, squatty kettle-form w/side knobs supporting the swing bail handle, Delicia Citrus patt. (ILLUS. right) **$900**

Cracker jar, cov., Celtic Harvest patt., spherical footed body decorated w/embossed fruit & sheaves of wheat, chromed metal cover, 6 1/2" h. (chrome wear).. **$173**

Cup & saucer, "Bizarre" ware, Autumn Crocus patt., Athens shape **$300**

Dinner service: four dinner plates, thirteen luncheon plates, fifteen soup bowls, eight fruit plates, seven appetizer plates, four dessert plates, seven cups & saucers, cov. sugar, creamer & serving bowl; Biarritz patt., the square plates w/deep rounded wells, the creamer & sugar w/upright flattened round shapes, each decorated w/concentric bands in black, maroon, taupe, gold & yellow on a cream ground, ca. 1929, marked, the set **$2,000**

Figures, "Bizarre" ware, flat cutouts, comprising two groups of musicians & two groups of dancing couples, all highly stylized & glazed in reddish orange, yellow, lime green, cream & black, printed factory marks, ca. 1925, 5 5/8 to 7" h., 4 pcs. ... **$35,000**

Jam jar, cov., cylindrical body, Melon patt., decorated w/a band of overlapping fruit, predominantly orange w/yellow, blue & green w/brown outline, ca. 1930, restoration to rim & side, marked, 4" h. **$690**

Pitcher, 5 3/4" h., "Fantasque" line, Melon patt., wide conical body w/solid triangular handle, orange & thin black bands flanking a wide central band of stylized melons in yellow, blue, green & orange, marked, ca. 1930 (tiny glaze nicks at rim & base, faint scratch in lower orange band) **$875**

Pitcher, 7" h., 7" d., "Bizarre" ware, tapering cylindrical body w/flat rim & wide pointed spout, flattened angled handle from rim to base, Sliced Fruit patt., wide band of abstract fruit in yellow, orange & red, stamped mark **$1,800**

Pitcher, 9 1/4" h., My Garden patt., wide rim tapering to a flared base w/embossed flowers ornamenting the handle in orange, green & brown on a light tan ground, post-1936 .... **$288**

Lotus Pitcher in Delicia Citrus Pattern

Pitcher, 12" h., "Bizarre" ware, Lotus shape, ringed ovoid body tapering to a wide cylindrical neck, heavy loop handle, Delicia Citrus patt., large stylized red, yellow & orange fruits around the top w/green leaves & streaky green on a cream ground (ILLUS.) **$2,200**

Pitcher, 12" h., jug-type, "Bizarre" ware, Trees & House patt., ovoid w/molded narrow rings, decorated w/wide bands of orange & black flanking a wide central band w/green-roofed houses & black & orange trees, marked, ca. 1930 .... **$2,000**

Plate, 7 3/4" d., Broth patt., predominantly orange w/bubbles & orange, purple & blue cobwebs (few glaze scratches) **$230**

Plate, 10" d., "Fantasque" line, Autumn (Balloon Trees) patt. w/blue, yellow,

green & purple trees & orange striped border bands, base stamped "Fantasque Hand Painted Bizarre by Clarice Cliff Newport Pottery England" **$1,725**

Sugar shaker, Autumn patt., sharply pointed conical form w/rows of small holes pierced around the top, decorated in pastel autumn colors, marked, 5 1/2" h. **$1,700**

Sugar shaker, "Bizarre" ware, Bonjour shape, flattened egg-shaped body set on two tiny log-form feet, Crocus patt., banded body w/a central row of stylized crocus blossoms, in yellow, blue, orange & purple, stamped mark, 2 1/2" w., 5" h. **$900**

Clarice Cliff Bizarre Ware Tumbler

Tumbler, Bizarre Ware, slightly flaring cylindrical form, half-round stylized large blossoms along edge of rim in orange, pale green & yellow w/matching narrow bands around the inner rim, minor glaze nicks, 3 5/8" h. (ILLUS.) **$115**

Tumbler, Sunray patt., conical form, polychrome decoration of a stylized sun, orange banding, marked, 3" h. **$800**

Vase, 5 1/4" h., "Bizarre" ware, Shape No. 341, squatty bulbous chalice-form, Delicia Citrus patt., bright fruits on a creamy ground (ILLUS. left w/cracker jar) **$900**

Vase, 8" h., "Bizarre" ware, Shape No. 362, ovoid upper body above a heavy ringed & waisted base, Delicia Citrus patt., brightly painted fruits on a cream ground (ILLUS. center w/cracker jar) **$900**

Crocus Pattern Vase

Vase, 8" h., "Bizarre" ware, Shape No. 386, swelled cylindrical base below the angled shoulder & tall gently flaring neck, Crocus patt., a yellow rim band & brown bottom section below a cluster of colorful crocus blossoms on a cream ground (ILLUS., previous page) **$1,000**

Vase, 9" h., 4 3/4" d., "Bizarre" ware, baluster-shaped, Original Bizarre patt., a wide middle band of multicolored triangles flanked by a dark blue rim band & yellow & orange base bands, No. 264, ink mark (minor wear) **$2,500**

Vase, 9 1/2" h., 6 1/2" d., "Bizarre" ware, Isis shape, ovoid body tapering to a wide, flat rim, decorated in the Melon patt., bold stylized abstract fruits in dark red, blue, orange, green & yellow around the middle flanked by wide dark orange bands, ink mark... **$3,200**

Vase, 12 1/4" h., gently flaring conical body on a wide round foot, molded in bold relief w/green & yellow budgie birds on a leafy branch against a light blue shaded to cream ground **$410**

Vases, 8" h., "Bizarre" ware, footed ovoid body w/flared rim, Crocus patt., orange, blue & purple crocuses, green, brown & yellow bands, small glaze chip, marked, pr. **$690**

Clewell Wares

Although Charles W. Clewell of Canton, Ohio, didn't operate a pottery, he is responsible for a category of fine art pottery through his development of a unique metal coating placed on pottery blanks obtained from Owens, Weller and others. By encasing objects in a thin metal shell, he produced copper- and bronze-finished ceramics. Later experiments led him to chemically treat the metal coating to attain the bluish green patinated effect associated with copper and bronze. Although he produced metal-coated pottery from 1902 until the mid-1950s, Clewell's production was quite limited, for he felt no one else could competently recreate his artwork, therefore operated a small shop with little help.

Clewell Wares Mark

Fine Clewell Table Lamp

Lamp, table-type, a hammered brass ringed foot supporting to tall baluster-form body w/a fine crusty bluish green finish, hammered- copper cap & eletrical fittings at the top, bottom signed "Clewell 277-6" & w/old paper label under the cap reads "$45.00," lamp body 15 3/4" h. (ILLUS.) ... **$978**

Clewell Presentation Mug

Mug, footed paneled ovoid form w/faux rivets along panels, presentation-type, panels on front read "APA - 1908," marked on base "Clewell Canton, O," 4 1/4" h. (ILLUS.).. **$150**

Clewell Vase with Vines & Berries

Vase, 8" h., cylindrical slightly flaring form molded in high relief w/vertical vines topped by leaves & berries, good original patina, minor lines (ILLUS.) **$374**

Simple Clewell Clad Vase

Vase, 9 7/8" h., squatty bulbous base tapering to a tall cylindrical neck, nicely patinated, incised "Clewell 266-2," few minor breaks in copper (ILLUS.) **$805**

Coalport

Coalport Porcelain Works operated at Coalport, Shropshire, England, from about 1795 to 1926 and has operated at Stoke-on-Trent as Coalport China, Ltd., making bone china, since then.

Box, cov., flat-bottomed spherical form, the domed cover w/a central "agate" panel surrounded by a gilt band enameled w/"ruby" jewels, radiating alternating cartouches of "agate" or turquoise "jewels," on an embossed gold ground w/overall tiny blue

Very Ornate Coalport Small Box

beading, each reserve against a pale blue band w/ornate gilt urn designs, the base w/matching decoration, interior & base in powdered gilt, dated 1893, green printed crown mark, overprinted gilt Chicago Exhibition mark, probably designed by T.J. Bott, 4 1/2" d. (ILLUS.) **$2,629**

Ornate Beaded Gold Coalport Ewer

Ewer, ring-footed baluster-form body tapering to a slender neck w/long arched spout & ornate gold C-scroll handle, creamy white ground, the side painted w/a small oval lakeside landscape against a wide embossed gold band decorated overall w/graduated turquoise beading, gilt scroll & band trim, ca. 1900, green crowned mark, Registration No. 283672, 7 3/8" h. (ILLUS.) **$956**

Very Ornate Coalport Loving Cup

Loving cup, three-handled, the tall domed, knopped & ringed pedestal base in cobalt blue w/ornate gold trim, supporting a large deep rounded trefoil bowl surrounded by three fancy gold C-scroll handles, the upper cobalt blue band centered by a small landscape medallion w/a lakeside view framed in gold & w/ornate gold scrolling above the creamy white lower body, green printed crowned mark, Pattern No. V5950, ca. 1900, 9" h. (ILLUS.) **$837**

Coalport China Canton Pattern Teapot

Teapot, cov., Canton patt., Kingsware line, footed squatty bulbous gently lobed body w/a wide mouth, domed cover w/arched loop finial, angled spout, C-scroll handle, part of the Wedgwood Group, England (ILLUS.).. **$90**

Vase, 5 3/4" h., the short flaring pedestal base in gold w/turquoise beading supporting the wide squatty bulbous body w/a deep ruby red ground painted on the front w/a quatrefoil panel w/a lakeside landscape within a border band of ornate gilt scrolling, large angular gold shoulder handles, the wide short cream-ground neck & domed cover w/overall turquoise blue beading, ca. 1900, printed green

Ruby Ground Ornate Coalport Vase

crowned mark, Pattern No. V6677, mark of retailer Bailey, Banks & Biddle, Philadelphia (ILLUS.) **$1,434**

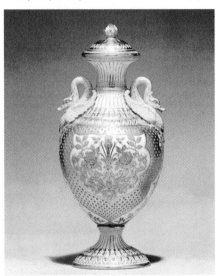

Outstanding Gold & Cream Coalport Vase

Vase, cov., 9 3/4" h., domed foot & short stem supporting the large ovoid body tapering to a trumpet neck w/domed cover & berry finial, cream ground, the gilt-trimmed cover above a collared gadrooned neck flanked by figural swan handles, the sides & central body decorated w/a meandering vine issuing cones, reserved on a shield-shaped embossed gold ground decorated w/graduated turquoise beading, ca. 1900, printed green crowned mark, Pattern No. V.2497 (ILLUS.)... **$1,912**

Cowan

R. Guy Cowan opened his first pottery studio in 1912 in Lakewood, Ohio. The pottery operated almost continuously, with the exception of a break during the First World War, at various locations in the Cleveland area until it was forced to close in 1931 due to financial difficulties.

Many of this century's finest artists began with Cowan and its associate, the Cleveland School of Art. This fine art pottery, particularly the designer pieces, are highly sought after by collectors.

Many people are unaware that it was due to R. Guy Cowan's perseverance and tireless work that art pottery is today considered an art form and found in many art museums.

Cowan Marks

Cowan Ashtrays, Flower Frog & Vase

Ashtray, model of a ram, green, designed by Edris Eckhardt, 5 1/4" l., 3 1/2" h. (ILLUS. lower left with chick ashtray/nut dish) **$225**

Ashtray/nut dish, ivory glaze, Shape No. 769, 1" h. **$20**

Cowan Clown Ashtrays & Vases

Ashtray/nut dish, figural clown Periot, blue or ivory glaze, designed by Elizabeth Anderson, Shape No. 788, 2 1/2 x 3", each (ILLUS. lower center) **$130**

Ashtray/nut dish, model of a chick, green glaze, Shape No. 768, 3 1/2" h. (ILLUS. bottom center, top next column)................. **$90**

Book ends, figural Art Deco-style elephant, push & pull, tan glaze, designed by Thelma F. Winter, one Shape No. 840 & one Shape No. 841, 4 3/4" h., pr...................... **$800**

Cowan Bookends & Model of Horse

Bookends, figural, model of a seated polar bear, front paws near face, ivory glaze, designed by Margaret Postgate, 6" h., pr. (ILLUS. left) **$1,200**

Bookends, figural, a little girl standing wearing a large sunbonnet & full ruffled dress, verde green, designed by Kat. Barnes Jenkins, Shape No. 521, 7" h., pr. **$350**

Bookends, figural, model of a unicorn, front legs raised on relief-molded foliage base, orange glaze, designed by Waylande Gregory, Shape No. 961, mark No. 8, 7" h., pr. (ILLUS. left, next page)............ **$1,200**

Variety of Cowan Animal Pieces

Bookends, figural, model of a ram, black, thick rectangular base w/slanted top, Shape No. E-3, designed by Waylande Gregory, 7 1/2" h., pr............................. **$1,800**

Cowan Bookends & Ashtray

Bookends, model of a stylized horse, back legs raised in kicking position, black, designed by Waylande Gregory, Shape No. E-1, 9" h., pr. (ILLUS. of one, with ashtray & boy & girl bookends)........................... **$2,000**

Bowl, miniature, 2" d., footed, flared body, Shape No. 514, mark No. 5, orange lustre... **$50**

Bowl, 7 1/2" w., octagonal, the alternating side panels hand-decorated w/floral design, brown & yellow glaze, Shape No. B-5-B **$300**

Bowl, w/drip, 3 x 9 1/2", blue lustre finish, Shape No. 701-A....................................... **$100**

Bowl, 3 x 11 1/4", designed to imitate hand molding, two-tone blue glaze, Shape No. B-827.. **$225**

Bowl, 3 x 10 x 11 1/2", leaf design, ivory & green, designed by Waylande Gregory..... **$175**

Bowl, 3 x 6 x 12 1/2" oblong, caramel w/light green glaze, Shape No. 683 .... **$60**

Bowl, 3 x 8 1/2 x 16 1/4", footed shallow form, flaring scalloped sides & rim, downcurved side handles, ivory exterior w/blue interior glaze, Shape No. 743-B **$125**

Bowl-vase, green & gold, Shape No. B-4, 11"... **$250**

Buttons, decorated w/various zodiac designs, by Paul Bogatay, 50 pcs................ **$500**

Candelabrum, "Pavlova," porcelain, two-light, Art Deco style, a footed squatty tapering central dish issuing at each side a stylized hand holding an upturned cornucopia-form candle socket, the center fitted w/a figure of a nude female dancer standing on one leg w/her other leg raised, her torso arched over & holding a long swirled drapery, Special Ivory glaze, stamped mark, 10" l., 7" h. (chip under rim of one bobeche) **$525**

Candleholder, figural, model of a Viking ship prow, green glaze, Shape No. 777, 5 1/4" h.. **$35**

Candleholders, ivory glaze, Shape No. 692, 2 1/4" h., pr... **$25**

Candleholders, footed, designed by R.G. Cowan, ivory, Shape No. 811, 2 3/8" h., pr... **$35**

Candleholders, semicircular wave design, white glaze, Shape No. 751, 4 3/4" h., pr. **$100**

Various Cowan Pieces

Candlestick, flared base below twisted column, blossom-form cup, green & orange drip glaze, Shape No. 625-A, 7 3/4" h. (ILLUS. far right) **$100**

Candlestick, figural, Byzantine figure flanked by angels, golden yellow glaze, designed by R.G. Cowan, 9 1/4" h. (ILLUS. left)......... **$325**

Byzantine Angel Candlesticks

Candlestick, figural, Byzantine figure flanked by angels, salmon glaze, designed by R.G. Cowan, 9 1/4" h. (ILLUS. right, previous page) $375

Cowan Figural Nude Candlestick

Candlestick, two-light, large figural nude standing w/head tilted & holding a swirling drapery, flanked by blossom-form candle sockets supported by scrolled leaves at the base, matte ivory glaze, designed by R.G. Cowan, Shape No. 745, 7 1/2" w., 9 3/4" h. (ILLUS.) $1,000

Candlestick/bud vase, tapering cylindrical shape w/flared foot & rim, blue lustre, Shape 530-A, 7 1/2" h. $70

Candlesticks, curled form, royal blue, 1 1/2" h., pr. $75

Candlesticks, figural grape handles, ivory glaze, 4" h., pr. $85

Candlesticks, w/loop handle, green, Shape No. 781, 4" h., pr. $65

Candlesticks, "The Girl Reserve," designed by R.G. Cowan, medium blue, Shape No. 671, 5 1/2" h., pr. $275

Centerpiece set, 6 1/4" h. trumpet-form vase centered on 8" sq. base w/candle socket in each corner, Princess line, vase Shape No. V-1, Mark No. 8, candelabra Shape No. S-2, Mark No. 8, black matte, 2 pcs., together w/four nut dishes/open compotes, green glaze, Shape No. C-1, Mark No. 8, the set $500

Charger, wall plaque, yellow, 11 1/4" d. $75

Charger, octagonal, hand-decorated by Thelma Frazier Winter, 13 1/4" $1,000

Cigarette/match holder, sea horse decoration, pink, No. 726, 3 1/2 x 4" $55

Clip dish, green, 3 1/4" d. (part of desk set, Shape PB-1)... $25

Console bowl, octagonal, stand-up-type, verde green, Shape No. 689, 3 x 8 x 8 1/2" $70

Console bowl, footed, low rounded sides w/incurved rim, orange lustre, Shape No. 567-B, 2 3/4 x 9 3/4" $40

Console bowl, April green, Shape No. B-1, 11 1/2" l., 2 1/4" h...................................... $75

Console bowl, ivory & pink glaze, Shape No. 763, 3 1/4 x 9 x 16 1/2"....................... $65

Console bowl, w/wave design, verde green, designed by Waylande Gregory, 2 3/4 x 9 x 17 1/2" $250

Console bowls, 3 3/4 x 4 1/2 x 11", two-handled, footed, widely flaring fluted sides, verde green, Shape No. 538, pr. $225

Console set: 6 1/2 x 10 1/2 x 17" bowl & pr. of candleholders; footed bowl w/figural bird handles, lobed sides, designed by Alexander Blazys, Shape No. 729, mottled blue glaze, the set $425

Console set: 9" d. bowl & pair of 4" h. candleholders; ivory & purple glaze, Shape Nos. 733-A & 734...................................... $150

Cowan Decanters & Wine Cups

Decanter w/stopper, figural King of Clubs, a seated robed & bearded man w/a large crown on his head & holding a scepter, black glaze w/gold, designed by Waylande Gregory, Shape E-4, 10" h. (ILLUS. left) $750

Decanter w/stopper, figural Queen of Hearts, seated figure holding scepter & wearing crown, Oriental Red glaze, designed by Waylande Gregory, Shape No. E-5, 10 1/2" h. (ILLUS. right with King of Clubs decanter)....................................... $700

Figurine, "Pierette," stylized figure of young woman wearing a short flaring skirt & holding a scarf behind her, russet & salmon glaze, designed by Elizabeth Anderson, Shape No. 792, 8 1/4" h. (ILLUS. center with polar bear bookends).......... $1,000

Figurine, kneeling female nude, almond glaze, 9" h. $325

Russian Tambourine Player Figurine

Figurine, Russian peasant, "Tambourine Player," white crackle glaze, designed by Alexander Blazys, Shape No. 757-760, 9" h. (ILLUS.) **$750**

Figurine, "Persephone," standing female nude holding a long scarf out to one side and near her shoulder, ivory glaze, designed by Waylande Gregory, Shape No. D-6, 15" h. **$2,750**

Figurine, "Nautch Dancer," female w/a flaring pleated skirt on rectangular base, semi-matte ivory glaze w/silver accents, incised "Waylande Gregory," impressed mark, 6 3/4 x 9 1/4", 17 3/4" h................ **$5,000**

Finger bowl, Egyptian blue, Shape No. B-19, 3"... **$75**

Flower frog, figural, Art Deco dancing nude woman leaning back w/one leg raised & the ends of a long scarf held in her outstretched hands, overall white glaze, impressed mark, 7 1/2" h. **$325**

Flower frog, figural, Art Deco nude scarf dancer, No. 35, ivory glaze, signed, 7 1/4" h... **$375**

Flower frog, figural, Art Deco style, two nude females partially draped in flowing scarves, each bending backward away from the other w/one hand holding the scarf behind each figure & their other hand joined, on an oval base w/flower holes, ivory glaze, designed by R.G. Cowan, Shape No. 685, 7 1/2" h. (ILLUS. lower right with "Repose" flower frog) **$600**

Flower frog, figural, "Diver," waveform base w/tall wave supporting nude female figure, back arched & arms raised over head, ivory glaze, designed by R.G. Cowan, Shape No. 683, 8" h. (ILLUS. right, top next column) **$800**

Flower frog, figural, "Fan Dancer," a standing seminude Art Deco woman, posed w/one leg kicked to the back, her torso bent back w/one arm raised & curved overhead, the other arm curved around her waist holding a long feather fan, a long drapery hangs down the front from her waist, on a rounded incurved broad leaf cluster base, overall Original Ivory glaze, designed by R.G. Cowan, Shape No. 806, stamped mark, 4" w., 9 1/2" h. **$2,000**

Cowan Female Form Flower Frogs

Flower frog, figural, "Marching Girl," Art Deco style, a nude female partially draped w/a flowing scarf standing & leaning backward w/one hand on her hip & the other raising the scarf above her head, on an oblong serpentine-molded wave base w/flower holes, ivory glaze, designed by R.G. Cowan, Shape No. 680, 8" h. (ILLUS. lower left with "Repose" flower frog) **$325**

Flower frog, figural, nude female, one leg kneeling on thick round base, head bent to one side & looking upward, one arm resting on knee of bent leg w/the other hand near her foot, ivory glaze, designed by Walter Sinz, 6" h. (ILLUS. left with Diver flower frog)... **$375**

Flower frog, figural, Pan sitting on large toadstool, ivory glaze, designed by W. Gregory, Shape No. F-9, 9" h. (ILLUS. with ram & chick ashtrays, page 164) **$650**

Various Cowan Flower Frogs

Flower frog, figural, "Repose," Art Deco style, a seminude sinewy woman standing & slightly curved backward, her arms away from her sides holding trailing drapery, in a cupped blossom-form base, ivory glaze, designed by R.G. Cowan, Shape No. 712, 6 1/2" h. (ILLUS. lower center, previous page) **$350**

Flower frog, figural, "Scarf Dancer," Art Deco-style nude dancing woman in a curved pose standing on one leg & holding the ends of a long scarf in her outstretched hands, ivory glaze, designed by R.G. Cowan, Shape No. 686, 7" h. (ILLUS. top with "Repose" flower frog, previous page) **$325**

Flower frog, figural, "Wreath Girl," figure of a woman standing on a blossom-form base & holding up the long tails of her flowing skirt, ivory glaze, designed by R.G. Cowan, Shape No. 721, 10" h. (ILLUS. center with Diver flower frog, previous page) **$650**

Flower frog, model of a deer, designed by Waylande Gregory, ivory glaze, Shape No. F-905, 8 1/4" h. (ILLUS. right with unicorn book ends, page 165)................... **$450**

Flower frog, model of a flamingo, orange glaze, designed by Waylande Gregory, Shape No. D2-F, 11 3/4" h. **$700**

Flower frog, model of a reindeer, designed by Waylande Gregory, polychrome finish, Shape No. 903, 11" h. (ILLUS. center with unicorn book ends, page 165) **$1,500**

Ginger jar, cov., blue lustre, Shape No. 513, 6 3/4" h. **$250**

Lamp, foliage decoration, 9" h...................... **$275**

Lamp, moth decoration, blue, w/fittings, 13" h., overall 22" h. **$425**

Lamp base, Art Deco style, angular, green, designed by Waylande Gregory, Shape No. 821, 8 3/8" h. **$250**

Cowan Lamp Base

Lamp base, round domed base below modernist teardrop-shaped body decorated w/nude female figure, ivory & brown glaze, designed by Waylande Gregory, 11" h. (ILLUS.) **$1,250**

Model of elephant, standing on square plinth, head & trunk down, rich mottled Oriental Red glaze, designed by Margaret Postgate, ca. 1930, faint impressed mark on plinth & paper label reading "X869 Elephant designed by M....et P....," 10 1/2" h... **$2,500**

Model of horse, standing animal on an oblong base, Egyptian blue glaze, designed by Viktor Schreckengost, 7 3/4" h. (ILLUS. right with polar bear bookends, page 164) **$3,000**

Model of ram, Oriental Red glaze, designed by Edris Eckhart, 3 1/2" h......................... **$250**

Pen base, maroon, Shape No. PB-2, 3 3/4" **$65**

Plaque, hand-decorated by Arthur E. Baggs, Egyptian blue, artist-signed "AEB," 2 1/2 x 12 1/2" **$2,200**

Strawberry jar w/saucer, light green, designed by R.G. Cowan, Shape No. SJ-6, 6" h., 2 pcs. **$250**

Trivet, round, center portrait of young woman's face encircled by a floral border, white on blue ground, impressed mark & "Cowan," 6 5/8" d. (minor staining from usage) **$225**

Cowan Urn w/Figural Grape Handles

Urn, cov., black w/gold trim & figural grape cluster handles, Shape No. V-95, 10 1/4" h. (ILLUS.) **$275**

Urn, Lakeware, blue, Shape V-102, 5 1/2" h. (ILLUS. left with vases, top next page).. **$75**

Vase, 4" h., bulbous ovoid tapering to cylindrical neck, Jet Black glaze, Shape No. V-5 (ILLUS. center w/urn, top next page) **$250**

Vase, 4" h., waisted cylindrical body w/bulbous top & wide flaring rim, mottled orange glaze, Shape No. 630 (ILLUS. second from left w/No. 625-A candlestick) **$75**

Vase, 4 3/4" h., bulbous body w/horizontal ribbing, wide cylindrical neck, green glaze, Shape No. V-30 (ILLUS. lower left with clown ashtrays)................................... **$50**

Vase, 4 3/4" h., bulbous body w/horizontal ribbing, wide cylindrical neck, mottled turquoise glaze, Shape No. V-30 .... **$75**

Cowan Lakeware Urn & Vases

Vase, 4 3/4" h., waterfall, designed by Paul Bogatay, maroon, hand-decorated, Shape No. V-77 .... **$950**

Vase, 4 3/4" h., wide tapering cylindrical body, mottled orange, brown & rust, Shape No. V-34 (ILLUS. second from right w/No. 625-A candlestick) **$60**

Vase, 5" h., fan-shaped, designed by R.G. Cowan, golden yellow, Shape No. V-801.... **$60**

Vase, 5 1/2" h., Lakeware, bulbous base w/wide shoulder tapering to wide cylindrical neck, blue glaze, Shape No. V-72 .... **$60**

Vase, 6 1/4" h., experimental, polychrome, designed by Arthur E. Baggs, Shape No. 15-A, artist signed "AEB" **$1,250**

Vase, bud, 6 1/4" h., flaring domed foot below ovoid body tapering to cylindrical neck w/flaring rim, plum glaze, Shape No. 916.. **$75**

Vase, 6 1/2" h., blue & green, Shape No. V-55 .... **$95**

Cowan Decorated Vases

Vase, 6 1/2" h., bulbous body w/short molded rim, black w/Egyptian blue bands & center decoration, designed by Whitney Atchley, Shape No. V-38 (ILLUS. right) **$1,600**

Vase, 6 1/2" h., footed, squatty bulbous base w/trumpet-form neck, flattened sides w/notched corners, green glaze, Shape No. V-649-A (ILLUS. right w/urn) **$100**

Vase, 6 1/2" h., mottled dark blue & green, Shape No. V-55 .... **$125**

Vase, 6 1/2" h., wide bulbous body, yellow glaze, Shape V-91 .... **$200**

Vase, 6 5/8" h., bright yellow glaze, Shape No. 797 .... **$75**

Vase, 7" h., fan-shaped w/scalloped foot & domed base decorated w/relief-molded sea horse decoration, pink glaze, Shape No. 715-A **$50**

Vase, 7" h., Lakeware, bulbous base w/trumpet-form neck, Oriental Red glaze, Shape No. V-75 .... **$125**

Vase, 7 1/4" h., footed slender ovoid body w/flaring rim, Oriental Red glaze, Shape No. V-12.. **$150**

Vase, 7 1/2" h., flared foot below paneled ovoid body, orange lustre glaze, Shape No. 691-A, mark No. 6 .... **$75**

Vase, 7 1/2" h., footed, tapering cylindrical body, green drip over yellow glaze, Shape No. 591, 8" h. (ILLUS. far right with clown ashtrays).................................... **$300**

Vase, 7 1/2" h., tall slender ovoid body w/short cylindrical neck, orange lustre, Shape No. 552 (ILLUS. lower right with chick & ram ashtrays) **$80**

Vase, 8" h., blue lustre, Shape No. 615 .... **$75**

Vase, 8" h., bulbous body tapering to cylindrical neck w/flaring rim, gold, Shape No. V-932 (ILLUS. far left w/No. 625-A candlestick).. **$175**

Vase, 8" h., bulbous body tapering to cylindrical neck w/flaring rim, black drip over Feu Rouge (red) glaze Shape No. V-932 (ILLUS. top with clown ashtrays) **$325**

Vase, 8" h., cylindrical body, black w/overall turquoise blue decoration, triple-signed (ILLUS. left with bulbous vase) **$750**

Vase, 8" h., footed bulbous body w/trumpet-form neck, yellow shading to green drip glaze, Shape No. 627 (ILLUS. top center w/No. 625-A candlestick) **$225**

Wine cups, Oriental Red glaze, Shape No. X-17, 2 1/2" h., each (ILLUS. of two, front left with decanter)...................................... **$35**

Dedham & Chelsea Keramic Art Works

This pottery was organized in 1866 by Alexander W. Robertson in Chelsea, Massachusetts, and became A.W. & H. Robertson in 1868. In 1872, the name was changed to Chelsea Keramic Art Works and in 1891 to Chelsea Pottery, U.S.A. About 1895, the pottery was moved to Dedham, Massachusetts, and was renamed Dedham Pottery. Production ceased in 1943. High-fired colored wares and crackle ware were specialties. The rabbit is said to have been the most popular decoration on crackle ware in blue.

Since 1977, the Potting Shed, Concord, Massachusetts, has produced quality reproductions of early Dedham wares. These pieces are carefully marked to avoid confusion with original examples.

Dedham & Chelsea Keramic Art Works Marks

Dedham Pottery Rabbit Pattern Bowl

Bowl, 9" d., 3 1/2" h., Rabbit patt., base marked "Registered," 1929-43 (ILLUS.).... **$288**

Dedham Rabbit Celery Tray

Celery tray, oval, Rabbit patt., base marked "Registered," 1929-43, 6 1/4 x 9 3/4" (ILLUS.) **$240**

Dedham Horse Chestnut Creamer

Creamer, squatty bulbous shape, Horse Chestnut patt., base marked "Registered," 1929-43, 4 1/2" d., 3 1/4" h. (ILLUS.) **$640**

Dedham Five-sided Rabbit Dish

Dish, five-sided shallow form, Rabbit patt., base marked "Registered," 1929-43, 7 1/2" w., 1 1/2" h. (ILLUS.)..................... **$360**

Early Chelsea Keramic Art Ewer

Ewer, footed squatty bulbous base w/a wide round shoulder centered by a tall cylindrical neck w/a tri-corner rim & high arched handle from the rim to the shoulder, overall mottled darak green & black majolica-like glaze, pre-1880 three-line mark "Chelsea Keramic - Art Work - Robertson and Sons," overall crazing, 11 3/8" h. (ILLUS.)................................... **$345**

Dedham Elephant Marmalade Jar

Marmalade jar, cov., barrel-shaped, Elephant patt., blue mark on base, cover w/3" slice off edge, 4" d., 3 3/4" h. (ILLUS.)........ **$403**

Plate, 4 3/8" d., butter size, Swan patt. **$259**

Dedham Duck Pattern Plate

Plate, 6" d., Duck patt., base marked "Registered," 1929-43, two rim hairlines (ILLUS.) ... **$96**

Plate, 6 1/8" d., bread & butter size, Horse Chestnut patt. **$144**

Plate, 7 1/2" d., salad size, Lobster patt....... **$288**

Dedham Turkey Pattern Plate

Plate, 8 1/2" d., Turkey patt., base marked "Registered," 1929-43 (ILLUS.)................. **$270**

Dedham Horse Chestnut Plate

Plate, 9 3/4" d., Horse Chestnut patt., impressed rabbit mark (ILLUS.) **$60**

Pair of Dedham Flower-decorated Plates

Plates, 6 1/4" d., unknown flower design, base marked "Registered," 1929-43, & impressed rabbit mark (ILLUS.) **$345**

Dedham Elephant Pattern Sugar Bowl

Sugar bowl, cov., squatty bulbous shaped w/wide flat rim, wide flattened cover w/button finial, Elephant patt., 2" slice off side of cover, in-the-making mark on rim, 4" d., 3" h. (ILLUS.) **$345**

Rare Dedham Rabbit Pattern Tureen

Tureen, cov., footed squatty bulbous oblong shaped w/small buttress end handles, domed cover w/figural rabbit finial, two bands of Rabbit patt. decoration, small chip inside rim, 7 1/2 x 11", 8" h. (ILLUS.) **$2,185**

Small Chelsea Keramic Art Vase

Vase, 3 3/4" h., 4 1/4" w., flattened pillow-shape on scroll feet, the sides carved in relief w/blue violets & green leaves on a bottle green ground, stamped "CKAW" & artist-signed "TT" or "TM," Chelsea Keramic Art Works (ILLUS., previous page) **$881**

Experimental Robertson Dedham Vase

Vase, 7 1/2" h., 4 1/2" d., simple ovoid shape w/a short cylindrical neck, experimental design covered in a matte green orange-peel glaze, by Hugh Robertson, firing lines in the base incised mark "Dedham Pottery - HCR" (ILLUS.) **$1,998**

Delft

In the early 17th century Italian potters settled in Holland and began producing tin-glazed earthenwares, often decorated with pseudo-Oriental designs based on Chinese porcelain wares. The city of Delft became the center of this pottery production and several firms produced the wares throughout the 17th and early 18th century. A majority of the pieces featured blue on white designs, but polychrome wares were also made. The Dutch Delftwares were also shipped to England, where eventually the English copied them at potteries in such cities as Bristol, Lambeth and Liverpool. Although still produced today, Delft peaked in popularity by the mid-18th century.

Large Dutch Delft Floral Charger

Charger, round shallow dished form w/a narrow flanged rim, the center w/a large rounded panel-sided reserve h.p. w/leafy scrolls around a round center w/a stylized leafy blossom, the border band decprated w/small oval reserves decorated w/scrolls & squiggles, a blue initial or X under the bottom, various glaze & rim chips, Holland, 18th c., 13 3/4" d. (ILLUS.) **$460**

Derby & Royal Crown Derby

William Duesbury, in partnership with John and Christopher Heath, established the Derby Porcelain Works in Derby, England about 1750. Duesbury soon bought out his partners and in 1770 purchased the Chelsea factory and six years later, the Bow works. Duesbury was succeeded by his son and grandson. Robert Bloor purchased the business about 1814 and managed successfully until illness in 1828 left him unable to exercise control. The "Bloor" Period, however, extends from 1814 until 1848, when the factory closed. Former Derby workmen then resumed porcelain manufacture in another factory and this nucleus eventually united with a new and distinct venture in 1878 which, after 1890, was known as Royal Crown Derby.

A variety of anchor and crown marks have been used since the 18th century.

Derby & Royal Crown Derby Marks

Royal Crown Derby Imari-style Candlesticks

Candlesticks, decorated in the Imari taste, squared foot w/incurved sides & a dolphin head at each corner, tapering to a tall baluster stem supporting a squatty socket w/a widely flaring dished bobeche, in shades of white, brick red, cobalt blue & gold, Royal Crown Derby mark, 10 1/2" h., pr. (ILLUS.) **$1,093**

Large Royal Crown Derby Dinner Service in Imari Patterns

Cup & saucer, cylindrical cup w/angled handle, painted in the "Japan" patt. in a bright Imari palette, Bloor era, ca. 1815-30, cup 2 3/4" h. **$161**

Dinner service: 12 dinner plates, six luncheon plates, five bread & butter plates, three large soup bowls, two small soup bowls, five cups & saucers, five oval vegetable bowls, four crescent-shaped bone dishes, two oval platters, one oval open vegetable dish, a cov. cigarette box & an English saucer in a similar design; composed of several very similar Imari patterns w/different factory marks, in shades of brick red, cobalt blue, white & gold, Royal Crown Derby, second quarter 20th c., the set (ILLUS., top of page) **$2,300**

by crown mark, crossed batons & "D" mark w/triangle, incised Model No. 195, attributed to J.J. Spengler, ca. 1775, 12 1/4" h. (ILLUS.) **$3,824**

Teapot, cov., Old Avesbury (gold Avesbury) patt., oblong cylindrical body w/narrow angled shoulder, domed cover w/flower finial, straight spout, angled scrolled handle, modern, part of Royal Doulton Tableware, Ltd., England (ILLUS, top next page.)... **$1,350**

Early Derby Bisque Figure Group

Figure group, bisque, modeled as two Classical maidens by a flowering tree pointing down at the sleeping figure of Cupid, his head resting on his quiver, his bow on the ground at his side, rockwork base w/scattered blossoms, incised Der-

Tall Very Ornate Royal Crown Derby Vase

Vase, 15 1/2" h., ringed pedestal foot supporting a tall ovoid body w/a slender trumpet neck w/rolled scalloped rim, long delicate double C-scroll gold handles from base of neck down the sides, cobalt blue ground w/scattered delicate gilt scrolls, the front & back each w/a large colorful floral bouquet within an ornate raised gilt acanthus leaf & bellflower scrolling cartouche, embossed roses above the round foot, Royal Crown Derby red crowned monogram mark, Shape No. 1492, artist-signed & dated 1920 (ILLUS.)................. **$3,107**

Quality Royal Crown Derby Modern Teapot

Doulton & Royal Doulton

Doulton & Co., Ltd., was founded in Lambeth, London, in about 1858. It was operated there until 1956 and often incorporated the words "Doulton" and "Lambeth" in its marks. Pinder, Bourne & Co., Burslem was purchased by the Doultons in 1878 and in 1882 became Doulton & Co., Ltd. It added porcelain to its earthenware production in 1884. The "Royal Doulton" mark has been used since 1902 by this factory, which is still in operation. Character jugs and figurines are commanding great attention from collectors at the present time.

John Doulton, the founder, was born in 1793. He became an apprentice at the age of 12 to a potter in south London. Five years later he was employed in another small pottery near Lambeth. His two sons, John and Henry, subsequently joined their father in 1830 in a partnership he had formed with the name of Doulton & Watts. Watts retired in 1864 and the partnership was dissolved. Henry formed a new company that traded as Doulton & Co.

In the early 1870s the proprietor of the Pinder Bourne Co., located in Burslem, Staffordshire, offered Henry a partnership. The Pinder Bourne Co. was purchased by Henry in 1878 and became part of Doulton & Co. in 1882.

With the passage of time the demand for the Lambeth industrial and decorative stoneware declined whereas demand for the Burslem manufactured and decorated bone china wares increased.

Doulton & Co. was incorporated as a limited liability company in 1899. In 1901 the company was allowed to use the word "Royal" on its trademarks by Royal Charter. The well known "lion on crown" logo came into use in 1902. In 2000 the logo was changed on the company's advertising literature to one showing a more stylized lion's head in profile.

Today Royal Doulton is one of the world's leading manufacturers and distributors of premium grade ceramic tabletop wares and collectibles. The

Doulton Group comprises Minton, Royal Albert, Caithness Glass, Holland Studio Craft and Royal Doulton. Royal Crown Derby was part of the group from 1971 until 2000 when it became an independent company. These companies market collectibles using their own brand names.

Royal Doulton Mark

Bunnykins Figurines

Footballer, DB 123, blue & white, 1991, limited edition of 250 .... **$650**
Fortune Teller, DB 218, red, black & yellow, white ball, produced only in 2001 .... **$55**

Bunnykins Friar Tuck

Friar Tuck, DB 246, brown w/green, 2001
(ILLUS., previous page) **$60**

Girl Skater, DB 153, green coat w/white
trim, pink dress, blue books, yellow
skates, 1995-97.. **$45**

Goalkeeper, DB 118, red & black, 1991,
special edition of 250 .... **$650**

Goalkeeper, DB 122, grey & black, 1991,
limited edition of 250 .... **$650**

Bunnykins Goodnight

Goodnight, DB 157, pink nightgown, reddish brown Teddy, blue & white base,
1995-99 (ILLUS.).. **$45**

Groom, DB 102, grey & burgundy, 1991-
2001 .... **$45**

Gymnasts, DB 207, 1999, limited edition of
2,500, the set (sold only in set of 5) **$625**

Happy Birthday, DB 21, red coat, blue
trimmed white tablecloth, 1983-97 .... **$50**

Harry, DB 73, blue, brown, white & yellow,
1988-93.. **$85**

Harry the Herald, DB 49, maroon, white &
tan, Royal Family series, 1986-90............. **$155**

Home Run, DB 43, blue, yellow & white,
1986-93.. **$90**

Ice Cream, DB 82, white, blue & green,
1990-93.. **$200**

Irishman, DB 178, green w/shamrocks,
1998, limited edition of 2,500 .... **$225**

Jester, DB 161, red, green & yellow, 1995,
limited edition of 1,500 .... **$495**

Jogging, DB 22, yellow, blue & white, 1983-
89 .... **$115**

John Bull, DB 134, grey, yellow, red, white
& blue Union Jack waistcoat, 1993, limit-
ed edition of 1,000.................................... **$550**

Judge, DB 188, red & white, 1999, RDICC
exclusive **$80**

Juggler, DB 164, blue suit, black pompons,
white ruff, 1996, limited edition of 1,500.... **$395**

King John, DB 45, red, yellow & blue, Royal
Family series, 1986-90............................. **$135**

King Richard, DB 258, grey w/yellow trim,
grey/green cloak, 2002.............................. **$60**

Little Bo Peep, DB 220, yellow & orange
dress, 2000 .... **$60**

Little Jack Horner, DB 221, maroon & yel-
low, 2000 .... **$60**

Little Miss Muffet, DB 240, blue dress,
green tuffet, 2002 .... **$60**

Maid Marion, DB 245, pink, yellow & green,
2001 .... **$60**

Mermaid, DB 263, 2003, limited edition of
3,000 .... **$125**

Milkman, DB 125, white, green & grey,
1992, limited edition of 1,000 .... **$750**

Mother and Baby, DB 167, brown, light
pink dress, red shoes, yellow blanket,
1997-2000.. **$45**

Mother's Day, DB 155, brown & blue, 1995-
2000 .... **$45**

Mr. Bunnykins at the Easter Parade, DB
51, blue tie & hat band, maroon coat, light
grey trousers, pink ribbon on package,
1986.. **$850**

Mr. Punch, DB 234, blue, red, yellow
stripes, 2002, limited edition of 2,500 ...... **$180**

Mrs. Bunnykins at the Easter Parade, DB
52, maroon dress, white collar, blue bow
on bonnet, multicolored bows on packag-
es, 1986 .... **$950**

Bunnykins Series

Bunnykins Aussie Explorer Teapot

Teapot, cov., Aussie Explorer patt., designed by Shane Ridge, limited edition of
2,500, introduced in 1996 (ILLUS.) **$225**

Teapot, cov., figural Geisha Girl model, designed by Martyn Alcock, limited edition
of 2,500, introduced in 1998 (ILLUS. of
two views, top of next page) **$225**

Bunnykins Lady of the Manor Teapot

Two Views of the Bunnykins Geisha Girl Teapot

Teapot, cov., figural Lady of the Manor, designed by Shane Ridge, limited edition of 1,500, introduced in 2003 (ILLUS., previous page) **$300**

Bunnykins USA President Teapot

Teapot, cov., USA President model, designed by Shane Ridge, limited edition of 2,500, introduced in 1995 (ILLUS.) **$250**

Bunnykins Lord of the Manor Teapot

Teapot, cov., Lord of the Manor patt., designed by Shane Ridge, limited edition of 1,500, introduced in 2003 (ILLUS.) **$300**

Burslem Art Wares

Early Royal Doulton Kingsware Tea Set

Tea set: cov. teapot, open sugar & creamer; Kingsware, each piece w/a different embossed figural scene, introduced in 1902, the set (ILLUS.) **$750**

Front & Back of the Sodden & Sobriety Figural Teapot

Teapot, cov., figural Sodden and Sobriety model, designed by Anthony Cartlidge, limited edition of 1,500, introduced in 2003 (ILLUS. of both sides, above).......... **$300**

Teapot, cov., Kingsware line, Dame patt. w/motto around base, introduced in 1901 (ILLUS.)... **$1,000**

Teapot, cov., Kingsware line, self-pouring style, relief-molded half-length portraits on side, J.J. Royle's Patent design, ca. 1900 (ILLUS., bottom of page).............. **$2,000**

Early Royal Doulton Kingsware Dame Pattern Teapot

Royal Doulton Kingsware Witch Teapot

Doulton Self-Pouring Kingsware Patent Teapot

Royal Doulton Morrisian Ware Teapot

Teapot, cov., Kingsware line, Witch patt., introduced in 1902 (ILLUS., previous page)
.... **$500**

Teapot, cov., Morrisian Ware, footed wide urn-shaped body w/a squared handle & serpentine spout, design of a dancing lady, ca. 1900 (ILLUS., top of page) **$1,000**

Royal Doulton Old Leeds Spray Pattern Teapot

Teapot, cov., Old Leeds Spray patt., squatty octagonal body, angled spout & squared handle, England, ca. 1912 (ILLUS.) **$100**

Royal Commemorative Urn-Vase

Urn-vase, royal commemorative, footed wide slightly waisted cylindrical shape flanked by long loop handles, made in 1937 to celebrate the coronation of King George VI & Queen Elizabeth, one side w/a large light gold portrait medallion surrounded by various royal emblems glazed in greens, cream, red, yellow & browns, special Royal Doulton base mark, No. 205 of 2,000 made, overall crazing, 10 1/2" h. (ILLUS.) **$345**

Fine Royal Doulton Sung Ware Vase

Vase, 5 1/2" h., Sung Ware, very wide bulbous ovoid body tapering sharply to a short cylindrical neck, bold mottled & streaky deep red & dark blue glaze, decorated by Charles Noke & Fred Moore, Royal Doulton, Sung & Noke marks (ILLUS.)
.... **$547**

Doulton Shaded Blue Titanian Vase

Vase, 5 7/8" h., Titanian Ware, footed ovoid body w/a short flaring neck, overall glossy shaded dark to teal blue crystalline glaze, Titanian logo mark on base, early 20th c. (ILLUS.) **$230**

Doulton Natural Foliage Ware Vase

Vase, 12 1/4" h., Natural Foliage Ware, tall baluster-form body w/a short neck w/cupped rim, mottled streaky yellowish tan & brown ground decorated w/long branches of mottled dark blue & green leaves, Doulton-Lambeth, Shape No. 6768 (ILLUS.).. **$230**

Vase, 12 1/2" h., Sung Ware, very wide bulbous ovoid body w/narrow cylindrical neck, stylized red, green & purple cherry blossoms interspersed w/lustered green, blue, red & tan drip glazes, decorated by Charles Noke, "Sung" & "Noke" in black slip & "7163," "4," & "46" impressed on bottom (restored drill hole in bottom) **$1,600**

Character Jugs

Gladiator, small, D 6553, 4 1/4" h. **$350**
Gone Away, miniature, D 6545, 2 1/2" h......... **$35**
Gone Away, small, D 6538, 3 3/4" h. **$45**
Granny, miniature, D 6520, 2 1/4" h................ **$55**

The Guardsman

Guardsman (The), large, D 6568, 6 3/4" h. (ILLUS.).. **$95**
Gulliver, miniature, D 6566, 2 1/2" h............. **$375**

Hamlet

Hamlet, large, D 6672, 7 1/4" h. (ILLUS.) **$150**
Henry V, flag decal, large, variation No. 3, D 6671, 7 1/4" h. **$90**

Izaac Walton Character Jug

Izaac Walton, large, D 6404, 7" h. (ILLUS., previous page) **$65**
Jester, small, D 5556, 3 1/8" h. **$45**
John Barleycorn, small, D 5735, 3 1/2" h. **$70**
John Doulton, small, two o'clock, D 6656, 4 1/4" h. **$40**

John Peel

John Peel, large, D 5612, 6 1/2" h. (ILLUS.)
.... **$115**
John Peel, tiny, D 6259, 1 1/4" h. **$125**
John Shorter, small, D 6880, 4 1/4" h. **$85**
King Charles I, large, D 6917, 7" h. **$275**

Figurines

Darling, HN 1985, white nightshirt, 1946-97 ... **$90**
Deborah, HN 2701, green & white, 1983-84
.... **$175**
Delight, HN 1772, red dress, 1936-67 .... **$225**
Delphine, HN 2136, blue & lavender, 1954-67 .... **$400**
Diana, HN 1986, red, 1946-75 .... **$175**
Discovery, HN 3428, matte white, 1992 .... **$125**
Dulcie, HN 2305, blue, 1981-84 .... **$225**
Easter Day, HN 2039, multicolored, 1949-69 .... **$425**
Elegance, HN 2264, green dress, 1961-85... **$230**
Eliza, HN 2543, gold, Haute Ensemble Series, 1974-79 .... **$300**
Eliza, HN 3179, red & lilac, 1988-92 .... **$175**

Ellen

Ellen, HN 3816, ivory & light blue dress, 1996-97 (ILLUS.) **$160**
Elyse, HN 2429, blue dress, 1972-95 .... **$225**
Emily, HN 3204, style 2, white & blue, 1989-93 .... **$135**
Enchantment, HN 2178, blue, 1957-82........ **$135**
Fair Lady, HN 2832, red gown, green sleeves, 1977-96.................................... **$205**
Fair Lady, HN 2835, coral pink, 1977-96 ...... **$225**
Fair Maiden, HN 2434, red gown, 1983-94..... **$75**
Falstaff, HN 2054, red jacket, brown belt & boots, 1950-92 .... **$140**
Fat Boy, M 44, blue & white, 1932-83............. **$65**
Fatboy (The), HN 2096, blue & cream, 1952-67 .... **$375**
Favourite (The), HN 2249, blue & white, 1960-90 .... **$205**
Fiona, HN 2694, red & white, 1974-81 .... **$175**
First Dance, HN 2803, pale blue dress, 1977-92 .... **$225**
First Steps, HN 2242, blue & yellow, 1959-65 .... **$475**
First Waltz, HN 2862, red dress, 1979-83 .... **$275**
Fleur, HN 2368, green dress, 1968-95.......... **$165**
Flora, HN 2349, brown & white, 1966-73 ...... **$225**
Flower Seller's Children, HN 1342, purple, red & yellow, 1929-93 .... **$575**

Fond Farewell

Fond Farewell, HN 3815, red, 1997-99 (ILLUS.) **$225**

Fortune Teller

Fortune Teller, HN 2159, multicolor, 1955-67 (ILLUS., previous page) **$550**
Forty Winks, HN 1974, green & tan, 1945-73 .... **$295**
Fragrance, HN 2334, blue, 1966 to present **$225**
Francine, HN 2422, green & white dress, 1972-81 .... **$105**
Gaffer (The), HN 2053, green & brown, 1950-59 .... **$425**
Genevieve, HN 1962, red, 1941-75 .... **$325**
George Washington at Prayer, HN 2861, blue & tan, 1977, limited edition of 750 .. **$2,750**
Gillian, HN 3042, green, 1984-91 .... **$125**

Lambing Time

Lambing Time, HN 1890, light brown, 1938-80 (ILLUS.)....................................... **$175**
Last Waltz, HN 2315, apricot dress, 1967-93 .... **$145**
Laura, HN 3136, dark blue & white, 1988 ..... **$225**
Leading Lady, HN 2269, blue & yellow, 1965-76 .... **$205**
Legolas, HN 2917, cream & tan, Middle Earth Series, 1981-84 .... **$205**
Lights Out, HN 2662, blue trousers & yellow spotted shirt, 1965-69 .... **$235**
Lilac Time, HN 2137, red, 1954-69 .... **$385**
Lisa, HN 2394, yellow & lilac, 1983-90 .... **$175**
Lizzie, HN 2749, green, white & red, 1988-91 .... **$205**
Lorna, HN 2311, green dress, apricot shawl, 1965-85 .... **$175**
Love Letter, HN 2149, pink & blue dress, 1958-76 .... **$375**
Lucy Locket, HN 524, yellow dress, 1921-49 .... **$775**
Lynne, HN 2329, green dress, 1971-96 .... **$175**
Madonna of the Square, HN 2034, light green-blue, 1949-51 .... **$1,100**
Margaret, HN 1989, red & green, 1947-49 ... **$500**
Marguerite, HN 1928, pink dress, 1940-49 ... **$600**
Marietta, HN 1341, black & red, 1929-49... **$1,650**
Marjorie, HN 2788, blue & white dress, 1980-84 .... **$325**

Mary, HN 3375, blue & white, Figure of the Year Series, 1992 .... **$575**
Melissa, HN 2467, purple & cream, 1981 to present **$250**
Melody, HN 2202, blue & peach, 1957-62 .... **$285**
Meriel, HN 1931, pink dress, 1940-49 .... **$1,650**
Michelle, HN 2234, green, 1967-94............. **$175**
Midsummer Noon, HN 2033, pink, 1949-55 .... **$700**
Minuet, HN 2019, white dress, floral print, 1949-71 .... **$285**
Miss Fortune, HN 1897, blue & white shawl, pink dress, 1938-49 .... **$1,000**
Monica, HN 1467, flowered purple dress, 1931-95 .... **$125**
Monica, M 66, shaded pink skirt, blue blouse, 1935-49 .... **$750**
Mr. Micawber, HN 1895, brown, black & tan, 1938-52... **$525**
Mr. Pickwick, HN 1894, blue, tan & cream, Dickens Series, 1938-42.......................... **$475**
My Love, HN 2339, white w/red rose, 1969-97 .... **$225**
Nicola, HN 2839, flowered lavender dress, 1978-95 .... **$275**
Nina, HN 2347, matte blue, 1969-76............. **$135**
Ninette, HN 2379, yellow & cream, 1971-97 .... **$225**
Noelle, HN 2179, orange, white & black, 1957-67 .... **$450**

Old Country Roses

Old Country Roses, HN 3692, red, 1995-99 (ILLUS.).. **$360**
Old Meg, HN 2494, blue & grey matte finish, 1974-76 .... **$215**
Olga, HN 2463, turquoise & gold, 1972-75 ... **$195**
Once Upon a Time, HN 2047, pink dotted dress, 1949-55 .... **$475**
Orange Vendor (An), HN 1966, purple cloak, 1941-49 .... **$950**
Owd Willum, HN 2042, green & brown, 1949-73 .... **$225**
Paisley Shawl, HN 1392, white dress, red shawl, 1930-49...................................... **$450**
Paisley Shawl, M 4, green dress, dark green shawl, black bonnet w/red feather & ribbons, 1932-45.................................... **$375**

Pamela, HN 3223, style 2, white & blue, 1989-89 .... $225

Pantalettes, HN 1362, green & blue, 1929-38 .... $625

Pantalettes, M 16, red skirt, red tie on hat, 1932-45 .... $425

Partners, HN 3119, black, blue & grey, 1990-92 .... $265

Paula, HN 3234, white & blue, 1990-96 .... $195

Pauline, HN 2441, peach, 1984-1989.......... $250

Pearly Boy, HN 2035, reddish brown, 1949-59 .... $195

Pearly Girl, HN 1483, red jacket, 1931-49.... $325

Pecksniff, HN 2098, black & brown, 1952-67 .... $375

Peggy, HN 2038, red dress, green trim, 1949-79 .... $125

Summertime, HN 3137, white & blue, 1987, RDICC Series... $225

Sunday Morning, HN 2184, red & brown, 1963-69 .... $425

Susan, HN 2952, blue, black & pink, 1982-93 .... $250

Suzette, HN 2026, 1949-59......................... $475

Sweet Anne, HN 1330, red, pink & yellow skirt, 1929-49 .... $325

Sweet Anne, HN 1496, pink & purple dress & hat, 1932-67... $275

Sweet April, HN 2215, pink dress, 1965-67 .... $425

Sweet Dreams, HN 2380, multicolored, 1971-90 .... $150

Sweet Lavender, HN 1373, green, red & black, 1930-49... $1,250

Sweet Seventeen, HN 2734, white w/gold trim, 1975-93.. $195

Sweet Sixteen, HN 2231, 1958-65 .... $375

Sweet Suzy, HN 1918, 1939-49................... $950

Sweet & Twenty, HN 1298, red & pink dress, 1928-69 .... $365

Sweeting, HN 1935, pink dress, 1940-73 ..... $135

Teresa, HN 1682, red and brown, 1935-49 .... $1,375

Thanks Doc

Thanks Doc, HN 2731, white & brown, 1975-90 (ILLUS.)...................................... $225

Tootles, HN 1680, pink, 1935-75.................. $105

Top O' The Hill, HN 1833, green & blue dress, 1937-71 .... $275

Top 'O The Hill

Top 'O The Hill, HN 2126, mauve & green, 1988, miniature (ILLUS.)............................ $125

Treasure Island, HN 2243, 1962-75............. $215

Tuppence a Bag, HN 2320, green dress, blue shawl, 1968-95.................................. $225

Valerie, HN 2107, red gown w/white apron, 1953-95 .... $95

Vanity, HN 2475, red, 1973-1992 .... $125

Veneta, HN 2722, green & white, 1974-81.... $165

Veronica, HN 3205, style 3, white & pink, 1989-92 .... $165

Victoria, HN 2471, patterned pink dress, 1973 to present $295

Victorian Lady (A), M 1, red-tinged dress, light green shawl, 1932-45....................... $500

Virginia, HN 1693, yellow dress, 1935-49 .... $1,300

Wendy, HN 2109, blue dress, 1953-95........... $80

Willy-Won't-He, HN 2150, red, green, blue & white, 1955-59 .... $235

Windflower, M 79, blue & green, 1939-49 .. $1,250

Winter, HN 2088, shaded blue skirt, 1952-59 .... $415

Winter's Walk (A), HN 3052, pale blue & white, 1987-95 .... $250

Wintertime

Wintertime, HN 3060, 1985, RDICC (ILLUS.,
   previous page) **$325**
Young Dreams, HN 3176, pink, 1988-92 ..... **$175**
Young Master, HN 2872, purple, grey &
   brown, 1980-89 .... **$250**
Yvonne, HN 3038, turquoise, 1987-92.......... **$155**

Flambé Glazes

Miscellaneous Pieces
Figurine, The Genie, HN 2999, Rouge
   Flambé, 1989-95 .... **$350**

Small Doulton Rouge Flambé Vase

Vase, 4" h., Rouge Flambé glaze, footed
   squatty bulbous body tapering sharply to
   a two-lobed upright rim, red ground &
   veining down through a dark ground,
   marked w/Flambé insignia (ILLUS.) **$138**

Silver-overlaid Rouge Flambé Vase

Vase, 4 1/8" h., Rouge Flambé glaze, wide
   squatty bulbous form tapering to a tiny
   flared neck, the deep red background
   decorated w/silver overlay, a thin medial
   band below undulating silver leafy vines
   below a pierced Greek key neck band &
   silver-covered neck, silver marked by
   the Gorham Mfg. Co., one silver leaf
   missing, some minor glaze rubs, early
   20th c. (ILLUS.) **$460**
Vase, 5 1/2" h., Sung Ware, bulbous ovoid
   body tapering to a short cylindrical neck,
   a Flambé glossy glaze in red mottled
   w/dark green & gold, signatures of deco-

Doulton Sung Ware Vase

rators Noke & Moore, early 20th c., base
chip (ILLUS.) **$173**

Doulton Flambé Rouge et Noir Vase

Vase, 10 3/4" h. Flambé Rouge et Noir Line,
   a simple swelled cylindrical body tapering
   to a small trumpet neck, most of the body
   in a glossy black glaze w/dark red at the
   shoulder & neck, No. 1619, fairly recent
   (ILLUS.).. **$230**

Vase with Special Rouge Flambé Glaze

Vase, 11 1/4" h., 4 3/4" d., Rouge Flambé glaze, slightly flaring rounded cylindrical form w/a rounded shoulder to the short flaring neck, an experimental swirling deep red & black glaze, marked on the bottom "Royal Doulton Flambé - 26 - AERO G. - Taylor - 11.2.69 - Flambé" (ILLUS., previous page) **$460**

Scenic Doulton Rouge Flambé Vase

Vase, 11 1/2" h., Rouge Flambé glaze, wide bulbous baluster form tapering to a wide flat mouth, decorated w/a black silhouetted Arabian landscape w/men on camels, marked on the bottom "Royal Doulton Flambé," early 20th c. (ILLUS.).... **$1,200-1,800**

Lambeth Art Wares

Doulton Lambeth H. Barlow Cracker Jar

Cracker jar w/silver rim, cover & swing bail handle, stoneware, barrel-shaped, the sides w/a wide white center band incised w/rabbits in a field highlighted in dark blue, base & rim bands w/a teardrop band design in dark blue & greenish gold, decorated by Hannah Barlow & dated

1885, Doulton Lambeth mark, 4 1/2" h. (ILLUS.).. **$1,840**

Early Doulton Lambeth Salad Set

Salad set: wide low squatty pottery flat-rimmed bowl w/a sterling silver rim band & matching pottery-handled sterling serving fork & spoon; the bowl w/a dark brown ground below a dark blue rim band, the sides decorated w/an undulating white petaled band w/blue trim, dated 1882, Doulton Lambeth & decorator marks, serving pieces 10 3/4" l., bowl 9" d., 4 1/2" h., the set (ILLUS.) **$490**

Doulton-Lambeth Faience Teapot

Teapot, cov., faience, rounded cylindrical body w/long serpentine spout, C-scroll handle & metal rim & hinged cover, stylized floral decoration, Doulton-Lambeth, ca. 1900 (ILLUS.) **$1,000**

Early Rare Figural Cameo Teapot

Teapot, cov., figural, crouching camel w/a heavy load, the Arab driver pulling from behind & forming the handle, ruby glaze, designed by the Moore Brothers, apparently made by Doulton, Doulton-Lambeth, ca. 1877 (ILLUS.) **$5,000**

Rare Doulton Marqueterie Ware Teapot

Teapot, cov., Marqueterie Ware, diamond lattice & swirl overall design, Doulton-Lambeth, ca. 1890 (ILLUS.).................. **$4,000**

Rare Doulton-Lambeth Marqueterie Teapot with Scene

Teapot, cov., Marqueterie Ware, low rectangular shape w/straight spout & angled loop handle, large design reserve w/scene of a child against a swirled background, Doulton-Lambeth, painted by Ada Dennis, ca. 1893 (ILLUS.) **$5,000**

Extremely Rare Royal Doulton Stoneware Toby Teapot

Teapot, cov., stoneware, figural Toby shape, designed by Harry Simeon, ca. 1925, extremely rare (ILLUS.)............... **$7,500**

Doulton-Lambeth Teapot with Scene

Teapot, cov., stoneware, tapering cylindrical body w/flaring rim, angled spout, large rectangular panel w/scene of Bladud, the founder of the City of Bath, made for R.S. Carey, Bath, Doulton-Lambeth, ca. 1894 (ILLUS.)..................... **$750**

Unusual Doulton Chiné Ware Umbrella Stand

Umbrella stand, Chiné Ware, a flared base below the slightly flaring cylindrical body w/a wide gently flaring cylindrical neck w/a molded rim, the base band & neck in dark burnt orange decorated w/a band of dark yellow stylized daisy blossoms, the main body decorated w/a special technique involving pressing dampened lace-like fabric onto the wet clay to form an overall floral lacy design in yellow on an orange background, various Doulton Lambeth marks, ca. 1900, small glaze chip in pattern near the base, 25 5/8" h. (ILLUS.).. **$690**

Pair of Doulton Vases

Vases, bulbous body w/foliate motifs, flared neck decorated w/stylized leaves & jewelwork, raised pedestal base, all-over green tones on deep brown ground accented by beige & brown, underside impressed w/marks & numbers "Doulton Lambeth, mm, 1870, CL, EAS - 318," ca. 1880-1895, 7 1/4" h., pr. (ILLUS.) **$350**

Series Wares

Bowl, 8 1/2" h., Gallent Fishers Series.......... **$200**
Candlestick, Old Moreton Series, low flaring round foot & slightly swelled cylindrical shaft below widely flaring flattened socket rim, color transfer of 16th c. gentleman titled "Old Moreton," impressed "7277," 6 3/8" h. **$80**
Chop plate, round w/flanged rim, Old Moreton Series, black transfer-printed design decorated in polychrome, a large center interior scene titled "Queen Elizabeth at Old Moreton 1589," early 20th c., 12 3/4" d. **$85**
Dish, oval, English Old Scenes Series, The Gleaners scene, 9 x 11 1/4, 2 1/8" h. **$55**

Old Wife Series Loving Cup

Loving cup, The Old Wife Series, tall waisted cylindrical body w/a long orange branch handles down the sides, molded relief decoration of flowers & a woodland, ca. 1940, 8" h. (ILLUS.) **$900-1,000**
Pitcher, Shakespeare Characters Series, Juliet, scene from Shakespeare's Romeo & Juliet **$150**

John Peel Hunting Scene Plate

Plate, John Peel Hunting Series color scene, No. D4340, 1924 (ILLUS.) **$70-90**

"Robin Hood" Series Plate

Plate, 7 1/2" sq., Under the Greenwood Tree Series, Friar Tuck Joins Robin Hood, natural-colored scene of Robin Hood & Friar Tuck standing & talking under large tree (ILLUS.) **$85**
Plate, 10 1/4" d., English Old Scenes Series, The Gleaners scene **$65**

Hunting John Peel Series Sugar Bowl

Sugar bowl, open, Hunting John Peel Series, wide flat bottom & slightly rounded cylindrical sides w/a lightly scalloped rim, 1915 (ILLUS.)... **$70-90**

Teapot, cov., Shakespeare Characters Series, scene of Hamlet, introduced in 1912 .... **$500**

Sketches from Teniers Series Teapot

Teapot, cov., Sketches from Teniers Series, landscape scene, introduced in 1905 (ILLUS.) **$1,000**

Landscape Scene on a Royal Doulton Woodland Series Teapot

Teapot, cov., Woodland Series, landscape w/trees & cottage, introduced in 1908 (ILLUS.) **$600**

Bird of Paradise Series Tobacco jar

Tobacco jar, cov., Bird of Paradise Series, wide cylindrical body w/a molded base & rim, Titanian decoration of an exotic bird perched among vines around the top on a greyish blue ground, ca. 1925, 11" h. (ILLUS.).. **$1,100-1,300**

Miniature Snowscenes Series Vase

Vase, 3 3/4" h., miniature, Snowscenes Series, baluster-form body slip-decorated w/a cottage in a snowy landscape, ca. 1910 (ILLUS.).................................... **$400-500**

Bird of Paradise Series Vase

Vase, 6 3/4" h., Bird of Paradise Series, ovoid body tapering to a small neck, Titanian decoration of a large exotic bird on a greyish tan ground, ca. 1925 (ILLUS.) **$700-900**

Pair of Doulton Ships Series Vases

Vases, 11 3/4" h., Ships Series, tall slender ovoid body w/a rounded shoulder & small rolled neck, decorated w/a large sailing ship slip-painted in shades of blue & white, ca. 19010, pr. (ILLUS.) **$2,000-3,000**

Dickens Ware Series

Dickens Ware Sam Weller Pitcher

Pitcher, jug-type, waisted cylindrical body w/a pointed angled handle, relief-molded scene of Sam Weller, No. D5864, Charles Noke, 1937 (ILLUS.) **$275-325**

Royal Doulton Dickensware Series Teapot

Teapot, cov., color scene of a man in front of shops, introduced in 1908 (ILLUS.) **$600**

Early Royal Doulton Old Charley Teapot

Teapot, cov., figural Old Charley model, designed by Charles Noke, introduced in 1939 (ILLUS.).. **$2,000**

Early Royal Doulton Sairey Gamp Teapot

Teapot, cov., figural Sairey Gamp model, designed by Charles Noke, introduced in 1939 (ILLUS.).. **$2,000**

Early Royal Doulton Tony Weller Teapot

Teapot, cov., figural Tony Weller model, designed by Charles Noke, introduced in 1939 (ILLUS.).. **$2,000**

Fiesta (Homer Laughlin China Co. -HLC)

Fiesta dinnerware was made by the Homer Laughlin China Company of Newell, West Virginia, from the 1930s until the early 1970s. The brilliant colors of this inexpensive pottery have attracted numerous collectors. On February 28, 1986, Laughlin reintroduced the popular Fiesta line with minor changes in the shapes of a few pieces and a contemporary color range. The effect of this new production on the Fiesta collecting market is yet to be determined.

Fiesta Mark

Ashtray cobalt blue $45
Ashtray ivory.. $45
Ashtray red $45
Ashtray turquoise.. $35
Ashtray yellow $35
Bowl, cream soup cobalt blue......................... $45
Bowl, cream soup ivory $45
Bowl, cream soup red..................................... $45
Bowl, cream soup turquoise $30
Bowl, cream soup yellow $30
Bowl, dessert, 6" d. ivory $40
Bowl, dessert, 6" d. turquoise........................ $30
Bowl, dessert, 6" d. cobalt blue $40
Bowl, dessert, 6" d. red $40
Bowl, dessert, 6" d. yellow............................. $30
Bowl, individual fruit, 5 1/2" d. ivory $25
Bowl, individual fruit, 5 1/2" d. turquoise...... $20
Bowl, individual fruit, 5 1/2" d. yellow........... $20
Bowl, nappy, 8 1/2" d. ivory $45
Bowl, nappy, 8 1/2" d. turquoise $30
Bowl, nappy, 8 1/2" d. red.............................. $45
Bowl, nappy, 8 1/2" d. yellow.......................... $30
Bowl, nappy, 8 1/2" d. cobalt blue $45
Bowl, nappy, 9 1/2" d. ivory $60
Bowl, nappy, 9 1/2" d. turquoise $55
Bowl, nappy, 9 1/2" d. cobalt blue $60
Bowl, nappy, 9 1/2" d. red.............................. $60
Bowl, nappy, 9 1/2" d. yellow......................... $55
Bowl, salad, large, footed cobalt blue $350

Bowl, salad, large, footed red $350
Bowl, salad, large, footed turquoise........... $275
Bowl, salad, large, footed yellow $275
Candleholders, bulb-type, pr. cobalt blue... $120
Candleholders, bulb-type, pr. ivory $120
Candleholders, bulb-type, pr. red.............. $120
Candleholders, bulb-type, pr. turquoise $80
Candleholders, bulb-type, pr. yellow........... $80
Carafe, cov. cobalt blue.............................. $275
Carafe, cov. ivory.. $275
Carafe, cov. red $275
Carafe, cov. turquoise................................. $250
Carafe, cov. yellow $250
Casserole, cov., two-handled, 10" d. cobalt
  blue $180
Casserole, cov., two-handled, 10" d. ivory ... $180
Casserole, cov., two-handled, 10" d. red $180
Casserole, cov., two-handled, 10" d. tur-
  quoise $150
Casserole, cov., two-handled, 10" d. yellow
  .... $150
Coffeepot, cov. cobalt blue $230
Coffeepot, cov. ivory $230
Coffeepot, cov. red...................................... $230
Coffeepot, cov. turquoise $180
Coffeepot, cov. yellow $180
Coffeepot, cov., demitasse, stick handle
  cobalt blue.. $500
Coffeepot, cov., demitasse, stick handle
  ivory $500
Coffeepot, cov., demitasse, stick handle
  red.. $500
Coffeepot, cov., demitasse, stick handle
  turquoise $400
Coffeepot, cov., demitasse, stick handle
  yellow.. $400
Compote, 12" d., low, footed cobalt blue.... $180
Compote, 12" d., low, footed ivory............. $180
Compote, 12" d., low, footed red............... $180
Compote, 12" d., low, footed turquoise $160
Compote, 12" d., low, footed yellow $160
Compote, sweetmeat, high stand cobalt
  blue $125
Compote, sweetmeat, high stand ivory...... $125
Compote, sweetmeat, high stand red $125
Compote, sweetmeat, high stand tur-
  quoise $95
Compote, sweetmeat, high stand yellow...... $95
Creamer cobalt blue...................................... $25
Creamer ivory.. $25
Creamer red.. $25
Creamer turquoise $20
Creamer yellow $20
Cup, demitasse, stick handle cobalt blue $80
Cup, demitasse, stick handle ivory.............. $80
Cup, demitasse, stick handle red $80
Cup, demitasse, stick handle turquoise........ $70
Cup, demitasse, stick handle yellow $70
Cup, ring handle cobalt blue $25
Cup, ring handle ivory $25
Cup, ring handle red $25
Cup, ring handle turquoise............................ $15
Cup, ring handle yellow $15
Cup & saucer, demitasse, stick handle
  cobalt blue.. $95
Cup & saucer, demitasse, stick handle
  ivory $95
Cup & saucer, demitasse, stick handle
  red.. $95

Cup & saucer, demitasse, stick handle
turquoise $85
Cup & saucer, demitasse, stick handle
yellow $85
Cup & saucer, ring handle cobalt blue......... $27
Cup & saucer, ring handle ivory.................. $27
Cup & saucer, ring handle red $27
Cup & saucer, ring handle turquoise $17
Cup & saucer, ring handle yellow $17
Egg cup cobalt blue $60
Egg cup ivory.. $60
Egg cup red $60
Egg cup turquoise $55
Egg cup yellow.. $55
Fork (Kitchen Kraft) cobalt blue.................. $150
Fork (Kitchen Kraft) light green $150
Fork (Kitchen Kraft) red.............................. $150
Fork (Kitchen Kraft) yellow $150
Gravy boat cobalt blue................................. $60
Gravy boat ivory $60
Gravy boat red $60
Gravy boat turquoise $40
Gravy boat yellow $40
Marmalade jar, cov. cobalt blue $365
Marmalade jar, cov. ivory............................ $365
Marmalade jar, cov. red $365
Marmalade jar, cov. turquoise..................... $350
Marmalade jar, cov. yellow $350
Mixing bowl, nest-type, size No. 1, 5" d. co-
balt blue.. $275
Mixing bowl, nest-type, size No. 1, 5" d.
ivory... $275
Mixing bowl, nest-type, size No. 1, 5" d. red
.... $275
Mixing bowl, nest-type, size No. 1, 5" d. tur-
quoise... $220
Mixing bowl, nest-type, size No. 1, 5" d.
yellow $220
Mixing bowl, nest-type, size No. 2, 6" d. co-
balt blue.. $125
Mixing bowl, nest-type, size No. 2, 6" d.
ivory... $125
Mixing bowl, nest-type, size No. 2, 6" d. red
.... $125
Mixing bowl, nest-type, size No. 2, 6" d. tur-
quoise... $100
Mixing bowl, nest-type, size No. 2, 6" d.
yellow $100
Mixing bowl, nest-type, size No. 3, 7" d. co-
balt blue.. $125
Mixing bowl, nest-type, size No. 3, 7" d.
ivory... $125
Mixing bowl, nest-type, size No. 3, 7" d. red . $125
Mixing bowl, nest-type, size No. 3, 7" d. tur-
quoise... $110
Mixing bowl, nest-type, size No. 3, 7" d.
yellow $110
Mixing bowl, nest-type, size No. 4, 8" d. co-
balt blue.. $150
Mixing bowl, nest-type, size No. 4, 8" d.
ivory... $150
Mixing bowl, nest-type, size No. 4, 8" d. red
.... $150
Mixing bowl, nest-type, size No. 4, 8" d.
yellow $110
Mixing bowl, nest-type, size No. 5, 9" d. co-
balt blue.. $190
Mixing bowl, nest-type, size No. 5, 9" d.
ivory... $190

Mixing bowl, nest-type, size No. 5, 9" d. red
.... $190
Mixing bowl, nest-type, size No. 5, 9" d. tur-
quoise... $175
Mixing bowl, nest-type, size No. 5, 9" d.
yellow $175
Mixing bowl, nest-type, size No. 6, 10" d.
cobalt blue.. $260
Mixing bowl, nest-type, size No. 6, 10" d.
ivory... $260
Mixing bowl, nest-type, size No. 6, 10" d.
red.. $260
Mixing bowl, nest-type, size No. 6, 10" d.
turquoise $230
Mixing bowl, nest-type, size No. 6, 10" d.
yellow $230
Mixing bowl, nest-type, size No. 7, 11 1/2"
d. cobalt blue $400
Mixing bowl, nest-type, size No. 7, 11 1/2"
d. ivory $400
Mixing bowl, nest-type, size No. 7, 11 1/2"
d. red.. $400
Mixing bowl, nest-type, size No. 7, 11 1/2"
d. turquoise $325
Mixing bowl, nest-type, size No. 7, 11 1/2"
d. yellow $325
Mug, Tom & Jerry style cobalt blue.............. $70
Mug, Tom & Jerry style ivory/gold................ $70
Mug, Tom & Jerry style red.......................... $70
Mug, Tom & Jerry style turquoise $50
Mug, Tom & Jerry style yellow $50
Mustard jar, cov. cobalt blue...................... $250
Mustard jar, cov. ivory................................ $250
Mustard jar, cov. light green $240
Mustard jar, cov. red.................................. $250
Mustard jar, cov. turquoise $240
Mustard jar, cov. yellow $240

Rare Fiesta Onion Soup Bowl

Onion soup bowl, cov. turquoise (ILLUS.)
.... $8,000
Pie server (Kitchen Kraft) cobalt blue $150
Pie server (Kitchen Kraft) light green.......... $150
Pie server (Kitchen Kraft) red $150
Pie server (Kitchen Kraft) yellow................ $150
Pitcher, water, disc-type chartreuse $200
Pitcher, water, disc-type cobalt blue $150
Pitcher, water, disc-type forest green $200
Pitcher, water, disc-type ivory.................... $150
Pitcher, water, disc-type medium green
.... $1,500
Pitcher, water, disc-type red $150
Pitcher, water, disc-type turquoise............. $100
Pitcher, water, disc-type yellow $100
Plate, 10" d. cobalt blue............................... $35

Plate, 10" d. ivory..	$35
Plate, 10" d. light green	$30
Plate, 10" d. medium green	$125
Plate, 10" d. red...	$35
Plate, 10" d. turquoise	$30
Plate, 10" d. yellow	$30
Plate, 6" d. cobalt blue	$5
Plate, 6" d. ivory..	$5
Plate, 6" d. red	$5
Plate, 6" d. turquoise	$4
Plate, 6" d. yellow	$4
Plate, 7" d. cobalt blue	$8
Plate, 7" d. ivory..	$8
Plate, 7" d. red..	$8
Plate, 7" d. turquoise	$7
Plate, 7" d. yellow	$7
Plate, 9" d. cobalt blue	$15
Plate, 9" d. ivory..	$15
Plate, 9" d. red..	$15
Plate, 9" d. turquoise	$10
Plate, chop, 13" d. cobalt blue	$45
Plate, chop, 13" d. ivory	$45
Plate, chop, 13" d. red...................................	$45
Plate, chop, 13" d. turquoise.........................	$40
Plate, chop, 13" d. yellow..............................	$40
Plate, chop, 15" d. cobalt blue	$90
Plate, chop, 15" d. ivory	$90
Plate, chop, 15" d. red...................................	$90
Plate, chop, 15" d. turquoise.........................	$70
Plate, chop, 15" d. yellow..............................	$70
Plate, grill, 10 1/2" d. cobalt blue	$40
Plate, grill, 10 1/2" d. ivory	$40
Plate, grill, 10 1/2" d. red	$40
Plate, grill, 10 1/2" d. rose............................	$35
Plate, grill, 10 1/2" d. turquoise.....................	$35
Plate, grill, 10 1/2" d. yellow.........................	$35
Platter, 12" oval cobalt blue	$50
Platter, 12" oval ivory	$50
Platter, 12" oval red	$50
Platter, 12" oval turquoise.............................	$40
Platter, 12" oval yellow...................................	$40
Relish tray w/five inserts cobalt blue	$355

Relish tray w/five inserts ivory	$355
Relish tray w/five inserts red	$355
Relish tray w/five inserts turquoise............	$310
Relish tray w/five inserts yellow..................	$310
Salt & pepper shakers, pr. cobalt blue	$25
Salt & pepper shakers, pr. ivory....................	$25
Salt & pepper shakers, pr. red	$25
Salt & pepper shakers, pr. turquoise.............	$22
Salt & pepper shakers, pr. yellow	$22
Soup plate, rimmed, 8" d. ivory....................	$50
Soup plate, rimmed, 8" d. red	$50
Soup plate, rimmed, 8" d. turquoise.............	$35
Soup plate, rimmed, 8" d. yellow	$35
Sugar bowl, cov. cobalt blue..........................	$60
Sugar bowl, cov. ivory....................................	$60
Sugar bowl, cov. medium green	$225
Sugar bowl, cov. red.......................................	$50
Sugar bowl, cov. turquoise	$50
Sugar bowl, cov. yellow	$50
Tea set: child's, cov. teapot, cov. sugar, creamer, one cup & saucer & plate; the teapot & plate in grey, the creamer & sugar in blue & the cup & saucer in purple, 1999 (ILLUS., bottom of page)..........	**$100-125**
Teapot, cov., cobalt blue, medium size (6 cup), Homer Laughlin China Co.	**$225**
Teapot, cov., forest green, medium size (6 cup), Homer Laughlin China Co.	**$325**
Teapot, cov., grey, medium size (6 cup), Homer Laughlin China Co.......................	**$325**
Teapot, cov., light green, medium size (6 cup), Homer Laughlin China Co.........	**$150-175**
Teapot, cov., large size (8 cup) cobalt blue	**$250**
Teapot, cov., large size (8 cup) ivory.........	**$250**
Teapot, cov., large size (8 cup) light green	**$210**
Teapot, cov., large size (8 cup) medium green..	**$1,200+**
Teapot, cov., large size (8 cup) red	**$250**
Teapot, cov., large size (8 cup) turquoise...	**$250**
Teapot, cov., large size (8 cup) yellow........	**$210**

Modern Fiesta Ware Child's Tea Set

Fiesta Teapot in Cobalt Blue

Teapot, cov., medium size (6 cup) cobalt blue (ILLUS.)	$200
Teapot, cov., medium size (6 cup) ivory	$200
Teapot, cov., medium size (6 cup) red	$200
Teapot, cov., medium size (6 cup) turquoise	$150
Teapot, cov., medium size (6 cup) yellow	$150
Tumbler, water, 10 oz. cobalt blue	$80
Tumbler, water, 10 oz. ivory	$80
Tumbler, water, 10 oz. red	$80
Tumbler, water, 10 oz. turquoise	$70
Tumbler, water, 10 oz. yellow	$70
Utility tray cobalt blue	$45
Utility tray ivory	$45
Utility tray red	$45
Utility tray turquoise	$45
Utility tray yellow	$40
Vase, 8" h. cobalt blue	$650
Vase, 8" h. ivory	$650
Vase, 8" h. red	$650
Vase, 8" h. turquoise	$600
Vase, 8" h. yellow	$600
Vase, bud, 6 1/2" h. cobalt blue	$100
Vase, bud, 6 1/2" h. ivory	$100
Vase, bud, 6 1/2" h. red	$100
Vase, bud, 6 1/2" h. turquoise	$75
Vase, bud, 6 1/2" h. yellow	$75

Flow Blue

Flow Blue ironstone and semi-porcelain was manufactured mainly in England during the second half of the 19th century. The early ironstone was produced by many of the well known English potters and was either transfer-printed or hand-painted (brush stroke). The bulk of the ware was exported to the United States or Canada.

The "flow" or running quality of the cobalt blue designs was the result of introducing certain chemicals into the kiln during the final firing. Some patterns are so "flown" that it is difficult to ascertain the design. The transfers were of several types: Asian, Scenic, Marble or Floral.

The earliest Flow Blue ironstone patterns were produced during the period between about 1840 and 1860. After the Civil War Flow Blue went out of style for some years but was again manufactured and exported to the United States beginning about the 1880s and continuing through the turn of the century. These later Flow Blue designs are on a semi-porcelain body rather than heavier ironstone and the designs are mainly florals. Also see Antique Trader Pottery & Porcelain Ceramics Price Guide, 5th Edition.

ABBEY (George Jones & Sons, ca. 1900)

Beeker, 3 1/2" d., 4" h.	$55
Bowl, 8" d., 4 1/2" h.	$85
Bowl, 9" d., 4 1/2" h.	$95
Hot water pot, 6" h.	$125

Abbey Punch Bowl

Punch bowl, 10 1/2" d., 6" h. (ILLUS.)	$750
Shredded wheat dish, 6 1/4" l., 5" w.	$65

ABBEY (Petrus Regout Co., Maastricht, Holland, date unknown)

Abbey Cup & Saucer

Farmer's cup & saucer, oversized, cup 5" d., 4" h. & saucer, 8" d. (ILLUS.)	$75

ABERDEEN (Bourne & Leigh), ca. 1900, Floral,

Butter pat, 3 1/2" d.	$40

ACME (Sampson Hancock & Sons, ca. 1900)

Plate, 9" d., five-sided	$55

Acme Plate

Plate, 9" d., scalloped (ILLUS., previous page) **$55**

ADDERLEY (Doulton & Company, ca. 1886), Floral
Vegetable bowl, open, round, 8 1/2" d., 2 3/4" h. **$125**

ALASKA (W.H. Grindley & Company, ca. 1891)
Bowl, berry, 5" d. **$45**
Creamer, 5 1/4" h. **$200**
Plate, 10" d., scalloped **$95**
Platter, 14" l. **$250**
Soup plate w/flanged rim, 9" d. **$90**

ALBANY (Johnson Bros., ca. 1900)
Plate, salad/dessert, 8" d. **$45**
Tea cup & saucer, cup, 2 1/2" h., 3 1/2" d, saucer, 6" d. **$85**

ALBANY (W.H. Grindley & Company, ca. 1899)
Butter pat, 3 1/2" d. **$40**
Plate, bread, 6 1/2 d. **$40**

Albany Platter

Platter, 14 1/2" l. (ILLUS.) **$275**

ALTHEA (Podmore, Walker & Company, ca. 1834-1859)

Althea Coffeepot

Coffeepot, cov., 11" d. (ILLUS.) **$650**
Creamer, 6" h. **$250**
Sugar, cov., footed, two-handled, 7" h. **$250**
Tea cup & saucer, cup, 4" d., 2 1/2" h., saucer, 5 3/4" d. **$125**

ALTON (W.H. Grindley & Co., ca. 1891)

Alton Platter

Platter, 18" l. (ILLUS.) **$325**

AMOUR (Societé Céramique, Dutch, ca. 1865)

Amour Footed Compote

Compote, footed, two-handled, 10" d. (ILLUS.) **$375**

ANDORRA (Johnson Bros., ca. 1901)

Andorra Vegetable Bowl

Vegetable bowl, open, round, 9 1/2" d. (ILLUS.) **$165**

ANEMONE (Lockhart & Arthur, ca. 1855)
Plate, 10 1/4" d. **$75**
Platter, 16" l. **$250**

ARGYLE (W.H. Grindley & Co., ca. 1896)

Argyle Platter

Platter, 16" l. (ILLUS.) $350
Platter, 18" l. $450

ARUNDEL (Doulton & Co., ca. 1891)
Ginger jar, cov., 8" h. $295

Arundel Pitcher

Pitcher, 8" h. (ILLUS.) $325

ASHBURTON (W.H. Grindley & Co., ca.1891)
Plate, salad/dessert, 8" d............................... $55

Plate, luncheon, 9" d. $60
Plate, dinner, 10" d.. $75
Platter, 12" l. $125
Platter, 14" l. $225

Ashburton Platter

Platter, 16" l. (ILLUS.) $275
Platter, 18" l. $300
Sauce ladle, 7" l. $295

ATALANTA (Wedgwood & Company, ca. 1900)

Atalanta Platter

Platter, 14" l. (ILLUS.) $175

ATLAS (W.H. Grindley and Co., ca. 1891)

Ten-piece Atlas Wash Set

Wash set: 13" h. x 10 1/2" w. pitcher, 15" d. wash bowl, cov. chamber pot, 13" h. cov. slop jar, soap dish without drainer, 4 1/2" h. shaving mug, 6" h. toothbrush holder; set of 10 (ILLUS., bottom previous page) **$2,800**

AULD LANG SYNE (Rowland & Marcellus, ca. 1891) - miscellaneous
Cup & saucer, farmer's, cup 5 1/2" d., 3 1/2" h., saucer, 7 1/2" d. **$195**

BALTIC (W.H. Grindley & Company, ca. 1891)
Compote, w/pedestal, 9 1/2" d., 3 1/4" h. **$300**
Creamer, 3 1/2" h. **$225**
Gravy boat, 7" l. **$125**
Plate, dinner, 10" d. **$75**
Sugar bowl, cov., 4 1/2" h. **$275**
Teapot, cov., , 5 1/2" h. **$575**

BAMBOO (Samuel Alcock & Co., ca. 1845)
Soup tureen, cov. **$650**

BEAUFORT (W.H. Grindley & Co., ca. 1903)

14" Oval Beaufort Platter

Platter, oval, 14" l. (ILLUS.) **$225**
Sugar bowl, cov., 7" handle to handle, 4" h.
.... **$250**
Underplate, for cov. butter, two-handled, 9" d. **$125**

BELMONT (Alfred Meakin, ca. 1891)
Teapot, cov., 8 1/2" handle to spout, 6" h.
.... **$300**

BELMONT (J.H. Weatherby & Sons, ca. 1892)
Plate, luncheon, 9" d. **$65**
Plate, dinner, 10" d. **$75**

BIMRAH (Flacket, Toft & Robinson, ca. 1857)
Covered vegetable, 10 1/2 x 12 1/4" handle to handle, 8" h. **$400**

BLUE BELL (Dillwyn-Swansea, Welsh, ca. 1840)
Syrup pitcher w/pewter lid, 8 1/2" h **$700**

BLUE DANUBE (Johnson Bros., ca. 1900)
Creamer, 4" h. **$175**

Blue Danube Luncheon Plate

Plate, luncheon, 9" d. (ILLUS.) **$80**
Plate, dinner, 10" d. **$75**
Soup bowl, luncheon, open, 9" d. **$65**
Soup tureen, cov., oval **$475**
Sugar, cov., 5" h. **$175**
Tea cup & saucer **$85**

BOLINGBROKE (The), (Ridgways, ca. 1909)

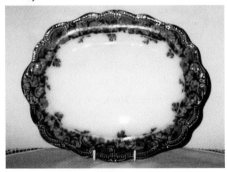

The Bolingbroke Platter

Platter, 13" l. (ILLUS.) **$250**

BOUQUET (Henry Alcock & Co., ca. 1895)

Bouquet Vegetable Dish

Vegetable dish, cov., footed, 12" l. (ILLUS.)
.... **$225**

CHISWICK (Wood & Baggaley, ca. 1850)

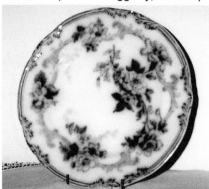

Chiswick Cheese Stand

Cheese stand, 12" d. (ILLUS.) $225

CHRYSANTHEMUM (Myott, Son & Co., ca. 1907)
Platter, 14" l $200

CHU-SAN (John Meir & Son, ca. 1840)

Chu-San Razor Box

Razor box, cov., 3 x 7 1/2" (ILLUS.) $250

CHUSAN (Francis Morley & Co., ca. 1850)
Comport, 9" d $450

CHUSAN (J. Clementson, ca. 1840)

Clementson Chusan Pattern Flow Blue Teapot

Teapot, cov., Long Hexagon body shape
  (ILLUS.) $650

CHUSAN (Podmore, Walker & Co., ca. 1834-1859)

Set of 8 Chusan Flow Blue Plates

Plates, 10 1/2" d., set of 8 .... $460

CLARENCE (W.H. Grindley & Co., ca. 1900)

Clarence Platter

Platter, 16" l. (ILLUS.) $250

CLAYTON (Johnson Bros., ca. 1902)
Chamber set: pitcher & bowl, chamber pot,
  shaving mug & small water pitcher; the
  set $1,500
Chamber set: pitcher & bowl, chamber pot,
  toothbrush holder & shaving mug; the set
  .... $1,500
Platter, 16" l. $250

Clayton Soup Plate

Soup plate w/flanged rim, luncheon, 9" d.
    (ILLUS.).. $85
Vegetable dish, open, oval, 9" l.................... $125

CLYTIE (Wedgwood & Co., ca. 1908)
Plate, dinner, 10" d., w/turkey design............ $150
Platter, 19" l., w/turkey design.................... $1,000

COLONIAL (J. & G. Meakin, ca. 1891)
Butter pat, 3 1/2" d.. $40
Vegetable bowl, open, oval, 9" l.................. $125

CONWAY (New Wharf Pottery & Co., ca. 1891)

Conway Vegetable Bowl

Vegetable bowl, open, round, 9 1/2" d.
    (ILLUS.) $85

DAISY (Burgess & Leigh, ca. 1897)

Daisy Soup Plate

Soup plate w/flanged rim, 9" d. (ILLUS.)....... $65

DELFT (Minton, ca. 1893)

Delft Oyster Plate

Oyster plate, 10" d. (ILLUS.) $185

Delft Platter

Platter, 14" l. (ILLUS.).................................. $175

DERBY (W.H. Grindley, ca. 1891) - Floral (this is a "polychrome" pattern)
Plate, 9" d... $65

Derby Platter

Platter, 14" l. (ILLUS.) $225
Soup plate w/flanged rim, 9" d. $85
Vegetable dish, cov., 12" l., 7" h. $225

DOT FLOWER (Unknown, ca. 1840) - Brush-stroke
Creamer, 5" h. $275

ECLIPSE (Johnson Bros., ca. 1891)
Demitasse cup & saucer, cup 2 1/2" h.,
    saucer 4 1/2" d. $125
Plate, 9" d... $80
Vegetable bowl, cov.................................... $250

FLENSBURG (James Edwards, England, ca. 1847)

Flensburg Pattern Flow Blue Teapot by Edwards

Teapot, cov., Six Sided Primary body shape
(ILLUS.)... **$450**

FLORA (Thomas Walker, ca. 1845)

Flora Plate

Plate, 10 1/2" d. (ILLUS.).............................. **$125**

FLORAL GAUDY (Mellor & Venables, England, ca. 1849)

Mellor & Venables Floral Gaudy Teapot

Teapot, cov., free-hand, Vertical Panel
Gothic body shape (ILLUS.)...................... **$650**

FLORIDA (Ford & Sons, ca. 1891)
Plate, 10 1/4" d... **$100**

Florida Platter

Platter, 17" l. (ILLUS.).................................. **$375**
Vegetable dish, cov., 12" w., 7" h................ **$225**

FLORIDA (Johnson Bros., ca. 1900)
Egg cup, 3 1/2" h. **$150**
Pitcher, 7" h. **$325**
Plate, 10" d.. **$115**
Platter, 14" l. **$250**

FORMOSA (T.J. & J. Mayer, ca. 1850)
Platter, 19" l. **$800**

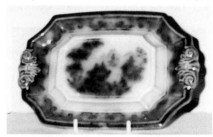

Formosa Undertray to Sauce Boat

Underplate to sauce boat, rectangular,
5 1/2 x 8 1/2" (ILLUS.).............................. **$250**

FORMOSA (W. Ridgway, England, ca. 1840s)

Formosa Pattern Flow Blue Teapot

Teapot, cov., Flat Panel Primary body
shape (ILLUS.).. **$600**

Godwin No. 26 Partial Child's Tea Set

GLOIRE DE DIJON (Doulton & Co., ca. 1895)

Gloire de Dijon Pitcher

Pitcher, belonging to pitcher/bowl wash set
   (ILLUS.).. **$350**

GODWIN NO. 26 (J. & R. Godwin, ca. 1834) - this pattern is found in child's tea set, not always marked; when it is, it's marked only w/"Godwin No. 26"
Tea set, child's: 3 3/4" h. cov. teapot,
   2 3/4" h. creamer, 4" d. x 2 3/4" h. waste
   bowl; partial set (ILLUS., top of page)....... **$675**

GRACE (W. H. Grindley & Co., ca. 1897)
Butter pat, 3 1/2" d. **$60**
Platter, 16" l. **$300**

GRECIAN SCROLL (T.J. and J. Mayer, ca. 1850)

Grecian Scroll Teapot

Teapot, 10" h. (ILLUS.) **$695**

HADDON (W. H. Grindley & Co., ca. 1891)
Butter pat, 3 1/2" d. **$45**
Butter w/insert, cov..................................... **$275**
Plate, 9" d.. **$65**
Plate, 10" d... **$75**
Platter, 12" l. **$150**

Haddon Tree Platter with Meat Well

Heath's Flower Creamer & Sugar

Platter w/meat well, 22" l. (ILLUS., bottom
previous page) **$750**
Vegetable bowl, cov., round, 11" d.,
6 1/2" h. **$200**
Vegetable bowl, open, oval, 9" d. **$125**

HEATH'S FLOWER (Thomas Heath, ca. 1830, brush stroke)

Creamer & cov. sugar, 5" h. creamer, 6" h.
sugar (ILLUS, top of page.) **$725**

Heath's Flower Plate

Plate, 9 1/2" d., 12-sided (ILLUS.) **$125**
Platter, 13 1/2" l. **$225**

HOLLAND (Johnson Bros., ca. 1891)

Gravy boat, 6 1/2" l. **$150**
Soup bowl, open, 8" d. **$85**
Vegetable dish, cov., footed, 12" l.,
6 1/2" h. **$225**

HONC (Petrus Regout, ca. 1858)

Honc Bedpan

Bedpan (ILLUS.) **$1,000**

INDIAN (F. & R. Pratt, ca. 1850)

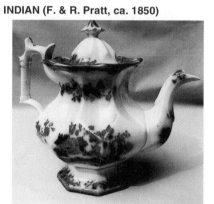

Indian Flow Blue Pattern Teapot

Teapot, cov., Inverted Diamond body shape
(ILLUS.) **$650**

INDIAN JAR (Jacob & Thomas Furnival, ca. 1843)

Creamer, 4 1/2" h. **$250**
Sauce tureen, cov. **$325**

1840s Indian Jar Pattern Flow Blue Teapot

Teapot, cov., Twelve Panel Ridged body
shape (ILLUS.) **$650**

LAHORE (Thomas Phillips & Son, ca. 1840)
Pitcher, 7" h. $375

LAKEWOOD (Wood & Sons, ca. 1900)
Butter pat, 3 1/2" d.. $40
Gravy boat w/underplate $165

Lakewood Dinner Plate

Plate, 10" d. (ILLUS.).................................... $100
Soup tureen, cov. $375
Tea cup & saucer, cup 4" h., 3 1/2" d., sau-
    cer 6" d... $85

LANCASTER (New Wharf Pottery & Co., ca. 1891)
Butter pat, 3 1/2" d.. $40

LANCASTER (New Wharf Pottery & Co., ca. 1891)

New Wharf Pottery Lancaster Pattern Teapot

Teapot, cov., squatty bulbous unnamed
    body shape (ILLUS.) $500

LAZULI (James Edwards, ca. 1842)

Lazuli Razor Box

Razor box, 9" w. (ILLUS.) $275

LORNE (W.H. Grindley & Co., ca. 1900)
Bowl, berry, 5" d.. $45
Platter, 12" l. $165

MANHATTAN (Henry Alcock & Co., ca. 1900)
Bowl, berry, 5" d.. $45
Butter dish w/insert, cov.............................. $250
Cake plate, two-handled $175
Plate, 8" d... $45
Plate, 9" d... $55
Platter, 14" l. $175
Platter, 16" l. $225
Soup plate w/flanged rim, 9" d..................... $65
Tea cup & saucer $65
Tea set: teapot, sugar & creamer; the set..... $900
Vegetable dish, cov., footed........................ $250

MARIE (W. H. Grindley & Co., ca. 1891)
Pitcher, 7" h. $275
Plate, 10 1/4" d... $75

MARLBOROUGH (W. H. Grindley & Co., ca. 1891)
Butter pat, 3 1/2" d. $45
Pitcher, 6" h. (ILLUS. right, top next page) ... $225
Pitcher, 8" d. (ILLUS. middle, top next
    page).. $250
Pitcher, 10" h. (ILLUS. left, top next page) ... $300

Marlborough Open Vegetable Bowl

Vegetable bowl, open, oval, 9" l. (ILLUS.) ... $125

MARTHA WASHINGTON (Unknown, ca. 1900 aka "Chain of States")
Plate, 9" d... $95

Marlborough Graduated Pitchers

MEISSEN (F.A. Mehlem, German, ca. 1891)

Meissen Vegetable Bowl

Vegetable bowl, open, 10" d. (ILLUS.) $95

MELBOURNE (W.H. Grindley & Co., ca. 1891)

Bowl, berry, 5" d... $45
Butter pat, 3 1/2" d... $55
Cake plate, 12" d., two-handled.................... $165
Plate, 6" d... $45
Plate, 8" d... $50
Plate, 9" d... $65

Melbourne Dinner Plate

Plate, 10" d. (ILLUS.) $75
Platter, 14" l. $225
Platter, 16" l. $295
Platter, 18" l. $350

Melbourne Soup Tureen

Soup tureen, cov., oval, footed, 14" l., 7 1/2" h. (ILLUS.) $650
Vegetable bowl, cov., oval $250
Vegetable bowl, open, round $125

MELROSE (Doulton & Co., ca. 1891)

Plate, 10 1/4" d.. $65
Platter, 20" l. $350

MIKADO (A.J. Wilkinson, ca. 1896)

Mikado Dinner Plate

Plate, 10 1/2" d. (ILLUS.) $75
Platter, 18" l. $325
Soup plate w/flanged rim, 10 1/2" d. $65

MURIEL (Upper Hanley Pottery, ca. 1895)

Muriel Platter

Platter, 14" l. (ILLUS.) **$250**

NANKIN (Mellor, Venables & Co. or Thomas Walker, ca. 1845)

Plate from Nankin Tea Set

Tea set: teapot, oversized cov. sugar, creamer, 6 cups w/no handles & 6 saucers, 6 9" d. plates; Primary body style, the set (ILLUS. of plate) **$2,500**

NON PAREIL (Burgess & Leigh, ca. 1891)
Butter pat **$55**

NON PAREIL (Burgess & Leigh - Middleport Potteries, ca. 1891)
Platter, 16" l. **$350**
Soup plate w/flanged rim, 9" d. **$95**

NORMANDY (Johnson Bros., ca. 1900)
Bowl, berry, 5" d. **$45**
Butter pat, 3 1/2" d. **$55**
Plate, 9" d. **$65**

Normandy Soup Plate
Soup plate w/flanged rim, 10" d. (ILLUS.)..... **$95**

OLD CURIOSITY SHOP (Ridgways, ca. 1910)

Old Curiosity Shop Platter

Platter, 16" l. (ILLUS.) **$295**
Vegetable bowl, open, oval, 10" l. **$125**

ORCHID (John Maddock & Sons, ca. 1896)
Platter, 16" l. **$250**
Platter, 18" l. **$275**

ORIENTAL (Samuel Alcock & Co., ca. 1840)
Plate, 9 1/2" d. **$125**
Plate, 10 1/2" d. **$175**
Platter, 16" l. **$450**

Oriental Underplate

Underplate, two-handled w/reticulated tab handles, 13" d. (ILLUS.)............................ **$450**

ORMONDE (Alfred Meakin, ca. 1891)
Plate, 8" d. **$45**
Plate, 10 1/4" d. **$65**

PAISLEY (Mercer Pottery Co., American, ca. 1890)

Paisley Platters, Bone Dishes, Gravy

Minton & Co. Flow Blue Tea Set

Bone dish, crescent-shaped (ILLUS. lower left, previous page) $85
Gravy boat (ILLUS. lower right, previous page) $150
Platter, 20" l. (ILLUS. upper right, previous page) $350
Relish dish, 9" l. $125
Soup tureen, cov., round $450

PEKIN (Johnson Bros., ca. 1891)

Pekin Dinner Plate

Plate, 10" d. (ILLUS.) $75

PEONY (Minton & Co., ca. 1875-1891)

Tea set: cov. teapot, open sugar, creamer, cup & saucer, tray; the teapot 6 1/2" h. x 9 1/2" w. from spout to handle, the sugar 2 1/2" h. x 5 1/2" w. from handle to handle, the creamer 2 1/2" h. x 4 1/2" w. from spout to handle, the cup 3" d. x 2 1/2" h., the saucer 5" d., the tab-handled tray 14 1/2" sq., only marked "Minton" w/crown above it, no patt. name, the set (ILLUS., top of page) **$1,200**

PERSIAN SPRAY (Doulton & Co., ca. 1885)

Bowl, 8" d. $165
Compote, 9" d. $250
Teapot, self-pouring $475

PLYMOUTH (New Wharf Pottery & Co., ca. 1891)

Plymouth Dinner Plate

Plate, 10" d. (ILLUS.) $65
Tea cup & saucer $65

POPPY (Doulton & Co., ca. 1902)
Jardiniere, 10" h. $450

POPPY (W. H. Grindley & Co., ca. 1891)

Poppy Dinner Plate

Plate, 10" d. (ILLUS.) $100

RHODES (possibly Samuel Ford & Co., ca. 1898-1929)

Rhodes 8" Plate

Plate, 8" d., marked "S.F. & Co." (ILLUS.)....... **$50**

RICHMOND I (Ford & Sons, ca. 1900)

Richmond Soup

Rim soup, flanged edge, 10" d. (ILLUS.) **$100**

RICHMOND (Johnson Bros., ca. 1900) - Floral

Richmond 8" Plate

Plate, 8" d. (ILLUS.)... **$65**
Platter, 16" l.. **$275**

Vegetable dish, open, 9" d. **$175**

RIO (Pountney & Co., Ltd., ca. 1893)
Platter, 13" l. **$200**
Vegetable dish, open, 10" d. **$150**

ROSE (Bourne & Leigh, ca. 1910)
Candlesticks, 5" h., pr. **$350**

ROSE & VINE (David Methven & Sons, ca. 1847)

Bowl in Rose & Vine Pattern

Bowl, 10 1/2" d. (ILLUS.) **$175**

ROSES (Unknown, ca. 1850)

Large Platter in Roses Pattern

Platter, 17 x 22", only has mark "F.B. Roses" & impressed mark "Newstone," which was used by Spode & Co. after 1830 (ILLUS.)... **$650**

ROSEVILLE (John Maddock & Sons, ca. 1891)

Roseville Celery Dish

Celery dish, 11" l. (ILLUS.)........................... **$125**

ROYAL BLUE (Balmoral) (Burgess & Campbell, American, ca. 1880)
Butter dish, cov. **$225**

SCINDE (J. & G. Alcock, ca. 1840)

Scinde Jam Jar

Jam jar w/attached tray, w/lion's head handles, only one of its kind (ILLUS.) **$6,000**

Scinde Platter

Platter, 18" l. (ILLUS.) **$750**

Scinde Teapot

Teapot, primary body style, 9" h. (ILLUS.) **$900**

SEVILLE (New Wharf Pottery & Co., ca. 1891)

Seville Dinner Plate

Plate, 10" d. (ILLUS.) **$75**

SHANGHAI (W.E. Corn, ca. 1900)

Shanghai Dinner Plate

Plate, 10" d. (ILLUS.) **$75**

SHUSAN (F. & R. Pratt & Co., ca. 1855)

Shusan Dinner Plate

Plate, 10 1/2" d. (ILLUS.) **$125**

SYRIAN (W. H. Grindley & Co., ca. 1892)

Syrian Chamber Pot

Chamber pot, cov., 11" w., 7" h. (ILLUS.) **$325**

TEMPLE (Podmore, Walker, ca. 1849)

Temple Pattern Flow Blue Teapot

Teapot, cov., Oval body shape (ILLUS.) **$800**

Temple Pattern Teapot in Varied Shape

Teapot, cov., Twelve Panel Bulbous body
shape (ILLUS.) **$750**

TOGO (F. Winkle & Co., ca. 1900) (Also known as Colonial)
Chamber pot **$250**
Pitcher, 7" h. **$150**

TOKIO (Johnson Bros., ca. 1900)

Tokio Luncheon Plate

Plate, 9" d. (ILLUS.) **$55**

TONQUIN (Wm. Adams & Son, ca. 1845)
Creamer, 6" h. **$375**
Rim soup, w/flanged edge, 9" d **$125**

Tonquin Pattern Flow Blue Teapot

Teapot, cov., Full Panel Gothic body shape
(ILLUS.) **$650**

TOURAINE (Henry Alcock & Co., ca. 1898)
Butter dish, cov. **$250**
Cake plate, w/tab handles, 9 1/2" d. **$175**

Alcock Touraine Pattern Flow Blue Teapot

Large Stanley Pottery Touraine Pattern Flow Blue Dinner Service

Teapot, cov., fluted urn-form unnamed body
shape (ILLUS., previous page) **$750**
Vegetable bowl, individual size, 5 1/2" w. **$100**

TOURAINE (Stanley Potteries, England - modern)
Teapot, cov., fluted urn-form unnamed body
shape, modern reproduction by the Stanley Potteries, England **$75**

TOURAINE (Stanley Pottery Co., ca. 1898)
Dinner service: eleven 10" d. dinner plates,
six soup plates, four small plain edge cereal bowls, eight 8" d. salad plates, 18
dessert plates, 16 dessert bowls, 16 teacups & 25 saucers, ten bread & butter
plates, eight crescent-shaped bone dishes, round sauce bowl, paneled round
sauce bowl, open oval 8 1/2" l. vegetable
dish, slightly larger open oval vegetable
dish, two oval 17" l. meat platters, four
ovoid open vegetable bowls, one slightly
smaller open vegetable dish, two handled cov. sugar bowls (repaired handles),
4 1/2" h. creamer & 5" h. pitcher, the set
(ILLUS., top of page)............................ **$3,450**

TRILBY (Wood & Sons, ca. 1891)

Trilby Cake Plate

Cake plate, w/tab handles, made for export
for "Holmes Luce & Co., Boston, Mass.,"

to be given away w/each purchase of furniture, the name of the company printed
on front, 10 1/2" d. (ILLUS.) **$150**

TROY (Charles Meigh, ca. 1840)
Teapot **$475**

TULIP (Copeland & Garrett, ca. 1845)

Tulip Fruit Compote

Fruit compote, footed, 10" d., 6" h.
(ILLUS.)... **$550**

TURKEY (Cauldon, Ltd., ca. 1905)

Turkey Dinner Plate

Plate, 10 1/2" d. (ILLUS.) **$150**

Very Large Doulton Turkey Platter

Rare Turkey Set by Wedgwood & Company

TURKEY (Doulton & Co., ca. 1900) (Doulton produced more than one design with a turkey)
Platter, 24" l. (ILLUS., top of page) **$1,200**

TURKEY (marked "La Belle China W.P." for La Belle China Co. & Wheeling Pottery Co. of Wheeling, West Virginia, when they merged; American, ca. 1893-1903)
Serving set: 18" l. platter & twelve 10" d. plates; the set **$1,800**

TURKEY (Ridgways, ca. 1900)
Turkey set: platter, 22" l., & 12 dinner plates, 10" d.; the set **$2,500**

TURKEY (Wedgwood & Co., ca. 1900)
Turkey set: 13 1/4 x 18" oval platter & twelve 10"d. dinner plates, floral border, the set (ILLUS., second from top) **$2,358**

TYROLEAN (Ridgway, ca. 1850)
Charger, 12 1/2" d. **$175**

VERMONT (Burgess & Leigh, ca. 1895)
Plate, 10" d. **$95**
Sauceboat w/underplate, 9" l., 5" h. **$275**

Vermont Pattern Flow Blue Teapot

Teapot, cov., ribbed pear-shaped unnamed body (ILLUS.) **$450**

VERONA (Wood & Sons, ca. 1891)
Plate, 10" d. **$95**

VIRGINIA (John Maddock & Sons, ca. 1891)

Virginia Platter

Platter, 16" l. (ILLUS.) **$275**

WATER NYMPH (Josiah Wedgwood, ca. 1872)

Bowl, footed, 8" d., 5" h................................. **$195**

WATTEAU (Doulton & Co., ca. 1891)

Oil lamp, converted to electric, 26" h. **$850**

Watteau Dinner Plate

Plate, 10 1/2" d. (ILLUS.)................................. **$95**

WAVERLY (John Maddock & Son, ca. 1891)

Waverly Platter

Platter, 16" l. (ILLUS.) **$275**

WENTWORTH (J. & G. Meakin, ca. 1907)

Butter pat, 3 1/2" d. **$40**

Wentworth Dinner Plate

Plate, 10" d. (ILLUS.) **$65**
Vegetable bowl, cov., 12" l., 6 1/2" h........... **$175**

Fulper Pottery

The Fulper Pottery was founded in Flemington, New Jersey, in 1805 and operated until 1935, although operations were curtailed in 1929 when its main plant was destroyed by fire. The name was changed in 1929 to Stangl Pottery, which continued in operation until July of 1978, when Pfaltzgraff, a division of Susquehanna Broadcasting Company of York, Pennsylvania, purchased the assets of the Stangl Pottery, including the name.

Fulper Marks

Nearly Spherical Fulper Vase

Vase, 5 1/2" h., flat-based nearly spherical shape w/an inward-rolled rim, overall mottled drippy green & brown matt glaze, vertical ink stamp mark (ILLUS.).............. **$288**

Squatty Bulbous Fulper Vase

Vase, 5 5/8" h., 9" d., wide squatty bulbous form tapering sharply to a small rolled neck, Butterscotch Flambé glaze in green shaded to light yellow, Shape No. 657, vertical ink stamp mark, some very minor grinding chips on base (ILLUS.)...... **$518**

Ringed Fulper Vase with Cucumber Glaze

Vase, 6" h., tapering cylindrical form composed of four wide rings, flat mouth flanked by looped vine-stype handles, Cucumber Crystalline glaze, vertical racetrack ink stamp mark (ILLUS.)............ **$345**

Very Bulbous Footed Fulper Vase

Vase, 6 1/4" h., footed nearly spherical slightly squatty body topped by a wide short cylindrical neck flanked by three small loop shoulder handles, overall dark purple Wisteria glaze, Shape No. 564, raised oval vertical mark, uncrazed (ILLUS.) **$345**

Fulper Vasekraft Flambé-glazed Vase

Vase, 8" h., 4" w., Vasekraft line, square tapering lower body below square flat sides, a stylized embossed coat-of-arms at the top of each side, Flemington Green Flambé glaze, rectangular ink mark (ILLUS.) **$1,035**

Aqua & Olive Flambé Fulper Vase

Vase, 8 1/2" h., 8" d., very wide bulbous ovoid body w/a wide shoulder centered by a short cylindrical neck flanked by arched shoulder handles, aqua & olive Flambé glaze, raised racetrack mark (ILLUS.)........ **$460**

Fulper Vase with Frothy Blue Glaze

Vase, 9 1/2" h., 7" d., wide heavy baluster-form body, fine frothy turquoise blue glaze, ink racetrack mark (ILLUS.)............ **$489**

Grey to Blue Flambé-glazed Fulper Vase

Vase, 10" h., 7" d., wide squatty rounded lower body below the wide steeply tapering cylindrical sides flanked by long flattened & angled handles, mouse grey to dark blue flambé glaze, raised racetrack mark (ILLUS.).. **$805**

Unusual Fulper Vaz-Bowl

Vaz-bowl, wide shallow rounded lobed dish w/four of the lobes pulled up into tapering strap handles that are joined above the center of the dish, mottled green matte glaze, vertical inkstamp mark & label from the Pan Pacific International Exposition, San Francisco, 1915, 6 1/2" d. (ILLUS.) **$863**

Gallé Pottery

Fine pottery was made by Emile Gallé, the multitalented French designer and artisan who is also famous for his glass and furniture. The pottery is relatively scarce.

Gallé Pottery Mark

Gallé Pottery Ewer with Praying Mantis

Ewer, footed wide squatty bulbous low body centered by a tall flaring & swelled neck w/a pinched spout & long angled handle from top to shoulder, a mottled glossy purple glaze decorated w/sponged gold & enameled w/a large & gangly praying mantis about to land on white spider mums on leafy stems below, all outlined in gold, base stamped in black "E+G déposé - E. Gallé" & a possibly obscured "Nancy," footring w/a few flat chips, 7 1/4" h. (ILLUS.) **$1,725**

Ewer, squatty bulbous body centering a very tall slender cylindrical neck, a long curved handle from the rim to the side of the shoulder, one side decorated w/a modeled mushroom-shaped flower, the opposite decorated w/a great raised blue & brown grasshopper, background w/splashes of blue, yellow, gold, rust & brown, signed on the bottom "E G Dé-

Unusual Modeled Gallé Pottery Ewer

posé" & signed "E Gallé Nancy," some
very minor crazing to glaze, 9 1/4" h.
(ILLUS.) **$1,495**

Gallé Vase with Barnyard Scenes

Vase, 7" h., 4 1/2 x 11 1/2", long flat-sided
oval form w/a long rectangular mouth
flanked by lion heads w/ring handles,
raised on four scroll feet, one side h.p.
w/a colorful scene of a hen & rooster
w/four chicks & a ladder, the other side
w/a scene of a chicken w/wheelbarrow &
broom on hay, base impressed w/loz-
enge mark "E.G.," mold number 244, artist-signed, late 19th c. (ILLUS.) **$518**

Vase, 7 1/8" h., footed wide squatty bulbous
body centered by a tall upright gently flaring & deeply crimped neck, overall flowing pink & blue glaze, the base h.p. w/a
scene of a quiet inlet village painted in
sepia tones, various sea sheels painted
around the neck & shoulder, base signed
"E. Gallé Fayencerie Nancy," crazed in-
side & out (ILLUS., top next column) **$1,093**

Squatty Gallé Vase with Village Scene

Rare Gallé Figural Wall Pocket

Wall pocket, round w/a large relief-molded
crescent man-in-the-moon face around
the border, the background h.p. Italian-
ate seascape, signed "E. Gallé à Nancy
195" & molded "EG" w/a Cross of Lorraine & "Mode...et décor dép...," ca.
1890s, 14" w., 13 1/2" h. (ILLUS.).......... **$5,736**

Geisha Girl Wares

*Geisha Girl Porcelain features scenes of Japa-
nese women in colorful kimonos along with the
flora and architecture of turn-of-the-century
Japan. Although bearing an Oriental motif, the
wares were produced for Western use in dinnerware and household accessory forms favored during the late 1800s through the early 1940s. There
was minimal production during the Occupied
Japan period. Less ornate wares were distributed
through gift shops and catalogs during the 1960s-
70s; some of these are believed to have been manufactured in Hong Kong. Beware overly ornate
items with fake Nippon marks that are in current
production today, imported from China. More*

than a hundred porcelain manufacturers and decorating houses were involved with production of these wares during their heyday.

Prices cited here are for excellent to mint condition items. Enamel wear, flaking, hairlines or missing parts all serve to lower the value of an item. Prices in your area may vary.

More than 275 Geisha Girl Porcelain patterns and pattern variations have been catalogued; others are still coming to light.

The most common patterns include:

Bamboo Tree

Battledore

Child Reaching for Butterfly

Fan series

Garden Bench series

Geisha in Sampan series

Meeting series

Parasol series

Pointing series

The rarest patterns include:

... And They're Off

Bellflower

Bicycle Race

Capricious

Elegance in Motion

Fishing series

Foreign Garden

In Flight

Steamboat

The most popular patterns include:

Boat Festival

Butterfly Dancers

By Land and By Sea

Cloud series

Courtesan Processional

Dragonboat

Small Sounds of Summer

So Big

Temple A

A complete listing of patterns and their descriptions can be found in The Collector's Encyclopedia of Geisha Girl Porcelain. Additional patterns discovered since publication of the book are documented in The Geisha Girl Porcelain Newsletter.

References: Litts, E., Collector's Encyclopedia of Geisha Girl Porcelain, Collector Books, 1988; Geisha Girl Porcelain Newsletter, P.O. Box 3394, Morris Plains, NJ 07950.

Bowl, 7" d., Garden Bench C patt., tri-footed, rose, cobalt blue border w/gold embellishments **$45**

Bowl, 8 1/2" d., Drum D patt., pale cobalt blue border, signed "Kutani"....................... **$55**

Box, manicure, Lady in Kaga patt., red border, 2 1/2" d... **$15**

Geisha Temple A Candlesticks

Candlesticks, Temple A patt., multicolor border, Noritake's green M-in-wreath Nippon mark, 5 3/4" h., pr. (ILLUS.) **$175**

Cup & saucer, cocoa, Bamboo Trellis patt., wavy red border w/gold lacing **$18**

Cup & saucer, tea, Parasol C patt., red border, marked "Japan"................................... **$10**

Dish, Garden Bench F patt., figural leaf shape, ornate multicolor border & highly gilded decoration....................................... **$25**

Egg cup, double, Playing Catch patt., red border... **$18**

Mustard jar w/lid & spoon, Lunchtime patt., blue-green border, marked "Made in Japan" **$30**

Geisha Girl Temple A Perfume Bottle

Perfume bottle, Temple A patt., multicolor border, R K Nippon mark, 4 1/2" h. (ILLUS.)... **$95**

Plate, 7 1/4" d., Parasol patt. variant, dark green border w/unusual raised white enamel detailing **$15**

Platter, 10" l., Duck Watching A patt., gold border, marked "Made in Japan" **$35**

Salt & pepper shakers, Lantern Boy patt., pine green border, 2 3/4" h., pr. **$15**

Teapot, cov., Bow B patt. in reserve on floral backdrop, cobalt blue border w/gold striping, gold upper edge & spout rim **$45**

Toothpick holder, Carp A patt., three-sided, red border w/interior gold lacing **$25**

Geisha Gardening Pattern Vase

Vase, 6 3/4" h., Gardening patt., red border w/interior band of gold lacing (ILLUS.) **$28**

Gonder

Lawton Gonder founded Gonder Ceramic Arts in Zanesville, Ohio, in 1941 and it continued in operation until 1957.

The firm produced a higher priced and better quality of commercial art potteries than many firms of the time and employed Jamie Matchet and Chester Kirk, both of whom were outstanding ceramic designers. Several special glazes were developed during the company's history and Gonder even duplicated some museum pieces of Chinese ceramic. In 1955 the firm converted to the production of tile due to increased foreign competition. By 1957 its years of finest production were over.

Increase price ranges as indicated for the following glaze colors: red flambé - 50 percent, antique gold crackle - 70 percent, turquoise Chinese crackle - 40 per cent, white Chinese crackle - 30 per cent.

Lamp, Keystone, Mold No. 4085, 9 1/4" w., 12 3/4" h. **$40-60**

Lamp, no number, "LG," 8 1/2" h., 6 3/8" w. **$75-100**

Lamp, Scroll, Mold No. 2255, 9 1/4" w., 12 3/4" h. **$40-60**

Lamp, Swirl, Mold No. 3060, 7 3/4" w., 5 1/2" h. **$40-60**

Lamp, Tall Bottle, Mold No. 5506, 17 1/2" h. **$125-150**

Lamp, Vine & Leaves, Mold No. 3031, 9 1/2" h. **$40-60**

Planter, twist shoe strap, Mold No. 585, hard to find, 4 5/8 x 10 5/8", 4" h. **$75-100**

Planter, Zig Zag, Mold No. 737, 11 3/4 l., 2 1/2" h. **$15-30**

Planter set, figurine of doe w/turned head, side planters, Mold No. 213, 3 x 4 1/2", 10 5/8" h., the set **$75-100**

Planter set: Oriental man & woman water bearers w/baskets; Mold No. 777, man 10 1/2" w., 14 1/8" h., woman 10 1/4" w., 14 1/4" h., each **$50-75**

Tray, 8-section, Mold No. 100, very hard to find, 10 15/16 x 19 1/4" **$150-200**

Tray, shell, Mold No. 865, very hard to find, 12 x 14" **$175-225**

Urn, Sovereign cigarette footed, Mold No. 801, 3 1/2" h. **$40-60**

Vase, applied leaf, Mold No. 370, E-70 ...... **$20-35**

Vase, large cylindrical, Mold No. 712 .... **$25-35**

Vase, modeled pillow, Mold No. 506 .... **$50-75**

Vase, pigtail handles, Mold No. H-608 ... **$100-150**

Vase, 2 1/2" h., square mini, Mold No. 407 .... **$15-20**

Vase, 3 1/2" h., footed Chinese rectangle, Mold No. 707 .... **$15-25**

Vase, 3 1/2" h., small round, Mold No. 745 **$15-20**

Vase, 5" h., small square footed, Mold No. 706 .... **$10-20**

Vase, 6 1/4" h., square banded, Mold No. 369, 703, E-69, E-369 .... **$20-30**

Vase, 6 1/2" h., large flat rectangular, Mold No. 708 .... **$15-25**

Vase, 6 1/2" h., metallic-look pitcher form, Mold No. 382 .... **$30-45**

Vase, 6 1/2" h., ribbon handle ewer, Mold No. 373, E-73, E-373 .... **$25-35**

Vase, 7" h., ribbed cornucopia, Mold No. 360 .... **$20-35**

Vase, 7" h., small flat horn, Mold No. 305, E-5 .... **$15-30**

Vase, 7 1/16" h., 6 1/2 x 6 3/8", 4-footed large flared square, Mold No. 750 .... **$25-35**

Vase, 7 3/4" h., bottle-form, Mold No. 1209 .... **$50-70**

Vase, 7 7/8" h., raised circular bud, Mold No. 1208 .... **$40-60**

Vase, 9" h., standing Oriental male, Mold No. 519 .... **$15-25**

Hall China

Founded in 1903 in East Liverpool, Ohio, this still-operating company at first produced mostly utilitarian wares. It was in 1911 that Robert T. Hall, son of the company founder, developed a special single-fire, lead-free glaze that proved to be strong, hard and nonporous. In the 1920s the firm became well known for its extensive line of teapots (still a major product), and in 1932 it introduced kitchenwares, followed by dinnerwares in 1936 and refrigerator wares in 1938.

The imaginative designs and wide range of glaze colors and decal decorations have led to the growing appeal of Hall wares with collectors, especially people who like Art Deco and Art Mod-

erne design. One of the firm's most famous patterns was the "Autumn Leaf" line, produced as premiums for the Jewel Tea Company. For listings of this ware see "Jewel Tea Autumn Leaf."

Helpful books on Hall include The Collector's Guide to Hall China by Margaret & Kenn Whitmyer, and Superior Quality Hall China - A Guide for Collectors by Harvey Duke (An ELO Book, 1977).

HALL CHINA

MADE IN U.S.A.

Hall Marks

Ashtray, triangular, deep, No. 683, turquoise..	**$15**
Ashtray w/match holder, closed sides, No. 618 1/2, cobalt...	**$20**
Baker, French Fluted shape, Blue Bouquet patt.	**$25**
Baker, French Fluted shape, Silhouette patt.	**$30**
Baker, French Fluted shape, Yellow Rose patt.	**$25**

Five Band Batter Bowl

Batter bowl, Five Band shape, Chinese Red (ILLUS.)	**$95**
Batter jug, Sundial shape, Blue Garden patt.	**$250**
Bean pot, cov., New England shape, No. 2 & No. 4, each	**$120-140**
Bean pot, cov., New England shape, No. 4, Blue Blossom patt.	**$225**
Bean pot, cov., New England shape, No. 4, Crocus patt...	**$325**
Bean pot, cov., New England shape, No. 4, Shaggy Tulip patt.	**$275**
Bean pot, cov., tab-handled, Sani-Grid (Pert) shape, Rose Parade patt.	**$115**
Bowl, 6" d., Medallion shape, Silhouette patt.	**$23**
Bowl, 6" d., Radiance shape, No. 4, Crocus patt..	**$25**
Bowl, 6" d., Radiance shape, Yellow Rose patt.	**$20**
Bowl, 6" d., Thick Rim shape, Blue Blossom patt.	**$40**
Bowl, 7" d., Medallion shape, Silhouette patt.	**$25**
Bowl, 7" d., Radiance shape, Crocus patt.......	**$40**

Butter dish, cov., Crocus patt., Zephyr shape, 1 lb.	**$1,200**
Cake plate, Primrose patt.	**$20**
Canister, cov., Radiance shape, Chinese Red	**$200**

Casserole with Chrome Base

Casserole, cov., Art Deco w/chrome reticulated handled base (ILLUS.)	**$75**
Casserole, cov., Five Band shape, Flamingo patt..	**$75**
Casserole, cov., Ribbed line, russet	**$45**
Casserole, cov., round, No. 76, Wild Poppy patt., 10 1/2" d.	**$75**
Casserole, cov., Sundial shape, No. 4, Chinese Red..	**$55**
Casserole, cov., tab-handled, Rose Parade patt.	**$42**
Coffeelator, cov., cobalt blue........................	**$125**
Coffeepot, cov., Drip-O-Later, Duse shape	**$50**
Coffeepot, cov., Drip-O-Later, Sash shape, red..	**$70**

Hall Coffeepots

Coffeepot, cov., Drip-O-Later, Jerry shape (ILLUS. left)...	**$50**
Coffeepot, cov., Drip-O-Later, Scoop shape, Wildflower patt.	**$40**
Coffeepot, cov., Drip-O-Later, Waverly shape	**$35**
Coffeepot, cov., Meltdown shape w/basket, Crocus patt..	**$90**

Crocus Pattern Coffeepot

Coffeepot, cov., Terrace shape, Crocus patt. (ILLUS., previous page) $80

Coffeepot, cov., Tricolator, Ritz shape, Chinese Red (ILLUS. right w/Jerry Drip-O-Lator).. $135

Coffeepot, cov., Waverly shape, Minuet patt. $65

Meadow Flower Cookie Jar

Cookie jar, cov., Five Band shape, Meadow Flower patt. (ILLUS.) $325

Cookie jar, cov., Flareware, Gold Lace design.. $75

Cookie jar, cov., Red Poppy patt. $500

Cookie jar, cov., Sundial shape, Blue Blossom patt. $400

Cookie jar, cov., Sundial shape, Chinese Red $235

Cookie jar, cov., Zeisel, Gold Dot design $95

Creamer, Art Deco, Crocus patt. $25

Creamer, Medallion shape, Silhouette patt. $18

Creamer, Modern, Red Poppy patt. $35

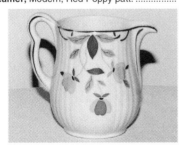

Creamer in Autumn Leaf Pattern

Creamer, Radiance shape, Autumn Leaf patt. (ILLUS.) $45

Creamer, individual, Sundial shape, Chinese Red, 2 oz. $65

Custard cup, straight-sided, Rose White patt. $25

Custard cup, Thick Rim shape, Meadow Flower patt. $35

Drip jar, cov., Radiance shape, Chinese Red (ILLUS., top next column) $60

Drip jar, cov., Thick Rim shape, Royal Rose patt. $25

Drip jar, open, No. 1188, Mums patt. $35

Gravy boat, Red Poppy patt. $125

Radiance Shape Drip Jar

Gravy boat, Springtime patt. $35

Leftover, cov., square, Crocus patt. $125

Zephyr Shape Leftover

Leftover, cov., Zephyr shape, Chinese Red (ILLUS.) $110

Fantasy Leftover

Leftover, cov., Zephyr shape, Fantasy patt. (ILLUS.) $225

Mixing bowl, Thick Rim shape, Royal Rose patt., 8 1/2" d. $30

Mug, beverage, Silhouette patt. $60

Mug, flagon shape, Monk patt. $45

Hall Commemorative Mug

Autumn Leaf Pitcher with Box

Mug, Irish coffee, footed, commemorative, "Hall China Convention 2000" (ILLUS., previous page) $40
Pie plate, Orange Poppy patt. $45
Pitcher, ball shape, Autumn Leaf patt., 1978, w/box (ILLUS., top of page) $65
Pitcher, ball shape, No. 3, Chinese Red $55
Pitcher, jug-type, Doughnut shape, cobalt blue $75

Doughnut-shape Jug-type Pitcher

Pitcher, jug-type, large, Doughnut shape, Chinese Red (ILLUS.) $135
Pitcher, jug-type, Loop-handle, Blue Blossom patt. $195
Pitcher, jug-type, Loop-handle, emerald green $65
Pitcher, jug-type, Medallion line, No. 3, Silhouette patt. $45
Pitchers, Sani-Grid (Pert) shape, Chinese Red, three sizes (ILLUS. of three, top next page) $35-55
Plate, salad, 8 1/4" d., No. 488 patt. $15
Plate, dinner, 9" d., Silhouette patt. $15
Plate, dinner, 10" d., Wildfire patt. $20
Platter, 11 1/4" l., oval, Springtime patt. $20
Platter, 13 1/4" l., oval, Mums patt. $50
Pretzel jar, cov., Crocus patt. $225

Pretzel jar, cov., Pastel Morning Glory patt. $125
Punch set: punch bowl & 10 punch cups; Old Crow, punch bowl reads "May YOU always - have an eagle in your pocket ...a turkey on your table - and Old Crow in your glass," the set $175
Salt & pepper shakers, canister style, red, pr. $90
Salt & pepper shakers, Five Band shape, Blue Blossom patt., pr. $75
Salt & pepper shakers, handled, range-type, Blue Blossom patt., pr. $80
Salt & pepper shakers, handled, Royal Rose patt., pr. $34

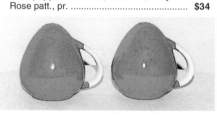

Pert Salt & Pepper Shakers

Salt & pepper shakers, Sani-Grid (Pert) shape, Chinese Red, pr. (ILLUS.) $35
Salt & pepper shakers, Sani-Grid (Pert) shape, Rose Parade patt., pr. $35
Salt & pepper shakers, Teardrop shape, Blue Bouquet patt., pr. $35
Soup tureen, cov., Clover style, Crocus patt. $350
Soup tureen, Thick Rim shape, Blue Bouquet patt. $300
Stack set, Radiance shape, Carrot patt. $125
Sugar bowl, cov., Art Deco, Crocus patt. $35
Sugar bowl, cov., Medallion line, Silhouette patt. $35
Syrup pitcher, cov., Five Band shape, Blue Blossom patt. $165
Tea tile, octagonal, art-glaze blue & white $65
Tea tile, round, Chinese Red $50

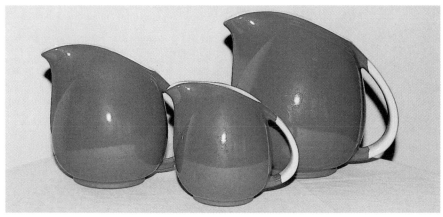

Pert Pitchers in Various Sizes

Teapot, cOv., Aladdin shape, oval opening, w/infuser, Cobalt Blue w/gold trim............. **$110**

Hall Adele Shape Teapot

Teapot, cov., Adele shape, Art Deco style, Olive Green (ILLUS.).................................. **$200**
Teapot, cov., Airflow shape, Chinese Red.... **$130**
Teapot, cov., Airflow shape, Cobalt Blue w/gold trim, 6-cup...................................... **$100**
Teapot, cov., Aladdin shape, Canary Yellow w/gold trim, w/infuser **$65**
Teapot, cov., Aladdin shape, Cobalt Blue w/gold trim, 6-cup...................................... **$125**
Teapot, cov., Albany shape, Mahogany w/gold trim, 6-cup... **$75**

Hall Automobile Shape Teapot

Teapot, cov., Automobile shape, Chinese Red (ILLUS.) **$800**
Teapot, cov., Baltimore shape, Ivory Gold Label line... **$125**
Teapot, cov., Basket shape, Cadet Blue w/platinum decoration **$150**
Teapot, cov., Basketball shape, Emerald Green w/gold decoration **$650**

Bellevue Shape Orange Poppy Teapot

Teapot, cov., Bellevue shape, Orange Poppy patt. (ILLUS.)..................................... **$1,800**

Birdcage Teapot with "Gold Special" Decoration

Teapot, cov., Birdcage shape, Canary Yellow w/"Gold Special" decoration (ILLUS.)
.... **$500**
Teapot, cov., Birdcage shape, Maroon w/"Gold Special" decoration, 6-cup **$400**
Teapot, cov., Boston shape, Canary Yellow, 2-cup **$45**
Teapot, cov., Boston shape, Chinese Red.... **$150**
Teapot, cov., Boston shape, Cobalt Blue w/gold Trailing Aster design, 6-cup........... **$150**

Tea-for-Two Teapot in Pink & Gold

Teapot, cov., Tea-for-Two shape, Pink
w/gold decoration (ILLUS.)........................ **$150**
Teapot, cov., Thorley series, Grape shape,
Ivory w/Special Gold & rhinestone deco-
ration **$295**
Teapot, cov., Thorley series, Starlight
shape, Pink w/gold & rhinestone decora-
tion **$125**
Teapot, cov., Windshield shape, Ivory Gold
Label line.. **$50**
Teapot, cov., Windshield shape, Turquoise
w/gold decoration **$68**
Twin-Tea set: cov. teapot, cov. hot water
pot & matching divided tray; art glaze
green.. **$125**
Twin-Tea set: cov. teapot, cov. hot water
pot & matching divided tray; Pansy patt.... **$225**
Vase, Edgewater, No. 630, cobalt blue **$25**
Vase, bud, Trumpet, No. 631, Chinese Red.... **$35**
Vase, bud, No. 631 1/2, maroon..................... **$15**
Vase, bud, No. 641, canary yellow **$10**

Blue Garden Water Bottle

Water bottle, cov., refrigerator ware line,
Zephyr shape, Blue Garden patt. (ILLUS.)... **$650**
Water server, cov., Montgomery Ward re-
frigerator ware, Delphinium blue **$55**
Water server, Plaza shape, Chinese Red **$135**
Water server w/cork stopper, Hotpoint re-
frigerator ware, Dresden blue...................... **$85**
Water server w/hinged cover, Westing-
house refrigerator ware, Hercules shape,
cobalt blue.. **$110**

Hampshire Pottery

*Hampshire Pottery was made in Keene, New
Hampshire, where several potteries operated as*
*far back as the late 18th century. The pottery now
known as Hampshire Pottery was established by
J.S. Taft shortly after 1870. Various types of
wares, including Art Pottery, were produced
through the years. Taft's brother-in-law, Cadmon
Robertson, joined the firm in 1904 and was
responsible for developing more than 900 glaze
formulas while in charge of all manufacturing.
His death in 1914 created problems for the firm,
and Taft sold out to George Morton in 1916.
Closed during part of World War I, the pottery
was later reopened by Morton for a short time and
manufactured white hotel china. From 1919 to
1921, mosaic floor tiles became the main production. All production ceased in 1923.*

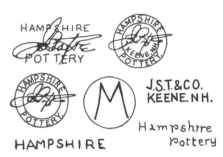

Hampshire Marks

Small Leaf-molded Hampshire Bowl

Bowl, 2 3/4" h., bulbous form molded overall w/overlapping leaves w/a blue & green
semi-matte glaze, marked, Shape No. 24
(ILLUS.)... **$683**

Green Melon-shaped Hampshire Pitcher

Pitcher, 8" h., bulbous ovoid melon shaped w/large leaves forming the neck & pointed spout, vine handle, overall green matte glaze, unmarked (ILLUS., previous page) **$288**

Bulbous Bluish Green Hampshire Vase

Vase, 4" h., 5" d., wide bulbous shape w/a wide short flat-rimmed neck, overall fine bluish green feathered glaze, marked (ILLUS.) **$558**

Small Paneled Green Hampshire Vase

Vase, 4 1/4" h., wide ovoid body w/a wide round shoulder centered by a short molded neck, large lightly molded arched panels around the sides, crystalline matte green glaze, marked "Hampshire Pottery 640 - 110" & impressed M in a circle (ILLUS.) **$432**

Fine Mottled Blue & Green Hampshire Vase

Vase, 5 1/4" h., squatty bulbous body w/a wide shoulder centered by a wide gently flaring short cylindrical neck, mottled blue & green matte glaze, designed by Cadmon Robertson & marked w/his monogram, Shape No. 118 (ILLUS.) **$690**

Hampshire Vase with Brownish Glaze

Vase, 6 1/4" h., bulbous ovoid body w/a wide tapering neck, overall brownish grey matte glaze, marked (ILLUS.) **$441**

Hampshire Green Crystalline Vase

Vase, 7 1/2" h., gently swelled cylindrical body w/an inward-rolled flat mouth, green crystalline matte glaze, marked (ILLUS.)` **$460**

Fine Hampshire Vase with Leathery Glaze

Vase, 8 3/4" h., 9 3/4" d., very wide squatty bulbous shaped w/a rounded shoulder centering a short wide neck w/flat rim, fine leathery green & blue matte glaze, incised mark (ILLUS., previous page).... **$2,703**

Harker Pottery

Harker Pottery was in business for more than 100 years (1840-1972) in the East Liverpool area of eastern Ohio. One of the oldest potteries in Ohio, it advertised itself as one of the oldest in America. The pottery produced numerous lines that are favorites of collectors.

Some of their most popular lines were intended for oven to table use and were marked with BAKER-ITE, COLUMBIA BAKERITE, HOTOVEN, OVEN-WARE, Bungalow Ware, Cameo Ware, White Rose Carv-Kraft (for Montgomery War) and Harkerware Stone China / Stone Ware brand names.

Harker also made Reproduction Rockingham, Royal Gadroon, Pate sur Pate, Windsong, and many souvenir items and a line designed by Russel Wright that have gained popularity with collectors.

Like many pottery manufacturers, Harker reused popular decal patterns on several ware shapes. Harker was marketed under more than 200 backstamps in its history.

Advertising, Novelty & Souvenir Pieces

Ashtrays, w/advertising, each..................... **$5-10**

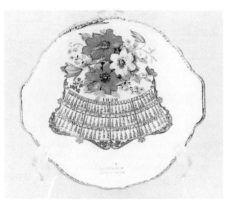

Harker 1929 Calendar Plate

Calendar plates, 1907 to 1930, later dates of lower value, each (ILLUS. of 1929 plate) **$25-35**
Souvenir plates, 6" d., 1890-1930, each... **$20-50**
Tea tile, "Townsend Plan" **$3-50**

Autumn Leaf

Harker made some Autumn Leaf for Jewel Tea before Hall China received the exclusive contract. The ware and decal are somewhat finer than that used by Hall China. Although some Autumn Leaf was unmarked, most was produced under the Columbia Chinaware (Statue of Liberty in color) trademark. Generally, prices for Harker Autumn Leaf are relatively high.

Cake plate, Virginia shape **$200-250**
Casserole, cov. **$75-100**

BakeRite, HotOven

Harker was one of the first American potteries to produce pottery that could go from the oven to the table. Most of this ware, made from the late 1920s to the late 1950s, features brightly colored decals that are popular with collectors today. Prices can vary widely, depending upon the decal pattern. Among the most popular designs are Countryside, Ruffled Tulip, Mallow, Red Apple, Silhouette, Jewel Weed, Carnivale, Crayon Apple, Whistling Teapots, Amy, Fire in the Fireplace, Lisa, Oriental Poppy, Ivy, Petit Point, and Pastel Posies. We will list examples of some of these patterns here.

Modern Age/Modern Tulip

This shape was created to celebrate Harker's 100 year anniversary. Hollowware pieces had surface etching on the body of the pieces resembling arrow shafts and fletchings (feathers) and with lids having the distinctive "Life-Saver" finials. This shape was manufactured with many decal patterns, including Red Apple, Tulip Bouquet, Silhouette, Cactus, Emmy, Shadow Rose, Southern Rose, Petit Point, English Ivy, Calico (Gingham), Tulip and Modern Tulip, to name a few.

Bowl, utility, 4" d., Zephyr shape (ILLUS. middle row, second from left)................... **$3-5**
Cake plate **$12-18**

Modern Age/Modern Tulip Pieces

Cookie jar, cov. (ILLUS. bottom row)......... **$20-30**
Creamer (ILLUS. top row center).................. **$3-5**
Custard cup, individual, Zephyr shape (ILLUS. second row, second from right)
.... **$4-6**
Pie baker (ILLUS. top right, left)................. **$18-24**
Pitcher, cov., square, jug-type (ILLUS. top row, right) **$35-40**
Plate, 6" d., plain round (ILLUS. middle row, far right)... **$2-4**
Sugar bowl, cov.. **$8-12**

Various Petit Point Pattern Pieces

Petit Point Pattern

Batter set: two covered Ohio Jugs, lifter & Virginia utility plate; the set **$80-110**

Bean pot, individual (ILLUS. top row, center front with other Petit Point pieces, top of page) **$5-8**

Bowls, utility, 3" to 5" d., nesting-type, Zephyr shape, each (ILLUS. of 3" d. size, bottom, second from left with other Petit Point pieces) **$10-15**

Butter dish, cov., 1 lb. **$50-60**

Cake/cheese plate, round **$20-25**

Casserole, cov. (ILLUS. top row, far left with other Petit Point pieces) **$30-40**

Cheese bowl, cov., Zephyr shape **$30-40**

Coffeepot, ball finial on cover **$50-60**

Cookie jar, cov., Modern Age shape **$40-50**

Cookie jar, cov., round............................. **$35-45**

Cup & saucer, plain round **$10-15**

Custard cup, individual **$4-6**

Custard cup set: six cups in a rack; the set **$50-60**

Grease/drips jar, cov., D'Ware shape **$15-20**

Grease/drips jar, cov., Skyscraper shape **$15-20**

Mixing bowl, w/pouring lip, 10" d.............. **$40-50**

Ohio jug, cov., pitcher-shaped, paneled shape, medium...................................... **$35-45**

Pie baker **$15-25**

Plate, 10" d., dinner, plain round (ILLUS. middle row, right with other Petit Point pieces).. **$5-8**

Salt & pepper shakers, Skyscraper shape, 4 1/2" h., pr. (ILLUS., top next column) **$20-25**

Scoop **$60-75**

Teapot, ball finial on cover **$35-45**

Trivet (tea tile), octagonal, (ILLUS. top row, center back, with other Petit Point pieces) **$25-35**

Utility plate, Virginia shape, 12" w. **$15-20**

Petit Point Hi-Rise Shape Shakers

Red Apple I & Red Apple II Patterns

Bowl, utility, 4" d., Red Apple I patt., Zephyr shape (ILLUS. front row, second from left with other Red Apple pieces) **$10-15**

Casserole, ball finial on cover, Red Apple I patt., Zephyr shape (ILLUS. far right with other Red Apple pieces, top next page) **$30-40**

Plate, 10" d., dinner, plain round, Red Apple II patt. (ILLUS. second from left with other Red Apple pieces, top next page) **$10-15**

Salt & pepper shakers, Red Apple II patt., Skyscraper shape, pr. **$20-25**

Teapot, cov., Red Apple II patt., Zephyr shape (ILLUS. far left with other Red Apple pieces, top next page)......................... **$50**

Other Patterns

Bean pot, Calico Tulip patt.......................... **$8-12**

Ohio jug, cov., paneled pitcher-shape, Silhouette patt., medium **$35-45**

Pitcher, cov., jug-type, Red Deco Dahlia patt., Hi-Rise style, GC shape................ **$45-60**

Utility plate, Calico Tulip patt., Virginia shape, 12" w. **$12-20**

Various Red Apple Pieces

Cameoware Pieces

Cameoware

This process was used by Bennett Pottery in Baltimore and when Bennett closed in 1936, the patent holder brought the process to Harker. Harker made Cameoware from about 1940-1948 in the Dainty Flower pattern with its design etched through to the white body. This is Harker's most widely collected pattern. The heaviest production was in blue with pink the next most popular color. Harker also made Dainty Flower in yellow, teal, gray, pumpkin, chartreuse and black but in much smaller quantities. These latter colors are the most rare and command the highest prices which greatly exceed those for blue and pink pieces.

About 1950 Harker made the "White Rose Carv-Kraft" pattern (in blue and pink) exclusively for Montgomery Ward. Though not as common as "Dainty Flower," "White Rose" has its own devoted fans.

A Variety of Dainty Flower Pieces

Ashtray, Dainty Flower patt., blue, Modern Age shape (ILLUS. far left with other Dainty Flower & Pear pattern pieces, second from top) **$18-24**

Berry set: square serving bowl & six small dishes; Dainty Flower patt., blue, the set **$35-50**

Bowl, 5" sq., berry or fruit, Dainty Flower patt., blue (ILLUS. top, far right with other blue Dainty Flower pieces)........................ **$5-8**

Bowl, 7" sq., cereal, Dainty Flower patt., blue **$10-12**

Bowl, 8" sq., soup, Dainty Flower patt., blue (ILLUS. bottom with other blue Dainty Flower pieces)....................................... **$10-18**

Bowl,, 9 1/2" d., Pear patt, Shell shape, blue (ILLUS. front center with ashtray)... **$20-30**
Casserole, cover w/ball finial, Dainty Flower patt., blue **$20-30**
Coffeepot, cov., Dainty Flower patt., blue.. **$50-60**
Cookie jar, cov., Dainty Flower patt., Zephyr shape, blue (ILLUS. far right with Dainty Flower ashtray).................................. **$35-45**
Creamer, round, Dainty Flower patt., blue, Shell shape **$10-15**
Cup & saucer demitasse, Dainty Flower patt., blue **$12-18**
Custard cup, Dainty Flower patt., blue or pink, each.. **$3-5**
Fork or spoon, serving-type, Dainty Flower patt., blue or pink, each........................... **$12-18**
Gravy boat, Dainty Flower patt., blue or pink, each... **$10-15**
Grease/drips jar, cov., Dainty Flower patt., D'Ware shape, blue or pink................... **$25-35**
Grease/drips jar, cov., Dainty Flower patt., Skyscraper shape, blue or pink , each ... **$20-25**
Lifter, pie or cake, Dainty Flower patt., blue or pink, each... **$12-19**
Mixing bowl, 9"-12" d., nesting-type, Dainty Flower patt., blue or pink, each **$25-45**
Pitcher, cov., jug-type, Dainty Flower patt., Hi-Rise style, GC shape, blue **$50-70**
Pitcher, cov., jug-type, Dainty Flower patt., Round Body shape, blue **$35-45**
Pitcher, jug-type, Dainty Flower patt., Square Body shape, blue...................... **$35-45**
Plate, 6" d., Swirl shape **$5-8**
Plate, 6" sq., Dainty Flower, blue (ILLUS. top row, far left with other blue Dainty Flower pieces).. **$2-4**
Plate, 7" d., Dainty Flower patt., Shell shape, blue (ILLUS. back row, left with blue Dainty Flower ashtray) **$3-5**
Plate, 7" sq., Dainty Flower patt., blue or pink, each.. **$4-6**
Plate, 9" sq., Dainty Flower patt., blue or pink, each.. **$4-6**
Platter, 14" l., oval, plain, Dainty Flower patt., blue or pink, each........................ **$25-35**
Rolling pin, Dainty Flower patt., blue or pink, each... **$60-75**
Salt & pepper shakers, Dainty Flower patt., Modern Age shape, blue or pink, pr......... **$8-12**
Salt & pepper shakers, Dainty Flower patt., Skyscraper shape, blue, pr. (ILLUS. top row, center front with other blue Dainty Flower pieces).................................... **$15-20**
Sugar bowl, cover w/ball finial, round, Dainty Flower patt., Shell shape, blue **$8-12**
Trivet (tea tile), Dainty Flower patt., blue .. **$15-25**
Vegetable bowl, 9" sq., Dainty Flower patt., blue **$12-15**

Children's Ware

Harker's Kiddo sets came in pink and blue with etched classic designs. The mugs had a toy soldier and a circus elephant on either side. Plates might have a duck with an umbrella, a bear with a ballon or a goat on a pull cart, facing either right or left. Related bowls might have a kitten or what looks like an early Donald Duck. Hot water feeder baby dishes were made with cavorting lambs, double ducks, bunny butts and baby ducks, all of which were made in blue or pink. Harker also made demitasse-style cups & saucers with baby ducks in both colors, though these are more rare.

Bowl, various animal designs, blue or pink, each **$20-25**
Hot water baby feeder, ceramic reservoir, various animal designs, blue or pink, each **$40-50**

Child's Mug & Plate

Mug, toy soldier decoration, blue, 3" h. (ILLUS. front with plate) **$12-15**
Plate, Teddy bear w/balloon decoration, blue (ILLUS. w/toy soldier mug) **$20-30**

Gadroon and Royal Gadroon

This shape, with its distintive scalloped edge, was extremely popular and was produced in several glaze colors, with the classic Chesterton grey and Corinthian green (which commands slightly higher prices) presenting an especially elegant table setting. Pate sur pate, though frequently used, is only one of several marks found on this ware. The Royal Gadroon shape was also decorated with numerous colorful decals, including Bridal Rose, Shadow Rose, Royal Rose, Wild Rose, Currier & Ives, Godey, Game Birds, Morning Glories, Violets and White Thistle (silk screened on yellow and pink glazed ware).

Gadroon
Bowl, berry or fruit.. **$2-4**
Bowl, cereal/soup, lug handles (ILLUS. middle right with Chesterton collection, top next page) **$3-5**
Cup & saucer (ILLUS. middle left with Chesterton collection, top next page) **$7-10**
Fork, serving **$10-15**
Gravy boat (ILLUS. middle row, center with Chesterton collection, top next page) **$5-8**
Gravy underplate (relish/pickle dish), ... **$3-5**
Lifter, cake or pie **$10-15**
Luncheon set: 7" sq. plate w/cup ring & matching cup; 2 pcs. **$8-12**
Platter, 12" l., oval...................................... **$10-12**
Salt & pepper shakers, pr............................. **$4-8**
Soup plate, flat rim....................................... **$6-9**
Teapot, cov. **$30-40**

Harker Chesterton Collection

Plate, 9" d., dinner, Magnolia patt., w/gray band (ILLUS. top row, center with other Royal Gadroon pieces, above) **$5-8**

Plate, 9" d., dinner, Violets patt. (ILLUS. top row, left with other Royal Gadroon pieces, to the left) **$8-10**

Platter, 15" l., oval, Vintage (Grapes) patt. (ILLUS. middle row, left with other Royal Gadroon pieces, to the left).................. **$35-50**

Teapot, cov., Ivy Vine patt. (ILLUS. bottom row, right with other Royal Gadroon pieces, to the left) **$35-45**

Later Intaglios

This is the technical name for the process used to make Cameo and more modern patterns in the 1960s and 1970s. Although highly popular during their time and quite plentiful on the market today, these patterns are not generally in high demand and prices reflect this. Colors include celadon green, blue, yellow, orange, black and pink cocoa. Some patterns that command higher prices include Brown-Eyed Susan and Wild Rice (in blue, gray & salmon). Modern Intaglio pattern names include Cock 0' Morn, Rooster, Coronet, Star-Life, Sun-Glo, Everglades, Rose on Cameo Blue, Mosaic, Patio, Country Cousins, Provincial, Petite Fleurs, White Daisy, Spring Time, Snow Leaf, Bamboo, Fruit, Wheat, Vintage I & II (a.k.a. Grapes), Orchard, Daisy Lane, Viking, Rocaille, Alpine, Fern, Lotus, Ivy Wreath, Spanish Gold, Acorns, Wreath and Russel Wright White Clover.

Harker Royal Gadroon Pieces

Royal Gadroon (decal decorations)

Bowl, cereal/soup, lug handles, Vintage patt. (ILLUS. bottom row, center with Royal Gadroon pieces, to the left)........... **$5-10**

Bowl, 4 1/2" d., berry or fruit, Cortland (a.k.a. St. John's Wort) patt. (ILLUS. middle row, center, with other Royal Gadroon pieces, above)................................ **$4-6**

Cake plate, Old Rose (a.k.a.Wild Rose) patt., 10" d. (ILLUS. bottom row, left with Royal Gadroon pieces, above)................. **$8-10**

Cake set: 9" or 10" d. cake plate w/six 6" d. matching serving plates & cake lifter; Currier & Ives patt., 8 pcs........................ **$25-45**

Plate, 6" d., luncheon, Bermuda patt. (ILLUS. top row, right with other Royal Gadroon pieces, above)............................. **$3-5**

Plate, 6" d., luncheon, Pheasants patt. (ILLUS. middle row, right with other Royal Gadroon pieces, above) **$3-5**

Creamer & sugar bowl, pr. **$8-20**
Cup & saucer **$4-8**
Plate, dinner **$3-10**
Platter 11" or 13"....................................... **$10-20**

Reproduction Rockingham

Harker Reproduction Rockingham was made in the early 1960s. This line included hound-handled pitchers (the only pieces actually made in the mid-19th century), hound-handled mugs, Jolly Roger jugs*, Daniel Boone jugs*, ashtrays, Armed Forces logo plates and ashtrays, soap dishes, candleholders (for rhw hound-handled mugs), tobacco leaf candy dish/ashtrays, Rebecca at the Well teapots, tidbit trays, Give Us This Day Our Daily Bread plates, octagonal trivets, a 7 1/2" h. bald eagle figure, 6" l. skillet spoon holders (unmarked), Jolly Roger pipes (extremely rare), and even a rolling pin (only one found to date). Colors included brown, gold (honey brown), and bottle green and a light creamy brown trivets and soap dishes have also turned up. Because some pieces have a date of "1840" and are not marked as reproductions, some confusion has resulted, but modern pieces should not confuse anyone familiar with mid-19th century wares and their glazes.

*(Harker called this "jugs" but they were really mugs.)

Bread tray, brown **$15-20**
Jug (mug), figural Jolly Roger head, brown
.... **$18-24**
Mug, figural hound handle, brown **$15-20**

Hound-handled Pitcher

Pitcher, jug-type w/figural hound handle, brown (ILLUS.) **$35-40**
Plate, relief-molded American eagle (Great Seal of the U.S.), brown **$5-8**

Stone China

This heavy ware, with its solid pink, blue, white or yellow glazes over a gray body, was manufacturered in the 1960s and 1970s. The glaze was mixed with tiny metallic chips, which many collectors call "Oatmeal." Later Harker created hand-decorated designs using the intaglio process to create several designs such as Seafare, Peacock Alley, MacIntosh and Acorns, to name a few.

Values listed here are for pieces in any of the four solid colors.

Bowl, 5" or 6" round, each **$3-5**
Bowl, 7" or 8" round, each **$8-12**
Butter dish, cov. **$18-24**
Casserole, cov. **$20-30**
Coffeepot, cov., jug-style **$30-40**
Cookie jar, cov. **$30-50**
Creamer, ... **$5-8**
Cruet set: two handled jugs w/covers, "O" for oil & "V" for vinegar, pr. **$20-30**
Cup & saucer **$3-5**
Pitcher with stopper lid, jug-type **$25-35**
Plate, 8" d. **$2-4**
Platter, 11" oval **$5-8**
Rolling pin **$150-200**
Tidbit tray, three-tier **$15-25**

Teapots - Miscellaneous

Pink Dainty Flower Teapot

Teapot, cov., Pink Dainty Flower patt., cylindrical body tapering in at shoulder, angled handle, serpentine spout, stepped base, pink w/cream-colored stylized floral design on body, cream finial on lid & line decoration on rim, part of Cameoware line, ca. 1935 (ILLUS.) **$40**

Harker Teapot in Pink Luster

Teapot, cov., Pink Luster patt., spherical body w/C-form handle & short serpentine spout, metallic lustre glaze in pink w/black highlights on rim, finial & lid, ca. 1900 (ILLUS.) **$40**

Harker's Rebecca at the Well Rockingham Reproduction Teapot

Teapot, cov., Rebecca at the Well patt., cylindrical body tapering in at shoulder, short foot & neck, domed inset lid w/turned finial, C-scroll handle w/thumbrest, turned serpentine spout, brown body embossed w/scene of Rebecca at the Well, part of Harker's line of Rockingham reproductions, the date of 1840 on bottom referring to the year Harker Pottery opened, ca. 1960 (ILLUS.) **$40**

Harker Red Apple Pattern Teapot

Teapot, cov., Red Apple patt., Zephyr shape, cylindrical body, angled handle, serpentine spout, stepped base, a horizontal band of decoration just below shoulder consisting of red apples & yellow pears w/green leaves & blue shading, red highlights on rim, lid, finial & spout, oven-to-table ware, ca. 1930 (ILLUS.) **$45**

Tulip Bouquet Teapot by Harker

Teapot, cov., Tulip Bouquet patt., Royal Gadroon shape, squatty lobed bulbous body w/piecrust rim, short foot, ribbed C-scroll handle & slightly serpentine spout, the conforming lid w/applied scroll loop handle, the body, spout & lid decorated w/small flowers in shades of turquoise, pink, blue, purple & orange w/green leaves on white ground, ca. 1940 (ILLUS.) ... **$20**

Vintage Teapot on Royal Gadroon Shape

Teapot, cov., Vintage patt., Royal Gadroon shape, squatty lobed bulbous body w/piecrust rim, short foot, ribbed C-scroll handle & slightly serpentine spout, the conforming lid w/applied scroll loop handle, the body & lid decorated w/horizontal bands of entwined grapevines w/purple fruit, the finial, spout & handle accented w/green line decoration, ca. 1940 (ILLUS.) **$25**

Harris Strong Designs

Harris Strong (b. 1920) is so identified with the decorative tiles produced by his company during the 1950s and 1960s that even unsigned tiles of that era are often attributed to him although the style may be markedly different.

Born in Wisconsin, Strong studied ceramics and chemical engineerings at North Carolina State University. In 1947, after working for Kelby Originals, a Brooklyn pottery, Strong and co-worker Robert Krasner founded Potters of Wall Street. Their new firm specialized in ceramic lamps, ashtrays and other decorative pieces, including tiles.

The tiles for which strong became famous were actually a secondary focus of his, created primarily to test glazes. However, their novelty, whether used as individual accent pieces or grouped together to form a tile "painting," caught on with the public. Buoyed by this success Strong opened his own firm in the Bronx in the early 1950s.

Strong's tile scenes, framed or mounted on burnished wood backings, proved popular with architects, interior decorators and consumers seeking contemporary wall art at affordable prices. Themes included portraits, abstracts and exotic locales as well as medieval and other period depictions. Strong's tile plaques are noted for their vibrant color combinations, the three-dimensionality of the figures and scenes and an attention to detail. Color and form are filtered through the precise parameters of ceramic tile as well as through Strong's own visual sense that encompasses both the primitive and the contemporary.

The sheer size of many Harris Strong plaques made them especially well suited to corporate, hotel and restaurant decor where they made arresting focal points in the interior. In essence, Strong created the early 1950s market for tile-based decorative wall hangings, adapting his designs for nearly every location: ship's lounges, office building facades, elevator interiors and even bowling alleys. One particularly challenging commissioin was the massive "Cathedral Wall" divider created for New York's Waldorf-Astoria Hotel which spanned the entire interior of the hotel's Marco Polo Club.

Attribution of Harris works has often been haphazard since paper labels were used on the back of his plaques rather than a permanent signature. In the absence of a label, one reliable indicator of a Strong plaque is the heart-shaped hooks used for hanging.

Harris G. Strong, Inc. relocated to Maine in 1970 and eventually phased out tile production, focusing instead on paintings, collages and other types of wall decor. For the company's 40th anniversity in 1992 a series of commemorative tiles were produced. The company ceased all production in 1999.

In looking back on his career, Mr. Strong noted "Nobody ever handled tiles the way we did because we regarded them as a piece of pottery; A lot of us worked together to achieve our goal. What I provided, I hope, was the continuing thread that went through all the years --- of quality, workmanship and good design. If I did that then that's enough.

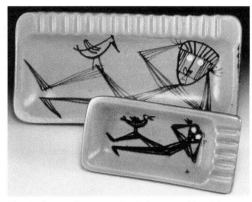

Two Harris Strong Rectangular Ashtrays with a Man and Bird

Advisor for this category, Donald-Brian Johnson, is an author and lecturer specializing in Mid-Twentieth century design. Photos are by his frequent collaborator, Leslie Pina.

Ashtray, rectangular, #C-35, a reclining man w/a bird in black on turquoise, 5 3/4" l. (ILUS. front with larger ashtray).. **$50-75**

Ashtray, rectangular, #C-35, a reclining man w/a bird in black on turquoise, 9" l. (ILUS. back with smaller ashtray, top of page) **$75-100**

Dish, triangular, #B-80, stylized birdcage design within a dark grey border, 8 1/8" l. (ILLUS. right with larger dish, top of page) **$100-125**

Dish, triangular, #B-75, stylized female musicians, 9 1/2" l. **$175-200**

Two Harris Strong Triangular Dishes

Dish, triangular, #B-77, red-domed building on a yellow ground within a green border, 11 3/4" l. (ILLUS. left with smaller dish) **$125-150**

Shadowbox with Dancing Stick Figures

Shadowbox, the central tile depicting dancing stick figures, 12 1/4" square (ILLUS.) **$175-200**

Strong Native Dancers Framed Tile

Tile, #A-43, a stylized design of native dancers wearing ceremonial masks in browns on a black ground, linen mat & white oak frame, 10 3/4" sq. (ILLUS.) **$150-175**

Tile, design of a ram figure in dark blue on a light blue ground, framed, 11" sq. **$150-175**

Tile, design of a sheep figure in dark blue on a light blue ground, framed, 11" sq. ... **$150-175**

Strong Tile Picture with a Industrial Scene of Buildings

Tile, #E-18, design of stylized penguins, framed, 10 3/4" sq. **$150-175**

Tile, #E-32, stylized design of swimming frogs, framed, 10 3/4" sq. **$150-175**

Tile, #E-78, two stylized fish, framed, 10 3/4" sq. **$150-175**

Tile, #O-81, abstract figures of a man & woman, 7" sq. **$125-150**

Tile, #O-82, abstract design of a mother bird feeding her young, framed, 7" sq. **$125-150**

Tile picture, rectangular, #1222, a dock scene composed of twelve tiles, framed, 19 x 43" **$600-700**

Tile picture, rectangular, #141, a landscape w/sailboats in a bay & mountains beyond, composed of six tiles, framed, 15 1/2" w., 21 1/2" h. **$300-400**

signed "Strong" on the front, framed, 10 x 22" (ILLUS., top of page) **$200-300**

Tile picture, rectangular, #332, part of the "Impressionist Series," a park scene composed of four tiles on a walnut plaque, 11 x 24" **$250-350**

Tile picture, rectangular, #540, a design of medieval flagbearers composed of five tiles on a walnut plaque, 12" w., 36" h. **$300-400**

Tile picture, rectangular, a stylized city skyline composed of four tiles, on a walnut plaque, 36" w., 9" h. **$200-300**

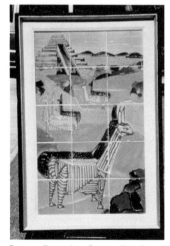

Strong Peruvian Scene Tile Picture

Tile picture, rectangular, #1503, fifteen square tiles in dark blue & black forming a scene of alpacas & Machu Picchu, framed, 1960, 24 x 36" (ILLUS.) **$600-700**

Tile picture, rectangular, #313, a long industrial scene showing a line of buildings in various colors, composed of three tiles,

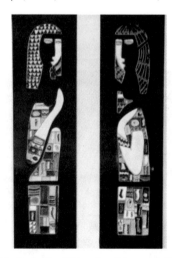

Tile Portraits of Egyptian Woman & Man

Tile picture on leather, rectangular, #L-101, a tall slender stylized image of an Egyptian woman in shades of brown, 11" w., 42 1/2" h. (ILLUS.left with Egyptian man picture) **$400-500**

Tile picture on leather, rectangular, #L-102, a tall slender stylized image of an Egyptian man in shades of brown, 11" w., 42 1/2" h. (ILLUS.right with Egyptian woman picture) **$400-500**

Tile picture on walnut, rectangular, #W-11, stylized portrait of a falconer, 9 1/2" w., 41 1/4" h. **$400-500**

Waller-design "Harlequin" Plaque

Tile plaque, rectangular, "Harlequin," P-15, half-length stylized portrait, a Marvin Waller design, 9" w., 14" h. (ILLUS.) **$800-900**

Haviland

Haviland porcelain was originated by Americans in Limoges, France, shortly before the mid-19th century and continues in production. Some Haviland was made by Theodore Haviland in the United States during the last World War. Numerous other factories also made china in Limoges. Also see LIMOGES.

Haviland Marks

Ashtray, rectangular, white w/gold Embassy eagle, 3 x 5" **$45**
Basket, mixed floral decoration w/blue trim, Blank No. 1130, 5 x 7 1/2" **$154**
Bonbon plate, w/three dividers, h.p., H & Co, 9 1/2" d. **$175**
Bone dishes, No. 146 patt., Blank No. 133, set of 4 .... **$100**
Bouillon cup & saucer, Ranson blank, Schleiger 42A, flared shape decorated w/pink roses **$50**
Bouillon w/saucer, cov., Marseilles blank, decorated w/blue flowers, H & Co **$75**
Bowl, 10" d., 3" h., salad, Schleiger 19, Silver Anniversary **$225**
Broth bowl & underplate, No. 448, 2 pcs. **$110**
Butter dish, cov., No. 271A patt., Blank No. 213 .... **$145**
Cake plate, square, CFH/GDM, decorated w/spray of yellow wildflowers, 9" sq. **$85**
Cake plate, handled, No. 1 Ranson blank, patt. No. 228, 10 3/4" d. **$95**
Cake plate, handled, Ranson blank No. 1 .... **$125**

Candlesticks, Marseille blank, h.p. floral decoration, 6 3/4" h., pr. **$275**
Celery tray, Baltimore Rose patt., Blank No. 207, 5 5/8 x 12" **$275**
Cereal, Schleiger 57A, Ranson blank, decorated w/pink roses & blue scrolls, 6 x 2" ... **$32**
Chocolate cup & saucer, No. 72A **$45**
Chocolate pot, cov., scallop & scroll mold w/floral decoration & gold trim, marked "Haviland Limoges, France," 9" h. **$275**
Chocolate set: cov. pot & eight cups & saucers; Schleiger 235B, decorated w/pink & green flowers & gold trim **$750**
Coffeepot, cov., demitasse, Osier, Blank No. 211, impressed "Haviland & Co. - Limoges - France" & English mark **$195**
Coffeepot, cov., Paradise, blue edge w/decoration of birds, Theodore Haviland, 8" h. **$225**
Coffeepot, cov., Sylvia patt., 1950s **$225**

Footed Comport with Reticulated Rim

Comport, pedestal on three feet w/ornate gold shell design, top w/reticulated edge, peach & gold design around base & top, 9" d. (ILLUS.) **$595**
Comport, Meadow Visitors patt., smooth blank, 5 1/8" h., 9 7/8" d **$225**
Cracker jar, cov., Marseille blank **$450**
Creamer, Schleiger 146, commonly known as Apple Blossom, Theodore Haviland, 4" **$60**
Creamer & open sugar, dessert, Cloverleaf patt., Schleiger 98, pr. **$145**
Creamer & sugar, Schleiger 223A, Blank 1, decorated w/pink flowers, pr. **$125**
Cup & saucer, coffee, Schleiger 39D, decorated w/pink roses & gold trim **$55**
Cup & saucer, tea, Schleiger 19, white w/gold trim **$45**
Cup & saucer, Rosalinde patt. **$45**

Meadow Visitors Cup & Saucer

Cups & saucers, Papillon butterfly handles w/Meadow Visitors decoration, six sets (ILLUS. of one set, previous page) **$900**

Cuspidor, smooth blank, bands of roses decorating rim & body, 6 1/2" h. **$350**

Dessert set: 8 1/2 x 15" tray & four 7 1/4" dishes; Osier Blank No. 637, fruit & floral decoration, the set.................................... **$325**

Fish set: 23" l. platter & six 9" d. plates; each w/different fish scene, dark orange & gold borders, Blank No. 1009, 7 pcs... **$1,250**

Plate from Fish Set

Fish set: 22" l. oval platter & twelve 8 1/2" d. plates; each piece w/a different fish in the center, the border in two shades of green design w/gold trim, h.p. scenes by L. Martin, mark of Theodore Haviland, 13 pcs. (ILLUS. of plate) **$2,750**

Fish set: 23 1/4" l. platter & twelve 7 3/8" plates; Empress Eugenie patt., No. 453, Blank No. 7, 13 pcs. **$3,500**

Gravy boat w/attached underplate, No. 98 patt., Blank No. 24..................................... **$145**

Haviland Hair Receiver

Hair receiver, cov., squatty round body on three gold feet, h.p. overall w/small flowers in blues & greens w/gold trim, mark of Charles Field Haviland (ILLUS.)................ **$150**

Ice cream set: tray & 6 individual plates; Old Pansy patt. on Torse blank, 7 pcs. **$395**

Jam jar w/underplate, cov., No. 577 patt., smooth blank.. **$325**

Mustard pot, cov., No. 266 patt. on Blank No. 9... **$225**

Nut dish, footed, No. 1070A patt. **$55**

Oyster plate, Ranson blank, Schleiger 42A, decorated w/pink roses **$175**

Oyster plate, The Princess patt., Schleiger 57C, 9 1/2" d. **$195**

Oyster plates, five-well, 72C patt., Blank No. 17, center indent for sauce, 9" d., pr. **$450**

Oyster tureen, Henri II Blank, decorated by Dammouse.. **$850**

Pickle dish, shell-shaped w/gold trim, leaf mold, 8 3/4" l. **$65**

Pin tray, rectangular, open handles, decorated w/pink roses, Blank 1, Schleiger 251, 3 x 5"... **$125**

Pitcher, 7" h., milk, Schleiger 98, Blank 12, Cloverleaf patt. **$195**

Pitcher with Anchor in Relief

Pitcher, 7" h., milk-type, tankard style w/tapering cylindrical white body w/a large relief-molded anchor under the heavy rope-twist loop handle, bright gold trim, old Haviland & Co. mark (ILLUS.)............... **$1,165**

Pitcher, 8 3/8" h., Ivy patt. w/gold trim **$175**

Pitcher, 8 5/8" h., Ranson blank No. 1.......... **$250**

Haviland Lemonade Pitcher

Pitcher, 9" h., lemonade-type, Schleiger 1026B variation, Blank 117, decorated w/lavender flowers & brushed gold trim, Theodore Haviland (ILLUS.) **$250**

Haviland Covered Sugar Bowl

Sugar bowl, cov., large cylindrical form w/small loop side handles & inset flat cover w/arched handle, white ground decorated w/sprays of pink daisies touched w/yellow & greyish brown leaves, variation of Schleiger No. 1311, 1 lb. size, Charles Field Haviland, marked "CFH/GDM" (ILLUS.)................................... $75

Tea set: cov. teapot, creamer & sugar bowl; floral & leaf mold w/gold trim, 3 pcs. $450

Tea & toast set: scalloped plate & cup; Marseilles blank, decorated w/pink roses, H & Co.. $175

Tea tray, round, Schleiger 29A, decorated w/pink flowers, unglazed bottom, 16" d..... $275

Teapot, cov., 4-cup, CFG/GDM, white w/gold, ribbon handle............................... $225

Toothbrush box, cov., Moss Rose patt. w/gold trim, smooth blank, ca. 1860s-70s, 8" l. $225

Vegetable dish, oval, Schleiger 142A, decorated w/pink daisy-like flowers, blue fences & scrolls, gold trim, Theodore Haviland, 8 x 10"... $85

Vegetable dish, cov., decorated w/small orange roses, Blank No. 24, 10" d. $145

Waste bowl, Schleiger 233A, The Norma, decorated w/tiny pink & yellow flowers & gold daubs, 5 x 3" $47

Head Vase Planters

Head Vase Planters were most popular and most abundant during the 1950s. Whereas some could be found prior to this period, the majority were Japanese imports and a direct product of Japan's postwar industrial boom. Sizes, shapes, styles and quality varied according to importer. American manufacturers did produce some head vase planters during this time, but high quality standards and production costs made it hard to compete with the less expensive imports.

Ardalt, No. 6039, Madonna w/both hands holding roses, pastel coloring in glossy bisque, planter, paper label, 6" h. $30

Ardco, No. C1248, high bouffant hair, dark green dress, earrings, necklace, paper label, 5 1/2" h. $75

Brinn, No. TP2071, molded blonde hair, painted eyes, earrings, right hand near face, 6" h. $125

Inarco, King w/full grey beard, red, yellow & black w/gold trim, 4 3/4" h. (small base flake) $100

Inarco, No. E1062, head turned to the right, gold clasps on black gown, earrings, necklace, closed eyes w/big lashes, paper label & stamp, 1963, 5 1/4" h. $125

Inarco, No. E1062, ringlet hair, earrings, closed eyes w/big lashes, black gloved right hand holding gilt decorated fan under right cheek, paper label & stamp, 1963, 6" h.. $225

Inarco, No. E1611, closed eyes w/big lashes, earrings, gold painted bracelet, left hand under face on right, 1964, 5 1/2" h. $600

Inarco, No. E1756, "Lady Aileen," gold & green tiara & matching painted necklace, paper label, 5 1/2" h. $275

Inarco, No. E1852, Jackie Kennedy wearing black dress & glove w/hand to cheek, paper label, 6" h. $350

Inarco, No. E193/M, applied pink rose in hair, light green dress, earrings, necklace, right hand on cheek, closed eyes w/big lashes, 1961, 5 1/2" h. $100

Inarco, No. E2254, black dress, pearl finish on hair, earrings, necklace, closed eyes w/big lashes, paper label, 6" h. $100

Inarco, No. E2322, black dress, black open-edged hat w/white ribbon, gloved hand by right cheek, earrings, necklace, paper label, 7 1/4" h. $250

Inarco, No. E2523, child w/blue scarf & dress, pigtails, painted eyes, high gloss, stamped, 5 1/2" h. $70

Inarco, No. E2735, soldier boy w/bayonet, closed eyes, stamped, 5 3/4" h. $55

Inarco, No. E5624, pink hat & blue dress, earrings, painted eyes, paper label & stamp, 5 1/2" h. $200

Inarco, No. E779, applied blonde hair & peach rose, peach dress, earrings, necklace, right hand by cheek, paper label & stamp, 1962, 6" h. $125

Inarco, No. E969/S, mint green hat & dress, painted closed eyes w/big lashes, 1963, 4 1/2" h. $65

Japan, No. 2261, black dress w/white collar, black bow in blonde hair, painted eyes, earrings, glazed finish, 7" h. $275

Lefton, No. 1086, white iridescent blouse, necklace, paper label, 6" h. $150

Lefton, No. 1343A, applied flowers on large brimmed hat & collar, painted features, raised right hand, paper label, glossy finish, 6" h. $105

Lefton, No. 2536, flower in hair, painted earrings & necklace, gloved right hand under chin, 5 1/4" h. $80

Lefton, No. 2796, blue blouse, blue sash on head, paper label, 6" h. $100

Lefton, No. 2796, pink blouse, pink sash on head, paper label, 6" h. $100

Lefton, No. 4596, green hat, scarf & coat, earrings, painted eyes, black gloved hand under cheek, partial Lefton's label, 5 1/2" h. $95

Lefton, No. 611B, Lefton paper label & Geo. Z. Lefton stamp, bird on pink floral hat, high collar, closed painted eyes, glossy finish, 6 1/4" h. $70

Manchu, Ceramic Arts Studio of Madison, Wisconsin, 7 1/2" h. $150

Napco, No. A5120, large pink hat, fur-trimmed pink dress w/blue daisy, closed eyes w/big lashes, paper label, 5" h. $75

Napco, No. A5120, orange bonnet w/bow & matching lace-trimmed dress, paper label, 5 1/4" h. $80

Napco, No. C1775A, green striped hat w/bow on top right, jeweled green dress, hand by cheek, big lashes, stamped, 1956, 7 1/4" h. $150

Napco, No. C2589A, wearing black dress & feather hat, gold painted earring, closed eyes w/big lashes, right hand under right side of chin, bracelet, paper label & stamp, 1956, 5" h. $65

Napco, No. C2632C, large lavender hat w/dark trim, matching lavender dress, hand to hat, earring in exposed ear, 7" h. $165

Napco, No. C2633C, black hat & dress, gold dots on white hat bow, earrings, necklace, closed eyes w/big lashes, 1956, 5 1/2" h. $85

Napco, No. C2634B, baby w/white bonnet, paper label, 5 1/2" h. $55

Napco, No. C2636B, flat white hat w/gold trim, dark green dress, left hand under chin, earrings, necklace, closed eyes w/big lashes, paper label, 1956, 6" h. $125

Napco, No. C2637C, white round flat hat, black dress, hand under left cheek, painted eyes, earrings, necklace, paper label & stamp, 1956, 7" h. $225

Napco, No. C2638C, earrings, painted eyes, molded necklace, stamped, 1956, 6" h. $100

Napco, No. C3205B, wearing crown of gold & white flowers, necklace, paper label, 5 1/2" h. $80

Napco, No. C3815, gold & white trim on blue hat, blue high collar jacket, earrings, closed eyes w/big lashes, paper label, 1959, 5 1/2" h. $85

Napco, No. C3959A, blue hat w/bow & high collar blouse, real lashes, earrings, paper label, 5 1/2" h. $75

Napco, No. C4556C, child wearing green hat, painted eyes, glossy finish, partial paper label, impressed, 1960, 5 1/4" h. $75

Napco, No. CX2707, Christmas girl, green w/red trimmed hat & dress, painted eyes, right hand under cheek, paper label & stamp, 1957, 5 1/2" h. $85

Napco, No. CX2708, Christmas girl, holly sprigs in hat, painted cross necklace, gloved right hand away from face, closed eyes w/big lashes, paper label & stamp, 1957, 6" h. $300

Napco, No. CX2709A, Christmas child in fur-trimmed hat & coat, holding song book, painted eyes, paper label & stamp, 1957, 3 1/2" h. (worn paint on back near base) $75

Napcoware, No. 8494, gold bow in long hair, gold dress w/white collar, left earring, painted eyes, 7 1/4" h. $225

Napcoware, No. C6428, three flowers on neck of blue gown, dark gloved hand on left cheek, earrings, closed eyes w/big lashes, stamped mark, 5 1/2" h.............. $125

Napcoware, No. C6429, molded bouffant hair, white floral collar on blue gown, closed eyes w/big lashes, earrings, dark blue glove, hand by cheek, 7" h. $250

Napcoware, No. C6985, green dress w/center jewel, closed eyes w/big lashes, earrings, necklace, 8 1/2" h...................... $350

Napcoware, No. C7472, dark blue blouse, necklace & earrings, paper label, 6" h. $85

Napcoware, No. C7473, head turned to right, applied floral decoration on right shoulder, earrings, necklace, painted eyes, 7 3/4" h. $165

Napcoware, No. C8493, long hair off to right side, gold bow & dress w/white collar, earring in left ear, painted eyes, 6" h. $100

Relpo, No. 2004, green dress & hair bow, painted eyes, earrings, paper label & stamp, 7" h. $250

Relpo, No. 2089, Marilyn, grey bow in hair on right, black halter dress, earrings, painted eyes, open lips, paper label & stamp, 7" h. (chip on top of bow, minor paint wear on chin & left cheek) $3,000

Relpo, No. 5634, Christmas girl, hood w/holly, fur-trimmed coat, painted eyes, gloved hand near face, Sampson Import Co., impressed, 1965, 7 1/2" h. $200

Relpo, No. K1175M, wearing hat & matching dress, w/hands folded under chin, open eyes, earrings, necklace, 5 1/2" h. $110

Relpo, No. K1633, Japan, black dress w/white decoration, gloved right hand touching chin & cheek, earring, necklace, painted eyes, 7" h. $200

Relpo, No. K1662, floral molded green & lavender hat & green dress, painted eyes, earrings, necklace, paper label & stamp, 6" h. $175

Relpo, No. K1696, wearing green in hair & matching top, earrings, necklace, paper label, 5 1/2" h. $100

Relpo, No. K1836, Japan, white hat w/blue edge & bow, blue dress w/white trim, painted eyes, right earring, 6 1/2" h. $500

Relpo, No. K1932, black bows in hair & black high collar dress, earrings, painted eyes, paper label & stamp, 5 1/2" h. $225

Ruben, multicolored clown in green & yellow, closed eyes, 5" h. $35

Ruben, No. 4123, white ruffled black dress, earrings, necklace, painted eyes, impression & paper label, 7" h. $75

Ruben, No. 4129, blonde ponytails, painted eyes, earrings, necklace, paper label, 5 1/2" h. $110

Ruben, No. 4185, braided blonde hair w/flower, green dress w/high white collar, impressed mark, 5 1/2" h. $110

Ruben, No. 484, heart-shaped grey hat, necklace, earrings, paper label, 5 3/4" h. ... $150

Ruben, No. 531, Japan, Lucy in top hat w/horse neck piece, shades of grey, stamped & painted lashes, flake in tie end, 7 1/2" h. **$450**

Rubens, No. 531, Japan, Lucy in top hat w/horse neck piece, yellow & green w/glazed finish, stamped & painted lashes, 7 1/2" h. **$450**

Ucagco, baby dressed in blue bonnet trimmed w/lace & blue bib, paper label, 6" h. **$45**

Velco, No. 3688, Japan, pink hair bow & dress, w/hand at cheek, paper label, 5 1/2" h. (missing one earring) **$110**

Velco, No. 3749, white bow on grey hat, black dress, rhinestone earrings, closed eyes w/big lashes, left hand near chin, paper label & stamp, 5 3/4" h. **$125**

Historical & Commemorative Wares

Numerous potteries, especially in England and the United States, made various porcelain and earthenware pieces to commemorate people, places and events. Scarce English historical wares with American views command highest prices. Objects are listed here alphabetically by title of the view.

Most pieces listed here will date between about 1820 and 1850. The maker's name is noted at the end of the entry.

Arms of Delaware platter, trumpet flower & vine border, dark blue, Thomas Mayer, ca. 1830, 17 1/8" l. (ILLUS., bottom of page) **$5,600**

Arms of Rhode Island plate, flowers & vines border, dark blue, T. Mayer, minor glaze scratches, 8 1/2" d. **$750-775**

Baltimore & Ohio Railroad, level (The) plate, shell border, dark blue, E. Wood,

10 1/8" d. (stains, minor roughness on table ring) **$990**

Battle of Bunker Hill platter, vine border, dark blue, R. Stevenson, 10 1/4 x 13".... **$8,625**

Scarce Boston Mails Wash Set

Boston Mails wash set: 13 1/4" d. wash bowl (under rim chips & crack), 12" pitcher (base chip), 6" h. chamber pot & cover (base crack), 7 1/4" l. toothbrush box base; black scenes of the gentleman's or ladies' cabins, J. & T. Edwards, the set (ILLUS.) **$920**

Boston State House basket & undertray, flowers & leaves border, basket w/reticulated sides & scalloped flaring rim, dark blue, J. Rogers, basket 6 1/2 x 9 1/4", the set (hairline cracks) **$2,760**

Boston State House dish, flowers & leaves on flanged rim, deep sides, dark blue, J. Rogers, 12 3/4" d. (minor glaze scratches) **$2,070**

Boston State House pitcher, Rose Border series, fully opened roses w/leaves border, dark blue, Stubbs, 6" h. (small chip on handle) **$978**

Boston State House sauce tureen, cover & undertray, flowers & leaves border, pedestal base w/upward looped handles, high domed cover, dark blue, J. Rogers, tureen 7 1/4 x 8 1/4", the set **$3,738**

Arms of Delaware Platter

The Capitol Washington - Beauties of America Platter

Cadmus Historical Cup Plate

Cadmus (so-called) cup plate, trefoil border, dark blue, Wood, tiny spot of glaze wear on rim, 3 11/16" d. (ILLUS.) **$275**

Cadmus (so-called) plate, shell border, irregular center, dark blue, Wood, 10" d. (light scratches) **$500-600**

Capitol, Washington (The) platter, Beauties of America series, flowers within medallions border, well-and-tree-style, dark blue, 15 1/2 x 20 1/2", Ridgway (ILLUS. top of page) **$1,315**

Capitol, Washington (The) serving bowl, vine border, embossed white rim, dark blue, Stevenson, 11" d. (glaze imperfections) **$2,645**

Castle Garden, Battery, New York cup plate, trefoil separated by knobs border, dark blue, 3 3/4" d., E. Wood (ILLUS. bottom row right with other cup plates, top next page) **$303**

Christianburg Danish Settlement on the Gold Coast, Africa platter, shell border, well-and-tree center, dark blue, E. Wood, 18 3/4" l. (minor glaze imperfections) **$3,220**

City Hotel, New York plate, oak leaf border, double portrait reserves at border of Washington & Lafayette, inset view of the Entrance to the Erie Canal, dark blue,

R. Stevenson, 8 1/2" d. (minor scratching) **$4,600**

Columbia College, New York plate, acorn & oak leaves border, portrait medallion at rim of "President Washington," inset of "View of the Aqueduct Bridge at Rochester," dark blue, R. Stevenson, 7 1/2" d. (minor scratches) **$8,625**

Commodore MacDonnough's Victory tea set, shell border, dark blue, cov. teapot, cov. sugar bowl & creamer, E. Wood, teapot 7 1/2 x 11", the set .... **$$1,275-1,325**

Court House, Baltimore plate, fruit & flowers border, dark blue, Henshall, Williamson & Co., 8 1/2" d. (light wear, hairline) .. **$470**

Dam & Water Works (The), Philadelphia (Sidewheel Steamboat) plate, fruit & flowers border, dark blue, Henshall, Williamson & Co., 9 7/8" d. **$646**

Doctor Syntax Amused with Pat in the Pond platter, flowers & scrolls border, dark blue, E. Wood, 14 1/4 x 19" (glaze scratches, scattered minor staining) **$1,840**

Entrance of the Erie Canal into the Hudson at Albany - View of the Aqueduct Bridge at Little Falls pitcher, floral border, dark blue, E. Wood, excellent condition, 6" h. **$1,500-1,725**

Esplanade and Castle Garden, New York - Almshouse, Boston pitcher, vine border, dark blue, R. Stevenson, 10" h. **$2,300**

Esplanade and Castle Garden, New York platter, vine border, dark blue, R. Stevenson, minor glaze scratches, 14 1/2 x 18 1/2" **$5,750**

Pink Historical Staffordshire Teapot

Group of Historical Cups Plates & a Toddy Plate

Fulton's Steamboat on the Hudson - Ship Cadmus teapot & cover, the squatty bulbous body w/a serpentine spout & C-scroll handle, white ground transfer-printed in rusty pink w/a scene on each side, the low domed cover & button finial w/further transfer scenes, pink lustre band trim on the rim, handle & spout, Staffordshire, England, ca. 1830-50, restoration to the base, end of spout & cover, 6" h. (ILLUS., previous page) **$303**

Fulton's Steamboat soup plate, floral border, dark blue, unknown maker, 10 1/4" d. (minor scratches & rim chips) **$875-900**

Highlands, Hudson River platter, shell border, dark blue, E. Wood, minor roughness on interior rim, 10 x 12 3/4" **$3,335**

Lake George, State of New York platter, shell border, dark blue, E. Wood, 16 1/2" l. (very minor glaze scratches) ... **$2,585**

Landing of General Lafayette at Castle Garden, New York, 16 August 1824 plate, primrose & dogwood border, dark blue, Clews, 8 7/8" d. **$300-350**

Landing of the Fathers at Plymouth, Dec. 22, 1620 cup plate, scrolls & leaves border, dark blue, 3 3/4" d., E. Wood (ILLUS. bottom row left with other cup plates) **$523**

Mount Vernon, The Seat of the Late Gen'l. Washington tea set: cov. teapot, cov. sugar bowl, creamer, waste bowl & handleless cup & saucer; large flowers border, dark blue, unknown maker, teapot, 10" l., 5" h., the set **$3,800-4,000**

Park Theatre, New York bowl, oak leaf border, dark blue, R. Stevenson, 8 3/4" d. **$2,500-2,600**

Park Theatre, New York plate, oak leaf border, four portrait medallions at the border of Jefferson, Washington, Lafayette & Clinton, inset of the Aqueduct Bridge at Little Falls, dark blue, R. Stevenson, 10" d. **$3,700-3,800**

Pennsylvania Hospital, Philadelphia platter, flowers within medallions border, Beauties of America series, dark blue, Ridgway, few minor scratches, 14 1/8 x 18 3/8" (ILLUS., top next page) **$1,880**

State House, Boston platter, spread-eagle border, dark blue, Stubbs, 14 3/4" l. **$1,250-1,300**

States series pitcher, building, two wings, water in foreground, border w/names of fifteen states in festoons separated by five-point stars border, dark blue, Clews, 6 3/4" h. (minor interior staining) **$975-1,000**

States series plate, two-story building w/curved drive, border w/names of fifteen states in festoons separated by five-point stars border, dark blue, Clews, 7 3/4" d. **$330-350**

States series platter, mansion, foreground a lake w/swans, names of states in festoons separated by five-point stars border, dark blue, Clews, ca. 1830, 16 3/4" l., ... **$2,280**

Pennsylvania Hospital Platter

Table Rock, Niagara plate, shell border - circular center, dark blue, E. Wood, 10 1/8" d. **$500-550**

Upper Ferry Bridge over the River Schuylkill platter, spread-eagle border, dark blue, Stubbs, 15 1/2 x 18 3/4" **$700-750**

Rare Brown View of Pittsburgh Platter

View of Pittsburgh platter, floral & scrolled leaves border, brown, Clews, 16 1/8 x 19 5/8" (ILLUS.) **$3,525**

Washington Standing at Tomb, scroll in hand waste bowl, floral border, dark blue, E. Wood, 6 1/4" d., 3 1/4" h. **$750-860**

West Point Military Academy platter, shell border, dark blue, E. Wood, 9 1/4 x 11 3/4" (minor glaze scratches) **$2,760**

Winter View of Pittsfield, Massachusetts platter, vignette views & flowers border, dark blue, Clews, glaze scratches, 14 x 16 1/2" **$3,450**

Winter View of Pittsfield, Massachusetts toddy plate, full border w/three medallions, dark blue, 4 5/8" d., flake on table

ring, Clews (ILLUS. top row left with cup plates) **$440**

Woodlands Near Philadelphia cup plate, partial leaf border, dark blue, E. Wood, 3 3/16" d. (ILLUS. top row right with other cup plates) **$330**

Ironstone

The first successful ironstone was patented in 1813 by C.J. Mason in England. The body contains iron slag incorporated with the clay. Other potters imitated Mason's ware, and today much hard, thick ware is lumped under the term ironstone. Earlier it was called by various names, including graniteware. Both plain white and decorated wares were made throughout the 19th century. Tea Leaf Lustre ironstone was made by several firms.

General

Cabinet plates, each w/a scalloped rim, "Japan" patt., floral border & center, painted in the Imari palette, Hick & Meigh, England, ca. 1830, 10 3/8" d., pr. (one w/hairline) **$235**

Cups & saucers, handleless, "gaudy" Blackberry patt. in underglaze-blue trimmed w/yellow & orange enamel & lustre, E. Walley mark, ca. 1850, some variation, set of 10 .... **$1,375**

Dessert service: 10 5/8" l. shaped dish, 5 3/4" h. open compote, four 10" l. leaf-shaped dishes & fourteen 9 1/4" d. plates; Imari-style designs w/shaped edges & deep green borders, Mason's, mid-19th c., the set **$3,680**

Dinner service: child's size; Moss Rose patt., by G. Scott, a few w/light discoloration, one inner lid chip, 16 pcs. (ILLUS., top next page) **$625**

Gravy boat, Long Octagon shape, all-white, ca. 1847, T.J. & J. Mayer........ **$125-140**

Mug, Gothic patt., all-white, ca. 1840s, James Edwards **$120-130**

G. Scott Moss Rose Pattern Children's Set

English Ironstone Imari-style Pitcher

Pitcher, 8 1/2" h., paneled ovoid shaped w/a wide flaring rim spout & ornate C-scroll handle, decorated w/a color Imari-style decoration, England, second half 19th c., glaze flaws at rim (ILLUS.) **$115**

Pitcher, 9 3/4" h., footed wide squatty bulbous body molded w/wide ribs & tapering to a wide mouth w/arched spout, high arched C-scroll handle, transfer decoration of birds in flowering trees & foliage w/polychrome enamel, mark of Ashworth Bros., England, ca. 1890 .... **$303**

Pitcher, 9 3/4" h., table-type, Grape Octagon shape, all-white, Pearson & Hancock **$150-180**

Plate, 8" d., twelve-sided, "gaudy" Bittersweet patt. w/underglaze flow blue & copper luster, impressed "Real Ironstone" (light stains) **$83**

Plate, 8 3/8" w., paneled shape, "gaudy" freehand Strawberry patt., underglaze-blue w/green & two shades of red enamel & copper lustre trim, mid-19th c. **$385**

Plate, 8 1/2" d., "gaudy" decoration, vintage grape vine design painted in underglaze-blue, black, ochre & two shades of green (wear, crazing) **$110**

Plate, 8 1/2" d., "gaudy" style, center w/urn in flow blue w/pink & red flowers & copper lustre highlights (stains) **$110**

Plate, 8 3/4" w., "gaudy" Strawberry patt., paneled shape w/underglaze-blue trimmed w/red, pink, green & copper lustre, impressed mark, mid-19th c. **$138**

Plate, 9 1/4" w., paneled shape, "gaudy" freehand Morning Glory patt., underglaze-blue trimmed w/two shades of green, red & black enamel, mid-19th c. **$303**

Plate, 9 1/2" d., Bordered Hyacinth/Lily shape, all-white, ca. 1860, W. & E. Corn **$50-65**

Plate, 9 1/2" w., paneled sides, "gaudy" Floral Urn freehand patt., underglaze-blue & green & trimmed w/two shades of red enamel & copper lustre, mid-19th c. (light stains, tiny enamel flake) **$330**

Plate, 9 5/8" d., "gaudy" Blackberry patt., underglaze-blue & black trimmed w/red, yellow & copper lustre, impressed "E. Walley - Niagara Shape," 1850s **$193**

Plate, 10 1/4" d., New York shape, all-white, ca. 1858, J. Clementson **$50-65**

Plate, 10 1/4" d., twelve-sided "gaudy" style w/strawberries, pink flowers & underglaze flow blue leaves **$248**

Plate, 10 1/2" d., Fig shape, all-white, ca. 1856, Davenport/Wedgwood **$60-75**

Plates, 8 1/2" d., decorated w/floral motif in blue & rust, marked "Ashworth Brothers Hanley," England, ca. 1890, set of 9 .... **$134**

Plates, 9 5/8" d., paneled edge, central transfer-printed garden landscape w/urn of flowers, flower & scroll border, Florilla patt., purple highlighted w/yellow, green, blue & red enamel, mid-19th c., set of 6 (stains) **$138**

Plates, 10 1/2" d., scalloped flanged rim, overall Imari-style transfer decoration in polychrome trimmed w/gold, mid-19th c., pr. **$303**

Platter, oval, 10" l., President shape, all-white, John Edwards **$30-40**

Platter, 13 1/2" l., octagonal, "gaudy" Strawberry patt., underglaze-blue w/red, pink & green enamel & luster trim, wear, stains & some enamel flaking **$770**

Various Red Cliff Pieces

Platter, 13 1/2" l., rectangular w/cut corners, "gaudy" freehand Morning Glory patt., underglaze-blue trimmed w/two shades of green, red & black, mid-19th c. (old red flaking, minor stains) **$385**

Platter, 11 3/8 x 14 1/8", rectangular, romantic transfer scene of a lakeside cabin w/boaters, marked "Cat, Albion" & "Turnbull, Stepney," light blue, mid-19th c. **$121**

Platter, 14 3/4" oval, "gaudy," blue transfer-printed War Bonnet patt. trimmed in red, orange & yellow, marked "Ironstone China," mid-19th c. (wear, scratches)............. **$165**

Platter, 15 3/4" l., rectangular w/cut corners, Florentine patt., light blue, T. Mayer, mid-19th c. (internal hairline) **$110**

Platter, oval, 16" l., Corn & Oats shape, all-white, Davenport/Wedgwood **$65-75**

Platter, rectangular, 16" l., Rolling Star shape, all-white, James Edwards......... **$90-100**

Platter, 16 1/4" l., oval w/lightly scalloped rim, "gaudy" freehand Strawberry patt., underglaze black, mid-19th c. (small chips on one corner) **$413**

Platter, 18 1/2" l., Indiana patt., ca. 1880, Wedgwood **$196**

Platter, 16 x 21", well-and-tree-type, oval, Rural Scenery patt., broad floral border surrounding a meadow landscape w/figures & animals, Davewell & Goodfellow, England (chips on foot, hairline)............... **$440**

Platter, 21 1/4" l., oval w/flanged rim, the center transfer-printed w/a large landscape scene of a dog holding a stick on the bank of a river w/figures rowing a boat, the river flanked by trees & a country house in the distance, wide floral border, blue & white, back w/printed mark of a ribbon-tied banner inscribed "British Views," mid-19th c................................. **$1,265**

Platter, 22" l., oval, polychrome floral decoration w/gilt trim, Stokes Works mark on base, 19th c.. **$863**

Punch bowl, footed deep rounded bowl, floral embellishments around the rim & base, twig urn w/flowers & bird at center & sides, in shades of cobalt blue, yellow, pink, orange & green w/gilt highlights, mid-19th c., 14 1/4" d., 6 1/2" h............. **$1,035**

Relish dish, 1851 Shell shape, all-white, ca. 1851, T. & R. Boote **$100-125**

Relish dish, Berlin Swirl, all-white, ca. 1856, Mayer & Elliot............................... **$65-75**

Relish dish, mitten-shaped, Moss Rose patt., marked "C.P.W." (some faded gold trim)... **$55**

Relish dish, plain, oval w/two tab handles, all-white, ca. 1870s, Wood, Son & Co. .. **$20-30**

Salt & pepper shakers, Boote's 1851 shape, all-white, ca. 1960s, Red Cliff, 4" h., pr. (ILLUS. far right & far left, top of page)... **$50-60**

Sauce ladle, Moss Rose patt. **$110**

Sauce tureen, cov., oblong form, decorated in color w/the Japanese Garden patt., molded butterfly handles & finial, England, 19th c., 5 3/4" h. **$173**

Soap box, cover & liner, plain oval, all-white, ca. 1872-87, Thomas Elsmore & Son, 3 pcs. **$40-45**

Soap box, cover & liner, President shape, all-white, John Edwards, 3 pcs. **$120-130**

Soap dish, open, plain hollow rectangular body w/drain holes in well & one on side for cleaning, all-white, various potters.... **$20-30**

Moss Rose Ironstone Soup Ladle

Soup ladle, Moss Rose patt., slight glaze wear (ILLUS.)... **$120**

Soup plate, flanged paneled rim, Paradise patt., purple floral transfer design w/polychrome trim, mid-19th c., 10 1/2" w. **$83**

Soup plate, Sharon Arch shape, all-white, Davenport, 9 1/2" d. **$50-60**

Soup tureen, cover, ladle & underplate, Stafford shape, all-white, ca. 1854, S. Alcock & Co., 4 pcs. **$750-800**

Soup tureen, undertray, cover & ladle, Vista England patt., footed deep tureen, grape leaf & vine border, cranberry, tray 14 3/4" l., tureen 10 1/2" h., the set.......... **$605**

Three Boote's 1851 Shape Pieces

Sugar bowl, cov., Favorite shape, Moss
Rose patt., glaze flake on cover rim,
Grindley **$180**

Alcock's Pear White Ironstone Teapot

Teapot, cov., all-white, Alcock's Pear
shape, by John Alcock, England, ca.
1860 (ILLUS.).................................... **$125-150**

Teapot, cov., all-white, Boote's 1851 shape,
adult size, by T. & R. Boote, England, ca.
1851 (ILLUS. left with other Boote's 1851
pieces, top of page)........................... **$300-325**

Teapot, cov., all-white, Boote's 1851 shape,
child's size, by T. & R. Boote,
England, ca. 1851 (ILLUS. center with
other Boote's 1851 pieces, top of page)
.... **$200-250**

Teapot, cov., all-white, Boote's 1851 shape
cov. creamer, a ca. 1960s reproduction
by Red Cliff, based on the early shape
(ILLUS. right with other Boote's 1851
pieces, top of page)............................... **$35-45**

Edwards Lily of the Valley Teapot

Teapot, cov., all-white, Lily of the Valley
shape, by James Edwards, England, ca.
1860s (ILLUS.)................................... **$200-225**

Edwards Pedestaled Gothic Teapot

Teapot, cov., all-white, Pedestaled Gothic
shape, by James Edwards, England, ca.
1845 (ILLUS.).................................... **$300-325**

American Moss Rose Teapot

Teapot w/hinged metal cover, spherical body, Moss Rose patt., small interior pit & stain, inside rim roughness, Knowles, Taylor & Knowles (ILLUS.) **$170**

Toothbrush vase, cylindrical w/ruffled rim, Moss Rose patt., Alfred Meakin (worn lustre) **$130**

Vegetable dish, cov., Scotia (Poppy) shape, oval, all-white, ca. 1870, F. Jones & Co., 9" l. **$100-120**

Victorian Mason's Ironstone Wash Set

Wash bowl & pitcher, footed wide paneled bowl w/vertical sides, the pitcher w/a bulbous paneled lower body & tall gently flaring wide paneled neck w/wide rim spout, ornate C-scroll handle, pitcher & bowl both printed w/colorful Oriental landscapes & flowers in shades of rust, cobalt blue, deep red & green on a white ground, blue Mason's mark w/crown & banner, second half 19th c., minor glaze flakes, bowl 16" d., 5 1/4" h., pitcher 11" h., the set (ILLUS.) **$288**

Washbowl & pitcher, miniature, Classic Gothic shape, all-white, Red Cliff, ca. 1960s, overall 4 1/2" h. (ILLUS. second from right w/salt & pepper shakers) **$50-75**

Washbowl & pitcher, miniature, Fig (registered Union shape), all-white, Red Cliff, ca. 1960s, overall 3 1/2" h. (ILLUS. second from left w/salt & pepper shakers) **$50-75**

Washbowl & pitcher, miniature, Sydenham shape, all-white, Red Cliff, ca.

1960s, overall 4 1/2" h. (ILLUS. center w/salt & pepper shakers) **$80-100**

Washbowl & pitcher, "Tudor" patt., transfer-printed overall w/stylized floral medallions, branches & berries in lilac on an ivory ground, William Brownfield & Sons, 1871-91, bowl 15" d., overall 10" h., 2 pcs. **$287**

Tea Leaf Ironstone

Basketweave Shape 3-Piece Butter

Butter dish, cover & insert, Basketweave patt., tiny glaze flaw inside, A. Shaw (ILLUS.) **$425**

Shaw Cable 3-Piece Butter Dish

Butter dish, cover & insert, Cable patt., A. Shaw (ILLUS.) **$195**

Butter dish, cover & insert, Lion's Head patt., Mellor Taylor (minor wear & crazing) **$200**

Cake plate, Daisy & Tulip patt., Wedgwood & Co. **$130**

Edge Malkin Tea Leaf Cake Plate

Cake plate, Edge Malkin (ILLUS.) **$125**

Cake plate, Prairie Flowers patt., gold Tea Leaf, Powell & Bishop **$130**

Chamber pot, open, Daisy n' Chain patt., Wilkinson.. **$110**

Coffeepot, cov., Lily-of-the-Valley patt., Anthony Shaw (small under rim chip on cover).. **$275**

Compote, open, 9 1/4" sq., Square Ridged patt., Wedgwood & Co. **$325**

Compote, open, domed foot below the ringed stem supporting the wide shallow round bowl w/rolled rim, Edge Malkin **$550**

Compote, open, round, small low round foot below the wide shallow round bowl, T. Furnival **$195**

Creamer, Chelsea patt., Alfred Meakin, 5" h. **$90**

Creamer, Favorite patt., Grindley................... **$90**

Creamer, Victory patt., Edwards, 5" h. (Some lustre wear)................................... **$100**

Creamer & cov. sugar bowl, Simple Pear patt., Alfred Meakin, pr. (lustre wear) **$340**

Cup & saucer, handled, white body, Edge Malkin **$50**

Gravy boat, Lily of the Valley patt., Anthony Shaw **$325**

Gravy boat & undertray, Chelsea patt., Alfred Meakin, 2 pcs. **$160**

Meakin Fishhook Table Pitcher

Pitcher, table size, Fishhook patt., mild discoloration, Alfred Meakin (ILLUS.) **$150**

Pitcher, water, Little Cable patt., square shape, T. Furnival **$200**

Pitcher, 6 3/4" h., Favorite patt., Grindley **$155**

Pitcher, 8" h., Hawthorn patt., A. Wilkinson **$95**

Pitcher, 8 1/2" h., Chelsea patt., Alfred Meakin (potting flaw under base rim) **$350**

Pitcher, 8 1/2" h., Daisy n' Chain patt., Wilkinson... **$125**

Posset cup, Lily-of-the-Valley patt., Anthony Shaw (ILLUS., top next column).... **$275-300**

Punch bowl, footed, deep rounded bowl w/flared rim, H. Burgess........................ **$1,100**

Relish dish, mitten-shaped, A. Wilkinson (slight crazing)... **$95**

Sauce dish, Lily of the Valley patt., Anthony Shaw **$50**

Sauce ladle, Alfred Meakin **$250**

Lily-of-the-Valley Posset Cup

Sauce ladle, Cable patt., A. Shaw **$255**

Sauce tureen, cover & undertray, Cable patt., Anthony Shaw, 3 pcs. **$120**

Shaving mug, Maidenhair Fern patt., Wilkinson (some lustre touch-up)............. **$400**

Shaving mug, Scroll patt., Alfred Meakin **$110**

Soap dish, cover & drainer, Simple Square patt., Wedgwood & Co. **$150**

Soap dish, cover & insert, Chinese patt., Anthony Shaw (small flakes & hairline) **$250**

Red Cliff Bullet Soup Tureen Set

Soup tureen, cover, ladle & undertray, Bullet patt., Red Cliff, ca. 1960s, the set (ILLUS.).. **$175**

Soup tureen, cover, ladle & undertray, Bullet patt., Red Cliff, ca. 1970, the set **$175**

Soup tureen, cover, ladle & undertray, Scroll patt., Alfred Meakin (hairline in cover) **$440**

Sugar bowl, cov., Lily-of-the-Valley patt., Anthony Shaw.. **$275**

Teapot, Cable patt., T. Furnival...................... **$90**

Teapot, cov., Fig Cousin patt., pink lustre trim, Davenport (lid crazing, small flake inside cover).. **$300**

Teapot, cov., Pagoda patt., H. Burgess, 8 3/4" h... **$275**

Davenport Rondeau Pattern Teapot

Teapot, cov. Rondeau patt., minor glaze
wear, spout repair, Davenport (ILLUS.) **$110**

Burgess Square Ridged Pattern Teapot

Teapot, cov., Square Ridged patt., minor
potting flaw, H. Burgess (ILLUS.) **$80**
Toothbrush vase, Chelsea patt., ovoid
shape, Alfred Meakin (moderate glaze &
lustre wear) **$275**

Rare Chrysanthemum Toothbrush Vase

Toothbrush vase, Chrysanthemum patt.,
unmarked H. Burgess (ILLUS.) **$1,325**

Toothbrush vase, Maidenhair Fern patt.,
ovoid body w/fluted rim, A. Wilkinson
(chip on upper rim) **$500**
Toothbrush vase, Square Ridged patt.,
Wedgwood & Co. **$225**

Rare Fig Cousin Brush Vase & Tray

Toothbrush vase & undertray, Fig Cousin
patt., pink lustre trim, minor crazing, Dav-
enport (ILLUS.) **$2,300**
Vegetable dish, cov., Hexagon patt., An-
thony Shaw, 13" w. **$75**
Vegetable dish, cov., oval, Coronet patt.,
W. & E. Corn, 12" l. (very minor crazing) **$70**
Vegetable dish, cov., round, Cable patt.,
Anthony Shaw, 11 1/2" d......................... **$175**

Pagoda Pattern Washbowl & Pitcher

Washbowl & pitcher, Pagoda patt., H. Burgess, base rim glaze flakes, tiny body
nick, the set (ILLUS.) **$300**

Tea Leaf Variants

Brush box, cov., oblong, Grape Octagon
shape, copper lustre band decoration, E.
Walley (small inside rim chip) **$200**
Butter dish, cover & insert, Twelve-Pan-
elled shape, copper lustre band trim,
Livesley & Powell (slight roughness in-
side cover) **$175**
Cake plate, Berry Cluster patt., cobalt blue
& lustre band decoration, Jacob Furnival.. **$275**

Teaberry Pattern Elegance Shape Mitten Relish Dish

Cake plate, Rose patt., Washington shape, Powell & Bishop **$325**

Chamber pot, open, Grape Octagon shape, lustre band trim, E. Walley **$130**

Compote, open, 9" h., tall paneled pedestal w/large paneled bowl flanked by scroll handles below the wide flaring rim w/flat molded edge, copper lustre band decoration, Livesley & Powell **$625**

Creamer, Morning Glory patt., Portland shape, Elsmore & Forster, 6" h. **$175**

Creamer, Teaberry patt., Grand Loop shape, J. Furnival..................................... **$375**

Tobacco Leaf Pattern Cuspidor

Cuspidor, Tobacco Leaf patt., Elsmore & Forster, long hairline, rim flake (ILLUS.) ... **$400**

Mug, child's, Morning Glory patt., unmarked (professional repair to rim hairline)............ **$425**

Teaberry Pattern Heavy Square Pitcher

Pitcher, 8 1/2" h., Teaberry patt., Heavy Square shape, Clementson Bros. (ILLUS.) **$500**

Punch Bowl with Primrose Scroll Design

Punch bowl, pedestal foot below the wide squatty rounded bowl w/a widely flaring rim, copper lustre primrose scroll decorated around the sides & inner rim, Livesley & Powell (ILLUS.) **$600**

Relish dish, mitten-shape, Teaberry patt., Elegance shape, one small pinprick, worn lustre, Clementson Bros. (ILLUS., top of page)... **$500**

Sauce tureen, cover, ladle & undertray, Nautilus shape, copper lustre band decoration, J. Clementson (hairlines, cover chip) **$650**

Soap dish, cov., Grape Octagon patt., copper lustre band decoration, unmarked (bottom inside rim flakes)......................... **$210**

Sugar bowl, cov., Cockscomb shape, pedestal base, copper lustre & cobalt blue band trim, J. Furnival **$475**

Sugar bowl, cov., Panelled Grape shape, lustre band & cobalt sprig decoration **$200**

Sugar bowl, cov., Pinwheel patt., Full Panelled Gothic shape **$125**

Sugar bowl, cov., Teaberry patt., Beaded Band shape, Clementson Bros. **$180**

Ceres Shape Lustre-trimmed Teapot

Teapot, cov., Ceres shape, lustre trim,
Elsmore & Forster (ILLUS.)...................... **$600**

Grand Loop & Blackberry Teapot

Teapot, cov., Grand Loop shape, decorated
w/a dark brown Blackberry transfer-printed design trimmed in copper lustre, sugar
bowl cover (ILLUS.).................................. **$175**
Teapot, cov., Pinwheel patt., Grape Octa-
gon shape **$375**
Teapot, cov., Wrapped Sydenham shape,
copper lustre band decoration, E. Walley
(slight crazing).. **$160**
Water pitcher, lustre band trim, New York
shape, J. Clementson (very slight lustre
wear) **$150**

Jewel Tea Autumn Leaf

*Though not antique this ware has a devoted
following. The Hall China Company of East Liverpool, Ohio, made the first pieces of Autumn Leaf
pattern ware to be given as premiums by the*

*Jewel Tea Company in 1933. The premiums were
an immediate success and thousands of new cus-
tomers, all eager to acquire a piece of the durable
Autumn Leaf pattern ware, began purchasing
Jewel Tea products. Though the pattern was
eventually used to decorate linens, glasswares
and tinware, we include only the Hall China
Company items in our listing.*

Autumn Leaf Bean Pot

Bean pot, one-handled, 2 1/4 qt. (ILLUS.).... **$950**
Bowl, cereal, 6 1/2" d. **$12**
Bowl, flat soup, 8 1/2" d. **$20**
Bowl, salad, 9" d. **$30**

Jewel Tea Butter Dish

Butter dish, cov., square top w/straight
finial, 1/4 lb. (ILLUS.) **$1,400**

Butter Dish with Butterfly Handle

Butter dish, cov., w/butterfly-type handle
(ILLUS.).. **$1,800**

Drip-type Coffee maker

Coffee maker, cov., all china, drip-type
(ILLUS.) **$325**

Autumn Leaf Electric Percolator

Coffeepot, cov., electric, percolator (ILLUS.)
.... **$300**
Cup & saucer **$14**
French baker, swirled soufflé-style, 2 pt.
.... **$120-130**
Gravy boat & undertray, the set.................... **$50**
Mixing bowl, 7" d., part of set **$20**
Pickle dish (gravy undertray)......................... **$25**
Pie baker, 10"... **$35**
Plate, dinner, 10" d... **$14**
Salt & pepper shakers, bell-shaped, small,
pr. **$35**
Salt & pepper shakers, regular size, bell-
shaped, pr. **$500**
Teapot, cov., Newport shape w/gold trim,
1978 version.. **$200**

Newport Autumn Leaf Teapot

Teapot, cov., Newport shape w/gold trim
(ILLUS.)... **$250**
Vegetable bowl, 10 1/2" oval **$30**

Limoges

*Limoges is the generic name for hard paste
porcelain that was produced in one of the Limoges
factories in the Limoges region of France during
the 19th and 20th centuries. There are more than
400 different factory identification marks, the
Haviland factory marks being some of the most
familiar. Dinnerware was commonly decorated by
the transfer method and then exported to the
United States.*

*Decorative pieces were hand painted by a fac-
tory artist or were imported to the United States
as blank pieces of porcelain. At the turn of the
20th century, thousands of undecorated Limoges
blanks poured into the United States, where any
of the more than 25,000 American porcelain
painters decorated them. Today hand-painted
decorative pieces are considered fine art. Limoges
is not to be confused with American Limoges.
(The series on collecting Limoges by Debby
DeBay, Living With Limoges, Antique Limoges at
Home and Collecting Limoges Boxes to Vases are
excellent reference books.)*

Cachepot, underglaze factory mark in
green "W.G.&Co." (William Guérin),
12" h. **$1,500**
Cake plate on pedestal, h.p., underglaze
factory mark in green "T&V Limoges
France Depose" (Tressemann & Vogt),
4 x 12"... **$395**
Candlesticks, h.p. roses, heavy gold, un-
derglaze factory mark in green "T&V,"
16" h., pr. **$600**
Charger, dramatic h.p. roses on dark
ground, gold scroll on rim, underglaze
factory mark in green "AK [over] D
France" (A. Klingenberg), 15" d. **$1,000**
Chocolate set: 12" pot, two cups, 12"
tray; h.p., underglaze factory mark in
green "J.P.L. France" (Jean Pouyat, Li-
moges), the set **$1,500**
Cracker jar, cov., barrel-shaped, h.p. large
roses, h.p., underglaze mark in green
"T&V Limoges France," 7 1/2" h. **$325**
Dresser set: tray, cov. jar & hair
receiver; h.p. by amateur artist, underglaze factory mark in green "W.G.&Co.,
France" (William Guérin), the set **$500**

Lovely Hand-painted Limoges Fish Set

Fish set: long narrow oval open-handled 10 x 24" platter, twelve 9 1/2" d. plates & an 8 1/4" l. sauceboat & understray; each piece w/a gently scalloped rim, the tray h.p. w/a large game fish in browns & greens swimming among lavender water plants against a pale blue ground, each plate & sauceboat h.p. w a different game fish w/similar water plants, greem mark of Latrille Freres, Limoges, France, ca. 1899-1913 & also red HC Limoges, France mark, the set (ILLUS.) **$1,898**

Outstanding Hand-painted Limoges Game Set

Game set: an oval 14 x 18 1/2" platter w/an ornate scalloped & scroll-molded gold border & panled sides, twelve 9 1/2" d. plates & two 6" d. sauce dishes; each large piece h.p. w/pairs of realistic game birds on a shaded ground, sauce dishes each h.p. w/pheasants, artist-signed, red mark of Lazeyras, Rosenfeld & Lehman, Limoges, early 20th c., the set (ILLUS., above)............ **$2,588**

Jardiniere, fluted pedestal base, fluted handles, h. p. large roses & leaves, underglaze factory mark in green "J.P.L. France" w/anchor, 12 x 14" **$2,500**

Planter, h.p. w/vibrant chrysanthemums, gilt handles & four feet, underglaze factory mark in green "D&Co.," 8 x 12 1/2" ... **$2,000**

Plate, 10 1/2" d., heavy gold rim & h.p. roses, underglaze factory mark in green "J.P.L. France," overglaze factory decorating mark w/pink & green wreath **$225**

Platter, 18" l., game-type, h.p. game birds & florals signed by factory artist "Dubois," "Limoges France" & star, Flambeau studio decorating mark **$2,000**

Large Limoges Platter Hand-painted with Game Dogs

Limoges Cider Pitcher with Roses

Pitcher, cider, 10 1/2" h., h.p. large deep pink roses & gold trim, signed by factory artist "Roby," underglaze factory mark in green "T&V France," "T&V" decorating mark in purple (ILLUS.) **$1,500**

Platter, 13 x 19", ovoid w/a scalloped gilt-banded rim & molded gold loop end handles, h.p. w/a scene of a brown & white Pointer dog at point w/a flying pheasant, another large brown dog behind it, in naturalistic brown & yellow grasses, artist-signed, greem mark of Lazeyras, Rosenfeld & Lehman, Limoges, early 20th c. (ILLUS.) **$805**

Punch bowl & undertray, rare mammoth blank w/three gold feet, h.p. w/dramatic roses by unknown artist, underglaze factory mark in green "J.P.L. France," 13 x 26", 2 pcs. **$5,500**

Fine & Complete Grape-decorated Limoges Punch Set

Punch set: large bowl & base, ten punch cups & a large round tray; the 14" d., 6 1/4" h.deep flaring rounded bowl w/a heavy gold scroll-molded rim above h.p. sides decorated w/purple grap clusters amid yellow, green & orange leaves, gold foot resting on the matching base w/large scroll-molded scroll feet, round handled cups each h.p. a berry sprig & on a gold foot, the 18" d. wide tray w/a shallow gold rim also h.p. in the center w/a grapevine design, marks of Tressemann & Vogt, ca. 1900, the set (ILLUS.)............................ **$1,725**

Tea set: cov. teapot, cups & saucers & round tray; tall urn-form teapot & tall conical cups, each piece h.p. w/bands of pink roses & green leaves, green factory mark "France - PM - De M Limoges" (Mavaleix mark 1), ca. 1908-14, the set (ILLUS., bottom of page)........................... **$600**

Tea set: cov. teapot, four cups & saucers & four dessert plates; squatty bulbous teapot w/gold C-form handle & loop finial on domed cover, serpentine spout, each piece h.p. w/bands composed of pairs of pink roses & green leafage, factory mark of Jean Pouyat, Limoges, France, 1891-1932, the set (ILLUS., top next page) **$700**

Limoges Set with Teapot, Cups & Saucers & Tray

Rose-decorated Teapot, Cups & Saucers & Dessert Plates

Elegant Gold & White Limoges Tea Set on Tray

Tea set: tall cov. teapot, cov. sugar bowl, creamer, six cups & saucers & a tray; the tall tapering teapot in white w/a scroll gold band around the neck below a wide gold rim band, matching band design on the other pieces, gold handles, spouts & covers, marks for Blakeman & Henderson, Limoges, France, ca. 1890s, teapot 6" h., the set (ILLUS., above) **$1,500**

Teapot, cov., tall cylindrical body w/a long serpentine spout, C-form handle & domed cover w/knob finial, decorated w/an oval reverse & a border band of grapevines, Bernadaud & Company, France, early 20th c. (ILLUS., next column) **$85**

Bernadaud & Co. Limoges Teapot

Simple Limoges Porcelain Teapot

Teapot, cov., wide bulbous body w/a long gold spout & C-form handle, domed cover w/pointed disk finial, marks of B & H Limoges, France & Legrand, Limoges, ca. 1920 (ILLUS.) **$50**

Tile, h.p. porcelain of woman & cherub, underglaze factory mark in green "T&V France," 11 x 14" **$3,000**

Tureen, cov., squatty bulbous form w/domed cover, loop end handles & scrolled base & feet, h.p. w/berries, artist signed "Andrew," underglaze factory mark in green "P&P" (Paroutaud Frères), 8 x 9" **$1,500**

Vase, 8" h., 13 1/2" d., low squatty round body w/a short rolled neck, h.p. roses, underglaze factory mark in green "T&V Limoges France" & artist signed "Vera Gray," unusual shape & size **$3,000**

Vase, 14" h., tapering waisted conical body, factory h.p. w/ roses & artist signed "Rouncon," underglaze mark in green "PBM DE M Limoges, France" (Malaleix), overglaze decorating mark in green "Coronet" in crown **$3,000**

One of Two Tall Limoges Vases

Vase, 22" h., tall slender ovoid body bolted on a pedestal base & w/a slender trum-

pet neck w/rolled rim, raised gold trim, one of a pair, h.p. w/roses & enameled w/raised gilt, underglaze factory mark in green "W.G.&Co.," ca. 1891-1900, each (ILLUS. of one) **$4,000**

Lotus Ware - Knowles, Taylor & Knowles (KT&K)

Knowles, Taylor & Knowles made Lotus Ware (bone china) for a very short time. Reference books differ on the starting date but it ranges between 1889 and 1892. There is agreement that production of the ware ceased sometime in 1896. KT&K tried to make Lotus Ware again in 1904 but it proved too costly and was soon abandoned. Many pieces of this ware were hand-painted and hand-decorated. Lotus Ware rivaled some of the finest European decorated bone china in quality and refinement of decoration and artwork. KT&K employed skilled artists, whose work is highly prized to this day by knowledgeable collectors.

Bowl, 4 3/4" d., 4 1/2" h., Columbia design, plain ovoid sides w/wide crimped rim (ILLUS. center with two other Columbia bowls, top next page) **$300-400**

Bowl, 6 1/2" d., 4" h., Columbia design, pinched ovoid body w/crimped rim & filigreed medallions on the sides (ILLUS. right with two other Columbia bowls, top next page) **$200-300**

Bowl, 6 1/2" d., 4 1/2" h., Columbia design, pinched ovoid shaped w/applied flowers & filigreed medallions on the sides (ILLUS. left with two other Columbia bowls, top next page) **$300-450**

Fine Lotus Ware Decorated Shell Bowl

Bowl, 10" w., Shell design, rough sheel embossing on the outsides w/blue & pink blush trim, smooth shell interior, red along inside edge, blue & pink blush, h.p. scene in the bottom of a sailing ship & gulls on rough seas crashing on a rocky shoreline (ILLUS.) **$600-800**

Three Lotus Ware Columbia Bowls

Lotus Ware Cracker Jar & Tuscan Vase

Cracker jar, cov., all-white, barrel-shaped body w/a low flared & scalloped rim, domed inset cover w/button finial, applied w/flowers, branches, vines & berries, 6 1/2" h. (ILLUS. right with Tuscan Vase)... **$200-350**

Two Lotus Ware Chestnut Creamers

Creamer, Chestnut design, all-white w/twig handle, 3 1/2" h. (ILLUS. left with other Chestnut creamer) **$150-200**

Creamer, Chestnut design, pale blue background, painted in gold below the spout w/the initials "JMD," h.p. purple violets & green leaves on the sides, 3 1/2" h. (ILLUS. right with other Chestnut creamer).. **$225-250**

Lotus Ware Souvenir-type After-dinner Cup & Saucer

Cup, after-dinner style, cylindrical cup w/a green transfer design titled "Holyrood Castle," 2 3/4" h. (ILLUS. right with matching saucer) **$75-100**

Cup & saucer, after-dinner style, Mecca design, all-white, cylindrical cup w/angled handle, lightly molded matching saucer, saucer 3" d., cup 2 3/8" h., the set (ILLUS. left with Globe cup & saucer, top next page) **$75-125**

Lotus Cup & Saucer with Frog Scene

Mecca After-dinner Cup & Saucer & a Globe Cup & Saucer

Two Lotus Ware Star Design Cups & Saucers

Cup & saucer, cylindrical cup w/ruffled rim, decorated in color w/a scene of a frog seated under an umbrella & fishing, titled, "Oregon Webfoot," w/a lotus pad-shaped saucer, saucer 4 3/4" d., cup 2 1/4" d., 1 5/8" h. (ILLUS., previous page) **$125-150**

Cup & saucer, Globe design, footed wide shallow cup & shallow saucer, saucer 6" d., cup 4 1/2" d., 1 1/2" h., the set (ILLUS. right with Mecca after-dinner cup & sauce, top of page) **$75-125**

Cup & saucer, Star design, all-white, cup 3 1/2" d., 1 5/8" h. (ILLUS. left with decorated Star design cup & saucer, second from top) **$75-100**

Cup & saucer, Star design, h.p. w/pink, blue & yellow flowers, cup 3 1/2" d., 1 5/8" h. (ILLUS. right with plain Star design cup & saucer, second from top) **$100-125**

Spherical Lotus Ware Flower Bowl

Flower bowl, footed spherical form w/a pierced closed rim, applied w/berries & leaves around the sides, 3 3/4" d., 4 1/2" h. (ILLUS.) **$250-300**

Lotus Ware Ivica Jar, Globe Pitcher & Thebian Vase

Two White Lotus Ware Nappies & a Salt Dip

Ornate Lotus Ware Deccan Jar

Jar, cov., Deccan Jar (a.k.a. Luxor Jar), all-white footed bulbous body decorated w/four filigreed medallions & applied teardrops & beaded strings, matching pierced cover (ILLUS.) **$400-600**

Jar, Ivica Jar, footed bulbous ovoid body w/a closed rim, large gold beads around the foot & rim, h.p. pink & white flowers & green leaves around the sides, missing the cover, 4 5/8" h. (ILLUS. left with a Globe pitcher & Thebian Vase, top of page).. **$250-350**

Nappy, scalloped oblong four-lobed all-white shape, twig feet, 4 x 5 1/8" (ILLUS. right with larger nappy & salt dip, second from top)... **$100-125**

Nappy, scalloped oblong four-lobed all-white shape, twig feet, 4 x 7" (ILLUS. left with smaller nappy & salt dip, second from top)... **$100-125**

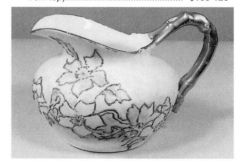

Decorated Globe Jug Pitcher

Pitcher, 3 1/8" h., 4 1/4" d., jug-style, Globe design, squatty bulbous body w/a wide low rim & spout, gold forked handle, bisque finish, the sides h.p. w/pink & yellow flowers & blue & green leaves all outlined in gold (ILLUS.)........................... **$125-150**

Pitcher, 5" h., 7" d., jug-type, Globe design, squatty bulbous body w/a wide low flaring rim & spout, gold forked handle, the sides h.p. w/burgundy & yellow roses (ILLUS. right with Ivica jar and Thebian Vase) **$400-600**

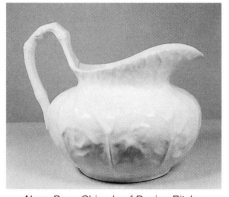

None-Bone China Leaf Design Pitcher

Pitcher, 6 1/4" h., 7 1/2" d., jug-style, Leaf design, all-white, squatty bulbous body lightly embossed w/a leaf design, made

from a Lotus Ware mold but not bone china (ILLUS.)... **$45-60**

Salt dip individual size, all-white, rounded scalloped shape, 1 1/2" d., 1/2" h. (ILLUS. in front of smaller nappy) **$30-50**

Saucer, shallow dished form, four panels printed in green "Holyrood Commandery - No. 32 - K.T. - Cleveland, Ohio 1899," 4 7/8" d. (ILLUS. left with matching afterdinner cup) **$50-75**

Gold-decorated Lotus Ware Sugar Bowl

Sugar bowl, cov., squatty bulbous body w/a domed cover & button finial, angled handle, molded gadroon body design, highlightover overall w/gold, 6" l., 4" h. (ILLUS.)... **$100-125**

Three Piece Lotus Ware Valiniennes Tea Set

Tea set: cov. teapot, cov. sugar bowl & creamer; Valinciennes design, each piece h.p. w/violets in panels between light purple applied fishnet, twig handles, creamer (some damage) 4" l., 3 1/8" h., sugar 5 1/2" l., 3 3/4" h., teapot 7" l., 4 1/4" h., the set (ILLUS.) **$475-600**

Violet-decorated Lotus Ware Valinciennes Tea Set

Tea set: cov. teapot, cov. sugar bowl & creamer; Valinciennes design, each piece h.p. w/violets, twig handles, creamer (some damage) 4" l., 3 1/8" h., sugar 5 1/2" l., 3 3/4" h., teapot 7" l., 4 1/4" h., the set (ILLUS.) **$300-400**

Venice Design Lotus Ware Tea Set

Tea set: cov. teapot, open sugar bowl & creamer; Venice design, oblong bodies w/lightly molded designs, gold banding, creamer 4" l., 3" h., sugar 5 1/2" l., 3" h., teapot 7" w., 4 1/4" h., the set (ILLUS., top of page) **$375-475**

Non-Bone China Teapot from Lotus Mold

Teapot, cov., squatty bulbous body w/swirled ribbing, domed cover w/knob finial, short spout & angled handle, blue blush ground h.p. w/pink & blue flowers on a brown transfer, gold-sponged throat & cover, from a Lotus Ware mold but not bone china, 7 1/2" l., 5" h. (ILLUS.)........ **$75-85**

Tray, shell-shaped, raised base, white ground w/a delicate brown vine decoration & gilt trim, 4 3/8" w., 4" h. (ILLUS. left front with two other shell-shaped trays, bottom of page) **$100-125**

Tray, shell-shaped, raised base, pale yellow blush ground decorated w/a band of small blue flowers & pink ribbons, gold trim, 5 3/8" w., 5" h. (ILLUS. right with two other shell-shaped trays) **$125-150**

Tray, shell-shaped, raised three-twig base, all-white, 8 1/2" w., 8" h. (ILLUS. left behind small shell-shaped tray, bottom of page) **$200-250**

Three Lotus Ware Shell-shaped Trays

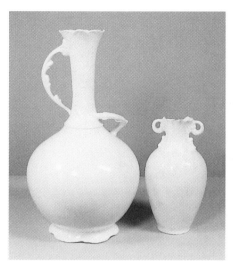

Cremoniam & Parmian Lotus Vases

Vase, 6" h., Cremoniam shape, all-white ovoid body tapering to a molded flaring neck flanked by small ring handles (ILLUS. right with Parmian vase) **$150-200**

Two Lotus Ware Grecian Vases

Vase, 6" h., Grecian design, ewer-form w/bulbous tapering ovoid body, pointed upright spout & angled white handle, embossed base & neck, the lower body h.p. w/pink & yellow flowers (ILLUS. left with other Grecian vase)........................... **$150-200**

Vase, 6" h., Grecian design, ewer-form w/bulbous tapering ovoid body, pointed upright spout & angled gold handle, embossed neck trimmed in gold, the lower pale blue body h.p. w/tiny blue flowers (ILLUS. right with other Grecian vase) **$150-200**

Vase, 8" h., Tuscan Vase, all-white, wide cylindrical body on three large ball feet, applied morning glory blossoms, vines & bugs (ILLUS. left with cracker jar) **$500-750**

Vase, 8 1/4" h., Thebian shape, double-gourd form w/angular handles from rim to

shoulder, bisque finish in pale yellow h.p. w/pink & yellow flowers (ILLUS. center with Ivica jar & Globe pitcher) **$400-600**

Vase, 10" h., Parmian shape, all-white, ruffled foot & bulbous nearly spherical body w/a tall slender cylindrical embossed neck w/flared rim, asymetric wine-like handles down around the neck (ILLUS. left with Cremoniam vase) **$200-300**

Majolica

Majolica, a tin-enameled glazed pottery, has been produced for centuries. It originally took its name from the island of Majorca, a source of figuline (potter's clay). Subsequently it was widely produced in England, Europe and the United States. Etruscan majolica, now avidly sought, was made by Griffen, Smith & Hill, Phoenixville, Pa., in the last quarter of the 19th century. Most majolica advertised today is 19th or 20th century. Once scorned by most collectors, interest in this colorful ware so popular during the Victorian era has now revived and prices have risen dramatically in the past few years.

Etruscan

Rare Etruscan Begonia Leaf Basket

Basket, Begonia Leaf patt., wicker-form forked overhead handle, wicker strap border band, 11 1/2" l. (ILLUS.) **$1,120**

Large Grouping of Varied Shell & Seaweed Pieces

Bowl, 7 1/2" d., Shell & Seaweed patt., great color (ILLUS. front row, far left with Shell & Seaweed cake stand, pitcher and other pieces) **$392**

Bowl, 8" d., Shell & Seaweed patt., minor glaze nick (ILLUS. front row right with other Shell & Seaweed pieces, top next page)... **$224**

Cake stand, Shell & Seaweed patt., good color, 9 1/4" d.,5" h. (ILLUS. top row, far right with Shell & Seaweed pitcher and other pieces, top next page) **$1,120**

Grouping of Etruscan Shell & Seaweed Pieces

Etruscan Pitchers, Syrup Pitchers and Other Pieces

Creamer, Corn patt. (ILLUS. front row, fourth from left with Etruscan pitchers and syrup pitchers)..................................... $67

Creamer, Shell & Seaweed patt., 3" h. (ILLUS. front row left with other Shell & Seaweed pieces)....................................... $134

Creamer, Shell & Seaweed patt., minor rim nick, 3 1/4" h. (ILLUS. front row center with other Shell & Seaweed pieces).......... $101

Creamer & cov. sugar bowl, Shell & Seaweed patt., large size, rim repair on creamer (ILLUS. center row left & right with other Shell & Seaweed pieces).......... $280

Cup & saucer, Shell & Seaweed patt., large size, minor rim repair on cup, w/extra saucer (ILLUS. middle row, right with Shell & Seaweed cake stand, pitcher & other pieces) $196

Mug, footed ovoid shape, Lily patt. (ILLUS. front row third from left with Etruscan pitchers and syrup pitchers) $179

Mustache cup & saucer, Shell & Seaweed patt., rim nicks on saucer (ILLUS. middle row, center with Shell & Seaweed cake stand, pitcher and other pieces) $179

Pitcher, 5" h., Sunflower patt., cream ground (ILLUS. center row, middle with Etruscan pitchers and syrup pitchers)....... $336

Pitcher, 5" h., Sunflower patt., cream ground, rim nicks (ILLUS. center row, far right with Etruscan pitchers and syrup pitchers) $196

Pitcher, 5" h., Wild Rose patt. w/butterfly spout (ILLUS. front row, third from right with Etruscan pitchers and syrup pitchers).. $168

Pitcher, 5 1/4" h., Sunflower patt., greenish grey ground, minor rim nicks (ILLUS. front row, second from left with Etruscan pitchers and syrup pitchers) $280

Pitcher, 6" h., Hawthorn patt. (ILLUS. front row, far left with Etruscan pitchers and syrup pitchers) $196

Pitcher, 7" h., Fern patt., hairline (ILLUS. front row, second from right with other Etruscan pitchers and syrup pitchers)....... $336

Pitcher, 7" h., Fern patt., nicks (ILLUS. front row, far right with other Etruscan pitchers and syrup pitchers) $196

Pitcher, 9" h., Wild Rose patt., butterfly spout (ILLUS. center row, far left with Etruscan pitchers and syrup pitchers) $252

Plate, 7" d., Shell & Seaweed patt. $134

Plate, 8" d., Shell & Seaweed patt. (ILLUS. back row, left with Shell & Seaweed cake stand and other pieces) $123

Platter, 13 1/2" oval, Shell & Seaweed patt., Albino Ware (ILLUS. front row, right with other platters, top next page) $179

Platter, 13 1/2" oval, Shell & Seaweed patt., lavender center, great color (ILLUS. back row, left with other platters, top next page).. $896

Platter, 13 1/2" oval, Shell & Seaweed patt., lavender center, very minor rim nicks on back, great color (ILLUS. back row, right with other platters, top next page)....... $672

Platter, 13 1/2" oval, Shell & Seaweed patt., yellow center, very minor rim nicks on back, great color (ILLUS. front row, left with other platters, top next page) $448

Spittoon, Shell & Seaweed patt., Albino Ware, colored trim, 6 1/4" h. (ILLUS. front row, right with Shell & Seaweed cake stand and other pieces, top of page)......... $392

Spooner, Shell & Seaweed patt., shell rim handles (ILLUS. center row middle with other Shell & Seaweed pieces, top of page) $202

Syrup pitcher w/hinged metal lid, Bamboo patt. (ILLUS. center row, second from left with Etruscan pitchers and syrup pitchers) $336

Syrup pitcher w/hinged metal lid, Sunflower patt., cobalt blue ground (ILLUS. back row, right with Etruscan pitchers and syrup pitchers) $392

Group of Etruscan Shell & Seaweed Platters

Syrup pitcher w/hinged metal lid, Sunflower patt., pink ground (ILLUS. back row, center with Etruscan pitchers and syrup pitchers, previous page) $392

Syrup pitcher w/hinged metal lid, Sunflower patt., pink ground, nice color, hairline (ILLUS. back row, left with Etruscan pitchers and syrup pitchers, previous page) $420

Tea set: cov. teapot, cov. sugar bowl, creamer & spooner; cov., Shell & Seaweed patt., straight spout teapot, sugar cover & handle repaired, wear on creamer & spooner rims, the set (ILLUS. far left with other Shell & Seaweed pieces, top previous page) $560

Tea set: cov. teapot, cov. sugar bowl, creamer & spooner; cov., Shell & Seaweed patt., crooked spout teapot, hairline in creamer, the set (ILLUS. far right with other Shell & Seaweed pieces, top previous page) $728

Teapot, cov., Shell & Seaweed patt., straight spout, good color, hairline (ILLUS. back row middle with other Shell & Seaweed pieces, top previous page) $364

Scarce Etruscan Vase and Wall Pocket

Vase, 5" h., Oak Leaf, Acorn & Basketweave patt., yellow ground, scarce, hairline (ILLUS. left with Etruscan wall pocket) $700

Wall pocket, Basketweave & Twig patt., yellow & brown, base chip, rare, 6 1/4" w., 6 1/4" h. (ILLUS. right with Etruscan vase) $252

General

Very Rare Beehive Cheese Keeper

Cheese keeper, cov., Beehive & Blackberry patt., modeled as a large straw beehive w/a vine loop top handle & blackberry vines wrapping around the sides, the base a square platform w/cut-corners raised on vine legs, Minton, England, ca. 1880s, hairline in base, very rare, 13" h. (ILLUS.) **$35,200**

Fine Victorian Storks & Leaves Compote

Large Minton Jarindiere with Figural Panels

Compote, open, 9 1/4" h., 10 1/2" d., the wide shallow dished top composed of large overlapping green leaves raised on a tall green stem framed by three standing storks w/their heads bent down touching their breasts & glazed in mottled yellow to dark brown, on a mottled brown & bluish green tripartite base, unmarked (ILLUS., previous page) **$518**

Jardiniere, deep oval form w/gently flaring paneled & scalloped sides, cobalt blue ground decorated on the sides w/oblong green scroll-framed panels enclosing colorful scenes of Classical figures & Cupids, Shape No. 1087, Minton, England, ca. 1880s, professional rim repair, 17 1/2" l., 7 3/4" h. (ILLUS., top of page) **$3,300**

Majolica Shell & Seaweed Tea Set

Tea set: cov. teapot, cov. sugar bowl & creamer; Shell & Seaweed patt., in mottled shades of grey, pink & brown w/green sea plants, late 19th c., some roughness to creamer rim, teapot 5 1/2" h., the set (ILLUS.).......................... **$374**

Reissued Minton Cockerel Teapot

Teapot, cov., figural Cockerel patt., produced by Minton, based on Victorian

original, limited edition of 2,500, introduced in 2000 (ILLUS.) **$700**

Reissued Minton Majolica Fish Pattern Teapot

Teapot, cov., figural Fish patt., produced by Minton, based on Victorian original, limited edition of 2,500, introduced in 2000 (ILLUS.)... **$750**

Very Rare Holdcroft Putto in Rowboat Teapot

Teapot, cov., Putto Rowing Boat patt., wide low squatty rounded body on three scroll feet, the body in cobalt blue w/a straight brown spout & C-form brown handle, the top modeled w/the figure of a winged putto seated in a model of a tan rowboat w/pale green interior & green oars, Holdcroft, England, third quarter 19th c., very rare, professional repair to arm of figure, 8" l., 6" h. (ILLUS.) **$15,680**

New Minton Figural Tortoise Teapot

Teapot, cov., Tortoise patt., produced by Minton, limited edition of 2,500, introduced in 1999 (ILLUS.) **$750**

Marblehead

This pottery was organized in 1904 by Dr. Herbert J. Hall as a therapeutic aid to patients in a sanitarium he ran in Marblehead, Massachusetts. It was later separated from the sanitarium and directed by Arthur E. Baggs, a fine artist and designer, who bought out the factory in 1916 and operated it until its closing in 1936. Most wares were hand-thrown and decorated and carry the company mark of a stylized sailing vessel flanked by the letters "M" and "P."

Marblehead Mark

Ovoid Blue Matt Marblehead Vase

Vase, 5" h., flaring ovoid body w/a wide flat mouth, blue matte glaze, company logo mark (ILLUS.) **$345**

Marblehead Green Crystalline Vase

Vase, 5 1/8" h., flaring ovoid body w/a wide flat mouth, green crystalline matte glaze, hand-thrown, company logo mark (ILLUS.) **$375**

Lavender Matte Glaze Marblehead Vase

Vase, 5 1/8" h., flaring ovoid body w/a wide flat mouth, lavender matte glaze, company logo mark (ILLUS.) **$432**

Marblehead Matte Blue Vase

Vase, 7 3/4" h., tapering cylindrical body w/a rounded base & thin flaring rim, dark blue matte glaze, impresed mark & original paper label (ILLUS.) **$460**

McCoy

Collectors are now seeking the art wares of two McCoy potteries. One was founded in Roseville, Ohio, in the late 19th century as the J.W. McCoy Pottery, subsequently becoming Brush-McCoy Pottery Co., later Brush Pottery. The other was also founded in Roseville in 1910 as Nelson McCoy Sanitary Stoneware Co., later becoming Nelson McCoy Pottery. In 1967 the pottery was sold to D.T. Chase of the Mount Clemens Pottery Co., who sold his interest to the Lancaster Colony Corp. in 1974. The pottery shop closed in 1985. Cookie jars are especially collectible today.

A helpful reference book is The Collector's Encyclopedia of McCoy Pottery, by the Huxfords (Collector Books), and McCoy Cookie Jars From the First to the Latest, by Harold Nichols (Nichols Publishing, 1987).

McCoy Mark

Book ends, decorated w/swallows, ca. 1956, 5 1/2 x 6" **$200-250**
Book ends, model of violin, ca. 1959, 10" h., pr. **$100-150**
Cachepot, double w/applied bird, ca. 1949, 10 1/2" l. **$35-45**

Bunch of Bananas Cookie Jar

Cookie jar, Bunch of Bananas, ca. 1948 (ILLUS.) **$150-250**
Cookie jar, Chipmunk, ca. 1960 (ILLUS., top next column) **$100-125**
Cookie jar, Christmas Tree, ca. 1959 (ILLUS., middle next column) .... **$1,000+**
Cookie jar, Corn (ear of corn), ca. 1958 .... **$150-175**

Chipmunk Cookie Jar

Christmas Tree Cookie Jar

Cookie jar, Hobby Horse, ca. 1948 .... **$100-150**

McCoy Indian Head Cookie Jar

Cookie jar, Indian Head, ca. 1954 (ILLUS.).. **$633**
Cookie jar, Tomato, ca. 1964 .... **$60-70**

Yellow Mouse Cookie Jar

Cookie jar, Yellow Mouse, ca. 1978
(ILLUS.).. **$35-45**
Figurine, head of witch, ca. early 1940s,
3" h... **$400-600**
Iced tea server, El Rancho Bar-B-Que
line, ca. 1960, 11 1/2" h. **$250-300**
Jardiniere, fish decoration, ca. 1958,
7 1/2" h... **$350-400**

Leaves & Berries Jardiniere & Pedestal

Jardiniere & pedestal base, Leaves & Berries design, ca. 1930s, overall 21" h., 2
pcs. (ILLUS.) **$250-350**
Jardiniere & pedestal base, ring
design, ca. 1930s, overall 29" h., 2 pcs.
.... **$450-550**

McCoy Cowboy Boots Lamp

Lamp w/original shade, model of pair of
cowboy boots base, original shade, ca.
1956 (ILLUS.).................................... **$150-200**

Model of Angelfish

Model of angelfish, aqua, ca. early 1940s,
Cope design, 6" h. (ILLUS.) **$300-400**
Model of cat, ca. 1940s, 3" h................ **$300-400**
Oil jar, bulbous ovoid body w/slightly flaring
rim, angled shoulder handles, red
sponged glaze, 18" h. **$300-400**
Pitcher, embossed w/parading ducks, ca.
1930s, 4 pt. **$90-125**
Pitcher, 7" h., Donkey, marked "NM," early
1940s **$300-350**
Pitcher, 10" h., Butterfly line **$150-225**
Pitcher-vase, 7" h., figural parrot, ca. 1952
.... **$200-225**

Rare Madonna Planter

Planter, figural, Madonna, white, ca. 1960s, rare, 6" h. (ILLUS.) **$200-250**

Planter, model of baby scale, ca. 1954, 5 x 5 1/2" **$35-50**

Planter, model of Cope monkey head, 5 1/2" h... **$100-200**

Fish Planter

Planter, model of fish, green, ca. 1955, 7 x 12" (ILLUS.)............................ **$1,000-1,200**

Planter, model of lemon, ca. 1953, 5 x 6 1/2" **$100-125**

Planter, model of pomegranate, ca. 1953, 5 x 6 1/2" **$125-150**

Planter, model of rooster on wheel of wheelbarrow, ca. 1955, 10 1/2" l. ... **$100-125**

Planter, model of snowman, ca. 1940s, 4 x 6" **$70-90**

Planter, model of stork, ca. 1956, blue & pink, 7 x 7 1/2" **$75-100**

Planter, model of "stretch" dachshund, 8 1/4" l. **$150-175**

Planting dish, rectangular, front w/five relief-molded Scottie dog heads, white, brown & green, ca. 1949, 8" l. **$50-60**

Platter, 14" l., Butterfly line, ca. 1940s **$250-600**

Porch jar, wide tapering cylindrical body w/ribbed base, embossed leaf & berry decoration below rim, green, marked "NM," ca. 1940s, 9 1/2 x 11" (ILLUS., top next column) **$200-250**

Spoon rest, Butterfly line, ca. 1953, 4 x 7 1/2" **$90-125**

Porch Jar

Sprinkler, model of turtle, green w/yellow trim, ca. 1950, 5 1/2 x 10" **$80-100**

Tea set: cov. teapot, creamer & open sugar bowl; Pine Cone patt., ca. 1946, 3 pcs. **$75-100**

McCoy Fireplace TV Lamp

TV lamp, model of fireplace, ca. 1950s, 6 x 9" (ILLUS.)..................................... **$75-100**

Umbrella Stand with Leaf Design

Umbrella stand, cylindrical w/applied handles, ribbed panels alternating w/embossed leaf design panels, glossy brown glaze, ca. 1940s, 19" h. (ILLUS.) **$250-350**

Vase, 6" h., footed, heart-shape w/embossed roses, ca. 1940s **$60-80**

Vase, 6" h., Hobnail line, Castlegate shape, ca. early 1940s **$150-200**

Vase, 8" h., footed bulbous base w/trumpet-form neck & scrolled handles, embossed peacock decoration, ca. 1948 .... **$40-60**

McCoy Magnolia Vase

Vase, 8 1/4" h., figural magnolia, pink, white, brown & green, ca. 1953 (ILLUS.) **$250-300**

Vase, 8 1/2" h., figural wide lily-form, white, brown & green, ca. 1956 .... **$100-125**

Vase, 14" h., Antique Curio line, ca. 1962 .... **$75-100**

Vase, 14" h., figural seated cat, matte black, ca. 1960 .... **$200-250**

Vase, 14 1/2" h., Tall Fan, ca. 1954 .... **$150-200**

McCoy Clown Wall Pocket

Wall pocket, figural, clown, white w/red & black trim, ca. 1940s, 8" l. (ILLUS.).... **$100-150**

Wall pocket, model of apple, ca. early 1950s, 6 x 7" **$200-225**

Wall pocket, model of bellows, ca. mid-1950s, 9 1/2" l. **$90-110**

Wall pocket, model of bird bath, late 1940s, 5 x 6 1/2" **$90-110**

Meissen

The secret of true hard paste porcelain, known long before to the Chinese, was "discovered" accidentally in Meissen, Germany by J.F. Bottger, an alchemist working with E.W. Tschirnhausen. The first European true porcelain was made in the Meissen Porcelain Works, organized about 1709. Meissen marks have been widely copied by other factories. Some pieces listed here are recent.

Meissen Mark

Two-tiered Meissen Centerpiece

Centerpiece, a domed round gadrooned base tapering to a knopped stem supported a two-tiered top w/each dished section w/reticulated edges & h.p. in blue w/three cartouches w/blue highlights & flowers, the top center mounted w/a figure of a standing woman holding up her apron full of flowers, overall blue trim, blue crossed swords mark on base, probably late 19th c., base dish 9" d., overall 16" h. (ILLUS.) **$450**

Meissen Figure of Young Boy Drinking

Figures of child, blond boy wearing white nightgown, blue socks & tan slippers, holding blue & white bowl or cup to lips, a horse toy on its back behind him, underglaze blue crossed-sword mark, 20th c., 7 1/2" h. (ILLUS.) **$1,035**

Satirical Figure of Baron Munchhaussen

Figurine, Baron Munchhaussen, in a satirical pose dressed as a cavalry office riding on the full moon, on a stepped ebonized wood base, blue crossed-swords mark, signed by Alexander Struck, ca. 1941, 13 1/4" h. (ILLUS.) **$5,975**

Plates, 9 1/2" d., three oblong rim reserves h.p. in dark blue w/a stylized blossom connected by reticulated basketweave section around the center w/a large blue floral decoration, blue crossed-swords mark, 19th c., set of 6 (ILLUS., top next column)....................................... **$805**

Set of Six Meissen Reticulated Plates

Unusual Figural Meissen Scent Bottle

Scent bottle w/stoppers, figural, modeled as the figure of a standing bearded man in a long brown hooded robe holding the neck of a white goose in one hand & a basket of colored fruit over his other arm, a long basket holding a small child, the head of the child & the man form a stopper, blue crossed-swords mark & impressed "2472," late 19th c., 3" h. (ILLUS.) **$1,323**

Meissen Teapot with Landscape Scenes

Pair of Extremely Ornate Meissen Potpourri Vases

Teapot, cov., slightly squatty nearly spherical body w/a molded fish-form spout & London-shape handle w/shell design, h.p. on each side in color w/a landscape w/cow & sheep framed by trellis & blossom bands, blue crossed-swords mark, ca. 1795, hairline in base (ILLUS., previous page) **$748**

Vases, cov., 29 7/8" h., potpourri-type, ornate Rococo style, each domed & pierced cover surmounted by a large bouquet of realistic flowers, the bulbous inverted pear-shaped body w/front & back panels finely decorated w/colorful floral bouquets, the sides very ornately encrusted w/a wide variety of large, colorful flowers & fruits, the flaring pedestal base trimmed in gold & green & mounted on one side w/the figure of a small putto or nymph, after a model by J.J. Kandler,

blue crossed-swords mark, ca. 1900, pr. (ILLUS., top of page).......................... **$10,755**

Mettlach

Ceramics with the name Mettlach were produced by Villeroy & Boch and other potteries in the Mettlach area of Germany. Villeroy and Boch's finest years of production are thought to be from about 1890 to 1910. Also see STEINS.

Mettlach Mark

Lovely Mettlach Gilt Bronze-Mounted Charger

Charger, gilt bronze-mounted, large round shallow dish w/the colorful Golden Pheasant & Flowers design in the center, the wide border decorated w/colorful flowers & butterflies, decorated by M. Hein, the back signed & numbered, dated 1887, No. 1676, the gilt-bronze rim band w/scrolling leaf & blossom handles, raised on a base w/four scrolled feet joined by floral swags, 23 1/2" d., 7 1/4" h. (ILLUS. of two views)
.... **$4,140**

Two Small Mettlach Vases

Vase, 5 1/4" h., ovoid body w/a short rolled neck, white ground transfer-printed & hand-enameled w/an overall design of crosses alternating w/florets in shades of green, yellow & red, No. 1016-3058 (ILLUS. right with other Mettlach vase).... **$242**

Vase, 6" h., wide ovoid body w/a narrow shoulder to the low flared neck, glazed in relief w/an Oriental-style decoration, a dark red ground w/lappet bands around the base & shoulder & a narrow center band flanked by opposing pairs of ornate lappets, all in shades of dark blue, pink & green, No. 1596 (ILLUS. left with other Mettlach vase).. **$242**

Unusual Mettlach Vase in Red & Green

Vase, 9 1/2" h., flat-bottomed bulbous lower body tapering to a wide cylindrical neck, painted under glaze w/green hops & leaves against a deep red ground, overall slightly iridescent glaze, No. 2541 (ILLUS.) **$253**

Minton

The Minton factory in England was established by Thomas Minton in 1793. The factory made earthenware, especially the blue-printed variety, and Thomas Minton is sometimes credited with the invention of the blue "Willow" pattern. For a time majolica and tiles were also important parts of production, but bone china soon became the principal ware. Mintons, Ltd., continues in operation today. Also see MAJOLICA.

Minton Marks

Ornate Sèvres-style Bottle Cooler

Bottle cooler, Sèvres-style, footed wide & deep cylindrical form w/a ring-molded wide flat rim, gilt-trimmed scroll handles, the lower body in turquoise blue decorated w/a band of tall gold leaves, a narrow shoulder band in blue decorated w/Classical figural reserves in white on black framed by gilt scrolls, narrower white bands w/delicate florals flanking it, based on a piece from a service made for Catherine the Great of Russia, gold crowned globe mark, ca. 1906, 7 1/2" h. (ILLUS.)... **$9,560**

Bowl, 9 1/2" d., Sèvres-style, a low footring below the wide rounded upright sides w/a wide flat rim, turquoise blue ground decorated on the front & back w/a large oval reserve of colorful exotic birds framed w/ornate gilt oak leaf banding & swags, gilt line rim & interior gilt dentil band, based on a service made by Sèvres for the Prince of Rohan, gold crowned globe mark, ca. 1900 (ILLUS., top next page).................. **$2,629**

Mintons Charger with Scene of Artemis

Ornate Sèvres-style Mintons Bowl

Charger, round, finely painted w/a celestial view of the nude Artemis standing before a tree w/a net ensnaring flying putti, one putto captured & tucked in her side satchel, in pastel colors, painted & impressed mark, decorated by Louis Marc Solon, 1872, 11 7/8" d. (ILLUS., previous page) **$5,736**

Rare Mintons Pate-sur-Pate Pilgrim Bottle

Pilgrim bottle, pate-sure-pate, the footed flattened round body topped by a cylindrical neck w/flared rim flanked by small gold loop shoulder handles, dark chocolate brown ground, a large round front reserve w/a border of pale blue bands w/a top bow centered by a green leaftip band, the center in cobalt blue decorated in white slip relief w/a seated Bacchante resting w/a wine ewer in her lap, spilling fruit & an upturned jug at her feet, gold crowned globe mark, decorated by Frederick Alfred Rhead, ca. 1875, 10" h. (ILLUS.) **$8,365**

Plate, 9 3/4" d., "Act of Union" commemorative, the wide deep pink border decorated w/three long reserves decorated w/plants representing England (roses), Scotland (thistles) & Ireland (shamrocks) all bordered in gilt floral scrolls, the white center h.p. w/the large entwined monogram "VR" for Queen Victoria below a

Mintons Art of Union Commemorative Plate

small crown, representing the Union of Great Britain, dated 1874, impressed uppercase mark (ILLUS.) **$3,107**

Set of Red & Gold Minton Service Plates

Service plates, white center w/a wide rim decorated w/a deep red band w/a heavy gold outer & inner rim bands, the red band decorated w/delicate lacy gold designs, bottoms marked "H3986 - Ovington's New York," ca. 1891-92, 10 1/2" d., set of 12 (ILLUS.) **$2,070**

Elegant Pair of Minton Turquoise Cloisonné-style Vases

Minton Art Nouveau-style Vases

gold rim, each mounted on the side w/a large scarab beetle in similar colors, Shape No. 1644, designed by Christopher Dresser, puce printed crowned globe mark, dated 1974, pr. (ILLUS., top of page) **$19,120**

One of Two Large Sèvres-style Vases

Vases, 9 1/2" h., 4" d., Art Nouveau style, tall slender ovoid body tapering to a small flat mouth, each decorated in the squeezebag style in a Secessionist design of undulating ribbons up around the sides highlighted w/stylized clusters of bubble-like devices, one in deep purple, dark blue & green, the other in deep red, maroon & white & green, one w/restoration to the base & small rim chip, stamped "Minton Ltd. - No. 1" (ILLUS.) **$805**

Vases, 10" h., decorated to resemble Oriental cloisonné, gold ring-footed bottle form w/tall slender tapering neck, turquoise blue ground decorated around the lower body w/an ornate band of stylized scrolls & leaves in shades of dark blue, brick red, white & pale green, a lappet band in white, blue & green on the upper neck below the

Vases, Sèvres classical style, a square foot & tapering ringed pedestal supporting the wide bulbous ovoid body tapering to a cylindrical neck w/a flared rim, molded gold rope swags around the neck & down the sides, dark green & gold on the base & lower body, the main body in white h.p. overall w/large colorful swags of flowers & leaves, a green band & bow at the top of the neck, ca. 1855, 12 5/8" h., pr. (ILLUS. of one) **$6,573**

Moorcroft

William Moorcroft became a designer for James Macintyre & Co. in 1897 and was put in charge of the art pottery production there. Moorcroft developed a number of popular designs, including Florian Ware, while with Macintyre and continued with that firm until 1913, when it discontinued the production of art pottery.

After leaving Macintyre in 1913, Moorcroft set up his own pottery in Burslem, where he continued producing the art wares he had designed earlier, introducing new patterns as well. After William's death in 1945, the pottery was operated by his son, Walter.

Small Dark Blue Moorcroft Vase

Moorcroft Marks

Wide Shallow Moorcroft Bowl

Bowl, 11" d., footed wide flat-bottomed shape w/rounded upright sides, loop side handles, Pomagranate patt. in reddish orange, golden brown & purple on a cobalt blue ground, some crazing on interior (ILLUS.).. **$390**

Miniature Moorcroft Orchids Vase

Vase, miniature, 2 5/8" h., Orchids patt., footed very wide squatty bulbous body centered by a short flaring neck, painted w/vivid deep rose & dark blue orchids & yellow & green leaves on a cobalt blue ground, marked (ILLUS.).......................... **$230**
Vase, miniature, 2 7/8" h., footed wide & low squatty body centered by a short flaring neck, overall mottled dark blue lustre glaze, impressed "Moorcroft M82 - Made in England" (ILLUS., top next column) **$173**

Miniature Moorcroft Grape & Leaf Vase

Vase, 3" h., miniature, Grape & Leaf patt., footed nearly spherical body w/a small short flared neck, a large green shaded to maroon leaf in front of a large cluster of dark blue red-tinted grapes on a dark blue ground, W. Moorcroft signature, ca. 1930s, some glaze anomalies & slight crazing, a few glaze pops (ILLUS.) **$196**

Miniature Moorcroft Florian Ware Vase

Vase, miniature, 3 1/2" h., Florian Ware, a wide flat-bottomed squatty ovoid body w/a wide shoulder centering a small trumpet neck, a white ground decorated w/a band of large blue poppies on delicate pale green leafy stems, dark blue interior, MacIntyre era, No. 63, ca. 1898-1905, mild crazing (ILLUS., previous page) **$1,265**

Squatty Moorcroft Pansy Vase

Small Moorcroft Hibiscus Vase

Vase, 5 1/8" h., Hibiscus patt., footed bulbous ovoid body tapering to a widely flaring trumpet neck, a large pink blossom & green leaves on a dark green ground, marked w/partial paper label, few minor glaze pits (ILLUS.)...................................... **$184**

Early Moorcroft Pomegranate Vase

Vase, 5 5/8" h., footed wide ovoid body w/a wide short finely ringed cylindrical neck, Pomegranate patt., large deep red fruits & yellowish green leaves among small red & blue fruits against a dark blue ground, impressed Cobridge factory mark, ca. 1913-16, Shape No. 102 (ILLUS.).............. **$490**

Vase, 7 1/4" h., 8" d., Pansy patt., footed very wide squatty bulbous body tapering to a short neck, cobalt blue ground decorated w/large deep purple, white & deep red pansies & pale green leaves, early 20th c. (ILLUS., top next column).............. **$748**

Anemone Pattern Moorcroft Vase

Vase, 8" h., footed nearly spherical bulbous body tapering to a wide rolled short neck, Anemone patt., large dark purplish blue & dark rose red blossoms & green leaves against a deep green to blue ground, painted by Walter Moorcroft, ca. 1945-49, light overall crazing (ILLUS.).............. **$432**

Morton Potteries

A total of six potteries were in operation at various times in Morton, Illinois, from 1877 to 1976. All traced their origins from the Morton Brick and Tile Company begun in 1877 by six Rapp brothers who came to America in the early 1870s to escape forced military service under Kaiser Wilhelm I. Sons, nephews and cousins of the founding fathers were responsible for the continuation of the pottery industry in Morton as a result of buyouts or the establishment of new and separate operations. The potteries are listed chronologically by beginning dates.

Morton's natural clay deposits were ideal for the Rapps' venture into pottery production. Local clay was used until it was depleted in 1940. That clay fired out to a golden ecru color. After 1940, clay was imported from South Carolina and Indiana.

It fired out snow white. The differences in clay allow one to easily date production at the Morton potteries. Only a few items were marked by any of the potteries. Occasionally, paper labels were used, but most of those have long disappeared. Glaze is sometimes a determinant. Early glazes were Rockingham brown, green and cobalt blue, or transparent, to produce yellowware. In the '20s and '30s colorful drip glazes were used. In the later years solid pastel and Deco colors were in vogue.

Most of Morton's potteries were short-lived, operating for twenty years or less. Their products are elusive. However, Morton Pottery Company was in operation for fifty-four years, and its products appear regularly in today's secondary market.

Rapp Brothers Brick & Tile Company & Morton Pottery Works (1877-1915) -

Morton Earthenware Company (1915-1917)

Baker, deep, yellowware, 10" d. **$125**
Bank, figural acorn, brown Rockingham glaze, no advertising **$50**
Churn, mottled brown Rockingham glaze, 4 gal. **$250**

Rapp Bros. Green-glazed Creamer

Creamer, waisted cylindrical form w/molded bark & flowers under a dark green glaze, 5" h. (ILLUS.) **$50**

Rapp Brothers Jardiniere

Jardiniere, tapering cylindrical form, embossed leaf design, green, 7" d. (ILLUS.) ... **$50**
Lapel button, model of an elephant w/embossed "GOP" on side, dark brown glaze, 1 1/8 x 1 3/4" **$95**

Rapp Bros. Turk's Turban Mold

Mold, food, Turk's turban shape, field tile clay w/dark brown glaze, 7" d. (ILLUS.) **$80**
Mug, cylindrical, w/lightly molded lappet rim band, brown Rockingham glaze, 3 1/4" h., each (ILLUS. left & center, bottom of page) **$55**
Mug, cylindrical, yellowware, 2 3/4" h. (ILLUS. right with other mugs, bottom of page) **$80**

Three Rapp Brothers Mugs

Bison Paperweight

Paperweight, model of a bison, advertises Rock Sand Company, brown Rockingham glaze, 2 7/8" l. (ILLUS.) **$70**

Rapp Brothers Dutch Jug Pitcher

Pitcher, jug-type, milk (Dutch jug), brown Rockingham glaze, 3 1/2 pt. (ILLUS.) **$80**

Rapp Bros. Sauerkraut Crock

Sauerkraut crock, cover/press, impressed mark, dark brown glaze, 4 gal., rare, 11" h. (ILLUS.) **$175**
Stein, barrel-shaped w/"Trinke was klar ist und rede was wahr ist" embossed around rim & base, green, 1 pt. **$65**
Teapot, cov., acorn-shaped, mottled brown Rockingham glaze, 3 3/4 cup size **$90**

Cliftwood Art Potteries, Inc. (1920-1940)

Figural Cow Creamer

Creamer, figural cow, standing, tail forms handle, chocolate brown drip glaze, 3 3/4 x 6" (ILLUS.) **$100**

Cliftwood Figure of a Billiken

Figure of a Billiken, seated, dark brown Rockingham glaze, 10 1/2" h. (ILLUS.) **$125**
Flower frog, figural turtle, holes pierced on back, bluish mulberry drip glaze, 4" l. **$30**

Cliftwood Art Deco Lamp Base

Lamp base, Art Deco style, spherical body on four square legs, pinkish orchid drip glaze, base 4" h. (ILLUS., previous page) ... **$50**

Lamp Base with Sailing Ships

Lamp base, waisted cylindrical form w/a stepped shoulder, embossed panels around the sides showing a sailing ship, herbage green glaze, round metal foot, 11" h. (ILLUS.) **$70**

Cliftwood Model of a Bison

Model of bison, natural colors of light & dark brown, 9 1/2" l., 6 1/2" h. (ILLUS.)..... **$200**

Cliftwood Model of German Shepherd

Model of dog, German shepherd, reclining, white, 8 1/2" l., 6" h. (ILLUS.) **$75**
Model of elephant, standing, chocolate brown drip glaze, 7 1/4 x 13 1/2"............... **$125**

Cliftwood Model of a Frog

Model of frog, seated, glass eyes, shaded green to white glaze, 5" h. (ILLUS.) **$50**
Model of lioness, standing, chocolate brown drip glaze, 16" h., 5" h. **$95**

Cliftwood Deco Vase with Drip Glaze

Vase, 8" h., Art Deco style, square gently flaring sides w/a widely flared rim, chocolate brown drip glaze (ILLUS.) **$75**

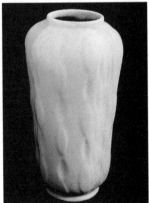

Cliftwood Vase with Chain Design

Vase, 10" h., footed, slightly flaring cylindrical body w/rounded base & shoulder w/a flat mouth, lightly embossed vertical chain bands, matte orchid glaze (ILLUS.) ... **$80**

Morton Pottery Canister Set

Vase, 16" h., footed baluster-form body w/flat rim, No. 114, bluish grey drip glaze ... **$85**

Vase, 18 1/4" h., urn form w/figural snakes swallowing fish handles, No. 132, chocolate brown drip glaze **$150**

Wall pocket, bullet-shaped w/handle on each side, matte turquoise & ivory glaze, 5" w., 7 1/2" h. **$70**

Wall pocket, elongated bell shape, No. 123, matte green glaze, 3 1/3" w., 8 3/4" h. **$50**

Morton Pottery Company (1922-1976)

Bank, figural, cat, sitting, yellow & white, 8 1/2" h. **$60**

Bank, figural, hen on nest, white w/red cold painted comb, black feather detail, yellow beak, 4" h. **$50**

Bank, figural, house, shoe-shaped, yellow w/green roof, 6 1/2" h. **$40**

Bank, figural, Little Brown Church, 2 5/8 x 3 5/8", 3 3/4" h. **$30**

Morton Pottery Teddy Bear Bank

Bank, figural, Teddy bear, seated w/legs outstretched, brown, pink, blue & black on white, 8" h. (ILLUS.) **$50**

Canister set: marked "Coffee," "Flour," "Sugar" & "Tea;" white cylindrical base w/yellow hat-shaped lid w/high button handle, 9" & 10" h., the set (ILLUS., top of page) **$55**

Cookie jar, cov., baby bird in blue & yellow spray over white **$60**

Cookie jar, cov., basket of fruit, green or brown basket w/colored fruit, No. 3720, each **$50**

Panda Bear Cookie Jar

Cookie jar, cov., panda bear, black & white, front paws crossed (ILLUS.) **$80**

Creamer & sugar bowl, model of chicken & rooster, black & white w/cold-painted red comb, pr. **$55**

Morton Pottery Egg Tray

Egg tray, hexagonal cluster of eggs & half-round eggs w/a figural chick in the center, 12" w. (ILLUS.).. **$45**

Figure of John F. Kennedy, Jr., standing on square base, right hand to head in salute position, gold paint trim, rare version, 7" h. **$125**

Grass grower, bisque, bust of "Jiggs," the comic strip character, 5" h. **$35**

Grass grower, bisque, model of a standing pig, 7 1/2" l., 3 3/4" h. **$20**

Head vase, woman w/1920s hairstyle, wide brim hat, white matte glaze **$75**

Head vase, woman w/1940s hairstyle, pill box hat, blue matte glaze **$65**

Head vase, woman w/upswept hairstyle, white w/red lips, bow in hair & heart-shaped locket **$40**

Morton Pottery Jardiniere

Jardiniere, squared form w/swelled sides, low rectangular mouth, tab side handles, small block feet, pink ground w/embossed floral sprig in blue & green, 4 1/2" h. (ILLUS.) **$30**

Morton Kerosene Lamp

Lamp, kerosene, brass fixture w/glass chimney, cylindrical body w/ribbed base & relief-molded swag design, white glaze (ILLUS.) **$70**

Morton Davy Crockett Lamp & Shade

Lamp, table, figural Davy Crockett w/bear beside tree, original shade (ILLUS.) **$200**

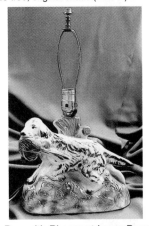

Dog with Pheasant Lamp Base

Lamp base, model of a black & white dog w/brown pheasant in mouth, relief-molded brown & green grassy base, double opening in planter, 5 x 10", 8 1/4" h. (ILLUS.) **$125**

Morton Pottery Bird Planter

Planter, model of a bird w/bright colors of yellow, blue, orange & red on a green grassy base, 5" h. (ILLUS.) **$24**

Morton Rooster on Rockers Planter

Planter, model of a rooster on rockers, yellow & pink sprayed glaze w/h.p. black & red trim, 4 1/2" h. (ILLUS.) **$30**

Morton Heart-shaped Vase

Vase, 12" h., model of a large & small red heart on an oval base, rare (ILLUS.) **$70**

Christmas Novelties

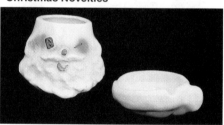

Figural Santa Claus Head Cigarette Box

Cigarette box, cov., figural Santa Claus head, hat cover becomes ashtray, cold painted red hat (ILLUS.) **$50**
Lollipop tree, w/holes to insert lollipops, green bisque, 9 1/4" h. **$60**
Model of a sleigh, Victorian style, white w/h.p. holly & berries, No. 3015 .... **$40**
Model of a sleigh, Victorian-style, red paint, No. 772 .... **$45**

Boston Terrier Planter

Planter, model of Boston terrier, sitting, black & white (ILLUS.) **$30**

Morton Santa Nut Dishes

Nut dish, oval, stylized Santa face, red background, rare, 2 1/2 x 3" (ILLUS. left) **$30**
Nut dish, oval, stylized Santa face, white background, rare, 2 1/2 x 3" (ILLUS. right) **$30**
Plate, 8", figural Santa Claus face, h.p. white w/blue eyes, pink cheeks, hat cold painted red **$50**
Plate, 12", figural Santa Claus face, white w/blue eyes, pink cheeks, hat cold painted red **$95**

Kitten & Fish Bowl TV Lamp

TV lamp, figural, black kitten seated on chartreuse stump base reaching for glass fish bowl, 9" h. (ILLUS.) **$75**
Vase, model of a tree trunk, matte green glaze, No. 260 .... **$30**

Morton Santa Claus Punch Set

Midwest Potteries Ducks

Punch set: punch bowl & 8 punch cups; figural Santa Claus head, white w/pink trim, green stone eyes, 9 pcs. (ILLUS. of part) **$295**

Midwest Potteries, Inc. (1940-1944)

Midwest Leaping Deer Book Ends

Book ends, Art Deco style, a stylized leaping deer against an upright disc, round foot, blue glaze, 7 3/4" h., pr. (ILLUS.) **$40**
Figure of baseball player, batter, grey uniform, 7 1/4" h. **$300**
Figure of baseball player, catcher, white uniform, 6 3/4" h. **$300**
Figure of baseball player, umpire, black uniform, 6 1/4" h. **$300**

Model of deer w/antlers, white w/gold trim, 12" h. **$50**
Model of ducks, three attached in graduated sizes, white w/yellow trim, 6" l. (ILLUS., second from top) **$36**
Model of flamingo, brownish green spray glaze, 10 1/2" h. **$50**

Midwest Potteries Flying Fish

Model of flying fish, stylized form in leaping pose, white glaze, 9 1/4" h. (ILLUS.) **$45**

Midwest Potteries Golden Pheasants

Pitcher, 4 1/2" h., figural, seated cow, brown & white drip glaze............................ **$30**

Midwest Potteries Deco-style Planter

Midwest Potteries Swan Model

Model of swan, large stylized bird w/tall upright curved & flared wings, long neck turned to back, dark brown & yellow drip glaze, 8" h. (ILLUS.) **$30**

Models of golden pheasants, white w/gold trim, male 4 3/4" h., female 4 1/2" h., pr. (ILLUS., top of page)................................... **$45**

Planter, figural, Art Deco style, standing draped nude woman flanked by globe-shaped planters, platinum glaze, 5 3/4" l., 5 1/2" h. (ILLUS.) **$55**

Planter, figural, Calico Cat, yellow & blue spatter on white, 7 1/2" h. (ILLUS. right, top next page) **$30**

Planter, figural, Gingham Dog, blue & yellow spatter on white, 7 1/2" h. (ILLUS. left with Calico Cat, top next page) **$30**

Midwest Potteries Hen & Rooster

Models of hen & rooster, white w/cold painted red & yellow trim, hen 7" h., rooster 8" h., pr. (ILLUS.) **$50**

Midwest Potteries Owl TV Lamp

TV lamp, model of an owl w/spread wings, sprayed brown on white ground, green eyes, 12" h. (ILLUS.)................................... **$95**

Calico Cat & Gingham Dog Planters

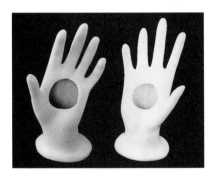

Midwest Potteries Hand Vases

Vase, 4 1/2" h., bud-type, model of an open
hand, white matte glaze (ILLUS. right)....... **$25**
Vase, 4 1/2" h., bud-type, model of open
hand, turquoise matte glaze (ILLUS. left) ... **$25**

American Art Potteries (1947-1963)

American Art Candlestick

Candlestick, three-light, open doughnut-
shaped ring fitted w/three sockets, wide
round foot, dark bluish green glaze, No.
140J, 7 1/2" w., 6 1/2" h. (ILLUS.).............. **$35**
Lamp, table, double cornucopia form, white
w/gold trim, 13" h. (ILLUS., top next col-
umn) **$50**

Double Cornucopia Table Lamp

French Poodle Table Lamp

Lamp, table, figural, model of a seated
French poodle, black ground w/sprayed
pink on bands of curls, 15" h. (ILLUS.) **$70**

Crouching Panther Table Lamp

Lamp, table, figural, stylized crouching panther on a tall tree trunk, rose & black spray glaze, 11 1/2" h. (ILLUS.) **$60**

American Art Bird on Stump Model

Model of bird on stump, white w/gold trim, 7" h. (ILLUS.) **$25**
Model of cockatoo on stump, natural colors, No. 315, 7" h. **$30**

Rearing Horse by American Art

Model of horse, rearing position, brown & green spray glaze (ILLUS.) **$25**
Model of pig, black w/white band, No. 89, 5 1/2" h. **$45**

Chunky Pony Figural Planter

Planter, figural, model of a chunky standing pony, dark streaky mauve & pink spray glaze, sticker on side, No. 49, 5 1/4" l., 4 3/4" h. (ILLUS.) **$15**

Bird on Stump Planter

Planter, figural, model of a long-tailed bird perched on a stump, green & brown spray glaze, 7" h. (ILLUS.) **$20**

Recumbent Deer Figural Planter

Planter, figural, model of a recumbent deer w/head turned over shoulder, green & brown spray glaze, 5" h. (ILLUS.) **$20**

Doe and Fawn Figural Planter

Planter, figural, model of a standing doe bending her head down to her reclining fawn, mottled brown glaze, No. 322J, 7 1/4" h. (ILLUS.) $25

Planter, figural, model of a swordfish, blue & mauve spray glaze, No. 307P, 7 1/2 x 11" $25

TV lamp, figural, model of a standing doe bending her head down to her reclining fawn, mottled brown glaze, No. 322J, 7 1/4" h. $50

Vase, 8" h., ewer-form, blue & mauve glaze w/gold trim, No. 209G $35

Vase, 10 1/2" h., double cornucopia form, white w/gold trim, No. 208B $30

Vase, 12" h., octagonal, pink & mauve spray glaze, No. 214G $25

Wall pocket, figural, model of a dustpan, white w/h.p. underglaze decoration, No. 81C... $24

Wall pocket, figural, model of a red apple on a green leaf, No. 127N $20

Wall pocket, figural, model of a teapot, white w/h.p. underglaze decoration, No. 79C... $24

Window sill box, arched diamond design, green & pink spray glaze, No. 32I, 3 1/2 x 4 x 10" $30

Window sill box, white w/h.p. ivy, No. 25D, 2 1/2 x 4 x 13" $30

Mulberry

Mulberry or Flow Mulberry ironstone wares were produced in the Staffordshire district of England in the period between 1840 and 1870 at many of the same factories that produced its close "cousin," Flow Blue china. In fact, some of the early Flow Blue patterns were also decorated with the dark blackish or brownish purple mulberry coloration and feature the same heavy smearing or "flown" effect. Produced on sturdy ironstone bodies, the designs were either transfer-printed or hand-painted (Brushstroke) with an Asian, Scenic, Floral or Marble design. Some patterns were also decorated with additional colors over or under the glaze; these are designated in the following listings as "w/polychrome."

Quite a bit of this ware is still to be found and is becoming increasingly sought-after by collectors, although presently its values lag somewhat behind similar Flow Blue pieces. The standard references to Mulberry wares is Petra Williams' book, Flow Blue China and Mulberry Ware, Similarity and

Value Guide and Mulberry Ironstone - Flow Blue's Best Kept Little Secret, by Ellen R. Hill.

ACADIA (maker unknown, ca. 1850)
Creamer, 6" h., Classic Gothic shape $300

Acadia Plate

Plate, 8" d. (ILLUS.) $200

AMERILLIA (Podmore, Walker & Co., ca. 1850)
Egg cup $200
Plate, 9 1/2" $75

Amerillia Covered Vegetable Dish

Vegetable dish, cov. (ILLUS.) $300

ATHENS (Charles Meigh, ca. 1845)
Creamer, 6", vertical-paneled Gothic shape
.... $150
Cup plate $100

Athens Pitcher

Pitcher, 6-paneled, 10" h. (ILLUS.)............... $350
Punch cup $125

Sugar, cov., vertical-paneled Gothic shape .. $200

ATHENS (Wm. Adams & Son, ca. 1849)
Cup plate $95
Plate, 8 1/2" d... $55
Soup Plate, w/flanged rim, 9" d...................... $75
Sugar, cov., full-paneled Gothic shape $200
Teapot, cov., full-paneled Gothic shape........ $275

AVA (T.J. & J. Mayer, ca. 1850)
Cup & saucer, handleless, w/polychrome $95
Plate, 9 1/2" d., w/polychrome........................ $85
Plate, 10 1/2" d., w/polychrome...................... $95
Platter, 16" l., w/polychrome $250

Ava Sauce Tureen & Undertray

Sauce tureen, cover & undertray, w/poly-
    chrome, 3 pcs. (ILLUS.) $500

BEAUTIES OF CHINA (Mellor Venables & Co., ca. 1845)
Cup plate $95
Plate, 7 1/2" d., w/polychrome........................ $65
Platter, 14" l., w/polychrome $225
Sauce tureen, cover, ladle & undertray,
    long octagon, 4 pcs. $650

BOCHARA (James Edwards, ca. 1850)
Creamer, full-paneled Gothic shape, 6" h. $150
Pitcher, 7 1/2" h., full-paneled Gothic shape
    .... $170
Plate, 10 1/2" d.. $75

Bochara (James Edwards, ca. 1850)

Bochara Flow Mulberry Teapot

Teapot, cov., Pedestaled Gothic shape
    (ILLUS.) $350

BRUNSWICK (Mellor Venables & Co., ca. 1845)
Plate, 7 1/2" d., w/polychrome........................ $65
Platter, 16" l., w/polychrome $275
Relish dish, stubby mitten-shaped, w/poly-
    chrome $150
Sugar, cov., Classic Gothic shape, w/poly-
    chrome $225

BRYONIA (Paul Utzchneider & Co., ca. 1880)
Cup & saucer, handled.................................. $50
Gravy boat $100
Plate, 7 1/2" d... $35

Bryonia Plate

Plate, 9 1/2" d. (ILLUS.) $40

CEYLON (Charles Meigh, ca. 1840)
Plate, 9 1/2" d... $75
Plate, 10 1/2" d., w/polychrome...................... $85
Platter, 14" l., w/polychrome $175
Vegetable bowl, open, small $125

CHUSAN (P. Holdcroft, ca. 1850)
Plate, 9 1/2" d... $80

Chusan Potato Bowl

Potato bowl, 11" d. (ILLUS.)......................... $250

CLEOPATRA (F. Morley & Co., ca. 1850)
Basin & ewer, w/polychrome........................ $600
Plate, 9 1/2" d... $60
Soap box, cover & drainer, 3 pcs.............. $300
Soup plate, w/flanged rim, 9" d..................... $75

COREA (Joseph Clementson, ca. 1850)
Cup & saucer, handleless $65
Sugar, cov., long hexagon $250
Teapot, cov., long hexagon......................... $350

COREAN (Podmore, Walker & Co., ca. 1850)
Cup plate $100
Cup & saucer, handled, large..................... $125
Relish, mitten-shaped $135
Sauce tureen, cover & undertray, 3 pcs.
.... $400

Corean Covered Sugar
Sugar, cov., oval bulbous style (ILLUS.)....... $350

COTTON PLANT (J. Furnival, ca. 1850)
Creamer, paneled grape shape, w/poly-
chrome, 6 5/8" h....................................... $200

Cotton Plant (J. Furnival, ca. 1850)

Cotton Plant Mulberry Teapot
Teapot, cov., cockscomb handle, trimmed
in polychrome (ILLUS.) $650

CYPRUS (Wm. Davenport, ca. 1845)
Cup plate $95

Cyprus Gravy
Gravy boat, unusual handle (ILLUS.) $200
Pitcher, 11" h., 6-sided $250

DORA (E. Challinor, ca. 1850)
Plate, 9 1/2" d.. $85

Dora (E. Challinor, ca. 1850)

Dora Baltic Shape Teapot
Teapot, cov., Baltic shape (ILLUS.) $650

FERN & VINE (maker unknown, ca. 1850)

Fern & Vine Creamer
Creamer, Classic Gothic style, 6" h. (ILLUS.) . $350
Plate, 7 1/2" d... $95

MARBLE (Mellor Venables, ca. 1845)
Plate, 9 1/2" d... $50
Teapot, cov., child's, Vertical Paneled Gothic shape.. $350

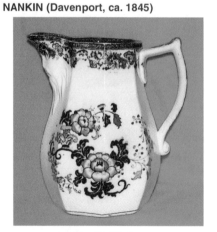

Marble Pattern Gothic Shape Teapot

Teapot, cov., Vertical Paneled Gothic shape (ILLUS.).. $600

MEDINA (J. Furnival, ca. 1850)
Cup & saucer, handleless $55
Gravy boat $135
Sugar, cov., cockscomb handle.................... $300

NANKIN (Davenport, ca. 1845)

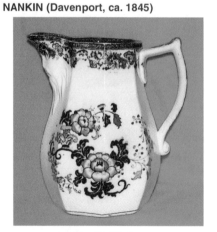

Nankin Pitcher

Pitcher, 8" h., mask spout jug w/polychrome (ILLUS.).. $350
Plate, 8 1/2" d., w/polychrome.......................... $75

NING PO (R. Hall, ca. 1840)
Cup & saucer, handleless $85
Plate, 10 1/2" d.. $95
Soup plate, w/flanged rim, 10" d.................... $95

PARISIAN GROUPS (J. Clementson, ca. 1850)
Plate, 7 1/2" d., w/polychrome......................... $60
Plate, 8 1/2" d., w/polychrome......................... $70
Sauce dish, w/polychrome............................. $65

Parisian Sauce Tureen & Undertray

Sauce tureen, cover & undertray, w/polychrome, 3 pcs. (ILLUS.).......................... $400

PELEW (Edward Challinor, ca. 1850)
Cup & saucer, handleless, pedestaled.......... $75
Plate, 7 1/2" d... $50
Plate, 10 1/2" d.. $70
Punch cup, ring handle................................ $100

Pelew Pumpkin-shaped Teapot

Teapot, c0v., pumpkin shape (ILLUS.).......... $450

PERUVIAN (John Wedge Wood, ca. 1850)

Peruvian Cup & Saucer

Cup & saucer, handleless, "double bulge" (ILLUS.).. $95
Gravy boat $145

Teapot, cov., 16-Paneled shape $400
Waste bowl, "double bulge" $150

PHANTASIA (J. Furnival, ca. 1850)

Phantasia Creamer

Creamer, w/polychrome, cockscomb han-
  dle, 6" h. (ILLUS.)..................................... $450
Cup plate, w/polychrome $95
Plate, 9 1/2" d., w/polychrome........................ $85
Sugar, cov., w/polychrome, cockscomb
  handle $500
Teapot, cov., w/polychrome, cockscomb
  handle $700

RHONE SCENERY (T.J. & J. Mayer, ca. 1850)
Gravy boat $150
Plate, 7 1/2" d.. $35
Plate, 10 1/2" d... $55
Sauce tureen, cover & undertray, 3 pcs.
  .... $300
Sugar, cov., full-paneled Gothic shape $200

SCINDE (T. Walker, ca. 1847)
Creamer, Classic Gothic shape, 6" h. $100
Plate, 9 1/2" d.. $70
Soup plate, w/flanged rim, 9" d...................... $80
Teapot, cov., Classic Gothic shape............... $300

SHAPOO (T. & R. Boote, ca. 1850)
Plate, 8 1/2" d.. $75
Sugar, cov., Primary shape........................... $300
Teapot, cov., Primary shape $450
Vegetable dish, cov., flame finial................. $300

TEMPLE (Podmore, Walker & Co., ca. 1850)
Cup plate $75
Cup & saucer, handled (ILLUS., top next
  column) $75
Plate, 8 1/2" d.. $55
Sugar, cov., Classic Gothic shape $200
Teapot, cov., Classic Gothic shape............... $300

VINCENNES (J. Alcock, ca. 1840)
Cup & saucer, handleless, thumbprint $95
Plate, 7 1/2" d.. $60
Plate, 10 1/2" d... $80

Temple Cup & Saucer

Vincennes Punch Cup

Punch cup (ILLUS.)..................................... $125
Soup tureen, cover & undertray, 10-sided,
  3 pcs. $2,000

VINCENNES (J. & G. Alcock, ca. 1845)

Vincennes Compote

Compote, Gothic Cameo shape (ILLUS.)..... $650

WASHINGTON VASE (Podmore, Walker & Co., ca. 1850)
Creamer, Classic Gothic shape, 6" h. $225
Cup & saucer, handleless $95
Plate, 10 1/2" d... $85
Soup plate, w/flanged rim, 9" d...................... $85
Vegetable bowl, cov.................................... $300

WHAMPOA (Mellor Venables & Co., ca. 1845)

Gravy boat $165
Plate, 10 1/2" d.. $95
Sauce tureen, cov., long octagon shape, 2
  pcs.. $300

WREATH (Thomas Furnival, ca. 1850)

Wreath Ewer

Ewer (ILLUS.)... $300
Plate, 9 1/2" d... $75

Newcomb College

This pottery was established in the art department of Newcomb College, New Orleans, Louisiana, in 1897. Each piece was hand-thrown and bore the potter's mark & decorator's monogram on the base. It was always a studio business and never operated as a factory. Its pieces are, therefore, scarce, with the early wares being eagerly sought. The pottery closed in 1940.

Newcomb College Pottery Mark

Small Quality Newcomb College Vase

Vase, 3 1/4" h., small bulbous ovoid body w/a wide flat mouth, oak trees & Spanish moss design in shades of dark blue & pink, by Anna Frances Simpson, potted by Jonathan Hunt, impressed logo & date code for 1929 (ILLUS.).......................... $3,105

Squatty Bulbous Floral Newcomb Vase

Vase, 5 1/4" h., footed wide squatty bulbous form tapering to a wide flat mouth, deeply carved around the shoulder w/a wide band of large stylized white blossoms & green leaves above a dark blue matte ground, potter Joseph Meyer, ca. 1925, professionally repaired rim chip (ILLUS.).......... $1,150

Extremely Rare Early Newcomb Vase

Vase, 5 1/2" h., 7 1/4" d., a wide low squatty bulbous body w/a wide shoulder tapering to a tiny cylindrical neck, finely painted w/a repeating design of large blue irises & stylized scrolling foliage, highlighted w/dark mustard yellow including a band of small irises around the small neck, glossy glaze, painted by Elizabeth Goelet Rogers, potted by Joseph Meyer, dated 1898 (ILLUS.)...................................... $19,550
Vase, 8" h., slightly swelled cylindrical form w/a rounded shoulder tapering to a short cylindrical neck, molded w/pale blue leaves & berry clusters drooping down

Newcomb Vase with Berries & Leaves

from the rim against a shaded dark blue matte ground, potter Joseph Meyer, Shape No. 250, 1923 (ILLUS.)............. **$3,220**

Very Rare Tulip-decorated Newcomb Vase

Vase, 8 1/4" h., baluster-form body w/a wide low mouth, modeled w/large dark blue tulip blossoms on tall dark green leafy stems around the sides against a white ground, glossy glaze, painted by Harriet Joor, ca. 1900 (ILLUS.) **$21,850**

Nippon

"Nippon" is a term used to describe a wide range of porcelain wares produced in Japan from the late 19th century until about 1921. It was in 1891 that the United States implemented the McKinley Tariff Act, which required that all wares exported to the United States carry a marking indicating their country of origin. The Japanese chose to use "Nippon," their name for Japan. In 1921 the import laws were revised and the words "Made in" had to be added to the markings. Japan was also required to replace the "Nippon" with the English name "Japan" on all wares sent to the United States.

Many Japanese factories produced Nippon porcelain, much of it hand-painted with ornate floral or landscape decoration and heavy gold decoration, applied beading and slip-trailed designs referred to as "moriage." We indicate the specific marking used on a piece, when known, at the end of each listing. Be aware that a number of Nippon markings have been reproduced and used on new porcelain wares.

Important reference books on Nippon include: The Collector's Encyclopedia of Nippon Porcelain, Series One through Three, by Joan F. Van Patten (Collector Books, Paducah, Kentucky) and The Wonderful World of Nippon Porcelain, 1891-1921 by Kathy Wojciechowski (Schiffer Publishing, Ltd., Atglen, Pennsylvania).

Nippon Humidor with Canoe Scene

Humidor, cov., three square block feet supporting the wide slightly tapering cylindrical body w/a slightly tapering cover w/large mushroom finial, the body decorated w/a lanscape of a man in a canoe w/a stag in green bushes on the shore, dark yellow to pale cream ground, the feet & top rim decorated w/geometric decorative bands w/stylized symbals, matching band around the cover, 7" h. (ILLUS.)... **$575**

Nippon Vase with Lady & Peacock Scene

Vase, 5 3/4" h., bulbous ovoid body tapering to a short flaring neck trimmed in gold & flanked by arched gold shoulder handles, the body centered by a large gold oval reserve painted w/a full-length portrait of an exotic young woman standing in front of a peacock, surrounded by an overal good lattice & pink rose decoration on the white ground, green Maple Leaf mark, minor gold wear (ILLUS., previous page) **$432**

Pretty Nippon Sharkskin Vase

Vase, 7 1/8" h., "sharkskin" technique, slender slightly tapering cylindrical body w/a narrow shoulder centered by a short neck w/widely flaring mouth, arched & pierced-loop gold shoulder handles, the sides h.p. w/a stylized landscape w/tall trees in the foreground & small houses & a lake in the distance, done in pastel shades of blue, yellow, green, lavender & orange, purple Cherry Blossom mark, tiny glaze nick in the base (ILLUS.) **$230**

Fine Nippon Tapestry-style Vase

Vase, 9 1/2" h., tapestry-type, tall gently tapering cylindrical body w/a flat rim, the upper body decorated w/a wide band of stylized geometric designs in shades of green, blue, rose red & gold & faux jewels, delicate gold beaded swags sus-

pended down the sides, blue Maple Leaf mark (ILLUS.) **$1,150**

Noritake

Noritake china, still in production in Japan, has been exported in large quantities to this country since early in the last century. Although the Noritake Company first registered in 1904, it did not use "Noritake" as part of its backstamp until 1918. Interest in Noritake has escalated as collectors now seek out pieces made between the "Nippon" era and World War II (1921-41). The Azalea pattern is also popular with collectors.

Noritake Mark

Ashtray, center Queen of Clubs decoration, 4" w. **$38**
Ashtray, center Indian head decoration, 5 1/2" w. **$275**

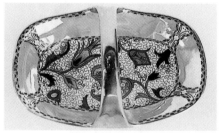

Noritake Basket with Flowers

Basket, oblong w/center handle, gold lustre ground, interior w/center stylized floral decoration & geometric design in each corner & around rim, 7 3/4" l., 3" h. (ILLUS.) **$85**
Basket-vase, 7 1/2" h. **$115**
Berry set: master bowl & 6 sauce dishes; decal & h.p. purple orchids, green leaves & pods decoration on green ground, 7 pcs. **$70**
Bonbon, raised gold decoration, 6 1/4" w. **$25**

Art Deco Bowl

Bowl, 6 1/2" d., 2" h., fluted sides of alternating light & dark grey panels w/pointed rims, center w/Art Deco floral decoration (ILLUS., previous page) **$160**

Art Deco Checkerboard & Roses Bowl

Bowl, 8 3/4" d., 2" h., Art Deco-style orange & white checkerboard ground decorated w/stylized dark brown roses & leaves outlined in grey & grey stems (ILLUS.) **$270**
Bowl, soup, Azalea patt. **$30**
Butter dish, cover & drain insert, Azalea patt., 3 pcs... **$80**
Cake plate, Sheridan patt., 9 3/4" d. **$20**

Noritake Oriental Scene Cake Plate

Cake plate, rectangular, open-handled, turquoise border w/oval center Oriental scene on black ground, 10" l. (ILLUS.)...... **$140**
Cake set: 14 x 6 1/4" oblong tray w/pierced handles & six 6 1/2" d. serving plates; white w/pale green & gold floral border, 7 pcs.. **$90**
Candlesticks, Indian motif decoration, 3 1/4" h., pr.. **$160**
Candy dish, octagonal, Tree in Meadow patt. **$60**
Candy dish, cov., figural bird finial, scalloped rim, blue lustre finish, 6 1/2 x 7 1/4" ... **$90**
Celery set: celery tray & 6 individual salt dips, decal & h.p. florals & butterflies decoration, 7 pcs... **$90**
Celery tray, Azalea patt. **$50**

Figural Swan Cigarette Holder

Cigarette holder, footed, figural swan, orange lustre w/black neck & head, black outlining on wing feathers & tail, 3" w., 4 1/2" h. (ILLUS.) **$310**

Cigarette Jar in Art Deco Style

Cigarette jar, cov., bell-shaped cover w/bird finial, Art Deco-style silhouetted scenic decoration of woman in chair & man standing, both holding cigarettes, 4 3/4" h., 3 1/2" d. (ILLUS.) **$575**
Coffee set: cov. coffeepot, creamer, cov. sugar bowl & four cups & saucers; greyish blue butterfly, pink florals & grey leaves decoration, 11 pcs. **$255**
Cologne bottle w/flower cluster stopper, Art Deco man wearing checkered cape, lustered sides, 6 3/4" h.............................. **$470**

Noritake Figural Condiment Set

Condiment set: cov. mustard jar & pr. salt & pepper shakers on handled tray; bulbous blue lustre mustard jar w/red rosebud finial, green leaves, ovoid shakers w/clown head tops, red, blue, orange & white lustre, blue lustre tray, 7" l., the set (ILLUS., previous page) $630

Condiment set: cov. mustard jar & pr. salt & pepper shakers on handled tray; lustre borders & tops, 5 1/2" w. tray, the set $75

Noritake Cracker Jar with Lake Scene

Cracker jar, cov., footed spherical body decorated w/a black band w/white swords & shields design & center oval yellow medallion w/scene of white sailboat on lake, white clouds in distance & blue stylized tree in foreground, black & white geometric design bands around rim & cover edge, orange lustre ground, 7" h. (ILLUS.) $210

Creamer, Azalea patt. $25

Creamer, Tree in Meadow patt. $20

Creamer & cov. sugar bowl, Azalea patt., pr. $75

Creamer & cov. sugar bowl, blue scenic decoration, brown borders, pr. $65

Creamer & Sugar in Art Deco Style

Creamer & open sugar bowl, Art Deco-style checked decoration in black, blue, brown & white, orange lustre interior basket-shaped sugar bowl w/overhead handle, creamer 3" h., sugar bowl 4 1/2" h., pr. (ILLUS.) $125

Scenic Creamer & Sugar Shaker Set

Creamer & sugar shaker, berry set-type, orange lustre interior, scenic decoration w/cottage, bridge & trees above floral cluster, blue lustre ground, 6 1/2" h., pr. (ILLUS.) $85

Noritake Floral Cruet Set

Cruet set w/original stoppers, the two conjoined globular bottles set at angles & joined w/a handle at the shoulder, shaded orange lustre ground decorated w/green & yellow clover leaves & stems, 6" l., 3 1/2" h. (ILLUS.) $130

Cup & saucer, demitasse, Tree in Meadow patt. $25

Cup & saucer, Tree in Meadow patt. $20

Desk set: heart-shaped tray w/pen rack at front & two cov. jars w/floral finials; decal & h.p. florals, 6 1/2" w. $385

Dinner bell, figural Chinaman, 3 1/2" h. $250

Dish, blue lustre trim, 5" sq. $20

Dresser box, cov., figural woman on lid, lustre finish, 5" h. $770

Figurine, maiden carrying a bundle of sticks on her head $55

Fish plates, h.p. & decal w/h.p. center fish decoration, gold borders, 8 1/2" d., pr. $125

Flower holder, model of bird on stump, base pierced w/four flower holes, 4 1/2" h. $95

Noritake Teapot with Stylized Flowers

Teapot, cov., footed bulbous ovoid body w/angled green shoulder & domed cover w/oval loop finial, C-scroll handle & long serpentine spout, large stylized blossoms on a slender leafy tree, in shades of blue, purple, green & brown, Noritake mark "27.1 DS," 8 1/4" l., 5 3/4" h. (ILLUS.)........... **$45**

Squatty Noritake Howo Pattern Teapot

Teapot, cov., Howo patt., squatty bulbous body w/serpentine spout & C-form handle, low domed cover w/arched loop handle, marked "Noritake - Howo - Made in Japan," ca. 1930s, 8" l., 4 1/2" h. (ILLUS.).................................. **$55-65**

Lovely Noritake Iris Pattern Teapot

Teapot, cov., Iris patt., Art Deco style, tall gently flaring body w/angled handle, tall angled spout, angled shoulder & peaked cover w/open diamond-shaped finial, blue iris & green leaves design, Noritake mark "54DS," 7 1/4" h. (ILLUS.) **$130**

Rare Noritake Lady & Bird Teapot

Teapot, cov., Lady & Bird in Garden patt., tall footed urn-form body w/long serpentine spout, tall arched black-trimmed blue handle, domed cover in red w/black urn-shaped finial, dark blue background w/an Art Deco-style scene of a crinolined lady holding a bird in one hand w/a birdcage in front of her, in shades of yellow, green, black, white, light blue & orange, Noritake mark "27.1 DS," 6 3/4" l., 6 1/4" h. (ILLUS.).................................... **$645**

Toast rack, two-slice, blue & yellow decoration **$45**

Tray, pierced handles, decal & h.p. fruit border, lustre center, 11" w. **$80**

Long Floral-decorated Noritake Tray

Tray, rectangular, pierced end handles, floral decoration on white ground, green edge trim w/brown trim on handles, 17 1/2" l. (ILLUS.)....................................... **$90**

Scenic Noritake Vase with Grape Handles

Vase, 4 1/4" h., 5 1/4" d., footed bulbous body w/figural leaf & grape cluster handles, gold & blue lustre ground decorated w/scene of trees & children (ILLUS.)......... **$365**

Vase, 7" h., fan-shaped w/ruffled rim, fruit & vines decoration, green & blue base.......... **$90**

Unusual Noritake Butterfly Vase

Vase, 8" h., footed ovoid body w/squared rim handles, butterfly decoration on shaded & streaked blue & orange ground (ILLUS.).. **$250**

Vase, 8 1/4" h., Indian motif & lustre decoration **$140**

Vegetable bowl, open, round, Tree in Meadow patt.. **$30**

Vegetable dish, cov., round, Azalea patt........ **$75**

Scenic Noritake Wall Plaque

Wall plaque, pierced to hang, silhouetted Art Deco-style scene of woman in gown w/full ruffled skirt, sitting on couch & holding mirror, white lustre ground, 8 3/4" d. (ILLUS.)... **$840**

Wall pocket, double, relief-molded floral cresting backplate, stylized florals & bird of paradise decoration, lustre border, 8" l.. **$200**

Wall pocket, single, h.p. tree & cottage lakeside scene on blue lustered ground, 8" h. **$90**

Waste bowl, Azalea patt. **$55**

Old Ivory

Old Ivory china was produced in Silesia, Germany, in the late 1800s and takes its name from the soft white background coloring. A wide range of table pieces was made with the various patterns, usually identified by a number rather than a name.

The following prices are averages for Old Ivory at this time. Rare patterns will command higher prices, and there is some variance in prices geographically. These prices are also based on the item being perfect. Cups are measured across the top opening.

Basket, handled, No. U2 Deco blank............ **$450**

Berry set: 10 1/2" master bowl & six small berries; No. 7 Clairon blank, the set......... **$300**

Berry set: 10 1/2" d. master bowl & six small berries; No. 15 Clairon blank, the set **$285**

Bonbon, inside handle, No. 62 Florette blank, rare, 6" l. **$500**

Bone dish, No. 16, Worcester blank, rare **$400**

Bouillon cup & saucer, No. 16 Clairon blank, 3 1/2" d. **$250**

Bowl, 5 1/2" d., No. 7 Clairon blank **$45**

Bowl, 5 1/2" d., waste, No. 11 Clairon blank **$285**

No. 84 Worchester Bowl

Bowl, 5 1/2" d., waste, No. 84 Worchester blank (ILLUS.) **$300**

Bowl, 6 1/2" d., No. 22 Clairon blank **$150**

Bowl, 10" d., No. 16 Clairon blank **$100**

Bowl, 10" d., No. 73 Empire blank **$250**

Old Ivory Bun Tray

Bun tray, oval w/open handles, No. 122 Alice blank, 10" l. (ILLUS.) **$300**

Butter pat, No. 15 Mignon blank, 3 1/4" d. ... **$150**

Cake plate, tab-handled, No. U15 Florette blank, 9 1/2" d. **$200**

Cake plate, open-handled, No. 200 Deco blank, 9 1/2" h. **$100**

Cake plate, open-handled, No. 10 Clairon blank, 10 1/2" d. **$125**

Pieces from No. 12 Clairon Cake Set

Cake set: 11" d. serving plate & 5 individu-
al plates; No. 12 Clairon blank, the set
(ILLUS. of two pieces) **$450**
Celery dish, No. 22 Clairon blank, 11 1/4" l.
.... **$300**
Celery dish, No. 28 Clairon blank, 11 1/4" l.
.... **$150**
Center bowl, No. 84 Deco Variant blank,
12 1/2" d. **$500**

No. 90 Clairon Charger

Charger, No. 90 Clairon blank, 13 1/2" d.
(ILLUS.) **$500**
Charger, No. 16 Clairon blank, 13" d. **$300**
Charger, 13 1/2" l., No. 75 Alice blank **$400**
Chocolate set: 9 1/2" h. cov. pot & six cups
& saucers; No. 53 Empire blank, rare, the
set **$1,500**
Chocolate set: 9 1/2" h. cov. pot & six cups
& saucers; No. 75 Empire blank, the set ... **$900**
Chowder cup & saucer, No. U29 Eglantine
blank, 4" d. **$300**
Cider cup & saucer, No. 16 Clairon blank,
3" d. **$150**

Empire Blank Demitasse Coffeepot

Coffeepot, cov., demitasse, No. 123 Em-
pire blank (ILLUS.) **$500-650**
Compote, 9" d., open, No. U11 Alice blank,
rare **$600**
Cracker jar, No. 11 Clairon blank, 8 1/2" h. .. **$400**
Cracker jar, cov., No. 33 Empire blank,
5 1/2" h. **$500**
Cracker jar, cov., No. 39 Empire blank, very
rare, 5 1/2" h. **$1,200**
Cracker jar, cov., No. 15 Clairon blank,
8 1/2" h. **$500**

No. 75 Deco Variant Creamer

Creamer, No. 75 Deco blank variant, ser-
vice, 5 1/2" h. (ILLUS.) **$195**
Creamer & cov. sugar bowl, No. 10
Clairon blank, 4" h., pr. **$175**
Creamer & cov. sugar bowl, service size,
No. 84 Deco variant blank, pr. **$400**
Creamer & cov. sugar bowl, service size,
No. U17 Eglantine blank, pr. **$500**
Creamer & cov. sugar bowl, No. 39 Em-
pire blank, rare, 3 1/2" & 5 1/2" h., pr. **$600**
Creamer & cov. sugar bowl, No. 99 Em-
pire blank, rare, 5 1/2" h., pr. **$500**

Louis XVI Blank Creamer & Sugar

Creamer & cov. sugar bowl, No. 76 Louis XVI blank, rare, pr. (ILLUS., bottom previous page) **$350-450**

Cup & saucer, demi, No. 10 Clairon blank, 2 1/2" d. **$135**

Cup & saucer, No. 22 Clairon blank, very rare, 3 3/4" d. **$500**

Cup & saucer, cov., bouillon-type, No. 73 Alice blank, rare, 3 1/2" d. **$400**

Cup & saucer, No. 99 Empire blank, rare, 3 1/2" d. **$450**

Cup & saucer, No. 16 Clairon blank, 3 1/4" d. **$75**

No. 90 Clairon Blank Cup & Saucer

Cup & saucer, No. 90 Clairon blank (ILLUS.) **$75-95**

Cup & saucer, No. 203 Deco blank, 3 1/4" d. **$95**

Cup & saucer, No. 82 Empire blank **$75-95**

Deco Variant Cup & Saucer & Teapot

Demitasse cup & saucer, No. 75 Deco variant blank (ILLUS. left) **$125-140**

Demitasse cup & saucer, No. 5 Elysee blank, rare, 2 1/2" d. **$200**

Demitasse pot, No. 97 Clairon blank, very rare, 7 1/2" h. **$2,000**

Demitasse pot, cov., No. 73 Clairon blank, 7 1/2" h. **$650**

Demitasse pot, cov., No. 62 Florette blank, very rare, 7 1/2" h. **$1,200**

Demitasse set: 7 1/2" pot & 4 cups & saucers; No. U22 Eglantine blank **$1,800**

Dish, tri-lobed, No. 202 Deco blank, 6" w. **$95**

Dish, tri-lobed, No. 204 Rivoli blank, 6" w. **$175**

Dresser tray, No. 90 Clairon blank, 11 1/2" l. **$350**

Dresser tray, No. 34 Empire blank **$250**

Egg cup, No. 84 Eglantine blank, very rare, 2 1/2" h. **$500**

Ice cream bowl, No. 6 Eglantine blank (ILLUS., top next column) **$300-400**

Jam dish, individual, No. 28 Alice blank **$150**

Eglantine Blank Ice Cream Bowl

Jam jar, cov., No. 137 Deco blank, 3 1/2" h. **$400**

Louis XVI Muffineer & Salt & Peppers

Muffineer, No. 84 Louis XVI blank (ILLUS. left) **$350-450**

Mustache cup & saucer, No. 4 Elysee blank, 3 1/2" d. **$500**

Mustard pot, cov., No. 12 Clairon blank, 3 3/4" h. **$425**

Olive dish, No. 75 Empire blank, 6 1/2" l. **$75**

Pickle dish, No. 32 Empire blank, 8 1/2" l. **$75**

Pin tray, No. U22 Eglantine blank **$350**

Acanthus Blank Water Pitcher

Pitcher, water, No. 84 Acanthus blank (ILLUS.) **$1,000-1,200.0**

Pitcher, 8" h., water, No. 11 Acanthus blank **$1,200**

Plate, 6 1/2" d., No. 121 Alice blank **$50**

Plate, 8 1/2" d., No. 60 Alice blank **$85**

Plate, 6 1/2" d., No. 10 Clairon blank **$45**

Plate, 7 1/2" d., No. 12 Clairon blank **$85**

Plate, 7 1/2" d., No. 4 Elysee blank **$65**

Old Ivory Etoile Teapot

Teapot, cov., Etoile blank, lobed ovoid body w/ruffled scalloped base w/embossed decoration & ruffled cutout rim, inset domed lid w/C-scroll finial, embossed C-scroll handle & serpentine spout, the body w/panels of embossing, the body & lid decorated w/pink-centered cream-colored roses & green leaves, line decoration on rim, marked "Old Ivory," Hermann Ohme, Germany, 7 1/2" h. (ILLUS.).......... **$850**

Old Ivory Mignon Teapot

Teapot, cov., Mignon blank, lobed bulbous body on ruffled foot, short flaring neck w/ruffled rim, peaked lid w/ornate cutout finial, ornate C-scroll handle w/thumbrest & serpentine spout, the body & lid decorated w/embossed decoration & sprigs of delicate green flowers & leaves, gold highlights on foot, rim, spout & handle, Hermann Ohme, Germany, 8" h. (ILLUS.) **$135**

Old Ivory Swirl Teapot

Teapot, cov., Swirl blank, footed bulbous body w/delicate swirled ribs, flaring lip, domed lid w/finial, applied ribbed scroll loop handle w/thumbrest, serpentine

spout, clear glaze, the body decorated w/large wine-colored floral design, the lid & spout w/wine-colored floral sprigs, the finial, rim, handle & base highlighted in gold, Hermann Ohme, Germany, 8 1/2" h. (ILLUS.)..................................... **$250**
Teapot, cov., No. 200 Deco blank, 8 1/2" l.... **$500**
Teapot, cov., No. 75 Deco variant blank (ILLUS. right w/demitasse cup & saucer) **$500-600**
Toothpick holder, No. 15 Clairon blank, 2 1/4" h.. **$295**
Toothpick holder, No. 73 Clairon blank, 2 1/4" h.. **$340**
Vase, 9" h., No. U12 blank **$1,700**
Vase, 5" h., No. 134 Deco variant blank........ **$385**
Vegetable dish, cov., No. 15 Clairon blank, 10 1/2" l. **$1,000**

Old Ivory Covered Vegetable Dish

Vegetable dish, No. 28 blank, 10 1/2" l (ILLUS.).. **$1,500**

Owens

Owens pottery was the product of the J.B. Owens Pottery Company, which operated in Ohio from 1890 to 1929. In 1891 it located in Zanesville and produced art pottery from 1896, introducing "Utopian" wares as its first art pottery. The company switched to tile after 1907. Efforts to rebuild after the factory burned in 1928 failed, and the company closed in 1929.

Owens Pottery Mark

Bulbous Utopian Vase with Pansies

Vase, 4 1/8" h., Utopian Line, bulbous ovoid body w/a wide shoulder centered by a short ringed neck, h.p. w/yellow & orange pansies against a shaded dark to light brown ground, decorated by Tot Steele, marked on base "J.B. Owens Utopian - 1110" (ILLUS., previous page) **$161**

Copper-clad Owens Pottery Vase

Vase, 5 3/4" h., copper-clad, wide bulbous ovoid body w/a scalloped base & four tab feet, a tiny cylindrical neck w/a flared rim, the sides incised w/large balloon-like panels outlined in double lines, marked w/an "N" inside & circle & the date 1905 (ILLUS.) **$500**

Owens Utopian Vase with Roses

Vase, 5 7/8" h., Utopian line, gently flaring cylindrical body w/a wide slightly rounded shoulder centering a small trumpet neck, decorated w/large deep red & pink wild roses & green leaves on a dark brown shaded to dark gold ground, artist-initials, some dry crazing (ILLUS.) **$173**

Vase, 6 1/2" h., wide bulbous ovoid body w/a wide rounded shoulder centered by a small rolled neck, molded w/four small open twisted twig handles around the neck continuing to relief-molded pine cones amid long pine needles, overall deep green matte glaze, impressed Owens mark, Shape No. 326 (ILLUS., top next column) **$1,093**

Rare Owens Matte Green Pine Cone Vase

Owens Aborigine Line Vase

Vase, 6 7/8" h., Aborigine line, a bulbous body tapering to a slightly flared mouth, decorated in a Native American style w/triangles & other geometric designs in brick red & tan outlined in black, incised "JBO - 32" (ILLUS.) **$184**

Three Handled Utopian Ware Vase

Vase, 6 7/8" h., Utopian Ware, footed ovoids body tapering to a flaring ruffled neck flanked by three large loop handles down the sides, decorated w/deep orange & red wide roses & green leaves against a shaded dark green ground, impressed base mark & indistinct artist signature, overall crazing (ILLUS.) **$138**

Green Matte Owens Pottery Vase

Vase, 8 7/8" h., squatty bulbous lower body w/four buttress feet, a double-ringed neck w/widely flaring rim, overall matte green glaze, marked, minor nicks on feet (ILLUS.)... **$500**

Utopian Ware Vase with Pansies

Vase, 10 1/4" h., Utopian Ware, tall cylindrical body w/a wide shoulder centering a tiny cylindrical neck, decorated w/orange & yellow pansy blossoms down the sides against a dark brown shaded to dark ground ground, signed by Harry Larzelere, base impressed "Owens - 2 - 1010" (ILLUS.)... **$173**

Vase, 11 1/2" h., Henri Deux line, large round & ornately molded black footed pedestal base supporting the wide cylindrical body w/a wide cupped mouth, the sides incised & decorated w/colored clays in greens, tans, gold & brown to form a stylized forest scene w/a maiden, unmarked, several chips at base, some small nicks (ILLUS., top next column)....... **$375**

Unusual Owens Henri Deux Line Vase

Unusual Malachite Beaded Utopian Vase

Vase, 13 3/8" h., Malachite Beaded Utopian Ware, a flaring ringed base tapering to a tall slender cylindrical body w/a bulbed top, a large bold orange blossom w/twig running up the side against a beaded dark green ground (ILLUS.) **$805**

Pennsbury Pottery

Henry Below and his wife, Lee, founded the Pennsbury Pottery in Morrisville, Pennsylvania, in 1950. The Belows chose the name because William Penn's home was nearby. Lee, a talented artist who designed the well-known Rooster pattern, almost the entire folk art designs and the Pennsylvania German blue and white hand-painted dinnerware, had been affiliated with Stangl Pottery of Trenton, New Jersey. Mr. Below had learned pottery making in Germany and became an expert in mold making and ceramic engineering. He, too, had been associated with Stangl Pottery, and when he and Lee opened Pennsbury Pottery, several workers from Stangl joined the Belows. Mr. Below's death in 1959 was unexpected, and Mrs. Below passed away in 1968 after a long illness. Pennsbury filed for bankruptcy in October 1970. In 1971 the pottery was destroyed by fire.

During Pennsbury's production years, an earthenware with a high temperature firing was used. Most of the designs are a sgraffito-type similar to Stangl's products. The most popular coloring, a characteristic of Pennsbury, is the smear-type glaze of light brown after the sgraffito technique has been used. Birds are usually marked by hand and most often include the name of the bird. Dinnerware followed and then art pieces, ashtrays and teapots. The first dinnerware line was Black Rooster, followed by Red Rooster. There was also a line known as Blue Dowry, which had the same decorations as the brown folk art pattern but done in cobalt.

Pennsbury
Pottery

Pennsbury
Pottery

morrisville, Pa.

Pennsbury Pottery Marks

Canister, cov., Black Rooster patt., w/black rooster finial, front reads "Flour," 9" h. **$125-175**
Desk basket, Two Women Under Tree patt., 5" h. **$15-20**
Model of chickadee, head down, on irregular base, model No. 111, signed "R.B.," 3 1/2" h. **$100-125**
Mug, beer-type, Barber Shop Quartet patt. **$15-25**

Amish Pattern Beer Mug

Mug, beer, Amish patt., dark brown rim & bottom w/dark brown applied handle, 5" h. (ILLUS.) **$15-25**
Pie plate, Dutch Haven commemorative, birds & heart in center, inscribed around the rim "When it comes to Shoo-Fly Pie - Grandma sure knew how - t'is the Kind of Dish she used - Dutch Haven does it now," 9" d. (ILLUS., top next column) **$90-100**

Commemorative Pie Plate

Pitcher, 5" h., Delft Toleware patt., fruit & leaves, white body w/fruit & leaves outlined in blue, blue inside **$40-50**

Amish Pattern Pitcher

Pitcher, 7 1/4" h., Amish patt. w/interlocked pretzels on reverse (ILLUS.) **$50-75**

Small Black Rooster Plate

Plate, 6" d., Black Rooster patt. (ILLUS.) ... **$30-40**
Plate, 8" d., Courting Buggy patt. **$30-40**

Large Red Rooster Pattern Plate

Plate, 10" d., Red Rooster patt. (ILLUS.) ... **$50-60**
Relish tray, Black Rooster patt., five-section, each w/different scene, Christmastree shape, 14 1/2" l., 11" w **$110-130**

Commemorative Plaque

Wall plaque, commemorative, "What Giffs, what ouches you?," reverse marked "NFBPWC Philadelphia, PA 1960," drilled for hanging, 4" d. (ILLUS.) **$20-30**

Plaque with Rooster

Wall plaque, Rooster patt., "When the cock crows the night is all," drilled for hanging, 4" d. (ILLUS.) **$20-30**

"It is Whole Empty" Plaque

Wall plaque, shows woman holding Pennsbury cookie jar, marked "It is Whole Empty," drilled for hanging, 4" d. (ILLUS.) **$20-30**

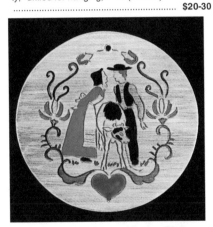

Amish Man & Woman Kissing Plaque

Wall plaque, Amish man & woman kissing over cow, drilled for hanging, 8" d. (ILLUS.) **$25-35**

Donkey & Clown Wall Pocket

Wall pocket, donkey & clown w/dark green border, ivory center, 6 1/2" sq. (ILLUS.) **$100-125**

Peters & Reed

In 1897 John D. Peters and Adam Reed formed a partnership to produce flowerpots in Zanesville, Ohio. Formally incorporated as Peters and Reed in 1901, this type of production was the mainstay until after 1907, when they gradually expanded into the art pottery field. Frank Ferrell, a former designer at the Weller Pottery, developed the "Moss Aztec" line while associated with Peters and Reed, and other art lines followed. Although unmarked, attribution is not difficult once familiar with the various lines. In 1921, Peters and Reed became Zane Pottery, which continued in production until 1941.

Peters & Reed Mark

Small Peters & Reed Landsun Vase

Vase, 4 3/4" h., Landsun line, baluster-form body w/a dark blue upper band above the mottled & streaked blackish brown, tan & yellow green lower body, unmarked, some burst glaze bubbles near base (ILLUS.) **$104**

Peters & Reed Small Landsun Vase

Vase, 5" h., Landsun line, flared foot & widely flaring trumpet-form body, decorated w/a band of upright swirled & pointed dark brown leaf-like devices around the bottom overlapping a band of transparent brown leaves over a dark green & yellow ground, unmarked, some small base chips (ILLUS.) **$81**

Peters & Reed Wilse Line Blue Vase

Vase, 7 1/4" h., Wilse line, gently tapering cylindrical body w/a wide cupped top, overall speckled glossy blue glaze, impressed Zane Ware mark (ILLUS.) **$69**

Interesting Shadow Ware Vase

Vase, 7 1/2" h., Shadow Ware, footed flaring trumpet-form body below the angled shoulder centered by a short molded neck, drippy streaks of blue, black & yellow down over a caramel ground, unmarked, overall crazing (ILLUS.) **$460**

Vase, 8" h., Landsun line, flared foot & swelled cylindrical body w/a wide ringed & molded wide flat mouth, overlapping angled streaky blue & brown bands around the sides against the pale green ground, impressed Zane Ware logo (ILLUS., next page) **$195**

Banded Landsun Line Vase

Peters & Reed Shadow Ware Vase

Vase, 9" h., Shadow Ware, simple ovoid body w/a short wide flaring mouth, black, blue & yellow dripping streaks down the sides against the creamy yellow glossy glaze, unmarked, overall crazing (ILLUS.).. **$219**

Tall Peters & Reed Marbleized Vase

Vase, 10" h., Marbleized line, flaring base tapering to a trumpet-form body, streaky bands of black & yellow on the brown ground, glossy glaze, unmarked, overall crazing (ILLUS.) **$127**

Pewabic

Mary Chase Perry (Stratton) and Horace J. Caulkins were partners in this Detroit, Michigan, pottery. Established in 1903, Pewabic Pottery evolved from their Revelation Pottery, "Pewabic" meaning "clay with copper color" in the language of Michigan's Chippewa Indians. Caulkins attended to the clay formulas and Mary Perry Stratton was artistic creator of forms & glaze formulas, eventually developing a wide range of colors for her finely textured glazes. The pottery's reputation for fine wares and architectural tiles enabled it to survive the Depression years of the 1930s. After Caulkins died in 1923, Mrs. Stratton continued to be active in the pottery until her death, at age 94, in 1961. Her contributions to the art pottery field are numerous.

Pewabic Pottery Mark

Miniature White & Blue Pewabic Vase

Vase, miniature, 2 3/4" h., baluster-form body w/a widely flaring trumpet neck, a drippy white & brown glaze around the neck & shoulder above a very dark blue mottled glaze on the lower body, round company sticker, very minor base grinding (ILLUS.) **$633**

Vase, miniature, 3 1/8" h., simple ovoid body w/a short wide neck, a drippy black glaze covering most of the lustrous grey base glaze, impressed round mark, flat chip on base (ILLUS., next page) **$460**

Miniature Pewabic Vase in Drippy Black

Small Experimental Pewabic Vase

Vase, miniature, 3 1/8" h., wide ovoid body w/a wide shoulder to the short, wide flat mouth, experimental type w/a drippy dark brown glaze down from the top over a moss green ground, incised mark & round paper label (ILLUS.) **$1,380**

Colorful Mottled Pewabic Vase

Vase, 4 7/8" h., a wide flat base below wide gently flaring short cylindrical sides w/a wide tapering shoulder to a short flat neck, glossy glaze w/mottled cream,

brick red & shades of green, unmarked, two chips at the base (ILLUS.) **$374**

Mottled Blue Pewabic Vase

Vase, 6 3/4" h., footed wide ovoid body w/a wide shoulder to the short flaring neck, mottled & swirled iridescent glaze in shades of dark & lighter blue, impressed logo (ILLUS.) **$1,035**

Fine Quality Pewabic Pottery Vase

Vase, 10 5/8" h., footed bulbous ovoid body w/a wide short cylindrical neck w/a flaring rim, copper red drippy glaze above a matte mauve lower body, impressed mark, very tight, faint line at rim (ILLUS.)
.... **$3,240**

Phoenix Bird & Flying Turkey Porcelain

Berry server, style "B," w/seven drain
  holes, 6" d. **$145**
Bouillon cup & saucer, cov. **$45**
Butter pat **$15**
Cann, w/handle, straight sides **$25**
Casserole, style #1, small oval **$75**
Celery, style #1, 13 1/2" l. **$125**
Cheese & cracker plate, tiered, style A **$135**
Chocolate pot, style #1, 8 3/4" h., 5 1/4" d.
.... **$125**
Coffeepot, cov., style No. 6 .... **$75**

Condensed milk jar, cov., style No. 1 .... $85
Cracker jar, cov., style No. 3 .... $165
Cup & saucer $7
Espresso cup & saucer $15
Gravy boat, style No. 6 .... $55
Gravy boat and underplate, style No. 6,
the set $75
Hot water pot cov., style No. 4 .... $55
Ice cream dish, w/inverted scallops, 7" l. $55
Lemonade glass, w/flared top $45
Lemonade pitcher $145
Mustard jar, cover & attached under-
plate, style No. 12, the set $55
Pancake, cov., w/two steam holes $135
Plate, 7 1/4" d. $7
Platter, 16 1/8" l., scalloped rim $95
Ramekin, style "A" $22
Ramekin, style "B" $18
Reamer, two-piece $195
Relish, style No. 12, double handles, 10" l. $145
Rice tureen, style No. 3-A $75
Salt dip, style No. 3, three round feet (Book
IV) $18
Syrup, cov., style No. 13 .... $55

marked "Made in Japan" within a double
circle, largest of three sizes, 8" l.,
5 1/2" h. (ILLUS.) $35

Rattan-handled Phoenix Bird Teapot

Teapot, cov., Phoenix Bird patt., bulbous
body w/a serpentine spout, overhead wo-
ven rattan swing bail handle (ILLUS.) **$35-55**

Phoenix Bird Wicker-handled Teapot

Teapot, cov., Phoenix Bird patt., bulbous
body w/serpentine spout & domed cover w/knob finial, overhead swing bail
handle of blue bands of wicker woven
w/uncolored wicker, marked w/six Japanese characters, ca. 1920s-30s,
5 1/4" h. (ILLUS. with liner) **$45**

Bulbous Phoenix Bird Pattern Teapot

Modern Phoenix (T-Bird) Teapot

Teapot, cov., Modern Phoenix (T-Bird)
patt., upright square body w/angled
spout, flat cover w/loop handle, swing
bail bamboo handle, marked w/a small
square & seven Japanese characters,
post-1970, 6" l., 6 3/4" h. (ILLUS.) **$30**

Phoenix Bird Teapot Found in Three Sizes

Teapot, cov., Phoenix Bird patt., bulbous
body w/a narrow shoulder & wide flat rim,
long serpentine spout & angled D-form
handle, low domed cover w/knob finial,

Teapot, cov., Phoenix Bird patt., footed bulbous body w/a serpentine spout & heavy ring handle w/small thumbrest, low domed cover w/knob finial, marked "Made in Japan," ca. 1920s-30s, 7 1/2" l., 4 1/2" h. (ILLUS., previous page) **$30**

Extra Large Phoenix Bird Teapot

Teapot, cov., Phoenix Bird patt., footed bulbous lower body & wide tapering shoulder w/a non-traditional design, long serpentine spout, angled handle w/small thumbrest, inset tapering cover w/knob finial, marked w/an "S" enclosed in a bulb above "Made in Japan," ca. 1920s-30s, extra large size, 10" l., 6 1/2" h. (ILLUS.) **$70**

Teapot, cov., Phoenix Bird patt., footed tapering ovoid body w/serpentine spout, C-form handle & domed cover, various Japanese marks, found in three sizes w/largest size illustrated, medium size, 7" l., 6 5/8" h. **$45-55**

Teapot, cov., Phoenix Bird patt., footed tapering ovoid body w/serpentine spout, C-form handle & domed cover, various Japanese marks, found in three sizes w/largest size illustrated, small size, 6" l., 6" h. **$35-45**

Delicate, Quality Phoenix Bird Teapot

Teapot, cov., Phoenix Bird patt., scalloped round foot supporting the wide squatty bulbous body w/a short spout & large ring handle, inset cover w/squared loop handle, delicate & fine quality, unmarked, ca. 1920s-30s, 7 3/4" l., 4 3/8" h. (ILLUS.) **$55**

Phoenix Bird HO-O Border Teapot

Teapot, cov., Phoenix Bird patt., squatty bulbous body w/low domed cover & knob finial, ring handle & short spout, w/HO-O heart-like variant border design, unmarked, 7 1/2" l., 4 3/4" h. (ILLUS.) **$45-50**

Teapot, cov., Phoenix Bird patt., tall tapering waisted body w/upright shaped spout & pointed loop handle, low domed cover w/button finial, marked w/a four-petaled flower on stem & "Japan," ca. 1920s-30s, 6 3/4" l., 5 1/2" h. (ILLUS. left with matching smaller teapot) **$35**

Two Upright Waisted Phoenix Bird Teapots

Teapot, cov., Phoenix Bird patt., tall tapering waisted body w/upright shaped spout & pointed loop handle, low domed cover w/button finial, marked w/a four-petaled flower on stem & "Japan," ca. 1920s-30s, 6 1/4" l., 4 1/4" h. (ILLUS. right with matching larger teapot) **$40**

"M in Wreath" Marked Teapot

Teapot, cov., Phoenix Bird patt., wide squatty bulbous body w/serpentine spout & D-form handle, low domed cover w/knob finial, "M in Wreath" Morimura Bros. mark & "Japan," ca. 1930s, 7 3/8" l., 3 3/4" h. (ILLUS.) **$20**

Quimper

This French earthenware pottery has been made in France since the end of the 17th century and is still in production today. Because the colorful decoration on this ware, predominantly of Breton peasant figures, is all hand-painted and each piece is unique, it has become increasingly popular with collectors in recent years. Most pieces offered today date from about the mid-19th century to the present. Modern potteries continue to operate today, with contemporary examples available in gift shops.

The standard reference in this field is Quimper Pottery A French Folk Art Faience by Sandra V. Bondhus (privately printed, 1981).

Quimper Marks

Baby's feeding pitcher, 4 1/2" h., tiny spout, decorated w/only a flower garland band, unsigned, 19th c., excellent............ **$150**

Bell, bagpipe shape w/original unglazed clapper, "Ivoire Corbeille" patt., bust portrait of man on front, half sunburst w/sponged circlets design on reverse, "HenRiot Quimper 73," 3 1/4" h., mint........ **$75**

Quimper Card Tray

Card tray, rococo amorphous form, "decor riche" patt., center decorated w/pair of Breton musicians surrounded by flower sprays of wild gorse & broom, "HenRiot Quimper 148," 13 x 10 1/2", mint (ILLUS.)
.... **$350**

Cigarette box, cov., image of woman w/flower branches on lid, geometric patt. on base, "HenRiot Quimper 116," 4 1/2" l., 3 1/4" w., mint **$100**

Cup & saucer, "croisille" style, the 4" lip-to-handle cup decorated w/image of seated woman in trefoil cartouche w/"tennis ball" latticework trim, 5" d. saucer, "HR Quimper," mint, pr. **$50**

Dish, fish shape, center w/design of woman wearing the costume of La Rochelle & surrounded by flower branches, "La Rochelle HenRiot Quimper 137," pierced for hanging, 10" l., 4 1/2" w., mint **$85**

Doll dish set: 4" d. cov. tureen, 4" d. charger, 3" l. gravy boat, two 2 3/4" d. plates & two 1 3/4" d. plates; each w/decoration of sailboat on waves, creamy buff glaze & rose pink sponged border, unsigned, attributable to HenRiot, excellent, set of eight (ILLUS., top of next page) **$125**

Doll plate, Modern Movement colors w/geometric stylized flower patt. in brown, yellow, blue & rose red, "HenRiot Quimper 106," 2 3/4" d., mint.................................... **$30**

Figure by "Fanch," wearing pantaloons & playing flute, Modern Movement colors, "HenRiot Quimper France 597," 3 1/2" h., mint **$175**

Figure group, Modern Movement bride & groom by artist Fanch, from "Noce Bigoudenne" group, the bride wears white dress & loaf coif painted w/yellow "embroidery" work, the groom a dark navy suit & red tie, "HB Quimper," mint **$200**

Figure of St. Yves, the patron saint of lawyers wears legal garb of the period, "HenRiot Quimper," 4 3/4" h., mint.................... **$100**

Holy water font, base w/figure of the Christ Child holding a cross in relief, the top adorned w/image of eye of God enclosed within radiant sun & two stars, Modern Movement colors, "HB Quimper 119," 5 1/2" l., mint **$150**

Inkwell, cov., square w/cut corners, design of peasant man w/flowers & red S-link chain border, w/original inset & lid, "HB Quimper 497," 3 1/2" sq., excellent.......... **$150**

Quimper Inkwell & Pen Tray

Inkwell w/pen tray, cov., oblong, w/four feet & center apron, "demi-fantasie" patt., scene on front of Bretonne woman balancing milk pail on her head surrounded by flowering branches & lattice work, original inset & knobbed lid, "HenRiot Quimper France 99," excellent (ILLUS.)
.... **$275**

Doll's Dish Set

Quimper Crown-shaped Jardiniere

Jardiniere, crown shape, "decor riche" patt. w/seated couple facing each other on front, back w/Crest of Brittany held by lions, "HenRiot Quimper 23," 11 1/2" l., one handle professionally restored (ILLUS.) **$650**

Handled "Decor Riche" Jardiniere

Jardiniere, oval shape w/cutout rim, short oval outcurved base, dainty scroll handles, "decor riche" patt., main cartouche shows seated woman holding a jug, reverse features crowned Crest of Brittany, "HB Quimper," 12 1/2 l., 7" h., mint (ILLUS.) **$500**

Knife rest, figural, Modern Movement-style form of reclining woman w/her head on her hands & her elbows extended, "HenRiot Quimper" and mark of artist C. Maillard, 4" l., mint **$100**

Liqueur set: barrel keg w/original wooden spigot, wooden stand & six original small handled cups; "Ivoire Corbeille" patt. w/bust portrait of woman in profile on side

"Ivoire Corbeille" Liqueur Set

of keg, "HenRiot Quimper," mint, the set (ILLUS.)... **$150**

Match holder, wall-mounted type, pocket features image of peasant woman w/flowers, back panel has lattice & dot geometric design, "HR Quimper," 3 x 2 1/2", mint **$150**

Artist-signed Flower Holder

Pique fleurs (flower holder), figural, Modern Movement-style image of a kneeling Bigoudenne lifting a basket of flowers, the basket w/holes for flower stems, "HenRiot Quimper" and signature of artist C.H. Maillard on base, 8" h., 9" l., mint (ILLUS.)... **$750**

"Decor Riche" Pattern Plates

Odetta Gresware Pitchers

First Period Porquier Beau Plate

Pitcher, 3" h., Odetta gresware w/concentric double diamond patt. in white & rich brown on navy blue/cobalt ground, "HB Quimper Odetta 494," mint (ILLUS. top right, w/other Odetta pitchers)................. **$150**

Pitcher, 3 3/4" h., Odetta gresware w/concentric double diamond patt. in white & rich brown on navy blue/cobalt ground, "HB Quimper Odetta 424," mint (ILLUS. bottom right, w/other Odetta pitchers)....... **$150**

Pitcher, 9 1/2" h., Odetta gresware w/a rich deep chocolate brown glaze over a light tan matte glaze "biscuit," bold geometric patt., "HB Quimper Odetta 423-1081+," mint (ILLUS. left, w/other Odetta pitchers)... **$300**

Plate, 8 3/4" d., "decor riche" patt. w/unusual scene of a Breton knight, Bertrand Duguesclin, "HR Quimper," mint (ILLUS. right, w/peasant plate, top of page).......... **$525**

Plate, 9 1/2" d., "decor riche" patt. w/scalloped border & pair of nicely detailed peasant folk, "HR Quimper," mint (ILLUS. left, w/Breton knight plate, top of page)..... **$350**

Plate, 9 1/2" d., First Period Porquier Beau, entitled "Ramasseur de goemon-Guisseny," scene of fisherman on shoreline holding a pike, w/Crest of Brittany above him in acanthus border, signed w/intersecting "PB" and name of scene, mint (ILLUS., top next column) **$1,250**

Plate, 9 3/4" d., "Broderie Bretonne" geometric patt., ten-pointed star on metallic gold background glaze, intricate raised-

to-the-touch heart-shaped patterns in border, "HB Quimper P.F. 163 D 708," mint **$100**

Plates, 8 1/2" d., "demi-fantasie" patt., w/different Breton peasant on each, marked w/"HenRiot Quimper France" and various two-digit numbers, mint, set of 5, each (ILLUS., top next page) **$100**

Platter, 13" l., 10" w., rectangular w/cut corners, decorated w/image of open basket w/bouquet of flowers, corners w/black ermine tails, "HenRiot Quimper France," excellent.. **$150**

"Croisille" Pattern Platter

Platter, 15" l., 10" w., ovoid, in the "croisille" style w/alternating panels of stylized dogwood blossom, finely detailed couple posed in conversation in the center, "HenRiot Quimper France 162," mint (ILLUS.) **$450**

Set of Five Peasant Plates

"Ivoire Corbeille" Fish Platter

Platter, 20 3/4" l., 10" w., oval fish platter, "Ivoire Corbeille" patt. w/portrait busts of young Breton couple framed w/Celtic motifs, "HenRiot Quimper," pierced for hanging, mint (ILLUS., middle of page)............ **$300**

Salt, open oval w/yellow glaze & flower sprig patt. on sides, "HenRiot Quimper," 2" l., mint **$25**

Tea set: 7" h. cov. teapot, creamer, five cups & six saucers; traditional peasant patt., decorative scalloped borders, "HR Quimper," excellent (ILLUS., bottom of page).. **$750**

Scalloped Tea Set

"Broderie Bretonne" Vase

Vase, 8 1/2" h., cylindrical form tapering in at top & in to short base, "Broderie Bretonne" patt., w/scene of standing peasants, a woman knitting, a man smoking a pipe, raised-to-the-touch Breton embroidery work on the sides, "HB Quimper," mint (ILLUS.) **$350**

Quimper "Demi-fantasie" Vase

Vase, 15" h., slightly ovoid cylindrical body, flaring to narrow neck w/outcurved rim, side loop handles, "demi-fantasie" patt., portly man smokes pipe on front panel, reverse shows bold double daisy w/wheat flower spray, "HenRiot Quimper France 73," mint (ILLUS.) **$300**

Wall pocket, bagpipe shape w/double blue bows, decorated w/image of peasant man holding walking stick & posed in an open field, "HB Quimper" beneath figure, 5 1/2" l., mint **$100**

R.S. Prussia & Related Wares

Ornately decorated china marked "R.S. Prussia" and "R.S. Germany" continues to grow in popularity. According to the Third Series of Mary Frank Gaston's Encyclopedia of R.S. Prussia (Collector Books, Paducah, Kentucky), these marks were used by the Reinhold Schlegelmilch porcelain factories located in Suhl in the Germanic regions known as "Prussia" prior to World War I, and in Tillowitz, Silesia, which became part of Poland after World War II. Other marks sought by collectors include "R.S. Suhl," "R.S." steeple or church marks, and "R.S. Poland."

The Suhl factory was founded by Reinhold Schlegelmilch in 1869 and closed in 1917. The Tillowitz factory was established in 1895 by Erhard Schlegelmilch, Reinhold's son. This china customarily bears the phrase "R.S. Germany" and "R.S. Tillowitz." The Tillowitz factory closed in 1945, but it was reopened for a few years under Polish administration.

Prices are high and collectors should beware of the forgeries that sometimes find their way onto the market. Mold names and numbers are taken from Mary Frank Gaston's books on R.S. Prussia.

The "Prussia" and "R.S. Suhl" marks have been reproduced, so buy with care. Later copies of these marks are well done, but quality of porcelain is inferior to the production in the 1890-1920 era.

Collectors are also interested in the porcelain products made by the Erdmann Schlegelmilch factory. This factory was founded by three brothers in Suhl in 1861. They named the factory in honor of their father, Erdmann Schlegelmilch. A variety of marks incorporating the "E.S." initials were used. The factory closed circa 1935. The Erdmann Schlegelmilch factory was an earlier and entirely separate business from the Reinhold Schlegelmilch factory. The two were not related to each other.

R.S. Prussia & Related Marks

R.S. Germany

Berry set: 9" master bowl & six matching 5 1/2" sauce dishes, Iris mold, decorated w/large red roses, 7 pcs. **$500-550**

Bowl, 10" d., decorated w/wild roses, raspberries & blueberries, glossy glaze **$125-175**

Bowl, large, Lettuce mold, floral decoration. lustre finish **$300-350**

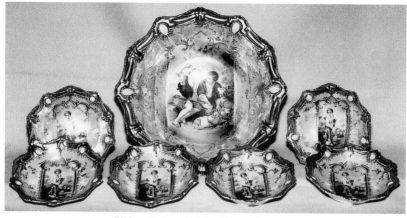

Ribbon & Jewel Melon Eaters Berry Set

R.S. Germany Cake Plate

Cake plate, double-pierced small gold side handles, decorated w/a scene of a maiden near a cottage at the edge of a dark forest, 10" d. (ILLUS.) **$275-325**

Creamer, Mold 640, decorated w/roses, gold trim on ruffled rim & ornate handle **$35-50**

Cup & saucer, demitasse, ornate handle, eight-footed **$75-100**

Mustard jar, cov., calla lily decoration **$65-100**

Plate, 7 1/4" d., poppy decoration **$30-50**

Salad set, 10 1/2" d. lettuce bowl & six 8" d. matching plates, Mold 12, Iris decoration on pearl lustre finish, 7 pcs. **$300-350**

Tray, handled, decorated w/large white & green poppies, 15 1/4" l. **$275-300**

R.S. Prussia

Bell, tall trumpet-form ruffled body w/twig handle, decorated w/small purple flowers & green leaves on white ground, unmarked, 3 1/2" l. **$300-350**

Berry set: master bowl & six sauce dishes; five-lobed, floral relief rim w/forget-me-nots & water lilies decoration, artist-signed, 7 pcs. **$400-450**

Berry set: master bowl & six sauce dishes; Ribbon & Jewel mold (Mold 18) w/Melon

Eaters decoration, 7 pcs. (ILLUS., top of page) **$3,500-3,800**

Bowl, 9 3/4" d., Iris variant mold, rosette center & pale green floral decoration **$250-300**

Bowl, 10" d., Mold 202, gold beaded rim, double swans center scene in shades of beige & white, unmarked **$200-225**

Bowl, 10 1/4" d., center decoration of pink roses w/pearlized finish, border in shades of lavender & blue w/satin finish, lavish gold trim (unlisted mold) **$400-450**

Bowl, 10 1/2" d., Countess Potocka portrait decoration, heavy gold trim **$4,000-4,300**

Bowl, 10 1/2" d., decorated w/scene of Dice Throwers, red trim **$900-1,200**

Bowl, 10 1/2" d., Iris mold, poppy decoration **$350-400**

Ornate Mold 211 Bowl with Roses

Bowl, 10 1/2" d., Mold 211, deeply fluted scalloped border, decorated w/large roses in pink, white & yellow, shadow flowers & blue trim around border (ILLUS.) **$250-300**

Bowl, 10 1/2" d., Point & Clover mold (Mold 82), decorated w/pink roses & green leaves w/shadow flowers & a Tiffany finish **$250-300**

Bowl, 11" d., 3" h., Sunflower mold, satin finish.. **$450-500**

Bowl, 11" d., Mold 22, four large jewels, satin finish.. **$250-300**

Bowl, 11" d., 3" h., Fishscale mold, decorated w/white lilies on purple & orange lustre ground, artist-signed **$325-375**

Bowl, 15" d., Icicle mold (Mold 7), Snow Bird decoration, scenic reserves around the rim, very rare **$12,000-14,000**

Butter dish, cover & insert, Mold 51, floral decoration, unmarked **$200-250**

Floral Decorated Cake Plate

Cake plate, open handled, decorated w/pink & white flowers, green leaves, pink & yellow ground, gold trim, 9 3/4" d. (ILLUS.)... **$225**

Cake plate, open-handled, Mold 155, hanging basket decoration, 10" d.............. **$325-350**

Cake plate, open-handled, Fleur-de-Lis mold, decorated w/a castle scene in rust, gold, lavender & yellow, 10 1/4" d. **$1,000-1,300**

Cake plate, Iris mold, yellow poppy decoration, 11" d. **$250-300**

Cake plate, open-handled, modified Fleur-de-Lis mold, floral decoration, beaded, satin finish, artist-signed, 11" d. **$175-225**

Cake plate, open handles, Mold 256, satin ground decorated w/flowers in blue, pink & white w/gold trim, 11 1/2" d. **$120-150**

Cake plate, open-handled, Mold 343, Winter figural portrait in keyhole medallion, cobalt blue inner border, gold outer border, 12 1/2" d..................................... **$400-450**

Cake plate, open-handled, Carnation mold, decorated w/multicolored roses **$300-350**

Celery dish, Hidden Image mold, colored hair, 5 x 12"....................................... **$400-450**

Celery tray, Mold 254, decorated w/green & pink roses, lavish gold tracery, artist-signed, 12" l. **$275-325**

Celery tray, Mold 255, decorated w/Surreal Dogwood decoration, pearlized lustre finish, artist-signed, 12 1/4" l. **$200-225**

Celery tray, Carnation mold, decorated w/pink & yellow flowers on lavender satin finish, 6 1/2 x 13 1/4".......................... **$300-350**

Chocolate cup & saucer, decorated w/castle scene... **$125-150**

Chocolate pot, cov., Icicle mold (Mold 641), rosebush decoration, 10" h. **$300-400**

Chocolate pot, cov., peacock & pine trees decoration **$650-750**

Chocolate set: cov. pot & four cups & saucers; sunflower decoration, the set **$700-750**

Chocolate set: 10" h. cov. chocolate pot & four cups & saucers; Ribbon and Jewel mold, scene of Dice Throwers decoration on pot & single Melon Eater scene on cups, the set............................... **$4,500-5,000**

Lebrun-decorated Chocolate Set

Melon Eaters Creamer & Sugar

Chocolate set: 10" h. cov. chocolate pot & six cups & saucers; Mold 517, Madame Lebrun portrait decoration, the set (ILLUS., bottom previous page) **$7,500-8,200**

Cracker jar, cov., Mold 540a, beige satin ground w/floral decoration in orchid, yellow & gold, 9 1/2" w. handle to handle, overall 5 1/2" h. **$300-350**

Cracker jar, cov., Mold 704, grape leaf decoration, 7" h. **$450-500**

Cracker jar, cov., Hidden Image mold, image on both sides, green mum decoration **$900-1,000**

Creamer & cov. sugar bowl, floral decoration, green highlights, pr. **$125-150**

Creamer & cov. sugar bowl, Ribbon & Jewel mold, single Melon Eaters decoration, pr. (ILLUS., top of page) **$1,500-1,800**

Cup & saucer, decorated w/pink roses, peg feet & scalloped rim, cup 1 3/4" h., saucer 4 1/4" d., pr. **$125-175**

Dessert set: pedestal cup & saucer, oversized creamer & sugar bowl, two 9 3/4" d., handled plates, eleven 7 1/4" d. plates, nine cups & saucers; plain mold, decoration w/pink poppies w/tints of aqua, yellow & purple, all pieces are matching, the set......................... **$2,200-2,500**

Dresser tray, Icicle mold, scenic decoration, Man in the Mountain, 7 x 11 1/2" **$600-700**

Hair receiver, cov., Mold 814, Surreal Dogwood decoration **$150-175**

Model of a lady's slipper, embossed scrolling on instep & heel & embossed feather on one side of slipper, a dotted medallion w/roses & lily-of-the-valley on the other, shaded turquoise blue w/fancy rim trimmed w/gold, 8" l. **$250-300**

Mug, rose decoration on pink satin finish **$125-175**

Mustard pot, cov., Mold 509a, decorated w/white flowers, glossy light green ground.. **$150-175**

Nut bowl, footed, Point & Clover mold, decorated w/ten roses in shades of salmon, yellow & rose against a pink, green & gold lustre-finished ground, 6 1/2" d. **$150-200**

Pin dish, cov., Hidden Image mold, floral decoration, 2 3/4 x 4 3/4" **$350-450**

Carnation - Summer Season Pitcher

Pitcher, tankard, 12 1/2" h., Carnation mold (Mold 526), Summer Season decoration, pink border trim (ILLUS.).............. **$7,000-8,000**

Pitcher, cider, 7" h., iris decoration w/green & gold background **$250-300**

Pitcher, tankard, 10" h., Mold 584, decorated w/hanging basket of pink & white roses **$700-750**

Pitcher, tankard, 12" h., Mold 538, decorated w/Melon Eaters scene (ILLUS. left, top next page) **$3,500-4,000**

Pitcher, tankard, 13" h., decorated w/scene of Old Man in Mountain & swans on lake (ILLUS. right w/other tankard pitcher, top next page) **$4,000-4,500**

Pitcher, tankard, 13 1/2" h., Carnation Mold, pink poppy decoration, green ground.. **$750-850**

Plaque, decorated w/scene of woman w/dog, 9 1/4 x 13" **$2,000-2,500**

Plate, 7 1/2" d., Carnation mold, decorated w/pink roses, lavender ground, satin finish **$200-250**

Plate, 8 1/2" d., Gibson Girl portrait decoration, maroon bonnet **$500-550**

R.S. Prussia Tankard Pitchers

Plate, 8 1/2" d., Mold 263, pink & white roses decoration................................. **$175-200**

Plate, 8 3/4" d., Mold 278, center decoration of pink poppies on white ground, green border.. **$150-175**

Mold 91 Rose-decorated Plate

Plate, 8 3/4" d., Mold 91, yellow roses decoration on pink ground, shiny yellow border (ILLUS.)....................................... **$150-200**

Plate, 9 3/4" d., Icicle mold, swan decoration **$800-900**

Plate, 11" d., Point & Clover mold, Melon Eater decoration............................ **$900-1,100**

Plate, dessert, Mold 506, branches of pink roses & green leaves against a shaded bluish green to white ground w/shadow flowers & satin finish **$100-125**

Relish dish, Iris mold (Mold 25), oval w/scalloped sides & end loop handles, Spring Season portrait surrounded by dark border w/iris, 4 1/2 x 9 1/2" **$1,200-1,400**

Relish dish, scene of masted ship, 4 1/2 x 9 1/2" **$250-300**

Relish dish, Mold 82, decorated w/forget-me-nots & multicolored carnations, six jeweled domes **$125-175**

Spooner/vase, Mold 502, three-handled, decorated w/delicate roses & gold trim, unsigned, 4 1/4" h. **$75-100**

Syrup pitcher & underplate, Mold 507, white & pink roses on a shaded brown to pale yellow ground, 2 pcs. **$200-250**

Tea set: cov. teapot, creamer & cov. sugar bowl; floral decoration, the set **$300-350**

Tea set: cov. teapot, creamer & cov. sugar bowl; pedestal base, scene of Colonial children, 3 pcs.................................... **$600-700**

Toothpick holder, ribbed hexagonal shape w/two handles, decorated w/colorful roses **$265-300**

Toothpick holder, three-handled, decorated w/white daisies on blue ground, gold handles & trim on top **$150-175**

Tray, pierced handles, Mold 82, decorated w/full blossom red & pink roses, gold Royal Vienna mark, 8 x 11 1/8"......... **$250-300**

Vase, 4" h., salesman's sample, handled, Mold 914, decorated w/large lilies & green foliage, raised beading around shoulder, gold handles, shaded green ground, artist-signed **$150-175**

Vase, 5 1/2" h., cottage & mill scene decoration, cobalt trim **$550-650**

Vase, 6 1/4" h., decorated w/brown & cream shadow flowers **$75-100**

Vase, 8" h., cylindrical body w/incurved angled shoulder handles, decorated w/parrots on white satin ground, unmarked **$2,200-2,600**

Vase, 8" h., ovoid body w/wide shoulder tapering to cylindrical neck w/flared rim, decorated w/scene of black swans (ILLUS. left, next page) **$1,200-1,500**

Vase, 10" h., ovoid body decorated w/scene of two tigers, pastel satin finish (ILLUS. right, next page) **$5,500-7,000**

R.S. Suhl Coffee Set with Romantic Scenes

R.S. Prussia Vases with Animals

Other Marks

Bowl, 10" d., Cabbage mold w/center rose decoration (R.S. Tillowitz) **$250-300**

Chocolate pot, cov., Art Nouveau decoration, glossy finish (R.S. Tillowitz - Silesia) **$55**

Coffee set: 6 5/8" l., 3 1/4" d., cov. ovoid coffeepot & two cups & saucers; each piece decorated w/a color oval reserve w/a different romantic scene within a thin gilt border & a deep burgundy panel against a creamy white ground trimmed w/gilt scrolls, a wide red & narrow dark green border band on each, saucers 2 3/4" d., cups 2 1/4" h., blue beehive & R.S. Suhl marks, the set (ILLUS., top of page) **$650**

Match holder, hanging-type on attached backplate decorated w/a scene of a man w/mug of beer & pipe (E.S. Prov. Saxe) **$175-200**

Plate, 7 3/4" d., Sunflower mold, rose pink & yellow roses w/Tiffany finish (Wheelock Prussia) **$125-150**

Plate, 10 1/2" d., lovely center portrait of Madame DuBarry, four cameos in differ-

ent poses on a deep burgundy lustre border band (E.W. Prov. Saxe) **$500-600**

E. Schlegelmilch Handled Server

Server, center-handled, decorated w/orange, white & pink poppies on a shaded bluish grey ground, w/a narrow gilt border band, 8 1/2" d., 3 3/4" h., E. Schlegelmilch - Thuringia (ILLUS.) **$100-150**

Tray, rectangular, open-handled, bright colored bird decoration, 5 x 14" (R.S. Tillowitz) **$75-100**

Vase, 6 3/8" h., 3" d., wide, ovoid, shouldered body tapering to slender, flaring cylindrical neck, Melon Eaters decoration surrounded by gold border w/reverse decorated w/heart-shaped area w/dainty pink roses on pastel ground, two-thirds of vase covered in purplish lustre w/fine gold leaves & flowers overall, neck in off white w/fine gold floral decoration, artist-signed in gold, Red Crown "Viersa" mark, Suhl or Tillowitz (ILLUS., next page) **$350-400**

Vase, 7 1/2" h., wide, squatty, bulbous base tapering sharply to a tall, slender, cylindrical neck w/an upturned four-lobed rim, long slender gold handles from rim to shoulder, decorated w/a center reserve of a standing Art Nouveau maiden w/her hands behind her head & a peacock behind her framed by delicate gold scrolls & beading & floral bouquets, all on a pearl lustre ground (Prov. Saxe - E.W. Germany) **$375-425**

Melon Eaters Vase

Vase, 9 1/4" h., gently tapering cylindrical body w/a wide, cupped, scalloped gilt rim, pierced gold serpentine handles from rim to center of sides, decorated around the body w/large blossoms in purple, pink, yellow & green on a shaded brownish green ground (Prove. Saxe)............... **$125-150**

Vase, 10" h., gold Rococo handles, scene of sleeping maiden w/cherub decoration (E.S. Royal Saxe)............................. **$350-400**

Vase, 13 1/2" h., twisted gold handles, portrait of "Goddess of Fire," iridescent burgundy & opalescent colors w/lavish gold trim (Prov. Saxe, E.S. Germany)........ **$650-700**

Red Wing

Various potteries operated in Red Wing, Minnesota, from 1868, the most successful being the Red Wing Stoneware Co., organized in 1877. Merged with other local potteries through the years, it became known as Red Wing Union Stoneware Co. in 1906, and was one of the largest producers of utilitarian stoneware items in the United States. After a decline in the popularity of stoneware products, an art pottery line was introduced to compensate for the loss. This was reflected in a new name for the company, Red Wing Potteries, Inc., in 1936. Stoneware production ceased entirely in 1947, but vases, planters, cookie jars and dinnerwares of art pottery quality continued in production until 1967, when the pottery ceased operation altogether.

Red Wing Marks

Art Pottery

Ash receiver, figural, model of a pelican, turquoise, embossed "Red Wing, USA," No. 880 .... **$195**

Basket with 75th Anniversary Seal

Basket, yellow & grey, embossed "Red Wing USA," No. 348, w/75th anniversary seal (ILLUS.) **$65**

Cookie jar, cov., Carousel shape, white, blue, red & brown, h.p., very rare, 8 1/2 x 8" **$575**

Cookie jar, cov., grape design, royal blue, 10" h.. **$220**

Cookie Jar with Peasants Design

Cookie jar, cov., Labriego design decorated w/incised dancing peasants, h.p., green, red & yellow, no markings, 9 1/2" h. (ILLUS.).................................... **$100**

Figures of cowboy & cowgirl, fully decorated, 11" h., pr. **$500**

Planter, hanging-type, No. M-1487................ **$45**

Planter in the Form of a Stove

Planter, in the form of a stove, green & cream, No. 765, 8" h. (ILLUS.) **$55**

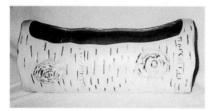

Planter in the Form of a Log

Planter, in the form of a white birch log, no markings, 11" l. (ILLUS.) **$110**
Vase, deer decoration, No. 1120 .... **$60**
Vase, figural elephant handle, ivory ground, matte finish, Rum Rill mark **$140**
Vase, No. 1079, blue glaze **$65**
Vase, No. 839, blue glaze **$100**
Vase, 7" h., expanding cylinder w/squared handles rising from narrow shoulder to mouth, No. 163-7, grey & tan glaze **$100**
Vase, 7" h., No. 1509-7, black satin matte glaze **$35**
Vase, 9" h., ribbed, No. 637 .... **$45**
Vase, 9 1/2" h., No. M1442-9 1/2, Colonial buff & salmon **$65**
Vase, 10" h., No. 902-10, lustre Dubonnet **$100**
Vase, 11" h., No. 1377/11, green & yellow glaze **$75**
Wall pocket, No. M 1630, brown glaze, 10" h. **$80**

Brushed & Glazed Wares
Vase, leaf decoration, buff & green, No. 1166 .... **$35**
Vase, 7" h., bulbous body tapering to a short cylindrical neck, angled handles, decorated w/acorn & oak leaf design, dark & light green, No. 149-7 .... **$165**
Vase, 8" h., flower design decoration, green & mauve, No. 1107 (minor base flake) **$75**

Matte Green & White Cemetery Vase

Vase, 10" h., cemetery vase, green & white, no markings (ILLUS.) **$125**
Vase, 15" h., swelling cylindrical body tapering to a flat rim, angled shoulder handles, green & yellow, No. 186-15 .... **$145**

Convention Commemoratives
Bowl, 1980 Red Wing Collectors Society commemorative **$800**
Cookie jar, 1996 Red Wing Collectors Society commemorative, grey line **$120**
Crock, 1977 Red Wing Collectors Society commemorative, salt glaze **$2,250**

Commemorative Ball Lock Jar

Jar, cov., ball lock, 2002 Red Wing Collectors Society 25th anniversary commemorative, white glaze (ILLUS.) **$90**
Mug, 1982 Red Wing Collectors Society commemorative, cherry band **$750**
Planter, 1995 Red Wing Collectors Society commemorative, in the form of a giraffe ... **$105**
Poultry waterer, 1993 Red Wing Collectors Society commemorative, bell-shaped w/saucer... **$110**

Dinnerwares & Novelties

Ash receiver, figural, model of a seated donkey w/mouth wide open, green glaze **$195**

Red Wing Bob White Casserole

Cookie jar, cov., Bob White patt. **$60**

Red Wing Dutch Girl Cookie Jar

Rare "Pretty Red Wing" Wing Ashtray

Ashtray, earthenware, "Pretty Red Wing" style, model of a large red-glazed wing embossed w/a bust profile of an Indian maiden (ILLUS.) **$400-450**

Beverage server w/stopper, Bob White patt. **$75**

Beverage server w/stopper, Smart Set patt. **$180**

Bowl, berry, Bob White patt. **$8**

Bowl, berry, Capistrano patt............................... **$9**

Bowl, berry, Tampico patt. **$10**

Bowl, cereal, Bob White patt. **$25**

Bowl, cereal, Tampico patt.............................. **$15**

Bowl, salad, Random Harvest patt., large....... **$40**

Bowl, soup, Bob White patt.............................. **$20**

Bowl, salad, 12" d., Capistrano patt. **$75**

Bowl, salad, 12" d., Tampico patt................... **$85**

Bread tray, Round Up patt. **$200**

Bread tray, rectangular, Bob White patt., 24" l. **$100**

Butter dish, cov., Bob White patt., 1/4 lb. **$75**

Butter warmer, Bob White patt. **$95**

Candlesticks, Magnolia patt., pr.................... **$50**

Carafe, cov., Bob White patt. **$185**

Casserole, Bob White patt., 2 qt. **$40**

Casserole, cov., French-style w/stick handle, Town & Country patt., peach glaze **$95**

Casserole, cov., Smart Set patt., 2 qt. **$68**

Casserole, cov., Bob White patt., 4 qt. (ILLUS., top next column) **$50**

Celery dish, Flight patt................................. **$175**

Cocktail tray, Bob White patt......................... **$40**

Coffeepot, cov., Village Green line **$35**

Cookie jar, cov., figural Katrina (Dutch girl), yellow glaze (ILLUS.) **$100**

Cookie jar, cov., figural monk, blue glaze..... **$100**

Cookie jar, cov., side handle & side top, red glaze **$225**

Creamer, Bob White patt................................ **$25**

Cruets w/stoppers, Bob White patt., pr........ **$175**

Cruets w/stoppers in metal rack, Bob White patt., the set **$325**

Cup & saucer, Bob White patt. **$9**

Cup & saucer, Capistrano patt. **$13**

French bread tray, Bob White patt., 24" l...... **$90**

Gravy boat, cov., Bob White patt................... **$55**

Gravy boat w/stand, Tampico patt., 2 pcs. **$60**

Hor d'oeuvres holder, Bob White patt., model of a bird pierced for picks **$50**

Mug, Bob White patt....................................... **$80**

Pitcher, jug-type, Tampico patt., 2 qt. **$65**

Pitcher, 12" h., Round Up patt. **$210**

Pitcher, water, Bob White patt., 60 oz. **$50**

Plate, salad, Flight patt.................................. **$60**

Plate, 6 1/2" d., Capistrano patt. **$5**

Plate, 6 1/2" d., Tampico patt. **$7**

Plate, bread & butter, 6 1/2" d., Bob White patt. **$6**

Plate, 8" d., Bob White patt. **$8**

Plate, 8 1/2" d., Tampico patt. **$12**

Plate, 10 1/2" d., Capistrano patt. **$10**

Plate, 10 1/2" d., Tampico patt. **$14**

Plate, dinner, 10 1/2" d., Bob White patt. **$13**

Platter, 13" oval, Bob White patt. **$85**

Platter, 20" l., Bob White patt. **$100**

Platter w/metal rack, Bob White patt., large, 2 pcs. **$160**

Relish, Bob White patt., three-part $70
Relish, Bob White patt., two-part $45
Relish, Tampico patt., 13" l. $35
Salt & pepper shakers, figural bird, Bob White patt., pr... $35
Salt & pepper shakers, figural pitcher, jug-type w/ice lip, red, Rum Rill mark, pr.......... $45
Salt & pepper shakers, figural Schmoo, bronze glaze, pr. $95
Salt & pepper shakers, figural Schmoo, cinnamon glaze, Rum Rill mark, pr. $65
Syrup pitcher, Town & Country patt., blue glaze... $75
Teapot, cov., Village Green patt..................... $60
Teapot, cover & stand, Bob White patt., the set $140
Tidbit tray, Random Harvest patt., original paper label $27
Tray on warmer, Smart Set patt., large, 2 pcs.. $145
Vegetable dish, open, divided, Capistrano patt. $24
Vegetable dish, open, divided, Smart Set patt... $65
Vegetable dish, open, divided, Tampico patt. $45

Specialty Items

Book, "The Clay Giants," 1st edition, history, stoneware of Red Wing, rare, mint, 1977 .... $175
Book, "The Clay Giants," 3rd edition, history w/price guide, stoneware of Red Wing, mint, 1987 .... $160
Bottle, w/iron bailed stopper, amber, embossed "Red Wing Brewing Co., Red Wing, Minn.," rare, 14" h. $105
Gunny sack, 100 pounds flour, "Red Wing, Minn." $85
Yard stick, advertising Hi-Park Guernsey Milk, Red Wing, Minn. $45

Stoneware & Utility Wares

Bean pot, cov., white & brown glaze, advertising, "Christmas Greetings from Christle's Cash Store, Brillion, Wis.," rare $145
Bean pot, cov., white & brown glaze, advertising "Geo. C. Radloff, Farmersburg, Iowa" $115
Beater jar, cylindrical, Sponge Band line $325
Beater jar, white glaze w/blue band, advertising "Schulenburg & Thom, Wells, Minn." $200
Bowl, 8" d., spongeware paneled, advertising "Swanson & Nelson, Chisago City" [sic], very rare.. $250
Bowl, Sponge Band line, South Dakota advertising in bottom, No. 7 .... $285

White-glazed Bowl with Pink & Blue Bands

Bowl, 7" d., deep rounded & ribbed sides, white-glazed & decorated w/pale pink & blue bands (ILLUS.) **$75-125**
Bowl, 7" d., Dunlap, brown & white glaze, advertising "Columbia Metal Products Co., Chicago, Ill." $45

Large Gray Line (Sponge Band) Bowl

Bowl, 9" d., Gray Line (Sponge Band) ware, deep rounded & ribbed sides w/a narrow sponged orange band flanked by thin blue bands (ILLUS.) **$175-225**
Butter crock, blue sponge glaze, no markings $325
Butter crock, white glaze, 4" wing mark, "20 lbs" stamped above wing, very rare **$1,100**
Churn, w/pottery lid & wooden dasher, white glaze, 4" wing mark, blue oval pottery stamp below wing, 5 gal. $450
Churn, w/pottery lid, white glaze, 4" wing mark, blue oval pottery stamp above wing, 6 gal.. $595
Churn w/wooden lid & dasher, swelled cylindrical body, Union Stoneware Co., large wing mark, 3 gal............................. $325

Red Wing Stoneware Iced Tea Cooler

Cooler, cov., iced tea, white glaze, wire handles, no wing, 5 gal. (ILLUS.).............. $500
Crock, white-glazed, big wing mark, 1 gal. ... $500
Crock, white glaze, embossed on base "Minnesota Stoneware, Red Wing, Minn.," no wing, 1 gal................................. $75
Crock, w/molded rim, white-glazed, large "2" over double birch leaves & oval marks, Red Wing Union Stoneware, 2 gal., 9 3/4" d. $85

Crock, white glaze, two "elephant ears," oval Union Stoneware Co. stamp in blue, 2 gal. **$125**

Crock, white-glazed, large wing mark, 50 gal. **$2,400**

Crock, white glaze, advertising "Ev-Re-Day Oleomargarine, Wisconsin Butterine Co.," no wing, 2 qt. **$75**

Fruit jar, cov., white glaze, blue or black stamp, "Stone - Mason Fruit Jar - Union Stoneware Co. - Red Wing, Minn.," very rare, 1 gal. **$1,100**

Fruit Jar with Screw-on Lid

Fruit jar, screw-on metal lid, cylindrical w/tapering shoulder, white-glazed, black stamp reads "Stone - Mason Fruit Jar - Union Stoneware Co. - Red Wing, Minn.," 2 qt. (ILLUS.) **$275**

Jar, cov., applesauce, white glaze, bail handles, ball lock, oval Union Stoneware stamp, 3 gal. **$325**

Jar, steam table jar, white glaze, cobalt blue #5 stamp, no wing **$50**

Minnesota Stoneware Brown Jug

Jug, beehive-shaped, overall dark brown glaze, mark on bottom for the Minnesota Stoneware Company, 1/2 gal. (ILLUS.) **$75-95**

Jug, brown glaze, embossed "Minnesota Stoneware, Red Wing" on base, 1 gal. **$95**

Jug, syrup, white glaze, cone-shaped top, embossed "Minnesota Stoneware Co." on base, 1 gal. **$75**

3-Gallon Beehive Jug with Leaves

Jug, beehive-shaped, white w/printed blue size number, double birch leaves & oval Union Stoneware Co. mark, 3 gal. (ILLUS.) **$400-450**

Jug, w/white-glazed shoulder, 4" wing above Red Wing oval mark, 3 gal. **$125**

Rare Red Wing Jug

Jug, beehive-shaped, small cylindrical neck, dark blue printed diamond w/Iowa advertising above the blue double birch leaf mark, 5 gal. (ILLUS.) **$2,900**

Jug, beehive-shaped, white-glazed, w/Portland, Oregon advertising, 5 gal. **$950**

Red Wing 5-Gallon Marked Jug

Jug, shoulder-style, cylindrical body w/rounded shoulder & small neck, white glaze, printed blue size number, oval Red Wing Union Stoneware mark & a 4" red wing, 5 gal., 18" h. (ILLUS.) **$173**

Jug, white-glazed shoulder, 4" wing mark, blue oval stamp, 5 gal. **$125**

Red Wing Stoneware "Koverwate"

"Koverwate" (crock cover-weight designed to keep the contents submerged under preserving liquid; bottom & side holes allowed brine to come to the top), white glaze, stamped "Koverwate - Red Wing, Minn.," 15 gal., 13 3/4" d. (ILLUS.) **$295**

Rare Sleepy Eye Advertising Verse Mug

Mug, Sleepy eye verse-type, cylindrical white glazed form w/double blue bands flanking Sleepy Eye advertising, a bust of Chief Sleepy Eye & a verse (ILLUS.) **$2,500-2,800**

Red Wing Packing Jar with Cover & Seal

Packing jar, cov., cylindrical w/rounded shoulder & cylindrical neck w/original ball-lock sealing mechanism & wire bail handle w/wooden grip, white glaze, a script "3" above the 4" red wing & oval Red Wing Union Stoneware marks, 3 gal. (ILLUS.) **$275-325**

Poultry feeder, KoRec chicken feeder, white glaze, 1 gal., 2 pcs. **$175**

Poultry waterer, w/end opening, "Eureka"-style, marked around opening "Patd. April 7, 1885," Red Wing marking on bottom **$250**

Refrigerator jar, stacking-type, short form w/a molded rim, white-glazed w/narrow blue bands & "Red Wing Refrigerator Jar" on the side, 5 1/2" d. **$225**

Salt box, cov., hanging-type, grey line....... **$1,800**

Trivet, advertising Minnesota Centennial 1858-1958 .... **$95**

Water cooler, cov., w/spigot, bail handles, white glaze, 4" wing mark, blue oval Red Wing stamp below wing, 3 gal. **$950**

Water cooler, cov., w/spigot, bail handles, white glaze, 4" wing mark, blue oval Red Wing stamp below wing, 10 gal. **$1,200**

Rookwood

Considered America's foremost art pottery, the Rookwood Pottery Company was established in Cincinnati, Ohio, in 1880 by Mrs. Maria Nichols Longworth Storer. To accurately record its development, each piece carried the Rookwood insignia or mark, was dated, and, if individually decorated, was usually signed by the artist. The pottery remained in Cincinnati until 1959, when it was sold to Herschede Hall Clock Company and moved to Starkville, Mississippi, where it continued in operation until 1967.

A private company is now producing a limited variety of pieces using original Rookwood molds.

Rookwood Mark

Rookwood Ashtrays with Moths

Ashtray, production-type, a rectangular dish w/a cigarette notch at each corner, a small upright rectangle at the back rim, the interior molded w/a band of moths, overall yellowish green Matte glaze, Shape No. 1669, 1910, 2 1/2 x 5" (ILLUS.).................. **$150**

Pair of Large Rook Rookwood Book Ends

Book ends, figural, modeled as a large rook perched on an open book, dark brown glossy glaze, Shape No. 2274, 1916, chip to to of flower next to one rook, 6" h., pr. (ILLUS.)... **$863**

Ivory Rookwood Galleon Book Ends

Book ends, modeled as galleons under full sail, designed by William McDonald, Ivory Mat glass, Shape No. 2695, 1936, 5 1/2" h., pr. (ILLUS.) **$230**
Chamberstick, vegetal form resembling an inverted large mushroom w/the cap forming the dished base incised w/fine lines & w/a looped mushroom-shaped ring edge handle, central stem w/socket resembles a mushroom stem, mottled Matte green glaze, Shape No. 331 Z, 1902, Anna Valentien, 4 3/8" h. (ILLUS., top next column).. **$748**

Inverted Mushroom Chamberstick

Bulbous Rookwood Standard Glaze Creamer

Creamer, four peg feet supporting the squatty bulbous body w/a closed rim, side spout & scrolled ring handle, Standard glaze, decorated w/golden clover & green leaves on a shaded green, gold & brown ground, Shape No. 616, 1897, Constance Baker (ILLUS.) **$230**

Early Rookwood Dull Finish Creamer

Creamer, low rectangular form w/swelled sides, a gilt rim spout at one end & an angled gilt handle at the over, the Dull Finish glaze in pale green decorated w/brick red stylized blossoms on twigs, Shape No. 43, 1885, Anna Marie Bookprinter, 2" h. (ILLUS.) **$173**

Unusual Standard Glaze Fernery

Fernery & separate liner, wide flat-bottomed dish w/a shallow swelled round lower body tapering to a low flaring & finely scalloped rim, taller wide cylindrical liner, Standard glaze, the dish decorated on the exterior w/dark orange pansies against a shaded dark brown to green ground, Shape No. 652 C, 1897, Lenore Asbury, 9" d., 2 3/4" h., 2 pcs. (ILLUS.) **$575**

Rookwood Blue Figural Flower Frog

Flower frog, figural, a stylized seated faun on a large turtle, light blue Matte glaze, Shape No. 2336, 1922, some crazing & mild peppering, 6 3/4" h. (ILLUS.) **$173**

Square Blue Rookwood Inkwell

Inkwell, cov., footed slightly tapering square form w/beveled corners, square flat cover w/button finial, dark blue Matte glaze, includes original ink cup, Shape No. 2747, 1924, 3 1/2" h. (ILLUS.) **$317**

Jug w/original stopper, ovoid body tapering to a small molded neck w/handle from rim to shoulder, pointed stopper, Standard glaze, decorated w/ears of golden corn & green leaves suspended from the top against a brown, dark green & brown shaded ground, Shape 512 A, 1899, Lenore Asbury, 10 1/4" h. (ILLUS., top next column) **$1,150**

Pitcher, 4 1/4" h., gently flaring cylindrical body w/a tricorner wide mouth, angular side handle, Green Matte glaze, incised w/a tall stylized dark blue peacock feather at each corner, Shape No. 259 E, 1907, Albert Pons (ILLUS., middle next column) **$748**

Standard Glaze Jug with Corn Decoration

Small Matte Green Peacock Feather Pitcher

Rare Rookwood Pitcher with Sprite

Pitcher, 10 5/8" h., tankard-type, tapering cylindrical form w/a ringed base, small pinched rim spout & angled handle down the side, Standard glaze, decorated w/a winged sprite riding on the back of an ominous looking winged dragon, blackish green shaded down to brown ground,

Shape No. 564, 1891, Kataro Shiraya-madani (ILLUS.) **$4,255**

Rookwood Blue Ship Pattern Teapot

Teapot, cov., Dinnerware line, Blue Ship patt., ten-sided slightly tapering cylindrical body w/a flat shoulder w/inset cover w/knob finial, squared spout & angular handle, Shape M-18, ca. 1920s, 3 3/4" h. (ILLUS.) **$115**

Standard Glaze Rookwood Teapot

Teapot, cov., footed wide squatty bulbous body w/a short angled spout, flat rim w/low domed cover sprig finial, an arched real bamboo swing bail handle, Standard Glaze, decorated w/dark golden yellow leafy & flowering branches on a shaded brown to dark green to mustard yellow ground, Shape No. 404W, 1894, Josephine Zettel, 7" l., 4" h. (ILLUS.) **$881**

Teapot, cov., tall Turkish-style pot, a narrow footring supporting the bulbous ovoid lower body tapering sharply to a tall cylindrical neck w/a domed cap cover & gold button finial, tall slender serpentine spout joined to the neck w/a delicate S-scroll bracket, long arched handle from the top of the neck to the shoulder, creamy ground h.p. on one side w/a scene of a blue frog seated on shore & holding a fishing pole, the reverse decorated w/a scene of sandcrabs, in shades of dark blue, tan & dark blue w/ornate gold trim, dull semi-matte glaze, mark attributed to M.L. Nichols, dated 1883, 11" h. (ILLUS., top next column) **$1,725**

Unusual Rookwood Turkish Teapot

Small Matte Glazed Nasturium Vase

Vase, 4 3/4" h., bulbous base tapering to a wide cylindrical neck, Matte glaze, decorated w/large pink & yellow stylized nasturium blossoms & green leafy stems on a turquoise blue ground, Shape No. 6101, 1939, Sallie Coyne (ILLUS.) **$460**

Rare Small Dark Iris Glazed Fish Vase

Vase, 5 1/4" h., wide ovoid body tapering to a wide flat mouth, Dark Iris glaze, decorated around the center w/three large swimming green fish in a salmon & white current, the top & bottom bands in shaded dark green, Shape No. 942 D, 1906, E.T. Hurley (ILLUS., previous page) **$10,063**

Matte Glazed Vase with Yellow Flowers

Vase, 5 3/8" h., footed flaring ovoid body w/a rounded shoulder to the short wide cylindrical neck, Matte glaze, decorated w/stylized smeary yellow & brown flowers & green leaves against a creamy ground, 1935, Jens Jensen (ILLUS.)...................... **$403**

Rookwood Production Vase with Flowers

Vase, 6 1/4" h., production-type, ovoid body w/a wide flat mouth, the top molded w/five large stylized daisy blossoms in indented panels around the rim w/a straight stem down the side, dark blue Matte glaze, Shape No. 2380, 1929 (ILLUS.) **$317**

Vase, 6 5/8" h., a production piece w/an ovoid body & small cylindrical neck w/a flared rim, molded in low relief w/stylized flower & overlapping leaves under a blue Crystalline Matte glaze, Shape No. 6467, 1934 (ILLUS., top next column) **$390**

Blue Crystalline Glaze Production Vase

Vellum Glazed Vase with White Swan

Vase, 6 7/8" h., gently swelled & tapering cylindrical body w/a flat mouth, Vellum glaze, decorated w/a large white swan swimming on shaded dark to light blue water w/dark green at the top, Shape No. 950 E, 1904, Carl Schmidt (ILLUS.)....... **$8,238**

French Red Glazed Floral Band Vase

Vase, 7" h., bulbous ovoid body w/a wide flat mouth, French Red glaze, a wide band around the shoulder w/deep pink blossoms clusters & green leaves flanked by a white della robbia-style bands all against a very dark grey ground, Shape No. 915 D, 1920, Sara Sax (ILLUS.)... **$6,613**

Vase, 7 1/4" h., 4 1/4" d., slightly tapering cylindrical body w/a wide flat mouth, Jewel Porcelain glaze, decorated w/large stylized peony blossoms in pink, blue & tan on brown leafy stems against a shaded grey ground, blue rim band, 1921, Arthur Conant (ILLUS.) **$5,750**

Vellum Glazed Vase with Landscape

Vase, 7 7/8" h., gently swelled cylindrical body w/a narrow flared rim, Vellum glaze, decorated w/a stylized landscape w/a house & barn in a wooded setting in shades of light & dark blue, lavender & green, Shape No. 808, 1923, Fred Rothenbusch (ILLUS.) **$3,910**

Rookwood Sea Green Vase with Cranes

Vase, 7 1/4" h., 3" d., footring below the slightly swelled cylindrical body w/a narrow shoulder to the thick flared rim, Sea Green glaze, decorated w/three standing cranes in black, white & a touch of red, among tall dark green grasses, against a dark green to pale yellowish green ground, small firing line at rim, 1894, Matthew Daley (ILLUS.) **$4,313**

Rare Sea Green Vase with Large Fish

Vase, 8 1/4" h., 4 1/2" d., Sea Green glaze, ovoid body tapering to a short trumpet neck, decorated w/large dark green fish swimming through white waves on a tan shaded to dark green ground, E. Timothy Hurley, 1901 (ILLUS.) **$23,000**

Jewel Porcelain Floral Vase

Large Standard Glaze Floral Vase

Vase, 13" h., large ovoid body tapering to a low rolled mouth, upturned loop shoulder handles, Standard glaze, decorated w/very large dark yellow & orange Cereus blooms on dark green stems against a shaded dark green ground, Shape No. 581 C, restoriation to one handle, 1894, Albert Valentien (ILLUS.) **$4,945**

Lovely Large Scenic Vellum Vase

Vase, 15" h., gently flared cylindrical body w/a narrow flat shoulder to a low cylindrical rim, Scenic Vellum glaze, decorated w/a misty landscape w/tall trees in the foreground & a wide waterway & meadow in the distance, in shades of dark & light greens, blues, pinks & cream, slight bruise at rim, light overall crazing, Shape No. 1369 B, 1912, Kataro Shirayamadani (ILLUS.)... **$8,050**

Rare Tall Rookwood Vase with Sprite

Vase, 14 1/2" h., footed wide squatty bulbous lower body tapering to a tall cylindrical neck w/a widely flaring rim, Standard glaze, painted w/a winged sprite riding a large green fish swimming through turbid water, dark blackish green shaded up to tan to gold neck, decorated by Kataro Shirayamadani, Shape No. 537, 1891 (ILLUS.)... **$5,750**

Rare Large Decorated Matte Vase

Vase, 22 5/8" h., very tall footed slender ovoid body w/a widely flaring neck, Decorated Matte glaze, lightly incised dark blue irises on dark green leafy stems against a shaded dark purple ground, highly textured surface, Shape No. 264 A, 1920, Elizabeth Lincoln (ILLUS.) **$9,780**

Rare Whiskey Jug with Snake Decoration

Smaller Rose Medallion Punch Bowl

Whiskey jug w/stopper, wide bulbous squatty tapering body w/a short flaring neck & handle from rim to shoulder, fitted w/a pointed button stopper, Standard glaze, decorated w/three shaded green entwined snakes a shaded dark to light brown ground, sterling silver overlay of leafy grapevines around the lower body w/solid silver on the neck, handle & stopper, Gorham Co. silver marks, Shape No. 675, 1893, Ed Abel, 7 1/8" h. (ILLUS.) ... **$4,600**

Rose Medallion & Rose Canton

The lovely Chinese ware known as Rose Medallion was made through the past century and into the present one. It features alternating panels of people and flowers or insects, with most pieces having four medallions with a central rose or peony medallion. The ware is called Rose Canton if florals and birds or insects fill all the panels. Unless otherwise noted, our listing is for Rose Medallion ware.

Fine Rose Medallion Teapot

Teapot, cov., small round raised foot supporting the deep rounded lower body w/a sharply angled gently angled shoulder centering the low flat mouth fittled w/a high domed cover, ornate C-scroll handle & serpentine spout, the sides & cover decorated w/alternating panels of colorful flowers or Chinese figures, mid-19th c., 8 1/4" h. (ILLUS.) **$1,093**

Large Rose Medallion Punch Bowl

Punch bowl, deep rounded sides w/colorful alternating panels of flowers & Oriental figures, late 19th c., 15" d., 6" h. (ILLUS.) ... **$1,668**
Punch bowl, rounded deep & flaring shape, decorated inside & out w/large alternating panels of flowers & Oriental figures, second half 19th c., 11 1/2" d., 4 3/4" h. (ILLUS., top next column) **$1,150**

Very Large Rose Medallion Palace Vase

Vase, palace-style, 35 1/2" h., 13 1/2" d., wide cylindrical body w/the rounded shoulder tapering to a large waisted neck w/a widely flaring flattened rim, the neck w/large figural Foo dog & ball handles, each side of the body & neck decorated w/large panels w/scenes of numerous people in buildings, detailed floral background & gold trim, one under rim chip, 19th c. (ILLUS., previous page) **$2,300**

Roseville

Roseville Pottery Company operated in Zanesville, Ohio, from 1898 to 1954, having been in business for six years prior to that in Muskingum County, Ohio. Art wares similar to those of Owens and Weller Potteries were produced. Items listed here are by patterns or lines.

Roseville

Roseville Mark

Apple Blossom (1948)
White apple blossoms in relief on blue, green or pink ground; brown tree branch handles.

Small Pink Apple Blossom Jardiniere

Jardiniere, wide bulbous body w/a molded flat mouth flanked by small twig handles, pink ground, No. 300-4", 4" h. (ILLUS.)....... **$69**

Cylindrical Green Apple Blossom Vase

Vase, 9 1/2" h., 5" d., asymmetrical handles, cylindrical w/disc base, green ground, No. 387-9" (ILLUS.) **$184**

Blue Apple Blossom Vase

Vase, 10" h., wide flaring foot w/base handles, trumpet-form body, blue ground, No. 388-10" (ILLUS.)................................ **$184**

Pink Cylindrical Apple Blossom Vase

Vase, 10" h., swelled cylindrical body w/shaped rim, disk base w/handles up the sides, pink ground, No. 389-10" (ILLUS.)
.... **$140-180**

Footed Cylindrical Apple Blossom Vase

Vase, 10" h., swelled cylindrical body w/shaped rim, disk base w/handles up the sides, green ground, No. 389-10" (ILLUS.) **$184**

Blue Apple Blossom Floor Vase

Vase, 15" h., floor type, double base handles, short globular base, long cylindrical neck, blue ground, No. 392-15" (ILLUS.) **$518**

Carnelian II (1915-31)
Intermingled colors, some with a drip effect, giving a textured surface appearance. Colors similar to Carnelian I.

Bulbous Carnelian II Vase

Vase, 7" h., footed, bulbous base tapering to wide cylindrical neck w/rolled rim, ornate handles from shoulder to below rim, mottled rose, grey & green glaze, No. 311-7" (ILLUS.) **$317**
Vase, 10" h., compressed globular form w/angled handles from mid-section to rim, mottled blue & green glaze, No. 323-10" (ILLUS., top next column) **$518**

Tall Carnelian II Blue-green Vase

Fanned Carnelian II Wall Pocket

Wall pocket, wide arched & fanned top w/panels down the sides, heavy loop side handles from under rim to near base, mottled blue & green glaze, No. 1252-8", 8 1/8" l. (ILLUS.) **$460**

Cherry Blossom (1933)

Terra Cotta Cherry Blossom 5" Vase

Vase, 5" h., bulbous ovoid body tapering to a small molded mouth flanked by small loop handles, terra cotta ground, No. 618-5" (ILLUS., previous page)................ **$288**

Pink & Blue Cherry Blossom 5" Vase

Vase, 5" h., bulbous ovoid body tapering to a small molded mouth flanked by small loop handles, pink & blue ground, No. 618-5" (ILLUS.) **$431**

Pink & Blue Cherry Blossom Ovoid Vase

Vase, 5" h., wide ovoid body tapering to a wide, slightly rolled mouth flanked by small loop handles, pink & blue ground, No. 619-5" (ILLUS.)........................... **$375-400**

Terra Cotta 5" Cherry Blossom Vase

Vase, 5" h., wide ovoid body tapering to a wide slightly rolled mouth flanked by

small loop handles, terra cotta ground, No. 619-5" (ILLUS.).................................. **$259**

Bulbous 6" Cherry Blossom Vase

Vase, 6" h., bulbous body, shoulder tapering to wide molded mouth, small loop shoulder handles, terra cotta ground, unmarked, No. 621-6" (ILLUS.).................... **$259**

Cosmos (1940)

Embossed blossoms against a wavy horizontal ridged band on a textured ground, ivory band with yellow and orchid blossoms on blue, blue band with white, and orchid blossoms on green or tan.

Tall Blue Cosmos Vase

Vase, 12 1/2" h., footed ovoid w/large loop handles from sides of short paneled neck to sides of shoulders, blue ground, No. 956-12"... **$260**

Dahlrose (1924-28)

Band of ivory daisy-like blossoms and green leaves against a mottled tan ground.

Small Spherical Dahlrose Jardiniere

Jardiniere, footed spherical body w/a wide low rolled neck flanked by small pointed handles, No. 614-4", 4 1/4" h. (ILLUS., previous page) **$173**

Bulbous Dahlrose Jardiniere

Jardiniere, footed, bulbous form w/a thick molded rim flanked by tiny squared rim handles, No. 614-6", 6" h. (ILLUS.).......... **$161**

Wide Bulbous Dahlrose Vase

Vase, 6" h., squatty bulbous body tapering to wide rolled rim, tiny angled handles from shoulder to rim, No. 364-6" (ILLUS.) **$288**

Dahlrose Rectangular Pillow Vase

Vase, 6" h., 8" l., flattened pillow-type, tall upright rectangular form w/small angled handles at the top ends, black paper label, No. 358-8" (ILLUS.)............................ **$489**

Rare Square Dahlrose Vase

Vase, 6 1/8" h., square flared foot below the slightly tapering square body w/a wide sharply flaring neck, black paper label, No. 372-6" (ILLUS.)................................... **$748**

Donatello (1915)
Deeply fluted ivory and green body with wide tan band embossed with cherubs at various pursuits in pastoral settings.

Rare Tall Donatello Vase

Vase, 12 1/2" h., tall waisted cylindrical body w/a wide flat mouth, long serpentine angled handles down the sides, restoration to rim & handles, rare shape (ILLUS.) **$375**

Freesia (1945)
Trumpet-shaped blossoms and long slender green leaves against wavy impressed lines, white and lavender blossoms on blended green, white and yellow blossoms on shaded blue, or terra cotta and brown.

Green Freesia Three-Piece Tea Set

Tea set: cov. teapot No. T, creamer No.6-C & open sugar bowl No.6-C; bulbous tapering shapes, green ground, No. 6, 3 pcs. (ILLUS.) **$250-300**

Blue Freesia 6" Vase

Vase, 6" h., baluster-form w/flat mouth & pointed angled handles, blue ground, No. 117-6" (ILLUS.) **$150**

Blue Freesia Vase No. 118-6"

Vase, 6 1/4" h., footed, squatty, bulbous base w/wide cylindrical neck, large angled base handles, blue ground, No. 118-6" (ILLUS.) **$104**

Freesia Vase with Tall Cylindrical Neck

Vase, 7" h., footed disk-form base w/angular base handles below the tall cylindrical neck, blue ground, No. 119-7" (ILLUS.) **$115**

Blue Freesia Bud Vase

Vase, bud, 7" h., handles rising from compressed globular base, long slender tapering neck, blue ground, No. 195-7" (ILLUS.) **$115**

Blue Footed Ovoid Freesia Vase

Vase, 8" h., footed, ovoid body flanked by D-form handles, blue ground, No. 121-8" (ILLUS., previous page) **$115**

Blue Footed Freesia Vase

Vase, 9 1/2" h., a short ringed pedestal base supporting a flaring half-round body w/an angled shoulder tapering slightly to a tall, wide cylindrical neck, down-curved angled loop handles from center of neck to rim of lower shoulder, blue ground, No. 123-9 (ILLUS.) **$115**

Fuchsia (1939)

Coral pink fuchsia blossoms and green leaves against a background of blue shading to yellow, green shading to terra cotta, or terra cotta shading to gold.

Vase, 6" h., footed ovoid w/handles rising from shoulder to short cylindrical neck rim, overall crazing, green ground, No. 892-6" **$104**

Iris (1938)

White or yellow blossoms and green leaves on rose blending with green, light blue deepening to a darker blue or tan shading to green or brown.

Small Blue Iris Jardiniere

Jardiniere, two-handled, footed squatty bulbous body w/a wide short cylindrical mouth, blue ground, No. 647-3", 3 1/2" h. (ILLUS.) **$92**

Tall Roseville Blue Iris Vase

Vase, 15 1/2" h., footed large ovoid body tapering to a paneled & scalloped neck flanked by loop handles, blue ground, No. 929-15" (ILLUS.) **$518**

Blue Iris Handled Wall Pocket

Wall pocket, two handles rising from base to below flaring rim, blue ground, No. 1284-8", 8" h. (ILLUS.) **$432**

Ixia (1930s)

Embossed spray of tiny bell-shaped flowers and slender leaves, white blossoms on pink ground, lavender blossoms on green or yellow ground.

Tall Cylindrical Yellow Ixia Vase

Vase, 12" h., cylindrical, closed upright shoulder handles, yellow ground, No. 864-12" (ILLUS.) **$200-300**

Luffa (1934)

Relief-molded ivy leaves and blossoms on shaded brown or green wavy horizontal ridges.

Bulbous Luffa Jardiniere

Jardiniere, large squatty bulbous body w/a wide flat rim flanked by tiny squared shoulder handles, brown ground, No. 631-7", 7" (ILLUS.) **$288**

Morning Glory (1935)

Delicately colored blossoms and twining vines in white or green with blue.

Spherical Morning Glory Urn-Vase

Urn-vase, bulbous nearly spherical body tapering to a wide flat mouth, squared shoulder handles, green ground, No. 269-6, 6" h. (ILLUS.) **$575**

Rare Tall Morning Glory Vase

Vase, 14 1/4" h., tapering cylindrical body w/flared rim, angled handles from shoulder to mid-section, green ground, No. 732-14" (ILLUS.) **$920**

Moss (1930s)

Green moss hanging over brown branch with green leaves; backgrounds are pink, ivory or tan shading to blue.

Pink & Blue Moss Urn-form Vase

Vase, 8 1/2" h., urn-form, flared foot, bulbous body w/pointed side handles & wide flaring rim, pink shading to blue ground, No. 779-8" (ILLUS.) **$288**

Mostique (1915)

Indian designs of stylized flowers and arrowhead leaves, slip decorated on bisque, glazed interiors. Occasional bowl glazed on outside as well.

Large Bulbous Mostique Jardiniere

Jardiniere, wide bulbous body w/a very wide flat rim, geometric designs in dark yellow, brown & blues alternating w/long dark & medium blue vertical leaf-like geometric designs on a light tan ground, No. 740-8", 8" d., 7" h. (ILLUS.) **$210**

Panel (Rosecraft Panel 1920)

Background colors are dark green or dark brown; decorations embossed within the recessed panels are of natural or stylized floral arrangements or female nudes.

Brown Rosecraft Panel Wall Pocket

Wall pocket, cylindrical w/rounded end, curved asymmetrical rim, long tan trailing leaves & berries down the front on a dark brown ground, 9" h. (ILLUS.) **$260**

Pine Cone (1935 & 1953)
Realistic embossed brown pine cones and green pine needles on shaded blue, brown or green ground. (Pink is extremely rare.)

Tall Green Pine Cone Basket

Basket, w/overhead branch handle, disk base, flaring rim, green ground, some glaze crazing, No. 338-10", 10" h. (ILLUS.) **$260**

Small Brown Pine Cone Jardiniere

Jardiniere, footed wide squatty bulbous body w/a wide flat mouth, small asymmetrical twig handles, brown ground, No. 632-4", 4" h. (ILLUS.) **$259**

Blue Pine Cone Footed Mug

Mug, footed, blue ground, few minor glaze puckers, No. 960-4", 4" h. (ILLUS.) **$316**

Brown Pine Cone Pattern Mug

Mug, footed, brown ground, No. 960-4", 4" h. (ILLUS.) **$316**

Large Ovoid Pine Cone Pitcher

Pitcher, 9 1/2" h., ovoid, small branch handle, brown ground, very slight glaze peppering, No. 708-9" (ILLUS., previous page) **$633**

Oblong Pine Cone Planter

Planter, oval upright sides w/flaring arched serpentine rim, an openwork pine needle & cone handle at one end & a small twig handle at the other, some glaze discoloration, few pinpoint glaze dimples, brown ground, No. 457-7", 4 1/2" h. (ILLUS.) **$207**

Blue Cupped Pine Cone Planter

Planter, a deep cup-shaped bowl set off-center on an oval foot w/a pine cone & pine needle handle extending from base to rim, another sprig on pine needles molded into the lower body, blue ground, No. 124-5", 5" h. (ILLUS.) **$288**

Cup-shaped Pine Cone Planter

Planter, deep cup-shaped bowl set off-center on an oval foot w/a pine cone & pine needle handle extending from base to

rim, another sprig on pine needles molded into the lower body, green ground, No. 124-5", 5" h. (ILLUS.) **$173**

Footed Brown Pine Cone Vase

Vase, 6" h., footed bulbous base w/wide cylindrical neck, handles from shoulder to mid-section of neck, brown ground, No. 839-6" (ILLUS.) **$230**

Blue Footed Bulbous Pine Cone Vase

Vase, 6" h., footed bulbous base w/wide cylindrical neck, handles from shoulder to midsection of neck, blue ground, No. 839-6" (ILLUS.) **$316**

Cylindrical Pine Cone Vase

Vase, 6 1/2" h., wide cylindrical body w/flaring rim, asymmetrical handles, brown ground, No. 838-6" (ILLUS.) **$259**

No. 479-7" Pine Cone Bud Vase

Vase, bud, 7 3/4" h., round disk foot w/upright slender ovoid body w/sprig handle from side to foot, brown ground, No. 479-7", 1950s version of No. 112-7" (ILLUS.) **$259**

Slender Blue Pine Cone No. 479 Vase

Vase, bud, 7 3/4" h., round disk foot w/upright slender ovoid body w/sprig handle from side to foot, blue ground, No. 479-7", 1950s version of No. 112-7" (ILLUS.) **$403**

Unusual Pine Cone Triple Bud Vase

Vase, 8" h., triple bud, domed foot w/twig handles w/a slender trumpet-form cen-

tral vase flanked by angled smaller cylindrical vases, green ground, No. 113-8" (ILLUS.) **$317**

Poppy (1930s)
Shaded backgrounds of blue or pink with decoration of poppy flower and green leaves.

Poppy Vase in Green & Pink

Vase, 8" h., footed, wide cylindrical form w/C-form handles, green ground, No. 871-8" (ILLUS.) **$115**

Primrose (1932)
Cluster of single blossoms on tall stems, low pad-like leaves; backgrounds are blue, tan, or pink.

Tall Blue Primose Vase

Vase, 14 5/8" h., footed tall ovoid body w/a wide flat mouth, low pointed angled handles at center of sides, blue ground, No. 772-14", silver foil sticker & original retailer sticker (ILLUS.) **$432**

Rozane (1900)
Dark blended backgrounds; slip decorated underglaze artware.

Roseville Rozane Vase with Iris

Vase, 7 3/4" h., bulbous ovoid body tapering to a tall slender neck w/widely flaring rim, h.p. with a large yellow & deep red iris & green leaves on a shaded dark brown to green ground, impressed mark "Rozane 838 5," overall crazing (ILLUS.).. **$173**

Snowberry (1946)
Brown branch with small white berries and green leaves embossed over spider-web design in various background colors (blue, green and rose).

Snowberry Shaded Rose Bud Vase

Vase, 7 1/2" h., bud, rectangular foot tapering to a tall, slender, flaring body w/angled rim, asymmetrical pointed loop handles at the base, shaded rose ground, No. 1V1-7" (ILLUS.) **$104**

Vase, 7 1/2" h., bulbous base w/tall cylindrical neck, pointed shoulder handles, shaded blue ground, No. 1V2-7" (ILLUS., top next column) **$104**

Vase, 9" h., large round disk foot supporting a tall cylindrical body w/a flared rim, down-turned pointed handles just above the foot, shaded green ground, No. 1V1-9" **$150-200**

Tall-necked Blue Snowberry Vase

Green Snowberry 9" Vase

Vase, 9" h., base handles, shaded green ground, No. 1V1-9" (ILLUS.) **$150**

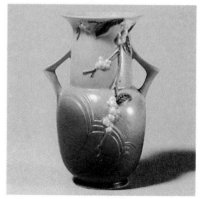

Shaded Rose 10" Snowberry Vase

Vase, 10" h., footed, bulbous lower body below a wide, cylindrical neck w/flaring rim, pointed handles from middle of neck to shoulder, shaded rose ground, No. 1V2-10" (ILLUS.) **$161**

Shaded Rose Baluster Snowberry Vase

Vase, 12 1/2" h., footed, tall, baluster-form body w/flaring rim, pointed angled handles at sides, shaded rose ground, No. IVI-12" (ILLUS.) **$200-300**

Sunflower (1930)

Tall stems support yellow sunflowers whose blooms form a repetitive band. Textured background shades from tan to dark green at base.

Wide Cylindrical Sunflower Vase

Vase, 5" h., wide, flat base w/gently flaring cylindrical sides & a rounded shoulder to the wide closed mouth, No. 486-5" (ILLUS.) **$863**

6" Roseville Sunflower Vase

Vase, 6" h., swelled cylindrical body w/short cylindrical neck flanked by small loop handles, No. 485-6" (ILLUS.) **$547**

Nearly Spherical Sunflower Vase

Vase, 6" h., bulbous, nearly spherical body, wide shoulder tapering to a short cylindrical neck, No. 488-6" (ILLUS.) **$900-1,000**

Swelled Cylindrical Sunflower Vase

Vase, 6 1/4" h., slightly swelled & flaring cylindrical body w/a wide, short, slightly flaring neck flanked by tiny loop handles, No. 494-6" (ILLUS.) **$575**

Sunflower Vase with Bulbous Base

Vase, 8" h., bulbous base, wide tapering cylindrical neck, No. 490-8" (ILLUS.) **$1,093**

Ovoid Sunflower Vase

Vase, 8 1/4" h., ovoid body w/a widely flaring rim flanked by small loop handles, No. 491-8" (ILLUS.) **$1,035**

Cylindrical Sunflower Vase

Vase, 10" h., swelled cylindrical body w/tiny shoulder handles, No. 492-10" (ILLUS.) ... **$920**

Sylvan (1918)

Tree bark textured exterior in shades of grey or sandy tan with incised forest scenes including hunting dogs, foxes and owls, sometimes with a scattering of leaves or acorns; glazed interior.

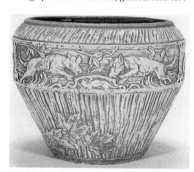

Sylvan Jardiniere with Hunting Dogs

Jardiniere, wide tapering ovoid form w/a wide flat mouth, light green band of hunting dogs decoration against a light brown

tree bark ground, some very small glaze nicks, No. 568, 10" h. (ILLUS.) **$375**

Tourmaline (1933)

Although the semi-gloss medium blue, highlighted around the rim with lighter high gloss and gold effect seems to be accepted as the standard Tourmaline glaze, the catalogue definitely shows this and two other types as well. One is a mottled overall turquoise, the other a mottled salmon that appears to be lined in the high gloss but with no overrun to the outside.

Pair Blue Tourmaline Candlesticks

Candlesticks, flared ribbed base, flaring nozzle, mottled blue ground, gold labels, No. 1089-4 1/2", 4 1/2" h., pr. (ILLUS.) **$127**

Gold Tourmaline Globular Urn

Urn, footed globular body w/embossed lines around shoulder interrupted w/some vertical bands, mottled gold, No. 238-5", 5 1/2" h. (ILLUS.) **$81**

Tourmaline Pink Pillow-type Vase

Vase, 6" h., rectangular pillow-type w/horizontally ribbed lower half flanked by small scroll handles, mottled pink w/pale blue upper band, gold foil sticker, No. A-65-6" (ILLUS., previous page).................... **$69**

Tourmaline Blue Pillow-type Vase

Vase, 6" h., rectangular pillow-type w/horizontally ribbed lower half flanked by small scroll handles, mottled blue w/drippy green upper band, No. A-65-6" (ILLUS.) **$92**

Spherical Pink Tourmaline Vase

Vase, 6" h., footed nearly spherical body w/a wide band of narrow rings just below the wide rolled rim, mottled pink, No. 611-6" (ILLUS.) **$81**

Spherical Blue Tourmaline Vase

Vase, 6" h., footed nearly spherical body w/a wide band of narrow rings just below the wide rolled rim, mottled blue, No. 611-6" (ILLUS.) **$115**

Simple Blue Tourmaline Vase

Vase, 7" h., footed swelled cylindrical body tapering to a short wide neck w/flared rim, mottled blue, No. A-308-7" (ILLUS.) .. **$159**

Blue Tourmaline Vase with Leaf Band

Vase, 8 1/4" h., footed flating cylindrical body w/a ringed base, tapering pointed tab handles at lower sides, the body molded in low-relief w/narrow ribbed strips joined around the top by a molded leaf band, mottled blue (ILLUS.) **$184**

Blue Tourmaline Vase in Scarce Shape

Vase, 9" h., flared foot below buttressed base, trumpet-form body, mottled blue glaze, No. A-429-9" (ILLUS., previous page) **$317**

Square Blue Tourmaline Vase

Vase, 9 1/2" h., footed gently flaring square form w/a narrow molded herringbone band below the flared rim, mottled blue ground, No. 615-9" (ILLUS.) **$260**

Tuscany (1928)

Marble-like finish most often found in a shiny pink, sometimes in matte grey, more rarely in a dull turquoise. Suggestion of leaves and berries, usually at the base of handles, are the only decorations.

Short Tuscany Turquoise Vase

Vase, 4" h., 6 1/2" w., bowl-form, footed widely flaring trumpet-form w/open handles from under rim to the foot, mottled turquoise, No. 67-4" (ILLUS.) **$92**

Pink Tuscany Conical Wall Pocket

Wall pocket, conical w/wide flaring half-round ringed rim, loop handles at sides molded w/small purple grape clusters &

pale green leaves, pink, No. 1254-7", 7" h. (ILLUS.) **$288**

Pink Tuscany 8" Wall Pocket

Wall pocket, long open handles, rounded rim, mottled pink glaze, paper label, short hairline from mounting hole to rim, No. 1255-8", 8" h. (ILLUS.)............................... **$173**

Vista (1920s)

Embossed green coconut palm trees & lavender blue pool against grey ground.

Tall Cylindrical Vista Vase

Vase, 12" h., 4 3/4" d., footed, bulbous base tapering to tall wide cylindrical neck w/flat rim, No. 125-12" (ILLUS.)......................... **$978**

Water Lily (1943)

Water lily and pad in various color combinations: tan to brown with yellow lily, blue with white lily, pink to green with pink lily.

Large Blue Water Lily Conch Shell

Model of a conch shell, shaded blue ground, No. 438-8", 8" l. (ILLUS., previous page) **$150-200**

Water Lily Shaded Blue Tea Set

Tea set: cov. teapot No. 5, open sugar bowl No. 5-S & creamer No. 5-C; squatty bulbous forms, shaded blue ground, the set (ILLUS.).. **$345**

Bulbous Blue Water Lily Vase

Vase, 8 1/4" h., footed, bulbous, ovoid body w/a short, wide, cylindrical neck flanked by angular handles, pale blue ground, No. 77-8" (ILLUS.).............................. **$175-225**

Footed Ovoid Blue Water Lily Vase

Vase, 9" h., footed, ovoid body w/wide, flat mouth, the sides w/pointed downswept handles, pale blue ground, No. 78-9" (ILLUS.) **$175-250**
Vase, 9" h., footed, ovoid body w/wide, flat mouth, the sides w/pointed downswept handles, pink shaded to green ground, No. 78-9" (ILLUS., top next column) .. **$250-350**

Pink Shaded to Green Water Lily Vase

No. 80-10" Water Lily Vase

Vase, 10 1/4" h., low foot below the widely flaring flattened lower body tapering to a tall waisted neck w/flaring rim, large angled handles from center of neck to edge of lower body, tan shading to brown ground, No. 80-10" (ILLUS.) **$200-300**

White Rose (1940s)
White roses and green leaves against a vertically combed ground of blended blue, brown shading to green, or pink shading to green.

Spherical Blue White Rose Jardiniere

Jardiniere, spherical w/wide notched rim flanked by small shoulder loop handles, blended blue ground, No. 653-10", 10" h. (ILLUS.).. **$200-250**

Tea set: cov. teapot, sugar bowl & creamer; brown shading to green ground, Nos. 1T, 1S, 1C, 3 pcs.. **$489**

White Rose Brown & Green Urn-Vase

Urn-vase, pedestal base below the wide, bulbous, ovoid body w/a wide cylindrical neck w/a notched rim, curved handles from rim to shoulder, brown shaded to green ground, No. 147-8", 8" h. (ILLUS.) **$150-175**

Wisteria (1933)

Lavender wisteria blossoms and green vines against a roughly textured brown shading to deep blue ground or brown shading to yellow and green; rarely found in only brown.

Tapering Cylindrical Wisteria Vase

Vase, 8" h., 6 1/2" d., wide, tapering, cylindrical body w/small angled handles flanking the flat rim, blue ground, No. 633-8" (ILLUS.).. **$1,265**
Vase, 8 1/2" h., flaring foot tapering to the gently flaring body bulging slightly below the flat rim, short handles from lower body to foot, brown shading to yellow & green ground, No. 635-8" (ILLUS., top next column)... **$575**

Rare Flaring Wisteria Vase

Rare Flaring Blue Wisteria Vase

Vase, 8 1/2" h., flaring foot tapering to the gently flaring body bulging slightly below the flat rim, short handles from lower body to foot, brown shading to yellow & green ground, gold foil label, blue ground, No. 635-8" (ILLUS.) **$1,035**

Ovoid Wisteria Vase with Tall Neck

Vase, 9 1/2" h., cylindrical ovoid body w/angular handles rising from shoulder to midsection of slender cylindrical neck, brown shaded to yellow & green ground, No. 638-9" (ILLUS.) **$690**

Cylindrical 10" Wisteria Vase

Vase, 10" h., cylindrical body w/closed rim, angled shoulder handles, brown shaded to yellow & green ground, silver foil sticker, No. 639-10" (ILLUS.) **$500**

Zephyr Lily (1946)
Tall lilies and slender leaves adorn swirl-textured backgrounds of Bermuda Blue, Evergreen and Sienna Tan.

Tall Terra Cotta Zephyr Lily Ewer

Ewer, footed flaring lower body w/angled shoulder tapering to a tall forked neck w/upright tall spout, long low arched handle, terra cotta ground, No. 23-10", 10 3/8" h. (ILLUS.) **$127**

Zephyr Lily Flowerpot & Saucer

Flowerpot w/saucer, terra cotta ground, No. 672-5", 5" h. (ILLUS.) **$150-175**

Royal Bayreuth

Good china in numerous patterns and designs has been made at the Royal Bayreuth factory in Tettau, Germany since 1794. Listings below are by the company's lines, plus miscellaneous pieces. Interest in this china remains at a peak and prices continue to rise. Pieces listed carry the company's blue mark except where noted otherwise.

Among the important reference books in this field are Royal Bayreuth - A Collectors' Guide and Royal Bayreuth - A Collectors' Guide - Book II by Mary McCaslin (see Special Contributors list).

Royal Bayreuth Mark

Corinthian
Cake plate, classical figures on black ground, 10" d... **$150**
Creamer & cov. sugar bowl, classical figures on black ground, pr. **$120**

Corinthian Pitcher

Pitcher, tankard, 6 7/8" h., 3 3/4" d., orange inside top, classical figures on black satin ground, gold bands w/black & white geometric design around neck & base (ILLUS.) **$150**
Planter, classical figures on red ground........ **$120**

Devil & Cards
Ashtray **$125-150**
Ashtray w/match holder **$250-275**
Salt dip, master size **$275-325**
Stamp box, cov., 3 1/2" l....................... **$550-600**
Sugar bowl, open, short **$300-350**

Mother-of-Pearl
Ashtray, Spiky Shell patt......................... **$75-100**

Creamer, grape cluster mold, pearlized white, 3 3/4" h. **$150-175**

Creamer & cov. sugar bowl, grape cluster mold, pearlized yellow, colorful foliage, pr. **$300-375**

Cup & saucer, demitasse, Oyster & Pearl mold **$300-350**

Hatpin holder, white pearlized finish **$150-175**

Sugar bowl, cov., footed, figural Spiky Shell patt., pearlized finish, 3 1/2" h. **$250-300**

Toothpick holder, Spiky Shell patt., pearlized finish **$150-175**

Rose Tapestry

Basket, rope handle, base & outer rim, three color roses, 4 1/4" w., 4" h. **$250-350**

Bowl, 10 1/2" d., shell- & scroll-molded rim, three-color roses **$950-1,050**

Chocolate pot, cov., apricot, white, pink & yellow roses, leaf finial, gold trim, 8 1/2" h. **$1,800-2,000**

Creamer & cov. sugar bowl, pink & white roses, pr. **$550-650**

Dessert set: large cake plate & six matching small serving plates; three-color roses, 7 pcs. **$1,000-1,200**

Nappy, tri-lobed leaf shape, decorated w/orange roses, 4 1/2" l. **$150-200**

Pitcher, 5 3/4" h., waisted shape, C-scroll handle angled at bottom, three-color roses **$350-500**

Vase, 4 1/2" h., ovoid body decorated w/clusters of small red roses at top & base, large yellow roses in center, short neck flaring slightly at rim **$200-300**

Sunbonnet Babies

Ashtray, babies cleaning **$250-275**

Candlestick, babies washing, 5" d., 1 3/4" h. **$275-300**

Creamer, babies ironing, 3" h. **$250-300**

Cup & saucer, babies washing **$250-350**

Tea set, child's **$750-900**

Miscellaneous

Ashtray, figural elk **$250-275**

Ashtray, figural shell, 4 1/2 x 4 1/2" **$50-75**

Ashtray, stork decoration, artist-signed, 4 1/2" l. **$75-100**

Basket, "tapestry," footed, bulbous body w/a ruffled rim & ornate gold-trimmed overhead handle, portrait of woman w/horse, 5" h. **$550-600**

Bell, scene of musicians, men playing a cello & mandolin **$300-350**

Bowl, 9 1/2" l., 3 3/4" h., raised enameled white roses & foliage on creamy ivory ground, flared, gently ruffled rim, four gold-trimmed reticulated reserves, four short gold feet **$225-350**

Bowl, 6 7/8" d., 2 1/2" h., footed, shallow slightly scalloped sides, Cavalier Musicians decoration, gold trim on feet **$100-125**

Cracker jar, cov., figural poppy, 6" h. **$800-1,000**

Creamer, figural clown, red suit **$400-450**

Creamer, figural eagle, grey.................. **$300-400**

Creamer, figural girl w/pitcher, red **$800-900**

Creamer, figural leopard **$6,000-6,500**

Creamer, figural oak leaf....................... **$200-250**

Creamer, figural Santa Claus, attached handle, red, 4 1/4" h..................... **$3,000-3,200**

Standing Trout Creamer

Creamer, figural trout, standing on tail, shaded brown to white w/reddish dots (ILLUS.).. **$4,500**

Creamer, flow blue, Babes in Woods decoration **$250-300**

Creamer, scene of girl w/basket, salmon color **$600-800**

Creamer, figural seashell, boot-shaped, 3 3/4" h. **$150-195**

Creamer & cov. sugar bowl, figural poppy, pr. **$300-350**

Creamer & cov. sugar bowl, figural strawberry, unmarked, pr. **$450-500**

Ewer, cobalt blue, Babes in Woods decoration, 6" h. **$600-650**

Hair receiver, cov., "tapestry," scene of farmer w/turkeys **$250-300**

Penguin Hatpin Holder

Hatpin holder, model of a penguin, in red, white & grey, signed (ILLUS.) **$800-900**

Model of a man's high top slipper **$250-300**

Cavalier Pitcher

Pitcher, 3 1/4" h., 2" d., decorated w/Cavalier scene, two Cavaliers drinking at a table, grey & cream ground, unmarked (ILLUS.) **$65**
Pitcher, miniature, 4 1/2" h., scene of a skiff w/sail **$100-125**
Pitcher, 5" h., figural crow **$175**

Royal Bayreuth Santa Pitcher

Pitcher, 5 1/4" h., figural, Santa Claus, pack on back serves as handle (ILLUS.)
.... **$3,500-4,000**
Pitcher, lemonade, 7 1/2 " h., figural apple
.... **$1,000-1,200**
Pitcher, milk, figural red & white parrot handle **$550-600**
Pitcher, milk, musicians decoration **$150-175**
Pitcher, water, tankard, 9 1/2" h., h.p. pastoral cow scene **$250-300**
Pitcher, water, 6" h., figural Santa Claus, red **$6,000-9,000**
Pitcher, water, 7 1/4" h., pinched spout, scenic decoration of cows in pasture . **$250-300**
Plate, 5 1/4" d., leaf-shaped, decorated w/small yellow flowers on green ground, green curved handle **$40**
Plate, 8 1/2" d., scene of man hunting.......... **$135**
String holder, hanging-type, figural rooster head **$400-550**
Toothpick holder, figural bell ringer, 3 1/2" h... **$200-250**
Toothpick holder, three-handled, scene of horse & wagon **$150-175**
Vase, 3" h., scene of children w/St. Bernard dog **$75-125**

Vase, 3 5/8" h., footed conical body tapering to a swelled neck flanked by four loop handles, decorated w/hunting scene, man & woman on horses, unmarked **$50-75**
Vase, 4" h., two-handled, decorated w/longtailed Bird of Paradise **$300-350**
Vase, 5" h., "tapestry," bulbous ovoid body tapering to a short slender flaring neck, "Castle by the Lake" landscape scene **$300-350**
Vase, 5 1/4" h., ovoid body w/short cylindrical neck, medallion portrait framed w/gold band in incised leaf design w/enamel trim..................................... **$200-250**
Vase, 7 3/4" h., mercury & floral finish, ca. 1919, artist-signed & signed "Kgl. Priv. Tettau"... **$250**
Vase, 8" h., bulbous body on short quatrefoil foot, side C-scroll handles w/decorative ends, short reticulated neck w/flaring rim, decorated w/waterfall scene **$200-250**
Vase, 8" h., decorated w/scene of hunter & dogs **$200-250**

Vase with Peacock

Vase, 9 1/2" h., peacock decoration, openwork on neck & at base, ornate scroll handles, lavish gold trim (ILLUS.) **$700-750**
Vase, double-bud, ovoid body w/two angled short flaring necks joined by a small handle, scene of Dutch children............... **$100-150**

Small Royal Bayreuth Vases

Vases, 3 1/8" h., 2 5/8" d., squatty bulbous lower body below the tall tapering sides ending in a ringed neck & flanked by loop handles, one w/scene of Dutch boy & girl playing w/brown dog & the other w/scene of Dutch boy & girl playing w/white & brown dog, green mark, pr. (ILLUS.).... **$75-125**

Royal Bonn & Bonn

Bonn and subsequently Royal Bonn china were produced in Bonn, Germany, in a manufactory established in 1755. Later wares made there are often marked "Mehlem" or bear the initials "FM" or a castle mark. Most wares were of the hand-painted type. Clock cases were also made in Bonn.

Royal Bonn & Bonn Mark

Another Royal Bonn Old Dutch Vase

Vase, miniature, 3 3/4" h., Old Dutch Line, spherical body w/a small trumpet neck, decorated w/a wide central band featuring an undulating thin green-striped ribbon entwined w/matching arches, against a dark brown ground w/deep purple leaf clusters, the shoulder w/a band of repeating arches in brown, yellow & dark blue below a thin dark blue band & the dark green & yellow neck, a matching arched band around the base, marked "Royal Bonn - Germany - Old Dutch - D60," late 19th c. (ILLUS.).................................. **$100-150**

Royal Bonn Old Dutch Line Vase

Vase, miniature, 3 3/4" h., Old Dutch Line, spherical body w/a small trumpet neck, decorated around the shoulder w/a band of colorful stylized blossoms in pink, white & brick red on a dark green & blue ground, white & yellow leafy stems up from the lower body against a dark brown ground, marked "Royal Bonn - Old Dutch - 7 3091/3 319," late 19th c. (ILLUS.)........ **$115**

Pair of Royal Bonn Vases with Pastoral Scenes of Watering Cattle

Vases, 11 1/2" h., ovoid form w/short neck & flaring lobed rim, studio decorated in the round w/h.p. scenes of cattle standing in shallow stream, w/trees & foliage in background & foreground, low hills in the distance, artist signed "J. Sticher," marked "Royal Bonn," Germany, late 19th c., pr. (ILLUS.).............................. **$2,300**

Pair of Royal Bonn "Tapestry" Vases

Vases, 12" h., "tapestry-type," ovoid body tapering to a tall cylindrical neck, h.p. overall w/an exotic woodland scene w/large colorful blossoms under a textured surface, marked on bottom, late 19th c., pr. (ILLUS.).................................. **$575**

Pair of Royal Bonn Portrait Vases

Vases, 14" h., cylindrical form tapering out to rounded shoulder w/short flaring neck, each w/h.p. scene of young woman w/flowing brown hair picking flowers in meadow w/trees & distant hills in background, one wearing green skirt & pink & white blouse, the other a white sleeveless dress w/green apron, the meadow in shades of yellow & light yellow-green, the base & neck of each turquoise w/gilt decoration, artist signed indistinguishably, printed marks, Germany, early 20th c., pr. (ILLUS.)... **$1,725**

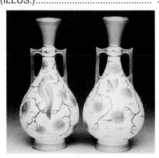

Fancy Royal Bonn Decorated Vases

Vases, 15 3/4" h., small tapering cylindrical foot supporting the bulbous ovoid body tapering to a tall slender trumpet neck flanked by wide squared gold handles, gold neck & gold base band on the foot, the creamy body h.p. on the front w/a large colorful parrot on entwined branches w/fan-shaped green leaves, the reverse w/a flying butterfly among the branches, heavy gold trim, marked on the base, late 19th c., pr. (ILLUS.) **$400-600**

Royal Copenhagen

Although the Royal Copenhagen factory in Denmark has been in business for over 200 years, very little has been written about it. That is not to say the very beautiful porcelain it produces is not

easily recognizable. Besides producing gorgeous dinnerware, such as "Blue Fluted" and "Flora Danica," it produced - and still does - wonderful figurines depicting animals and people. The company employs talented artists as both modelers and painters. Once you become familiar with the colors, glazes and beauty of these figurines, you will have no trouble recognizing them at a glance.

Collecting these magnificent figurines seems as popular now as in the past. As with most objects, and certainly true of these figurines, value will depend on the complexity, size, age and rarity of the piece. There is other Danish porcelain on the market today, but the Royal Copenhagen figurines can readily be recognized by the mark on the bottom with the three dark blue wavy lines. Accept no imitations!

Royal Copenhagen Mark

Boy with Teddy Bear Figure Group

Figure group, boy & Teddy bear, toddler standing wearing blue romper, holding tan bear behind him, No. 3468, 3 1/2" w., 7" h. (ILLUS.) **$150**

Girl Feeding Calf Figure Group

Figure group, girl feeding calf, a farm girl bending over to feed a calf from a pail, green oblong base, No. 779, 6 1/2" l., 6 1/2" h. (ILLUS., previous page) **$250**

Figure group, Hans Clodhopper, boy seated astride a billy goat, No. 1228, 5 1/2" l., 6 3/4" h. **$175**

Royal Copenhagen Harvest Group

Figure group, Harvest Group, young farmer & farm girl standing close together, each leaning on a hoe, No. 1300, small, 4" w., 7 1/2" h. (ILLUS.)............................. **$250**

Shepherd Boy and Dog

Figure group, shepherd boy w/dog, standing boy wearing cap & long blanket cloak, No. 782, 3 1/2" w., 7 1/2" h. (ILLUS.) **$175**

Faun on Tortoise Figure Group

Figure group, young faun seated astride a large tortoise, No. 858, 3 1/2" l., 4" h. (ILLUS.) **$145**

Young Children & Puppy Figure Group

Figure group, young girl & boy hugging brown puppy, No. 707, 5 1/2" l., 5 3/4" h. (ILLUS.)... **$250**

Figure of a boy, February Boy Juggler, standing wearing a top hat & holding a baton to juggle, No. 4524, 6 1/2" h. **$150**

Royal Copenhagen Sandman Figure

Figure of boy, Sandman (Wee-Willie-Winkie), standing on white square stepped base & leaning on an umbrella, holding

another, dressed in grey, No. 1145, 6" h.
(ILLUS.) **$75**

Model of bird, Budgie on Gourd, white bird
w/blue trim on dark blue gourd, No. 4682,
4 x 5 1/2" **$125**

Royal Copenhagen Sandman Figure

Figure of boy, Sandman (Wee-Willie-
Winkie,) standing wearing a long white
nightgown & pointed blue cap, a closed
umbrella under one arm, opening a
brown vial in his hands, No. 1145,
6 3/4" h. (ILLUS.)... **$75**

Model of a Fat Robin

Model of bird, Fat Robin, rounded baby
robin in blue, white & rust red, No. 2266,
3" h. (ILLUS.) **$55**

Royal Copenhagen Model of a Grebe

Model of bird, Grebe, handsome swimming
bird w/blue crest & grey & white body,
No. 3263, 7" l., 4" h. (ILLUS.)...................... **$95**

Royal Copenhagen Boy on Gourd

Figure of boy on gourd, young barefoot
boy wearing white shirt & blue overalls
seated astride a large green gourd, No.
4539, 4 1/4 x 4 1/2" (ILLUS.)....................... **$75**

Royal Copenhagen Icelandic Falcon

Model of bird, Icelandic Falcon, large bird
w/speckled bluish grey & white feathers,
No. 263, 8 1/2" l., 11" h. (ILLUS.).............. **$350**

Figure of Young Man Eating Lunch

Figure of young man eating lunch, reclining position, eating from a lunch box, No.
865, 7" l., 4" h. (ILLUS.) **$150**

Model of Finches

Model of birds, pair of blue, white & grey
finches perched close together, No.
1189, 5" l., 2" h. (ILLUS.) **$45**

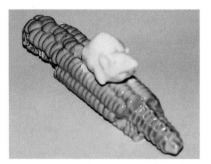

Mouse on Ear of Corn Figure

Model of mouse, white & pink mouse perched on an ear of brown corn, No. 512, 5" l., 2" h. (ILLUS.) **$48**

Royal Copenhagen Panda Figure

Model of panda, seated eating bamboo, No. 662, 5 1/2" w., 7" h. (ILLUS.) **$175**

Royal Copenhagen Penguins

Model of penguins, two birds seated side by side, No. 1190, 4" h. (ILLUS.) **$75**
Model of piglets, pair of piglets fused together, white w/grey spots, pink snout, No. 683, 2 1/2 x 4 1/2" **$75**

Small Royal Copenhagen Rabbit

Model of rabbit, seated upright eating leaf, No. 1019, small size, 3 1/2" h. (ILLUS.) **$48**

Royal Copenhagen Sea Lion

Model of sea lion, head raised, shades of tan & grey, No. 265, 7 x 12" (ILLUS.)........ **$275**

Royal Copenhagen Rose Bowl

Rose bowl, squatty spherical form w/wide flat mouth, dark blue ground painted w/large white blossoms & green leaves, No. 424, 8" d., 6" h. (ILLUS.).................... **$125**

Royal Copley

Royal Copley was a trade name used by the Spaulding China Company of Sebring, Ohio, during the 1940s and 1950s for a variety of ceramic figurines, planters and other decorative pieces. Similar Spaulding pieces were also pro-

duced under the trade name "Royal Windsor," or carried the Spaulding China mark.

Dime stores generally featured the Royal Copley line, with Spaulding's other lines available in more upscale outlets.

The Spaulding China Company ended production in 1957, but for the next two years other potteries finished production of its outstanding orders. Today these originally inexpensive wares are developing a dedicated collector following thanks to their whimsically appealing designs.

Figurines

Airedale Figurine

Airedale, seated, brown & white, 6 1/2" h.
(ILLUS.).. **$40-45**
Cockatoos, 7 1/4" h. **$5o-60**
Deer & Fawn, 8 1/2" h............................... **$60-70**
Dog, 8" h.. **$40-45**
Hen & Rooster, Royal Windsor mark, 6 1/2"
& 7" h., pr. **$120-140**
Kingfishers, 5" h....................................... **$40-50**

Oriental Boy & Girl Figurines

Oriental Boy & Oriental Girl, standing,
7 1/2" h., pr. (ILLUS.) **$35-55**
Sea Gulls, 8" h. **$35-55**
Swallow with extended wings, 7" h. **$110-130**
Thrushes, 6 1/2" h. **$20-25**
Wrens, 6 1/4" h... **$20-25**

Planters

Angel on Star Planter

Angel on Star, white relief figure on creamy
yellow ground, 6 3/4" h. (ILLUS.) **$30-40**
Balinese Girl, 8 1/2" h. **$50-60**
Big Hat Chinese Boy & Girl, 7 1/2" h., pr. **$50-60**
Cinderella's Coach, 6" h., 3 1/4" h........... **$25-30**
Cocker Spaniel, 8" h. **$30-35**

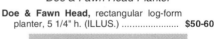

Doe & Fawn Head Planter

Doe & Fawn Head, rectangular log-form
planter, 5 1/4" h. (ILLUS.) **$50-60**

Dog with Raised Paw Planter

Dog with Raised Paw, 7 1/2" h. (ILLUS.).. **$70-80**
Dogwood, oval, 3 1/2" h. **$30-35**

Duck with Mailbox, 6 3/4" h. $70-80
Dutch Boy & Girl with Buckets, 6 1/4" h.,
     pr. $60-85

Elf and Shoe Planter

Elf and Shoe, 6" h. (ILLUS.) $60-70
Fighting Cock, 6 1/2" h............................. $60-70

Girl on Wheelbarrow Planter

Girl on Wheelbarrow, 7" h. (ILLUS.) $50-55
High Tail Rooster, 7 3/4" h. $60-70

Kitten and Book Planter

Kitten and Book, 6 1/2" h. (ILLUS.) $45-55
Mallard Duck, standing, 8" h. $20-25
Mature Wood Duck, 7 1/4" h..................... $35-45
Oriental Boy with Basket on Back & Ori-
     ental Girl with Basket on Back, 8" h.,
     pr. $140-150
Peter Rabbit, 6 1/2" h. $90-100

Reclining Poodle Planter

Poodle, reclining, white w/black nose &
     eyes, 8" l. (ILLUS.) $80-90

Ribbed Star Royal Windsor Planter

Ribbed Star, all-white, "Royal Windsor"
     sticker, 4 3/4" h. (ILLUS.) $35-40

Stuffed Animal Elephant Planter

Stuffed Animal Elephant, pale green &
     white, 6 1/2" h. (ILLUS.) $90-100
Tanagers, 6 1/4" h. $30-40
Teddy Bear, white, 8" h. $85-100

Rare Teddy Bear with Concertina

Teddy Bear with Concertina, rare, 7 1/4" h. (ILLUS.) **$120-145**

Tony Head Planter

Tony Head, man wearing large blue hat, 8 1/4" h. (ILLUS.) **$60-85**
Woodpeckers, 6 1/4" h. **$30-40**

Miscellaneous

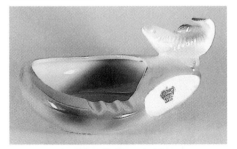

Leaping Salmon Ashtray

Ashtray, Leaping Salmon, oblong boat-shaped bowl w/figural salmon on rim, 5 x 6 1/4" (ILLUS.) **$35-45**
Bank, Teddy Bear, 7 1/2" h. **$120-140**
Pitcher, Floral Beauty, 8" h. **$80-95**
Vase, 5 3/4" h., Fish, open center **$55-70**
Vase, 6 1/4" h., footed pillow-shape, ivy decoration **$25-30**
Vase, 7 1/4" h., Deer, open center **$40-45**

Vase, 8 1/4" h., Dogwood........................... **$35-45**
Wall plaque-planters, Hen & Rooster, 6 3/4" h., pr... **$140-170**

Island Man Wall Pocket

Wall pocket, Island Man, black head wearing white turban, 8" h. (ILLUS.) **$150-170**
Wall pocket, Spice Box, 5 1/2" h. **$90-100**

Royal Dux

This factory in Bohemia was noted for the figural porcelain wares in the Art Nouveau style it exported around the turn of the 20th century. Other notable figural pieces were produced through the 1930s. The factory was nationalized after World War II.

Royal Dux Marks

Royal Dux Bull & Farmer Group

Figure group, a large cream-colored bull being held on a rein by a standing farmer wearing a hat, long-sleeved sheet, pants & boots, on a naturalistic rectangular base, decorated in dark gold, pink trian-

gle mark & impressed number, late 19th
- early 20th c., 13" l., 11" h. (ILLUS.)......... **$748**

Royal Dux Arab & Camel Figure Group

Figure group, an Arab man wearing a hood
& flowing robes seated atop a tall walking
camel, a half-naked young boy below
struggling w/two large bags, decorated in
shades of deep red, brown, tan, cream &
gold, pink triangle & Made in Czecho-
slovkia marks on base, 6 x 14", 18" h.
(ILLUS.)... **$480**

Maiden at Poolside Figure

Figure of a maiden, Classical figure wearing a long deep red robe & leaning
against a large tree & bending down
holding a water pot above a pool, oval
base, trimmed in gold & pale green, pink
triangle mark & impressed number, late
19th - early 20th c., 8 1/2" l., 16 1/2" h.
(ILLUS.)... **$720**
Figure of a maiden, Classical standing fig-
ure wearing an off-the-shoulder long gold
robe, holding two red roses to her face
w/one hand & carrying a basket of roses
in the other, pink triangle mark & impressed number, late 19th - early 20th c.,
20 1/4" h. (ILLUS., top next column) **$450**
Figure of an Arab man, walking bearded
figure wearing loose robes & a turban,
carrying a water jug in one hand & the other arm raised to support a large boat-
shaped container across his shoulders,

Royal Dux Maiden with Roses

Royal Dux Figure of an Arab Man

overall gold on cream ground, pink triangle mark on base, on a round rockwork
base, 28" h. (ILLUS.)............................... **$840**

Royal Dux Peasant Man & Woman

Figures, peasant man & woman, he standing wearing a wide-brimmed hat, gold shirt & brown pants & holding a bag over one shoulder & a net in the other, on a round naturalistic base w/stump & chain she wearing a short-sleeved blouse & vest & long deep red dress w/one hand holding up her gold apron full of apples & a jug over her arm, on a matching rounded base, pink triangle & impressed triangle marks w/numbers, 20" & 22" h., pr. (ILLUS., previous page) **$720**

Royal Dux Lamp with Horse & Boy

Lamp, figural table model, the oblong base enclosed in a brass frame & mounted w/the model of a large creamy white work horse carrying a removable young farm boy wearing a cap, shirt & rolled up pants, trimmed in dark gold, pink triangle mark & impressed "1602," metal upright at back w/electric fitting & decorated creamy silk shade, early 20th c., figure 12" l., 14" h. (ILLUS.) **$690**

Royal Dux Mirror with Maiden Figure

Mirror, figural table-type, an upright oval beveled edge mirror set along one side w/a curved flower & vine support raised on a tree trunk base, a tall classical maiden standing to the side wearing long deep red robes, squared dished base, pink triangle mark, late 19th - early 20th c., base 16" w., overall 17" h. (ILLUS.) .. **$1,323**

Royal Dux Floral Art Nouveau Vase

Vase, 20 1/2" h., 11 1/2" d., Art Nouveau style, footed wide squatty base section below the tall gently tapering upper body tapering to a wide cupped rim, molded down the sides & around the base section w/realistic leaves & blossoms w/undulating loop handles down the sides, dusted black finish & gold trim, pink triangle & impressed numbers, late 19th - early 20th c. (ILLUS.) **$518**

Pair of Royal Dux Figural Vases

Vases, 12" h., figural, a large cylindrical molded tree trunk form, one applied w/a the figure of a boy playing a lyre & the other w/the figure of dancing girl w/a lamb, cream ground w/heavy gold trim, pink triangle marks & impressed numbers, late 19th - early 20th c., pr. (ILLUS.) **$408**

Royal Vienna

The second factory in Europe to make hard paste porcelain was established in Vienna in 1719 by Claud Innocentius de Paquier. The factory underwent various changes of administration through the years and finally closed in 1865. Since then, however, the porcelain has been reproduced by various factories in Austria and Ger-

many, many of which have also reproduced the early beehive mark. Early pieces, naturally, bring far higher prices than the later ones or the reproductions.

Royal Vienna Mark

Marie Antoinette Royal Vienna Plate

Plate, 9 1/2" d., cabinet-type, a central color bust portrait of Marie Antoinette, signed by Wagner, the cobalt blue border band ornately decorated w/gold panels, scrolls & florals (ILLUS.).................................... **$1,150**

Lovely Royal Vienna Portrait Plate

Plate, 9 1/2" d., cabinet-type, the center w/a finely painted bust portrait of a Renaissance era noblewoman w/a feathered headdress, the cobalt blue border band ornately decorated w/undulating panels of fancy florals, mounted in a deep giltwood shadowbox frame lined in deep red velvet, overall 16" sq. (ILLUS.)............... **$1,725**

Ornate Royal Vienna Urn, Cover & Stand

Urn, cover & stand, the domed stand on shaped gold tab feet & a gold border, the cobalt blue ground ornately decorated w/overall bands of delicate floral vines centering a round reserve h.p. in color w/a scene of a Greek god & goddess, the urn w/a tapering pedestal below the wide urn-form body, cobalt blue ground decorated overall w/gold bands & ornate delicate leafy vines, a large central oval reserve h.p. in color w/a group of Greek gods & goddesses, long angled gold handles flanking the shoulder & the tapering domed cover w/a pointed gold finial & h.p. w/another color reserve, late 19th - early 20th c., overall 21 1/4" h., the set (ILLUS.).. **$5,581**

Pretty Royal Vienna Portrait Vase

Vase, 5" h., ovoid body tapering to a slender neck w/a flaring rim, gilt openwork vine-like gold handles from the center neck to shoulder, a large gold oval enclosing a color portrait of a young maiden w/brown hair, background in pale shaded green w/ornate gilt decoration, artist-signed, marked on the base "Germany - Sincerity - 3666," tiny flat nick on the rim (ILLUS.) $575

Slender Royal Vienna Vase with Maiden

Vase, 7" h., footed bulbous base tapering to a tall slender cylindrdical body w/a bulbed forked mouth, gold ruffled loop handles on center of the blue neck trimmed w/gilt florals & a Greek key band, the main body decorated w/a color scene of a young maiden seated looking at a pair of doves w/a cherub by her side, artist-signed, blue Beehive mark on the base (ILLUS.) $863

Russel Wright Designs

The innovative dinnerware designed by Russel Wright and produced by various companies beginning in the late 1930s was an immediate success with a society that was turning to a more casual and informal lifestyle. His designs, with their flowing lines and unconventional shapes, were produced in many different colors, which allowed a hostess to arrange creative tables.

Although not antique, these designs, which we list here by line and manufacturer, are highly collectible. In addition to dinnerwares, Wright was also known as a trendsetter in the design of furniture, glassware, lamps, fabric and a multitude of other household goods.

Russel Wright Marks

American Modern (Steubenville Pottery Co.)

Baker, glacier blue, small $55
Bowl, child's, black chutney $100
Bowl, fruit, lug handle, cedar green $30

Group of American Modern Pieces

Bowl, fruit, lug handle, chartreuse (ILLUS. left) $20
Bowl, salad, cedar green $100
Bowl, soup, lug handle, bean brown $35
Butter dish, cov., white................................. $365
Carafe w/stopper, bean brown..................... $500
Coaster, granite grey $20
Coffee cup cover, black chutney.................. $175
Coffeepot, cov., after dinner, coral $120
Coffeepot, cov., black chutney $250
Coffeepot, cov., seafoam blue...................... $275
Creamer, cedar green...................................... $30
Cup & saucer, coffee, cantaloupe $40
Cup & saucer, demitasse, cantaloupe........... $60
Gravy boat, chartreuse................................... $20
Gravy liner/pickle dish, seafoam blue.......... $25
Hostess plate & cup, cedar green, pr. $90
Ice box jar, cov., black chutney $225
Mug (tumbler), black chutney......................... $90
Pitcher, cov., water, cedar green .... $400+
Pitcher, water, 12" h., bean brown................ $150
Pitcher, water, 12" h., seafoam blue............. $125
Plate, salad, 8" d., seafoam blue.................... $18
Plate, dinner, 10" d., cantaloupe $40
Plate, chop, 13" sq., chartreuse $30
Plate, child's, coral $60
Platter, 13 3/4" l., oblong, granite grey........... $30
Ramekin, cov., individual, bean brown $250
Relish dish, divided, raffia handle, coral....... $175
Relish rosette, seafoam blue $250
Salad fork & spoon, white, pr. $300
Sauceboat, coral... $40
Shaker, single, glacier blue............................ $20
Stack server, cov., cedar green (ILLUS. back, with fruit bowl) $300
Stack server, cov., granite grey................... $250
Sugar bowl, cov., granite grey........................ $20
Teapot, cov., seafoam blue............................ $135
Tumbler, child's, granite grey......................... $125
Vegetable bowl, cov., coral, 12" l................. $40
Vegetable dish, open, divided, cedar green (ILLUS. right front, with fruit bowl)............. $130
Vegetable dish, open, oval, granite grey, 10" l. $25

Casual China (Iroquois China Co.)

Bowl, 5" d., cereal, ripe apricot $15
Bowl, 5 3/4" d., fruit, oyster grey.................... $20
Butter dish, cov., brick red, 1/4 lb............ $1,000+
Butter dish, cov., pink sherbet....................... $75
Carafe, oyster grey...................................... $900+
Casserole, deep tureen, lemon yellow......... $250
Coffeepot, cov., nutmeg brown.................... $140

Coffeepot, cov., sugar white $200
Coffeepot, cov., after dinner, lemon yellow .. $125
Cover for cereal/soup bowl, nutmeg
brown $30
Cover for water pitcher, ripe apricot............. $60
Creamer, family-style, pink sherbet................. $40
Cup & saucer, coffee, original, oyster grey
(ILLUS. front center w/other cups & sau-
cers & shakers) $30
Cup & saucer, coffee, redesigned, lemon
yellow $25
Cup & saucer, original, avocado yellow $20

Casual Cups & Saucers & Shakers

Cup & saucer, demitasse, avocado yellow
(ILLUS. front left w/other cups & saucers
& shakers)... $150-175
Cup & saucer, demitasse, sugar white......... $225
Gravy, redesigned w/cover which becomes
stand, sugar white $250
Gravy stand, ice blue.................................... $40
Gravy w/attached stand, avocado yellow.... $100
Gumbo soup bowl, cantaloupe, 21 oz.......... $60
Gumbo soup bowl, ice blue, 21 oz. $40
Mug, original design, pink sherbet (ILLUS.
left with two other mugs) $60-85
Mug, restyled, ice blue $100
Pepper mill, lemon yellow.......................... $300+
Pitcher, cov., ice blue, 1 1/2 qt..................... $150
Plate, bread & butter, 6 1/2" d., lettuce
green... $10
Plate, luncheon, 9 1/2" d., pink sherbet.......... $17
Plate, chop, 13 7/8" d., ice blue..................... $50
Platter, 10 1/4" oval, individual, lettuce
green $50
Platter, 12 3/4" oval, parsley green................ $40
Salt & pepper shakers, stacking-type, ice
blue, pr. $25
Salt & pepper shakers, stacking-type, oys-
ter grey, pr. (ILLUS. right rear, with cups
& saucers)... $60
Salt shaker & pepper mill, redesigned,
lemon yellow, pr. (ILLUS. left rear, with
cups & saucers) .... $500+
Soup, cov., redesigned, 18 oz....................... $30
Sugar, redesigned, brick red...................... $225+
Sugar, stacking-type, sugar white, family
size.. $40
Tumbler, iced tea, Pinch patt., seafoam
blue, Imperial Glass Co., 14 oz. $50
Vegetable dish, open, cantaloupe, 10" d........ $85
Vegetable dish, open, nutmeg brown,
8 1/8", 36 oz. $35

Iroquois Casual Cookware
Casserole, 3 qt.. $225+
Dutch oven .... $500+

Fry pan, cov. .... $500+
Sauce pan, cov. .... $500+
Serving tray, electric, 12 3/4 x 17 1/2" .... $2,000+

Sascha Brastoff

*An endlessly inventive mind, a flair for dra-
matic illustration and unerring promotional
skills made Sascha Brastoff (1918-1993) one of
the best known ceramics designers of the 1950s
and '60s. Brastoff's varied projects embraced
everything from the practical, such as candela-
braa and cigarette boxes, to purely art objects
such as wall plaques and decorative obelisks as
well as lines of china and earthen dinnerwares.
Every item carried his signature and was brought
to the public's attention through intense promotional efforts by the artist. His name recognition
was so widespread that, even after ill health force
his retirement in the early 1960s, the Brastoff
company continued to successfully turn out pieces
in his style for ten more years. (Items with a full
"Sascha Brastoff" signature were decorated by
Brastoff himself; those with only a "Sascha B."
signature or the Brastoff name and a 'rooster
stamp' were products of the decorating staff.*

*Born Sanuel Brostofsky, Brastoff trained briefly
at Cleveland's Western Reserve School of Art, then
moved to New York. Following military service during World War II, his flair for theatrical design
found an outlet at 20th Century Fox where he
designed costumes for, among others, Carmen
Miranda. His ongoing ceramic work attracted the
attention of philanthropist/investor Winthrop
Rockefeller, who became Brastoff's patron, an association that lasted throughout the artist's career.*

*The 35,000-foot Brastoff studio in Los Angeles,
which opened in 1953, became a mecca for tour-
ists and movie stars. An endless array of ceramic
products was on view, from ashtrays and lamps
to enameled wares and sculptures done in such
fanciful designs as "Star Steed" and "Rooftops."
Brastoff supervised all design, turning out over
400 new items yearly.*

*The "designer extraordinaire," as his firm's
publicity called him, worked in a variety of
media. Included in his output were freeform
metal sculptures, mosaic wall masks, terra cotta
figurines, fabric and even a line of "hologram
jewelry." Popular with the movie community,
Brastoff's designs eventually found their way into
films; his "Illusion" sculpture can be seen in the
movie "Forbidden Planet."*

*Although Sascha Brastoff's mercurial creative
interests led him in many directions, one element
remains constant in his work: the presentation is
always highly theatrical and laced with whimsy.
A signature element was the use of unusual color
combinations, sometimes metallic or with metallic accents. As his enduring popularity indicates,
Bratoff had a keen ability to make the extraordinary commercially and artistically appealing.*

*Advisor for this category, Donald-Brian
Johnson, is an author and lecturer specializing in
Mid-Twentieth Century design. Photos are by his
frequent collaborator, Leslie Pina.*

Group of Brastoff Rooftops Pattern Pieces

Ashtray, free-form, No. F 2, Rooftops patt., 8 1/2" w. (ILLUS. front, far left with other Rooftops pattern pieces) **$70-80**

Ashtray, hooded pyramidal form, gold glaze, No. H 6, 6 1/4" h. (ILLUS. back right with domed ashtray) **$25-35**

A Domed & Two Hooded Ashtrays

Ashtray, low domed shape, No. H 1, black & orange glaze, 6" d. (ILLUS. front left with two hooded ashtrays) **$25-35**

Ashtray, No. O 16, Poodle patt., 11" d. (ILLUS. back row with bowls, Alaska cigarette container, Star Steed dish & Alaska egg-shaped box, bottom of page) **$65-75**

Brastoff Jeweled Peacock Ashtray & Vase

Ashtray, round, Jeweled Peacock patt., 7" d. (ILLUS. left with Jeweled Peacock vase) **$65-75**

Poodle Pattern Ashtray and Various Other Brastoff Pieces

Group of Brastoff Aztec-Mayan Pieces

Ashtray, round, leaf decoration, full signature, large **$350**

Ashtray, rounded freeform, No. F-33, Aztec-Mayan patt., 13" w. (ILLUS. back row right with Aztec-Mayan bowl, Aztec-Mayan box, Aztec-Mayan egg & Aztec-Mayan ewer, top of page) **$60-70**

Ashtray, square, No. O 3, Rooftops patt., 6 1/4" w. (ILLUS. front, second from left with other Rooftops pieces, bottom of page) **$50-60**

Ashtray, hooded pyramidal form, gold glaze, No. H 3, 4 1/4" h. (ILLUS. back left with domed ashtray, top of page) **$25-35**

Sascha Brastoff Mosaic Bowl

Bowl, banana shape, Mosaic design outside, solid color inside (ILLUS.) **$65**

Bowl, 5 5/8" d., footed, swirled yellow & gold, each (ILLUS. of two, front row far left with Poodle ashtray & other pieces, top of page 363) **$25-35**

Bowl, 7 1/4" d., No. 63, Aztec-Mayan patt. (ILLUS. front, far right with other Aztec-Mayan pieces, top of page) **$30-40**

Box, cov., Jewel Bird decoration, No. 020 ...... **$85**

Box, cov., long rectangular shape, No. 0 23, Aztec-Mayan patt., 9 1/4" l. (ILLUS. front, second from left with other Aztec-Mayan pieces, top of page) **$50-75**

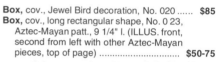

Brastoff Chop Plate, Vase & Egg Box

Chop plate, Aztec-Mayan patt., 16 1/2" d. (ILLUS. left with Abstract Originals vase & egg box, top of page) **$175-200**

Cigar tray, oblong, No. 78, Persian patt., 17 3/4" l. (ILLUS. back with two other Persian pieces, bottom of page) **$90-100**

Cigar tray, slightly curved rectangular form, No. F 8A, Rooftops patt., 14 1/2" l. (ILLUS. back with other Rooftops pieces, top of page 363) **$100-120**

Persian Pattern Cigar Tray, Dish & Model of a Pipe

Cigarette box, cov., Rooftops patt., No. 021, 8" l. **$100**

Cigarette container, small tapering cylindrical shade, Alaska patt., 2 5/8" h. (ILLUS. front row, far right with Poodle ashtray & other pieces, bottom of page 363) **$20-30**

Compote, polar bear decoration, No. 085 .... **$75**

Dish, free-form, No. F 2, Persian patt., 8 1/2" l. (ILLUS. right front with Persian cigar tray, bottom of page 364) **$50-60**

Dish, three-footed, fish-shaped (flounder), house decoration, 8 1/4 x 8 1/2" **$125**

Egg box, cov., Abstract Originals patt., banded design, 7 1/2" h. (ILLUS. right with Aztec-Mayan chop plate & Abstract Originals vase) **$75-90**

Egg box, cov., No. O 44A, Aztec-Mayan patt., 7 1/2" h. (ILLUS. front, second from left with other Aztec-Mayan pieces, top of page 364) **$75-90**

Egg box, cov., No. O 44H, Alaska patt., 7 1/2" h. (ILLUS. front, second from right with Poodle ashtray & other pieces, top of page 363) **$75-90**

Ewer, No. O 68, spherical body w/high arched spout, Aztec-Mayan patt., 10 1/2" h. (ILLUS. back, with other Aztec-Mayan pieces, top of previous page) ... **$80-100**

Lamp base, mosaic tile, 27" h. **$350**

Model of a pipe, No O 81, Persian patt., 4 1/2" h. (ILLUS. front right with two other Persian pieces, bottom previous page).. **$50-75**

Model of a pipe, No. O 8D, Rooftops patt., 4 1/2" h. (ILLUS. front, second from right with other Rooftops pieces, top of page 363) **$50-75**

Model of rooster, mosaic design, 15" h. **$575**

Obelisk, cov., full signature, 21" h. **$950**

Plate, square, vegetable decoration, full signature **$300**

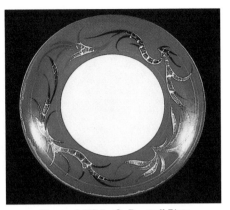

Brown & White S. Brastoff Plate

Plate, 9 1/2" d., wide brown rim w/abstract design, white center, full signature (ILLUS.) **$750**

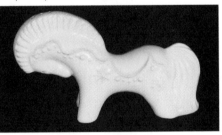

Sascha Brastoff Horse Salt Shaker

Salt shaker, model of a horse, white, produced in 1947-1948, 5 1/4" l., 3 1/4" h. (ILLUS.) **$150**

Vase, 10" h., tapering ovoid shape w/a small mouth, No. F 24, Rooftops patt. (ILLUS. front row, far right with other Rooftops pieces, top of page 363) **$90-110**

Vase, 13 1/2" h., tapering cylindrical freeform, Jeweled Peacock patt. (ILLUS. right with Jeweled Peacock ashtray, bottom of page 363) **$100-125**

Vase, 17 1/8" h., No. O 84, Abstract Originals patt., banded design (ILLUS. center with Aztec-Mayan chop plate & Abstract Originals egg box) **$80-90**

Wall pocket, Rooftops patt., No. 031, 20" h. **$550**

Satsuma

These decorated wares have been produced in Japan since the end of the 18th century. The early pieces are scarce and high-priced. Later Satsuma wares are plentiful and, with prices rising, are also becoming highly collectible.

Sascha Brastoff Plate

Plate, 8" d., w/house & tree design (ILLUS.) ... **$20**

Fine Satsuma Plate and Vases

Finely Decorated Satsuma Jar

Fine Dragon-trimmed Satsuma Teapot

Jar, cov., bulbous ovoid body w/the shoulder tapering to a short rolled neck & domed cover w/a gold pointed button finial, the sides h.p. w/a wide continuous band showing scenes of children involved in various activities, pink shoulder & cover decorated w/ornate cloud designs w/gold trim, late 19th - early 20th c., unmarked, 6" h. (ILLUS.) **$403**

Plates, 7 1/2" d., dessert, each finely painted w/landscapes & figures w/Mt. Fuji in the background, Meiji period, ca. 1920, set of 6 (ILLUS. of one at right with two vases, top of page).................................. **$748**

Teapot, cov., footed squatty spherical body w/a wide shoulder centered by a tall cylindrical neck fitted w/a small domed cover, a long gold dragon wrapped around the base of the neck w/the neck & head forming the spout & the arched tail forming the handle, the creamy background h.p. w/exotic birds among colorful flowering plants in shades of red, blue, white & purple w/heavy gold trim, black & gold chop mark on the base, late 19th - early 20th c., 6 3/4" h. (ILLUS., top next column) **$1,006**

Large Decorative Satsuma Floor Vase

Vase, 25" h., floor-type, footed baluster form w/a tall neck w/widely flared ruffled rim & foo dog & ring shoulder handles, dark blue background painted w/pink & blue blossoms & surrounded a large panel showing two Geisha against a dark gold ground, unmarked, ca. 1900 (ILLUS.) **$250-300**

Fine Satsuma Floor Vase

Vase, 29" h., 10" d., floor-type, tall slightly tapering body w/a slightly bulbed base band w/three cut-outs, the angled shoulder tapering to a cylindrical neck, the neck & shoulder decorated w/diaper panels & stylized florals, the upper body divided into a band of large arched panels each h.p. w/a different flower plant, the lower body decorated w/various geometric designs & floral panels, all in shades of gold, tan, rose red & light blue, 19th c. (ILLUS.).. **$390**

Vases, 7 1/4" h., simple ovoid form w/a flat gold mouth, each h.p. in color w/family scenes of mothers & children in front of a red house, flowering trees, waters & mountains in the distance, some gilt wear, signed, Meiji period, ca. 1900, pr. (ILLUS. left with a dessert plate) **$748**

Satsuma Vases with Buddhist Saints

Vases, 9 1/2" h., 4 1/2" d., footed ovoid six-sided body w/a short flaring neck, the sides decorated w/groups of Buddhist saints in color w/heavy gold trim, figural elephant shoulder handles, painted chop mark on the base, probably late 19th c., pr. (ILLUS.).. **$259**

Schafer & Vater

Founded in Rudolstadt, Thuringia, Germany in 1890, the Schafer and Vater Porcelain Factory specialized in decorative pieces of porcelain usually in white or colored bisque. It produced many novelty figural items such as creamers, toothpick holders, boxes and hatpin holders, and also a line of jasper ware with white relief decoration in imitation of the famous Wedgwood jasper wares. The firm also decorated whiteware blanks.

The company ceased production in 1962, and collectors now seek out its charming pieces, which may be marked with a crown over a starburst containing the script letter "R."

Schafer & Vater Mark

Bottle, figural, a figure of a male golfer in color & wearing a white outfit w/knickers & a cap leaning over a large brown flat-sided round flask w/a short neck projecting at an angle, the flask inscribed "Golf and Good Spirits Make a Good Highball," 4 1/2" h. (missing stopper) **$322**

Bottle, figural, a skeleton standing enveloped in a sheet marked on the front "Gift!" (Poison), white w/brown trim, No. 6109, 9 1/2" h.. **$334**

Bottle, figural, large rounded head of a young man w/wild hair wearing an inverted funnel for a hat, the funnel inscribed "Nurnberger Trichter," overall glossy washed blue glaze, No. 6218, 8" h. **$403**

Bottle set: figural bottle, six cups & tray; bottle in the form of a comical short, fat doctor w/curled wig standing beside a large upright syringe, six small cylindrical cups w/names of medicines around the base resting on a round tray, pointed tip of syringe forms bottle stopper, overall glossy washed blue glaze, bottle 9 3/4" h., the set.. **$575**

Figural Chinese Man Creamer

Creamer, figural, in the form of a Chinese man wearing a long orange robe, holding a large white goose by the feet while it tries to fly away, thus forming the spout w/the open beak for pouring, the man's long black pigtail forming the handle, unmarked, 2 1/4" w., 4" h. (ILLUS., previous page) **$135**

Figurines, Sun Ladies & Moon Men, two w/a smiling cream-colored sun head on the body of a seated late-Victorian woman, one w/her arms away from her body, wearing a black jacket, white dress & red slippers w/a red handbag in her lap, the other w/a matching outfit but playing a banjo; the three men w/a cream crescent moon head, one head smoking a pipe & attached to the body of a reclining late-Victorian man wearing a short white coat w/black collar & white knee breeches, a second man wearing a similar outfit but kneeling & holding out a bouquet w/one hand & a pink hat in the other, the third man reclining on his stomach w/his lower legs in the air, No. 3150 through 3155, 3 1/2 to 4 1/2" l., the set of 5 (two women w/minor chip repairs) **$1,380**

Schafer & Vater Sugar Shaker

Sugar shaker w/original metal top, bisque, a slender waisted cylindrical white form w/a band of embossed scrolls around the wide bottom & a molded lappet band at the top, the body molded in relief w/figures of Grecian women tinted grey w/an altar in pink & foliage in green, 3 1/4" d., 6 1/8" h. (ILLUS.) **$135**

Tea set: cov. teapot, cov. sugar bowl, creamer & two cups & saucers; figural, all in pink bisque w/grey-green trim, the teapot body formed by the wide deep skirt of a woman, a slender ribbed spout at the front, the cover formed by the torso of the woman wearing a ruffled collar & balloon sleeves, a tall ribbon on her head, the handle formed by a slender, elongated figure of a bent-over gentleman wearing a tall top hat, the figural sugar bowl in the form of a similar lady but w/small scroll handles at the sides, the open creamer in the form of a wide skirt w/the handle in the form of the bent-over gentleman,

each cup w/a gentleman handle & on a ruffled saucer, all pieces w/molded ornate scrolls & swags, No. 3861, 3862 & 3863, 4" to 7" h., the set (few small chips, repaired lines) **$834**

Sèvres & Sèvres-Style

Some of the most desirable porcelain ever produced was made at the Sèvres factory, originally established at Vincennes, France, and transferred, through permission of Madame de Pompadour, to Sèvres as the Royal Manufactory about the middle of the 18th century. King Louis XV took sole responsibility for the works in 1759, when production of hard paste wares began. Between 1850 and 1900, many biscuit and soft-paste pieces were made again. Fine early pieces are scarce and high-priced. Many of those available today are late productions. The various Sèvres marks have been copied, and pieces listed as "Sèvres-Style" are similar to actual Sèvres wares but not necessarily from that factory. Three of the many Sèvres marks are illustrated here.

Sèvres marks

Plates, 9 1/4" d., white ground w/the center of each h.p. w/a different colorful butterfly enclosed by double rings of delicate tiny pink rose sprigs, the wide border hand decorated w/a continuous band of blue floral swags alternating w/small pink rose drops, thin leaf & gilt border bands, blue Sevres marks & decorator initials, late 19th c., five w/bottom rim chips, one w/a repair, two w/upper rim chips, set of 18 (ILLUS., top next page) **$4,370**

Set of Bird & Branch-Painted Sevres Plates

Plates, 9 1/2" d., white center w/a central gold starburst w/filigree, the wide border band h.p. w/small reserves h.p. w/small colorful birds & insects bordered by flowering leafy branches, a small oval border reserve w/the gilt monogram "LP" above a crown, blue mark in circle & additional wreath & crown "Chateau de Fontaineb-leau" mark, late 19th c., two w/rim chips, set of 12 (ILLUS.) **$1,323**

Outstanding Set of Sevres Plates with Butterflies & Floral Bands

Sevres-style Tea Set with Spurious Factory Marks

Tea set: cov. teapot, cov. sugar bowl, creamer, two cups & saucers & an undertray; Sevres-style, the serving pieces w/bulbous ovoid bodies tapering to flat mouths & domed covers w/fluted pointed finials, each w/a cobalt blue ground centered on the front w/a large rounded gold-bordered reserve featuring a bust portrait of a court beauty of the late 18th c., the four-lobed tray centered by a color half-length portrait of Louis XVI, each piece further trimmed w/ornate delicate gold scrolls, spurious Sevres & chateau marks, France, early 20th c., tray 11 7/8" w., the set (ILLUS. of part) **$2,350**

Fine Sevres-style Porcelain Tea Set with a Pink Ground

Tea set: tete-a-tete style, cov. teapot, cov. sugar bowl, creamer, two cylindrical cups & saucers & a scalloped round footed undertray; Sevres-style, teapot w/ovoid body, creamer w/tapering ovoid body raised on four gold legs, cylindrical sugar bowl, all w/a pink ground elaborately painted w/overall bands of long gold arabesques highlighted w/delicate turquoise blue, deep red & pink "jeweling," spurious gilt interlaced Ls mark, France, mid- to late 19th c., undertray 8 7/8" d., the set (ILLUS., bottom previous page) **$3,760**

Shawnee

The Shawnee Pottery Company of Zanesville, Ohio, opened its doors for operation in 1936 and, sadly, closed in 1961. The pottery was inexpensive for its quality and was readily purchased at dime stores as well as department stores. Sears, Roebuck and Co., Butler Bros., Woolworth's and S. Kresge were just a few of the companies that were longtime retailers of this fine pottery.

Shawnee Pottery Company had a wide array of merchandise to offer, from knickknacks to dinnerware, although Shawnee is quite often associated with colorful pig cookie jars and the dazzling "Corn King" line of dinnerware. Planters, miniatures, cookie jars and Corn King pieces are much in demand by today's avid collectors. Factory seconds were purchased by outside decorators and trimmed with gold, decals and unusual hand painting, which makes those pieces extremely desirable in today's market and enhances the value considerably.

Shawnee Pottery has become the most sought-after pottery in today's collectible market.

Reference books available are Mark E. Supnick's book Collecting Shawnee Pottery, The Collector's Guide to Shawnee Pottery by Duane and Janice Vanderbilt or Shawnee Pottery - An Identification & Value Guide by Jim and Bev Mangus.

Shawnee
U.S.A.
Shawnee Mark

Shawnee Figural Ashtrays

Ashtray, figural kingfisher, parrot, bird, fish, terrier or owl, marked "U.S.A.," dusty rose, turquoise, old ivory, white or burgundy, 3" h., each (ILLUS. of fish, kingfisher & bird)... **$45-50**

Shawnee Figural Banks

Bank, figural bulldog, 4 1/2" h., unmarked (ILLUS. left)....................................... **$150-175**
Bank, figural tumbling bear, unmarked, 4 3/4" h. (ILLUS. right) **$150-175**
Bank-cookie jar, figural Smiley Pig, chocolate or butterscotch base, marked "Patented: Smiley Shawnee 60 U.S.A.," 10 1/2" h. (ILLUS. left w/Winnie Pig bank-cookie jar) **$350-375**
Bank-cookie jar, figural Winnie Pig, chocolate or butterscotch base, marked "Patented: Winnie Shawnee 61 U.S.A." 10 1/2" h. (ILLUS. right w/Smiley Pig bank-cookie jar, below) **$350-375**

Winnie Pig & Smiley Pig Banks/Cookie Jars

Shawnee Figural Book Ends

Book ends, figural, full figure of a man at
potter's wheel, brown, marked "Crafted
by Shawnee Potteries Zanesville, Ohio
1960," 9" h., pr. (ILLUS.) **$400-500**

Indian Motif Cigarette Box

Cigarette box, cov., embossed Indian ar-
rowhead on lid, brown, marked "Shaw-
nee," 3 1/4 x 4 1/2" (ILLUS.) **$400-450**
Coffeepot, cov., Pennsylvania Dutch patt,
marked "U.S.A. 52," 42 oz.................. **$125-150**
Coffeepot, cov., Sunflower patt, marked
"U.S.A.," 42 oz.................................... **$125-150**
Cookie jar, cov., figural ear of corn, Corn
King line, No. 66, 10 1/2" h. **$200-225**
Cookie jar, cov., figural fruit basket, marked
"Shawnee U.S.A. 84," 8 1/2" h. **$75-100**
Cookie jar, cov., figural Jo-Jo the clown,
marked "Shawnee U.S.A. 12," *repro-
duction alert, 9" h. **$125-150**

Muggsy Cookie Jar

Cookie jar, cov., figural Muggsy dog, blue
bow, gold trim & decals, marked "Patented Muggsy U.S.A.," 11 3/4" h. (ILLUS.)
.... **$450-475**
Cookie jar, cov., figural Puss 'n Boots, long
tail, burgundy bow, marked "Patented
Puss N Boots U.S.A.," 10 1/2" h. **$100-125**
Cookie jar, cov., figural sailor boy, decorated w/decals & gold trim, marked "U.S.A.,"
11 1/2" h. **$500-550**

Pink Elephant Cookie Jar/Ice Bucket

Cookie jar-ice bucket, cov., figural elephant, pink, marked "Shawnee U.S.A.
60" or "Kenwood U.S.A. 60" (ILLUS.) .. **$95-100**

Dutch-style Creamer & Pitcher

Various Shawnee Figurines

Creamer, ball-type, Dutch style, decorated w/tulip & blue around neck, marked "U.S.A.," 4 1/4" h. (ILLUS. left w/pitcher, bottom previous page) **$175-200**

Creamer, White Corn line, airbrushed & gold trim, marked "U.S.A.," 4 3/4" h. (ILLUS. third from left, front row, with White Corn Line pieces) **$95-125**

Figural Elephant Creamer

Creamer, figural elephant, w/gold decoration & decals, marked "Patented U.S.A.," 4 3/4" h. (ILLUS.) **$175-200**

Creamer, Lobster Ware, charcoal grey, figural lobster handle, marked "U.S.A. 909," 4 1/2" h. **$35-45**

Valencia Line Dealer's Display Sign

Dealer's display sign, figural Spanish dancers, "Valencia" embossed across base, tangerine glaze, 11 1/4" h. (ILLUS.) **$400-450**

Figurine, model of deer, no mark, 3" h. (ILLUS. far right w/various figurines, top of page) **$175-200**

Figurine, model of Pekingese, no mark, 2 1/2" h. (ILLUS. center w/various figurines, top of page) **$50-55**

Figurine, model of puppy, no mark, 3" h. (ILLUS. second from left w/various figurines, top of page) **$45-50**

Figurine, model of rabbit, sitting, no mark, 3" h. (ILLUS. second from right w/various figurines, top of page) **$55-65**

Figurine, model of squirrel, no mark, 2 1/2" h. (ILLUS. third from right w/various figurines, top of page) **$45-50**

Figurine, model of Teddy bear, no mark, 3" h. (ILLUS. third from left w/various figurines, top of page) **$45-50**

Figurine, model of tumbling bear, no mark, 3" h. (ILLUS. far left w/various figurines, top of page) **$65-75**

White Corn Line Pieces

Shawnee Fern Matchbox Holder

Matchbox holder, embossed Fern patt.,
marked "U.S.A.," 5 1/2" h. (ILLUS.)...... **$75-100**
Pitcher, ball-type, Dutch style, w/painted
tulips & embossed blue rope decoration
around neck, marked "U.S.A.," 64 oz.
(ILLUS. right w/Dutch-style creamer,
bottom of page 371) **$300-350**
Pitcher, 7" h., ball-type, Valencia line, burgundy, green, cobalt, orange or yellow,
marked "U.S.A." **$45-65**
Pitcher, 7 1/2" h., figural Boy Blue, gold
trim, marked "Shawnee U.S.A. 46"
.... **$225-250**
Pitcher, 7 1/2" h., figural Chanticleer roost-
er, marked "Patented Chanticleer U.S.A."
.... **$50-65**
Pitcher, 7 3/4" h., figural Smiley Pig, peach
or burgundy flower decoration, marked
"Patented Smiley U.S.A." **$125-150**
Pitcher, 8" h., White Corn line, airbrushed &
gold trim, marked "U.S.A." (ILLUS. back
row, left w/White Corn pieces) **$195-250**

Shawnee Clown Planter

Planter, figural clown w/blocks, marked
"Shawnee U.S.A.," 4 1/2" h. (ILLUS.)... **$85-100**

Fox & Bag Planter

Planter, model of a fox & bag, marked
"U.S.A.," 4 1/2" h. (ILLUS.).................... **$50-65**

Flower & Fern Salt Box

Salt box, cov., Flower & Fern patt., yellow,
green or blue, marked "U.S.A.," 4 3/4" h.
(ILLUS.)... **$95-125**
Salt & pepper shakers, figural cottage, pr.
.... **$200-250**

Figural Smiley & Winnie Shakers

Salt & pepper shakers, figural Smiley Pig &
Winnie Pig, clover blossom decoration,
3", pr. (ILLUS.) **$65-85**
Salt & pepper shakers, White Corn line,
airbrushed & gold trim, no mark, 3" h., pr.
(ILLUS. front row, far right, in front of larger shakers, w/White Corn pieces) **$40-50**
Salt & pepper shakers, White Corn line,
airbrushed & gold trim, no mark,
5 1/4" h., pr. (ILLUS. front row, far right,
behind smaller shakers, w/White Corn
pieces) **$85-100**

Yellow & Blue Shawnee Elephant Teapots

Lobster Ware Snack Jar/Bean Pot

Snack jar-bean pot, cov., Lobster Ware, tab-handled, figural lobster finial on lid, marked "Kenwood U.S.A. 925," 8" h. (ILLUS.) **$275-300**

Sugar bowl-grease jar, cov., figural cottage, marked "U.S.A. 8," 4 1/2" h. **$350-375**

Sugar bowl-grease jar, cov., White Corn line, airbrushed & gold trim, marked "U.S.A." (ILLUS. front row, far left, w/White Corn pieces, page 372) **$95-125**

Sugar shaker, White Corn line, airbrushed & gold trim, marked "U.S.A.," 5 1/4" h. (ILLUS. front row, second from left, w/White Corn pieces, page 372) **$350-375**

Teapot, cov., figural Elephant patt., blue or yellow glaze, marked "U.S.A.," 6 1/2" h., each (ILLUS., top of page) **$150-200**

Teapot, cov., figural Elephant patt., green glaze, marked "U.S.A.," 6 1/2" h. **$175-225**

Rare Airbrushed Granny Ann Teapot

Teapot, cov., figural Granny Ann, airbrushed decoration w/blue apron & burgundy shawl, marked "Patented Granny Ann U.S.A.," each (ILLUS.) **$500-650**

Clover Blossom Shawnee Teapot

Teapot, cov., Clover Blossom patt., embossed decoration, marked "U.S.A.," 6-cup, 6 1/2" h. (ILLUS.) **$125-150**

Rare Version of Tom the Piper's Son Teapot

Teapot, cov., figural Tom the Piper's Son, airbrushed matte reddish orange & greenish yellow w/gold trim, marked "Tom the Piper's Son Patented U.S.A. 44" (ILLUS., previous page) **$325-375**

Teapot, cov., Flower & Fern patt., gold-trimmed, 5-cup size, 5 1/4" h.................. **$75-85**

Horizontal Ribbed Shawnee Teapot

Teapot, cov., Horizontal Ribbed patt., h.p. floral vine decoration, marked "U.S.A.," 6" h. (ILLUS.) **$35-45**

Shawnee Pennsylvania Dutch Teapot

Teapot, cov., Pennsylvania Dutch patt., marked "U.S.A. 10," 10 oz., two-cup size, also found in 14 oz., 18 oz., 27 oz. & 30 oz. sizes, each (ILLUS. of 10 oz. size)... **$50-65**

Teapot, cov., Sunflower patt., marked "U.S.A.," 30 oz., 6 1/4" h. **$65-85**

Swirl Pattern Teapot by Shawnee

Teapot, cov., Swirl patt., turquoise blue glaze, marked "U.S.A.," 6 1/2" h. (ILLUS.) **$25-30**

Teapot, White Corn line, airbrushed & gold trim, marked "U.S.A.," 30 oz. (ILLUS. back row, right w/White Corn pieces) **$250-275**

Scotty Dog Wall Pocket

Wall pocket, Scotty dog head, green, burgundy, cobalt, yellow or white, unmarked, 9 1/2" h. (ILLUS.) **$45-55**

Wall pocket, Sunflower patt., marked "U.S.A.," 6 3/4" h. **$40-50**

Shelley China

Members of the Shelley family were in the pottery business in England as early as the 18th century. In 1872 Joseph Shelley formed a partnership with James Wileman of Wileman & Co. who operated the Foley China Works. The Wileman & Co. name was used for the firm for the next fifty years, and between 1890 and 1910 the words "The Foley" appeared above conjoined "WC" initials.

Beginning in 1910 the Shelley family name in a shield appeared on wares, although the firm's official name was still Wileman & Co. The company's name was finally changed to Shelley in 1925 and then Shelley China Ltd. after 1965. The firm changed hands in the 1960s and became part of the Doulton Group in 1971.

At first only average quality earthenwares were produced, but in the late 1890s new shapes and better quality decorations were used.

Bone china was introduced at Shelley before World War I, and these fine dinnerwares became very popular in the United States and are increasingly popular today with collectors. Thin "eggshell china" teawares, miniatures and souvenir items were widely marketed during the 1920s and 1930s and are sought-after today.

Shelley Mark

Shelley Begonia Teapot in Dainty Big Floral Shape

Teapot, cov., Dainty Big Floral Shape, Begonia patt. No. 13427, from the Best Ware group, 1943 (ILLUS.) **$180-280**

Trailing Violets Teapot in Dainty Kettle Garlands Shape

Teapot, cov., Dainty Kettle Garlands Shape, Trailing Violets patt. No. 9056, shaded style, from the Best Ware group, 1897 (ILLUS.)..................................... **$180-380**

Shelley Regency Teapot in Dainty Plain Shape

Teapot, cov., Dainty Plain Shape, Regency patt. No. 785, from the Special group, 1945 (ILLUS.)..................................... **$150-250**

Shelley Rosebud Teapot in Dainty Repeat Shape

Teapot, cov., Dainty Repeat Shape, Rosebud patt. No. 13426, from the Best Ware group, 1943 (ILLUS.) **$250-350**

Her Majesty Teapot in Dainty Shape by Shelley

Teapot, cov., Dainty Scenic Shape, Her Majesty (tractor) patt., from the Souvenir Ware group, 1920 (ILLUS.).................. **$50-150**

Popular Shelley Dainty Blue Teapot

Teapot, cov., Dainty Shape, Dainty Blue patt., the original & most sought-after Shelley design, 1896-1966+ (ILLUS.)......... **$500-600**

Teapot, cov., Daisy Shape, Jungle Print patt., Wileman & Co., 1885-1914, 7 1/4" l., 6 1/8" h. (ILLUS., top next page) **$400-600**

Dorothy Teapot with Tea Tile

Teapot, cov., Dorothy Shape, patt. No. 8063, w/matching tea tile w/earlier Wileman backstamp, teapot overall 9 5/8" l., 6 1/4" h., the set (ILLUS.).................. **$200-500**

Empire Shape Teapot with Bold Red & Blue Florals

Wileman Jungle Print Tall Teapot

Marguerite Teapot & Other Pieces in Henley Shape

Teapot, cov., Empire Shape, patt. Wileman & Co., No. 0888, shape introduced in 1893 (ILLUS., previous page) **$600-900**

Gainsborough Drifting Leaves Teapot

Teapot, cov., Gainsborough Shape, Drifting Leaves patt. No. 13848, from the Contemporary group, 1957 (ILLUS.) **$80-150**

Teapot, cov., Globe Shape, Daffodil Time patt. No. 13370, Scenic style, from the Best Ware group, 1942 (ILLUS., top next column) **$100-200**

Shelley Daffodil Time Teapot

Globe Teapot with Flower Basket

Teapot, cov., Globe Shape, white ground decorated w/a colorful basket of flowers, undated (ILLUS., previous page) **$100-200**

Teapot, cov., Henley Shape, Marguerite patt. No. 13688, Chintz style, from the Best Ware group, 1949, teapot only (ILLUS. w/stand & sugar & creamer - add at least $100 for stand & about $150 for sugar & creamer, middle of previous page) **$150-250**

Mode Art Deco Pot with Pink Florals

Teapot, cov., Mode Shape, floral decoration w/pink blossoms, light blue trim, factory second, 1929-34, 9 1/8" l., 4 7/8" h. (ILLUS.) **$350-500**

New York Shape Floral Decor Teapot

Teapot, cov., New York Shape, decorated w/delicate bands of colorful flowers, 1890-1905 (ILLUS.) **$150-250**

Shelley London Crested Teapot in New York Shape

Teapot, cov., New York Shape, London patt., Crested style, from the Souvenir Ware group, 1910 (ILLUS.) **$50-150**

New York Teapot with Blue Sprigs

Teapot, cov., New York Shape, scattered blue floral sprigs, 1890-1905 (ILLUS.)... **$75-125**

Black Cloisonne Teapot & Other Pieces in Queen Anne Shape

Teapot, cov., Queen Anne Shape, Black Cloisonne patt. No. 8321, Chintz style, from the Best Ware group, 1910, teapot only (ILLUS. w/stand & other pieces - add at least $100 for stand) **$500-700**

Tall Teapot Made for Ideal China Co.

Teapot, cov., tall trumpet shape w/ring handle & finial, made for the Ideal China Co., Canada, registration number 781613, overall 7 1/4" h. (ILLUS.) **$250-400**

Basket of Fruit Teapot in Tulip Shape

Teapot, cov., Tulip Shape, Basket of Fruit patt. No. 8204, Floral style from the Stenciled group, 1918 (ILLUS.) **$120-160**

Spongeware

Spongeware's designs were spattered, sponged or daubed on in colors, sometimes with a piece of cloth. Blue on white was the most common type, but mottled tans, browns and greens on yellowware were also popular. Spongeware generally has an overall pattern with a coarser look than Spatterware, to which it is loosely related. These wares were extensively produced in England and America well into the 20th century.

Blue Spongeware Covered Canister

Canister, cov., cylindrical w/molded rim & inset flat cover, light blue fine overall sponging on cream, very tight hairline through bottom, stack mark on cover, late 19th - early 20th c., 7" h. (ILLUS.) **$303**

Miniature Blue Sponged Chamber Pot

Chamber pot, miniature, cream w/overall light blue sponging, ca. 1900, 1 1/2" h. (ILLUS.) **$88**

Spongeware Creamer with Molded Design

Creamer, bulbous wide body tapering to a wide cylindrical neck w/wide spout & loop handle w/pointed thumb rest, the lower body molded in relief w/a scene of a heron holding a snake in its beak in a garden setting, dark blue overall sponging on white, late 19th - early 20th c., 5 1/2" h. (ILLUS.) **$495**

Master potty (slop jar), wide baluster-form body tapering to a flat rim w/a stepped domed cover w/button finial, small vertical loop handles at upper sides, overall dense dark blue sponging on white w/two narrow white bands flanking a dark blue band near the base, excellent condition, late 19th - early 20th c., 13" h. **$963**

Spongeware Pitcher with Pointed Handle

Pitcher, 6 1/2" h., cylindrical body w/molded rim & pointed rim spout, pointed scroll loop handle, overall dark blue sponging on white, minor interior stains, late 19th - early 20th c. (ILLUS., previous page)........ **$201**

Spongeware Pitcher with Angled Handle

Pitcher, 9" h., swelled bottom below the cylindrical body w/a pointed rim spout & angled loop handle, overall blue sponging on white, minor glaze flake at spout, late 19th - early 20th c. (ILLUS.) **$303**

Small Advertising Sponged Syrup Jug

Syrup jug, advertising-type, bulbous beehive-shaped w/short rim spout & wire bail handle w/black turned wood grip, overall blue sponging w/lower oval reserve stenciled "Grandmother's Maple Syrup of 50 Years Ago," relief-molded vine design around top half, bottom molded in relief "Mfg'd by N. Weeks - Style XXX Pat. Pending - Akron, O.," surface chips on spout, late 19th - early 20th c., 5 1/4" h. (ILLUS.).. **$495**

Spongeware Combination Salt & Pepper

Salt & pepper shaker, one-piece, ovoid body divided into two halves w/two short spouts w/metal caps, overall blue & brown sponging on white, some small cap dents, excellent condition, early 20th c., 3" h. (ILLUS.).. **$154**

Rare Blue Spongeware Toothbrush Vase

Toothbrush vase, footed baluster-form, wide dark blue on white sponged bands alternating w/two narrow white bands, excellent condition, late 19th - early 20th c., 5" h. (ILLUS.).. **$440**

Umbrella stand, tall cylindrical form, decorated w/four wide bands of fine banded blue sponging on white, sponged bands separated by three bands composed of two white bands flanking a narrow blue center band, late 19th - early 20th c., excellent condition, 20 1/2" h. **$770**

Blue Sponged Washbowl & Pitcher Set

Washbowl & pitcher, bulbous ovoid pitcher tapering to a wide flaring neck, C-scroll handle, matching bowl w/rolled rim, the pitcher w/overall coarse blue sponging on white w/a wide band in blue & white around the bottom, sponged rim & base bands on the bowl flank the wide blue & white bands, attributed to Red Wing, Minnesota, early 20th c., minor hairline & glaze flake on pitcher, pitcher 12" h. (ILLUS.) **$633**

Stoneware

Stoneware is essentially a vitreous pottery, impervious to water even in its unglazed state, that has been produced by potteries all over the world for centuries. Utilitarian wares such as crocks, jugs, churns and the like were the most common productions in the numerous potteries that sprang into existence in the United States during the 19th century. These items were often enhanced by the application of a cobalt blue oxide decoration. In addition to the coarse, primarily salt-glazed stonewares, there are other categories of stoneware known by such special names as basalt, jasper and others.

Jar, cov., wide low pedestal base & ovoid body w/a molded rim flanked by eared handles, a high domed cover w/an acorn finial, the body incised & trimmed in blue w/narrow bands & the inscription "Mrs. Anna Munson - 1885" framed w/a leafy wreath & a large leaf, edge chips, hairline in base, 18 1/4" h. (ILLUS., top next column) **$7,475**

Large Inscribed Covered Jar

Radam's Microbe Killer Jug

Jug, flat-bottomed beehive shape w/small cylindrical mouth & strap handle, impressed mark reading "Wm. Radam's Microbe Killer Co.," trimmed in blue, ca. 1890-1900, 10 3/8" h. (ILLUS.) **$96**

Pitcher, 10" h., ovoid body tapering to a wide cylindrical neck w/pinched spout, impressed 3/4 capacity mark below the spout & above a cobalt blue brushed cluster of cherries decoration, unsigned but probably from New Jersey or Pennsylvania, glaze burn & mottled clay color, ca. 1850 (ILLUS., next page) **$990**

Preserve jar, cov., cylindrical body tapering to a wide, low cupped rim w/inset flat cover w/button finial, overall mottled dark green alkaline glaze, unsigned, ca. 1860, excellent condition, 1 qt., 5 3/4" h. **$55**

Tall Stoneware Pitcher with Cherries

Preserve jar, advertising-type, gently swelled cylindrical form tapering to a molded rim, cobalt blue brushed double plain bands & a squiggle band around the top & a single plain band around the base, the whole center of the side stenciled in cobalt blue w/inscription reading "From Ood's Hardpan Crockery - Lockhaven, PA," the oversized "C" & "Y" in "Crockery" flanking the center part of the inscription, a stenciled size number flanked by leafy scrolls below the inscription, unknown maker, excellent condition, ca. 1870, 2 gal., 11 1/2" h... **$1,705**

Preserve Jar with Blue Inscription

Preserve jar, cov., cylindrical body tapering to a flaring flat neck & inset cover w/disk finial, large cobalt blue slip-quilled "2 Quarts" in script below a round blue-trimmed tooled & impressed circle mark for a Cortland, New York factory, ca. 1860, 2 qt., 7 1/2" h. (ILLUS.) **$303**

Unusual Stoneware Strainer-Jug

Strainer-jug, cylindrical body tapering to a short wide molded mouth, no handle, pierced overall w/strips of small holes down the sides, possibly an oyster strainer, unmarked, stack marks at base, some minor use staining, ca. 1870, 2 gal., 13 1/2" h. (ILLUS.) **$358**

Water cooler, cov., wide cylindrical form relief-molded around the sides w/a scene of an elk in a forest setting, overall cobalt blue glaze, pine boughs & cones around the cover, metal spigot at the front base, minor chips under the cover, late 19th - early 20th c., 14 3/4" h. **$345**

Teco Pottery

Teco Pottery was actually the line of art pottery introduced by the American Terra Cotta and Ceramic Company of Terra Cotta (Crystal Lake), Illinois, in 1902. Founded by William D. Gates in 1881, American Terra Cotta originally produced only bricks and drain tile. Because of superior facilities for experimentation, including a chemical laboratory, the company was able to develop an art pottery line, favoring a matte green glaze in the earlier years but eventually achieving a wide range of colors including a metallic lustre glaze and a crystalline glaze. Although some hand-thrown pottery was made, Gates favored a molded ware because it was less expensive to produce. By 1923, Teco Pottery was no longer being made, and in 1930 American Terra Cotta and Ceramic Company was sold. A book on the topic is *Teco: Art Pottery of the Prairie School*, by Sharon S. Darling (Erie Art Museum, 1990).

Teco Mark

Nice Green Crystalline Teco Vase

Vase, 9 3/8" h., ovoid lower body w/a rounded shoulder to the tapering cylindrical neck, long handles from the edge of the rim to the shoulder, nicely charcoaled crystalline green glaze, Shape No. 283, designed by Fritz Albert, two impressed marks on the base (ILLUS.) **$1,115**

Tall Teco Squared & Lobed Vase

Vase, 15 3/4" h., squatty bulbous base below the slender tall squared four-column sides w/a flared mouth, nicely charcoaled green matte glaze, designed by W.D. Gates & Fritz Albert, two impressed marks on base (ILLUS.) **$2,645**

Tiles

Tiles have been made by potteries in the United States and abroad for many years. Apart from small tea tiles used on tables, there are also decorative tiles for fireplaces, floors and walls. This is where present collector interest lies, especially in the late 19th century American-made art pottery tiles.

American Encaustic Water Mill Tile

American Encaustic Tiling Co., Los Angeles, California, branch, square, lightly embossed water mill scene covered w/a golden greenish brown glossy glaze, marked, some small corner chips & crazing, 6" w. (ILLUS.) **$150**

American Encaustic Portrait Tile

American Encaustic Tiling Co., Los Angeles, California, branch, square, molded bust profile portrait of a bearded Renaissance era man wearing a large plumed hat, medium blue glossy glaze, marked, crazing, 6" w. (ILLUS.) **$184**

Framed Cambridge Art Portrait Tiles

Interesting American Encaustic Tile

Columbia Victorian Lady Portrait Tile

American Encaustic Tiling Co., Los Angeles, California, branch, square, advertising-type, a central molded bust portrait of a classical lady enclosed by a scrolled banner reading "Dedication: A.E. Tile Works - Zanesville, O. - April 19, 1892," shaded dark blue glossy glaze, marked on the back "detimLloCL-TEA - AET Co. Limited," crazing, 4 1/8" w. (ILLUS.) **$150**

Cambridge Art Pottery, Cambridge, Ohio, square, a bust profile portrait of a young Victorian girl wearing a sailor-style cap & a bust profile portrait of a young Victorian boy wearing a hat w/visor, both w/a yellowish green glossy glaze, each marked on the back, facing pair, in new frame, minor edge nicks, some surface nicks, 6 x 12", the pair (ILLUS., top of page)
.... **$432**

Columbia Tile Company, Anderson, Indiana, square, molded w/a profile bust portrait of a young Victorian lady wearing a large boater-style hat & dress w/a ruffled collar, shaded deep rose glossy glaze, marked, crazing, notch cut in back, 6" w. (ILLUS., top next column) **$173**

Colorful Delft Commemorative Tile

de Porceleyne Fles, Delft, Holland, rectangular, a colorful incised & painted interior scene of a pottery shop w/potters at work, in shades of blue, brown, green, white & black, a light blue base band impressed w/the factory logo flanked by the

Pair of Trent Tiles with Young Victorian Girls

dates 1900 & 1950, probably a special commemorative for the factory, framed, 6 x 8 1/4" (ILLUS.)..................................... **$345**

Delft Wartime Commemorative Tile

de Porceleyne Fles, Delft, Holland, rectangular, an vertical landscape incised w/a scene of a woman & child standing & waving at a large war plane passing overhead, a large rising sun & small village in the distance, glazed in shades of blue, white, yellow, green, orange & brown, rectangular base panel inscribed in Dutch "Voedsel, Vrede, Vryheid" (Food, Peace, Freedom) & the dates April 29 to May 5, 1945, company logo on the back, very minor back edge chips, framed, 6 x 8 1/4" (ILLUS.).................................... **$317**

Trent Tile Company, Trenton, New Jersey, square, one w/a bust profile portrait of a very young Victorian girl w/a ribbon in her hair & wearing a lace-trimmed dress, a second w/a bust profile portrait of a very young Victorian girl wearing a lace-trimmed dress, both w/a shaded blue glossy glaze, newly framed, un-

marked, minor surface nicks, 6 x 12", facing pair (ILLUS., top of page)............... **$403**

Toby Mugs & Jugs

The Toby is a figural jug or mug usually delineating a robust, genial drinking man. The name has been used in England since the mid-18th century. Copies of the English mugs and jugs were made in America.

For listings of related Character Jugs see DOULTON & ROYAL DOULTON.

Nice Rockingham-glazed Toby Jug

Rockingham-glazed Toby, seated Mr. Toby w/a high tricorn hat, wearing a jacket, vest & kneebreeches, a grapevine-molded back handle, overall dark brown mottled glaze, unmarked, possibly Bennington, Vermont, 19th c., 6 1/2" h. (ILLUS.)..................................... **$210**

Staffordshire Toby, seated man wearing brown tricorn hat, brown jacket, blue vest, tan breeches & brown boots, legs apart seated on a large block, arms away from body, one hand holding tumbler, the other holding a bottle, Prattware-style, late 18th c., minor chips, 11 3/8" h. **$780**

Fine Staffordshire Toby with Pitcher

Staffordshire Toby, seated Mr. Toby wearing a black tricorn hat, orange jacket, tan kneebreeches & holding a deep red pitcher on one knee & a white glass in the other hand, script "3" on the bottom, probably 19th c., 10" h. (ILLUS.) **$230**

Torquay Pottery

In the second half of the 19th century several art potteries were established in the South Devon region of England to take advantage of a belt of fine red clay there. The coastal town of Torquay gives its name to this range of wares, which often featured incised sgraffito decoration or colorful country-style decoration with mottos.

The most notable potteries operating in the Torquay area were the Watcombe Pottery, The Torquay Terra-cotta Company and the Aller Vale Art Pottery, which merged with Watcombe Pottery in 1901 and continued production until 1962. Other firms whose wares are collectible include Longpark Pottery and The Devonmoor Art Pottery.

Early wares feature unglazed terra cotta items in the Victorian taste including classical busts, statuary and vases and some painted and glazed wares including examples with a celeste blue interior or highlights. In addition to sgraffito designs, other decorations included flowers, Barbotine glazes, Devon pixies framed in leafy scrolls and grotesque figures of cats, dogs and other fanciful animals, produced in the 1890s.

The dozen or so potteries flourishing in the region at the turn of the 20th century introduced their most popular product, Motto Wares, which became the bread and butter line of the local industry. The most popular patterns in this line included Cottage, Black and Colored Cockerels and Scandy, based on Scandinavian rosemaling designs. Most of the mottoes were written in English, with a few in Welsh. On early examples the sayings were often in Devonian dialect. These Motto Wares were sold for years at area seaside resorts and other tourist areas, with some pieces exported to Australia, Canada and, to a lesser

extent, the United States. In addition to standard size teawares and novelties, some miniatures and even oversized pieces were offered.

Production at the potteries stopped during World War II, and some of the plants were destroyed in enemy raids. The Watcombe Pottery became Royal Watcombe after the war, and Longpark also started up again but produced simpler patterns. The Dartmouth Pottery, started in 1947, produced cottages similar to those made at Watcombe and also developed a line of figural animals, banks and novelty jugs. The Babbacombe Pottery (1950-59) and St. Marychurch Pottery (ca. 1962-69) were the last two firms to turn out Motto Wares, but these later designs were painted on and the pieces were lighter in color, with less detailing.

Many books on the various potteries are available, and information can be obtained from the products manager of the North American Torquay Society.

Torquay Pottery Marks

Rare Aller Vale Miniature Teapot

Teapot, cov., miniature, colored scrolling B-1 decoration, Aller Vale Pottery, 5 1/4" l., 3 1/2" h. (ILLUS.) **$350-400**

Miniature Longpark Crocus Teapot

Teapot, cov., miniature, Crocus patt., wide low tapering cylindrical body w/wide shoulder tapering to conical cover w/knob finial, straight spout, C-form handle, Longpark Pottery, 4 1/4" l., 2 1/2" h. (ILLUS.) **$250**

Mini Royal Watcombe Sailing Ship Teapot

Teapot, cov., miniature, Sailing Ship patt., spherical body w/angled spout, C-form handle & inset cover w/knob finial, Royal Watcombe Pottery, 4 7/8" l., 3" h. (ILLUS.) **$180-250**

Miniature Black Cockerel Teapot

Teapot, cov., Motto Ware, Black Cockerel patt., miniature size, wide squatty bulbous tapering body w/angled spout & C-form handle, conical cover w/button finial, reads "Duee drink a cup a tay," Longpark Pottery, 4 1/2" l., 2 1/2" h. (ILLUS.) **$250-295**

Small Blue Spikey Tail Cockerel Teapot

Teapot, cov., Motto Ware, Blue Spikey Tail Cockerel patt., wide squatty body w/inset domed cover w/knob finial, angled spout & high C-form handle, reads: "Guid morn!," Aller Vale Pottery, small size (ILLUS.) **$125**

Old English Cock Fight Faience Teapot

Teapot, cov., Motto Ware, Cock Fight patt., faience, wide flat bottom w/slightly tapering cylindrical sides & narrow angled shoulder, inset cover w/knob finial, reads: "Old English Cock Fight," Watcombe Pottery, 6 1/2" l., 4 1/4" h. (ILLUS.) **$295**

Uhl Pottery

Original production of utilitarian wares began at Evansville, Indiana, in the 1850s and consisted mostly of jugs, jars, crocks and pieces for food preparation and preservation. In 1909, production was moved to Huntingburg, Indiana, where a more extensive variety of items was eventually produced including many novelty and advertising items that have become highly collectible. Following labor difficulties, the Uhl Pottery closed in 1944.

Unless it is marked or stamped, Uhl is difficult to identify except by someone with considerable experience. Marked pieces can have several styles of ink stamps and / or an incised number under glaze on the bottom. These numbers are die-cut and impressed in the glazed bottom. Some original molds were acquired by other potteries. Some production exists and should not be considered as Uhl. These may have numbers inscribed by hand with a stylus and are usually not glazed on the bottom.

Many examples have no mark or stamp and may not be bottom-glazed. This is especially true of many of the miniature pieces. If a piece has a "Meier's Wine" paper label, it was probably made by Uhl.

While many color variations exist, there are about nine basic colors: blue, white, black, rose or pink, yellow, teal, purple, pumpkin and browns / tans. Blue, pink, teal and purple are currently the most sought after colors. Animal planters, vases, liquor / wine containers, pitchers, mugs, banks, kitchenware, bakeware, gardenware and custom-made advertising pieces exist.

Similar pieces by other manufacturers do exist. When placed side by side, a seasoned collector can recognize an authentic example of Uhl Pottery.

A Variety of Uhl Marks

Ashtray, #199, in the form of a dog lifting its leg at a hydrant, marked (ILLUS. top row, left w/Uhl Pottery pieces) **$550**
Ashtray, green, hand-turned mark, 3" d. **$150**
Bank, figural, large grinning pig, yellow, unmarked **$400**
Bean pot, brown/blue, marked "Boston Bean Pot" **$170**
Bowl, basketweave, blue, unmarked **$90**

Bowl, 5" d., shouldered mixing bowl, unmarked **$140**

Bowl, 8" d., luncheon, blue, marked............... **$70**

Canteen, commemorative of Uhl Collectors Society, 1988 .... **$275**

Casserole, cov., blue, #528 & marked........... **$60**

Churn, 4-gal., cov., white, acorn mark, solid lid... **$185**

Creamer, light tan, hand-turned square mark, 5 1/2" h.. **$150**

Flowerpot, ribbed, yellow, no attached saucer, unmarked, 6" **$25**

Jar, 1-gal., white, acorn mark **$50**

Jar, 3-gal., tan, Evansville, Ind., mark **$360**

Jar, 6-gal., white, acorn mark **$75**

Jar, cov., cottage cheese, white, metal lid embossed "UHL"....................................... **$500**

Jug, 3-gal., light tan, Evansville, Ind., mark... **$360**

Jug, 5-gal., blue/white, marked "Dillsboro Sanitarium, Dillsboro, Ind."....................... **$700**

Jug, 6-gal., light tan, Evansville, Ind., oval mark **$120**

Various Uhl Pottery Items

Jug, blue & white, "Colonial Mineral Springs, Martinsville, Indiana" (ILLUS. top left w/various Uhl Pottery items)....... **$1,400**

Jug, brown/white, miniature shoulder, front acorn mark **$550**

Uhl Pottery Pieces

Jug, form of football, large, 5" l., rarer than smaller version (ILLUS. middle row, left w/Uhl Pottery pieces) **$225**

Jug, form of softball, Meier's label, 3 3/8" d. (ILLUS. middle row, right w/Uhl Pottery pieces) **$250**

Jug, miniature acorn, marked "Acorn Wares" **$70**

Jug, miniature, marked, 1" h. **$100**

Jug, red/green, "1940 Merry Christmas," marked "Uhl Pottery Company," 2 3/8" h. . **$225**

Lamp, Liberty Bell **$145**

Model of cat, potter's name engraved, unmarked **$1,000**

Model of cowboy boot, marked (ILLUS. bottom row, right w/Uhl Pottery pieces) **$150**

Model of dog & hydrant, similar to ashtray #199, two separate pieces, no marks (ILLUS. top row, center & right w/Uhl Pottery pieces) **$350**

Model of military boot, marked (ILLUS. bottom row, center w/Uhl Pottery pieces) ... **$95**

Model of shoe, miniature woman's slipper, marked (ILLUS. of two bottom row, left w/Uhl Pottery pieces) **$130**

Model of shoes, white, marked #2, pr......... **$110**

Mug, coffee, blue, marked............................. **$65**

Mug, coffee, pink, marked **$60**

Mug, "Homestead Hotel, No. 7 Water" (ILLUS. bottom right w/various Uhl Pottery items) **$150**

Mug, "West Baden Springs Hotel" (ILLUS. bottom left w/various Uhl Pottery items) **$145**

Pepper shaker, dark blue, unmarked **$35**

Pitcher, barrel-shaped, blue, marked............. **$65**

Pitcher, barrel-shaped, brown, unmarked....... **$40**

Pitcher, bulbous grape, pumpkin, #183 .... **$55**

Pitcher, Hall Boy, blue & white, unmarked **$1,500**

Pitcher, miniature, blue, marked "Norristown, Tenn.".. **$180**

Pitcher, squat grape, blue, unmarked........... **$160**

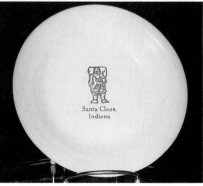

Rare Uhl Plate

Plate, 6 3/4" d., stamped "Santa Claus, Indiana," very rare, only three known to exist (ILLUS.)... **$600+**

Stein, 3-oz., miniature, brown, marked **$80**

Stein, miniature, w/box, commemorative of Uhl Collectors Society, 1987 .... **$500**

Teapot, 2-cup, blue, marked #131 .... **$200**

Three Sizes of the Uhl Pottery Teapot

Teapot, cov., spherical body w/long serpentine spout, C-form handle, low rim w/inset flattened cover w/knob finial, one of three sizes made, marked w/the circle mark on the bottom & also usually an incised number, made in various colors including white, yellow, brown, at least three shades of blue, a scarce shade of green, dark blue, pink, teal, black or purple are most desirable today, value depends on color, large size, 8-cup (ILLUS. in dark blue at far right with other Uhl teapots, top of page) **$100**

Teapot, cov., spherical body w/long serpentine spout, C-form handle, low rim w/inset flattened cover w/knob finial, one of three sizes made, marked w/the circle mark on the bottom & also usually an incised number, made in various colors including white, yellow, brown, at least three shades of blue, a scarce shade of green, dark blue, pink, teal, black or purple are most desirable today, value depends on color medium size, 4-cup (ILLUS. in light blue in the center with other Uhl teapots, top of page) **$125**

Teapot, cov., spherical body w/long serpentine spout, C-form handle, low rim w/inset flattened cover w/knob finial, one of three sizes made, marked w/the circle mark on the bottom & also usually an incised number, made in various colors including white, yellow, brown, at least three shades of blue, a scarce shade of green, dark blue, pink, teal, black or purple are most desirable today, value depends on color, small size, 2-cup (ILLUS. in dark blue at far left with other Uhl teapots, top of page) **$200**

Tulip bowl, yellow, marked #119 .... **$70**

Vase, blue, hand-turned mark **$700**

Vase, dark blue, marked #154 .... **$90**

Vase, waisted form, "Merrill Park Florist, Battle Creek, Mich.," extremely rare (ILLUS. top right w/various Uhl Pottery items) .... **$price unknown**

Vase, 4 3/4" h., bud vase, #107, hard to find, price depends on color, w/blue & especially purple being most popular (ILLUS. center w/various Uhl vases) **$45-75**

Various Uhl Vases

Vase, 5" h., handled, #152, very hard to find, marked, price depends on color, w/blue & especially purple being most popular (ILLUS. bottom left w/various Uhl vases) **$45-75**

Vase, 5 1/4" h., fan-shaped w/scalloped rim, #157, hard to find, price depends on color, w/blue & especially purple being most popular (ILLUS. bottom right w/various Uhl vases) **$55-75**

Vase, 5 1/4" h., flaring ribbed neck, #158, incised, hard to find, price depends on color, w/blue & especially purple being most popular (ILLUS. top left w/various Uhl vases) **$45-75**

Vase, 5 1/4" h., side handles, #156, incised, hard to find, price depends on color, w/blue & especially purple being most popular (ILLUS. top right w/various Uhl vases) **$45-75**

Water cooler, 5-gal., cov., white, acorn mark **$225**

Van Briggle

The Van Briggle Pottery was established by Artus Van Briggle, who formerly worked for Rookwood Pottery, in Colorado Springs, Colorado, at the turn of the century. He died in 1904, but the pottery was carried on by his widow and others. From 1900 until 1920, the pieces were dated. It remains in production today, specializing in Art Pottery.

Early Van Briggle Pottery Mark

Small Mulberry Van Briggle Bowl-Vase

Bowl-vase, footed wide squatty rounded lower sides below the wide sharply angled shoulder to a wide flat mouth, the shoulder molded w/repeating looping vine-like design, overall mulberry matte glaze, Shape No. 735, early 20th c., 3 3/8" d. (ILLUS.).... **$173**

Fine Small Brown Van Briggle Vase

Vase, 3 7/8" h., wide squatty bulbous ovoid form w/a wide short cylindrical neck, the sides w/lightly molded arched panels each enclosing a maple leaf, overall brown matte glaze, Shape No. 626, 1915 (ILLUS.) **$575**

Large Bulbous Van Briggle Vase

Vase, 10" h., wide bulbous ovoid body w/the round shoulder tapering to a wide flat mouth, the neck & shoulder molded fanned stylized flowers w/the stems down the sides, dark blue shaded to dark maroon matte glaze, an Anna Van Briggle design, late teens or early 1920s (ILLUS.) **$633**

Vernon Kilns

The story of Vernon Kilns Pottery begins with the purchase by Mr. Faye Bennison of the Poxon China Company (Vernon Potteries) in July 1931. The Poxon family had run the pottery for a number of years in Vernon, California, but with the founding of Vernon Kilns, the product lines were greatly expanded.

Many innovative dinnerware lines and patterns were introduced during the 1930s, including designs by such noted American artists as Rockwell Kent and Don Blanding. In the early 1940s items were designed to tie in with Walt Disney's animated features "Fantasia" and "Dumbo." Various commemorative plates, including the popular "Bits" series, were also produced over a long period of time. Vernon Kilns was taken over by Metlox Potteries in 1958 and completely ceased production in 1960.

Vernon Kilns Mark

"Bits" Series
Plate, 8 1/2" d., Bits of Old New England Series, The Cove **$30**
Plate, 8 1/2" d., Bits of the Old South Series, Cotton Patch **$40**
Plate, chop, 14" d., Bits of the Old Southwest Series, Pueblo **$75**

Dinnerwares
Bowl, chowder, tab handle, Gingham patt.
.... **$15-18**
Bowl, soup, Coronado patt......................... **$15-20**
Bowl, 13" d., salad, Homespun patt........... **$75-85**
Butter dish, cov., Casual California patt.... **$25-30**
Butter dish, cov., Tickled Pink patt........... **$30-40**
Candleholders, teacup form w/metal fittings, Tam O'Shanter patt., pr............ **$100-125**
Casserole, cov., Heavenly Days patt......... **$45-60**
Casserole, cov., Tam O'Shanter patt......... **$50-70**
Coaster, Gingham patt.............................. **$25-30**
Coffeepot, cov., Heavenly Days patt., 8-cup ... **$65**
Creamer, Modern California patt............... **$10-15**
Cup & saucer, after-dinner size, Early California patt., red or cobalt blue, each (ILLUS. front, top next page)............... **$25-30**
Egg cup, Early California patt., turquoise (ILLUS. with Early California cups & saucers, top next page) **$20-25**
Gravy boat, Gingham patt. **$20-25**
Mixing bowls, nesting set, Gingham patt., 5" to 9" d., five pcs. **$175-200**

Early California Egg Cup & After Dinner Cups & Saucers

Mug, Barkwood patt., 9 oz............................. **$25**
Pepper mill, Homespun patt. **$150-175**

Hawaiian Coral Streamline Pitcher

Pitcher, Streamline shape, Hawaiian Coral
  patt., 1 qt. (ILLUS.)................................ **$45-55**
Pitcher, 5" h., Streamline shape, Barkwood
  patt., 1/2 pt. **$25-30**
Plate, 7 1/2" d., Frontier Days patt. **$35-45**
Plate, 9 1/2" d., luncheon, Organdie patt.... **$10-12**
Plate, 9 1/2" d., Trader Vic patt. **$100-125**
Plate, 10 1/2" d., dinner, Calico patt............... **$25**
Plate, chop, 12" d., Frontier Days patt.... **$150-175**
Plate, chop, 14" d., Gingham patt.............. **$35-40**
Platter, 12" d., round, Organdie patt. **$20-25**
Relish dish, leaf-shaped, four-part, Native
  California patt.. **$50-75**
Salt & pepper shakers, large size, Tam
  O'Shanter patt., pr................................. **$45-65**
Salt & pepper shakers, regular size, Ging-
  ham patt., pr. **$20**
Spoon rest, Organdie patt. **$75-85**

Tweed Pattern Sugar Bowl

Sugar bowl, cov., Tweed patt. (ILLUS.)..... **$30-35**
Teacup & saucer, jumbo size, Homespun
  patt. **$45-55**
Teacup & saucer, Winchester '73 patt. **$45-50**

Santa Barbara Pattern Teapot

Teapot, cov., Santa Barbara patt. (ILLUS.)
  .... **$75-95**
Teapot, cov., Tam O'Shanter patt. **$45-55**
Tumbler, Bel Air patt. **$20-25**

Portion of Rockwell Kent Salamina Pattern Dinner Service

Tumbler, Tickled Pink patt. **$20**

Disney "Fantasia" & Other Items
Bowl, 8" d., soup, Flower Ballet patt. **$50**
Figure of Baby Weems, No. 37, 6" h. ... **$150-175**
Tray, hors d'oeuvre, May & Vieve Hamilton
  design, 16" d. **$400-600**
Vase, 12" h., carved handles, May & Vieve
  Hamilton design .... **$1,500+**

Don Blanding Dinnerwares
Cup & saucer, Coral Reef patt., blue......... **$40-50**
Sugar bowl, cov., Coral Reef patt., blue.... **$85-95**
Tumbler, Hilo patt., #4, 5 1/2" h. **$125-150**

Rockwell Kent Designs
Bowl, chowder, "Our America" series, coco-
  nut tree, blue **$60-70**
Cup & saucer, Moby Dick patt., maroon.... **$45-50**
Dinner service: four 9 1/2" d. luncheon
  plates, four 6 3/4" w. chowder bowls, four
  6 1/4" d. bread & butter plates, four cups
  & saucers, an 8" d. bowl & a 9" d. bowl;
  Salamina patt., ca. 1935, one chowder
  bowl repaired, the set (ILLUS. of part, top
  of page) **$920**
Plate, 6 1/2" d., "Our America" series,
  steamship, blue **$45-50**
Plate, 9 1/2" d., Moby Dick patt., blue **$110-145**
Sugar bowl, cov., Moby Dick patt., blue .. **$85-105**
Teapot, cov., Moby Dick patt., Rockwell
  Kent Designs, blue, 6-cup **$150-175**

States Map Series - 10 1/2" d.
Plate, Texas **$40-45**

States Picture Series - 10 1/2" d.
Plate, North Dakota, multicolored................... **$25**
Plate, Virginia, maroon **$18-20**

Miscellaneous Commemoratives
Cup & saucer, after-dinner size, Niagara
  Falls.. **$25**
Plate, 10 1/2" d., Christmas Tree patt.
  (ILLUS. w/Christmas Tree teacup &
  saucer, next column) **$65-75**
Plate, 10 1/2" d., Hollywood Stars, blue **$70-80**

Christmas Tree Pattern Pieces

Plate, 10 1/2" d., Notre Dame University,
  brown **$20-25**
Plate, Statue of Liberty, multicolor............. **$50-75**
Teacup & saucer, Christmas Tree (ILLUS.
  with Christmas Tree plate) **$30-35**

Warwick

*Numerous collectors have turned their atten-
tion to the productions of the Warwick China
Manufacturing Company that operated in Wheeling, West Virginia, from 1887 until 1951. Prime
interest seems to lie in items produced before 1911
that were decorated with decal portraits of beautiful women, monks and Native Americans. Fraternal Order items, as well as floral and fruit
decorated items, are also popular with collectors.*

*Researcher John R. Rader, Sr. has recently
determined that the famous "IOGA" and helmet
mark was used by Warwick from April 1903 until
December 1910. "Ioga" is a Native American word
meaning "Beautiful."*

"Tudor Rose" Sugar & Creamer

Warwick Mark

Salesman's Sample Ashtray

Ashtray, salesman's sample, white trimmed in gold w/"Warwick China" in script & knight's helmet in black, no mark on back, ca. 1940s, 4 3/4" l., 3 1/2" w. (ILLUS.).. **$75**

Creamer & cov. sugar, white w/red "Tudor Rose" decor patt. (rare), marked w/Warwick knight's helmet in green, ca. 1940s, creamer 4 1/2" h., sugar 5" d., pr. (ILLUS., top of page)............................ **$95**

Warwick Ewer with Hazelnuts

Ewer, matte brown & tan w/hazelnuts, gold trim, marked w/IOGA knight's helmet in green, decor code M2, ca. 1908, 11" h. (ILLUS.).. **$150**

Humidor with B.P.O.E. Elk Logo

Humidor, cov., brown & tan w/elk's head & clock, "Cigars" on back, marked w/IOGA knight's helmet in grey & "Warwick China" in black, decor code A-13 in red, scarce, ca. 1903, 6 1/2" h., 4 1/2" d. (ILLUS.) **$260**

Mug, cylindrical, decorated w/the head of an elk & the "BPOE" emblem.......................... **$45**

Pitcher, 6 1/2" h., Tokio #3, brown shaded to brown ground, decorated w/color portrait of Native American, A-12 .... **$300**

Pitcher, 7 3/4" h., Tokio #1 shape, overall red ground w/color portrait of fisherman in yellow slicker, No. E-3.......................... **$155**

Lemonade Pitcher with Woman

Pitcher, 9 3/4" h., lemonade shape, overall pink ground w/color "Gibson Girl" type bust portrait of a young woman w/dark hair in a bouffant style & holding purple flowers, No. H-1 (ILLUS., previous page)... **$265**

Platter in "June Bride" Pattern

Platter, 22" l., white w/small pink flowers & gold rim in "June Bride" decor patt., marked w/Warwick knight's helmet in maroon, decor code #B2062, ca. 1940s (ILLUS.).. **$25**

Portrait Spirits Jug

Spirits jug, matte tan & brown w/woman in low-cut gown & flowing hair, marked w/IOGA knight's helmet in green, decor code M-1 in red, scarce, ca. 1908, 6 1/4" h. (ILLUS.) **$225**

VP Style Stein with Bulldog

Stein, VP style, brown & cream w/photo-graphic transfer of bulldog, "Ch. l'Almas-

sadeur," marked w/IOGA knight's hel-met, decor code A-32, ca. 1906, 2 2/4" d., 4 1/2" h. (ILLUS.) **$75**

Teapot, cov., h.p. portrait, "Gibson Girl" de-cor, turquoise & pink, matte finish, signed "H. Richard Boehm," marked w/IOGA knight's helmet in green, decor code M5, rare in this color, ca. 1910, 7 1/2" h. **$425**

Vase, 4" h., Pansy shape, yellow shading to green ground, color portrait of Anna Po-taka, K-1 .... **$200**

Vase, 8 1/4" h., Victoria style, white w/gold rim, two herons, marked w/IOGA knight's helmet in grey, decor code D-1 in red, ca. 1909 .... **$190**

Vase, 9 1/2" h., Penn shape, overall green color w/no decoration, matte finish, No. M-6 .... **$270**

Vase, 9 1/2" h., Thelma style, pink w/h.p. "Gibson Girl" decal, signed "H. Richard Boehm," marked w/IOGA knight's hel-met, decor code H-1, scarce, ca. 1909 ..... **$245**

Vase, 9 1/2" h., Verbenia #1 shape, brown shaded to brown ground, color floral dec-oration, No. A-6.. **$165**

Vase, 9 3/4" h., Iris shape, brown shaded to brown ground, nut decoration, No. A-64 .... **$150**

Vase, 10" h., baluster form w/scroll handles, brown w/pink roses, marked w/IOGA knight's helmet, decor code A-12 in red, scarce, ca. 1904 .... **$205**

Vase, 10" h., Flower shape, brown shaded to brown ground, color floral decoration, No. A-6 .... **$135**

Vase, 10" h., Henrietta shape, brown shad-ed to brown ground, color portrait of a seminude young woman, No. A-30 .... **$275**

Vase, 10" h., Magnolia style, grey w/picture of partially nude woman, signed "Car-reno," marked w/IOGA knight's helmet, decor code #C-2 in red, ca. 1905 .... **$850**

Portrait Vase with Gypsy Girl

Vase, 10 1/4" h., Bouquet #2 portrait style in tan & brown, bust portrait of Gypsy girl in red dress & headscarf, marked w/IOGA knight's helmet in green, decor code M-1 in red, ca. 1908 (ILLUS.)........................... **$240**

Warwick Vase with Poppies

Vase, 12 1/2" h., baluster form, brown w/pink poppies, marked w/IOGA knight's helmet in green, decor code A40, scarce, ca. 1904 (ILLUS.) **$200**

Commercial china

Warwick B&O Railroad Platter

Platter, 8 1/4" l., white w/22k gold decorative band on rim & B&O Railroad symbol, marked w/Warwick knight's helmet in green, ca. 1938 (ILLUS.) **$175**

Warwick "Sumter Hospital" Sugar Bowl

Sugar bowl, cov., white w/two green bands, "Sumter Hospital" logo, 3 3/4" h. (ILLUS.) ... **$25**

Tray, oval, white w/"The Washington" logo, 3 1/2 x 9 3/4" **$30**

Dinnerwares

Bowl, oval, Pattern No. 2000 .... **$25**
Cup & saucer, Pattern No. 9903, Grey Blossom decoration **$18**

Warwick Demitasse Cup & Saucer

Demitasse cup & saucer, Gray Blossom decor patt. w/platinum rim, saucer only marked w/Warwick knight's helmet in gold w/patt. name "Gray Blossom - Pat. #9903," ca. 1940, 2 1/4" h. cup, 5" d. saucer, cup & saucer (ILLUS.)............................ **$26**
Pitcher, 8" h., buttermilk-type, white ground w/floral decoration of small pink flowers **$45**
Plate, 6 1/2" d., bread & butter, Pattern No. 9437-M, Windsor Maroon decoration............ **$5**
Plate, 6 1/2" d., bread & butter, Pattern No. E-9450 .... **$15**
Plate, 9" d., Pattern No. B-9059 .... **$15**
Plate, 10" d., dinner, Pattern No. 9584, Bird of Paradise decoration w/single bird **$10**
Platter, 13" l., Pattern No. B-9272, coin gold trim **$40**
Vegetable bowl, handled, Pattern No. 2062 ... **$30**

Watt Pottery

Founded in 1922, in Crooksville, Ohio, this pottery continued in operation until the factory was destroyed by fire in 1965. Although stoneware crocks and jugs were the first wares produced, by 1935 sturdy kitchen items in yellowware were the mainstay of production. Attractive lines like Kitch-N-Queen (banded) wares and the hand-painted Apple, Cherry and Pennsylvania Dutch (tulip) patterns were popular throughout the country. Today these hand-painted utilitarian wares are "hot" with collectors.

A good reference book for collectors is Watt Pottery, An Identification and Value Guide, by Sue and Dave Morris (Collector Books, 1933)

Watt Pottery Mark

Baker, cov., Open Apple patt., No. 110, 8 1/2" d. **$165**
Baker, open, White Daisy patt., 7" **$25**
Baker, cov., Rooster patt., No. 67, 8 1/4" d..... **$85**
Baker, cov., Apple patt., No. 96, 8 1/2" d., 5 3/4" h. **$55**

Watt Pottery Apple Pattern Bowls

Baker, Tear Drop patt., rectangular, No. 85, 9" w. (minor hairline in base).................... $210

Bean cup, Apple patt., individual, No. 75, 3 1/2" d. 2 1/4" h... $155

Bean cup, Tear Drop patt., individual, No. 75, 3 1/2" d. 2 1/4" h.................................... $10

Bean pot, cov., two-handled, Star Flower (four petal) patt., No. 76, 7 1/2" d., 6 1/2" h.. $85

Bowl, 4 1/4" d., 2" h., Starflower (four-petal) patt., ribbed, No. 04.................................... $30

Bowl, 4" d., 1 1/2" d., Apple patt., No. 602 (ILLUS. far left, top of page)...................... $30

Bowl, 4 1/4" d., 2" h., Starflower (five-petal) patt., ribbed, No. 04.................................... $10

Bowl, 4 1/4" d., 2" h., Apple patt., ribbed, No. 04.. $20

Bowl, 5" d., Eagle patt., ribbed, No. 5............. $75

Bowl, 5" d., individual cereal or salad, Apple patt., No. 68.. $40

Bowl, 5" d., 1 3/4" h., Tear Drop patt., No. 68.. $30

Bowl, 5" d., 2" h., Apple patt., No. 603 (ILLUS. center left, top of page) $45

Bowl, cov., 5 " d., 2 1/2" h., Apple patt., No. 05.. $35

Bowl, 5 1/2" d., 2" h., Reduced Decoration Apple patt., No. 74 .... $20

Bowl, 5 3/4" d., Apple patt., No. 23 .... $18

Bowl, 5 3/4" d., Cut-Leaf Pansy (Rio Rose) patt., No. 23... $15

Bowl, 6" d., 1 3/4" h., cereal or salad, Apple patt., No. 94... $25

Bowl, 6" d., 1 3/4" h., cereal or salad, Autumn Foliage patt., No. 94.......................... $10

Bowl, 6" d., 2 1/2" h., Apple patt., No. 604 (ILLUS. center, top of page)...................... $30

Bowl, cov., 7 1/2"d., Apple patt., w/Iowa advertising, No. 66 .... $60

Bowl, 8" d., Cross-Hatch Pansy (Old Pansy) patt., small spaghetti, No. 44.............. $165

Bowl, 8" d., Cut-Leaf Pansy (Rio Rose) patt., small spaghetti, No. 44...................... $15

Bowl, cov., 8 1/2" d., Butterfly patt., No. 67 (hairline in base).. $375

Bowl, 9 1/2" d., 4" h., salad, Apple patt., No. 73 .... $20

Bowl, 10 3/4" d., 3 1/2" h., footed salad, Apple patt., No. 106.. $125

Bowl, 11 3/4" d., 4" h., Apple (two-leaf) patt., No. 55.. $50

Bowl, 13" d., Apple (two-leaf) patt., spaghetti, No. 39 (ILLUS., top next column) $60

Bowl, 13" d., Starflower (five-petal) patt., spaghetti, No. 39 .... $25

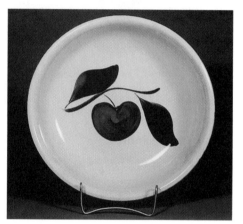

Two-leaf Apple Spaghetti Bowl

Canister, cov., Dutch Tulip patt., large, No. 72, 7 1/4" d., 9 1/2" h. (chip inside cover rim)... $195

Canister, cov., Tear Drop patt., large, No. 72, 7 1/4" d., 9 1/2" h. $200

Casserole, cov., Apple patt., individual, French handled, No.18, 8" l. $125

Casserole, cov., Autumn Foliage patt., individual, French handled, No.18, 78" l. $105

Casserole, cov., Black Moonflower patt., individual, French handled, No. 18, 8" l. $20

Casserole, cov., Dutch Tulip patt., individual, French handled, tab handle on cover, No. 18, 8" l. $95

Casserole, cov., Raised Pansy patt., individual, French handled, No.18, 8" l. $15

Casserole, cov., Tear Drop patt., individual, French handled, No.18, 8" l. $65

Casserole, cov., Morning Glory patt., cream-colored, No. 94, 8 1/2" d. (missing cover)........ $95

Casserole, cov., Apple patt., w/advertising, on metal stand, No. 96, 8 1/2" d., 5 1/2" h. $65

Casserole, cov., Double Apple patt., No. 96, 8 1/2" d., 5 1/2" h. $95

Chip-n-Dip set, Apple patt., No. 110 & 120 bowls, the set $110

Cookie jar, cov., Cross-Hatch Pansy (Old Pansy) patt., No. 21, 7 1/2" h. $200

Cookie jar, cov., Cut-Leaf Pansy (Rio Rose) patt., No. 21, 7 1/2" h..................... $105

Creamer, Apple (two-leaf) patt., No. 62, 4 1/4" h.. $55

Autumn Foliage Creamer & Pitchers

Rooster Pattern Creamer & Pitchers

Creamer, Apple (two leaf) patt., No. 62 w/advertising, 4 1/4" h. **$55**

Creamer, Autumn Foliage patt., No. 62, 4 1/4" h. (ILLUS. right w/Autumn Foliage pitchers, top of page) **$30-50**

Creamer, Double Apple patt., No. 62, 4 1/4" h. **$195**

Creamer, Dutch Tulip patt., No. 62, 4 1/4" h. **$115**

Creamer, Morning Glory patt., cream-colored, No. 97, 4 1/4" h. **$425**

Creamer, Rooster patt., No. 62, 4 1/4" h. (ILLUS. left w/pitchers, second from top) .. **$125**

Cup & saucer, Cross-Hatch Pansy (Rio Rose) patt., No. 40, the set **$135**

Dip bowl, slanted sides, Autumn Foliage patt., No. 120, 5" d., 2" h. **$20**

Grease jar, cov., Apple patt., w/South Dakota advertising, No. 01, 5 1/2" h. **$200**

Mixing bowl, Double Apple patt., No. 64, 7 1/2" d., 5" h. **$50**

Mixing bowl, Tear Drop patt., No. 64, w/Minnesota advertising, 7 1/2" d., 5" h. (ILLUS.) **$40**

Mixing bowl, Pansy patt., ribbed, w/Minnesota advertising, No. 8, 8" d., 4 1/2" h. **$20**

Mixing bowl, Autumn Leaf patt., w/advertising, No. 9, 9" d., 5" h. **$40**

Mug, Star Flower (four-petal) patt., barrel-shaped, No. 501, 4 1/2" h. **$30**

Mug, Apple patt., cylindrical w/angled handle, No. 701, 3 3/4" h. **$300**

Mug, Apple patt., tapering cylindrical form, No. 121, 3 3/4" h. **$105**

Mug, Autumn Foliage patt., cylindrical waisted shape, No. 121, 3 3/4" h. **$75**

Pie plate, Apple patt., No. 33, 9" d. **$50**

Pie plate, Cross-Hatch Pansy (Old Pansy) patt., No. 33, 9" d. **$175**

Tear Drop No. 64 Mixing Bowl

Starflower Four-Petal No. 15 Pitcher

Pitcher, 5 1/2" h., Starflower (four-petal) patt., No. 15 (ILLUS., previous page).......... **$30**

Pitcher, 6 1/2" h., Apple patt., w/advertising, No. 16.. **$50**

Pitcher, 8" h., 8 1/2" d., refrigerator-type, square-shaped, Apple (two-leaf) patt., No. 69.. **$300**

Pitcher, 5 1/2" h., Autumn Foliage patt., No. 15 (ILLUS. center w/Autumn Foliage creamer).. **$30**

Pitcher, 5 1/2" h., Dutch Tulip patt., No. 15 .... **$100**

Pitcher, 5 1/2" h., Rooster patt., No. 15 (ILLUS. center w/Rooster creamer & pitcher)... **$65**

Pitcher, 5 1/2" h., Tear Drop patt., No. 15 .... **$25**

Pitcher, 5 1/2" h., Tulip patt., No. 15 .... **$400-500**

Pitcher, 6 1/2" h., Autumn Foliage patt., No. 16 (ILLUS. left w/Autumn Foliage creamer)... **$30**

Pitcher, 6 1/2" h., Cherries patt., No. 16 .... **$65**

Pitcher, 6 1/2" h., Dutch Tulip patt., No. 16 (rub on spout)... **$50**

Pitcher, 6 1/2" h., Rooster patt., No. 16 (ILLUS. right w/Rooster creamer & pitcher).. **$50-100**

Pitcher, 7" h., 7 3/4" d., Cross-Hatch Pansy (Rio Rose), old style **$175**

Pitcher, 8" h., Apple patt., w/ice lip, No. 17 (nick on spout)... **$85**

Plate, 10" d., Cut-Leaf Pansy (Rio Rose) patt., No. 101... **$40**

Pink on Black Moonflower Plate

Plate, 10" d., Moonflower patt., pink on black, No. 101 (ILLUS.)............................... **$65**

Plate, 10 1/2" d., divided, Dutch Tulip patt. **$700**

Platter, 12" d., Apple patt., No. 49 .... **$105**

Platter, 12" d., Cherry patt., No. 49 (ILLUS., top next column)....................................... **$95**

Platter, 12" d., Pansy patt., No. 49................. **$30**

Platter, 15" d., Cherries patt., No. 31 .... **$65**

Watt Cherry Pattern 12" Platter

Platter, 15" d., Cross-Hatch Pansy (Rio Rose) patt., No. 31................................... **$105**

Apple Hourglass Salt & Pepper Shakers

Salt & pepper shakers, Apple patt., hourglass shape, w/Iowa advertising, No. 117 & No. 118, pr. (ILLUS.) **$145**

Salt & pepper shakers, Autumn Foliage patt., hourglass shape, No. 117 & No. 118, pr. **$75**

Salt & pepper shakers, Starflower (five-petal) patt., barrel-shaped, w/advertising, No. 45 & No. 46, 4" h., the set **$35**

Salt & pepper shakers, Tear Drop patt., barrel-shaped, No. 45 & No. 46, 4" h., pr. . **$265**

Salt & pepper shakers, Tear Drop patt., hourglass shape, No. 117 & No. 118, each **$135**

Salt shaker, Cherries patt., barrel-shaped, No. 45, 4" h. **$45**

Sugar bowl, cov., Apple patt. w/advertising, No. 98 .... **$170**

Sugar bowl, cov., Autumn Foliage patt., No. 98 .... **$45**

Sugar bowl, cov., Morning Glory patt., w/advertising, cream-colored, No. 98, 4 1/4" h. **$195**

Teapot, cov., Apple (three-leaf) patt., No. 112, rare, spout professionally repaired,

6" h. (ILLUS. right with other Apple teapot) **$1,400**

Wedgwood

Reference here is to the famous pottery established by Josiah Wedgwood in 1759 in England. Numerous types of wares have been produced through the years to the present.

WEDGWOOD

Early Wedgwood Mark

Basalt

Fine Wedgwood Basalt Ewer

Ewer, Classical urn-form body on a square foot & ringed & reeded pedestal, the body w/a fluted lower body & narrow molded band below large molded grapevine swags, the angled shoulder w/a cylindrical neck & high arched spout w/the figure of a crouching satyr reaching around the base of the spout to grasp the horns of a goat mask below the spout, the loop handle issuing from the shoulders of the satyr, 19th c., 15 1/2" h. (ILLUS.) **$863**

Wedgwood Basalt Figure of Nude Male

Figure of a nude male, standing w/legs crossed & playing a flute, leaning against a tall tree trunk w/his cloak pinned at one shoulder & draping down around the stump, 19th c., 17 1/4" h. (ILLUS.) **$920**

Miscellaneous

Wedgwood Fairland Lustre Boston Cup

Boston cup, Fairyland Lustre, a low cylindrical footring supporting the wide rounded bowl, the exterior decorated w/the Leaping Elves patt., yellowish brown upper sides decorated w/fairing w/transparent gold wing frolicking on a green & blue ground w/mushroom, the upper section sprinkled w/printed gold stars; the interior decorated w/the Elves on a Branch patt. w/two small elves perched on a prickly branch w/black bat & bird around the leafy rim, base w/the Portland Vase mark & "ZXXXX," 5 1/4" d. (ILLUS.) **$1,725**

Miniature Wedgwood Lustre Bowl

Bowl, miniature, 2 1/4" w., Lustre Ware, footed octagonal shape, the exterior w/a mottled orange lustre glaze decorated w/various gold mythological beasts between gold rim & base bands, the dark blue mottled interior decorated w/a stylized spider (ILLUS.) **$260**

Rare Fairyland Lustre Willow Bowl

Fine Wedgwood Fairyland Lustre Octagonal Bowl

Bowl, 8"w., Fairyland Lustre, footed deep octagonal shape decorated in the Willow patt., the exterior in Coral & Bronze decorated w/a printed gold Willow Ware style decoration, the interior w/a Willow patt. in the bottom & a blue leafy band around the rim, Portland Vase mark & "Z5406" (ILLUS., previous page) **$3,450**

Bowl, 9 3/8" w., 4 1/2" h., Fairyland Lustre, footed octagonal shape, Fairy in a Cage patt., the exterior w/each side w/a lacy gold border enclosing a landscape scene, the interior deocrated w/fantastic creatures in an exotic landscape, No. Z5125 (ILLUS., top of page) **$3,450**

Woodland Elves VI Fairyland Lustre Bowl

Bowl, 8" w., Fairyland Lustre, footed octagonal form, the exterior in the Woodland Elves VI patt., the Fiddler in Tree aginst a midnight blue lustre background, the interior decorated w/the Ship & Mermaid patt. against a white lustre ground, some minor scratches to interior bottom (ILLUS.)....... **$4,600**

Fairyland Lustre Poplar Trees Bowl

Bowl, 10 3/4" d., 4 3/4" h., Fairyland Lustre, a narrow footring supports the deep rounded sides, exterior Poplar Tree patt. decorated w/a fanciful landscape of stylized trees against a midnight blue lusre ground, interior decorated w/the Woodland Elves V, Woodland Bridge patt., some minor scratches on the interior (ILLUS.).. **$5,175**

Woodland Elves VI Fairyland Bowl

Bowl, 8 1/2" d., 4" h., Fairyland Lustre, Woodland Elves VI patt., a narrow footring supports the octagonal bowl, the exterio w/a continuous design of tree trunks in dark bluish green & all the elves in brown on a flame lustre background of orange over crimson, the interior w/the Ship & Mermaid patt. w/a flame lustre center, Pattern No. Z5360 (ILLUS.) **$7,475**

Garden of Paradise Fairyland Lustre Bowl

Bowl, 11" d., Fairyland Lustre, wide rounded shape, the interior decorated w/the Garden of Paradise (Variation I) patt.

Fairyland Lustre Daventry Bowl

w/daylight lustre, the arch in the design is missing but the black pillars remain against a mother-of-pearl sky, two different idol figures appear in violet & the dancing beetle faces the opposite way, the green " Cake" tree w/a companion tree w/a curvaceious black trunk & copper brown foliage, the exterior w/the Flight of Birds patt. printed in gold outline on a very dark green & blue lustre ground encircling the sides, the under rim & foot decorated w/gold pebble & grass border, signed on the base, Pattern No. Z4968 (ILLUS. of interior, previous page) **$4,600**

Bowl, 13" d., 5 1/4" h., Fairyland Lustre, Daventry patt., a low pedestal round foot supporting the wide bowl w/sharply flaring sides, the interior w/a design in four panels done in bluish lavender lustre over-printed w/a crimson lustre thorn diamond, border flower inserts covered w/orange lustre & the narrow surrounding the panels in green, the panel designs & center design in brown outlined in gold, the exterior decorated w/a ground of orange lustre over-printed w/a crimson or brown pheasant eye diaper & a wide band w/an Oriental landscape in solid brown outlined in gold (ILLUS., top of page) **$4,600**

Jar, cov., Fairyland Lustre, malfrey pot Shape No. 2312, bulbous ovoid body fitted w/a domed cover, the exterior includes various patterns including Demon Tree, Roc Bird, Bat in the Demon Tree, Black Toad & Dwarf, Red Monkeys & the Scorpion w/a long yellow tail & spines,a narrow dragon bead border around the base & rim of the collar, inside of collar decorated in the Pan-Fei border, the cover decorated w/Owls of Wisdom w/purple bodies & bright copper-colored faces, blue eyes & red pupils, the cover w/a Red Fei border band & the Scorpion, cover also w/a Pan-Fei border around the inside surrounding Elves on a branch in the center, Pattern No. Z-4968, very light wear to gold cover trim, 14" h. (ILLUS.) **$57,500**

Set of 12 Wedgwood Lustre Plates

Plates, 11" d., Lustre decoration, octagonal w/eight alternating panels of gold geometric designs alternating w/panels showing Oriental men, the figures in gold against a dark blue lustre ground, Portland Vase mark & retailer mark for William H. Plummer & Co., New York, sete of 12 (ILLUS.).. **$900**

Extremely Rare Fairyland Lustre Jar

Fairyland Lustre Lahore Punch Bowl

Punch bowl, Fairyland Lustre, wide flaring foot supporting the wide deep rounded bowl, exterior decorated w/the Lahore patt. featuring swags of brilliant colors & hanging lanterns, the interior decorated w/three elephants, two of which have riders, a camel, a war horse w/lancer & a flying goose in the center, all figures in black mother-of-pearl outlined in gold against a yellow lustre ground, Pattern Z5266, 11" d., 5 5/8" h. (ILLUS., previous page) **$8,625**

Fairyland Lustre Butterfly Woman Vase

Vase, 8" h., Fairyland Lustre, a flaring base tapering to a tall trumpet-form body, the sides decorated w/two large portraits of the beautiful Butterfly Woman seated in a colorful tree against a dark blue ground, the outer rim & base decorated w/lacy gold bands, colorful inner rim decoration, Wedgwood mark & incised "0187," black slip-painted "249 68," minor interior rim stains (ILLUS.) **$2,100**

Fairyland Lustre Willow Pattern Bowl

Vase, 8 1/2" h., Fairyland Lustre, Willow patt., baluster-form body w/a short flaring neck, finely decorated w/violet tree trunks & flower spikes, green leaves & lanterns of red & yellow w/orange lustre that are surrounded by a view of sky & water of blue lustre over a rich bluish green shade, the houses in black w/torches of crimson & the conventional "Candle Lighthouse" on the bridge reflected in orange ripples, a group of violet gnomes shelter under black toadstool umbrellas at the base, the chestnut leaflets not hatched in gold print but have both Flame & Moonlight Fairyland Lustre, Pattern No. Z5228 (ILLUS.) **$6,900**

Fairyland Lustre Tree Serpent Vase

Vase, 11" h., Fairyland Lustre, Serpent Tree patt., a flaring base tapering to a tall cylindrical body w/a flaring rim, the abstract tree & landscape design in bright colors against a flame lustre sky, base signed, Pattern No. Z4968 (ILLUS.) **$7,475**

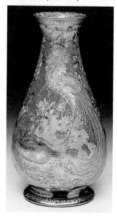

Fairyland Lustre Chinese Pheasant Vase

Vase, 12" h., Fairyland Lustre, Argus shape, Chinese Pheasant patt., footed bulbous baluster-form body w/a flaring rim, decorated w/a large strutting Chinese pheasant in crimson & pink w/gold-trimmed feathers on both the front & back, birds surrounded by other water & shorebirds & is standing on a green grassy round w/leafy flowers in red & pink, foot & rim surrounded w/a gold dragon border, base marked "Wedgwood - Made in England Argus" (ILLUS., previous page).............. **$6,325**

Rare Tree Serpent Fairyland Lustre Vase

Vase, 12" h., Fairyland Lustre, Tree Serpent patt., tall simple ovoid body tapering to a short cylindrical neck w/a flared rim, a full-length scene of the tree, which hides the initials "SMJ," in a bazaar landscape w/the baby done in white resting on green grass on both sides, green Imps walking across a bridge below a large flying bat on one side, Shape No. 3150, Pattern No. Z5360 (ILLUS.) **$17,250**

Tall Extremely Rare Fairyland Lustre Vase

Vase, 17" h., Fairyland Lustre, footed squatty bulbed base band below the tall slightly flaring cylindrical body, decorated w/daylight lustre background w/crimson & violet Imps crossing a red bridge w/a light yellow top against green bushes, the sky in reddish pink & the river in deep blue w/a yellow canoe, the bubbles boy & bat

are black & the Roc bird is vermilion, the base band w/a blue lustre background w/a green flaming wheel border, the treehouse above the bridge w/a green roof w/yellow, red & black walls, signed on the base & numbered "Z4968" (ILLUS.)..... **$43,125**

Weller

This pottery was made from 1872 to 1945 at a pottery established originally by Samuel A. Weller at Fultonham, Ohio, and moved in 1882 to Zanesville. Numerous lines were produced, and listings below are by pattern or line.

Reference books on Weller include The Collectors Encyclopedia of Weller Pottery by Sharon & Bob Huxford (Collector Books, 1979) and All About Weller by Ann Gilbert McDonald (Antique Publications, 1989).

WELLER
Weller Marks

Ardsley (1928)
Various shapes molded as cattails among rushes with water lilies at the bottom. Matte glaze.

Bulb bowl, lobed blossom form base w/leaf-form openwork top, pale green leaves on white, 4 7/8" h. **$69**

Ardsley Console Bowl & Flower Frog

Console bowl & flower frog, the widely flaring shallow round bowl molded overall w/cattails, the figural flower frong w/a large lavender blue fish above the round domed base, inkstamp marks, restoration to the fish tail & edge of bowl, bowl 12" d., 2 pcs. (ILLUS.).............................. **$345**

Ardsley Double Vase

Vase, double, 10" h., two angled clusters of cattails connected at the top by a pointed branch handle, a molded white pond lily blossom at the base, marked w/half kiln ink stamp mark (ILLUS., previous page) **$115-130**

Aurelian (1898-1910)
Similar to Louwelsa line but with brighter colors and a glossy glaze. Features bright yellow/orange brush-applied background along with brown and yellow transparent glaze.

Weller Aurelian Mug with Seed Pods

Mug, flared ringed base below the tall slightly tapering sides, large C-form handle, h.p. large deep orange mountain ash seed pods w/green leaves on a long stem against a shaded dark brown & golden yellow ground, artist-signed, marked "Aurelian Weller 435," 6 1/4" h. (ILLUS.).......... **$184**

Aurelian Mug with Dark Fruits

Mug, slightly tapering cylindrical body w/a heavy C-form handle, decorated w/large very dark blue grapes w/a brown stem & green & yellow leaves against a slightly mottled dark blackish green ground, artist-signed, marked "Weller Aurelian 562 12," 6" h. (ILLUS.) **$150**

Tall Aurelian Vases with Irises

Vase, 14 3/8" h., tall ovoid body w/a rounded shoulder to the short rolled neck, h.p. deep yellow & orange-red irises on green leafy stems against the dark brown to yellow & tan ground, impressed Aurelian mark & "334," small glaze nick on edge of base, artist-signed (ILLUS.) **$1,150**

Baldin (about 1915-20)
Rustic designs with relief-molded apples and leaves on branches wrapped around each piece.

Baldin Vase with Red Apple at Base

Vase, 7" h., squatty bulbous base tapering to a tall slightly flaring cylindrical neck, twisted branch down the sides w/a red apple & green leaves at the base, unmarked (ILLUS.)... **$127**

Barcelona (1920s)
A line of simple peasant-style pieces with a golden tan background hand-painted with colorful stylized floral medallions.

Colorful Weller Barcelona Bowl

Bowl, 9" d., 2 1/8" h., wide shallow round form, h.p. center four-petal blossoms surrounded by small red blossoms & green & yellow leaves, dark green border band, original paper label (ILLUS.) **$104**

Weller Barcelona Vase

Vase, 7 1/4" h., baluster-form w/a wide flat rim flanked by heavy C-form shoulder handles, Weller inkstamp mark & portion of paper label (ILLUS.) **$115**

Bedford Glossy (ca. 1915)
Simple shapes generally molded around the top w/a band of molded blossoms in pastel colors above a dark shaded ground. Bedford Matte is a similar line with a matte finish.

Weller Bedford Glossy Vase

Vase, 8 1/4" h., slightly waisted cylindrical body w/molded alternating bluish pink & yellow blossoms around the top above a streaky dark green ground, unmarked, stilt pull on base & some minor burst glaze bubbles, overall crazing (ILLUS.)
.... **$104**

Blue & Decorated Hudson (1919)
Handpainted lifelike sprays of fruit blossoms and flowers in shades of pink and blue on a rich dark blue ground.

Blue & Decorated Floral Cluster Vase

Vase, 9 5/8" h., a gently swelled cylindrical body w/a rounded shoulder to a short flat neck, a lighter blue shoulder band decorated w/a long trailing cluster of dark rose, pink & white blossoms & green leaves, block letter mark, crazing (ILLUS.) **$317**

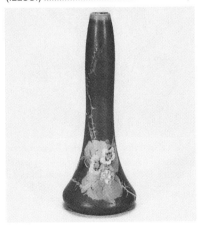

Blue & Decorated Hudson Bud Vase

Vase, 10" h. bud-type, the flaring base tapering sharply to a tall slender cylindrical body, decorated around the base w/a cluster of blossoming blackberry plant, block letter mark (ILLUS.) **$184**

Tall Blue & Decorated Hudson Vase

Vase, 10 1/2" h., a disk foot below the tall cylindrical body w/a widely flaring trumpet-form top, decorated w/a long cluster of small pink & white blossoms on a green leafy stem down the side, block letter mark, light crazing (ILLUS.) **$184**

Brighton (1915)
Various bird or butterfly figurals colorfully decorated and with glossy glazes.

Model of a butterfly, small figure w/wings open & decorated in color, 3" w. **$144**

Coppertone (late 1920s)
Various shapes with an overall mottled bright green glaze on a "copper" glaze base. Some pieces with figural frog or fish handles. Models of frogs also included.

Scarce Coppertone Figural Flower Frog

Flower frog, model of lily pad bloom enclosing a seated frog, raised on a rounded footed base w/flower holes, 4 3/8" h. (ILLUS.) **$518**

Fine Large Coppertone Vase

Vase, 8" h., bulbous ovoid body w/molded rim, figural frog shoulder handles, ink stamp mark (ILLUS.) **$2,100**

Cornish (1933)
Simple shapes with a mottled tan, deep rust red or dark blue ground molded near the rim with two or three long pointed leaves suspending a small cluster of blue berries.

Weller Blue Cornish Console Set

Console set: bowl & pair of short candlesticks; the 7 1/4" d., 3" h. bowl w/a wide flat bottom & upright cylindrical sides w/small rosette knob rim handles, 3 1/4" h. candlesticks w/a domed base w/small knob handles & a cylindrical socket, mottled blue, impressed script mark, the set (ILLUS.) **$196**

Ovoid Weller Cornish Vase

Vase, 7 1/4" h., large ovoid body w/tiny rosette knob shoulder handles & a short cylindrical neck, mottled rust, incised mark (ILLUS.)... **$127**

Dechiwo (1908)

This was the original name for the Burnt Wood line. Since this name was hard to remember Weller changed it to Burnt Wood in 1908. Dechiwo pieces can have a glossy or matt glaze.

Rare Green-glazed Dechiwo Vase

Vase, 6 1/2" h., a bulbous ovoid shape tapering to a thick flat molded mouth, incised w/a continuous scene of children in early 20th clothing playing beneath an upper band of green leaf clusters w/red apples at the centers, overall shaded light to dark green glossy glaze, block letter mark, a line at the rim, overall crazing (ILLUS.).. **$3,940**

Dickensware 2nd Line (early 1900s)

Various incised "sgraffito" designs, usually with a matte glaze. Quality of the artwork greatly affects price.

Dickensware 2nd Line Pillow Vase

Vase, 8 7/8" h., pillow-type, four knob feet supporting the flattened rounded body w/a low, long oblong mouth, colorful incised design of two men in Colonial attire seated at a tavern table playing checkers, against a shaded dark green ground, signed by John Herold, incised Weller mark on base (ILLUS.)............................. **$683**

Unusual Glossy Dickensware Vase

Vase, 10 5/8" h., tall cylindrical body w/a narrow shoulder below the short cylindrical rolled neck, incised scene of a church interior w/a monk kneeling before the altar, in black, white & yellow against a dark redding brown ground, unusual glossy glaze, impressed "Dickens Ware Weller 604-7," fine overall crazing (ILLUS.).................... **$1,150**

Vase, 16 1/4" h., tall ovoid body tapering to a flared rim, incised w/a colorful scene of Satan being cast out of Heaven by the Archangel Michael, all against a dark blue ground, signed by Charles Babcock Upjohn, marked on the base "X 270 1," inscribed on the side "Satan Smitten by Michael," rare (ILLUS., next page)......... **$3,795**

Large Rare Dickensware 2nd Line Vase

Dickensware 3rd Line (1904)
Similar to Eocean line. Various fictional characters molded and slip-painted against pale background colors. Glossy glaze.

Dickinsware Mug with Comic Man

Mug, tapering cylindrical body w/C-form handle, relief image of a skinny man wearing a floppy yellow hat, large red bow tie & blue jacket, against a dark green shaded to blue ground, light crazing, 5 1/4" h. (ILLUS.)............................. **$230**

Eldora-Chelsea (pre-1920)
Pieces decorated around the upper body with a wide molded band of stylized floral rosettes in light blue and red with green leaves. The lower body molded with green-tinted vertical ribbing.

Vase, 8 3/4" h., footed ovoid body tapering to a wide flat mouth, impressed mark, overall crazing & staining on interior (ILLUS., top next column)... **$104**

Weller Eldora-Chelsea Vase

Eocean and Eocean Rose (1898-1925)
Early art line with various handpainted flowers on shaded grounds, usually with a clear glossy glaze. Quality of artwork varies greatly.

Squatty Weller Eocean Vase

Vase, 5 1/4" h., footed wide squatty bulbous body centered by a wide cylindrical neck w/a molded rim, decorated w/a large deep rose nasturtium blossom & green leafy vine against a very dark green shaded to cream ground, artist-signed, marked "Eocean Weller R 63 C - D 206," overall crazing (ILLUS.) **$207**

Fine Eocean Ovoid Vase

Vase, 6 3/8" h., bulbous ovoid body tapering to a short wide cylindrical neck, decorated w/deep red nasturtium blossoms & green leaves against a very dark green shaded to cream ground, signed by Sarah McLaughlin, marked "Eocean Weller X 508," light crazing (ILLUS., previous page) **$460**

Etched Floral (ca. 1905)
Various simple shapes decorated with incised flowers or berries outlined in black and usually against solid backgrounds in green, orange, yellow, beige, or pink.

Rare Tall Etched Floral Vase

Vase, 12 1/4" h., tall slender ovoid body w/a small flat mouth, deeply carved white & orange irises & pale green leaves against a light tan matte ground, impressed mark, overall crazing (ILLUS.)................ **$1,380**

Etna (1906)
Colors similar to Early Eocean line, but designs are molded in low relief and colored.

Etna Jardiniere & Pedestal with Pansies

Jardiniere & pedestal, bulbous ovoid jardiniere swelled around the top below the wide rolled rim, dark green rim shading to blue to cream, molded around the top w/red pansies on tall stems w/leaves around the base, the match pedestal w/red pansies on a dark blue shaded to cream ground, impressed mark, some minor chips, overall 24" h., 2 pcs. (ILLUS.) **$432**

Weller Etna Vase with Large Roses

Vase, 10" h., tall slender ovoid body tapering to a short cylindrical neck, molded on the shoulder w/large deep red roses w/leafy green stem down the side, against a deep purple shaded to white shaded to pink ground, block letter mark, overall crazing (ILLUS.) **$184**

Fleron (late '20s)
Green glaze, made to look hand turned (called Ansonia if blue or grey). Middle period.

Weller Fleron Batter Pitcher

Batter pitcher, tall ovoid body w/a flat molded rim, short angled cylindrical spout on shoulder, curved handle from rim edge to center of side, marked, 10 3/8" h. (ILLUS.).................................... **$184**

Floretta (ca. 1904)

An early line with various forms molded with clusters of various fruits or flowers against a dark brown, shaded brown or sometimes a dark grey to cream ground. Usually found with a glossy glaze but sometimes with a matte glaze.

Floretta Tankard Pitcher with Grapes

Pitcher, 10 3/4" h., tankard-type, tall slightly tapering cylindrical body w/a small rim spout & D-form handle, a molded cluster of large light purple grapes against a shaded green to pink matte ground, unmarked (ILLUS.) **$115**

Floretta Vase with Grape Cluster

Vase, 5 5/8" h., tapering cylindrical sides below a bulbous four-lobed top, a molded cluster of reddish purple grapes on the side against a dark green shaded to cream ground, circular Floretta Weller mark, Shape No. 10, moderate overall crazing (ILLUS.) **$81**

Glendale (early to late 1920s)

Various relief-molded birds in their natural habitats, lifelike coloring.

Gate-form Glendate Double Bud Vase

Vase, double-bud, 4 3/4 x 8", gate-form, square shaped vases joined by openwork fence, wren & grapevine decoration (ILLUS.) **$403**

Glendale Vase with Large Marsh Bird

Vase, 6" h., cylindrical w/narrow shoulder to a short cylindrical neck, large standing marsh bird (ILLUS.) **$375**

Glendale Vase with Marsh Bird

Vase, 6 1/2" h., footed bulbous ovoid w/flared rim, embossed w/polychrome marsh scene of marsh bird & nest (ILLUS.) **$460**

Glendale Vase with Flying Bird

Vase, 6 1/2" h., ovoid body w/slightly tapering neck & a flat rim, decorated w/outdoor
scene of a bird in flight (ILLUS.) **$460**

Greora (early 1930s)
*Various shapes with a bicolor orange shaded
to green glaze splashed overall with brighter
green. Semigloss glaze.*

Large Greora Strawberry Pot

Strawberry pot, bulbous baluster-form
body w/flaring neck & half-round cupped
opening around the middle of the sides,
script mark & partial paper label, 8 1/4" h.
(ILLUS.) **$260**

Hudson (1917-34)
*Underglaze slip-painted decoration, "parch-
ment-vellum" transparent glaze.*

Vase, 8 7/8" h., ovoid body w/a narrow
shoulder to the short rolled neck, h.p.
around the shoulder w/clusters of small
lavender flowers w/yellow centers on
green leafy stems, shaded purple to
cream ground, block letter mark, minor
grinding roughness on base, overall craz-
ing (ILLUS., top next column) **$288**

Hudson Vase with Lavender Flowers

Hudson Vase with Blue & White Blossoms

Vase, 8 7/8" h., slightly ovoid body w/a narrow shoulder & low wide neck, decorated
w/large white & blue blossoms & light
green leafy stem against a light blue
shaded to cream ground, signed by Sarah McLaughlin, block letter mark, overall
crazing (ILLUS.) **$460**

Tapering Square Weller Hudson Vase

Vase, 9 3/8" h., slightly tapering tall square creamy body, a thin black rim band & a wide grey & black body band decorated w/tight scrolls in pale blue & pink, block letter mark, minor glaze bubbles, overall crazing (ILLUS., previous page)............... **$317**

Weller Hudson Vase with Daisies

Vase, 9 1/2" h., slightly tapering hexagonal form w/a small rounded shoulder & short cylindrical neck, the neck & shoulder in purple shaded to pink above a fine black scalloped line above a narrow purple band trimmed w/large stylized yellow daisies all against a creamy ground, block letter mark, overall crazing (ILLUS.).......... **$230**

Hudson Vase with Trailing Floral Band

Vase, 9 5/8" h., slightly swelled cylindrical form tapering slightly to a flat rim, creamy ground h.p. around the shoulder w/narrow black bands & trailing pink, green & yellow florals, block letter mark, overall crazing (ILLUS.)...................................... **$161**

Vase, 10 1/2" h., tall slightly tapering hexagonal body w/a narrow shoulder to the short cylindrical neck, cream ground h.p. around the rim & down the sides w/a long brown branch & small red & mauve berries, block letter mark, overall fine crazing (ILLUS., top next column) **$317**

Weller Hudson Vase with Long Branch

Weller Hudson Vase with Tulips

Vase, 11 1/8" h., slender ovoid body tapering to a small molded mouth, lavender tulip blossoms & pale green leaves against a purple shaded to cream ground, block letter mark, couple of tiny nicks, overall crazing (ILLUS.) **$260**

Wild Roses on Hexagonal Hudson Vase

Vase, 11 1/2" h., tall hexagonal form, narrow black bands around the rim trimmed w/trailing red wild roses blossoms down the creamy lower body, block letter mark, overall crazing (ILLUS.)............................ **$207**

Weller Hudson Vase with Roses

Vase, 13" h., simple ovoid body w/a narrow rounded shoulder centered by a short flaring neck, h.p. large white roses & pale green leaves against a purple shaded to green shaded to cream ground, Weller block letter mark, overall crazing (ILLUS.).. **$288**

Tall Cylindrical Hudson Vase

Vase, 13 1/4" h., tall center cylindrical form, a dark blue upper band above the creamy lower portion, h.p. trailing design of small purple blossoms & green leaves on a black stem from the rim down the side, block letter mark, grinding nick on base, overall crazing (ILLUS.).................. **$317**

Vase, 23 1/8" h., very large ovoid body tapering to a short widely flaring & flattened neck, decorated w/large white, gold & pink peony blossoms on a leafy stem against a dark blue shaded to cream ground, decorated by Hester Pillsbury, ink stamp logo, a patch of bubbles & peppering on the back (ILLUS., top next column).. **$4,830**

Huge Weller Hudson Peony Vase

Ivory (1910 to late 1920s)

Ivory-colored body with various shallow embossed designs with rubbed-on brown highlights.

Sand jar, wide cylindrical shape w/a scroll-molded upper border band & leaf scroll bottom band, the side molded w/bold leafy scrolls centering large scroll cartouches, catalog No. 67, 19" h. **$207**

Klyro (early to late '20s)

Most pieces feature molded wood framing around panels topped by double pink blossoms and dark purple berries against a finely ribbed ground, often trimmed in tan, brown, cream or olive green.

Weller Klyro Wall Pocket

Wall pocket, long tapering rectangular form w/an openwork fence top band above a pair of deep rose molded blossoms above a cluster of blue berries, green ground, overall crazing, 7 1/2" l. (ILLUS.)
.... **$115**

Knifewood (late teens)

Pieces feature deeply molded designs of dogs, swans, and other birds and animals or flowers in white or cream against dark brown grounds.

Knifewood Wall Pocket with Daisies

Wall pocket, bullet-shaped w/flat rim, large Shasta daisies on green leafy stems against a finely ribbed tan ground, light crazing, 8 1/4" l. (ILLUS.) **$207**

L'Art Nouveau (1903-04)

Various figural and floral-embossed Art Nouveau designs.

Tall L'Art Nouveau Vase with a Poppy

Vase, 11 5/8" h., tall cylindrical lower body below the wide swelled top curving to a closed rim, the rim molded w/a large orange poppy blossom, the rim & base in pale green shading to a pinkish cream ground, impressed round mark, slight discoloration above the base (ILLUS.) **$230**

Lamar (1923)

A metallic luster ware in a deep red decorated with black luster scenery. Never marked except with a paper label.

Vase, 12 3/4" h., widely flaring base tapering to a tall cylindrical waisted body, black silhouetted island palm tree landscape on a dark red ground, original paper label **$431**

Lasa (1920-25)

Various landscapes on a banded reddish and gold iridescent ground. Lack of scratches and abrasions important.

Lamp base, bulbous ovoid form tapering to a small mouth w/electric fitting, fitted on a round flaring metal base, decorated w/a landscape of tall pine trees in iridescent shades of gold, green & maroon, signed, 13" h. (some finish wear) **$489**

Lasa Vase with Tree Decoration

Vase, 8 5/8" h., swelled cylindrical body tapering to a flaring trumpet neck, decorated w/a tall leafy tree against a banded iridescent background in shades of deep rose, gold, blue & pink, signed on the side (ILLUS.) **$547**

Fine Lasa Vase with Palm Trees

Vase, 9 1/4" h., footed bulbous ovoid body tapering sharply to a small flat mouth, tropical scene of tall green palm trees against a banded iridescent ground in gold, deep rose, purple & blue, some minor scratches (ILLUS.) **$978**

Lonhuda Faience (1894-1895)

William Long, founder of the Lonhuda Pottery, joined the Weller Pottery with this line in 1894. It was a hand-decorated Standard Glaze ware very similar to Rookwood pottery of that era. After Long left Weller they introduced the Louwelsa and Aurelian lines to take its place.

Weller Lonhuda Faience Ewer

Ewer, short squatty bulbous body tapering to a short neck w/widely rolled tri-lobed rim & delicate C-scroll handle, decorated w/deep red tulips & green leaves against a dark green shaded to a mottled yellow & orange ground, Lonhuda shield mark, initialed by decorator, overall crazing, 8 7/8" h. (ILLUS.) **$805**

Squatty Weller Lonhuda Powder Box

Powder box, cov., squatty rounded double-lobed box w/conforming domed cover, the cover decorated w/orange blossoms & green leafy stems on a shaded dark green to yellow & orange ground, mottled dark green & orange box, Lonhuda block letter & shield mark, Shape No. 209, fine overall crazing, 2 1/2" h. (ILLUS.) **$490**

Louwelsa (1896-1924)

Handpainted underglaze slip decoration on dark brown shading to yellow ground; glossy yellow glaze.

Tall Louwelsa Vase with Fruits

Vase, 10 1/4" h., tall slender slightly swelled cylindrical body w/a narrow shoulder & short rolled neck, decorated w/a very dark blue & golden fruit w/large green leaves near the top against a nearly black shaded to very dark green ground, artist-signed & marked, normal crazing (ILLUS.) **$184**

Two Large, Unusual Louwelsa Vases

Vase, 12 1/4" h., tall ovoid body tapering to a small flaring neck w/flattened rim, decorated w/a portrait of a small Benji-esque dog against a dark brown shaded to dark gold ground, signed by Lisabeth Black, marked "Louwelsa Weller K 539 2" & w/partial factory sticker, crazing (ILLUS. lower left with Indian portrait vase) **$1,150**

Vase, 13 5/8" h., wide ovoid body w/a rounded shoulder & short rolled neck, decorated w/a fine half-length portrait of a Native American chief in full regalia, signed by Anthony Dunlavy in 1901, marked "Weller Louwelsa 11 - K 227 5," crack at neck, overall crazing (ILLUS. upper right with dog portrait vase)............. **$2,185**

Large Louwelsa Vase with Owl & Mice

Vase, 15 1/8" h., large bulbous ovoid body tapering to a short flaring neck, decorated w/a dark golden yellow owl perched on a branch & ready to pounce down on two small mice below, all against a very dark brown to tan ground, signed by Ed Abel, Louwelsa Weller logo, Shape No. 506, light crazing (ILLUS.)...................... **$2,990**

Manhattan (early 1930s-'34)
Simple modern shapes embossed with stylized leaves or leaves and blossoms and glazed in shades of green or brown.

Vase, 8" h., wide squatty rounded lower body tapering gently to wide cylindrical sides & a wide flat mouth, molded around the bottom w/three overlapping bands of short rounded leaves, molded ribs up the sides, light brown matte glaze.................... **$92**

Vase, 8 1/2" h., wide squatty rounded lower body tapering gently to wide cylindrical sides & a wide flat mouth, molded around the bottom w/three overlapping bands of short rounded leaves, molded ribs up the sides, mottled bluish green matte glaze.... **$230**

Matt Green (ca. 1904)
Various shapes with slightly shaded dark green matte glaze and molded with leaves and other natural forms.

Small Weller Matt Green Jardiniere

Jardiniere, four knob feet supporting the slightly tapering hexagonal body w/a thick molded rim, molded swirling poppy flowers & vines around the sides, tiny chip on one foot, 3 5/8" h. (ILLUS.)........... **$230**

Muskota (1915 - late 1920s)
Figural pieces with human figures, birds, animals or frogs. Matte glaze.

Muskota Frog & Lotus Flower Frog

Flower frog, figural frog emerging from a lotus blossom, block letter mark, crazing, 4 1/2" h. (ILLUS.) **$230**

Roma (1912-late '20s)
Cream-colored ground decorated with embossed floral swags, bands or fruit clusters.

Weller Roma Flowerport

Flowerpot, tapering cylindrical sides w/a wide molded fruit & leaf band below the wide rolled & gadrooned tan-tinted rim, crazing, 5 1/2" h. (ILLUS.)........................... **$92**

Weller Roma Square Planter

Planter, low square form w/concave sides molded w/rose swags & molded at each corner w/a tan lion head holding a ring, removable liner, impressed mark, 6 3/8" w., 3 3/8" h. (ILLUS., previous page) **$69**

Wall pocket, conical, incised vertical lines & decorated w/roses & grape cluster near top, green leaves w/yellow center at base, cream ground, 8 1/4" h. **$92**

Sicardo (1902-07)
Various shapes with iridescent glaze of metallic shadings in greens, blues, crimson, purple or coppertone decorated with vines, flowers, stars or freeform geometric lines.

Sicardo Vase with Peacock Feathers

Vase, 7 1/4" h., simple cylindrical form, decorated w/tall peacock feathers in iridescent greenish gold against an iridescent bronze ground, signed (ILLUS.) **$863**

Simple Cylindrical Sicardo Vase

Vase, 10 3/4" h., simple cylindrical form w/a flat molded mouth, bluish green iridescent glazed w/golden-copper leaf design, Shape No. 602 (ILLUS) **$518**

Silvertone (1928)
Various flowers, fruits or butterflies molded on a pale purple-blue matte pebbled ground.

Silvertone Vase with Small Blossoms

Vase, 7 3/4" h., ovoid body tapering to a short cylindrical neck flanked by handles from rim to shoulder, molded cluster of stylized deep rose & white blossoms & green leaves w/a brown branches against a pale lavender ground, inkstamp mark, crazing (ILLUS.) **$260**

Tall Silvertone Vase with Poppies

Vase, 11 3/4" h., ovoid body tapering down to a flared base, the wide mouth w/a deeply ruffled rim, thick shoulder handles, large stylized pink poppies & green leaves w/a yellow butterfly against the pale lavender ground, inkstamp mark, some dry crazing (ILLUS.) **$432**

Sydonia (1931)
Pleated blossom or fan shapes on a leaf-molded foot. Mottled blue or dark green glaze.

Weller Sydonia Footed Bowl

Bowl, 6 1/2" l., 2" h., rectangular green foot supporting a long shallow flaring & ribbed blue bowl, script mark (ILLUS., previous page) **$58**

Pair of Blue Weller Sydonia Vases

Vases, 5 1/4" h., forked fan shape w/pleated sides, mottled blue body on green rectangular foot, marked, pr. **$75-100**

Turada (1897)

Turada was an early ware used to produce lamps, mugs, vases & various other decorative items. The dark glossy background was glazed in shades of brown, orange, blue, olive green & claret and highlighted with applied bands of delicate ivory or white pierced scrolling. Pieces were often marked with the line name.

Bowl, cov., 6" d., wide half-round bowl in dark brown decorated w/blue flowers & ivory vines, the domed cover in ivory & blue w/a wide pierced scroll band flanked by raised scroll bands & topped w/a knop finial, impressed mark (repaired) **$201**

Velva (1933)

Simple forms with a dark green, blue or shaded tan ground decorated with a full-length rectangular panel down the side molded in low-relief with large stylzed green leaves & small creamy blossoms.

Tall Weller Velva Covered Urn

Urn, cov., footed tall ovoid body w/small scroll shoulder handles, short cylindrical neck w/a fitted high domed cover w/button finial, shaded tan, impressed script mark, 11" h. (ILLUS.) **$260**

Zona (1911 to 1936)

Red apples and green leaves on brown branches, all on a cream-colored ground; some pieces with molded florals or birds with various glazes. A line of children's dishes was also produced featuring hand-painted or molded animals. This is referred to as the "Zona Baby Ware."

Zona (about 1920)

Zona Baby Ware Small Pitcher

Pitcher, 4" h., Baby Ware, tapering cylindrical body w/an arched rim spout & loop handle, cream ground ground w/a seated brown rabbit looking up at a bluebird on a leafy branch, impressed script mark (ILLUS.) **$69**

Wheatley Pottery

Thomas J. Wheatley was one of the original founders of the art pottery movement in Cincinnati, Ohio, in the early 1880s. In 1879 the Cincinnati Art Pottery was formed, and after some legal problems it operated under the name T.J. Wheatley & Company. Its production featured Limoges-style handpainted decorations, and most pieces were carefully marked and often dated.

In 1882 Wheatley dissociated himself from the Cincinnati Art Pottery and opened another pottery, which was destroyed by fire in 1884. Around 1900 Wheatley finally resumed making art pottery in Cincinnati, and in 1903 he founded the Wheatley Pottery Company with a new partner, Isaac Kahn.

The new pottery from this company featured colored matte glazes over relief work designs; green, yellow and blue were the most often used colors. There were imitations of the well-known Grueby Pottery wares as well as artware, garden pottery and architectural pieces. Artwork was apparently not made much after 1907. This plant was destroyed by fire in 1910 but was rebuilt and run by Wheatley until his death in 1917. Wheatley artware was generally unmarked except for a paper label.

Wheatley Marks

Wheatley Vase with Ochre Glaze

Vase, 10 1/2" h., 8 1/2" d., architectural style w/wide bullet-form body supported by four buttressed feet & w/wide upright band of embossed leaves around the upper half, matte ochre glaze, chip on one foot, WP mark (ILLUS.) **$1,150**

Tall Green Handled Wheatley Vase

Vase, 17 3/4" h., tall slightly tapering cylindrical body w/a wide rolled rim issuing four long rope-like handles down the sides, fine matte green glaze, base marked "TWP - 606 - B," small chip low on body (ILLUS.) **$3,040**

Willow Wares

This pseudo-Chinese pattern has been used by numerous firms throughout the years. The original design is attributed to Thomas Minton about 1780, and Thomas Turner is believed to have first produced the ware during his tenure at the Caughley works. The blue underglaze transfer print pattern has never been out of production since that time. An Oriental landscape incorporating a bridge, pagoda, trees, figures and birds supposedly tells the story of lovers fleeing a cruel father who wished to prevent their marriage. The gods, having pity on

them, changed them into birds, enabling them to fly away and seek their happiness together.

Blue

Ashtray, figural whale, ca. 1960, Japan..... **$25-30**
Ashtray, unmarked, American **$15**
Bank, figural, stacked pigs, ca. 1960, Japan, 7" h. **$50-55**
Batter jug, frosted, Hazel Atlas Glass, 9" h.
.... **$75-95**
Batter jug, Moriyama, Japan, 9 1/2" h. .. **$100-125**
Bell, modern, Enesco, Japan **$15**
Bone dish, ca. 1890, unmarked, England
.... **$40-45**

Blue Willow Bone Dish

Bone dish, Buffalo Pottery, 6 1/2" l. (ILLUS.)
.... **$60-70**
Bowl, berry, Allertons, England
.... **$12-15**
Bowl, berry, Japan **$8**
Bowl, berry, milk glass, Hazel Atlas............... **$15**
Bowl, cereal, Royal China Co. **$11**
Bowl, individual, 5 1/4" oval, J. Maddock........ **$20**
Bowl, soup, 8" d., Japan **$18-20**
Bowl, soup w/flanged rim, 8 1/4" d., Royal China Co. **$10**
Bowl, 6 1/2 x 8 1/4", Ridgways, England ... **$45-50**
Bowl, salad, 10" d., Japan **$75**
Butter dish, in wood holder, 6" d. **$50-75**
Butter dish, cov., for stick, Japan, rectangular, 7" l. **$60-70**
Butter dish, cov., 8" d., England.................. **$100**
Butter pat, Buffalo Pottery **$25**
Butter pat, Wood & Sons.............................. **$20**
Cake plate, Green & Co., 8" sq................. **$40-45**
Canister, cov., round, tin, 5 3/4" h. **$20-25**

Blue Willow Coffee Canister

Canister, labeled "Coffee," marked "Willow," Australia, ca. 1920s, 5 3/4" h. (ILLUS.) ... **$35-40**
Canister set: cov., "Coffee," "Flour," "Sugar," "Tea," barrel-shaped, ca. 1960s, Japan, the set **$275-300**
Chamber pot, Wedgwood, 9" d. **$175-200**
Charger, 11 3/4" d., Moriyama, Made in Japan **$65-85**
Charger, 12" d., Buffalo Pottery **$75-95**
Cheese dish, cov., rectangular, unmarked, England **$150**

Blue Willow Cheese Stand

Cheese stand, J. Meir & Sons, England, 8 1/2" d. (ILLUS.) **$175-200**
Condiment cruet set: cov. oil & vinegar & mustard cruet, salt & pepper; carousel-type base w/wooden handle, Japan, 7 1/2" h., the set **$175-200**

Blue Willow Cracker Jar

Cracker jar, cov., silver lid & handle, Minton, England, 5" h. (ILLUS.) **$175**
Creamer, Allerton, England............................ **$40**

Blue Willow Cow-shaped Creamer

Creamer, cow-shaped, W. Kent, England, 1920s-50s (ILLUS.)........................... **$250-300**
Creamer, individual, Shenango China Co.. **$25-30**
Creamer, John Steventon **$30**

Blue Willow Figural Cow Creamer

Creamer w/original stopper, figural cow standing on oval base, mouth forms spout & tail forms handle, ca. 1850, unmarked, England, 7" l., 5" h. (ILLUS.) **$500-600**
Cruets w/original stoppers, oil & vinegar, Japan, 6" h., the set **$55**
Cup & saucer, Booth **$40-45**
Cup & saucer, Buffalo Pottery **$40-45**
Cup & saucer, child's, ca. 1900, unmarked, England **$50**
Cup & saucer, demitasse, Copeland, England **$40**
Cup & saucer, "For Auld Lang Syne," W. Adams, England, oversized **$100-125**
Cup & saucer, Japan................................. **$10-15**
Drainer, butter, ca. 1890, England, 6" sq........ **$75**
Egg cup, Booths, England, 4" h................ **$40-45**
Egg cup, Japan, 4" h. **$20-25**
Egg cup, Allerton, England, 4 1/2" h. **$40-45**
Ginger jar, cov., Japan, 5" h. **$30**
Ginger jar, cov., Mason's, 9" h. **$50-60**
Gravy boat, Buffalo Pottery **$65-75**

Blue Willow Gravy Boat

Gravy boat, ca. 1890, unmarked, England, 7" l. (ILLUS.)... **$50-60**
Gravy boat w/attached underplate, double-spouted, Ridgways, England **$60-70**
Hot pot, electric, Japan, 6" h.......................... **$75**
Invalid feeder, ca. 1860, unmarked, England **$150-175**
Knife rest, ca. 1860, unmarked, England . **$85-95**
Ladle, pattern in bowl, unmarked, England, 6" l... **$125-135**
Ladle, pattern in bowl, floral handle, unmarked, England, 12" l. **$175-185**
Lamp, w/ceramic shade, Japan, 8" h. **$50**

Buffalo Pottery Blue Willow Pitcher

Pitcher, cov., 5 1/2" h., Buffalo Pottery
(ILLUS.) **$150-175**
Pitcher, 6" h., scalloped rim, Allerton, En-
gland **$100**

Blue Willow "Chicago Jug"

Pitcher, 7" h., "Chicago Jug," ca. 1907, Buffalo Pottery,p3 pt. (ILLUS.)................. **$200-225**
Pitcher, 8" h., glass, Johnson Bros., En-
gland **$35-40**
Pitcher w/ice lip, 10" h., Japan..................... **$100**

Blue Willow Place card Holder

Place card holder, unmarked, England, ca.
1870s, 2 1/2" d. (ILLUS.)...................... **$85-100**
Place mat, cloth, 16 x 12" **$18-20**
Plate, bread & butter, Allerton, England..... **$12-15**
Plate, bread & butter, Japan.......................... **$5-7**
Plate, child's, 4 1/2" d., Japan **$10-15**
Plate, "Child's Day 1971," sandman w/wil-
low umbrella, Wedgwood **$50-60**

Plate, dinner, Booth's, England **$40-45**

Buffalo Blue Willow Dinner Plate

Plate, dinner, Buffalo Pottery, 1911 (ILLUS.)
.... **$30-35**
Plate, dinner, ca. 1870, unmarked, England
.... **$35-40**
Plate, dinner, Cambridge, blue patt. on clear
glass... **$40-50**
Plate, dinner, flow blue, Royal Doulton **$65-75**
Plate, dinner, Holland................................ **$18-20**
Plate, dinner, Japan **$10-15**
Plate, dinner, Mandarin patt., Copeland, En-
gland **$35-40**
Plate, dinner, modern, Royal Wessex........... **$6-8**
Plate, dinner, Paden City Pottery **$30-35**
Plate, dinner, restaurant ware, Jackson..... **$15-20**
Plate, dinner, Royal China Co. **$10-15**
Plate, dinner, scalloped rim, Allerton, En-
gland **$30-35**
Plate, grill, Allerton, England **$45-50**
Plate, luncheon, Wedgwood, England **$20-25**
Plate, luncheon, Worcester patt. **$35-40**
Plate, 7 1/2" d., Arklow, Ireland **$20**
Plate, 10" d., tin, ca. 1988, Robert Steffy ... **$10-12**
Plate, grill, 10" d., Japan **$18-20**
Plate, 10 1/4" d., paper, Fonda **$1-2**
Plate, grill, 10 1/2" d., Holland **$18-20**

Blue Willow Wedgwood Platter

Platter, 9 x 11" l., rectangular, Wedgwood
& Co., England (ILLUS.) **$100-125**
Platter, 8 1/2 x 11 1/2" l., oval, scalloped
rim, Buffalo Pottery **$100-125**
Platter, 9 x 12" l., oval, American.............. **$15-18**

Mintons Blue Willow Teapot

Teapot, cov., squatty bulbous body tapering to flaring asymmetrical neck, slightly domed cover w/trefoil finial, C-scroll handle, slightly serpentine spout, dark blue handle, spout & finial, Mintons, England, ca. 1900 (ILLUS.).................. **$175-200**

Royal Corona Ware Teapot

Teapot, cov., squatty ovoid body on short foot, flattened dome cover w/button finial, C-form handle, gently serpentine spout, dark blue spout, handle & finial, gold highlights, Royal Corona Ware, S. Hancock & Sons, England, early 20th c. (ILLUS.) **$225-250**

Hammersley & Co. Blue Willow Teapot

Teapot, cov., squatty ovoid body on short foot, incurved neck, C-scroll handle, slightly serpentine spout, inset cover tapering to peaked circular finial, decorated w/bands of gold beading at shoulder & on cover, gold decoration on rim, handle, spout & finial, Hammersley & Co., England, ca. 1912-39 (ILLUS.)........... **$150-175**

Royal Worcester Blue Willow Teapot

Teapot, cov., squatty ovoid body tapering in at shoulder to gently peaked cover w/knob finial, straight spout, C-scroll handle, Royal Worcester porcelain, England, ca. 1920s (ILLUS.)............. **$150-175**

Doulton & Co. Blue Willow Teapot

Teapot, cov., squatty ovoid body tapering in at shoulder to short cylindrical neck, slightly tapering inset cover w/disk finial, angled handle, slightly curved spout, shoulder reads "We'll tak a cup o' kindness yet, for days o' auld lang syne," Doulton & Co., England, ca. 1882-91 (ILLUS.)................... **$200**

Miles Mason Blue Willow Teapot

Teapot, cov., squatty ovoid body tapering in at shoulder to short neck, C-scroll handle, slightly serpentine spout, tapering cover w/disk finial, embellished w/silver line decoration & band of silver grapevine decoration at shoulder & on cover, Miles Mason, England, ca. 1807-13 (ILLUS.)............ **$300-350**

Miniature Blue Willow Teapot

Teapot, cov., miniature, lobed ovoid body,
domed inset cover w/finial, C-scroll handle, serpentine spout, gold line decoration on handle, spout, rim & finial, Windsor China, England, 3 3/4" h. (ILLUS.,
previous page) **$15-20**
Teapot, cov., individual, Moriyama, Japan,
4 1/2" h... **$75-100**
Teapot, cov., Sadler, 4 3/4" h.................... **$40-45**

Blue Willow Teapot & Trivet

Teapot, cover & trivet, spherical body on
short tapering foot, short neck w/inset
cover w/button finial, C-scroll handle, serpentine spout, on matching round trivet,
Grimwades, England, early 20th c., tea-
pot 6" h., 2 pcs. (ILLUS.) **$250-275**

"Yorkshire Relish" Tip Tray

Tip tray, "Yorkshire Relish," England, 4" d.
(ILLUS.)... **$40-50**

Blue Willow Tip Tray

Tip tray, "Schweppes Lemon Squash," En-
gland, 4 1/2" d. (ILLUS.)......................... **$40-50**

Blue Willow Toby Jug

Toby jug, w/Blue Willow jacket, unmarked,
England, 6" h. (ILLUS.) **$300-400**
Toby jug, w/Blue Willow jacket, W. Kent,
England, 6" h...................................... **$300-400**
Toothbrush holder, Wedgwood, England,
5 1/4" h.. **$50-75**
Tray, round, brass, 6" d. **$50**
Vegetable bowl, open, Japan, 10 1/2" oval.... **$35**
Warmer for butter, round, holds candle, Ja-
pan **$50-60**
Wash pitcher & bowl, ca. 1890, unmarked,
England, the set **$400-500**

Blue Willow Wash Bowl & Pitcher

Wash pitcher & bowl, Royal Doulton, the
set (ILLUS.).. **$500-750**

Other Colors

Butter dish, rectangular, for stick, red, Ja-
pan, 7"... **$65-75**
Butter pat, red, Japan.................................... **$20**
Charger, brown, Buffalo China, 11" d. **$60-70**
Coffeepot, cov., ca. 1890, brown, un-
marked, England, 8 3/4" h.................. **$175-200**

Purple Willow Ware Cup

Cup, purple, handleless, unmarked, England (ILLUS., previous page) **$50-75**
Cup & saucer, red, ca. 1930, Buffalo China **$30-35**
Egg cup, red, England, 4 1/2" h................ **$35-40**

Red Willow Ware Pitcher

Pitcher, 5" h., red, "Old Gustavsberg," Sweden (ILLUS.)... **$50-60**
Plate, 2 3/4" d., green, miniature, modern, Coalport, England **$20-25**

Brown Willow Ware Child's Plate

Plate, 4 3/4" d., brown, child's, E.M. & Co. (ILLUS.)... **$40-50**
Plate, 6" d., restaurant ware, brown, Buffalo China.. **$15**
Plate, 9" d., ca. 1890, brown, John Meir & Son... **$20-25**

Copeland Red Mandarin Pattern Plate

Plate, 9" d., Mandarin patt., red, Copeland (ILLUS.)... **$35-40**
Plate, 9" d., purple, Britannia Pottery **$35-40**
Plate, bread & butter, 6" d., green, Japan.. **$18-20**
Plate, dinner, red, Japan **$15-20**
Plate, grill, 11 1/4" d., green, Royal Willow China... **$25-30**
Platter, 9", brown, early, unmarked, England **$90-100**
Platter, 9", red, Petrus Regout, Holland..... **$35-45**
Platter, 9 1/4 x 11 1/4", rectangular, red, Allerton, England.................................... **$150-175**
Platter, 11 x 19" l., rectangular, green, John Steventon & Sons **$125-150**
Sugar bowl, red, Japan **$25-35**
Teapot, cov., purple, Britannia Pottery... **$175-200**
Teapot, cov., red, child's, E.M. & Co., England **$125-150**
Teapot, cov., red, restaurant ware, Sterling China... **$75-85**
Vegetable bowl, cov., round, green, Victoria Porcelain **$100-125**
Vegetable bowl, red, Allertons, 7" d. **$50-60**
Vegetable bowl, red, cov., Japan, 10" d........ **$30**

Zeisel (Eva) Designs

One of the most influential ceramic artists and designers of the 20th century, Eva Zeisel began her career in Europe as a young woman, eventually immigrating to the United States, where her unique, streamlined designs met with great success. Since the 1940s her work has been at the forefront of commercial ceramic design, and in recent decades she has designed in other media. Now in her ninth decade, she continues to be active and involved in the world of art and design.

Castleton - Museum Ware

Bowl, 11" d., salad, White **$160**

Castleton - Museum Ware Coffee Set

Coffeepot, cov., tall, slender form w/C-scroll handle (ILLUS. second from left w/coffee set).. **$500**
Creamer, handleless (ILLUS. second from right w/coffee set)..................................... **$300**
Cup & saucer, flat, Mandalay **$20**
Cup & saucer (ILLUS. far left w/coffee set) **$150-200**
Plate, 8 1/4" sq., salad, White **$135**
Plate, 10 1/2" d., dinner, White...................... **$50**
Sugar, cov., handleless (ILLUS. far right w/coffee set).. **$250**

Hall China Company - Kitchenware

Golden Clover Cookie Jar

Cookie jar, cov., Golden Clover (ILLUS.) **$65**
Marmite, Casual Living **$30**

Tri-tone Nested Mixing Bowls

Mixing bowls, nested, Tri-tone, set of 5 (IL-
LUS.) **$250**
Refrigerator jug, cov., Tri-tone **$150**
Sugar, Tri-tone **$60**

Tri-tone Teapot

Teapot, cov., 6-cup, Tri-tone, ca. 1954
(ILLUS.) **$85**

Hallcraft - Century Dinnerware

Creamer, Fern... **$35**
Gravy boat & ladle, Fern............................... **$95**
Plate, 10" d., dinner, Sunglow **$25**
Relish, divided, White **$90**

White Vegetable Bowl

Vegetable bowl, 10 1/2" d., White (ILLUS.).... **$35**

Hollydale

Hollydale Chop Plate

Chop plate, 14" l., brown (ILLUS.)................. **$60**
Gravy bowl, bird-shape **$85**
Sauce dish, bird-shape, yellow/turquoise..... **$200**
Tureen & ladle, bird design, the set............. **$300**

Hyalyn "Z Ware"

Bowl, cereal, oxblood, commercial
grade/restaurant ware **$40**

Satin Black "Z Ware" Coffee Server

Coffee server, cov., satin black w/white lid
(ILLUS.).. **$150**
Creamer, handleless, autumn gold,
4 3/4" h... **$85**

Johann Haviland

Bowl, fruit, Wedding Ring patt. **$12**
Creamer & cov. sugar, Wedding Ring patt. ... **$60**
Cup & saucer, Wedding Ring **$20**
Dinnerware set, Wedding Ring, 20-pc. ser-
vice for 4 .... **$200-250**
Plate, bread & butter, Wedding Ring patt....... **$10**
Platter, oval, Wedding Ring patt. **$60**
Serving bowl, round, Wedding Ring patt. **$40**
Tureen/vegetable bowl, cov., White **$80**

Monmouth Dinnerware

Butter pat, Pals, 4" **$25**
Creamer, Lacy Wings..................................... **$50**

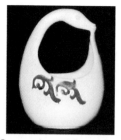

Goose-shaped Gravy Boat

Gravy boat, goose shape, Lacey Wings
   (ILLUS.)... **$175**
Sugar, cov., bird lid, Blueberry........................ **$25**

Monmouth Bird-shaped Sugar

Sugar, cov., bird lid, Lacey Wings (ILLUS.) **$50**

Lacey Wings Teapot with Bird Decoration

Teapot, cov., Lacey Wings patt., wire handle w/ceramic grip, Prairie Hen, w/bird
   decoration, ca. 1952 (ILLUS.) **$150**
Vegetable bowl, 9 1/2" d. **$65**

Norleans Dinnerware by Meito
(pieces marked "Made in Occupied Japan" are worth 25% more)

Fairfield Cup & Saucer

Cup & saucer, Fairfield (ILLUS.) **$8**

Livonia Dinner Plate

Plate, dinner, Livonia (ILLUS.) **$12**
Service for six, Livonia, 36-piece set........... **$200**

Riverside

Riverside Bowl

Bowl, 8 1/2" d., celadon & moss yellow
   (ILLUS.)... **$600**
Plate, dinner, yellow & olive green **$60**

Schmid Dinnerware
Casserole, cov., bird lid, 9 1/2 x 8" **$150**

Schmid Dinnerware Coffeepot

Coffeepot, cov., Lacey Wings/Rosette
   (ILLUS.).. **$125**

Schmid Dinnerware Pitcher

Pitcher, 10" h., Lacey Wings & Sunburst (ILLUS., previous page) **$85**

Schmid Bird-shaped Teapot

Teapot, cov., bird-shaped, rattan handle, Lacey Wings, 1950s (ILLUS.) **$85**

Schramberg

Schramberg Triangular Ashtray

Ashtray, triangular, Gobelin 13 (ILLUS.)....... **$160**
Cup & saucer, Gobelin 13 .... **$75**

Mondrian Covered Jar

Jar, cov., terraced, Mondrian, 5" (ILLUS.).. **$1,000**
Pitcher, 4 1/2" h., Mondrian **$225**
Plate, 7 1/2" d., dessert, Gobelin 13................ **$60**

Gobelin 13 Teapot

Teapot, cov., Gobelin 13 patt., Germany, 1930s (ILLUS.)... **$900**

Gobelin 8 Vase

Vase, 6" h., offset oval, Gobelin 8 (ILLUS.) **$200**

Stratoware

Stratoware Candlestick

Candlestick, brown trim (ILLUS.) **$120**

Stratoware Cup & Saucer

Cup & saucer, gold interior (ILLUS.) **$50**

Stratoware Shakers

Shakers, green trim, pr. (ILLUS.)................... **$85**

Lazy Susan Relish Set

Town and Country Dinnerware - for Red Wing Potteries

Lazy Susan relish set w/mustard jar
(ILLUS., top of page)................................. **$600**
Mustard jar, cover & ladle, dusk blue, the
set (ILLUS., bottom of page).................... **$250**
Pitcher, jug-type, rust, 3 pt............................ **$250**
Plate, 10 1/2" d., dinner, bronze..................... **$55**

Town and Country "Yawn" Creamer
Creamer, "yawn," bronze (ILLUS.) **$70**

Large & Small "Schmoo" Shakers

Town and Country Mustard Jar

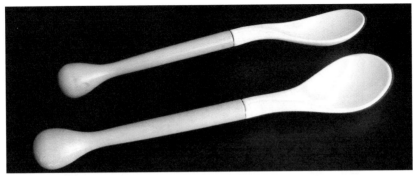

Salad Serving Spoons

Shaker, large "schmoo," Ming green (ILLUS. right w/small "schmoo" shaker, previous page) **$75**
Shaker, small "schmoo," rust (ILLUS. left w/large "schmoo" shaker)............................ **$40**
Spoons, salad servers, white, the set (ILLUS., top of page)............................... **$1,700**

Town & Country Covered Soup Tureen

Tureen, cov., soup, sand (ILLUS.) **$850**

Watt Pottery

Watt Pottery Drip Glaze Bowl

Bowl, 8 1/4" d., blue drip glaze (ILLUS.) **$25**
Chop tray, Mountain Road, 14 1/2" **$210**
Teapot, cov., rattan handle, Animal Farm patt., ca. 1954 .... **$650**

Zsolnay

This pottery was made in Pecs, Hungary, in a factory founded in 1862 by Vilmos Zsolnay. Utilitarian earthenware was originally produced, but by the turn of the 20th century ornamental Art Nouveau-style wares with bright colors and lustre decoration were produced; these wares are especially sought today. Currently Zsolnay pieces are being made in a new factory.

Zsolnay Marks

Zsolnay Domed Box

Box, cov., rectangular, w/domed lid, Ivory Ware medieval design w/later metallic eosin glaze, incised Zsolnay factory mark, unknown form number, ca. 1900, 3 1/4" h. (ILLUS.) **$400-600**
Bust, "Luna" by Sandor Apati Abt, realistic portrait of woman w/long hair & closed eyes, various metallic eosin glazes, incised Zsolnay factory mark, incised form number 5494, exhibited at the Paris Exposition in 1900, ca. 1899, 11" h. (ILLUS., top next page)................................. **$25,000-30,000**

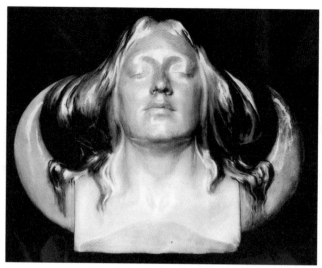

"Luna" Portrait Bust by Zsolnay

Very Rare Large Zsolnay Plaque with Scene of Eve in the Garden

Charger, large round shallow form, h.p. w/a large scene of a nude Eve w/long brown hair in the Garden of Eden, a field of tall white lilies at one side & a group of large threatening snakes on the other, done in vibrant Eosin metallic colors of dark brown, tan, white, dark green & rose, painted by Sandor Apati Abt, 1899, h.p. Zsolnay logo on back w/other markings, cast holes in back for hanging, 14 3/4" d. (ILLUS.)....... **$20,700**

Zsolnay Cock-form Pitcher

Pitcher, 18" h., in the form of a crowing cock w/stylized feathers on oval base, open beak forms spout, pale green eosin glaze, incised Zsolnay factory mark, incised form number 1132, ca. 1903 (ILLUS.)
.... **$4,000-5,000**

Zsolnay Plaque-like Tile

Tile, rectangular plaque form w/oval cartouche w/relief decoration of idyllic setting w/Art Nouveau-style female dancer & Pan-like figures playing musical instruments, multicolored eosin glazes, designed by Lajos Mack, incised Zsolnay factory mark, incised form number 7892, ca. 1906, 8 1/4 x 10 3/4" (ILLUS.)
.... **$7,500-9,500**

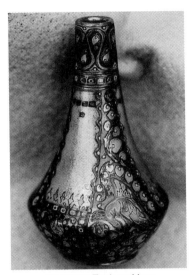

Miniature Zsolnay Vase

Vase, miniature, 4" h., wide base tapering to ring foot & long neck, richly decorated w/Hungarian folkloric designs in gold & blue/green eosin glazes, incised Zsolnay factory mark, ca. 1912 (ILLUS.) ... **$1,000-1,250**

Egyptian Decor Zsolnay Vase

Vase, 5" h., cylindrical, tapering out toward top, then in toward short neck w/small opening, Art Deco Egyptian decor, designed by Teréz Mattyasovszky-Zsolnay, printed Zsolnay factory mark, ca. 1915 (ILLUS.)....................................... **$1,250-1,500**

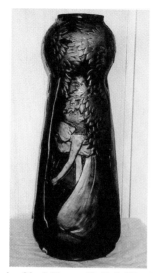

Lajos Mack Vase with Relief Design

Vase, 28" h., tapering cylindrical form w/squat ovoid neck, decorated w/relief design of figures in forest setting including Pan-like form, various eosin metallic glazes, designed by Lajos Mack, incised Zsolnay factory mark, incised form number 5902, ca. 1900 (ILLUS.)..... **$25,000-30,000**

CHARACTER COLLECTIBLES

Numerous objects made in the likeness of or named after comic strip and comic book personalities or characters abounded from the 1920s to the present. Scores of these are now being eagerly collected and prices still vary widely. Also see DISNEY COLLECTIBLES and TOYS and "ANTIQUE TRADER TOY PRICE GUIDE."

Amos 'N' Andy Fresh Air Taxi Toy

Amos 'N' Andy Fresh Air Taxi toy, lithographed tin jalopy w/the two characters, Marx, ca. 1930s, some fading to one side of figures, 8" l. (ILLUS.)............................ **$575**

Archies (The) juice glass, pictures of Betty & Vernonica, titled "Betty and Veronica - Fashion Show," 1971, 4 1/4" h................ **$8-15**

Archies (The) lunch box & thermos, steel box illustrated w/the characters, plastic thermos, Aladdin, 1969 .... **$150-350**

Archies (The) record, cardboard cereal box cut-out, "The Archies," 33 1/3 rpm, 1970s **$15-35**

"Everthing's Archie" Record Album

Archies (The) record album, "Everything's Archie - The Archies," color photo of teens dancing on the sleeve, by Calendar-Kirschner, 1969 (ILLUS.) **$8-20**

"The Archies - Jingle Jangle" Album

Archies (The) record album, "The Archies - Jingle Jangle," color photo on the sleeve, by Kirschner, 1969 (ILLUS.) **$7-15**

Batman modil kit, Batmobile, 1/32 scale, Aurora, in original box, 1966 (ILLUS., top next page) **$100-275**

Betty doll (The Archies), vinyl, sealed in original package w/pictures of the main cartoon characters, Marx, 1976 (ILLUS., next page) **$65-125**

Batmobile Model Kit by Aurora

Captain Marvel toy, Lightning Race Car, Automatic Toy Co., 1947, 4" l. **$100-200**

Betty Doll from The Archies

Chairry Chair from Pee Wee Herman

Chairry (Pee Wee Herman) chair, child's size, stuffed cloth, w/tag, Matchbox, 1988 (ILLUS.)..................................... **$200-350**

Scarce Charlie McCarthy - Mortimer Snerd Auto Toy

Charlie McCarthy & Mortimer Snerd toy, wind-up toy, "Charlie McCarthy - Mortimer Snerd Private Car," long stylized sleek auto painted in bright yellow, black & red w/the heads of Charlie & Mortimer poking from the top, heads spin & auto bounces back & forth when wound, some paint wear, Marx, 1939, 16" h. (ILLUS.).......... **$1,150**

Cowboy Curtis (Pee Wee Herman) action figure, on original card, Matchbox, 1988, 6" h... **$25-45**

Figure of Bill from Fat Albert

Bill (Fat Albert) figure, soft PVC plastic, made in Hong Kong, early 1970s, 3 1/4" h. (ILLUS.) **$12-20**

Dick Tracy Board Game

Dick Tracy game, board-type, "Dick Tracy - The Master Detective Game," SeeRight - Selchow & Righter, 1962 (ILLUS.) **$75-125**
Dick Tracy toy, windup tin Dick Tracy Police Station w/car, Marx, 1950s, 3 1/2 x 8" **$300-600**

Figure of Dumb Donald from Fat Albert

Dumb Donald (Fat Albert) figure, soft PVC plastic, made in Hong Kong, early 1970s, 3 1/4" h. (ILLUS.) **$12-20**

Fat Albert figure, soft PVC plastic, made in Hong Kong, early 1970s, 3 1/4" h. **$12-20**
Fat Albert game, board-type, Milton Bradley, 1973 .... **$25-40**
Fat Albert lunch box, steel, King Seeley, 1973 .... **$25-45**
Fat Albert puzzle, jigsaw-type, 125 pieces, Whitman, 1974, 20" d............................ **$15-25**

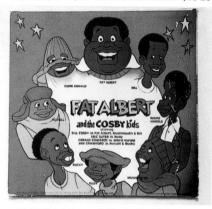

Fat Albert Record Album Back Cover

Fat Albert record album, "Halloween Starring Fat Albert and the Cosby Kids," LP, Kid Stuff Records, 1980 (ILLUS. of back cover) **$8-15**
Fat Albert thermos bottle, plastic, King Seeley, 1973 .... **$8-20**
Felix the Cat figure, jointed wood body w/leather ears, black & white w/his name on his chest, full original decal under on foot, Schoenhut, copyright 1924, restrung, 8" h. **$115**
Garfield the Cat telephone, figural plastic, eyes move when receiver lifted off his back, Tyco, 1981 (ILLUS., below).......... **$25-65**

Garfield the Cat Figural Telephone

Early Harold Lloyd Wind-up Bell Toy

Harold Lloyd bell toy, wind-up tin, colorful lithographed tin head of the early comedian w/a bell below, faces moves & bell rings when wound, mechanism needs adjustment, ca. 1920s, 6 1/2" h. (ILLUS.).... **$454**

Jonathan Livingston Seagull 1st Edition

Jonathan Livingston Seagull book, hardcover w/just jacket, first edition, MacMillan, 1970 (ILLUS.)................................. **$40-75**

Jonathan Livingston Seagull Game

Jonathan Livingston Seagull game, board-type, "Jonathan Livingston Seagull Game of Individual Challenge," Mattel, 1973 (ILLUS.).. **$20-40**
Miss Yvonne (Pee Wee Herman) action figure, on original card, Matchbox, 1988, 5" h.. **$15-35**

Red from Fraggle Rock Plush Toy

Muppet Show (The) toy, figure of Red from Fraggle Rock, plush, Hasbro, 1985, 14" h. (ILLUS.) **$10-30**

Uncle Matt Muppet Show Plush Toy

Muppet Show (The) toy, figure of Uncle Traveling Matt from Fraggle Rock, plush, Hasbro, 1985, 14" h. (ILLUS.)............... **$25-50**

Peanuts Lucy Felt Banner

Peanuts banner, orange felt printed in black w/a picture of Lucy & "Bleah! - Lucy," other designs available, 1971, 15 x 33" (ILLUS.).................................... **$15-35**

Pee Wee Herman action figure, on original card, Matchbox, 1988, 6" h. **$10-15**

Pee Wee Herman Lunch Box

Pee Wee Herman lunch box & thermos, "Pee-Wee's Playhouse," applied cartoon scene on cover, red or pink plastic, Thermos, 1987, each (ILLUS.) **$25-40**

Pee Wee Herman trading card set, "Pee-Wee's Playhouse Fun Pak," 123 pieces including cards, tattoos, toys, stickers, etc., in original package, Topps, 1989, the set **$50-150**

Pigs in Space Muppet Show Lunch Box

Pigs in Space (The Muppet Show) lunch box, steel, King Seeley, 1977 (ILLUS.)... **$50-80**

Popeye Riding Large Motorcycle Toy

Popeye toy, cast iron, Popeye riding a motorcyle w/a large rear compartment, cycle in red w/three black rubber tires, ca. 1930s, 5 1/2" l. (ILLUS.)............................ **$690**

Popeye on Motorcycle Toy

Popeye toy, cast iron, Popeye riding a red motorcycle w/three rubby tires, Hubley, probably a later reproduction, 8 1/4" l. (ILLUS.)... **$403**

Rare Popeye Basket Ball Player Toy

Popeye wind-up tin toy, "Mechanical Popeye the Basket Ball Player," figure of Popeye holding a ball & standing standing beneath the hoop, colorful decoration, all-original & near mint w/original colorful cardboard box, Line-Mar, ca. 1950s, 9" h. (ILLUS.).............................. **$1,553**

Robin, The Boy Wonder Model Kit

Robin (Batman) model kit, plastic figure of Robin, The Boy Wonder, 1/12 scale, Aurora, 1966, w/original box (ILLUS.) **$45-85**
Scooby Doo bank, bubble gum bank, plastic figural head of Scooby Doo, 1970s, 9 1/2" h... **$40-65**
Scooby Doo cup, red plastic w/picture of Scooby Doo, 1971, 4 1/4" h. **$15-25**

Scooby Doo lunch box & thermos, green plastic box w/decal & green plastic thermos, King Seeley, 1973 .... **$25-40**
Scooby Doo lunch box & thermos, steel box & green plastic thermos, King Seeley, 1973 .... **$50-70**
Scooby Doo magnet, puffy vinyl, various characters, Taiwan, 1978, each.............. **$5-10**

Scooby Doo Magnet Display Board

Scooby Doo magnet display board, flat metal rectangular form w/flat cut-out magnets of the various characters, original package, 1978 (ILLUS.) **$25-40**
Scooby Doo toy, diecast car w/plastic figure of Scooby Doo, on original card, Corgi, 1981 .... **$20-30**

Superman Aurora Model Kit

Superman model kit, plastic, 1/8 scale, painting-style box cover art, Aurora, 1963, 4 x 13" box (ILLUS.).................. **$75-225**

Toonerville Trolley Wind-up Toy

Toonerville Trolley toy, wind-up tin model of the trolley complete w/driver & attachments, copyright markings, made by Nifty, ca. 1920s, 5" l. (ILLUS.) **$460**

1920s Uncle Wiggily's Parade Drum

Uncle Wiggily drum, child's, lithographed tin sides w/wooden upper & lower bands joined by string, the sides printed in color w/cartoon characters, one carrying a large drum marked "Uncle Wiggily's Parade," also marked w/U.S. patent information & the date 1924, paint wear to wooden bands, 7 1/2" d., 6 1/2" h. (ILLUS.) **$460**

Uncle Wiggily Crazy Car Wind-up Toy

Uncle Wiggily toy, wind-up tin crazy car, colorfully printed, Uncle Wiggily drives a jalopy that spins & turns while his head turns, Marx, copyright 1935, overall very good condition & working (ILLUS.) **$345**

Weird Harold (Fat Albert) figure, soft PVC plastic, made in Hong Kong, early 1970s, 4" h. **$12-20**

CHASE BRASS & COPPER COMPANY

From 1930 until 1942, the Chase Brass & Copper Co. of Waterbury, Connecticut, produced an acclaimed line of Art Deco-inspired metal houseware items. These Chase "Specialties" encompassed six general categories, each designed to meet a particular household need: table electrics, buffet service articles, decorative items, drinking accessories, smokers' articles, and miscellaneous housewares. An additional Chase division operating during the same period produced lamps and lighting fixtures.Primary finishes for Chase Specialties included brass, copper, and the company's signature "Chase Chrome."

The company contracted with prominent industrial designers of the time, and among those credited with Chase pieces are Walter Von Nessen, Ruth and William Gerth, Lurelle Guild, Russel Wright, Rockwell Kent, Dr. Albert Reimann, and Harry Laylon.

Chase metal giftwares proved particularly popular during the Depression era of the 1930s, since they conveyed the look of elegance at an economical price, and were easy to maintain. Chase also popularized the vogue for at-home entertaining with its buffet service line, enlisting the promotional efforts of etiquette expert Emily Post. At the height of the firm's popularity in the mid-1930s, Chase wares were displayed in the lavishly decorated showrooms of New York City's Chase Tower.

With the onset of World War II, Chase closed its Specialty division, devoting efforts to wartime production. The company now specializes in the production of brass rods for industrial use. Although the 12-year "Specialty" period was only a brief interlude in the history of Chase (the firm was established in 1876), more than 500 Specialty items were released, as were an equal number of lamps and lighting fixtures. Most are readily identifiable by the presence of the Chase logo: the engraved figure of a centaur and the words "CHASE U.S.A." Today's collectors prize Chase pieces for the same qualities that initially attracted buyers: eye-catching Deco-inspired designs, easy care, and good value for the investment. The Chase Collectors Society website can be accessed at: www.public.asu.edu/~icbly/chase.htm.

References on the Chase Brass & Copper Co. include a four-volume series by Donald-Brian Johnson and Leslie Pina, released by Schiffer Publishing: Chase Complete (1999); 1930s Lighting: Deco & Traditional by Chase (2000); The Chase Catalogs: 1934 & 1935 (1998), and The Chase Era (2001). Photos for this category are by Dr. Pina.

Buffet Service Articles

Brittany table bell, No. 13002 .... **$70-80**

Chase Cocktail Canape Server #28001

Cocktail canape server, No. 28001, 13 3/4" h. (ILLUS.) **$175-200**
Cold meat platter, "Quiet Pool," No. 27004, Lurelle Guild design, 9 1/2 x 15" **$60-70**

Wright-designed Individual Coffee Set

Individual coffee set, No. 90073, three-part cylinder w/side handles, Russel Wright design, 6 1/4" h. (ILLUS.)........ **$110-125**
Tidy crumber w/brush, No. 90147, Harry Laylon design **$40-50**

Decorative Items

Book ends, Cat design, No. 17042, Walter Von Nessen design, 7 3/8" h., pr. **$475-500**
Candlepiece, No. 21005, single unit for four candles, Albert Reimann design .. **$1,200-1,500**

Davey Jones & Pilot Book Ends

Davey Jones book ends, No. 90142, model of an anchor, Harry Laylon design, 6" h., pr. (ILLUS. back with Pilot book ends) **$50-60**

Four-Tube Chase Bud Holder

Four-tube bud holder, No. 11230, Ruth and William Gerth design, 8 1/4" h. (ILLUS.) ... **$25-50**
Pilot book ends, No. 90138, model of a ship's wheel, 6 3/8" h., pr. (ILLUS. front with Davey Jones book ends) **$75-85**

Chase Taurex Uneven Candlesticks

Taurex candlestick, No. 24003 - Even, 7 1/8" h., or No. 24004 - Uneven, 9 3/4" h., Walter Von Nessen design, each (ILLUS. uneven set) **$75-80**
Tom Thumb plant pots, No. 04010, Harry Lylon design, 2 9/16" h., set of 5............ **$20-30**

Drinking Accessories

Antarctic ice bowl, No. 17108, Russel Wright design, 7" d............................ **$100-125**
Doric cocktail cup, No. 90101, blue or white Bakelite base **$20-30**
Ice servidor, No. 90001, satin silver finish, Ruth & William Gerth design, 8 1/4" d.
.... **$175-200**

Lamps

Colonel & Colonel's Lady Lamps

Colonel & Colonel's Lady lamps, No. 27013 & No. 27014, stylized comic-like figures in red, Lurelle Guild designs, 9 3/8" h., each (ILLUS. of both).......... **$250-275**

Three Chase Glow Lamps

Glow Lamp, No. 01001, spherical base & conical shade, Ruth Gerth design, 8 1/4" h., each variation (ILLUS. of three) **$50-100**

Miscellaneous

Airalite pocket flashlight, No. 22003, August Mitchell design **$75-85**
Mirror Top box, No. 21003, Albert Reimann design, 5 3/4" d. **$900-1,000**
Sailboat weathervane, No. 90136, 15 1/2" h. **$225-250**

Smoker's Articles

Chase Antelope Ash Receiver

Antelope ash receiver, No. 881, etched glass base, 4 1/2" d. (ILLUS.) **$110-120**
Autumn Leaf ash receiver, No. 28009, 5 7/16" l. **$40-45**
Flip-Top ash receiver, No. 871, Harry Laylon design (ILLUS. lower right with Snuffer ashtray & Riviera ashtray, bottom of page)... **$65-75**
Riviera ashtray, No. 885, Howard Reichenbach design (ILLUS. left with Flip-Top ash receiver & Snuffer ashtray, bottom of page)... **$40-50**
Snuffer ashtray, No. 845, George Burton design, gold fish in center for extinguishing the cigarette (ILLUS. upper right with Flip-Top ash receiver & Riviera ashtray, bottom of page)...................................... **$60-70**
Steeplechase cigarette box, No. 17098, Harry Laylon design, 9 1/16" l. **$125-150**

Chase Snuffer & Riviera Ashtrays & Flip-Top Ash Receiver

Table Electrics

Comet coffee maker, No. 17084, Walter
Von Nessen design **$110-125**
Table butler, No. 17100, w/glass baking
dish, 8 5/8" d. **$200-225**
Table Chef chafing dish, No. 17087,
Walter Von Nessen design, 10" d. **$150-175**

CHILDREN'S BOOKS

Daniel Boone - Opening of the Wilderness

Daniel Boone - The Opening of the Wilderness, by John Mason Brown, illustrated by Lee J. James, one of a series from Landmark Books, published by Random House, New York, 1952 (ILLUS.) **$15**

Dave Dawson on the Russian Front

Dave Dawson on the Russian Front, The War Adventure Series, by R. Sidney Bowen, Saalfield Publishing, New York, New York, & Akron, Ohio, hard cover w/dust jacket, 1943 (ILLUS.) **$18**
Davy Crockett L'Invincible (The Invincible), a Walt Disney illustrated stamp book for the French-speaking market,

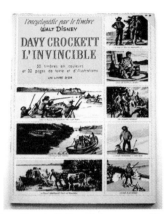

Davy Crockett French Language Book

Western Publishing, Racine, Wisconsin, 32 pp. of text, 1955 (ILLUS.) **$50**

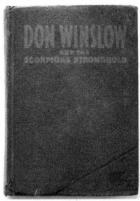

Don Winslow - The Scorpion's Stronghold

Don Winslow and The Scorpion's Stronghold, by Frank Martinck, brown cloth covers, based on the radio & movie serial hero, Whitman Publishing, Racine, Wisconsin, 1940 (ILLUS.) **$20**

Let's Go Shopping Wonder Book

Let's Go Shopping, Wonder Book, by Gunyon Brooke, illustrated by Nancy Meyerhoff, 1958 (ILLUS., previous page) **$10-15**

Mike Mars Flies the Dyna-Soar

Mike Mars Flies The Dyna-Soar, by Donald A. Wollheim, illustrated by Albert Orbaan, part of a series, great color dust jacket, Doubleday and Co., Garden City, New York, 1962 (ILLUS.) **$35**

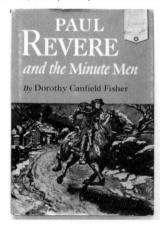

Paul Revere and the Minute Men

Paul Revere and the Minute Men, by Dorothy Canfield Fisher, illustrated by Norman Price, Landmark Book from Random House, original dust jacket, 1950 (ILLUS.)... **$10**

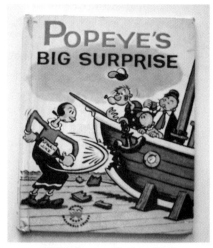

1960s Popeye Cartoon Book

Popeye's Big Surprise, based on the comic strip, hard cover w/color scene of Popeye, Olive Oyl, Swee' Pea & Wimpy, Wonder Books, New York, New York, 1962 (ILLUS.)... **$8**

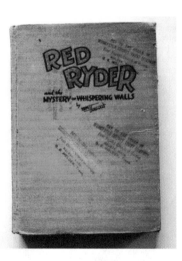

Red Ryder - Mystery of Whispering Walls

Red Ryder and the Mystery of Whispering Walls, by R.R. Winterbotham, based on the comic strip, hard cover w/defacing stamped markings, 1941 (ILLUS.) **$10-15**

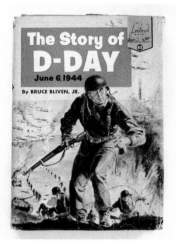

The Story of D-Day Book

The Story of D-Day - June 6, 1944, by Bruce Bliven, Jr., illustrated by Albert Orbaan, part of the Landmark Series, dramatic color dust jacket art, Random House, 1956 (ILLUS.) **$20**

The Young Pitcher by Zane Grey

The Young Pitcher, by Zane Grey, damaged original dust jacket w/a scene of a baseball player sliding into home base, Grosset and Dunlop, New York, New York, 1939 (ILLUS.) **$35**

Little Golden Books

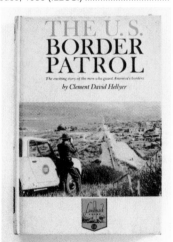

The U.S. Border Patrol Book from 1963

The U.S. Border Patrol - The Exciting Story of the Men Who Guard America's Borders, by Clement David Hellyer, hard cover w/photo of a Border Patrolman on duty, a Landmark Series book, Random House, 1963 (ILLUS.) **$6**

Reissued The Night Before Christmas

"Night Before Christmas (The)," No. 20, 1949 (1970s reissue), illustrations by Corinne Malvern, written by Clement C. Moore, 28 pp., some cover scuffing & wear (ILLUS.) **$2-4**

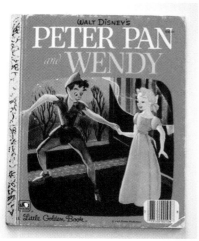

Walt Disney's Peter Pan and Wendy

"Peter Pan and Wendy (Walt Disney's),"
No. 104-51, 1952 (later reissue), by An-
nie North Bedford, illustrated by Eywind
Earle, some cover wear (ILLUS.) **$1-2**

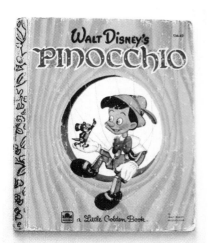

Pinocchio 1979 Reissue

"Pinocchio (Walt Disney's)," No. 104-2,
1979, 46th edition, illustrated by Camp-
bell Grant, some cover wear (ILLUS.) **$1-2**
**"Rudolph - The Red-Nosed Reindeer (Ri-
chard Scarry's),"** No. 452-11, 1958
(1990s reissue), by Barbara Shook
Hazen, adapted from story by Robert L.
May, illustrated by Richard Scarry, 24 pp.
(ILLUS., top next column) **$1-2**
"Saggy Baggy Elephant (The)," No. 385,
1947 (1959 reissue), by Kathryn & Byron
Jackson, illustrated by Gustaf Tenggren,
42 pp., slight cover wear (ILLUS., middle
next column)... **$2-4**

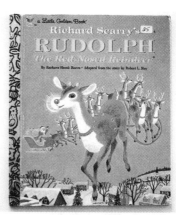

Reissue of Rudolph, The Red-Nosed Reindeer

The Saggy Baggy Elephant Reissue

Disney's Santa's Toy Shop

"**Santa's Toy Shop (Walt Disney's),**" No. 451-10, 1950, by Al Dempster, Walt Disney Studios illustrations, slight cover wear, pencil mark (ILLUS.) **$1-2**

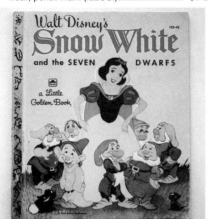

Snow White and the Seven Dwarfs

"**Snow White and the Seven Dwarfs (Walt Disney's),**" No. 103-42, 1948 (1980s re-issue), illustrated by Ken O'Brien (ILLUS.) **$1-2**

Tom and Jerry's Merry Christmas

"**Tom And Jerry's Merry Christmas,**" No. 457-42, by Peter Archer, illustrated by Harvey Eisenberg, 1954, slight cover wear (ILLUS.) **$3-5**

CHRISTMAS COLLECTIBLES

Starting in the mid-19th century, more and more items began to be manufactured to decorate the home, office or commercial business to celebrate the Christmas season.

In the 20th century the trend increased. Companies such as Coca-Cola, Sears and others began producing special Christmas items. The inexpensive glass, then plastic Christmas tree decorations began to appear in almost every home. With the end of World War II the toy market moved into the picture with annual Santa Claus parades and the children's visits to Santa.

In the 21st century this trend continues, and material from earlier Christmas seasons continues to climb in value.

Early Standing Santa Claus Figure

Figure, standing Santa Claus w/a cloth body & red & white suit, molded mask painted face, composition black boots, beaded necklace w/bells, lightly soiled, denting to face, early 20th c., 24" h. (ILLUS.) **$58**

Rare Glass Christmas Flask

Flask, clear glass, footed flattened round shape w/original screw-on metal cap, smooth base, decorated on the side w/a round multicolored paper label showing a songbird on a blossoming branch w/the words "A Very Merry Christmas - Happy New Year," ca. 1880-1910, 4 7/8" h. (ILLUS.) **$784**

Rare Hubley Santa Claus Sleight Pull-toy

Santa Claus Lantern Head in Blue

Lantern, papier-maché Santa Claus head, pierced eyes & mouth, blue hood, wire bail handle, trimmed w/mica, near mint, missing paper eyes & teeth, Germany, early 20th c., 6" h. (ILLUS.)............. **$900-1,000**

Santa Claus Lantern Head in Red

Lantern, papier-maché Santa Claus head, pierced eyes & mouth, red hood, wire bail

handle, trimmed w/mica, near mint, missing paper eyes & teeth, Germany, early 20th c., 6" h. (ILLUS.)............................. **$1,150**

Pull-toy, cast iron, Santa Claus seated in a large ornate white & gold sleigh pulled by two white reindeer on red wheels, very fine condition, Hubley, early 20th c., 16" l. (ILLUS., top of page)............................. **$2,300**

Early Santa on Nodding Donkey Toy

Toy, Santa riding a nodding-head donkey, papier-maché brown donkey w/a small Santa wearing red & white felt clothing, early 20th c., 8" h. (ILLUS.)...................... **$173**

Early Santa on Nodding Elephant

Toy, Santa riding a nodding-head elephant, papier-maché grey elephant w/a small Santa wearing red & white papier-maché clothing & holding a small feather tree, original "Made in Germany" decal, possible marriage of figures, early 20th c., 8" h. (ILLUS., previous page) **$180**

Rare Schoenhut Roly Poly Santa Toy

Toy, Santa roly poly, jovial Santa dressed in red, white & green, Schoenhut, ca. 1930s, 11 1/2" h. (ILLUS.)...................... **$1,380**

Christmas Seal Collectibles

For collectors of Christmas items, the classic Christmas Seal still offers an inexpensive collectible. First introduced in 1907, they have been produced during the Christmas season ever since. Although individual unused seals are fairly common, attached groups or full sheets are scarcer and very early seals are much harder to find.

There are also crossover Christmas seal items such as pinback buttons, placemats and even gift tags. We list a variety of Christmas Seal items below.

Bond certificate, early paper bond printed "The Crusade of the Double Barred Cross - $5 - Christmas Seal Bonds," values can vary, this example **$25**

Bookmark, 1992, issued by the American Lung Association, printed "Christmas Seals - The #1 Hope for the #3 Killer: Lung Disease," 1 3/4 x 5".............................. **$3**

Early Christmas Seal Pinback Button

Pinback button, 1920s, color image of the head of Santa Claus w/"Health For All" across the top, 1 1/4" d. (ILLUS.)............... **$45**

Christmas Seals Place Mat Showing Seals from 1907 to 1973

Place mat, rectangular paper printed in blue & red w/rows of seals dating from 1907 to 1973, Christmas seals logo & advertising in the lower left corner, 10 x 14" (ILLUS.)... **$9**

1970 Paper Place Mat with Seals from 1907 to 1970

Place mat, rectangular paper printed in green & red w/rows of seals dating from 1907 to 1970, Christmas seals logo & advertising in the lower left corner, 10 x 14" (ILLUS., top of page) **$10**

Seal, 1930, pictures Santa Claus carrying a Christmas tree & printed "Merry - Christmas," red border w/cross of Lorraine logo, single **$20**

Seal, 1934, image of a smiling Santa Claus, printed "Season's - Greetings" & the date w/the cross of Lorraine logo, single............. **$17**

Seal, 1951, image of Santa Claus on a green ground, cross of Lorraine logo in lower left, single **$4**

Single 1961 Christmas Seal

Seal, 1961, color image of a father hanging a wreath w/his daughter & young son helping, "Christmas 1961" at the bottom w/red cross of Lorraine logo, single (ILLUS.) **$2**

1967 Toy Train Car Christmas Seal

Seal, 1967, yellow & blue toy train car, marked "Christmas 1967" at top & bottom w/red cross of Lorraine logo, single (ILLUS.) **$2**

Seal, 1980, American Lung Assoc. of Massachusetts, color scene of children around a Christmas tree, single **$1**

1937 Christmas Seal on an Envelope

Seal on envelope, 1937, color image of a Colonial bell ringer w/a house in the background w/the red cross of Lorraine, printed "Greetings - 1937," single (ILLUS.) **$10**

Two 1981 Norman Rockwell Seals

Seals, 1981, color image by Norman Rockwell showing a grandfather & grandson on a rocking horse, printed across the top "American Lung Association 1981" w/red cross of Lorraine," "Merry Christmas" across the bottom, each (ILLUS. of two)....... **$3**

Two 1982 Christmas Seals

Seals, 1982, color image of Santa Claus chasing a dog carrying a gift in its mouth, "American Lung Association" across the top & "Season's Greetings 1982" at the bottom w/the red cross of Lorraine logo, each (ILLUS. of two) **$1**

Set of Three 1983 Canadian Christmas Seals

Seals, 1983, series of three, one w/a boy & girl looking at the star atop a Christmas tree, the second w/Santa Claus checking his list & the third w/showing a snowy mailbox full of cards, Canadian, set of 3 (ILLUS.).. **$3**

Seals, 1983, strip of eight seals, color portrait of Santa's head, American Lung Assoc. symbol in lower right, also issued in sheets of 36 seals & gift tags, packageof seals & tags (ILLUS. of seals, top next column) **$12**

Group of 1983 Christmas Seals

Set of Six 1986 Mouse Christmas Seals

Seals, 1986, set of six w/four different color images of a mouse in a Santa suit, each printed "The Christmas Seal People - Season's Greetings 1986," the set (ILLUS.) **$3**

Full Sheet of 1976 Christmas Seals forming a Winter Landscape

Sheet of seals, 1976, full sheet of 54 seals illustrating an expansive winter landscape w/a village & houses on snowy hillsides w/Santa & his reindeer & an angel in the sky, each seal w/tiny print & the red cross of Lorraine logo, mint sheet (ILLUS.) **$15**

Set of 10 Commemorative Millenium Seals from 2000

Sheet of seals, 2000, set of 10 seals marked across the top "Commemorative Millenium Edition" in English & French, each seal reproduces an earlier Christmas seal including ones from 1939, 1935, 1945 & other years, complete sheet (ILLUS., above) **$3**

CLOCKS

ALSO SEE "Antique Trader Clocks Price Guide," 2003.

Art Deco neon clock, octagonal stainless steel frame enclosing a black dial w/white Arabic numerals & hands, a red neon band along the inside of the outer frame, marked "Say It In Neon - Buffalo, N.Y.,"

working, ca. 1940, 33" w. (ILLUS., next column) **$690**

Unusual Art Deco Neon Clock

Early Massachusetts Banjo Clock

Banjo clock, Massachusetts, Federal style mahogany & mahogany veneer case, top round brass bezel & door opening to the white dial w/Roman numerals, the tall slender neck inset w/a floral-decorated églomisé panel above the rectangular lower section w/a larger églomisé panel w/narrow white & gold borders framing a deep green ground centered by a small oval pendulum window, ca. 1820 (ILLUS.) **$940**

Early American-made Banjo Clock

Banjo clock, probably Boston area, Federal-style, decorated giltwood, the top w/a round dial case topped by a small eagle finial, the dial w/Roman numerals & two service names & a small oval sticker marked "Wm. Senter & Co. 51 Exchange Street, Portland, Maine,"the tall slightly tapering narrow rectangular throat flanked by slender curved & pierced brass bars,

the throat w/the sides decorated w/tiny ropetwist bands flanking the gold églomisé panel decorated w/a black leaf band, the rectangular lower case w/further ropetwist trim around a larger rectangular églomisé panel decorated w/a sea battle between the Constitution & Guerriere w/a central title "Hull," the bottom edge mounted w/a row of small ball drops & a tapering reeded & pointed drop panel, weight, pendulum & key present finial replaced, brass movement, ca. 1815-25, some restoration (ILLUS.) **$1,725**

Lovely Enameled Swiss Boudoir Clock

Boudoir clock, Gubelin, Lucerne, Switzerland, gilt-bronze & enamel, a wide roundd & ringed foot w/guilloché blue enamel tapering to the slender matching ringed standard supporting the round dial w/a narrow white-enameled outer chapter ring w/Roman numerals & delicate painted flowers, the center dial w/further guilloché blue enamel decoration, signed in script on the backplate, early 20th c., 8 1/2" h. (ILLUS.) **$1,380**

Rare Early English Bracket Clock

Bracket clock, Etherington (George), London, England, an upright ebonized wood case, the four-sided tapering domical top fitted w/a shaped brass bail handle, the top w/a molded border above the case w/arched & glazed front & side panels, the front door opens to the ornate dial w/gilt pierced spandrels w/a small strike-silent dial above the large main dial w/Roman numerals, flaring molded base band, key & pedulum present, very early 18th c., 19th c. repairs on the movement, some minor damage to the case, 8 1/2 x 11 1/4", overall 20 1/2" h. (ILLUS., previous page) **$3,450**

Tiffany & Co. Marked Carriage Clock

Carriage clock, upright brass frame enclosing a front beveled glass front over the enameled dial w/Arabic numerals & marked "Tiffany & Co.," beveled glass sides expose the movement, arched swing handle across the top, back of movement stamped "DG" inside an oval, case monogrammed, seconds hand missing, dial w/two hairlines, overall 6 3/4" h. (ILLUS.) **$230**

Decorated French Carriage Clock

Carriage clock, upright brass frame enclosing a front beveled glass front over the enameled dial w/small Roman numerals, each side w/a porcelain panel decorated w/a figure of a woman holding a sheaf of wheat & a sickle, probably French, some wear & discoloration to brass, 6" h. (ILLUS.) **$863**

Cherry Late Federal Grandfather Clock

Grandfather clock, Cate (Simeon) attribution, Sanborton, New Hampshire, Federal style cherry case, the arched molded crest w/squatty turned wood corner finials above slender swelled turned colonettes flanking the arched glazed door opening to a white-painted wooden dial w/Roman numerals, a scrolling cartouche at the top center & floral-painted spandrels, the tall central case w/quarter-round reeded columns flanking a tall plain door, a tall simple stepped-out lower case w/a serpentine apron & French feet, thirty-hour wooden movement, ca. 1834, imperfections, 83" h. (ILLUS.) **$1,410**

Grandfather clock, Elite, Germany, mahogany Chippendale-Style case, a high broken-scroll crest fitted w/three turned wood ovoid finials w/pointed tops above the arched glazed door opening to the dial w/an upper moon phase dial above the steel dial w/brass Arabic numerals & pierced gilt-brass corners, flanked by small free-standing colonettes above a flared cornice above the tall stepped-in case w/quarter-round side columns flanking the tall glazed door showing the pendulum & two large weights, a lower molded border above the paneled lower body raised on squatty paw feet, works w/plaque marked "Elite Germany 301," early 20th c., 16 x 24", 101" h. (ILLUS., next page)....... **$2,703**

Fine German Grandfather Clock

Very Rare Louis XV-Style Tall Clock

Grandfather clock, Morbier, France, Louis XV-Style after a model by Julien Le Roy & Charles Cressent, Kingwood, tulipwood & bronze doré case, the asymmetrical cartouche-form bonnet top surmounted by a gilt-bronze allegorical figure of Time holding a scythe, the round

enameled dial calibrated in Roman & Arabic numerals & framed by a scalloped brass bezel, the bold serpentine-sided case mounted w/gilt-bronze side scrolls & a large oblong Zephyr mask mount above a narrow rectangular metal band over a gilt-bronze scrolling heart-shaped glazed opening showing the sunburst pendulum bob, the wider lower case w/gilt-bronze scroll-mounted projecting bracket legs w/cartouche paw foot mounts, the whole case w/fine parquetry inlay including diamond lattice panels, all atop a rectangular serpentine-sided platform base, the original of this model in the British Royal Collection, ca. 1880, 11 1/2 x 29", 104"h. (ILLUS.) **$17,250**

Early Pennsylvania Grandfather Clock

Grandfather clock, Pennsylvania, Federal style cherry & mahogany case, the hood w/a broken-scroll pediment fitted w/three turned wood urn finials above the arched glazed pane flanked by slender swelled colonettes, the white-painted iron dial w/Arabic numerals below a moon phase panel & sunburst-painted spandrels, the tall central case w/a tall door framed w/banded inlay & w/a serpentine top, the stepped-out lower case w/a scroll-cut apron & slender French feet, brass eight-day weight-driven movement, old surface, works of different origin, early 19th c., 91 3/4" h. (ILLUS.)............................ **$2,820**

Grandfather clock, Queen Anne style, black lacquer decorated case, the top w/a rectangular deep curved cornice w/gilt decorative bands above a glazed front & sides within a gilt-decorated red & black molding w/a colonette at each cor-

Queen Anne Decorated Grandfather Clock

ner, the silvered steel dial w/Roman numerals & two keywind holes framed by spandrels w/cherub heads, another flaring stepped cornice band above the tall stepped-in body centered by a tall paneled door decorated w/an Oriental scene of ships, swans, people & a pagoda, the stepped-out base section w/similar decorated molding & a rectangular center panel w/a red ground w/a man & bird in gold, on a molded base w/a serpentine front apron, unsigned works, England, 18th c., weights & pendulum present, oveall 65 1/2" h. (ILLUS.) **$4,485**

Grandfather clock, Whiting (Riley), Winstead, Connecticut, Federal style pine case, a low broken-scroll pediment above the arched glazed door opening to a white-painted dial w/Arabic numerals & h.p. floral spandrels, the tall central case w/a tall simple door, plain stepped-out lower case w/simple bracket feet, thirty-hour weight-driven works, refinished, imperfections, ca.1825, 86" h. (ILLUS., top next column) **$1,410**

Lyre wall clock, Brown (J.C.) & Co., Bristol, Connecticut, rosewood scroll-sided case w/a scroll-cut top section framing a small molded rectangular glazed door opening to the white-painted zinc dial w/Roman numerals, the long lower case w/a waisted tall glazed door reverse-decorated w/a color scene of the Merchant's Exchange, Philadelphia, opening to original label reading "Eight Day Spring Timepiece Manufactured by J.C. Brown & Co., Bristol, Conn.," eight-day ladder-type spring

Riley Whiting Grandfather Clock

Rare Lyre-style Eight-day Wall Clock

movement, minor imperfections, ca. 1850, 13" w., 28 1/4" h. (ILLUS.)........... **$15,275**

Three Classical Lyre Wall Clocks

Lyre wall clock, Massachusetts, Classical-style carved mahogany case, a carved fleur-di-lis style finial above the round brass bezel opening to a painted iron dial w/Roman numerals, the long lyre-form body carved w/leafy scrolls above the stepped rectangular bottom w/tapering pointed base drop, brass eight-day weight-driven movement, refinished, ca. 1825, minor imperfections, 39" h. (ILLUS. left with two other Lyre clocks, top of page) **$31,725**

Lyre wall clock, probably Massachusetts, Classical style carved mahogany case, a large fleur-de-lis carved finial above the round wood bezel opening to a painted iron dial w/Roman numerals & inscribed "Smith," the central body w/boldy carved acanthus leaf scrolls flanking an églomisé panel decorated w/a central stripe in red & gold flanked by green scrolls & cornucopia on a white ground, the long low rectangular lower section inset w/another églomisé panel w/stylized large red & green leaves & small gold cornucopias on a white ground centered by an oval pendulum window, tapering base drop w/half-round pointed drop finial, brass eight-day weight-driven movement, ca. 1825, refinished, replaced glass panels, 41" h. (ILLUS. center with two other Lyre clocks) **$5,288**

Lyre wall clock, probably Massachusetts, Classical style mahogany & mahogany veneer case, a turned acorn finial above the round molded wood bezel opening to a painted metal dial w/Roman numerals, the main body w/narrow S-scrolls flanking

a large églomisé panel w/a small red & gold stripe & delicate gold floral swags & cornucopias against a white ground, the narrow rectangular lower section w/a conforming églomisé panel decorated w/dark gold & red leafy scrolls framing an oval pendulum window, tapering base drop, brass eight-day weight-driven movement, restored, ca. 1825, 38 3/4" h. (ILLUS. right with two other Lyre clocks) **$1,243**

Comical Man Novelty Alarm Clock

Novelty clock, alarm-type, cast-metal, a comical figure of a smiling man w/a brass bell forming his top hat, his arms & lower body encircling a brass bezel around the dial w/Arabic numerals & a subsidiary seconds dial, his feet supporting the front of the case, original painted surface, Germany, pre-1900, non-working, 8" h. (ILLUS., previous page) **$810**

Novelty Owl Clock with Moving Eyes

Novelty clock, cast-bronze & wood, the front cast as an owl w/moving eyes & a round metal dial w/Arabic numerals inset into its chest, the wooden back w/a sheet-metal back panel, probably German, ca. 1905, 6 1/2" h. (ILLUS.)........ **$417**

Novelty Cast-metal Monkey Clock

Novelty clock, cast-metal, a bronze-finished metal figure of a seated monkey holding a book, moving eyes & mouth,

atop a squared black-finished base w/incised lines centered by a round dial w/Arabic numbers, Germany, late 19th - early 20th c., non-working, 9 1/2" h. (ILLUS.) **$766**

Cast-Brass Novelty Walking Rabbit Clock

Novelty clock, figural, a cast-brass case in the shape of a walking rabbit w/a stick cane & carrying the round clock on his back, the white dial w/Arabic numerals, late 19th - early 20th c., 6 5/8" h. (ILLUS.) **$201**

Unusual Highwheeler Bike Clock

Novelty clock, figural, cast as a young man in cyclist garb riding a highwheeler bicycle w/the smaller rear wheels formed by the round clock case w/brass bezel around the dial w/Roman numerals, fine detailing, ca. 1885, 9 1/2" h. (ILLUS.)
.... **$1,180**

Regulator wall clock, Howard (E.) & Co., Boston, Massachusetts, Model No. 70, oak case, a large round molded top over the large signed white dial w/Roman numerals, the long rectangular lower case w/a mid-molding over a rectangular molding enclosing a reverse-painted glass panel in deep red bordered in black, brass eight-day weight-driven movement, late 19th c. (ILLUS., next page) **$1,645**

Fine E. Howard Oak No. 70 Regulator

Fine Waltham Oak Wall Regulator

Regulator wall clock, Waltham Clock Co., Waltham, Massachusetts, oak case, arched & scroll-cut pediment above a narrow flaring cornice above a wide squared frame w/corner fan carving & a large round glazed opening over the signed white dial w/Roman numerals, the long rectangular lower case w/a glazed front showing the wooden pendulum & large brass pendulum bob, molded tapering base drop, brass eight-day spring-drive movement, early 20th c. (ILLUS.) **$3,173**

Regular Clock Attributed to S.B. Terry

Regulator wall clock, Terry (S.B.) & Co. attribution, Terryville, Connecticut, rosewood case, large round molded top section enclosing the large white dial w/Roman numerals, the long lower case w/a large glazed door reverse-painted & stenciled w/a central scrolled gilt band centering an oval pendulum winder, a tapering molded base drop, brass eight-day double-weight drive movement, ca. 1852 (ILLUS.)... **$999**

Unusual Oak-cased Mantel Clock

Shelf & mantel, Boston Clock Company, Boston, Massachusetts, oak case w/the flat top centered by a low flaring rectangular crest above the rounded top corners, the upper frieze band carved w/ornate leafy scrolls above pairs of small columns flanking narrow spindled panels on either side of the recessed front panel centered by the dial w/a brass bezel & a brass pierced grille over porcelain w/black Arabic numerals, the blocked flat bottom centered by a rectangular leaf-carved panel, spring movement, late 19th - early 20th c., 6 x 18", 15 1/2" h. (ILLUS.) **$403**

Rare Gothic Double-Steeple Clock

Shelf or mantel, Birge & Fuller, Bristol, Connecticut, Gothic-style 'candlestick' double-steeple mahogany & mahogany veneer case, the pointed top above a two-pane door w/the upper pane opening to the white-painted zinc dial w/Roman numerals & the lower pane reverse-painted w/a diamond, florette & fan design in gold, white & black, each side w/two slender turned tapering pointed steeples, the wider rectangular lower case w/a long horizontal rectangular door w/another reverse-painted glass panel decorated in gold, white & black w/a cross & quatrefoil design, raised on small bun feet, eight-day time & strike movement marked "J. Ives Patent Accelerating Lever Spring," ca. 1845, 4 x 13 3/4", 26" h. (ILLUS.) **$8,225**

Rare Rosewood Acorn Shelf Clock

Shelf or mantel, Forestville Mfg. Company, J.C. Brown, Bristol, Connecticut, acorn-style rosewood case, the boldly shaped

case w/the upper section in the shape of an inverted acorn enclosing a glazed panel over the conforming white-painted zinc dial w/Roman numerals & delicate floral sprigs, the tall lower case w/deeply waisted narrow wood molding enclosing a conforming reverse-painted panel decorated w/a color primitive landscape w/a boat on a lake & a home in the distance, the case supported by slender sharply serpentine uprights w/small acorn finials, all raised on a narrow rectangular stepped platform base, eight-day time & strike wood barrel fusee spring movement, ca. 1850, imperfections, 5 1/2 x 15", 24 1/2" h. (ILLUS.) **$5,581**

Fine Neoclassical Marble & Bronze Clock

Shelf or mantel, gilt-bronze & red marble, a long rectangular stepped red marble base on gilt-bronze disk feet & trimmed w/gilt-bronze banding & an applied pierced bronze plaque featuring a goddess riding in a chariot drawn by peacocks & surrounded by putti, the top centered by a tall arched red marble case applied w/another bronze plaque showing classical lovers, a round dial w/Roman numerals above, enclosed by a bronze bezel, the clock section centered between large patinated bronze figures of Psyche & Cupid, after a model of Antonio Canova, France, mid-19th c., retailed by Tiffany & Co., New York, 30 1/2" h. (ILLUS.) **$9,200**

Shelf or mantel, Ingraham (E.) Company, Bristol, Connecticut, kitchen shelf-style, ornate pressed oak case, decorated w/a Labor & Industry theme, the top w/a high crest centered by a large roundel w/a raised sheaf of grain insignia flanked by wide serpentine winged figures of cherubs working machinery & tending plants, the paneled arched glazed door opening to a white dial w/Roman numerals, the lower door panel gilt-stenciled w/a lattice & tropical garden scene, smaller serpen-

Unusual Labor & Industry Oak Clock

tine winged figures of cherubs flanking
the bottom of the door, all raised on a
deep flaring molded flat base, ca. 1890s
(ILLUS.).. **$373**

Art Nouveau Pewter Clock by Liberty & Co.

Shelf or mantel, Knox (Archibald) for Liberty & Co., London, England, pewter &
enamel, Art Nouveau style, the upright
tapering pewter case cast in the lower
panel w/a stylized leafy tree below the
rounded & pointed upper section enclosing the dial w/a chapter ring marked
w/Roman numerals & mottled purple &
green enamel in the center, marked, ca.
1902-05, 7 3/4" h. (ILLUS.) **$8,365**

Nice Terry Pillar & Scroll Clock

Shelf or mantel, Terry (Eli & Samuel), Plymouth, Connecticut, Pillar & Scroll style,
mahogany & mahogany veneer, the
scroll-cut crest decorated w/three small
blocks topped by small brass urn finials,
the upright case w/small colonettes flanking the two-part glazed door w/the large
upper pane over the painted wood dial
w/Roman numerals, the small rectangular lower pane reverse-painted w/a colorful landscape featuring a large house &
stairway to water w/a boat, also a small
central oval pendulum window, thin molded base over the serpentine apron & tiny
French feet, original back label, original
wooden works, key & pendulum present,
major restoration to base & top of case,
painted panel may be a replacement, ca.
1820s, 17 1/2" w., 31 1/4" h. (ILLUS.).... **$1,035**

Unusual Classical-style Shelf Clock

Shelf or mantel, Willard (Aaron), Grafton,
Massachusetts, Classical-style mahogany & mahogany veneer case, a flat narrow rectangular top above a square ve-

neered glazed door opening to the engraved brass dial w/Roman numerals & floral designs & signed by the maker, large ring-, baluster- and knob-turned columns at the sides, the wider lower case w/large columns flanking a tall central panel pierced w/two small round glazed holes, flat base, brass weight-driven thirty hour movement, ca. 1775-1825, imperfections, 3 1/2 x 9 1/4", 18" h. (ILLUS.) **$4,700**

Ansonia Cast-iron Temple-style Clock

Shelf or mantel clock, Ansonia Clock Co., Ansonia, Connecticut, cast-iron temple-style case, the pedimented top centered by a dome w/a gilt-brass flame-form finial, a gilt-brass mount at the front above the large round brass bezel door opening to a dial w/Arabic numerals, pairs of freestanding reeded columns at each side, deep rectangular platform base centered at the front w/a large gilt-brass pierced scrolling mount, black enameled finish, ca. 1900, 13 1/2" h. (ILLUS.) **$219**

Ansonia Oak "Tunis" Model Clock

Shelf or mantel clock, Ansonia Clock Co., Ansonia, Connecticut, "Tunis" model oak case, an arched notch-cut crest centered by a crown-form cutout block above a conforming incised frieze band over the round stamped brass bezel enclosing the brass dial w/Arabic numerals, flat pilasters flank the dial, on a rectangular base w/angled sides, eight-day movement, time & strike, original varnished finish, paper label on back, ca. 1880-1900, 5 1/4 x 11 1/2", 14" h. (ILLUS.) **$250-300**

Shelf or mantel clock, Atkins Clock Co., Bristol, Connecticut, cottage-style w/rosewood case, paneled arched top over a conforming door w/two glass panes, the top pane over the white dial w/Roman numerals & some paint loss, lower pane reverse-painted w/a colorful floral bouquet against a black ground, ogee molded base, small piece of veneer missing on right base, 30-hour movement, time only, ca. 1865, 10 1/4" h. **$179**

French Multi-dial Mantel Clock

Shelf or mantel clock, Bourdin, France, black marble rectangular case w/molded pediment topped by bronze sculpture of retriever signed "P.J. Mene," a glass pane over the rectangular decorated gilt dial surround w/round time dial & two oblong dial cartouches w/two subsidiary dials each, all white w/black numerals/text, the time dial w/Roman numerals & subsidiary seconds dial, the panels containing dials w/days of the week, months & dates of the month & moon phases in Arabic numerals, dial signed "Bourdin, Hr. Bté , Rue de la Paix 28, a Paris," the beveled block base on short beveled feet, time & strike movement also signed "Bourdin, à Paris, Nr. 3802," small chip to marble, ca. 1880, 19" h. (ILLUS.)........... **$5,880**

Fancy French Porcelain & Ormolu Clock

Shelf or mantel clock, Japy Freres Cie., France, Rococo style porcelain & ormolu case, upright porcelain case w/a domed front topped by a pierced ornate scroll ormolu finial above a crest w/arching ormolu leafy scrolls above a pale blue arched panel above the brass bezel enclosing the porcelain dial w/Roman numerals, the lower case w/two free-standing porcelain columns w/gold capitals & bases flanking a wide flat central panel h.p. w/a Romanic 18th c. garden landscape w/two ladies & a gentleman in formal attire, the flaring case base enclosed w/ornate ormolu leafy scrolls extending to form scroll feet, the painting signed "Petit," back of case marked "Made in France," brass works marked "Made in France 7252 81," some crazing & minor hairlines to case, early 20th c., 14 1/2" w., 21" h. (ILLUS.)...................... **$2,530**

Victorian Walnut Kitchen-style Clock

Shelf or mantel clock, kitchen-style, walnut 'gingerbread' type case, a high arched & lobed scroll-cut & line-incised crest above the tall arched door w/the upper round section showing the round dial w/Roman numerals, the lower door stenciled w/fancy gilt leafy scrolls & banding w/an oval gold & red medallion in one corner, scroll-trimmed brass pendulum showing, side scroll base brackets above the deep molded base w/a serpentine & line-incised apron, late 19th c., 21" h. (ILLUS.)............. **$173**

Victorian Walnut 'Gingerbread' Clock

Shelf or mantel clock, kitchen-style, walnut 'gingerbread' type case, the high arched, scroll-cut & line-incised crest decorated w/two roundels above the arched molded tall glazed door w/the upper round section showing the white dial w/Roman numerals, the lower section stenciled overall w/ornate gold flowers, scrolls & bands, sawtooth-cut side brackets above the molded platform base w/a notch-cut apron, late 19th c., 21" h. (ILLUS.)............ **$184**

Walnut 'Gingerbread' Clock with Alarm

Shelf or mantel clock, kitchen-type w/walnut 'gingerbread' style case, the high arched crest deeply notch-cut & line-incised, above the tall glazed door w/angular top molding opening to the white-painted dial w/Roman numerals, the lower door stenciled w/ornate gilt decoration & showing the flowerhead brass pendulum bob, deep molded & canted platform base, time & strike mechanism w/alarm, late 19th c., 21" h. (ILLUS., previous page) **$127**

Fine Louis XVI-Style Shelf Clock

Shelf or mantel clock, Mougin (A.D.), France, Louis XV-Style, faux tortoiseshell & ormolu, the tall upright waisted case w/a small domed platform top supporting the ormolu figure of a standing angel holding a fern leaf in one hand, the arched case front bordered w/narrow ormolu scrolls & a winged sphinx head at the top above the large round brass dial inset w/white porcelain plaques w/black Roman numerals, enclosed by an arched ormolu bezel & above a panel of very ornate pierced leafy scrolls, the serpentine ormolu scroll base band continues to scroll front feet, sunburst & face pendulum, brass works marked by maker & "E.M. 12970:7.7," late 19th - early 20th c., 6 x 15 1/2", 29" h. (ILLUS.) **$1,783**

Shelf or mantel clock, New Haven Clock Co., New Haven, Connecticut, kitchen-type w/oak 'gingerbread' style case, the very tall arched & fanned crest w/a peaked center & overall line-incised scrolls & leaves, the tall glazed door w/an angular top molding opening to the worn white-painted dial w/Roman numerals, a diamond-shaped brass pendulum bob, scroll-cut base side brackets above the base w/a deep canted apron w/a shell & leaf design & scalloped rim, late 19th, 22 1/2" h. (ILLUS., top next column) **$100-150**

Oak New Haven Kitchen-type Clock

Extremely Rare Pillar & Scroll Clock

Shelf or mantel clock, Nicholl (John), Belvidere, New Jersey, Pillar & Scroll Classical-stype mahogany & mahogany veneer case, the broken-scroll pediment w/three turned & pointed finials above the wide, tall door w/two glazed panels, the upper panel opening to the painted dial w/Roman numerals & fan-painted spandrels & signature of the maker, the lower shorter panel reverse-painted w/a primitive landscape w/four red-roofed houses & a central oval window, the sides each w/a spiral- and ring-turned & a plain turned colonette, platform base raised on carved paw front feet, ca. 1830, small areas of repair & minor flaking to painted panel, 5 x 15", 29" h. (ILLUS.) **$64,400**

Finely Carved Swiss Wooden Clock

Shelf or mantel clock, Switzerland, carved wood, the tall ornately carved case topped w/the figures of two large chamois on rockwork w/three carved birds below the projecting round wood dial w/Roman numerals, projecting round base feet carved as holes w/a rabbit looking out of one & another rodent in the other, overall finely carved floral details, pendulum missing, ca. 1890, 23 1/2" w., 33" h. (ILLUS.)... **$5,175**

Terry Federal Pillar & Scroll Shelf Clock

Shelf or mantel clock, Terry (Eli & Samuel), Plymouth, Connecticut, Federal style Pillar & Scroll mahogany & mahogany veneer case, the broken-scroll pediment fitted w/three urn-turned finials above the wide tall door w/two glass panels, the upper panel opening to the large white-painted dial w/Roman numerals & delicate floral spandrels, the short lower panel reverse-painted w/a landscape

w/trees & a Classical brick house at the left, slender colonettes down the sides, a narrow molded base w/a serpentine apron & slender French feet, labeled, ca. 1825, small areas of repair & some paint flaking, 4 1/2 x 16 3/4", 32" h. (ILLUS.).. **$2,415**

Tiffany Bronze Doré Mantel Clock

Shelf or mantel clock, Tiffany (Louis C.), gold doré bronze case w/a pointed top, the pediment decorated w/a fine twisted rope design w/a round & triangular insets of red enamel, the squared front w/matching rope design & four enamel panels framing the round dial w/Arabic numerals, molded front edges & set on a molded base raised on tiny cushion feet, dial marked w/the Tiffany Furnaces logo, the bottom marked "Louis C Tiffany Furnaces, Inc. 651," works marked "Chelsea Clock Co. Boston USA 154955," early 20th c., 7 1/2" h. (ILLUS.) **$6,900**

Waterbury "Bruno" Model Clock

Shelf or mantel clock, Waterbury Clock Co., Waterbury, Connecticut, "Bruno" model, black cast-iron & gilt-metal case,

the large domed top mounted w/an ornate gilt-brass scrolling crest continuing
down the waisted sides to the wide oblong base w/further ornate scroll mounts,
the large brass bezel over the fancy
brass dial w/inset porcelain plaques
w/black Arabic numerals, late 19th c.,
13" h. (ILLUS.) **$230**

U.S.S. Kearsarge Ship's Clock

Ship's clock, round wide molded mahogany case centering a white dial w/Arabic
numerals & marked "U.S.S. Kearsarge,"
dial appears to be repainted, overall
15 1/4" d. (ILLUS.) **$374**

Fine Quality Enameled Swiss Clock

Table clock, Swiss enamel, a paneled
white onyx plinth base supporting the
domed guilloché green enameled foot
painted w/small oval color portraits of
18th c. ladies, a silvered metal & enameled stem supporting to large upright
egg-shaped matching green enameled
case w/large oval colored portrait panels
& delicate gold scrolls, silvered metal gadrooned bands above & below the time
indicator band w/Arabic & Roman numerals, bands joined by short baluster-
shaped posts, each suspending a stone
teardrop connected by slender chain

swags, the domed top w/a metal & enameled finial, Switzerland, late 19th c., 7" h.
(ILLUS.).. **$4,313**

Nice Oak-cased Simplex Time Clock

Time clock, Simplex Time Recorder Company, Gardner, Massachusetts, wall-
mounted, the long oak case w/a wide flaring stepped cornice & frieze band above
the arched glazed front over the white
time & strike dial w/Arabic numerals
above the large brass pendulum, company name in gilt script below the dial on the
glass, the projecting base compartment
w/a hinged lid opening to the time recorder mechanism, base molding & narrow
scalloped apron, key & pendulum
present, late 19th - early 20th c., 18" w. at
top, overall 15 1/2" h. (ILLUS.)................. **$920**

Rare Old Bangor Electric Wall Clock

Wall clock, Bangor Electric Clock Company, Bangor, Maine, oak case, the flaring
stepped cornice w/an arched central
shell-carved crest above a long rectangular case decorated w/carved swags

above the large round steel dial w/black Arabic numerals, the lower throat w/a rectangular glazed panel showing the pendulum, the bottom mounted w/a small rectangular bowl w/a carved wreath to enclose the battery for producing electricity, brass works signed, w/brass pendulum, late 19th - early 20th c., 17" w., overall 43 1/2" h. (ILLUS.) **$3,565**

French Box Wall Clock with Chimes

Wall clock, box-style, long walnut case w/a spindled top gallery trimmed w/a scroll-cut crest & flanked by turned finials, pairs of slender colonettes down the sides flanking the long door w/a round opening over the silvered metal dial w/Arabic numerals, the lower door w/three narrow vertical glass panes showing the pendulum & brass bob, molded base w/corner drop finials & short center drop, eight-day time & strike movement w/Westminster chimes, France, ca. 1910-20, 15" w., 36" h. (ILLUS.) **$1,800-2,000**

Decorative Ceramic Wall Clock

Wall clock, ceramic case, squared form w/cut corners, wide dark blue panels alternating w/small white panels w/pink flower sprigs, round dial w/Arabic numerals, eight-day movement, time only, ca. 1935-55, 9 3/4" w. (ILLUS.) **$50-60**

Wall clock, Empire Clock Co., England, round gallery timepiece, oak frame w/stripped finish, white painted dial w/some chips, Roman numerals, movement marked "Made in England," cylindrical pendulum, ca. 1930, 16" d. (ILLUS., top next column) **$123**

1930s English Wall Clock

Furtwangler German Wall Clock

Wall clock, Furtwangler (Lorenz) & Sohne, Germany, Berliner-style solid & veneered oak case w/Art Nouveau detailing, a high crestrail pierced & carved w/scrolls & stylized leaves above a flaring molded cornice above the molded sides enclosing a square glass front over an engraved silver & gold metal dial w/Arabic numerals, a simple scroll apron above shaped side brackets & a long scroll-pieced backboard framing the free-hanging pendulum w/shaped & stamped brass bob, eight-day time & strike movement strikes the hours & half hours on a gong, ca. 1900, 17" w., 36" h. (ILLUS.) **$2,000-2,500**

Mauthe Berliner Fancy Wall Clock

Wall clock, Mauthe Clock Co., Germany, Berliner-style, carved light walnut case , the high carved & pierced central crestrail w/a molding over a carved iris flanked by corner blocks & turned finials over a flat stepped cornice above half-round ring-turned columns flanking the wood dial frame w/carved leaves at each corner around the brass bezel enclosing the dial w/a celluloid chapter ring w/Arabic numerals around an embossed brass center, a narrow scalloped front apron & short turned corner drop finials, scalloped brackets & a long pierce-carved backboard framing the pendulum & embossed brass bob, eight-day time & strike movement, ca. 1890-1900, 15" w., 35" h. (ILLUS.)...................................... **$1,400-1,500**

Wall clock, Mauthe (F.), Schwenningen, Germany, R-A-type, softwood & walnut-veneered case in a dark finish, the gallery crest carved w/leaves, turned supports & turnip-form finials, reeded side columns w/turned capitals & bases flank the long door over the porcelain dial w/Roman numerals & a brass gridiron pendulum w/large brass bob, drop pendants at the bottom corners of the case, eight-day spring-wound time & strike movement, ca. 1900-10, 15" w., 37" h. **$800-950**

Wall clock, New Haven Clock Co., New Haven Connecticut (works only), English oak short-drop case, large round frame around the dial w/Roman numerals & the printed name of the English retailer, pierced leafy scroll side brackets flank the small rectangular glazed door w/beaded edge trim over the decorative brass pendulum bob, long coved base drop w/slender horizontal rods w/finials, refinished, late 19th c., 5 x 16", 26 1/2" h. **$600-700**

Terry Clock with Iron Case

Wall clock, Terry Clock Co., Waterbury, Connecticut, round-topped black iron case w/a deep rectangular base, most of the original gold scroll & line decoration remains, original brass bezel around the dial w/Roman numerals, some paint chips on sides of case, 30-hour movement, time-only, ca. 1875, 8 1/4" h. (ILLUS.) **$190**

Thomas Oak Schoolhouse Clock

Wall clock, Thomas (Seth) Clock Co., Plymouth, Connecticut, oak short drop schoolhouse-style case, wide octagonal top framing the heavy brass bezel & painted dial w/Arabic numerals, the short pointed drop w/a small conforming glass window showing the brass pendulum bob, eight-day time-only movement, ca. 1920s, 15" w., 22" h. (ILLUS.)............ **$500-600**

Thomas "Office No. 11" Wall Clock

Wall clock, Thomas (Seth) Clock Co., Plymouth, Connecticut, "Office No. 11" model, square flat oak frame enclosing a brass bezel & painted dial w/Arabic numerals & sweep seconds hand, 30-day movement, ca. 1920-25, 15" w. (ILLUS.) **$1,200-1,500**

Wall clock, Waltham Clock Co., Waltham, Massachusetts, a very tall unique fancy jigsaw-cut late Victorian case, the large pediment w/a rectangular top w/low front openwork gallery supporting the tall scroll-cut crest w/turned urn finial above a deep frieze band pierce-carved w/delicate leafy scrolls above another spindled band above the tall rectangular front w/cut-out scrolls above the arched glazed door opening to a white time-and-strike dial w/Roman numerals above a long metal pendulum, long pierce-cut serpentine panels down the sides above another lower spindled band on a projecting rectangular shelf above the long lower case composed of a tapering panel pierce-cut w/ornate scrolls & pierced scroll ears over a bottom three-spindle gallery over a small arched section flanked by the cut-out long bracket supports, late 19th c., one repaired fretwork break on door, missing the hands, late 19th c., 14" w., 49" h. (ILLUS., next page) **$633**

Unique Tall Waltham Jigsaw-cut Clock

Tall Oak Waterbury Wall Clock

above the wooden pendulum w/brass bob, molded shelf-form base w/a narrow scalloped front apron & an arched & notched bottom backboard, brass double weight-driven movement, late 19th - early 20th c. (ILLUS.)...................................... **$1,175**

Waterbury "Galesburg" Wall Clock

Wall clock, Waterbury Clock Co., Waterbury, Connecticut, "Galesburg" model, tall oak case w/a high arched crest centered by a block & turned finial flanked by turned corner finials on the molded cornice, short blocks & turned finials at the top & bottom corners of the front flanking the tall arched & glazed door w/wood molding enclosing the brass bezel & paper dial w/Roman numerals, the glass showing the long pendulum & large brass bob, original label inside case, eight-day spring-wound time & strike movement, ca. 1900-10, 15" w., 52" h. (ILLUS.)...................................... **$1,900-2,250**

Wall clock, Waterbury Clock Co., Waterbury, Connecticut, long oak case w/a broken-scroll pedimented top molding above the tall molding-framed front enclosing a large arched glass panel showing the large white dial w/Roman numerals

Early Waterbury Short-drop Wall Clock

Wall clock, Waterbury Clock Co., Waterbury, Connecticut, mahogany & mahogany veneer case, the wide octagonal top framing the glazed opening over the white dial w/Roman numerals, the short drop case w/a small rectangular glass panel stenciled w/gilt scrolls & flanked by carved scrolls, beveled lower case drop, brass spring-driven movement, ca. 1865 (ILLUS.)...................................... **$235**

Renaissance Revival Rosewood Clock

Wall clock, Welch, Spring & Co. attribution, Forestville, Connecticut, carved rosewood Victorian Renaissance Revival style case, the broken-scroll crest w/a center roundel & three small ball finials above a narrow flaring cornice w/blocked corners above a square top door flanked by slender double baluster-turned spindles & opening to the large white dial w/Roman numerals, the lower case w/a larger rectangular glazed door also flanked by slender double baluster-turned spindles & w/a reverse-painted panel in black centered by a gilt portrait medallion above a rectangular-framed pendulum window, molded flat base w/beveled front corners, brass eight-day weight-driven movement, ca. 1875 (ILLUS.) **$1,410**

Interesting Old French Lantern Clock

Wall-mounted lantern clock, French, a projecting round brass dial w/black Roman numerals & a single steel hand w/a heart cut-out, the top of the dial w/a pierced brass crest w/a rooster, cherubs w/horns & a woman's head, the bottom w/a narrow band of pierced florals, dial attached to a metal case w/brass wheels w/a striking pendulum, all mounted on a backboard w/a pointed arched top & a long acorn-shaped lower section, pendulum & weight present, early, sides & one wheel loose, dial 8" d., overall 12 1/2" h. (ILLUS.) **$720**

CLOISONNÉ & RELATED WARES

Cloisonné comes from the French term cloison (cell). Standard cloisonné has a metal body covered with motifs made of wire cells filled with enamels.

Standard Cloisonné: A sheet of metal is bent and hammered into the desired shape. An artist paints the design onto the metal. The wires are bent into shapes and placed on their edges to form partitions (cells) or cloisons. A layer of enamel (powdered glass) is sifted over the wires and gently fired to secure them in place. The cells are packed with enamel in powdered form. The color of the fused enamel depends upon the mixture of natural minerals with the crushed glass. The cells are packed again and refired until the cells are filled to the top or reach the height of the wires. The piece is polished with stones of various coarseness and then with charcoal and finally powdered horn mixed with oil until the proper finish is obtained.

Chinese Cloisonné: Chinese cloisonné is termed Ching tai lan after the period in the Ming Dynasty in which it was developed. Pieces can have a gold, bronze, copper or brass body. There can be the presence of pitting. Ground coloring includes rust, black, ox blood, white, turquoise, green, etc. In addition to the prime motif there can be background designs of diapers (repetitive patterns). Objects include animals, figures, water pipes and snuff bottles as well as ornamental, occasional and functional wares. Chinese cloisonné can be marked with Reign Marks (period markings).

Japanese Cloisonné: The body of an object can be silver, brass, ceramic (pottery or porcelain), bronze, copper, papier-maché or lacquer. Japanese cloisonné can have fancy marks, artists signatures or seals. Enamels can be opaque, transparent or translucent. Designs are naturalistic and do not have to cover the entire piece. Objects include netsuke, belt buckles, tsuba, pins and inro as well as ornamental and functional wares. Japanese cloisonné, also termed Shippo Yaki, includes the following techniques: Yusen - wires; Musen - wireless; Yu Musen - wire and wireless; Shotai (plique-à-jour) - transparent enamels with the body etched away; Moriage (cameo) - a motif in relief; Totai - ceramic bodies; Ginbari - silver coin wrapped around a metal body having translucent or trans-

parent enamel; *Akasuk (Pigeon Blood)* - red. *Saiyu:* The design is embossed by pressing and hammering, and the enamel is applied on the raised parts.The term *goldstone* applies to the enamel, which has iron pyrite and/or copper filings added to it so that it glitters like gold. *Fishscale* simply refers to a repetitive motif that resembles the scales of a fish.*Counter enameling* is found on both Japanese and Chinese cloisonné. Usually used inside and/or on bases to counteract the expansion and contraction of the enamel and metal, it strengthens the body.*Repoussé* is relief formed by pressing or hammering a motif from the back.*Basse Taille:* A translucent enamel over metal, the metal having motifs in various heights of relief. This is produced by the Chinese and usually machine made.*Champlevé:* A technique in which the metal body is engraved, etched, stamped or chiseled with sunken designs, with enamels used to fill the depressions, leaving divisions in relief. It is devoid of wires.

Cloisonné

Chinese Cloisonné Foo Dog Bowl

Bowl, a small footring supporting the wide deep rounded bowl w/a flaring scalloped rim, decorated inside & out w/a design of stylized Foo dogs & vines in red, white, green & black on a light blue ground, marked under the base, China, 19th c., 10" d., 5" h. (ILLUS.) **$288**

Fine Chinese Cloisonné Candlesticks

Candlesticks, pricket-style, a brass foot on the bell-shaped base joined by a knop to a wide dished drip pan below a tall cylindrical shaft w/small knops below the pricket socket, decorated overall w/colorful stylized flowers on a light blue ground, marked

under the base, China, late 18th - early 19th c., 6" d., 13 1/4" h., pr. (ILLUS.) **$3,163**

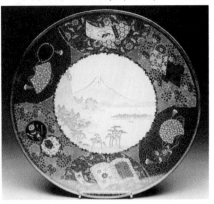

Large Cloisonné Scenic Charger

Charger, footed round form, the top centered by a round scenic panels featuring Mt. Fuji w/water & forested hills in the foreground all in shades of grey & white, the wide border band composed of large half-round panels each decorated w/different Oriental symbols in shades of red, white, blue & black on deep red or purple grounds, the underside in blue w/the base decorated inside w/a colorful bird on a hanging bracket, Japan, late 19th - early 20th c., 18" d. (ILLUS.)..................... **$920**

Chargers, large round dished form, decorated w/a red lattice-like design on a blue ground in the center within a light blue & white circle, the outer band composed of swirled panels in shades of red, blue, green & white, Japan, 19th c., 18" d., pr. (ILLUS., top next page) **$1,434**

Lovely Russian Cloisonné Cigarette Case

Cigarette case, flattened square hinged case in silver ornately decorated w/light blue scrolls & dots & red, white & blue blossoms, a wide diagonal band decorated w/a chain-like design of scrolls in red, white & blue, Vassily Rukavishnikov, Moscow, Russia, 1890-1908, 3 1/2" w. (ILLUS.)... **$403**

Japanese Cloisonné Chargers

Green Chinese Cloisonné Ginger Jars

Ginger jars, cov., bulbous ovoid body tapering to a short neck w/a high domed cover, dark green ground decorated w/pale yellow scrolls & large stylized flowers & leaves in white, red, pink, black & green, China, late 19th - early 20th c., 6" d., 7" h., pr. (ILLUS.) **$518**

Japanese Koro with a Purple Ground

Koro, cov., ball-shaped body decorated w/colorful flowers & butterflies on a dark purple ground, the domed cover w/a similar decoration & a small metal finial, on three pointed feet, Japan, Meiji period, 19th c., 4" d., 4 1/2" h. (ILLUS.) **$288**

Early Chinese Cloisonné Incense Burner

Incense burner, two-part, the base section composed of two bell-shaped cups joined by a central disk, decorated w/stylized vines & flowers on a light blue ground, the matching domed cover w/four small cylindrical smoke vents centered by a large ball finial, interior of base stamped w/four Chinese characters, China, probably late 18th c., 5" d., 10" h. (ILLUS.)...................... **$805**

Japanese Ball-shaped Koro & Cover

Koro, cov., ball-shaped body decorated w/dropped shaped panels of birds & other design, the intricate cover border w/geometric designs, the bottom w/glistening goldstone decoration, all resting on three small gold feet, decorative cover finial, Japan, Meiji period, 19th c., 4 1/2" d., 5" h. (ILLUS.) **$575**

Pretty Bird & Branches Cloisonné Vases

Pair Black Floral Cloisonné Vases

Vases, tall slightly flaring cylindrical body w/a wide shoulder tapering to a short trumpet neck, black ground decorated w/delicate tall chrysanthemums on leafy stems in shades of white, pink, deep red, yellow & green, metal foot & rim band, some silver loss to rim bands, Japan, late 19th - early 20th c., 7 1/4" h. (ILLUS.)....... **$489**

Japanese Cloisonné Vase with Chickens

Vases, footed ovoid body tapering to a short neck w/a wide shallow cupped rim, black ground decorated overall w/colorful flowers & birds w/a hen & rooster below, one w/restoration on the side, Japan, late 19th c., 7 1/2" h., pr. (ILLUS. of one) **$1,560**

Vases, wide bulbous body on a silver footring curving up to a short cylindrical neck w/a silver rim, the background in pale blue & white decorated w/large leafy branches in blues & greens w/small red berries & w/pairs of small tan, white & black birds perched, Japan, late 19th - early 20th c., 7 1/2" d., 7 1/2" h., pr. (ILLUS., top of page) **$1,840**

Pair of Chinese Cloisonné Vases

Vases, ovoid body tapering to a trumpet neck, decorated w/reserve panels of chrysanthemums & Foo dogs against a goldstone ground, the reserve panels against a black ground decorated w/butterflies & a goldstone band w/phoenix & floral decoration at the shoulder, China, ca. 1890, 11 3/4" h., pr. (ILLUS.) **$690**

COCA-COLA ITEMS

Coca-Cola promotion has been achieved through the issuance of scores of small objects through the years. These, together with trays, signs and other articles bearing the name of this soft drink, are now sought by many collectors. The major reference in this field is Petretti's Coca-Cola Collectibles Price Guide, 11th Edition, by Allan Petretti (Antique Trader Books). An asterisk (*) indicates a piece which has been reproduced.

Calendar, 1922, "Coca-Cola," color lithographed cardboard, three-quarter length portrait of a young lady wearing a pink dress & hat & holding a glass while leaning on a bench, baseball players in background, 12 x 32" **$7,700**

1931 Rockwell Coca-Cola Calendar

Calendar, 1931, "The Barefoot Boy," color lithographed cardboard, Norman Rockwell artwork of a young boy in straw hat seated by tree eating sandwich & drinking from a bottle, his dog watching, mild rust on four staples, some mild fold marks, very light ripples, light to medium soiling, full page, 12 x 24" (ILLUS.) **$770**

Calendar, 1934, "Carry Me Back to Old Virginny," artwork by Norman Rockwell of an elderly Southern gentleman seated on a large porch w/a pretty young woman wearing a long yellow gown & playing a guitar seated on the steps in front of him, matted & framed under glass, light soiling, tiny closed margin tears, few strong creases & fold marks at bottom, light soiling, 12 x 24" **$1,150**

1954 Coca-Cola Calendar

Calendar, 1954, "Coca-Cola," color lithographed paper, a month at the top & bottom w/the bust portrait of a young woman holding a bottle of Coca-Cola in the center w/a background portrait of a leaping basketball player to the right, only slight soiling, six pages (ILLUS.) **$143**

Two Metal Coke Calendar Holders

Calendar holder, die-cut metal, red double fishtail logo at the top above a tapering white section printed in red "Coke Refreshes You Best" above a striped background & attached paper calendar pages, 1963, slightly ambered, few shallow dents & scratches (ILLUS. left with other calendar holder) **$275**

Calendar holder, metal, vertical rectangular shape w/rounded corners, white ground printed in red at the top "things go better with Coke" above a red Coke button logo & attached partial paper calendar pages for 1952, only light wear & ambering, 15" h. (ILLUS. right with other metal Coca-Cola calendar holder) **$121**

Modern Coca-Cola Promotional Can

Can, cylindrical color-printed metal w/fitted flat red top, various action sports scenes around the sides w/Coca-Cola advertising in the background, 1990, 6" h. (ILLUS.) **$10**

Very Rare Early Leaded Glass Coca-Cola Hanging Lamp Shade

Clock, electric wall type, light-up style, glass, metal & plastic, horizontal rectangular shape w/dark border, large red double fishtail Coca-Cola logo in the center, numerals only at 12, 2, 4, 6, 8 & 10, sweep seconds hand, made by Swihart, few minor marks & some wear, 1960s, 13 x 16" **$253**

Very Rare Coca-Cola Clock & Sign

Clock & sign, countertop neon light-up style, a round clock dial at the top in black on white w/"Drink Coca-Cola" in red on a stepped frame above a long rectangular sign in red banded w/chrome & featuring a white neon tube around a yellow circle w/a six-pack of Coca-Cola & white wording "Drink Coca-Cola - Take home a carton," domed clock cover may be a replacement, some motors & transformers updated, minor paint & edge wear, 1930s (ILLUS.).. **$13,750**
Leaded glass shade, hanging-type, wide cylindrical flat sides w/panels formed by

narrow bands of green slag glass enclosing deep ruby glass inset w/the Coca-Cola name in white glass script, the wide angled top & flaring crown band composed of white glass section, metal band at crown stamped "Property of The Coca-Cola Company - To Be Returned On Demand," 1920s, one piece of green slag broken other very good condition, 16" d. (ILLUS., top of page)............................. **$4,030**

Very Rare 1905 Lillian Nordica Sign

Sign, color-printed cardboard, a full-length portrait of singer Lillian Nordica holding a large black feather fan & leaning on a gold pedestal w/a glass of Coca-Cola, black background printed in white at the top "Coca-Cola - At Soda Fountains - 5¢," decorative gold border w/panels at the bottom printed "Delicious - Coca-Cola - Refreshing," orginal wide brown molded plaster frame, 1905, few small paper chips, some mild stains, bit of professional restoration, 26 x 46" (ILLUS.) **$19,600**

Scarce Triangular Coca-Cola Sign

Sign, porcelain, two-sided triangular design, dark green arched top band & border enclosing a pale green ground w/a red panel printed in white "Drink Coca-Cola," a bottle of Coke flanked by "Ice Cold" in green below, 1935, nearly perfect, mild discoloration, few touched up chips (ILLUS.) **$3,630**

1914 Unused Coca-Cola Sign

Sign, rectangular embossed & enameled tin, red & dark green bands at one side printed in white "Ice Cold - Coca-Cola - Sold Here," a color picture of an early Coca-Cola bottle at the left side, new old stock w/portions of original separation paper intact, 1914, 19 1/27 1/2" (ILLUS.) **$1,265**

Thermometer, Masonite, rectangular, the red & white Coca-Cola button at the top above a color picture of a bottle beside a long thermometer in white, dark & light green ground w/"Thirst knows no season" at the bottom, 1944, only minor marks & soiling, 7 x 17" (ILLUS., top next column) **$523**

1940s Masonite Coca-Cola Thermometer

1939 Canadian Coca-Cola Thermometer

Thermometer, porcelain, oblong, round logo in gold, red & white at the top reading "Drink Coca-Cola" above a long dark green center panel printed in yellow "Thirst knows no season" next to the thermometer & over a yellow & green silhouette of lady drinking from bottle, Canadian, ca. 1939, few small chips, clear-coated w/some touch-up, tube appears to be a replacement, 5 1/2 x 18" (ILLUS.) **$715**

1959 Round Coca-Cola Thermometer

Thermometer, round w/domed glass, black letters & red & white center logo on white ground read "Drink Coca-Cola Be Really Refreshed!," Pam-type dial, 1959, only minor marks, few minor bends to metal face, 12" d. (ILLUS.) **$935**

Thermometer, round w/domed glass, red letters on white ground read "things go better with Coke," Robertson-type dial, 1964, light soiling & minor marks, light oxidation on gold needle, 12" d. **$358**

Thermometer, round w/domed glass, white letters on red ground read "Drink - Coca-Cola - In Bottles," Robertson-type dial, 1950s, 12" d. (some scratches on glass cover) **$80**

Round Coca-Cola Thermometer Variation

Thermometer, round w/domed glass, white letters on red ground read "Drink - Coca-Cola - In Bottles," Robertson-type dial, 1950s, only very light soiling, 12" d. (ILLUS.) **$165**

Rare Version of Round Thermometer

Thermometer, round w/domed glass, white letters on red ground read "Drink - Coca-

Cola - Sign of Good Taste," Robertson-type dial, 1950s, minor scratches, marks & gloss variations, 12" d. (ILLUS.) **$743**

Thermometer, round w/domed glass, white letters & shadow of bottle in center logo on white ground read "Drink Coca-Cola," dark green border band w/black numbers, Pam-type dial, 1948, 12" d. **$825**

Thermometer, tin, cigar-shaped vertical oblong form, arched red top printed in white "Drink Coca-Cola - Sign of Good Taste," oblong white reserve framing the thermometer & printed in red at the bottom "Refresh yourself," 1950s, only minor marks, 30" l. **$330**

1930s Bottle-Shaped Coke Thermometer

Thermometer, tin, die-cut bottle-shaped, reads "Coca-Cola - Trade Mark Registered - Bottle Pat'd Dec. 25, 1923," small thermometer at the bottom, small marks & minor wear, 1930s, 5 x 17" (ILLUS.)...... **$275**

Thermometer, tin, oval w/narrow gold border & red ground, embossed gold Coca-Cola bottle enclosing a small thermometer, 1937, few minor crimps & rust spots, light wear, 6 1/2 x 16".............................. **$138**

Scarce 1915 Coca-Cola Thermometer

Very Rare 1912 Coca-Cola Trolley Sign

Thermometer, wood, long rectangular form w/rounded top, dark green border band & white ground printed in red at the top "Drink Coca-Cola - Delicious and Refreshing" above the thermometer w/large red numbers & "5¢" at the bottom, ca. 1915, some soiling, chips, nick & scratches, 5 x 21" (ILLUS., previous page) **$605**

1939 Oval Tin Coca-Cola Thermometer

Thermometer, tin, "Drink Coca-Cola - Delicious and Refreshing," red ground circle above thermometer & black-on-white silhouette of girl drinking from bottle in circle below, 1939, minor marks, some edge chinks, 6 1/2 x 16" (ILLUS.) **$358**

Trolley sign, cardboard, printed in color w/a pretty young woman reclining in a hammock & holding up a glass of Colca-Cola, sepia-toned background, reads across the bottom "Have a Drink of Coca-Cola - Deliciously Refreshing," 1912, matted &

framed, minor edge marks & crimps, 11 x 20 1/2" (ILLUS., top of page) **$11,550**

COMPACTS & VANITY CASES

A lady's powder compact is a small portable cosmetic make-up box that contains powder, a mirror and puff. Eventually, the more elaborate compact, the "vanity case," evolved, containing a mirror, puffs and compartments for powder, rouge and/or lipstick. Compacts made prior to the 1960s when women opted for the "au natural" look are considered vintage. These vintage compacts were made in a variety of shapes, sizes, combinations, styles and in every conceivable natural or man-made material. Figural, enamel, premium, commemorative, patriotic, Art Deco and souvenir compacts were designed as a reflection of the times and are very desirable. The vintage compacts that are multipurpose, combined with another accessory—the compact/watch, compact/music box, compact/fan, compact/purse, compact/perfumer, compact/lighter, compact/cane, compact/hatpin—are but a few of the combination compacts that are not only sought after by the compact collector but also appeal to collectors of the secondary accessory.

Today vintage compacts and vanity cases are very desirable collectibles. There are compacts and vanities to suit every taste and purse. The "old" compacts are the "new" collectibles. Compacts have come into their own as collectibles. They are listed as a separate category in price guides, sold in prestigious auction houses, displayed in museums, and several books and many articles on the collectible compact have been written. There is also a newsletter, Powder Puff, written by and for compact collectors. The beauty and intricate workmanship of the vintage compacts make them works of fantasy and art in miniature.

For additional information on the history and values of compacts and vanity cases, readers should consult Vintage and Vogue Ladies' Compacts by Roselyn Gerson, Collector Books.

Century of Progress Compact-Bracelet

Compact-cuff bracelet, souvenir-type, silvertone w/the red-enameled lid centered by a raised round logo button reading "A Century of Progess - 1934," from the Chicago World's Fair of 1933-34, interior reveals a metal mirror, puff & perforated swiveling powder well (ILLUS.) **$225**

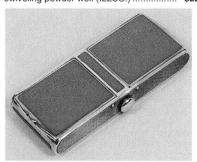

Rare German Combination Compact & Watch

Compact-watch, rectangular sterling silver case enameled in red w/side-by-side compartments, one side opens to reveal a powder compartment, puff, mirror & slide-out lipstick, the other side opens to review a small watch, Germany (ILLUS.) **$600**

Deck of cards compact, flat rectangular design, the top decorated in blue enamel w/the Bicycle playing cards design, the bottom enameled in red as the ace of Hearts, interior contains a framed mirror, puff & powder compartment (ILLUS., top next column) **$175**

Deck of Cards Compact

Lovely Enameled Compact & Lipstick

Enameled compact & lipstick set, antique vermeil sterling silver enameled pieces, the oblong compact w/engraved gilt banding centering an oval panel painted w/two lady musicians framed by dark green & black panels, the matching long rectangular lipstick w/a similar enameled scene & a blue cabochon stone on the latch, the compact w/a gilded interior w/a beveled mirror, the lipstick tub opens to reveal a small mirror, lipstick $150 & powder compact (ILLUS. of compact & lipstick) ....,.............. **$750**

Estee Lauder Art Deco-style Compact

Estee Lauder compact, "Golden Age" design, rectangular brushed goldtone, lid embossed w/an Art Deco style face of a lady, 1994 (ILLUS.) **$80**

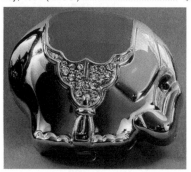

Estee Lauder Elephant-shaped Compact

Estee Lauder compact, "Little Prince" design, stylized goldtone model of an elephant, the back of the elephant w/a red enemaled blanket trimmed w/a rhinestone-set border (ILLUS.).......................... **$100**

German silver armor mesh vanity bag, extension gate top w/carrying chain, round compact w/convex mirror located on outer cover **$225**

German silver fluted chatelaine, oval/locket pin container, oblong stamp holder, round compact, oval coin holder, & oblong memo pad all suspended from 1 1/4" ring... **$700**

Fine Art Deco Cartier Gold Compact

Gold, silver gilt & enamel compact, Art Deco style, long rectangular case in gold incised w/thin bands & centered by a black enamel square w/further trim at each end, opening to a mirrored interior w/lipstick & two compartments, diamond thumbpiece, hallmark of Cartier, Paris & French gaurantee stamps (ILLUS.)........ **$1,998**

Goldtone compact, oblong, deeply incised cover decorated w/polished goldtone strip w/small applied goldtone knots set w/colored stones, interior powder well & mirror, Hattie Carnegie............................. **$155**

Goldtone compact, round, enameled goldfish underneath plastic domed cover, Melissa **$75**

Goldtone compact, round, the cover decorated w/painted courting scene, signed "I. Peynet," beveled glass bottom, interior reveals mirror & puff, Miref........................ **$125**

Goldtone compact, square, cover decorated w/a red, white & blue enameled Union Jack flag, the reverse centered w/an applied goldtone "Dieu et Mon Droit" emblem, Evans **$125**

Roulette Spinning Wheel Compact

Goldtone & enamel compact, round, made to resemble a spinning roulette wheel, goldtone cover decorated w/red & black spaces w/white numbers on them revealed under glass top, instructions in German on how to play "Spielregel Roulette" included (ILLUS.) **$400**

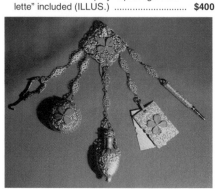

Goldtone Engraved Belt

Goldtone filigree engraved belt chatelette, decorated w/applied green four-leaf clover decoration, matching button hook, round compact, perfume or smelling salts container, writing slate & pencil suspended on filigree chain from belt hook (ILLUS.) **$450**

Goldtone jeweled powder compact, round, cover set w/round mobe pearl framed by pronged faceted turquoise stones, compact w/a twist closure, Germaine Monteil **$45**

Goldtone vanity, shaped as hand mirror, filigree lid & lipstick tube enhanced w/red stones, interior opens to reveal mirror, powder & rouge compartments, lipstick slides out of filigree handle, large faceted red stone centered on lid & on the end of the lipstick tube **$250**

Hand Mirror-shaped Vanity Case

Goldtone vanity case, in the shape of a hand mirror, the round filigree lid & lipstick tube handle enhanced w/red stones, compact interior opens to a mirror & powder & rouge compartments, lipstick slides out of handle, a large faceted marquise-cut red stone at the center of the lid & end of the handle (ILLUS.) **$175**

Fancy French Goldtone Vanity Case

Goldtone vanity case, the matte goldtone case w/an enameled lid encrusted w/prong-set blue & pink cabochon stones, w/a carrying chain & suspending a goldtone tassel, goldtone interior w/a mirror & compartments for powder, lipstick & eye make-up, France (ILLUS.) **$225**

Powder & Perfume Canister Container

Powder & perfume canister container, goldtone & red enamel canister, the outside bottom lid opens & contains a mirror that opens to reveal a powder well & puff, the pointed top unscrews to reveal a miniature perfume vial, France (ILLUS.) **$125**

Two Collectible Colorful Powderettes

Powderettes, dark green or yellow tapering cylindrical plastic containers, operated by unscrewing the top & filling w/powder & reattaching the top, press the pointed button in the top to release the powder against a powder puff, each (ILLUS. of two) **$50**

Sterling Silver Compact/Vinaigrette Pendant

Silvertone compact, round, lid decorated w/goldtone, silvertone & bronze neo-classical high-relief discs........................... **$175**

Zephyr Roulette Spinning Wheel Compact

Silvertone & enamel compact, round, made to resemble a spinning roulette wheel, silvertone ground decorated w/black enamel outer lid centered w/red, black, green & white numbered sections, interior reveals powder puff w/Zephyr logo (ILLUS.)... **$350**

Silvertone pendant/compact, oblong, cut-off corners, white enameled cover decorated w/black silhouette of period lady, back opens to reveal metal mirror & powder well, complete w/silvertone chain (ILLUS., next column)..................... **$125**

Silvertone triple compact, square, compact comes complete w/two lipsticks, one for daytime & one for evening wear, either one can be snapped tandem to compact, cover of compact centered w/sepia photo, interior metal mirror separates rouge from powder compartment, comes complete w/original presentation box, Yardley **$250**

Silvertone Pendant/Compact

Sterling silver compact, square, "window wiper" style, the cover decorated w/inscribed sunburst pattern, monogram on lower lid, interior reveals beveled mirror, powder well, puff, Tiffany & Co. **$350**

Sterling silver compact/vinaigrette pendant combination, round, lavender enamel, first opening reveals convex compartment w/perforations around rim of vinaigrette section, complete w/sterling neck chain, shown closed & opened, Vanuette (ILLUS., top of page) **$425**

Sterling silver hallmarked necessaire, octagonal, silhouettes on cover & front of necessaire, w/a wrist carrying cord & tassel, sliding lipstick in center front, top lid opens to reveal mirror & compartment for powder, second opening for small articles, bottom opening has mirror on the lid & a rouge compartment **$1,200**

Volupté "Petite Boudoir" Compact & Presentation Box

Volupté compact, "Petite Boudoir," silver-tone model of a vanity table w/collapsible cabriole legs, a mirror on the outside top of lid, interior w/powder compartment & signed puff, complete w/original presentation box (ILLUS. of compact & box) **$175**

Volupté political compact, round goldtone enameled on the lid w/red, white & blue bands printed in white & blue "Re-Elect - Roosevelt - President," 1930s, very rare (ILLUS.).. **$250**

Volupté Palette-shaped Compact

Volupté enameled compact, in the shape of an artist's palette, the white lid applied w/the raised, enameled figures of marching band musicians (ILLUS.) **$75**

Whiting & Davis Enameled "El-sah" Vanity Bag

Whiting & Davis vanity bag, silvertone "El-sah" mesh enameled in a lattice design in shades of green, yellow & white, comes w/a carrying chain & a Van Dyke-style bottom edge, top of compact mesh lid enameled w/pink & green flowers, compact opens to a round lidded powder well, "El-sah" imprint on attached interior metal tag, early 20th c. (ILLUS.) **$450**

CURRIER & IVES PRINTS

This lithographic firm was founded in 1835 by Nathaniel Currier, with James M. Ives becoming a partner in 1857. Current events of the day were portrayed in the early days, and the prints were hand-colored. Landscapes, vessels, sport and hunting scenes of the West all became popular subjects. The firm was in existence until 1906. All prints listed

Rare Volupté Political Compact

*are hand-colored unless otherwise noted. Numbers
at the end of the listings refer to those used in Currier & Ives Prints - An Illustrated Checklist, by Frederick A. Conningham (Crown Publishers).*

American Country Life - October Afternoon

**American Country Life - October After-
noon,** large folio, N. Currier, 1855, framed,
122, toning, stains, framed (ILLUS.) **$1,410**

The Cares of a Family

Cares of a Family (The), large folio, 1856,
N. Currier, framed, 814, repaired margin tear, light toning, mat stains, framed
(ILLUS.) **$2,468**
City of New York (The), large folio, 1870,
bird's-eye view looking north, framed,
1105, bands of pale staining, repaired
tears at lower margin, minor margin
damage & repairs (ILLUS., bottom of
page) **$8,963**
**Destruction of the Tea at Boston Harbor
(The),** small folio, N. Currier, 1846, unframed, 1571 (some stains, soiling &
creases) **$632**

Early General Tom Thumb Print

**General Tom Thumb...Now Performing
with Barnum's Travelling Museum
and Menagerie,** small folio, 1849, N.
Currier, standing on chair w/six small
views up each side, evenly toned, framed
(ILLUS.) **$231**
Grand Drive (The) - Central Park, N.Y.,
large folio, 1869, framed, 2481, light stains
in lower margin, light toning (ILLUS., next
page) **$4,700**

Rare City of New York View Print

The Grand Drive - Central Park, N.Y.

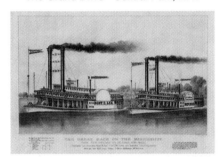

Great Race on the Mississippi Print

Great Race on the Mississippi from New Orleans to St. Louis (The), large folio, 1870, unframed (ILLUS.)........................ **$3,738**

Hunter's Shanty (The), large folio, 1861, in a narrow modern frame, overall toning & foxing, No. 2993 (ILLUS., next column) **$1,035**

The Hunter's Shanty Print

Currier & Ives Landscape, Fruit and Flowers Print

Landscape, Fruit and Flowers, large folio, 1862, 3440, framed, top corners reinforced, minor toning (ILLUS.)................ **$2,820**

Rare The Life of a Hunter Currier & Ives Print

Life of a Hunter (The) - A Tight Fix, large folio, 1861, 3522, repair to margin, framed (ILLUS.) **$44,063**

The Splendid Naval Triumph Print

Splendid Naval Triumph on the Mississippi, April 24, 1862 (The), large folio, 1862, framed, 5659, repaired tear in margin, slight abrasions, part of bottom title trimmed (ILLUS.)................................... **$1,058**

The Western Farmer's Home Print

Western Farmer's Home (The), small folio, 1871, framed, 6619, some staining, (ILLUS.) **$161**

The Whale Fishery - Sperm Whale "In a Flurry"

Whale Fishery, (The) - Sperm Whale "In a Flurry," large folio, 1852, 6627, repaired tear in margin, light staining (ILLUS.)..... **$8,813**

Winter in the Country - The Old Grist Mill

Winter in the Country - The Old Grist Mill, large folio, 1864, framed, repaired tear in lower title, light mat stain (ILLUS.) **$8,813**

Winter Morning

Winter Morning, medium folio, 1861, framed, 6740, mat stains, minor foxing in sky (ILLUS.) **$2,233**

DECOYS

Decoys have been used for years to lure flying water fowl into target range. They have been made of carved and turned wood, papier-mâché, canvas and metal. Some are in the category of outstanding folk art and command high prices.

Black Duck, Augustus Wilson, South Portland, Maine, carved & painted wood, combination rocking head & feeding pose, head mortised & pinned through the body to allow it to swivel up & down, fine original paint, flaws in wood on back & breast, second quarter 20th c. (ILLUS., top next page) **$5,750**

Black Duck with Rocking Head by Augustus Wilson

Large Oversized Canada Goose Decoy by James Whitney

A. Moak Canvasback Drake & Hen Decoys

Canada Goose, James Whitney, Falmouth, Maine, large oversized carved & painted wood, natural flaw in wood on back now plugged, branded w/name of maker (ILLUS., middle of page) **$150**

Canada Goose, Philippe Sirois, Arrowsic, Maine, one-fourth size, carved & painted wood w/relief wing carving, original paint w/minor discoloration & wear, small tail chips, crude repair to crack in neck, third quarter 20th c. (ILLUS. center with two Old Squaw Drake decoys, above) **$250**

Canvasback drake & hen, Augustus Moak, Tustin, Wisconsin, carved & painted wood, hollow-carved w/original paint w/minor discoloration & wear, several small dents, hend w/slightly turned head, second quarter 20th c., pr. (ILLUS., above) **$5,225**

Loon, Goldeneye Hen & Eider Drake Decoys

Eider drake, carved & painted wood w/inlet head attached w/a small dowl, good bill carving, restored paint, small chip from underside of bill, numerous cracks & shot marks, central Maine coast (ILLUS. right with Loon and Goldeneye Hen decoys, top of page) **$1,050**

Goldeneye drake & hen, hollow-carved wood w/open bottoms & keels, old paint & glass eyes, by an anonymous Ontario, Canada carver, 15 3/4" l., pr. **$55**

Goldeneye hen, George Huey, Friendship, Maine, carved & painted wood, original paint w/average wear, think crack in underside, first quarter 20th c. (ILLUS. center with Loon & Eider Drake decoys, top of page) **$1,500**

Loon, hollow-carved wood, original paint w/moderate wear, crack in neck, several small dents, Maine, third quarter 20th c. (ILLUS. left with Goldeneye Hen & Eider Drake, top of page) **$600**

Mallard drake, carved & painted wood, very thin shelled, light weight w/serrated mandibles & good bill carving, original paint w/minor shrinkage & wear, slight roughness on tail edge, minor structural wear, Ontario, Canada, last quarter 19th c. (ILLUS., middle of page) **$10,725**

Mallard drake & hen, both w/incised detail & glass eyes, brown, tan, white, black & blue paint, unsigned by Frank Schmidt, 16 1/2" & 15 1/2" l., pr. (one missing keel) **$2,585**

Mallard drake & hen, Charles Perdew, Henry, Illinois, both branded "LORIE KORSEN," both retain Perdew weights, old repaint, second quarter, 20th c., pr............. **$1,210**

Mallard hen, Hiram Hotze, Peoria, Illinois, hollow carved body w/fine detail, original paint protected by original coat of varnish, weight missing, very rare, second quarter, 20th c. **$6,325**

Mallard hen, Mason Decoy Factory, Detroit, Michigan, hollow Premier grade, original paint, first quarter 20th c. (part of a knot on one side missing at body seam, tight age line on body) **$1,925**

Mallard hen, original brown & ochre paint, brown glass eyes, 16" l., 7" h. **$440**

Ontario-carved Mallard Drake Decoy

Fine Merganser Drake by George Huey

Old Squaw Drake & a Small Canada Goose Decoys

Merganser drake, George Huey, Friendship, Maine, carved & painted wood, fine dry original paint w/patinated surface, bill broken off & reattached, carved into bottom "Builder, G.R. Huey" w/a carved flying bird, 20th c. (ILLUS., bottom previous page) **$13,750**

Old Squaw drake, carved & painted wood, old repaint, several small dents, from Sullivan, Maine (ILLUS. left with small Canada Goose & Old Squaw drake with glass eyes, top of page) **$450**

Old Squaw drake, carved & painted wood w/glass eyes & inlet head, original paint w/minor wear, several tiny dents, last quarter 19th c. (ILLUS. right with other Old Squaw decoy & small Canada Goose decoy, top of page) **$1,450**

DISNEY COLLECTIBLES

Scores of objects ranging from watches to dolls have been created showing Walt Disney's copyrighted animated cartoon characters, and an increasing number of collectors now are seeking these, made primarily by licensed manufacturers.

ALSO SEE Antique Trader Toy Price Guide.

Wind-up Tin Ferdinand the Bull & Matador Toy

Ferdinand the Bull toy, wind-up tin, a brown & white flat cut-out Ferdinand raised on a two-wheeled tin platform & charging the jointed matador perched on another two-wheeled platform, good working condition, copyrighted 1935, 8 1/2" l. (ILLUS.) **$316**

Ceramic Jiminy Cricket Figurine

Jiminy Cricket (from Pinocchio) figurine, ceramic, colorful, 2 3/4" h. (ILLUS.) **$10-20**

Mickey & Minnie Mouse Seesaw Toy

Mickey & Minnie Mouse seesaw toy, celluloid & metal, rubber band-activated, celluloid figures of Mickey & Minnie riding a seesaw raised on a metal post, elastic-strung arms & legs, marked "Made in Japan," ca. 1950s, very find condition, original elastic no longer stretches, 5 1/4" h. (ILLUS.) **$690**

Rare Early Mickey Mouse Band Fisher Price Push Toy

Mickey Mouse & Pluto push toy, "Mickey Mouse Band," lithographed paper on wood figures of Mickey & Pluto on a rectangular blue wood platform on small yellow wheels, Mickey plays a drum & cymbol when pushed by the long slender rod handle, Fisher Price No. 530, ca. 1934, very fine condition, 12" l. (ILLUS.) **$1,840**

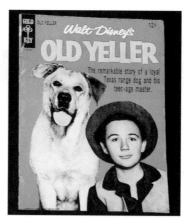

Disney Old Yeller Comic Book Reprint

DOLLS

"Susie-Q" & "Bobby-Q" Cloth Dolls

Minnie Mouse Knitter Toy

Minnie Mouse toy, windup tin, "Minnie Mouse Knitter," Minnie sitting in rocking chair knitting, colorful, Line Mar, Japan, 1950s, mechanism works but skips, 6 1/2" h. (ILLUS.) **$288**

Old Yeller comic book, photo of characters on cover, Gold Key reprint, 1966 (ILLUS., top next column)...................................... **$8-20**

Pinocchio doll, jointed wood body w/a painted composition head, cloth collar & bow tie, original chest decal & impressed Disney mark on back of head, Ideal, ca. 1940, 8" h. **$58**

Alexander (Madame) "Susie-Q" & "Bobby-Q," marked "Susie Q [Bobby Q] - by Madame Alexander, N.Y. - All Rights Reserved" on clothing tag, also cardboard tag in shape of purse (Susie Q) and book (Bobbie Q), cloth heads w/mask faces, painted blue eyes to side, single-stroke brows, closed mouths, painted cherry cheeks, yarn hair, cloth bodies jointed at shoulders only, mitten hands, striped fabric on legs for stockings, black felt feet for shoes, wearing original matching outfits of blue skirt or shorts, gold felt jackets w/blue buttons, white collar, white felt spats, buckram hats, Susie carries black parasol, 13", pair (ILLUS.)...................... **$1,600**

Madame Alexander W.A.V.E. Doll

Alexander (Madame) W.A.V.E., marked "Mme. Alexander" on back of head, "W.A.V.E. - Madame Alexander - New York - All Rights Reserved" on clothing tag, composition head, blue sleep eyes w/real lashes, painted lower lashes, single-stroke brows, closed mouth, original auburn mohair wig, five-piece composition body wearing original W.A.V.E. uniform including leatherette shoulder bag, hat, socks & shoes, 14" (ILLUS.) **$600**

All-bisque "Mignonnette" with Clothes

All-bisque "Mignonnette" child, marked "12," bisque socket head w/set blue eyes, closed mouth, original blonde mohair curly wig, jointed shoulders & hips, molded & painted white-ribbed socks & black two-strap shoes, wearing original blue print dress w/lace trim & ribbon at waist, matching beret-style hat w/ribbon, original lace-trimmed underclothes, Germany, early 20th c., 4 1/2" (ILLUS.) **$550**

Cute All-Bisque Girl Doll

All-bisque girl, marked "150/3," stiff-necked, jointed arms & legs, blue glass sleep eyes, blonde mohair wig on plaster pate, chunky legs w/pink stocking & painted black shoes, wearing a fancy lace outfit, 8 1/2" (ILLUS.) **$575**

Armand Marseille Flapper Lady Doll

Armand Marseille bisque head "Flapper" lady, marked "M.H. A 300 M," bisque head w/blue glass sleep eyes, pouty closed mouth, blonde mohair wig, five-piece composition Flapper-style body, wearing original underwear & black lace-trimmed dress, painted gold shoes, small chip to composition at neck, 9" (ILLUS.) **$1,035**

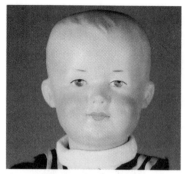

Armand Marseille Boy Character Doll

Armand Marseille character boy, Model 500, bisque head w/blond molded hair, intaglio blue eyes & dimples, on a jointed composition body, wearing an older replacement felt sailor suit, 13 1/2" (ILLUS.).. **$345**

Armand Marseille Queen Louise Doll

Armand Marseille "Queen Louise," bisque head w/brown glass sleep eyes, dirty blonde mohair wig, open mouth w/upper teeth, wearing an antique white dress w/brocade piping, antique leather shoes, 29" (ILLUS.) **$288**

Girl Playing Piano Automaton

Automaton, child playing piano, bisque head w/blonde mohair wig & glass eyes, seated at an upright piano, wearing a wide red dress w/thin black & gold bands & black lace trim, when engaged music plays & she moves her hands across the keys while turning her head, possibly 1930s, fine original condition, on deep platform base, 7 1/2" h. (ILLUS.).............. **$748**

Young Chef Automaton

Automaton, standing young chef w/a Size 1 bisque Tete Jumeau head w/brown glass paperweight eyes, in all-original clothing & holding a copper saucepan in one hand & should have a ladle in the other, when activated music plays & his right hand strikes the copper pan w/the ladle while turning his head, on a squared red velvet-covered base w/wear, some fraying to outfit, late 19th c., 16" h. (ILLUS.) **$4,715**

Georgene Averill Bonnie Babe Doll

Averill (Georgene) bisque head Bonnie Babe, marked "Copr. by - Georgene

Averill - 1005 - 3652 - Germany," solid dome flange head, brown sleep eyes, open laughing mouth w/tongue, two lower teeth, molded dimples in cheeks, lightly molded & painted hair, cloth mamadoll-type body w/composition arms & lower legs, wearing possibly original white organdy print baby dress w/lace trim, organdy bonnet, cotton slip, diaper, socks, original shoes, very tiny chip on lower rim of left eye, arms & legs repainted, 16" (ILLUS.) **$440**

Georgene Averill Nurse Jane Doll

Averill (Georgene) Nurse Jane, molded cloth, character from the Uncle Wiggily stories, wearing original costume w/blue duster cap, blue & red floral-printed dress & white apron, very minor face soiling, 13" (ILLUS.) **$316**

Bahr & Proschild bisque socket head Belton type girl, marked "204 - 11" on head, set brown eyes, heavy feathered brows, painted lashes, open closed mouth, pierced ears, old mohair brown wig, jointed wood & composition body w/straight wrists, wooden upper arms & upper legs, wearing white factory chemise trimmed w/blue lace, pants, new black socks & shoes, 17 1/2" (slight wear, flaking, missing left middle finger) **$1,400**

Belton-faced Bisque Head Lady Doll

Belton-faced bisque head lady, swivel neck, blue glass eyes, typical "Belton Bru" open-closed mouth, replaced blonde mohair wig, kid body w/bisque lower arms, wearing original silk gown w/lace trim, one earring hole pulled through, other chipped, deterioration to silk outfit, replacement shoes, 13" (ILLUS.) **$748**

Belton-type Bisque Head Lady Doll

Belton-type bisque head lady, blue paperweight eyes, closed mouth, straight-wristed jointed composition body, wearing a long dress of crushed velvet & satin w/matching hat, 12" (ILLUS.) **$633**

Fine Painted Bisque Shoulder-head Lady

Bisque shoulder-head lady, unmarked, tinted bisque w/painted blue eyes w/red lid line, single stroke brows, closed mouth w/accent line, pierced-in ears, finely molded tightly curled painted blonde hair w/blue ribbon, kid body w/bisque lower arms, gussets at elbows, pin joints at hips & knees, wearing antique two-piece outfit w/velvet panel on top & skirt, antique pants, corset, new socks & shoes, 21" (ILLUS.) **$715**

Flat-Top China Head Lady Doll

China shoulder head lady, painted blue
eyes w/molded lids, red lid line, closed
mouth w/accent line between lips, molded & black-painted 'flat-top' hairstyle
w/side curls, original home-made heavy
cloth body w/individually-stitched fingers,
wearing probably original red print dress
w/black velvet ribbon trim, lace collar,
original slip, paints made w/old fabric,
new black socks & antique leather shoes,
29" (ILLUS.) **$358**

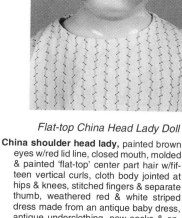

Flat-top China Head Lady Doll

China shoulder head lady, painted brown
eyes w/red lid line, closed mouth, molded
& painted 'flat-top' center part hair w/fif-
teen vertical curls, cloth body jointed at
hips & knees, stitched fingers & separate
thumb, weathered red & white striped
dress made from an antique baby dress,
antique underclothing, new socks & antique shoes, replaced body w/some age,
23" (ILLUS.) **$550**

Covered Wagon China Head Lady

China shoulder head lady, painted blue
eyes w/red lid line, closed mouth w/white
space between lips, molded & painted
'covered wagon' style center-part black
hair w/thirteen vertical curls, cloth body
w/kid arms, wearing a new purple print
two-piece outfit, white muslin pinafore,
two short antique half slips, antique
pants, no socks or shoes, arms in poor
condition, 21" (ILLUS.) **$523**

Scarce Door of Hope Girl Doll

Door of Hope girl, carved wood hands,
elaborate silk costume & matching head-

band, slight fabric fading, China, early 20th c., 6 1/2" h. (ILLUS.)....................... **$1,610**

Early Door of Hope Woman Doll

Door of Hope woman, a middle-aged woman w/a bun in rear of head, wearing a finely made replica clothes in patterned red & blue silk, earlier model w/cloth mitt hands, aging & discoloration to head, China, early 20th c., 11 1/2" (ILLUS.) **$460**

Scarce Dora Petzold Girl Doll

Dora Petzold girl, molded composition head w/painted blue eyes & red closed mouth, blonde wig, all-original w/velvet clothing & blue leather shoes, some distressing to painted hat & cuffs, Germany, ca. 1920s, 20" h. (ILLUS.).... **$1,265**

Pretty Gaultier Bisque Head Girl

Gaultier (Francois) bisque socket-head girl, marked "9 - F.G. (in scroll)," large blue paperweight eyes, heavy feathered brows, open-closed mouth w/tip of tongue, pierced ears, original brown h.h. wig w/French label, jointed wood & composition body w/jointed wrists, redressed in a lavish rose silk-type dress trimmed w/lace & ruffles, matching bonnet w/antique flowers, new full slip, old half-slip & pants, new stockings & shoes, two flakes at neck opening, 23" (ILLUS.) **$1,540**

Fine Gaultier French Fashion Lady

Gaultier (Francois) Fashion Lady, bisque head w/blue threaded paperweight eyes, closed mouth, sandy blonde h.h. wig, gusseted kid French fashion body, wearing a cotton print dress, red leather boots, 18" (ILLUS.) **$2,875**

Fine Near Mint Beloved Belindy Doll

Georgene "Beloved Belindy" cloth doll, near mint w/painted face & button eyes, red kerchief & red & white dress w/original paper hang tag, in original cardboard box w/end label, Georgene Novelties, New York City, 15" (ILLUS.).................. **$3,278**

German Bisque Head Character Girl

German bisque socket head character girl, marked "B - 2 - 0 - Germany," bisque head w/set green eyes, open-closed mouth, molded crease lines around mouth, replaced brown h.h. wig, joined wood & composition body, wearing an antique dress w/a pink skirt & lace bodice, antique underclothing, socks & new shoes, fine small inherent firing line at outside corner of one eye, 16" (ILLUS.)
.... **$825**

Lovely German Lady Fashion Doll

German bisque socket head Fashion Lady, marked "3," head w/bisque shoulder plate, set cobalt blue eyes, feathered brows, closed mouth, pierced ears, original blonde mohair wig, kid body w/gussets at elbows, hips & knees, individually stitched fingers, wearing lovely pale green silk taffeta dress w/flower trim at neckline, slip, antique pants, socks & shoes, fine crack at right earring hole, small hole at left elbow & right lower leg, 13" (ILLUS.) **$1,980**

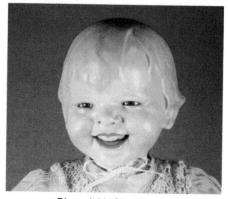

Bisqueloid "Gladdie" Doll

"Gladdie" child doll, bisqueloid character head w/heavily molded blonde hair & large widely smiling mouth w/teeth & tongue, inset glass eyes, cloth & composition body, wearing older pink dress w/replacement shoes & socks, fine crazing on head, heavier crazing on arms & legs, 23" (ILLUS.)...................................... **$510**

Heinrich Handwerck No. 109 Girl

Handwerck (Heinrich) bisque socket head girl, marked "109-7 1/2 - H - 1," blue sleep eyes, feathered brows, open mouth w/accented lips & four upper teeth, pierced ears, replaced brown h.h. wig, jointed wood & composition body, wearing white lawn dress trimmed w/lace & tucks, underclothing, black cotton socks, antique shoes & blue bonnet, old replaced hands, 16 1/2" (ILLUS.).............. **$495**

Handwerck (Heinrich) bisque socket head girl, marked "Germany - Heinrich - Handwerck - Simon & Halbig - 0 1/2" on head, "Heinrich Handwerck - Germany" on right hip, blue sleep eyes, feathered brows, open mouth w/four upper teeth, pierced ears, original mohair wig, jointed wood & composition body, wearing ecru dress trimmed w/lace & ribbons, underclothing, antique socks & shoes, 16 1/2" (edge chipped around neck socket) **$375**

Large Heinrich Handwerck Girl

Handwerck (Heinrich) bisque socket head girl, marked "16 - 99 - DEP - Ger-

many - Handwerck - 7" on head, "Heinrich Handwerck - Germany" in faint stamp on right hip, brown sleep eyes, molded & feathered brows, open mouth w/accented lips & four upper teeth, pierced ears, original brown h.h. wig, jointed wood & composition Handwerck body, wearing antique white dress trimmed w/tucks & eyelet, underclothing, socks & antique shoes, 33" (ILLUS.) **$950**

Handwerck Bisque Socket Head Girl

Handwerk (Heinrich) bisque head girl, marked "69-6 - Germany - Handwerck - 01 - 2," socket head w/blue sleep eyes, open mouth w/outlined lips & four upper teeth, pierced ears, replaced brown h.h. wig, joined wood & composition Handwerck body, redressed in an orange silk dress w/lace collar & trim, matching hair ribbon, underclothing made of old fabric, new socks & shoes, 15" (ILLUS.).............. **$495**

Blonde Handwerck Girl with Fur Brows

Handwerk (Heinrich) bisque head girl, marked "Germany - Heinrich Handwerck - Simon & Halbig - 5," socket head w/brown sleep eyes w/real lashes, original fur brows, open mouth w/outlined lips & four upper teeth, pierced ears, original blonde h.h. wig, jointed wood & composition body, wearing probably silk dress w/net overlay, original underclothing, socks & high-button shoes, 24 1/2" h. (ILLUS., previous page) **$413**

Tall Handwerck 109 Girl Doll

Handwerk (Heinrich) bisque head girl, marked "Handwerck," Model 109, brown glass sleep eyes, open mouth w/upper teeth, new long blonde h.h. wig, composition body, wearing an older cream-colored muslin dress w/a knit sweater, 28" (ILLUS.) **$345**

Karl Hartman Socket Head Girl

Hartman (Karl) bisque socket head girl, marked "30.5 - K/4" inside large "H" on back of head, brown sleep eyes, molded & feathered brows, painted lashes, open mouth w/four upper teeth, replaced synthetic wig, jointed wood & composition body, redressed in drop-waist blue dress w/lace bodice trim & ribbon belt, antique underclothing, socks & old fabric shoes, some touchups, old tape residue on lower torso, 24 1/2" (ILLUS.) **$225**

Hertel, Schwab All-bisque Girl Doll

Hertel, Schwab & Co. all-bisque girl, marked "208 - 5" on back of head & "Made in Germany" on the back & "208 - 5" on legs, head w/stiff neck, blue sleep eyes, open/closed mouth w/white space between lips, brown mohair wig, all-bisque body jointed at shoulders & hips, molded & painted white socks & black one-strap shoes, redressed in pink silk crepe dress w/lace trim, matching hat, slip & pants made from antique fabric, 7" (ILLUS.) **$220**

Hertel, Schwab & Co. solid dome bisque socket head baby, marked "151 - 7," blue intaglio eyes w/feathered "flyaway" brows, open mouth w/molded tongue & two painted upper teeth, lightly molded & brush-stroked hair, bent-limb composition baby body w/jointed wrists, wearing old pink baby dress, slip & diaper, 15 1/2" (body is repainted, wear & chips around neck socket, which is lined w/leather) **$225**

Heubach (Ernst) bisque socket head baby, marked "Heubach - Koppelsdorf - 342 - 6 - Germany," blue sleep eyes w/real lashes, feathered brows, open mouth w/two upper teeth & spring tongue, original brown mohair wig, composition baby body, wearing antique baby dress w/lace inserts, antique baby bonnet & underclothing, 18 1/2" (ILLUS., next page) **$303**

Ernst Heubach Bisque-head Baby

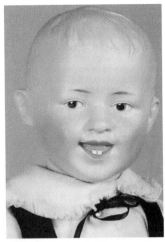

Fine G. Heubach Character Boy

Heubach (Gebruder) bisque head character boy, marked "(sunburst) GH (entwined) - 76 DEP - 04 - 7 - Germany," socket head w/blue intaglio eyes w/molded lids, open-closed laughing mouth w/two lower teeth, molded dimples, molded & lightly tinted hair, joined composition toddler body w/joints at shoulders, elbows, wrists, hips & knees, wearing knit underwear, white lace-trimmed shirt, black velvet pants, new black socks & shoes, body finish wear, 15" (ILLUS.) **$688**

Nice Ernst Heubach Boy Doll

Heubach (Ernst) bisque socket head body, marked "Heubach - Koppelsdorf - 320-7 - Germany," blue sleep eyes w/real lashes, open mouth w/accented lips & four upper teeth, pierced nostrils, original brown mohair wig, jointed wood & composition body, well dressed in a white shirt w/bow tie, brown wool pants, knit underclothing, maroon knit vest, reddish brown felt hat, matching socks, new lace-up boots, 26" (ILLUS.) **$578**

Lovely G. Heubach Character Lady

Heubach (Gebruder) bisque head character lady, Model 7926, blue glass eyes, stiff turned neck, cloth lady-style body w/long, slender bisque arms (replaced?), open mouth w/four upper teeth, dirty blonde mohair wig w/black bead tiara, wearing elaborate deep red fashion-style gown w/train, lady collar & black trim, 21" (ILLUS., previous page) **$1,610**

Gebruder Heubach "Baby Stuart"

Heubach (Gebruder) bisque socket head "Baby Stuart," marked "5 - 79 [sunburst] 77 - DEP - Germany," head w/molded bonnet painted w/pink flowers & green leaves, blue intaglio eyes, closed pouty mouth, composition toddler body w/straight legs, wearing baby dress made w/old fabric, matching slip, diaper & booties, 8" (ILLUS.) **$495**

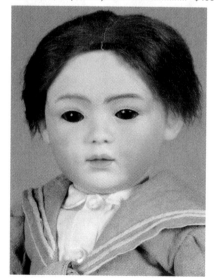

Gebruder Heubach Bisque Head Boy

Heubach (Gebruder) bisque socket head boy, marked "7407 - 6 - Germany," brown sleep eyes, feathered brows, closed mouth w/accent line between lips, molded dimples, original short brown mohair wig, jointed wood & composition body w/wooden upper arms & legs, wearing a white shirt, blue sailor shirt over it, black short pants, black socks & new black shoes, large chip & small flakes at neck opening, right lower leg replaced, repaired & repainted, left arm socket cracked & worn, left little finger replaced, 17" (ILLUS.) **$3,850**

Huret bisque shoulder head lady, body stamped w/"Huret Blvd Haussman" mark, lidded eyes painted blue, closed mouth, rosy cheeks, original blonde skin wig, articulated jointed gutta percha body, bisque hands, wearing white cotton undergarments & blouse, period red plaid wool dress w/black velvet trim, w/watch, jack-knife & pair of green gloves, ca. 1860s, 17" (wig thinning, wear at joints, broken off at right knee)... **$17,625**

Huret painted bisque head lady, Huret stamp on kid strip of torso, painted eyes, closed mouth, old blonde mohair wig, fully articulated embossed leather brown kid body, unclothed, ca. 1860s, 17" (some color loss to neck) **$22,325**

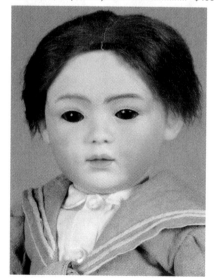

Jumeau Open-mouthed Girl

Jumeau (Emile) bisque head girl, marked "5," socket head w/blue paperweight eyes, feathered brows, open mouth w/six upper teeth, pierced ears, antique blonde mohair wig on cardboard pate, jointed wood & composition French body, wearing a dress of antique gold silk w/light blue piping & trim, matching bonnet, underclothing made w/antique fabric, new socks & older replacement shoes, hand & lower legs repainted, 16" (ILLUS.)...... **$1,760**

Rare First Series Jumeau Portrait Girl

Jumeau (Emile) first series bisque head Portrait girl, marked "3/0," large almond-shaped eye cut-outs w/blue threaded glass eyes, closed mouth, original blonde mohair wig w/curls draped down her back, on proper eight ball-jointed Jumeau body, original spring in the head, original burgundy & sea foam green dress, blue-trimmed straw hat, Jumeau-marked shoes, 13" (ILLUS.) **$14,375**

Rare Long-Faced Jumeau Girl

Jumeau (Emile) long-face girl, Size 9, huge blue paperweight eyes & sorrowful expression, closed mouth, brown h.h. wig, eight ball-jointed straight-wristed marked Jumeau body, wearing an antique shie cotton dress w/satin & lace trim, brown leather boots, original spring in her head, U-shaped hairline about 1" into forehead w/piece glued back in

place, another hairline down towards bridge of nose, 20" (ILLUS.) **$5,175**

*Fine K*R Character Toddler*

K (star) R bisque socket head character toddler, marked "K*R - S & H - 115 - A 42," blue sleep eyes, feathered brows, closed pouty mouth, original blonde mohair wig on original cardboard pate, jointed wood & composition body w/straight wrists, wearing probably original two-piece suit, knit undershirt w/ribbon tie, original socks & shoes, 16" (ILLUS.)...... **$4,070**

*Rare K*R Gretchen Character Girl*

K (star) R bisque socket head Gretchen character girl, marked "K*R 114 - 57 cm," painted blue eyes, closed slightly pouty mouth, blonde mohair wig, on a fat, chunky pink composition body, wearing original pale pink dress & underclothing, replaced shoes, 22" (ILLUS., previous page) **$4,600**

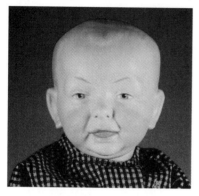

Kammer & Reinhardt Character Baby

K [star] R (Kammer & Reinhardt) bisque socket head character baby, molded face w/painted blue eyes & open mouth w/tongue, lightly molded & tinted hair, pink jointed composition child body, wearing an antique houndstooth romper outfit, 15" (ILLUS.) **$460**

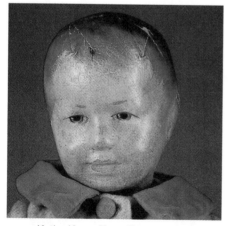

Kathe Kruse-Type Character Boy

Kathe Kruse-type character boy, possibly by Heine & Schneider, swivel neck molded head w/painted features on an all-felt straw-filled body w/side hip joints & shoulders, minimal head wear, some moth damage on body, replacement clothing, 15" (ILLUS.) **$390**

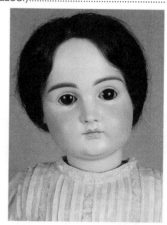

Kestner Bisque Head Baby Jean

Kestner (J.D.) bisque head Baby Jean baby, marked "J.D.K. - made in 14 Germany," solid dome head w/blue sleep eyes, feathered brwos, open mouth w/outlined lips & two upper teeth, lightly molded & brushed hair, composition Kestner baby body, wearing antique long white baby dress, shirt, diaper, socks & booties, 17" (ILLUS.)... **$770**

Tall Kestner Closed-mouth Girl

Kestner (J.D.) bisque head girl, marked "18," socket head on bisque shoulder plate, brown sleep eyes, feathered brows, closed mouth w/outlined lips & accent line between lips, antique brown h.h. wig, kid body w/bisque lower arms, gussets at elbows, hips & knees, wearing antique white low-waisted child's dress, antique underclothing, socks & velvet shoes, small chip at inside corner upper right lid, repairs to all gussets, kid repair at left ankle, 34" (ILLUS.)............. **$1,650**

Nice Closed-Mouth Kestner Girl

Kestner (J.D.) bisque socket-head girl, unmarked, turned head, brown sleep eyes, feathered brows, closed mouth w/accent line between lips, antique brown mohair wig, kid body w/bisque lower arms, gussets at hips & knees, wearing antique brown plaid jumper light blue antique blouse w/lace collar, straw bonnet w/silk pleated sun ruffle in back, antique underclothing & socks, no shoes, 13" (ILLUS.) **$550**

Kestner (J.D.) solid dome bisque socket head baby, marked "J.D.K. - made in 12 Germany," blue sleep eyes, feathered brows, open mouth w/accented lips & two lower teeth, Kestner bent-limb baby body, wearing antique white baby dress, slip & diaper, 15" **$375**

Rare 12" Kestner Kewpie

Kestner Kewpie, bisque socket head w/brown set eyes looking to left, single-

stroke brows, closed smiling mouth, ball jointed composition body w/"starfish" hands, finger replaced on right hand, pinkie missing on left, 12" (ILLUS.) **$9,200**

Pretty Bisque Head Lori Baby

Lori Baby bisque head body, attributed to Swaine and Compnay, blue glass sleep eyes, molded open-closed mouth, near mint composition baby body wearing an antique white baby gown, hairline on left side behind ear, head 14" c. (ILLUS.) **$575**

Mary Hoyer Composition Doll

Mary Hoyer Doll Mfg. Company girl, composition, red mohair wig, handmade red knit ski outfit w/skis & poles, slight chip to lip paint, 14" (ILLUS.) **$489**

Morimura Brothers Bisque Head Baby

Morimura Brothers bisque head baby, blue sleep eyes, open mouth w/upper teeth, short light brown wig, voice box in head, composition baby body, wearing newer blue baby dress & lacy bonnet, Japan, ca. 1918, 15" (ILLUS.).................. **$230**

Early French Papier-maché Lady

Papier-maché lady doll, Beidermeier-type, molded head w/inset glass eyes & open mouth w/upper & lower teeth, brown h.h. wig, gusseted kid body, wearing an embossed silk outfit w/matching bonnet, antique brown leather shoes, complete w/a small trunk w/extra dress & other assorted garments & accessories, winner of various show ribbons, France, first half 19th c., 20" (ILLUS.).............................. **$1,955**

Unusual Early Papier-maché Lady Doll

Papier-maché lady, head w/molded hairdo & inset h.h. black curls, wearing wonderfull all-original outfit, most of the shoulder plate missing for many years, straight-legged kid body, wooden feet w/painted shoes, in old box w/history written on it reading "Sent to Lucy Coyt Cleveland cousin to Grover Cleveland - July 1827," 16" (ILLUS.) **$1,725**

Early Glass-eyed Papier-maché Lady

Papier-maché lady doll, molded shoulder head w/set glass pupilless eyes, single stroke brows, closed mouth, molded & painted hair w/long curls to shoulders, cloth body jointed at hips & knees, individually stitched fingers, wearing antique blue & white dress, underclothing, socks, shoes & black lace-trimmed bonnet, Europe, first half 19th c., possible fine repair or touch-up to top of head, large flakes on front bottom of shoulder plate, 19" (ILLUS.).................................... **$715**

Early Papier-maché Milliner Model

Papier-maché milliner model lady, molded head w/black hair pulled back into a bun, painted features, wearing a fine cotton print dress w/green fringe trim, minor paint touch-up on china, some shoulder plate crazing, 13 1/2" (ILLUS.) **$259**

Papier-mâché shoulder head girl, brown painted eyes, dark painted molded hair w/nine long curls falling onto shoulders behind exposed ears, Sarah Robinson 1883 patented fully articulated body, long curved kid arms w/separate fingers, wearing pink sprigged cotton dress, probably America, mid-19th c. (pupils touched in) **$2,703**

Papier-mâché shoulder head milliner's model, unmarked, painted brown eyes, single-stroke brows, closed mouth, molded & painted hair w/long curls on sides, small bun in back w/curls below on neck, exposed ears, kid body w/wooden lower arms & lower legs, painted green shoes, wearing original black & white dress w/bustle, original underclothing, 12 1/2" (few minor strips of paint off legs) **$850**

All-original Parian Head Lady

Parian head lady, molded blonde hair w/center part, blue glass eyes, pink lips & cheeks, cloth body w/parian lower arms & lower legs w/boots, wearing great pink silk dress w/train, 13" (ILLUS.) **$460**

Black Lady Rag Doll

Rag doll, black folk art type lady in sateen w/applied facial features including double button eyes, applied nappy black hair, wearing simple white cotton dress & holding cotton buds, late 19th - early 20th c., 23" (ILLUS.) **$518**

S.F.B.J. #301 Girl Doll

S.F.B.J. (Société Francaise de Fabrication de Bebes et Jouets) bisque socket head girl, marked "S.F.B.J. - 301 - Paris - 7," blue sleep eyes w/real lashes, feathered brows, open mouth w/accented lips & four upper teeth, pierced ears, replaced brown wig, jointed wood & composition body labeled "Bebe Jumeau - Diplome d-Honneur," w/working mama-papa crier, wearing a lace blouse, brown jumper w/velvet ribbon at waist, underclothing made from antique fabric, sockes & antique German shoes, 17 1/2" (ILLUS.) **$495**

Schmidt (Franz) bisque socket head baby, marked "1295 - F.S. & Co. - 60" on back of head, blue sleep eyes w/remnants of real lashes & painted upper & lower lashes, heavy feathered brows, open mouth w/protruding spring tongue, original mohair fabric wig, bent-limb composition baby body wearing antique white baby dress w/lace trim, antique

Franz Schmidt Bisque Socket Head Baby

bonnet, slip, diaper, wool socks & wool felt baby shoes, flaking around arm joints, 23" (ILLUS.) **$475**

Schoenau & Hoffmeister masquerade set in box, marked "4000 5/0 - S PB [in star] H - 10" on head, "F" on backs of legs, "Germany" stamped on bottoms of shoes, bisque socket head w/walking mechanism to legs, set brown eyes, single-stroke brows, open mouth w/four upper teeth, antique mohair wig, five-piece composition body w/walking mechanism, wearing original pastel dress w/pale green ribbon trim, original gauze-type underclothing, socks, leather shoes w/black pompons, doll is tied in red cardboard box w/two lace-trimmed compartments, the other compartment holding blue Pierrot costume trimmed w/black & white ruffled collar, large black buttons, matching cone-shaped hat, black face mask w/lace trim, 13 1/2" **$525**

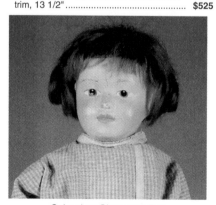

Schoehut Character Boy

Schoenhut character boy, molded head w/painted eyes & pouty mouth, original reddish tosca wig, wearing blue-checked romper suit, replacement shoes & socks, untouched paint, on original wooden body, 13" (ILLUS.)..................................... **$460**

Schoenhut "Tootsie Wootsie" character toddler, illegible partial impressed mark on head, "Schoenhut Doll - Pat. Jan. 17, '11, U.S.A. - & Foreign Countries" impressed on back, wooden socket head w/brown intaglio eyes, feathered brows, open-closed mouth w/two upper teeth & molded tongue, old mohair wig, spring-jointed wooden body w/joints at shoulders, elbows, wrists, hips, knees & ankles, redressed in copy of Schoenhut outfit of two-piece sailor suit, new socks & tie shoes, 15" (repaint on face, wig added, hands repainted) **$1,500**

Schoenhut Pouty Boy in Beige Outfit

Schoenhut wooden socket head boy, marked "Schoenhut Doll - Pat. Jan. 17th 1911 - U.S.A." on oval label on back, painted blue intaglio eyes, closed pouty mouth, original blond mohair wig, wooden body spring-jointed at shoulders, elbows, wrists, hips, knees & ankles, redressed in beige two-piece outfit w/matching hat, new socks & lace-up shoes, some light wear, 21" (ILLUS.)
.... **$880**

Schoenhut wooden socket head boy, marked "H.E. Schoenhut - © - 1913" on round label on head, "Schoenhut Doll - Pat. Jan. 17th 1911 - U.S.A." on oval label on back, painted blue eyes, closed mouth, original mohair wig, wooden body spring-jointed at shoulders, elbows, wrists, hips, knees & ankles, wearing black velvet two-piece boy's suit w/matching hat, antique white shirt, socks & leatherette shoes, 14" (brows missing, original wig cut on right side & in back) **$300**

Simon & Halbig Model 1079 Girl

Simon & Halbig 23 1/2" Girl

Simon & Halbig bisque socket head girl, marked "S & H - 1079 - Germany - DEP - 12," set blue eyes, feathered brows, open mouth w/accented lips & four upper teeth, pierced ears, replaced blonde h.h. wig, jointed wood & composition body, wearing a black taffeta dress w/wide crocheted collar, underclothing made from antique fabric, new socks & old shoes, small flake at right earring hole, 24 1/2" (ILLUS.).. **$440**

Simon & Halbig bisque socket head girl, marked "1039 - Germany - Simon & Halbig - S&H - 10" on head, "R D" on key (for winding walking mechanism) at left hip, blue flirty eyes w/real lashes, feathered brows, open mouth w/four upper teeth, pierced ears, h.h. wig, jointed wood & composition body w/working keywind walking mechanism, wearing lacy satin dress, antique underclothing, high button boots, 19 1/2" (repainted torso has repairs around right arm socket & on back, stockings are glued to front of legs) **$1,050**

Simon & Halbig bisque socket head girl, marked "12 SH 1039 - DEP," light blue sleep eyes, feathered brows, open mouth w/accented lips & four upper teeth, pierced ears, replaced h.h. wig, jointed wood & composition body, wearing antique white dress w/shirred panel, eyelet trim, antique underclothing, new white socks, leatherette shoes, 23 1/2" (ILLUS., top next column) **$850**

Simon & Halbig #739 Lady Bride

Simon & Halbig bisque socket head lady, marked "S 9 H 739 DEP," bisque head on shoulder plate, set brown eyes, feathered brows, open mouth w/six upper teeth, pierced ears, replaced white caracul wig, kid body w/cloth torso, rivet joint at elbows, bisque lower arms, gussets at hips & knees, wearing lovely wedding gown made w/antique fabric, veil, antique underclothing, cotton socks, antique pink cloth shoes, flake at earring hole, tiny flake inside corner left eye, repairs to gussets, 18" (ILLUS.) **$880**

Simon & Halbig Oriental Girl

Simon & Halbig bisque socket head Oriental girl, marked "Simon & Halbig - Germany - 1329 - 8," head w/olive skin tone, brown sleep eyes, molded & feathered brows, open mouth w/accented lips & four upper teeth, pierced ears, replaced black h.h. wig, jointed wood & composition body w/yellowish tone, wearing original Oriental print kimono w/multicolored woven ribbon at waist, white blouse, white flannel shirt, pants, undershirt, antique red socks & tan leather shoes, 21" (ILLUS.)... **$2,310**

Simon & Halbig Oriental Lady Doll

Simon & Halbig Oriental lady, marked "1329 - Germany - Simon & Halbig - S&H -

4" on back of head, bisque socket head w/olive complexion, brown sleep eyes w/real lashes & painted upper & lower lashes, feathered brows, open mouth w/four upper teeth, pierced ears, original black mohair wig in Geisha-type style, jointed wood & composition body w/olive finish, wearing original kimono, underclothing, socks, brown sandals, & original hair decorations, turquoise necklace & earrings, original kimono is very fragile & has been lined to stabilize it, 15" (ILLUS.)............... **$3,100**

Rare Black Simon & Halbig Girl

Simon & Halbig socket head black girl, body marked w/"Le Petit Parisian" label, brown paperweight eyes, feathered brows, open mouth w/four upper teeth, original short black mohair wig, fully jointed brown body w/original finish, wearing antique silk dress w/matching bonnet & white leather shoes, some cracking to finger joints, minor wear, 22" (ILLUS.)....... **$1,680**

Rare Steiner Walking-Crying Girl

Steiner bisque head gigoteur walking girl, blue paperweight eyes, open mouth w/two rows of teeth, original blonde wig, wearing a creamy silk dress w/pleats, ribbons & layers of lace, original underwear, French-style socks, tan leather shoes w/buckles, 20" (ILLUS.)......................... **$2,300**

Vogue Ginny in Original Clown Outfit

Vogue "Ginny," hard plastic, painted blue eyes, closed mouth, original blonde mohair wig, five-piece hard plastic body, wearing original tagged red & white taffeta clown suit w/matching hat, gathered tulle collar, original red & white oilcloth shoes, unplayed-with, 7 1/2" (ILLUS.)....... **$303**

Norah Wellings Boy Doll

Wellings (Norah) boy, molded cloth, the head w/painted blue eyes & red lips, short blond wig, wearing original velvet outfit w/tam-type cap & blue leather shoes, slip chip under chin, England, early 20th c., 20" (ILLUS.) **$805**

WPA Czechoslovakian man & woman, each w/hand-modeled shoulder head w/painted features, well-modeled ears, molded & painted hair, cloth bodies, stitched fingers & separate thumbs, the woman wearing a white peasant blouse w/embroidery at the neck & sleeves, lace trim at neck & end of sleeves, a multi-colored silk brocade vest w/red ribbon edg-

WPA-made Czech Man & Woman Dolls

ing, red flower print skirt w/multi-colored ribbon trim, four panels of embroidered linen w/crocheted lace trim, two slips, pants, leather boots & red embroidered hat, the man wearing a white linen shirt w/embroidered trim at neck, front panel, shoulders & cuffs, black vest w/embroidery & button trim, black wool pants w/blue decorative panels in front, black leather boots & black felt cap w/red tassels, both w/a nose repair, on wooden stands w/labels, 1930s, 15 1/2 & 17", pr. (ILLUS.)... **$358**

DOORSTOPS

Bathing Girls, two stylized long-legged 1920s Flappers seated side by side under a small umbrella, marked w/the name of the artist, "Fish," Hubley, 1920s, some wear to original paint, 11" h...................... **$690**

Dog, German Shepherd, full-bodied, looking straight ahead, original paint, 9 3/4" h. (some paint flaking) **$230**

Cast-iron Terrier with Old Red Paint

Dog, terrier, full-bodied, standing w/head turned to side & short tail erect, original worn overall red paint, early 20th c., 8 1/2" h. (ILLUS., previous page) **$127**

Owl, tall perched bird, original paint, mold No. 7797, Bradley & Hubbard, 16" h. **$1,898**

Fine Spanish Girl Doorstop

Spanish Girl (Flamenco Dancer), round base, dancer w/a swirling bright red dress w/a black & yellow bodice, holding an open yellow & black fan, a tall comb in her black hair, marked "WS," original paint w/some rust spots, 9 3/4" h. (ILLUS.) **$575**

Squirrel, figure of bushy-tailed squirrel sitting on a log & holding nut to mouth w/front paws, attributed to Hubley, old black repaint, 11 1/4" h. **$413**

Stag, recumbent animal w/one front leg raised, head facing viewer, on oblong base, old dry black repaint, 8" l., 9" h. **$440**

Top, redware, hollow, in the form of an upside down top, w/original red & white paint & dark gold stripes, wear & edge chips, 6 1/2" d., 6" h. **$358**

DRUGSTORE & PHARMACY ITEMS

The old-time corner drugstore, once a familiar part of every American town, has now given way to a modern, efficient pharmacy. With the streamlining and modernization of this trade, many of the early tools and store adjuncts have been outdated and now fall in the realm of "collectibles." Listed here are some of the tools, bottles, display pieces and other ephemera once closely associated with the druggist's trade.

Three Early Blown Apothecary Bottles

Apothecary bottles w/stoppers, free-blown spherical amethyst glass w/a tall neck & ball stopper, ground base pontil, each w/a painted gold band decorated in black w/the contents, labels read "Liq. Calc. Chl.," "Ess. Zingh" & "Tr. Chiratae," Europe, late 18th - early 19th c., some minor loss to labels, 9 1/2" d., 15 1/2" h., set of 3 (ILLUS.) **$1,800**

Art Deco-Style Apothecary Show Globe

Apothecary show globe w/original stopper, hanging-type, Art Deco style, a large clear glass teardrop-shaped globe w/a stepped shoulder, short cylindrical neck & tall oblong stopper, suspended in a three-arm ribbed cast-aluminum frame hung from chains, designed to hold colored water in a drugstore window, made by Owens-Illinois Co., ca. 1930s, globe 18" h. (ILLUS.) **$360**

Rare Pair of Early Blown Show Globes

Apothecary show globes w/original stoppers, hanging-type, each a large long mold-blown pointed teardrop form w/a spiraled rib design & tall flared neck suspended from a fancy cast-iron crown ring & chains, one in dark green & the other in dark red, 19th c., globe 22" h., pr. (ILLUS.) **$2,300**

Apothecary show jars w/original stoppers, clear blown glass, a round disk foot supporting a short stem below the very wide ovoid body tapering to a tall slender ringed neck w/a flared rim, the neck fitted

EPERGNES

One of a Pair of Rare Show Jars

w/a matching much smaller jar attached to the stopper & completed w/original hollow blown & knopped stopper, late 19th - early 20th c., some interior residue, overall 36 1/2" h., pr. (ILLUS. of one)............ **$2,185**

Rare Early Western Drugstore Bottle

Drugstore bottle, embossed "Geo. P. Morrill - Apothecary - Virginia City," cylindrical w/short cylindrical neck & applied top, deep bluish green aqua, Virginia City, Nevada, late 19th c., 7" h. (ILLUS.) **$3,300**

Epergnes were popular as centerpieces on tables of the 19th century. Many have receptacles of colored glass for holding sweetmeats, fruit or flowers. Early epergnes were made entirely of metal, including silver.

Cranberry glass, four lily, a very tall slender & gently flaring central lily w/a wide flared & ruffled top & a spiral of applied clear rigaree near the top, flanked by three matching much shorter lilies alternating w/three tall upright curled clear ropetwist canes each suspending a matching cranberry basket, all above the wide shallow crimped cranberry bowl base, ca. 1900, some arms reset, 20" h. (ILLUS. right with two other cranberry epergnes) **$978**

Cranberry glass, four lily, a very tall slender & gently flaring central lily w/a wide flared & ruffled top applied w/a clear pointed rim band & a spiral of applied clear rigaree near the top, flanked by three matching much shorter lilies alternating w/three tall upright curled clear ropetwist canes each suspending a clear basket, all above the wide shallow crimped cranberry bowl base w/an applied clear rigaree rim, ca. 1900, 23" h. (ILLUS. center with two other cranberry epergnes) **$1,265**

Cranberry glass, three lily, a very tall slender & gently flaring central lily w/a wide flared & ruffled top & a spiral of applied clear rigaree near the top, flanked by two matching much shorter lilies alternating w/tall upright curled clear ropetwist canes each suspending a matching cranberry basket, all above the wide shallow crimped cranberry bowl base, ca. 1900, 21" h. (ILLUS. left with two other cranberry epergnes, top next page) **$748**

Fancy English Silver Plate & Cut Glass Epergne

Cut glass & silver plate, an ornate silver plate stand w/a three-legged scroll-cast domed base below a grape cluster-trimmed knob issuing four long slender reeded serpentine arms each ending in a small platform supported on four in-

Three Fancy Victorian Cranberry Glass Epergnes

curved open leaf-cast bands & fitted w/a small shallow scalloped cut glass dish, the center knob topped by a tall paneled trumpet-form column decorated w/overall delicate engraved scrolls & cast grape & scroll around the rim, topped by a large shallow scalloped cut glass bowl, a crossed arrow mark under the base, bowls replaced, England, late 19th c., 26" w., 23" h. (ILLUS.)............................ **$2,530**

English Neo-Classical Epergne

Cut glass & silver plate, Neo-Classical Revival style, a trefoil base fitted w/cast figures of hippocampi surrounding a central fluted columnar stem supporting a large frame w/a large cut glass bowl at the top center & three upswept pierced scroll arms each supporting a matching smaller

cut glass bowl, decorated w/beading, shells, scrolls, rosettes & cast rams' heads, England, registration mark for 1861, 14 1/2" w., 21 3/4" h. (ILLUS.)...... **$1,438**

Green Opalescent Epergne with Baskets

Green opalescent glass, three lily, a very tall slender & gently flaring center lily shading from pale green to dark opalescent green at the flaring ruffled rim, the sides w/an applied spiral band of clear rigaree, surrounded by two matching shorter lilies alternating w/two tall clear ropetwist canes each suspending a matching green opalescent basket, all above the matching wide shallow ruffled bowl base, ca. 1900, 23" h. (ILLUS.) **$1,265**

Pale yellow opalescent glass, six lily, a domed optic ribbed round foot below a knob w/holes supporting six matching up-turned flaring lily-form vases centered by a tall central trumpet-form vase, probably England, late 19th c., 10" d., 16 3/4" h... **$2,185**

Webb Satin Glass Four-Lily Epergne

Satin glass, four lily, cranberry mother-of-pearl satin in the Diamond Quilted patt., consisting of a clear squared glass block base issuing a tall center stem support-ing a wide squatty bulbous satin bowl-form lily w/a crimped mouth, three frost-ed arms supporting smaller matching satin vases w/applied front pointed drop finials alternating w/three clear arched rigaree leaves, all resting on a round mirror plateau, attributed to Thomas Webb & Son, England, late 19th c., 10" h. (ILLUS.) **$1,840**

Exceptional 18th Century English Sterling Silver Epergne

Sterling silver, basket-style, the frame sup-ported on three openwork foliate feet & clad w/laurel & berry garlands, support-ing six leaf-clad scroll branches w/round baskets pierced w/pales amid drapery & flowerheads, the central shaped circular large basket similarly decorated, marks of Orlando Jackson, London, England, 1772, 19" w., 16 1/4" h. (ILLUS.).......... **$14,340**

EYEWEAR

For many years eyewear was regarded as a necessary evil, with the emphasis on serviceability rather than style. By the mid-twentieth century, however, consumers were in the mood for some-thing more flattering. In 1930, eyeglasses made their debut in a major New York fashion show and 1939 swa the arrival of the "Harlequin" frame. This Altina Sanders creation, predecessor of the upswept "cat-eyes" of the 1950s, was the recipient of an America Design award.

Then, following World War II, cellulose acetate emerged as an inexpensive, workable frame com-ponent, leading to the 1948 introduction of the first molded frames. Finally, eyeglass designers could let their imaginations run wild.

Eyewear advertising soon focused on the appeal of glasses as a desirable fashion accessory. Different eye fashions were now specifically geared for work, for play, for dress and for every-thing in between. Bausch & Lomb ran an entire campaign based on the premise that "one pair of glasses is not enough," and 1954s "Miss Beauty in Glasses" declared "modern frames for various occasions are as much a part of fashion today as shoes, hats, or jewelry."

Short-lived eyeglass innovations included "radio glasses," which came with a built-in tran-sistor radio; "headband glasses," "earring glasses," "eyelash glasses," --- enven "awning glasses" equipped with mini-shades to ward off raindrops.

Achieving a longer lifespan was the "cat-eye." Although its swooping brow edges were almost uniformly unflattering, the style remains firmly identified with the 1950s. Variations included the "double cat-eye," the "trimple cat-eye" and even vesions with yellow, blue or green lenses.

Also popular were "highbrows," among the most imaginative (and most expensive) of eyewear designs. Liberally dotted with rhinestones, pearls and other decorative accents, highbrows came in a variety of fanciful shapes. some were built up like sparkling tiaras, others took on the form and patterning of colorful butterflies or had brow edges reminiscent of soaring bird wings.

Vintage eyeglass frames continue to grow in popularity. Their revival began as far back as the late 1960s when "The Outasight Co." capitalized on the Hippie look by marketing round metal frames from the late 19th century as "the orignial granny glasses." More recently, those with an eye for recycled fashion acquire period framed, than have the original lenses replace with a new pre-scription or restylzed as sun glasses. Today, eye-wear of the 1950s and '60s continues to make an extravagant fashion statement all its own.

A comprehensive overview of collectible eye-wear is included in Specs Appeal: Extravagant 1950s & 1960s Eyewear by Leslie Pina and Donald-Brian Johnson (Schiffer Publishing Ltd., 2001). Photos for this category are by Dr. Pina with text by Mr. Johnson.

Frames, "Hands" design, black w/jeweled fingernails.. **$400-425**

Frames, "Highbrow" style w/black & rhinestone plumes on clear plastic, by Frame France... **$600-650**

Frames, Lumar w/clear stripe design....... **$90-105**

Frames "Mona Lisa" style looped brow design in cream w/silver studs, made in France... **$275-300**

Frames, "Wraparound" style, rhinestone-covered **$550-600**

Glasses, "Anglo American for Sir Winston," red w/triple bow shape, by Frame England **$375-400**

Fancy Black & Gold Mesh-framed Glasses

Glasses, black & gold mesh frames w/pearl & blue rhinestone brow clusters (ILLUS.) **$120-140**

Glasses, "Cat-eyes" frames in light blue w/clear cutaways & rhinestone trim........ **$70-80**

Dr. Scholl's Health Glasses

Glasses, "Dr. Scholl's Health Glasses," amber frames w/black lens w/an overall dotted design (ILLUS.) **$25-35**

Yellow "Earring Chains" Glasses

Glasses, "Earring Chains" design, yellow frames also found in a black & white check, 1960s (ILLUS.)........................ **$120-160**

Glasses, "Eyelash Glasses" design, fringed brow **$350-375**

Tura Gold Floral Vines Framed Glasses

Glasses, gold frames w/floral vines at temples, by Tura (ILLUS.)........................ **$275-325**

Glasses, 'granny glasses,' gold metal frames w/a blue & pearl cloisonné border, by Christian Dior **$150-200**

Glasses, "Headband" design, tortoiseshell frames **$250-275**

Glasses, "Highbrow" style, antennae-shaped frames w/Aurora Borealis rhinestone decoration, France **$375-400**

Highbrow Feathered Black Glasses

Glasses, "Highbrow" style, feather-shaped in black w/rhinestone decoration (ILLUS.) **$275-300**

Glasses, "Highbrow" style, 'Monarch Butterfly' design frames in black w/gold stripes & multi-colored rhinestones ... **$500-550**

Glasses, loop browed frames, Raphael, Paris, France, 1930s......................... **$140-160**

Glasses, May "Bandoleers," leather thong temples on the frames **$50-60**

Glasses, young girl's size, "Miss Terry Red" design in pink & red **$30-40**

Glasses & bracelet set, by Stendahl, the set **$150-200**

Glasses stand, Lucite, back-carved w/a floral design **$15-20**

Black Rhinestone-trimmed Lorgnette

Lorgnette, black frames w/rhinestone decoration (ILLUS., previous page) **$70-80**

"Anne Marie" Rhinestone Sun Glasses

Sunglasses, "Anne Marie," rhinestone unibrow design, made in France (ILLUS.)
.... **$110-120**

Golden Framed Schiaparelli Sunglasses

Sunglasses, clear yellowish gold framed mounted at the corners w/fruit clusters, Schiaparelli (ILLUS.) **$230-250**
Sunglasses, "Radio" style frames, by Spectra **$50-60**

FABERGÉ

The creations of Carl Fabergé (1846-1920), goldsmith and jeweler to the Russian Imperial Court, are recognized as the finest of their kind. He made a number of enamel fantasies, including Easter eggs, for the Imperial family and utilized precious metals and jewels in other work.

Fabergé Ashtray & Cigarette Case

Ashtray, silver & silver-gilt, square w/rounded corners & a thin acanthus leaf border, the silver-gilt center enclosing a silver coin depicting the profile of Empress Catherine II, on four tiny ball feet, marked under the base by the workmaster Julius Rappoport, St. Petersburg, Russia, 1899-1908, in original fitted case stamped w/Fabergé logo, 2 5/16" w. (ILLUS. top with cigarette case) **$8,365**

Small Fabergé Lapis Lazuli Box

Box, cov., jeweled gold lapis lazuli & enamel, long octagonal shape w/a hinged, flat cover, the lapis lazuli body set w/a gold ribbon-tied laurel leaf mount within white opaque enamel panels, a rose-cut diamond thumbpiece, marked inside w/the Fabergé mark & that of Workmaster Henrik Wigstrom, St. Petersburg, Russia, 1908-17, 2 1/8" l. (ILLUS.) **$77,675**

Small Fabergé Silver & Enamel Box

Box, cov., silver & enamel, the squatty round silver body adorned w/floral sprigs, the flat hinged cover enameled in translucent mint green over a sunburst ground & centered by a cabochon ruby surrounded by silver openwork laurel garlands within a hexagonal design, the edge of the cover w/beading, base marked w/the Fabergé mark in Cyrillic, the Imperial Warrant & a partial scratched inventory number, Moscow, Russia, 1899-1908, 84 standard silver, 2 1/2" d. (ILLUS.) **$5,750**

Two Fabergé Gold Charka

Charka (footed cup), gem-set gold, of campana form, raised on a spreading squared chased & engraved acanthus leaf foot, the lower body gadrooned, the upper body w/repoussé stylized arrowhead design & complex scroll rim, a coiled serpent handle w/an emerald-set head, fully marked, Workmaster Alfred Thielemann, St. Petersburg, Russia, ca. 1890, 2" h. (ILLUS. left with other charka, top of page) **$14,350**

Charka (footed cup), three-color gold, the body of compressed amphora form, the integral stand raised on four hoof feet, the body w/four chased & engraved ram's heads, suspending two-color gold ribbon-tied laurel swags, a cylindrical reeded rim & figural harpy handle, the interior of darker colored gold, marked on the rim, Workmaster Alfred Thielemann, St. Petersburg, Russia, ca. 1890, 2 1/4" h. (ILLUS. right with other charka, top of page) **$14,340**

nassiev, St. Petersburg, Russia, 1898-1903, 2" d. (ILLUS.) **$17,925**

Cigarette case, jeweled two-color gold, thin rectangular form w/rounded corners, overall engraved w/a reeded design, a cabochon sapphire thumbpiece, marked inside w/the mark of the workmaster Albert Holtrom, St. Petersburg, Russia, 1908-17, 3 5/8" l. (ILLUS. bottom with ashtray, previous page) **$7,140**

Fine Fabergé Enameled Frame

Frame, silver-gilt & guilloché enameled wood, the rectangular acanthus leaf rim enclosing a reeded ribbon-tied circular bezel, mounted on a panel of translucent green enamel over a moiré ground, set in the lower part w/a ribbon-tied wreath & swags, mounted on a wood panel w/a wooden back strut, marked on the rim, Workmaster Anders Nevalainen, St. Petersburg, Russia, 1908-17, 6 3/4" h. (ILLUS.) **$31,070**

Small Guilloché Enamel Cigar Cutter

Cigar cutter, jeweled two-color gold silvergilt & guilloché enamel, short circular form w/a flat top, decorated overall w/translucent purple enamel over the guilloché sunburst ground, the rim w/a two-color gold laurel leaf band, the round blade opening in the center top w/a gold-mounted cabochon moonstone stopper, on a gold raised base, marked under base, Workmaster Fedor Afa-

Rare Fabergé Silver Model of a Lizard

Fabergé Miniature Triptych Icon

Fabergé Nephrite & Silver Pencil Holder

FIRE FIGHTING COLLECTIBLES

American fire fighting "antiques" are considered those items over 100 years old that were directly related to fire fighting, whereas fire fighting "collectibles" are items less than a century old. Pieces from both eras are very sought-after today.

Foreign-made fire fighting antiques and collectibles have a marketplace of their own and, for the most part, are not as expensive and in demand as similar American pieces.

Icon, miniature triptych-style, silver, flattened arched case w/two hinged doors, decorated overall w/Pan-Slavic scrolls & geometric designs, the center painted w/a miniature icon of Kazan Mother of God, in original fitted case w/removable stand w/stamped Fabergé marks, Moscow, 1908-17, 2 3/8" h. (ILLUS.) **$8,365**

Model of lizard, silver, realistically modeled in an alert pose w/head raised, the head hinged, the mouth forms as a tapermount, marked under tail, Moscow, ca. 1890, 7 1/8" l. (ILLUS., top of page) **$59,750**

Pencil holder, silver-mounted nephrite, tall slightly swelled upright nephrite body on a raised silver base w/acanthus leaf rim within beaded borders engraved in Russian "Proletarians of all countries unite," the top w/a similar silver acanthus rim, marked on rim & under base, Workmaster Julius Rappoport, St. Petersburg, Russia, 1896-1908, 5 1/8" h. (ILLUS., top next column) **$10,755**

Rare American Decorated Fire Bucket

1930 Seagrave Model 6DT Fire Engine

Fire bucket, painted leather, slightly flaring cylindrical form, deep red rim & base bands, the main body in old dark green paint w/yellow dashes & large ovals enclosing black wording "August B - Tappan No. 2 - 1827," replaced black leather handle, 8" d., without handle 12" h. (ILLUS., previous page) **$2,185**

Fire engine, 1930 Seagrave Model 6DT, nearly complete w/original red & gold paint & hoses but no ladders, marked in gold "Brunswick Fire Department Engine No. 2," odometer reads 6,737 miles, unrestored (ILLUS., top of page) **$6,268**

Fire horn, silver plated, presentation-type, the trumpet-form body engraved overall w/a floral motif, the hose nozzle, spiked sticks & two engraved panels reading "Geo. ..Becker 2nd Asst. Chief Presented by Phoenix Hose No. 5 1909," misshapen rim, silver plate wear, early 20th c., 19 1/4" l. (ILLUS., next column) **$518**

Silver Plate Presentation Fire Horn

FIREARMS

Gallager Civil War Percussion Carbine

Carbine, Gallager Civil War standard percussion model, .54 cal., pinched front sight & two-position flip rear sight, straight grip walnut stock w/smooth steel carbine buttplate, sling bar & ring on lieft side of wrist, patchbox containing a spare nipple on right side of butt, round 22 1/2" l. round barrel (ILLUS.) **$2,415**

Maynard Second Model Civil War Carbine

Sharps & Hankins Saddle Ring Carbine

Spencer Model 1865 Carbine

Carbine, Maynard Second Model Civil War percussion model, martially-marked, .50 cal., pinched front sight, two-leaf three-position rear sight, stock without patch-box, date 1865, barrel w/90% bluing, buttstock w/several small crude scratched drawings, octagonal to round 20" barrel (ILLUS., bottom of previous page) **$2,645**

Carbine, Sharps & Hankins saddle ring model, .52 cal., missing sights, the lever catch & a chunk of the stock, also missing sling swivel on stock, main spring broken, round barrel 19" l. (ILLUS., top of page) **$690**

Carbine, Spencer Model 1865 model, .50 cal., "ESA" cartouche on left side of stock behind sling ring bar, traces of finish, round barrel 20" l. (ILLUS., second from top) **$2,128**

Carbine, Starr Civil War percussion model, .54 cal., unusual configuration w/a stepped round barrel w/blade front side & two-position flip rear sight, small forearm w/straight stock & semi-crescent carbine brass buttplate, usual markings on lock-plate & top tang, no original finish, barrel 20 3/4" l. (ILLUS., first below) **$2,013**

Musket, Colt Special Model 1861, .58 cal., dated 1863 on lockplate, overall rust brown patina, w/bayonet w/broken locking ring, partially octagonal barrel 40" l. (ILLUS., middle below)........................... **$1,323**

Musket, Harpers Ferry Model 1842, .69 cal., barrel dated 1852, faint inspector mark, overall grey patina, w/bayonet, barrel 42" l. (ILLUS., bottom of page) **$978**

Starr Civil War Percussion Carbine

Colt Special Model 1861 Musket with Bayonet

Harpers Ferry Model 1842 Musket

Mason Model 1863 Musket

Ohio Surcharge German Model Musket

Musket, Mason Model 1863, .58 cal., barrel dated 1863 on the lock, nipple welded into place, rear side & swing swivels missing, ramrod & bayonet replacements, moderate to heavy pitting, stock repaired, barrel 48" l. (ILLUS., top of page) **$633**

Musket, Ohio surcharage German model, .74 cal., barrel dated 1831, lockplate engraved "Saarn." & "OHIO" stamped at the wrist & left side of stock, correct 18 3/4" l. bayonet, rear sling swivel missing, rust brown patina on barrel, bayonet rusted, partially octagonal barrel 41 1/4" l. (ILLUS., second from top) **$1,158**

Colt Model 1849 Pocket Revolver

Revolver, Colt Model 1849 pocket type, .31 cal., one-piece walnut grip, octagonal barrel w/two-line New York address marking, small brass front sight, silver plated trigger guard & back strap, fine condition, Serial No. 24484, barrel 4" l. (ILLUS.) **$1,035**

Rare & Early Colt Model 1860 Army Model Revolver

Revolver, Colt Model 1860 Army model, .44 cal., rare early Army model w/Navy frame, round barrel, rebated cylinder w/"Colt's Patent" on left side of frame, brass trigger guard & back strap w/the left flat of the trigger guard stamped "36 CAL," Navy-sized one-piece walnut

grips, no original finish, one of frame pins missing, barrel 7 1/2" l. (ILLUS.) **$5,175**

Colt Model 1878 Revolver

Revolver, Colt Model 1878 DA model, .45 cal., blued finish w/7 1/2" l. barrel, attached ejector rod, black hard rubber grips & a lanyard loop in the butt, refinished, 90 percent of old reblue, right grip w/large chip in heel, Serial No. 11734 (ILLUS.) **$633**

Colt Single-action Revolver

Revolver, Colt single-action, handle w/applied bone plaques, one side carved w/a steer head, produced in 1891, 10 1/8" l. (ILLUS.) **$1,725**

Remington Beals Army Revolver

Revolver, Remington Beals Army model, .44 cal., standard Beals Army w/octagonal barrel, dovetailed cone German silver front sight w/two-piece walnut grips, usual markings on top of barrel, brass trigger guard, one of only 1900 produced, worn but legible markings, replaced rammer screw, missing large chip from right side, barrel 8" l. (ILLUS.) **$2,128**

volver, cylindrical pin stamped "24," barrel 8" l. (ILLUS.) **$1,265**

Remington New Model Army Revolver

Revolver, Remington New Model Army, .44 cal., martially marked w/blue finish, two-piece walnut grips, outline of a cartouche on the left grip & small inspector initials on various parts, overall good condition, brass trigger guard w/inspector initial from a smaller frame Navy re-

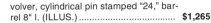

Rogers & Spencer Percussion Revolver

Revolver, Rogers & Spencer percussion model, .44 cal., octagonal barrel, cone front sight, reproduction two-piece walnut grips, small "B" inspector mark on various parts, Serial No. 2738, barrel 7 1/2" l. (ILLUS.) **$1,093**

Frank Wesson Tip-up Model Rifle

Rifle, Frank Wesson tip-up model, .38RF cal., tang sight missing, barrel sights replacements, oil-stained stock, octagonal barrel 24" l. (ILLUS.) **$460**

Maynard Model 1873 Improved Hunters No. 8 Rifle

Rifle, Maynard Model 1873 Improved Hunters No. 8 single-shot model, .35-30 cal., blued finish, pinched front sights w/two position V-notch rear sight, straight stock w/carbine-type smooth steel buttplate, octagonal to round 26" barrel (ILLUS.) **$1,035**

Remington Rolling-Block Military Rifle

Rifle, Remington rolling-block military model, .50/70 cal., standard markings on upper tang, action w/the New York safety but no markings, bayonet & ramrod replaced, round barrel 36" l. (ILLUS.) **$518**

Ribbons, Kendall & Lawrence Model 1842 Mississippi Rifle

Springfield Model 1855 Cadet Rifle

Rifle, Robbins, Kendall & Lawrence Model 1842 Mississippi, .54 cal. dated 1847 on the lockplate, "WAT" cartouche on left side of stock, spare nipple in patchbox, overall greyish brown patina, round barrel 33" l. (ILLUS., bottom previous page) **$1,955**

Rifle, Springfield Model 1855 Cadet model, .60 bored out cal., barrel & lock dated 1869, overall grey patina, ramrod a short replacement, stock including forearm tip 49 1/2" l. (ILLUS., top of page)............... **$1,438**

FIREPLACE & HEARTH ITEMS

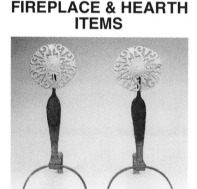

Early Andirons with Brass Medallions

Andirons, brass & wrought iron, iron base w/arched front legs ending in penny feet, supporting a flattened swelled gooseneck upright w/a large pierced brass flower & scroll medallion, late 18th - early 19th c., possibly Europe, 17" l., 21" h., pr. (ILLUS.)... **$1,093**

Unusual Flower-decorated Andirons

Andirons, cast iron, arched front legs w/penny feet support w/slender central post topped by a large flaring cut-out spray of flowers & leaves w/colorful paint, early 20th c., 16" l., 19 1/2" h., pr. (ILLUS.) **$288**

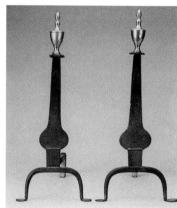

Iron & Brass Federal Andirons

Andirons, iron & brass, Federal style, a tall turned brass urn-shaped finial above a flattened iron steel blade upright rounded near the base where it joins the arched front legs w/penny feet, found in Maine, early 19th c., 23 1/2" h., pr. (ILLUS.)...... **$1,035**

Rare Miniature Federal Andirons

Andirons, miniature, brass, Federal style w/a bold ring-turned & tapering front post raised on openwork almond-shaped legs joined by a matching stretcher, wrought iron log bar, 6 1/2" l., 7 3/4" h., pr. (ILLUS.) **$1,093**

Early Federal Era Fireplace Fender

Unusual Dog-form Iron Andirons

Andirons, wrought iron, modeled as stylized stick-form dogs, arched rear legs w/penny feet, straight log bar to straight splayed front legs w/penny feet, front top angled log stop mounted w/a flat stylized dog head, some rust, probably 19th c., 7" w., 15 1/2" l., pr. (ILLUS.)...................... **$460**

Unusual Wrought-iron Bird Spit

Bird spit, wrought iron, three flattened arched legs w/penny feet supporting a very tall upright rod fitted w/a spring-adjusted oval rack w/four two-prong spike, early, 25 1/2" h. (ILLUS.)....................... **$1,150**

Fireplace fender, Federal style, brass & wire, long half-round brass top rail fitted w/three bulbous turned brass finials above the iron bar & wire screen w/scrolled wire trim, some bends & missing wire, early 19th c., 37" l., 13" h. (ILLUS., top of page) **$805**

Unusual Early Brass Fireplace Reflector

Fireplace reflector, hand-wrought brass & iron, a large half-round shield form w/an arched band of buttons around the high domed répoussé center decorated w/stylized shell & leafy scroll designs, a wide bottom band w/raised bottons, all raised on three twisted iron legs joined by a bowed lower stretcher base & ending in slender scrolled feet, dark toning & some surface rust, probably 18th c., 21" w., 24" h. (ILLUS.) **$345**

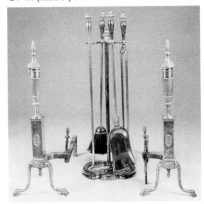

Unusual Federal-Style Fireplace Set

Fireplace tool set: consisting of a pair of urn-top andirons w/matching log stops supported on cabriole front legs w/hoof feet, a similar tool rack w/an L-shaped poker, broom, shovel & tongs & a folding wire fire screen; Federal-Style, all in silver plate, the screen w/a tag reading "Wm. H. Jackson Company, New York," late 19th - early 20th c., one screen finial missing, minor silver loss, andirons 24" h., the set (ILLUS.).............................. **$920**

Unusual Early Iron Fireplace Trivet

Fireplace trivet, wrought iron, rectangular form w/long flat side bars raised on scroll-tipped legs, eight crossbars, the back w/a curved upright strap handles w/heart-shaped top w/a hanging hole, early, 9 x 13" (ILLUS.)... **$201**

FOXY GRANDPA COLLECTIBLES

Foxy Grandpa first appeared in a comic strip in the New York Herald newspaper in the early 20th century. Drawn by Carl E. Schultze, who often used the pen name "Bunny," this foxy comic character often looked a bit like a clown. The comic strip ran for sixteen years in several newspapers. Merchandise representing this early comic character is treasured today for its age and rarity.

Advertising sheet, cut-out style for a grocery store promotion, 1903 .... **$60**
Book, "Adventures of Foxy Grandpa," published by Stokes, 1903................................. **$86**
Book, "Foxy Grandpa - Child's Paint Book," Donohue & Co., 1914................................. **$18**

1905 "Foxy Grandpa Flip-Flaps" Book

Book, "Foxy Grandpa Flip-Flaps" by Bunny, color cover w/Foxy Grandpa doing a hand-stand, by Donohue & Co., 1905 (ILLUS.) **$80**

Book, "Foxy Grandpa - Fun on the Farm," 1908 .... **$71**
Book, "Foxy Grandpa Plays Santa Claus,," 1908 .... **$45**
Book, "Foxy Grandpa's Frolics," 1906 .... **$50**
Book, "Foxy Grandpa's Mother Goose," 1910 .... **$35**
Book, "Foxy Grandpa's Triumphs," by Bunny, comic book w/hard covers.................. **$167**
Book, "Foxy Grandpa's Up-To-Date Book," Hearst Publishing, 1903............................. **$60**
Book, "The Latest Adventures of Foxy Grandpa," 1905... **$75**
Book, "The Latest Larks of Foxy Grandpa," early 1905 .... **$65**
Book, "The Merry Pranks of Foxy Grandpa" **$55**
Candy container, papier-maché, Foxy Grandpa seated on a chick **$225**
Candy container, papier-maché, Foxy Grandpa seated on an Easter egg........... **$125**
Candy container, papier-maché, model of Foxy Grandpa riding a pig...................... **$1,570**
Card game, complete w/40 cards, mint in the box, early 1900s................................. **$78**
Christmas card, scene of Foxy Grandpa, signed by Bunny, 1924 .... **$22**
Christmas tree ornament, feather tree figure of Foxy Grandpa w/annealed legs, Germany **$101**

Early Foxy Grandpa Cigarette Papers Wrapper

Cigarette papers wrapper, "Foxy Grandpa - A pack of pleasure for Pipe or Cigarette - A Good Smoke," printed in red & black & illustrating a packet of Foxy Grandpa Tobacco, Roth Tobacco Co. (ILLUS.)......... **$30**

Foxy Grandpa Head Container

Container, papier-maché head of Foxy Grandpa in color, no markings (ILLUS.) **$50**
Doll, carved wood rather grotesque figure of Foxy Grandpa, by Schoenhut **$2,550**

Early Foxy Grandpa Clapper Doll

Early Printed Cloth Foxy Grandpa Doll

Doll, clapper-type, Foxy Grandpa w/a papier-maché head, wooden feet & hands holding cymbals, wearing rough cloth shirt & pants (ILLUS.) **$225**

Doll, crudely made figure of Foxy Grandpa, dressed, early 20th c. **$27**

Doll, Foxy Grandpa w/a papier-maché head on a straw-stuffed cloth body w/papier-maché arms & lower legs, 12" h. **$99**

Close-up of Early Foxy Grandpa Doll

Miss Muffet & Foxy Grandpa Hanky

Doll, Foxy Grandpa w/composition head & limbs, in original clothes, 17" l. (ILLUS. of head) **$511**

Doll, stuffed printed cloth, 18" h. (ILLUS., top next column) **$195**

Dolls, composition, Foxy Grandpa & the Boys, boys 8 1/2" h., Grandpa 12" h., the group **$4,312**

Drawing, original pen & ink picture of Foxy Grandpa on scrap paper, signed "Bunny" ... **$45**

Figure, handmade composition Foxy Grandpa dressed in cloth clothing, 6 1/2" h. **$40**

Figure, hollow bisque figure of Foxy Grandpa, painted trim, early 20th c., 5" h. **$125**

Figure, jointed all-composition, Foxy Grandpa, painted trim, 4 1/2" h. **$100**

Handkerchief, square, printed cloth w/a poem about Little Miss Muffet & Foxy Grandpa, color scene of Foxy Grandpa driving fast past Miss Muffet & running over the spider (ILLUS.) **$62**

Newspaper comics, single-page, from the New York Herald, March 10, 1901 .... **$35**

Newspaper comics, single-page, from the New York Herald, March 24, 1901 .... **$53**

Newspaper supplement, Christmas 1901 color cover scene of Foxy Grandpa, Los Angeles Herald **$45**

Newspaper supplement, Foxy Grandpa & bobsled, uncut, dated January 11, 1903 .... **$54**

Nodder figure, Foxy Grandpa by Kenton Hardware, 10 1/2" h. **$950**

Early Foxy Grandpa Nodder Figure

Nodder figure, Foxy Grandpa w/an oversized nodding head w/rabbit fur side-
burns, 1915, 8 1/2" h. (ILLUS.) **$50**

Early Foxy Grandpa Pinback Button

Pinback button, celluloid, color bust portrait of Foxy Grandpa & the boys, 1901
(ILLUS.) **$27**
Pipe, clay, featuring Foxy Grandpa & the
boys, Germany, 6" l. **$85**
Pitcher, china, color picture of Foxy Grand-
pa printed on the side................................. **$25**

Early Foxy Grandpa Easter Postcard

Postcard, "Easter Greetings to All," embossed color scene of Foxy Grandpa
opening a large box full of baby chicks,
dated 1908 (ILLUS.).................................... **$10**
Postcard, heat-transfer design of Foxy
Grandpa, reads "Hello Boy," 1906 .... **$15**
Poster, full-color newspaper, 1902,
15 x 20".. **$250**
Rubby stamp set, different character on
each, early 20th c., boxed set **$80**

Foxy Grandpa 1902 Sheet Music

Sheet music, "The Submarine Boat," color
cover of Foxy Grandpa seated on the
edge of a rowboat at dock w/two boys beside him, 1902 newspaper supplement
(ILLUS.)... **$39**

Early Foxy Grandpa Still Bank

Still bank, cast iron, standing figure of Foxy
Grandpa w/his hands on his hips, original
paint (ILLUS.) **$130**
Toy, molded papier-maché roly-poly figure
of Foxy Grandpa, by Schoenhut (ILLUS.,
next page) **$750**
Toy, squeeze-type, figure of Foxy Grandpa
.... **$392**

Schoenhut Foxy Grandpa Roly-Poly Toy

"Foxy Grandpa's Multiplier" Toy

Toy, wheel-shaped educational-type, "Foxy Grandpa's Multiplier," yellow ground w/picture of Grandpa & the boys, souvenir of the 1904 Louisiana Purchase Exposition in St. Louis (ILLUS.)............................ **$63**
Toy, windup tin, Foxy Grandpa skater, Germany, ca. 1910................................... **$611**

German Wind-up Foxy Grandpa Toy

Toy, windup-type, a composition figure of Foxy Grandpa wearing real cloth clothing, lead feet, made in Germany, ca. 1915, 6" h. (ILLUS.) **$550**
Toy, windup-type, waddling figure of Foxy Grandpa, ca. 1910, 7 1/2" h. **$1,157**
Toys, pipsqueaks, papier-maché figures of Foxy Grandpa & Mrs. Foxy, made in Germany, w/original box, ca. 1910, the set..... **$630**

1906 Tuck Foxy Grandpa Valentine

Valentine, color die-cut of Foxy Grandpa & the boys, published by Tuck, 1906 (ILLUS.) **$105**

FRAMES

Large Pierced & Carved Norwegian Frame

Carved giltwood, rectangular, shadowbox style, the wide coved sides w/serpentine scroll-molded edges & pierced cartouches at each corner, the top centered by a large crown crest, trace of a label, probably for Maler & Forgylder of Norway, encloses a print of Frans Gustav Oscar in a military uniform, late 19th c., 25 1/2 x 34 3/4" (ILLUS.)....................... **$1,380**

Large Norwegian Victorian Frame

Carved giltwood, rectangular, wide shadowbox style, the wide serpentine sides decorated w/molded scrolls & flowering vines w/the top centered by a large laurel leaf & crown crest, paper label reading "Vicolai Bing - Maler & Forgylder - i - Christiana," enclosed a black & white print of a royal gentleman, Norway, late 19th c., 27 x 40" (ILLUS.)...................... **$1,725**

Folk Art Frame with Carved Hearts

Carved wood, folk art criss-cross-style, the sides composed of flat narrow boards w/criss-cross corners & w/a carved heart applied at each corner, dark stain finish, fitted w/an old mirror, Pennsylvania, mid-19th c., some wear on mirror, 7 3/4 x 10 1/2" (ILLUS.)............................ **$431**

Labeled Late Victorian Giltwood Frame

Giltwood & gesso, rectangular narrow shadowbox style w/a narrow molded rim band, labeled "Otto Scheibal's Art Store, Philadelphia," late 19th c., overall 34 x 39" (ILLUS.)...................................... **$230**

Signed Late Victorian Gilt Gesso Frame

Giltwood & gesso, rectangular, shadowbox style, the deep sides molded w/delicate sprays of flowers, back inscribed "Samuel Little," small gesso loss, late 19th c., overall 30 1/4 x 36" (ILLUS.) **$288**

Victorian Gilt Plaster Frame with Liner

Giltwood & gesso, rectangular, shadowbox-style, the side molded overall w/delicate bands of leaves & flowers, red velvet liner, late 19th c., overall 23 1/4 x 31 3/4" (ILLUS.).. **$288**

Ornate French Victorian Frame

Giltwood & plaster, deep shadowbox style boldly carved in the Barbizon style w/alternating curling leaves & flowerhead clusters, France, late 19th c., 53 x 74" (ILLUS., previous page) **$2,070**

FURNITURE

Furniture made in the United States during the 18th and 19th centuries is coveted by collectors. American antique furniture has a European background, primarily English, since the influence of the Continent usually found its way to America by way of England. If the style did not originate in England, it came to America by way of England. For this reason, some American furniture styles carry the name of an English monarch or an English designer. However, we must realize that, until recently, little research has been conducted and even less published on the Spanish and French influences in the area of the California missions and New Orleans.

After the American revolution, cabinetmakers in the United States shunned the prevailing styles in England and chose to bring the French styles of Napoleon's Empire to the United States and we have the uniquely named "American Empire" (Classical) style of furniture in a country that never had an emperor.

During the Victorian period, quality furniture began to be mass-produced in this country with its rapidly growing population. So much walnut furniture was manufactured, the vast supply of walnut was virtually depleted and it was of necessity that oak furniture became fashionable as the 19th century drew to a close.

For our purposes, the general guidelines for dating will be: Pilgrim Century - 1620-85 William & Mary - 1685-1720 Queen Anne - 1720-50 Chippendale - 1750-85 Federal - 1785-1820 Hepplewhite - 1785-1820 Sheraton - 1800-20 American Empire (Classical) - 1815-40 Victorian - 1840-1900 Early Victorian - 1840-50 Gothic Revival - 1840-90 Rococo (Louis XV) - 1845-70 Renaissance - 1860-85 Louis XVI - 1865-75 Eastlake - 1870-95 Jacobean & Turkish Revival - 1870-95 Aesthetic Movement - 1880-1900 Art Nouveau - 1890-1918 Turn-of-the-Century - 1895-1910 Mission (Arts & Crafts movement) - 1900-15 Art Deco - 1925-40

All furniture included in this listing is American unless otherwise noted.

Bedroom Suites

Classical style: double sleigh bed, large rectangular ogee-framed mirror, chest-of-drawers & commode: all mahogany & mahogany veneer, the chest w/two small handkerchief drawers w/wooden knobs on the rectangular top above a long ogee-front drawer slightly projecting above the lower case w/three long flat drawers w/turned wood knobs flanked by tall ogee pilasters ending in heavy C-scroll feet, the commode w/a white marble backsplash & rectangular marble top above a long ser-

Four-Piece Classical Bedroom Suite

pentine drawer above a pair of paneled doors over the serpentine apron & casters, ca. 1840, the set (ILLUS.) **$978**

Victorian Faux Bamboo: double bed, chest of drawers, octagonal side table & pair of side chairs; turned wood & bird's-eye maple, the high-backed bed w/a tall rectangular headboard w/a top low gallery of bamboo-turned spindles above the bird's-eye maple headboard w/a large oval recessed panel, the bamboo-turned side stiles topped w/large ball finials, the side rails w/bamboo-turned trim & the low footboard matching the highboard, the chest of drawers w/a large oval mirror swiveling between bamboo-turned uprights above the rectangular case w/three long graduated drawers, attributed to R. J. Horner & Co., New York, New York, ca. 1875, bed 60 x 81", 68" h., the set (ILLUS. of the bed, top next page) **$13,800**

Canopied French Renaissance Revival Bed

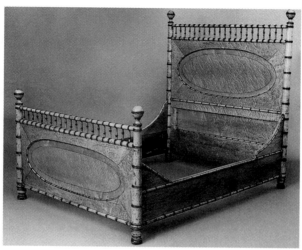

Victorian Vaux Bamboo Bed from a Suite

Victorian Renaissance Revival substyle: canopied double bed & mirrored armoire; ebonized beech, the bed hearboard w/a broken-scroll crestrail centered by a scroll-carved plaque centered by a classical female mask, low spindled galleries on each side between the blocked stiles w/turned finials, all above an arched frieze band over a solid panel, the low footboard w/a flat top rail above two large rectangular raised panels centered by large roundels & flanked on each side by slender columns, the bed w/an appropriate giltwood canopy frame cnetered w/a scroll & palmette finial, Napoleon II Era, France, ca. 1860, bed 60 x 82", 72" h. (ILLUS. of bed, previous page) **$11,213**

Ornate Renaissance Revival Bed

Victorian Renaissance Revival substyle: high-backed double bed & chest of drawers; walnut & burl walnut, the bed w/a tall palmette-and-scroll-carved center crest flanked by scrolls above the molded broken-arch pediment above triangular raised burl panels over a wide section w/scroll-carved sides flanking a large center oval burl panel surrounded by small triangular raised burl panels all flanked by urn-form finials on the block-carved sides flanking three tall vertical rectangular panels, the low footboard w/matching carving & panels; the chest of drawers w/a matching crest above wide tapering scroll-carved sides w/candle shelves flanking a tall rectangular mirror over the drop-well white marble top, the case w/pairs of small burl drawers over a single long drawer w/raised burl panels flanking a center roundel, ca. 1875, original finish, bed 60 x 80", 8' 4" h., 2 pcs. (ILLUS. of bed) **$6,500**

Victorian Renaissance Revival substyle: queen-sized bed & chest of drawers; walnut & flame-grained cherry veneer, both pieces w/matching crestrails centered by a long rectangular flaring block-form crest above scroll cutouts over a small arched cherry burl panel flanked by a broken-arch pediment, the headboard w/shaped scroll-carved sides centering a large burl cherry panel, a matching low footboard & deep side boards; the chest crest above a large rectangular mirror flanked by shaped supports w/small rounded shelves over the rectangular white marble top & a case of three long burl-paneled drawers, all on flattened bun feet, original finish, ca. 1880, chest overall 8' 7" h., 2 pcs. (ILLUS., top next page) **$4,500**

Two-piece Renaissance Revival Bedroom Suite

Beds

One of Two Classical Low-Poster Beds

Classical low-poster beds, twin-sized, each w/a headboard topped w/a round crest bar ending in leafy scrolls raised above serpentine sides flanked by ring-, knob- and baluster-turned headposts topped by carved pineapple finials, matching footboard w/the posts joined by an baluster-, ring- & knob-turned blanket rail & a flat lower rail, first half 19th c., 39 x 75", 49" h., pr. (ILLUS. of one) **$1,006**

Classical sleigh bed, carved mahogany, twin-sized, the head- and footboards of the same height, each w/trefoil carvings atop the side stiles joined by figured veneer panels, the ends w/applied carving

American Classical Sleigh Bed

& molding, joined by highly figured veneered siderails, ca. 1840, 37 x 82", 43 1/2" h. (ILLUS.) **$920**

French Classical Sleigh Bed

Classical sleigh bed, mahogany, matching head- and footboards w/outscrolled sides w/delicate carved scrolls flanking plain panels, deep molded siderails & long block feet on casters, France, first half 19th c., 45 x 80", 43" h. (ILLUS.)............ **$1,610**

Fine Carved Classical Tall Poster Bed

Classical tall-poster canopy bed, carved mahogany, the headboard w/a pair of scroll-carved crests w/a small bobbin-turned top bar above a narrow reeded panel over a plain panel flanked by headposts spiral-carved w/ribbons & acanthus leaves & ending in large blocks above the baluster-form leaf-carved legs, matching footposts, all supporting the canopy frame, square side rails, restoration & alterations, ca. 1830, 62 x 84", 94" h. (ILLUS.) **$13,800**

Mahogany Classical Canopy Bed

Classical tall-poster canopy bed, mahogany, the rectangular canopy frame w/rounded corners & deep ogee sides & lined w/fabric, raised atop four heavy columns w/a tapering ring-turned top sec-

tions above heavy paneled posts above tall square corner blocks raised on heavy turned legs on disk & peg feet, the headboard w/a simple arched molded crestrail above a plain panel, the siderails & footboard w/shaped corner brackets, Mississippi Valley, ca. 1840, 67 x 86", 97" h. (ILLUS.)... **$6,325**

Fine Southern Classical Canopy Bed

Classical tall-poster canopy bed, mahogany, the rectangular full canopy w/rounded corners & deep ogee rails & lined w/radiating fabric, resting atop tall tapering clustered-column posts w/plain round lower sections on disk feet, the headboard w/a flat molded crest flanked by scroll-carved sides over a large plain rectangular panel, the deep siderails & footboard w/scrolling leaf-carved corner brackets, probably New Orleans, ca. 1840, 69 x 90", 120" h. (ILLUS.) **$16,675**

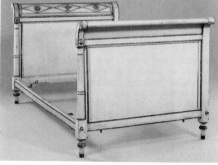

French Directoire-Style Sleigh Bed

Directoire-Style sleigh bed, painted & decorated wood, the matching head- and footboards w/out-scrolled crestrails decorated w/a band of dark green diamonds enclosing small classical motifs on a deep cream ground, simple turned columns flank the plain head- and footboard panels in deep cream w/dark green trim, narrow siderails, short turned disk & peg feet, France, mid-19th c., 50 x 82 1/2", 45" h. (ILLUS.) **$2,155**

Fine American Federal Canopy Bed

Federal tall-poster canopy bed, mahogany, a low arched headboard joining simple square tapering headposts, the footposts turned tapering shape w/reeding above tall square tapering legs, square siderails, full arched canopy frame, ca. 1800, 60 x 80", 67 1/2" h. (ILLUS.) **$7,170**

Simple American Federal Canopy Bed

Federal tall-poster canopy bed, maple & pine, simple arched headboard between simple turned & tapering headposts w/urn-turned finials, matching low arched footboard & footposts, swelled tapering turned legs, full arched canopy frame, old repairs, first half 19th c., 49 1/2 x 78 1/8", 82" h. (ILLUS.) **$1,000**

Green & Gold Louis XVI-Style Twin Bed

Louis XVI-Style bed, painted & decorated, twin-size, a high arched headboard w/a gilt imbricate-carved crestrail above an upper panel carved w/a thin raised arched rectangular panel framing leafy swags centered by a bow suspending crossed quivers all on a pale green ground & flanked by ring-and-knob-turned & reeded posts w/ball finials, the slightly lower matching footboard decorated w/a large arched panel enclosing ornate gilt leafy scrolls centered by a ribbon bow suspending a large oval figural medallions, toupie feet, France, ca. 1900, 40 1/2 x 79", 60 1/2" h. (ILLUS.) **$3,220**

Elaborate Renaissance-Style Canopy Bed

Renaissance-Style canopy bed, carved mahogany, the large rectangular canopy frame w/a flaring molded cornice above scroll-carved sides w/florette-carved corner blocks, raised on tall heavy spiral twist-turned posts, the high headboard w/an arched crestrail w/ornate floral carving above three square panels carved w/shaped panels & roundels above two plain panels, the lower footboard w/a long rectangular upper panel incised w/delicate scrolls above a mid-molding & a long lower panel boldly carved w/leafy scrolls centered by a large roundel, the deep siderails w/matching scroll carving, a narrow flaring gadroon-carved base molding above the large flat-tened bun feet, Portugal, mid-19th c., 58 1/2 x 85 1/2", 117" h. (ILLUS.) **$8,625**

Simple Renaissance Revival Walnut Bed

Victorian Renaissance Revival substyle bed, carved walnut, the low headboard w/an arched crestrail w/a broken-scroll crest above a cartouche flanked by leafy scrolls & tapering raised panels all over a plain panel, tapering shaped stiles, a slightly shorter matching footboard, original siderails, ca. 1875, 54 x 68", 53" h. (ILLUS.)... **$405**

Fine Renaissance Half-Tester Bed

Victorian Renaissance Revival substyle half-tester bed, carved walnut, the half-tester w/a serpentine frame mounted at the front w/an arched pierced scroll-carved crest & large turned bulbous finials, raised on angled serpentine brackets above the tall square tapering headposts & tall square legs w/block feet, the tall headboard w/an arched broken-scroll crest center w/a carved cartouche finial & carved scrolls & raised panels above an arched rail over a pair of tall arched oblong burl panels below a cluster of scroll carving, the low footboard w/a raised arched central panel over a large molded roundel flanked by raised asymmetrical panels, curved corner panels w/scroll-carved finials & feet, ca. 1875, 67 x 82 1/2", 112" h. (ILLUS.) **$3,680**

Very Fine Carved Renaissance Revival Half-tester Bed

Victorian Renaissance Revival substyle half-tester bed, walnut & burl walnut, the large rectangular half-tester frame w/a bowed front rail centered by a large blocked panel topped w/a carved palmette crest, small corner palmette finials, the flaring top molding above narrow raised burl panels, the tester supported by large pierced & carved curved panels decorated w/raised burl panels, joined to the tall square tapering headposts trimmed w/raised burl panels & roundels, the very high headboard w/a large blocked & arched crestrail topped by a carved palmette finial & small end finials above small raised burl panels all above a large rectangular molded burl panel flanked by narrow vertical raised burl panels, a large bottom rectangular burl panel, the low arched footboard w/the crestrail centered by a carved palmette &

small burl panels above a pair of small rectangular burl panels, heavy square footposts w/paneled caps, raised burl panels & heavy block feet, the wide siderails w/narrow raised burl panels & quarter-round corner brackets, ca. 1865, 72 x 88", 129" h. (ILLUS.) **$8,625**

High-backed Renaissance Revival Walnut & Burl Walnut Bed

Victorian Renaissance Revival substyle high-backed bed, walnut & burl walnut, the head headboard w/an arched & molded crestrail centered w/a large blocked panel topped by a large carved palmette finial, all above narrow raised burl panels & small blocks over a large rectanular burl panel, the square sideposts w/a blocked & banded design w/a roundel, the lower footboard w/a simple stepped crestrail above blocks & raised burl panels over two smaller rectangular burl panels, capped square footposts w/raised burl panels, heavy block feet, the wide siderails w/long raised burl panels & corner brackets w/burl panels, ca. 1875, 67 1/2 x 89", 86" h. (ILLUS.) **$1,840**

Fine Rococo Revival Mahogany Bed

Victorian Rococo Revival substyle bed, carved mahogany, the high arched headboard topped by a large carved shell crest above a large knob & floral swags & scroll-carved edging above a long rectangular burl panel w/cut-corners, the ring- and rod-turned head posts topped by disk-turned finials, the low footboard w/a low arched top above raised panels flanked by rounded corners w/floral carving, original sideboards, old surface, posts now shortened, mid-19th c., 70 x 83", 87 1/2" h. (ILLUS.) **$4,600**

Black Lacquer Victorian Rococo Bed

Victorian Rococo Revival substyle bed, gilt-decorated black lacquer, double-size, the arched serpentine headboard w/a molded edge decorated w/gilt trim above the smooth panel decorated under the arch w/a band of delicate gold florals & chinoiserie designs including birds & arabesques, simple serpentine stiles above the blocked legs w/black feet, the low footboard w/a heavy flat molded crestrail & tapering blocked corner posts w/half-round spindles above the stepped block feet, probably Philadelphia, ca. 1850-60, 66 x 78", 4' 9" h. (ILLUS.) **$1,380**

Very Elaborate Rococo Rosewood Full-tester Bed

Fine Rococo Substyle Bed Attributed to Prudent Mallard

Victorian Rococo Revival substyle tall-poster full-tester bed, carved rosewood, the large tester frame decorated on each side w/an ornate arched & scroll-carved crestrail centered by a shell cartouche above a flared cornice band over a paneled frieze band w/a central roundel, raised on four heavy paneled knob-and ring-turned posts above heavy paneled legs ending in heavy paneled feet, the fairly low headboard w/a simple central arched crest above a plain panel, the paneled side rails centered by a florette & trimmed on top w/scroll-carved corner brackets & a central serpentine-carved crest, America or France, ca. 1850, 84 x 89", 10' h. (ILLUS., previous page) **$13,800**

Victorian Rococo substyle high-backed bed, carved rosewood, the headboard w/a high arched broken-scroll pediment w/pierced scrolls below the large foral-carved cartouche over a simple arched crestrail & panel, the square sideposts topped by tall paneled posts w/large ring-and knop-turned finials, the simple arched footboard w/simple molded panels & curved corners w/scrolls & curved panels, the deep siderails w/molded rectangular panels, scroll-carved end feet, formerly a half-tester bed now reduced in height, probably from New Orleans & the shop of Prudent Mallard, ca. 1855, 69 1/2 x 87", 84 1/2" h. (ILLUS., top of page)............. **$19,550**

Benches

Bucket (or water) bench, painted pine, a long narrow rectangular top board above single-board ends w/arched cut-out feet & sloping at the front above two

Early Painted Bucket or Water Bench

open shelves, two back braces, mortised construction, crusty old reddish brown paint, mid-19th c., 12 x 37 1/4", 34 1/2" h. (ILLUS.)................................. **$2,013**

Simple Country Pine Bucket Bench

Large Victorian Oak Hall Bench & Mirror Set

Bucket (or water) bench, pine, the rectangular top above a closed lower shelf flanked by single-board bootjack ends, 19th c., 36" l., 23" h. (ILLUS., previous page) **$104**

Simple Country-Style Hardwood Bench

Country-style bench, hardwood, a long flat crestrail above a spindled back flanked by square stiles continuing to the rear legs, shaped open arms on low turned supports flanking the long plank seat, ring- and rod-turned tapering front legs, 19th c., 71" l. (ILLUS.) **$1,016**

Hall bench & mirror, late Victorian style, oak, the bench w/a tall rectangular back w/a flat crestrail ending in rosette ends above a large central beveled square panel flanked by pairs of smaller panels all flanked by heavy reeded & scrolled end arms on large reeded ball arm supports above the rectangular seat w/a lift-top above the deep apron w/double front panels & single end panels, heavy flaring molded base on large bun feet, together w/a matching wall mirror w/a flaring flat cornice w/a dentil-carved crestrail above a frieze band centered by a scroll-carved panel panel above a large rectangular mirror w/heavy molding, late 19th - early 20th c., mirror 50 x 52 1/4", bench 20 x 55", 43" h., the pair (ILLUS., top of page) **$2,070**

Simple Painted Kneeling Bench

Kneeling bench, painted wood, long narrow rectangular top w/narrow side aprons, short bootjack legs, original worn green paint, possibly Shaker-made, 19th c., 7 x 30" lo., 8 1/2" h. (ILLUS.) **$403**

Louis XVI-Style window bench, giltwood, the padded rectangular top w/padded & outscrolled upholstered low ends, above a narrow apron centered by a cornucopia-carved pendant, raised on eight tapering fluted legs ending in peg feet, France, mid-19th c., 22 x 48", 18 1/2" h. (ILLLUS., top next page) **$4,830**

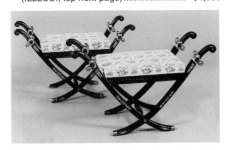

French Neoclassical Cross-Sword Benchs

Neoclassical benches, parcel-ebonized & gilt beech, 'crossed-sword' design, a rectangular upholstered seat on a narrow carved seatrail raised on realistically-carved cross-sword supports on each side, France, 19th c., 17 x 40", 26 1/2" h., pr. (ILLUS.) **$1,035**

Fine Louis XVI-Style Giltwood Window Bench

Leather-covered Regency-Style Bench

Regency-Style window bench, upholstered mahogany, the long U-shaped top
w/inscrolled ends & raised on arched flat
legs covered overall w/ tufted & tack-
trimmed brown leather, England, late 19th
- early 20th c., 18 x 36", 24" h. (ILLUS.)
.... **$1,495**

Regency-Style window benches, faux
bois & giltwood, the long U-shaped seats
w/inscrolled ends upholstered on the interior & exterior, the seatrails w/mahoga-
ny-grained panels trimmed w/giltwood &
centered by a rosette & leaf-carved panel, the scrolling outswept legs headed by
large gilt leaf clusters & ending in scroll
feet w/a gilt rosette, England, late 19th -
early 20th c., 18 x 46 1/2" h., 24 1/2" h.,
pr. (ILLUS., bottom of page) **$2,530**

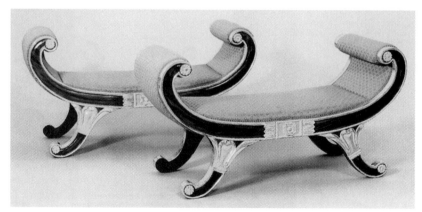

Pair of Fine Regency-Style Window Benches

Bookcases

Arts & Crafts Revolving Bookcase

Arts & Crafts bookcase, oak, revolving-style, the square top w/a narrow molded edge over three open graduated shelves separated by cut-out inner panels & three-rail corners, revolving on a four flat cast-iron cabriole legs on a X-form platform, two small chips, repair to base & rails, signed by John Danner, Canton, Ohio, ca. 1890, 23" sq., 51 1/4" h. (ILLUS.)............... **$633**

Handsome Biedermeier-Style Bookcase

Biedermeier-Style bookcase, blonde wood, a plain rectangular top above an open compartment w/three adjustable wood shelves flanked by free-standing ebonized columns above the lower case w/a pair of large plain cupboard doors centered by a small lion mask & ring pulls, narrow molded base on low bracket feet, Europe, late 19th - early 20th c., 13 x 49", 63" h. (ILLUS.) **$2,070**

Simple Large Classical Bookcase

Classical bookcase, mahogany & mahogany veneer, a high arched & scroll-carved crest on the rectangular top w/a deep flaring cornice above a case w/a pair of tall doors w/large glazed panes above recessed panels opening to wooden shelves, the stepped-out base w/a pair of deep drawers w/simple turned wood knobs above a deep platform base w/thin block feet, shrinkage cracks in side panels, veneer chips, ca. 1850, 18 3/4 x 48 1/4", 74" h. (ILLUS.) **$633**

Nice Classical-Style Mahogany Bookcase

Classical-Style bookcase, carved mahogany & mahogany veneer, the rectangular top w/blocked ends & a narrow flaring cornice above a wide frieze band & a pair of tall geometrically-glazed doors opening to wooden shelves, all flanked by free-standing ring- and leaf-carved columns resting on paw-carved front feet, ca. 1890, 21 1/4 x 48", 72 1/4" h. (ILLUS.).............. **$1,840**

English Edwardian Revolving Bookcase

Edwardian bookcase, mahogany, revolving-style, the square top above a cornice w/line-incised decoration above four slender turned & reeded corner columns framing the two shelf inner revolving bookcase w/angled corner panels, a narrow apron & small tapering corner block legs on casters, minor veneer chip, England, ca. 1900, 20" sq., 31 1/4" h. (ILLUS.)............ **$1,265**

Fine George III Hanging Bookcase

George III bookcase, mahogany, hanging-type, composed of five graduated open shelves supported by a flat back rail & joined at the sides w/ornate pierce-carved rails, England, ca. 1810, 6 3/4 x 37 1/4", 45 1/2" h. (ILLUS.) **$3,105**

Golden Oak bookcase, rectangular top w/thin flared cornice above serpentine corner brackets flanking a tall glazed door w/angled carved top corner brackets, opening to three adjustable shelves, glass sides, molded apron on simple cabriole legs, ca. 1900, 30" w. 5' 3" h. **$604**

Simple Late Victorian Mahogany Bookcase

Late Victorian bookcase, mahogany, two-part construction: the upper section w/a rectangular top w/a deep flaring cornice above a banded frieze band over a pair of tall glazed doors opening to four wooden shelves & double-paneled sides; the lower section w/a mid-molding over a pair of drawers w/simple bail pulls over the deep platform base, last quarter 19th c., 19 x 67 1/2", 93" h. (ILLUS.) **$1,438**

Victorian Eastlake Revolving Bookcase

Victorian Eastlake substyle bookcase, inlaid mahogany, revolving-style, the square top w/a line-incised molding above two open shelves separated on each side w/cut-out panels & trimmed w/three narrow rails at each corner, satin wood inlay trim, rotating atop a cross-form base on casters, late 19th c., 21" sq., 32" h. (ILLUS.)................................. **$1,610**

Cabinets

Fine Victorian Oak & Glass Cane Cabinet

Cane cabinet, oak & glass, tall upright rectangular form, the oak framework topped w/a hinged curved glass top & glass sides opening to a mirrored back & a stick-band-ball grid w/78 square cane holes, the tall lower case w/a mirrored back & glass front & sides, raised on a deep stepped oak base on metal casters, ca. 1880, 18 1/4 x 36", 48" h. (ILLUS.).. **$1,840**

Tall Rectangular Victorian Cane Cabinet

Cane cabinet, oak & glass, the tall rectangular cabinet w/an oak framework & rectangular oak hinged top opening to a removable grate w/a decorative metal center section for holding 65 canes, all four sides composed of two large glass panes, ca. 1880, 14 1/2 x 30", 44 3/4" h. (ILLUS.).. **$1,265**

Large Chippendale-Style China Cabinet

China cabinet, Chippendale-Style, mahogany & mahogany veneer, breakfront-style, the rectangular top w/a projecting central section, the narrow flaring bead-carved cornice above a conforming blind fret-carved frieze band above a wide tall glazed central door opening to three long wood shelves & flanked by tall narrow geometrically-glazed doors & glazed side panels above the slightly stepped-out base cabinet w/a gadrooned band above a blind fret-carved frieze band above a pair of center doors decorated w/veneered panels framing a large oval reserve carved in relief w/Chinese figures & a small temple, flat side doors decorated w/veneered panels & a diamond-shaped burl center panel, narrow molded base raised on four carved ogee bracket feet, England, early 20th c., 19 1/2 x 60 1/2", 81" h. (ILLUS.) **$5,750**

Mission Oak China Cabinet with Crest

China cabinet, Mission-style (Arts & Crafts movement), oak, the rectangular top w/a low arched carved crest above the case w/a tall rectangular glazed center door flanked by tall narrow arched glass panels, glass sides, door opens to three wooden shelves, flat apron w/beaded band, square stile legs w/curved & pierced front corner brackets, legs joined by an H-stretcher, branded number on the back, earl6 20th c., 19 x 44", 63 1/2" h. (ILLUS., previous page) **$345**

Simple Golden Oak China Cabinet

China cabinet, Victorian Gold Oak style, the half-round top mounted by a long low flat back rail centered by a small pierced arch scroll crest, the flat-centered conforming case w/a tall glass door opening to four wooden shelves & flanked by curved glass side panels, molded base raised on four simple flattened cabriole legs on casters, ca. 1900, 35" w., 69" h. (ILLUS.) **$863**

China cabinet, Victorian Rococo substyle, ebonized oak, the top w/a very tall arched & ornately carved crest in a broken-scroll design centered by a shell finial above a large cartouche flanked by ornate ribbon & flower carving, the small projecting round top corners fitted w/squatty turned finials, the long chamfered front cabinet sides w/carved details flanking the tall glazed door w/a large oval of glass surrounded by a twig-carved molding & opening to three glass shelves & an oval mirrored back, the flat molded base rail w/a scroll-carved center drop, all raised on cabriole legs ending in pad feet, original black finish, by G.W. Horrix Company, Gravenhage, mid-19th c., 16 x 42", overall 82 1/2" h. (ILLUS., top next column) **$1,610**

Unusual Ebonized Rococo Cabinet

Ornate Tall Japanese Curio Cabinet

Curio cabinet on stand, carved & decorated handwood, Oriental, the tall upper cabinet w/a rectangular top w/a narrow scroll-carved cornice above a pair of small projecting cupboard doors decorated w/panels in dark blue applied w/carved bone figures of people, birds, flowers & trees, each trimmed w/pierce-carved bands & flanking a pair of similar smaller recessed doors, the projecting narrow side sections each w/two open compartments w/decorative figural panels or pierce-carved panels above another pair of decorated doors at the bottom, the wider central section below the upper doors composed of two long rectangular open compartments backed by figural panels & another pair of small cupboard doors over an open backless compartment, three small drawers across the bottom; the high platform base w/a pierce-carved narrow frieze above a leaf-carved apron continuing into flat scrolling front legs joined by a long delicate scroll-carved bracket, Japan, Meiji period, ca. 1880, some repairs & missing applied pieces, 15 1/2 x 59 1/4", 86" h. (ILLUS.) .. **$3,910**

Chinese Chippendale-Style Curio Cabinet

Curio cabinet on stand, carved & lacquered wood, Chinese Chippendale-Style, two-part construction: the upper section w/a rectangular top above a pair of tall flat doors opening to shelves, decorated overall w/green lacquer panels painted in gold & black w/stylized Chinese landscape & trimmed w/fancy pierced & chased metal strapwork hinges & keyhole escutcheons; the lower section w/a shell-carved mid-molding above a serpentine scroll-carved narrow apron raised on leaf-carved cabriole legs ending in scroll & peg feet, England, late 19th - early 20th c., 19 x 38", 62" h. (ILLUS.) **$1,610**
Curio cabinet on stand, mother-of-pearl inlaid hardwood, Moorish-Style, two-part construction: the upper section w/a very tall pierced spearpoint-carved crestrail inlaid w/small stars above the very deep cornice frieze composed of carved tiered spearpoints above a cabinet w/a pair of small carved & star-inlaid panels flanking a pierced lattice-carved rectangular panel above a raised panel inlaid w/Arabic script above a pair of tall latticework doors framed by an inlaid leafy vine, flanked on each side by two open compartments w/Moorish arches carved w/incised designs & decorative inlay, the

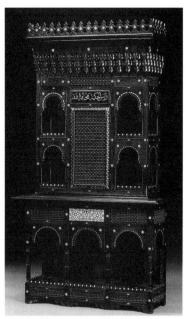

Elaborate Tall Moorish-Style Cabinet

sides w/matching Moorish arch compartments; the stepped-out lower cabinet w/a rectangular top overhanging a case w/a pair of rectangular pierced lattice panels flanking a single geometrically-inlaid drawer above three tall Moorish arches raised on simple turned columns, the sides w/matching pierced panels & arches, the deep platform base w/a scalloped top band w/button inlay above three carved & lattice-pierced rectangular panels, scroll-cut bracket feet, ca. 1890, 17 1/2 x 47 1/4", 88 1/4" h. (ILLUS.) **$7,768**

Tall Late Victorian Music Cabinet

Music cabinet, mahogany-finished hardwood, tall upright form w/an arched crestrail carved w/a rondel & pierced scrolls above a narrow open shelf raised on pairs of slender spiral-turned spindles above a back panel fitted w/a rectangular beveled mirror, the projecting case w/a rectangular top flanked by simple end galleries above a narrow carved front edge over a pair of tall narrow paneled doors each carved w/stylized leaves & berries centered by a carved harp, narrow half-round spiral-carved pilasters down the sides above an open bottom compartment above the flat reeded legs ending in scallop-cut feet, doors open to six birch or maple pull-out drawers, patent-dated tag in the lower drawer dated 1892, some wear to finish, 14 1/2 x 19 1/2", 62" h. (ILLUS., previous page) **$1,080**

Unusual Early Jacobean Style Cabinet

at each side, the front supported by two heavy knob- and baluster-turned supports above the plain trapazoidal lower shelf, the solid back divided into four recessed panels, the flat base apron w/shallow leafy scroll carving & resting on two small bun feet, Europe, probably 18th c. or possibly 17 th c., dark finish, 19 1/2 x 33", 32" h. (ILLUS.) **$1,035**

Side cabinet, polychromed & bone-inlaid walnut, Renaissance-Style, a long rectangular top above a case w/a central arch-paneled door opening to three drawers & above a bottom drawer, the door flanked by a stack of three drawers on either side, the outer frame inlaid w/a zig-zag band, the arched door panel w/carved & inlaid stylized colums, each drawer centered by an inlaid six-point star flanked by small inlaid panels, raised on ring-turned bun feet, Spain, late 18th - early 19th c., 13 x 35", 22" h. (ILLUS., top next page) **$3,450**

Rare Gustav Stickley Music Cabinet

Music cabinet, oak, Mission-style (Arts & Crafts movement), the rectangular top w/a low three-quarters mortised gallery above a single tall 12-pane glazed door w/hammered amber glass panes, stamped copper door pull, opening to shelves, flat base w/simiple cut-out sides, mint original finish, one replaced glass pane, branded mark of Gustav Stickley & evidence of a paper label, 16 x 20", 54 1/2" h. (ILLUS.) **$16,100**

Side cabinet, hardwood, Jacobean style, the flat two-board trapazoidal top tapers toward the front above a wide frieze band w/the sides finely carved w/scrolls & scallops, the front w/a single drawer w/a metal teardrop pull & decorated w/a repeating scroll band, flanked by small scrolled leaf-carved panels, the case above open sides w/arched top brackets

Provincial French Empire Cabinet

Side cabinet, provincial Empire-Style, fruitwood, the long rectangular top w/molded edges above a concealed long drawer over two paneled cupboard doors flanked by engaged columns w/ormolu mounts, on short turret feet, France, mid-19th c., 21 x 51", 35" h. (ILLUS.)............ **$1,955**

Elaborately Carved, Inlaid & Painted Early Spanish Side Cabinet

Fine Victorian Aesthetic Side Cabinet

heavy baluster- and ring-turned posts resting on an large open shelf w/a paneled board back & flaring stepped & carved apron raised on squatty bun feet, late 19th c., 14 x 46", 72" h. (ILLUS.)..... **$2,070**

Ornate French Renaissance Side Cabinet

Side cabinet, Victorian Aesthetic Movement style, mahogany, in the Renaissance taste, the tall superstructure w/an ornate arched crestrail pierce-carved w/a pair of birds & leafy scrolls flanking a medallion above a cornice molding over a long low rectangularr mirror flanked by large scroll-carved ends all raised on stepped gadroon-carved rails, the rectangular top w/molded edges overhanging the case w/end doors w/rectangular beveled glass doors flanking reeded & carved pilasters flanking the large central solid door carved w/ornate scrolls & a central urn, the end stiles carved w/bold caryatids, beveled glass end panels, all above a long narrow scroll-carved central drawer flanked by carved masks above a serpentine scroll-carved apron raised on

Side cabinet, Victorian Renaissance Revival substyle, parcel giltwood & bronze-mounted ebonized wood, the rectangular top w/incurved sides & a blocked front trimmed w/stepped brass banding above a fluted cornice & egg-and-dart frieze, the wide cabinet door w/a large double-band gold-outlined panel centered by an arched bronze relief plaque of the toilette of Venus framed by boldly carved arched scrolls & columns, fancy gilt-bronze latch, projecting spiral-carved columns at each corner flanking the concave side panels w/a thin rectangular metal panel enclosing long beribboned floral gilt-bronze pendants, the wide conforming molded base banded w/gilt-bronze gadrooning & a shell & leaf central panel, raised on short disk- and knob-turned feet, France, Napoleon III era, ca. 1860-70, 20 x 40", 44" h. (ILLUS.) **$8,050**

Rosewood Renaissance Side Cabinet

Side cabinet, Victorian Renaissance Revival substyle, rosewood, nearly square top inset w/marble, ovolu front corners over ring-and-rod-turned reeded corner posts flanking a single drawer w/leaf-carved cartouche & wood pulls over a single raised-panel door w/scroll-carved keyhole escutcheon, carved front apron flanked by projecting round corners, refinished, ca. 1870, 17 x 18", 28" h. (ILLUS.)............... **$1,800**

Charles II-Style Side Cabinet

Side cabinet on stand, Charles II-Style, the upper black-lacquered cabinet w/a rectangular top over two doors decorated w/polychrome Japanese landscape scenes & fitted w/brass strap hinges & ornate lock mounts, the doors opening to an arrangement of ten drawers, composed of mid-19th century elements, raised on a late 19th century rectangular stand w/a paneled apron & square paneled legs joined by a flat X-stretcher & ending in square tapering feet, England, late 19th c., 18 1/2 x 35 1/2", overall 4' 10" h. (ILLUS.) **$2,070**

Victorian Upright Store Spool Cabinet

Spool cabinet, cherry, upright revolving store-type, the square top w/a notched pediment above the molded cornice, the front fitted w/a stack of narrow spool drawers w/pull-down glass fronts over two narrow bottom drawers, the sides & back fitted w/mirrors, revolving on a short base, late 19th c., 18" sq., 38" h. (ILLUS.) **$1,093**

Victorian Two-Drawer Spool Cabinet

Spool cabinet, walnut, store counter-type style, the square top w/an inset panel overhanging the short case fitted w/two shallow drawers w/turned pulls flanking an inset oval glass panel, one printed in gold on black "Goff's," the other "Braid," narrow molded flat base, late 19th c., 17 1/4" sq., 7 1/2" h. (ILLUS.) **$173**

Rare Figural Cast-Iron Umbrella Stand

Umbrella/cane stand, cast iron, the upright section cast as a realistic small dog standing on its rear legs & holding a long double-loop whip in its mouth, all painted in naturalistic colors, raised on a cast-iron base w/a blue cylindrical pedestal above the wide fanned & scroll-cast base w/a drip tray cast as large blue leaves, some paint wear, second half 19th c., 12 x 24", 24" h. (ILLUS.) **$3,220**

Fine Louis XV-Style Vitrine Cabinet

Vitrine cabinet giltwood, Louis XV-Style, the half-round paneled top mounted by a high central arched broken-scroll crest decorated w/leaves above the triple-arched molded cornice, the front w/a tall flat glazed door w/an arched top opening to two half-round wooden shelves, the angled sides w/arched glazed panels, the stiles each carved w/floral pendants & narrow raised panels, the lower section

w/a gadrooned mid-molding over the conforming apron decorated w/bold shell & leaf carvings, raised on four tapering square legs topped by large leafy scroll & rosette sections & ending in pointed block feet, the legs joined by a flattened cross-stretcher centered by a small bulbous turned finial, France, late 19th c., 14 x 36 1/2", 84" h. (ILLUS.) **$4,600**

Chairs

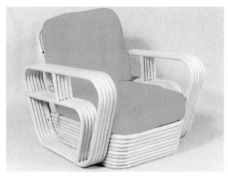

Art Deco Bent Bamboo Armchair

Art Deco armchair, bamboo, the back w/a squared bent bamboo frame fitted w/a large cushion, the large five-layered bent bamboo pretzel-style arms enclosing further bamboo rails, the deep oblong seat frame made of five-layered bent bamboo, deep cushion seat, after a design by Paul Frankl, 30" h. (ILLUS.) **$150-300**

Art Deco armchairs, mahogany, a slightly flaring rectangular back panel w/bone white linen upholstery raised above the over-upholstered seat flanked by curved open wood arms, raised on slender square tapering slightly shaped front legs, in the style of Emile-Jacques Ruhlmann, ca. 1930, 32" h., pr. (ILLUS., top next page) .. **$2,990**

Large Flemish Baroque-Style Armchair

Pair of Fine Art Deco Armchairs

Wonderfully Carved Swiss Armchairs

Baroque-Style armchair, carved walnut, the large squared & arched back upholstered in a needlepoint tapestry material above the serpentine open arms on incurved arm supports above the wide tapestry-upholstered seat, serpentine front legs & square rear legs joined by an H-stretcher, Flemish, mid-19th c., 48" h. (ILLUS., previous page) **$1,495**

Baroque-Style armchairs, carved walnut & marquetry, Black Forest-style, the large ballon-shaped back boldly carved overall w/naturalistically carved branches, clusters of grapes & leaves amid scrolls & centered by a small oval panel inlaid w/floral designs in light wood, the long scroll-carved open arms on C-scroll supports above the wide shaped seat w/gadroon-carved edges, heavy cabriole front legs carved w/leaf designs & leaf-carved serpentine rear legs, Switzerland, late 19th c., 43" h., pr. (ILLUS., middle of page) **$3,738**

One of Two Country Chippendale Chairs

Chippendale country-style side chairs, mahogany, the serpentine crest above the pierced vasiform splat above the upholstered slip seat, square Marlborough front legs & square canted rear legs joined by box stretchers, refinished, minor imperfections, possibly Virginia, late 18th c., 37 1/2" h., pr. (ILLUS. of one) ... **$2,938**

Finely Carved Chippendale-Style Chair

Chippendale-Style armchair, carved mahogany, the shaped crestrail centered by a high arched scroll-carved crest w/a central shell above the pierce-carved Gothic-style back splat flanked by the molded & gently outswept stiles, shaped open arms ending in scroll grip raised on incurved arm supports above the over-upholstered wide seat, square front legs carved w/Gothic panels, square canted rear legs, all joined by an H-stretcher, ca. 1890, 54" h. (ILLUS.) **$920**

One of Two Chippendale Side Chairs

Chippendale side chairs, carved mahogany, the serpentine crest centered by a carved shell above the pierced scroll-carved splat, upholstered slip seat, square Marlborough front legs & canted square rear legs, joined by box stretchers, old refinish, minor imperfections, Boston or Salem, Massachusetts, 1755-85, 38" h., pr. (ILLUS. of one) **$4,113**

Set of Oak Chippendale-Style Chairs

Chippendale-Style dining chairs, oak, a serpentine crest w/eared corners above a scroll- and bar-pierced splat flanked by stiles above an over-upholstered seat, square legs on casters joined by an H-stetcher, late 19th - early 20th c., 38" h., five side chairs & one armchair, set of 6 (ILLUS.)... **$920**

Set of Bird's-Eye Maple Classical Side Chairs

Classical country-style side chairs, bird's-eye maple, the crestrail w/a rolled center & rounded ends above the vasi-form splat & curved back stiles, caned seat above sabre-style front legs & outswept rear legs, curved flat front rung & turned side & back stretchers, ca. 1830, three w/no seat caning, one w/a back repair, 33" h., set of 4 (ILLUS., top of page) **$518**

Unusual Landscape-decorated Classical Side Chairs

Classical country-style side chairs, painted & decorated, the wide gently curved crestrail h.p. w/a stylized rustic landscape over a narrow pierced knob band & raised above a smaller knob band slat between the decorated stiles, round-fronted caned seat raised on ring- and baluster-turned front legs joined by a flat front stretcher centered by a large flat rosette in gold, simple turned side & back stretchers, each crestrail w/a different landscape, probably New York State, ca. 1820-30, 35" h., set of 4 (ILLUS., above) **$9,560**

Classical rocking chair w/arms, mahogany, Grecian-style, the tall serpentine-shaped upholstered back flanked by padded open arms on large open-scroll arm supports flanking the over-upholstered seat, the carved flat seatrail on flat curved front legs joined to the shorter rear legs by the long rocker, ca. 1830-40, 41" h. (ILLUS., to the right) **$920**

American Classical Grecian Rocker

Pair of Duncan Phyfe Classical Side Chairs

Classical side chairs, carved mahogany, a narrow curved flat crestrail above a large pierced harp-shaped splat raised on a narrow lower rail, flanked by the scrolled & reeded stiles continuing down to flank the upholstered slip seat, incurved acanthus-carved front legs ending in hairy paw feet, canted square rear legs, attributed to Duncan Phyfe, New York, New York, ca. 1815-25, 32 3/4" h., pr. (ILLUS., top of page) **$19,120**

One of Two Boston Classical Side Chairs

Classical side chairs, carved mahogany, a narrow rectangular crestrail carved w/incised bands & flanked above & below by narrow gadroon-carved bands, raised above a lower pierce-carved slat between the reeded stiles continuing down to frame the upholstered slip seat & form the incurved front legs, square canted rear legs, Boston, ca. 1815-20, 33 1/2" h., pr. (ILLUS. of one) **$1,175**

Early Painted Banister-back Side Chair

Early American "banister-back" side chair, painted hardwood, the arched & scroll-cut crestrail above four tall split balusters flanked by tall baluster- and block-turned stiles topped w/turned finials & raised above the woven rush seat, baluster-, ring- and rod-turned front legs joined by two swelled turned front stretchers, double side & a single back stretcher, old dark brown paint w/gilt stencil & color floral designs, New England, second half 18th c., 44" h. (ILLUS.)........................... **$1,058**

Early American "ladder-back" armchair, painted wood, the back w/three arched slats between the knob- and rod-turned stiles continuing down to from the back legs & topped by large ball finials, simple turned open arms joining knob- and rod-turned front supports continuing down to form the front legs joined by two swelled

Fine Early "Ladder-back" Armchair

& ring-turned front stretchers, woven rush seat, double side & single rear stretchers, worn old black paint, second half 18th c., 44 3/4" h. (ILLUS.)............. **$2,415**

Early Painted "Ladder-back" Highchair

Early American "ladder-back" highchair, painted wood, three arched slats flanked by the heavy turned stiles forming the rear legs & topped by knob-turned finials, shaped open arms on baluster-turned supports continuing down to form the front legs, old woven rush seat, two worn front stretchers, turned plain side stretchers & one back stretcher, old & possibly original black paint, late 18th c., 41 1/2" h. (ILLUS.) **$1,035**

Delaware Valley "Ladder-back" Highchair

Early American "ladder-back" highchair, turned wood, the back w/four narrow arched slats between heavy turned stiles continuing to form the back legs & topped by knob-turned finials, shaped open arms raised on baluster-turned arm supports continuing into the front legs, woven rush seat, a flattened upper front stretcher above a plain turned lower stretcher, double side stretchers & a single back stretcher, Delaware River-style, natural finish, late 18th - early 19th c., 38" h. (ILLUS.) **$575**

George III-Style Fancy Armchairs

George III-Style armchairs, mahogany, a shell-carved crestrail on the balloon back centered by a solid scroll-carved splat & flanked by serpentine open arms terminating in a carved, curled bird head above an S-scroll arm support, the wide oblong slip seat in a molded shell-carved seatrail raised on cabriole front legs w/shell-carved knees & ending in claw-and-ball feet, England, late 19th - early 20th c., 41" h., pr. (ILLUS.) **$1,035**

English George III-Style Wing Chair

George III-Style wing chair, the tall arched upholstered back flanked by tall tapering & rolled upholstered wings above rolled upholstered arms w/incurved scroll-carved arm supports, a cushion seat above the egg-and-dart-carved seatrail raised on heavy cabriole legs w/leaf-and-cartouche-carved knees & compressed ball-and-claw feet, England, mid-19th c., 4' 4" h. (ILLUS.) **$3,450**

Georgian Upholstered Side Chair

Georgian side chair, mahogany, a tall rounded upholstered back above the squared over-upholstered seat, on carved cabriole legs w/leaf-carved knees & ending in pad front feet, gros point & petit point fabric w/floral panels, England, probably late 18th c., small patches & repairs to upholstery, 23 x 24 1/2", 43" h. (ILLUS.) **$1,430**

Georgian side chair, the tall squared upholstered back above a wide upholstered seat, the front cabriole legs w/acanthus-carved knees, shaped hairy ankles & scroll-carved returns, deeply carved four-toe feet w/talons, rear legs w/pad feet, needlepoint upholstery probably later 19th c., England, mid-18th c., missing several returns, foot of proper right rear leg off but present, frame loose under upholstery, extensive fading to upholstery, 37" h. **$2,090**

One of Two Louis XV-Style Fauteuils

Louis XV-Style fauteuils (open-arm armchairs), fruitwood, the wide upholstered back w/an arched serpentine crestrail centered by a floral-carved crest & continuing down to form the shaped back frame, open padded arms on incurved arm supports above the wide upholstered seat, serpentine molded seatrail centered by a floral-carved reserve, cabriole front legs w/floral-carved knees & ending in simple peg feet, France, ca. 1900, 38 1/2" h., pr. (ILLUS. of one) **$1,840**

Louis XV-Style Provincial "ladder-back" dining chairs, fruitwood, the side chairs w/tall backs w/serpentine floral-carved crestrails above two lower slats flanked by serpentine stiles above the woven rush seats, curved & scalloped seatrails centered by floral carving, cabriole front legs w/floral-carved knees & ending in raised scroll toes, baluster-, ring- and plaque-carved front stretchers, w/two matching armchairs w/lower backs, France, late 19th c., 34" h., set of 6 (ILLUS., top next page) **$1,725**

Louis XV-Style French Provincial Dining Chairs

Louis XV-Style side chairs, hardwood, the oval back frame enclosing a leather panel raised above leather seats w/brass tack decoration, cabriole front legs w/scroll feet, France, late 19th c., minor stains, wear to leather seats, 36 1/2" h., set of 6 .... **$3,080**

Louis XVI-Style Upholstered Armchair

Louis XVI-Style armchair, painted wood, a wide arched upholstered back w/the frame decorated w/narrow ribbon carving & a top central pierced ribbon & flower-carved crest, closed padded & upholstered arms w/carved & incurved arm supports flanking the wide upholstered seat w/a narrow ribbon-carved bowed seatrail, ring- and rod-turned tapering front legs w/knob & peg feet, light brown w/dark brown highlights, splits on the legs, France, early 20th c., 44" h. (ILLUS.) **$259**

Louis XVI-Style bergères (closed-arm armchairs), beechwood, gently arched & carved crestrail w/ribbon & floral deco-

ration continuing down to frame shallow wings & closed padded arms w/acanthus carving & incurved arm supports, the cushion seat above a carved seatrail raised on tapered & fluted legs, striped upholstery, France, early 20th c., one leg repaired, separations, small losses, 43" & 46" h., set of two similar chairs **$1,650**

Giltwood Louis XVI-Style Side Chair

Louis XVI-Style side chair, giltwood, the arched & stepped crestrail above a large pierced lyre splat flanked by canted fluted stiles w/a floral finial, the upholstered seat on a molded seatrail above the turned, tapering & fluted front legs ending in peg feet, simple turned stretchers, France, late 19th c., 33 1/2" h. (ILLUS.)

.... **$489**

Pair of Modern "Wasily" Pattern Armchairs

Unusual Large Mission Oak Armchair

Mission-style (Arts & Crafts movement) armchair, oak, the angled slated back fitted w/a large black leather cushion & flanked by wide flat arms raised on flat supports w/corbels, the deep frame w/heavy square front legs, a long black leather spring cushion seat, cleaned original finish, Charles Limbert Furniture Co., unmarked, early 20th c., 32 x 37", 33" h. (ILLUS.) **$4,888**

Plycraft 1970s Lounge Chair & Ottoman

Modern-style armchair & ottoman, lounge-style, laminated & bent walnut & black vinyl upholstery, the tall rectangular tufted upholstered back & seat flanked by out-scrolled wood arms, raised & swiveling on a low cross-form base, matching upholstered ottoman, designed by George Mulhauer for Plycraft, ca. 1970, 34" h. (ILLUS.) **$288**

Modern-style armchairs, chromed steel & leather, "Masily" patt., the rectangular back frame composed of tubular steel fitted w/brown leather straps & suspended in a tubular steel frame w/squared side supports w/narrow brown leather straps & a wide leather seat panel, designed in 1925 by Marcel Breuer for use at the Bauhaus, these made by Knoll International, late 20th c., one w/Knoll paper label, 29" h., pr. (ILLUS., top of page) **$1,955**

1950s Bamboo "Pretzel" Armchair

Modern-style "Pretzel" armchair, bent bamboo, the angled bamboo-framed back & seat flanked by high rounded & looping sides forming the arms & legs, bamboo stretchers, later upholstered cushions, ca. 1955, 26" w., 31" h. (ILLUS.).............. **$200-300**

Nice Country Queen Anne Side Chair

Fine Massachusetts Queen Anne Chair

tion, Massachusetts, ca. 1740-60, 39 3/4" h. (ILLUS.) **$4,406**

Queen Anne side chairs, carved walnut, the shaped crestrail centered by a carved shell above the tall vasiform splat flanked by the shaped stiles above the balloon slip seat in a conforming seatrail raised on cabriole front legs w/scroll-carved returns & ending in pad feet, canted rear legs, baluster- and block-turned stretchers, probably Boston, 1750-1770, 39 1/4" h., pr. (ILLUS., top next page) **$41,825**

Fine Philadelphia Queen Anne Side Chair

Queen Anne side chair, maple, the serpentine crestrail w/flared ears above the vasiform solid splat flanked by the flat stiles & raised above the upholstered slip seat, a narrow serpentine front seatrail raised on tall cabriole front legs ending in simple claw-and-ball feet joined by a swelled front stretcher, canted rear legs, simple turned side & rear stretchers, Fussel-Savery School, Philadelphia, 18th c., 40 1/2" h. (ILLUS.) **$5,019**

Queen Anne side chair, the simple oxyoke crest continuing to the flat backswept stiles flanking a tall vasiform solid splat, ballooned upholstered drop seat w/the conforming seatrail raised on cabrole front legs w/scroll-carved returns & ending in pad feet, square canted rear legs, legs joined by baluster- and block-turned box stretchers, refinished, minor restora-

Queen Anne-Style Chair from a Set

Queen Anne-Style side chairs, mahogany, a simple shaped crestrail continuing into the tall gently curved stiles flanking the vasiform splat, trapezoidal slip seat raised on cabriole front legs ending in pad feet, turned swelled H-stretchers, old dark finish, late 19th - early 20th c., 40 3/4" h., set of 4 (ILLUS. of one)............ **$575**

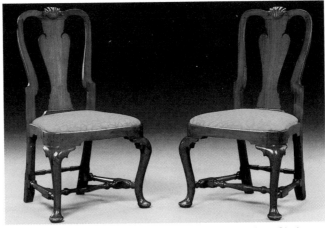

Rare Pair of New England Walnut Queen Anne Side Chairs

Set of Six Simple 1920s Queen Anne-Style Side Chairs

Queen Anne-Style side chairs, oak, the arched crestrail above a plain rectangular splat above the upholstered slip seat, raised on simple tapering cabriole front legs w/pad feet, slender square canted rear legs, simple box stretchers, ca. 1920s, 41" h., set of 6 (ILLUS., above) **$288**

Queen Anne-Style Wing Chairs

Queen Anne-Style wing chairs, tall arched upholstered back flanked by tall flared rounded side wings above the out-scrolled upholstered arms flanking the over-upholsterd seat, cabriole front legs w/acanthus leaf-carved knees, square canted rear legs, early 20th c., 52" h., pr. (ILLUS.) **$1,100**

Regency-Style armchair & rocker, mahogany & leather, each w/a tall back-swept back upholstered in red tufted leather & continuing down to form deep curved seats flanked by padded scrolled open arms, flattened arched legs joined by simple turned stretchers, England, early 20th c., armchair 38 1/2" h., the set (ILLUS., top next page) **$1,265**

Nice Regency-Style Mahogany & Leather Chairs

Set of Victorian Baroque Revival Dining Chairs

Victorian Baroque Revival dining chairs, oak, each w/a high arched crestrail carved w/fancy scrolls & neoclassical designs between columnar stiles, the side chairs w/a shaped back panel upholstered in black leather & raised on a rail above the over-upholstered leather seat, the armchair w/padded open arms w/incurved supports, molded & scroll-carved seatrails, the side chairs w/square tapering legs joined by an H-stretcher & on casters, the armchair w/urn-turned front legs joined to the rear legs w/a curved X-stretcher all on casters, ca. 1880s, seven side chairs & one armchair, armchair 48" h., the set (ILLUS.).......................... **$1,725**

Victorian Baroque-Style Side Chairs

Victorian Baroque Style side chairs, oak, the arched crestrails carved w/designs of fruit & flowers above upholstered back panels above the upholstered seat, heavily turned legs & stretchers, probably cane originally, possibly England or Europe, ca. 1880, 34" h., set of 8 (ILLUS.).. **$800**

Victorian Gothic Revival Hall Chair

Victorian Gothic Revival hall chair, carved walnut, the tall pointed crest pierced w/Gothic trefoils & quatrefoils & topped by three small turned finials, the tall spiral-turned stiles w/turned pointed finials flank a tall rectangular central upholstered panel w/scroll-carving down the frame & above the raised stretcher above the over-upholstered seat, spiral-turned front legs w/knob feet, square rear legs, third quarter 19th c., 44" h. (ILLUS.)........... **$460**

Fine Belter-type Rococo Armchair

Victorian Rococo Revival armchair, pierced & carved laminated rosewood, the high balloon back w/a floral-carved crest above the serpentine pierced scroll-carved side panels flanking the large ser-

pentine oblong tufted upholstered back panel, open padded arms w/scroll-carved incurved arm supports flanking the over-upholstered tufted upholstery seat w/the serpentine scroll-carved seatrail centered by a floral-carved drop, front cabriole legs w/carved grapes at the knees & ending in scroll feet on casters, canted square rear legs on casters, attributed to John H. Belter, New York, New York, ca. 1855, 44" h. (ILLUS.)....................................... **$5,520**

Decorative Rococo Papier-maché Chair

Victorian Rococo Revival side chair, black-lacquered inlaid papier-maché, the balloon back w/a wide scrolling center splat above a small lower splat, wide caned seat w/a serpentine seatrail above simple cabriole front legs, the back decorated w/inlaid mother-of-pearl florals & ornate gilt trim, ca. 1860-70, 33" h. (ILLUS.).. **$920**

Unusual Rosewood Rococo Armchair

Nice Heywood-Wakefield Wicker Armchairs

Victorian Rococo substyle armchair, carved laminated rosewood, the high back w/a simple arched crestrail enclosing a long shaped upholstered panel flanked by pierce-carved leafy scroll panels continuing into the padded arms w/incurved arm supports, the wide over-upholstered seat w/a serpentine seatrail carved w/a center scroll reserve, carved details at the top of the demi-cabriole front legs ending in scroll feet, on casters, attributed to John Henry Belter, New York, New York, ca. 1855, one back leg repaired, veneer chip, some cracks in the back, 39" h. (ILLUS., previous page) **$1,265**

the upholstered seat over the serpentine matching seatrail & cabriole front legs ending in scroll feet, stamped on underside "Jennens & Bettridge," England, ca. 1850, 37" h. (ILLUS.) **$2,185**

Wicker armchairs, a tightly woven pointed arched crestrail continuing down & around to form the flat arms, a lattice-woven back w/tight weaving under the arms, a tightly woven apron w/a lower arched panel w/loose lattice & tight weaving, added back & seat cushions, labeled by Heywood-Wakefield, several breaks & minor damages, ca. 1915-30, 42 3/4" h., pr. (ILLUS., top of page) **$1,035**

Fine English Papier-Maché Chair

Victorian Rococo "tub" chair, black-lacquered papier-maché, the high arched solid back sloping down to form low rolled arms & decorated overall w/ornate gilt scrolls & inlaid mother-of-pearl accents,

William & Mary Country-style Armchair

William & Mary country-style "ladderback" armchair, painted wood, the back w/three double-arch slats between the block- and baluster-turned stiles w/small ring-turned finials, slender shaped open arms on canted ring- and baluster-turned arm supports above the wide woven rush

Yellow-painted & Decorated Windsor Bamboo-turned Side Chairs

seat, block- and knob-turned legs on button feet w/double turned stretchers at the front & sides, worn bluish paint, probably Canadian, 18th c. (ILLUS.)...................... **$4,541**

Ornate William & Mary-Style Armchairs

William & Mary-Style armchairs, carved walnut, a very tall back w/the arched wide framework ornately pierce-carved w/leafy scrolls enclosing a long narrow oval upholstered panel & flanked by spiral-turned stiles, long serpentine open arms w/scrolled hand grips raised on incurved arm supports above the wide upholstered seat, the serpentine scroll-carved front seatrail continuing into front cabriole legs ending in scroll feet, late 19th c., 51 1/4" h., pr. (ILLUS.) **$604**

Windsor bamboo-turned side chairs, yellow-painted & decorated, each w/a long gently arched crestrail decorated w/a stenciled design of purple fruits & green leaves flanked by dark gold banding, the tapering backswept stiles flanking simple turned spindles above the shaped plank seat w/dark banding, canted bamboo-turned legs joined by box stretchers, probably from Maine, first half 19th c., some touch-up or repaint, some old repairs, 32 1/2" h., set of 8 (ILLUS., top of page)... **$2,013**

One of a Pair of Fine Bow-Back Windsors

Windsor "bow-back" armchairs, the arched crestrail continuing down to form the narrow arms all above eleven simple turned spindles, canted ring-and-baluster-turned arm supports above the shaped saddle seat, raised on four canted baluster- and ring-turned legs joined by a shaped H-stretcher, probably Rhode Island, old grain-painted finish, late 18th - early 19th c., 37" h., pr. (ILLUS. of one) **$3,450**

Very Fine "Comb-back" Windsor Armchair

Windsor "comb-back" armchair, painted hardwood, the slender serpentine crestrail above seven tall turned spindles continuing through the U-shaped medial rail, the flat narrow shaped arms raised on two more spindles & a canted baluster-turned arm support, the oval shaped seat on widely canted baluster- and ring-turned legs joined by a swelled H-stretcher, old worn red paint over yellow & early paints, overall 41 1/4" h. (ILLUS.) **$20,700**

Nice Windsor "Comb-back" Armchair

Windsor "comb-back" armchair, the narrow serpentine & curved crestrail above eight tall simple turned spindles continuing through a medial rail extending to form the shaped arms raised on two short spindles & a baluster-turned canted arm support, wide shaped saddle seat, canted baluster-, ring- and rod-turned legs joined by a swelled H-stretcher, old refinish w/traces of old paint, old label w/provenance, late 18th c., 43" h. (ILLUS.) **$1,725**

Fine Philadelphia "Fan-back" Side Chair

Windsor "fan-back" side chair, painted wood, narrow serpentine crestrail w/scroll-carved ears above eight slender spindles & tall baluster-turned stiles over the shaped saddle seat, raised on canted baluster-, ring- and rod-turned legs joined by a swelled H-stretcher, old dark green paint over original lighter green, Philadephia origin, late 18th c., 36 1/2" h. (ILLUS.).. **$2,875**

Chests & Chests of Drawers

Unusual Old Pine Apothecary Chest

Apothecary chest, country-style, pine, hanging or table-type, the scroll-carved three-quarters gallery top above two rows of four square drawers w/white porcelain knobs above a pair of rectangular doors fitted on the interior w/bottle racks, flat bottom, complete w/eleven apothecary jars & spices, 19th c., 7 3/4 x 21 1/2", 23" h. (ILLUS.) **$863**

Country-style Chippendale Blanket Chest

Blanket chest, Chippendale country-style, yellow pine & poplar chest w/original painted surface decorated w/swags & tassels, on walnut, tulip poplar & yellow pine frame w/short cabriole legs w/trifid feet in front & tapered rear legs, scalloped side & front skirts, cut-nail construction, North Carolina, replaced hinges, restoration to feet, some fading & losses to paint, surface chips, scratches & scuffs, 26 1/2 x 42 x 18" (ILLUS., above) **$14,300**

Simple Cherry Country Blanket Chest

Blanket chest, country-style, cherry, the rectangular top w/a molded edge opening to a deep well, paneled sides raised on turned bun feet, original finish, mid-19th c., 37 1/2" l., 22" h. (ILLUS.).............. **$345**

Fine Grain-painted Blanket Chest

Blanket chest, country-style, painted & decorated, the hinged rectangular lid w/molded edges opening to a deep well, a molded base raised on shaped bracket feet, decorated overall w/grain painting w/a yellow ground covered w/red burl-style graining, Maine, 1820-40, 21 1/2 x 51 1/2", 27" h. (ILLUS.) **$5,975**

Early Grain-painted Blanket Chest

Blanket chest, grain-painted wood, six-board construction w/a rectangular top opening to an interior fitted w/one lidded till & eight drawers w/small turned knobs, original locks, raised on four short turned knob feet, all original mustard yellow-outlined panels w/simulated mahogany graining, probably from Maryland, early 19th c., 20 1/2 x 41 1/2", 21 3/4" h. (ILLUS.) **$1,150**

Chippendale "reverse-serpentine" chest of drawers, mahogany & mahogany veneer, the rectangular top w/a string-inlaid serpentine front edge above a conforming case w/four long graduated drawers w/butterfly brasses & keyhole escutcheons, molded base on boldly carved claw-and-ball feet, Massachusetts, ca. 1780, old replaced brasses, refinished, minor imperfections, 19 1/2 x 35", 33 1/4" h. (ILLUS., next page)............... **$9,988**

Reverse-serpentine Chippendale Chest

Maple Chippendale Tall Chest of Drawers

Chippendale tall chest of drawers, maple, a rectangular top w/a molded edge above a case w/a row of three small drawers above four long graduated thumb-molded drawers, all w/oval brasses, molded base w/scroll-cut bracket feet, old brasses, refinished, some restoration, New England, late 18th c., 17 3/4 x 39", 4' h. (ILLUS.) **$2,233**

Chippendale Revival Tall Chest of Drawers

Chippendale Revival tall chest of drawers, mahogany & mahogany veneer, rectangular top w/a wide coved cornice above a frieze band over a case w/a row of three small drawers above five long graduated drawers all w/butterfly pulls, narrow molded case on heavy foliate-carved ball-and-claw feet, some cockbeading missing on one drawer, minor veneer cracks, probably mid-19th c., 24 x 47 1/2", 5' 4" h. (ILLUS.) **$2,185**

Fine Chippendale-Style Block-front Desk

Chippendale-Style "block-front" chest of drawers, mahogany, the rectangular top w/molded edges & a double-blocked front above a conforming blocked case w/four long graduated drawers w/brass butterfly pulls & shield-shaped brass keyhole escutcheons, molded base w/scroll-cut corner blocks & short cabriole legs w/ball-and-claw feet, unsigned, fine quality, early 20th c., 18 x 32", 32" h. (ILLUS.) **$1,150**

Fine Classical State of Maine Chest

Classical chest of drawers, mahogany grain painting & mahogany veneer, the top w/a very high scroll-carved arched crest w/brass florettes at the scroll tips, above a two-tier section w/a pair of very narrow drawers above a pair of slightly deeper drawers all on the rectangular top slightly overhanging the case w/a projecting long curve-fronted top drawer above three set-back long graduated mahogany-veneered drawers, all drawers w/old pressed lacy glass pulls, the lower drawers flanked by turned black columns, molded base raised on tall heavy ring- and baluster-turned legs w/large ball feet, tiered drawers & case sides decorated w/red & black mahogany graining, State of Maine, first half 19th c., 20 1/2 x 44", overall 64" h. (ILLUS.)....... **$4,313**

Classical country-style chest of drawers, curly maple & walnut, the rectangular top w/a flat backsplash w/taller blocked ends,

above the base w/a row of three small curly maple drawers w/early pressed opalescent pulls above a deep long false-front drawer w/hinged front & matching pulls slightly projecting above a stack of three long graduated matching drawers flanked by full-round baluster- and spiral-turned columns resting on projecting blocks above the tapering turned double-knob front feet, fold-down compartment enclosing six pigeonholes & a central door opening to a compartment & hidden drawer, first half 19th c., 23 1/4 x 47 1/2", 4' 10" h. (interior hinge needs screws) ... **$1,870**

Fine New York Classical Silver Chest

Classical silver chest, mahogany & mahogany veneer, a thin rectangular top above a case w/three long graduated drawers w/round brass pulls, raised on four ropetwist-turned legs w/ring-turned sections & ending in brass caps w/casters, New York, New York, ca. 1800-20, 20 1/2 x 29 1/2", 36 1/2" h. (ILLUS.) **$3,585**

Very Rare Decorated Pennsylvania Dower Chest

Dower chest, painted & decorated, the rectangular hinged top w/a molded edge opening to a well, the front elaborately decorated w/brightly painted Pennsylvania Dutch designs, a large central twelve-point star in red & yellow below a facing pair of birds & w/tulips & starflowers below, a rearing unicorn at each side below a large parrot & a cluster of a star, tulip blossoms & starflowers at each end, a German inscription across the top front, all on a dark blue ground, a dark red base molding on dark blue scroll-cut ogee bracket feet, attributed to John Flory (1754-after 1824), Rapho Township, Lancaster County, Pennsylvania, dated 1794, 22 x 51 3/4", 22 1/2" h. (ILLUS., bottom of previous page) **$45,410**

Fine New Hampshire Federal Chest

Federal "bow-front" chest of drawers, cherry & burled birch, rectangular top w/a projecting ovolo corners & bowed front above a conforming case w/four long graduated drawers each w/banded & paneled veneer & oval brasses, ring-turned & reeded side stiles continue into the ring- and baluster-turned legs w/peg feet, New Hampshire, early 19th c., 19 1/2 x 43 1/2", 38" h. (ILLUS.) **$7,475**

Nicely Inlaid Federal Bow-front Chest

Federal "bow-front" chest of drawers, inlaid cherry & maple, the rectangular top w/a gently bowed front & ovolo corners projecting above a ring-turned segment over a tall reeded corner column flanking the case w/four gently curved long graduated drawers, each w/a long narrow oval central panel & oval brasses, a scroll-cut serpentine apron, turned tapering legs w/peg feet, probably Massachusetts, ca. 1815, replaced brasses, old refinish, minor imperfections, 21 3/4 x 44", 42" h. (ILLUS.) **$5,581**

Federal "bow-front" chest of drawers, inlaid mahogany, the rectangular top w/a bowed front above four long graduated dovetailed & cockbeaded bow-front drawers w/string & canted corner inlay & round brass pulls, biscuit corners w/conforming reeded columns, scalloped skirt above ring-turned legs, America, late 18th - early 19th c., one leg w/repaired split, minor restorations, replaced drawer runners, top drawer bottom replacement, added support pieces on side panels, 21 1/2 x 42 1/2", 37" h. **$2,640**

Federal chest of drawers, inlaid mahogany, rectangular top above four long graduated dovetailed & cockbeaded drawers w/original brass pulls & line inlay, drawer fronts w/book-matched figured mahogany, scalloped skirt on French feet, America, early 19th c., old refinishing, feet & skirt later replacements, 18 1/2 x 37 1/2", 36 1/2" h. **$1,540**

Fine Early Federal Chest of Drawers

Federal chest of drawers, mahogany & satin birch veneer, rectangular top w/projecting blocked corners above reeded square styles flanking the case w/four long drawers each w/two round brass pulls & oval keyhole escutcheons & decorated w/double rectangular panels of satin birch veneer, scroll-cut apron, raised on baluster- and ring-turned legs w/peg feet, original hardware, early 19th c., 19 1/2 x 44 3/4", 39" h. (ILLUS.) **$4,025**

Federal chest-on-frame, tiger stripe maple, a rectangular top w/a narrow coved cornice above a case w/five long graduated thumb-molded drawers w/brass batwing pulls & keyhole escutcheons, molded base raised on a gently shaped apron w/bracket feet, old refinish, probably Rhode Island, late 18th - early 19th c., 19 x 38 1/4", 47 1/4" h. (replaced brasses, surface imperfections) **$2,350**

Early English Jacobean Oak Chest

Jacobean chest, carved oak, long rectangular hinged top opening to a deep well, the front divided into three panels, a narrow carved dart panel across the top, the matching end panels carved w/two small crosses in the center within a molded rectangle w/projecting corners, the center section w/an upper rectangular panel carved w/"AT," the lower panel carved w/rectangular bands & two elongated crosses, thin beaded bands down each front edge, flat base, on bun feet, shrinkage cracks, refinished, normal wear, England, late 17th - early 18th c., 26 1/4 x 63 3/4", 34 1/2" h. (ILLUS.)
.... **$690**

Louis XV-Style chest of drawers, inlaid hardwood, rectangular serpentine-sided mottled brown & ivory marble top w/biscuit corners above a conforming case w/two hand-dovetailed drawers w/hand-planed surfaces & original locks, decorated w/elaborate floral & vine inlay, ormolu mounts w/extensive scrolled & raised openwork surfaces w/14" ormolu mounts at tops of legs, scrolled ormolu feet & apron, paper label on back of top drawer reading "Hirsch Antiquities, 32 Rue du Grinelle, Paris," France, 19th c., repairs to legs, various separations & veneer losses, missing ormolu on proper left side of top drawer, several panels loose under top, marble top broken, w/two large pieces present, repairs to marble, metal frame to reinforce marble, 25 x 63 1/2", 36" h. **$5,280**

Louis XVI-Style bachelor's chest, figured veneers w/h.p. floral & gilt decoration, red, grey & white shaped marble top w/small gallery at rear holding two small drawers, body w/reeded legs & pilasters w/raised acanthus leaves & banding around door & drawer panels, holding 18 drawers including four on each side behind the doors, two in the bottom, & two at the center w/concave fronts, by "Slack Rassnick & Co, New York," 24 1/2 x 48 1/2", 4' 6" h. (ILLUS., top next column) **$1,150**

Louis XVI-Style Bachelor's Chest

Mule chest (box chest w/one or more drawers below a storage compartment), early American country-style, pine, rectangular one-board top w/edge molding opening to a deep well above a long bottom drawer w/edge molding, board ends w/bootjack cut-outs, constructed w/mostly early T-head nails, old refinish, New England, 18th c., 18 1/4 x 48", 32 1/2" h. (minor age splits, iron batwing keyhole escucheon replacement) **$770**

Mule chest (box chest w/one or more drawers below a storage compartment), pine, rectangular top w/molded edges above two long false drawer fronts fitted w/butterfly brasses & keyhole escutcheon above two long working drawers w/matching hardware, base molding above simple shaped bracket feet, top opening to a well w/a till, wrought-iron hinge pins, refinished, probably late 18th c., New England, 17 1/2 x 37 1/2" (replaced brasses, edge wear, bottom drawer damaged & w/replaced bottom board, lower backboard replaced).................... **$1,595**

Cradles

Victorian Renaissance Revival Cradle

Victorian Renaissance Revival "trestle-style" cradle, carved walnut, the cradle w/eight pierced slats on each side decorated w/circle carvings, the ends w/pierced scroll carving & applied decorative molding, supported by an iron hanger at each end & hanging between turned posts above the trestle-style framed w/flattened serpentine legs joined by a flat cross stretcher, ca. 1870, one leg w/repaired split, 19 1/4 x 41", 38 1/2" h. (ILLUS.) **$300-500**

Cupboards

Nice Federal Country Corner Cupboard

Corner cupboard, Federal country-style, pine, two-part construction: the upper section w/a flat top & blocked coved cornice above stepped reeded pilasters down the front flanking an arched frieze band of small ovals centered by a keystone all above the wide arched door w/geometric glazing opening to three shelves; the lower section w/a mid-molding above a pair of shorter paneled cupboard doors flanked by the continued reeded pilasters, flat base raised on knob-turned front legs, old refinish, Pennsylvania, early 19th c., 24 x 47", 7' 7" h. (ILLUS.) **$6,463**

Pennsylvania Walnut Corner Cupboard

Corner cupboard, Federal country-style, walnut, one-piece construction, the flat top w/a coved cornice above a pair of two-panel cupboard doors opening to three shaped shelves above a mid-molding & a pair of shorter paneled cupboard doors, molded base on scroll-cut bracket feet, Pennsylvania, first half 19th c., 26 x 39", 6' 4 1/2" h. (ILLUS.)................. **$3,025**

Corner cupboard, Federal style, walnut, two-part construction: the upper section w/a cove-molded cornice above two 8-pane glazed doors opening to three shelves; the lower section w/a medial astragal molding above a pair of two-panel cupboard doors, molded base on scroll-cut bracket feet w/reeded faces, original "H" hinges, vertical yellow pine backboards w/original hand-wrought nails, Piedmont, North Carolina, late 18th or early 19th c., wear on hinges, one side front of skirt off but present, missing other side, missing several pieces of door molding, 21 x 54", 7' 11" h. (ILLUS., next page).. **$5,280**

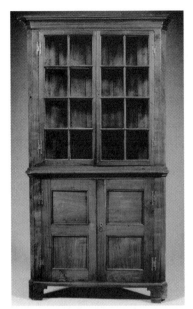

Fine Federal Corner Cupboard

Very Fine Nutting-Made Corner Cupboard

Corner cupboard, Nutting-signed Federal-Style, inlaid mahogany, two-part construction: the upper section w/a high molded broken-scroll crest w/rosettes flanking a tall center urn-turned finial, the frieze band inlaid w/an oval paterae above the tall arched 14-pane glazed door w/a fine light inlaid border band & opening to three shelves, the angled sides also inlaid w/long panels; the lower section w/a medial band above a case w/a single long rectangular door opening to a single shelf & w/light inlaid banding & a central paterae, the angled sides also inlaid w/short double panels, molded base w/scroll-cut bracket feet, w/original key, back branded "Wallace Nutting," early 20th c., 15 1/4 x 32 1/2", overall 85 1/2" h. (ILLUS.) **$5,750**

Fine Painted Country Jelly Cupboard

Jelly cupboard, painted & decorated country-style, rectangular top w/a deep flaring cornice above a single tall & wide four-panel door w/turned wood knob opening to three shelves, flat base raised on heavy ring- and knob-turned legs, original lock, remnants of early red paint under grain painting, probably from Pennsylvania or Ohio, mid-19th c., 21 x 40", 61 1/2" h. (ILLUS.) **$3,738**

Nice Painted Pie Safe

Walnut & Cherry Pie Safe

Pie safe, painted poplar & chestnut, the long rectangular top above a single long drawer w/wooden knobs over a pair of doors each set w/two punched-tin panels decorated w/a pinwheel & quarter-round design, two matching tin panels in each side, flat apron, square stile legs, original reddish brown paint, 19th c., 17 1/2 x 42", 44 3/4" h. (ILLUS., previous page) **$2,013**

Pie safe, walnut & cherry, mortise-&-tenon construction, the rectangular top above two dovetailed drawers w/cut-nail construction above two doors each fitted w/four punched-tin panels, each panel w/designs of urns & grapes & star corners, punched-tin panels in sides, turned legs, original brass hinges, vertical backboards w/cut nails, attributed to Rich family shop, Wythe County, Virginia, 1830-80, old refinishing, drawer bottoms w/chips, traces of old blue paint, top w/stains & small separations, 17 x 50", 4' 3" h. (ILLUS., top of page) **$6,600**

Pie safe, walnut, the rectangular top above a pair of deep drawers w/replaced oval brasses above a pair of tall doors each w/three replaced pierced-tin panels, old matching tin panels in the sides, flat apron raised on baluster- and ring-turned legs w/knob feet, mouse hole & chips on drawer front & openings, refinished, 19th c., 18 1/2 x 42", 4' 6 1/2" h. (ILLUS., top next column).. **$575**

Old Walnut Pie Safe

Side cupboard, painted & decorated poplar, rectangular top w/a shaped three-quarter gallery above a wide single board-and-batten door w/cast-iron thumb latch, one-board ends, curved bracket front feet, old brown graining, interior shelves, found near Richmond, Indiana, second half 19th c. 19 1/4 x 27 3/4", overall 32 1/2" h. (strip added to door)...... **$715**

Rare Chippendale Step-back Cupboard

Step-back wall cupboard, Chippendale, cherry, two-part construction: the upper section w/a rectangular top over a very deep stepped & flaring cornice w/a lower dentil-carved band above a pair of large six-pane glazed cupboard doors w/brass H-hinges & latches above a low pie shelf; the lower stepped-out section w/a row of three drawers w/butterfly pulls above a pair of double-paneled cupboard doors w/brass H-hinges & latches, narrow molded base on small ogee bracket feet, Pennsylvania, 1760-80, 20 x 59", 7' 2" h. (ILLUS.) **$5,736**

Grain-painted Wall Cupboard

Step-back wall cupboard, country-style, hardwood, two-part construction: the top section w/a molded cornice above a pair of paneled cupboard doors over a row of three narrow drawers above a high open pie shelf w/a narrow open shelf at the back; the base w/a row of three dovetailed drawers over two paneled doors beside a

stack of three small drawers on the left, porcelain drawer pulls & iron latches probably original, original grain-painted surface w/yellow graining, faux burlwood panels on doors & drawer fronts, probably Pennsylvania, 19th c., chips, stains & losses to painted surface, 21 3/4 x 52", 73" h. (ILLUS.) **$1,210**

Simple Old Pine Step-back Cupboard

Step-back wall cupboard, country-style, pine, one-piece construction: the upper case w/a rectangular top w/a molded cornice above a pair of tall two-panel cupboard doors opening to shelves above a pair of narrow drawers above a stepped-out shelf above a pair of shorter two-panel cupboard doors w/cast-iron latches, refinished, couple of later supports added to base, second half 19th c., 19 3/4 x 51", 6' 9 1/4" h. (ILLUS.) **$1,035**

Early Pennsylvania Step-back Cupboard

Fine French Art Deco Applewood & Parquetry Desk

Step-back wall cupboard, country-style, softwood, two-part construction: the upper section w/a rectangular top & widely stepped flaring cornice above a pair of large six-pane glazed cupboard doors w/brass latches above an open pie shelf; the stepped-out lower section w/a row of three drawers w/wooden knobs slightly projecting above a pair of paneled cupboard doors w/brass hardware flanked by half-round columns, on short heavy turned feet, replaced hardware & top board, Pennsylvania, mid-19th c., 19 x 52", 7' 1" h. (ILLUS., previous page) **$3,850**

Desks

Art Deco desk, horn-mounted applewood & parquetry, the rectangular top above a case w/a pair of small drawers w/round brass pulls flanking a long center drawer w/two angled brass bar pulls over the kneehole opening flanked by parquetry doors opening to reveal three parquetry-front drawers w/horn tadpole-shaped mounts, one replaced, France, ca. 1930, 30 x 55 1/2", 30 1/4" h. (ILLUS., top of page) **$3,650**

Chippendale slant-front desk, mahogany, the narrow top above a wide hinged slant-front opening to a three-part fan-

Chippendale Slant-Front Desk

carved interior, the case w/pull-out supports flanking a narrow long top drawer over three long graduated drawers all w/brass butterfly pulls, molded base raised on short cabriole legs w/ball-and-claw feet, the apron w/a central shell-carved drop, probably American, late 19th c., restored, crack on side, lip damage, holes in the top for missing gallery, 18 3/4 x 40 1/2", 42" h. (ILLUS.) **$1,438**

Fine Chippendale-Style Parnter's Desk

Oak Jacobean-Style English Desk

Chippendale-Style partner's desk, mahogany & mahogany veneer, the large rectangular top w/three tooled green leather inserts, the case fitted on each side w/a stack of two narrow drawers w/simple bail pulls flanking the arched serpentine kneehole opening w/a single drawer, scroll-carved cabriole legs w/claw-and-ball feet, late 19th - early 20th c., 48 x 72", 32" h. (ILLUS., bottom previous page) **$4,715**

Fine Federal-Style Tambour Desk

Federal-Style tambour desk, inlaid mahogany, two-part construction: the upper section w/a rectangular top w/a narrow molded cornice above mahogany-veneered frieze band & thin molding over two square tambour sliding doors opening to six cubby holes & two small drawers all flanked by narrow band-inlaid side panels & centered by a small door w/banded inlay surrounding a large inlaid flower-filled urn, the door opening to two cubby holes & a drawer; the lower section w/a medial molding above a narrow fold-out writing ledge above a case w/narrow drawer slides flanking the long drawer w/inlaid line banding & oval brass pulls above a deeper long drawer w/matching inlay & pulls, the sides inlaid w/long bellflower swags & line inlay continuing down the square tapering legs, American-made, early 20th c., 18 x 36", overall 45 1/2" h. (ILLUS.)........................ **$805**

Jacobean-Style desk, carved oak, the rectangular top w/an elaborately carved edge band & molded edges above a deep apron w/a long front drawer elaborately carved w/leafy scrolls centered by a grotesque mask pull, a bold carved grotesque mask at each corner above the bold baluster- and ring-turned legs w/further leafy scroll carving & ending in carved blocks joined by a heavy knob-and rod-turned H-stretcher w/reeding & leaf carving on bun feet, England, ca. 1900, 28 x 42", 30" h. (ILLUS., top of page) **$1,093**

Louis XV country-style desk, hardwood, long rectangular two-board top w/framed sides overhanging a case w/a center kneehole opening flanked by single deep drawers w/simple bail pulls, raised on flattened rectangular simple cabriole legs, some repairs & restoration, Europe, probably 19th c., 27 x 68 1/4", 29 1/4" h. (ILLUS., top next page)........................ **$1,150**

Louis XV Country-style Desk

Fine Louis XVI-Style Lady's Desk

Louis XVI-Style lady's desk, ebonized wood & boulle, the narrow rectangular top w/a low pierced brass gallery above the slanted hinged front w/a long rectangular inlaid boulle panel & gilt-brass banding opening to drawers, a storage well & a leather-inset writing surface, the serpentine apron & sides w/further ornate inlaid boulle panels, raised on simple cabriole legs w/gilt-brass scrolled knee mounts & ending in gilt-brass foot caps, Napoleon III-era, France, ca. 1870, 25 1/2" w., 36" h. (ILLUS., left) **$1,725**

Louis XVI-Style library desk, mahogany & parquetry, the banded rectangular top inset w/a leather writing surface above an apron w/a long central drawer flanked by a deeper drawer, all inset w/parquetry-inlaid panels, raised on square tapering inlaid legs ending in brass caps, France, early 20th c., 28 3/4 x 50 1/2", 30" h. (ILLUS., bottom of page)... **$3,220**

French Louis XVI-Style Mahogany & Parquetry Desk

Dry Sinks

Early New England Painted Dry Sink

Painted pine, the deep rectangular top well above a mid-molding above a single flat door, original old grey paint, originally built-in so no back, New England, 19th c., 17 x 28 1/2", 26 1/2" h. (ILLUS.) **$1,783**

Early Dry Sink with Nice Old Finish

Stained hardwood, the rectangular top well w/dovetailed construction above a case w/a pair of tall paneled cupboard doors opening to a shelf, low arched apron & simple bracket feet, nice weathered old finish, open crack in one side, mid-19th c., 16 1/2 x 38 1/2", 41" h. (ILLUS.).......... **$460**

Garden & Lawn

Italian 20th Century Stone & Iron Garden Suite

Garden suite: table, bench & two armchairs; the long table w/a rectangular Pietra Dura style decorated slate top featuring scrolled ivory-colored acanthus leaves & raised on scrolling wrought-iron end legs topped by pierced spiraling brass balls, the long rectangular bench w/an upholstered top & double-scroll ends legs joined by a long stretcher, each armchair w/a low back w/a long rectangular panel of wide fabric bands, flat serpentine arms above the woven cloth seat supported on slender U-shaped iron frames & wide arched iron bar legs, Italy, mid-20th c., table, 30 x 57", 29" h., the set (ILLUS.).. **$2,415**

Two Neoclassical Garden Settees with Double-Diamond Backs

Settee, Neoclassical taste, a narrow reeded flat crestrail above the openwork back composed of two large double-diamond panels, serpentine end arms continuing down to form the front legs, long rectangular slat seat, legs joined by stretchers & bar braces, old cream paint, 19th c., 60" l., 38" h. (ILLUS. front with matching settee) **$2,185**

Settee, Neoclassical taste, a narrow reeded flat crestrail above the openwork back composed of two large double-diamond panels, serpentine end arms continuing down to form the front legs, long rectangular slat seat, legs joined by stretchers & bar braces, old cream paint, 19th c., 60" l., 38" h. (ILLUS. back with matching settee) **$2,990**

Victorian Arch-backed Garden Settee

Settee, the leaf-cast serpentine crestrail above the long back composed of rows of small openwork arche, the stepped &

canted end arms composed of upright C-scrolls, pierced-scroll long seat on S-scroll cabriole front legs, old white paint, late 19th c., 44" l. (ILLUS.) **$1,135**

Scrolling Victorian Garden Settee

Settee, the long low back composed of en-twined openwork leafy scrolls centered by a large grape clusters, long oblong pierced seat w/a matching pierced scroll apron & floral- and leaf-cast outswept front legs joined by curved bar stretchers to the rear legs, worn white paint, late 19th c., 42 1/2" l. (ILLUS.) **$956**

Three-piece English Garden Set with Gothic Motifs

Settee & armchairs, each w/a back cen-tered by a large round openwork medal-lion above a back composed of entwined Gothic arches, downswept arms com-posed of leafy scrolls, planked bead-board seats, Gothic arch-form openwork end legs, dark green paint, England, mid-19th c., the set (ILLUS.) **$1,955**

Double Gothic Arch Victorian Garden Settees

Settees, double chair-back style w/the back composed of two large open Gothic Arch-

es made of flattened iron straps, simple curved strap end arms above the long rectangular open slat seat raised on six flat bar legs joined by H-stretchers, green paint, 19th c., 42" l., 39" h., pr. (ILLUS.).... **$748**

Late Victorian Laurel Pattern Garden Settees

Settees, Laurel patt., the long scallop-topped back composed of openwork panels of large vertical leafy branches curving around to tapering scrolled arms, the long half-round seat composed of leafy scrolls, the front legs in the form a bird head & large wing curving down to a claw foot, old white paint, ca. 1900, 42" l., 29" h., pr. (ILLUS.) **$5,520**

Settees, the long arched back composed of entwining leafy vines w/various birds all centered by a large relief-molded oval plaque showing a seated classical nymph, the cast-iron slatted seat above curved legs ending in hoof feet, painted black, second half 19th c., 24 x 63", 38" h., pr. (ILLUS. of one, top next page) **$8,050**

One of Two Arch-backed Settees

Settees, the serpentine crestrail composed of leafy scrolls & florals above a back panel composed of repeating small open arches, the high stepped arms com-posed of slender C-scrolls, the ornate pierced seat above a scrolling pierced apron & scrolling cabriole legs, white paint w/overall rusting, 19th c., 43" l., pr. (ILLUS. of one) **$1,150**

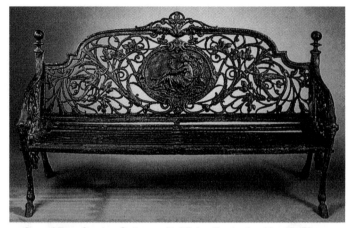

One of Two Garden Settees with Vining Backs & a Nymph Plaque

*One of a Pair of English Fern Pattern
Garden Settees*

Settees, the wide arched back composed of large pierced scrolling fern leaves curving around to form the end arms flanking the wooden slat seat, outswept fern-cast legs, old green paint, England, 19th c., 15 1/2 x 58", 35" h., pr. (ILLUS. of one) **$1,955**

Round Pierced Garden Table

Table, round top pierced overall w/tight leafy scrolls, supported on tall double C-scroll legs headed by pierced lattice pan-

els & joined by a pierced round lower shelf, 39" d., 27" h. (ILLUS.)...................... **$717**

Hall Racks & Trees

Unusual Bamboo-style Hall Rack

Hall rack, Victorian bamboo-style, composed of three tall crossed bamboo-turned legs joined at the bottom w/a triangular metal drip tray & side stretchers, each stick fitted w/coat hooks & topped w/a pointed metal halberd blade, late 19th c., overall 90 1/2" h. (ILLUS.) **$230**

Fine Classical-Style Mahogany Hall Tree

Hall tree, Classical-Style, carved mahogany, a tall post ornately decorated w/carved acanthus leaves & ring-turnings & capped by a brass ball & eagle finial, fitted w/serpentine lotus-carved hooks, raised on four scroll-carved heavy paw feet, late 19th c., 88" h. (ILLUS.) **$2,990**

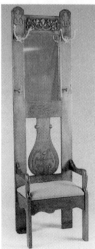

Tall Victorian Golden Oak Hall Tree

Hall tree, Victorian Golden Oak style, the very tall back w/a short leafy scroll-carved flat crest flanked by tall flat side stiles w/arched tops w/leaf carving & flanking a long rectangular mirror above a vasiform-lower splat w/scroll carving, the stile mounted w/two double & two single hat hooks, low shaped open arms

flanking the upholstered seat, serpentine apron, flat stile front legs, ca. 1890s, 15 x 21 3/4", 80 1/2" h. (ILLUS.) **$259**

Fancy Victorian Walnut Hall Tree

Hall tree, Victorian Renaissance Revival style, walnut, the tall base w/an arched pierced-scroll crest above a frieze band w/notched pegs flanking a small rectangular burl panel & w/hat posts at each side, the main upper section w/stepped & pierce-carved sides w/four hat pegs surrounding an upright rectangular mirror w/rounded corners, the narrower stepped & pierce-carved lower section w/a small candle shelf above an oblong rack w/side openings flanking a small square marble top, two rectangular front uprights to a base shelf fitted w/two cast-iron drip trays, a split in one of the umbrella ring holders, ca. 1890, 11 1/2 x 29", 89" h. (ILLUS.) **$604**

Highboys & Lowboys

Highboys
Chippendale bonnet-top highboy, carved mahogany, two-part construction: the upper section w/a broken swan's-neck pediment terminating in carved rosettes flanked by & centering urn-and-flame finials, above a central shell-carved long drawer w/ornate scrolling tendrils & flanked by two small drawers over a pair of drawers above three long graduated drawers all flanked by engaged quarter columns; the lower section w/a mid-molding over a long drawer over a deep central drawer w/a carved shell flanked by ornate leafy scrolls & flanked by two small drawers, the scalloped apron centered by a carved shell, raised on cabriole legs w/shell-carved knees & ending in claw-and-ball feet, Philadelphia, 1760-80, 25 1/2 x 47", 7' 11 1/4" h. (finials replaced) **$163,500**

Cherry Queen Anne "Married" Highboy

Queen Anne flat-top highboy, cherry, two-part construction: the upper section w/a rectangular flat top w/a deep coved cornice above a case w/a pair of drawers over four long graduated drawers all w/brass butterfly pulls; the lower married section w/a medial rail above a case w/a single long narrow drawer above two deep square drawers flanking a wide center deep drawer w/a fan-carved front, shaped front apron w/two turned drops, cabriole legs ending in raised pad feet, New England, 18th c., restored, top left cornice missing section of back, base 19 1/2 x 38 1/8", overall 78" h. (ILLUS.) ... **$4,025**

Nice "Married" Queen Anne Highboy

Queen Anne flat-top highboy, tiger stripe maple & cherry, two-part construction: the top section w/a rectangular top w/a deep flaring stepped cornice above a case w/five long graduated drawers

w/brass butterfly pulls & keyhole escutcheons; the married lower section w/a medial molding above a case w/two deep square drawers flanking a short central drawer above a high serpentine apron w/two turned drops, simple cabriolge legs ending in pad feet, replaced brasses, New England, late 18th c., base 17 3/4 x 39", overall 76" h. (ILLUS.) **$2,300**

English Burl Walnut Queen Anne Highboy

Queen Anne flat-top highboy, walnut & burl walnut, two-part construction: the upper section w/a flat top w/a narrow cornice above a pair of drawers over three long graduated drawers; the lower section w/a wide flared molding above a narrow center drawer flanked by deep side drawers all w/butterfly pulls & round keyhole escutcheons, arched & serpentine apron raised on cabriole legs ending in raised pointed pad feet, replaced hardware, England, ca. 1720, 40" w., 5' 3" h. (ILLUS.) **$8,050**

Love Seats, Sofas & Settees

European Jacobean-Style Carved Mahogany Chaise Longue

Fine Louis XV-Style Caned Chaise Longue

Chaise longue, Jacobean-Style, carved mahogany, the angled end backrest of square form w/a wide heavily pierce-carved frame of scrolls, leaves & shells centering a caned panel & flanked by spiral- and block-turned stiles, the long rectangular caned seat in a plain frame raised on six spiral- and block-turned legs on ball feet & joined by long flat pierced & scroll-carved side rails, Europe, late 19th c., 22 x 71", 35" h. (ILLUS., previous page) **$1,725**

Chaise longue, Louis XV-Style, carved gilt-wood, one end w/a caned back w/a gently arched crestrail centered w/shell carving & flanked by scrolling foliage, low curved caned arms w/acanthus leaf grips, on a scroll-carved & molded apron raised on carved cabriole legs ending in scroll feet & joined by U-form stretchers, w/a tapestry cushion, France, late 19th - early 20th c., 30 x 64", 39 1/2" h. (ILLUS., top of page) **$2,990**

Mahogany & Cane Louis XVI-Style Daybed

Daybed, Louis XVI-Style, carved mahogany, the gently arched long back w/a narrow molded & floral-carved crestrail above the paneled & caned back, the high arched & caned end arms w/tapering leaf-carved outswept arm supports above the long deep cushion seat, straight molded seatrail centered by a carved floral reserve, carved rounded

corner blocks raised on turned & tapering front feet, France, late 19th c., 31 x 81 1/2", 43" h. (ILLUS.) **$3,220**

Fine Louis XVI-Style Painted Daybed

Daybed, Louis XVI-Style, painted wood, the matching low head- and footboards w/a molded arched crestrail above upholstered panels flanked by reeded columnar stiles w/top & base blocks & topped by acorn-carved finials, raised on turned & tapering carved feet, narrow siderails, old creamy paint, fitted w/mattress & bolsters, France, late 19th c., 39 x 78", 34" h. (ILLUS.) **$6,325**

Fine Louise XV-Style Duchesse Brisée

Duchesse brisée, Louis XV-Style, gilt-wood, composed of a wingback armchair w/a rounded crest above the large cushion seat, the serpentine scroll-carved apron & cabriole legs in gilt, w/a matching large rectangular stool w/a large cushion, upholstered in fine claret damask, France, late 19th c., stool 20 1/2" h., chair 37" h., 2 pcs. (ILLUS.) **$2,185**

Fine American Classical Carved Mahogany Récamier

Récamier, Classical style, carved mahogany, the long narrow curved back crestrail over a tapering upholstered panels, one end of a high out-scrolled upholstered arms w/a diamond point-carved arm support w/scrolled tip & at the other end w//a large inscrolled low arm w/a carved tightly scroll diamond point-carved supports, the long narrow rounded seatrail supported by large carved spread-winged eagles raised on outswept carved paw feet, New York City, ca. 1820-30, 25 x 91", 30" h. (ILLUS.) **$4,780**

Fine Empire-Style French Récamier

Récamier, Empire-Style, ormolu-mounted mahogany, the padded end back w/an outscrolled swan's-neck crest above the long padded seat, the foot slightly raised & scrolled back to carved swans' necks, raised on a griffin- and Bacchus-applied apron raised on winged sphinx legs ending in ormolu paw feet, France, late 19th c., 27 x 70", 36" h. (ILLUS.) **$2,970**

Louis XV-Style Giltwood Recamier

Récamier, Louis XV-Style, carved giltwood, one end w/a long arched serpentine scroll-carved crestrail tapering into two panels at the back & curving to form the end arms w/an inscrolled arm support, long padded rectangular seat w/a serpentine front above the conforming seatrail carved w/delicate scrolls & raised on cabriole legs ending in scroll & peg feet, France, late 19th c., 24 x 53", 33" h. (ILLUS.) **$1,035**

Victorian Country-style Tiger Maple Settee

Settee, country-style, tiger stripe maple, a wide flat backboard w/rolled top joining the ends, each composed of a short ring- and rod-turned front & rear posts topped by a cannonball w/a heavy ring-turned rail joining the balls, the posts raised on blocks above the turned tapering legs w/knob- and peg-feet, round front & back rails pierced w/holes for looping rope, American, mid-19th c., nice alligatored finish, 25 x 72 1/2" l., 26" h. (ILLUS.) **$288**

Elizabethan Revival Rosewood Settee

Settee, Elizabethan Revival style, carved rosewood, the long back crestrail composed of ornate pierce-carved scrolls above three large upholstered panels flanked by further scroll panels, all flanked by spiral-turned stiles w/ring-turned finials above corner blocks, the shaped open arms w/scrolled hand grips raised on incurved arm supports flanking the long over-upholstered seat w/a narrow seatrail ending in scroll-carved front cabriole legs w/scroll feet on casters, England, mid-19th c., 25 x 60", 47" h. (ILLUS.) **$1,150**

Nice Country Federal Decorated Settee

Settee, Federal country-style, painted & decorated poplar, the long two-section flat crestrail w/rounded corner sections above two lower rails over a row of short turned spindles, the downswept S-shaped open arms on turned spindles & flanking the long plank seat raised on eight turned & canted legs joined by box stretchers, old red & black graining w/the crest stenciled w/baskets of fruit, blue line trim, ca. 1840-50, 23 x 70", 34" h. (ILLUS., top of page).............................. **$633**

Louis XVI-Style Giltwood Settee

open arms on incurved arm supports above the long upholstered seat, the flat molded two-part seatrail w/central carved panels, raised on tapering fluted front legs w/peg feet, France, early 20th c., 59 1/2" l., 37" h. (ILLUS.) **$978**

Settee, Windsor-style, the long wide flat crestrail above a two-section back composed of fifteen bamboo-turned spindles centered by a heavier turned stile, bamboo-turned open arms on three small spindles & a larger canted arm support, long plank seat raised on six canted bamboo-turned legs joined by box stretchers, nice old worn brown surface, some old repairs, first half 19th c., 44" l., 35 3/4" h. **$2,588**

Settle, Spanish Colonial, carved hardwood, a long scrolling foliate-carved crestrail centering religious cartouche flanked by stiles topped w/tall ring-turned finials, the lower back w/a shaped panel raised on pairs of knob-turned spindles, wide flat serpentine arms above floral-inlaid supports & legs flanking the long plank seat, the six-leg trestle-form base w/a flat floral-carved front stretcher, missing much mother-of-pearl inlay, round burn mark on right side of seat, 18th c., 26 x 81 7/8", 43 1/2" h. (ILLUS., top next page)......... **$6,325**

Fine Federal-Style Double-Back Settee

Settee, Federal-Style, carved mahogany, double-back style, two shield-shaped openwork panels joined by a pierced central panel, the shaped open arms on incurved arm supports above the over-upholstered bowed seat & seatrail, square tapering legs, minor nicks, late 19th - early 20th c., 44 1/2" l., 36 1/2" h. (ILLUS.).. **$1,115**

Settee, Louis XVI-Style, giltwood, the long oval upholstered back enclosed by a narrow carved frame topped by a small carved musical crest, shaped & padded

Unusual Carved Hardwood Spanish Colonial Settle

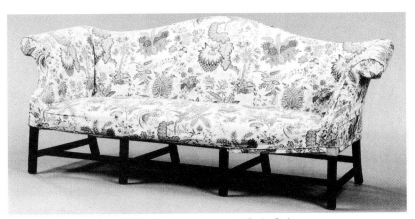

Chippendale Camel-back Style Sofa

Sofa, Chippendale camel-back style, mahogany, the long serpentine upholstered back flanked by outswept scrolled upholstered arms above the long upholstered seat, raised on eight square legs joined by box stretchers, late 18th c., 88" l. (ILLUS.) **$5,019**

Long Classical Country-style Sofa

Sofa Classical country-style, inlaid & veneered mahogany & bird's-eye maple, the wide & long flat round-fronted crestrail & short end stiles above the low upholstered back flanked by heavy low upholstered C-scroll arms flanking the seat w/a long upholstered cushion, the wide strait ogee seatrail raised on long heavy S-scroll legs, some veneer banding missing, attributed to Thomas Day (1801-61), 26 x 93", 30" h. (ILLUS.) **$690**

Sofa, Classical-Style, carved mahogany, the long rod-form crestrail w/leaf-carved inward-scrolled ends above a flat rail raised on serpentine ends above the deep outscrolled upholstered arms w/carved swan's-neck arm supports, the long ogee-molded seatrail w/blocked ends raised on large wings & outswept carved paw feet, old black horsehair upholstery, late 19th c., 64 1/2" l., 35 1/2" h. **$2,530**

High-backed Regency-Style Fruitwood Sofa

Sofa, Regency-Style, fruitwood, the triple-arched crestrail over the high upholstered back flanked by downswept closed arms above the long over-upholstered seat, four tall scrolled front legs joined by high serpentine front stretchers & lower serpentine H-stretchers, England, late 19th c., 75" l., 40 1/2" h. (ILLUS.).................... **$3,220**

Fine Regency-Style Mahogany Sofa

Sofa, Regency-Style, mahogany, the long narrow crestrail above the upholstered back flanked by high upholstered arms w/baluster- and ring-turned reeded front posts, a long cushion seat on an upholstered seatrail, four baluster-turned reeded front legs ending in peg feet, England, early 20th c., 29 x 76", 31" h. (ILLUS.)... **$1,495**

Sofa, Renaissance-Style, carved oak, the long back w/a very high & ornately pierce-carved crestrail composed of fruit & flowers w/a center oval medallion flanked by griffins, the back framed further carved along the sides & bottom & enclosing a tufted brown leather panel, the back blanked by spiral-turned open stile w/small turned finials, the padded open arms raised on short spiral-turned supports flanking the long leather seat raised on eight block-carved legs joined

by spiral-carved stretchers, France, late 19th c. **$1,380**

Small Renaissance Revival Walnut Sofa

Sofa, Victorian Renaissance Revival substyle, walnut & burl walnut, a double-back style, the double arched & burl-paneled crestrail centered by a tall pointed burl panel cartouche, the two upholstered back panels separated by an openwork shaped flat bar, outswept low upholstered arms w/incurved front rails flanking the upholstered seat w/a gently curved seatrail centered by a burl panel over a low arched drop, ring-turned tapering front legs & canted square rear legs, ca. 1875, 55" l., 41" h. (ILLUS.)........ **$316**

Meeks "Stanton Hall" Rococo Sofa

Sofa, Victorian Rococo style, carved & laminated rosewood, the long serpentine crestrail pierce-carved w/ornate scrolls & centering a higher central section w/a gadrooned rail centered by a large shell- and flower-carved crest, the crestrail curving down & enclosing the tufted upholstered back above closed scrolled arms w/incurved arm supports, a long upholstered seat w/a serpentine molded seatrail centered by a carved reserve, on demi-cabriole front legs on casters, the "Stanton Hall" pattern by J.& J.W. Meeks, New York City, ca. 1855, 27 x 66", 4' 1/2" h. (ILLUS.).................................. **$5,520**

Triple-back Victorian Rococo Sofa

Sofa Victorian Rococo substyle, carved rosewood, three-part back, the central shield-shaped panel w/a high arched & ornate scroll-carved crest & tufted upholstered panel flanked by curved upholstered side panels w/wide scroll-carved crestrail curving down the low upholstered arms w/incurved scroll-carved arm supports, the long upholstered seat w/a double-serpentine seatrail w/two carved floral & scroll panels, demi-cabriole front legs w/ornately carved knees, raised on four casters, original cut-plush upholstery, ca. 1860, 28 x 68", 43" h. (ILLUS.)............... **$1,380**

Victorian Rococo-Style Sofa

Sofa, Victorian Rococo-Style, carved walnut, medallion-back style w/the large central oval tufted upholstery panel topped by a floral-carved crest, the molded & arched side crestrail curving around & down over the tufted upholstered back & long outswepted upholstered arms w/scroll-carved arm supports, simple serpentine seatrail continuing into the demi-cabriole front legs, mid-20th c. (ILLUS.).... **$518**

Mirrors

Adams-Style wall mirror, carved giltwood, the large oval molded frame w/narrow egg-and-dart rim band topped by a tall carved urn & plume finial flanked by long delicate leafy scrolls continuing down the sides to floral-carved swags, the bottom decorated w/carved fabric swags centered by a leaf- and disk-carved pendant drop, England, early 20th c., restored

English Adams-Style Wall Mirror

split in crest, 23 1/2" w., 42" h. (ILLUS.)
.... **$460**

Chinese Chippendale English Mirror

Chippendale Rococo wall mirror, carved giltwood, in the Chinese taste, the tall rectangular mirror enclosed by a very ornat pierce-carved frame, the wide serpentine crestrail w/carved & pierced wide scrolls centering an openwork pagoda, the crest continuing down into the scrolling openwork sides w/narrow reeded pilasters, the serpentine bottom rail w/further pierced leafy scrolls & a central scrolled panels, in the manner of Thomas Johnson (1714-78), England, late 18th c., 32" w., 56" h. (ILLUS.)...................... **$2,070**

Chippendale Mahogany Wall Mirror

Chippendale wall mirror, parcel-gilt mahogany, the high arched & pierced scroll-cut crestrail centered by an open circle mounted w/a giltwood spread-winged phoenix, a narrow molded rectangular frame w/gilt liner enclosing the rectangular mirror, scroll-carved arched bottom crest, American or English, late 18th c., 29" h. (ILLUS.) **$1,673**

Fine Chinese Chippendale-Style Mirror

Chippendale-Style overmantel mirror, carved mahogany in the Chinese taste, the long, high serpentine crestrail composed of a large central pierce-carved pagoda flanked by pierced latticework panels topped by scrolls all above the three-part mirror plate w/narrow vertical side panels flanked by stiles carved w/entwining leafy berry vines, the arched base rail also pierce-carved w/long leafy scrolls, England, ca. 1900, 57" w., 76" h. (ILLUS.) **$3,450**

Charming Classical Country-style Mirror

Classical country-style wall mirror, painted & turned wood, the rectangular frame w/a long side rails composed of half-round ring- and rod-turned columns in gold & black, the two & bottom rails w/simple half-round posts in black & gold, the two section w/a rectangular reverse-painted glass pane w/a primitive homestead landscape w/a large two-story house flanked by trees along a road, each corner block w/a small brass rosette, all-original, ca. 1830-40, some paint flecking in landscape, 11 3/4 x 24 1/4" (ILLUS.).......................... **$230**

Eagle-topped American Classical Mirror

Classical overmantel mirror, carved giltwood, a large, wide molded shadowbox frame topped by a large model of a spread-winged American eagle perched on an American shield & flanked by leafy branches & ribbon bands, ca. 1840-60, 54 3/4" w., 74" h. (ILLUS.)...................... **$7,820**

Fine American Classical Giltwood Overmantel Mirror

Classical overmantel mirror, giltwood, the long low flaring crestrail w/blocked ends above corner blocks joined by a three-section spiral-turned columnar rail w/matching two-section columns down the sides, a wide upper frieze band decorated w/long panels of double leafy scrolls flanking a large central mirror all above the three-section mirror plate, a narrow flat bottom rail, ca. 1835, 64" l., 37 1/2" h. (ILLUS.) **$2,875**

Nice American Classical Overmantel Mirror

Classical overmantel mirror, giltwood, the wide rectangular frame w/a rosette block at each corner joined by sides decorated w/a narrow outer ribbon-and-leaf band & an inner thin gadrooned band enclosing the three-part mirror, ca. 1820, 60" l., 31 1/2" h. (ILLUS.) **$2,300**

Nice Carved Mahogany Classical Mirror

Classical wall mirror, carved mahogany, the flat-topped stepped narrow cornice w/blocked corners above central panel flanked by lyre-carved blocks above the sides carved w/a long acanthus leaf above a spiral-carved split baluster flanking the mirror plate, the molded & blocked base w/side blocks decorated w/ormolu rosettes flanking a narrow panel decorated w/a thin ormolu leaf mount, one carved lyre w/some damage, probably American, ca. 1815-30, 24 1/2" w., 47 1/2" h. (ILLUS.) **$345**

Classical Mirror with Inscribed Banner

Classical wall mirror, giltwood & gesso, the flat pediment w/a flaring cornice & large blocked ends above a wide frieze band w/central leaf cluster flanked by side blocks w/rosettes above an upper reverse-painted glass panel w/a scene of a red-coated Colonial era soldier w/a town & other soldiers in the background as well as a blue banner printed w/"A. Doolittle. N.H. 1788," above the tall rectangular mirror all flanked by half-round ring-turned & fan-carved pilasters ending in bottom corner blocks joined by a smaller ring-turned half-column at the bottom, attributed to Amos Doolittle, ca. 1830, reverse-painting badly flaked, small corner missing & mirror corner cracked, 25 3/4" w., 44 1/2" h. (ILLUS.)............... **$1,208**

One of Two Rare American Classical Mirrors

Classical wall mirrors, giltwood, the flat flaring blocked pediment decorated w/a row of acorn-shaped drops above a frieze band decorated w/small panels w/a florette & four small balls flanking a central bow & swag design, the sides w/decorated top corner blocks above half-round ropetwist pilasters resting on plain bottom corner blocks joined by a plain molded bottom rail, fitted w/a tall two-part rectangular mirror, ca. 1810-20, 27 1/2" w., 50" h., pr. (ILLUS. of one, previous page) **$14,340**

Fine Federal Era Girondole Mirror

Federal girandole wall mirror, giltwood, a round deeply molded frame enclosing a ring of gilt balls around the convex mirror, the top centered by a large spread-winged carved gilt eagle looking to the right & flanked by large arched ornate open scrolls, the bottom w/a narrow pleated ribbon band & center drop, England or America, early 19th c., section of gesso missing at bottom, 26 1/2" w., 38" h. (ILLUS.) **$2,070**

Small Federal Mahogany Wall Mirror

Federal wall mirror, carved mahogany, the flat flaring pediment w/blocked sides above a narrow rectangular reverse-painted glass panel decorated w/a primitive landscape w/two houses above the

tall rectangular mirror plate, slender reeded pilasters down the sides above the blocked flaring bottom rail, ca. 1820, 18 1/2" w., 33 3/4" h. (ILLUS.).................. **$374**

Federal Mirror with Églomisé Panel

Federal wall mirror, giltwood, the flat narrow projecting crest above projecting corner blocks over reeded side columns w/shaped capitals, flanking a top rectangular églomisé panel in black & gold on a white ground, the center w/a rectangular panel showing a woman holding a cornucopia w/raised hand toward a ship sailing away, flanked by delicate squares enclosing a circle around a feathered pinwheel, top & bottom thin leafy vine band above the rectangular mirror plate, molded base band w/projecting corner blocks, early writing on the back indicating a London, England origin, early 19th c., 18" w., 26 1/2" h. (ILLUS.) **$1,610**

Nice Federal-Style Mahogany Mirror

Federal-Style wall mirror, mahogany & gilt gesso, a wide, high broken-scroll crest trimmed w/gilt gesso banding & rosetttes centered by a squatty urn finial issuing arching wheat & flower stems, the top block corners w/suspending pierced gilt gesso leaf swags, the large rectangular mirror plate framed w/narrow gilt bands, a wide serpentine-carved bottom rail, restoration to urn, first half 20th c., 26 3/4" w., 55" h. (ILLUS.)......................... **$403**

English George III-Style Pier Mirror

George III-Style pier mirror, giltwood, Neoclassical style, a widely flaring stepped flat cornice w/blocked corners above a narrow band of buttons over a blocked frieze band carved w/a narrow raised rectangular block w/an open book motif flanked by leafy scrolls & wreathes, the molded flat leafy-vine decorated side pilasters decorated w/scroll-carved capitals & urn-shaped bases, the deep flaring plinth base decorated w/a bold scroll band, England, late 19th - early 20thc., 43" w., 55" h. (ILLUS.)............................... **$633**

Georgian-Style Cheval Mirror

Georgian-Style cheval mirror, mahogany, a tall rectangular molded frame enclosing a mirror & swiveling between tall tapering

reeded columnar uprights w/turned tapering finials & leaf-carved base sections, above a trestle base w/reeded outswept legs on casters joined by a slender turned stretcher, England, ca. 1900, 36 1/2" w., 5' 9" h. (ILLUS.)................... **$2,300**

Nice Victorian Oak Cheval Mirror

Late Victorian cheval mirror, oak, the central upright framework w/an arched & scroll-carved crestrail above the central long swiveling beveled mirror flanked by matching swing-out mirrors, raised on an arched trestle base w/an arched & carved panel cross stretcher, decal label of the Bele Heckey Mfg. Co. Store Outfitters, St. Louis, Missouri, original finish, one finial missing, late 19th c., open 73" w., 6' 7" h. (ILLUS.)......................... **$1,035**

Late Victorian Long Oval Wall Mirror

Late Victorian wall mirror, gilt plaster, long narrow oval frame molded w/a continuous band of laurel leaves & berries, ca. 1900, 30 x 50" (ILLUS.)............................. **$403**

Louis XVI Provincial wall mirror, carved giltwood, the high arched crestrail carved w/an open oval ribbon ring over further ribbons & ornate carved flowers centered by a beaded heart reserve, the rectangular narrow frame sides carved w/flower sprigs, southern France, late 18th c., 34" w., 5' h. (ILLUS., next page) **$1,955**

Provincial Louis XVI Wall Mirror

Rare French Modern Style Wall Mirror

Modern style wall mirror, giltwood 'talosel' style, in the form of an oval sunflower w/a reeded inner frame surrounded by oyster shell-type petals, marked "Line Vautrin France," ca. 1955, 8 1/4" h. (ILLUS.) **$8,963**

Louis XVI-Style Overmantel Mirror

Louis XVI-Style overmantel mirror, carved giltwood, the tall molded rectangular frame w/rounded top corners centered by a large leafy scroll-carved crest w/two putti flanking a small oval mirror, France, late 19th c., 33" w., 5 6 1/2" h. (ILLUS.).. **$1,840**

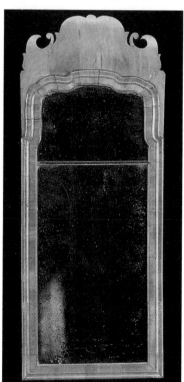

Early English Queen Anne Wall Mirror

Queen Anne wall mirror, mahogany, the high arched crest w/scroll-cut details above a shaped arched molding continuing around the sides & enclosing a two-part mirror plate, a flat molded bottom rail, England, first half 18th c., 12 1/2" w., 32" h. (ILLUS.) **$956**

One of Two Rare Aesthetic Mirrors

Victorian Aesthetic Movement overmantel mirrors, giltwood, the long gently arched crestrail centered by a low pierced rectangular gallery above a low rectangular recessed panel molded w/ornate stylized blossoms, the narrow flaring beaded cornice above an narrow frieze panel decorated w/additional floral designs flanked by blocked top corners above the flattened reeded side pilasters resting on flower-decorated bottom corner blocks joined by a blocked molded & stepped bottom rail, original stenciled label on the back reads "L Uter Dealer in Looking Glasses - N. 17 Royal Street - New Orleans," late 19th c., 60 1/2" w., 79 1/2" h., pr. (ILLUS. of one) **$7,763**

English Renaissance Revival Mirror

Victorian Renaissance Revival substyle overmantel mirror, carved giltwood, the

narrow molded crestrail w/blocked ends mounted in the center by an arched crest composed of floral swags enclosing a blue & white faux-Jasper ware medallion decorated w/a portrait of a Renaissance era lady, the sides composed of slender reeded pilasters above blocked & scroll-carved bottom corners joined by a thin bottom rail, England, late 19th c., 61" w., 71" h. (ILLUS.) **$1,610**

Very Fine Victorian Rococo Pier Mirror

Victorian Rococo pier mirror, carved mahogany, the very high arched & scroll-carved curved crest topped by a large scallop over a profile of a man & two lion heads & other scroll detail above the very tall arched mirror flanked by sides carved w/simple half-round columns & a leaf-carved central panels, the bottom w/scroll carving above the narrow projecting half-round serpentine shelf w/a pierced scroll-carved apron centered by a cartouche & raised on two short front cabriole legs, ca. 1850s, 12 x 32", overall 102" h. (ILLUS.) **$2,185**

Ornate Rococo Giltwood Overmantel Mirror

Victorian Rococo substyle overmantel mirror, giltwood, the arched crest composed of very ornate entwined leafy scrolls above the molded arched frame enclosing the large mirror, the bottom corners w/further leafy scrolls, ca. 1855, 56" w., 7' h. (ILLUS., previous page)...... **$6,900**

Fine American Victorian Rococo Mirror

Victorian Rococo substyle pier mirror, giltwood, the arched serpentine crestrail centered by a large shell-carved crest framed by large open scrolls continuing down around the top corners to the deep molded sides further decorated w/flowers & leafy scrolls ending in more large pierced corner scrolls at the bottom joining the lower frame rail, all resting on a narrow arched serpentine white marble shelf above a conforming deep apron ornately decorated w/a band of large beads & leafy scrolls, raised on large scroll feet, ca. 1850-60, 50" w., 122 1/2" h. (ILLUS.)............................. **$6,900**

Fine Labeled Rococo Pier Mirror

Victorian Rococo substyle pier mirror, giltwood, the tall scrolled pediment above a narrow rondel band over a large cabochon flanked by large scrolling corners over the tall rectangular mirror flanked by engaged columns decorated w/clusters of pendent flowers, the later base console w/a serpentine outlined marble top raised upon a conforming frieze on cabriole legs, label on the back for McClees Galleries, Philadelphia, mid-19th c., 33" w., 9' 5 1/2" h. (ILLUS.).................. **$4,313**

Parlor Suites

French Scrolling Art Nouveau Style Parlor Suite

Art Nouveau style: settee, armchair & side chair; carved giltwood, the settee w/a long serpentine crestrail centered by a pierced scroll-carved crest & w/fanned scroll round corners enclosing the upholstered back, open serpentine arms curving into the narrow serpentine scroll-carved seatrail enclosing the upholstered seat, long C-scroll outswept front legs on scroll & peg feet on casters, the chairs w/matching frames, some rubbing to gilt, fabric worn, France, ca. 1890s, settee 51 1/2" l., 37 1/2" h., 3 pcs. (ILLUS.)............... **$600**

Sofa and Chairs from Fine Louis XVI-Style Parlor Suite

Louis XVI-Style: two sofas, two open-arm armchairs & two side chairs; carved gilt-wood, the sofa w/a long narrow & gently arched crestrail centered by carved scrolls atop the rectangular frame enclosing a tapestry-upholstered back featuring scenes from "The Fables of Fontaine," padded open arms w/incurved & reeded arm supports above the tapestry-upholstered seat w/a narrow gently arched molded seatrail raised on four turned tapering & reeded front legs ending in knob-and-peg feet, the chairs of matching design, France, late 19th c., 6 pcs. (ILLUS. of one sofa and the chairs **$6,613**

Nice French Victorian Renaissance Revival Parlor Suite

Fine Renaissance Revival Sofa from Large Parlor Suite

Victorian Renaissance Revival: sofa, two armchairs & four side chairs; walnut & burl walnut, the triple-back sofa w/each upholstered shield-form back panel topped by an arched crestrail w/a carved palmette crest above pierced scroll brackets centering a large rondel, the large center panel w/a classical female face carved in the rondel, each back section separated by an ornately carved urn-form device, upholstered open arms w/the armrests carved as classical female busts, over-upholstered seat on a burl-paneled & line-incised serpentine seatrail w/three drops between the four bulbous turned & tapering front legs on casters, the chairs all w/matching backs & detailing, attributed to John Jelliff, Newark, New Jersey, ca. 1870, sofa 72" l., 46" h., the set (ILLUS. of the sofa) **$4,025**

Victorian Renaissance Revival substyle: sofa, one armchair & four side chairs; ebonized beechwood, the sofa w/a long narrow gently arched crestrail centered by carved crossed torches & a quiver tied w/a ribbon & bow, the raised back frame w/rounded lower corners framing the tufted upholstery back, open padded arms w/incurved arm supports above the long gently curved upholstered seat on a conforming three-section seatrail w/a small carved shell centering each, raised on disk-turned and fluted tapering legs, the chairs w/matching shield-shaped backs, France, ca. 1860-70, sofa 70" l., 43" h. (ILLUS. in two photos) **$1,840**

Victorian Rococo: sofa, a pair of armchairs & a pair of side chairs; pierced & carved laminated rosewood, each piece w/a high pierced & scroll-carved crestrail w/a central diamond-shaped scroll-carved medallion flanked by bead-carved rails continuing to curving pierce-carved scrolls curving down to the low upholstered or padded arms, incurved carved arm supports & deep over-upholstered

Restrained Rococo Rosewood Parlor Suite

Victorian Rococo Stanton Hall Pattern Sofa

seat, serpentine scroll-carved seatrails w/a central medallion, semi-cabriole front legs on casters, Stanton Hall patt. attributed to J. & J.W. Meeks, New York New York, settee 47 1/2" h., the set (ILLUS. of sofa) **$16,655**

Victorian Rococo: sofa, armchair & four side chairs; carved rosewood, the sofa w/a long upholstered serpentine back w/a narrow conforming crestrail w/low carved crests, padded & closed upholstered arms w/incurved arm supports, long serpentine seatrail w/a carved trim above four demi-cabriole front legs, matching chairs w/shaped balloon backs, original finish, ca. 1860, sofa 66" l., the set (ILLUS., top of page) **$2,300**

Victorian Rococo substyle: armchair & three side chairs; carved & laminated rosewood, the armchair w/a high arched back w/an ornate flower- and fruit-carved crestrail continuing to scroll-carved waisted sides enclosing a tufted upholstery panel, the curved open arms on incurved molded arm supports above the wide upholstered seat w/a serpentine front above the conforming seatrail carved w/fruits & flowers, demi-cabriole front legs on casters & square canted rear legs on casters, the side chairs of matching design, attributed to John Henry Belter, New York City, ca. 1855, each 45" h., 4 pcs. (ILLUS., below) **$8,625**

Fine Suite of Carved & Laminated Rosewood Victorian Rococo Chairs

Fine & Rare Victorian Rococo Carved & Laminated Rosewood Parlor Suite

Victorian Rococo substyle: sofa, armchair & two side chairs; pierce-carved & laminated rosewood, the long sofa w/double high chair backs flanking a lower long arched central back section, the central section w/a high arched serpentine crestrail ornately pierce-carved w/scrolls & centered by large carved face w/a leaf-form tongue, the high arched chair backs w/higher matching serpentine carved crestrail also centered by carved faces, padded incurved arms on heavy pierced & scroll-carved sides, the long serpentine seat w/a scroll-carved serpentine seatrail centered by a carved face, on demi-cabriole front legs w/leaf-carved feet on casters, canted square reeded legs on casters, each chair w/a high arched back matching the sofa backs, attributed to Charles Boudoine, New York City, ca. 1855,   sofa 82" l., 42 1/4" h., the set (ILLUS., above) **$29,900**

Screens

Very Rare Art Deco Iron Firescreen

Firescreen, gilded wrought iron, a large upright circle composed of bold openwork scrolls centered by a diamond-shaped lattice panel, raised on a fanned support resting on a narrow oval platform on outswept low scroll legs, designed by Gilbert Poillerat in 1929, manufactured by Baudet, Donon et Roussel, France, ca. 1946, top 26 3/4" d., overall 32 1/4" h. (ILLUS.) **$57,360**

English Jacobean-Style Firescreen

Firescreen, Jacobean-Style, carved walnut, the pierced leafy scroll-carved crestrail centered by a crown & supporting a pierce-carved framework enclosing an armorial needlework panel over a caned lower panel, all supported by spiral-twist side stiles w/upper & lower corner blocks & turned top finials, on a trestle-style base w/arched scrolled legs joined by a small turned stretcher & a long spiral-turned cross stretcher, England, late 19th c., 17 x 31", 44" h. (ILLUS.) **$403**

Louis XV-Style Needlework Firescreen

Firescreen, Louise XV-Style, carved walnut, the rectangular molded frame w/molded sides & rounded corners topped by a central shell-carved crest & top corner scrolls, enclosing a fine needlework panel w/a portrait of a French aristocrat surrounded by ornate florals on a brown ground, trestle base w/inwardly scrolled & leaf-carved feet, France, third quarter 19th c., 27 1/2" w., 46" h. (ILLUS.) **$431**

Napoleon III Era Fire Screen

Firescreen, Napoleon III era, ebonized wood, a slender arched crestrail centered by a carved wheat sheaf & tools above a large velvet panel in a framework supported by slender turned side columns w/turned finials, a trestle-form base

w/arched & acanthus leaf-carved legs w/scrolled toes, France, third quarter 19th c., 43 1/2" h. (ILLUS.) **$518**

Colorful Victorian Glass Fire Screen

Firescreen, Victorian leaded & stained glass, an upright rectangular brass frame w/trestle feet & a row of open spindles across the bottom encloses a large glass panel, the central stained oval decorated w/a bust portrait of a young Victorian maiden holdinf pale yellow roses, surrounded by a narrow red border & a fleur-de-lis wider band w/four blue half-circles at the top & sides, the triangular corner panels stained w/clusters of whites flowers & golden brown leaves & berries against a pale gold ground, the center section w/a wide border band in black & gold & inset w/leaded glass squares "jewels" in deep red, light & dark blue, ca. 1880s, few small cracks in edge pieces, 20" w., 33" h. (ILLUS.) **$748**

Rococo Firescreen with Needlework

Firescreen, Victorian Rococo style, pierce-carved rosewood, a narrow square molding enclosing the original needlepoint panel all framed by ornate scrolls, raised on ring- and knob-turned supports joined by an upper scroll-carved stretcher & a simple baluster- and knob-turned lower stretcher between the scrolled shoe feet, original finish, ca. 1850s, 24" w., overall 44" h. (ILLUS.) **$1,000**

Lacquered & Painted Oriental Screen

Folding screen, four-fold, Oriental, lacquered wood & painted canvas, each panel w/a flat rectangular gilt frame enclosing a narrow rectganular upper panel w/a gilt background painted w/a different flowering branch above a tall vertical panel w/a black background decorated in gold & color w/a different garden scene, each outer corner w/an embossed brass bird & leaf mount, China, early 20th c., some losses, overall 96" w., 69" h. (ILLUS.)...................... **$250-400**

Ornately Carved Chinese Screen

Folding screen, four-fold, pierced & carved hardwood, Oriental style, eached tall panel topped w/an arched & pierce-carved crest above a narrow rectangular lattice-carved panel above a tall central

solid panel carved in relief w/a serpentine dragon, a bottom short rectangular panel w/floral carving, the framework carved w/characters & a bamboo-carved edge, scrolled arched base to each panel, China, late 19th c., overall 84" w., 78 1/4" h. (ILLUS.).. **$1,035**

Victorian Screen with Landscape Designs in the Japanoesque Taste

Folding screen, four-fold, Victorian Japonesque taste, each tall rectangular panel decorated w/a gold background highlighted w/asymmetrically arranged geometric reserves each painted w/a different landscape & framed w/various flowers & fruits, the largest panels representing the four seasons, English or American, late 19th c., overall 88" w., 70 1/2" h. (ILLUS.) **$1,610**

English Screen with Exotic Landscape

Folding screen, three-fold, Aesthetic taste, the three fabric panels painted w/a large continuous exotic landscape full of birds & leafy trees around a lake, the reverse painted in monochrome claret, scattered small rents & losses, England, ca. 1900, overall 66" w., 65" h. (ILLUS.)................ **$1,840**

Ornately Painted Louis XIV-Style Screen

Folding screen, four-fold, Louis XIV-Style, painted & gilt-trimmed continuous design of colorful exotic birds, flowering vines & fruit-filled scrolls, on an antiqued gold ground, France, ca. 1900, 88" w., 6' 6" h. (ILLUS.)... **$2,530**

Pair of English Victorian Pole Screens

Secretaries

Rhode Island Chippendale Secretary

French Screen with Oriental Decoration

Folding screen, four-fold, Napoleon III era, Oriental taste, colorfully painted overall w/a continuous Chinese landscape w/figures & buildings against a black ground, the reverse w/outlined panels, France, third quarter 19th c., overall 90" w., 7' h. (ILLUS.)... **$3,220**

Pole screens, inlaid mahogany, each w/a large oval shield enclosing an embroidered panel of floral design centered by a cartouche w/a romantic scene, supported & adjusting on a slender square pole w/a thicker tapering base section above the stepped square base, banded edge inlay, wear & losses to embroidery, some inlay loss, England, late 19th c., 10 1/4" sq. base, 55 1/2" h., pr. (ILLUS., top of next column)... **$546**

Chippendale secretary-bookcase, birch & maple w/some curl, two-part construction: the upper section w/a rectangular top w/a flaring stepped cornice above a pair of raised-panel cupboard doors opening to a divided interior; the lower section w/a hinged slant front opening to an interior fitted w/two small drawers & pigeonholes, the lower case w/four long graduated drawers w/brass butterfly pulls & keyhole escutcheons, molded base w/a narrow serpentine apron & scroll-cut bracket feet, old replaced brasses, old glued foot restorations, hinged replaced w/pieced restorations, attributed to Rhode Island, old mellow refinishing, late 18th c., 19 1/2 x 37 1/4", 76 1/2" h. (ILLUS.)........ **$3,738**

Rare Chippendale Secretary-Bookcase

Chippendale secretary-bookcase, cherry, two-part construction: the upper section w/a rectangular top w/a flaring stepped cornice above a pair of tall paneled cupboard doors opening to four small drawers; the lower section w/a fold-down slant front opening to an interior fitted w/a central prospect door enclosing four small shelves flanked by pigeonholes, the lower case w/four long graduated drawers w/butterfly brasses & keyhole escutcheons, molded base on scroll-cut ogee bracket feet, some foot restorations, Pennsylvania, 1760-80, 21 1/2 x 39", 84" h. (ILLUS.) **$14,340**

American Classical Secretary-Bookcase

Classical secretary-bookcase, mahogany & mahogany veneer, three-part construction: the upper section w/a rectangular top & removable widely flaring stepped cornice above a pair of tall glazed cupboard doors opening to three wooden shelves; the stepped-out lower section

w/a fold-down drawer front opening to three small drawers w/bird's-eye maple fronts below eight pigeonholes; the lower case w/a pair of paneled doors opening to two shelves & flanked by pilasters on blocks above the bun feet, ca. 1830, 19 1/4 x 41", 84" h. (ILLUS.) **$2,013**

Early Classical Two-Part Secretary

Classical secretary-bookcase, mahogany & mahogany veneer, two-part construction: the upper section w/a rectangular top w/a deep widely flaring flat cornice above a flat frieze band w/end blocks above a pair of heavy columns flanking a pair of tall Gothic arch paneled cupboard doors opening a two adjustable shelves above a pair of narrow drawers w/turned wood knobs; the lower stepped-out section w/a fold-out writing surface above a long ogee-front drawers over heavy end columns w/carved capitals flanking the set-back long flat drawers w/turned wood knobs, on simple turned legs w/knob feet, probably New England, first-half 19th c., 20 x 42 1/4", 70" h. (ILLUS.) **$805**

Fine New York Classical Secretary

Classical secretary-bookcase, mahogany & mahogany veneer, two-part construction: the upper section w/a rectangular top & low flaring ogee cornice above an arched frieze above a pair of tall set-back geometrically-glazed cupboard doors opening to shelves & flanked by tall turned columns; the lower case w/a hinged fold-out writing surface projecting above a recessed square center door flanked by narrower quarter-round doors all flanked by serpentine front pilasters above the heavy C-scroll front feet, similar to examples produced by Joseph Meeks & Sons, New York, New York, ca. 1830s, 26 x 53", 83" h. (ILLUS., previous page) **$9,200**

American Signed Rosewood Secretary

Classical secretary-bookcase, rosewood veneer, two-part construction: the upper section w/a rectangular top w/a widely flaring low ogee cornice above a pair of tall glazed cupboard doors w/pierced scroll-cut corner brackets opening to two shelves; the lower section w/a rectangular top above a projecting long fold-down drawer front opening to an interior fitted w/drawers & pigeonholes, two long lower drawers flanked by serpentine pilasters & heavy scroll-form feet, back signed "J. Alsop, Carlisle, PA," ca. 1830s, 19 1/2 x 43 1/2", 78" h. (ILLUS.) **$1,610**

Classical-Style secrétaire à abattant, walnut & burl walnut, the rectangular top w/a narrow flaring cornice above a frieze band flanked by chamfered blocks above a long narrow drawer w/a raised burl panel & a serpentine brass bail pulls above the wide flat fold-down writing panel opening to an interior fitted w/an arrangement of eleven small inlaid drawers centered by a tall open compartment, the lower case w/three long burl-veneered drawers w/matching brass pulls, the side pilasters w/small carved urns above fluted columns over tall blocks resting on disk-turned front

Classical-Style Secrétaire à Abattant

feet, Europe, late 19th c., 23 1/4 x 43 1/4", 64 1/2" h. (ILLUS.) **$1,495**

Rare Federal Three-Part Secretary

Federal secretary-bookcase, inlaid mahogany & mahogany veneer, three-part construction: the top section w/a low cornice centered by a square block w/banded veneer & topped by a carved spread-winged eagle finial & w/small corner blocks w/small turned wood urn-form finials all above a pair of cupboard doors each w/two arched glazed panels over small blocks & panels; the center section w/a pair of flat cupboard doors centered by a narrow small door; the bottom section w/a narrow fold-out writing surfaced above a case of four long graduated drawers w/oval brass pulls, serpentine apron on tall French feet, Northshore, Massachusetts, ca. 1815, 20 x 41", 81" h. (ILLUS.) **$13,145**

Nice New England Federal Secretary

Federal secretary-bookcase, inlaid mahogany & mahogany veneer; two-part construction: the upper section w/a flat rectangular top over a frieze band & a pair of squared geometrically-glazed cupboard doors over two narrow line-inlaid drawers; the lower section w/a fold-out baize-lined writing surface above a case w/three long graduated drawers w/oval brass pulls, serpentine apron & tall French feet, probably Portsmouth, New Hampshire, late 18th - early 19th c., 17 1/2 x 35", 57" h. (ILLUS.) **$2,760**

New England Mahogany Secretary

Federal secretary-bookcase, inlaid mahogany & mahogany veneer, two-part construction: the upper section w/a low cornice centered by a banded rectangular panel w/a round brass ball finial topped by a small eagle, small corner blocks also w/round brass ball finials above a frieze band over a pair of wide geometrically-glazed cupboard doors opening to two shelves above a narrow row of three drawers; the lower section

w/a fold-out writing surface above a case of three long graduated drawers w/period oblong brass pulls, serpentine apron on tall French feet, New England, late 18th c., 17 1/2 x 40", 76" h. (ILLUS.).............. **$5,750**

Rare Philadelphia Federal Secretary

Federal secretary-bookcase, mahogany & mahogany veneer, two-part construction: the upper section w/a rectangular top & flaring cornice above a pair of tall diamond-glazed cupboard doors above an arrangement of six small narrow drawers; the stepped-out lower section w/a cylinder tambour front opening to an interior fitted w/eight pigeonholes & twelves small drawers w/figured maple facings over a velvet & mahogany writing surface, the lower case w/a row of three drawers above a pair of drawers flanking an arched kneehole opening, raised on slender turned & reeded legs w/peg feet, Connelly-Haines School, Philadelphia, ca. 1800-10, 26 x 42", 95" h. (ILLUS.) **$38,240**

Nice English Georgian Secretary

George III secretary-bookcase, mahogany, two-part construction: the upper section w/a broken-scroll crest w/carved rosettes above the flaring stepped cornice w/dentil-carved narrow bands above a pair of tall geometrically-glazed cupboard doors opening to three shelves; the lower section w/a wide hinged slant lid opening to an interior fitted w/small drawers & pigeonholes centering a central cupboard door above a case w/four long thumb-molded graduated drawers w/simple bail pulls, the molded base on ogee bracket feet, England, late 18th c., 24 1/2 x 48", 103" h. (ILLUS., previous page) **$8,050**

Nice George III-Style Secretary

George III-Style secretary-bookcase, red-lacquered & decorated, two-part construction: the upper section w/a low broken-scroll pediment on the rectangular top above a pair of tall solid cupboard doors decorated overall w/gilt Chinese figural & landscape scenes; the lower section w/a hinged fold-out slant front w/Chinese designs opening to an interior fitted w/pigeonholes above a pair of square paneled cupboard doors w/further Chinese style decoration, molded base on scroll-cut bracket feet, England, ca. 1900, 16 1/2 x 44", 92" h. (ILLUS.)................................ **$4,370**

Queen Anne-Style secretarty-bookcase, painted & decorated, two-part construction: the upper section w/a double-arched molded crestrail centered by a large scrolled cartouche finial & w/urn-carved corner finials above a pair of tall arched doors fitted w/beveled mirrors separated & flanked by reeded pilasters; the lower case w/a hinged slant front opening to an interior fitted w/a center prospect door flanked by pigeonholes over four small drawers, the lower case w/four thumbmolded long graduated drawers w/butterfly brasses, molded base on large bun feet, the whole decorated soft green w/gold trim on the top &

English Queen Anne-Style Secretary

gilt Chinese-style figural scenes on the slat front & drawers, cinnabar-colored desk interior, England, late 19th c., 19 1/2 x 36", 81 1/2" h. (ILLUS.) **$8,050**

Nice Victorian Rococo Secretary

Victorian Rococo secretary-bookcase, mahogany & mahogany veneer, two-part construction: the upper section w/an arched molded cornice above a frieze band centered by a scroll-carved band above a pair of arched glazed doors w/narrow molding & carved scrolls in the top center corners & opening to two shelves; the lower section w/a stepped-back upper section w/a row of three narrow drawers over a single long drawer above a stepped-out fold-out writing surface above a pair of cupboard doors decorated w/raised squared molding forming a panel, serpentine scroll-carved apron & bracket feet, ca. 1850s, 21 x 47", 91 1/2" h. (ILLUS.)..................... **$2,990**

Nice Rococo Rosewood Secretary

Victorian Rococo secretary-bookcase, rosewood, two-part construction: the upper section w/a deep flaring coved cornice w/rounded corners above a wide conforming ogee frieze band over a pair of tall glazed Gothic arch designed doors carved w/leafy scrolls; the projecting lower section w/a cyma-shaped fold-out writing surface opening to a fitted interior above a pair of paneled cupboard doors w/carved scroll banding, flat apron on short bracket feet, ca. 1860, possibly made for the Southern market, 23 x 54", 7' 11 1/2" h. (ILLUS.)............................. **$3,680**

Nice Victorian Rococo Walnut Secretary

Victorian Rococo secretary-bookcase, walnut, two-part construction; the upper section w/an arched serpentine wide crestrail topped by a high arched pierced & scroll-carved crest w/medallion above a conforming frieze band w/molding above a pair of tall serpentine-topped glazed doors opening to three wooden shelves & flanked by chamfered corners w/applied quarter-round carved drops; the lower section w/a medial molding above the serpentine slant-top opening to a maple & rosewood segmented interior above a pair of narrow drawers projecting above a pair of short paneled base doors flanked by turned drops & base brackets above the flat molded base on casters, ca. 1870, 22 x 45", 101 1/2" h. (ILLUS.) **$3,450**

Shelves

Finely Carved Walnut Magazine Shelf

Magazine shelf, hanging folding-type, carved walnut, the wide pointed backboard w/florets above a finely carved panel of daisy-like flowers among leaves, the fold-out front board held by a side chain & also finely carved w/a design of trumpet flowers, Cincinnati Art Club, ca. 1880s, 16" w., 16" h. (ILLUS.)................... **$345**

Blue-painted Plate Shelves

Plate shelves, hanging-type, painted wood, dovetailed construction, three shelves, the narrow rectangular top above graduated sides flanking two upper shelves each w/a front cross rail, a short narrow bottom shelf, old blue paint, some stains, 19th c., 8 1/2" to 4 1/2", 41" w., 32" h. (ILLUS.) **$460**

Very Rare American Figural Eagle Giltwood Wall Shelves

Wall shelves, carved giltwood, each w/a rectangular platform top w/a fruit & floral-carved edge supported atop a large spread-winged eagle w/head slightly bent down & perched on rockwork, probably Boston, ca. 1815, 12 1/2" h., pr. (ILLUS.)
.... **$28,680**

Colorful Wall Shelves with Cabinet Base

Wall shelves, corner-style, painted & decorated, tall tapering backboard w/serpentine edges flanking three quarter-round shelves, painted bright yellow w/Chinese style florals, the bottom shelf above a quarter-round two-door cabinet opening to a shelf, painted deep red w/each door decorated w/a Chinese landscape w/figures, flat base, some wear & paint loss, one shelf w/old repaint & scattered insect holes, probably Europe, 19th c., 18" w., 36" h. (ILLUS.) **$210**

Prince of Wales Plumes Giltwood Shelf

Wall shelves, giltwood, a half-round top shelf w/molded edge supported on tall carved Prince of Wales plumes tied at the base w/a bow & ribbons, England, early 19th c., 8 x 16 1/2", 15" h., pr. (ILLUS. of one) **$431**

Rare Painted & Decorated Wall Shelves

Wall shelves, painted & decorated pine, a high top backrail w/a flat center crest & rounded corners above two large hanging holes, decorated w/the original red & black graining & further painted w/a pair of large pink & white blossoms & green leaves, three open graduated shelves each w/slightly canted scallop-cut aprons w/further graining & blossoms & supported by scallop-cut bowed supports, gold banding, one side near crest w/minor damage & touch-up, Maine, first half 19th c., 4 1/2 x 15 1/2", 22 1/2" h. (ILLUS., previous page) **$7,130**

Early Shelves with Spoon Rack

Wall shelves, painted maple, the narrow top board carved as a spoon rack above triple-scalloped graduated sides flanking three shelves each w/a narrow front cross rail, yellowish brown finish, 18th c., 21" h. (ILLUS.) **$777**

Country Painted Wall Shelves

Wall shelves, painted walnut & pine, a rectangular top w/a dentil-carved cornice

above a single open shelf above the molded base w/dentil band, old mellow brown finish, some empty nail holes on the sides, found in Maine, 19th c., 9 x 20 3/4", 29 1/2" h. (ILLUS.) **$575**

Sideboards

Fine French Art Deco Mahogany Sideboard

Art Deco sideboard, gilt-bronze-mounted mahogany, the long rectangular top w/rounded front corners inset w/a long black marble slab above the case w/two large square paneled doors w/round brass hardware, long low pedestal base, France, ca. 1930, 20 1/2 x 67", 40" h. (ILLUS.) **$4,600**

Baroque-Style server, carved walnut, the long narrow rectangular black marble top above a round-fronted narrow apron w/leaf-carved panels raised on two clusters of four bulbed square tapering legs w/detailed carving & joined by flat serpentine oblong stretchers, each front pair of legs flanking a large half-round pierce-carved drop centered by a large shell, the apron enclosing three silver flatware drawers, some loss to carvings, mark of John Colby & Sons, ca. 1910, 25 x 87", 37" h. (ILLUS., top next page) **$690**

Fine American Classical Server

Classical server, mahogany & mahogany veneer, the rectangular white marble top aobve a long ogee-front drawer projecting over a pair of arch-paneled cupboard

Long Baroque-Style Marble-topped Walnut Server

doors flanked by free-standing white marble columns w/ormolu capitals & bases, the top of each paneled end fitted w/a pull-out work surface, the front w/bulbous squared tapering block feet, ca. 1830s, marble top replaced, 26 x 48 3/4", 41" h. (ILLUS.) **$1,955**

Unusual Classical-Style Server

Classical-Style server, mahogany & mahogany veneer, a long half-round top w/narrow beaded edge above the conforming apron centered by a long drawer w/two brass lion head & ring pulls, the top supported at each end by three free-standing reeded columns flanking an open serpentine medial shelf & a kidney-shaped base raised at each end on three large ball feet on casters, early 20th c., 18 1/4 x 48", 34" h. (ILLUS.) **$518**

American Classical-Style Sideboard

Classical-Style sideboard, mahogany & mahogany veneer, the rectangular top above a pair long curved-front drawers w/small pulls projecting over four flat cupboard doors above a long, deep bottom drawer, all flanked by free-standing turned columns w/carved capitals & bases raised on heavy carved paw feet, ca. 1890, 24 1/8 x 59 7/8", 40 7/8" h. (ILLUS.) **$500**

French Empire-Style Lacquered Credenza

Empire-Style credenza, gilt-bronze inlaid ebonized lacquer, the long top inset w/white marble w/rounded ends & a blocked front, the conforming case w/a narrow frieze band decorated w/scroll-inlaid central panel flanked by small gilt-bronze mounts above a large paneled door elaborately decorated w/a large scene of floral baskets & scrolled acanthus in chased bronze & mother-of-pearl, gilt-bronze mounts around the door frame, flanked by narrow vertical panels w/additional inlaid basket & scroll designs, urn- and columnar-turned corner columns w/gilt-bronze capitals, feet & leaf mounts, the curved sides w/further gilt-bronze mounts, the conforming blocked apron w/further mounts & raised on disk- and peg-turned tapering feet, France, ca. 1950, 18 x 55", 45" h. (ILLUS.) **$2,300**

Victorian Centennial Federal-Style Inlaid Mahogany Sideboard

Federal-Style sideboard, inlaid mahogany & mahogany veneer, the long rectangular top w/a projecting serpentine center section above a conforming case w/a large deep wine drawer at one end & a matching door at the other end, each inlaid w/rectangular border banding & a thin central oval enclosing the oval brass pull, the serpentine center section w/a single long line-inlaid drawer above a long arched inlaid apron, raised on six square tapering legs w/spade feet, ca. 1880, 28 1/4 x 75", 35" h. (ILLUS., top of page) **$5,865**

Fine Early Federal-Style Sideboard

Federal-Style sideboard, inlaid mahogany, the long rectangular top w/a bowed front decorated w/line-inlay along the edge above the conforming case w/a pair of curved short drawers w/line-inlay flanking a long flat line-inlaid central drawer, all w/oval bail brasses, the lower case w/curved & line-inlaid end doors flanking a pair of flat line-inlaid central doors, the front divided by four line-inlaid stiles continuing down to tapering square line-inlaid legs, branded mark "C. Dodge Furniture Co. - Since 1841 - Manchester, Mass.," late 19th - early 20th c., 22 x 62", 41" h. (ILLUS.) **$1,265**

French Provincial Cherry Buffet

French Provincial buffet, cherry, the rectangular top w/rounded front corners above a case w/a pair of narrow drawers w/small turned wood knobs above a pair of paneled cupboard doors, flat base raised on paneled block feet, France, late 19th c., 19 1/4 x 43 1/4", 39 1/2" h. (ILLUS.) **$546**

Carved Oak French Provincial-Style Long Sideboard

French Provincial-Style sideboard, carved oak, the long rectangular top w/a stepped-out central section, the back mounted w/a long low & gently arched crestrail centered by a carved fanned scroll crest, the cased fitted at the ends w/a single scroll-carved paneled drawer above a scroll-arched & leafy scroll-carved panel & centered by a pair of matching projecting doors, the serpentine scroll- and lattice-carved apron raised on short cabriole legs, France, early 20th c., 24 x 93 3/4", 50 1/2" h. (ILLUS.) **$1,150**

Very Ornate Georgian-Style Sideboard

Georgian-Style sideboard, inlaid rosewood, two-part construction: the tall upper section w/an ornate arrangement of shelves & mirrors topped by a tall projecting central section w/a broken-scroll crest w/floral inlays above an inlaid frieze band over a tall geometrically-glazed cabinet door above a set-back tapering inlaid panel flanked by curved vertical mirror panels, each side of the top w/a half broken-scroll inlaid crest above an arrangement of projecting open shelves supported by slender turned columns & backed by mirrored panels above scroll-inlaid panels, the rectangular top w/a deep concave central section above a conforming case, each end fitted w/a narrow flat inlaid drawer above an urn-and-scroll-inlaid cupboard door above a open compartment w/a turned corner spindle & low front gallery, the concave section w/a serpentine top shelf above narrow inlaid drawers over a three-part serpentine apron raised on turned spindles & a deep open compartment above three inlaid lower doors, all raised on six ring-turned front legs, some inlay restoration, England, ca. 1880, 18 x 60", 94 1/2" h. (ILLUS.).. **$3,450**

Louis XVI-Style Server with Marble Top

Louis XVI-Style server, figured veneers w/h.p. floral designs, red, grey & white shaped marble top over three drawers across the top, two lower drawers w/fronts w/concave arches w/sunburst design & ribbon crest, serpentine doors on either side conceal three drawers each, by "Slack Rassnick & Co., New York," late 19th c., 24 1/2 x 56 1/2", 33 1/2" h. (ILLUS.) **$1,495**

Fine Charles Limbert Mission-style Oak Sideboard

Mission-style (Arts & Crafts movement) sideboard, oak, the long rectangular top backed by a low arched plate rail, the case fitted w/two paneled cupboard doors flanking two small drawers over two long drawers w/hammered copper pulls, a very long drawer w/hammered copper pulls across the bottom, gently arched apron, mortised stile legs, Charles Limbert Furniture Co. branded mark, original finish, water damage to top, small chip to plate rail, early 20th c., 25 x 66", 46" h. (ILLUS.) **$3,450**

Mission-style (Arts & Crafts movement) sideboard, oak, the rectangular top mounted w/a tall superstructure w/a narrow top shelf on curved brackets above a long rectangular mirror, the case w/a pair of tall paneled cupboard doors mounted w/long hammered copper strap hinges flanking a stack of four drawers w/rectangular hammered copper pulls, a long bottom drawer w/hammered copper pulls, paneled ends & square stile legs, new finish, unmarked, L. & J.G. Stickley - Onondaga Shops, early 20th c., 24 1/4 x 53 1/4" l., 62 1/4" h. (ILLUS., next page) **$4,600**

Nice L. & J.G. Stickley Mission Sideboard

Unique Renaissance-Style Sideboard

carved brackets centered by a four-panel back; the lower section w/a rectangular top w/curved ends above a conforming case w/a long carved drawer over a pair of diamond- and scroll-carved cupboard doors flanked by tall carved blocks, the rounded ends w/a single scroll-carved drawer over an open compartment w/two rounde shelves, deep blocked plinth base, Europe, late 19th c., 17 1/2 x 70", 95" h. (ILLUS.) **$1,840**

Decorative Queen Anne-Style Server

Queen Anne-Style server, black lacquered & decorated, the long rectangular top w/molded edges mounted at the back w/a long arched & scroll-cut crestrail decorated w/painted Chinese figures & landscape scenes, the case fitted w/a pair of long rectangular paneled doors each decorated w/Chinese-style floral designs within a narrow raised molding, the doors separated & flanked by narrow vertical panels further decorated w/stylized flowers & leaves, a narrow serpentine decorate apron above the cabriole front legs ending in pad feet, square rear legs, shrinkage crack in the top, Europe, ca. 1880, 18 1/8 x 48 1/4", 39 7/8" h. (ILLUS.) **$1,265**

Renaissance-Style sideboard, carved oak, two-part contruction: the massive superstructure w/a very large broken-scroll pediment flanking low carved scrolls above the deep flaring, stepped & blocked cornice above a deep frieze w/a long central panel ornately carved w/a large wreath & floral swags flanked by projecting blocks & curved & carved side panels, supported on very heavy scroll-

Italian Renaissance-Style Sideboard

Renaissance-Style sideboard, carved walnut, two-part construction: the upper section w/a long rectangular top w/a widely flaring stepped cornice above a row of three rectangular paneled doors finely carved w/ornate scrolls & medallions & flanked at the side by turned columns, all projecting above a narrow scroll-carved back panel & caryatid-carved supports; the lower section w/a long rectangular top w/a molded edge above a frieze fitted w/three narrow carved drawers over three large paneled cupboard doors w/ornately carved scrolls & medallions all flanked by turned & carved corner columns, the gadroon-carved base raised on carved paw front feet, 16th-century Italian Tuscan-style, Italy, late 19th c., 23 x 81", 81" h. (ILLUS.) **$1,610**

Very Long Ornately Carved Rococo-Style Server

Rococo-Style server, carved mahogany, the long narrow top w/projecting rounded ends & molded edges above a deep apron decorated w/a very ornately pierce-carved design of Rococo scrolls & leaves, raised on cabriole legs w/floral-carved knees & ending in scroll feet on pegs, dark finish, early 20th c., 25 x 74", 30" h. (ILLUS.) **$1,150**

American Victorian Baroque-Style Sideboard

Victorian Baroque-Style sidboard, carved oak, the long rectangular top w/a low rectangular back crest ornately carved w/scrolling leaves centered by a cabochon, the apron w/a pair of curved-front drawers ornately carved w/leafy scrolls & flanked at each end by a carved lion head block, raised on heavy scroll- and leaf-carved cabriole front supports resting on a lower shelf w/a serpentine front & backed by a large rectangular mirror, raised on heavy carved paw feet, ca. 1900, 27 x 48 1/2", 36" h. (ILLUS.) **$1,150**

Victorian Elizabethan-Style sideboard, carved oak, two-part construction: the high upper section w/three large carved panels, the raised central horizontal panel topped by an arched scroll- and leaf-carved crest above a heavily chip-carved frame inscribed at the top "I And My House Will Serve The Lord" over the relief-carved panel showing the "Judgment of Christ," all above a projecting narrow shelf w/the narrow apron inscribed "Ye Yeare of Jubilee - 1614" supported on carved seated lions holding a shield flanking a cupboard w/tapering carved panel sides & a small carved panel door, the large vertical side panels each w/a flaring cornice w/scroll-carved crest above a carved frame, one inscribed at the top "Thomas Machen" & the other "Christian Machen," each panel ornately carved w/an arch & floral pilasters enclosing a large shield & floral scrolls; the lower section w/a long rectangular top above a narrow projecting apron fitted w/a row of narrow drawers carved w/a repeating band of round knobs, rectangular blocks & diamond blocks, supported on five pairs of slender knob-turned & fluted columns supported on blocks along the open bottom shelf backed by large back panels carved w/rosettes, sunbursts, a large diamond & scrolls, raised on five heavy bun feet, England, late 19th c., 22 x 90", 98" h. (ILLUS., bottom of page) **$4,830**

Unique Elizabethan-Style Carved & Inscribed Oak Sideboard

Very Ornate Golden Oak Carved Sideboard

Fantastically Detailed Victorian Golden Oak Sideboard

Victorian Golden Oak sideboard, oak, two-part construction: the tall superstructure w/a serpentine low crestrail centered by a large shell-carved crest flanked by griffin heads over a rounded gadroon-carved band & a pair of low arched mirrored panels centered by a carved female head all flanked by heavy rounded end brackets, a narrow open shelf raised on turned columnar supports over a long rectangular horizontal mirror; the lower section w/a rectangular brown Tennesse marble top above a case w/a long drawer w/two ornate brass pulls beside a small matching drawer all above a pair of small drawers over squared cupboard doors w/a large roundel flanking the very large central door ornately carved w/winged devices above an arched panel carved w/a large shell suspending long leafy scrolls, the side stiles w/curved blocks & ring- and urn-turned columns, a long line-incised apron, on casters, ca. 1890s, 26 1/2 x 70 1/2", 92 1/2" h. (ILLUS.) **$3,220**

Victorian Golden Oak sideboard, three-part construction: the long half-round top w/a removable fan-carved crest centered by pair of small carved putti flanking a shield; the upper section w/rounded ends each w/two curved & leaded glass panels flanking a pair of central clear leaded glass doors centered by pink leaded blossoms & raised at the front by large carved C-scrolls each supporting a full-figure winged lady, the back panel fitted w/a long beveled mirror; the lower section w/wide rounded corners each composed of a curved & leaded glass end panel & a curved, leaded glass door flanking the center swelled cabinet fitted w/a pair of small drawers w/simple bail pulls above a pair of large flat doors decorated at the center w/delicate scrolls above a single long drawer, the front raised on short cabriole legs w/paw feet, square back legs, ca. 1900, 22 x 61", overall 83" h. (ILLUS.) **$11,213**

Very Ornately Inlaid Victorian Renaissance Revival Credenza

Victorian Renaissance Revival credenza, inlaid rosewood, the long rectangular top inset w/white marble w/side concave ends above the conforming case w/a dentil-carved top band above the concave ends each w/a line-inlaid panel above large concave panels w/rectangular molding enclosing a light burl panel centered w/an entwined loop inlay, the flat front section w/two long very shallow drawers w/inlaid bands & small brass teardrop pulls above large cabinet doors w/border molding enclosing delicate inlaid rectangles centered by a large inlaid oval w/a very ornate design of multiple birds among branches, the conforming deep base raised on thin disk front feet, attributed to Herter Brothers, ca. 1880s, 20 x 65", 42" h. (ILLUS., previous page) **$4,830**

Signed Victorian Renaissance Server

Victorian Renaissance Revival server, ebonized & carved oak, the top back w/an ornately carved crestrail w/a tall center cartouche flanked by ornate scrolls & floral swags connecting at each side to full-figure carved winged putti, the rectangular top w/blocked front corners above a conforming apron w/florette-carved corner blocks flanking a singled long drawer carved w/a windflower & vines, the front supported by tall caryatid-carved uprights supporting two long open shelves, the lower shelf w/a molded border raised on two front bun feet, by W.B. Moses & Sons, Washington, D.C., marked w/a metal tag on back of the removable crest, ca. 1870, 21 x 44", overall 51 1/2" h. (ILLUS.) **$1,035**

Victorian Renaissance Revival server, gilt-incised & marquetry-inlaid walnut, the very tall superstructure w/a high stepped & arched cornice decorated w/line-incised flower & scrolls & carved drapes flanked by small tapering raised burl panels, a narrow decorative frieze band above a tall central ebonized panel inlaid w/large ribbon-tied cluster of objects representing

Rare American Renaissance Server

the Arts, each tall side section w/a central arched burl panel mounted w/two tiered half-round shelves & flanked by double turned colonettes, the rectangular top of tan marble above a case w/a narrow frieze drawer flanked by carved blocks above a large paneled cupboard doors w/ebonized molding enclosing a raised burl panel boldly carved w/drapery swags suspending a flower & fruit cluster, raised blocked & narrow raised burl side panels above the deep blocked plinth base, ca. 1870s, 21 x 42", 98" h. (ILLUS.) **$5,750**

Renaissance Revival Game-carved Sideboard

Fine Early English Oak Low Welsh Dresser

Victorian Renaissance Revival side-board, carved walnut, two-part construction: the tall superstructre w/an arched crestrail above scroll-acrved stepped sides centered at the top w/a large boldly carved hanging game cluster flanked by small half-round open shelves all above a narrow rectangular shelf raised on scroll-carved brackets flanking two rectangular molded panels; the lower section w/a rectangular white marble top w/molded edges above a case w/a pair of drawers w/raised rectangular molding & scroll-carved pulls over a medial band & a pair of large paneled cupboard doors w/raised square molding panels centering scroll-carved cartouches, the deep flat apron on thin rounded bracket feet on casters, ca. 1870s, 21 1/2 x 54", 83" h. (ILLUS., previous page) **$2,990**

Fine Renaissance Revival Sideboard with Carved Scrolls & Fruit

Victorian Renaissance Revival side-board, carved walnut, two-part construction: the upper superstructure w/an arched & scroll-molded crestrail over a large fruit-carved cluster above the long

narrow half-round shelves raised on heavy S-scroll fruit-carved supports, the stepped S-scroll-carved sides also carved w/fruit clusters; the lower section w/a long white marble top w/rounded ends above a conforming case w/a pair of flat paneled drawers w/turned wood knobs over a pair of paneled cupboard doors centered by large carved fruit clusters, the rounded ends each w/a drawer above a curved paneled door, flat molded apron on thick block feet, ca. 1870, 21 x 70 1/2", 73" h. (ILLUS.) **$3,220**

Welsh dresser, oak, the long rectangular top fitted w/a low four-panel backrail, the flaring molding above a pair of long drawers w/the original engraved brass pulls above a mid-molding over the two-part serpentine apron raised on six simple cabriole legs ending in pad feet, old patina, England, 19th c., 20 x 65 1/2", 33 1/2" h. (ILLUS., top of page) **$4,600**

Stands

Chippendale Tilt-top Candlestand

Group of Five Federal Candlestands

Candlestand, Chippendale, mahogany, tilt-top style, the large square top w/serpentine edges tilting above a vase- and ring-turned pedestal on a tripod base w/flattened cabriole legs ending in arris pad feet on platforms, old finish, very minor imperfections, Massachusetts, late 18th c., 28" w., 28 3/4" h. (ILLUS., previous page) **$4,113**

Candlestand, Federal style, butternut & maple, the long octagonal top w/applied molded edges raised on a ring- and knob-turned pedestal above the tripod base w/flattened cabriole legs, New England, 18th c., traces of old red paint, old refinish, imperfections, 17 x 17 1/2", 28" h. (ILLUS. back row right with four other Federal candlestands, top of page) **$1,528**

Candlestand, Federal style, cherry, nearly square top w/serpentine edges & rounded corners raised on a baluster-turned pedestal over a tripod base w/cabriole legs ending in pad feet, New England, ca. 1790, old refinish, imperfections, 16" w., 24 3/4" h. (ILLUS. front row left with four other Federal candlestands, top of page) **$764**

Candlestand, Federal style, cherry, round top above a single double-sided candle drawer raised on baluster- and ring-turned pedestal over a tripod base w/flattened cabriole legs ending in pad feet, old dark stain, New England, late 18th - early 19th c., alterations, repairs, 16 1/2" d., 26 1/4" h. (ILLUS. front row right with four other Federal candlestands, top of page) **$823**

Candlestand, Federal style, cherry, the nearly square top w/serpentine edges & rounded corners raised on a baluster-turned pedestal over a tripod base w/cabriole legs ending in arris pad feet, Connecticut River Valley, ca. 1790, refinished, minor restoration, 18" w., 26" h.

(ILLUS. center back row with four other Federal candlestands, top of page) **$2,938**

Candlestand, Federal style, inlaid cherry, rectangular top w/a string-inlaid edge raised on a baluster-turned pedestal above a tripod base w/cabriole legs ending in arris pad feet, probably Connecticut, imperfections, ca. 1790, 13 3/4 x 15", 26 3/4" h. (ILLUS. far left with four other Federal candlestands, top of page) **$1,116**

English Regency-Style Canterbury

Canterbury (music stand), mahogany, Regency-Style, rectangular frame fitted w/four slotted compartments & a carrying handle divided by flat slats & bamboo-turned corner posts w/button finials, the apron w/a single paneled drawer w/round brass pulls, raised on ring- and baluster-turned legs on brass casters, England, late 19th c., 15 x 18 1/2", 23 1/2" h. (ILLUS.) **$345**

Nice Limbert Mission Magazine Stand

Magazine stand, Mission-style (Arts & Crafts movement), oak, the tall tapering sides w/two squared cut-outs joined by five long graduated open shelves above a narrow apron, branded mark of the Charles Limbert Furniture Company, early 20th c., 13 x 23 1/2", 40" h. (ILLUS.) .. **$3,450**

Victorian Stick & Ball Music Stand

Music stand, late Victorian, stick-and-ball construction w/four open stick shelves joining the tall stick sides w/the corner posts topped by ball finials & raised on ball feet, late 19th - early 20th c., 18" w., 38" h. (ILLUS.) **$196**

Nighstands, Victorian Renaissance Revival substyle, carved rosewood, a nearly square white marble top w/canted front corners above a conforming case w/a small drawer w/a scroll-carved pull above a cupboard door centered by a tall scroll-carved panel, the bottom of the canted corners mounted w/a scroll-carved bracket above the blocked plinth base on casters, France, ca. 1870s, 16 x 17", 30" h., pr. (ILLUS., top next column) **$2,760**

French Renaissance Revival Nightstands

Fine Renaissance Revival Nightstand

Nightstand, Victorian Renaissance Revival substyle, walnut & burl walnut, the rectangular white marble top w/projecting rounded corners above the case w/a single drawer w/pierced brass butterfly pulls above a short door w/a large arched burl panel all flanked by boldly carved caryatids at the canted front corners, paneled sides, deep platform base w/blocked corners, on casters, ca. 1875, 18 3/4 x 24 3/4", 28" h. (ILLUS.) **$1,265**

Unusual Reverse-painted Parlor Stand

Parlor stand, Victorian Renaissance Revival substyle, walnut & reverse-painted
glass, the tilting round top w/a molded
scalloped wood frame enclosing a large
round reverse-painted glass panel decorated in the center w/an oval reserve
h.p. w/a seascape w/boats & castle surrounded by a wide black border decorated w/large delicate lacy, lattice & swag
gilt designs, tilting above the four-sec-
tion base w/molded S-scroll supports
joined to a central post w/an urn-turned
finial & turned drop supports by four
molded flat S-scroll legs, some flaking to
painted panel, mid-19th c., 23" d.,
29 1/2" h. (ILLUS., previous page............ **$690**

Unusual Ceramic & Iron Art Deco Stand

Plant stand, Art Deco style, ceramic &
wrought iron, the round ceramic top
glazed w/a yellow background highlighted w/a bright abstract geometric band in
shades of blue, green, yellow & orange, a
tall ceramic conical matching base
mounted in a wrought-iron stand w/out-
swept scrolling curl legs, marked "Made
in Italy," ca. 1930s (ILLUS.) **$259**

Victorian Picture & Print Stands

Picture stand, carved rosewood, a tapering
upright framework w/flattened legs joined
by a rectangular raised-panel box
backed w/a hinged swing-out back leg,
England, ca. 1900, 29 1/2" w., 62 1/2" h.
(ILLUS. left with ebonized print stand) **$978**

Oak 17th Century Trestle-base Stand

Pilgrim century stand, oak, a rectangular
top w/cut corners raised on a trestle base
w/flat scalloped end legs joined just under the top w/a rectangular stretcher &
four angled braces, stepped shoe feet,
probably England or Europe, 17th c.,
18 x 33", 29" h. (ILLUS.) **$978**

Early Moorish-style Plant Stand

Plant stand, Arts & Crafts style, oak, the
small, nearly square top w/a molded
edge overhanging a deep apron centered by a pierced oblong opening above
the high Moorish arch edge, the canted
corners decorated w/a band of chevron

inlay continuing down the slender square
& outswept legs, ca. 1900, 11 x 12",
34 1/2" h. (ILLUS.) **$288**

Carved & Inlaid Oriental Plant Stand

Plant stand, carved & inlaid rosewood, Oriental style, the round top inlaid w/pink
marble above the deep curved apron
pierce-carved w/scroll panels alternating
w/panels inlaid w/mother-of-pearl vines,
raised on notch-carved cabriole legs ending in paw feet & joined by a cross-
stretcher, China, early 20th c., 44 1/2" h.
(ILLUS.).. **$431**

Fine Late Victorian Oak Plant Stand

Plant stand, carved oak, late Victorian style,
a square foot w/a thick ringed base below
the tall heavy column w/a spiral-carved
lower section below the plain cylindrical
upper section w/a scroll-carved capital below the small square top, ca. 1890-1900,
12" sq. top, overall 37" h. (ILLUS.) **$805**
Plant stand, Classical style, rosewood, circular top above tapered & turned pedestal w/tripod scrolled feet, England, 19th
c., minor surface chips & abrasions,
base w/several minor separations, top
band w/veneer loss, 18 1/2" d.,
29 1/2" h. (ILLUS., top next column)........ **$990**

English Classical Style Plant Stand

Early Spiral-twist Turned Plant Stand

Plant stand, late Victorian, carved hardwood, the small round top raised on a
bold spiral-twist turned column above a
leaf-carved knob above the dished round
base on small knob feet, ca. 1900, 12" d.,
41 1/2" h. (ILLUS.) **$345**

Victorian Carved & Turned Plant Stand

Plant stand, late Victorian, turned & carved oak, a small round top raised on a tall ornately ring-turned pedestal topped by a full-relief carved classical woman's head, on a round foot w/small knob feet, late 19th - early 20th c., 35 1/2" h. (ILLUS., previous page) **$230**

Late Victorian Turned Plant Stand

Plant stand, late Victorian, turned oak, the thin round top raised on a slender pedestal w/two fluted columns joined by a central knob w/four pointed disks, supported on a domed, stepped round base on small outswept feet, late 19th - early 20th c., 19" d, 33 1/2" h. (ILLUS.) **$219**

Rare French Victorian Neo-Grec Stand

Plant stand, parcel-gilt bronze-mounted & ebonized wood, Victorian Neo-Grec style, a round black Belgian marble top framed w/a narrow gadrooned band w/shell drops & raised on a tripod base composed of carved full-body satyr-topped monopodi-

ae joined by a central slender post w/a central disk over scrolls, the outswept legs w/hoof feet resting on a tripartite base, by Charpentier et Cie., Paris, France, ca. 1867, 41 1/2" h. (ILLUS.) **$22,705**

Print stand, ebonized wood, the top composed of rectangular lattice adjustable panels raised on a trestle-style base w/projecting frames on each side above the arched base on cushion feet joined by a ring- and baluster-turned stretcher, England, early 20th c., 28" w., 44" h. (ILLUS. right with rosewood picture stand).............. **$805**

American Classical Walnut Sewing Stand

Sewing stand, Classical style, walnut, the rectangular hinged lid w/a raised center w/a thin hinged lid, the apron w/two long narrow drawers above the arched scroll-cut front apron, raised on tall slender squared serpentine legs joined by a cross-stretcher, drawers w/bird's-eye maple dividers, ca. 1830-40, 16 x 21", 30" h. (ILLUS.) **$460**

Fine Gothic Revival Shaving Stand

Shaving stand, Victorian Gothic Revival style, carved rosewood, the top w/a small Gothic arch frame enclosing a mirror swiveling between slender bobbin-turned uprights supported on a pedestal above a rectangular white marble top over a single small drawer supported on a tall paneled column ending in a paneled post supported on a tripod base w/outswept C-scroll legs, marble repaired, second quarter 19th c., 16" w., overall 6' h. (ILLUS., previous page)..... **$2,760**

Fine Renaissance Shaving Stand

Shaving stand, Victorian Renaissance Revival style, walnut & burl walnut, a rectangular mirror in a molded frame w/corner blocks & a scroll-and-shell-carved crest swiveling between scroll-tipped uprights & a pierced tapering panel over a small half-round shelf, the rectangular white marble top w/molded edges above a narrow burl veneered drawer, raised on a slender rod- and urn-turned pedestal on center post supported by four arched & scroll-trimmed legs, refinished, ca. 1870s, 14 x 16", 5' 10" h. (ILLUS.)......... **$2,800**

Side stands, Louis XVI-Style, mahogany, rectangular tops of amber, ivory & mottled beige marble, w/three-quarters openwork brass gallery over single dovetailed drawer above door w/old leather book spines, tapered legs, France, early 20th c., extensive separations, losses to veneer, chips to leather spines, missing brass cuffs, 11 x 15", 30" h., pr. **$880**

Washstand, Classical, carved mahogany, a serpentine & scroll-carved high three-quarters gallery on the top surrounding a bowed top centered by a round bowed opening & w/two tiny drawers flanking the central bowed section, raised on ring- and rod-turned back supports & bold carved & molded S-scroll front supports terminating in floral-carved scrolls resting on a medial shelf w/a concave front over a conforming drawer w/round brass pulls, all raised on baluster-, knob- and ring-turned legs, refinished, probably Boston, ca. 1800-25, 16 1/2 x 19 1/2", 38" h. (minor restorations)..................... **$1,880**

American Classical Mahogany Washstand

Washstand, Classical style, mahogany & mahogany veneer, the rectangular black marble top fitted w/a three-quarters gallery w/a high scroll-carved backsplash & outswept low scrolled sides, the case w/a long ogee-front drawer over a pair of paneled cupboard doors flanked by simple pilasters, C-scroll front feet, ca. 1830s, 18 1/2 x 40 1/2", 43" h. (ILLUS.) **$1,150**

Classical Washstand with Mirror

Washstand, Classical style, mahogany & mahogany veneer, the rectangular white marble top fitted w/a large oval mirror swiveling in a long U-shaped support raised on a low pedestal base, the case w/a long narrow drawer above a pair of flat cupboard doors, deep plinth base raised on ball-shaped front feet, probably New York City, ca. 1830, 20 x 42", 67" h. (ILLUS.).. **$2,185**

Victorian Aesthetic Style Washstand

Washstand, Victorian Aesthetic Movement substyle, walnut, the rectangular top fitted w/a brass bar gallery above a single narrow drawer w/two rectangular aluminum bail pulls over a single raised panel door w/line-incised floral decoration, slender square reeded stile legs, late 19th c., 16 x 24", 34" h. (ILLUS.).............. **$185**

Victorian Renaissance Revival Washstand

Washstand, Victorian Renaissance Revival substyle, walnut & burl walnut, the rectangular white marble top w/a rectangular backsplash fitted w/two small half-round shelves, the case w/a long drawer w/a narrow raised burl panel & carved leaf pulls above a pair of cupboard doors centered by raised rectangular burl panels, canted front corners w/scroll-carved

mounts, deep plinth base on casters, 16 x 29", 36 1/2" h. (ILLUS.) **$250-450**

Victorian Marble-topped Washstand

Washstand, Victorian Renaissance Revival substyle, walnut, the white marble rectangular top w/a serpentine splash guard above the case w/a single long drawer trimmed w/two raised-molding panels w/leaf-carved pulls & a central round molded circle, the lower cabinet w/a pair of cupboard doors w/arched raised molding panels, deep molded base on casters, ca. 1870, 17 1/2 x 31 1/2", 36" h. (ILLUS.) **$345**

Grain-painted Federal One-drawer Stand

Federal country-style one-drawer stand, painted & decorated, nearly square top overhanging the apron fitted w/a single drawer w/a small turned wood knob, on four tall slender square tapering legs, original black swirling w/red grain painting, first half 19th c., 17 3/4 x 18 3/4", 30 1/2" h. (ILLUS.) **$863**

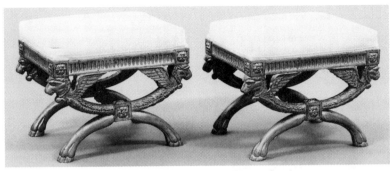

Pair of Fine Empire-Style Giltwood Stools

Fine Federal Two-drawer Stand

Federal country-style two-drawer stand,
cherry & bird's-eye maple, rectangular
top blanked by wide hinged drop leaves
above an apron fitted w/two small bird's-
eye maple drawers w/large early lacy
glass pulls, on ring- and rod-turned legs
w/tall peg feet raised on original brass
casters, first half 19th c., open
20 x 34 1/2", 27 3/4" h. (ILLUS.) **$1,495**

Stools

French Baroque Style Walnut Stool

Baroque style stool, carved walnut, the
rectangular needlepoint-upholstered top
raised on four bold S-scroll legs joined by
a double-scroll carved H-stretcher,

France, late 18th - early 19th c., 18 x 19",
17" h. (ILLUS.) **$1,150**
Empire-Style stools, giltwood, upholstered
square top above a narrow reeded apron
raised on X-form side legs headed by
winged lion heads & ending in paw feet,
late 19th c., 22" w., 18" h., pr. (ILLUS.,
top of page)... **$2,760**

Rare American Federal Piano Stool

Federal piano stool, mahogany, the round
seat missing the upholstery adjusting
above the round reeded apron raised on
slightly canted legs w/ring- and ball-
turned upper sections over tapering
reeded sections on ring-turned feet fitted
w/brass ball caps, central wood threaded
column w/a slender turned long drop finial, New York City, ca. 1800-20, 20 1/2" h.
(ILLUS.)... **$3,585**

Nice Tobey Furniture Mission Oak Stool

Mission-style (Arts & Crafts style) footstool, oak & leather, the rectangular curved leather top w/tack trim mounted on a rectangular frame w/square legs joined by box stretchers, medallion mark of the Tobey Furniture Co. on the side of the top rail, replaced leather, early 20th c., 20 x 22", 16" h. (ILLUS., previous page) **$690**

Fine Gustav Stickley Mission Footstool

Mission-style (Arts & Crafts style) footstool, the rectangular top w/replaced burgundy upholstery w/tack trim along the slight arched aprons, square corner legs w/slightly tapering feet joined by a flat cross-stretcher, cleaned & waxed original finish, faint signature of Gustav

Stickley, early 20th c., 17 x 20", 17" h. (ILLUS.).. **$5,750**

French Napoloen III Upholstered Stool

Napoleon III stool, upholstered mahogany, the padded square top above a concave upright base raised on a carved base band & small bun feet, France, late 19th c., 13 1/2" w., 19" h. (ILLUS.)................... **$259**

Regency stool, upholstered mahogany, the long rectangular top w/tufted upholstery raised on bulbous ring-turned & reeded legs on brass casters, England, early 19th c., 27 x 53", 18 1/2" h. (ILLUS., below) **$1,495**

English Regency Upholstered Long Stool

Pair of Victorian Aesthetic Movement Upholstered Stools

Victorian Aesthetic Movement substyle stools, upholstered mahogany, hexagonal upholstered top & side panels alternating w/vertical scroll-incised wood panels, on wooden casters, late 19th c., 15" w., 14" h., pr. (ILLUS., bottom of previous page) **$1,350**

French Renaissance Revival Stool

Victorian Renaissance Revival substyle stool, polychromed & ebonized beech, the square upholstered top above a pierced apron decorated w/carved pendants, raised on four square tapering legs on outswept feet joined by a turned cross-stretcher joined by a central ball, France, ca. 1865, 13" w., 19" h. (ILLUS.) ... **$518**

William & Mary-Style Upholstered Stool

William & Mary-Style stool, walnut, the rectangular upholstered top w/tack trim raised on knob- and block-turned legs w/knob feet & joined by baluster- and knob-turned side stretchers & a baluster- and knob-turned H-stretcher, England, late 19th - early 20th c., 17 x 20", 17" h. (ILLUS.) **$633**

Early American Windsor Footstool

Windsor footstool, turned hardwood w/pine top, long oval top raised on four canted knob-, ring- and tapering rod-

turned legs joined by a swelled H-stretcher, old worn black or brown-stained surface, top underside branded "B.B. T.," 18th c., 11 1/2 x 19 1/2", 8" h. (ILLUS.)..... **$633**

Tables

Art Deco Half-round Bamboo End Tables

Art Deco end tables, bent bamboo, a half-round wood top raised on a conforming bamboo rood rail & end upright above a matching lower wood shelf & curved bamboo base, ca. 1930s, 21" h., pr. (ILLUS.) ... **$431**

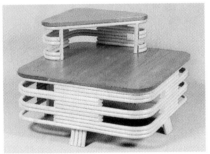

Art Deco Bent Bamboo Corner Table

Art Deco lamp table, corner-style, bent bamboo, the upper triangular wooden corner shelf on a low bent bamboo rod frame resting on the squared wooden top w/rounded corners raised on a deep openwork bamboo rod apron on short bamboo feet, ca. 1930s, 26" h. (ILLUS.)... **$431**

Rare French Art Deco Side Table

Art Deco side table, sycamore & chrome, a round top above three offset round wooden trays raised on a chrome cylindrical rod mounted at one side of the round base, France, ca. 1930, 18 1/8" d., 28 7/8" h. (ILLUS., previous page) **$5,736**

Clematis Art Nouveau Side Table

Art Nouveau side table, carved mahogany, "Clematis" patt., the round top inset w/tan marble, the border carved w/a band of Art Nouveau florals above the shaped apron carved w/clematis blossoms & vines continuing down the three tapering molded legs joined by a triple-arched stretcher, designed by Louis Majorelle, France, ca. 1900, 24 1/4" d., 32" h. (ILLUS.) **$7,170**

Small Hexagonal Art Nouveau Side Table

Art Nouveau side table, stamped oak, the hexagonal top overhanging flat sides each stamped w/an Art Nouveau design of pairs of poppies on leafy vines above Moorish arch legs, ca. 1900 (ILLUS.)........ **$172**

Arts & Crafts Side Table

Arts & Crafts side table, oak, a narrow rectangular top raised on slender flaring flat legs joined by two narrow shelves w/an X-form back brace & splat side panels, after a design by Rohfs Ross, scuffs & scratches, original finish, early 20th c., 13 x 29 1/2", 29 1/2" h. (ILLUS.) **$748**

Carved Indian Elephant Head Table

Asian side table, carved teak, the round top decorated w/inlaid camels & elephants in ivory circling a central carved elephant relief w/a border of vine, leaves & berries, raised on four figural carved elephant head legs w/trunks forming the legs, each w/inlaid ivory eyes & tusks, joined by a cross-stretcher w/a dish center, India, first half 20th c., some inlay missing, 15" d., 19" h. (ILLUS.) **$201**

Baroque-Style library table, fumed oak, the rectangular top w/a molded edge overhanging a geometrically carved apron & raised on heavy upright rectangular panel legs carved on the outside edges w/full-figure caryatids above a shell-carved band that continues around the cross-stretcher, raised on low scroll- and shell-carved feet, Holland, ca. 1900, 42 1/2 x 82", 32" h. (ILLUS., top next page) **$978**

Dutch Baroque-Style Oak Library Table

Extremely Rare American Classical Mahogany Dining Table

Classical dining table, mahogany, extension-type w/accordian action, the rectangular top w/rounded corners above an accordian-action base w/six baluster- and spiral-turned posts atop flat wide arched rails continuing into downswept square reeded sabre legs ending in brass toes on casters, w/six mahogany leaves stored in their original box, New York City, ca. 1800-1810, open 60 x 167", 30" h. (ILLUS., above)........................ **$339,500**

Classical parlor center table, carved mahogany, the round black marble to above a plain veneered apron raised on a tapering triangular pedestal carved at the base w/three swans resting on the tripartitie base w/disk feet on casters, professional restoration to break in marble top, ca. 1830, 38 1/2" d., 29 1/2" h. (ILLUS, to the right.) **$2,645**

Fine Classical Parlor Center Table

One of a Pair of Very Rare American Classical Pier Tables

Classical pier tables, mahogany & mahogany veneer, a rectangular white marble top above a flat apron raised on large front column supports w/gilt-brass capitals & bases & joined by a concave shelf backed by a large retangular mirror, raised on gilt acanthus leaf-carved turned feet, New York City, ca. 1815-30, 17 x 42", 35" h., pr. (ILLUS. of one)
.... **$35,850**

Fine New England Classical Work Table

Classical work table, japanned & decorated, the rectangular top decorated w/gilt Chinoiserie landscape w/buildings & opening to a fitted interior, the coved apron fitted w/a single drawer further decorated w/Chinese motifs, raised on a trestle-style base w/flattened baluster-shaped end uprights on arched scroll-tipped feet joined by a pair of slender baluster- and knob-turned stretchers, New England, ca. 1835, 20 x 24", 29" h. (ILLUS.)................ **$2,875**

Large Classical-Style Dining Table

Classical-Style dining table, carved mahogany, extension-type, the round divided top w/a foliate-carved edge band above the plain apron, raised on a heavy short pedestal w/a large reeded & flaring bulbous base issuing four outswept acanthus leaf-carved legs ending in paw feet on casters, late 19th c., original finish, one small cylindrical hold in the top, 54" d. (ILLUS.) **$1,560**

Simple Federal Mahogany Card Table

Federal card table, carved mahogany, the D-shaped fold-over top above a deep ogee apron, raised on a heavy baluster-turned & leaf-carved pedestal supported by four long outswept C-scroll legs ending in brass paw feet on casters, probably New York, first quarter 19th c., 17 3/4 x 36", 28 1/4" h. (ILLUS.) **$805**

Fine Mahogany Federal Console Table

Federal console table, mahogany & mahogany veneer, long demi-lune top decorated w/radiating crotch grain mahogany above the paneled veneer panels separated by for raised panels decorated w/oval inlaid paterae, four square tapering legs ending in stepped square feet, underside of skirt w/a glued piece of a 19th c. Boston newspaper, American-made, possibly Boston or Baltimore, some veneer damage, repairs & loss, top w/section of missing veneers & cracks, 24 1/4 x 51 1/4", 33" h. (ILLUS., previous page) **$2,588**

Rare Rhode Island Federal Pembroke Table

Federal Pembroke table, inlaid mahogany, the rectangular top w/bowed ends flanked by half-round drop leaves, the apron w/a line-inlaid working drawer at one end & a false drawer at the other, raised on square tapering legs headed by inlaid blocks above narrow long inlaid banded triangles, Newport, Rhode Island, ca. 1795, 20 1/2 x 34", 27 1/2" h. (ILLUS.)... **$16,730**

American Federal Sofa Table

Federal sofa table, ebony-inlaid mahogany, rectangular top flanked by wide D-form drop leaves w/reeded edges, the apron fitted w/a pair of drawers w/line & circle inlay, testle base w/end uprights supported on outswept inlaid legs ending in brass paws on casters, flat cross-stretcher, coastal New England, ca. 1800-15, refinished, 25 x 59 1/2" open, 28" h. (ILLUS.) **$3,910**

Irish George III Waiter

George III waiter, mahogany, the round banded top joined to a lower shelf by turned brass uprights, raised on a turned & reeded pedestal on a tripod base w/reeded outswept legs ending in brass caps on casters, Ireland, ca. 1800, 24" d., 39 1/2" h. (ILLUS.) **$1,840**

Long George III-Style Side Table

George III-Style side table, mahogany, the long rectangular top raised on cabriole legs w/shell-carved knees & ending in hairy paw feet, England, late 19th c., 20 1/2 x 57", 35" h. (ILLUS.) **$633**

Nice English Jacobean-Style Oak Refectory Table

George III-Style Tea Table

George III-Style tea table, mahogany, the large round top above a baluster-turned pedestal on a tripod base w/cabriole legs ending in pad feet, England, late 19th c., 33" d., 30" h. (ILLUS.) **$1,610**

Georgian-Style Oak Dining Table

Georgian-Style dining table, oak, the narrow rectangular top w/rounded ends flanked by wide half-round drop leaves, a scalloped apron raised on straight turned legs ending in pad feet, England, mid-

19th c., open 44 x 54", 27 1/2" h. (ILLUS. closed) **$1,265**

Jacobean-Style refectory table, carved oak, the large rectangular plank top above a deep scroll- and leaf-carved apron raised on four large turnip-shaped leaf-carved legs above blocks joined by flat rails, England, ca. 1900, 33 1/2 x 72", 29 1/2"h. (ILLUS., top of page) **$1,265**

Louis XVI-Style dining table, ormolu-mounted mahogany, extension-type, the oval top w/matchbook veneers & rosewood banding above a paneled apron w/ormolu banding, raised on fluted tapering legs raised on ormolu peg feet, w/one folding leaf, France, early 20th c., open 43 x 100", 31" h. (ILLUS. open, top next page).. **$2,990**

Louis XVI-Style side table, gilt hardwood, cartouche-shaped top, gilt & carved frieze, tapered stop-fluted legs, one dovetailed drawer, cross-stretcher base, France, probably early 20th c., trace of original gilding, ivory & blue paint, extensive chips & losses to painted surface, 22 x 37", 30" h.. **$1,870**

Louis XVI-Style Small Oval Table

Fine Louis XVI-Style Ormolu-mounted Mahogany Dining Table

Louis XVI-Style side table, mahogany, the oval top inset w/brown & white marble & framed w/a low pierced brass gallery, raised on shaped & pierced side uprights joined by two brass-banded oval lower shelves above the trestle base w/shoe feet, France, third quarter 19th c., 10 3/4 x 21 3/4", 29 1/2" h. (ILLUS., previous page).. **$575**

Rare Gustav Stickley Director's Table

Pair of Louis XVI-Style Marble-topped Side Tables

Louis XVI-Style side tables, giltwood, a rectangular grey & maroon marble top above an apron carved w/a band of florettes centered by a carved maiden head on two sides, raised on turned & tapering fluted legs w/knob feet, France, 19th c., 28 x 56", 38" h., pr. (ILLUS.) **$2,990**

Mission-style (Arts & Crafts movement) director's table, oak, the large rectangular top overhanging a deep pegged & slightly canted apron raised on heavy square slightly canted legs on thick shoe feet w/beveled ends, refinished, paper label of Gustav Stickley, early 20th c., 42 x 84", 29 1/2" h. (ILLUS., top next column)... **$10,925**

Early Gustav Stickley Round Lamp Table

Mission-style (Arts & Crafts movement) lamp table, oak, round top fitted onto square legs joined by a mortised cross-stretcher, original finish, 1902-03 decal mark of Gustav Stickley, 23 1/2" d., 28" h. (ILLUS.) **$5,750**

Extremely Rare Frank Lloyd Wright-designed Side Table

Modern style side table, oak, three-tier 'flower table,' a thick rectangular top over-hanging a framework w/a short narrow top shelf raised on four square supports enclosing a medial shelf & joined to four square legs w/outswept feet & joined by a wider bottom shelf, designed by Frank Lloyd Wright in collaboration w/George Mann Niedecken of Niedecken-Walbridge, for the Second Story Hall of the Avery Coonley House, Riverside, Illinois, ca. 1910, 16 x 29 7/8", 25 1/4" h. (ILLUS.) ... **$59,750**

Small Neoclassical Side Table

Europe, mid-19th c., 13 1/2 x 19 1/2", 30" h. (ILLUS.) **$1,265**

Napoleon III Rococo Parlor Table

Napoleon III parlor center table, Rococo-style, ebonized wood, the grey marble "turtle top" above a conforming apron w/applied ormolu mounts & beading continuing to cabriole legs joined by a serpentine cross-stretcher centered by a large urn-form post w/ormolu finial, France, third quarter 19th c., 30 x 43", 27" h. (ILLUS.) **$920**

Neoclassical side table, inlaid mahogany, the rectangular top w/canted corners decorated w/rosewood banding above the conforming apron w/a single narrow rosewood-banded drawer, raised on square tapering legs ending in brass caps on casters & joined by a cross-stretcher centered by a small oval shelf,

Nutting-made William & Mary Table

Nutting-signed William & Mary-Style side table, wide rectangular top above the trestle base w/block- and knob-turned legs joined by two block-, baluster- and knob-turned cross stretchers, shaped shoe feet, block letter branded signature under the top, 13 x 18 3/4", 26 3/4" h. (ILLUS., previous page) **$518**

Carved Chinese Side Table

Oriental side table, carved & painted hardwood, a rectangular frame & panel top w/exposed joinery, the case w/a pair of drawers over a long drawer all w/strap metal pulls, flanked by scrolling pierced side brackets, on flat rectangular stile legs, old reddish paint, scorched areas on top, China, late 19th c., 32 x 42 1/2", 34" h. (ILLUS.) **$575**

Ornately Carved Chinese Rosewood Table

Oriental side table, carved rosewood, the round top inset w/rose marble & w/a beaded border & an incurved band above the deep apron ornately pierce-carved w/scrolls & bars, raised on four heavy cabriole legs headed by a mask & carved shell & ending in heavy paw feet, joined by a cross stretcher, China, late 19th - early 20th c., top 17" d., 19" h. (ILLUS.)
.... **$316**

Queen Anne country-style tea table, painted, three-board oval top w/a center

Country Queen Anne Tea Table

cleat above the deep gently arched apron raised on turned & tapering legs ending in small round pad feet, red paint not original, restoration to feet & top, first half 18th c., 26 1/2 x 32", 28" h. (ILLUS.)......... **$920**

Large Renaissance-Style Carved Library Table

Renaissance-Style library table, carved mahogany, long rectangular top w/molded edges overhanging a narrow scroll-carved apron raised on a trestle base w/heavy scroll-carved end legs on scroll-carved shoe feet & joined by a medial shelf, ca. 1900, professionally refinished, 24 1/2 x 72", 30 1/2" h. (ILLUS.) **$1,380**

Renaissance-Style library table, carved mahogany, the long rectangular top w/a molded edge above a deep rounded leaf-carved apron w/two drawers on one side, raised on wide ornately carved trestle-style end legs w/carved winged griffins at each side flanking a finely carved panel centered by a female mask resting on carved shoe feet joined by a wide ornately carved flat stretcher, the underside of the top center decorated w/two long flat tapering carved drop panels w/turned drop finials, Europe, late 19th c., 30 x 50", 31" h. (ILLUS., top next page)
.... **$2,300**

Fine European Renaissance-Style Carved Library Table

Pretty Little Rococo-Style Side Table

Aesthetic Movement Parlor Table

Rococo-Style side table, inlaid mahogany, the triangular top flanked by three half-round drop leaves opening to form a three-lobe clover-form, each leaf inlaid w/a wreath of sprays of vines & flowers, raised on three simple cabriole legs w/a leaf-carved knee, metal scroll mounts on the feet, Europe, late 19th - early 20th c., top w/open cracks, 20" d. open, 28" h. (ILLUS.).. **$403**

Victorian Aesthetic Movement parlor center table, carved walnut, the square top w/molded edges & rounded corners above a line-incised apron w/curved corner blocks w/large turned pointed bulbous drops, two sides fitted w/a small central drawer w/a crosshatch-carved front, raised on four brackets above carved bulbous segments & spiral-carved columns, resting on a cross-form platform raised on four angled & scroll-carved legs raised on casters, late 19th c., 30" sq., 30" h. (ILLUS., next column) ... **$431**

Large Square Baroque Revival Oak Dining Table

Victorian Baroque Revival dining table, quarter-sawn oak, extension-type, the square top w/a block band-carved deep apron w/florette-carved corners, raised on four serpentine acanthus leaf-carved legs resting on heavy brass caps on casters, joined by a scroll-carved serpentine cross stretcher centered by a raised octagonal platform supporting four bulbous short pedestals, refinished, ca. 1895, w/six leaves, 54" w., 30" h. (ILLUS.) **$3,200**

Nicely Carved Oak Baroque Library Table

Victorian Baroque Revival library table, carved quarter-sawn oak, the rectangular top w/a gadrooned edge above a flat apron w/a single drawer w/brass teardrop pulls on one side, rosette-carved corner blocks, raised on heavy S-scroll carved corner supports topped by a short ring-turned column & resting on bun feet, each joined by a wide ornately pierced scroll-carved support joined by a heavy medial shelf, original finish, ca. 1895, 24 x 48", 30" h. (ILLUS.) **$1,200**

Simple Victorian Eastlake Dining Table

Victorian Eastlake dining table, quarter-sawn oak, extension-type, the divided square top above a reeded apron raised on five heavy square reeded legs w/curved brackets under the apron, on casters, ca. 1900-1910, w/three 13 3/4" w. leaves, closed 48" sq., 29 1/2" h. (ILLUS.) **$575**

Early Victorian Gothic Revival Table

Victorian Gothic Revival card table, mahogany, the fold-over rectangular top w/serpentine edges above a deep apron bordered w/Gothic arches & rounded corners w/small turned drops, raised on four slender bobbin-turned legs resting on arched trestle feet joined by a bobbin-turned stretcher, ca. 1840-50, closed 16 x 31 1/2", 29" h. (ILLUS.) **$230**

Victorian Jacobean-Style Library Table

Victorian Jacobean-Style library table, oak, the rectangular top w/a faux-painted marbleized insert & gadrooned edge band above the apron w/florette-carved corner blocks flanking two long leaf-carved drawers w/carved lion mask handles, raised on four heavy spiral-turned legs joined by a spiral-turned H-stretcher, carved block & bun feet, dark medium color, ca. 1900, 32 x 48", 29 1/2" h. (ILLUS.) **$748**

Nice Victorian Renaissance Revival Dining Table

Victorian Renaissance Revival substyle dining table, carved mahogany, extension-type, the oval top overhanging a deep apron raised on heavy ring-turned & tapering fluted legs w/disk ankles on brass & porcelain casters, w/two leaves, ca. 1870, open 64 x 106", 29 1/2" h. (ILLUS. open, bottom previous page) **$1,955**

Rare Victorian Rococo Parlor Center Table Attributed to Meeks

Victorian Rococo substyle parlor center table, carved & laminated rosewood, the shaped "turtle-top" w/a later inset top above a conforming apron w/each deep serpentine side pierced & carved w/ornate scrolls centering a floral cartouche, raised on four serpentine cabriole legs w/floral-carved knees & ending in scroll feet on casters, legs joined by four arched & pierced scroll-carved stretchers joined by a central post w/a large carved fruit-filled compote, attributed to J. & J.W. Meeks, New York, New York, ca. 1855, 30 x 46", 31 1/2" h. (ILLUS.) **$20,700**

Rococo Marble-topped Parlor Table

Victorian Rococo substyle parlor center table, carved rosewood, the inset tan marble "turtle-top" w/a conforming gadrooned edge above a conforming apron w/ornate scroll-carved serpentine sides, raised on four bold ornately carved S-scroll legs on casters joined by four ornate S-scroll stretchers centered by a short post w/a turned drop finial & a large carved compote-shaped finial, ca. 1860, 32 x 51", 29" h. (ILLUS.) **$8,050**

Nice Victorian Rococo Parlor Table

Victorian Rococo substyle parlor center table, walnut, the white marble "turtle-top" above a deep conforming apron carved at the side centers w/bold scrolls & corner blocks w/small turned drops, raised on a very bulbous octagonal pedestal above four long outstretched ornate S-scroll legs on casters, ca. 1855, 27 1/2 x 38", 28" h. (ILLUS.) **$920**

William IV Mahogany Library Tabl

William IV library table, mahogany, the rectangular top inset w/a gilt-tooled leather writing surface, the apron fitted w/three drawers on each side, raised on reeded curule-style legs joined by a long turned stretcher, England, mid-19th c., 46 1/2 x 72", 30" h. (ILLUS.) **$2,760**

Extremely Rare William & Mary Dining Table from Long Island

William & Mary dining table, maple, a long rectangular top w/slightly rounded ends flanked by wide half-round drop leaves, raised on a shaped apron w/a drawer at one end raised on baluster- and ring-turned legs & a swing-out leg support, all on blocks joined by knob-turned stretchers above compressed feet, Hempstead,

Long Island, New York, 1700-20, drawer & one leaf old replacements, closed 20 1/2 x 48", 28" h. (ILLUS.) **$35,850**

William & Mary Maple Dining Table

William & Mary dining table, maple, the narrow rectangular figured maple top w/rounded ends flanked by two wide half-round drop leaves above the apron w/one drawer raised on baluster- and ring-turned legs w/swing-out gateleg support, baluster- and ring-turned stretchers, probably Massachusetts or Connecticut, early 18th c., some old repair & restoration, open 42 x 49", 26 1/2" h. (ILLUS.) **$1,265**

Wardrobes & Armoires

Ornate Anglo-Colonial Carved Rosewood Armoire

Armoire, Anglo-Colonial style, pierced & carved rosewood, the long rectangular breakfront top w/beaded edges & six small turned pointed finials above a conforming fruit & leaf-carved frieze band over four tall doors each w/ornate scroll carving around a large arched panel pierce-carved w/intricate scrolling tree-of-life-style designs, two center doors opening to pull-out shelves & two short drawers over two long drawers, the outer doors opening to pull-out shelves, the deep flaring leaf-carved base raised on carved paw feet, possibly Burma, mid-19th c., 24 x 98", 78 1/2" h. (ILLUS.)...... **$6,638**

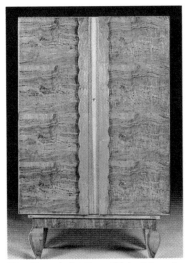

Fine French Art Deco Walnut Armoire

Armoire, Art Deco style, brass-inlaid walnut veneer, the rectangular top above a pair of tall cupboard doors w/decorative veneering & vertical scalloped veneer bands along the inner edges, an inset plinth base raised on short bulbous stylized cabriole legs, Andre Sornay, France, ca. 1935, 17 1/2 x 39 1/2", 64" h. (ILLUS.)... **$7,170**

Fancy Baroque-Style Walnut Armoire

Armoire, Baroque-Style, walnut & burl walnut, the long rectangular top w/a widely flaring coved cornice above a pair of tall wide doors decorated w/pairs of patterned burl panels, flanked by narrow vertical side panels w/further burl panels & centered by a narrow paneled stile, the bottom w/a pair of long burl-paneled drawers over the rounded base molding raised on thin bun feet, Europe, mid-19th c., 27 x 78", 77" h. (ILLUS.)................... **$5,520**

Large Three-part Baroque-Style Armoire

Armoire, Baroque-Style, walnut, the long breakfront-case w/an arched serpentine cornice above a projecting wide arched center section fitted w/a wide arched mirrored door above a long paneled drawer, the tall narrow sides sections w/tall mirrored doors over smaller paneled drawers, plinth base raised on four bun feet, repair to left rear leg, Europe, late 19th - early 20th c., 26 1/2 x 94 1/2", 100" h. (ILLUS.)... **$1,380**

Classical Transitional Rosewood Armoire

Armoire, Classical Transitional style, rosewood, the rectangular top w/a widely projecting stepped cornice above a wide ogee frieze band over the tall rectangular door w/raised molding enclosing a tall mirror & flanked by slender bead-carved corner bands above a single long bottom drawer w/further bead-carved banding, a deep platform base w/a narrow slipper

drawer on block feet, possibly made in New Orleans, ca. 1850, 36 x 52", 96" h. (ILLUS.)... **$4,600**

Fine Carved French Provincial Armoire

Armoire, French Provincial, carved oak, the rectangular top w/a wide flaring cornice above a leaf- and scroll-carved frieze band above a pair of tall arched three-panel cupboard doors, the top panels carved w/fancy flowers & leaves, the central panel carved w/a paneled cartouche w/more leafy scrolls & the bottom panel decorated w/a plain arched panel framed by leafy scrolls, five-panel sides, a wide flaring & stepped base raised on thin bun feet, France, early 19th c., 22 x 51", 80" h. (ILLUS.) **$2,070**

Large French Provincial-Style Armoire

Armoire, French Provincial-Style, carved walnut, the wide arched crestrail centered by a large scroll-carved crest above a conforming molded frieze band over a pair of tall mirrored cupboard doors flanked by chamfered front corners w/scroll carving, the molded base band above a deep serpentine apron carved in the center w/a large scrolling cartouche, short scroll-carved cabriole front legs, feet cut off, top of large crest missing, France, ca. 1890, 24 x 59", 101" h. (ILLUS., previous page) **$2,530**

Nice Renaissance Revival Armoire

Armoire, Victorian Renaissance Revival substyle, rosewood veneer, the rectangular top w/a deep flaring cornice above a frieze band w/a narrow raised burl panel above a pair of tall paneled cupboard doors inset w/tall mirrors & flanked by slender half-round columns over a mid-molding & a pair of bottom drawers w/raised burl panels & round brass bail pulls, flat plinth base on thin blocked feet, ca. 1870, 25 x 67", 97" h. (ILLUS.).......................... **$2,760**

American Rococo Fancy Armoire

Armoire, Victorian Rococo substyle, carved mahogany, the arched flaring cornice topped by a long high arched crestrail pierce-carved w/ornate scrolls flanked by disk-turned corner finials above the arched frieze band carved w/a long scroll band w/fruit & leaves centering a face, the tall arched doors w/large scroll-carved corner panels above the tall inset mirrors, flanked by slender spiral- and baluster-turned quarter-round corner columns, a mid-molding above a pair of bottom drawers w/scroll-carved pulls, the low scroll-carved apron w/rounded front corners, retaining original interior partition & shelving, ca. 1855, 25 x 66", 118 1/2" h. (ILLUS.) **$5,520**

English Chippendale-Style Wardrobe

Wardrobe, Chippendale-Style, mahogany, the rectangular top w/a narrow flaring cornice above a pair of tall cupboard doors each w/three raised panels opening to shelves, flat molded base raised on high scroll-cut bracket feet, refinished, restorations w/replacements, England, late 19th - early 20th c., 24 x 53 3/4", 78" h. (ILLUS.) **$1,495**

Wardrobe, country-style, blue-painted & decorated, a narrow arched & molded cornice above a pair of tall arched cupboard doors w/two raised panels, the top two painted in color w/figures in landscapes, the lower two painted w/flower-filled vases, each panel framed by ornate gilt scrolls, wide canted front corners w/further painted scrolls, deep plinth base w/further painted scrolls, old woodworm damage, Europe, possibly Portugal, 19th c., 21 x 60", 75" h. (ILLUS., next page).. **$2,645**

Colorfully-painted Country Wardrobe

Simple Victorian Walnut Wardrobe

Wardrobe, Victorian country-style, walnut, the rectangular top w/a flaring stepped cornice above a pair of tall double-panel doors, flat molded base on thin block feet, second half 19th c., 21 x 64 1/4", 86" h. (ILLUS.) **$1,076**

Whatnots & Etageres

Rare Victorian Rococo Rosewood Etagere

Etagere, Victorian Rococo substyle, carved rosewood, the tall superstructure w/a wide arched scroll-carved & pierced crest above a half-round narrow serpentine top shelf raised on slender S-scroll carved front supports & flanked by S-scroll

European Painted Country Wardrobe

Wardrobe, country-style, painted & decorated, a rectangular top w/a flaring cornice painted w/a blue & white band above a blue frieze band painted w/a row of small white arches above a molding over a pair of tall paneled doors decorated w/a tall central blue diamond framed by white fan carving, a thick blue & white mid-molding above the deep plinth base raised on square legs, Europe, 19th c., 20 7/8 x 47 3/4", 71 1/2" h. (ILLUS.) **$863**

carved side flanking a mirrored back all above a matching larger lower shelf & mirrored back resting on the half-round serpentine-edged sienna marble top above a conforming cabinet base w/a serpentine-fronted scroll-carved top drawer above a conforming wide door centered by an oval panel, flanked on each side by two open quarter-round shelves w/scroll-carved brackets, the deep conforming apron w/ornate scroll carving, ca. 1850-60, 20 3/4 x 49 1/2", 73 1/2" h. (ILLUS.) **$8,050**

Rare Chinese Chippendale-Style Etageres

Etageres, Chinese Chippendale-Style, carved mahogany, in the form of tall pagodas, a top cupola shelf over four graduated open shelves each w/a full pierced gallery, the upright w/blind fret carving, raised on cabriole legs ending in paw feet, late 19th - early 20th c., 20 1/2" sq., 70" h., pr. (ILLUS.) **$4,140**

GAMES & GAME BOARDS

Fine Early Decorated Game Board

Game board, painted & decorated wood, square form w/old decoration w/a dark red ground decorated w/black, green & cream, the center w/a small checkerboard surrounded by panels & diamonds w/"1878" & triangles w/stars, applied color decals of hunters in the corners, minor splits, a corner chip, 18 1/4" sq. (ILLUS.) **$2,415**

Game board, painted pine, rectangular, executed in black, white & pink w/a checkerboard headed by a woman on one end & a man on the other, each flanked by barns, America, 19th c., 18 1/2 x 25 3/4" **$4,183**

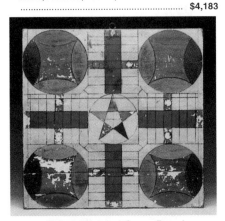

Colorful Painted Game Board

Game board, painted wood three-board square w/breadboard ends, one side w/a colorful Parcheesi board, the reverse w/a checkerboard, the Parcheesi side centered by a five-point star in green, red, brown, blue & gold, the large corner circles in the same colors against a white ground, checkerboard in black & red, some overall paint loss, late 19th - early 20th c., 18" sq. (ILLUS.) **$805**

Little Black Sambo Board Game

"Little Black Sambo," board-type, colorful board shows Sambo & his adventures, colorful box cover shows Sambo w/his umbrella, ca. 1945, near mint w/box, box 10 x 20" (ILLUS.) **$52**

Early Marble Toy with Children

Marble game, lithographed paper on wood figure of Victorian children dancing around a maypole topped w/American flags & wrapped w/a metal spring, marble rolls down through the spring, possibly European, late 19th c., excellent condition w/minor paper loss on right side, 15" h. (ILLUS.) **$633**

Parker Bros. Nodding Nancy Game

"Nodding Nancy - A Party Game," a figure of a black woman w/a lithographed paper on wood head above a simple cloth-covered body, her smiling mouth holding a projecting wooden pipe, object of game is to toss wooden rings over the pipe, Parker Bros., w/original box, early 20th c., toy near mint, box w/damaged sides, box 12" l. (ILLUS.) **$230**

1970s The Wizard of Oz Game

Wizard of Oz Game (The), board-type, Cadaco Storybook Class Game, based on the 1939 MGM movie & television favorite, color drawings of the main characters on the box top, 1974, still sealed in box (ILLUS.) **$20-30**

GARDEN FOUNTAINS & ORNAMENTS

Ornamental garden or yard fountains, urns and figures often enhanced the formal plantings on spacious lawns of mansion-sized dwellings during the late 19th and early 20th century. While fountains were usually reserved for the lawns of estates, even modest homes often had a latticework arbor or cast-iron urn in the yard. Today garden enthusiasts look for these ornamental pieces to lend the aura of elegance to their landscaping.

Fine Figural Two-part Lead Fountain

Fountain, cast lead, two-art, the top cast as a mermaid boy riding atop a large dolphin w/the mouth fitted forming the foutain outlet, sitting in a wide shallow shell-shaped base, some outdoor use, late 19th - early 20th c., shell base 19" w., figure 13 3/4" h., 2 pcs. (ILLUS.)............... **$1,265**

One of Two French Terra Cotta Tubs

Tree tubs, terra cotta, in the late Louis XVI-Style, wide cylindrical form molded w/winged & helmeted female masks joined by large floral swags around the body, molded shoulder band & flaring gadrooned rim, supported on small recumbent lion feet, France, 19th c., 41" d., 32" h., pr. (ILLUS. of one) **$4,370**

Urn, cast-iron, four-piece including reservoir, rectangular plinth w/raised panel signed "Hay," short ribbed, ringed pedestal on stepped foot, wide shallow bowl w/ornate applied scrolled leaf handles, worn white paint, 29 1/2" w., 36" h. **$440**

Urns, bronze, classical form w/moulded flared rim, ram's head handles, raised on square pedestal base, 20" d., 26" h., pr. **$2,128**

One of Two English Garden Urns

Urns, cast iron, tall neoclassical style w/the body cast in relief w/Classical figures below the gadrooned shoulder, wide short cylindrical neck w/a rolled gadrooned rim flanked by upright serpent-entwined handles each enclosing a small mask, worn polychrome paint, England, 19th c., 76" h., pr. (ILLUS. of one) **$4,600**

GLASS

Amberina

Amberina was developed in the late 1880s by the New England Glass Company and a pressed version was made by Hobbs, Brockunier & Company (under license from the former). A similar ware, called Rose Amber, was made by the Mt. Washington Glass Works. Amberina-Rose Amber shades from amber to deep red or fuchsia and cut and plated (lined with creamy white) examples were also made. The Libbey Glass Company briefly revived blown Amberina, using modern shapes, in 1917.

Amberina Label

Plated Amberina Lobed Bowl

Bowl, 7 3/4" d., Plated Amberina, low rounded form w/five-lobed sides (ILLUS.) **$8,050**

Amberina Butter Dish

Butter dish, cov., wide flat-topped flaring cylindrical top w/an applied curl finial, Inverted Thumbprint patt., on a deeply ruffled fuchsia base, 7 1/2" d., 5" h. (ILLUS.) **$575**

Amberina Inverted Thumbprint Creamer

Creamer, rounded squatty base w/sharply tapering cylindrical sides to a tricorner rim, Inverted Thumbprint patt., applied amber handle, 4 1/2" h. (ILLUS.) **$460**

Cruet w/original stopper, Plated Amberina, bulbous body tapering to a cylindrical neck w/tricorner rim, applied amber handle, facet-cut amber stopper, 7 1/4" h. (ILLUS., next page) **$6,900**

Rare Pressed Amberina Ice Cream Set

Rare Plated Amberina Cruet

Ice cream set: large shallow oblong bowl in a fancy footed silver plate stand & twelve 5 3/4" w. square side dishes; pressed Daisy & Button patt., very minor roughage to large bowl & chip on one side dish, large bowl 9 1/4 x 17" l., the set (ILLUS., top of page) **$2,185**

Plated Amberina Punch Cup

Punch cup, Plated Amberina, rounded tapering cup w/applied amber handle, 2 1/2" h. (ILLUS.) **$2,875**

Finely Enameled Amberina Punch Set

Pair of Deep Ruby Amberina Goblets

Goblets, a round foot & slender stem w/a swelled top supporting a large bulbous knop below the deep rounded bowl w/a flat rim, deep red to amber bowl, w/a typed note indicating they may have come from the New England Glass Co., 8 1/2" h., pr. (ILLUS.) **$518**

Punch set: cov. punch bowl & eight punch cups; the large footed bowl w/a rounded base & wide cylindrical sides, fitted w/a wide domed cover w/a tall panel-cut pointed finial, the sides enameled w/a large bouquet of large, colorful flowers, matching cylindrical cups w/applied amber handles & white-enameled blossoms, one enameled flower petal w/a chip, roughness at edge of ladle opening in cover, some gilt wear, late 19th c., bowl 8" d., 14" h., the set (ILLUS.) **$805**

Egg-shaped Amberina Vase

Vase, 5 1/2" h., egg-shaped w/tricorner rim, on three applied amber reeded feet, Diamond Quilted patt., ground pontil (ILLUS.)... **$578**

Vase, 6" h., lily-form w/tricorner rim, New England Glass Co. **$532**

Libbey Amberina Lily-form Vase

Vase, 10 3/4" h., lily-form, ruffled rim, ground pontil & signed by Libbey, ca. 1917 (ILLUS.).. **$575**

Decorated Amberina Water Set

Water set: 8 3/4" h. pitcher & five cylindrical 4 1/2" h. tumblers; the pitcher w/an ovoid body & cylindrical neck, ornate enameled w/designs of flowers, butterflies & insects, applied reeded amber handle, each tumbler w/enameled insect decoration, some wear to gold trim, the set (ILLUS.)... **$600**

Animals

Americans evidently like to collect glass animals. For the past sixty years, American glass manufacturers have turned out a wide variety of animals to please the buying public. Some were produced for long periods and some were later reproduced by other companies, while others were made for only a short period of time and are rare. We have not included late productions in our listings and have attempted to date the productions where possible. Evelyn Zemel's book, American Glass Animals A to Z, will be helpful to the novice collector. Another helpful book is Glass Animals of the Depression Era by Lee Garmon and Dick Spencer Collector Books, 1993.

Blue Jay, flower frog, clear, Cambridge Glass Co., 5 1/2" h. **$145**

Cat, bottle w/shot glass lid, clear, Cambridge Glass Co., 8 3/4" h. **$58**

Chanticleer (rooster), black, Fostoria Glass Co., 10 3/4" h. **$650**

Deer, reclining, clear, Fostoria Glass Co., 2 1/2" h.. **$38**

Fish, book end, clear, Heisey Glass Co., 6 1/2" h., pr... **$295**

Fish, bowl, clear, A.H. Heisey & Co., 9 1/2" h. **$450**

Heisey Clear Clydesdale Horse

Horse, Clydesdale, clear, Heisey Glass Co., 7" l. (ILLUS.)... **$475**

Rearing Fostoria Horse in Satin Clear

Horse, rearing, satin clear, Fostoria Glass Co., 7 3/4" h. (ILLUS., previous page) **$65**

Heisey Mallards, Wings Down & Up

Mallard, wings down, clear, A. H. Heisey & Co., 4 1/2" h. (ILLUS. right with other Mallard) **$325**

Mallard, wings up, clear, A. H. Heisey & Co., 4 1/2" h. (ILLUS. left with other Mallard) **$185**

Mama bear, clear, No. 488, New Martinsville Glass Co., 6" l., 4" h. **$195**

Clear Fostoria Owl Book End

Owl, book end, clear, Fostoria Glass Co., 7 1/2" h. (ILLUS.) **$170**

Parlour Pup, Bulldog, milk glass, Imperial Glass Co., 3" h. **$65**

Imperial Amber Scottie Parlour Pup

Parlour Pup, Scottie, amber, Imperial Glass Co., 2 1/2" h. (ILLUS.) **$28**

Pheasant, head down, Copen Blue, Tiffin Glass Co., 16" l. **$245**

Pig, clear, Fenton Art Glass Co., 2 1/2" h. **$27**

Piglet, walking, clear, A. H. Heisey & Co., 7/8" h. **$120**

Sea horse, clear, Fostoria Glass Co., 8" h.... **$135**

Squirrel on log, black, Viking Glass Co., 5 1/2" h... **$68**

Imperial Caramel Slag Woodchuck

Woodchuck, caramel slag, Imperial Glass Co., 4 1/2" h. (ILLUS.) **$52**

Blown Three Mold

This type of glass was entirely or partially blown in a mold and was popular from about 1820 to 1840. The object was formed and the decoration impressed upon it by blowing the glass into a metal mold, usually of three—but sometimes more—sections hinged together. Mold-blown glass actually dates back to ancient times. Recent research reveals that certain geometric patterns were reproduced in the 1920s; some new pieces, usually sold through museum gift shops, are still available. Collectors are urged to read all recent information available. Reference numbers are from George L. and Helen McKearin's book, American Glass.

Pieces are clear unless otherwise noted.

Bar bottle, geometric, globular body tapering to a tall neck w/outward rolled ring mouth, pontil scar, greenish aqua, Kent Glassworks, Kent Ohio, ca. 1830, 8 7/8" h. **$4,480**

Celery vase, baroque, thick applied base w/ringed stem supporting the tall trumpet-form bowl molded w/repeating long scrolls, possibly Boston & Sandwich Glass Co., 1820-40, clear, some wear & scratches & possible crizzling, 8 3/4" h., GV-21 .... **$420**

Decanter w/no stopper, geometric, bulbous body molded w/three round starbursts in circles separated by curved ribbing, a tall tapering ribbed neck w/flattened mouth, very pale greyish green, attributed to Boston & Sandwich Glass Co., GV-10, qt. **$840**

Decanter w/no stopper, geometric, bulbous body tapering to a tall neck w/sheared mouth, Keene, New Hampshire, bright golden yellow shaded to golden amber, pt., GIII-16 .... **$784**

Decanter w/no stopper, geometric, clubform w/diamond point & ribbed bands & ribbed neck w/flared mouth, pontil scar, aqua, attributed to the Kent Glass Works, Kent, Ohio, 1820-40, small burst bubble, tiny spider crack in upper band, 7 1/4" h., GII-6 .... **$784**

Decanter w/no stopper, geometric, flat-bottomed ovoid body tapering to a tall neck w/sheared mouth, pontil scar, bright forest green, Keene Marlboro Glassworks, Keene, New Hampshire, ca. 1830, some minor in-the-making roughness, pint, GIII-16 .... **$1,064**

Decanter w/no stopper, geometric, flat-bottomed ovoid body tapering to a tall neck w/sheared mouth, pontil scar, bright yellowish olive, Keene Marlboro Glassworks, Keene, New Hampshire, ca. 1830, pint, GIII-16 .... **$1,120**

Decanter with Original Blown Stopper

Geometric Decanter with Acorn Stopper

Decanter w/original blown acorn stopper, geometric, a wide band of diamond point & starbursts in squares flanked by ribbed bands, flared rim, pontil scar, clear, 10 1/2" h., GIII-5 (ILLUS.)............... **$258**

Decanter w/original blown stopper, geometric, wide flat bottom & bulbous sides w/a wide band of diamonds below swirled ribbing up the neck, swirled rib stopper, pontil scar, clear, tiny flake at edge of lip, 10 1/4" h., GIII-2, type 1 (ILLUS., top next column) **$202**

Baroque-style Decanter with Stopper

Decanter w/original pressed wheel stopper, baroque, flat-bottomed, bulbous body w/a wide band of ribbing around the bottom below an entwined chain band & heart-shaped scrolls enclosing palmettes, pontil scar, clear, 10 5/8" h., GV-13 (ILLUS.).. **$190**

branches, late 19th c., 9" h. (ILLUS., top
next column) **$180**

Geometric Decanter with Wheel Stopper

**Decanter w/original pressed wheel stop-
per,** geometric, bulbous body w/a wide
diamond point & starburst in square band
around the center between ribbed bands,
tapering neck w/flared rim, pontil scar,
clear, 9 1/8" h., GIII-16 (ILLUS.)............... **$157**
Inkwell, geometric, short cylindrical form
w/pen hole in the top center, pontil scar
w/ringed base, medium forest green,
Keene Marlboro Street Glassworks,
Keene, New Hampshire, ca. 1830,
2 1/4" d., 1 1/2" h., GII-18 .... **$840**
Mug, geometric, cylindrical w/fancy applied
clear reeded handle, clear, pontil scar,
overall crizzling, probably Boston &
Sandwich Glass Co., ca. 1830, 3 1/8" h.,
GII-18 .... **$504**
Pitcher, 7 1/4" h., baroque-style, footed
bulbous body molded w/bands of stylized
flowerheads flanking a wavy body band,
tooled rim w/pinched spout, applied strap
handle, clear, crack under & to sides of
lower handle, GV-16 .... **$560**

Bohemian

*Numerous types of glass were made in the
once-independent country of Bohemia and fine
colored, cut and engraved glass was turned out.
Flashed and other inexpensive wares also were
made; many of these, including amber- and ruby-
shaded glass, were exported to the United States
during the 19th and 20th centuries. One favorite
pattern in the late 19th and early 20th centuries
was Deer & Castle. Another was Deer and Pine
Tree.*

Chalice, blown moss green w/a widely flaring round, ringed foot & ringed knop stem
below the tall cylindrical bowl applied
w/prunts around the bottom, the sides
enameled in color w/the figure of a working man holding a small train under one
arm & a raised torch in the other, framed
w/a white scroll banner & green leafy

Blown Bohemian Chalice with Figure

Bohemian Vase on a Figural Base

Vase, 6 1/2" h., a wide waisted cylindrical
form w/a widely flaring four-lobed rim, iridescent verre de soie ground applied
around the sides w/amethyst vines dotted
w/leaf pods, the base nestled into a
bronzed metal dish flanked by nude kneeling children all set upon a thin round brown
& white marble base, attributed to the Pall-
me-Konig firm, base 9" d. (ILLUS.) **$207**

Colorful Iridescent Bohemian Vase

Vase, 12 3/4" h., squatty bulbous base below the tall cylindrical sides w/a widely flaring folded rim pulled into four points, wine red decorated w/dark iridescent blue, green & gold pulled designs, attributed to the Rindskopf firm (ILLUS.) **$260**

Burmese

Burmese is a single-layer glass that shades from pink to pale yellow. It was patented by Frederick S. Shirley and made by the Mt. Washington Glass Co. A license to produce the glass in England was granted to Thomas Webb & Sons, which called its articles Queen's Burmese. Gundersen Burmese was made briefly about the middle of the 20th century, and the Pairpoint Company is making limited quantities at the present time.

Fine Four-piece Burmese Caster Set

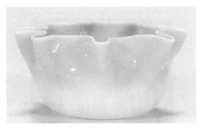

Small Glossy Burmese Bowl

Bowl, 5 1/2" d., 2 3/4" h., rounded bottom w/upright flaring & crimped sides, glossy finish, Mt. Washington Glass Co. (ILLUS.) **$288**

Small Satin Burmese Bowl

Bowl, 5 3/4" d., 2 3/4" h., rounded bottom w/upright flaring & crimped sides, satin finish, Mt. Washington Glass Co. (ILLUS.) **$260**
Caster set: two shakers, a cruet w/facet-cut pointed stopper & a mustard pot w/a hinged silver plate cover; the shakers & cruet w/ribbed cylindrical sides, the mustard w/a swelled cylindrical ribbed body, all fitted in a silver plate frame w/a tall central handle w/a large loop handle & a flattened base w/ruffled rim, frame marked "Pairpoint Mfg. Co. - Quadruple Plate - 751," stopper neck reduced, one shaker w/tiny neck nick, two holder rings rejoined, mustard 3 1/4" h., shakers 3 7/8" & 4" h., cruet 5 1/4" h., the set (ILLUS., top next column) **$1,495**

Rare Burmese Centerpiece Bowl

Centerpiece, a wide triangular-shaped glass bowl w/rounded upturned sides w/wide flaring & tightly crimped edges, the exterior enameled w/continuous vines of tiny flowers, raised on a silver plate base w/a ringed pedestal support above the round engraved base on three pointed & pierced outswept wide feet, silver w/Pairpoint Mfg. Co. trademark, bowl 11" w., overall 11" h. (ILLUS.) **$4,370**

Burmese Breakfast Creamer & Sugar

Creamer & open sugar bowl, breakfast-size, tall tapering cylindrical creamer w/a tightly crimped rim w/spout, applied yellow handle, squatty bulbous sugar tapering to a widely flaring crimped rim, satin finish, Mt. Washington Glass Co., sugar bowl 2 7/8" h., creamer 5 1/2" h., pr. (ILLUS., previous page) **$633**

Fine Decorated Burmese Cruet

Cruet w/original stopper, squatty bulbous ribbed body tapering to a slender neck w/a high arched spout, applied yellow handle w/red striping, red rim line & matching lines on the pointed ribbed stopper, the body h.p. w/a white mum on a green & brown leafy stem, satin finish, Mt. Washington Glass Co., 6 3/4" h. (ILLUS.) **$2,185**

Webb Burmese Cups & Saucers

Cups & saucers, footed deep rounded cup w/applied pale yellow handle, matching shallow saucer, satin finish, Thomas Webb & Son, cup 2 3/8" d., saucer 5 1/2" d., pr. (ILLUS.) **$230**

Epergne, single-lily, a long slender tapering ovoid Burmese vase w/a wide flaring & ruffled rim & enameled w/yellow blossoms & leafy green stem, fitted in a silver plate frame w/upright slender S-scrolls enclosing the vase & resting on a flat gently scalloped round base etched w/raspberry sprigs on small ball feet, Thomas Webb & Son, silver plate marked "Bramwell & Co. - Sheffield "EPNS 4297," vase 6 1/2" h., overall 8 1/2" h. (ILLUS., top next column) **$633**

Lovely Burmese & Silver Plate Epergne

Tall Tapering Cylindrical Burmese Pitcher

Pitcher, 11 1/4" h., a round foot & short stem below the tall round-bottomed tapering cylindrical body w/a flat rim & pinched spout, applied yellow handle low on the side, satin finish, Mt. Washington Glass Co., w/a museum exhibit label from the New Bedford Whaling Museum (ILLUS.)... **$575**

Set of Webb Burmese Plates

Plates, 7 5/8" d., shallow rounded form, satin finish, Thomas Webb & Son, set of 4 (ILLUS., previous page) **$207**

Unusual Mt. Washington Punch Cup

Punch cup, waisted cylindrical shape w/a flattened Hobnail patt., applied yellow handle, glossy finish, Mt. Washington Glass Co., exhibit label from the New Bedford Whaling Museum, 2 3/4" h. (ILLUS.) ... **$460**

Glossy Burmese Hobnail Rose Bowl

Rose bowl, nearly spherical body w/a molded flattened Hobnail patt., tapering to a short flaring & ruffled rim above an applied band of yellow rigaree, glossy finish, Mt. Washington Glass Co., w/a museum exhibit label from the New Bedford Whaling Museum, 4 1/4" h. (ILLUS.) **$805**

Rare Decorated Burmese Syrup Jug

Syrup jug w/original hinged metal cap & collar, gently tapering ovoid body w/an applied angular yellow handle, h.p. small white & yellow blossoms & green leafy vines around the sides, the domed hinged cover embossed w/flowers & butterflies, satin finish, 6 1/4" h. (ILLUS.).... **$4,600**

Decorated Burmese Toothpick Holder

Toothpick holder, bulbous squatty body w/a wide flaring gently ruffled neck, enameled w/lavender blossoms & green & lavender leaves & stems, satin finish, Thomas Webb & Son, 2 5/8" h. (ILLUS.) **$432**

Miniature Webb Burmese Vase

Vase, miniature, 3" h., bulbous body tapering to a flaring five-crimped rim w/folded edges, base marked "Thomas Webb & Sons - Queen's Burmese Ware - Patented" (ILLUS.) **$260**

Simple Ovoid Satin Burmese Vase

Vase, 9 1/2" h., simple ovoid body curving up to a small closed mouth, satin finish, Mt. Washington, small carbon particles (ILLUS., previous page) **$575**

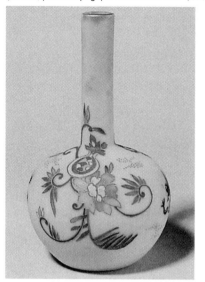

Beautifully Decorated Burmese Vase

Vase, 9 5/8" h., bottle form, the spherical body centered by a tall stick neck, beautifully enameled in color w/two black Japanese dragons prancing through bouquets of stylized blossoms & leafy vines, outlined in raised gold, satin ground, Mt. Washington (ILLUS.) **$2,415**

Tall Aster-decorated Burmese Vase

Vase, 11 1/2" h., squatty bulbous body tapering sharply to a stick neck, pale

ground enameled w/delicate aster blossoms on threadlike stems, gilt rim band, satin finish, Mt. Washington (ILLUS.) **$978**

Tall Burmese Lily Vase

Vase, 18 1/2" h., lily-form, satin finish, Mt. Washington Glass Co., (ILLUS.) **$575**

Glossy Burmese Water Set

Water set: tankard pitcher & two tumblers; all w/glossy finish, tumblers 3 3/4" h., pitcher 7 1/2" h., the set (ILLUS.) **$1,265**

Cambridge

Cambridge Glass operated from 1902 until 1954 in Cambridge, Ohio. Early wares included numerous pressed glass patterns in imitation of cut glass, often clear and bearing an impressed mark of "NEAR CUT" in the inside center of the object. Later products included color, stylized shapes, animals and hand-cut and decorated tableware. Particularly popular with collectors today are the Statuesque line, popularly called Nude Stems, and a pink opaque color called Crown Tuscan. When marked, which is infrequently, the Cambridge mark is the letter "C" in a

Cambridge Bridge Tumbler Set

triangle. Other authors have been wise to remind us not to confuse this 20th century company with the earlier New England Glass Company of Cambridge, Massachusetts, at times called "Cambridge Glass."

 NEAR CUT   TUSCAN

Cambridge Marks

Etched Rose Point Pattern

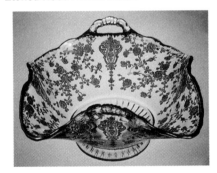

Gold Encrusted Rose Point Basket

Basket, squared upturned sides, footed, two-handled, Gold Encrusted, 6" w. (ILLUS.) $55
Cocktail shaker, cov., No. 98, Crystal w/chrome lid, 46 oz. $265
Plate, 18" d., punch bowl underplate, clear $750

Miscellaneous Patterns
Bowl, 12" w., four-footed, flared, etched Wildflower patt., No. 3400/4, Crystal $62
Bridge tumbler set, clear swelled cylindrical bowl on black or red feet in the shape of different card suits, 5" h., the set (ILLUS., top of page) $220
Candle blocks, Cambridge Square patt., clear, 2" w., 2 1/2" h., pr. (ILLUS., top next column) $26

Clear Cambridge Square Candle Blocks

Candleholders, two-light, keyhole stem, etched Candlelight patt., pr. $145
Champagne, etched Apple Blossom patt., No. 3035 stem, Topaz $35
Champagne, etched Chantilly patt., No. 3126 stem, gold-encrusted clear $60
Cocktail, Statuesque (No. 3011) line, Crystal bowl, clear Nude Lady stem, 4 1/2 oz., 6 1/2" h. $120
Cocktail icer, w/liner, etched Wildflower patt., Crystal $70

Etched Diane Compote in Chrome Stand

Crown Tuscan Cigarette Box & Cover

Compote, open, 5" d., 7 1/2" h., etched Diane patt., Crystal, fitted in a Farberware chrome frame (ILLUS., previous page) **$68**

Console set: 12" d. rolled edge bowl & pair two-light candleholders; Everglades patt., Crystal, the set **$245**

Crown Tuscan bowl, flower or fruit, 10 1/2" l., footed, Statuesque line, Flying Lady patt., seashell bowl w/nude lady at one end, h.p. Charleton Rose decoration **$455**

Crown Tuscan Sea Shell Candy Dish

Crown Tuscan candy dish, cov., Sea Shell patt., shell-shaped, gold trim, 6" h. (ILLUS.) **$78**

Crown Tuscan candy dish, cov., three-part, etched Portia patt., gold-encrusted, 7" w. **$135**

Crown Tuscan cigarette box, cov., rectangular Sea Shell shape w/dolphin feet, gold trim, 4 3/4" l., 3 3/4" h. (ILLUS., top of page) **$82**

Crown Tuscan compote, open, 8" h., Sea Shell patt., shell-shaped bowl, Charleton Rose decoration **$250**

Ivy ball w/keyhole stem, Carmen optic ribbed ball on Crystal stem, 8 1/2" h. (ILLUS., top next column) **$95**

Model of a swan, Emerald, 8" l. **$130**
Model of a swan, Green, 10" l. **$360**

Carmen & Crystal Ivy Ball

Model of a top hat, brim turned down on two sides, etched Chantilly patt., Crystal, 4" h. **$240**

Oil bottle & stopper, footed, etched Diane patt., No. 3400/161 shape, Crystal **$135**

Pitcher, 11" h., footed, etched Cleo patt., Green **$325**

Salt & pepper shakers, all-glass ball, individual, pressed Caprice patt., Moonlight Blue, pr. **$165**

Tumbler, flat, etched Chantilly patt., No. 3900/115 stem, 13 oz., Crystal **$70**

Vase, 8" h., flip-style, etched Wildflower patt., Crystal **$160**

Vases, cornucopia-shaped in sterling bases, etched Chantilly patt., Crystal, pr. . **$290**

Carnival

Earlier called Taffeta glass, the Carnival glass now being collected was introduced early in the 20th century. Its producers gave it an iridescence that attempted to imitate that of some Tiffany glass. Collectors will find available books by leading authorities Donald E. Moore, Sherman Hand, Marion T. Hartung, Rose M. Presznick, and Bill Edwards.

Acanthus (Imperial)
Bowl, 8" to 9" d., purple, deep sides **$215**
Bowl, 8" to 9" d., smoky **$55**

Advertising & Souvenir Items
Bowl, souvenir, "Millersburg Courthouse," purple $800

Basket (Fenton's Open Edge)
Aqua, w/two rows, two sides turned up $45
Blue $25
Green, jack-in-the-pulpit shape $85
Red, jack-in-the-pulpit shape $145
Smokey lavender, two-sides up $45

Beaded Cable (Northwood)
Rose bowl, aqua opalescent $185
Rose bowl, purple $50
Rose bowl, purple, Rayed interior $35

Captive Rose
Bowl, 8" d., amethyst, three-in-one edge $60
Bowl, 8" to 9" d., green, candy ribbon edge .. $115
Bowl, 8" to 9" d., purple, candy ribbon edge ... $65

Diamond Lace (Imperial)

Diamond Lace Pitcher

Pitcher, water, purple (ILLUS.) $150-250
Tumbler, purple $35

Double Star or Buzz Saw (Cambridge)
Cruet w/stopper, marigold, large, clear stopper, 6" $75
Cruet w/stopper, green, large, 6" $175

Dragon & Lotus (Fenton)

Dragon & Lotus Green Ruffled Bowl

Bowl, 8" to 9" d., green, ruffled (ILLUS.) $50
Bowl, 8" to 9" d., green, three-in-one edge $70
Bowl, 8" to 9" d., marigold, ruffled $35
Bowl, 8" to 9" d., peach opalescent, three-in-one edge $450
Bowl, 9" d., blue, ice cream shape, collared base $45

Good Luck (Northwood)
Bowl, 8" to 9" d., blue, piecrust edge, ribbed back $225
Bowl, 8" to 9" d., blue, ruffled, ribbed back ... $195
Bowl, 8" to 9" d., purple, ruffled, Basketweave back $165

Grape & Cable (Northwood)
Berry set: master bowl & 6 sauce dishes; green, 7 pcs. $145
Hatpin holder, marigold $225-275
Hatpin holder, purple $135
Plate, 6" d., turned-up handgrip, purple $75
Plate, 7 1/2" d., turned-up handgrip, purple $150-175
Plate, 9" d., Basketweave exterior, purple $110
Plate, 9" d., marigold, spatula-footed $30
Powder jar, cov., green $105

Grape & Cable Marigold Punch Bowl

Punch bowl & base, marigold, 14" d., 2 pcs. (ILLUS.) $800
Punch set: 11" bowl, base & 6 cups; purple, 8 pcs. (ILLUS., top next page) $350

Grape & Gothic Arches (Northwood)
Water set: pitcher & 5 tumblers; marigold, 6 pcs. $95
Water set: pitcher & 6 tumblers; blue, 7 pcs. $550

Grape Leaves (Northwood)
Bowl, 9" d., horehound, ruffled $20
Bowl, 9" d., green, ruffled $25

Hearts & Flowers (Northwood)
Bowl, ruffled w/ribbed back, ice blue, light iridescence $145
Bowl, ruffled w/ribbed back, purple $300
Compote, 6 3/4" h., ice blue $300
Compote, 6 3/4" h., marigold $95

Grape & Cable Eight-piece Purple Punch Set

Hearts & Flowers Ice Blue Plate

Plate, 9" d., ice blue (ILLUS.) **$1,100**

Heavy Grape (Dugan, Diamond Glass or Millersburg)
Bowl, 6" d., lime green, deep sides................ **$20**

Heavy Grape (Imperial)
Plate, 7" to 8" d., green **$25**
Plate, 7" to 8" d., purple................................. **$145**
Plate, chop, 11" d., marigold **$70**

Holly, Holly Berries & Carnival Holly (Fenton)
Bowl, 8" to 9" d., blue, very flat w/three-in-
one edge **$75**
Bowl, 8" to 9" d., blue w/silvery iridescence,
three-in-one edge....................................... **$40**
Bowl, 8" to 9" d., lime green, three-in-one
edge **$65**
Bowl, 8" to 9" d., ruffled, amber **$145**
Bowl, 8" to 9" d., ruffled, powder blue
w/marigold overlay **$85**
Bowl, 8" to 9" d., ruffled, white **$60**

Rare Holly Red Ice Cream Shape Bowl

Bowl, 8" to 9" d., ice cream shape, red
(ILLUS.) **$3,300**
Bowl, 8" to 9" d., ruffled, green **$50**
Dish, hat-shaped, red, crimped rim, 5 3/4".... **$125**

Horse Heads or Horse Medallions (Fenton)
Bowl, 7" d., ice cream shape, marigold.......... **$30**
Bowl, jack-in-the-pulpit shaped, flattened,
amber... **$45**
Plate, 7" to 8" d., marigold............................. **$130**

Imperial Grape (Imperial)
Pitcher, water, marigold **$50**
Pitcher, water, purple..................................... **$125**
Plate, 6" d., green... **$30**
Plate, 6" d., purple... **$105**

Kittens (Fenton)
Dish, turned-up sides, blue **$600**

Lotus & Grape (Fenton)
Plate, 9" d., amethyst **$1,150**

Orange Tree (Fenton)
Bowl, 8" to 9" d., ruffled, white $75
Bowl, ice cream shape, blue $200
Creamer, blue, individual size $55
Dish, whimsey w/ruffled rim made from a
   sherbet, marigold $75
Mug, light amethyst $25
Plate, 9" d., flat, blue, tree trunk center $450
Powder jar, cov., blue $100
Punch set: bowl, base & 7 cups; blue, 9
   pcs... $375
Tumbler, blue... $75

Peach (Northwood)
Spooner, white... $65
Sugar bowl, cov., white $85

Peacock at Fountain (Northwood)

Peacock at Fountain Marigold Orange Bowl

Blue Peacock at Fountain Fruit Bowl

Bowl, fruit, blue (ILLUS.).............................. $550
Bowl, fruit, marigold w/light color $135

Peacock at Fountain Master Ice Cream

Bowl, master ice cream-shape, blue w/elec-
   tric iridescence (ILLUS.)......................... $2,100
Bowl, orange, three-footed, marigold
   (ILLUS., top next column) $300
Bowl, 6" d., blue w/great iridescence, flat-
   tened-shape $650
Sauce dish, blue, ice cream-shaped $60
Sauce dish, green, ice cream-shape $350
Tumbler, blue w/eletric iridescence $45
Tumbler, ice blue $65

Peacock & Grape (Fenton)
Bowl, 8" d., ice cream shape, marigold,
   spatula-footed $20
Bowl, 9" d., ruffled, amethyst $50
Bowl, 8" d., spatula-footed, blue $50
Plate, 9" d., flat base, marigold $350

Persian Garden (Dugan)
Bowl, 11" d., ice cream shape, white $130
Plate, 6" to 7" d., marigold............................. $35
Plate, 6" to 7" d., purple................................ $210

Persian Medallion (Fenton)
Bonbon, two-handled, blue............................. $25
Bowl, 10" d., green, three-in-one rim $135

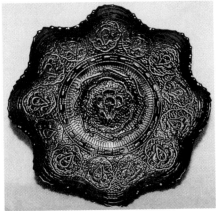

Rare Red Persian Medallion Bowl

Bowl, 8" to 9" d., red, ruffled rim (ILLUS.).. $1,000
Hair receiver, marigold $25

Peter Rabbit (Fenton)
Bowl, 8" d., green, ruffled........................... $1,100

Scales
Bowl, 7" d., blue opalescent, ruffled............... $45
Bowl, 7" d., marigold on milk glass, ruffled $35

Stag & Holly (Fenton)
Bowl, 8" d., footed, ice cream shape, blue...... $95
Bowl, 8" d., footed, ice cream shape, mari-
   gold $75
Bowl, 9" to 13" d., ball-footed, deep sides,
   ruffled rim, blue $155

Bowl, 10" to 11" d., three-footed, ruffled, blue **$150**

Central Glass Works

From the 1890s until its closing in 1939, the Central Glass Works of Wheeling, West Virginia, produced colorless and colored handmade glass in all the styles then popular. Decorations from etchings with acid to hand-painted enamels were used.

The popular "Depression" era colors of black, pink, green, light blue, ruby red and others were all produced. Two of its 1920s etchings are still familiar today, one named for the then President of the United States and the other for the Governor of West Virginia - these are the Harding and Morgan patterns.

From high end Art glass to mass-produced plain barware tumblers, Central was a major glass producer throughout the period.

Central Green Frances Ash Receiver

Ash receiver, cov., Frances patt., green, 5" d., 2 3/4" h. (ILLUS.) **$125**
Basket, art glass-type, amethyst w/applied white handle & rim, 10" l., 12" h. **$395**
Bowl, 9" d., rolled edge, three-footed, Frances patt., pink **$65**
Candleholders, Frances patt., pink, 3 1/2" h., pr. **$120**
Candleholders, low, #2000 line, Smetak etching, amber, pr. **$49**
Candy dish, cov., diamond-shaped, green **$88**
Candy dish, cov., diamond-shaped, Morgan etching, pink **$795**
Cigarette jar, footed, clear optic bowl on amber foot, gold-encrusted Dunn's Parrot etching **$75**
Cordial, #1900 Winslow line, clear bowl, green stem & foot .... **$**
Cup & saucer, Harding etching, clear, the set **$75**
Goblet, #1428 stem, Balda etching, Orchid (lavender pink) **$60**
Goblet, #1447 stem, Linda etching, blue **$62**
Goblet, wafer stem, Morgan etching, pink **$120**
Mayonnaise bowl, rolled edge, #2001 line, Morgan etching, amber **$85**
Pitcher, flat squatty shape, Thistle etching, clear **$85**
Pitcher, milk, Linda etching, clear **$88**
Plate, 10" d., dinner, Balda etching, pink......... **$48**

Tumbler, ice tea, flat, handled, Oak etching, clear **$78**

Vase with Dunn's Parrot Etching

Vase, 8" h., fan-shaped, gold-encrusted Dunn's Parrot etching, black (ILLUS.)....... **$175**

Orchid-colored Frances Pattern Vase

Vase, 10" h., flat bottom w/cylindrical sides flared & deeply ruffled at the top, Frances patt., Orchid (ILLUS.) **$150**

Crown Milano

This glass, produced by Mt. Washington Glass Company late in the 19th century, is opal glass decorated by painting and enameling. It appears identical to a ware termed Albertine, also made by Mt. Washington.

Printed Crown Milano Mark

Crown Milano Squatty Bulbous Ewer

Ewer, wide squatty bulbous body tapering to a short neck w/a rim spout, gilt reeded scroll shoulder handle, the white sides enameled around the shoulder w/heavy gilt scrolls & a lattice design on a pale yellow ground all highlighted w/a clusters of pink flowers, Crown Milano mark, 6 1/2" h. (ILLUS.) **$2,500-3,000**

Scarce Crown Milano Mustard Pot

Mustard pot w/hinged silver plate cover & handle, a bulbous lobed body w/each white lobe bordered by pink & h.p. w/tiny blue forget-me-nots w/green leaves, domed petaled cover w/knob finial, slight silver wear, two flower dots missing, 2 3/4" h. (ILLUS.) **$690**

Pitcher, 9" h., jug-shaped, a very wide bulbous ovoid body w/a short divided neck w/a wide arched neck & a coiled snake handle trimmed in gold, the sides decorated overall w/a peach & pale green scrolling ground decorated w/heavy gilt florals & applied beaded trailing around the sides, Crown Milano mark (ILLUS., top next column).................................... **$4,485**

Finely Decorated Crown Milano Pitcher

Cut

Cut glass most eagerly sought by collectors is American glass produced during the so-called "Brilliant Period" from 1880 to about 1915. Pieces listed below are by type of article in alphabetical order.

Hawkes, Hoare, Libbey and Straus Marks

Bowls

Bowl Cut with Buttons & Hobstars

Button and hobstar-cut widely flaring shallow form w/a six-scallop notch-cut rim, panels of button cutting alternating w/pointed pointed arches over large hobstars, 9 1/2" d. (ILLUS.)........................... **$150**

Hawkes-signed Bowl with Hobstars

Hawkes-signed, widely flaring sides w/a six-scallop notch-cut rim, the sides cut w/groupings of four hobstars alternating w/diamonds & fans, 8" d. (ILLUS.) **$161**

Long Oval Hobstar & Fan Cut Bowl

Hobstar and fan-cut flat-bottomed oval shape w/widely flaring flattened sides, cut w/large hobstars alternating w/fan-cut border panels, 11 3/4"l. (ILLUS.).............. **$184**

Flat-sided Hobstar-cut Bowl

Hobstar-cut, wide flat bottom w/vertical sides & a scalloped & notch-cut rim, cut w/large hobstars alternating w/long diamond-shaped panels enclosing small hobstars, 8" d. (ILLUS.)..................... **$150-200**

Libbey-signed Hobstar-cut Bowl

Libbey-signed, widely flaring sides w/six-scallop notch-cut rim, cut w/a design of large hobstars alternating w/wide V-shaped devices over fans, 8" d. (ILLUS.) **$100-200**

Libbey-signed Cut & Engraved Bowl

Libbey-signed, deep rounded sides w/a flat rim, cut around the rim & base w/bands of fine diamond point cutting, the rim band over a scallop-cut band w/the sides engraved w/a wide band of blossom & leaf clusters, ca. 1910, 9"d. (ILLUS.) **$259**

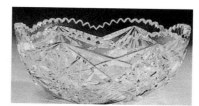

Tuthill-signed Bowl with Hobstars

Tuthill-signed, widely flaring sides w/six-scallop notch-cut rim, cut w/a design of large hobstars alternating w/wide V-shaped devices over fans, 8" d. (ILLUS.).. **$125-150**

Compotes

Hobstar-cut Tall Compote

Hawkes-attributed, round shallow bowl cut w/hobstars raised on a tapering paneled & notched stem above the round ray-cut foot, 7 1/4 " d., 8 1/8" h. (ILLUS.) **$150-200**

Decanters

Fine Ruby Cut to Clear Whiskey Decanter

Cranberry cut to clear, flattened spherical body tapering to a small cylinddrical neck w/thin flared rim, applied clear shoulder handle, bulbous stopper, the body w/a rectangular reserve at the center engraved "Whiskey" & flanked by leafy floral bands, deep cut straight bands & small squares cut w/alternating punties or crosses, stopper w/matching cutting, late 19th c., overall 10 1/2" h . (ILLUS.) **$250-500**

Tall Green to Clear Cut Baluster Decanter

Green cut to clear, tall baluster-shaped body tapering to a tall panel-cut neck w/an arched spout, tall egg-shaped green to clear stopper, applied facet-cut clear shoulder handle, panel-cut around the base below a body cut overall w/swirled fanned leaves & large drooping blossoms, attributed to Stevens & Williams, England, late 19th c., heat check to handle, overall 15" h. (ILLUS.) **$2,300**

Large Rare Green to Clear Cut Decanter

Green cut to clear, upright oblong paneled sides w/a rounded shoulder centered by a small neck w/pinched spout, green to clear bubble stopper, small applied clear shoulder handle, the sides & stopper cut overall w/swirling leaves & large feathery flowers, attributed to Stevens & Williams, England, late 19th c., 10 1/2" h. (ILLUS.) **$2,875**

Dishes, Miscellaneous

Pitkin & Brooks-signed Celery Dish

Celery dish, long oval shape w/upturned sides, cut w/fans & hobstars at the ends continuing to vesicas & starbursts, a hobstar-cut band across the center, Pitkin & Brooks-signed, 12" l. (ILLUS.) **$100-150**

Lamps

Scottish Lamp with Cut Glass Shade

Table, domed mushroom-shaped 10" d. shade cut w/staggered bands of large hobstars trimmed w/fan-cutting, raised on a silver plate ring above the slender columnar silver plate base w/a flaring ringed round foot, base marked "Hamilton & Inches Goldsmiths Edinburgh - D&B - E.P.N.S.," Scotland, early 20th c., overall 17" h. (ILLUS.) **$805**

Table, high domical mushroom-shaped 11 1/2" d. shade cut w/a band of large pinwheels, in a brass shade ring suspending long facet-cut prisms, raised on a slender baluster-shaped cut base w/a panel-cut stem above the domed foot cut w/small hobstars within diamonds, roughness on base foot, early 20th c., overall 19" h. (ILLUS., next page) **$1,035**

Cut Glass Lamp with Pinwheel Shade

Miscellaneous

Pair of Crosshatch-Cut Decanters

Decanters with metal covers, crosshatch cutting, flattened spherical body tapering to a tall plain cylindrical neck fitted w/a silver-plate chased collar w/flaring rim & long arched spout & hinged dome cover w/finial, a leafy scroll long handle down the back, the sides cut simply w/two wide line panels forming a large square-cut central design, some very minor edge roughness, some staining to interior bottoms, late 19th c., 10 1/2" h., pr. (ILLUS.)... **$259**

Nice Waffle Cut Ice Cream Set

Ice cream set: rectangular tray w/rounded corners & eleven 5" d. dishes; all cut overall w/a fine waffle design, one small dish w/rim chip, late 19th - early 20th c., tray 7 1/2 x 12", the set (ILLUS.)............... **$390**

Strawberry Diamond-cut Whiskey Set

Whiskey set: tall cylindrical decanter w/a tapering neck to a ringed top fitted w/a domed bulbous facet-cut stopper & four matching whiskey taster tumblers; each piece cut w/the strawberry diamond design, the tall decanter neck panel-cut w/six sides, two tasters w/small rim chips, tasters 2 3/4" h., decanter 15 1/4" h. (ILLUS.)............................ **$250-350**

Perfumes & Colognes

Libbey-signed Waisted Perfume Bottle

Libbey-signed perfume, slender waisted cylindrical base cut around the base w/a band of swirled bands, the sides cut w/large flashed stars below the panel & zipper-cut neck, tall cut drum-form stopper, both pieces marked, overall 6 1/2" h. (ILLUS.)... **$175-275**

Double hobstar and fan-cut, flat-bottomed cylindrical body w/rounded shoulder to the ring-cut neck & arched spout, applied notch-cut handle, the sides cut w/panels of double hobstars alternating w/pointed vertical narrow panels centered by a small hobstar & topped by pairs of fans, 8 1/2" d., 10" h. (ILLUS., next page) **$863**

Pitchers

Fine Double Hobstar & Fan Cut Pitcher

Stripe-cut Tall Tankard Pitcher

Tankard, tall tapering conical shape w/a high arched rim spout, applied notch-cut handle, the sides cut w/long narrow zipper- and -block-cut stripes, large hobstars below the spout, 10" h. (ILLUS.)....... **$316**

Punch bowls

Large Cane-cut Two-Part Punch Bowl

Cane-cut, two-part, the wide deep rounded bowl w/a notched flattened rim cut overall w/a bold Cane design, on a matching pedestal base w/a top ring above the widely flaring sides & notched & scalloped rim, three chips to points, minor flea bites, late 19th - early 20th c., 9" d., overall 12" h., 2 pcs. (ILLUS.) **$575**

Fan-cut Dome-based Punch Bowl

Fan and hobstar-cut, two-part, the wide domed base cut w/wide arched fan-cut panels below small hobstars & a ring-cut top & short pedestal, the wide upper bowl w/deep sides cut w/large flaring cut fans alternating w/hobstars, 12" d., 11" h. (ILLUS.)... **$920**

Fine Hawkes-Signed Punch Bowl & Base

Hawkes-signed, two-part, the large bowl cut w/a repeating design of large arches enclosing a large hobstar over pairs of fan-cut panels alternating around the scalloped & notched rim w/small hobstars in diamond-shaped panels, on a matching tall widely flaring pedestal base w/a ring-cut top band, chip to cutting in fan design, several chips to hobstar on bottom of bowl, chip to rim of base, late 19th c., 15" d., overall 13 3/4" h. (ILLUS.)............ **$1,093**

Nice Hobstar-cut Two-Part Punch Bowl

Hobstar-cut, two-part, the deep rounded bowl w/a deeply scalloped & notched rim, the sides cut w/a design of large circles enclosing multiple smaller hobstars separated by flaring panels topped by a large hobstar, the matching pyramidal base w/a ring-cut neck & narrow cut rim band, several notches on bowl rim ground, top of base w/two ground chips, late 19th - early 20th c., 14" d., 13 1/4" h. (ILLUS.).... **$863**

Vases

Tall Cylindrical Cut Glass Vase

Cylindrical, 10" h., slightly flared base & flaring notched & scalloped rim, cut up the sides w/alternating wide & narrow bands of hobstars w/fans cut around the base, very minor flea bites, late 19th - early 20th c. (ILLUS.) **$230**

D'Argental

Glass known by this name is so-called after its producer, who fashioned fine cameo pieces in St. Louis, France in the late 19th century and up to 1918.

D'Argental Mark

Small D'Argental Vase with Thistles

Cameo vase, 3 7/8" h., ovoid body tapering to a waisted cylindrical neck, pale green ground overlaid w/dark green & cameo cut w/leafy prickly thistles around the body, cameo signature, slight polishing to rim edge (ILLUS.).................................. **$345**

D'Argental Cameo Lily-of-the-Valley Vase

Cameo vase, 4 3/4" h., footed ovoid body tapering to a flaring cylindrical neck, deep amber ground overlaid in white & dark green & cameo-carved w/lily-of-the-valley blossoms among tall leaves, signed in cameo "D'Argental St. Louis" (ILLUS.)... **$1,840**

Small D'Argental Cameo Vase

Cameo vase, 4 3/4" h., wide cushion foot supporting a small ovoid body w/a short cylindrical neck, orange shaded to amethyst ground overlaid w/dark reddish brown & cameo cut overall w/a leafy raspberry vine w/three berries, cameo signature (ILLUS.) **$432**

Small D'Argental Berry & Leaf Vase

Cameo vase, 5" h., baluster-form body tapering to a short flared mouth, citron yellow ground overlaid w/russet & cameo-carved w/large clusters of berries on leafy vines, signed in cameo on the side (ILLUS.)... **$748**

D'Argental Cameo Vase with Hops

Cameo vase, 11 5/8" h., simple ovoid body tapering gently to a wide flat rim, medium frosted orange ground overlaid w/dark brown & cameo-cut w/leafy hop vines wrapped around the sides, signed in cameo, inclusion in the interior (ILLUS.) **$1,150**

D'Argental Tropical Island Cameo Vase

Cameo vase, 12" h., tall ovoid body tapering to a flat mouth, cream ground overlaid in browns & cameo-carved w/a tropical island scene w/scattered tall palm trees, signed on the side (ILLUS.) **$2,070**

Daum Nancy

This fine glass, much of it cameo, was made by Auguste and Antonin Daum, who founded a factory in 1875 in Nancy, France. Most of their cameo and enameled glass was made from the 1890s into the early 20th century.

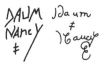

Daum Nancy Marks

Fine Daum Nancy Cameo Basket

Cameo basket, flat-bottomed oval shape w/deep flat & slightly flaring sides, a high arched mottled yellow handle from side to side, deep orange & yellow mottled body cameo-etched & enameled w/a snowy woodland landscape enameled in shades of white, black, brown & green, signed on the bottom, overall 7" h. (ILLUS.) **$6,900**

Daum Cameo Winter Landscape Bowl

Cameo bowl, 5 3/4" d., 4 1/2" h., squatty bulbous pale blue body curving to an undulating wide rim, cameo-etched w/a continuous winter landscape w/a village in the distance, enameled in shades of black, white, brown & gold, signed on the bottom (ILLUS.) **$5,463**

Very Rare Daum Boat-shaped Cameo Bowl

Cameo bowl-vase, a round cushion foot supporting a large elongated boat-shaped bowl w/pointed ends, mottled deep orange & yellow ground cameo-etched & enameled w/a snowy winter landscape w/trees in black, brown & green & white around the cushion foot, enameled on base "Daum Nancy S71," 14" l., 5 1/4" h. (ILLUS.) **$12,650**

Daum Winter Scene Cameo Creamer

Cameo creamer, footed squatty bulbous boat-shaped form w/a long pointed spout, deep golden yellow ground cameo-etched & enameled w/a snowy winter landscape in white, black & browns, applied deep yellow handle, signed on bottom, 5 1/2" l. (ILLUS.) **$2,588**

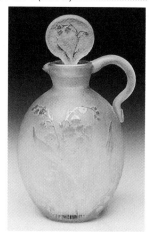

Daum Nancy Cameo Floral Cruet

Cameo cruet w/original stopper, bulbous ovoid body tapering to a short cylindrical neck w/a small pinched spout, round disk stopper & applied shoulder handle, frosted clear ground cameo-etched w/delicate flowering stems & long leaves trimmed w/gilt, etched signature on the side, one nick on upper rim of stopper, overall 7" h. (ILLUS.) **$1,495**

Daum Nancy Cameo Powder Box

Cameo powder box, cov., squared squatty body w/rounded corners fitted w/a low domed cover, mottled white & pink cover & mottled white to greenish yellow base, cameo cut & enameled w/bright deep rose red small blossoms on slender leafy stems, base rim polished & w/a pin nick on design, inside rim nicks on cover, cameo signature on the base, 4" w., 2 1/2" h. (ILLUS.) **$1,840**

Daum Cameo Vase with Orchids

Cameo vase, 5 3/4" h., a round cushion foot tapering to a trumpent-form body w/an irregular shaped rim pulled into a spout at one side, mottled yellow shaded to motted dark brown cameo-etched w/wild orchids on tall leaft stems w/a flying bee, enameled in shades of pink, green, black & gold, signed on the bottom, some wear to gilding on the foot (ILLUS.) **$8,625**

Daum Cameo Aesop Fable Vase

Cameo vase, 8" h., footed ovoid body tapering sharply to a narrow cylindrical neck, deep bluish green shading to a frosted ground cameo-etched w/a wreath of small leaves decorated w/green & yellow enamel & encircling a black enameled scene illustrating the Aesop fable of "The Crow and the Fox," gilt signature on the bottom (ILLUS.).............................. **$3,220**

Tall Daum Nancy Cameo Vase

Cameo vase, 13" h., very tall slender ovoid body tapering to a very slender gently flaring cylindrical neck, mottled white to yellow ground cameo cut & enameled w/long leafy rose branches laden w/slender reddish orange rose hips, cameo signature on the side (ILLUS.)................... **$2,945**

Colorful Large Daum Center Bowl

Center bowl, a wide black disk foot supporting a very wide shallow flaring round bowl in mottled & swirls russet & brown w/gold foil inclusions. carved signature on the base, early 20th c., 12 1/4" d. (ILLUS.) **$374**

Delicate Enameled Daum Cup & Saucer

Cup & saucer, the delicate round stepped cup w/applied handle & matching gently scalloped saucer each enameled w/florals & a dragonfly all highlighted w/gold, both signed, saucer 4 1/2" d., cup 2" h., pr. (ILLUS.) **$805**

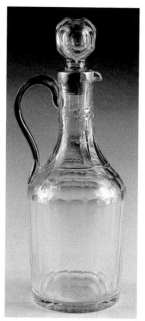

Fine Daum Cut Crystal Decanter

Decanter w/original facet-cut stopper, clear cylindrical panel-cut body w/a rounded shoulder tapering to the panel-cut neck w/a small rim spout, round panel-cut stopper, long applied C-scroll handle, trimmed in gold & signed in gold, 10" h. (ILLUS.) **$345**

DeLatte

Andre de Latte of Nancy, France, produced a range of opaque and cameo glass after 1921. His company also produced light fixtures but his cameo wares are most collectible today.

Small DeLatte Cameo Vase with Cherries

Cameo vase, 4" h., nearly spherical body w/a small flared neck, mottled white to pale green to amethyst ground overlaid in pale blue & cameo cut w/long leafy branches w/cherries, cameo signature, some glasss impurities (ILLUS.) **$317**

DeLatte Cameo Vase with Thorny Branches

Cameo vase, 6" h., ovoid body tapering to a short flaring neck, mottled white shading to light purple ground overlaid in dark amethyst & cameo cut w/an overall design of large thorny branches & leaves & oblong fruits, cameo signature (ILLUS.) **$575**

Tall Slender DeLatte Cameo Vase

Cameo vase, 13 1/2" h., disk foot below the tall flaring cylindrical body w/a tapering neck & molded mouth, mauve & white mottled ground overlaid in maroon & cameo-cut w/tall stems of flowers up the sides, signed in cameo (ILLUS.) **$978**

Depression

The phrase "Depression Glass" is used by collectors to denote a specific kind of transparent glass produced primarily as tablewares, in crystal, amber, blue, green, pink, milky-white, etc., during the late 1920s and 1930s when this country was in the midst of a financial depression. Made to sell inexpensively, it was turned out by such producers as Jeannette, Hocking, Westmore-

land, Indiana and other glass companies. We compile prices on all the major Depression Glass patterns. Collectors should consult Depression Glass references for information on those patterns and pieces that have been reproduced.

Cloverleaf, Hazel Atlas Glass Co., 1931-35 (Process-etched)

Ashtray w/match holder in center, black, 5 3/4" d.	$60
Bowl, 4" d., dessert, green	$35
Bowl, 4" d., dessert, pink	$24
Bowl, 4" d., dessert, yellow	$24
Bowl, 5" d., cereal, green	$30
Bowl, 5" d., cereal, yellow	$40
Bowl, 7" d., salad, deep, green	$60
Bowl, 7" d., salad, deep, yellow	$65
Bowl, 8" d., green	$85
Candy dish, cov., green	$75
Candy dish, cov., yellow	$125
Creamer, footed, black, 3 5/8" h.	$15
Creamer, footed, green, 3 5/8" h.	$8
Creamer, footed, yellow, 3 5/8" h.	$12
Cup & saucer, black	$15
Cup & saucer, green	$10
Cup & saucer, pink	$10
Cup & saucer, yellow	$12
Plate, 6" d., sherbet, black	$20
Plate, 6" d., sherbet, green	$8
Plate, 6" d., sherbet, yellow	$7
Plate, 8" d., luncheon, black	$12
Plate, 8" d., luncheon, clear	$2
Plate, 8" d., luncheon, green	$8
Plate, 8" d., luncheon, pink	$9
Plate, 8" d., luncheon, yellow	$12
Plate, 10 1/4" d., grill, green	$30
Plate, 10 1/4" d., grill, yellow	$28
Salt & pepper shakers, black, pr.	$85
Salt & pepper shakers, green, pr.	$40
Salt & pepper shakers, yellow, pr.	$110
Sherbet, footed, pink 3" h.	$6
Sherbet, footed, yellow, 3" h.	$8
Sherbet, footed, black, 3" h.	$15
Sherbet, footed, clear, 3" h.	$2
Sherbet, footed, green, 3" h.	$8
Sugar bowl, open, footed, black, 3 5/8" h.	$15
Sugar bowl, open, footed, green, 3 5/8" h.	$8
Sugar bowl, open, footed, yellow, 3 5/8" h.	$12
Tumbler, green, 4" h., 9 oz.	$65
Tumbler, flared, green, 3 3/4" h., 10 oz.	$48
Tumbler, flared, pink, 3 3/4" h., 10 oz.	$35
Tumbler, footed, green, 5 3/4" h., 10 oz.	$32
Tumbler, footed, yellow, 5 3/4" h., 10 oz.	$38

Georgian or Lovebirds, Federal Glass Co., 1931-36 (Process-etched)

Bowl, 4 1/2" d., berry	$8
Bowl, 6 1/2" d., deep	$55
Bowl, 7 1/2" d., berry	$58
Bowl, 9" oval vegetable	$55
Butter dish, cov.	$75
Creamer, footed, 3" h. (ILLUS. left, top of next column)	$8
Creamer, footed, 4" h.	$12
Cup & saucer (ILLUS. center w/creamer, top next column)	$8
Hot plate, center design, 5" d.	$65
Lazy susan, 18 1/4" wooden base w/seven hot plate inserts	$800
Plate, 6" d., sherbet	$4

Georgian Creamer, Sugar & Cup & Saucer

Plate, 8" d., luncheon	$8
Plate, 9 1/4" d., dinner	$20
Plate, 9 1/4" d., center design only	$18
Platter, 11 1/2" oval, closed handles	$55
Sherbet	$8
Sugar bowl, cov., footed, 3" h.	$45
Sugar bowl, cov., footed, 4" h.	$50
Sugar bowl, open, footed, 3" h. (ILLUS. right, top of column)	$8
Sugar bowl, open, footed, 4" h.	$12
Tumbler, 4" h., 9 oz.	$60
Tumbler, 5 1/4" h., 12 oz.	$135

Holiday or Buttons and Bows, Jeannette Glass Co., 1947-mid '50s (Press-mold)All items in pink unless otherwise noted.

Bowl, 5 1/8" d., berry	$12
Bowl, 7 3/4" d., flat soup	$48
Bowl, berry, 8 1/2" d.	$28
Bowl, 9 1/2" oval vegetable	$24
Butter dish, cov.	$60
Cake plate, three-footed, 10 1/2" d.	$95
Candlesticks, 3" h., pr.	$98
Console bowl, 10 3/4" d.	$145
Creamer, footed	$6
Cup & saucer, plain or rayed base	$10
Pitcher, milk, 4 3/4" h., 16 oz.	$65
Pitcher, milk, 4 3/4" h., 16 oz., iridescent	$25
Pitcher, 6 3/4" h., 52 oz.	$40
Plate, 6" d., sherbet	$5
Plate, 9" d., dinner	$22
Plate, 13 3/4" d., chop	$95
Platter, 8 x 11 3/8" oval	$24
Platter, 8 x 11 3/4" oval, iridescent	$10
Sandwich tray, 10 1/2" d.	$16
Sherbet	$6
Sugar bowl, cov.	$30
Sugar bowl, open	$8
Tumbler, footed, 4" h., 5 oz.	$40
Tumbler, footed, iridescent, 4" h., 5 oz.	$10
Tumbler, footed, 6" h., 9 oz.	$145
Tumbler, 4" h., 10 oz.	$20

Lace Edge or Open Lace, Hocking Glass Co., 1935-38 (Press-mold)

Bowl, 6 1/2" d., cereal, clear	$5
Bowl, 6 1/2" d., cereal, pink	$24
Bowl, 7 3/4" d., ribbed, clear	$45
Bowl, 7 3/4" d., ribbed, pink	$45
Bowl, 7 3/4" d., salad or butter dish bottom, clear	$28
Bowl, 7 3/4" d., salad or butter dish bottom, pink	$28
Bowl, 9 1/2" d., plain or ribbed, clear	$8

Variety of Manhattan Pattern Pieces

Bowl, 9 1/2" d., plain or ribbed, pink............... $24
Bowl, 10 1/2" d., three-footed........................ $245
Butter dish or bonbon, cov., clear............... $20
Butter dish or bonbon, cov., pink.................. $65
Candlesticks, pink, pr..................................... $350
Candlesticks, pink frosted, pr......................... $50
Candy jar, cov., ribbed, clear, 4" h. $25
Candy jar, cov., ribbed, pink, 4" h. $60
Candy jar, cov., ribbed, pink frosted, 4" h. $25
Compote, cov., 7" d., footed, pink.................. $65
Compote, open, 7" d., footed, clear $10
Compote, open, 7" d., footed, pink $24
Compote, open, 9" d., footed, pink $450
Console bowl, three-footed, clear, 10 1/2" d.. $
Console bowl, three-footed, pink, 10 1/2" d.. $245
Console bowl, three-footed, pink frosted, 10 1/2" d...................................... $48
Cookie jar, cov., clear, 5" h. $30
Cookie jar, cov., pink, 5" h. $75
Creamer, clear $20
Cup & saucer, clear....................................... $8
Cup & saucer, pink... $25
Fish bowl, clear, 1 gal., 8 oz........................ $35
Flower bowl w/crystal block, pink.............. $28
Flower bowl without crystal block, pink....... $16
Plate, 7 1/4" d., salad, clear........................... $2
Plate, 7 1/4" d., salad, pink........................... $20
Plate, 8 1/4" d., luncheon, clear..................... $2
Plate, 8 1/4" d., luncheon, pink...................... $22
Plate, 10 1/2" d., dinner, clear....................... $20
Plate, 10 1/2" d., dinner, pink........................ $30
Plate, 10 1/2" d., grill, pink............................ $22
Plate, 13" d., solid lace, clear .... $
Plate, 13" d., solid lace, pink $50
Platter, 12 3/4" oval, clear............................... $8
Platter, 12 3/4" oval, pink.............................. $45
Platter, 12 3/4" oval, five-part, clear.............. $12
Platter, 12 3/4" oval, five-part, pink $38
Relish dish, three-part, deep, clear, 7 1/2" d... $12
Relish dish, three-part, deep, pink, 7 1/2" d.. $60
Relish plate, three-part, pink, 10 1/2" d. $24
Relish plate, four-part, solid lace, clear, 13" d.. $12
Relish plate, four-part, solid lace, pink, 13" d.. $60
Sherbet, footed, clear...................................... $6
Sherbet, footed, pink..................................... $95

Sugar bowl, open, pink.................................. $20
Tumbler, pink, 3 1/2" h., 5 oz........................ $125
Tumbler, pink, 4 1/2" h., 9 oz........................ $28
Tumbler, footed, pink, 5" h., 10 1/2 oz........... $95
Vase, 7" h., pink $450
Vase, 7" h., pink frosted $65

Manhattan or Horizontal Ribbed, Anchor Hocking Glass Co., 1938-43 (Press-mold)

Ashtray, clear, 4" d. $6
Ashtray, clear, 4 1/2" sq. $12
Ashtray, clear w/gold trim, 4 1/2" sq. $14
Bowl, 9" d., salad, clear $28
Bowl, 4 1/2" d., sauce, two-handled, clear........ $8
Bowl, 5 3/8" d., berry, two-handled, clear $12
Bowl, 5 3/8" d., berry, two-handled, pink $14
Bowl, 5 1/2" d., cereal, clear $60
Bowl, 7 1/2" d., large berry, clear (ILLUS. far right with other Manhattan pieces, top of page).. $12
Bowl, 8" d., two-handled, clear $20
Bowl, 8" d., two-handled, pink........................ $24
Bowl, 9" d., salad, clear $28
Bowl, 9 1/2" d., fruit, clear.............................. $32
Bowl, 9 1/2" d., fruit, pink............................... $38
Candleholders, clear, 4 1/2" sq., pr.............. $20
Candlesticks, double, clear, 4 1/4" h., pr. $30
Candy dish, cov., clear................................... $24
Candy dish, open, three-footed, clear.............. $6
Coaster, clear, 3 1/2" d. $12
Compote, 5 3/4" h., clear (ILLUS. second from left with other Manhattan pieces)........ $28
Compote, 5 3/4" h., pink $40
Creamer, oval, clear.. $6
Creamer, oval, pink.. $8
Cup & saucer, clear.. $12
Pitcher, juice, 24 oz., ball tilt-type, clear $30
Pitcher, juice, 24 oz., ball tilt-type, ruby $475
Pitcher w/ice lip, 80 oz., ball tilt-type, clear.... $45
Pitcher w/ice lip, 80 oz., ball tilt-type, pink..... $65
Plate, 6" d., sherbet or saucer, clear $2
Plate, 8 1/2" d., salad, clear $12
Plate, 10 1/4" d., dinner, clear $24
Plate, 10 1/4" d., dinner, pink $125
Plate, 14" d., sandwich, clear $20
Relish tray, five-part, clear w/clear inserts, 14" d.. $55
Relish tray, five-part, clear w/pink inserts, 14" d.. $65

Relish tray, five-part, clear w/ruby inserts, 14" d. (ILLUS. far left with other Manhattan pieces, top previous page) $65
Relish tray, five-part, pink w/pink inserts, 14" d. $65
Salt & pepper shakers, square, clear, 2" h., pr. $28
Salt & pepper shakers, square, pink, 2" h., pr. $40
Sherbet, clear $8
Sherbet, pink $10
Sugar bowl, open, oval, clear $6
Sugar bowl, open, oval, pink $8
Tumbler, footed, clear, 10 oz. $15
Tumbler, footed, green, 10 oz. $16
Tumbler, footed, pink, 10 oz. $18
Vase, 8" h., clear (ILLUS. second from right with other Manhattan pieces, top previous page) $18
Wine, clear, 3 1/2" h. $5

Old Cafe, Hocking Glass Co., 1936-40 (Press-mold)
Bowl, 3 3/4" d., berry, clear $3
Bowl, 3 3/4" d., berry, pink $5

Old Cafe Ruby Berry Bowl

Bowl, 3 3/4" d., berry, ruby (ILLUS.) $8
Bowl, 5" d., nappy, handled, clear..................... $3
Bowl, 5" d., nappy, handled, pink..................... $10
Bowl, 5 1/2" d., cereal, clear $10
Bowl, 5 1/2" d., cereal, pink $28
Bowl, 5 1/2" d., cereal, ruby $18
Bowl, 9" d., handled, clear $8
Bowl, 9" d., handled, pink $24
Bowl, 9" d., handled, ruby $28
Candy dish, clear, 8" d. $6
Candy dish, pink, 8" d. $16
Candy dish, ruby, 8" d. $18
Cup & saucer, clear $3
Cup & saucer, pink $10
Cup & saucer, ruby cup, clear saucer $10
Lamp, clear $85
Lamp, pink $95
Lamp, ruby $125
Olive dish, clear, 6" oblong.............................. $5
Olive dish, pink, 6" oblong $10
Pitcher, 6" h., 36 oz., clear.............................. $20
Pitcher, 6" h., 36 oz., pink $85
Pitcher, 8" h., 80 oz., pink $125
Plate, 6" d., sherbet, clear $2
Plate, 6" d., sherbet, pink $6
Plate, 10" d., dinner, clear $15
Plate, 10" d., dinner, pink $55
Sherbet, low foot, clear $2
Sherbet, low foot, pink $12
Sherbet, low foot, ruby $14
Tumbler, juice, clear, 3" h. $5

Tumbler, juice, pink, 3" h. $12
Tumbler, juice, ruby, 3" h................................. $10
Tumbler, water, clear, 4" h............................... $5
Tumbler, water, pink, 4" h................................ $18
Tumbler, water, ruby, 4" h................................ $20
Vase, 7 1/4" h., clear $10
Vase, 7 1/4" h., pink $45
Vase, 7 1/4" h., ruby $50

Pineapple & Floral or Number 618 or Wildflower, Indiana Glass Co., 1932-37 (Press-mold)
Ashtray, clear, 4 1/2" l. $5
Bowl, 4 5/8" d., cream soup, amber................. $8
Bowl, 4 5/8" d., cream soup, clear $8
Bowl, 4 3/4" d., berry, clear............................. $6
Bowl, 6" d., cereal, clear $12
Bowl, 7" d., salad, amber................................ $3
Bowl, 7" d., salad, clear $3
Bowl, 10" oval vegetable, amber $6
Compote, diamond-shaped, amber.................. $4
Compote, diamond-shaped, clear.................... $4
Creamer, diamond-shaped, amber................... $3

Pineapple & Floral Creamer & Sugar

Creamer, diamond-shaped, clear (ILLUS. with open sugar bowl) $3
Cup & saucer, amber $4
Cup & saucer, clear... $4
Plate, 6" d., sherbet, amber............................. $2
Plate, 6" d., sherbet, clear............................... $2
Plate, 8 3/8" d., salad, amber $3
Plate, 8 3/8" d., salad, clear $3
Plate, 9 3/8" d., dinner, amber......................... $6
Plate, 9 3/8" d., dinner, clear........................... $6
Plate, 11 1/2" d., sandwich, amber................... $7
Plate, 11 1/2" d., sandwich, clear $7
Plate, 11 1/2" d., w/indentation, clear............... $8
Platter, 11", closed handles, amber $10
Platter, 11", closed handles, clear $10
Relish, divided, clear, 11 1/2" $6
Sherbet, footed, amber $4
Sherbet, footed, clear...................................... $4
Sugar bowl, open, diamond-shaped, amber.. $3
Sugar bowl, open, diamond-shaped, clear (ILLUS. with creamer) $3
Tumbler, clear, 4 1/4" h., 8 oz.......................... $8
Tumbler, iced tea, clear, 5" h., 12 oz. $12
Vase, 12 1/2" h., cone-shaped, clear $18

Queen Mary or Vertical Ribbed, Hocking Glass Co., 1936-49 (Press-mold)
Ashtray, clear, 3 1/2" d. $2
Ashtray, ruby, 3 1/2" d. $6
Ashtray, clear, 2 x 3 3/4" oval.......................... $2
Ashtray, pink, 2 x 3 3/4" oval $3
Bowl, 4" d., nappy, clear $3
Bowl, 4" d., nappy, pink $6
Bowl, 4" d., nappy, single handle, clear $3

Bowl, 4" d., nappy, single handle, pink $5
Bowl, 5" d., berry, clear................................... $4
Bowl, 5" d., berry, pink $8
Bowl, 5 1/2" d., two-handled, clear.................. $5
Bowl, 5 1/2" d., two-handled, pink................... $20
Bowl, 6" d., cereal, clear $5
Bowl, 6" d., cereal, pink................................. $22
Bowl, 7" d., nappy, clear $6
Bowl, 7" d., nappy, pink................................. $8
Bowl, 8 3/4" d., large berry, clear................... $20
Bowl, 8 3/4" d., large berry, pink.................... $15
Butter (or jam) dish, cov., clear $25
Butter (or jam) dish, cov., pink $125
Candlesticks, two-light, clear, 4 1/2" h., pr..... $20
Candlesticks, two-light, ruby, 4 /12" h., pr...... $45
Candy dish, cov., clear $20
Candy dish, cov., pink $45
Celery (or pickle) dish, pink, 5 x 10" oval $15
Cigarette jar, clear, 2 x 3" oval $4
Cigarette jar, pink, 2 x 3" oval........................ $6
Coaster, clear, 3 1/2" d. $2
Coaster, pink, 3 1/2" d.................................. $3
Coaster-ashtray, clear, 4 1/4" sq.................... $3
Coaster-ashtray, pink, 4 1/4" sq...................... $5
Coaster-ashtray, ruby, 4 1/4" sq. $6
Compote, 5 3/4" d., clear $6
Compote, 5 3/4" d., pink $18
Creamer, oval, clear...................................... $4
Creamer, oval, pink....................................... $8
Cup & saucer, clear...................................... $4
Cup & saucer, pink....................................... $6
Plate, 6" d., sherbet, clear............................. $1
Plate, 6" d., sherbet, pink.............................. $2
Plate, 6 5/8" d., clear.................................... $2
Plate, 6 5/8" d., pink..................................... $3
Plate, 8 1/2" d., salad, clear........................... $4
Plate, 9 3/4" d., dinner, clear.......................... $14
Plate, 9 3/4" d., dinner, pink $38
Plate, 12" d., sandwich, clear $10
Plate, 12" d., sandwich, pink $14
Plate, 14" d., serving, clear............................ $8
Plate, 14" d., serving, pink............................. $16
Relish, three-part, clear, 12" d. $6
Relish, four-part, clear, 14" d. $8
Relish, four-part, pink, 14" d. $12
Salt & pepper shakers, clear, pr. $15
Sherbet, footed, clear.................................... $3
Sherbet, footed, pink..................................... $8
Sugar bowl, open, oval, clear $4
Sugar bowl, open, oval, pink $8
Tumbler, juice, clear, 3 1/2" h., 5 oz. $2
Tumbler, juice, pink, 3 1/2" h., 5 oz. $8
Tumbler, water, clear, 4" h., 9 oz. $4
Tumbler, water, pink, 4" h., 9 oz. $12
Tumbler, footed, clear, 5" h., 10 oz................ $15
Tumbler, footed, pink, 5" h., 10 oz. $45

Ribbon, Hazel Atlas Glass Co., early 1930s (Press-mold)
Bowl, 4" d., berry.. $20
Bowl, 8" d... $28
Bowl, 8" d., black.. $16
Candy dish, cov... $35
Creamer, footed $8
Creamer, footed, black.................................... $12
Cup & saucer $5
Plate, 6 1/4" d., sherbet................................. $2
Plate, 8" d., luncheon $6
Plate, 8" d., luncheon, black............................ $12
Salt & pepper shakers, black, pr. $35

Salt & pepper shakers, pr............................... $20
Sherbet, footed $6
Sugar bowl, open, footed $8
Tumbler, 6" h., 10 oz...................................... $30

Ring or Banded Rings, Hocking Glass Co., 1927-33 (Press-mold)
Bowl, 5" d., berry, clear.................................... $2
Bowl, 5" d., berry, clear w/multicolored bands $4
Bowl, 5" d., berry, green $6
Bowl, 7" d., soup, clear $6
Bowl, 7" d., soup, clear w/multicolored bands $6
Bowl, 7" d., soup, clear w/platinum trim $5
Bowl, 7" d., soup, green $8
Bowl, 8" d., large berry, clear.......................... $5
Bowl, 8" d., large berry, clear w/multicolored bands $8
Bowl, 8" d., large berry, green $10
Butter tub, clear.. $8
Butter tub, clear w/multicolored bands.......... $10
Butter tub, green $20
Cocktail shaker, clear $12
Cocktail shaker, clear w/multicolored bands $15
Cocktail shaker, clear w/platinum trim $12
Cocktail shaker, green $18
Creamer, footed, clear $3
Creamer, footed, clear w/multicolored bands $4
Creamer, footed, green $10
Cup & saucer, clear.. $4
Cup & saucer, clear w/multicolored bands $5
Cup & saucer, clear w/platinum trim................ $5
Cup & saucer, green $6
Cup & saucer, green w/platinum trim $5
Decanter w/stopper, clear.............................. $15
Decanter w/stopper, clear w/multicolored bands $18
Decanter w/stopper, green $24
Goblet, clear, 7 1/4" h., 9 oz. $6
Goblet, clear w/multicolored bands, 7 1/4" h., 9 oz. $8
Goblet, clear w/platinum trim, 7 1/4" h., 9 oz. $6
Goblet, green, 7 1/4" h., 9 oz. $10
Ice bucket w/tab handles, clear....................... $13
Ice bucket w/tab handles, clear w/multicolored bands $28

Green Ring Pattern Ice Bucket

Ice bucket w/tab handles, green (ILLUS., previous page) $24
Pitcher, 8 1/2" h., 80 oz., pink $30
Pitcher, 8" h., 60 oz., clear............................ $12
Pitcher, 8" h., 60 oz., clear w/multicolored bands $15
Pitcher, 8" h., 60 oz., green $24
Pitcher, 8 1/2" h., 80 oz., clear...................... $12
Pitcher, 8 1/2" h., 80 oz., clear w/multicolored bands $15
Pitcher, 8 1/2" h., 80 oz., green $30
Plate, 6 1/4" d., sherbet, clear $1
Plate, 6 1/4" d., sherbet, clear w/multicolored bands $2
Plate, 6 1/4" d., sherbet, green........................ $3
Plate, 6 1/2" d., off-center ring, clear............... $3
Plate, 6 1/2" d., off-center ring, clear w/multicolored bands............................... $4
Plate, 6 1/2" d., off-center ring, clear w/platinum trim $3
Plate, 6 1/2" d., off-center ring, green.............. $5
Plate, 8" d., luncheon, clear............................ $3
Plate, 8" d., luncheon, clear w/multicolored bands $4
Plate, 8" d., luncheon, clear w/platinum trim $3
Plate, 8" d., luncheon, green $4
Plate, 8" d., luncheon, green w/platinum trim $3
Plate, 8" d., luncheon, red.............................. $12
Salt & pepper shakers, clear, 3" h., pr......... $12
Salt & pepper shakers, clear w/multicolored bands, 3" h., pr............................ $16
Salt & pepper shakers, green, 3" h., pr. $35
Sandwich server w/center handle, clear $10
Sandwich server w/center handle, clear w/multicolored bands $16
Sandwich server w/center handle, clear w/platinum trim.. $8
Sandwich server w/center handle, green..... $16
Sherbet, low, clear $3
Sherbet, low, clear w/multicolored bands $8
Sherbet, low, green... $8
Sherbet, footed, clear, 4 3/4" h. $2
Sherbet, footed, clear w/multicolored bands, 4 3/4" h. $8
Sherbet, footed, green, 4 3/4" h....................... $6
Sugar bowl, open, footed, clear........................ $3
Sugar bowl, open, footed, clear w/multicolored bands $4
Sugar bowl, open, footed, green $10
Tumbler, whiskey, clear, 2" h., 1 1/2 oz........... $3
Tumbler, whiskey, clear w/multicolored bands, 2" h., 1 1/2 oz. $6
Tumbler, whiskey, green, 2" h., 1 1/2 oz......... $10
Tumbler, clear, 3 1/2" h., 5 oz......................... $3
Tumbler, clear w/multicolored bands, 3 1/2" h., 5 oz. $6
Tumbler, green, 3 1/2" h., 5 oz. $8
Tumbler, clear, 3 3/4" h., 8 oz......................... $5
Tumbler, clear w/platinum trim, 3 3/4" h., 8 oz. $6
Tumbler, clear, 4 1/4" h., 9 oz......................... $3
Tumbler, clear w/multicolored bands, 4 1/4" h., 9 oz. $5
Tumbler, green, 4 1/4" h., 9 oz. $8
Tumbler, green, 4 3/4" h., 10 oz. $10
Tumbler, clear, 5 1/8" h., 12 oz....................... $8
Tumbler, clear w/multicolored bands, 5 1/8" h., 12 oz. $6

Tumbler, green, 5 1/8" h., 12 oz. $8
Tumbler, pink, 5 1/8" h., 12 oz. $8
Tumbler, cocktail, footed, clear, 3 1/2" h. $3
Tumbler, cocktail, footed, clear w/multicolored bands, 3 1/2" h.................................... $4
Tumbler, cocktail, footed, green, 3 1/2" h. $8
Tumbler, water, footed, clear, 5 1/2" h............. $4
Tumbler, water, footed, clear w/multicolored bands, 5 1/2" h.................................... $6
Tumbler, water, footed, green, 5 1/2" h. $10
Tumbler, iced tea, footed, clear, 6 1/2" h. $5
Tumbler, iced tea, footed, clear w/multicolored bands, 6 1/2" h................................ $6
Tumbler, iced tea, footed, clear w/platinum trim, 6 1/2" h... $4
Tumbler, iced tea, footed, green, 6 1/2" h. $8
Vase, 8" h., clear $8
Vase, 8" h., clear w/multicolored bands $18
Vase, 8" h., green $24

Roulette or Many Windows, Hocking Glass Co., 1935-39 (Press-mold)
Bowl, 9" d., fruit, clear.................................... $6
Bowl, 9" d., fruit, green.................................. $18
Cup & saucer, clear.. $2
Cup & saucer, green $5
Cup & saucer, pink $5
Pitcher, 8" h., 65 oz., clear............................ $15
Pitcher, 8" h., 65 oz., green $30
Pitcher, 8" h., 65 oz., pink............................. $30
Plate, 6" d., sherbet, clear $1
Plate, 6" d., sherbet, green $2
Plate, 6" d., sherbet, pink $2
Plate, 8 1/2" d., luncheon, clear $2
Plate, 8 1/2" d., luncheon, green $5
Plate, 8 1/2" d., luncheon, pink $5
Plate, 12" d., sandwich, clear $5
Plate, 12" d., sandwich, green......................... $12
Sherbet, clear $2
Sherbet, green $5
Sherbet, pink $5
Tumbler, whiskey, clear, 2 1/2" h., 1 1/2 oz. $5
Tumbler, whiskey, green,. 2 1/2" h., 1 1/2 oz. $8
Tumbler, whiskey, pink, 2 1/2" h., 1 1/2 oz. $8
Tumbler, juice, clear, 3 1/4" h., 5 oz. $2
Tumbler, juice, green, 3 1/4" h., 5 oz. $15
Tumbler, juice, pink, 3 1/4" h., 5 oz. $15
Tumbler, Old Fashioned, clear, 3 1/4" h., 7 1/2 oz. $8
Tumbler, Old Fashioned, green, 3 1/4" h., 7 1/2 oz. $20
Tumbler, Old Fashioned, pink, 3 1/4" h., 7 1/2 oz. $20
Tumbler, water, clear, 4 1/8" h., 9 oz. $10
Tumbler, water, green, 4 1/8" h., 9 oz. $16
Tumbler, water, pink, 4 1/8" h., 9 oz. $16
Tumbler, footed, clear, 5 1/2" h., 10 oz........... $10
Tumbler, footed, green, 5 1/2" h., 10 oz. $20
Tumbler, footed, pink, 5 1/2" h., 10 oz. $20
Tumbler, iced tea, clear, 5 1/8" h., 12 oz. $12
Tumbler, iced tea, clear, 5 1/8" h., 12 oz. $24
Tumbler, iced tea, pink, 5 1/8" h., 12 oz. $24

Royal Ruby, Anchor Hocking Glass Co., 1939-60s (Press-mold)
Ashtray, 4 1/2" sq... $6
Bowl, 4 1/4" d., berry....................................... $8
Bowl, 4 3/4" sq... $5
Bowl, 5 1/4" d. $8

Bowl, 6 1/2" d., scalloped	$10
Bowl, 7 3/8" sq.	$12
Bowl, 7 1/2" d., soup	$14
Bowl, 8" oval vegetable	$24
Bowl, 8 1/2" d., berry	$20
Bowl, 10" d., popcorn, deep	$40
Bowl, 11 1/2" d., salad	$35
Candy dish	$10
Creamer, flat	$5

Creamer, Sugar & Cup & Saucer

Creamer, footed (ILLUS. top with sugar & square cup & saucer)	$6
Cup, round	$6
Cup, square	$6
Cup & saucer, round	$5
Cup & saucer, square (ILLUS. bottom right with creamer & sugar bowl)	$6
Goblet, ball stem	$12
Lamp, Old Cafe patt.	$65
Pitcher, 22 oz., tilted or upright	$38
Pitcher, 3 qt., tilted or upright	$48
Plate, 6 1/2" d., sherbet	$3
Plate, 7" d., salad	$5
Plate, 7 3/4" d., luncheon	$8
Plate, 8 3/8" sq.	$12
Plate, 9" d., dinner	$15
Plate, 13 3/4" d.	$35
Playing card or cigarette box, divided, clear base	$48
Punch bowl	$45
Punch bowl base	$35
Punch cup	$3
Sherbet, footed	$6
Sugar bowl, flat	$5
Sugar bowl, footed (ILLUS. bottom left with creamer & cup & saucer)	$6
Sugar bowl w/slotted lid, footed	$15
Tumbler, cocktail, 3 1/2 oz.	$5
Tumbler, juice, 5 oz.	$6
Tumbler, water, 9 oz.	$8
Tumbler, water, 10 oz.	$8
Tumbler, iced tea, footed, 6" h., 12 oz.	$12
Tumbler, iced tea, 13 oz.	$14
Vase, various styles, large	$20
Vase, 4" h., ball-shaped	$5
Vase, 5" h., ball-shaped	$8
Vase, bud, 5 1/2" h., ruffled top	$8
Vase, 6 1/2" h., bulbous	$8
Wine, footed, 2 1/2 oz.	$6

Sandwich, Anchor Hocking Glass Co., 1939-64 (Press-mold)

Bowl, 4 5/16" d., clear	$3

Bowl, 4 5/16" d., green	$5
Bowl, 4 7/8" d., berry, amber	$3
Bowl, 4 7/8" d., berry, clear	$4
Bowl, 4 7/8" d., berry, pink	$5
Bowl, 4 7/8" d., berry, ruby	$12
Bowl, 5" d., crimped, clear	$6
Bowl, 5 1/4" d., ruby	$18
Bowl, 5 1/4" d., scalloped, amber	$5
Bowl, 5 1/4" d., scalloped, clear	$5
Bowl, 6 1/2" d., smooth or scalloped, amber	$6
Bowl, 6 1/2" d., smooth or scalloped, clear	$6
Bowl, 6 1/2" d., smooth or scalloped, green	$20
Bowl, 6 1/2" d., smooth or scalloped, ruby	$26
Bowl, 6 3/4" d., cereal, amber	$8
Bowl, 6 3/4" d., cereal, clear	$12
Bowl, 7" d., salad, clear	$6
Bowl, 7" d., salad, green	$45
Bowl, 8" d., scalloped, clear	$8
Bowl, 8" d., scalloped, green	$48
Bowl, 8" d., scalloped, pink	$20
Bowl, 8" d., scalloped, ruby	$60
Bowl, 8 1/2" oval vegetable, clear	$8
Bowl, 9" d., salad, amber	$20
Bowl, 9" d., salad, clear	$18
Butter dish, cov., clear	$35
Cookie jar, cov., amber	$25
Cookie jar, cov., clear	$24
Creamer, clear	$4
Creamer, green	$10
Cup & saucer, amber	$5
Cup & saucer, clear	$3
Cup & saucer, green	$18
Custard cup, clear	$3
Custard cup, green	$5
Custard cup, ruffled, clear	$8
Custard cup liner, clear	$6
Custard cup liner, green	$3
Pitcher, juice, 6" h., clear	$40
Pitcher, juice, 6" h., green	$125
Pitcher w/ice lip, 2 qt., clear	$50
Pitcher w/ice lip, 2 qt., green	$195
Plate, 7" d., dessert, amber	$10
Plate, 7" d., dessert, clear	$6
Plate, 8" d., clear	$4
Plate, 9" d., dinner, amber	$8
Plate, 9" d., dinner, clear	$15
Plate, 9" d., dinner, green	$85
Plate, 9" d., snack, clear	$4
Plate, 12" d., sandwich, amber	$8
Plate, 12" d., sandwich, clear	$18
Punch bowl, clear	$15
Punch bowl, opaque white	$8
Punch bowl & base, clear	$25
Punch bowl & base, opaque white	$10
Punch cup, clear	$2
Punch cup, opaque white	$1
Sherbet, footed, clear	$4
Sugar bowl, cov., clear	$18
Sugar bowl, open, clear	$4
Sugar bowl, open, green	$10
Tumbler, juice, clear, 3 oz.	$4
Tumbler, juice, green, 3 oz.	$5
Tumbler, clear, 5 oz.	$5
Tumbler, green, 5 oz.	$6
Tumbler, footed, amber, 9 oz.	$45
Tumbler, footed, clear, 9 oz.	$20
Tumbler, water, clear, 9 oz.	$6
Tumbler, water, green, 9 oz.	$8

Spiral, Hocking Glass Co., 1928-30 (Press-mold)

Bowl, 4 3/4" d., berry, green	$4

Bowl, 7" d., green.. $12
Bowl, 8" d., berry, green.................................. $10
Creamer, flat or footed, green $6
Cup & saucer, green $5
Ice or butter tub, green $24
Pitcher, 7 5/8" h., 58 oz., green...................... $28
Plate, 6" d., sherbet, green.............................. $2
Plate, 8" d., luncheon, green $3
Platter, 12" l., oval, green................................ $18
Preserve, cov., green...................................... $20
Salt & pepper shakers, green, pr.................. $40
Sandwich server, w/center handle, green...... $24
Sherbet, green $4
Sugar bowl, flat or footed, green $6
Tumbler, juice, green, 3" h., 5 oz..................... $4
Tumbler, water, green, 5" h., 9 oz.................... $8

Swirl or Petal Swirl, Jeannette Glass Co., 1937-38 (Press-mold)

Ashtray, pink, 5 3/8".. $6
Bowl, 5 1/4" d., cereal, Delphite...................... $12
Bowl, 5 1/4" d., cereal, pink............................ $10
Bowl, 5 1/4" d., cereal, ultramarine $15
Bowl, 9" d., salad, Delphite $26
Bowl, 9" d., salad, pink................................... $18
Bowl, 9" d., salad, ultramarine $29
Bowl, 10" d., fruit, closed handles, footed,
   ultramarine... $35
Bowl, 9" d., rimmed, pink $20
Bowl, 9" d., rimmed, ultramarine.................... $28
Butter dish, cov., pink.................................. $195
Butter dish, cov., ultramarine $225
Candleholders, double, pink, pr. $60
Candleholders, double, ultramarine, pr......... $65
Candy dish, cov., pink $110
Candy dish, cov., ultramarine....................... $165
Candy dish, open, three-footed, pink,
   5 1/2" d.. $12
Candy dish, open, three-footed, ultrama-
   rine, 5 1/2" d.. $18
Coaster, pink, 3 1/4" d., 1" h. $10
Coaster, ultramarine, 3 1/4" d., 1" h. $14
Console bowl, footed, pink, 10 1/2" d............ $18
Console bowl, footed, ultramarine,
   10 1/2" d... $35
Creamer, Delphite $8
Creamer, pink.. $6

Swirl Ultramarine Creamer & Sugar Bowl

Creamer, ultramarine (ILLUS. with sugar
   bowl) $12
Cup & saucer, Delphite $12
Cup & saucer, pink... $10
Cup & saucer, ultramarine $14
Pitcher, 48 oz., footed, ultramarine........... $1,800
Plate, 6 1/2" d., sherbet, Delphite.................... $4
Plate, 6 1/2" d., sherbet, pink $4
Plate, 6 1/2" d., sherbet, ultramarine............... $5
Plate, 7 1/4" d., pink $6
Plate, 7 1/4" d., ultramarine............................. $8
Plate, 8" d., salad, Delphite $6
Plate, 8" d., salad, pink................................... $5
Plate, 8" d., salad, ultramarine $10
Plate, 9 1/4" d., dinner, Delphite.................... $10

Plate, 9 1/4" d., dinner, pink $12
Plate, 9 1/4" d., dinner, ultramarine............... $18
Plate, 10 1/2" d., Delphite.............................. $20
Plate, 12 1/2" d., sandwich, pink $20
Plate, 12 1/2" d., sandwich, ultramarine $24
Platter, 12" oval, Delphite $32
Salt & pepper shakers, ultramarine, pr......... $45
Sherbet, pink... $12
Sherbet, ultramarine $18
Soup bowl w/lug handles, pink $24
Soup bowl w/lug handles, ultramarine......... $40
Sugar bowl, open, Delphite............................. $8
Sugar bowl, open, pink.................................... $6
Sugar bowl, open, ultramarine (ILLUS.
   with creamer) $12
Tumbler, footed, pink, 9 oz. $12
Tumbler, footed, ultramarine, 9 oz................. $38
Tumbler, pink, 4" h., 9 oz............................... $16
Tumbler, ultramarine, 4" h., 9 oz. $32
Tumbler, pink, 4 5/8" h., 9 oz......................... $15
Tumbler, pink, 5 1/8" h., 13 oz....................... $30
Tumbler, ultramarine, 5 1/8" h., 13 oz. $115
Vase, 6 1/2" h., pink $18
Vase, 8 1/2" h., ultramarine........................... $30

Tea Room, Indiana Glass Co., 1926-31 (Press-mold)

Banana split dish, flat, clear, 7 1/2".............. $28
Banana split dish, flat, green, 7 1/2".............. $85
Banana split dish, flat, pink, 7 1/2" $85
Banana split dish, footed, clear, 7 1/2"........... $24
Banana split dish, footed, pink, 7 1/2" $60
Bowl, 8 3/4" d., salad, green $75
Bowl, 8 3/4" d., salad, pink............................. $75
Bowl, 9 1/2" oval vegetable, green $55
Bowl, 9 1/2" oval vegetable, pink $55
Candlesticks, green, pr. $50
Candlesticks, pink, pr..................................... $50
Celery or pickle dish, green, 8 1/2" $28
Celery or pickle dish, pink, 8 1/2" $28
Creamer, green, 3 1/4" h................................ $18
Creamer, pink, 3 1/4" h. $18
Creamer, clear, 4" h... $
Creamer, green, 4" h....................................... $18
Creamer, pink, 4" h. $18
Creamer, footed, amber, 4 1/2" h................... $24
Creamer, footed, green, 4 1/2" h.................... $20

Tea Room Creamer & Sugar Bowl

Creamer, footed, pink, 4 1/2" h. (ILLUS.
   with sugar bowl) $20
Creamer, rectangular, green........................... $20
Creamer, rectangular, pink.............................. $20
Cup & saucer, green $40
Cup & saucer, pink $40
Finger bowl, green $48
Finger bowl, pink.. $48
Goblet, clear, 9 oz.. $25
Goblet, green, 9 oz. $55
Goblet, pink, 9 oz... $55
Ice bucket, green $65
Ice bucket, pink $65

Lamp, electric, clear, 9"	$60
Lamp, electric, green, 9"	$145
Lamp, electric, pink, 9"	$145
Marmalade w/notched lid, clear	$60
Marmalade w/notched lid, green	$145
Marmalade w/notched lid, pink	$145
Mustard, cov., clear	$60
Mustard, cov., green	$150
Mustard, cov., pink	$150
Parfait, clear	$25
Parfait, green	$85
Parfait, pink	$85
Pitcher, 64 oz., amber	$200
Pitcher, 64 oz., clear	$175
Pitcher, 64 oz., green	$185
Pitcher, 64 oz., pink	$185
Plate, 6 1/2" d., sherbet, green	$20
Plate, 6 1/2" d., sherbet, pink	$20
Plate, 8 1/4" d., luncheon, green	$28
Plate, 8 1/4" d., luncheon, pink	$28
Plate, 10 1/2" d., two-handled, green	$40
Plate, 10 1/2" d., two-handled, pink	$40
Plate, sandwich, w/center handle, green	$60
Plate, sandwich, w/center handle, pink	$60
Relish, divided, green	$24
Relish, divided, pink	$24
Salt & pepper shakers, green, pr.	$85
Salt & pepper shakers, pink, pr.	$85
Sherbet, low, flared edge, clear	$12
Sherbet, low, flared edge, green	$28
Sherbet, low, flared edge, pink	$28
Sherbet, low footed, green	$30
Sherbet, low footed, pink	$30
Sherbet, tall footed, clear	$20
Sherbet, tall footed, green	$40
Sherbet, tall footed, pink	$40
Sugar bowl, cov., green, 3" h.	$35
Sugar bowl, cov., pink, 3" h.	$35
Sugar bowl, open, footed, amber, 4 1/2" h.	$45
Sugar bowl, open, footed, clear, 4 1/2" h.	$6
Sugar bowl, open, footed, green, 4 1/2" h.	$18
Sugar bowl, open, footed, pink, 4 1/2" h. (ILLUS. with creamer, previous page)	$18
Sugar bowl, open, rectangular, green	$20
Sugar bowl, open, rectangular, pink	$20
Sundae, footed, ruffled, clear	$16
Sundae, footed, ruffled, green	$38
Sundae, footed, ruffled, pink	$38
Tray, rectangular, for creamer & sugar bowl, green	$40
Tray, rectangular, for creamer & sugar bowl, pink	$40
Tray w/center handle, for creamer & sugar bowl, green	$45
Tray w/center handle, for creamer & sugar bowl, pink	$45
Tumbler, footed, clear, 6 oz.	$16
Tumbler, footed, green, 6 oz.	$38
Tumbler, footed, pink, 6 oz.	$38
Tumbler, green, 4 3/16" h., 8 oz.	$85
Tumbler, footed, amber, 5 1/4" h., 8 oz.	$95
Tumbler, footed, green, 5 1/4" h., 8 oz.	$35
Tumbler, footed, pink, 5 1/4" h., 8 oz.	$35
Tumbler, pink, 4 3/16" h., 8 1/2 oz.	$38
Tumbler, footed, clear, 11 oz.	$18
Tumbler, footed, green, 11 oz.	$45
Tumbler, footed, pink, 11 oz.	$45
Tumbler, footed, clear, 12 oz.	$20
Tumbler, footed, green, 12 oz.	$65
Tumbler, footed, pink, 12 oz.	$65
Vase, 6 1/2" h., ruffled rim, green	$80
Vase, 6 1/2" h., ruffled rim, pink	$80

Vase, 9 1/2" h., ruffled rim, amber	$80
Vase, 9 1/2" h., ruffled rim, clear	$18
Vase, 9 1/2" h., ruffled rim, green	$95
Vase, 9 1/2" h., ruffled rim, pink	$95
Vase, 9 1/2" h., straight, green	$75
Vase, 9 1/2" h., straight, pink	$75
Vase, 11" h., ruffled rim, clear	$60
Vase, 11" h., ruffled rim, green	$160
Vase, 11" h., ruffled rim, pink	$160
Vase, 11" h., straight, green	$110
Vase, 11" h., straight, pink	$110

Twisted Optic, Imperial Glass Co., 1927-30 (Press-mold)

Bowl, 4 3/4" d., cream soup, amber	$8
Bowl, 4 3/4" d., cream soup, green	$12
Bowl, 4 3/4" d., cream soup, pink	$12
Bowl, 5" d., cereal, amber	$4
Bowl, 5" d., cereal, green	$6
Bowl, 5" d., cereal, pink	$6
Bowl, 7" d., soup or salad, amber	$5
Bowl, 7" d., soup or salad, green	$10
Bowl, 7" d., soup or salad, pink	$10
Candlesticks, amber, 3", pr.	$15
Candlesticks, green, 3", pr.	$28
Candlesticks, pink, 3", pr.	$28
Candlesticks, yellow, 3", pr.	$30
Candy jar, cov., amber	$18
Candy jar, cov., green	$24
Candy jar, cov., pink	$24
Candy jar, cov., yellow	$35
Creamer, amber	$4
Creamer, green	$6
Creamer, pink	$6
Creamer, yellow	$8
Cup & saucer, amber	$3
Cup & saucer, green	$6
Cup & saucer, pink	$6
Cup & saucer, yellow	$8
Pitcher, 64 oz., clear	$28
Pitcher, 64 oz., green	$38
Pitcher, 64 oz., pink	$38
Plate, 6" d., sherbet, amber	$1
Plate, 6" d., sherbet, green	$3
Plate, 6" d., sherbet, pink	$3
Plate, 6" d., sherbet, yellow	$4
Plate, 7" d., salad, amber	$2
Plate, 7" d., salad, green	$4
Plate, 7" d., salad, pink	$4
Plate, 8" d., luncheon, amber	$3
Plate, 8" d., luncheon, green	$6
Plate, 8" d., luncheon, pink	$6
Plate, 8" d., luncheon, yellow	$8
Plate, 9 x 7 1/2" oval, w/indentation, yellow	$10
Preserve jar w/slotted lid, amber	$14
Preserve jar w/slotted lid, green	$28
Preserve jar w/slotted lid, pink	$28
Sandwich server, two-handled, amber	$8
Sandwich server, two-handled, green	$12
Sandwich server, two-handled, pink	$12
Sandwich server, two-handled, yellow	$18
Sandwich server w/center handle, amber	$10
Sandwich server w/center handle, green	$18
Sandwich server w/center handle, pink	$18
Sandwich server w/center handle, yellow	$24
Sherbet, amber	$3
Sherbet, green	$4
Sherbet, pink	$4
Sherbet, yellow	$6
Sugar bowl, open, amber	$4
Sugar bowl, open, green	$6
Sugar bowl, open, pink	$6

Tumbler, green, 4 1/2" h., 9 oz. $8
Tumbler, pink, 4 1/2" h., 9 oz. $8
Tumbler, amber, 5 1/4" h., 12 oz. $8
Tumbler, green, 5 1/4" h., 12 oz. $10
Tumbler, pink, 5 1/4" h., 12 oz. $10

Duncan & Miller

Duncan & Miller Glass Company, a successor firm to George A. Duncan & Sons Company, produced a wide range of pressed wares and novelty pieces during the late 19th century and into the early 20th century. During the Depression era and after, they continued making a wide variety of more modern patterns, including mold-blown types, and also introduced a number of etched and engraved patterns. Many colors, including opalescent hues, were produced during this era, and especially popular today are the graceful swan dishes they produced in the Pall Mall and Sylvan patterns.

The numbers after the pattern name indicate the original factory pattern number. The Duncan factory was closed in 1955. Also see ANIMALS.

American Way Basket

Basket, applied handle, American Way patt., clear, 7 1/4 x 11 1/4" (ILLUS.) $55
Basket, Canterbury patt., blue opalescent, 9"h. $115
Basket, Hobnail patt., blue opalescent, 9 x 14" $220

Clear Hobnail Pattern Candleholders

Candleholders, one-light, Hobnail patt., clear, 3 3/4" h., pr. (ILLUS.) $28
Candy dish, cov., footed, Canterbury patt., ruby w/clear foot $155
Cigarette box cov., rectangular, Sculptured Line, Dogwood patt., clear satin, 5" l. $175
Compote, open, 7" h., 8" d., Diamond Ridge patt., clear $70

Cornucopia, No. 121, pink opalescent, 13" l. $295
Decanter w/stopper Mardi Gras patt., clear $175
Deviled egg plate, Early American Sandwich patt., clear, 12" d. $100

Alden Pattern Blue Goblet

Goblet, Alden patt., blue, 6 1/2" h. (ILLUS.).... $24
Goblet, Early American Sandwich patt., clear w/amber stain on rim & stem $40

Indian Tree Etched Goblet

Goblet, Indian Tree etching, clear, 7 3/4" h. (ILLUS.) $30
Model of swan, Viking, yellow opalescent, 9" l. $375

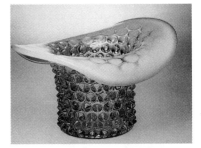

Blue Opalescent Hobnail Top Hat

Model of top hat, Hobnail patt., blue opalescent, 2 1/2" h. (ILLUS.) $34
Pitcher, tankard style, Mardi Gras patt., clear $255
Pitcher, 7 1/2" h., Toby patt., clear $275

Blue Opalescent Dogwood Plate

Plate, 14 1/2" d., Sculptured Line, Dogwood
patt., blue opalescent (ILLUS.)................. **$295**

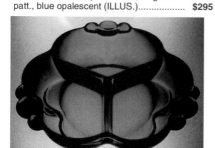

Canterbury Pattern Ruby Relish

Relish, three-part, Canterbury patt., ruby,
7 1/2" w. (ILLUS.)...................................... **$45**
Vase, 10" h., footed, crimped, Caribbean
patt., blue **$270**
Vase, three-footed, No. 12 patt., ruby **$260**
Vase, 7" h., footed, Shell & Tassel patt.,
clear **$95**
Vase, 8" h., flip style, Puritan patt., green........ **$85**
Vase, 10 1/2" h., footed, Venetian No. 126
patt., ruby **$270**

Durand

*Fine decorative glass similar to that made by
Tiffany and other outstanding glasshouses of its
day was made by the Vineland Flint Glass Works
Co. in Vineland, New Jersey, first headed by Victor Durand Sr. and subsequently by his son, Victor Durand Jr., in the 1920s.*

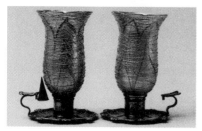

Candle Lamps with Durand Shades

Candle lamps, rounded metal base w/side
C-scroll upright handle & center cylindrical socket supporting a tall tulip-form Durand shade in iridescent gold decorated
w/green & white pulled-feather design &
applied w/random gold threading, one
snuffer missing, somne threading miss-
ing, 8 1/2" h., pr. (ILLUS.) **$978**

Durand Shaded Luminaire

Luminaire, Moorish-style, a ribbed trumpet-
form gold iridescent sahde w/a textured
surface mounted on a brass-colored metal round base w/four figural dolphin feet,
electric, 7" h. (ILLUS.) **$374**

Small Nearly Spherical Durand Vase

Vase, 4" h., nearly spherical body w/a small
flat mount, green & burnt orange ground
decorated w/an overall wavy platinum iridescent King Tut design, signed, one mi-
nor scratch (ILLUS.).............................. **$1,150**

Fine Unsigned Leaf & Vine Durand Vase

Vase, 7" h., flat-bottomed ovoid body w/a
short widely flaring neck, orange ground
w/overall green iridescent heart leaf &
vine decoration, unsigned (ILLUS.)........ **$1,495**

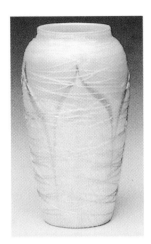

Durand Pulled-Feather & Threaded Vase

Vase, 8" h., simple ovoid body w/a narrow
shoulder to the low wide flat mouth, citron
ground decorated w/a blue & gold pulled-
feather design up the sides, applied overall w/fine random threading, unsigned,
some thread loss (ILLUS.) **$230**

Durand Vase with Heart Leaf & Vine Design

Vase, 8 3/4" h., simple ovoid body w/a
rounded shoulder & short wide trumpet
neck, overall green vine & heart leaf design on a golden iridescent ground, gold
iridescent interior, unsigned (ILLUS.) **$920**
Vase, 27 1/2" h., baluster-shaped body w/a
green King Tut vine & leaf design around
the golden iridescent body, now mounted
as a lamp on a gilt-brown round base &
electric fittings, base drilled (ILLUS., top
next column) **$1,380**

Tall Durand Vase Mounted as Lamp

Fenton

*Fenton Art Glass Company began producing
glass at Williamstown, West Virginia, in January
1907. Organized by Frank L. and John W. Fenton, the company began operations in a newly
built glass factory with an experienced master
glass craftsman, Jacob Rosenthal, as their factory
manager. Fenton has produced a wide variety of
collectible glassware through the years, including
Carnival. Still in production today, its current
productions may be found at finer gift shops
across the country.*

*William Heacock's three-volume set on Fenton,
published by Antique Publications, is the standard reference in this field.*

Fenton Mark

Ruby Snow Crest Bonbon

Bonbon, heart-shaped, handled, Ruby
Snow Crest, 6 1/2" d. (ILLUS.) **$58**
Bowl, 6" d., crimped, Hobnail patt., green
opalescent **$28**
Bowl, 8 1/2" d., art glass, Mosaic Inlaid **$1,100**
Bowl, 11 1/2" d., double crimped, Flame
Crest **$165**

Butter dish, cov., 1/4 pound, Cactus patt.,
   topaz opalescent **$235**
Candleholder, art glass, one-loght, ring
   handle, Mosaic Inlaid, 5 1/2" h. **$875**
Candleholders, one-light, cornucopia No.
   951, Gold Crest, pr. **$72**

Modern Fenton Glass Chalice

Chalice, stepped blue foot supported the
tall cup-form bowl in blue cased in white
& decorated w/a dark blue vining heart
leaf design, signed by artist Dan Fitty, impressed "DLF Fenton" & dated 2004,
6 3/4" h. (ILLUS.)` **$115**

Aqua Crest Cologne Bottle & Stopper

Cologne bottle & stopper, No. 192, Aqua
   Crest, 5" h. (ILLUS.) **$125**
Cup & saucer Aqua Crest **$65**

Figural Hen Deviled Egg Plate

Deviled egg plate, figural hen cover, oval,
   milk glass w/amethyst head, 12 1/2" l.
   (ILLUS.) **$365**
Flower frog set, figural No. 1645 Nymph
   figure w/separate flower frog & petal bowl
   in Jade green on black five-footed base,
   4 pcs. **$325**

Modern Ruby & White Fenton Goblet

Goblet, a deep ruby foot below the knopped
stem & large bell-shaped bowl in deep
ruby cased in white & decorated w/a design of overall ruby vines & heart leaves,
artist signed by Dan Fitty & dated 2004,
impressed mark "DLF Fenton," 5 3/4" h.
(ILLUS.) **$150**
Plate, 10" d., Emerald Crest **$49**
Punch bowl, Persian Pearl (white Stretch
   glass), 12" d. **$345**
Tray, center handle, Lincoln Inn patt., ruby
   .... **$175**
Tumbler, flat iced tea, Polka Dot patt., cran-
   berry opalescent, 12 oz. **$74**

Jade Green Dolphin-Handled Vase

Vase, 5 1/2" h., fan-shaped, dolphin-handled, No. 1533, Jade green (ILLUS.) **$60**

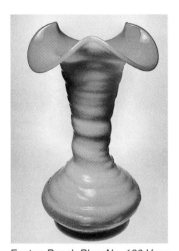

Fenton Peach Blow No. 186 Vase

Vase, 6 1/2" h., three-crimp rim, No. 186,
Peach Blow (ILLUS.) **$48**

Fenton Ivy Overlay Vase

Vase, 7 1/2" h., three crimp rim, No. 3001,
Ivy Overlay (ILLUS.) **$52**

Custard Vase with Underwater Scene

Vase, 8 1/4" h., limited edition, h.p. underwater scene, Custard (ILLUS) **$245**

Late Fenton Satin Glass Vase

Vase, 10 1/2" h., deep rose mother-of-pearl
satin glass in the Raindrop patt., small foot
below the widely flaring bulbous body
w/the wide shoulder tapering to a short
trumpet neck w/widely flaring crimped rim,
second half 20th c. (ILLUS.) **$104**

Fenton Milk Glass Hobnail Swung Vase

Vase, 19" h., footed, swung, Hobnail patt.,
milk glass (ILLUS.) **$35**

Fostoria

*Fostoria Glass company, founded in 1887, pro-
duced numerous types of fine glassware over the
years. Its factory in Moundsville, West Virginia,
closed in 1986.*

Fostoria Label

Book ends, Lyre-shaped, pr. **$95**
Bowl, 10" l., oval, scroll handled, No. 2395,
Oak Leaf Brocade etching, pink **$265**

Colony Pattern Footed Bowl

Bowl, 10 1/2 " d., 5 1/2" h., low footed, Colony patt., clear (ILLUS.) **$75**
Bowl, 12" d., rolled edge, Versailles etching, green **$129**
Bowl, 12" l., oval, Heirloom patt., pink opalescent... **$70**
Cake stand, Coin patt., amber..................... **$130**
Cake stand, Colony patt., clear.................... **$148**

Fostoria No. 2383 Candleholder

Candleholder, three-light, No. 2383, Rose (ILLUS.)... **$38**
Candleholders, one-light, low, No. 2375, Oakwood Brocade etching, blue, 3" h., pr. **$175**
Candleholders, one-light, tall, Rebecca-at-Well patt., blue satin, 10" h., pr. **$270**
Candleholders, one-light, tall, Vesper etching, amber, 9" h., pr.................................. **$170**

Green Optic Ribbed Candy Dish

Candy dish, cov., footed flaring optic ribbed base w/molded scroll handles at the bot-

tom, low pyramidal cover w/knob finial, Green, 5 1/2" h. (ILLUS.) **$50**

American Pattern Clear Candy Dish

Candy dish, cov., low, flat, three-part, American patt., clear, 6" d. (ILLUS.) **$74**

Windsor Crown Covered Chalice

Chalice, cov., Windsor Crown patt., yellow, 8 1/2" h. (ILLUS.) **$55**

Fostoria Contrast Line Champagne

Champagne, Contrast line, black foot & stem, white bowl, 5 3/4" h. (ILLUS.)............ **$28**
Console set: No. 1412 low footed bowl, & pr. No. 2412 candleholders; bowl w/ green stem & foot & clear bowl, green candleholders, Queen Anne patt., candleholders 9" h., 3 pcs.............................. **$695**
Cream soup bowl, Vesper etching, amber..... **$24**
Cream soup bowl & underplate, June etching, pink, 2 pcs. **$105**

Cup & saucer, flat cup, Vesper etching, amber, set **$18**

Fostoria No. 4101 Decanter & Stopper

Decanter & stopper, No. 4101 shape, Rose (ILLUS.) **$82**

Argus Pattern Goblet & Sherbet

Goblet, Argus patt, blue (ILLUS. left with sherbet) **$20**

Goblet, Captiva patt., frosted blue shell stem w/blue bowl, 1980s............................. **$17**

Ice dish w/liner, American patt., clear, 4 oz. ... **$75**

Ice tub w/liner, American patt., clear, 6 1/2" d., 4 1/2" h.. **$120**

No. 2451 Green Icer

Icer, w/fruit cocktail liner, No. 2451, green, 2 pcs. (ILLUS.) **$34**

Jewel box, cov., American patt., clear, 2 1/4 x 5 1/4", 2" h...................................... **$400**

Ketchup (condiment) bottle w/stopper, American patt., clear, 6 1/4" h. **$160**

Blue Coin Lamp & Original Chimney

Lamp & original chimney, electric, handled courting, Coin patt., blue (ILLUS.)..... **$175**

Amber Coin Lamp & Original Chimney

Lamp & original chimney, oil, handled courting, Coin patt., amber (ILLUS.) **$125**

Mayonnaise bowl w/ladle, American patt.,
divided, clear, 3 1/4" d., 6 1/4" h., 2 pcs. **$65**
Mayonnaise bowl w/underplate, Colony
patt., clear, 2 pcs. **$40**
Mayonnaise bowl w/underplate, Ro-
mance etching, clear, 2 pcs. **$60**
Mayonnaise dish & liner, Fairfax patt., Na-
varre etching, clear, 2 pcs. **$74**
Mustard jar, cover & spoon, American
patt., clear, 3 pcs. **$65**
Nappy, American patt., flared, green,
4 1/2" d. **$75**
Nappy, American patt., tri-cornered, han-
dled, clear, 5" w. **$15**
Nappy, Baroque patt., handled, flared,
clear, 5" d. **$15**
Nappy, Century patt., handled, clear,
4 1/2" d. **$10**
Novelty, model of a top hat, American patt.,
clear, 3" h. **$35**
Olive dish, American patt., clear, 6" l. **$15**
Oyster cocktail, American Lady patt., clear,
4 oz., 3 1/2" h. **$14**
Oyster cocktail, American patt., clear,
4 1/2 oz. **$13**
Oyster cocktail, Beverly etching, amber **$20**
Oyster cocktail, Chintz etching, clear **$25**
Oyster cocktail, Versailles etching, Azure **$50**
Parfait, June etching, blue, 5 1/2" h. **$125**
Pickle dish, Century patt., clear, 8 3/4" l. **$22**
Pickle dish, Colony patt., clear **$25**
Pickle jar w/silverplated lid, cov., Ameri-
can patt., clear, 6" h. **$550**
Pitcher, Coin patt., emerald green **$260**
Pitcher, footed, No. 5000, Oakwood Bro-
cade etching, azure blue **$1,100**
Pitcher, Hermitage patt., Wisteria, 1 pint,
5" h. **$85**
Pitcher, 5 3/8" h., Coin patt., ruby **$125**
Pitcher, 5 3/4" h., American patt., single
serving, clear, pint **$40**
Pitcher, 6 1/2" h., Coin patt., clear **$89**
Pitcher, 7 1/2" h., Jamestown patt., pink **$195**
Pitcher, Jenny Lind patt., milk glass **$125**
Pitcher, Priscilla patt., footed, green **$100**
Pitcher, Vesper etching, No. 5100, footed,
amber **$310**
Plate, 10 " d., Captiva patt, frosted blue
shell design, 1980s **$17**
Relish dish, three-part, round, Pioneer
patt., amber, 8" d. **$13**
Sherbet, Argus patt., blue (ILLUS. left with
Argus goblet) **$15**
Tumbler, footed juice, Captiva patt, frosted
shell stem, blue bowl **$15**
Vase, 6" h., footed & flared, Colony patt,
Charleston rose decoration, clear **$135**
Vase, 8" h., flip-style, June etching, pink **$425**

Fry

*Numerous types of glass were made by the H.C.
Fry Company of Rochester, Pennsylvania. One of
its art lines was called Foval and was blown in
1926-27. Cheaper was its milky-opalescent oven-
ware (Pearl Oven Ware), made for utilitarian purposes but also now being collected. The company
also made fine cut glass.*

*Collectors of Fry glass will be interested in the
recent publication of a good reference book, The
Collector's Encyclopedia of Fry Glassware, by The
H.C. Fry Glass Society (Collector Books, 1990).*

Aquarium, amber, 14" d., 9" h. **$450**
Bowl, 8" d., flat soup, gold etching band on
rim, Foval line **$165**
Champagne, "Cactus" stem, diamond optic
bowl design, Rose **$95**
Goblet, "Modernistic" patt., blue **$95**

Fry Paneled Blue Goblet

Goblet, paneled, blue, 9" h. (ILLUS.) **$55**
Ivy ball, black w/ clear swirl connector, 7" h. . **$120**
Pitcher, footed, Japanese Maid etching,
clear **$750**

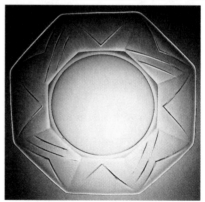

Fry "Modernistic" Blue Plate

Plate, 8" w., octagonal, "Modernistic" patt.,
blue (ILLUS.) **$20**
Plate, 10 1/2" d., grill-type, Pearl Art line **$48**
Tumbler, footed juice, Foval line, w/jade
green foot **$95**
Tumbler, iced tea, handled, Foval line,
w/jade green handle **$118**
Tumbler, iced tea, handled, Japanese Maid
etching, clear **$89**

Vase, 8" h., crimped, clear w/controlled bubbles, green threading around top **$130**
Vase, 13 1/2" h., "Radio Wave" patt., opal w/jade green loops & jade green foot..... **$2,500**
Wine, green "Cactus" stem, clear bowl **$160**
Wine, paneled, clear w/black petal foot, 4 3/4" h. **$24**

Gallé

Gallé glass was made in Nancy, France, by Emile Gallé, a founder of the Nancy School and a leader in the Art Nouveau movement in France. Much of his glass, both enameled and cameo, is decorated with naturalistic motifs. The finest pieces were made in the last two decades of the 19th century and the opening years of the 20th.

Pieces marked with a star preceding the name were made between 1904, the year of Gallé's death, and 1914.

Various Gallé Marks

Unusual Gallé Cameo Scent Bottle

Cameo scent bottle w/original stopper, footed flaring cylindrical body w/a wide rounded shoulder centering a small cylindrical neck w/a pointed stopper, pale green & opalescent white ground overlaid in green & cameo-cut w/stylized Queen Anne's lace blossoms trimmed in white & green leafy stems, cameo-signed, 6 1/2" h. (ILLUS.) **$1,323**

Gallé Cameo Vase with Landscape

Cameo vase, 6 3/4" h., banjo-style, bulbous flattened base tapering to a tall slender stick neck w/small cupped rim, frosted pale yellow shaded to dark blue ground overlaid in dark purple & cameo cut around the lower body w/a landscape w/large leafy trees in the foretground & a river & mountains in the distance, cameo signature on the back (ILLUS.) **$1,725**

Scarce Gallé Blown-out Cameo Vase

Cameo vase, 7" h., round foot below the ovoid body tapering slightly to the molded flat mouth, mottled citrine yellow & frosted ground w/an applied blown-out design of deep purple leaves suspending long pale pods, molded signature (ILLUS.)
.... **$5,405**

Gallé Cameo Stick Vase

Gallé Cameo Forest Landscape Vase

Cameo vase, 7" h., wide swelled & slightly tapering cylindrical body w/a thin rolled rim, yellow shaded to frosted white background overlaid in brown & green & deeply cameo-cut w/a stylized forest landscape w/large leafy trees in the foreground, cameo signature on the side (ILLUS.) **$2,990**

Gallé Cameo Landscape Vase

Cameo vase, 8 1/4" h., a round ringed cushion foot supporting a very wide bulbous ovoid body tapering to a short flaring neck, mottled amber & frosted white ground overlaid in dark brown & pale green & cameo-cut w/a landscape of leafy trees around a lake, etched signature on side (ILLUS.) **$2,300**

Gallé Cameo Vase with Poppies

Cameo vase, 7 1/2" h., cushion foot tapering to a large ovoid body w/a flat mouth, frosted white shaded to dark blue ground overlaid in orange, pink & dark green & cameo cut w/a design of large pink poppies above green leafy stems, cameo signature w/star on the side (ILLUS.)
.... **$1,610**

Cameo vase, 8 1/8" h., a round cushion foot below the tall slender stick body, shaded pink to white frosted ground overlaid in amethyst & cameo cut w/a cascading wisteria vine, cameo signature on top of the foot (ILLUS., top next column) **$740**

Tall Gallé Cameo Leaves & Pods Vase

Cameo vase, 15" h., flat-bottomed bulbous spherical lower body tapering sharply to a very tall gently flaring cylindrical neck, mottled salmon pink & frosted white ground overlaid in green & chartreuse & cameo-cut w/long leafy stems & seed pods, signed in cameo on the side (ILLUS., previous page) **$2,185**

Pair of Gallé Enameled Fleur-de-Lis Cups

Cups, clear flat-based cylindrical shape w/an applied twisted rope handle, overall enameled decoration of fleurs-de-lis w/a gilded rim, engraved "E. Gallé Nancy," late 19th c., 2" h., pr. (ILLUS.)................... **$345**

Rare Gallé Marquetry Floral Pitcher

Pitcher, 9 3/4" h., Marquetry-style, a low squatty round lower body tapering to bell-shaped sides below the high cylindrical neck w/rim spout, marquetry-carved body decorated w/stylized pink magnolia flowers & green leaves against a lightly martelé clear to white mottled background, long applied peach-stained handle, engraved signature in one of the leaves (ILLUS.) **$18,400**

Heisey

Numerous types of fine glass were made by A.H. Heisey & Co., Newark, Ohio, from 1895. The company's trademark, an H enclosed within a diamond, has become known to most glass collectors. The company's name and molds were acquired by Imperial Glass Co., Bellaire, Ohio, in 1958, and some pieces have been reissued. The glass listed below consists of miscellaneous pieces and types. Also see ANIMALS.

Heisey Diamond "H" Mark

Heisey No. 360 Ashtray

Ashtray w/match holder, No. 360, Flamingo (pink), 6" d. (ILLUS.) **$75**
Bowl, 12" d., crimped, Lariat patt., clear **$60**
Bowl, 11" d., Warwick patt., Cobalt Blue....... **$595**

Classic Pattern Candelabra

Candelabra w/prisms, one-light, Classic patt., clear, 16" h., pr. (ILLUS.) **$750**
Candleblock, pineapple-shaped, Plantation patt., clear **$85**
Candleholders, one-light low (nappy-type), Lodestar patt., Dawn (light grey), pr......... **$170**
Candleholders, three-light, Plantation patt., clear, pr. **$300**

Heisy Patrician Pattern Toy Candleholders

Candleholders, toy one-light, Patrician patt., clear, 4 1/2" h., pr. (ILLUS., previous page) $89

Candleholders, two-light, Lariat patt., clear, pr. $70

Candleholders, two-light, Warwick patt., Sahara (light yellow), pr. $195

Cocktail, Chanticleer patt., clear, 3 1/2 oz. $62

Cocktail, Creole patt., Alexandrite (lavender) $92

Cream soup, two-handled, Empress patt., Alexandrite $120

Heisey Stanhope Pattern Cup & Saucer

Cup & saucer, Stanhope patt., clear w/black plastic knob in handle (ILLUS.) $32

Goblet, blown, Plantation patt. w/Ivy etching, clear $90

Ice Bucket, chrome handle, Empress patt., Lotus Vesta etching, clear $145

Matchbox, cov., Banded Flute patt., clear $250

Mayonnaise bowl, footed, handled, Twist patt., w/cutting, Moongleam (light green), 5 1/2" d., 4 1/2" h. $78

Mayonnaise bowl, dolphin feet, Old Colony etching, Sahara, 5 1/2" d. $68

Mayonnaise bowl & spoon, dolphin-footed, Minuet etching, Queen Ann blank, clear, 2 pcs. $100

Mint bowl, Queen Ann patt., dolphin-footed, clear, 6" d. $18

Mug, eight-sided w/elephant head & trunk forming handle, amber $925

Mug, Pineapple & Fan patt., emerald green...... $90

Mustard jar, cov., Crystolite patt., clear $35

Mustard jar, cov., Narrow Flute patt., clear $50

Nappy, Whirlpool (Provincial) patt., clear, 5 1/2" $15

Nut cup, Empress patt., Flamingo $35

Nut dishes, Octagon patt., Moongleam, set of 7 .... $120

Oil cruet & stopper, Pleat & Panel patt., Moongleam, 3 oz. (ILLUS., top next column) $80

Oil cruet & stopper, Stanhope patt., clear w/red plastic knob in handle, 3 oz. $295

Oyster cocktail, Victorian patt. (No. 1425), clear, 5 oz... $16

Parfait, Albemarle patt., clear bowl w/Moongleam foot, 1 1/4 oz. $35

Parfait, Old Glory patt., clear........................ $15

Perfume bottle w/stopper, Ridgeleigh patt., clear, 5 oz....................................... $250

Pitcher, flat w/bulbous bottom, No. 3434, Orchid etching, clear $450

Pleat & Panel Moonbleam Cruet

Pitcher, Minuet etching, No. 4164, 1/2 gal., clear $350

Pitcher, tankard type, Bead Swag patt., ruby-stained, late 1890s............................ $150

Pitcher, water, Puritan patt., clear, 3 qt......... $250

Pitcher w/ice lip, blown, Crystolite patt., crystal, 1/2 gal... $155

Plate, 5" d., Beehive patt., Zircon (pale blue) ... $85

Plate, 6" d., Tudor patt., clear........................ $10

Plate, 6" w., New Era patt., clear $15

Plate, 7" d., Empress patt., clear $12

Plate, 7" d., Empress patt., Tangerine $165

Plate, 7" d., Minuet etching, clear.................. $22

Plate, 7 1/2" d., Empress patt., Sahara $20

Plate, 8" d., Fandango patt., clear................. $50

Plate, 8" d., Ipswich patt., Sahara $35

Plate, 8" d., Orchid etching, clear.................. $28

Plate, 8" sq., Empress patt., Sahara $22

Plate, 8" sq., No. 1489 Puritan patt., crystal.... $15

Plate, 8 1/4" d., Rose etching, clear $28

Plate, 8 1/2" d., Empress patt., Tangerine $150

Plate, 10 1/2" d., dinner, Rose etching, Waverly blank, clear...................................... $225

Plate, 10 1/2" d., serving type, Lariat patt., clear $30

Plate, 10 1/2" w., dinner, square, Old Colony etching, Empress blank, clear $100

Queen Ann Orchid Etched Plate

Plate, 11" d., demi-torte type, Orchid etching, Queen Ann blank (ILLUS.) $78

Plate, 13" d., Ridgeleigh patt., clear $50

Plate, 13" d., torte type, rolled rim, Lariat
patt., clear $40

Plate, 14" d., torte type, Rose etching, Wa-
verly blank, clear $100

Plate, 14" d., torte type, Rose etching, Wa-
verly blank, clear $100

Pretzel jar, cov., etched Fisherman patt. $750

Puff box, cov., Winged Scroll patt., emerald
green, late 19th c. $225

Punch bowl, spherical, Ridgeleigh patt.,
clear, 11" d. $225

Punch bowl & base, Banded Flute patt.,
clear, 2 pcs. $395

Punch cup, Pillows patt., clear, ca. 1900 .... $35

Punch cup, Pinwheel & Fan patt., clear $25

Punch cup, Prince of Wales patt., clear,
early 1900s $20

Punch cup, Prison Stripe patt., No. 357,
clear $35

Punch cup, Victorian patt., crystal $10

Punch ladle, two-spouts, bowl w/ground
bottom, crystal, 13" l. $135

Punch set: bowl, base & eleven cups;
Greek Key patt., clear, 13 pcs. $595

Punch set: bowl, base & ten cups; Beaded
Panel & Sunburst patt., No. 1235, clear,
12 pcs. $425

Punch set: bowl & twelve cups; Puritan
patt., clear, 13 pcs. $320

Relish dish, five-part, Colonial patt., clear $55

Relish dish, four-part, clover leaf-shaped,
Crystolite patt., clear $36

Relish dish, four-part, Plantation patt.,
clear, 8" l. $95

Relish dish, oval, Crystolite patt., crystal,
6" l. $25

Three-Part Empress Pattern Relish Dish

Relish dish, three-part, Empress patt., Alexandrite, 7" d. (ILLUS.) $250

Relish dish, three-part, Fern patt., Zircon $275

Relish dish, three-part, Lariat patt., clear,
10" l. $45

Relish dish, three-part, Lariat patt., clear,
12" l. $45

Relish dish, three-part, Orchid etching, Waverly blank, clear, 11" l. $80

Relish dish, four-part, round, Rose etching,
Waverly blank, crystal, 9" d. $75

Relish tray, five-part, Crystolite patt., crys-
tal $45

Rose bowl, Fancy Loop patt., clear, late
1890s, 4" h. $65

Salt dip, individual size, Ridgeleigh patt.,
crystal $15

Salt & pepper shakers, footed, Old Sand-
wich patt., Sahara, pr. $85

Salt & pepper shakers w/original metal
tops, Pineapple & Fan patt., clear, late
1890s, pr. $100

Salt & pepper shakers w/original metal
tops, Pineapple & Fan patt., emerald
green w/gold, late 1890s, pr. $300

Salt & pepper shakers w/original tops,
Bead Swag patt., clear, late 1890s, pr. $50

Salt & pepper shakers w/original tops,
Empress patt., Sahara, pr. $150

Sherbet, blown, Plantation patt. w/Ivy etch-
ing, clear $40

Vase, 9" h., Warwick patt, Sahara $200

Higgins Glass

*Fused glass, an "old craft for modern tastes"
enjoyed a mid-20th century revival through the
work of Chicago-based artists Frances and
Michael Higgins of the Higgins Glass Studio.
Although known for thousands of years, fusing
had, by the 1940s, been abandoned in favor of
glassblowing. A meticulous craft, fusing can best
be described as the creation of a "glass sandwich."
A design is either drawn with colored enamels or
pieced with glass segments on a piece of enamel-
coated glass. Another piece of enameled glass is
placed over this. The "sandwich" is then placed on
a mold and heated in a kiln, with the glass
"slumping" to the shape of the mold. When complete, the interior design is fused between the
outer glass layers. Additional layers are often utilized, accentuating the visual depth. Sensing that
fused glass was a marketable commodity, the
Higginses opened their studio in 1948 and
applied the fusing technique to a wide variety of
items: tableware such as bowls, plates, and servers; housewares, ranging from clocks and lamps
to ashtrays and candleholders; and purely decorative items, such as mobiles and jewelry. With its
arresting mix of geometric and curved lines and
bold use of color, Higgins glass transformed the
ordinary into decor accent pieces both vibrant
and exciting.*

*Unlike many of their contemporaries, the Hig-
ginses received national exposure thanks to an
association with Chicago industrial manufacturer Dearborn Glass Company. This collaboration, lasting from 1957 through 1964, resulted in
the mass marketing of "higginsware" worldwide.
Since nearly every piece carried the lower-case
signature "higgins," name recognition was both
immediate and enduring.*

*The Dearborn demand for new Higgins pieces
resulted in more than 75 identifiable production
patterns with such buyer-enticing names as
"Stardust," "Arabesque," and "Barbaric Jewels."
Objects created in these patterns included ashtrays of every size (4" "Dinner Dwarfs" to 15"
jumbo models), "rondelay" room dividers and an
extensive line of tableware. (As evidenced by Dearborn promotional postcards, complete dining
tables could literally be set with Higgins glass).*

*In 1965, the Higginses briefly moved their base
of operations to Haeger Potteries before opening
their own studio in Riverside, Illinois, where it
has been located since 1966. Although Michael
Higgins died in 1999 and Frances Higgins in*

2004, the Studio today continues under the leadership of longtime artistic associates Louise and Jonathan Wimmer. New pieces celebrate and expand on the traditions and techniques of the past.Higgins pieces created from 1948 until 1957 are engraved on the reverse with the signature "higgins" or the artist's complete name. A raised "dancing man" logo was added in 1951. Pieces created at Dearborn or Haeger (1957-65) bear a gold "higgins" signature on the surface or a signature in the colorway. The marking since 1966 has been an engraved "higgins" on the reverse of an object, with the occasional addition of the artist's name. Pieces produced since the death of Frances Higgins are signed "higgins studio."

Once heralded as "an exclamation point in your decorating scheme," Higgins glass continues, nearly 60 years since its inception, to enchant collectors with its zest and variety.

References on Higgins glass include the Schiffer books Higgins: Poetry in Glass (2005), and Higgins: Adventures in Glass (1997), both by Donald-Brian Johnson and Leslie Pina. Photos for this category are by Dr. Pina.

The Higgins Glass Studio is located at 33 East Quincy Street, Riverside, IL 60546 (708-447-2787), www.higginsglass.com.

Price ranges given are general estimates covering all available patterns produced at Dearborn Glass Company and Haeger Potteries (1957-1965). The low end of the scale applies to the most commonly found patterns (e.g., "Mandarin," "Siamese Purple"), the upper end to those found less frequently (e.g., "Gemspread," "Carousel").

Ashtray, rectangular, Cyclamen Pink patt., 5 x 7" **$75-100**
Ashtray, circular, Roulette patt. only in 5 1/2" d. size **$50-75**
Ashtray, geometric, Gemspread patt. only, two sides 5 3/4" **$275-325**
Ashtray, circular, various patterns, 7" d., each **$100-125**
Ashtray, Rogue Freeform Ashtrays Set #1, Butterflies patt., 7" longest side **$150-200**
Ashtray, rectangular, Forget-Me-Not patt., 7 x 10" **$100-175**
Ashtray, geometric, various patterns, two sides 7 1/4" **$125-175**
Ashtray, footed, Birdcages patt., 8" longest side... **$300-400**
Ashtray, circular, Barbaric Jewels patt., 8 1/4" to 8 1/2" d. **$100-150**
Ashtray, circular, Buttercup patt., 8 1/4 to 8 1/2" d. **$100-150**
Ashtray, circular, Sunburst patt., 8 1/4" to 8 1/2" d. **$100-150**
Ashtray, Rogue Freeform Ashtrays Set #2, Balloons patt., 9" longest side........... **$175-225**
Ashtray, Rogue Freeform Ashtrays Set #1, Butterflies patt., 9 1/2" longest side .. **$175-250**
Ashtray, rectangular, Variation patt., 10 x 14" **$150-250**
Ashtray, geometric, Barbaric Jewels patt. only, two sides 10 1/4" **$200-250**
Ashtray, Rogue Freeform Ashtrays Set #2, Balloons patt., 10 1/2" longest side **$200-250**

Ashtray, circular, scalloped edge, Stardust patt. only, 11 1/2" d. **$150-200**
Ashtray, Rogue Freeform Ashtrays Set #1, Butterflies patt., 12" longest side....... **$250-300**
Ashtray, Rogue Freeform Ashtrays Set #2, Balloons patt., 15" longest side **$250-350**
Ashtray-dish, square, Dinner Dwarf patt., 4" w. **$50-95**
Ashtray-dish, square, various patterns, 5" w. **$75-100**
Ashtray-dish, square, Barbaric Jewels patt. only, 6" w.................................... **$85-125**
Ashtray-dish, square, various patterns, 7" w. **$100-150**
Ashtray-dish, square, various patterns, 9" to 10" w. **$150-250**
Bonbon, various patterns, 6 1/2" h. **$225-400**
Bowl, 3 1/2" d., circular, various patterns... **$50-95**
Bowl, 5 1/4" w., squarish, various patterns **$100-150**
Bowl, 6" d., circular, various patterns..... **$100-175**
Bowl, 7" w., squarish, various patterns **$125-225**
Bowl, 7" w., squarish w/lip, various patterns **$175-300**
Bowl, 7 1/4" to 7 1/2" d., scalloped rim, various patterns **$125-200**
Bowl, 8 1/4" d., various patterns **$175-300**

Round Controleld Bubble Higgins Bowl

Bowl, 9" d., round, controlled bubble pattern, green & yellow, by Frances Higgins (ILLUS.)... **$700-750**
Bowl, 10" w., squarish, various patterns **$300-400**
Bowl, 10 3/4" d., circular, various patterns **$250-300**
Bowl, 11" w., squarish w/lip, various patterns **$225-400**
Bowl, 12 1/4" d., various patterns **$225-350**
Bowl, 14" w., squarish w/lip, Riviera patt. **$400-600**
Bowl, 17" d., circular, various patterns **$550-750**
Butter dish, various patterns, 3 3/4 x 7 1/2" **$95-125**
Cake or jelly stand, circular, various patterns, 10" to 12" d............................. **$175-300**
Cakestand, squarish, various patterns, 10" w. **$175-300**

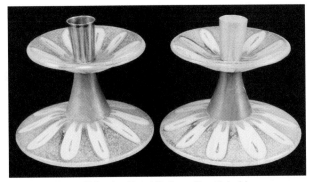

Pair of Higgins Petal Pattern Candleholders

Cakestand, squarish, various patterns, 13" w. **$200-350**

Candleholders, Petal patt., 2 1/2" h., pr. **$100-150**

Candleholders, Petal patt., 4 1/2" h., pr. (ILLUS., top of page)......................... **$150-225**

Candleholders, Colonial patt., 6 1/2" h., pr. **$150-250**

Candleholders, Dinner patt., 8 1/2" h., pr. **$250-400**

Candleholders, Mandarin patt., 8 1/2" h., pr. **$250-400**

Candy dish, cov., various patterns, 8" d. **$350-550**

Cigarette box, cov., rectangular, various patterns, bases, in order of increasing value, are of glass, walnut or glass & metal, 4 x 7" **$200-300**

Higgins Modern Style Gold & Black Clock

Clock, wall or table, gold & black, General Electric, 1954, 8" d. (ILLUS.)........... **$900-1,000**

Clock, wall-type, Carnival patt., 11 1/2" sq. **$500-550**

Dipster, various patterns, 12" d.............. **$250-400**

Dish, four-sided geometric, various patterns, 10 x 12" longest sides **$150-250**

Epergne, three-tier, circular, various patterns **$350-500**

Fruit & nut server, two-tier, circular, various patterns **$250-400**

Goblet/vase with lip, various patterns, 7 3/4" d... **$150-225**

Hanging baskets, various patterns, 7 1/2" d. **$200-300**

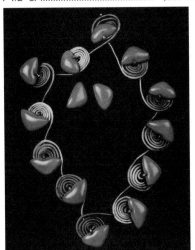

Higgins Glass Jewelry Set

Jewelry set: necklace & earrings; coral glass nuggets & brass spirals, the set (ILLUS.) **$900-1,000**

Green-Eyed Snowy Cat Face Oblong Plaque

Plaque, oblong, "Green-Eyed Snowy," cat face design, by Frances Higgins, 4 1/2 x 7" (ILLUS., previous page) **$350-400**

Rare Framed Ugly Duchess A Plaque

Plaque, rectangular, "Ugly Duchess A" patt., by Michael Higgins, framed, 12 x 20" (ILLUS.)......................... **$3,500-3,750**
Plate, 6" d., various patterns **$100-150**
Plate, 7 1/4" w., squarish, various patterns
.... **$75-125**
Plate, 8 1/4" d., circular, various patterns
.... **$125-225**
Plate, 10 1/2" w., squarish, various patterns
.... **$100-200**
Plate, 12 1/4" d., circular, various patterns
.... **$200-300**
Plate, 12 1/4" d., circular, various patterns
.... **$200-300**
Plate, 13 1/2" w., squarish, various patterns
.... **$150-250**
Plate, 14" square, various patterns **$200-300**
Plate, 16 3/4" d., circular, various patterns
.... **$400-575**

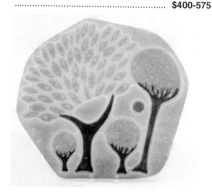

Large "Summer Trees" Platter

Platter, 15" l., irregular shape, "Summer Trees" patt., by Frances Higgins (ILLUS.)
.... **$3,500-3,750**
Posy pocket, various patterns, 5 x 7"
.... **$250-400**
Posy pocket, various patterns, 7 x 10"
.... **$300-475**

Relish server, circular, various patterns, 15" d.. **$300-475**

Higgins Glass "Bubbles" Sculpture

Sculpture, "Bubbles" patt., multi-colored glass circles & chip glass, brass stem, by Frances Higgins, 13" h. (ILLUS.)
.... **$1,500-1,700**
Server, double-sided rectangular form, various patterns, 7 x 14" **$150-250**
Server, squarish, two-tier, various patterns
.... **$250-400**
Server, circular, three-pocket, various patterns, 9 1/2" d................................. **$150-225**
Server, circular, three-pocket, various patterns, 13 1/2" d................................ **$200-300**
Server, circular, six-pocket, various patterns, 18" d.. **$400-600**
Trifle dish or "Long John," various patterns, 7 x 10" **$400-500**

Very Rare Signed Frances Higgins Vase

Vase, 7 3/4" h., dropout style, signed "Frances Stewart Higgins, 1967" (ILLUS.)
.... **$5,000-5,500**

Large Higgins Dropout Style Vase

Vase, 11" h., 14" d., oversized dropout style, multi-colored (ILLUS.)......... **$1,500-1,750**

Honesdale

The Honesdale Decorating Company, Honesdale, Pennsylvania, was originally founded to decorate glass for the C. Dorflinger & Sons firm. Purchased in 1918 by C.F. Prosch, the firm then bought other glass blanks which they etched and decorated. The factory closed in 1932.

Honesdale Green to Clear Art Nouveau Vase

Cameo vase, 9 3/4" h., flaring base tapering to a tall trumpet-form body, clear frosted ground cased in lime green & cut w/an Art Nouveau design of tall stylized leafy flowers & scrolling vines, gold highlights, signed in gold on the bottom, minor gold wear (ILLUS.) **$300-500**

Honesdale Floral Cameo Vase

Cameo vase, 11" h., very slightly tapering cylindrical body w/a slightly flared flat rim, frosted clear overlaid in golden orange & etched w/an overall design of stylized flowers & scrolling leafy vines highlighted in gold, bottom signed in gold (ILLUS.)..... **$575**

Fine Golden Honesdale Art Nouveau Vase

Vase, 14 1/2" h., tapering cylindrical lower body w/a large bulbed top below a very wide flaring & flattened mouth, decorated around the top w/Art Nouveau orange & yellow scrolls w/vines down the sides to panels of scrolls around the base, against a frosted clear ground, signed on the base (ILLUS.) **$1,840**

Imperial

From 1902 until 1984 Imperial Glass of Bellaire, Ohio, produced hand made glass. Early pressed glass production often imitated cut glass and may bear the raised "NUCUT" mark in the interior center. In the second decade of the 1900s Imperial was one of the dominant manufacturers of iridescent or Carnival glass. When glass collecting gained popularity in the 1970s, Imperial again produced Carnival and a line of multicolored slag glass. Imperial purchased molds from closing glass houses and continued many lines popularized by others including Central, Heisey and Cambridge. These reissues may cause confusion but they were often marked.

Later Imperial Marks

Candlewick
Bowl, 8 1/2" d., two-handled, No. 400/72, Viennese Blue... $88
Calendar holder, oblong, clear..................... $245
Cream soup bowl, two-handeld, No. 400/50, clear, 5" d. $40
Cup & saucer, demitasse, No., 400/77, clear, 2 pcs. $30
Hurricane lamp, two-piece, No. 400/79, clear w/hand painted decorations, the set $425
Muddler, clear, 4" l. $36
Parfait, No. 3400, clear, 6 oz. $85
Punch set: bowl, base & twelve cups; gold-encrusted, 14 pcs. $8,000
Sugar bowl, open, beaded handles, No. 400/30, clear w/gold handles $15

No. 400/123 Clear Toast Plate

Toast plate w/glass dome lid, No. 400/123, clear, 8" d., 2 pcs. (ILLUS.)........ $425

Cape Cod

Cape Cod Square Decanter

Decanter w/stopper, square, No. 160/212, clear (ILLUS.).. $75
Jar, cov., peanut-type, handled, No. 160/210, clear, 12 oz. $89

Free-Hand Ware

Black & Orange Imperial Blown Vase

Vase, 7 1/4"h., footed baluster-form w/a widely flaring rim, cobalt blue exterior decorated w/an iridescent orange design of random threading & heart-shaped leaves, unsigned (ILLUS.)......................... $978
Vase, 9" h., cylindrical, cobalt blue, orange iridescent interior...................................... $230
Vase, 9" h., cylindrical, cobalt blue & white swirls, orange iridescent interior $325

Pulled-feather Orange Iridescent Vase

Vase, 9 1/4" h., bulbous ovoid lower body tapering to a cylindrical neck w/a very wide rolled rim, overall blue & white pulled-feather design decorated w/orange iridescence, iridescent orange interior, unsigned (ILLUS.).............................. $920

Miscellaneous Patterns & Lines
Basket, red slag, 10" h................................... $90

Imperial No. 1961/110 Clear Candy Dish

Candy dish cov., low, flat, three-part, No. 1961/110, clear, 9" d. (ILLUS.).................. **$36**

Logo sign, "Handcrafted Imperial from the makers of Lenox China," clear, 4" l. **$135**

Big Shot Pattern Ruby Mug

Mug, Big Shot patt., ruby, 4 1/2" h. (ILLUS.) **$35**

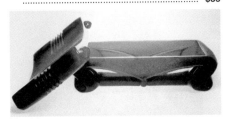

Cathay Line Jade Green Pillow Box

Pillow box, cov., Cathay Line, jade green, 4" x 8" (ILLUS.) **$18**

Sherbet, Chroma patt., dark green, 4 1/2" h. (ILLUS., top next column) **$18**

Tumbler, iced tea, flat Big Shot patt., green **$22**

Tumbler, whiskey, flat, Little Shot patt., green **$22**

Chroma Pattern Dark Green Sherbet

Kew Blas

In the 1890s the Union Glass Works, Somerville, Massachusetts, produced a line of iridescent glasswares closely resembling Louis Tiffany's wares. The name was derived from an anagram of the name of the factory's manager, William S. Blake.

Small Pulled-feather Kew Blas Vase

Vase, 5" h., simple ovoid body w/a very widely flaring rim, a gold iridescent pulled-feather design on a white ground, a gold iridescent interior, signed (ILLUS.) **$460**

Fine Pulled-feather Kew Blas Vase

Vase, 5 3/8" h., footed nearly spherical body tapering to a short flaring & ruffled neck, decorated w/a green & gold pulled-feather design against an ivory ground, gold iridescent interior, signed (ILLUS.) **$1,783**

Kew Blas Vase with Pulled Feathers

Vase, 7" h., a wide cushion foot tapering sharply to gently flaring sides w/a rounded shoulder centered by a short flaring & scalloped neck, delicate green & gold iridescent pulled-feather design on an ivory ground, gold iridescent interior, signed on the polished pontil (ILLUS.).............. **$1,208**
Vase, 7 3/4" h., gently waisted cylindrical body w/a small shoulder tapering to a low flaring neck encircled by a band of bright gold rigaree, gold iridescent pulled-feather design on an ivory exterior, gold iridescent interior, signed on the pontil, slight wear to base rim (ILLUS., next column).............. **$1,323**

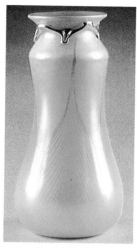

Kew Blas Gold Pulled-feather Vase

Lalique

Fine glass, which includes numerous extraordinary molded articles, has been made by the glasshouse established by René Lalique early in the 20th century in France. The firm was carried on by his son, Marc, until his death in 1977 and is now headed by Marc's daughter, Marie-Claude. All Lalique glass is marked, usually on or near the bottom, with either an engraved or molded signature. Unless otherwise noted, we list only those pieces marked "R. Lalique," produced before the death of René Lalique in 1945.

R. Lalique France N:3152

R LALIQUE

FRANCE

Lalique Marks

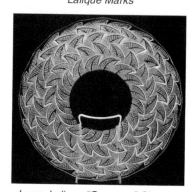

Large Lalique "Ormeaux" Charger

Charger, "Ormeaux," frosted clear molded around the wide sides w/overlapping leaves, stenciled block mark "R. Lalique France," 13 5/8" d. (ILLUS.) **$547**

Lalique Arys Perfume Bottle

Perfume bottle with original stopper, "Arys," flattened wide tapering sides pressed w/a feather design, the pointed stopper w/a matching design, bottle & stopper patinated in light blue, original sticker on the side reads "Faisons un Reve ARYS," signed on the base in raised letters "ARYS - R. Lalique," flake on bottle lip, 4 3/4" h. (ILLUS.) **$805**

Lalique D'Orsay Amber Perfume Bottle

Perfume bottle with original stopper, "D'Orsay," tall slightly tapering square deep amber bottle w/a molded figure of a standing woman wearing a long gown at each corner, the flattened square stopper molded w/florals, signed on the foot "Ambre D'Orsay -Lalique," 5" h. (ILLUS.) **$1,495**

Perfume bottle with original stopper, "Duflores," frosted & clear colorless body molded in the shaped of overlapping blossoms, dotted blossom-form stopper, R. Lalique etched signature, 3 1/2" h. (ILLUS., top next column) **$690**

Lalique Duflores Perfume Bottle

Lalique Ibis Pattern Vase

Vase, 6 1/2" h., "Ibis," widely flaring trumpet form w/eight panels of narrow vertical ribs w/an impressed head of wheat at the base of each panel, clear w/light blue patination, signed "R. Lalique - France" (ILLUS.) **$1,020**

Green Lalique "Gui" Vase

Vase, 6 5/8" h., "Gui," small foot below the wide nearly spherical body w/a small flat mouth, emerald green molded overall w/berried mistletoe branches, signed in block letters "R. Lalique France," Model No. 948 (ILLUS., previous page)........... **$2,300**

Lalique Blue Danaides Vase

Vase, 7 1/4" h., "Danaides," footed wide ovoid body w/a wide flat rim, molded around the sides w/standing nude maidens each holding a large urn on her shoulder & pouring water from it, clear w/blue patination, signed "R. Lalique" (ILLUS.)
.... **$4,140**

Lalique Blue-colored Ajaccio Vase

Vase, 7 3/4" h., "Ajaccio," flat-bottomed wide trumpet-form body, deeply molded around the base w/a band of recumbent sleeping impalas below overall graduated stars against a dark blue patinated background, signed "R. Lalique - France" (ILLUS.)... **$2,300**

Brown-patinated Lalique Plumes Vase

Vase, 8" h., "Plumes," flat-bottomed wide squatty bulbous body tapering sharply to a small cylindrical neck, molded overall w/swirling ostrich plumes, clear w/a dark reddish brown patination, signed "R. Lalique" (ILLUS.)... **$2,160**

Lalique Domremy Pattern Vase

Vase, 8 1/2" h., "Domremy," flat-bottomed wide ovoid body w/a rounded shoulder & short flaring neck, molded overall w/large spherical flower tops on spiney leafy stems, clear w/light blue patination, signed "R. Lalique - France" (ILLUS.) **$1,720**

Le Verre Francais

Glassware carrying this marking was produced at the French glass factory founded by Charles Schneider in 1908. A great deal of cameo glass was exported to the United States early in the 20th century and much of it was marketed through Ovingtons in New York City.

Various Le Verre Francais Marks

Rare Le Verre Francais Cameo Coupe

Cameo coupe, Art Deco style, a round cushion foot supporting a tall slender flaring stem flaring into the wide cupped top, mottled white to pale blue ground, overlaid w/deep orange at the top shading to dark blue & cameo-cut w/a design of fuschia blossoms around the bowl supported to tall leafy stems, signed in script, 15 1/4" h. (ILLUS.) **$3,335**

Rare Le Verre Francais Escargot Lamp

Cameo lamp, "Escargot" patt., 8 1/2" d. domical shade in deep yellow overlaid w/dark brown shaded to orange & cam-

eo-cut w/a design of large snails on arching foliage, raised on a matching urn-form base w/a knopped stem & round orange foot w/another snail, engraved signature on the foot, overall 13" h. (ILLUS.) **$5,160**

Art Deco Le Verre Francais Cameo Vase

Cameo vase, 7 1/4" h., the tall amphora-form body w/a flaring rim cased in bright red shading to deep burgundy & cameo cut w/an Art Deco design of stylized flowers & foliage on a lemon yellow ground, made to fit into a contemporary handled iron stand, signed (ILLUS.) **$575**

Spherical Le Verre Francais Cameo Vase

Cameo vase, 11" h., footed spherical body tapering to a widely flaring low trumpet neck, mottled peach & yellow ground overlaid w/deep orange shading to deep purple & cameo-carved around the bottom w/a band of grass issuing a band of very slender stems topped by bold five-petaled blossoms, signed "Le Verre Francais- France" (ILLUS.) **$3,360**

Fine Le Verre Francais Fuschia Vase

Cameo vase, 12" h., Art Deco style, footed bulbous ovoid body tapering to a small flat mouth flanked by small applied deep purple loop handles, shaded mottled white to blue ground overlaid w/mottled orange to indigo blue & cameo-cut w/a design of stylized fuschia blossoms above a band of leaves, etched signature on foot rim (ILLUS.).............................. **$3,960**

Unusual Striped Le Verre Francais Vase

Cameo vase, 13 3/4" h., Art Deco style, large cushion foot & compressed knob supporting a vase w/a widely flaring flattened lower body to a wide medial band continuing to sharply tapering upper sides topped by a large trumpet neck, soft yellow mottled ground overlaid w/cobalt blue shading to medium orange around the middle & back to cobalt blue below, the upper & lower angled sides

cameo-cut w/narrow knobby stripes, the orange medial band etched w/stylized flowerheads, dark blue neck, signed in script (ILLUS.) **$2,645**

Unusually Shaped Le Verre Francais Vase

Cameo vase, 14" h., a bell-shaped body tapering to a very tall & slender tapering neck w/a tiny flaring rim, mottled pale yellow ground overlaid in mottled orange & yellow shading down to mottled orange & blue & cameo-carved around the body w/stripes of stylized berry swags, neck uncarved (ILLUS.).................................. **$1,440**

Tall Charder-Le Verre Francais Vase

Cameo vase, 18 1/2" h., Art Deco style, a large round cushion foot supporting the very tall swelled cylindrical body w/a widely flaring, flattened rim, mottled pale yellow & orange ground overlaid w/deep raisin brown shading to bright orange & cameo-cut around the top w/short vines & large leaf clusters suspending long trumpet-shaped flowers, signed "Charder" in cameo & "Le Verre Francais" in script (ILLUS.) **$3,795**

Monumental Le Verre Francais Vase

Cameo vase, 22" h, a cushion foot & squatty knob support the tall baluster-form body w/a flaring rim, mottled yellow ground overlaid w/bright orange shading down to dark raisin brown & cameo-cut w/a stylized floral design of large blossoms on tall leafy stems, signed in script (ILLUS.).. **$3,335**

Legras

Cameo and enameled glass somewhat similar to that made by Gallé, Daum Nancy and other factories of the period was made at the Legras works in Saint Denis, France, late in the 19th century and until the outbreak of World War I.

Legras Cameo Vase with Landscape

Tall Slender Legras Landscape Vase

Vase, 16" h., a cushion foot below the tall slender tapering body w/a small flaring rim, clear ground enmaled up the sides in mottled orange & yellow & then enameled in shades of dark green & brown w/tall leafy trees in the foreground & a lake w/sailboats & forest in the distance, signed on the foot (ILLUS.) **$518**

Loetz

Iridescent glass, some of it somewhat resembling that of Tiffany and other contemporary glasshouses, was produced by the Bohemian firm of J. Loetz Witwe of Klostermule and is referred to as Loetz. Some cameo pieces were also made. Not all pieces are marked.

Typical Legras Mark

Cameo vase, 5 7/8" h., round-based tapering cylindrical body w/a bulbed top, a mottled orange & red upper body shading to dark mottled purple, a design of a foggy low river valley cameo cut in the foreground w/a tall weathered tree enameled in brown w/green leaves & grass below, a swollen river below, signed in enamel on the side (ILLUS., top next column)....... **$633**

Loetz, Austria

Loetz Mark

Squatty Loetz Handled Bowl-Vase

Bowl-vase, squatty bulbous body tapering to a four-lobed rim, arched reeded applied handles from the rim to lower body, overall gold iridescent oil spot decoration, unsigned, 4 1/2" h. (ILLUS.) **$510**

Loetz Tree Trunk-style Iridescent Vase

Vase, 5 1/2" h., 6 1/2" d., wide cylindrical tree trunk-style form w/a cushion foot, deep random ruffling on the rim, tooled lines & indentations around the sides, gold w/an overall iridescent finish w/platinum oil-spot decoration (ILLUS.) **$690**

Small Iridescent & Silver Overlay Loetz Vase

Vase, 4 5/8" h., pinched & undulating cylindrical form w/flared mouth, peach decorated overall w/salmon & silvery blue wavy iridescent bands, the base further decorated w/silver overlay leafy scrolling vines & a silver rim band, signed on the bottom (ILLUS.) **$2,070**

Very Rare Decorated Loetz Vase

Vase, 7 1/8" h., footed wide squatty bulbous lower body tapering sharply to the widely flaring neck, apricot ground decorated overall w/horizontal silvery blue wavy bands & applied w/nine long raindrop prunts applied down the sides in dark blue w/silvery iridescent stripes, engraved script signature in the polished pontil (ILLUS.) **$11,500**

Loetz Papillon & Silver-overlay Vase

Vase, 9 1/2" h., tapering conical lower body below the large bulbed neck w/a flaring rim, green w/an overall Papillon style platinum ribbon decoration, the bottom decorated w/a wide band of silver overlay scrolling leaves & blossoms, glass signed (ILLUS.) **$2,990**

Twisted & Ruffled Blue Loetz Vase

Vase, 10" h., tall cylindrical form w/pinched-in & twisted design below the widely flaring inverted three-lobe neck, amethyst w/overall silvery blue oil spot iridescence, unsigned (ILLUS.) **$720**

Vase, 10 1/4" h., Papillon style, a tapering ovoid body w/a gently flaring wide cylindrical neck, ruby red decorated overall w/silvery blue oil spot decoration & enclosed by openwork pewter Art Nouveau looping vines, long looping & undulating pewter handles down the sides from the rim to the base, metal w/impressed number 4530 (ILLUS., top next column) **$2,185**

Loetz Vase with Pewter Overlay

Lustres

Lustres were Victorian glass vase-like decorative objects often hung around the rim with prisms. They were generally sold as matched pairs to be displayed on fireplace mantels. A wide range of colored glasswares were used in producing lustres and pieces were often highlighted with colored enameled decoration.

Later Czechoslovakian Cut Lustres

Cased & cut white to cranberry glass, a wide round base domed in the center below the tall trumpet-shaped top w/a flaring crown-form rim, white cut around the foot & lower body w/rows of printies, the sides cut w/long narrow oval panels w/a band of small cut circles on the swelled shoulder below the flaring top cut w/a band of small ovals below pairs of narrow sliver cuts, further highlighted w/enameled floral & leaf bands in red & green, paper label marked "Made in Czechoslovakia," ca. 1950s, 16" h., pr. (ILLUS.) **$805**

Two Pairs of Cut Glass Victorian Lustres

Fancy Cranberry Lustres with Prisms

Cranberry glass, a ringed stepped hollow base supporting a columnar stem w/a top ring below the bulbous squatty top body w/a flaring crown-form scalloped top, the bowl & rim h.p. w/tiny enameled white flowers w/gold & blue leaves & stems, long facet-cut spearpoint prisms hung from the bowl, very minor chipping, late 19th c., 14 1/4" h., pr. (ILLUS.) **$540**

Cut glass, a domed round foot & baluster-shaped stem supporting a wide cup-shaped top cut w/simple diamond bands & a pointed notch rim, long triangular prisms suspended from the base of the top bowl, ca. 1870, three replaced prisms, 14" h., pr. (ILLUS. center with two taller cut lustres, top of page) **$978**

Cut glass, a hexagonal foot & ring- and knob-cut stem continuing to a trumpet-shaped top w/a widely rolled cut rim hung w/long spearpoint prisms, fitted w/a boboche & a tall tulip-shaped leaf-etched chimney shade, late 19th c., several replaced prisms, 18 1/2" h., pr. (ILLUS. left & right with other cut glass lustres) **$460**

Pink cased glass, round cushion foot tapering to a ringed baluster-form pedestal supporting the upper bowl w/a com-

Pink Cased Glass Victorian Lustres

pressed ring below the slightly flaring cylindrical sides & point-cut rim, the bowl enameled w/alternating panels of purple & blue flowers & gold floral designs, the bowl suspending long triangular cut spearpoint prisms, late 19th c., 11 1/4" h., pr. (ILLUS.) **$200-300**

Enameled Pink Cased Lustres

Pink cased glass, round cushion stepped foot below a tapering columnar pedestal supporting a squatty bulbous & ringed top w/tall cylindrical sides & a notched rim, the cylindrical top enameled w/gilt panels enclosing alternating designs of white flowers & blue leaves & blue & white crosses, shoulder rings suspending long facet-cut spearpoint prisms, Bohemian, late 19th c., one prism missing, 13 1/2" h., pr. (ILLUS.) **$690**

McKee

The McKee name has been associated with glass production since 1834, first producing window glass and later bottles. In the 1850s a new factory was established in Pittsburgh, Pennsylvania, for production of flint and pressed glass. The plant was relocated in Jeanette, Pennsylvania, in 1888 and operated there as an independent company almost continuously until 1951, when it sold out to Thatcher Glass Manufacturing Company. Many types of collectible glass were produced by McKee through the years including Depression, Pattern, Milk Glass and a variety of utility kitchenwares. See these categories for additional listings.

                 PRESCUT

Early McKee Mark, ca. 1880, McKee Prescut Mark

Kitchenwares
Butter dish cov, rectangular, Red Ships patt. **$68**

Seville Yellow Flour Shaker

Flour shaker, original metal cover, Seville Yellow (ILLUS.) **$37**
Flour shaker, red lid, white w/red vertical line decal **$43**
Measuring cup, Custard, four-cup (ILLUS., top next column) **$55**
Measuring cup, two spout, Chalaine blue, one-cup **$750**

McKee Custard Measuring Cup

Sugar shaker w/metal lid, black, Closed Badge patt., Jade **$200**
Teapot, cov., Glasbake, clear w/ colored rings **$35**

Rock Crystal Pattern
Bowl, 8 1/2" d., center-handled, red **$195**

McKee Rock Crystal Candlestick

Candlestick, one-light tall, amber, 8 1/4" h. (ILLUS.) **$62**
Goblet, clear, 7 1/2 oz. **$22**
Oil bottle & stopper, clear, 6 oz. **$75**
Plate, 8 1/2" d., scalloped edge, pink **$18**
Vase, 11" h., footed, green **$155**

Miscellaneous Patterns & Pieces
Berry set: one 8 3/8" bowl & four 4 3/4" bowls; Wiltec patt., clear, 5 pcs. **$38**
Candleholders, one-light, octagonal, low rolled edge, Brocade patt., green, pr. **$82**
Creamer, child's, Laurel patt., Jade w/Scottie dog decal **$235**
Plate, 9" d., grill-type, Laurel patt., Jade **$26**
Tumbler & coaster, "Bottoms Up," Jade, 2 pcs. **$325**

Vases, automobile-type, w/metal holders,
  Vaseline, pr. **$160**
Vegetable bowl, oval, Laurel patt., Ivory,
  9 3/4" l. **$28**

Rare Jolly Golfer Whiskey Set

Whiskey set: "Jolly Golfer," figural decanter
  in the form of a stocky male golfer wearing knickers & cap & grasping a golf club,
  cap form the stopper, togehter w/four
  matching head-shaped glasses w/cap-
  shaped lids, frosted pink, marked "Pat.
  Applied For" on smooth base of decanter,
  some tiny checks & bruise, late 1930s,
  decanter 11 5/8" h., the set (ILLUS.) **$616**

Morgantown (Old Morgantown)

*Morgantown, West Virginia, was the site where
a glass firm named the Morgantown Glass Works
began in the late 19th century, but the company
reorganized in 1903 to become the Economy Tumbler Company, a name it retained until 1929. By
the 1920s the firm was producing a wider range
of better quality and colorful glass tablewares; to
reflect this fact, it resumed its earlier name, Morgantown Glass Works, in 1929. Today its many
quality wares of the Depression era are growing
in collector demand.*

Ritz Blue Janice Pattern Bowl

Bowl, 13" d., flared, No. 4335 Janice patt.,
  Ritz Blue [burgundy cobalt] (ILLUS.) **$175**
Box, cov., No. 1413 High Mushroom patt.,
  white w/ruby cover, 11" h. **$225**
Candleholders, one-light, Golf Ball stem,
  ruby, pr. **$250**
Finger bowl, 4 1/2" d., footed, Virginia etch-
  ing, Golden Iris [pale amber] (ILLUS., top
  next column) **$30**
Flowerlite bowl & frog, No. 9920 Noval
  patt., Burgundy w/clear frog, the set **$38**
Goblet, American Beauty etching, pink **$90**

Virginia Etched Finger Bowl

Goblet, Brilliant patt., Spanish Red **$45**
Goblet, Golf Ball stem, clear **$25**

Coronett Pattern Hurricane Lamp

Hurricane lamp, slant cut, Coronet patt.,
  Gypsy Fire decoration (ILLUS.) **$32**
Pitcher, Crinkle Ockner-shape, pink, 50 oz. ... **$55**
Pitcher, footed, No. 7621 1/2 Corona patt.,
  pink, 54 oz. **$295**
Pitcher, No. 19 Flemish patt., w/Bramble
  Rose etching, clear, 9 1/4" h. **$135**
Plate, 6" d., Springtime etching, clear **$13**
Salt & pepper shakers, No. 6 Bowman-
  shape, Jade Green, pr. **$70**

Betsy Ross Pattern Juice Tumbler

Tumbler, juice, footed, Betsy Ross patt., cobalt foot, white stem, ruby bowl (ILLUS.) **$97**

Camilla Pattern Footed Juice Tumbler

Tumbler, juice, footed, No. 7661 Camilla patt., needle etching, clear w/jade green foot (ILLUS.)... **$35**

Vase, 6 1/2" h., No. 70 Saturn-shaped, Jade Green **$350**

Engagement Shape Jade Green Vase

Vase, 9 1/2" h., footed, No. 58 1/2 Engagement-shape, Jade Green w/ebony connector (ILLUS.)... **$325**

Moser

Ludwig Moser opened his first glass shop in 1857 in Karlsbad, Bohemia (now Karlovy Vary, in the former Czechoslovakia). Here he engraved and decorated fine glasswares especially to appeal to rich visitors to the local health spa. Later other shops were opened in various cities. Throughout the 19th and early 20th century lovely, colorful glasswares, many beautifully enameled, were produced by Moser's shops and reached a wide market in Europe and America. Moser died in 1916 and the firm continued under his sons. They were

forced to merge with the Meyer's Nephews glass factory after World War I. The glassworks were sold out of the Moser family in 1933.

Unusual Moser Blue Chamberstick

Chamberstick, a domed foot below the baluster-form stem below a wide deep bowl-form drip pan centered by the cylindrical socket w/a flattened rim, a long C-scroll gilt handle from rim of pan to stem, pale blue w/heavy paneled gold designs & gold florals on the drip pan & garlands around the foot, annealing lines where handle meets drip pan, 4 5/8" h. (ILLUS.).............. **$288**

Tall Ornately Decorated Moser Ewer

Ewer, dark blue, round low domed foot w/a short stem supporting a bulbous body tapering to a very tall slender cylindrical neck w/a flared arched spout, applied amber handle, the body decorated overall w/enameled branches of blue, yellow & brown swirling oak leaves & lacy gold stems w/a large applied flying bird in color on the front, late 19th c., chip & one area of repair on foot, 17 3/4" h. (ILLUS.)........ **$3,565**

Gilt & Enameled Moser Goblets

Finely Decorated Moser Goblet

Moser Pitcher Decorated with Poppies

Small Moser Cranberry Scent Bottle

Goblet, a round foot supporting a very tall slender stem w/upper ball knob below the bell-shaped bowl, clear foot & stem finely enameled w/delicate florals & gold, the deep cranberry bowl enameled overall w/lacy gold scrolls & tiny blossoms, berries & leaves in blues, greens & pinks, minor gold wear, 7 7/8" h. (ILLUS.) **$460**

Goblets, a domed ringed foot supporting an ornate ringed & bulbed stem supporting a deep rounded bowl, champagne color, the bowls ornately decorated w/tiny exotic flowers on scrolling vines enameled & filled in w/silver & lilac lustre, gold decoration down the stem also trimmed w/applied prunts, an overall wash of mother-of-pearl lustre, 7 1/4" h., set of 10 (ILLUS., top of page) **$2,645**

Pitcher, 8 1/2" h., bulbous ovoid optic ribbed body w/a short neck below the wide cupped rim w/pinched spout, applied clear handle, body in clear shaded to deep green at the base & enameled w/large white, pink & purple poppies on leafy green stems, nearly invisible heat check at handle, minor fogginess (ILLUS., top next column) **$547**

Scent bottle w/original brass cap & finger ring, tusk-form, cranberry decorated around the top w/a wide band of gold enameled w/tiny blossoms, the sides decorated w/gold fern leaves, some gold wear, 3" l. (ILLUS.) **$546**

Sherbet & underplate, the pedestal-based sherbet w/a deep rounded bowl w/a swirled & crimped rim, the round underplate w/a matching rim, pale aqua ornately decorated w/gold swags & florals, underplate 4 5/8" d., sherbet 3 3/8" h., 2 pcs. (ILLUS., next page) **$230**

Moser Sherbet & Underplate

Ornate Miniature Moser Pillow Vase

Vase, 2 3/4" h., miniature pillow style, gold tightly coiled scroll feet supporting the flattened rounded cranberry body w/an arched rim, the sides colorfully enameled w/stylized floral vines & insects, signed & numbered on the bottom (ILLUS.)............. **$575**

Miniature Gold Moser Vase

Vase, 3 1/8" h., miniature, three gold scroll feet supporting the squatty bulbous body tapering to a flared & scalloped rim, overall gold decorated w/purple & blue sprigs of blossoms w/green leaves, slight gold wear (ILLUS.) **$230**

Lobed & Engraved Moser Vase

Vase, 4 3/4" h., footed bulbous six-lobed clear body w/a short flaring neck, each lobe ornately engraved w/delicate florals around a ruby-flashed oval reserve in each lobe further engraved w/a floral bouquet, gold trim, signed on the base (ILLUS.)... **$420**

Mt. Washington

A wide diversity of glass was made by the Mt. Washington Glass Company of New Bedford, Massachusetts, between 1869 and 1900. It was succeeded in 1900 by the Pairpoint Corporation. Miscellaneous types are listed below.

Ornately Molded Mt. Washington Box

Jewelry box w/hinged cover, squatty bulbous base ornately molded w/leafy scrolls trimmed in gold & brown framing smooth panels decorated w/pink florals on a green ground, metal neck & cover fittings, bottom marked "4652-1219," 7 1/2" d., 5 3/4" h. (ILLUS.) **$1,150**

Mt. Washington Figural Fig Shakers

Salt & pepper shakers, figural figs, one w/a pale blue ground h.p. w/white blossoms & green & brown leaves, the other with a white ground w/pink lines on the ribs & h.p. pinl blossoms w/green & brown leaves, 2 1/2" h., pr. (ILLUS.) **$460**

Pretty Mt. Washington Cockle Shell Shaker

Salt shaker w/original top, figural cockle shell, decorated w/pink roses & green leafy stems on a pale green ground, original shell cap, 2 3/4" l. (ILLUS.) **$460**

Rare Small Mt. Washington Lava Vase

Vase, 3 3/4" h., "Lava," footed squatty bulbous body tapering sharply to a widely flaring neck, black ground w/scattered bright bits of glass in red, blue, green & white, glossy finish (ILLUS.) **$2,645**

Muller Freres

The Muller Brothers made acid-etched cameo and other fine glass at Luneville, France, starting in 1910 and until the outbreak of World War II in Europe.

Muller Freres Mark

Miniature Muller Cameo Landscape Vase

Cameo vase, 2" h., miniature, squatty bulbous body tapering to a small cupped neck, peach ground heavily overlaid in deep purple & teal & cameo-carved w/tall trees against a stylized landscape background, cameo-signed, tiny bit of grinding on upper lip (ILLUS.) **$780**

Large Muller Freres Cameo Pillow Vase

Cameo vase, 7 1/2" h., 10 3/8" l., oblong pillow form w/rounded upright sides & a slightly flared rim, cased in shades of mulberry, green, orange & yellow & cameo cut w/a continuous design of leafy brambles of blackberries against an opal ground, engraved signature on bottom, two small open bubbles (ILLUS., bottom previous page) **$2,300**

Lovely Cameo Scene on Muller Freres Vase

Cameo vase, 9 3/4" h., a narrow base tapering gradually up to a rounded shoulder & short flaring neck, mottled almond, tangerine & chocolate brown cased in dark brown & cameo cut w/a landscape seen in the distance through tall conifer trees in the foreground, cameo signature (ILLUS.) **$1,093**

Muller Cameo Oriental Landscape Vase

Cameo vase, 9 3/4" h., flared foot tapering to a tall gently flaring body w/a rounded shoulder centered by a short cylindrical neck, dark mottled green & yellow shad-

ing to brown ground cameo-cut w/an Oriental winter landscape w/a tall bare tree &a man wearing a heavy fur coat & cooley hat on a snow-covered hill w/numerous huts, enameled in shades of white & brown, enameled signature "Muller Fres. Luneville," rubbed area to enamel, grind to top rim (ILLUS.) **$5,175**

Muller Chrysanthemums Cameo Vase

Cameo vase, 11 3/4" h., tall ovoid body tapering to a short flaring neck, light mottled amber ground overlaid in dark & medium brown & cameo-carved w/large chrysanthemum blossoms on leafy stems, cameo-signed on the side "Muller Fres Luneville" (ILLUS.) **$2,530**

Colorful Satin Muller Freres Vase

Vase, 8" h., squatty bulbous base tapering to a tall cylindrical stick neck, bright yellow mottled w/burgundy & tangerine, satin finish & acid-etched mark (ILLUS., previous page) **$316**

Unusual Muller Fres. Paperweight Vase

Vase, 12" h., Art Deco paperweight-style, bulbous ovoid body tapering to a flat molded mouth, composed of bold mottled bands of colors in sunset tones of orange, yellow & green w/gold fleck inclusions, bottom signed in script "Muller Fres Luneville France" (ILLUS.) **$1,020**

Nice Art Deco Muller Freres Vase

Vase, 12" h., Art Deco style, flat-bottomed thick gently flaring cylindrical form, a clear ground w/overall mica fleck inclusions decorated around the sides w/diamonds & zig-zag bands in pale yellow & orange, base signed "Muller Fres Luneville France" (ILLUS.) **$960**

Nailsea

Nailsea was another glassmaking center in England where a variety of wares similar to those from Bristol, England were produced between 1788 and 1873. Today most collectors think of Nailsea primarily as a glass featuring swirls and loopings, usually white, on a clear or colored ground. This style of glass decoration, however, was not restricted to Nailsea and was produced in many other glasshouses, including some in America.

Glass Bellows Bottle Whimsey

Bellows on pedestal cranberry red body w/white loop pattern throughout & applied clear glass rigaree, pedestal & foot, pontil scarred foot, applied mouth & neck rings, America or England, ca. 1860-90, 8 3/4" h. (ILLUS.) **$420**

Nailsea-style Blown Sugar Bowl Base

Sugar bowl base, clear heavy disk foot & short ringed pedestal supporting a bulbous bowl w/a tooled rim in milk white decorated overall w/dark blue looping, pontil scar, Pittsburgh district, ca. 1840-60, some white casing lost in manufacture, 5 3/4" h. (ILLUS.) **$504**

Rare White & Red Nailsea Vase & Ball

Vase & witch ball, 12" h., free-blown vase w/a flaring funnel pedestal base supporting a squatty bulbous body below the tall widely flaring trumpet neck, milk glass decorated overall w/cranberry looping, supporting a round matching ball, American, possibly New England, ca. 1850-70, 2 pcs. (ILLUS.) **$2,240**

Vase & witch ball, 13 1/2" h., free-blown vase of trumpet form w/cushion foot, clear w/white loopings, supporting a round clear ball w/white loopings, probably New Jersey, ca. 1850-70, 2 pcs. **$840**

Small Blown Nailsea Wine Glass

Wine glass, free-blown w/an aqua cup-shaped bowl w/white looping, applied to a simple aqua pedestal base, probably South Jersey, ca.1840-60, 3 1/8" h. (ILLUS.) **$448**

New Jersey Nailsea Witch Ball on Stand

Witchball on stand, round ball w/white loopings on clear, matching trumpet-form base w/cushion foot, New Jersey, 1850-70, overall 12 1/4" h., 2 pcs. (ILLUS.) **$952**

Nakara

Like Kelva, Nakara was made early in this century by the C.F. Monroe Company. For details see WAVE CREST.

Unusual Nakara Broomholder

Broomholder, cylindrical ribbed glass container w/a green ground decorated w/pink & white flowers, mounted in a gilt-brass frame w/an ornately pierced & scrolling backplate, unsigned, 7" w., 9 1/2" h. (ILLUS.) **$1,955**

Fine Rose-decorated Nakara Box

Dresser box w/hinged cover, round w/a flat cover, pale blue ground h.p. on the cover w/large pink & white roses & green leaves, gilt brass fitting & scrolling footed base, unsigned, 3 3/4" d., 3" h. (ILLUS., previous page) **$1,438**

Nash

A. Douglas Nash, a former employee of Louis Comfort Tiffany, purchased Tiffany's Corona Works in December 1928 and began his own operation there. For a brief period Nash produced some outstanding glasswares, but the factory closed in March of 1931 and Nash then became associated with Libbey Glass of Toledo, Ohio. This quality glass is quite scarce.

Orange & Clear Banded Nash Plate

Plate, 6 1/2" d., shallow form w/wide gently flared rim, alternating narrow clear & wide orange bands radiating from the center, unsigned (ILLUS.) **$115**

Bulbous Nash Chintz Pattern Vase

Vase, 7 1/2" h., Chintz patt., footed very wide squatty bulbous body w/a the wide shoulder centered by a short flared neck, alternating stripes in dark green & speckled brown, clear applied foot, unsigned (ILLUS.) **$863**

Green & Blue Striped Nash Chintz Vase

Vase, 7 1/2" h., Chintz patt., swelled & waisted cylindrical body tapering to a closed rim, narrow stripes of dark blue joined by swagged light green speckled band all in a clear ground, unsigned (ILLUS.) ... **$800-1,200**

New Martinsville

The New Martinsville Glass Mfg. Co. opened in New Martinsville, West Virginia, in 1901 and during its first period of production came out with a number of colored opaque pressed glass patterns. Also developed was an art glass line named "Muranese," which collectors refer to as "New Martinsville Peach Blow." The factory burned in 1907 but reopened later that year and began focusing on production of various clear pressed glass patterns, many of which were then decorated with gold or ruby staining or enameled decoration. After going through receivership in 1937, the factory again changed the focus of its production to more contemporary glass lines and figural animals. The firm was purchased in 1944 by The Viking Glass Company (later Dalzell-Viking).

Basket, Radiance (No. 42) patt., blue, 6 1/2" **$149**
Beverage set: decanter w/ beehive stopper & four wines, No. 15, cobalt blue, 5 pcs.... **$230**
Bowl, 6 3/4" d., flat soup, Moondrops patt., cobalt blue.. **$100**

No. 415 Flame Pattern Candleholder

No. 34 New Martinsville Creamer and Sugar Bowl

Candleholder, one-light, No. 415 Flame patt., clear, 5" w., 6 1/2" h. (ILLUS., previous page) **$25**
Candleholders, nappy-style, cupped, Radiance patt., star cut, clear, 5" d., pr. **$120**
Cocktail shaker w/chrome lid, handled, Moondrops (No. 31) patt., cobalt blue **$145**
Condiment set: tray, sugar, creamer, salt & pepper; Radiance patt., blue, 5 pcs. **$195**
Cordial, Radiance patt., ruby, 1 oz. **$38**
Creamer, footed, No. 34, ruby (ILLUS. right w/sugar bowl, top of page) **$18**
Decanter w/ fan stopper, No. 15 Line, amber... **$65**

New Martinsville Clear Swan

Ribbon Etched No. 24 Line Decanter

Decanter w/ fan stopper, No. 24 Line, Ribbon etching, amber (ILLUS. right w/ juice tumbler) **$95**
Model of swan, "sweetheart" shape, w/cutting, clear, 6" l. (ILLUS., top next column) **$32**
Perfume & stopper, "Rocket" style, footed, amethyst... **$895**

"Wise Owl" Green Satin Pitcher

Pitcher 4 1/2" h., figural "Wise Owl," green satin w/ enamel decoration (ILLUS.) **$65**
Relish dish, oval, five-part, Prelude etching, clear, 14" l. **$59**
Sugar bowl, open footed No. 34, cobalt blue (ILLUS. left w/creamer) **$18**
Tumbler, juice, footed, Moondrops patt., Ribbon etching, amber (ILLUS. left w/decanter).. **$22**
Tumbler, water, footed Janice patt., ruby **$32**

Tumbler, whiskey, Moondrops patt., cobalt
blue **$20**
Vase, 14" h., Radiance patt., blue **$162**
Vase, 10" h., three-footed, jade green **$195**

Paden City

The Paden City Glass Manufacturing Com-
pany began operations in Paden City, West Vir-
ginia, in 1916, primarily as a supplier of blanks
to other companies. All wares were handmade,
that is, either hand-pressed or mold-blown. The
early products were not particularly noteworthy,
but by the early 1930s the quality had improved
considerably. The firm continued to turn out high
quality glassware in a variety of beautiful colors
until financial difficulties necessitated its closing
in 1951. Over the years the firm produced, in
addition to tablewares, items for hotel and restau-
rant use, light shades, shaving mugs, perfume
bottles and lamps.

Bar bottle w/ stopper, No. 69 Georgian
patt., Royal Blue **$148**
Batter set: black rectangular tray, clear bat-
ter pitcher w/ black cover & clear syrup
pitcher w/ black cover, 5 pcs. **$275**
Bowl, 8" w., square, footed, Crow's Foot
patt., orchid etching, ruby **$225**

Glades Pattern Bowl with Frost Etching

Bowl, 11 1/2" d., flared, three-footed, Glades
patt., Frost etching, clear (ILLUS.) **$48**
Candleholder, one-light, Crow's Foot patt.,
silver overlay, clear, 5" h. **$45**
Candleholders, one-light, No. 113, Ruby,
7" h., pr. **$155**
Candleholders, two-light, No. 220, Largo
patt., Ruby, pr. **$175**
Candy dish, cov., footed, Cupid etching,
Green, 5 1/4" h. **$325**

No. 210 Regina Green Candy Dish with Cutting

Candy dish, cov., low flat, No. 210 Regina
patt. w/cutting, Green (ILLUS.) **$54**

Eleanor-etched Cocktail Shaker

Cocktail shaker, cover & rooster stopper,
Eleanor etching, clear, 3 pcs. (ILLUS.) **$145**
Cup & saucer, No. 555, "Mr. B" patt., Baby
Orchid etching, clear, 2 pcs. **$24**
Decanter, chrome holder & stopper, Eden
Rose etching, Green **$265**

Glades Pattern Ruby Cordial Decanter

Decanter w/ stopper, tilt cordial style ruby
body w/ silver overlay, clear stopper,
Glades patt., 12 oz. (ILLUS.) **$95**
Ice bowl, gold metal holder & tongs, No.
900, Cavalier label, Emerald-Glo Line, for
the Rubel Company, set **$62**
Luncheon set: six cups & saucers, six 8"
plates, creamer & sugar; Ardith etching,
green, 14 pcs. **$750**
Plate, 8" d., Crow's Foot patt., Ruby **$16**
Plate, 10 1/2" d., two-handeld, Peacock re-
verse etching, Ruby **$125**

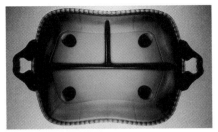

Gadroon Pattern Mulberry Relish Dish

Relish dish, three-part, Gadroon patt, Mulberry, 8 x 10" (ILLUS.) **$55**
Salt & pepper shaker, flat, No. 191, Party Line patt., Ruby, pr. **$95**
Samovar set: cov. "percolator," base & five stemmed wines w/ cutting, Neptune Blue, 8 pcs. **$495**
Server, center-handled, No. 221, Maya patt., Copen Blue, 11" d. **$68**

Pate de Verre

Pate de Verre, or "paste of glass," was molded by very few artisans. In the pate de verre technique, powdered glass is mixed with a liquid to make a paste which is then placed in a mold and baked at a high temperature. These articles have a finely pitted or matte finish and are easily distinguished from blown glass. Duplicate pieces are possible with this technique.

Pate De Verre Marks

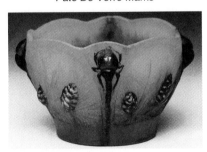

Very Rare Walter Pate de Verre Bowl

Bowl, 3 1/2" h., flat-bottomed flaring bulbous shape w/a scalloped rim, molded up the sides w/four large locusts in amber & dark blue against the mottled green & blue ground also molded w/yellow & green pine cones & green pine needles, signed on side of foot "A. Walter Nancy" (ILLUS.) **$8,913**
Bowl, 6 3/4" d., 3 1/2" h., figural, flat-bottomed w/wide flattened flaring sides in deep terra cotta, a large black amethyst model of a large iguana molded on the rim, signed "Berge SC - A. Walter Nancy" (ILLUS., top next column) **$345**

Walter Pate de Verre Iguana Bowl

Unusual Pate de Verre Night Light

Night light, round thin ribbed cast-iron foot supporting the swelled cylindrical body w/a wide cylindrical cast-iron rim fitted w/a flat cover w/a tiny melon-shaped finial, deep mottled green, red & yellow molded w/large roses & leaves around the upper body, side molded "G. Argy-Rousseau," & "France" on the top rim, original metal hardware, overall 7 1/2" h. (ILLUS.) **$4,680**

Pate-de-Verre Block Moths Paperweight

Paperweight, a square upright shape molded on the top w/two moths, one green & one w/a bluish purple spinde, the main block in deep lime green w/brown swirls, signed on the side "G. Argy-Rousseau," 1 7/8" w., 2 3/4" h. (ILLUS., previous page) **$2,185**

Pate de Verre Figural Mouse Paperweight

Paperweight, figural, an oblong thick brown-streaked white base topped by a large molded mottled dark greyish black mouse, side of rock engraved w/circular "DeCorchemont" mark, France, early 20th c., 2 1/4" l. (ILLUS.) **$1,438**

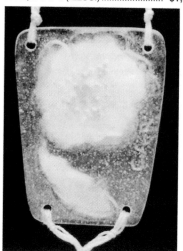

Argy Rousseau Pate de Verre Pendant

Pendant, flattened trapazoidel shape w/a mottled clear ground molded w/a large white flower w/yellow stamens, white cord at bottom holes & hanging cords at the top, signed "G.A.R.," 2 1/4" l. (ILLUS.) **$1,150**

Pendant, oval form cast in the shape of a cicada in colors of raspberry pink & mulberry blue, molded monogram of Gabriel Argy-Rousseau, 2 1/2" h. (ILLUS., top next column) **$1,150**

Pate de Verre Cicada Pendant

Pate de Verre Floral Picture Frame

Picture frame, rectangular w/a wide flat border molded w/large stylized red & blue blossoms on a white ground, rectangular metal band around the picture opening, signed on top left "G. Argy-Rousseau," 4 x 4 3/4" (ILLUS.) **$3,278**

Fine Argy Rousseau Deco-style Vase

Vase, 6 1/4" h., Art Deco style, swelled cylindrical body w/a short cylindrical neck flanked by large inward-scrolled molded handles w/notched border design, the body molded w/full-length narrow incised triangular panels w/zig-zag borders, in rich brown shaded to magenta & pink w/orange highlights at the top, signed on the side "G. Argy-Rousseau" (ILLUS.) ... **$4,920**

Rare Pate de Verre Libations Vase

Vase, 11 3/4" h., "Libations" patt., simple ovoid body tapering to a short wide flared rim, mottled deep orange & yellow ground, a wide raised center band composed of rows of wheel-like devices in orange, yellow & charcoal flanking a large rectangular vertical panel enclosing a half-length portrait of a female carrying a water jug on her shoulder done in shades of dark orange, deep yellow & charcoal, signed on the side "G. Argy-Rousseau" & "France" on the bottom, ca. 1920s, drill hole in bottom (ILLUS.) **$14,950**

Rare Walter Pate de Verre Vide Poche

Vide poche (figural dish), flat-bottomed shallow oval dish in mottled yellowish green molded in relief at one end w/a deep green fish, signed "Berge SC - A. Walter Nancy," 5 x 7 1/2" (ILLUS.) **$6,038**

Pattern

Though it has never been ascertained whether glass was first pressed in the United States or abroad, the development of the glass pressing machine revolutionized the glass industry in the United States, and this country receives the credit

for improving the method to make this process feasible. The first wares pressed were probably small flat plates of the type now referred to as "lacy," the intricacy of the design concealing flaws.

In 1827, both the New England Glass Co., Cambridge, Mass., and Bakewell & Co., Pittsburgh, took out patents for pressing glass furniture knobs; soon other pieces followed. This early pressed glass contained red lead, which made it clear and resonant when tapped (flint.) Made primarily in clear, it is rarer in blue, amethyst, olive green and yellow.

By the 1840s, early simple patterns such as Ashburton, Argus and Excelsior appeared. Ribbed Bellflower seems to have been one of the earliest patterns to have had complete sets. By the 1860s, a wide range of patterns was available.

In 1864, William Leighton of Hobbs, Brockunier & Co., Wheeling, West Virginia, developed a formula for "soda lime" glass that did not require the expensive red lead for clarity. Although "soda lime" glass did not have the brilliance of the earlier flint glass, the formula came into widespread use because glass could be produced cheaply.

An asterisk (*) indicates a piece which has been reproduced.

Actress
Cake stand, frosted rim & border on top, 9 3/4" d. **$170**
Champagne, clear bowl, frosted stem & foot, 5" h. **$450**
Champagne, frosted under bowl & in narrow band above pattern, 5" h. **$400**
Champagne, unfrosted, 5" h. **$300**
Goblet, unfrosted, 6 1/4" h. **$90**

Bellflower
Butter dish, cov., single vine, fine rib **$160**
Celery vase, single vine, fine rib, scalloped & pointed rim, rayed to edge of rim, rayed foot, 8" h. **$425**
Compote, cov., 8 d., single vine, fine rib, high stand **$1,000**
Compote, open, 9 3/4" d., 8" h., single vine, fine rib, scallop & point rim, octagonal hollow stem, domed patterned foot, wafer construction **$325**
Creamer, double vine, fine rib, applied handle **$110**
Creamer, single vine, fine rib, applied handle **$170**
Creamer, single vine, fine rib, molded handle, unpatterned rim & lower bowl bands, short stem, starred foot, 5 1/2" h. **$600**
Decanters w/original stoppers, single vine, fine rib, three rows of thumbprints around shoulder, pt., 11" h., pr. (traces of interior residue) **$300**
Goblet, barrel-shaped, single vine, fine rib, knob stem, rayed base, 5 7/8" h. **$80**
Goblet, single vine, fine rib, plain rim band, plain stem, 6 1/8" h. **$80**
Lamp, kerosene-type, all-glass, single vine, fine rib, squatty bulbous font applied to a high waisted & paneled pedestal on a round scalloped foot, 7 1/2" h. **$200**

Horn of Plenty Larger Creamer, Washington Head Butter & Celery

Pitcher, water, 8 3/4" h., double vine, fine
rib $350
Sugar bowl, cov., double vine, fine rib......... $120
Tumbler, single vine, fine rib, vines flow to
right, ribbed to rim, 3 1/2" h. $70-80

Bull's Eye with Diamond Point
Goblet 6 3/4" h., polished pontil $150-200
Wine, 4 3/4" h., (nick on one point of knop)... $209

Bull's Eye With Fleur De Lis
Goblet, 6 3/8" h. $150

Bull's Eye with Fleur De Lis
Lamp, whale oil, ovoid font attached w/wa-
fer to a paneled stem & hexagonal foot,
8 7/8" h. $325

Cable
Champagne $350
Decanter w/bar lip, qt. $170
Decanter w/stopper, pt., 11 1/2" h. (some
flaking on lower stopper) $210
Goblet 5 1/2" h., small................................ $143
Goblet 6 3/8" h., large $121
Lamp, whale oil, all glass, paneled pedestal
& hexagonal foot, 10" h. $400
Lamp, whale oil, all glass, paneled pedestal
& hexagonal foot, 7 3/4" h. $200
Molasses jug w/hinged tin lid, footed
base, applied handle, 6" h........................ $275
Pitcher, milk, high arched spout, applied
handle, 8 1/2" h. $650
Tumbler, footed (some under foot flakes)..... $200
Wine $180

Corona - see Sunk Honeycomb Pattern

Diamond Point
Decanter w/original stopper, pt.,
11 1/2" h. $90
Jelly glass, 5 1/4" h., 2 1/4" d., rim,
2 1/2" d. foot, polished pontil $77
Pitcher, water, cylindrical sides & high
arched spout, applied handle, 9" h. $230

Excelsior
Creamer, applied handle, made from footed
tumbler, 4 1/2" h. rim, 4 3/4" h. handle,
3 3/8" d. rim, 2 5/8" d. foot....................... $550

Egg cup, double, clear................................ $71
Tumbler, water, flat base, 3 3/4" h. $99

Fine Rib
Celery vase, plain rim, six panels below
bowl w/single step to hexagonal stem &
circular foot, 8 3/4" h, 3 5/8" d. rim $121
Champagne, 5 1/8" h................................... $121
Goblet, 6 1/8" h. $55
Salt dip, master size, barrel-shaped, hexag-
onal stem & plain round foot $90

Gothic
Celery vase plain flared rim, hexagonal
stem w/lower knop & circular foot, wafer
construction, 9 1/2" h, 4 7/8" d., rim,
4 1/2" d. foot... $385
Compote, open, 8 1/4" d., 5 1/2" h., wide
bowl w/scalloped rim, paneled high stan-
dard on plain round foot $425

Hamilton
Champagne, 4 3/4" h................................. $165
Pitcher, water, applied handle, 9" h. $850
Tumbler, water.. $80

Horn of Plenty (McKee's Comet)
**Butter dish & cover w/Washington's
head finial** (ILLUS. center with large
creamer and celery vase, top of page) .. $2,600
Cake stand, six-lobed stem, high stand,
9" d. $1,650
Celery vase, flared scalloped rim, plain
round foot (ILLUS. right with large creamer and Washington Head butter dish) $240
Compote, open, 7 1/8" d., deep bowl
w/scalloped rim, hexagonal high stan-
dard w/round patterned foot $150
Compote, open, 9 1/4" d., scalloped rim,
hexagonal high standard on round pat-
terned foot... $180
Compote, open, oval top, high stand, top
6 1/2 x 9 1/4"... $1,650
Compote, open, oval top, high stand, top
8 1/4 x 11 1/4"....................................... $3,500
Compote, cov., sweetmeat-style, 6 1/4" d.,
7 1/2" h. $385
Compote, open, 7" d., scalloped rim, low
stand $100

Magnet & Grape with Frosted Leaf Celery Vase, Champagne & Goblet

Compote, open, 8" d., scalloped rim, six-paneled high standard on round patterned foot (several flakes under foot) $130

Creamer, large, eight-lobed foot w/Inverted Diamond Point patt. underneath, applied handle, 6 1/2" h. (ILLUS. left with Washington Head butter dish and celery vase).. $467

Creamer, applied handle, 5 1/2" h................. $275

Creamer, large, applied handle, 7" h............. $220

Horn Of Plenty (McKee's Comet)
Goblet, large goblet, 6 1/4" h., w/polished pontil.. $77

Goblet, large goblet, 6 3/8" h., w/polished pontil.. $77

Horn of Plenty (McKee's Comet)
*Lamp, whale oil-type, all-glass, hexagonal stem & base, 9 1/2" h. $260

Peppersauce bottle w/no stopper, paneled & scalloped shoulder, no name on blank panel, 4 1/4" h. $300

Pitcher, water, 9" h.. $880

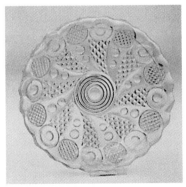

Rare Canary Horn of Plenty Plate

Plate, 6 1/4" d., canary (ILLUS.)................ **$1,150**

Salt dip, master size, oval............................ $110

Sugar bowl, cov., pagoda-shaped cover, 7 1/4" h.. $140

Tumbler, whiskey, 3" h. $468

Tumbler, whiskey, handled, 3" h.................. $800

Wine, flared rim, 4 1/2" h.............................. $150

Lion & Baboon
Butter dish, cov. $355

Celery vase $165

creamer, cov. $275

pitcher $550

Sauce dish $30

Spooner, frosted clear $225

Sugar bowl, cov... $325

Magnet & Grape with Frosted Leaf
Celery vase, scalloped rim, 8 1/2" h. (ILLUS. right with champagne and goblet, top of page) **$240-250**

Champagne (ILLUS. with celery vase & goblet) $253

Goblet, 6 1/2" h. (ILLUS. with celery vase & champagne) $88

Tumbler, footed, plain rim, 5 3/4" h................ $80

Tumbler, water, 3 1/2" h. $120

Wine, 3 7/8" h.. $110

Magnet & Grape with Frosted Leaf and American Shield
Goblet, 6 1/2" h. $286

McKee's Comet - see Horn of Plenty Pattern

Pillar
Goblet, polished pontil, 6 1/4" h. $77

Jelly Glass, polished pontil, 6 1/4" h., 2 3/8" d. rim, 2 1/2" d. foot.......................... $50

Roman Key (Roman Key with Flutes or Ribs)
Celery vase, scalloped rim, 8 3/4" h. $110

Ruby Thumbprint Castor Set & Partial Water Set

Champagne $80
Compote, open, 8 1/4" d., 7 1/4" h., flat rim, high faceted stem on a round foot............ $110
Goblet, frosted, 5 3/4" h. $50
Salt dip, master size $70
Tumbler, footed, 5 1/8" h. $80
Tumbler, water, 3 1/2" h................................. $100
Wine, frosted, 3 3/4" h....................................... $39
Wine, frosted keys, lower horizontal ribs and area above vertical ribs, 3 3/4" h.......... $44

Ruby Thumbprint
Bowl, 8 3/4" d., 3 1/4" h., scalloped rim, engraved leaf & berry decoration $120
Castor set, 4-bottle, in clear glass frame, wire loop center handle, minor flakes on frame, one shaker w/minor pattern flake, 9 1/2" h. (ILLUS. left with water set, top of page) $280
Pitcher, water, bulbous, 8 1/4" h................... $200

Engraved Ruby Thumbprint Pitchers

Pitcher, milk, tankard, 8 3/8" h., engraved souvenir inscription dated 1900 (ILLUS. right with engraved water pitcher $90
Pitcher, milk, tankard, 8 3/8" h. $110
Pitcher, water, tankard, 11" d., w/engraved leaf & berry band (ILLUS. left with engraved milk pitcher).................................. $240
Water set, bulbous pitcher & 3 tumblers, pitcher 8" h., 4 pcs. (ILLUS. of part, right with castor set) $275

Sunk Honeycomb (Corona)

Group of Ruby-stained Sunk Honeycomb Pieces

Cake stand, ruby-stained, 8 1/2" d., 5 1/4" h. (ILLUS. far left with other Sunk Honeycomb pieces) $275
Compote, cov., 7 1/8"" d., 11" h., ruby-stained (ILLUS. second from left with other Sunk Honeycomb pieces)................. $1,450
Cruet w/original stopper, ruby-stained & enameled w/leaves & flowers, 6 1/2" h. (ILLUS. second from right with other Sunk Honeycomb pieces) $120
Decanter w/original stopper, ruby-stained, 13 5/8" h. $120
Decanter w/original stopper, ruby-stained & engraved leaf & vine design, 13 5/8" h. $160
Goblets, ruby-stained, 6" h., set of 6 .... $310
Syrup jug w/original tin top, ruby-stained, 6" h. $260
Wines, rudy-stained & enameled leaf & flower decoration, 4" h., set of 4 (ILLUS. of one, far right with other Sunk Honeycomb pieces)...................................... $120

Thumbprint, Early (Bakewell, Pears & Co.'s "Argus")
*Cake stand, 7 1/2" d., low standard, one-piece construction $130
Celery vase, scalloped rim, paneled & stepped stem on plain round foot, 10 1/4" h.. $90
Compote, cov., 7 1/4" d., high hexagonal knopped stem on a plain round foot (minor rim roughness).................................... $300
Compote, open, 10 1/4" h., 8 7/8" d., deep cup-shaped bowl w/scalloped rim on a high hollow fluted stand on a patterned round foot (very shallow chip on top of foot)... $325

Compote, open, 12 3/4" d., 11" h., flaring
bowl on a fluted hollow standard on patterned round foot (minor edge nick on
one scallop).. $550
Decanter w/bar lip, qt., applied neck ring,
10 3/4" h.. $100
Goblet, barrel, goblet, 6 1/2" h. $88
Goblet, small goblet, 5 3/4" h. $88
*Tumbler, footed, 4 3/8" h................................ $45

Tree of Life - Portland
Compote, open, 7 3/4" d., foot signed "P.G.
and Co. Patent"... $70
Creamer & cov. sugar bowl, footed, pr. $110
Goblet, "P.G.Co. Patent" embossed under
foot, 6 5/8" h. $77

Tulip with Sawtooth
Decanter w/tulip-form stopper, pt.,
10 3/4" h.. $80
Decanter w/tulip-form stopper, pt.,
11 1/2" h.. $120
Decanter w/tulip-form stopper, qt., 15" h.
.... $80-100
Goblet, 6 1/2" h. $88

Waffle
Creamer, footed, applied handle................... $110
Goblet, polished pontil, 4 3/8" h. $77
Goblet, polished pontil, 6 1/4" h. $99
Sugar bowl w/pagoda-style cover (flake
on finial).. $50-75
Tumbler, whiskey, handled, 3 1/8" h............. $550

Waffle and Thumbprint
Champagne, 5 1/2" h. $99
Compote, open, 10" d., flared plain rim,
high hollow hexagonal standard onn a
lightly paneled round foot......................... $110
Decanter w/matching stopper, pt., panel-
cut neck, 11 3/4" h. $125
Goblet, polished pontil, 6 3/4" h. $121
Goblet, small, polished pontil, 6 1/4" h. $99
Jelly Glass, flared rim, polished pontil,
5 1/4" h., 2 3/8" d. rim, 2 1/2" d. foot $110
Lamp, whale oil-type, finger-type w/tapering
cylindrical font w/applied strap handle,
original brass collar & brass & tin double-
burner, 4 1/4" h. $176
Lamp, whale oil-type, font raised on a high
pressed hexagonal standard on a hexagonal foot, early brass collar, 10 1/4" h.
(minor flake on lower base corner)........... $165
Tumbler, water, polished pontil, 3 1/2" h.
(base flake) $242

Washington
Champagne, 4 7/8" h. $187
Goblet, 5 7/8" h. $110
Goblet, small, 5 1/2" h. $88
Goblet, small, w/floral & fruit engravings in
oval panels, 5 1/2" h................................. $550
Wine, 4" h... $66

Peach Blow

*Several types of glass lumped together by col-
lectors as Peach Blow were produced by half a
dozen glasshouses. Hobbs, Brockunier & Co.,
Wheeling, West Virginia, made Peach Blow as a
plated ware that shaded from red at the top to yellow at the bottom and is referred to as Wheeling
Peach Blow. Mt. Washington Glass Works produced an homogeneous Peach Blow shading from
a rose color at the top to pale blue in the lower
portion. The New England Glass Works' Peach
Blow, called Wild Rose, shaded from rose at the
top to white. Gundersen-Pairpoint Co. also reproduced some of the Mt. Washington Peach Blow in
the early 1950s and some glass of a somewhat
similar type was made by Steuben Glass Works,
Thomas Webb & Sons and Stevens & Williams of
England. New England Peach Blow is one-lay-
ered glass and the English is two-layered.*

*Another single-layered shaded art glass was
produced early in the 20th century by the New
Martinsville Glass Mfg. Co. Originally called
"Muranese," collectors today refer to it as "New
Martinsville Peach Blow."*

Gundersen - Pairpoint

Gundersen Peach Blow Satin Compote

Compote, open, 7 1/4" d., 6 3/4" h., a
round foot & slender baluster-shaped
stem below a twisted knop below the
wide shallow bowl w/a six-ruffle rim, sat-
in finish (ILLUS.)...................................... $288

Tall Gundersen Peach Blow Lily Vase

Vase, 9" h., lily-style, round foot & tall very slender stem to the flaring & inwardly-folded tricorner rim, deep rose to white, satin finish (ILLUS., previous page) **$173**

New England

New England Peach Blow Punch Cup

Punch cup, deep rounded bowl w/applied reeded white handle, satin finish, 2 3/4" h. (ILLUS.) **$150**

Mt. Washington Peach Blow Sugar Bowl

Sugar bowl, open, squatty bulbous form w/lightly molded ribbing & wide flat rim, applied white handles, 4 1/2" w., 2 3/4" h. (ILLUS.) **$120**

Wheeling

Drape Pattern Wheeling Peach Blow Creamer

Creamer, footed squatty bulbous body in the Drape patt., a flaring squared neck w/in the Drape patt., applied clear reeded handle, glossy finish, 4 1/2" h. (ILLUS.) **$345**

Wheeling Peach Blow Cruet

Cruet w/stopper, ovoid body tapering to small cylindrical neck w/arched spout, applied amber handle, facet-cut stopper, glossy finish, 7" h. (ILLUS **$748**

Rare Wheeling Griffin Vase Holder

Griffin vase holder, for the Morgan vase, pressed amber glass w/five griffin heads around the cylindrical center, satin finish, chips to interior heads of griffins, 3 1/8" h. (ILLUS.).. **$1,265**

Wheeling Peach Blow Salt & Pepper

Salt & pepper shakers, spherical body w/origional metal lid, glossy finish, 2 1/2" h., pr. (ILLUS.) **$748**

Wheeling Peach Blow Ovoid Vase

Vase, 6 1/4" h., bulbous ovoid body taper-ing to a short cylindrical neck, glossy fin-ish (ILLUS.) **$805**

Wheeling Peach Blow Bottle-form Vase

Vase, 9" h., bottle-form, tall ovoid body taper-ing to tall stick neck, glossy finish (ILLUS.)
.... **$1,200-1,800**

Pillar-Molded

This heavily ribbed glassware was produced by blowing glass into full-sized ribbed molds and then finishing it by hand. The technique evolved from earlier "pattern moulding" used on glass since ancient times, but in pillar-molded glass the ribs are very heavy and prominent. Most exam-ples found in this country were produced in the Pittsburgh, Pennsylvania, area from around 1850 to 1870, but similar English-made wares made before and after this period are also available. Most American items were made from clear flint glass, and colored examples or pieces with colored strands in the ribs are rare and highly prized. Some collectors refer to this as "steamboat" glass, believing it was made to be used on American riverboats, but most likely it was used anywhere that a sturdy, relatively inexpensive glassware was needed, such as taverns and hotels.

Compote, 5 3/4" d., 4 1/4" h., cobalt blue, ten ribs in deep rounded bowl w/flaring

flattened folded rim, applied baluster-shaped ribbed pedestal on an applied misshapen round foot, pontil scar, proba-bly Pittsburgh district, ca. 1830-50 .... **$1,232**
Pitcher, 9" h., eight-rib, slightly tapering cy-lindrical body w/widely flaring mouth & pinched spout, applied strap handle, ground pontil, clear, probably Pittsburgh, ca. 1840 .... **$420**
Sugar bowl, cov., eight-rib, an applied disk foot & knopped stem supporting the squatty bulbous ribbed body tapering to a galleried rim, matching domed cover w/knob finial, ground pontil, Pittsburgh district, ca. 1840, 9" h. **$4,200**

Quezal

In 1901, Martin Bach and Thomas Johnson, who had worked for Louis Tiffany, opened a com-peting glassworks in Brooklyn, New York. The Quezal Art Glass and Decorating Co. produced wares closely resembling those of Tiffany until the plant's closing in 1925.

Quezal

Quezal Mark

Gold Iridescent Quezal Toothpick Holder

Toothpick holder, small bulbous body w/deeply pinched-in sides below the short widely flaring neck, overall gold iri-descence w/magenta highlights, signed, 2 3/8" h. (ILLUS.) **$518**

Miniature Ribbed Gold Quezal Vase

Vase, 2 1/4" h., miniature, a footed squatty flaring ribbed body w/an angled shoulder below the four-petal rolled rim, overall

gold iridescence w/reddish pink highlights, tiny short scratches on rim, signed
(ILLUS.).. **$460**

Miniature Gold Quezal Vase

Vase, 4 1/8" h., miniature, a round cushion
foot below the slender stem flaring to a
wide ruffled rim, overall gold iridescence
w/magenta highlights, engraved "Quezal
K597" (ILLUS.) **$1,035**

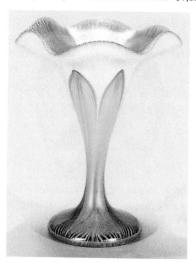

Quezel Pulled Feather Sweet Pea Vase

Vase, 5 7/8" h., sweet pea-type, the round
cushion foot tapering to a slender stem
below the widely flaring six-petal rim,
green w/gold iridescence pulled feathers
on a white ground up the sides, gold iridescent interior, engraved "Quezal 285"
(ILLUS.)... **$1,725**

Slender Gold Quezal Bud Vase

Vase, 6" h., bud-type, a round foot below
the very slender gently flaring sides to a
bulbed shoulder & widely flaring flattened
& gently ruffled rim, overall gold iridescence w/amethyst highlights, signed on
the bottom (ILLUS.).................................... **$518**

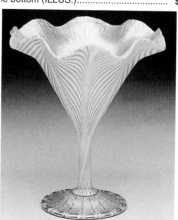

Fine Quezal Flora-form Vase

Vase, 6 3/4" h., flora-form, a round foot below a slender stem & widely flaring &
deeply ruffled body, exterior w/a cream &
green pulled-feather design, gold iridescent interior, iridescent green & gold zipper foot, signed on bottom (ILLUS.)....... **$3,163**

Large Group of Colorful Victorian Satin Glass

Extremely Rare Decorated Quezal Vase

Vase, 14 1/4" h., 6 1/4" d., flat-bottomed ovoid shape tapering to a short flaring neck, the bottom half decorated w/a band of wide pulled feathers in green & gold, the shoulder decorated w/large five-petal green blossoms on a cream ground w/random gold threading with gold heart-shaped leaves, signed, ca. 1908 (ILLUS.)
.... **$17,925**

Vase, 18 1/2" h., a rounded domed bronze foot base w/entwined snakes supporting a very tall slender trumpet-form vase w/a gently ruffled rim, vase w/overall bright gold iridescence, glass signed, bronze base marked "Copyright 1913..." (ILLUS., top next column) **$3,163**

Very Tall Quezal Vase with Bronze Base

Satin

Satin glass was a popular decorative glass developed in the late 19th century. Most pieces were composed of two layers of glass with the exterior layer usually in a shaded pastel color. The name derives from the soft matte finish, caused by exposure to acid fumes, which gave the surface a "satiny" feel. Mother-of-pearl satin glass was a specialized variety wherein air trapped between the layers of glass provided subtle surface patterns such as Herringbone and Diamond Quilted. A majority of satin glass was produced in England, Bohemia and America, but collectors *should be aware that reproductions have been made for many years.*

Bowl & underplate, wide squatty bowl w/an eight-crimp rim on a matching ruffled underplate, mother-of-pearl Diamond Quilted patt. in deep crimson shaded to peach, underplate 6 1/2" d., bowl 3" h., 2 pcs. (ILLUS. bottom row, second from left, top of previous page)........................ **$978**

Celery vase, deeply waisted lobed body in mother-of-pearl Herringbone patt. in dark blue shaded to white, 5" h. (ILLUS. middle row, far right with other satin pieces, top of previous page) **$173**

Creamer & open sugar bowl, footed bulbous creamer w/a flaring crimped & ruffled neck w/applied frosted rim band & applied frosted thorn handle, footed deep wide rounded sugar w/an upright crimped rim, both in mother-of-pearl Diamond Quilted patt. in deep rose shaded to pink, sugar 4 1/2" d., creamer 4 1/2" h., pr. (ILLUS. botton row far right with other satin pieces, top of previous page).. **$345**

Rose bowl, footed squatty bulbous body w/five pinched rim lobes, mother-of-pearl Zipper patt. in yellow cased inn pale green, marked w/English registry mark, Stevens & Williams, ca. 1890s, 4 1/2" d., 3 1/2" h. (ILLUS. back row, far right, top of previous page) **$690**

Rose bowl, spherical w/eight-crimp rim, mother-of-pearl Herringbone patt., shaded deep rose to pink, 3 1/2" h. (ILLUS. middle row, second from right with other satin pieces, top of previous page) **$75-150**

Vase, 5" h., footed ovoid body w/a short trumpet neck, mother-of-pearl Fleur-de-Lis patt., shaded deep yellow to pale yellow, enameled in colorful leafy vines & insects (ILLUS. bottom row, far left with other satin pieces, top of previous page) .. **$518**

Small Blue Swirl Pattern Satin Vase

Vase, 5 1/4" h., wide ovoid body w/a rounded shoulder to the shoulder flattened flaring neck, mother-of-pearl Swirl patt., dark shaded to light blue (ILLUS.)..................... **$259**

Vase, 7" h., baluster-form w/a tall waisted neck, mother-of-pearl Swirl patt., deep

rose shaded to dark yellow, Stevens & Williams, England (ILLUS. middle row, far left with other satin pieces, top of previous page) **$1,150**

Vase, 7" h., bulbous baluster-form body w/a widely flaring & crimped forked neck, mother-of-pearl Diamond Quilted patt., dark blue shaded to white & applied w/two enameled leafy stems & blossoms around the sides, English registry numbers on the bottom (ILLUS. middle row, second from left with other satin pieces, top of previous page) **$489**

Amethyst Satin Vase with Prunus

Vase, 7 3/4" h., bulbous body w/pinched-in sides below a short, whtie cylindrical neck, shaded amethyst to white exterior enameled w/white prunus blossoms on brown stems, the neck decorated w/a gold enamel band, lined in white, unsigned by numbered "III/115," England, late 19th c. (ILLUS.) **$345**

Vase, 8 1/4" h., large ovoid body tapering to a short ringed neck w/flaring rim, mother-of-pearl Swirl patt., deep pink cased in white, Stevens & Williams, England (ILLUS. back row, far left with other satin pieces, top of previous page) **$489**

Vase, 9" h., bottle-form body w/round indentations around the base, tall stick-form neck, mother-of-pearl Coinspot patt., caramel shading to white (ILLUS. back row, second from left with other satin pieces, top of previous page).... **$150-250**

Vase, 9 1/2" h., tall footed ovoid body tapering to a short flaring & crimped neck w/an applied frosted rim band, applied angled froste clear thorn handles, mother-of-pearl Diamond Quilted patt., dark shaded to pale yellow (ILLUS. back row, second from right with other satin pieces, top of previous page) **$288**

Schneider

This ware is made in France at Cristallerie Schneider, established in 1913 near Paris by Ernest and Charles Schneider. Some pieces of cameo were marked "Le Verre Francais" and others were signed "Charder."

Schneider Mark

Unusual Schneider Cameo Leafy Vase

Cameo vase, 5 1/2" h., a round clear foot applied w/a slender amethyst cylindrical stem supported a wide squatty bulbous body w/a very wide sloping shoulder centered by a short cylindrical neck, bowl w/a frosted mottled ground overlaid around the lower body wide rounded overlapping amethyst leaves trimmed w/dark yellow veining, signed w/a pink, blue & white striped cane on the underside (ILLUS.) **$1,560**

Rare Tall Schneider Cameo Vase

Cameo vase, 15 1/2" h., round foot & disk below tall flaring cylindrical body tapering to wide flaring neck, orange & burnt sienna mottled ground overlaid in deep pur-

ple & cameo cut w/large grape clusters, signed on foot (ILLUS.) **$12,075**

Deep Red Mottled Schneider Ewer

Ewer, large nearly spherical body tapering to a squatty bulbed neck w/a high arched & pointed spout, deep raspberry mottled on orange w/a small applied angular black shoulder handle, etched signature on side, 7" h. (ILLUS.) **$748**

Small Schneider Sweetmeat Dish

Sweetmeat dish, round thick foot supporting the wide cylindrical bowl w/a widely flaring rim, mottled golden orange shading into mulberry w/cobalt blue inclusions, small scratch on body, 5" d., 2 3/4" h. (ILLUS.) **$173**

Steuben

Most of the Steuben glass listed below was made at the Steuben Glass Works, now a division of Corning Glass, between 1903 and about 1933. The factory was organized by T.G. Hawkes, noted glass designer Frederick Carder, and others. Mr. Carder devised many types of glass and revived many old techniques.

AURENE

Steuben Marks

Acid Cut-Back

Acid Cut-back Vase with Gazelles

Vase, 10 1/2" h., wide bulbous ovoid Ivory body w/a wide shoulder centered by a short flaring neck, acid-cut overall w/the Art Deco Stamford patt. of leaping gazelles, satin finish, unsigned (ILLUS.).... **$2,530**

Amber

Unusual Steuben Amber Stump Vase

Vase, 6" h., stump-type, composed of three slender bumpy tree stumps in amber raised on a round Pomona green foot, Shape No. 2744, marked, stress lines near rim of one stump, rare color combination (ILLUS.) **$978**

Amethyst

Steuben Amethyst Deep Bowl

Bowl, 7 1/2" w., 4 1/4" h., a thin foot supporting the very deep rounded four-panel sides w/a rolled rim, a faint diagonally swirled optic rib design in the glass, base marked w/the Steuben fleur-de-lis mark (ILLUS.) **$489**

Pair of Steuben Amethyst Candlesticks

Candlesticks, flattened round optic ribbed foot support an applied cushioin wafer below the optic ribbed baluster-form double-knobbed stem below the tall ovoid socket w/a wide flattened rim, etched Steuben mark in block letters, 10" h., pr. (ILLUS.).. **$805**

Steuben Amethyst Console Set

Console set: compote & pair of candlesticks; the compote w/a deep amethyst round foot & clear stem supporting the shallow widely flaring ribbed bowl, each candlestick w/a domed ribbedd foot supporting the knopped baluster-form stem w/an applied clear disk supporting the tall tulip-form amethyst socket w/flaring flattened rim, each piece signed on the bottom in block letters, compote 8" d., 3 3/4" h., candlesticks 7 3/4" h., the set (ILLUS.).. **$863**

Deep Amethyst Steuben Stump Vase

Vase, 8" h., stump-style, composed of three tiered bumpy stumps on a round foot, Shape No. 2744 (ILLUS., previous page) **$432**

Aqua Marine

Scarce Steuben Aqua Marine Vase

Vase, 6" h., stump-style, composed of three tiered bumpy stumps on a round foot, Shape No. 2744 (ILLUS.) **$748**

Steuben Aqua Marine Urn-form Vase

Vase, 8 5/8" h., footed ovoid urn-form w/a wide flattened rim, Shape No. 938 (ILLUS.) **$288**

Aurene

Atomizer, a flaring base tapering to a tall slender stick-form body fitted w/a gilt-metal atomizer top, gold iridescence w/blue highlights & an engraved leafy floral design around the bottom, base signed "DeVilbiss," 9 1/4" h. (ILLUS., top next column) **$690**

Bowl, 3 7/8" d., 2 1/8" h., cylindrical base band below the wide squatty bulbous body w/a closed gently scalloped mouth, gold cover w/a greenish gold iridescence & decorated w/millefiori white blossoms & green leaves joined by criss-crossing gold vines, signed "Aurene 677," tiny scratch

on side, pin-sized open bubble near one leaf (ILLUS., middle next below) **$1,725**

Steuben Aurene DeVilbiss Atomizer

Aurene Bowl with Millefiori Blossoms

Gold Aurene & Calcite Candlestick

Candlestick, a flaring gold iridescent pedestal foot w/blue highlights supporting a cylindrical socket w/a Calcite exterior & a very wide flaring gold iridescent rim & interior, unsigned, 6" h. (ILLUS.) **$489**

Steuben Aurene & Calcite Sherbet Sets

Steuben Gold Aurene Candlesticks

Candlesticks, a wide round foot supporting the slender swelled stem w/a twisted top supporting the tall tulip-form socket, gold iridescence, base signed "Steuben Aurene 686," 8" h., pr. (ILLUS.) **$1,553**

Sherbets & matching underplates, each sherbet w/a Calcite foot & slender stem supporting the bell-shaped bowl w/gold iridescent Aurene interior, the shallow round matching underplate w/a Calcite bottom & gold Aurene top, underplates 6" d., sherbets 4" h., set of 8 (ILLUS., top of page) **$1,320**

Vase, 2 1/2" h., miniature, wide tapering ovoid body w/a short widely flaring neck, overall gold iridescence w/blue & reddish highlights, signed, Shape No. 2648 (ILLUS.) **$575**

Small Blue Aurene Flaring Vase

Vase, 4 7/8" h., a small foot below the bulbous squatty lower body w/a widely flaring trumpet top, overall dark iridescent blue, engraved signature, Shape No. 220 (ILLUS.).. **$518**

Miniature Steuben Gold Aurene Vase

Bulbous Steuben Blue Aurene Vase

Vase, 6" h., wide bulbous ovoid body tapering to a short widely flaring & flattened neck, deep blue iridescence decorated around the shoulder w/a narrow band of white heart leaves & undulating vines, bottom signed "Steuben Aurene 6299" & w/original Steuben paper label (ILLUS., previous page) **$7,015**

Blue Aurene Flora-form Steuben Vase

Vase, 8 1/4" h., 6" d., flora-form, a round foot supported a slender stem continuing to a widely flaring & ruffled rim, deep blue iridescence w/strong gold, purple & green highlights, base signed "Aurene 346" (ILLUS.).. **$1,265**

Large Gold Aurene Ovoid Vase

Vase, 8 1/2" h., wide bulbous ovoid body tapering to a short flaring neck, overall gold iridescence w/purple & blue highlights, base signed "Steuben Aurene 2683" (ILLUS.) **$805**

Cylindrical Steuben Aurene Vase

Vase, 9 3/4" h., cylindrical body w/a neck tapering to a flat rim flanked by delicate angled handles, overall gold iridescence w/magenta highlights, signed, minor surface scratches (ILLUS.) **$1,150**

Rare Blue Aurene Steuben Vase

Vase, 10 1/4" h., a flaring foot supporting the tall funnel-shaped vase in blue iridescence w/purple highlights   decorated w/an upper band of applied white heart leaves & wavy vines, signed "Steuben Aurene 1278" (ILLUS.).......................... **$5,175**

Large Bulbous Gold Aurene Vase

Vase, 11 1/4" h., wide bulbous ovoid body w/a wide rounded shoulder to a short flaring neck, overall gold iridescence w/magenta highlights, Shape No. 2683, iridescence irregular, short scratch on shoulder (ILLUS.) **$1,955**

Very Large Gold Aurene Steuben Vase

Vase, 16" h., flaring foot below the large ovoid body w/a wide shoulder centering a large trumpet neck, overall bright gold iridescence w/red & platinum highlights, base signed "Steuben Aurene 3285," very minor scratches (ILLUS) **$2,530**

Calcite
Bowl, 10" d., footed deep widely flaring sides, Calcite exterior & gold Aurene interior, ca. 1920, unmarked **$316**
Vase, 2 7/8" h., 5 5/8" d., mushroom-shaped form, a squatty bulbous Calcite body tapering to a very widely flaring & rolled rim, gold iridescent Aurene interior, Shape No. 3262, engraved "F. Carder" (ILLUS., top next column) **$575**

Small Mushroom-form Calcite Vase

Celeste Blue

Large Urn-form Celeste Blue Vase

Vase, 11" h., footed large bulbous urn-form body w/a narrow neck & wide low flaring rim, unsigned (ILLUS.) **$518**

Cluthra

Rare Large Steuben Cluthra Bowl in Frame

Bowl, 15" d., 8" h., a deep widely flaring inverted conical form w/a flat rim, white w/overall clear bubbles, resting in a scrolling wrought-iron Art Deco style holder, Shape No. 6169, scratches on interior (ILLUS.) **$2,070**

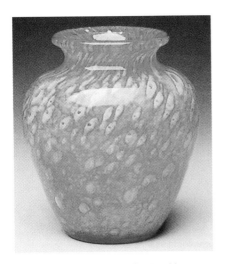

Deep Pink Steuben Cluthra Vase

Vase, 6 1/4" h., wide bulbous ovoid body tapering to a short widely flaring neck, deep pink & white swirled trapped air decoration, ground pontil, etched fleur-de-lis Steuben mark (ILLUS.) **$1,035**

Plum-colored Steuben Cluthra Vase

Vase, 10" h., footed ovoid body tapering gently to a flared rim, mottled plum & white air-trapped bubbles design, signed on the bottom w/the Steuben fleur-de-lis mark (ILLUS.)... **$1,035**
Vase, 10 1/2" h., wide bulbous ovoid body w/the wide shoulder centered by a short flaring neck, overall mottled blue & white trapped-air design, bottom drilled & plugged (ILLUS., top next column)............ **$660**

Large Bulbous Blue Cluthra Vase

Green

Steuben Green Vase in Metal Holder

Vase, 11 1/4" h., a narrow upright rectangular deep green vase fitted in a black metal holder w/four long leaf-shaped prongs resting on a four-petal foot w/curled tips, vase signed w/Steuben fleur-de-lis mark (ILLUS.).. **$403**

Grotesque

Steuben Grotesque Green to Clear Vase

Bowl-vase, deep rounded form w/widely flaring rim pulled into four points, shaded green to clear, Shape No. 7277, small flat chip beneath the base, 10 1/4" w., 6 1/2" h. (ILLUS., previous page) **$403**

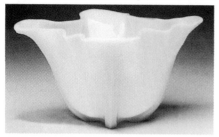

Steuben Ivory Steuben Bowl-Vase

Bowl-vase, deep rounded Ivory hander-chief-style form w/the pinched & ruffled sides pulled into four points, ground pontil, unsigned, 10 1/2" w., 5 1/2" h. (ILLUS.) **$748**

Long Grotesque Ivory Steuben Vase

Vase, 6 1/2" h., 12" l., an upright long fan-shaped Ivory body w/pinched & ruffled sides, w/original Steuben paper label (ILLUS.) **$345**

Tall Green to Clear Grotesque Vase

Vase, 10 3/4" h., a round foot supporting the tall flaring pinched & ruffled vase pulled into four points, green shaded to clear, signed w/the Steuben fleur-de-lis mark, some interior staining (ILLUS.).................. **$345**

Ivory

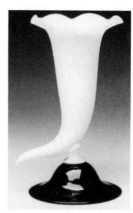

Steuben Ivory Cornucopia Vase

Cornucopia vase, a tall upright Ivory horn-shaped vase w/a flaring ruffled rim, resting on a domed black amethyst foot, marked w/the Steuben fleur-de-lis mark, 8" h. (ILLUS.) **$460**

Steuben Ivory Stump Vase

Vase, 6 3/8" h., stump-style, composed of three tiered bumpy stumps on a round foot, Shape No. 2744 (ILLUS.)................. **$633**

Bulbous Ovoid Steuben Ivory Vase

Vase, 8 1/2" h., wide bulbous ovoid body w/a wide rounded shoulder centering a short flaring neck, ground pontil, un-signed (ILLUS.) **$345**

Jade

Steuben Ivory Three-prong Vase

Vase, 10" h., three-prong grotesque design, a round foot applied w/a crimped star-shaped wafer supporting three staggered flaring triangular vases (ILLUS.)............. **$1,380**

Large Bulbous Steuben Ivory Vase

Vase, 10 1/2" h., wide bulbous ovoid body w/a wide rounded shoulder centered by a short flaring & flattened neck, 3original Steuben paper label on the bottom (ILLUS.).. **$450**

Lamp, table model, upright rectangular yellow Jade body acid-cut w/a large design of chrysanthemum buds on a leafy stem, a gilt-metal Greek key band raised on an Oriental-style footed base, gilt-metal overlapping leaf fitting below the electric socket at the top, w/fine cloth shade, body 4" w., 5 3/4" h. (ILLUS., top next column) **$2,070**

Plate, 8 1/2" d., Green Jade, dished center w/a wide flattened rim, base signed "F. Carder Steuben" (ILLUS., middle next column) **$150**

Fine Steuben Yellow Jade Lamp

Green Jade Steuben Plate

Pair Green Jade Slender Bud Vases

Vases, 8 1/4" h., bud-type, a round Alabaster foot supporting the tall slender stick-form Green Jade vase, some roughness inside one lip, pr. (ILLUS., previous page) **$288**

Pomona Green

Steuben Pomona Green Candlesticks

Candlesticks, a flaring optic ribbed foot supporting an optic ribbed baluster-shaped double-knobbed stem below the ovoid socket w/a wide flattened rim, Steuben fleur-de-lis mark on one, 10" h., pr. (ILLUS.).. **$575**

Rosaline

Miniature Steuben Rosaline Creamer

Creamer, miniature, squatty bulbous Rosaline body tapering to a wide mouth w/an arched spout, applied Alabaster handle, ground pontil, unsigned, 1 3/4" h. (ILLUS.) **$259**

Vases, 8 1/4" h., bud-type, a round Alabaster foot supporting the tall slender Rosaline cylindrical body, one signed w/the Steuben fleur-de-lis mark, some minor roughness on the inside lip of one, pr. (ILLUS., top next column) **$633**

Pair of Slender Rosaline Bud Vases

Topaz

Rare Steuben Topaz & Celeste Blue Bowl

Bowl, cov., 10 1/4" d., domed applied Celeste Blue foot w/a scalloped rim supporting the wide rounded Topaz bowl w/a wide flattened rim w/an applied rim band in Celeste Blue, the domed & pierced rigaree cover composed of alternating bands of Topaz and Celeste Blue w/a Topaz finial composed of four leaves curled in & joined at the top (ILLUS.)............... **$1,093**

Steuben Topaz & Pomona Green Bowl

Center bowl, a Pomona green flaring funnel base supporting the wide shallow Topaz optic ribbed bowl w/a rounded stepped bottom below the wide flattened rim, marked, Shape No. 3230, 4 1/2" h., 12" d. (ILLUS.) **$403**

Tyrian

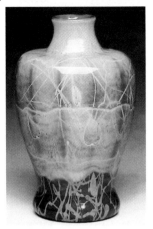

Very Rare Steuben Tyrian Vase

Vase, 7 1/2" h., a swelled botton tapering to a wide bulbous ovoid body w/a wide round shoulder tapering to a short tapering neck, an opal greenish blue ground at top shading to purplish grey at the bottom, decorated overall w/a gold heart leaf & random vine decorated, signed on the bottom "Tyrian," rare (ILLUS.) **$17,250**

Verre de Soie

Large Steuben Verre de Soie Bowl

Bowl, 11 3/4" d., 4 1/4" h., a footed very widely flaring rounded form w/a flat rim, resting on a low domed black glass base w/minor nicks (ILLUS.) **$345**

Steuben Verre de Soie Salt Dip & Sppon

Salt dip, a round foot below the deep bell-shaped bowl, overall gold iridescence, Steuben mark, accompanied by a Gorham sterling silver salt spoon, 1 5/8" h. (ILLUS.) **$115**

Verre de Soie Steuben Urn-form Vase

Vase, 8 7/8" h., footed wide urn-forn body w/a wide low rolled neck, Shape No. 938 (ILLUS.) **$288**

Stevens & Williams

This long-established English glasshouse has turned out a wide variety of artistic glasswares through the years. Fine satin glass pieces and items with applied decoration (sometimes referred to as "Matsu-No-Ke") are especially sought after today. The following represents a cross-section of its wares. Also see SATIN GLASS.

Small Stevens & Williams Satin Bowl

Bowl, 4" d., 2 3/8" h., squatty rounded form w/a wide pleated rim, mother-of-pearl ribbed satin in deep rusty red shaded to rose, creamy interior (ILLUS.) **$1,133**

Unusual Stevens & Williams Spangle Vase

Vase, 5 1/8" h., a wide flattened oblong bulbous body below a unique pulled up &

out arched neck, white interior cased
w/shaded pink spangle (ILLUS.) **$345**

Tiffany

*This glassware, covering a wide diversity of
types, was produced in glasshouses operated by
Louis Comfort Tiffany, America's outstanding
glass designer of the Art Nouveau period, from
the last quarter of the 19th century until the early
1930s. Tiffany revived early techniques and
devised many new ones.*

Various Tiffany Marks & Labels

Tiffany Gold Iridescent Candle Lamp

Candle lamp, the gold iridescent base w/a
flaring base tapering sharply to a swirled
rib cylindrical standard supporting a
cupped top holding the green glass candle w/a green pulled-feather design &
gilt-metal top fitting, the matching gold iridescent open-topped umbrella shade
w/a ruffled rim, original chimney w/gold iridescent finish, original metal hardware
stamped "The Twilight," shade & base
marked "L.C.T.," shade w/chip at top,
lamp drilled & electrified, overall 15" h.
(ILLUS.) **$1,725**

Pale Pastel Tiffany Candlesticks

Candlesticks, a wide clear iridescent round
foot below a slender clear stem topped
by a wafer supporting a pale pastel green
optic ribbed socket w/a widely flaring &
slightly cupped rim, base signed "LCT
Favrile C1890," 4" h., pr. (ILLUS.) **$1,093**

Gold Tiffany Center Bowl & Flower Frog

Center bowl, a wide flat-bottomed shallow
form w/upturned sides, centered by a cylindrical two-tier looped flower frog, overall gold iridescence, frog signed "L.C. Tiffany Favrile 7997 - 2," base of bowl
w/same signature, 10 1/4" d. (ILLUS.) ... **$1,610**

Gold Tiffany Favrile Champagne Flute

Champagne flute, a thin round gold iridescent foot & slender swelled stem supporting the wide swelled gold iridescent tulip-
form bowl, signed "Q5326 L.C. T.,"
8 3/4" h. (ILLUS.) **$978**

Tiffany Lemon Yellow Pastel Compote

Compote, open, 4 1/2" h., round clear foot w/a thin opalescent rim band, a slender applied clear stem supporting the widely flaring shallow lemon yellow pastel bowl w/a molded white feather design, signed "1701 L.C. Tiffany Favrile" (ILLUS.) **$1,208**

Tiffany Pastel Folded-side Dish

Dish, Pastel line, white opalescent foot supporting wide rounded sides w/two opposing sides folding up toward the center, deep bluish green shading to white opalescence w/radial stripes & an iridescent finish, signed on the bottom "Louis C Tiffany Favrile," 6" l. (ILLUS.) **$863**

Tiffany Blue & Pale Green Parfaits

Parfaits, a bright blue optic ribbed round foot supporting a tall elongated pear-shaped optic ribbed bowl in pale green w/light iridescence, signed on bottom "L.C.T. Favrile 31," 6" h., set of 4 (ILLUS.) **$920**

Pitcher, 6 1/4" h., cameo-type, a slightly tapering cylindrical body, a wide plain green iridescent top band above the white cameo wheel-carved body w/large peony-type flowers above leaves, applied white handle w/pale gold iridescence & wheel-carved fluting, signed on the bottom "3313P L.C. Tiffany - Favrile,"

Very Rare Cameo-Carved Tiffany Pitcher

also museum accession numbers, very rare (ILLUS.) **$14,375**

Tiffany Fuschia Pastel Plate

Plate, 8 3/4" d., Pastel line, shallow dished center w/a very wide flattened & gently scalloped rin, deep fuschia shading to clear decorated w/radiating white opalescent panels, signed on the bottom (ILLUS.) **$690**

Vine-decorated Tiffany Punch Cup

Punch cup, footed wide squatty bulbous shape slightly flared at the rim, gold iri-

descence w/purple highlights decorated
w/a band of stylized green heart leaf &
vine, applied iridescent gold handle,
base signed, 4" w. (ILLUS.) **$460**

Unusual Blue Favrile Tiffany Urn

Urn, cov., a round stepped dome foot below
the large ovoid body w/a wide flat mouth
fitted w/a tall tapering pointed cover w/a
knob finial, overall blue iridescence, base
signed "X236 8274L - L.C. Tiffany Favrile
B," cover signed "X236 9408L A," overall
9 1/2" h. (ILLUS.) **$2,933**

Tiny White Opal Tiffany Vase

Vase, 2 3/4" h., miniature, ovoid body tapering to a small flared mouth, tiny integral
loop handles at the sides, iridescent white
opal shading to clear, signed (ILLUS.) **$345**
Vase, 4" h., small flat-bottomed wide ovoid
body tapering to a wide flat mouth, iridescent gold decorated w/a green heart leaf
& vine design, base signed "L.C.T.
W3928" (ILLUS., top next column)......... **$1,208**
Vase, 6" h., bud-type, squatty bulbous wide
base tapering to a tall slender stick neck,
overall blue iridescent finish, signed
"1029-2432N - LC Tiffany Inc. Favrile"
(ILLUS., middle next column)................ **$2,070**

Small Tiffany Vase with Leaf & Vine Design

Blue Iridescent Favrile Bud Vase

Small Tiffany Ovoid Gold Vase

Fine Venetian Blown Stemware Set

Vase, 6" h., round foot & tall ovoid body tapering to a small trumpet neck, overall rich gold iridescence w/flashes of pink, base signed "L.C. Tiffany Favrile 2318J" (ILLUS., previous page) **$450**

Very Tall Decorated Tiffany Favrile Vase

Vase, 19 3/4" h., tapering conical lower body continuing to a very tall slender cylindrical neck, dark gold iridescence decorated around the base w/a band of dark green pulled-feather designs, signed "1970L L.C. Tiffany Favrile" (ILLUS.) **$4,313**

Pair of Tiffany Gold Wine Glasses

Wine glasses, rounded gold iridescent foot & very slender stem supporting the deep rounded gold iridescent bowl wheelcarved around the rim w/a fleur-de-lis band, one w/reddish iridescence, the other w/green iridescence, one signed "L.C.T.," the other "L.C.T. Favrile," 5 3/4" h., pr. (ILLUS.) **$1,208**

Venetian

Venetian glass has been made for six centuries on the island of Murano, where it continues to be produced. The skilled glass artisans developed numerous techniques, subsequently imitated elsewhere.

Modern Artist-done Venetian Sculpture

Sculpture, a large upright disc w/a flat base, a design cased in colorless glass representing a stylized fiery red sun being swallowed by the enclosing dark blue to black sky & turbulent water, by Romano Dona, ca. 2003, weight of 50 lbs., 14"w., 15" h. (ILLUS.)............................ **$1,725**

Stemware set: ten red-wine goblets, thirteen white-wine goblets, eight sherbets & eleven bowl-form champagnes; each w/swirled flaring green gilt iridized bowls & feet joined by gilt serpent-form stems, early to mid-20th c., the set (ILLUS. of part, top of page).................................. **$3,680**

Vase, 10 1/2" h., spherical body tapering to a short flaring neck, smoky ground internally decorated w/amber pulled & leaf-form designs & gold leaf, probably 20th c. **$690**

Pair of Swirled Venetian Vases

Vases, 11" h., footed baluster-form body w/a tall flaring trumpet neck w/ruffled rim, the clear funnel base supporting the body composed of swirling alternating bands of aventurine & white, probably 20th c., pr. (ILLUS.).. **$150-250**

Verlys

Verlys originated in France in the mid-1930s and was produced by the French Holoplane Co. A branch, Verlys in America, soon was opened in Newark, Ohio, and produced wares similar to the French examples but less expensive. Various Art Deco designs, some resembling Lalique glass, were blown or molded in clear, frosted clear and colors. Between 1955-57 the Heisey Company used some Verlys molds.

A Verlys France

French Verlys Mark

Verlys Vase with Chinese Man Design

Vase, 9 1/8" h., footed cylindrical colorless body w/a wide flat rim, molded in relief w/the tall figure of a Chinese man carry-ing a parasol & walking through a garden, Greek key design around the foot, signed on base (ILLUS.).. **$173**

Pair of Verlys Four Seasons Vases

Vases, 8 1/8" h., colorless slightly flaring cylindrical form w/wide flat rim, each molded on two sides w/female figures, a total of four representing the four seasons, each artist-signed by Carl Schmitz & signed in script, pr. (ILLUS.) **$317**

Wave Crest

Now much sought after, Wave Crest was produced by the C.F. Monroe Co., Meriden, Connecticut, in the late 19th and early 20th centuries from opaque white glass blown into molds.

It was then hand-decorated in enamels and metal trim was often added. Boudoir accessories such as jewel boxes, hair receivers, etc., predominated.

WAVE CREST WARE

Wave Crest Mark

Wave Crest Cracker Jar

Cracker jar, cov., Helmschmeid Swirl mold, pink ground decorated around the top w/white daises & green leafy stems, ruffled silver plate rim, domed cover & bail handle, 7 1/4" h. (ILLUS)........................ **$431**

Wave Crest Egg Crate Dresser Box

Dresser box w/hinged cover, Egg Crate mold, alternating turquoise & white panels decorated w/pink-stemmed yellow flowers, four footed embossed brass base, 5" w, 5 1/2" h. (ILLUS.)................ **$1,265**

Wave Crest Rare Egg Crate Dresser Box

Dresser box w/hinged cover, Egg Crate mold, shaded dark brown to tan ground decorated w/yellow & white mums, ornate ruffled brass collar & brass base w/scroll feet molded w/ cupid faces, marked, 6 3/4" w., 6 3/4" h. (ILLUS.)...... **$3,795**

Large Wave Crest Jewelry Box

Jewelry box w/hinged cover, Baroque Shell mold, white ground decorated on the cover w/small pink & white blossoms

& green leafy stems, brass fittings, unsigned, 7" d. (ILLUS.)................................ **$345**

Wave Crest Letter Holder

Letter holder, Egg Crate mold, upright rectangular shape w/brass scroll-trimmed rim band, shaded white & pink ground decorated w/red, white & pink flowers & pale green leaves, 4" h. (ILLUS.).............. **$403**

Fine Decorated Wave Crest Muffineer

Muffineer, Helmschmied Swirl mold, bulbous ovoid shape w/original silver plate lid, h.p. w/large white & deep rose blossoms & green leaves, unmarked, 3 1/8" h. (ILLUS.) **$345**

Webb

This glass is made by Thomas Webb & Sons of Stourbridge, one of England's most prolific glasshouses. Numerous types of glass, including cameo, have been produced by this firm through the years. The company also produced various types of novelty and "art" glass during the late Victorian period. Also see BURMESE.

Cameo vase, 4 3/4" h., in the Japonesque taste, ovoid body tapering to ringed cylindrical neck w/flared rim, wheel-cut w/ flowers & dragonflies revealing embedded swimming foil fish & a caged foil canary, the ground stipple-finished & gilt, the neck heavily enameled w/floral banding, enameling probably by J. Kretschman & the gilding by Jules Barbé, impressed on the pontil w/segmented fan-frammed reserve centering "Webb" (ILLUS., next page)............................. **$23,000**

Very Rare Webb Cameo Vase

Rare Webb Gem Cameo Vase

Cameo vase, 8 1/4" h., small knob feet support the squatty bulbous lower body decorated around the base & top w/cameo-cut bands w/florette diamonds & triangular enameled in gold & pink, the main body decorated w/five large oval cameo-cut panels w/a feathered leaf & link design in heavy gold & separated by a continuous undulating band of green leafy vines, the lower body centered by a tall cylindrical neck decorated w/four tall pointed arch panels each carved w/spiraling vines of green leaves & pink & yellow blossoms, the panels surrounded by heavy gold borders carved w/scrolling acanthus leaf vines, decorated by Jules Barbé, signed "Thomas Webb & Sons - Gem Cameo" (ILLUS.) **$9,775**

Westmoreland

In 1890 Westmoreland opened in Grapeville, Pennsylvania, and as early as the 1920s was producing colorwares in great variety. Cutting and decorations were many and are generally under appreciated and undervalued. Westmoreland was a leading producer of milk glass in "the antique style." The company closed in 1984 but some of their molds continued in use by others.

Early Westmoreland Label & Mark

Animal covered dish, dog, ribbed base, blue & white milk glass................................. **$95**

Basket, molded handle, "Woolworth" patt., green.. **$32**

Candleholders, low one-light, Ring & Petal patt., Bermuda Blue, 3 1/2" h., pr. (ILLUS., top next page).. **$36**

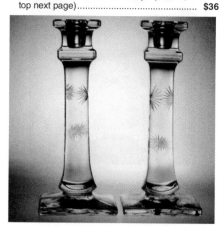

No. 1012 Line Candleholders

Candleholders, tall, one-light, No. 1012 Line w/cutting, clear, 7 1/2" h. (ILLUS.)....... **$48**

Figural Mantel Clock Candy Container

Ring and Petal Bermuda Blue Candleholders

Candy container, figural Mantel Clock patt., Brandywine Blue, 2 1/2" w., 3" h. (ILLUS., previous page) **$27**

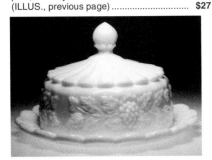

Paneled Grape Pattern Milk Glass Cheese Dish

Cheese dish, cov., round, Paneled Grape patt., milk glass, 7" d. (ILLUS.).................... **$58**
Cigarette box, cov., figural turtle, amber stain... **$42**

Ball Stem Compote

Compote, 7 1/2" h., 8" d., ball stem, spray-cased black, amber stain, cut to clear (ILLUS.) **$150**

Sawtooth Pattern Golden Sunset Compote

Compote bowl, 13" d., flared & high footed, Sawtooth patt., Golden Sunset (ILLUS.)..... **$75**
Creamer & open sugar, footed, English Hobnail patt., pink, pr. **$48**
Model of a revolver, solid, black, 5" l. **$175**
Pitcher bulbous, English Hobnail patt., ruby, 38 oz. **$295**

Milk Glass Pitcher with Monk Decor

Pitcher, 9" h., tankard-type w/ringed base & stag horn-shaped handle, milk glass w/a painted brown background decorated w/a black decal decoration of a monk playing a violin, early 20th c. (ILLUS., previous page) **$145**

Plate, 8 1/2" d., scallooped, Woolworth patt., pink... **$26**

Server, octagonal w/center dolphin-shaped handle, Blue Mist.. **$95**

Vase (straw jar), 10" h., English Hobnail patt., pink.. **$225**

GLOBE MAPS

English Signed Celestial Globe

Celestial globe, the openwork round framework enclosing an Earth-centered solar systam, the octagonal platform frame decorated w/celestial motifs w/bone edging raised on four square tapering reeded legs ending in gilt paw feet & joined by four square stretchers, Woodward, London, 19th c., 32" d., 51" h. (ILLUS.) **$4,830**

Belgian Terrestrial Globe on Stand

Terrestrial globe, large hand-colored globe in a four-legged ebonized fruitwood stand w/baluster- and ring-turned legs joined by a turned cross-stretcher, w/a medial zodiac ring, Merzback and Falk, Brussels, Belgium, 19th c., 16" d., 18" h. (ILLUS.)... **$546**

Louis XV-Style Globe Map

Terrestrial globe, Louis XV-Style, the Provincial style carved & turned oak stand w/cabriole legs joined by three turned stretchers joined by a central drop post, the serpentine apron carved w/scrolling florals, the globe w/a metal-banded meridian band, France, late 19th c., 23" d., 30" h. (ILLUS.) **$316**

Small American-Made Globe Map

Terrestrial globe, paper mat cover a wooden core, round maker mark to the left of North America, D.C. & A. Murdock, West Boylston, Massachusetts, ca. 1835-40, some stains, some rub marks, holes at end for mounting in a stand, 5" d. (ILLUS.)........ **$862**

HALLOWEEN COLLECTIBLES

Although Halloween is an American tradition and holiday, we must credit the Scottish for bringing it to the United States. The earliest symbols of Halloween appeared around the turn of the 20th century. During Victorian times, Halloween parties became popular in the United States. Decorations were seasonal products, such as pumpkins, cornstalks, vegetables, etc. Many early decorations were imported from Germany, only to be followed by increased demand in the United States during World War I, when German imports ceased.

Today Halloween collectibles are second in demand only to Christmas collectibles. Remembering the excitement one felt as a child dressing up in costume, going treat or treating, carving pumpkins, bobbing for apples, etc., the colors of orange and black trigger nostalgia for our youth for many of us.

The variety of Halloween collectibles is immense. Whether it be noisemakers, jack o' lanterns, candy containers, paper or plastic goods, candy molds or costumes, with the availability, the choice is yours.

Remember to buy the best, be it the very old or not so old. Search antiques shops, flea markets and house sales.

Goblin, Cat & Pumpkin Candy Container

Candy container, composition, figure of a goblin & black cat on a pumpkin, colorful paint, Germany, some flaking on cat, early 20th c., 5" h. (ILLUS.) **$863**

Pumpkin-head Witch Candy Container

Candy container, all-composition, figure of a pumpkin-headed witch w/a pointed black hat, red dress w/yellow bow & white apron, carrying a real broom, head removes, early 20th c., 5" h. (ILLUS.) **$403**

Colonial Veggie Man Candy Container

Candy container, composition, figure of a veggie man seated on a log wearing colorful colonial-style clothing w/black hat, orange & red shirt & green paints, early 20th c., 4 1/4" h. (ILLUS.)......................... **$575**

Boy on Jack-o'-Lantern Candy Container

Candy container, composition, figural boy seated atop a grinning Jack-o'-lantern, early 20th c., 3 1/2" h. (ILLUS.) **$460**

Pumpkin-head Sailor Candy Container

Candy container, composition pumpkin-
headed body wearing a blue & white sail-
or suit, some separation at back of neck,
small chip on rear of leg, early 20th c.,
5 1/2" h. (ILLUS., previous page) **$460**

Pumpkin Head Old Lady Candy Container

Candy container, composition, pumpkin-
headed old lady holding a closed umbrella, painted in orange, white, black, red &
lavender, small chip to underside of
head, early 20th c., 3" h. (ILLUS.) **$288**

Cat Pulling Pumpkin Coach Candy Container

Candy container, figural, composition, a
standing black cat pulling a large pumpkin-
shaped coach container, all- original, Germany, early 20th c., 3 1/2" h. (ILLUS.) **$633**

Candy container, figural, composition
pumpkin-headed veggie girl wearing a
black dress & pulling a large pumpkin-
shaped coach container on green molded wheels, stem broken on pumpkin
coach, container missing outer lid, early
20th c., 3 1/4" h. (ILLUS., top of next col-
umn) **$460**

Candy container, papier-mache, black cat
seated atop an orange pumpkin, original
paper stopper marked "Germany," early
20th c., 6" h. (ILLUS., middle of next col-
umn) **$374**

Veggie Girl & Coach Candy Container

Black Cat & Pumpkin Candy Container

Fine Witch on Shoe Candy Container

Candy container, papier-maché & composition, large witch w/composition head &
felt clothing atop a large brown & green
Dutch-style shoe, early 20th c., possible
hat repaint, 4" h. (ILLUS.) **$978**

Veggie Man on Tree Stump Decoration

Decoration, papier-maché, figural comic seated veggie man atop a large brown & green tree trunk, chip on bottom of tree stump, early 20th c., 3 3/4" h. (ILLUS.) **$345**

Rare Pumpkin Man Spherical Figure

Decoration, pumpkin man w/a spherical molded paper head on a large spherical body w/wire & wood arms & legs, crepe paper collar, rattles when shaken, early 20th c., standing 10" h. (ILLUS. sitting) **$978**

Rare Kneeling Pumpkin Man Lantern

Lantern, composition, a large Jack-o'-lantern head w/original paper inserts above a kneeling body in orange, white & green, early 20th c., 5 1/2" h. (ILLUS.) **$920**

Jack-o'-Lantern with Hat Lantern

Lantern, papier-maché Jack-o'-lantern w/original colored paper insert & string hair, wearing a black Pilgrim-style top hat w/a wire bail handle, early 20th c., 6" h. (ILLUS.) **$661**

Halloween Jack-in-the-box Toy

Toy, Jack-in-the-box, a lime green composition veggie head on cloth body springs from wooden box covered in printed paper w/a scene of Victorian girls on the front, minor losses & chipping, late 19th c., closed 4" h. (ILLUS. open) **$270**

Halloween Jack-in-the-Box Toy

Toy, Jack-in-the-box, flesh-toned pumpkin-headed figure w/a cloth body pops out of a wooden box covered w/red-patterned paper w/a color lithograph on the front of a young Victorian boy & girl, early 20th c., 4" h. (ILLUS., previous page) **$288**

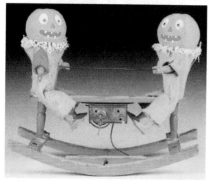

Rare Pumpkin Figures on Seesaw Windup Toy

Toy, windup seesaw-type, two composition pumpkin-headed figures w/carved wood bodies dressed in cloth outfits sit at each end of a wooden rocker base, working, early 20th c., 7 1/2" l., 6" h. (ILLUS.)...... **$2,040**

HORSE COLLECTIBLES

Pot Metal Souvenir Horse

Model of horse, copper tone pot metal, w/molded saddle, bridle & reins, souvenir of Betsy Ross House, Philadelphia, 3 1/2" (ILLUS.) **$18-25**

Flocked Horse

Model of horse, flocked, black w/white hair tail & braided red saddle & braided orange mane, 1960s, 3 3/4" (ILLUS.)........ **$15-25**

Durham Industries Draft Horse

Model of horse, metal, draft horse painted grey w/white hooves & pinned mane, darker grey tail, Durham Industries, 1977, 3" (ILLUS.) **$10-15**

Reproduction Ching Dynasty Horse

Model of horse, metal on wood base, reproduction of Ching Dynasty model, Alva, Art Institute of Chicago, 1960s, 2 1/2" (ILLUS.)....................................... **$30-40**

Reproduction of Mesopotamian Horse

Model of horse, metal on wood base, reproduction of Mesopotamian model, Alva - Art Institute of Chicago, 1 3/4" (ILLUS., previous page) **$30-40**

Mexican Pottery Horse

Model of horse, Mexican pottery, long, dachshund-shaped body, decorated w/colorful painted floral designs in yellow, green, blues, reds & white, Mexico, 3 3/4" (ILLUS.) **$8-15**

Plastic Appaloosa Horse

Model of horse, plastic, appaloosa, Hong Kong, 1960s, 5 1/4" (ILLUS.) **$15-20**

Hartland Plastics Appaloosa

Model of horse, plastic, appaloosa w/glossy painted finish, Hartland Plastics, 1960s, 6 1/2 x 7" (ILLUS.) **$12-20**

Hartland Plastics Buckskin Horse

Model of horse, plastic, buckskin w/black mane, tail & stockings, Hartland Plastics, 1960s, 5 1/2 x 7 1/2" (ILLUS.) **$8-15**

Hartland Plastics Model of "Silver"

Model of horse, plastic, white horse w/black saddle bridle & reins, small version of "Silver," Hartland Plastics, 4 1/2" (ILLUS.), ... **$12-20**

Miniature Running Horse

Model of horse, stainless steel, miniature of running horse, 1980s, 3/4" (ILLUS.)... **$15-20**

INDIAN ART & ARTIFACTS

Items are based on prehistoric stone artifacts of the Northeastern United States. Values are of whole, complete specimens. Breaks would knock prices down. Colorful flint or stone would increase the value as will any item with line designs or effigies involved.

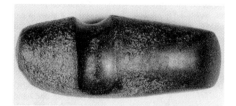

Early Hohocum Stone Adz-Axe

Adz-ax, Hohocom, hand-worked stone, 7 1/2" l. (ILLUS.).. **$345**

Maria & Julian San Ildefonso Bowl

Bowl, San Ildefonso, pottery, blackware squatty bulbous form w/a wide flat mouth, matte swag & leaf design around the mouth, signed "Maria and Julian," ca. 1940, 4" d., 3" h. (ILLUS.)........................ **$748**

Navajo Blanket with Yei Figure

Blanket, Navajo, Yei design, tightly woven in handspun wool, in natural ivory & deep brown bands, centering a single standing female figure wearing a brown dress & vibrant red shoes, only normal wear, 20th c., 16 x 30" (ILLUS.)................................. **$316**

Santa Clara Bowl by Madeline Naranjo

Bowl, Santa Clara, pottery, blackware w/a deeply incised serpent & arrow design around the body, signed "Madeline Sta Clara," by Madeline Naranjo, 8" d., 5 1/2" h. (iLLUS.)...................................... **$575**

Large Grouping of Indian Basketry Bowls & Jars

Bowl, Mono, coiled basketry, four sets of stacked arrows or quail topknots form the design, first half 20th c., 8 1/2" d., 4 1/4" h. (ILLUS. bottom row right with large group of basketry pieces)............................... **$259**

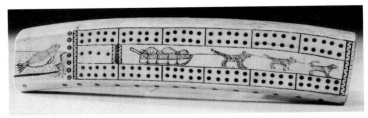

Early Inuit Ivory Engraved Cribbage Board

Bowl, Southwestern, possibly Papago or Pima, coiled basketry, flat bottom w/flaring cylindrical sides, a repeating design of dogs & human figures, laced rim, slight stitch loss on base, first half 20th c., 12 1/2" d., 7" h. (ILLUS. top row left with large group of basketry pieces, bottom previous page) **$863**

Bowl, Pima, coiled basketry, wide shallow form w/a repeated design of complex fret motifs emanating from four directions & centered w/floating square elements, first half 20th c., 13 1/8" d., 3 1/2" h. (ILLUS. middle row center with grouping of basketry pieces, bottom previous page)

.... **$776**

Bowl, San Carlos Apache, coiled basketry, wide shallow form w/a saguaro & cross motif emanating from a center surrounded by human & dog designs, complex fret band w/cross & bar designs around the rim, first half 20th c., 15" d., 3" h. (ILLUS. middle row right with large grouping of basketry pieces, bottom previous page)

.... **$3,680**

Bowl, Western Apache, coiled basketry, a double floral center design, a band of human figures beneath a mountain band border, mark of maker evident, body & rim damage, first half 20th c., 15" d., 4 1/2" h. (ILLUS. middle row left with large grouping of basketry pieces, bottom previous page) **$1,380**

Cribbage board, Inuit, carved ivory, flattened tusk engraved w/a dog sled & seal on one side & a cityscape, possibly Nome, Alaska, on the other, inscribed "Nome Alaska 1903," 8 3/4" l. (ILLUS., top of page) **$575**

San Ildefonso Pottery Jar by Tonita

Jar, San Ildefonso, pottery, blackware, widely flaring round bottom half w/a sharply tapering shoulder decorated w/a feather design around the wide flat mouth, signed "Tonita," 7" d., 4 1/4" h. (ILLUS.)... **$460**

Jar, Panamint, coiled basketry, squatty bulbous body w/an angled shoulder & wide cylindrical neck, a complex fret design around the neck & a complex chuckualla & cross design around the sides, mark of maker evident, first half 20th c., 6 1/2" d., 5 1/8" h. (ILLUS. bottom row left with large grouping of basketry pieces, bottom previous page) **$1,092**

Jar, Papago, split-stitch basketry, widely flaring round sides w/a rounded shoulder to the wide, short flaring neck, decorated w/cross designs separating radiating lightning designs & a whirling log on the bottom rim, first half 20th c., 9 1/2" d., 7 1/4" h. (ILLUS. top row right with large grouping of basketry pieces, bottom previous page) **$460**

Model of a canoe, Woodlands, birch bark, traditional design w/wrapped seams, orange rim band & painted stylized blossoms, ca. 1940, 22 3/4" l., 6 1/2" h. (ILLUS., bottom of page)........................... **$345**

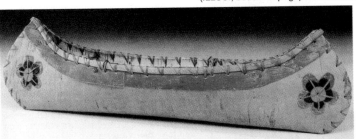

Model of Large Birch Bark Canoe

Navajo Squash Blossom Necklace

Necklace, Navajo, "squash blossom" design in silver & turquoise, 15" l. (ILLUS.) **$288**

Early Beaded Pouch & Tobacco Bag

Rare Large & Boldly Decorated Laguna Pottery Olla

Olla, Laguna, pottery, large squatty bulbous shape tapering to a wide flat mouth, decorated w/orange parallelograms pendant from the rim, stylized birds & leafed berry designs, checkered & foliate medallions separated by Chaco-scroll designs, red band on interior & at base, portion of rim missing, rim repair, small puncture hole on girth, first half 20th c, 13 1/2" d., 11 1/2" h. (ILLUS.) **$11,500**

Pouch, Southern Plains, beaded leather, dispatch-style flat bag w/beaded lazy stitched panel in white heart red, greasy yellow, dark blue & dark green on a white bead bround, reuse of commercially tanned leather, flap w/nickle silver concho & leather tie, leather handle & decorative rawhide ties at sides, possibly Sioux or Kiowa or Arapaho, 19th c., 8 1/4" w., 19" l. (ILLUS. right with beaded tobacco bag, top next column) **$3,335**

Navajo Rug with Diamond Designs

Rug, Navajo, Western Reservation, a large zigzag diamond center design flanked by smaller diamond & cross designs, in natural, dark brown & light brown, ca. 1930, 57 x 75" (ILLUS.) **$200-400**

Tapestry, Navajo, Yeibechai-type, woven male dancers led by Talking god, tones of blue w/brown & russet w/white & black wool on a grey wool ground, 24 x 25" (ILLUS., next page) **$460**

Tobacco bag, Plains, beaded leather, sinew-sewn lazy stitched in white heart red, dark blue, green, sky blue beads on a white bead ground, stylized star w/stepped tepee motif & feathers, reverse w/a geometric design panel & feathers, tin cone dangles w/horsehair, quilled panel missing some quills, small amount of bead loss, late 19th c., 7" w., 30" l. (ILLUS. right with beaded pouch, previous page) **$2,415**

Navajo Yeibechai Tapestry Weaving

JEWELRY

Antique (1800-1920)

Ornate Edwardian Bar Pin

Bar pin, diamond, seed pearl & platinum, composed of openwork arched & oblong side panels centered by a narrow bar all centered by a wheel-like ring, mounted overall w/bead- and bezel-set old European-cut diamond mélée & seed pearls, platinum-topped 14k gold mount, Edwardian, England, early 20th c. (ILLUS.) **$1,528**

Gold & Enamel Art Nouveau Barrette

Barrette, plique-a-jour enamel & 14k yellow gold, Art Nouveau style, long oval shape enclosing undulating gold leaves & an iris

blossoms highlighted by a small diamond & framed by lavender enamel, hallmark of Riker Bros., early 20th c., 5/8 x 1 7/8" (ILLUS.) **$1,528**

Ornate Gem-set Gold Belt Buckle

Belt buckle, gem-set 14k yellow gold, Art Nouveau style, the two lobed & rounded sections stamped w/scrolling designs of stylized fish & cattails, accented w/old mine-cut diamonds & small circular-cut red spinels, hallmark of Sloan & Co., late 19th - early 20th c. (ILLUS.) **$1,293**

Bracelet, beryl, seed pearl & gilt-metal, composed of a large oval central plaque flanked by scrolling pierced links & small plaques, each plaque centered by a large emerald-cut foil-backed pale green beryl surrounded by a circle of green pastes & highlighted w/seed pearls, gilt-metal mount, 19th c., 7" l. (ILLUS. of part, bottom of page) **$999**

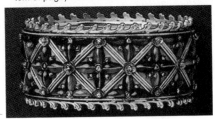

Rare Renaissance-style French Bracelet

Bracelet, chrysoberyl, enamel, diamond & gold, cuff-style, Renaissance Revival style, the wide band set w/cat's-eye quatrefoil designs punctuated by rose-cut diamond florettes joined by applied wirework on a pale blue enameled ground, white & black enamel accents, gadrooned edge, hallmark of Falize Freres, France & French guarantee stamps, enamel loss, one diamond & cat's-eye missing, 19th c., inside circumference 6 1/2" (ILLUS.) **$56,400**

Early Beryl & Seed Pearl Bracelet

Bracelet, peridot & 14k yellow gold, bangle-type, Art Nouveau style, the openwork gold frame decorated w/stylized looping leaves alternating w/six bezel-set step-cut peridot, Whiteside & Blank hallmark, early 20th, interior circumference 7 5/8" d. (ILLUS. top with other Art Nouveau bangle bracelet)........................... **$1,293**

Bangle-style Spinel & Diamond Bracelet

Bracelet, red spinel, diamond & gold, bangle-type, a narrow hinged mount prong-set on the top w/a band of graduating oval-cut spinels alternating w/pairs of small old mine-cut diamond mélée, silver-topped 14k gold mount, 19th c. (ILLUS.) **$1,763**

Bracelet, seed pearl, sapphire & 18k yellow gold, composed of rectangular foliate links w/lines of seed pearls spaced by bezel-set French-cut sapphires, ca. 1900, 7 3/8" l. **$1,998**

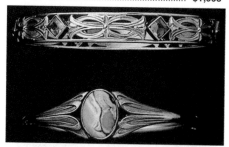

Two Art Nouveau Bangle Bracelets

Bracelet, turquoise & gold, bangle-type, Art Nouveau style, a large central oval bezel-set turquoise cabochon flanked by stylized lotus blossoms, Sloan & Co. hallmark & dated 1887 (ILLUS. bottom with other Art Nouveau bangle bracelet) **$1,058**

Russian Enamel & Gold Locket-Bracelet

Bracelet with locket, enamel, diamond & gold, bangle-style, the top w/a large round hinged locket decorated in the center w/a round blue enamel boss w/a leaf sprig design highlighted w/small rose-cut diamonds enclosed by a scalloped flora-form frame, the tapering

sides engraved w/delicate florals, Russian assay marks, 19th c., interior circumference 5 3/4" (ILLUS.).................. **$1,410**

One of Two Early Enameled Bracelets

Bracelets, enamel & gold, bangle-style, engraved floral & foliate devices on a black enameled background, 18k yellow gold mount, 5 7/8" interior diameter, Victorian, pr. (ILLUS. of one) **$1,645**

Fine Edwardian Amethyst & Diamond Brooch

Brooch, amethyst & diamond, oblong quatrefoil design centered by a clipped-corner amethyst within a pierced frame bead- and bezel-set overall w/old mine-, single- and European-cut diamonds, platinum & 18k gold mount, in a fitted box marked "Jays of London," Edwardian, missing brooch attachment (ILLUS.)...... **$5,405**

Victorian Amethyst & Seed Pearl Brooch

Brooch, amethyst, ruby, seed pearl & 18k yellow gold, centered by a large oval-cut amethyst framed by split seed pearls & circular-cut rubbies, gold mount, in original fitted box, Victorian (ILLUS.) **$823**

Krementz & Co. Amethyst & Pearl Brooch

Brooch, amethyst, seed pearl & 14k yellow gold, a large oval facet-cut amethyst enclosed in an openwork looped gold mount accented by seed pearls, hallmark of Krementz & Co., late 19th - early 20th c. (ILLUS., previous page) **$705**

Diamond & Gem-set Butterfly Brooch

Brooch, diamond, gem-set & gold, model of a butterfly, the wings & body bead-set w/opals, rose-cut diamonds & circular-cut sapphires, emerald & ruby mélée, silver-topped 14k yellow gold mount, one mélée w/chip, ca. 1910 (ILLUS.) **$1,763**

Art Nouveau Calla Lily Blossoms Brooch

Brooch, enamel & 18k yellow gold, Art Nouveau style model of a calla lily, the pale shaded blue to white enameled petal centered by a stamen & base bead-set w/yellow full-cut diamond mélée, early 20th c. (ILLUS.) **$1,116**

Antique Garnet & Diamond Bow Brooch

Brooch, garnet, diamond & 18k yellow gold, designed as a bow centered by a faceted rectangular garnet w/the ribbon set w/old European-, single- and mine-cut diamonds, two cultured pearl accents, gold mount, late 19th - early 20th c. (ILLUS.) **$823**

Large Garnet & Pearl Spider Brooch

Brooch, garnet, pearl & diamond, model of a large spider, a large cabochon almandite garnet forming the body, a pearl head & rose-cut diamond eyes & gold legs, 14k yellow gold mount, ca. 1920 (ILLUS.) **$588**

Art Nouveau Gold Medallion Brooch

Brooch, gold (14k yellow), Art Nouveau style, a round medallion depicting a profile bust of Hermes framed by openwork loop frame, the reverse depicting an oval on a fruiting branch, European hallmark, late 19th - early 20th c. (ILLUS.) **$588**

Fine Victorian Diamond Flower Brooch

Brooch, opal, diamond, ruby & 14k yellow gold, modeled as a long-stemmed flower, the carved six-petal opal flower centered by an old European-cut center surrounded by a small ring of ruby mélées, a second stem topped by a teardrop-shaped opal, a pair lof large serrated leaves set w/old mine cut diamonds, the double stems & ribbon wrap band also set w/diamonds, backing w/silver-topped 14k yellow gold, late 19th c. (ILLUS.) **$3,163**

Outstanding Opal & Diamond Brooch

Brooch/pendant, opal, diamond & demantoid garnet, centered by a large oval Australion peacock opal framed by two narrow rows of bead-set single- and old European-cut diamonds, w/calibre-cut demantoid garnets in four crossed bands, platinum-topped 14k gold mount, removable brooch fittings, ca. 1910 (ILLUS., previous page) **$18,800**

Buckle pin, gold (14k), Art Nouveau style, flattened & slightly curved wide oval form w/low-relief sinuous vine motifs, a pair of narrow bars extending across the top from one end, a hinged pin closure at the back, inscribed w/owner's name, also signed by maker Drosten, ca. 1900 .... **$558**

Victorian Shell Cameo with Landscape

Cameo brooch, carved shell, oval, cameo-carved w/a landscape showing a medieval man leading a rearing stallion, a stone castle in the background, in a gold-plated mount, late 19th - early 20th c. (ILLUS.) **$316**

Lovely Hardstone Portrait Cameo

Cameo brooch, hardstone, a large deeply carved profile bust of a classical lady

w/a floral garland in her hair against the dark brown background, in a delicate scrolling 14k gold frame accented w/seed pearls, French guarantee stamp, 19th c. (ILLUS.) **$2,703**

Early Hardstone Cameo in Fancy Mount

Cameo pendant, carved hardstone, enamel & 18k yellow gold, the oval cameo boldly carvedd w/the bust portrait of a classical lady, the gold frame trimmed w/polychrome champlevé enamel on the front & back, nick on the cameo face, 19th c. (ILUS.) **$1,116**

Cameo pendant, hardstone & 14k gold, a carnelian agate cameo within an oval frame w/applied foliate designs & a flexible fringe, suspended on a gold chain, Victorian, 18" l. (pendant bail missing suspended element) **$441**

Lovely Victorian Hardstone Cameo

Cameo pendant, hardstone & 14k yellow gold, the oval cameo w/a black ground boldly carved w/a large profile bust of a classical lady w/fabric headwrap trimmed w/a dark brown floral sprig, in a wide oval mount w/a twisted wire band, boxed, 19th c. (ILLUS.) **$1,880**

Rare Gem-set Gold Art Nouveau Choker

Early Turquoise & Gold Choker

Rare Cameo in Gem-set Enameled Frame

Cameo pendant, the oval shell cameo carved w/a scene of a classical woman driving a chariot, mounted in a flaring oval frame decorated w/polychrome champleve enamel & suspending a pearl, hung on two thin gold chains from a top segment centered by a cabochon ruby & suspending a smaller pearl, further enameling on the back, 20k yellow gold mount, 19th c. (ILLUS.) **$2,820**

Choker, gem-set 14k yellow gold, Art Nouveau style, composed of openwork looped & serpentine links highlighted w/seed pearls, diamonds, rubies, sapphires or turquoise, joined by trace link chains, American hallmark, late 19th - early 20th c., 13" l. (ILLUS. of part, top of page) **$3,819**

Choker, turquoise & 14k yellow gold, composed of six large oval turquoise cabochons joined by triple delicate trace link chains, ca. 1900, 13" l. (ILLUS. of part, second from top) **$764**

Cross pendant, gem-set 18k gold, the top center & end of each arm bezel-set w/a large circular-cut amethyst or emerald, four pearls near the center, applied bead & wirework accents, 19th c. **$2,938**

Gold Art Nouveau Cuff Links

Cuff links, gold (14k yellow), Art Nouveau style, a double-link design w/the oval segments stamped w/the head of a roaring lion, partial American hallmark, possibly Krementz & Co., pr. (ILLUS.) **$470**

Gold & Ancient Coin Cuff Link

Cuff links, gold (18k) & ancient coin, each set w/a silver denarius depicting a helmeted Roma, signed by Wiese, partially worn French guarantee stamps, pr. (ILLUS. of one, previous page) **$1,998**

Early Quartz-set Gold Cuff Links

Cuff links, quartz & 14k yellow gold, the oval top set w/gold quartz tablets, signed "H & Co.," one link w/a dent in terminal, 19th c., pr. (ILLUS.)................................... **$323**

Victorian Pink Coral Carved Earrings

Earrings, pink coral, the top carved as a small fly above a suspended carved flower over three teardrops, gilt-metal mounts, 19th c., pr. (ILLUS.) **$294**

Fine Art Nouveau Gold Hair Comb

Hair comb, tortoiseshell, 14k yellow gold & seed pearl, Art Nouveau style, the top w/a curved rectangular gold frame enclosing a blossom & leaf vine accented w/seed pearls, the long-toothed comb of tortoiseshell, hallmark of Sloan & Co., ca. 1900 (ILLUS.)... **$1,645**

Aquamarine, Pearl & Diamond Lavaliere

Lavaliere, aquamarine, pearl & diamond, designed w/two white pearl drops suspending small leaves set w/old mine-cut diamonds all above the large cushion-cut aquamarine drop, millegrain accents, platinum-topped 14k gold mount, completed w/a delicate platinum trace link chain, Edwardian, England, early 20th c., 16" l. (ILLUS.)... **$1,645**

Lovely Edwardian Diamond Lavaliere

Lavaliere, diamond & platinum, an openwork heart-shaped top bead- and bezel-set w/old European- and mine-cut diamonds suspending an openwork teardrop further set w/diamonds & suspending a large diamond solitaire, on a delicate trace link chain, Edwardian, England, early 20th c., 15 1/2" l. (ILLUS.) **$3,290**

Gold & Turquoise Snake Bracelet

Necklace, turquoise & 18k gold, snake-form, composed of flexible links, bezel-set w/turquoise cabochons, circular-cut ruby eyes, very minor solder evidence at pin near head, Victorian, 15 3/4" l. (ILLUS. of part) **$3,055**

Victorian Garnet Necklace & Pendant

Necklace & pendant, garnet, the necklace composed of clusters of rose-cut garnets, together w/a detachable oval pendant of rose-cut garnets, a glass compartment on the back, gilt-metal mounts, 19th c., 12" l. (ILLUS. of part) **$1,058**

Pendant, emerald, diamond & enamel, Art Nouveau style, a large central cabochon emerald & a teardrop emerald drop, the cabochon within a gold scroll mount framed by 47 old European-cut diamonds, platinum-topped 18k gold mount, chased & engraved on the reverse, by Marcus & Co., later pin stem, some enamel loss (ILLUS., top next column) **$17,625**

Rare Art Nouveau Emerald Pendant

Pendant, gold (18k), guilloché enamel & diamond, the 18k gold locket w/pale blue guilloché enamel in a radiating design set in the center w/an old European-cut diamond surrounded by an open ring w/leaf sprigs further set w/diamonds, a narrow outer rim band further set w/small rose- and old European-cut diamonds, suspended from a platinum chain w/blue enamel baton links trimmed w/seed pearls, Edwardian era, locket w/French guarantee stamp, chain 20" l. **$2,705**

Fine Ivory, Diamond & Emerald Pendant

Pendant, painted ivory, emerald, diamond & gold, a large central oval ivory plaque h.p. in color w/a scene of the circumcision of Christ, enclosed in an openwork scrolling gold frame & bail set w/old mind-cut diamonds & bezel-set step-cut emeralds, silver-topped 14k gold mouth, 19th c., 1 3/4 x 2 1/2" (ILLUS.) **$823**

Edwardian Pendant with Large Amethyst

Pin, platinum, diamond & amethyst, the flexibly set oval-cut large amethyst framed by a double ring of old European-, rose- and single-cut diamonds, suspended from a diamond-set looped circle & fancy link chain, millegrain accents, Edwardian, England, early 20th c., 28 1/4" l. (ILLUS.)..................... **$4,348**

Antique Enamel & Seed Pearl Locket

Pendant-locket, enamel, seed pearl & silver-gilt, the oval center panel enameled w/a scene of Eros w/his quiver & a basket of flowers framed by bands of small seed pearls within a thin black & white-dotted enamel border band, a seed pearl-set bow pin at the top, French assay stamp & partial hallmark, 19th c. (ILLUS.)............ **$1,175**

Pendant-necklace, gold (14k yellow) & seed pearl, the shield-shaped pendant w/fine applied bead & wirework scroll designs & seed pearl accents w/a locket compartment in the back, the fancy link chair engraved w/scroll & floral designs, Victorian (ILLUS. of part, top next column) **$764**

Pin, 10k yellow gold & black enamel, oval cartouche-shaped floral & scroll-etched gold frame w/black enamel border band, frames a half-length Daguerreotype portrait of a young female child, ca. 1850s, 1 5/8 x 2" **$132**

Victorian Gold & Seed Pearl Pendant-Necklace

Lovely Art Nouveau Enameled Pink

Pin, diamond, enamel & 18k gold, Art Nouveau style, designed as a pair of large scrolled leaves enameled in bluish green & framed by looping leaves & arching blossoms & buds bead-set w/single-cut diamond, suspending a freshwater pearl drop, early 20th c. (ILLUS.)................... **$2,233**

Fine Edwardian Diamond Pendant

Pin, diamond, the openwork form of foliate designs bead- and bezel-set overall

w/old European- and single-cut diamonds, millegrain accents, platinum-
topped 18k gold mount, Edwardian, En-
gland, early 20th c. (ILLUS.) **$4,230**

Rare Hedges Wasp-shaped Pin

Pin, enamel & gem-set 14k yellow gold, in
the shape of a flying wasp, the long wings
w/polychrome basse taille enamel studded w/old European-cut diamond mélée,
long gold body & legs, small demantoid
garnet eyes, hallmark of A. J. Hedges,
Newark, New Jersey, late 19th - early
20th c., 2 1/8" w. (ILLUS.) **$3,290**

American Seed Pearl Starburst Pin

Pin, seed pearl, diamond & gold, a starburst
design centered by an old European-cut
diamond mélée, the arms pavé-set
w/seed pearls, American hallmark, 19th
c. (ILLUS.) **$382**

Old Diamond-set Gold Ring

Ring, diamond & 18k yellow gold, the top
composed of thin bands mounted
w/twenty-seven old European-, old mine-
and single-cut diamonds, total weight
1.60 cts. (ILLUS.) **$646**

Ring, pearl, diamond & 18k gold, set w/five
pearls interspersed w/rose-cut diamonds, the gallery w/engraved C-scrolls,
19th c., size 5 1/4 .... **$999**

Edwardian Pearl & Diamond Ring

Ring, pearl, diamond & 18k yellow gold, a
center white pearl framed by a ring of old
European-cut diamond mélée, gold
mount, pearl possibly natural, by Theodore B. Starr, Edwardian, England, ear-
ly 20th c., size 6 1/4 (ILLUS.) **$1,293**

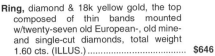

Fine Edwardian Turquoise & Diamond Ring

Ring, turquoise, diamond & 14k yellow gold,
the oblong top centered by an oval turquoise cabochon surrounded by old European-cut diamonds, Edwardian, England, early 20th c., size 2 3/4 (ILLUS.)
.... **$646**

Tiara, diamond & platinum, designed as
three intersecting floral garlands set
throughout w/old European- and single-
cut diamonds, w/a white metal tiara mount
& later brooch attachment, evidence of
solder, Edwardian, England, early 20th c.,
diamonds 7 1/4 cts. (ILLUS., bottom of
page) **$15,275**

Rare Edwardian Diamond Tiara

Victorian Garnet Vinaigrette-Pendant

Vinaigrette-pendant, garnet & gilt-metal, oval w/the wide top frame composed of cast spiral rings centered by a large cabochon garnet, opens to a perforated compartment, late 19th c. (ILLUS.) **$382**

Carnelian Puppy in Basket Watch Fob

Watch fob, carnelian, silver & gold, the top carved as a seated carnelian puppy w/red stone eyes in a basket of silver & 18k gold decorated w/navette & fleur-de-lis designs, the bottom set w/a carnelian intaglio depicting a pair of hunting hounds in an English landscape, 19th c. (ILLUS.) **$940**

Figural Gold & Hardstone Watch Fob

Watch fob, hardstone & 18k yellow gold, the top designed as the figure of a gold prospector w/pick, shovel, pan & rifle, bottom w/a hardstone seal engraved w/a name, 19th c. (ILLUS.) **$411**

Sets

Unusual Chinese Carved Hornbill Jewelry Set with Original Box

Bracelet, choker, brooch & earrings, carved Hornbill, each piece composed of oval segments set w/floral-carved hornbill alternating w/gold bird-decorated plaques, China, ca. 1860, complete w/original fitted velvet-lined camphorwood box carved on the top w/a central landscape scene w/figures & temples, the corners w/delicate floral-carved panels, hallmarked, necklace, the set (ILLUS.) **$5,288**

Victorian Coral Shell-carved Set

Brooch & earrings, pink coral & 18k yellow gold, each piece carved as a scallop shell centering a coral bead, w/original fitted box from Howard & Co., Victorian, the set (ILLUS.) **$2,115**

Fine Carved Coral Victorian Set

Brooch & earrings, pink coral, the brooch of squared shape boldly carved in the center w/the head of a classical lady framed by leafy roses & carved at each side w/another classical profile, suspending three carved coral teardrops, the longest central one carved w/a classical head, the matching earrings w/the small top carved as a classical head suspending a larger tapering carved plaque carved w/another classical head & suspending three carved coral teardrops, 14k yellow gold mounts, Victorian, the set (ILLUS.) **$2,350**

Early Turquoise & Yellow Gold Set

Necklace, pendant & earrings, turquoise & 18k yellow gold, the cross-form pendant w/rounded arms set w/teardrop-shaped turquoise-set teardrops & a central ring, the necklace composed of graduated circular turquoise & wirework florette links, matching teardrop-shaped earrings, 19th c., boxed, small losses, 19th c. (ILLUS. of part) **$4,700**

Coral Floral-carved Pendant from Set

Pendant & earrings, bi-color coral, the pendant carved as a large finely-petaled flower blossoms below a cluster of small carved flowers, matching earrings, gilt-metal mounts, 19th c., one flower blud detached, the set (ILLUS. of pendant) **$529**

Costume

Costume Jewelry refers to jewelry made of inexpensive materials. It was originally designed to accessorize designer's clothing collections, and was meant to be discarded along with the clothing when it went out of style. Women saved this jewelry for its beauty, and today it is a very important collectible. It was inexpensive in its time, and was made in the most up-to-the-minute designs. Today collectors can pay more for certain costume jewelry than for some precious jewelry.

Sterling & Gemstone Sterling Bar Pin

Bar pin, sterling silver & gemstone, Edwardian-style, the oblong openwork ornate frame centered by a large chrysoprase cabochon w/smaller carnelian, amber & amethyst cabochons around the sides, 1 x 2 3/4" (ILLUS.) **$185-215**

Leaf-carved Yellow Bakelite Belt Buckle

Belt buckle, Bakelite, round ring design w/stylized yellow carved leaves, 2 3/4" d. (ILLUS., previous page) **$40-55**

Belt buckle, Bakelitte, Art Deco style, two-part, black w/rayed design, 3 1/2" l., 2" h. **$50-65**

Black Celluloid & Rhinestone Belt Buckle

Belt buckle, black celluloid, two-piece, in the shape of an angular belt buckle pavé-set overall w/rhinestones, 2 1/2" l., 1 5/8" h. (ILLUS.) **$25-35**

Belt buckle, celluloid, two-piece, carved as red leaves, ca. 1935, 3 3/8" l., 1 1/2" h. **$30-40**

Two Agate Bead Bracelets

Bracelet, agate beads, pinkish orange marbleized beads on orange elastic, 3/8" w. (ILLUS. left with aventurine bracelet) **$25-35**

Bracelet, aventurine beads, mottled green on matching elastic, 3/8" w. (ILLUS. right with agate bead bracelet) **$25-35**

Bracelet, enameled goldplate, hinged bangle-style, decorated w/black enamel, belt & buckle-style, 3/8" l. **$40-55**

Bracelet, onyx & pearl, small black onyx beads & fresh water pearls w/gold spacers, 6 1/2" l. **$35-50**

Bracelet, sterling silver, hinged bangle-style, plain design, signed "Mexico JPH," 1 1/8" l. **$100-125**

Bracelet, sterling silver, hinged bangle-style, plain design w/pointed top, hallmarked & signed by DePercin **$100-125**

Bracelet, white metal & rhinestone, hinged bangle-style, the top pavé-set w/rhinestones, w/safety chain, 3/4" l. **$45-60**

Bracelet, white metal & rhinestone, hinged bangle-style, the top pavé-set w/rhinestones w/curved metal spacers, openwork back, signed "Lisner," 1/2" l. **$60-75**

White Metal & Colored Stone Bracelet

Bracelet, white metal & stone, flat links each set w/a different colored semi-precious stone alternating w/loop links, 3/8" w., 5 3/4" l. (ILLUS.).............. **$30-45**

Charm bracelet, sterling chain suspending charms in the shape of birds & hearts decorated w/turquoise & enamel, signed "Meka, Denmark," 7" l. **$50-65**

Triangular Bakelite Dress Clip with Flower

Dress clip, Bakelite, long narrow black triangle decorated w/an applied gilt-metal flower & leaf sprig centered by a pearl, 2" l. (ILLUS.)... **$40-60**

Dress clip, brass, Victorian-style design w/acorns & oak leaves, 1 7/8" h............ **$40-65**

Dress clip, rhinestone, Art Deco style, openwork shield shape, 1 7/8" h. **$30-45**

Dress clip, rhinestone, leaf-shaped & pavé-set w/rhinestones, 1 3/8" h. **$25-40**

Dress clips, rhinestone, Art Deco duette-type, converts to a pair of clips when removed from the pin frame, 2 5/8" w. **$65-85**

Dress clips, rhinestone, white metal bows set w/triangular & baguette rhinestone accents, 1 x 1", pr. **$35-50**

Earrings, art glass, millefiore-style mauve drops, gold ear wires, 1 5/8" l., pr. **$25-35**

Earrings, goldplate, designed as flowers, clip-on type, signed "Jomaz," 1 1/4" d., pr... **$60-75**

Earrings, goldplate & pearl, flower-shaped w/the center set w/a 1/4" d. cultured pearl, signed "Kramer N.Y.," pr. **$45-60**

Earrings, pearl & rhinestone, round rhinestone-set form accented w/pearls, clip-in type, on original card marked "Metaphor," 3/4" d., pr. **$20-30**

Green Peking Glass Earrings

Earrings, Peking glass, mottled light & dark green drops, screw-backs, ca. 1925, 2 1/4" l., pr. (ILLUS.) **$65-80**

1950s Loop Rhinestone Earrings

Earrings, rhinestone, hoop-type, the ring & clip set w/rhinestones, clip-on type, ca. 1955, 1 7/8" d., 2 1/4" h., pr. (ILLUS.) **$65-80**

Earrings, rhinestone & pearl, a baguette rhinestone-set feather-shaped mount centered by a pearl, screw-on type, ca. 1955, 3/8" w., 7/8" h., pr......................... **$30-40**

Fur clip, rhinestone & enamel, a white enameled flower set w/red & clear square rhinestone trim, "trembling" center of w/rhinestones, 2 1/4" h.......................... **$60-85**

Fur clip, rhinestone, Retro style, large marquise & emerald-shaped clear stones set in an openwork white metal mount, signed "Eisenberg Original," 3 1/8" h.
.... **$275-300**

Necklace with Bi-color Art Glass Beads

Necklace, art glass, bi-colored oblong flattened beads in shades of red, yellow, green & blue, beads alternate w/silvered metal chains, 36" l. (ILLUS.) **$35-50**

Necklace, Aurora Borealis crystal beads, graduated strand, 21" l. w/3" extensioin chain **$60-80**

Necklace, faux pearl, choker-style, double-strand cultured-type, a large faux pearl centering the rhinestone-set round clasp, signed "Ciner," 14" l. **$50-75**

Necklace, glass beads, composed of coral-colored graduated beads strung on a sterling silver chain, ca. 1940, 16" l........ **$80-96**

Necklace, glass beads, sections of coral- and turquoise-colored beads alternating w/smaller black beads, 37" l................... **$45-60**

Necklace, goldplate & glass beads, metal chain set w/five glass beads in purple & yellow each ending in fringe, signed "LCI," 42" l. **$55-75**

Necklace, goldplate & glass, composed of faux ancient Roman goldplate coins each w/a yellow glass insert, goldplate & glass beads, metal chain set w/five glass beads in purple & yellow each ending in fringe, signed "LCI," 42" l. **$95-110**

Goldplate & Rhinestone Retro Necklace

Necklace, goldplate & rhinestone, Retro-style small stylized flowers & leaves w/rhinestone centers & joined by rhinestone-set links, signed "Trifari," 12" l. w/3" extender chain (ILLUS.) **$55-75**

Necklace, mother-of-pearl beads, graduated white oval beads, w/a 14k white gold-filled clasp, 18" **$40-60**

Necklace, quartz beads, tranluscent white beads, sterling silver clasp, 26" l........... **$45-60**

Necklace, rhinestone, a clear single strand w/a center w/five graduated rows, signed "H.," 15" l. w/3 1/4" extender chain......... **$35-50**

Necklace, rhinestone, composed of large individually set multi-colored stones, 14" l. w/3" extension chain **$45-60**

Necklace, sterling silver, composed of double-leaf links alternating a smooth finish & striped finish, signed "Van Dell," 14" l. w/2" extender chain............................... **$75-95**

Necklace, sterling silver & rhinestone, choker-type, the flat chain w/center domed design set w/square rhinestones, unfastens at either end of the center design, signed "EB," 14" l. **$80-100**

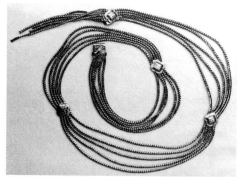

Christian Dior White Metal Necklace

Necklace-belt, white metal, composed of sections of five slender flat chains in a festoon style separated w/diamond-shaped floral mounts, hook closure w/tassel, can be used as a belt for a small waist, signed "Christian Dior," 26" l. (ILLUS.)............... **$65-85**

Egyptian Green Pendant

Pendant, glass, molded Egyptian green 3" scarab on 24" chain w/green beads between chain segments (ILLUS.) **$55-75**
Pendant, gold-filled & stone, a chain composed of 12k gold-filled round links alternating w/long slender pierced links, suspending a large octagonal mount in brush gold set w/a large translucent black emerald-cut stone, signed "Winard," pendant 1 1/2" l., chain 21" l. **$95-120**
Pendant, white metal & stone, metal chain w/an openwork drop enclosing a large oval black stone that changes colors to green, yellow, blue or black depending on wearer's mood, chain 16" l. **$20-35**

German Enameled Brass Pendant/Box

Pendant-box, enamel & brass, the oval brass box enameled on the top w/pink enamel against a guilloche ground h.p. w/small pink roses & green leaves, signed "Germany," 1 x 1 1/2" (ILLUS.)... **$70-95**
Pin, agate in ornate goldplate frame, oval, brown, 1 3/8" white center stone, ca. 1910, overall 1 1/2 x 1 3/4" **$125-150**

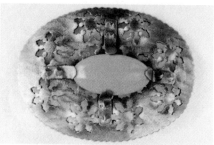

Brass Floral Design Pin

Pin, brass openwork floral design w/large 1 1/4" oval turquoise stone, used to hold sashes in place, ca. 1910, 2 1/4 x 3" (ILLUS.) **$55-75**

Orchid Pin

Pin, enamel, model of an orchid in deep and light pink, small aurora borealis rhinestone accents, pearl center, signed "Joan Rivers," 2 1/2" h., 2 1/4" w. (ILLUS.)
.... **$65-80**

Goldplate Lion Head & Scroll Pin

Pin-pendant, goldplate & rhinestone, designed as a large lion head mask w/green rhinestone eyes surrounded by large tight scrolls, signed "Goldette," 3 1/4" w., 3 3/4" h. (ILLUS.) **$85-110**

Ring, beadwork, hand-made, sivler beads w/blue Aurora Borealis flower front **$20-30**

Goldstone & Red Stone Adjustable Ring

Ring, goldplate, rhinestone & colored stone, ornate goldplate mount w/a deep scrolling sides highlighted w/small rhinestones & centering a large red cabochon stone, opens on a hinge, adjustable size, signed "Art" (ILLUS.) **$35-50**

Scarf clip, goldplate, a textured seashell design, signed "Pauline Rader," 2 1/2" w., 1 1/2" h. **$60-75**

Sets

Necklace & bracelet, goldplate, Retro-style openwork leaf-shaped links form each piece, signed "Monet Jewelers," bracelet, 7/8" w., 7" l., necklace 14" l. , 2 pcs. **$75-95**

Enameled Goldplate Saint Laurent Set

Necklace, bracelet & earrings, enameled goldplate, the necklace a tapering band decorated w/large gold crosses alternating w/bright red enameled panels, matching hinged bangle bracelet & round clip-on earrings, signed "YSL" (Yves Saint Laurent), the set (ILLUS.) **$125-150**

Necklace & earrings, sterling silver & rhinestone, Retro-style design set w/clear round & baguette stones, on a chain set w/round rhinestones, screw-on earrings, signed "Carl-Art," earrings 1 1/4" l., necklace 13" l, the set **$135-155**

White Metal & Green Art Glass Set

Necklace & earrings, white metal & art glass, the chain necklace w/oval metal oval spacers & filigree beads alternating w/swirled green glass beads ending in a double drop, matching teardrop-shaped screw-on earrings, earrings 1 1/8" l., necklace 25" l. w/a 4 1/2" l. double drop, the set (ILLUS.) **$70-95**

Modern (1920-1960s+)

Bracelet, amethyst & 14k yellow gold, Retro style, composed of pairs of step-cut amethysts joined by arched gold bar links, 7 1/4" l. (ILLUS. of part, bottom of page) **$2,233**

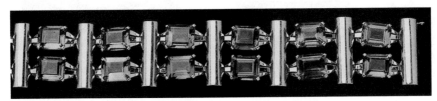

Retro Style Amethyst & Gold Bracelet

Very Rare Caldwell Art Deco Diamond & Platinum Bracelet

Bracelet, diamond & platinum, Art Deco style, a long narrow form w/double bands divided by three oval segments, set overall w/162 old European-, single-cut & baguette diamonds w/millegrain accents, signed by J. E. Caldwell, ca. 1930s, 7 1/4" l. (ILLUS.) **$16,450**

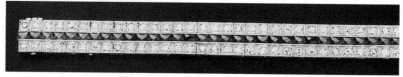

Fine Art Deco Diamond & Synthetic Sapphire Bracelet

Bracelet, diamond & synthetic sapphire, Art Deco style, a long narrow band centered by a line of French-cut synthetic sapphires flanked by lines of bead-set old European-cut diamonds & millegrain accents, platinum mount, ca. 1930s, 7" l. (ILLUS. of part, above) **$4,700**

Bracelet, enamel & 14k yellow gold, Art Deco style, composed of oblong links decorated in green & black champlevé enamel w/a dragon, hallmark of Enos Richardson & Co., ca. 1930, 7 1/2" l. (ILLUS. of part, bottom with other Art Deco bracelet) .. **$823**

Two Art Deco Enameled Gold Bracelets

Bracelet, enamel & 14k yellow gold, Art Deco style, composed of slightly arched white & navy blue striped champlevé enamel links joined by ribbed spacers, hallmark of Wordley, Allsopp & Bliss, ca. 1930, 7 1/4" l. (ILLUS. of part, top with other Art Deco bracelet) **$999**

Bold Amethyst & Gold 1950s Brooch

Brooch, amethyst & 14k yellow gold, a large abstract floral form composed of nine large prong-set pear- and oval-cut

amethysts w/thin gold extending from the top & base, ca. 1950s (ILLUS.) **$1,116**

Retro Style Bi-color Gold Bow Brooch

Brooch, bi-color 14k gold, Retro style, in the shape of a large bow, 2 3/4" l. (ILLUS.) **$470**

Very Fine Cartier Diamond Bow Brooch

Brooch, diamond & platinum, Art Deco style, model of a long bow set w/about 500 old European-, mine- and transitional-cut diamonds, signed by Cartier, ca. 1930s (ILLUS.) **$47,000**

Rare Art Deco Diamond & Sapphire Brooch

Brooch, diamond, sapphire & platinum, Art Deco style, oval slender openwork scrolling frame set w/old European- and rose-cut diamonds centering a large oval double cabochon sapphire, French guarantee stamp, ca. 1930s, 1 x 1 3/4" (ILLUS.)
.... **$9,988**

Fine Hardstone Art Deco Earrings

Earrings, chalcedony, coral, marcasite & onyx, Art Deco style, each designed as a shaped blue chalcedony tablet suspended from a marcasite pagoda form w/coral bead accents, cabochon onyx tops, silver mounts, hallmark of Theodor Fahrner, ca. 1930, pr. (ILLUS.) **$2,938**

Earrings, diamond & 18k yellow gold, the asymmetrical form prong-set w/single-cut diamonds suspending two gold tassels, ca. 1940, pr. **$705**

Art Deco Black Opal & Diamond Pendant

Pendant, black opal, diamond & platinum, Art Deco style, suspended from a earlier Edwardian diamond-set floral & ribbon swag pin, the oval pendent centered by a large black opal cabochon framed by old European- and single-cut diamonds, ca. 1930s (ILLUS.) **$4,818**

Pendant, emerald, diamond & 18k gold, designed w/a top prong-set square step-cut diamond weighint 3.00 cts. suspending a flexibly-set large pear-shaped emerald framed by twenty graduated old European-cut diamonds, early 20th c. (ILLUS., top next column)................................. **$76,375**

Unique Emerald & Diamond Pendant

Pablo Picasso Gold Face Pendant

Pendant, gold (23k yellow), flattened rounded shape decorated as a stylized human face, designs & signed by Pablo Picasso, No. 6/20 & 1434, French maker's mark "Ste MH," w/original box (ILLUS.) **$9,988**

Pendant necklace, jade & platinum, Art Deco style, the oblong green jade pendale carved & pierced w/gourds among leafy vines suspended from a platinum & diamond bail & silk necklace trimmed w/jadeite beads, pis & seed pearls, ca. 1930s, 33" l. **$5,170**

Fine Art Deco Diamond & Pearl Pin

Pin, diamond, pearl & platinum, Art Deco circle-style, the scrolling ring joined by two three-leaf clusters, bead-set overall w/old European- and mind-cut diamond mélée & centered by a white pearl, ca. 1930s (ILLUS.)....................................... **$2,115**

Retro Ring with Large Citrine

Ring, citrine, ruby, diamond & 14k yellow gold, Retro-style, a large step-cut square citrine flanked by single-cut diamonds & step-cut ruby shoulders, size 5 1/2 (ILLUS.) **$999**

Tiffany Diamond & Platinum Ring

Ring, diamond & platinum, Art Deco style, the oblong top centered by a bezel-set transitional-cut diamond weighing .50 cts. within a pierced mount set overall w/old European- and transitional-cut diamonds & millegrain accents, signed by Tiffany & Co., ca. 1930s (ILLUS.) **$2,938**

Art Deco Ring with Large Sapphire & Diamonds

Ring, diamond, sapphire & platinum, Art Deco style, the oblong top centered by a large bezel-set cushion-cut sapphire flanked by two large old mine-cut diamonds, the openwork mount further set w/thirty full-cut diamonds & millegrain accents, size 6 3/4 .... **$2,468**

Art Deco Sapphire & Diamond Ring

Ring, diamond, sapphire & platinum, Art Deco style, the rounded almond-shaped top centered by a bezel-set cushion-cut sapphire within an openwork frame bead-set w/ten old European-cut diamonds, millegrain accents (ILLUS.) **$6,463**

Pink Sapphire & Diamond Art Deco Ring

Ring, pink sapphire, diamond & platinum, Art Deco style, the square top centered by a bezel-set octagonal pink sapphire framed by bands of old European- and transitional-cut diamonds, the shoulders w/oval pink sapphire highlights, millegrain accents, ca. 1930s, size 6 (ILLUS.)......... **$5,288**

Unusual Sapphire & Diamond 1950s Ring

Ring, sapphire & diamond, bead-set w/three pear-cut sapphires in side lobes framed by diamonds & extending from the diamond-set top, w/five full-cut, thirty single-cut & twelve bauguette diamonds, platinum mounts, ca. 1950, size 4/3/4 (ILLUS.).. **$8,225**

Sapphire, Diamond & Platinum Ring

Ring, sapphire, diamond & platinum, mounted w/a 5.5 mm round blue sapphire flanked by four old European-cut diamonds in a platinum mount, ca. 1920s, size 6 3/4 (ILLUS.) **$990**

Ring, sapphire, diamond & platinum, Retro style, a central band channel-set w/a graduated line of square step-cut sapphires flanked by triangular section pave-set w/single-cut diamonds, platinum mount, ca. 1950, size 5 1/2 .... **$1,998**

Art Deco Turquoise & Ivory Ring

Ring, turquoise, ivory & gold, Art Deco style, bezel-set w/a turquoise-in-matrix cabochon framed by an ivory band, shoulders w/interlocking circle motifs, silver & gold mount, ivory band w/breaks, size 6 1/4 (ILLUS.) **$588**

Sets

Cuff Links from Cartier Dress Set

Man's dress set: oval cuff links & two shirt studs; platinum & black diamond, the oval cuff links each bezel-set w/an old European-cut black diamond joined by trace links sto an old European-cut black diamond & onyx baguette baton, matching shirt studs, signed by Cartier, New York, w/original fitted box, ca. 1930, the set (ILLUS. of part) **$9,400**

Modern Tiffany & Co. Petal-form Necklace & Earrings

Necklace & earrings, gold (18k yellow), the necklace composed of overlapping leaf-form rose petals, matching petal-shaped earrings, designed by Angela Cummings, Tiffany & Co., ca. 1979-80, necklace 15 1/2" l., the set (ILLUS.) **$6,463**

Necklace & two bracelets, composed of rock crystal beads bound by engraved silver bands, ca. 1920, necklace 22 1/2" l., the set (later jump ring closures) **$881**

KITCHENWARES

Coffee Mills

Coffee mills, commonly called grinders, are perfectly collectible for many people. They are appealing to the eye and are frequently coveted by interior decorators and today's coffee-consuming homeowners. Compact, intricate, unique, ornate, and rooted in early Americana, coffee mills are intriguing to everyone and are rich and colorful.

Coffee milling devices have been available for hundreds of years. The Greeks and Romans used rotating millstones for grinding coffee and grain. Turkish coffee mills with their familiar cylindrical brass shells appeared in the 15th century, and perhaps a century or two later came the earliest spice and coffee mills in Europe. Primitive mills were handmade in this country by blacksmiths and carpenters in the late 1700s and the first half of the 19th century. These were followed by a host of commercially produced mills, which included wood-backed side mills and numerous kinds of box mills, many with machined dovetails or finger joints. Characterized by the birth of upright cast-iron coffee mills, so beautiful with their magnificent colors and fly wheels, the period of coffee mill proliferation began around 1870. The next 50 years saw a staggering number of large and small manufacturers struggling to corner the popular home market for box and canister-type coffee mills. After that, the advent of electricity and other major advances in coffee grinding and packaging technology hastened the decline in popularity of small coffee mills.

Value-added features to look for when purchasing old coffee grinders include:

• *good working order and no missing, broken, or obviously replaced parts*

• *original paint*

• *attractive identifying markings, label or brass emblem*

• *uncommon mill, rarely seen, or appealing unique characteristics*

• *high quality restoration, if not original.*

—Mike White

Box Mills

Parker National Box Mill

Box mill, iron cover w/gear opening & crank & sunken hopper, on wooden box w/pull-out drawer in front, Parker National (ILLUS.) **$100**

Logan & Strobridge Brighton No. 1180 Box Mill

Box mill, iron crank & side handle on wooden box w/pull-out drawer in front, 1 lb. capacity, Logan & Strobridge Brighton No. 1180 (ILLUS.) **$150**

Decorative Moravian Box Mill

Box mill, raised brass hopper & crank, Moravian base & inlaid drawer, signed by maker (ILLUS.) **$200**

Norton Painted Tin Box Mill

Box mill, raised iron hopper & crank on tin canister w/picture of woman painted on front, drawer in back, patented Norton (ILLUS.) **$650**

Arcade Favorite No. 357 Box Mill

Box mill, raised iron hopper w/patented partial cover design & crank on wooden box w/pull-out front drawer, Arcade Favorite No. 357 (ILLUS.) **$100**

Side Mills

Kenrick Patented Side Mill

Side mill, iron, sliding cover, Kenrick patented, England (ILLUS.) **$110**

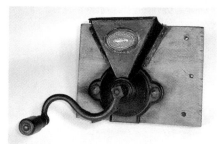

Peck Smith Mfg. Side Coffee Mill

Side mill, tin hopper on wood backing, brass emblem reads "Peck Smith Mfg." (ILLUS., previous page) **$100**

Upright Mills

Rare Large Enterprise Floor Model Mill

Upright mill, cast iron, Enterprise No. 218 floor model w/double 35" wheels & large brass hopper w/spread-winged eagle finial, original painted base & tin handled decorated bing, 50-70% original paint, late 19th c., 35" w., 70" h. (ILLUS.) **$3,393**

L.F. & C. Universal Coffee Mill

Upright mill, cast iron, L.F. & C. New Britain, Conn. Universal, overall green paint w/gold highlights, hand crank w/wooden grip, slide-out base drawer, mounted on wooden board, all-original & like new, late 19th c., 11 1/2" h. (ILLUS.) **$320**

Upright two-wheel mill, cast iron, miniature model for children, two 2"-h. wheels, Arcade No. 7, rare, overall about 2 1/2" h. (ILLUS., top next column) **$350**

Miniature Upright Coffee Mill

Coles No. 4 Upright Coffee Mill

Upright two-wheel mill, cast iron, pivoting lid on hopper, two 12"-h. wheels, Coles No. 4 (ILLUS.) **$950**

Clawson & Clark No. 1 Upright Mill

Upright two-wheel mill, cast iron, single wheel, cup, patented Clawson & Clark No. 1 model (ILLUS.) **$1,000**

Enterprise No. 7 Upright Coffee Mill

Upright two-wheel mill, cast iron, w/17" wheels, pivoting cover on hopper, original red paint, decals & pin striping, 1898 patent date marked on grinding burrs, Enterprise #7 (ILLUS.) **$1,500**

Children's Ceramic Wall Canister Mill

Wall-mounted canister mill, ceramic, children's model, glass measure, "Cafe" on front, Europe, about 6" h. (ILLUS.)............ **$420**

Enterprise No. 4 Upright Coffee Mill

Upright two-wheel mill, cast iron, w/nickel-plated brass hopper, 10 3/4" wheels, Enterprise No. 4 (ILLUS.) **$1,800**

Wall-Mounted Canister Mills

Douwe-Egberts Koffie Wall Mill

Wall-mounted canister mill, ceramic w/glass measure, marked on front "Douwe-Egberts Koffie," Europe (ILLUS.) **$140**

One-of-a-Kind Wall Mill

Wall-mounted canister mill, cast iron, decorative design based on Ami Clark's 1833 patent, w/adjusting thumbscrew in back & two-sided grinding burr, only known example (ILLUS.)........................ **$2,500**

Red Iron Clamp-on Wall Mill

Wall-mounted canister mill, iron, clamp-on type, w/pivoting lid, red, rare National Specialty No. 0 (ILLUS.) **$310**

L.F. & C. Universal No. 24 Wall Mill

Wall-mounted canister mill, iron & glass, w/2-qt. jar, L.F. & C. Universal No. 24 (ILLUS.) **$190**

Rare Hollis Telephone Wall Mill

Cow Creamers

Bennington Pottery Cow Creamer

Bennington pottery, platform-type, Rockingham glaze, rare, missing lid, chip on one horn, tail repair, expect damage as this creamer is a rare find in any condition, 5 x 7" (ILLUS.) **$450-550**

Bisque Cow Creamer

Bisque porcelain, highly textured bisque body, black spots, pink bow, w/yellow bell at neck, all glazed, "Japan" paper label, 4 1/4 x 5 3/4" (ILLUS.) **$20-24**

Black Ceramic Cow Creamer

Bronson-Walton Holland Beauty Wall Mill

Wall-mounted canister mill, litho-printed tin, decorated w/picture of woman in period clothing, Bronson-Walton Holland Beauty (ILLUS.)... **$510**

Wall-mounted canister mill, wood, w/side crank, rare patented Hollis Telephone model (ILLUS., top next column) **$1,100**

Ceramic, black high-gloss glaze over red clay pottery, highly detailed, cold-painted features, maker unknown, 5 x 5 1/2" (ILLUS., previous page) **$39-44**

Blue Painted Japanese Cow Creamer

Ceramic, blue painted flowers on both sides, molded green bell around neck, flowers in various colors, ink stamped "Japan" on bottom, 5 1/4 x 7 3/4" (ILLUS) **$32-35**

Blue Polka-dotted Cow Creamer

Ceramic, blue polka-dots on white glazed pottery, molded bell at neck, eyes accented w/long lashes, unmarked, maker unknown, 5 1/2 x 5 3/4" (ILLUS.) **$49-55**

Brahma Cow Creamer

Ceramic, Brahma, laying down, black at top, graduating to reddish brown over cream pottery, highly glazed, unusual bottom, very unusual, maker unknown, 3 3/4 x 8 3/4" (ILLUS.) **$39-45**

Brown & White Cow Creamer

Ceramic, brown markings on white glazed ceramic, h.p. eyes, tail curls down & connects to back hind leg forming handle, unmarked, 4 x 7" (ILLUS.) **$21-24**

Common Cow Creamer

Ceramic, brown markings over highly glazed white ceramic, ink stamped number "B544" underneath, common, 3 1/2 x 5 3/4" (ILLUS.) **$22-26**

Brown & White Bull Creamer

Ceramic, bull, brown & white, grey hooves & facial shading, tail curls under to form handle, ink stamped "K393," maker unknown, 4 1/2 x 7 3/4" (ILLUS.) **$29-35**

Grouping of Bull Creamers

Ceramic, bull creamers, also found w/matching salt & pepper shakers, stamped "Made in Japan," also "Occupied Japan," 3 x 3", each (ILLUS.) **$19-24**

Ceramic, bull creamers, also found w/matching salt & pepper shakers, stamped "Made in Japan," also "Occupied Japan," larger sizes, each **$24-35**

Cow Creamer Bust

Ceramic, bust-form, brown markings on white w/pink ears, cheeks & mouth, bulging eyes, yellow horns & bell at neck, commonly found in various other animal shapes, h.p. marked "Japan," 4 x 4" (ILLUS.) **$24-28**

Blue Floral Cow Creamer

Ceramic, dark & light blue flowers on white glaze, w/blue nose & ears, tail curled up over back to form handle, "Cream" stamped on one side, bottom ink stamp "E-3801," 4 1/4 x 7" (ILLUS.) **$39-46**

Flat-Bottomed Cow Creamer

Ceramic, flat bottom, turquoise spots on cream glazed pottery w/brown accents, molded bell at neck, rouge painted jaw area, unmarked, unglazed bottom, 5 1/2 x 7" (ILLUS.) **$65-69**

Handpainted Cow Creamer

Ceramic, h.p. floral on white, molded bell at neck, many found with "Souvenir" label from places visited, Japan, 3 1/4 x 5 1/4" (ILLUS.).. **$14-19**

Holly Ross Cow Creamer

Ceramic, h.p. flower on one side, bud on reverse, facial features, hooves & ribbon in gold, w/gold under glaze bottom marks, artist signed "Holly Ross, LaAnna, PA. Made in the Poconos," 5 x 7 1/2" (ILLUS.) **$39-45**

Otagiri Cow Creamer

Ceramic, h.p., w/gold foil label "M O C Japan, Otagiri 1981," embossed underneath, foil label on side, "Handpainted," still being produced, common, by Otagiri, 3 x 5 1/2" (ILLUS.).................................. **$12-15**

Black Cow Creamer

Ceramic, highly-glazed black over red clay, cold-painted features in pink, blue & gold, pottery bell w/painted flower attached by metal chain, original lid w/tip of tail ornamental to top, unmarked, 5 1/2 x 6" (ILLUS.) **$34-39**

Cow Creamer with Eyes Shut

Ceramic, lying down, eyes shut, yellow crown, pink nose, highlighted in brown on white glazed pottery, tail curled up to form handle loop over rear, impressed branding iron marking "R" within a "G" on

back side, unglazed pottery bottom, maker unknown, 5 x 6 1/2" (ILLUS.) **$42-45**

Black & White Lustre Cow Creamer

Ceramic, lying down, feet tucked under, lustreware w/black spots & gold accented horns, red ink stamp "Made in Japan," 4 x 6" (ILLUS.).. **$27-32**

Gold Accented Cow Creamer Pitcher

Ceramic, pitcher, black high gloss w/22 kt. gold detailed accents, bottom stamped in gold "Pearl China Co., hand decorated, 22 kt. Gold, U.S.A.," impressed "#635," larger than usual cow creamer, 6 1/2 x 6 1/2" (ILLUS.)............................ **$29-35**

Kenmar Purple Cow Creamer

Ceramic, purple glazed, small tin bell attached at neck w/fine wire, gold foil label marked "Kenmar, Japan," various colors, common, mint w/bell, 4 1/2 x 6 1/2" (ILLUS.) **$25-29**

Cow Creamer w/Pink Flowers

Ceramic, reddish brown on cream, pink flowers at base, unmarked, w/flat bottom base, 1950-60, 3 3/4 x 5 1/2" (ILLUS.)... **$19-25**

Common Japanese Cow Creamer

Ceramic, reddish brown over cream, Japanese, mass-produced before, during & after the war, found in many sizes, colors & various markings, common, 3 1/2 x 5 1/4" (ILLUS.)............................ **$25-28**

Brown & Cream German Cow Creamer

German porcelain, brown on cream porcelain, black accented tail, horns & hooves, red ink stamped "Germany," 3 1/2 x 5" (ILLUS.)... **$55-59**

German Green Reclining Cow Creamer

German porcelain, lying, w/tail curled up to form handle, impressed "Germany 1391" on back side, unusual light green color, mint, 3 1/2 x 7 1/2" (ILLUS.)............... **$114-120**

Brown-spotted Goebel Cow Creamer

Goebel china, brown markings on white, original tin bell on cord, full "Bee" blue ink stamp, "Germany," 5 x 7 1/2" (ILLUS.)... **$74-79**

Ironstone China Cow Creamer

Ironstone china, lying, w/legs tucked under, burgundy floral transfer on both sides, backstamp reads "Charlotte Royal Crownford Ironstone England," commonly found mold w/markings of different companies in various colors, marked "Made in England," 3 1/2 x 7" (ILLUS.) .. **$39-45**

Black Platform-Style Cow Creamer

Jackfield pottery, high-gloss black glaze over red clay w/gold trim, on platform w/lid, Shropshire, England, 4 1/2 x 6 1/4" (ILLUS.)... **$139-145**

Jackfield Cow Creamer

Jackfield pottery, platform base, high-gloss black glaze over red clay, gold details, w/original lid, Shropshire, England, 5 x 7 1/4" (ILLUS.).............................. **$195-225**

Limoges Porcelain Cow Creamer

Limoges porcelain, solid white, highly glazed, stamped in green ink inside top opening "Limoges, France," common mold, used for some souvenir items, 4 1/2 x 6 1/2" (ILLUS.)............................ **$25-29**

Rare Occupied Japan Cow Creamer

Occupied Japan china, lying down, legs folded underneath, irregular spots, graduating colors of greens & brown on cream, ink stamped "Made in Occupied Japan," rare, mint, 5 1/4 x 7" (ILLUS.) ... **$69-75**

Japanese Cow Creamer w/Lacy Collar

Porcelain, grey on white w/gold accents, very delicate & lacy collar around neck w/bell attached, eyes shut, red ink stamp "Japan" on hoof, 3 3/4 x 4 1/2" (ILLUS.).. **$21-24**

Pottery Cow Creamer

Pottery, pink accents on cream, green dots around neck forming a bow, lock handle tail, unmarked, 3 1/2 x 5" (ILLUS.) **$14-19**

Fine Early Staffordshire Cow Creamer

Staffordshire pottery, cov., platform-type, sponged dark brown & orange over white pottery, milkmaid seated on green base, facing forward, ca. 1810-20, 6 1/2" l. (ILLUS.) **$1,200-1,400**

Purple Sponged Cow Creamer

Staffordshire pottery, cov., sponged purple lustre over cream glazed pottery, orange backstamp "Old Staffordshire Ware, England," 1910-20, small chip on ear, 6 1/2" l. (ILLUS.) **$165-179**

Staffordshire pottery, cov., standing, sponged in manganese & yellow, milkmaid seated performing her task at oblong platform base, facing left, ca. 1780, repair, 6 3/4" l. **$1,400-1,800**

Later Staffordshire Cow Creamer

Staffordshire pottery, pink floral transfer on white, w/yellow bell at neck, unmarked, England, 20th c., 5 x 8" (ILLUS.) **$80-95**

English Sterling Silver Cow Creamer

Sterling silver, cov., ornate flowers around lid w/fly perched on top, marks "RC" w/"M" in a shield, lion w/raised paw facing left, leopard's head, letter "e," English, ca. 1960, still being produced, expect to pay more for earlier versions, 5.2 oz., 4 x 6" (ILLUS.) **$500-700**

White Lusterware Cow Creamer

White lustreware china, w/gold horns & tail, opening highlighted in gold, unmarked, mint, 4 3/4 x 6 1/2" (ILLUS.) **$74-79**

Yellowware pottery, cov., standing on a platform, lid w/little or no repair, similar to the Bennington cow creamer, very rare
.... **$1,500-2,000**

Egg Cups

Ceramic egg cups were a common breakfast table accessory beginning about the mid-19th century and were used for serving soft-boiled eggs. Ceramics egg "hoops" or "rings" were used for many years before the cup-form became common. Egg cups continue to be produced today, and

modern novelty and souvenir types are especially collectible.

The descriptions and values listed here were provided by collector Dr. Joan M. George, who notes that values for older egg cups are based on their marks, rarity and recent sales results.

Bucket-style, blue monogram "EIIR," for Queen Elizabeth II, England, 1950s **$22**

Bucket-style, commemorates death of Princess Diana, England, 1997 .... **$35**

Bucket-style, souvenir of Portsmouth, England w/picture of the HMS Victory, England, 1996 .... **$8**

English Gollywog Egg Cup

Bucket-type, colored design of a Gollywog pointing to a stove, Robertsons & Sons, England, ca. 1960s (ILLUS.) **$35**

Bjorn Wiinblad Designed Egg Cup

Bucket-type, colorful stylized modernistic design, Bjorn Wiinblad, Rosenthal, Germany, 1985 (ILLUS.) **$45**

Double, decorated w/a chick & a green stripe, Roseville Pottery, ca. 1919 .... **$250**

Singapore Bird Pattern Egg Cup

Double, Singapore Bird patt., Oriental-style design of birds & flowering branches on a celadon green ground, Adams, England, ca. 1950s (ILLUS.) $25

Double, souvenir of Caesar's Palace, Las Vegas, Nevada, brown design, 1993 .... $18

Early Staffordshire Egg Hoop

Hoop-style, green transfer-printed design of people & houses, Staffordshire, England, 19th c. (ILLUS.) $65

Hoop-style, white decorated w/green garland band & gilt scrolls, Haviland, Limoges, France, 1990s $85

W.H. Goss Crest Egg Cup

Single, banner w/crest marked "Ye Ancient Port of Seaford," W.H. Goss, England, 1930s (ILLUS.) $20

French Bart Simpson Egg Cup

Single, Bart Simpson bust, yellow w/blue base, France, 1997, large (ILLUS.)............. $25

Single, Bayeux Tapestry, white ground w/a picture showing a portion of the tapestry, Limoges, France, 1998 .... $15

French Bellhop Egg Cup

Single, bellhop wearing blue hat & coat, cigarette in his mouth, France, ca. 1920 (ILLUS.) $70

Rare Betty Boop Egg Cup

Single, Betty Boop head, red dress, grey lustre hair, Germany, ca. 1930s (ILLUS., previous page) **$300**

Single, commemorates the wedding of Princess Grace & Prince Rainier of Monaco, France, 1956 .... **$95**

Souvenir Cup with Dutch Children

Single, color scene of Dutch children around the sides, printed in gold at the top "Souvenir Holland," unmarked, 1930s (ILLUS.) **$32**

Charles & Diana Divorce Egg Cup

Single, commemorating the divorce of Prince Charles & Princess Diana, Coronet Pottery, England, 1996 (ILLUS.) **$30**

Early Goebel Boy's Head Egg Cup

Single, comical boy's head, painted features, high collar below chin, Goebel, Germany, ca. 1930s (ILLUS.) **$140**

Meissen Blue Orchid Egg Cup

Single, deeply scalloped rim, Blue Orchid patt., Meissen, Germany, 1988 (ILLUS.) **$95**

Goebel Girl's Head Egg Cup

Single, comical girl's head, painted features, ruffled collar & pink hair band, Goebel, Germany, ca. 1930s (ILLUS.) **$140**

French Faience Egg Cup

Single, faience, h.p. w/colorful blue & yellow florals & scrolls, France, ca. 1920s (ILLUS.) **$45**

Single, figural Swee'pea, from Popeye cartoons, KFS Vandor Imports, Japan, 1980, large size $55

Single, figural ugly man's face in grey clay, large nose & blue & white eyes, England, 1999 .... $15

Unusual Humpty Dumpty Egg Cup

Single, Humpty Dumpty body in blue, sitting on a wall titled "Humpty Dumpty Egg Cup," egg would form the head, unmarked, ca. 1920s (ILLUS.) $45

Jemima Puddleduck Egg Cup

Single, Jemima Puddleduck standing beside a bush-form cup, one from a set of Beatrix Potter characters, Enesco, 1999, each (ILLUS.) $35

Single, King Edward VII coronation commemorative, portrait wearing crown, England, 1901 .... $85

Single, King George V of England coronation commemorative, England, 1911 .... $65

Royal Albert, England Egg Cup

Single, Lady Carlyle patt., decorated w/large clusters of flowers below a scal-

loped pink rim band, Royal Albert, England, ca. 1950s (ILLUS.) $35

Rare Early Minnie Mouse Egg Cup

Single, Minnie Mouse, pointed nose & large ears, wearing orange skirt & blue blouse on a green base, Japan, ca. 1930s (ILLUS.) $55

Modern Cow-form Egg Cup

Single, model of a cow, round, painted black & white over green grass, Knobler, U.S., 1987 (ILLUS.).................................... $15

Royal Doulton Nanking Egg Cup

Single, Nanking patt., band of stylized colorful flowers & blue ribbons, Royal Doulton, England, ca. 1930s (ILLUS.) $28

Single, Niagara Falls picture titled "Niagara Falls Prospect Point Canada," Japan, 1930s $28

Single, Rhodes, Greece, white w/picture,
2000 .... **$6**

Modern Wedgwood Egg Cup

Single, rim band in blue & gold w/tiny red
blossoms, Wedgwood, England, 1990s
(ILLUS.).. **$25**
Single, Royal Copenhagen "Flora Danica"
patt., hand-painted, Denmark, current **$475**
Single, Royal Doulton example decorated
w/roses & gold garlands, England, 1927..... **$50**

Chintz "Welbech" Pattern Egg Cup

Single, Royal Winton Chintz "Welbech"
patt., England, 1999 (ILLUS.)...................... **$35**
Single, "Running Legs," white cup attached
to legs w/yellow shoes, Carlton Ware,
England, 1970s **$40**
Single, scalloped bottom, black transfer-
printed scene of "Porta Nigra, Tier," oldest city in Germany, Germany, 1998.......... **$15**

Rare Disney Snow White Egg Cup

Single, Snow White, standing beside cup
marked w/her name, Walt Disney Enter-
prises, part of a set, Japan, 1937 (ILLUS.).. **$225**

Winston Churchill-VE Day Egg Cup

Single, Winston Churchill portrait against
the Union Jack, commemorates 50th Anniversary of VE Day, Norwich Bone Chi-
na, England, 1995 (ILLUS.) **$55**

Shy Lady Egg Cup by Goebel

Single, woman w/center-parted brown hair
pulled into a bun, shy smile & side-glanc-
ing eyes, yellow bow at neck, Goebel,
Germany, ca. 1930s (ILLUS.) **$140**

Egg Timers

*A little glass tube filled with sand and
attached to a figural base measuring between 3"
and 5" in height was once a commonplace kitchen
item. Although egg timers were originally used to
time a 3-minute egg, some were used to limit the
length of a telephone call as a cost saving measure.*

*Many beautiful timers were produced in Ger-
many in the 1920s and later in Japan, reaching
their heyday in the 1940s. These small egg timers
were commonly made in a variety of shapes in
bisque, china, chalkware, cast iron, tin, brass,
wood or plastic.*

*Egg timers had long been considered an essen-
tial kitchen tool until, in the 1920s and 1930s, a
German pottery company, W. Goebel, introduced
figural egg timers. Goebel crafted miniature china
figurines with attached glass vials. After the Great*

Depression, Japanese companies introduced less detailed timers. The Goebel figural egg timers are set apart by their trademark, delicate painting and distinctive clothes. It is best to purchase egg timers with their original tube, but the condition of the figure is most important in setting prices.

Goebel Baker Egg Timer

Baker, ceramic, Goebel (ILLUS.) **$50**
Bellhop, ceramic, Oriental, wearing red out-
fit, marked "Germany" **$35**
Bird, ceramic, sitting on nest, wearing white
bonnet w/green ribbon, Josef Originals
sticker **$35**

Bird & Egg Near Stump Egg Timer

Bird, ceramic, standing next to stump w/egg
at base, shades of brown w/green grassy
base & leaves on stump, Japan (ILLUS.).... **$50**

Black Baby Egg Timer

Black baby, ceramic, sitting w/left arm hold-
ing timer (ILLUS.) **$75**

Black chef, ceramic, sitting w/arm up holding timer, variety of sizes, Germany....... **$65-95**

Black Chef with Fish Egg Timer

Black chef, ceramic, standing w/large fish,
timer in fish's mouth, Germany, 4 3/4" h.
(ILLUS.).. **$125**
Boy, ceramic, skiing pose, marked "Germa-
ny," 3" h. **$35**

Wooden Cat Egg Timer

Cat, wooden, black cat w/yellow eyes & red
collar on domed yellow base, timer lifts
out of back (ILLUS.) **$25**
Chef, ceramic, holding blue spoon, marked
"Germany".. **$50**
Chef, ceramic, winking, white w/black shoes
& trim, turning figure on its head activates
sand, 4" h. **$35**
Chef, composition board, black chef holding
platter of chicken, w/pot holder hooks........ **$25**
Chef, composition, w/cake, Germany............. **$65**

Egg Timer with Chef Holding Egg

Chef, porcelain, white & blue, holding reddish orange egg, supporting timer, Germany (ILLUS., previous page) $50

Chef, wood, "Time Your Egg" $20

Chick, ceramic, white, yellow & purple chick, marked "Japan" $35

Chick with cap, ceramic, Josef Originals $35

Clockman Planter

Clock, ceramic, clock face, w/man's plaid suit & tie below, w/planter in back, Japan (ILLUS.) $25

Clown Egg Timer

Clown, ceramic, Germany (ILLUS.) $95

Clown on phone, ceramic, standing, full-figured, Japan $48

Colonial lady with bonnet, ceramic, variety of dresses & colors, Germany, 3 3/4" h., each $48

Colonial man, ceramic, yellow & white, Japan $48

Dog, ceramic, Dachshund, red w/hole in back for timer, label on back reads "Shorty Timer" $35

Dog, ceramic, lustre ware, white w/brown ears & tail, Japan (ILLUS., top of next column) $50

Dog, ceramic, Pekingese, standing brown & white dog, marked "Germany" $48

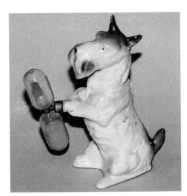

Lustreware Dog

Goebel Dutch Boy & Girl Egg Timer

Dutch boy & girl, ceramic, double-type, timer marked w/3-, 4- & 5-minute intervals, Goebel, Germany, 1953 (ILLUS.) $75

Dutch girl, ceramic, talking on telephone, Japan $35

Dutch girl, ceramic, w/red heart on apron, Germany $35

Dutch girl w/flowers, chalkware, walking, unmarked, 4 1/2" h. $50

Elephant, ceramic, white, sitting w/timer in upraised trunk, marked "Germany" $50

Elf by Well Egg Timer

Elf by well, ceramic, Manorware, England (ILLUS., previous page) **$25**

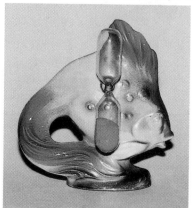

English Bobby Egg Timer

English Bobby, ceramic, Germany (ILLUS.) ... **$75**

Lustreware Fish Egg Timer

Fish, ceramic, lustre ware, burgundy, yellow & green, Germany (ILLUS.) **$65**

Fisherman Egg Timer

Fisherman, ceramic, standing, wearing brown jacket & hat, tall black boots, carrying a large white fish on his shoulders, timer attached to mouth of fish, Germany (ILLUS.)... **$85**

Friar Tuck, ceramic, single, Goebel, Germany, 4" h... **$48**

Frog, ceramic, multicolored frog sitting on egg, marked "Japan".................................. **$50**

Happy the Dwarf, ceramic, from "Snow White & the Seven Dwarfs," Maw Co., England.. **$75**

Honey bear, ceramic, brown & white, w/timer in mouth made to resemble milk bottle, Cardinal China Co., No. 1152 .... **$48**

Little Boy Egg Timer

Little boy, ceramic, standing wearing black shorts & shoes & large red bow tie, Germany (ILLUS.) **$50**

Little girl on phone, ceramic, sitting w/legs outstretched, pink dress, Germany **$50**

Goebel Little Girl & Chick Egg Timer

Little girl with chick on her toes, ceramic, Goebel, Germany (ILLUS.).................... **$125**

Mammy, tin lithographed, mammy cooking on gas stove, w/pot holder hooks, unmarked, 7 3/4" h...................................... **$125**

Mouse Chef Egg Timer

Mouse, ceramic, sitting & holding timer, brown w/white apron marked "Chef" in red letters, Josef Originals (ILLUS.) **$35**

Mrs. Claus Egg Timer

Mrs. Claus, ceramic, in yellow dress w/green collar, cuffs & hem, w/red bag full of gifts & black bag w/timer (ILLUS.) **$50**
Newspaper boy, ceramic, Japan, 3 1/4" h...... **$48**
Oliver Twist, ceramic, wearing red pants & vest, brown jacket, black hat, marked "Germany" **$75**

Goebel Owl Egg Timer

Owl, ceramic, Goebel, Germany (ILLUS.)....... **$50**
Parlor maid with cat, ceramic, Japan **$50**
Penguin, glazed chalkware, standing on green & white base w/"Bagnor Regis" painted on front, marked "Manorware, England".. **$35**
Rabbits, ceramic, double-type, various color combinations, Goebel, Germany, 4" h. ... **$50**
Rooster, wood, multicolored, standing on thick base... **$25**
Sailboat with sailor, ceramic, lustre ware, Germany **$50**
Scotsman with bagpipes, plastic, England, 4 1/2" h. **$28**

Sea Gull Egg Timer

Sea gull, ceramic, timer in beak, Germany (ILLUS.).. **$50**
Telephone, ceramic, black, Japan.................. **$25**
Vegetable person, ceramic, Japan **$95-125**
Veggie man or woman, bisque, Japan, 4 1/2" h., each **$95-125**

Waiter Egg Timer

Waiter, ceramic, standing next to ovoid holder for timer, black & white, Germany (ILLUS.).. **$50**
Welsh woman, ceramic, Germany, 4 1/2" h. **$35**

Napkin Dolls

Until the 1990s, napkin dolls were a rather obscure collectible, coveted by only a few savvy individuals who appreciated their charm and beauty. Today, however, these late 1940s and 1950s icons of postwar America are hot commodities.

Ranging from the individualistic pieces made in ceramics classes to jeweled Japanese models and the wide variety of wooden examples, these figures are no longer mistaken as planters or miniature dress forms. Of course, as their popularity has risen, so have prices, putting smiles on the faces of collectors who got in on the ground floor and stretching the pocketbooks of those looking to start their own collections.

Bobbie Zucker Bryson is co-author, with Deborah Gillham and Ellen Bercovici, of the pictorial price guide Collectibles For The Kitchen, Bath & Beyond - Second Edition, published by Krause Publications. It covers a broad range of collectibles including napkin dolls, stringholders, pie birds, figural egg timers, razor blade banks, whimsical whistle milk cups and laundry sprinkler bottles. Bryson can be contacted via e-mail at Napkindoll aol.com.

Ceramic, figure of a woman w/brown hair in a Colonial-style hairdo, wearing a long green off-the-shoulder dress, hands held up & clasped, marked "Frances - Edith King Originals, 1953," 11 1/2" h. **$75-95**

Ceramic, figure of a woman, wearing a green off-the-shoulder dress w/flowers on the front, her floppy-brimmed hat forming a candleholder, marked "Kreiss and Company," 10" h. **$65-85**

Ceramic, figure of a woman, wearing a long dress decorated w/maroon flowers & green leaves, also a blue hat, holding a blue toothpick holder bowl, signed "Helen Lewis, 1959," 9 1/2" h. **$95-135**

Ceramic, figure of a woman wearing a pink iridescent dress & black & pink wide-brimmed hat, white toothpick holder on each hip, marked "4059," 9 1/2" h. **$60-75**

Ceramic, figure of a woman, wearing a white dress w/yellow bodice & trim, holding out her skirt w/one hand, the other hand on her hip, marked "Tina," Mallory Studios, 9 1/2" h. **$75-85**

Ceramic, figure of a woman, wearing a yellow & white dress, yellow pigtails, holding a white lily, Atlantic Mold, 11" h. **$65-75**

Ceramic, figure of a young girl, aqua & white dress w/a black bodice & black bows on front & back of skirt, large pockets for napkins, marked "3475" on bottom, 7 7/8" h. **$75-95**

Ceramic, figure of a young girl, wearing a pink dress w/white ruffle trim, white picture hat w/pink rose & candleholder in the top, marked "Sunbonnet Miss - Holt Howard 1958," 5" h. **$125-150**

Ceramic, figure of an angel, pink & white & holding a bouquet, slits in shoulders for wings & in the rear, Japan paper sticker, 5 3/8" h. **$100-115**

Ceramic, figure of angel, blonde, wearing blue & white dress w/gold trim, holding maroon flowers w/green leaves, gold halo on head, two slits in shoulders for napkins to form "wings," 5 3/8" h. **$100-135**

Bartender/Waiter Napkin Doll & Shakers

Ceramic, figure of bartender/waiter, w/black mustache, red & white checked apron, black bow tie & shoes, holds a tray that serves as candleholder, foil sticker w/"Viking Handmade, Made in Japan," w/matching salt & pepper shakers, 8 3/4" h. (ILLUS.) **$135-140**

Ceramic, figure of genie, dressed in white robes trimmed in gold, jewel-decorated turban, holds a gold lantern, label reads "Genie at Your Service," Enesco, 8" h. **$100-135**

Byron Molds Napkin Doll

Ceramic, figure of girl holding flowers, red hair, yellow dress w/matching hair bow, arms clutch flowers to chest, marked "copyright Byron Molds," 8 1/2" h. (ILLUS.) **$55-75**

Atlantic Mold Napkin Doll

Ceramic, figure of girl holding lily, mouth
   open as if singing, brown bobbed hair
   w/yellow headband, bright yellow dress
   w/green leaf design, holds a blue lily in
   arms, Atlantic Mold, 11" h. (ILLUS.) **$50-65**
Ceramic, figure of "Miss Versatility," woman
   in red & white dress w/red scallop trim &
   matching red picture hat that serves as
   candleholder, one hand held behind
   back, California Originals, 13" h. **$60-75**
Ceramic, figure of Santa Claus, n red suit
   w/black belt & shoes, toothpick holes in
   hat, marked "Japan," w/a "Sage Store" la-
   bel, 6 3/4" h. **$95-150**

Holt Howard Napkin Doll

Ceramic, figure of "Sunbonnet Miss," red-
   haired little girl in yellow dress w/white
   shoulder ruffle, matching yellow picture
   hat w/pink rose serves as candleholder,
   one hand pats hair, other arm is extended,
   marked "© Holt Howard 1958" (ILLUS.)
   .... **$135-165**

Uncle Sam Napkin Holder

Ceramic, figure of Uncle Sam, dressed in
   red, white & blue w/matching top hat,
   gold star buttons on vest, holding cloth
   American   flag,   Lillian   Vernon
   Corporation, ca. 2003, 9" h. (ILLUS.) **$12**

Spanish Dancer Napkin Holder

Ceramic, figure of woman, black-haired
   Spanish dancer holding tambourine in
   one hand, the other holding skirt, wearing pink dress w/brown bodice, the skirt
   decorated w/yellow sunflowers, 17" h.
   (ILLUS.) **$130-150**

Napkin Holder/Toothpick Holder

Ceramic, figure of woman holding tray, blonde, wearing black off-the-shoulder dress, one hand on hip, other holding pink covered tray, the lid w/holes to hold toothpicks, 8 1/2" h. (ILLUS.) **$75-95**

Woman in Hat Napkin Holder

Ceramic, figure of woman in hat, in dress w/yellow drop waist & purple skirt, yellow & purple hat w/upturned brim, marked "Cal. Cer. Mold," 12 1/2" h. (ILLUS.) **$65-85**
Ceramic, figure of woman w/black hair wearing white dress w/red trim, balancing tray on head, 10" h. **$75-95**

Napkin Doll with Toothpick Holder

Ceramic, figure of woman w/brown hair in a bun, wearing brown dress w/white collar & cuffs, holding green heart w/holes for toothpicks, 6 1/2" h. (ILLUS.) **$65-85**

Holland Mold Napkin Holder

Ceramic, figure of woman w/daisy, black hair w/bangs, dressed in blue & white dress & long white gloves, one hand fixes daisy behind ear, ca. 1958, marked "Holland Mold," 7 1/4" h. **$75-95**

Napkin Doll Holding Fan

Ceramic, figure of woman w/fan, in 18th-c. white dress w/blue trim on bodice & sleeves & blue bows on front of dress & in her dark hair, one hand holds up white fan w/blue trim, marked "Jam. Calif. ©" (ILLUS.).. **$55-65**

Napkin Doll with Glossy Finish

Ceramic, figure of woman w/long black hair wearing white dress w/gold neckline & cuffs & holding white & gold pitcher in both hands, applied lavender roses w/green leaves on one shoulder & on pitcher, glossy finish, handmade, 11" h. (ILLUS., previous page) **$95-115**

Atlantic Mold Napkin Doll

Ceramic, figure of woman w/open mouth & brown hair, wearing vivid green & orange skirt & white blouse, holding yellow lily, Atlantic Mold, 11" h. (ILLUS.) **$65-75**

Handmade Atlantic Mold Napkin Doll

Ceramic, figure of woman w/open mouth & yellow bobbed hair, wearing full-skirted gown in shades of green & matching headband, holding orange lily, handmade from Atlantic Mold, 11" h. (ILLUS.) **$65-75**

Ceramic, figure of woman w/poodle, blonde, dressed in pink dress trimmed in black, matching hat serves as candle-holder, blue jeweled eyes, crystal jeweled necklace & red jewel on finger, holds a white poodle, marked "Kreiss & Co.," 10 3/4" h. **$115-135**

Ceramic, figure of woman w/toothpick tray, bobbed hair, white dress w/yellow scalloped trim, holds oblong toothpick tray attached at waist, 10 3/4" h. **$60-75**

Woman with Bird Napkin Doll

Ceramic, figure of woman w/toothpick tray, brown hair, green lustre dress decorated w/pink roses, one arm holds a toothpick tray w/similar decoration on her head, pink bird perches on other arm, 10 1/2" h. (ILLUS.) **$75-95**

Pie Birds

A pie bird can be described as a small, hollow device, usually between 3 1/2" to 6" long, glazed inside and vented from the top. Its function is to raise the crust of a pie to allow steam to escape, thus preventing juices from bubbling over onto the oven floor while providing a flaky, dry crust.

Originally, in the 1880s, pie birds were funnel-shaped vents used by the English for their meat pies. Not until the turn of the 20th century did figurals appear, first in the form of birds, followed by elephants, chefs, etc. By the 1930s, many shapes were found in America.

Today the market is flooded with many reproductions and newly created pie birds, usually in many whimsical shapes and subjects. It is best to purchase from knowledgeable dealers and fellow collectors.

Advertising, "Kirkbrights China Stores Stockton on Tees," ceramic, white, England **$60**

Advertising, "Lightning Pie Funnel England," ceramic, white, England................. **$75**

Advertising, "Paulden's Crockery Department Stretford Road," ceramic, white, England **$50**

Advertising, "Roe's Patent Rosebud," ceramic, England, 1910-30 .... **$50**

Bird, ceramic, black on white base, yellow feet & beak, Nutbrown, England **$25**

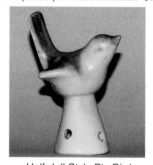

Camark Pottery Pie Bird in Blue

Bird, ceramic, Camark Pottery, Camden, Ark., ca. 1950s-60s, depending on color, 6 1/2" h. (ILLUS.) **$125-400**

Half-doll Style Pie Bird

Bird, ceramic, half-doll style, blue & yellow on conical base, USA (ILLUS.) **$350**

Bird, ceramic, "Midwinter," black, England...... **$35**

Rowe Pottery Pie Bird

Bird, ceramic, two-piece w/detachable base, 1992, Rowe Pottery (ILLUS.) **$25**

Bird, ceramic, w/flowers, Chic Pottery, ca. 1930s-60s, hard to find **$175**

Bird, pottery, "Scipio Creek Pottery, Hannibal, MO" **$15**

Rare Bird on Nest Pie Bird

Bird on nest w/babies, ceramic, Artisian Galleries, Fort Dodge, Iowa (ILLUS.). **$400-700**

Black Chef with Blue Smock

Black chef, ceramic, full-figured, blue smock, "Pie-Aire," USA, w/original tag (ILLUS.).. **$125**

Black chef, ceramic, full-figured, green smock, "Pie-Aire," USA **$175**

Very Large Black Pie Bird

Blackbird, ceramic, very large, 2 1/2" w x 5" h., English (ILLUS.) **$75**

Blackbird, ceramic, w/yellow trim on brown base **$65**

Wide-Mouth Blackbird Pie Bird

Blackbird, ceramic, wide mouth, yellow beak, fat, English (ILLUS.) **$150**
Blackbird, clay w/black & yellow glaze, ca. 1960s-70s **$35**
Blackbird, red clay w/black glaze, ca. 1930s-40s **$35**
Bluebird, ceramic, Japan, post-1960 .... **$35**
Chef, ceramic, "A Lorrie Design, Japan," Josef Originals, 1980s **$85**

"Benny the Baker" Pie Bird

Chef, ceramic, "Benny the Baker," w/tools & box, Cardinal China Co., USA (ILLUS.) **$125**

Chef, ceramic, half-figure, all-white, England **$65**
Cherry, apple & peach, ceramic, ca. 1950s, in original box, set of three **$350-450**

Chick with Dust Cap

Chick, ceramic, w/dust cap, Josef Originals (ILLUS.) **$65**
Chick, ceramic, yellow w/pink lips, Josef Originals **$40**

Rare Donald Duck Pie Bird

Donald Duck, ceramic, "Walt Disney" marked on one side & "Donald Duck" on the other, rare (ILLUS.) **$1,000**

English Dragon Pie Birds

Dragons, ceramic, various shapes & colors, 1980s-1990s, England, each (ILLUS. of three, bottom previous page) **$50**

Elephant, all-grey w/trunk up, ca. 1930s, Nutbrown, England (ILLUS.) **$200**
Elephant, ceramic, white, ca. 1930s **$125**

"Fred the Flour Grader" Pie Bird

Brown English Duck Pie Bird

Duck, ceramic, brown w/white & yellow beak, black trim, white base, England (ILLUS.) **$95**
Duck, ceramic, pink, blue or yellow, full-bodied, USA, each **$50**

"Fred the Flour Grader," ceramic, black & white, from Homepride Flour, ca. 1978 (ILLUS.).. **$65-100**

Kookaburra Pie Bird

Kookaburra, ceramic, light blue, Australia (ILLUS.)... **$195**

Dutch Girl Multipurpose Pie Bird

Dutch girl, ceramic, doubles as pie vent, measuring spoon holder and/or receptacles for scouring pads & soap, Cardinal China, rare (ILLUS.) **$100-135**
Dwarf Dopey, ceramic, Disney **$300-450**

Luzianne Mammy Pie Baker

Luzianne Mammy, ceramic, black woman dressed in yellow shirt & green skirt, carrying a red tray w/coffee service, white turban on head (ILLUS.) **$65**

Grey Nutbrown, England Elephant

Puff-chested Songbird Pie Bird

Songbird, ceramic, lavender & brown trim, puff-chested, ca. 1940s (ILLUS.) **$300-400**

Thistle-shaped Pie Bird

Thistle-shaped, ceramic, blue, England (ILLUS.) **$125**
Unusual pie vent, ceramic, "The Bleriot Pie Divider," white, 1910-20 .... **$450**

Yankee Pie Bird with Package

Yankee pie bird, ceramic, Millford, New Hampshire, ca. 1960s, w/original package (ILLUS.) **$35**

Reamers

Clown Reamer in Aqua & Maroon

Ceramic, two-piece figure of a clown, aqua & white body w/maroon hands & black feet, maroon, black & white conical reamer hat, marked "Japan," 5 1/2" h. (ILLUS.) **$55-65**
Ceramic, two-piece, figure of a native woman w/brown face & wide red lips, wearing gold hoop earrings & a bandana on her head, yellow & white conical reamer hat, marked "Made in Germany" on the base, 2 3/4" h. **$175-200**
Ceramic, two-piece, in the form of a lemon, yellow w/green leaves, brown stem, white cone, marked "House of Speyer," 4 1/2" h. **$50-60**
Ceramic, two-piece, in the form of a man's face, red w/white top, 3 1/2" h. **$45-60**

"Orange for Baby" Reamer

Ceramic, two-piece, in the form of an orange, yellow w/pebbled surface resembling orange peal, white & yellow cone top, front reads "Orange for Baby," marked "Registered Germany," 4" h. (ILLUS.) **$75-90**

A Pale Blue & Amberina-colored Reamer by Edna Barnes

Orchid-form Reamer

Ceramic, two-piece, in the form of an orchid, pink & white w/green handle & bottom, 3" h. (ILLUS.) **$100-115**

Figural Orange Two-Piece Reamer

Goebel Orange-shaped Reamer

Ceramic, two-piece, model of a realistic orange w/green leaf spout & brown branch handle, white top & reamer cone, marked "Goebel," Germany, 4 1/2" h. (ILLUS.)... **$65-75**

Ceramic, two-piece, model of an orange w/a green loop handle, marked "Japan" on the base, 3 3/4" h. (ILLUS., top next column) **$45-55**

Glass, saucer-type, deep orangish Amberina-type color, limited edition by Edna Barnes, marked on the bottom w/a "B" in a circle, 2 1/2" d. (ILLUS. right with pale blue opaque reamer, top of page) **$15-20**

Glass, saucer-type, pale blue opaque, limited edition by Edna Barnes, marked on the bottom w/a "B" in a circle, 2 1/2" d. (ILLUS. left with Amberina-colored reamer, top of page)...................................... **$15-20**

Green Glass Criss-Cross Reamer

Glass, saucer-type, raised ringed foot w/crisscross pattern saucer & a swirled rib reamer cone, green, Anchor-Hocking Glass Co., 6 1/8" d. (ILLUS.)................. **$25-30**

Glass, saucer-type, transparent pink glass embossed on the side "SUNKIST" & marked "Pat. No. 18764 Made in USA - McKee Glass Co.," 6" d......................... **$60-75**

Glass, saucer-type, transparent red color, Fenton Art Glass Co., 6 3/8" h. **$1,300-1,500**

Glass, saucer-type w/loop handle, milk glass w/embossed fleur-de-lis emblem on the front, 6 1/4" d............................ **$85-115**

Glass, saucer-type w/tab handle, pink, 5 7/8" d... **$45-55**

Glass, saucer-type w/tall pointed reamer cone, black opaque color, embossed "Saunders," 6 1/8" d. **$1,500-2,200**

Glass, saucer-type, yellow opaque glass embossed on the side "SUNKIST" &

marked "Pat. No. 18764 Made in USA - McKee Glass Co.," 6" d.......................... **$50-55**

Glass, straight sides w/ribbing, table handle w/hole, light green, Fry Glass Co., 6 1/4" d... **$35-40**

Glass, two-piece 4-cup pitcher-type, pink, part of the Paden City "Party Line Measuring Set," 8 3/4" h. **$150-200**

Edna Barnes Red Glass Reamer

Glass, two-piece, dark transparent red, paneled base & round reamer top, limited edition by Edna Barnes, marked on the bottom w/a "B" in a circle, 3 1/2" h. (ILLUS.) **$35-40**

Glass, two-piece, two-cup capacity bottom, pink, U.S. Glass Company, 5" h............. **$50-65**

Glass, two-piece, two-cup capacity bottom, white milk glass w/red stripe, 5 3/8" h. **$25-35**

Glass, two-piece two-cup measuring cup-type, milk glass w/red stripe trim, 5 3/8" h... **$45-55**

Glass, two-piece w/removable reamer cone, square loop handle, clear, marked "Jerrie Juicer - Avoid Hot Water"........ **$550-600**

Glass, two-piece w/two handles, milk glass w/printed color images of Jack & Jill on the side, 4 1/2" h. **$60-70**

Glass & metal, amber glass footed base & a metal reamer top, a Paden City Party Line cocktail shaker, overall 10 1/2" h. **$190-225**

Metal, countertop screw-on type, green enamel trim, 9" h. **$35-55**

Metal, countertop tilting screw-on type, marked "Seald Sweet Juice Extractor," 13" h. **$55-65**

Metal, w/red enamel base, Juice-O-Mat Single Action model, 8 1/2" h. **$12-15**

Metal, white enamel base w/chrome body, top & handle, marked "Juice-O-Mat Tilt Top," 7" h. **$10-12**

Metal & plastic, metal top w/bottom cranks, gold plastic base, marked "L.E. Mason Co., Boston, Mass. - Mason Seald Sweet Juicer," 7 1/2" h. **$15-25**

One-piece, saucer shape w/lipped spout and shell-form handle, white ground w/pink & magenta flowers, green leaves & gold bead trim, marked "Hand Painted Japan" (ILLUS., top of next column) **$150-175**

Floral Ceramic Reamer

Reamer with Lattice Strainer

One-piece, saucer shape w/spout & side handle, round seed dam w/lattice strainer, white ground w/design of red cherries & green leaves, gold trim, 3" h. (ILLUS.) **$85-115**

Gold-trimmed Reamer

One-piece, saucer shape, white w/gold trim, w/figures of tree, swan, butterfly & flowerpot, marked "Made In France - Limoges France," 3 1/2" d. (ILLUS.) **$75-95**

Hall Ceramic Reamer

One-piece, simple round shape w/lip & side tab handle, green outside, white inside,

marked "Hall," 6" h. (ILLUS., previous
page) **$550-600**

Souvenir Ceramic Reamer

One-piece, souvenir, saucer shape w/spout
& side handle, blue, rust & cream,
w/painted image of Victorian woman
w/parasol on one side of bowl & mass of
flowers on the other, marked "Made in
England, A Present From Dobercourt,"
3 1/4" d. (ILLUS.) **$85-125**
Three-piece, teapot shape, orange & white
w/gold trim, cone sits under gold-handled
lid, 3 1/2" h. **$50-60**
Three-piece w/tray, ceramic w/sterling sil-
ver trim, white ground w/orange flowers,
green leaves, rust trim, marked "France,"
5" h. **$225-250**
Two-piece, figure of duck w/white lustre
body, blue head, orange beak, yellow top
knot, marked "Made In Japan," 2 3/4" h.
.... **$35-50**

Oriental Man's Head Reamer

Two-piece, in the shape of an Oriental
man's head, w/collar as base, hat as
lid/reamer, light blue w/dark grey highlights, incised "9496," 5 3/4" h. (ILLUS.)
.... **$125-150**
Two-piece, model of lemon slice, yellow
w/green handle, marked "Japan,"
6 3/4" h. **$35-45**

Reamer with Basketweave Design

Two-piece, pitcher shape w/C-form handle,
basketweave design in dark green w/or-
ange & maroon flowers & light green
leaves, yellow top & cone, black trim,
marked "Maramotoware Hand Painted
Japan," 4" h. (ILLUS.) **$40-50**

Squat Pitcher-form Reamer

Two-piece, squat pitcher form w/lip & circular handle, white ground w/maroon & yellow flower design, gold trim, marked
"Hand Painted Japan," 3 3/4" h. (ILLUS.)
.... **$75-95**

Tall Pitcher-form Reamer

Two-piece, tall pitcher form w/lip, C-form
handle & short outcurved base, pale pink
ground w/painted floral decoration in
pinks, blues, yellows & greens, thin green
rim decoration, marked "Pantry Bak-In
Ware by Crooksville," 8 1/4" h. (ILLUS.)
.... **$125-175**

Two-piece, teapot shape on three legs, white ground w/color photograph of Westminster Abbey, marked "Foreign," 3 1/2" h. **$100-125**

Figural Painted Ceramic Reamer

Two-piece, teapot shape, with earthtone & purple pansy-type flowers on white ground, green lustre trim on handle & rim of body, lid & spout, ribbed lid w/holes for liquid to pass through, reamer in the form of a head with yellow ribbed cone hat, marked "Made in Japan," 6" h. (ILLUS.)......................... **$75-125**

String Holders

String holders were standard equipment for general stores, bakeries and homes before the use of paper bags, tape and staples became prevalent. Decorative string holders, mostly chalkware, first became popular during the late 1930s and 1940s. They were mass-produced and sold in five-and-dime stores like Woolworth's and Kresge's. Ceramic string holders became available in the late 1940s through the 1950s. It is much more difficult to find a chalkware string holder in excellent condition, while the sturdier ceramics maintain a higher quality over time.

Apple, ceramic, handmade, 1947 .... **$35**
Apple w/face, ceramic, "PY" **$95**
Apple with berries, chalkware, common........ **$20**

Apple with Worm String Holder

Apple with worm, chalkware, "Willie the Worm," ca. 1948, Miller Studio (ILLUS.) **$35**
Art Deco woman, chalkware, green beret & scarf **$95**

Baby, chalkware, frowning **$125**
Balloon, ceramic, variety of colors, each **$25**
Bananas, chalkware, ca. 1980s-present **$25**

Goebel Bears Egg Timer

Bears, ceramic, brown & tan, white base, Goebel (ILLUS.) **$75**
Betty Boop, chalkware, original **$400**
Bird, ceramic, green, "Arthur Wood, England," also found in blue & brown............. **$15**

"String Swallow" Bird String Holder

Bird, ceramic, in birdhouse, "String Swallow" (ILLUS.) **$35**
Bird, ceramic, yellow bird on green nest, embossed "String Nest Pull," Cardinal China, U.S.A. **$35**
Boy, w/top hat and pipe, eyes to side, chalkware **$30**
Brother Jacob and Sister Isabel, chalkware, newer vintage, each **$50**

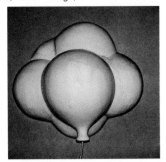

Bunch of Balloons String Holder

Bunch of balloons, ceramic, green, pink & blue, ca. 1983, Fitz & Floyd (ILLUS.) **$25**

Butler, ceramic, black man w/white lips & eyebrows, Japan, hard to find **$150**

Cabbage String Holder

Cabbage, ceramic, Japan (ILLUS.) **$85**
Campbell Soup boy, chalkware, face only... **$175**

Black Cat with Gold Bow

Cat, ceramic, black w/gold bow, handmade (ILLUS.) **$25**
Cat, ceramic, climbing a ball of string **$50**
Cat, ceramic, full-figured w/flowers & scissors **$25**

Cat with Ball of String Holder

Cat, ceramic, white, full-figured on top of ball of string (ILLUS.) **$35**

Cat on Ball of String String Holder

Cat, chalkware, grinning, on a ball of string, Miller Studio, 1952 (ILLUS.) **$30**
Cat, chalkware, on ball of string, Miller Studio, 1948 .... **$45-65**
Cat, chalkware, w/bow, holding ball of string ... **$25**
Chef, ceramic, "Gift Ideas Creation, Phila., Pa.," w/scissors in head **$25**

Chef with Rosy Cheeks

Chef, ceramic, w/rosy cheeks, marked "Japan" (ILLUS.) **$28**
Chef, chalkware, "Little Chef," Miller Studio **$95**

Chef with Bushy Eyebrows

Chef, chalkware, unusual version of chef w/bushy eyebrows **$75**

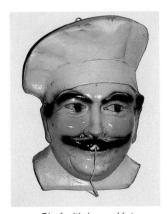

Chef with Large Hat

Chef, chalkware, w/large hat facing left (ILLUS.) **$75**

Bunch of Cherries String Holder

Cherries, chalkware, bunch on leafy stem (ILLUS.)... **$150**
Chicken, ceramic, "Quimper of France," found in several patterns, still in production **$50**
Chicken, ceramic, unmarked **$35**

Chipmunk String Holder

Chipmunk's head, ceramic, white & brown, red & white striped hat & bow, bow holds scissors, Japan (ILLUS.) **$35**

Clown, ceramic, full-figured, "Pierrot," hand holds scissors **$65**
Dog, ceramic, "Bonzo," comic character dog w/bee on chest... **$75**

Bonzo Face String Holder

Dog, ceramic, Bonzo face,comic character dog, marked "Japan," rare (ILLUS.) **$275**
Dog, ceramic, full-figured Shaggy Dog, w/scissors as glasses, marked "Babba-combe Pottery, England" **$20**

Westie with Bow String Holder

Dog, chalkware, Westie, bow at neck (ILLUS.)... **$85**

Westie with Studded Collar

Dog, chalkware, Westie, white w/studded color **$75**

Dog, wood, "Sandy Twine Holder," body is
ball of string **$20**

Dog with Black Eye

Dog w/black eye, ceramic, w/scissors holder in collar, right eye only circled in black, England (ILLUS.).. **$25**
Dove, ceramic, Japan..................................... **$25**
Dutch Boy, chalkware, w/cap **$75**

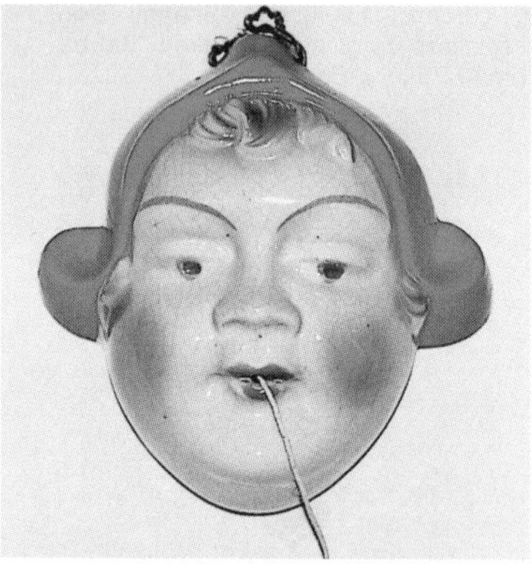

Ceramic Dutch Girl String Holder

Dutch Girl, ceramic, head only, Japan
(ILLUS.) **$25**

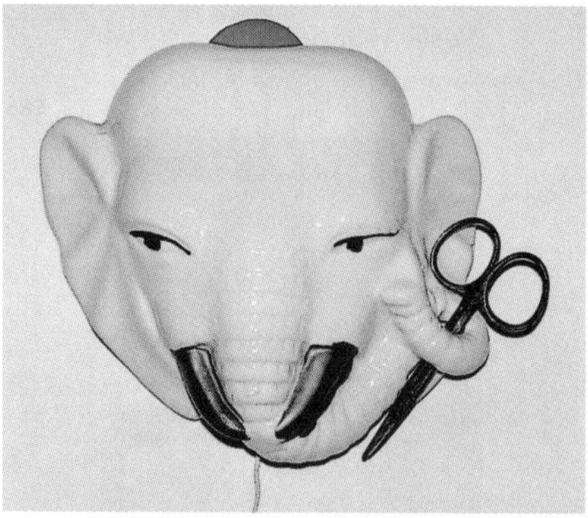

Elephant Pincushion-String Holder

Elephant, ceramic, white w/gold tusks, pincushion on head, Japan (ILLUS.)................ **$28**

Father Christmas String Holder

Father Christmas, ceramic, Japan (ILLUS.) ... **$95**
Flowerpot, ceramic, yellow, w/measuring
spoon holder **$50**

Chalkware Chef String Holder

French chef, chalkware, w/scarf around
neck (ILLUS.) **$85**
Funnel-shaped, w/thistle or cat & ball, ceramic **$45**
Gollywog, bisque, England........................... **$165**
Gourd, chalkware.. **$50**
Granny, ceramic, full-figured, top of nose
holds scissors that look like glasses **$25**

Puffed Heart String Holder

Heart, ceramic, puffed, heart reads "You'll always have a 'pull' with me!" California Cleminsons (ILLUS., previous page) **$35**

Humpty Dumpty String Holder

Humpty Dumpty, ceramic, sitting on wall, white & yellow (ILLUS.) **$35**

Indian in Headdress String Holder

Indian w/headdress, chalkware, brightly colored (ILLUS.) **$100**
Iron w/flowers, ceramic **$45**
Ladybug, chalkware....................................... **$85**

Cleminsons House String Holder

Latchstring house, ceramic, California Cleminsons (ILLUS.) **$50**

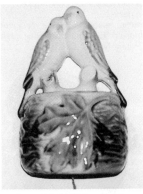

Loverbirds String Holder

Lovebirds, ceramic, Morton Pottery (ILLUS.) **$35**
Maid, ceramic, Sarsaparilla, 1984 .... **$35**
Mammy, ceramic, full-figured, plaid & polka dot dress, Japan **$60**

Mammy String Holder

Mammy, ceramic, full-figured, w/arms up & scissors in pocket (ILLUS.) **$100**

Mammy Holding Flowers

Mammy, chalkware, full-figured, holding flowers, marked "MAPCO" (ILLUS.)............ **$95**

Mammy, chalkware, head only, marked "Ty-Me" on neck **$125**
Man, ceramic, head only, drunk, designed by & marked "Elsa" on back, Pfaltzgraff, York, Pennsylvania **$50**

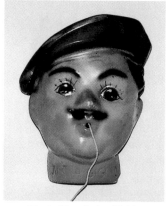

Gigolo Man String Holder

Man, chalkware, head only, marked across collar "Just a Gigolo" (ILLUS.).................... **$50**

Mexican Man with Flowered Hat

Mexican man, chalkware, head only, flower-trimmed hat (ILLUS.) **$60**
Mexican woman, chalkware, head only, w/braids & sombrero **$95**
Monkey, chalkware, sitting on ball of string, found in various colors **$95**
Mouse, ceramic, countertop-type, Josef Originals sticker... **$25**
Mouse, ceramic, England.............................. **$20**
Oriental man, ceramic, w/coolie hat, Abingdon Pottery **$250**
Owl, Babbacombe Pottery, England **$20**

Porter String Holder9

Porter, clay, without teeth, marked "Fredericksburg Art Pottery, U.S.A." (ILLUS.)......... **$95**
Prayer lady, ceramic, by Enesco................... **$95**
Rooster, porcelain, head only, Royal Bayreuth.. **$225**

Sailboat Lustre-glazed Egg Timer

Sailboat, ceramic, lustre ware, tan boat w/white sails, Germany (ILLUS.)................ **$50**
Sailor Boy, chalkware.................................... **$85**
Sailor Girl (Rosie the Riveter), chalkware .. **$145**
Santa Claus, ceramic, sitting, unmarked **$50**

Snail String Holder

Snail, ceramic, dark brown (ILLUS., previ-
ous page) $20
Soldier, chalkware, head only, w/hat $30
Southern gentleman with ladies, ceramic.... $35
Strawberry, chalkware, w/white flower,
green leaves & no stem $45
Susie Sunfish, chalkware, Miller Studio,
1948 .... $95
Teapot, ceramic, w/parakeet, Japan $35

Tomato String Holder

Tomato, ceramic (ILLUS.)............................... $35
Tomato, chalkware.. $35
Tomato chef, ceramic, eyes closed, "Ja-
pan".. $50
Witch in pumpkin, ceramic, winking $95

Woman in Flowered Dress String Holder

Woman, ceramic, full-figured, blue dress
w/white & red flowers, Japan (ILLUS.) $50

Utensils

Cherry pitter, tin, a flat tray base centered
by a narrow upright rectangular compartment below the flaring feeding bin, the
upper section w/moveable plungers,
spring-loaded mechanism for pitting
eight cherries at a time, 19th c., 10" w.,
13" h. (ILLUS., top next column) $288

Unusual Old Tin Cherry Pitter

Unusual Patented Iron Cork Extractor

Cork extractor, cast iron, a tall arched body
decorated w/ornate delicate scrolls, a
hinged turned wood handle, large hand-
grips at the sides of the bottom, adjustable extracting mechanism on the front,
marked "Champion," patent-dated in
1898, 9" h. (ILLUS.) $316

Victorian Mechanical Food Charger

Food charger, mechanical, a large wheel-operated cast-iron mechanism w/an arm fitting into a deep cylindrical copper container, all mounted on a rectangular board base, second half 19th c., 16" l. (ILLUS.).. **$258**

Canvas & Iron Folding Water Bucket

Water bucket, folding-type, canvas over a steel frame, stenciled base marked "Planet Co.," wire bail handle, late 19th c., 9 3/4" h. (ILLUS.).................................... **$58**

LACQUER

Most desirable of the lacquer articles available for collectors are those of Japanese and Chinese origin, and the finest of these were produced during the Ming and Ching dynasties, although the Chinese knew the art of fashioning articles of lacquer centuries before. Cinnabar is carved red lacquer.

Ornate Inlaid Lacquer Victorian Stand

Stand, tilt-top style, the large rectangular top w/an ornately scalloped edge in black centered w/an inlaid design of a tall vase holding a large floral bouquet done in mother-of-pearl & paint, a grapevine border band in white & gold, raised on a six-sided baluster-form pedestal in black decorated w/orante gilt scrolls, the molded tripartite black base on outswept wide scroll legs w/gold decoration & on casters, mid-19th c., 22 1/2 x 27", 29" h . (ILLUS.)......... **$633**

Large Oriental Lacquer Tea Set

Tea set: two cov. teapots, cov. sugar, creamer, six cups & saucers, six small plates & six small bowls w/spoons; ovoid & bulbous black bodies decorated w/designs of dragons in orange & gold, gilt interiors, Oriental, early 20th c., the set (ILLUS.) **$196**
Tray, cartouche shaped, inlaid black lacquer tray w/elaborate mother-of-pearl inlay, gilt decoration, w/design of turreted buildings surrounded by palm trees, urns w/flowers, 31 1/2" l., on later faux bamboo cross-stretcher base, minor chips & losses to tray surface, minor border separations **$990**

LIGHTING DEVICES

Early Non-Electric Lamps & Lighting

Miniature Lamps

Our listings are generally arranged numerically according to the numbers assigned to the various miniature lamps pictured in the following reference books: Frank R. & Ruth E. Smith's book Miniature Lamps, now referred to as Smith's Book I (Smith I) and Ruth Smith's sequel, Miniature Lamps II (Smith II), and Marjorie Hulsebus' books, Miniature Victorian Lamps (Hulsebus I or H-II) and Miniature Lamps of the Victorian Era (Hulsebus II or H-II).

Clear Handy Night Lamp & Reflector

Clear, squatty rounded font embossed "The Handy Night Lamp," w/cork-type burner & small tin reflector, overall 5 3/4" h., Smith I, Fig. 5, right (ILLUS.) **$60-70**

Little Fire Fly Clear Mini Lamp

Clear, bulbous font embossed "Little Fire Fly" w/arched design, milk glass chimney, Olmsted-type burner, overall 4 1/2" h., Smith I, Fig. 7, right (ILLUS.)............... **$150-170**

Little Pearl Clear Finger Lamp

Clear, finger lamp embossed "Little Pearl" on font, Hornet sized burner, 2 7/8" h., Hulsebus I, Fig. 19 (ILLUS.)............... **$125-150**

Twilight Clear Stem Mini Lamp

Clear, stem-style, flaring stem & slightly flaring cylindrical font embossed "Twilight," Olmsted-type burner, missing milk glass chimney that would add $50 to value, overall 5 1/2" h., Smith I, Fig. 19 (ILLUS. with no chimney) **$125**

Milk Glass Finger Lamp with Florals

Milk glass, finger-type, waisted cylindrical font w/h.p. florals around the font & pink on the top, Nutmeg burner, 3" h., Smith I, Fig. 39 (ILLUS.)................................. **$100-115**

Lamp with Metal Band & Ring Handle

Milk glass, finger-type, footed cylindrical font w/an embossed design & a metal band w/finger ring, 1896 catalog called it the "Brownie," Acorn burner, 3" h., Smith I, Fig. 53 (ILLUS.).................................. **$75-85**

Clear Stem Lamp with Strawberries

Clear, stem lamp w/embossed strawberries & vines, painted inside base stem,

Nutmeg burner, 6" h., Hulsebus I, Fig. 69 (ILLUS.) **$100-115**

Little Beauty Mountable Lamp

Nickel-plated brass, mountable-type, a milk glass beehive shade on a long curved metal arm ending in a round mounting plate, for table or wall mounting, original hang tag reads "Little Beauty Night Lamp," 4 1/2" h., Smith I, Fig. 77 (ILLUS.).. **$75-90**

Milk Glass Lamp with Rust Vines

Milk glass, footed spherical font, base & chimney shade decorated w/a rust-colored vine design, called "Will-O'-the-Wisp" in early ad, Nutmeg burner, 7 7/8" h., Hulsebus II, Fig. 89 (ILLUS.)............... **$200-225**

Clear, stem-type, embossed Bull's-eye patt., Acorn burner, 5" h., Smith I, Fig. 111 (ILLUS., top next column) **$85-95**

Blue opaque, bulbous base & shade, both w/embossed flower & leaf decoration over a lattice field, clear chimney, Nutmeg burner, small flake on edge of shade, 7 1/2" h., No. 229 (ILLUS., middle next column)... **$259**

Clear Bull's-eye Stem Lamp

Blue Opaque Flower & Lattice Lamp

Light Green Opaque Miniature Lamp

Light green opaque, bulbous tapering ovoid base w/molded scrolls, matching ball shade, clear chimney, Nutmeg burner, 8 1/4" h., Smith 1, Fig. 234 (ILLUS.).... **$518**

Frosted Clear Snail Pattern Mini Lamp

Frosted clear, Snail patt., a squared waisted scroll-embossed base & matching open-topped umbrella-form shade, Nutmeg burner, 8" h., Smith 1, Fig. 242 (ILLUS.) **$633**

Ribbed Blue Satin Miniature Lamp

Blue satin, footed bulbous ribbed base & matching open-topped umbrella shade, clear chimney, Nutmeg burner, thin flake on bottom edge of shade, 8 1/2" h., Smith 1, Fig. 299 (ILLUS.) **$518**

Cased Yellow Cosmos Miniature Lamp

Cased yellow, Cosmos patt., base & umbrella shade w/pink-stained band & colored florals, Nutmeg burner, flake in top edge of shade, 7 1/2" h., Smith 1, No. 286 (ILLUS.) **$403**

Milk Glass Mini Lamp with Flowers

Milk glass, footed spherical base & ball shade h.p. shaded pink w/burgundy flowers & green leaves, Nutmeg burner, clear chimney, 8 1/2" h., Smith I, Fig. 308 (ILLUS.) **$345**

Red Satin Floral-embossed Mini Lamp

Red satin, low squatty bulbous base molded w/roses, matching ball shade, clear chimney, P&A Victor burner, roughage & tiny flakes on shade top, 11 3/4" h., Smith 1, Fig. 288 (ILLUS.) **$230**

Pan-American Expo Souvenir Lamp

Milk glass, footed bulbous font & ball shade painted light blue & decorated w/the color logo & inscription for the "Pan-American Exposition - 1901 - Buffalo, N.Y.," Nutmeg burner, 9" h., Smith I, Fig. 309 (ILLUS., previous page) **$450-500**

Milk glass, footed bulbous font & clear frosted chimney shade, both w/a light blue ground decorated w/a transfer-printed cherub, Hornet burner, 9" h., Smith I, Fig. 325 .... **$350-400**

Floral-embossed Pink Opaque Lamp

Pink opaque, footed spherical base & chimney-form shade both embossed w/a floral & vine design, Hornet burner, 8 1/4" h., Smith I, Fig. 373 (ILLUS.).................. **$450-500**

Pink Cased Satin Lamp & Shade

Pink cased satin, squatty squared footed base & a bulbous artichoke pattern shade, Nutmeg burner, 8 3/4" h., Smith I, Fig. 385 (ILLUS.).............................. **$400-450**

Blue Cased Satin Molded Lamp & Shade

Blue cased satin, melon-lobed base & molded pansy design ball shade, Nutmeg-type burner, 7" h., Smith I, Fig. 389 (ILLUS.).. **$1,150**

Tomato Soup Red Lamp with Gilt Trim

Cased tomato soup red, waisted cylindrical base & domed open-top shade each w/fired-on gold floral designs, glossy finish, Acorn burner, clear chimney, 8 1/2" h., Smith I, Fig. 391 (ILLUS.)..... **$700-750**

Cased Yellow Miniature Lamp

Cased yellow, cylindrical font base w/ringed base & top, domed open-topped shade, gold floral decoration, Nutmeg burner, flake on edge of shade, Smith I, Fig. 391 (ILLUS.)......................... **$575**

Satin-finished Milk Glass Lamp

Milk glass satin, double-gourd ribbed base & ribbed domed shade, h.p. w/colored flowers, Nutmeg burner, clear glass chimney, 7 3/4" h., Smith I, Fig. 393 (ILLUS.) **$300-350**

Yellow Consolidated Pine Cone Lamp

Cased yellow, spherical body & domed shade in molded Pine Cone patt., glossy finish, made by Consolidated Lamp & Glass Co., clear glass chimney, 8" h., Smith I, Fig. 394 (ILLUS.).................. **$400-450**

Lamps, Miscellaneous

Argand lamp, gilt-brass, the round domed base cast w/leaves supporting the cut crystal baluster-form standard topped by a rolled crystal crown suspending long facet-cut prisms & centered by an upper gilt-brass post w/two straight arms each ending in a metal font & burner fitted w/tall tulip-shaped shades, the upper shaft topped by another cut crystal section supporting a gilt-brass band suspending additional prisms, Johnston Brooke & Company, first quarter 19th c., electrified, 16" w., 22" h. (ILLUS., top next column).. **$3,910**

Fine Early Signed Argand Lamp

Rare Early American Astral lamps

Astral lamps, a stepped marble & brass square base supporting a tall reeded standard topped by the font & shade ring hung w/long prisms & fitted w/a finely frosted & etched mushroom-shaped shade, American, early 19th c., electrified, 31 1/2" h., pr. (ILLUS.) **$5,750**

Pair of Blue Glass Banquet Lamps

Banquet lamps, kerosene-type, blue opaque glass base w/a round foot & tapering reeded column supporting a ringed cylindrical font decorated w/a Greek key band, kerosene burner w/chimney, ca. 1870, 15" h., pr. (ILLUS., previous page) ... **$230**

Interesting Old Iron Betty Lamp

Betty lamp, wrought iron, a flat-bottomed two-lobed rounded oblong tray lamp w/a hinged lid & short cylindrical end spout for wick, the end w/a high arched iron bar handle fitted w/a flat hanging bar w/hook end, possibly Pennsylvania, 19th c., 5" l., without hook 4 1/4" h. (ILLUS.) **$173**

Old Wrought-Iron Crusie Lamp

Crusie lamp, wrought iron, a serrated back stud supporting the upper shallow pointed oblong reservoir that can adjust as the fuel is consumed w/the longer matching lower reservoir collecting the drip, the top w/a long hook-ended hanging bar, probably 19th c., 6" l., without hook 6" h. (ILLUS.) **$100-150**

Cut-overlay banquet lamp, white cut to clear cut to blue alabaster, a stepped marble base trimmed w/brass supporting a tall waisted cylindrical standard cut w/ovals fitted w/a ringed brass connector to the inverted bell-shaped font cut w/bands of ovals, brass collar, attributed to Boston & Sandwich Glass Co., ca. 1870, very minor shedding to blue layer, upper most brass stem mount had leaves removed, 17" h. (ILLUS., top next column) **$6,600**

Fine Cut-Overlay Banquet Lamp

Rare Dolphin-based Cut-Overlay Lamp

Cut-overlay lamp, round pressed clam-broth triple-dolphin base w/gilt trim below a brass connector supporting the inverted pear-shaped font in white cut to clear w/dots & ovals & decorated w/gold leafy scrolls, Boston & Sandwich Glass Co., ca. 1870, 11 3/4" h. (ILLUS.) **$7,150**

Group of Four Hobbs' Coin Dot Pattern Kerosene Lamps

Group of Four Raymond Swirl Pattern Glass Kerosene Lamps

Finger lamp, kerosene-type, Hobbs' Coin Dot - No. 326 Windows patt., cranberry opalescent squatty bulbous font w/applied clear handle, early clear chimney w/pie-crest rim, 1880s, 3" h. (ILLUS. second from right with three other Coin Dot lamps, top of page) **$1,650**

Finger lamp, kerosene-type, pressed Raymond Swirl patt. in blue, short pedestal base & flaring swirled font, side finger handle, early clear pie-crust rim chimney (ILLUS. second from left with other Raymond Swirl lamps)..................................... **$275**

Finger lamp, kerosene-type, pressed Raymond Swirl patt. in vaseline, short pedestal base & flaring swirled font, side finger handle, early clear pie-crust rim chimney (ILLUS. far left with other Raymond Swirl lamps) **$358**

Gone-with-the-Wind table lamp, kerosene-type, a leafy-scroll cast-brass base supporting the squatty bulbous milk glass font decorated w/large red mums & green leaves on a shaded deep blue ground, a matching ball shade on top, electrified, ca. 1900, 15" h. (ILLUS., next column) **$150-200**

G.W.T.W. Lamp with Red Mums

Lion Mask Gone-with-the-Wind Lamp

Gone-with-the-Wind table lamp, kerosene-type, the ball globe & matching squatty glass base molded in bold relief w/lion head masks alternating w/lobed panels, dark brown w/each smooth panel printed w/a desert oasis scene against a shaded yellow ground, cast-brass scrolling arched base, brass font shoulder & burner, late 19th c., non-electric, 14" h. (ILLUS.).. **$575**

Rose-decorated Gone-with-the Wind Lamps

Gone-with-the-Wind table lamps, kerosene-type, the ball globe & matching ovoid glass base decorated w/a shaded pale blue, pink & cream ground painted w/rose sprays, brass pierced scroll base & font rim w/burner, late 19th c., non-electric, 17 1/2" h., pr. (ILLUS.) **$1,265**

Hall lamp, kerosene-type, a high domical mold-blown optic swirled rib blue shade w/a domed base cap w/ring finial & a small brass top collar hung from chains, complete w/font, burner & chimney, ca. 1900, overall 12" h. (ILLUS., next column) **$230**

Blue Optic Swirled Rib Hall Lamp

Cranberry Optic Swirled Rib Hall Lamp

Hall lamp, kerosene-type, a high domical mold-blown optic swirled rib cranberry shade w/a domed base cap w/ring finial & a small brass top collar hung from chains, ca. 1900, overall 12" h. (ILLUS.) **$250-350**

Pink Satin Glass Hall Lamp

Hall lamp, kersoene-type, a bulbous ovoid pink satin glass shade w/a brass base cap w/finial & brass top collar hung from chains, ca. 1900, electrified, overall 13 1/2" h. (ILLUS.) **$288**

Brass Parlor Lamp with Hobnail Shade

Hanging parlor lamp, kerosene-type, a brass bulbous lower section w/base ring supported by pairs of long brass scrolls & supporting the squatty bulbous brass font & pierced shade ring hung w/faceted prisms, a domed milky white shading to pink opalescent Hobnail patt. shade, openwork link chains & upper crown, clear glass chimney, ca. 1890 (ILLUS.) **$978**

Hanging Lamp with Purple Flowers

Hanging parlor lamp, kerosene-type, a leafy scroll brass frame supporting the squatty bulbous milk glass font decorated w/purple flowers & green leaves below a brown rim band, a matching domical shade in a pierced brass shade ring hung w/faceted prisms, pierced brass crown & upper ring hung w/faceted prisms, complete w/adjusting mechanism, ca. 1900, electrified, 14" d. (ILLUS.)... **$259**

Hanging Parlor Lamp with Tapering Shade

Hanging parlor lamp, kerosene-type, a cast-brass arched frame w/pierced triangular flanges & a base finial all set w/a blue jewel, a squatty cylindrical ribbed clear pressed glass font, a wide conical milk glass shade h.p. w/large flowers & green leafy stems, pierced brass crown & smoke bell, clear glass chimney, complete w/adjusting mechanism, ca. 1880, 14" d. (ILLUS.) **$345**

Rare Cranberry Opalescent Hobnail Lamp

Hanging parlor lamp, kerosene-type, a squatty bulbous cranberry opalescent Hobnail patt. font w/a pierced brass ring drop & brass font collar, a rare rubina Hobnail patt. chimney, the stamped & pierced shade ring hung w/faceted prisms & supporting the domical cranberry opalescent Hobnail shade w/a pierced brass crown & upper ring hung w/prisms, ca. 1890, complete w/adjusting mechanism, 14" d. (ILLUS.) **$1,725**

Ornate Brass French Sanctuary Lamp

Hanging sanctuary lamp, brass, a squatty bulbous paneled top stamped w/florette & leaf designs above the long paneled tapering pointed base drop w/fleur-de-lis drop finial, large ornately scrolling pieced handles at the side hung from openwork link chains, France, second half 19th c., overall 49" h. (ILLUS.) **$748**

Very Unique Victorian Piano Lamp

Piano lamp, kerosene-type, a floral-painted milk glass globe shade & clear chimney above the bulbous embossed brass font raised on a very tall brass standard w/two tall columnar sections cast w/delicate leafs connected by a bulbous decorative

knob, all raised on four arched lobster-style legs w/open claws & beady eyes, late 19th c., overall 63 1/2" h. (ILLUS.)... **$2,530**

Reproduction Sandwich Glass Lamps

Sandwich glass-style table lamps, pressed transparent green glass w/an octagonal foot & three-printie block font, 20th c. reproductions, ca. 1930s, 9 1/2" h., pr. (ILLUS.) **$46**

Scarce Early Sinumbra Lamp

Sinumbra lamp, square brass stepped base & slender reeded columnar standard w/arms supporting the shade ring & squatty brass font covered by the squatty clear frosted & ethed umbrella shade, ca. 1850, electrified, 22 1/2" h. (ILLUS.) **$2,271**

Solar lamp, kerosene-type, a square stepped cast brass base & tall reeded columnar standard supporting the brass font & ring suspending long prisms, topp by a frosted glass open-topped pear-shaped shade etched w/swirling leaves & berries, electrified, missing solar cap, ca. 1850, 28 1/4" h. (ILLUS. second from right with another solar lamp & two kerosene table lamps).................................... **$920**

Solar lamp, kerosene-type, a square white marble foot & tapering ringed brass standard below the bulbous brass font w/a shade ring hung w/long spearpoint prisms & supporting a frosted & clear etched glass tulip-shaped shade, Cornelius & Baker, Philadelphia, ca. 1850, 20" h. (ILLUS. far left with two kerosene & another solar lamp) **$575**

Double Student Lamp with Lithophane Shades

Student lamp, kerosene double-font style, a round decorated brass base centering a tall slender brass stem fitted w/two straight adjustable arms & a large bulbous inverted pear-shaped brass font, each arm ending in a small bulbous brass font & burner supporting a shade ring fitted w/a domical four-panel porcelain lithophane shade, two panels decorated w/a hunter speaking to a maiden by a fence, a third w/a hunter speaking to a maiden on a footbridge & the fourth showing the hunter & maiden walking over the bridge, one burner signed "Dardonville New York," & the other signed "B & H Duplex," electrified, late 19th c., 25" w., 25" h. (ILLUS.) **$7,188**

Double Student Lamp with Green Shades

Student lamp, kerosene double-font style, a round lappet-engraved domed foot below a slender rod standard & an elongated acorn-shaped brass font w/engraved lap-

pets & a ring finial, two straight ring-turned side arms each ending in an acorn-shaped brass font w/burner & shade ring supporting a cased dark green shade, one glass chimney, base marked "Bailey, Banks & Biddle Co. - Phila. PA," second half 19th c., 21" h. (ILLUS.) **$825**

Table lamp, kerosene-type, a pierced & domed cast-brass base below a wide flaring cylindrical frosted clear base etched w/large flower blossoms, a domed stamped brass collar font & burner w/a wide shade ring supporting the wide umbrella-form matching glass shade, clear glass chimney, ca. 1880, electrified, 24" h. (ILLUS. second from left with other kerosene & solar lamps) **$345**

Tall Kerosene Lamp with Bird Shade

Table lamp, kerosene-type, a round cast-brass base w/tab feet supporting a short blue opaque glass baluster-shaped stem & brass connnector below the squatty onion-form clear pressed glass font w/a swirl & block design, the burner w/a spider support for the open-topped domed milk glass shade h.p. w/a large red, blue & white bird perched on a blossoming branch against a shaded blue & pink ground, ca. 1890, 21" h. (ILLUS.) **$345**

Table lamp, kerosene-type, Hobbs' Coin Dot - No. 326 Windows patt., cranberry opalescent squatty bulbous font on a tall flaring clear reeded standard, 1880s, minor foot bruises, 9" h. (ILLUS. second from left with three other Coin Dot lamps) **$715**

Table lamp, kerosene-type, opalescent squatty bulbous font on a tall black glass Eason patt. pedestal, 1880s, minor foot flakes, 9" h. (ILLUS. far right with three other Coin Dot lamps) **$264**

Table lamp, kerosene-type, pressed Raymond Swirl patt. in amber, tall pedestal base & flaring swirled font, early clear pie-crust rim chimney (ILLUS. far right with other Raymond Swirl lamps) **$154**

Group of Kerosene and Solar Lamps

Table lamp, kerosene-type, pressed Raymond Swirl patt. in vaseline, tall pedestal base & flaring swirled font, early clear pie-crust rim chimney (ILLUS. second from right with other Raymond Swirl lamps) **$319**

Table lamp, kerosene-type, scroll-pierced cast-brass domed base supporting the ovoid base in deep red decorated w/applied green leaves & flanked by pierced leafy scroll side handles, a decorative brass shoulder & inset font, topped by a shaded light cranberry ball shade cameo-cut w/large white blossoms & long leaves, Bradley & Hubbard, ca.1890, electrified, 22" h. (ILLUS. far right with other kerosene & solar lamps, top of page) **$345**

Table lamp, kerosene-type, Hobbs' Coin Dot - No. 326 Windows patt., cranberry opalescent squatty bulbous font on a tall flaring clear reeded standard, 1880s, 8 1/4" h. (ILLUS. far left with three other Coin Dot lamps) **$1,100**

Three Painted Glass Victorian Vase Lamps

Vase lamp, kerosene-type, a cast & stamped brass footed round base supporting a cylindrical milk glass sleeve h.p. w/large flowers & leaves, the brass collar & removable font w/a burner & small shade ring supporting an open-topped frosted & clear etched ball shade, tall clear glass chimney, font drilled & professionally repaired, ca. 1880, 9" h. (ILLUS. center with two other vase lamps) **$143**

Vase lamp, kerosene-type, a cast & stamped brass footed round base supporting a cylindrical milk glass sleeve h.p. w/white & purple flowers on leafy green stems, the brass collar & removable font w/a burner & small shade ring supporting an open-topped frosted & clear etched squatty bulbous shade, clear glass chimney, font drilled & professionally repaired, ca. 1880, 10 3/4" h. (ILLUS. right with two other vase lamps) **$165**

Vase lamp, kerosene-type, a cast & stamped brass footed round base supporting a cylindrical milk glass sleeve h.p. w/a brown & white winter landscape w/cottage, the brass collar & removable font w/a burner & small shade ring supporting an open-topped frosted & clear etched squatty bulbous shade, clear glass chimney, font drilled & professionally repaired, ca. 1880, 10 1/2" h. (ILLUS. left with two other vase lamps) **$242**

Whale oil lamp, clear pressed & blown glass, a tall pressed four-sided lacy glass base molded w/tall ribbed C-scrolls ending in paw feet & topped w/applied ring wafers below the applied tall tapering bulbous blown font w/early pewter collar, possibly Boston & Sandwich Glass Co., ca. 1830, 10 1/2" h. (ILLUS. left with two other whale oil lamps, next page)....... **$880**

Whale oil lamp, clear pressed & blown glass, a tall pressed four-sided stepped pressed base w/rounded corners & internal ribbing topped by an applied ringed wafer & blown hollow knob w/another ringed wafer supporting the blown ovoid font w/a flattened shoulder centered a brass collar & forked camphene burner w/caps, possibly Boston & Sandwich Glass Co., ca. 1830-40, 10 1/2" h. (ILLUS. right with two other whale oil lamps, below) **$660**

Three Early Glass Whale Oil Lamps

Whale oil lamp, clear pressed & blown glass, the inverted pressed lacy glass cup plate base in Lee & Rose No. 32 patt. supports an applied ringed stem applied w/a tall tapering conical font fitted w/a tin whale oil burner, rough pontil mark, Boston & Sandwich Glass C. ca. 1830, minute base chips & flakes, edge of font burner disk trimmed, 6 7/8" h. (ILLUS. center with two other whale oil lamps) **$980**

Early Brass Whale Oil Lamps

Whale oil lamps, brass, egg-shaped font atop a urn- and three-knob-turned standard above the flaring round foot, early tin whale oil burners, attributed to Webb of Portland, Maine, some repair, mid-19th c., 9"h., pr. (ILLUS.) **$403**

Electric Lamps & Lighting

Handel Lamps

The Handel Company of Meriden, Connecticut (1885-1936) began as a glass and lamp shade decorating company. It became a major producer of decorative electric lamps which have become very collectible today.

Unusual Gold-Washed Handel Lamp

Boudoir lamp, 9 1/2" d. tapering pyramidial frosted glass shade fitted w/a metal cap, the shade exterior covered in a gold-wash & etched w/a delicated overall scrolling design, raised on a slender ribbed gilt-metal standard & round foot cast w/a design of triangles, shade signed ""Handel 7271," some wear on gold wash, roughness to shade fitter, overall 13 1/2" h. (ILLUS.)........................ **$345**

Handel Floor Lamp with Treasure Island Shade

Floor lamp, 10" d. domical reverse-painted shade decorated w/the Treasure Island patt. featuring a moonlit harbor w/a sailing ship & palm trees, suspended from a high arched bronze harp atop a tall slender standard on a tripod base w/cabriole legs ending in scroll feet, shade signed "Handel 6574," overall 57" h. (ILLUS.)............ **$7,475**

Fine Handel Hall Lamp with Parrots

Hall lamp, a spherical ball shade w/a gold ground painted w/a large dark blue & green parrots among green & orange leafy vines, fitter rim signed "Handel 6996 ED," w/original cast-metal base drop tassel & top metal cap & hanging chain, one very minor chip to lower rim, shade 10" d., overall 41" h. (ILLUS.)................. **$3,600**

Handel Floral & Landscape Table Lamp

Table lamp, 18" d. domical reverse-painted shade decorated around the border w/large clusters of deep red & pinks blossoms & green leaves, a background of low hills in deep purple & greenish yellow & w/tall slender trees in the foreground w/stippled green & yellow leaves, signed "7106 Handel R," raised on a bulbous tapering ovoid bronze base cast w/Art Nouveau looping & ending in four thick square feet, base w/worn Handel signature, one chip to shade rim,, overall 27" h. (ILLUS.).. **$4,888**

Rare Handel Hydrangea Plants Lamp

Table lamp, 16" d. domical reserve-painted shade decorated w/large hydrangea plants w/large shaded pink florals & shaded dark to light green leaves, chipped ice exterior, raised on a footed bulbous ovoid bronze base w/tiny scroll rim handles, overall 22" h. (ILLUS.)
.... **$14,950**

Rare Handel Jungle Birds Lamp

Table lamp, 18" d. domical reverse-painted shade decorated in the Jungle Bird patt., two large brightly colored macaws perched among tropical foliage, reverse w/a single macaw in flight, shade signed "Handel 6874," raised on a bronze Chinese-style base w/a paneled ovoid body on a disk foot raised on openwork scrolls, 23" h. (ILLUS.) **$25,300**

Handel Lamp with Parrots Shade

Table lamp, 18" d. domical reverse-painted shade, decorated w/a pair of large parrots in dark blue, yellow, white & brown perched among tan & yellow flowering leafy branches & scattered butterflies against a black ground, raised on a slightly tapering cylindrical polychromed base w/a round, ringed foot, shade signed "Handel 7449 Palme," base w/cloth Handel Lamps label on felt, moderate chipping to the base, overall 23 1/4" h. (ILLUS.) **$10,638**

Handel Lamp with Sunset Scene Shade

Table lamp, 18" d. domical reverse-painted shade decorated w/a tropical landscape w/plam trees flanking a lake w/the setting sun in the background, raised on a bronze tapering ovoid basketweave designed base w/four projecting block feet, shade signed "Handel 6322" & diamond logo, base unsigned & w/copper patina worn off the main body, 25 1/2" h. (ILLUS.) **$6,900**

Mid-Century Modern Lighting

White Bubble Lamp Designed by George Nelson for Howard Miller Co.

Bubble lamp, white covering stretched over metal ribs, hangs from ceiling on white plastic cord, designed by George Nelson for Howard Miller Co., 24" d. (ILLUS.) **$250-400**

String Art Ceiling Fixture

Ceiling fixture, string art ice block in metal tongs, ca. 1960s (ILLUS.) **$175-300**

White Glass Globe Ceiling Light

Ceiling light, white glass globe suspended on white vinyl cord, white metal fittings, 1960s, 11" d. (ILLUS.)............................. **$45-75**

Cobra Lamp, white resin with swivel top, cobra-shaped, interior reflector, by Elio Martinelli for Luce, Italy, 1968, 15" h. **$300-400**

Aqua Fiberglass Desk Lamp

Desk lamp, aqua fiberglass base and shade w/ gooseneck and pen holder, 1950s, 14" h. (ILLUS.)............................ **$35-50**

Chrome & White Shade Desk Lamp

Desk lamp, Mod metal design, white metal shade, adjusts up & down on chrome pole, 1960s, 14" h. (ILLUS.).................. **$35-65**

Painted Metal Globe Shade Desk Lamp

Desk lamp, painted metal, curved stand w/jointed adjustable globe shade, 9" h. (ILLUS.)... **$35-55**

Egg lamp, white frosted glass table lamp, egg shape, no base, by Gio Ponti for Fontana Arte, 1950s, 24" h. **$200-350**

Fiber Optic Fountain Spray Lamp

Fiber optic lamp, fountain of fiber optic stands forming spray from silber plastic base, on-off switch underneath, 1970s, 13" h. (ILLUS.) **$20-35**

Metal & Shaggy Fiberglass Floor Lamp

Floor lamp, gold metal w/wood accent, shaggy fiberglass globe & shade, 1950s, 5' h. (ILLUS.) **$175-250**

Mini Arch Lamp Floor Lamp

Floor lamp, mini-version of Arch Lamp, V-shaped heavy base supports a curved chrome pole w/chrome globe shade on the end, 1960s, diagonal height 5' (ILLUS., previous page) **$75-125**

Aluminum & White Shade Floor Lamp

Floor lamp, polished aluminum w/frosted white glass globe shade, marked "C5062" on base, 1960s, 6' h. (ILLUS.) **$145-195**

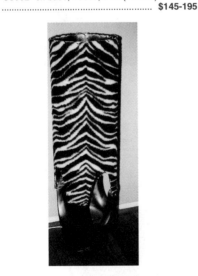

Zebra Faux Fur Floor Lamp

Floor lamp, tall vertical cylindrical zebra faux fur shade over black & gold plaster base, gold interior w/pull string inside, Pieri, 1967, 36" h. (ILLUS.) **$175-275**

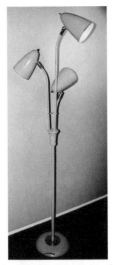

Floor Lamp with Adjustable Shades

Floor lamp, yellow-painted metal w/three adjustable metal shades on poles of varying heights, 1960s, 62" h. (ILLUS.) **$45-95**

Panthella Lamp, mushroom-shaped table lamp by Verner Panton for Louis Poulsen, Denmark, 1970, 27" h. **$200-275**

Robot lamp, male, female, & child versions, poseable bodies made of chrome spheres, Torino, Italy, 1960, female 37" h., each **$750-1,500**

Sputnik ceiling light, chrome poles jut out from center glove, original bulbs were spiked, 1950s, 30" w. **$250-450**

Black & Orange Pierced Ball-Shaped Swag Lamps

Swag lamp, black ceramic ball shade pierced w/round holes over a white cloth cylinder, gold chain, 1960s, 10" h. (ILLUS. right with orange ball lamp) **$90-150**

Swag lamp, orange ceramic ball shade pierced w/round holes over a white cloth cylinder, gold chain, 1960s, 14" h. (ILLUS. left with orange ball lamp) **$175-250**

1950s Abstract Gray Table Lamp

Table lamp, abstract gray ceramic base on black pedestal, Aladdin, 1950s, without base 15" h. (ILLUS.).............................. **$50-90**

Basketweave Plastic Table Lamp

Table lamp, basketweave molded plastic vertical shade on wooden tripod base, 1950s, 14" h. **$30-50**

Ceramic Lamp with Tiered Shade

Table lamp, ceramic stylized flame & scroll base holds extra flame bulb, retangular tiered shade w/attached gold metal gold star accents, aqua, gold & white, Majestic, 1950s 30" h. (ILLUS.) **$125-175**

Boomerang Base Table Lampdf

Table lamp, footed boomerang-shaped base supporting three lamp poles w/patterned cylindrical shades, Majestic, 1950s, 37" h. (ILLUS.)........................ **$200-300**

Tapering Cylindrical Table Lamp

Table lamp, tapering cylindrical plastic shade on wooden tripod base, 1960s, 12" h. **$30-60**

Table Lamp with S-Shaped Bars

Table lamp, three-metal S-shaped bar base between black rectangles, original rectangular mottled shade, Majestic, 1950s, 31" h. (ILLUS.) **$150-225**

Table lamp, white plastic shade on orange plastic base, Lightolier, 1960s, 22" **$55-100**

Table lamp, yellow plastic cylinder holds white plastic shade, Lightolier, 1960s, 18" h. **$90-150**

Conch Shell & Shell Flower Souvenir TV Lamp

TV lamp, conch shells hide interior bulbs; smaller shells, fake flowers and marbled plaster base complete the design, Sea Shell City, USA sticker on front, 1950s, 13" w. **$35-65**

Figural Siamese Cats TV Lamp

TV lamp, figural, cermanic model of two Siamese cats w/aqua rhinestone eyes, Lane & Co., 1958, 12" w., 12" h. (ILLUS.) **$40-85**

Seashell & Flamingo TV Lamp

TV lamp, seashells around figural pink plastic flamingo, marbled plaster base, 1950s, 10" h. (ILLUS.) **$20-45**

Z-Lamp, curving, zig-zag shape, brass & black-painted wood w/two tambourine-style printed shades, Majestic, 1950s, 26" h. **$450-650**

Moss Lamps

Moss, "the lamps that spin," were the work of San Francisco's Moss Manufacturing Co. The best-known of these plexiglass creations of the 1940s and '50s are those that incorporate motorized revolving platforms into their design. Figurines by many prominent ceramics firms of the time - among them, Ceramic Arts Studio, Yona, Hedi Schoop, Lefton, and deLee Art - adorn the platforms. The overall styling of each lamp complements the theme and costuming of the figurine utilized.

The choice of plexiglass as the base material for Moss lamps grew out of World War II metal rationing. Company co-owner Thelma Moss served as the guiding force and inspiration for the lamp designs, which were then realized by staff designers Duke Smith and John Disney. Plexiglass proved easy to work with and particularly suitable for the fanciful Moss creations; the striking visual impact was often highlighted by gigantic "spun glass" shades. Moss quickly built on its reputation for novelty with unique and at times bizarre additions to the line: aquarium lamps, fountain lamps, intercom lamps, and even motorized "double shade" lamps with the shades rotating independently in opposite directions.

The final Moss lamps were produced in 1968. Today, these prime examples of mid-20th century whimsy make attention-grabbing focal points in any decor. The lamps also have a dual appeal for those who collect specific figural ceramics of the era.

Moss Lamps of California is an msn.com group site devoted to the lamps. Complete information on Moss Manufacturing and its extraordinary product line is included in Moss Lamps: Lighting the '50s by Donald-Brian Johnson and Leslie Pina (Schiffer Publishing Ltd., 2000). Photos for this category are by Dr. Leslie Pina.

Floor lamp, "Ballet Man," No.2354, Decoramic Kilns figurines, 4' 10" h. **$475-500**

Floor lamp, "Floor to Ceiling" design, No. 2369, two spun glass globes, 8' 9" h.. **$425-450**

Floor lamp, "Leaf" design, No. 2250, white plexiglas, 5' 4" h. **$175-200**

Floor lamp, No. 2306, two angled stems, dual fluorescent tubes, 5" h............... **$225-250**

Floor lamp, No. 2318, birdcage lantern design, No. 2295, 5' 1" h. (ILLUS.)......... **$250-275**

Multifunction lamp, "Aquarium Cocktail Table," No. 1, fluorescent tubing, 2' 2" x 4' 2", 1' 4" h. **$700-800**

Multifunction lamp, "Cocktail Girl" music box lamp, No. XT 848, Decoramic Kilns figurine, 2' 9" h. **$250-275**

Multifunction lamp, "Lady in Cage" table lamp w/double revolve shade, No. T 686 .... **$400-425**

Multifunction lamp, "Masked Ballerina" table lamp, No. XT 850, w/Comedy & Tragedy faces on plexiglas spinner, 2' 8" h. **$275-300**

Multifunction lamp, "Poodle Girl" radio lamp, No. XT 852, Hedi Schoop figurine, 2' 10" h. **$350-375**
Multifunction lamp, "Snarling Panther" TV lamp, No. XT 851 .... **$150-175**
Multifunction lamp, "Water Wheel" lamp, No. No. T 726, 4' 2" h. **$1,200-1,300**

Moss Siamese Dancer Partner Lamp

Partner lamp, "Siamese Dancer," No. XT 815, no clock, deLee Art female figurine, 2' 11" h. (ILLUS.)................................. **$200-225**
Room divider, No. 2272, spun glass gong, 2' 6" w., 5' 4" h................................ **$750-1,000**

Bali Dance Corner Table Lamp

Table lamp, "Bali Dancer," No. T 681, corner table-type, double rectangular shades, Decoramic Kilns figurine, 3'4" h. (ILLUS.)... **$300-325**
Table lamp, "Bell Girl," No. T 544, corner table-style, triple pod shades, Decoramic Kilns figurine, 2' 10" h. (ILLUS., top next column) **$300-325**

Moss Bell Girl Table Lamp

Table lamp, "Dancer on Turquoise Cloud," No. XT 823, 2' 10" h. **$200-225**
Table lamp, "Egyptian Woman," No. XT 821, 2' 8" h. **$200-225**

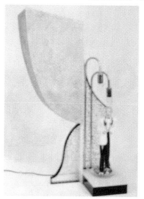

Escort Table Lamp with Torchere Shade

Table lamp, "Escort," No. XT 827, torchere shade, Decoramic Kilns figurine (ILLUS.) **$375-400**
Table lamp, "Fire Woman," No. XT 859, Ceramic Arts Studio of Madison figurine, 1' 7 1/2" h. **$350-375**
Table lamp, "Kneeling Woman in Gold," No. XT 829, 1' 11" h. **$150-175**
Table lamp, "Medieval Figure with Mandolin," No. XT 820, 3' h. **$175-200**
Table lamp, "Nubian," No. XT 818, 2' 5" h. **$125-150**
Table lamp, "Red Turbanned Guard with Gong," No. XT 825, 2' 2" h. **$150-175**
Table lamp, "Water Man," No. XT 809, Ceramic Arts Studio of Madison figurine, 2' 4" h... **$350-375**
Table lamp, "Woman with Dragon," No. XT 854, 2' 3" h. **$150-175**
Table lamp, "Woman with Panther," No. XT 828, 2' 7" h. **$125-150**

Table lamp, "Woman with Two Lanterns,"
No. T 690, attributed to Jean Manley, 2'
7 1/2" h... **$175-200**
Table lamps, "Lantern Man & Woman," No.
XT 808, Hedi Schoop figurines, 2' 8" h.,
pr... **$500-550**
Table lamps, "Oriental Boy & Girl," No. T
633, Decoramic Kilns figurines, 2' 6" h.,
pr... **$300-350**

Pairpoint Lamps

*Well known as a producer of fine Victorian art
glass and silver plate wares between 1907 and
1929, the Pairpoint Corporation of New Bedford,
Massachusetts, also produced a wide range of fine
quality decorative lamps.*

Pairpoint Puffy Boudoir Lamp

Boudoir lamp, 7" d. squatty open-topped
"Puffy" reverse-painted "Concord" shade,
molded w/large black & red butterflies
among large red flowers & green leaves
against a pink ground, raised on a silver
plate ringed urn-form base w/a heavy
square foot, base signed w/Pairpoint seal
& "B3070," 10 1/2" h. (ILLUS.) **$3,450**

Pairpoint Boudoir Lamp with Roses

Boudoir lamp, 8" w. domical paneled
"Portsmouth" patt. shade reverse-painted w/large red roses & green leafy stems
against a ground of vertical tinted stripes
alternating white & pale yellow, the exterior w/black outlining the designs, marked
shade, on a slender gilt-metal baluster-
form base on a stepped paneled foot also
marked, needs rewiring, overall
14 1/2" h. (ILLUS.) **$748**

Unusual Pairoint Art Deco Radio Lamp

Radio lamp, composed of a large upright
flat glass panel w/cut-corners reverse-
painted w/bold & colorful stylized Art
Deco florals in shades of blue, green, yellow, brown, red & orange, fitted onto a
brass-plated metal ribbed Art Deco platform base, base signed "Pairpoint
E3035" w/diamond logo, overall
10 1/2" h. (ILLUS.) **$1,610**

Pairpoint Poppy Lamp with Pink Poppies

Table lamp, 13" d., domical "Puffy" reverse-
painted "Poppy" shade, large molded
shaded pink poppy blossoms among
light & dark green leaves, raised on a
three-arm ring atop a bronze base w/the
slender cylindrical standard cast w/flower
& leaf clusters above the squatty disk foot
w/four scroll feet, shade w/Pairpoint signature, base marked "Pairpoint 3093,"
20" h. (ILLUS.) **$17,250**

Pairpoint Lamp with Poppy Shade

Table lamp, 13" d., domical "Puffy" reverse-painted "Poppy" shade, large molded red, orange & pink poppy blossoms among light & dark green leaves, raised on a three-arm ring & slender bronze squared base w/long teardrop panels above the rectangular ribbed & shell-cast foot, base signed "Pairpoint B3020," 20" h. (ILLUS.) **$17,825**

Fine Pairpoint "Puffy" Poppy Lamp

Table lamp, 14 1/2" d., domical "Puffy" reverse-painted "Poppy" shade, large molded red & orange poppy blossoms among light & dark green leaves, raised on a three-arm poppy-cast ring above the tall pyramidal bronze base cast in bold relief w/large poppy flowers & stems on each side, base signed "Pairpoint Mfg. Co. 3049" w/company logo, overall 21 1/2" h. (ILLUS.) **$20,700**

Pairpoint Lamp with Sunset Scene Shade

Table lamp, 17" d. domical reverse-painted "Exeter" shade decorated w/a continous sunset landscape w/green & yellow fields & black trees silhouetted against the deep orange, cream & purple sky, raised on a silver plate base w/a ring & leaf-cast section above a trumpet-form urn above the domed leaf-cast round foot, 21" h. (ILLUS.).. **$2,875**

Pairpoint Jungle Bird Variation Lamp

Table lamp, 18" d. domical reverse-painted "Carlisle" shade decorated in the Jungle Bird patt., painted on one side w/two exotic birds perched among tropical foliage, the other side depicts a single colorful bird resting on a branch w/another single bird among the tropical foliage, an unusual design variation, painted in shades of deep red, yellow, blue, green & cream, raised on a bronzed base composed of three serpentine supports resting on a tripartite base, shade & base signed "Pairpoint Corp.," overall 21" h. (ILLUS.) **$5,750**

Pairpoint Lamp with Floral Band Shade

Table lamp, 18" d. domical reverse-painted "Touraine" shade decorated w/pastel blue & yellow flowers & medallions on a pale pink ground above a dark green border band painted w/scrolling leaves & birds in blue, pink & yellow, shade signed inside rim, on a signed silver plate base w/a tall slender ringed standard above a cup-shaped base w/scroll fit, pierced silver plat cap, 22 1/2" h. (ILLUS.) **$2,588**

Tiffany Lamps

Pair of Tiffany Favrile Candle Lamps

Candle lamps, a round stepped gilt-bronze foot supporting a tall cylindrical Favrile glass standard in white opal decorated w/an iridized blue pulled-feather design, an electric brass cap w/drip tray, metal fittings stamped w/logo & "Louis Tiffany Furnaces Inc. - 756," one standard w/hairline, 13" h., pr. (ILLUS.) **$2,070**

Tiffany Desk Lamp with Damascene Shade

Desk lamp, 10" d., domical open-topped damascene shade in green iridescent w/rich blue & gold iridescent wavy lines, vertically ribbed w/a white interior casing, raised on a three-arm single-socket base bronze base tapering down to an artichoke-cast foot, gold patina, shaded signed "L.C.T.," base stamped "Tiffany Studios - New York - 445," replaced socket & minor wear on base, overall 16 1/2" h. (ILLUS.) **$4,560**

Tiffany Bronze Grapevine Desk Lamp

Desk lamp, 6" d. domical bronze shade lined w/green glass & pierced w/the grapevine design, suspended on an electric socket supported in a tall looped harp raised on a slender bronze pedestal above the domed & fluted base w/small ball feet, bronze w/fine greenish brown patina, shade signed "Tiffany Studios New York," base signed "Tiffany Studios New York - 424," patina on base enhanced, glass in shade appears to have been re-blown, overall 17" h. (ILLUS.) ... **$3,960**

Tiffany Acorn Pattern Table Lamp

Table lamp, "Acorn," 14" d. domical leaded glass shade, composed of an upper section of graduated striated green & white segments above a wide band of undulating acorns in green & orange striated segments, the border band w/three narrow bands of striated green & white segments, raised on a three-arm bronze base w/slender standard & round base w/wide ribs, shade signed "Tiffany Studios New York," base signed "Tiffany Studios New York" w/Tiffany Glass & Decorataing monogram, socket, support arms & ball appear to be modern replacements, several tiles w/hairlines, one acorn poorly replaced, shade slightly warped, overall 19 1/4" h. (ILLUS.) **$6,960**

Tiffany Lamps,

Rare Tiffany Bellflower Table Lamp

Table lamp, "Bellflower," 18" d. domical leaded glass shade composed of mottled light & dark green swirled leaves above a border band of red bellflowers, raised on a bulbous urn-form bronze

base raised on four slender curved & reeded legs ending on a squared foot w/rounded corners, shaded marked w/Tiffany Studios tag, base stamped "Tiffany Studios New York 299714" & company monogram, overall 22" h. (ILLUS.)
.... **$38,240**

Tiffany Geometric Shade Table Lamp

Table lamp, "Geometric," 16 1/2" d. domical leaded glass shade composed of panels of graduated mottled yellow tiles w/a narrow border band of small tiles, raised on a slender paneled gilt-bronze standard w/a round foot, shade signed "Tiffany Studios New York - 1901," base signed "Tiffany Studios New York - 539," 21" h. (ILLUS.) **$10,350**

Fine Tiffany Lemon Leaf Table Lamp

Table lamp, " Lemon Leaf," 18" d. domical leaded glass shade composed of an upper section of graduated mottled dichroic green & orange segments above a narrow band of swirled leaves, the drop border band composed of four bands of rectangular segments, raised on a slender ribbed & waisted standard on a domed ribbed base on ball feet, shade signed "Tiffany Studios New York 1470," base signed "Tiffany Studios New York 370," overall 23" h. (ILLUS.) **$29,900**

Twelve-light Tiffany Lily Lamp

Table lamp, "Lily," twelve-light, a gilt-bronze lily pad & blossoms base issuing twelve upright arching stems each ending in a gold iridescent blossom-form shade, shades signed, base signed "Tiffany Studios New York - 322," five shades w/fitted chips, one w/a cracked fitter (ILLUS.) .. **$27,600**

Rare Tiffany Peacock Table Lamp

Table lamp, "Peacock," 18 3/4" d. domical open-topped leaded glass shade composed of colored glass segments forming twenty peacock eyes arranged in two rows the encircle the middle of the shade, each eye w/a sapphire blue center surrounded by teal & green segments surrounded by orange & green striated segments, the upper portion made entirely of rippled glass in amethyst shading to or-

ange, the middle portion of the background graduated to feathers comprised of soft teal green & orange above two small horizontal bands of rippled glass over the apron continuing the feather design, raised on an original bronze peacock feather designed ovoid base tapering down to a scalloped bottom w/each scallop enclosing a peacock feather eye, three-arm shade support, shade & base unsigned, overall 25" h. (ILLUS.) **$120,750**

Very Rare Tiffany Poinsettia Lamp

Table lamp, "Poinsettia," 15 3/4" d. domical leaded glass shade composed of an upper band of mottled deep orange & yellow tiles above a wide band of dark red & blue poinsettia flowers on green leafy stems, narrow bands of mottled orange & green at the bottom rim, raised on a bulbous ovoid bronze base w/lightly cast stylized leaves above foot composed of upright trumpet-form blossoms, shade signed "Tiffany Studios New York - 1557," base signed "Tiffany Studios New York - 26846" & company monogram, 18 3/4" h. (ILLUS.) **$59,750**

Tiffany Whirling Leaves Table Lamp

Table lamp, "Whirling Leaf," 18" d. domical leaded glass shade composed of an upper band of graduated mottled tan blocks above a wide band of swirling green leaves leaves on a mottled tan ground, the wide lower border composed of bands of narrow rectangular tan blocks, riased on a three-spider above the bulbous sharply tapering bronze teardrop base raised on a three-legged framework on a round disk foot, shade marked w/a Tiffany Studios tag, base stamped "Tiffany Studios New York 190," two cracked tiles, missing top cap, one leg restored, socket cluster probably a copy, overall 23" h. (ILLUS., previous page) **$17,250**

Lamps, Miscellaneous

Unusual Aladdin Painted Boudoir Lamp

Aladdin boudoir lamp, 9 3/4" d., domical frosted glass shade painted w/a bold stylized country landscape w/a cottage among trees in shades of deep gold & green w/a white background, raised on a cast-metal Aladdin-signed base w/a trumpet-form standard above the leaf-cast round foot & finished w/a creamy white enamel (ILLUS.)............................. **$210**

Art Deco Czech Glass Boudoir Lamp

Art Deco boudoir lamp, the pointed conical frosted glass shade decorated w/raised stylized red & white blossoms & pale green leaves & stems, fits on a matching footed squatty spherical glass base, Czechoslovakia, 1920s, 10 1/2" h. (ILLUS.) **$259**

Quezal-Bradley & Hubbard Lamp

Art Nouveau accent lamp, a tulip-shaped signed Quezal glass shade in green w/gold & white pulled-feathers, raised on an electric socket attached to a Bradley & Hubbard lamp w/a cylindrical copper shaft & round foot, both parts signed, early 20th c., overall 13 1/2" h. (ILLUS.) **$720**

Art Nouveau Style Figural Lamp

Art Nouveau table lamp, the oval black marble base supporting a patinated bronzed metal figure of a scantially clad Art Nouveau maiden seated on grass, her arms outstretched & holding the ends of a long scarf, an upright metal stem behind her issuing leafy stems & topped by a large petaled electric socket fitted w/a flame-form bulb, metal base medallion tag reads "Fabrication Francaise, Paris - Made in France," ca. 1920s, base 10" d., overall 13" h. (ILLUS.)............................... **$460**

Early Electric Partner's Desk Lamp

Desk lamp, partner's-style, brass, the square base w/a central tapered paneled post topped by two long rectangular brass shades, each light w/an individual switch & bulb socket, early 20th c., 15" l., 15 1/2" h. (ILLUS.) **$259**

Duffner & Kimberly Wide-shade Lamp

Duffner & Kimberly leaded glass table lamp, 20" d. leaded glass shade w/a wide gently angled top & narrow drop border, the top composed of triangular & diamond-shaped mottled yellow & green slag glass w/dark green lobes around the top, the narrow border composed of an arrangment of rounded triangular mottled yellow & green slag tiles, raised on a slender bronzed tiered standard on a round ribbed foot, 24" h. (ILLUS.) **$3,450**

Duffner & Kimberly Poppy Shade Lamp

Duffner & Kimberly leaded glass table lamp, 24" d. domical leaded glass shade composed of mottled red, orange & yellow poppies on undulating green leafy stems against a ground of mottled green tiles, uneven lower edge, raised on a bronze base w/a very slender standard above the round petal-cast foot, slight separation, 23 1/2" h. (ILLUS.) **$5,750**

Heintz Art Metal Boudoir Lamp

Heintz Art Metal boudoir lamp, a flat-bottomed squatty bulbous bronze base w/a mottled green & brown patina w/sterling silver decoration of large flowers on leafy stems, the conical metal shade w/four cut-out panels w/a floral design matching the base, shade lined in salmon colored silk fabric, early 20th c., shade 8 1/2" d., overall 9 1/2" h. (ILLUS.) **$690**

Jefferson Lamp with Landscape Shade

Jefferson table lamp, 18" d. domical reverse-painted shade decorated w/a pretty landscape w/pairs of tall leafy trees & small wooded hills in the foreground & meadows in the distance, done in shades of yellow, blues, greens & brown, signed "2680 Jefferson Co. FH," raised on a rare large baluster-form glass base acid-etched w/a Chinese dragon design against a chipped-ice background & covered in a copper-colored patina, overall 24 1/2" h. (ILLUS.) **$1,725**

w/three candle lights on bulbous frosted glass sockets raised on upturned silver plate arms joined to a tapering triangular frosted glass base (ILLUS.) **$3,162**

Floral-bordered Leaded Glass Lamp

Leaded glass table lamp, 18" d. domical leaded glass shade composed of a wide upper section of geometric caramel slag tiles above a wide border band of large red, yellow & pink blossoms among green leaves & flanked by narrow red bands, raised on a bronze metal base w/a slender reeded standard & paneled & ribbed foot, 24" h. (ILLUS.) **$2,300**

Fine Art Nouveau Style Leaded Lamp

Leaded glass table lamp, 20" d. domical leaded glass shade composed of caramel slag, green slag & orange slag segments in an Art Nouveau design of long swirling leaves radiating from the top & around the rim & framing orange & cream stylized iris blossoms, raised on a very

Unusual Jefferson Lamp & Shade

Jefferson table lamp, tapering drum-shaped reverse-painted shade decorated w/a continuous sunset landscape w/tall trees near a lake in shades of yellow, orange, dark green & brown w/a frosted & textured lower border band & glass ball finial, raised on a candelabra-style base tall slender bronzed metal ribbed shaft issuing from a lobed & scrolled footed base, unsigned, early 20th c., overall 30" h. (ILLUS.) **$3,120**

Moe Bridges Lamp with Nasturiums

Moe Bridges table lamp, 15" d. domical reverse-painted shade decorated w/large nasturium blossoms in tangerine, scarlet & crimson & green leaves against a deep yellow shaded to brown ground, simple slender bronzed-metal base w/a rounded undulating & ribbed foot, shade & base properly signed & numbered, touched up chip on inside lower rim of shade, several tiny chips on flat of rim, overall 20 3/4" h. (ILLUS.) **$1,898**

Moe Bridges Autumn Landscape Lamp

Moe Bridges table lamp, 18" d. domical reverse-painted shade decorated w/an autumnal landscape w/a wide path winding through fields w/clusters of slender trees w/golden brown & green leaves, a lakeshore & high mountains in the distance, a pale yellow sky background, shade signed

"Moe Bridges Co. 192," raised on a Moe Bridges bronzed metal tapering paneled base w/a paneled flaring foot, all w/incised angular lines, overall 22" h. (ILLUS.)........ **$3,163**

Unusual Muller Fres. & Iron Deco Lamp

Muller Freres glass & iron table lamp, Art Deco style, composed of a round slightly domed iron foot supporting a large upright iron ring framing bands of tight scrolls, an electric socket suspended at the top center supporting a long tapering cylindrical Muller Freres glasss shade in mottled white w/a mottled lavender & pink rim band, shade signed "Muller Fres Luneville," base unsigned, overall 11" h. (ILLUS.)... **$288**

Pittsburgh Lamp with Jungle Scene Shade

Pittsburgh table lamp, 14" d. domical reverse-painted shaded decorated w/a continuous border jungle landscape w/palm trees & flowers against a deep tan to yellow sky, raised on a copper-finished metal base w/a paneled & dimpled design, 22" h. (ILLUS.) **$1,150**

Pittsburgh Lamp & Painted Shade

Pittsburgh table lamp, 18" d. domical reverse-painted shade in the "Call of the Wild" patt. showing a tepee & campfire camp site among trees beside a moonlit lake, raised on a bulbous melon-form bronze base w/small molded leaves around the base & small loop handles at the top, overall 22 1/2" h. (ILLUS.) **$4,025**

Figural Lamp with Elk-decorated Shade

Reverse-painted & figural table lamp, 11" d. domical reverse-painted shade

decorated w/a landscape of a bull elk grazing in a meadow in shades of red, pink, green & brown, raised on a bronzed metal ring above a tree-form standard resting on a green onyx foot also mounted w/a bronzed metal model of a large standing moose, shade signed "A. Frederick," reportedly an artist for Pairpoint, horns on moose repainted, 23 1/2" h. (ILLUS.) **$4,600**

Lamp with Bent Panel & Filigree Shade

Slag glass bent-panel table lamp, 20" d. umbrella-shaped shade composed of six wide panels of bent white glass w/light caramel highlights, each panel w/delicate ornate scrolling filigree, raised on a gilded cast-metal baluster-, ring- and knob-cast standard w/molded leaves above a cross-form foot, some gilt wear, early 20th c., 29 3/4" h. (ILLUS.) **$1,380**

Simple Bent Panel Slag Glass Lamp

Slag glass bent-panel table lamp, the domical 15" w. six-panel shade composed of six wide tapering caramel slag panels fitted in a gilt-metal framework w/a fanned lattice shell at the base of each panel, raised on a slender cast white metal bronzed base w/a slender standard w/acanthus leaves above the round foot w/a bellflower design, early 20th c., sockets replaced, overall 21 1/2" h. (ILLUS.) **$374**

Pretty Green Slag Glass Table Lamp

Slag glass table lamp, 13 1/4" w. pyramidal octagonal shade composed of panels of green & white slag glass mounted in a brass frame w/scrolling filigree bands at the top & rim, raised on a slender columnar bronzed cast white metal standard above the round low domed foot cast w/three sections of florals, early 20th c., overall 18 1/2" h. (ILLUS.) **$431**

Fine Banker's Lamp with Steuben Shades

Steuben banker's lamp, an oval footed bronzed metal base cast w/delicate scrolls centering a bulbed knob & tall

slender shaft issuing two arched side arms each ending in an electric socket fitted w/a signed domed gold Aurene Steuben shade, each shade 6 3/4" d., lamp overall 22" h. (ILLUS.) **$2,415**

Fine Double Harvard Student Lamp

Student lamp, Harvard double-light, round ringed brass base supporting a tall central rod supporting the cylindrical fuel font & two projecting adjustable arms each ending in a burner & ring supporting a domed open-topped cased ruby glass shade, overall 22 1/2" h. (ILLUS.) **$1,955**

One of Two Classical Style Tole Lamps

Tole-painted table lamps, the base w/a round domed foot & ringed pedestal below the large urn-form body flanked by lion mask ring handles, the concave top tapering to a slender stem & shade support, a large open-topped pyramidal shade, base & shade in black decorated in gold w/borders of Greek key & a wide band of dancing Grecian figures, overall 29" h., pr. (ILLUS. of one) **$518**

Wilkinson Lamp with Leaded Shade

Wilkinson leaded glass table lamp, 18" d. domical leaded glass shade composed of a wide upper section of dark & light green mottled slag graduating blocks above a wide border band of stylized flowers in ruby, pink, & mottled green slag, raised on a gilt-metal base w/a slender paneled standard ending in scrolls atop the round foot (ILLUS.)................... **$3,450**

Other Lighting Devices

Chandeliers

Unusual Three-light Antler Chandelier

Antler, 3-light, composed of a tall intertwined cluster of real antlers w/three curving out at the bottom to support a candle-form electric socket, iron hanging hook, probably Europe, late 19th - early 20th c., 40" w., 35" h. (ILLUS.).............. **$2,875**

Chrome & Degué Glass Chandelier

Art Deco, 4-light, glass & chrome, three long bars form the frame supporting a large frosted glass deep clam shell-shaped shade, the sides w/three chrome bands of graduated rings each arching up & ending in a socket fitted w/a frosted molded bell-shaped shade, embossed "Degué" mark on glass, electric fitting missing, France, ca. 1925, 20" w., 37 1/2" h. (ILLUS.) **$978**

Dramatic Arts & Crafts Chandelier

Arts & Crafts, bronze & glass, a wide cylindrical hammered bronze ring w/pierced geometric designs hung from four heavy chains, suspends four short chains ending in electric sockets each fitted w/a gold iridescent ribbed tulip-form blown glass shade, possibly by Steuben, ca. 1930, 14 1/2" d., 18" h. (ILLUS.) **$1,380**

Brass Chandelier with Steuben Shades

Brass & glass, five-light, the brass fixture topped by a fluted crown ring suspending five curved short arms each suspending a tall shield-shaped upright joining a lower ring w/five arched flattened arms each ending in an electric socket fitted w/a Steuben gold Aurene ribbed bell-shaped shade, early 20th c., overall 34" h. (ILLUS.) **$3,105**

Fine Cut Glass 12-Light Chandelier

Cut glass, 12-light, in the 18th c. style, the multi-tiered central shaft composed of cut crystal baluster-form segments alternating w/cupped bobeches each suspending cut triangular spearpoint prisms, the bottom section issuing twelve serpentine ropetwist arms each ending in a candle socket w/crystal bobeche suspending additional cut prisms, trimmed w/swags of cut jewels, England, 19th c., electrified, 28" d., 38" h. (ILLUS.) **$3,220**

Leaded Basket & Berry Chandelier

Leaded glass, 24 1/2" domical shade w/an open flaring pointed petal green slag glass top, the upper sides composed of graduated green slag blocks above a repeating design of large pink bows atop white baskets overflowing w/deep red berries & joined by trailing dark green leaves, uneven rim, some repairs & replaced segments, some tight hairlines, late 19th - early 20th c., 16" h. (ILLUS.).... **$403**

Leaded Chandelier with Jeweled Grapes

Leaded glass, 28" d. domical umbrella-form shade tapering to a small open top w/small flaring pointed caramel slag petals, the sides composed of light caramel slag blocks decorated around the top opening & the wide rim w/grape clusters composed of dark red & purple cabochon "jewels" & joined by dark green & blue slag leaves, few tight hairlines, late 19th - early 20th c., 15" h. (ILLUS.) **$489**

Unusual 5-Light Leaded Chandelier

Leaded glass, 5-light, a large tall gilt-iron cylindrical top fitting issuing four flattened & gently arched arms each suspending a chain & leaf-form electric sockeet, the top center fitted w/a large ball-shaped leaded glass shade composed of random caramel panels & centered by a triple band of tiny square mottled green & caramel tiles, each hanging socket w/a domical leaded shade of similar design, framed marked "The Morreau Co.," ca. 1925, 20" d., 20" h. (ILLUS.) **$1,093**

Tiffany-signed Ball-shaped Chandelier

Tiffany-signed, a large ball-shaped shade in creamy white decorated around the middle w/a wide band of gold pulled-feather design w/pale green edging, the top open fitter rim suspected in a three-hook bronze ring & three fine chains, shade signed, extensive crack from hold in bottom nearly to the top, 14" d. (ILLUS.) **$805**

Early French Neoclassical Chandelier

Neoclassical, 4-light, painted tin, a tall wide harp-shaped central section painted white w/gilt leaves & topped by a gilt ball above three brass rods, the tapering cylindrical base drop issuing four straight tubullar arms ending in cylindrical metal fonts w/half-round clear glass base globes, each arm also fitted w/an upright frame supporting a conical metal shade w/a pierce top band, some glass globes missing, wear, some rust, France, early 19th c., 16" w., 22" h. (ILLUS.).............. **$2,703**

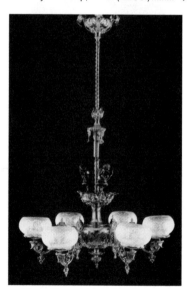

Fine Enameled Pairpoint Chandelier

Pairpoint-signed, a wide squatty bulbous lobed bowl-form shape w/a soft pink background ornately enameled in white w/scrolling leaves, lattice panels & flying cherubs, suspended by four brass chains joined to a center brass cap, shade signed in black "The Pairpoint Corp'n," 14" d. (ILLUS.) **$3,163**

Rare Signed Victorian Gasolier

Victorian Rococo Revival gasolier, 6-light, gilt-lacquered spelter, bronze & brass, the top canopy w/foliate mounts, the long stem w/spiral-twist sections over latticework & foliate pendants over a trio of bronzed metal figural cupids w/bows & a foliate-mounted bowl joined to six foliate & latticework arms each ending in a burner & six bulbous bowl-shaped frosted & etched shades, mounts labeled by Cornelius and Baker, ca. 1860-70, 78" d., 62 1/2" h. (ILLUS.) **$16,675**

Lanterns

One of Two Shaker Candle Lanterns

Candle lanterns, hanging-type, grey-painted tin, a hanging loop above a widely flaring conical tin shade w/a curved strap from side to side centered by a small candle socket, Shaker-made, Hancock, Massachuseets, mid-19th c., scattered paint loss & corrosion, 12 1/4" d., 11 1/4" h., pr. (ILLUS. of one) **$4,230**

Pair of Victorian Carriage Lanterns

Carriage lanterns, tin & glass, a rectangular vent top above a rectangular frame w/glass sides & a reflective metal back centered by a burner, long cylindrical tube fonts below, 19th c., 9" w., 18" h., pr. (ILLUS.) **$150**

Ornate Louis XVI-Style Hall Lantern

Hall lantern, 5-light, gilt wrought iron, Louis XVI-Style, a top center conical crown issuing four arms composed of C-scrolls & a long central shaft ending in five candle sockets, the five-sided framework w/arched sections fitted w/glass panes & decorated w/small pineapple base drops, electrified, France, late 19th - early 20th c., 16 1/2" w., 34" h. (ILLUS.) **$403**

Ribbed Blown Glass English Hall Lantern

Hall lantern, blown glass, a wide clear blown glass smoke bell above three chains connected to the rim of a deep cylindrical bowl-shaped lattern w/a ribbed design & a brass base cap, fitted w/a trio of interior lights, England, in the late Georgian style, electrified, late 19th c., 14" d., 36" h. (ILLUS.) **$1,360**

Fine French Louis XVI-Style Lantern

Hall lantern, gilt-brass & glass, Louis XVI-Style, four tapering rectangular beveled glass sides in the metal framework w/the base joined by four serpentine braces joined to a central post & fitted w/pomegranate drop finials, the upper frame w/a pomegranate finial at each corner & four arched braces joined to an upper crown, the center of each top edge centered by a pierced shell-form mount, France, 19th c., electrified, 35" h. (ILLUS.) **$1,380**

Wrought-iron Rococo Hall Lantern

Hall lantern, wrought iron & glass, Rococo taste, the top composed of six long tapering acanthus leaves suspending the tapering square lantern frame fitted w/beveled & etched glass panels, leafy S-scrolls around the base & forming an openwork pendant drop, probably Europe, 19th., 27" w., 49" h. (ILLUS.) **$2,990**

Unusual Figural Bronze Wall Lantern

Wall lantern, bronze, two-piece, a wall-mounted bracket w/the back plate made of two lion heads flanking an urn of fire & w/a small shellf supporting a large figural 14" h. winged dragon w/an open outh, the dragon's mouth suspends a large ring holding a six-panel lantern w/beveled glass panes centered by a post for three lights, one pane cracked, one missing a corner, dragon jar w/repaired breaks, 19th c., overall 27 1/2" h., lantern 22" h., 12" w. (ILLUS.) **$1,955**

Shades

Unusual Gold Crackle Durand Shade

Durand, a wide squatty bulbous stepped shape w/a long pierced leaf-shaped metal center pendant drop, heavily crackled gold iridescent surface, chips to fitter rim, fitter 4" d., 6 1/2" h. (ILLUS.) **$300**

Quezel Blue Pulled-feather Shade

Quezel-signed, long tulip-form, blue & gold pulled-feather design on white, iridescent gold interior, 4 7/8" d., 6" h. (ILLUS.) **$1,438**

Rare Fine Quality Quezel-signed Shade

Quezel-signed, tall trumpet form, the exterior w/a platinum zipper pattern over a dark green pulled-feather design in light green, dramatic deep purple & blue iridescence, gold iridescent interior, signed on the fitter rim, fitter rim 3 1/4" d., 8 1/4" h. (ILLUS.) **$2,703**

Sets of Signed Steuben & Tiffany Shades

Steuben-signed, bell-shaped w/a brownish gold iridescent exterior w/an intarsia border of alternating brown & white w/a platinum iridescent finish, white iridescent interior, 5" h., set of 6 (ILLUS. top with four Tiffany shades)...................................... **$4,370**

Steuben Shade in White & Green Band

Steuben-signed, small fitter opening above a cushion-form band over the wide umbrella-shaped sides, white Calcite exterior decorated w/an undulating band of green vining & florettes, iridescent gold interior, 5" d., 4 1/4" h. (ILLUS.) **$1,150**

Tulip-shaped Signed Tiffany Shade

Tiffany-signed, a simple lightly ribbed tulip form, overall gold iridescence, fitter rim signed "L.C.T.," 5" h. (ILLUS.) **$840**

Unusual Tiffany Pulled-feather Shade

Tiffany-signed, bulbous ovoid ribbed form w/a flat incurved rim, heat reactive glass decorated w/a lemon yellow & red pulled-feather exterior decoration, probably originally a candlestick shade, numbered "X2175," fitter 2 1/8" d., 4 1/2" h. (ILLUS.) **$1,955**

Tiffany-signed, cylindrical linen-fold design w/rich overall gold iridescence w/blue & purple highlights, 4 3/4" h., set of 4 (ILLUS. bottom with set of Steuben-signed shades) **$4,485**

Fine Tiffany Green Damascene Shade

Tiffany-signed, domical lightly ribbed open-topped damascene glass w/a rich green ground decorated w/overall wavy gold iridescent band decoration w/purple & blue highlights, signed w/initials inside the rim, 5 1/2" d. (ILLUS.) **$5,175**

Domical Butterscotch Tiffany Shade

Tiffany-signed, domical open-topped form w/a butterscotch iridescent exterior cased in white, signed "L.C.T.," chips to fitter rim, 8" d. (ILLUS. inverted, previous page) **$1,150**

Leaded Glass Tiffany-signed Shade

Tiffany-signed, leaded glass, wide tapering flat sides composedd of alternating narrow & wide green slag panels swirled w/blues & orange, the flattened top composed of narrow double slag glass bands around the center opening, signed "Tiffany Studios New York 1587," numerous cracks in the large panels, 11" w. (ILLUS.) **$2,013**

LIPSTICK TUBES

Forerunners of the lipstick tube as we know it now included lip and rouge pots and lipstick matches. The push-up lipstick tube preceded the swivel lipstick tube. In between the use of the lip and rouge pot and the modern type of lipstick tube, there were many ingenious lipstick tubes were devised with unique mechical devices for raising and lowering the lipstick.

Lipstick tubes have been produced in precious metals, enamel, metal alloys, Bakelite, papier-maché, wood, mother-of-pearl, cord and cardboard. These can be further enhanced with crystals, precious gems, fur, sparkles, colored rhinestones and petit-point. Most lipstick tubes are square or round with a flat base.

Many manufacturers of vintage lipstick tubes also had matching compacts. Costume jewelry and haute couture designers, including Paul Flato, Salvador Dali, Halston and Christian Dior, created delightful lipsticks that are now very coveted by collectors.

My personal favorite lipstick tubes are designed to resemble figurals, dolls, etc., and the gadgetry whimsical lipstick tubes that are combined with a secondary accessory such as a watch, whistle, flashlight, cigarette case, jewelry, a pen or a perfume vial. These dual-purpose collectibles are very desirable and are sought by both lipstick tube collectors and those who collect the various accessory items.

Lipstick tubes, both the vintage and contemporary examples, are beautiful , affordable and fun vanity collectibles.

For additional information on the history and values of lipsticks, consult the book Vintage and Contemporary Purse Accessories by Roselyn Gerson (Collector Books).

Atomette Owl & Rhinestone Lipstick

Atomette lipstick tube, polished goldtone decorated in relief w/an owl trimmed w/rhinestones, the top w/tiered bands of rhinestones around the flat mirror top (ILLUS.) **$125**

Christian Dior Crystal Obelisk Lipstick

Christian Dior crystal lipstick tube, modeled as an obelisk on a pedestal base, the first lipstick created by Dior in 1956, made as a smaller vesion of his famous perfume bottles (ILLUS.) **$200**

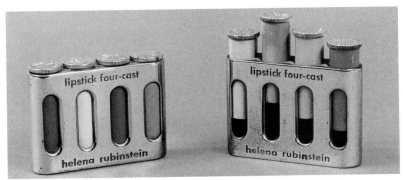

Two Helena Rubinstein Four-Case Lipstick Tubes

Helena Rubinstein, Four-Case lipsticks, four brightly colored enameled lipstick tubes indicating the shades of lipstick encased in the polished goldtone holder, each (ILLUS. of one open & one closed) .. **$125**

ed in Mexico, each (ILLUS. in pink & blue) **$65**

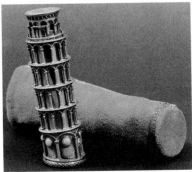

Leaning Tower of Pisa Lipstick & Case

Leaning Tower of Pisa lipstick tube, a model of the famous tower in vermeil sterling silver trimmed w/cabochon turquoise stones, comes w/a turquoise velvet case decorated w/gold trim, Rome, Italy (ILLUS.) **$300**

Revlon Flapper Doll Lipstick Case

Revlon lipstick case, designed to resemble a 1920s Flapper, trimmed in gold cloth & wrapped in black velvet (ILLUS.) **$85**

Two Papier-maché Lipstick Dolls

Papier-maché lipstick dolls, cylindrical w/decorated doll-shaped tops, handcraft-

Revlon Sphinx Doll Lipstick Case

Revlon lipstick case, figural design of a sphinx-shaped doll complete w/a gold & black headpiece (ILLUS.)......................... **$225**

MARBLES

Scarce Colorful Lutz Onionskin Marble

Lutz onionskin, colorful swirled core w/thin bands in black, blue, orange, yellow, red & pink mixed w/coppery Lutz swirls, near mint, 1" d. (ILLUS.) **$201**

Colorful Swirled Lutz Onionskin

Lutz onionskin, fine swirled ribbons in yellow, black, white, blue, green & orange w/lines of gold between each color & 17 coppery Lutz swirls, polished, 13/16" d. (ILLUS.) **$127**

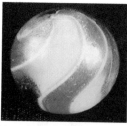

Lutz Ribbon Core Yellow & Copper Marble

Lutz ribbon core, yellow swirled ribbons alternating w/coppery swirled ribbons, light chips & scratches, fair condition, 7/8" d. (ILLUS.) **$115**

Four-panel Onion Skin in Red, White & Blue

Onion skin, four-panel design alternating speckled bands in red & white & blue &

white, light chips & scratches, early 20th c., 2 1/8" d. (ILLUS.) **$96**

Four-Panel Onion Skin with Mica

Onion skin, four-panel design w/alternating swirled panels in speckled red & white or red & yellow w/overall large mica flecks, polished w/some chips, early 20th c., 2 3/16" d. (ILLUS.) **$144**

Four-Panel Red, White & Green Onionskin

Onion skin, four-panel design, wide alternating panels in red & white & green & white, polished w/some light chips, 2 1/16" d. (ILLUS.) **$115**

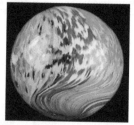

Six-Panel Colorful Onion Skin Marble

Onion skin, six-panel design w/alternating speckled swirled bands in blue & white, red & yellow, red & white & green & white, polished, a few chips, early 20th c., 2 1/8" d. (ILLUS.) **$180**

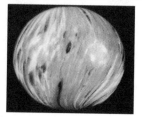

Colorful Six-Panel Onionskin Marble

Onion skin, six-panel design w/two panels each in speckled green & white, pink & yellow & pink & white, both pontils & straw marks, lightly buffed, early 20th c., 1 3/4" d. (ILLUS., previous page) **$201**

Red, White & Blue Onion Skin Marble

Onion skin, speckled red, white & blue w/blots of red & blue over a white ground, very fine overall mica flecks, fair condition w/chips, 1 5/8" d. (ILLUS.) **$72**

Four-panel Colorful Onion Skin Marble

Onion skin, two panels of red & white alternating w/two panels of turquoise & white, light chips overall, lightly buffs, w/pontil, early 20th c., 2 3/16" d. (ILLUS.) **$86**

Opaque Black & Swirled Lutz Marble

Opaque Lutz, wide swirled black bands alternating w/thin swirled green bands & coppery Lutz bands, w/both pontils, buffed w/a few light chips, 3/4" d. (ILLUS.) **$127**

METALS

Brass

Bed warmer, a round brass pan w/a hinged cover decorated w/a chased scrolling decoration & several small air holes, long well-turned baluser- and knob-turned handle in mustard yellow, red & black grain paint, pan 10" d., overall 40" l. (ILLUS.) **$345**

Early Brass Bed Pan with Long Handle

Early Decoraitve Pierced Brass Brazier

Brazier, two-part, a high domed cover ornately pierced w/delicate lattice swags, leaf bands & a lower Greek key band & topped by a tall turned finial, the stepped & widely flaring base w/a pierced Greek key apron & raised on tall flat legs w/paw feet, probably Europe, 19th c., 30" d., 32" h. (ILLUS.) **$1,495**

English Victorian Brass Coal Scuttle

Coal scuttle & shovel, L-shaped body w/a domed top w/a carrying handle & a hinged slanted front cover, small metal shovel fits into slot at the top back, raised on turned walnut ball feet, England, 19th c., 11 x 18", 18" h. (ILLUS.)...................... **$115**

Old Brass Eagle Door Knocker

Door knocker, modeled as a spead-winged American eagle w/a shield on the breast & arrows or laurel branches in the talons, a long U-form knocker bar, early 20th c., 6 x 7" (ILLUS.)... **$460**

Frying pan, round shallow pan w/a slender long iron handle ending in a long turned wood grip, mid-19th c., pan 11" d. (ILLUS. left with copper candy pan) **$633**

Two Views of a Rare 18th Century Brass Horn Book

Horn book, tablet-form w/top tab handle w/hanging hole, the front cast in relief w/capital alphabet letters arranged in seven rows, the back inscribed "St Pauls Infant School AD. 1729," 18th c., table 2 1/2 x 5" (ILLUS. of front & back) **$4,025**

Rare 18th Century English Wax Jack

Wax jack, a round brass base w/an ornate scroll projecting handle, centered by a slender round supporting a swiveling arm to hold the end of the spiraling band of wax, turned brass post finial, England, 18th c, 5 1/2" h. (ILLUS.)........................ **$6,573**

Bronze

Japanese Bronze Linen-form Basket

Basket, trompe l'oeil-style, footed bulbous form designed to resemble crumpled linen applied w/florals & insects & a woven handle, gilt finish, unmarked, Japan, 19th c., 10 1/4" h. (ILLUS.)................................ **$345**

Tiffany Bronze Card Tray

Card tray, an oblong rockwork form w/a reclining semi-nude maiden lying across the top ledge, signed "Tiffany Studios New York," early 20th c., 5 1/4" w. (ILLUS.) **$920**

Ornate Figural Bronze Compote

Compote, Baroque-style, the oval four-footed base cast w/small masks supporting a large dolphin ridden by a figure of Neptune forming the pedestal & carrying the large nautilus shell-shaped bowl pulled by a hypocampus & ridden by a winged cherub, unmarked, France, 19th c., 15" h. (ILLUS.) **$1,150**

Pairpoint-signed Bronze Compote

Compote, open, a domed round foot & large ball stem below the wide shallow rounded bowl, hand-hammered, dark exterior pati-

na, shiny gold enamel interior, marked under the foot w/the Pairpoint logo & "Pairpoint 7 - 1/2 G1461," 7 1/2" d. **$115**

French Bronze Coupe with Snake Handles

Coupe, Restauration-style, a wide shallow body wrapped around the rim w/snakes forming the handles & raised on a turned flaring pedestal resting atop a tall square Sienna marble pedestal base w/a square bronze foot, chip at bottom corner, France, late 19th c., 11 1/2" h. (ILLUS.).... **$431**

Chester Beach Dish with Scene

Dish, shallow rounded form, relief-cast in the interior w/a scene of a three-headed lion attaching a nude hunter w/a long bow, signed "Beach 1925 - Knust Foundry N.Y.," Chester Beach (American, 1881-1956), 4" d. (ILLUS.) **$780**

Tiffany Bronze Jewel Casket

Jewel casket, rectangular w/a flat hinged cover, large top & side panels cast w/Japanese garden scenes, bright gold finish, interior fitted w/two velvet-lined boxes, one w/a ring tray, the other open, bottom signed "Tiffany Studios New York 1102," 3 5/8 x 5 7/8" (ILLUS., previous page) **$920**

Bronze Plaque with Satyrs & Nymph

Plaque, oval, cast in high-relief w/the figures of two satyrs carrying off a nude nymph, gilt finish, unsigned, late 19th c., 10" h. (ILLUS.) **$690**

One of Two Ornate Chinese Urns

Urns, a ringed pedestal base below the bulbous body cast in relief around the sides w/scenes of birds, Foo dogs & foliage below the tall widely flaring trumpet neck wrapped w/a serpentine dragon, figural elephant head handles, rich chocolate brown patina, China, ca. 1900, 24" h., pr. (ILLUS. of one)... **$748**

Japanese Art Nouveau Bronze Vase

Vase, Art Nouveau style, footed wide ovoid body tapering to a short flaring trumpet neck, the sides cast in full-relief w/iris blossoms on leafy stems, signed, Japan, late 19th c., 13 1/2" h. (ILLUS.)................ **$330**

French Neoclassical Bronze Urn-vase

Vase, Neoclassical urn-form, square foot & stepped round pedestal below the tall ovoid body cast around the upper half w/a relief band of classical figures, wide cylindrical vine-cast neck w/rolled egg-and-dart rim flanked by upright cast scroll handles ending in bird heads, Napoleon III era, France, second half 19th c., 10" h. (ILLUS.)... **$863**

Copper

Cake mold, turk's turban design w/swirled ribbing, late 19th c., 8 1/2" d., 3 3/4" h. (ILLUS. right with lobed food mold)........... **$575**

Nice Roycrofters Copper Candlesticks

Candlesticks, hand-hammered, Arts & Crafts style, a square base supporting to slender square stems below the dished drip pan & short cylindrical candle socket, impressed Roycrofters mark, early 20th c., good patina, 7 1/2" h., pr. (ILLUS.).... **$1,208**

Candy pan, shallow round flat-bottomed pan w/angled open brass rim handles, folded rim, 19th c., 20" d., 7" h. **$2,300**

Rare Ornate Copper Chafing Dish

Chafing dish, cover, undertray & burner, the shallow flat-bottomed dish w/a flanged rim & decorated w/a thin applied silver band, the low domed cover w/a large ornate four-loop finial centered by a ball, a long projecting handle at one side w/a turned-wood grip, raised on three slender S-scroll legs further mounted w/a large standing figural rabbit, all resting on a copper-covered round oak board base, a footed round copper burner dish w/projecting handle under the center of the main dish, designed by Joseph Heinrich, Europe, ca. 1910, monogrammed, 11" h., the set (ILLUS.)........................... **$3,585**

Ewer, cov., Turkish-style, flat-bottomed ovoid body tapering sharply to a very tall slender neck topped by a bulbous hinged cap w/silver fitting, the bottom of the neck decorated w/sterling silver band stamped w/exotic roundel & floral designs, a very tall upright serpentined spout & a long C-form handle fitted w/two ivory heat rings, bottom marked "Gorham Co E40" & a date letter for 1881. Gorham Mfg. Co., Providence, Rhode Island, 13" h. (ILLUS., top next column) **$1,150**

Rare Gorham Copper & Silver Ewer

Early Classical Copper Hot Water Urn

Hot water urn, cov., classical-style, a square base on four small ball feet supporting a tapering pedestal & tall ovoid pot w/a long brass spigot at the front bottom, a thin decorative shoulder band below the low trumpet-form neck w/an inset cover & disk-turned finial, arched bar shoulder handles w/ring ends, Europe, 1800-20, 18 1/2" h. (ILLUS.) **$1,553**

Rare Early Copper Peanut Boiler

Peanut boiler, cov., deep rectangular dou-
ble-lined base w/a body band below a
rounded shoulder fitted w/a slender cylindrical spout, a four-sided tapering domed
cover w/a brass ball finial, 19th c.,
13 1/2 x 18", 21" h. (ILLUS., previous
page) **$2,530**

Simple Copper Civil War Powder Flask

Powder flask, simple flattened teardrop
form w/short cylindrical spout & small curl
lever handle, American, Civil War era,
small dents & stains, 7 3/4" l. (ILLUS.)...... **$104**

Two Early Copper Molds

Pudding mold, molded domed shape
w/lobed sides centered at the top by a six-
point star, 19th c., 10" d., 5 1/2" h. (ILLUS.
left with turk's turban cake mold) **$604**

Squatty Bulbous Roycrofters Vase

Vase, hand-hammered, Arts & Crafts style,
wide squatty bulbous flat-bottomed form
w/a wide shoulder centered by a short
flaring cylindrical neck, old patina, impressed Roycrofters mark, early 20th c.,
6 3/4" d., 4 1/2" h. (ILLUS.) **$748**

Iron

Charming Figural Iron Boot Scraper

Boot scraper, cast, figural, the openwork
upright ends cast w/the figure of a long-
legged elegantly dressed frog wearing a
long red & black tuxedo w/prancing
through tall green grass, a flat metal base
plate joins the sides, original paint, early
20th c., 7 3/4" h. (ILLUS.)......................... **$345**

Rare Early Iron Trammel Fat Lamp

Fat lamp, trammel-style, a long hanging bar
w/an adjustable sawtooth trammel bar
suspending a shallow Y-shaped fat lamp
w/a central twisted post w/a decorative
top hook area, probably 19th c., trammel
23 12" l., extends to 34 1/2" l. (ILLUS.)
.... **$1,380**

Old Cast-Iron Jockey Hitching Post

Hitching post, cast, figure of a white jockey wearing black boots, white pants & a red shirt & cap, one arm extended holding a black iron ring, on a thick square iron base, some rust & paint loss, late 19th - early 20th c., 31" w., 48" h. (ILLUS.) **$460**

Pair of Cast Iron Rabbit Ornaments

Models of rabbits, seated animal w/open front legss & upright ears, painted white, 20th c., some rust, 10 1/2" h., pr. (ILLUS.) .. **$805**

Early Cast-iron Dog Nutcracker

Nutcracker, cast, model of a large standing dog on a rectangular platform base, hinged long tail operates the nut-cracking jaws, traces of gold paint, late 19th c., 4 1/2 x 7 1/4", 5" h. (ILLUS.) **$294**

Oven peel, hand-wrought, the flat rectangular blade w/a small heart cut-out, long rounded bar handle ending in a heart-shaped loop, some rusting & pitting, early, blade 4 1/2" w., overall 19" l. (ILLUS., top next column) **$518**

Fine Early Wrought-iron Oven Peel

Nice Early Iron Pipe Tongs

Pipe tongs, hand-wrought, long tongs w/a spring-type looped-over handle, a central spike for cleaning the pipe, a knob stand below the handle on the side marked "IX XII," late 18th - early 19th c., 23" l. (ILLUS.) **$690**

Early Iron Skewer Holder & Skewers

Skewer holder & skewers, hand-wrought, the holder w/the flattened top composed of an oval loop above a triangular loop ending in two slender projecting arms w/upturned ends, each arm suspending three long slender skewers, early, skewers 7 1/2" to 9 1/2" l., holder 4 1/4 x 4 1/4", the set (ILLUS.)... **$330**

Nice Early Wrought-iron Sppon

Spoon, hand-wrought, deep tapering oblong bowl w/a long squared handle w/a tight ram horn curved end, very early, 7 1/4" l. (ILLUS.)...................................... **$403**

Early Wrought-iron Toasting Rack

Toasting rack, hand-wrought, the revolving rack composed of two open squares enclosing scrolled hearts, revolving on a three-legged bar base w/a long curved handle w/a hanging hole in the diamond point end, late 18th - early 19th c., overall 16" l. (ILLUS.)... **$575**

Unusual Old Trammel with Figural Fish

Trammel, hand-wrought, two long narrow rods linked w/chain w/a 7" l. figural fish-form adjustment w/a round loop handle & several hooks for hanging, unusual form, adjusts from 41" to 70" (ILLUS.)............... **$805**

Large Early Hand-wrought Iron Trivet

Trivet, hand-wrought, a flat rectangular plate w/angled back corners, raised on three iron bar legs joined by a T-form stretcher, a long twisted iron handle w/loop end projecting from the back edge, early 19th c., 12 3/4 x 30", 8 3/4" h. (ILLUS.)... **$288**

Pewter

Early Queen Anne Style Candlesticks

Candlesticks, Queen Anne style, a deep flaring octagonal base w/overhanging top plate centered by the tall baluster-and ring-turned shaft w/a tall cylindrical socket w/a very wide flaring rim, touch marks under bases, possibly England, first half 18th c ., base 4 1/4" w., 7" h., pr. (ILLUS.) **$316**

Candlesticks, round foot w/a tall slender trumpet-form standard & tall waisted cylindrical socket, touch mark of Henry Hopper, New York City, 1842-47, one base w/battering, polished, some solder repair, 10" h., pr. (ILLUS. top row, far left & right with large grouping of pewter, top next page) **$403**

Large Grouping of American Pewter

Large 19th Century European Flagon

Flagon, cov., a rounded stepped & domed foot below the wide ovoid body tapering to a wide cylindrical neck fitted w/a domed hinged cover w/a large ball thumbrest & a long slender scroll handle, upright serpentine spout w/a small hinged tip cover, hallmarks & the date of 1805 inside the cover, worn but sound, Europe, early 19th c., 13" h. (ILLUS.) **$518**

Flagon, cov., flaring ringed base & tall ringed cylindrical body w/a hinged stepped domed cover w/serpentine thumbrest, closed rim spout, long double-C-scroll handle, touchmark of Boardman & Hart, New York City, ca. 1850, 3 qt., 13" h. (ILLUS., top next column) **$3,055**

Lavabo, hanging-type, a tall oblong container w/domed cover & base spigot at the bottom edge, engraved w/a family crest, designed to hang above the matching round deep bowl w/flanged rim, Europe, 19th c., bowl 14" d., 2 pcs. (ILLUS., bottom next column) **$161**

Fine Boardman & Hart Tall Flagon

Two-Piece European Pewter Lavabo

Graduated Set of Old Pewter Measures

Measures, footed graduated baluster-form pieces w/a flaring neck, long S-scroll handle, some dents, range from 1/12th pt. to 1 qt., graduated set of 5 from 2 1/4" h. to 6 1/4" h., the set (ILLUS., top of page) **$230**

Group of Three Early American Pewter Mugs

Mug, flared base & slightly tapering cylindrical body, tapering S-scroll handle, touchmark of Samuel Hamlin, Hartford, Connecticut, late 18th c., minor wear, 1 qt., 5 7/8" h. (ILLUS. left with two other mugs) **$3,819**

Mug, flared base & slightly tapering cylindrical body, tapering S-scroll handle, touchmark of Samuel Hamlin, Hartford, Connecticut, late 18th c., minor wear & pitting, 1 qt., 5 7/8" h. (ILLUS. right with two other mugs) **$4,113**

Mug, flared base & slightly tapering cylindrical body, tapering S-scroll handle, touchmark of Joseph Danforth, Sr., Middletown, Connecticut, 1780-88, minor wear, 1 qt., 6" h. (ILLUS. center with two other mugs) **$4,700**

Early English Pewter Mug

Mug, footed ringed cylindrical sides w/S-scroll handle, interior w/touch mark "90 St. George...," bottom w/engraved writing, monogram & marked "Quart," England, early 19th c., 6 1/2" h. (ILLUS.) **$230**

Pitcher, cov., baluster-shaped body w rim spout, angled handle & hinged domed cover, touchmark of Boardman& Hart, New York City, ca. 1830s-50s, polished, small dent, 10" h. (ILLUS. center top row with large grouping of pewter) **$690**

Plate, round w/flanged rim, touchmark of James H. Putnam, Malden, Massachusetts, 1830-35, wear, minor dents, 5 1/4" d. (ILLUS. bottom row, third from right with large grouping of pewter) **$345**

Plate, round w/flanged rim, touchmark of Blakslee Barns, Philadelphia, ca. 1812-17, polished, some scratches, 7 7/8" d. (ILLUS. bottom row, third from left with large grouping of pewter) **$403**

Thomas & Sherman Boardman Porringer

Porringer, round bowl w/fancy scrolling crown-style handle, touchmark of Thomas D. & Sherman Boardman, Hartford, Connecticut, 1810-30, 5" d. (ILLUS.) **$588**

Porringer, round bowl w/ornate crown-form handle, touchmark of Thomas D. & Sherman Boardman, Hartford, Connecticut, 1810-30, polished, some wear, 5" d. (ILLUS. top row, second from right with large grouping of pewter) **$288**

Porringer, round bowl w/simple rounded tab handle w/hanging hole, unmarked by probably from Pennsylvania, scratch-carved date "1781," wear, 5 1/4" d. (ILLUS. top row, second from left with large grouping of pewter) **$1,035**

Teapots, cov., one w/a footed spherical body & short flaring neck w/low domed cover & ornate C-scroll handle, the other w/a footed squatty half-round body w/a wide shoulder & short flaring neck w/domed cover & painted ornate C-scroll handle, both w/touchmarks of Sellow & Co., Cincinnati, Ohio, ca. 1830-60, both w/some damage & repair, one w/replaced cover, 7 1/4" h., the two (ILLUS. bottom row, far left & far right with large grouping of pewter) **$316**

Sheffield Plate

Early Sheffield Telescoping Candlesticks

Candlesticks, telescoping-type, round flaring fluted base tapering to an adjustable fluted stem below the fluted trumpet-form candle socket, marked "Mortons Patent," England, early 19th c., 8 1/4" h., pr. (ILLUS.) **$518**

Two Early Sheffield Plate Entree Dishes

Entree dishes, cov., rounded rectangular form w/a gadrooned edge, matching flat-topped domed cover w/detachable leafy scroll loop handle, engraved arms & crowned heart armorial, England, ca. 1815, 8 1/4 x 11 1/2", 5" h., pr. (ILLUS.) **$575**

Hot water urn, cov., classical-style, the tall urn-shaped body supported by four reeded columnar legs ending in paw feet, opposing high arched & reeded side handles, tall tapering cover w/flared top & urn-shaped finial, a reeded spigot w/fan-shaped bone handle near the base, all raised on a square plinth base on small bracket feet & centering a round platform supporting the urn-shaped burner, ca. 1785, 10 1/2" d., 22" h. (ILLUS., top next column) **$1,840**

Fine 18th Century Hot Water Urn

Boulton Sheffield Plate Hot Water Urn

Hot water urn, cov., the large bulbous ovoid body w/oak leaf & shell-mounted loop handles, a down-turned spigot w/double C-scroll handle, a waisted lid w/an acanthus bud finial, raised on a ringed pedestal on a domed square base w/a pierced lower gallery all supported on four ball-and-claw feet, Matthew Boulton, Sheffield, England, ca. 1790, 11"d., 21"h. (ILLUS.) **$1,840**

Unusual Sheffield Plate Covered Platter

Platter, cov., rectangular rounded form w/a thin gadrooned rim band w/scrolled sections, the matching flat-sided cover w/a raised rectangular gadrooned center section w/a blossom-form finial, ca. 1830, 13 x 17", 9" h. (ILLUS., previous page) **$2,300**

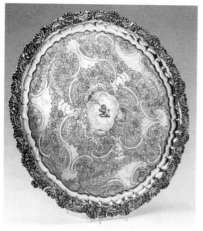

Large Early Sheffield Plate Platter

Platter, round w/a wide applied acanthus leaf scroll & flower rim band, the center engraved overall w/elaborate rococo C-scrolls & acanthus leaves centered by a rampant lion crest, raised on three fluted acanthus scroll feet, ca. 1790, some wear, 24 1/2" d., 2" h. (ILLUS.) **$978**

Unusual Three-pot Sheffield Plate Tea and Coffee Machine

Tea & coffee machine, comprising a spherical hot water urn & two tea or coffee urns, resting on a platform raised on five ball feet, the hot water urn on a swivel platform & w/a burner, each urn w/bright-cut engraved band of foliage & baskets, w/lion mask ring side handles, the small covers w/ball finials, the spouts w/ivory taps, unmarked, ca. 1800, overall 25 1/4" h. (ILLUS.) **$8,365**

Early Sheffield Plate Covered Urn

Urn, cov., a large pointed spiral-twist finial on the stepped domed cover chased w/floral & gadrooned bands, resting on a double-handled squat urn-form body w/reeded & chased floral scrolls centering a cartouche w/a crest & motto, flaring round foot, unknown maker's mark, ca. 1760, some wear, base of one handle bent, 12" h. (ILLUS.) **$1,093**

Silver

American (Sterling & Coin)

Fancy Footed Coin Silver Basket

Basket, coin, domed oval foot w/beaded edge band & répoussé florals tapering to the deep oblong boat-shaped body decorated w/ornate répoussé scrolls centering a cartouche w/engraved initials, arched swing handle across the top stamped w/the figure of a young boy climbing a beanstalk, impressed mark of Tenney, New York, New York, mid-19th c., 6" l., overall 6 1/2" h. (ILLUS.)............. **$489**

Medallion Pattern Creamer & Sugar

Creamer & open sugar bowl, sterling, Medallion patt., Neoclassical design, the helmet-shaped creamer on a low pedestal & round foot, a lappet band around the top w/a classical medallion face on each side, a pointed upright forked rim handle, the matching open oval sugar basket w/a classical mask at each end, a lappet rim band w/large roundels at the ends of the shaped overhead swing handle, John R. Wendt & Co., New York City, ca. 1865, creamer 6 1/2" h., sugar 6 3/4" h., pr. (ILLUS.)....... **$1,093**

Tiffany Neoclassical Creamer & Sugar

Creamer & open sugar bowl, sterling, Neoclassical-style, the creamer w/a round gadrooned foot & ovoid body applied w/an upper band w/a classical head, a wide arched spout & long angled handle, the matching rounded sugar w/fancy loop rim handles w/acorn drops, Tiffany & Co., ca. 1873, sugar 5" h., creamer 6" h., pr. (ILLUS.) **$805**

Ewer, coin, the tapering round pedestal base decorated w/repoussé flowers & scrolls, the bulbous body tapering to a tall cylindrical neck w/a wide rim spout & decorated overall w/ornate repoussé flowers & scrolls, a high ornate S-scroll handle, single letter monogram, Robert Rait, New York City, ca. 1840-50, some minor dents around monogram, 16 1/2" h. (ILLUS., top next column) **$2,185**

Tall Ornately Decorated Coin Ewer

Simple Boat-shaped Sterling Gravy Boat

Gravy boat, sterling, simple classical boat-shape w/a high looped end handle, raised on three shell-topped paw feet, Meriden Britannia Co., Connecticut, ca. 1920, 7 1/4" l., 4" h. (ILLUS.) **$230**

Rare Gorham Iceberg-shaped Ice Bowl & Ice Tongs

Ice bowl, sterling, figural design w/the bowl designed to resemble ice blocks hung w/icicles & chased w/frost on a flaring comforming base, the top of each end mounted w/a small model of a polar bear, Gorham Mfg. Co., Providence, Rhode Island, ca. 1870, 11 1/4" h. (ILLUS. top with ice tongs) **$17,925**

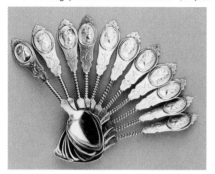

Set of Medallion Pattern Ice Cream Spoons

Ice cream spoons, coin, Medallion patt., each flattened oblong bright-cut handle stamped at the top w/an oval medallion w/a Roman warrior head, the twisted stem ending in a pointed bowl, engraved name of the owner on the handle back, mark of Duhme, Cincinnati, Ohio, ca. 1865, 6" l., set of 11 (ILLUS.) **$575**

Ice tongs, sterling, the slender handles modeled as harpoons wrapped w/rope, the arched top mounted w/a tiny model of a polar bear, a pointed spade-shaped ornately pierced spoon & three-barb harpoon-shaped fork, Gorham Mfg. Co., Providence, Rhode Island, ca. 1870, 12 1/4" l. (ILLUS. bottom with Gorham ice bowl, previous page) **$11,353**

Tiffany Sterling Silver Julep Cups

Julip cups, sterling, flared base & ringed gently flaring cylindrical body, monogrammed, Tiffany & Co., New York, late 19th c., 3 1/4" d., 5" h., set of 6 (ILLUS.) **$1,045**

Mug, coin, slightly tapering cylindrical form w/a ringed base & rim band, an engraved oblong leaf- and scroll-bordered cartouche w/an engraved presentation dated 1853, bottom stamped "Pure Silver Coin," made by Lincoln & Foss, Boston, Massachusetts, 3 3/4" h. (ILLUS., top next column) **$1,150**

Fine Dated Coin Silver Mug

Mug with Stonewall Jackson Portrait

Mug, sterling, slightly tapering cylindrical sides w/a zigzag & beaded base band, the sides engraved w/Egyptian Revival columns topped by sphinx heads forming arched panels, one panel enclosing the applied profile bust portrait of General Stonewall Jackson, also engraved w/a name & 1868 presentation date, applied hollow ear-shaped handle, retailed by E.A. Tyler, New Orleans, Louisiana, probably made by Baldwin & Company of New York City, 3 3/4" h. (ILLUS.).............. **$633**

Kirk Sterling Nut Bowl & Spoon

Nut bowl & spoon, sterling, a shallow round form w/swirled ribs centered by a repoussé fruit & nut design, the matching spoon w/a shallow round bowl etched w/fruits & a beaded handle, the bowl raised on three small ball feet, both pieces marked by S. Kirk & Son, late 19th c., bowl 5 3/4" d., 1 1/2" h., the set (ILLUS., previous page) **$173**

Tiffany Olympian Pattern Water Pitcher

Pitcher, water, sterling, Olympian patt., squatty bulbous body decorated w/a wide band ornately chased w/an elaborate mythical hunting scene, the wide cylindrical neck w/a narrow band chased w/scrolling leaves, hollow angular handle from rim to body, monogrammed on front & w/a base inscription dated 1894, Tiffany & Co., New York, 8" d., 8 1/4" h. (ILLUS.) **$4,025**

Rare Neoclassical Coin Silver Pitcher

Pitcher, water, coin, Neoclassical style, the round foot w/an egg-and-dart band below the low ringed pedestal & bulbous body decorated around the base & shoulder w/lappet bands, a wide arched spout w/beaded rim, high arched C-scroll han-

dle w/applied leaf designs, Baldwin Gardiner, New York City, ca. 1830, 13 1/2" h. (ILLUS.) **$5,463**

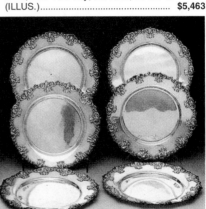

Set of Art Nouveau Dessert Plates

Plates, dessert, sterling, Art Nouveau style, the wide flanged rim decorated w/a scalloped repeating iris flower & scroll border, Whiting Mfg. Co., New York, New York, ca. 1905, 9 3/8" d., set of 12 (ILLUS. of part) **$2,185**

Rare Colonial Era Silver Punch Bowl

Punch bowl, coin, a high footring supporting the wide deep rounded bowl, maker's mark "IM," probably for John Moulinar, New York City, ca. 1750, later engraved on side & base "C*V*D" & "K*N*M," ca. 1750, 8 3/4" d. (ILLUS.) **$4,780**

Early Coin Silver Punch Ladle

Punch ladle, coin, a large deep oval bowl & long slender gently curved handle w/fiddle end, tip engraved w/two intertwining snakes, handle back marked "ED & SB," early 19th c., 14" l. (ILLUS.) **$173**

20th Century Kirk Salt & Pepper Shakers

Salt & pepper shakers, sterling, three small scroll feet supporting the bulbous base below tall tapering sides & a tall pierced & domed cap, overall stamped lush floral designs, base impressed "S. Kirk & Son - 11 oz. - 103," 20th c., 5 1/4" h., pr. (ILLUS.) **$500**

Rare Antebellum Southern Sugar Basket

Sugar basket, coin, the oval pedestal base w/a beaded rim band, the boat-shaped oval body orantely chased w/rococo leafy scrolls & flowers forming a cartouche on each side, beaded rim band, pierced serpentine swing handle w/beaded banding, James Conning, Mobile, Alabama, ca. 1855, 4 5/8 x 6 1/4", 6 3/4" h. (ILLUS.) **$2,530**

Fine Pilgrim Century American Tankard

Tankard, cov., coin, wide, gently tapering cylindrical body, the foot applied w/a meander wire below a stiff-leaf cut-card border, the body engraved w/an elaborate foliate cartouche w/pendant fruit & centering a coat-of-arms, the hinged flat-domed cover & corkscrew thumbpiece & serrated rim engraved w/foliage, the cover engraved w/a leafy band w/phoenixes & a winged cherub mask enclosing a foliate border w/a mirror cypher, the scroll handle applied at the grip w/a lion couchant & a cast cherub head terminal, the underside of cover rim engraved about 1800 w/"New York 1695," marked twice near handle by Jacobus van der Spiegel, New York City, ca. 1695, 7 1/4" h. (ILLUS.) **$339,500**

Tea service: tall coffeepot, open sugar & creamer on oval tray; sterling, the coffeepot w/a tall swelled cylindrical body w/pierced leafy scroll band at the bottom above the round foot, short rim spout, hinged cover w/scroll & flower bud finial, angled black wood handle, sugar & creamer of similar design, the tray w/pierced leafy scroll end handles, pieces engraved w/an initial, Tiffany & Co., New York, New York, 1947-56, tray 12 1/2" l., coffeepot 9 3/4" h., the set **$7,768**

Early Classical American Coin Silver Tea Service

Tea set: cov. teapot, cov. coffeepot, cov. sugar bowl, creamer & waste bowl; coin, Classical style, each piece raised on a ringed pedestal base supporting the tall bulbous body tapering to a swelled ringed tall shoulder tapering to a ringed neck & domed hinged cover w/flower finial, each piece w/narrow applied bands of acorn, grape & bellflowers, pots w/high arched C-scroll wooden handles & long serpentine leaf-clad spouts, each w/engraved monogram, mark of Curry & Preston, Philadelphia, ca. 1835, coffeepot 9 3/4" h., the set (ILLUS.)....................... **$2,868**

Tea set: cov. teapot, cov. coffeepot, cov. teakettle on stand, cov. sugar bowl, creamer, waste bowl & oval tray; sterling, ornate rococo designs on the footed squatty bulbous baluster-form bodies, each piece chased w/cornucopias w/fruit, flowers & foliage, a cartouche on each side, pots w/insulator spacers, the tray w/open scroll handles, Reed & Barton,

Fine Reed & Barton 20th Century Sterling Tea & Coffee Service

Taunton, Massachusetts, 1946, tray 31" l., teakettle overall 13 1/2" h., the set (ILLUS.).. **$22,705**

Victorian Coin Silver Kettle on Stand

Teakettle on stand, cov., coin, the wide squatty inverted pear-shaped body raised on leafy scroll legs, the low domed cover w/a flowerhead finial, ornate scroll-cast spout, scrolled overhead swing bail handle, resting on a round platform base centered by a burner & raised on tall leafy scroll legs w/shell feet, the shoulder engraved w/a monogram & crest, mark of Grosjean & Woodward, New York, New York, retailed by Lincoln & Foss, Boston, ca. 1850, overall 14 1/2" h. (ILLUS.)........... **$1,434**

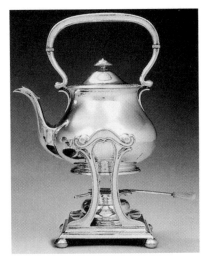

Early 20th Century Kettle on Stand

Teakettle on stand, cov., sterling, footed pear-shaped body w/flaring rim & hinged domed cover w/button finial, overhead swing bail handle w/ivory insulators, leaf-capped serpentine spout, raised on open arched scroll supports above a square platform centered by a squatty bulbous burner, stepped base on ball feet, mark of Arthur J. Stone, Gardner, Massachusetts, & craftsman's mark of Arthur L. Hartwell, ca. 1910, overall 13 1/4" h. (ILLUS.)................................. **$1,912**

Tiffany Silver Teakettle on Stand

Teakettle on stand, cov., sterling, rectangular body w/concave corners & rounded bottom, conforming stepped shoulder & hinged domed cover w/disk finial, paneled serpentine spout, swing bail handle at top, raised on paneled arched supports above a conforming platform base centered by a burner, marked "Tiffany &

Co. - Makers - Sterling Silver - 18389,"
2 3/4 pints, early 20th c. (ILLUS.)........... **$1,430**

Teakettle on stand, sterling, the kettle of a deep rectangular rounded form chased overall w/dense flowers & leaves, a short angled leaf-clad spout, a high fixed angular handle w/sea creature base joins & ivory insulators, the top center formed by a pair of facing dolphins, the rectangular flat cover w/a figural seated Chinese man finial, raised on a stand w/four leafy scroll legs ending in shell feet & centering an oblong floral-chased rectangular burner w/removable cover & two hinge pins, Samuel Kirk & Son, Baltimore, 1880-90, 13 1/4" h., the set (ILLUS. right with Kirk claret jug) **$2,868**

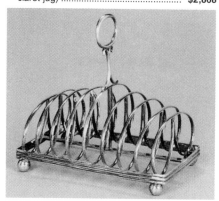

Unusal American Coin Toast Rack

Toast rack, coin, rectangular base band on four small ball feet, graduated arched loops form the rack centered by an upright handle w/a ring finial, J.B. Jones and Co., Boston, Massachusetts, marked "Pure Silver Coin," first half 19th c., 6 3/4" l., 6 1/2" h. (ILLUS.)................. **$1,912**

Fine Neoclassical Coin Silver Tureen

Tureen, cov., coin, Neoclassical design, the low oval pedestal foot trimmed w/a Greek key band, the long low flaring oval body w/a gadrooned band at the bottom below a plain band engraved w/an oval wreath, lion head & ring end handles, the high domed cover gadrooned at the top & fitted w/a figural lion head finial, cover w/an engraved monogram, R. & W. Wilson,

Philadlephia, ca. 1825-50, 10 1/4" l., 7 1/2" h. (ILLUS.) **$2,530**

American Coin Silver Waste Bowl

Waste bowl, coin, Neoclassical style, the round low pedestal base decorated w/a palmette rim band, the squatty bulbous body fluted around the lower half, w/a widely flaring rolled rim w/a palmette band, retailed by Canfield & Bro., B+altimore, made by Eoff and Shepherd, New York City, ca. 1850, 7" d., 5 1/2" h. (ILLUS.) **$575**

English & Other

Late 18th Century English Sterling Bowl

Bowl, footed, deep round sides w/a swelled shoulder band w/engraved scrolls above an engraved wreath w/a monogram, hallmark of Robert & David Hennell, London, England, 1799, 7" d., 4" h. (ILLUS.) **$840**

Ornate Silver Box for the French Market

Box, cov., rectangular form w/an arched lid, the whole decorated w/embossed columns, gadroon-and-shell banding, vitruvian scrolls & griffins, centering on plaques depicting Poseidon, Amphitrite & Aphrodite, the hinged cover opening to an indigo velvet-lined interior, probably German made for L. Oudry et Cie, Paris, France, ca. 1900, 6 x 11", 7 1/2" h. (ILLUS.).................................. **$2,530**

Unusual French Rooster Chocolate Pot

Chocolate pot, cov., figural, modeled in the shape of a large rooster w/the head & neck forming the spout, the squatty bulbous feathered body resting on large bent-in legs, a tall waisted cylindrical neck cast w/hanging bunches of fruit topped by a domed cover w/similar decoration, the large handle formed by the tail feathers, French marks, probably late 18th c., 9" w., 9" h. (ILLUS.).................. **$4,888**

English Sterling Coffeepot, Circa 1800

Coffeepot, cov., squared foot w/notched corners & short pedestal support the tall paneled baluster-form body w/a hinged domed cover w/disk finial, long serpentine spout & long angular ivory handle, side engraved w/a coat-of-arms w/a banner w/a Latin inscription, hallmark possibly of Samuel Hennell, London, England, 1802, 11 3/4" h. (ILLUS.) **$1,320**

Mexican Silver Jewelry Box

Jewelry box, figural, in the shape of a dome-top trunk w/a hinged cover, marked "Clavel Sterling - 0.950," Mexico, 2 x 2 1/2" (ILLUS.)..................................... **$395**

Rare Large German Model of a Hare

Model of a hare, the realistically cast & chased animal seated on its haunches, German marks on the base w/later Dutch control marks, ca. 1890, 10 3/4" h. (ILLUS.)................................. **$5,378**

Unusual English Lobed Muffin Dish

Muffin dish, cov., round shallow base w/a wide everted rim composed of a band of broad waterleaves, the conforming high domed & melon-lobed cover w/a wide band of leaves all topped by a melon-shaped finial, body & cover w/an engraved crest, marks of Charles Fox, London, England, 1831, 9 1/2" d. (ILLUS.).... **$2,629**

English 18th Century Salt Cellars

Salt cellars, squatty bulbous round form raised on short legs w/paw feet, a flared gadrooned rim, gilt interior, marks of Alexander Johnston, London, England, 1747, w/four later sterling salt spoons, 3" d., set of 3 (ILLUS.)............................... **$403**

English Victorian Silver Kettle & Stand

Teakettle on stand, cov., Victorian, wide bulbous inverted pear-shaped body elaborately chased w/rococo scrolls & floral designs, a serpentine ribbed spout, low domed cover w/chased leaftips & a pointed spiral finial, overhead handle w/ornate scroll uprights joined by a flat strap grip, on a stand w/an ornate openwork flower & scroll apron raised on three leafy-scroll legs joined by braces to a center ring now missing the burner, mark of Charles Stuart Harris, London, England, 1898, 10" w., overall 12 1/2" h. (ILLUS.) **$2,415**

Teapot, cov., East Indian, inverted melonform fluted body chased w/large scrolling acanthus leaves, a flaring leaf-cast neck & fluted hinged domed cover w/blossom finial, raised on leafy scroll feet, leaf-cast serpentine spout, ornate leafy C-scroll handle, mark of Hamilton & Co., Calcutta, India, ca. 1850, overall 12" l. (ILLUS. second from left with three other teapots, middle next column) **$1,315**

English Teapot by Hester Bateman

Teapot, cov., Neoclassical oval upright body w/flat top & domed hinged cover w/pine cone finial, straight angled spout, C-scroll wooden handle, engraved w/swags of flowers centered by an oval cartouche w/an animal, mark of Hester Bateman, England, 1785, 10" l., 6" h. (ILLUS.) **$2,588**

Teapot, cov., oblong paneled body & shoulder w/conforming hinged domed cover w/blossom finial, serpentine spout & C-scroll wooden handle, the sides chased w/a large floral medallion, mark of Moitinho de Almeida, Porto, Portugal, ca. 1815,

overall 11 3/4" l. (ILLUS. second from right with other three teapots, middle this column) **$1,000-1,500**

Fine Paul Storr Silver Teapot

Teapot, cov., round melon-lobed body resting on leafy feet, the hinged leaf-cast cover w/a removable blossom finial, leaf-trimmed twig handle w/ivory insulators, twig spout w/leaves, the body engraved w/flowers & leaves & a monogram & crest on each side, marked by Paul Storr, London, 1838, 6" h. (ILLUS.) **$2,987**

Teapot, cov., Spanish Colonial, bulbous nearly spherical body tapering to a domed cover w/a baluster-form finial, serpentine spout, overhead swing strap bail handle, engraved initials on the side, marked on the base w/a later French control mark, late 18th - early 19th c., 6 1/2" h. (ILLUS. far right with other three teapots, below) **$1,434**

Group of Four Foreign-made Silver Teapots

Teapot, cov., squatty bulbous body w/a fluted lower half, the upper half ornately embossed w/flowers, scrolls & shells, small fluted cover w/figural fruit finial, short branch-form spout, looped branch-form handle w/ivory insulators, base engraved "Palermo, 23 Febraro 1829. Giovanni Fecarotta fece," Italian, overall 9 1/2" l. (ILLUS. far left with three other teapots) **$3,585**

Teapot, cover & stand, pot w/upright serpentine oval shape & straight angled spout, hinged domed cover, C-scroll black wood handle, the body bright-cut w/floral festoons & oval cartouches, one side engraved w/a ship, the conforming stand w/a beaded border & raised on four pad feet, mark of Robert Pinkney & Robert Scott, Newcastle, England, teapot 1783, stand 1784-86, teapot 9 1/2" l., 2 pcs. **$2,868**

Rare Queen Anne English Silver Teapot

Teapot, cover & stand, Queen Anne era, wide bulbous pear-shaped body w/a high domed hinged cover w/knob finial, paneled scroll spout, C-scroll wooden handle, one side engraved w/a coat-of-arms, w/a round stand on three scrolled feet & pierced w/vertical flutes & w/a baluster-turned side wood handle, teapot w/mark of Richard Bayley, London, England, 1711, stand w/mark of Lewis Mettayer, London, England, 1706, teapot overall 7 1/4" l., 2 pcs. (ILLUS. of teapot) **$26,290**

Early English Sterling Silver Footed Tray

Tray, shallow rounded dished form w/serpentine edge & narrow beaded edge band, raised on small claw-and-ball feet, the center engraved w/a crest in an oval cartouche, unattributed mark for London, England, second half 18th c., 12 1/2" d. (ILLUS.)... **$6,573**

Sterling Silver (Flatware)

LOVE DISARMED (Reed and Barton)
Service for 12: twelve dinner forks; twelve salad forks; twelve teaspoons; twelve dinner knives; twelve ice cream spoons; a gravy ladle; one sugar spoon; one tomato server; one serving spoon; one slotted serving spoon; one large serving fork; one small serving fork; one master butter knife; one cheese scoop; one asparagus server; one cracker scoop; complete w/fitted wooden case, early 20th c., 86 pcs. (ILLUS. of one handle, top next column) **$18,400**

A Handle in the Love Disarmed Pattern

ROSE (The Stieff Company)

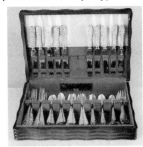

Part of a Set of Rose Pattern Silver

Boxed set: ten 8 3/4" knives; twelve 7" forks; nine 6" salad forks; twelve 5 3/4" ice cream forks; eight 5 3/4" teaspoons; twelve 5 1/2" spoons; 9 3/4" pie server; monogrammed, in wooden hinged case w/velvet liner, 64 pcs. (ILLUS. of part) ... **$1,725**

SHELL AND THREAD (Tiffany & Company)

Partial Set of Shell and Thread Flatware

Boxed set: eighteen 6" forks; six 6" hors-d'oeuvre forks; seven 5 3/4" flat-handled butter knives; one 7" spoon; six 6 3/4" soup spoons; six 9" knives & eighteen 7 1/2" knives; monogrammed, 62 pcs, (ILLUS. of part, previous page) **$2,300**

STRASBOURG (Gorham Mfg. Co.)

Part of a Strasbourg Flatware Set

Service for 12: twelve dinner knives; twelve hollow-handle butter knives; twelve dinner forks; twelves dessert forks; twelve soup spoons; twelve teaspoons, one meat fork, one large serving spoon, no monogram, in mahogany one-drawer lift-lid case, 74 pcs. (ILLLUS. of part) **$1,610**

WILLIAMSBURG SHELL (Colonial Williamsburg)

Boxed Set of Williamsburg Shell

Boxed set: eight 7 1/2" forks; eight 6 1/2" forks; eight 6 3/4" spoons; eight 6" teaspoons; eight 9 3/4" pistol-handled knives; six 7" pistol-handled butter knives; in a felt-lined mahogany case, 46 pcs. (ILLUS.) **$1,725**

Silver Plate (Hollowware)

Unusual Ebonized Beverage Pitcher

Beverage pitcher, cov., wide flaring round base band below the tapering cylindrical ebonized body mounted on each side w/a large bold-relief medieval battle scenes w/knights on horseback, a plain rim band & cast mask spout, leafy C-scroll handle, the hinged domed cover w/a figural finial, Europe, late 19th c. (ILLUS.) **$460**

English Silver Plate Bisquit Box

Bisquit box, upright hinged & divided shell-shaped container resting on scrolling legs within a scrolling frame, England, early 20th c., 6 x 8", 10" h. (ILLUS.) **$259**

Unusual Silver Plate & Wood Fish-shaped Carving Board

Carving board, silver plate & wood, model of a fish w/a metal head & tail & wooden body,silver marked "Chife Escoda - Made in Spain Alpaca," 7 1/2 x 36" (ILLUS.) **$546**

Large Christofle Victorian Silver Plate Center Bowl

Centerpiece bowl, oblong shallow bowl w/wide pierced sides composed of a lattice & leaf design, supported by four full-figure kneeling cupids, mark of Christofle & Cie., Paris, France, ca. 1890, 20 1/2" l., 5 1/4" h. (ILLUS.) **$5,019**

Victorian Heating Platter & Cover

Heating platter & cover, oval well-and-tree platter w/a hot water compartment, scroll-cast edges & looped end handles, raised on four leaf scroll feet, the matching high domed & lobed cover w/a leaf-style handle, second half 19th c., 14 3/4 x 20" (ILLUS.) **$748**

Unusual English Silver Plate Heated Serving Station

Serving station, heated-type, the round lazy Susan heated tray stand fitted w/a large central two-handled cov. soup tureen surrounded by three cov. round serving dishes, three shakers, three open footed salt dips w/cobalt blue glass liners, two cov. mustard pots w/cobalt blue glass liners & three tall shakers, each piece decorated w/a wide reeded band, tureen marked "Made in Sheffield, England," early 20th c., tray 27" d., the set (ILLUS.)... **$1,610**

Silver Plate & Cranberry Glass Sugar Bowl

Sugar bowl, cov., an open silver frame w/four pierced tab feet & pierced pointed side handles joined by a top band fitted

Unusual Hot Water Lazy Susan Set

Lazy Susan set: a low round pedestal base supporting a wide deep round hot water reservoir tray w/open scrolled side handles w/wood grips, fitted w/three oval covered serving dishes, two glass-lined sauce pots & a shaker around a central footed covered soup tureen & ladle, 20th c., overall 23" w., 18" h., the set (ILLUS.) ... **$920**

w/pairs of prongs to hold teaspoons, a cranberry glass bowl insert in the Inverted Thumbprint patt. fitted w/a domed silver plate cover w/a flatted tab finial, complete w/various sterling & plated teaspoons, ca. 1890, 8 1/2" h. (ILLUS.) **$518**

Meriden Silver Plate Tea & Coffee Service on Handled Tray

Tea & coffee service: a 13" h. cov. coffee-pot, a 12" h. cov. teapot, an 11 1/2" h., cov. teapot, cov. sugar bowl, spoon holder, creamer & waste bowl, on a large oval tray w/scrolled end handles; serving pieces w/footed baluster-form bodies w/beaded rims & foot rims, ornate scroll handles & ribbed serpentine spouts, all serving pieces marked by the Meriden Britannia Company, late 19th - early 20th c., hole in one teapot handle, tray 23 x 34", the set (ILLUS.) ... **$518**

Gorham Silver Plated Tea & Coffee Set

Tea & coffee set: cov. teapot, cov. coffee-pot, cov. sugar bowl, creamer & waste bowl; bulbous squared bodies w/each side decorated w/répoussé large leafy scrolls, squared necks & covers w/reeded button finials, hollow loop handles, Gorham Mfg. Co., Providence, Rhode Island, 1888, cof-feepot 7" h., the set (ILLUS.) **$460**

Teakettle on stand, the large squatty bul-bous kettle w/a long serpentine spout & high arched serpentine fixed handle, flat lid w/flower finial, the body engraved over-all w/scrolling leafy florals, on a three-foot-ed stand w/font but no burner, marked "Munday John St. Oxford St.," England, probably 19th c., some wear, 11" w., over-all 15 1/4" h., the set (ILLUS., next col-umn) **$316**

English Silver Plate Teakettle & Stand

English Silver Plate Willow Ware Teapot

Teapot, cov., Willow Ware design, flattened bulbous body on four ribbed button feet, flat lid w/ebony finial, straight spout, C-form ebony handle held in place w/two silver plate grips, engraved overall w/geometric designs around center me-dallion of Willow Ware design, unmarked, England, late 19th c. (ILLUS.)............ **$250-275**

Secessionist Silver Plate Pot on Stand

Teapot on stand, cov., the domical plated hand-hammered copper teapot w/a domed cover & knop finial, serpentine spout, angular loop raffia-wrapped han-dle, raised on a platform stand w/four flat panel supports on the flaring round base centered by a hinged sterno burner, the teapot & stand decorated w/embossed Germanic Secessionist floral medallions, base stamped "WMF/91," Wurttember-gische Metallwarenfabrik, Esslingen, Germany, early 20th c., 11" d., 11 1/2" h. (ILLUS.)... **$646**

Fine Large American Victorian Silver Plate Tray

Tray, oval, a cast large bead rim band, scroll-cast loop end handles, the center engraved w/a broad band of acanthus & lattice scrollwork quartered by cartouches depicting rural scenes including a stag, hound & buildings, by Rogers, Smith & Co., Hartford, Connecticut, 1857-62, 23 1/4 x 35 1/2" (ILLUS.) **$1,035**

Large Silve Plate Tray with Gallery Edge

Tray, oval w/a low reticulated gallery edge w/beading, the center engraved w/a castle tower scene enclosed by deep floral & leaf engraving, large ring loop end handles, raised on six small scroll feet, bottom marked "KH & Co.," English, overall 21 1/2 x 31 1/2", 2 1/2" h. (ILLUS.) **$748**

Tray, oval w/applied scroll, shell-and-floral design rim & end handles, the center w/an engraved field, marked on bottom "LBS 940," American-made, early 20th c., 22 x 30" (some plating wear) **$431**

Ornate Tureen on Attached Undertray

Tureen on attached undertray, cov., the oval tray w/a gadrooned rim & figural ram head end handles, the oval tureen base w/a gadrooned rim band below the deep oval body decorated overall w/embossed stripes centering a monogrammed cartouche, ram head handles & a gadrooned rim band, the matching domed cover w/upright loop handle, unmarked but

probably Europe, 19th c., 9 1/2" l., 7 1/2" h. (ILLUS.) **$1,035**

Tall Neoclassical Silver Plate Urns

Urns, cov., Necoclassical style, square foot & tapering pedestal chased w/scrolls & leaves, the tall urn-form body chased overall w/ornate scrolls foliage, birds & plain panels, cast ram head & ring rim handles, tall conical coverfs w/further chased decoration, England, 19th c., 15" h., pr. (ILLUS.) **$1,495**

Unusual European Plated Vanity Mirror

Vanity mirror, an oval plateau mirror inset into a conforming base decorated w/reeded banding & chased flower bands, two rear plinths supporting reeded columns flanking an oval swiveling mirror w/a reeded & ribbon-trimmed border & a bow & leaf sprig crest, Europe, ca. 1920, 11 x 14 1/2", 18" h. (ILLUS.) **$1,093**

Fine Silver Plate & Milk Glass Water Pitcher

Water pitcher, cov., an ornate silver plate frame w/a chased flaring base & rim bands joined by a wide pierced ornate handle w/a fish & flower design & a long dolphin-shaped spout, low domed cover w/pierced fanned finial, the frame enclosing a milk glass cylinder decorated on each side w/a winter landscape in shades of brown, tan, white & black, ca. 1880s, 13 1/2" h. (ILLUS., previous page) **$920**

Fine Victorian Silver Plate Water Set

Water pitcher set: large lined water pitcher w/hinged cover tilting in a silver plate stand w/a high arched handle , the round flaring base fitted w/two small rounded shelves each w/a pedestal-based water goblet, all pieces w/engraved scroll bands & winged cherubs, by Simpson, Hall, Miller & Company, Connecticut, ca. 1885-95, pitcher 12 1/2" h., overall 22 1/2" h., the set (ILLUS.) **$350-550**

Unusual English Cannon Wine Trolley

Wine trolley, modeled as a cannon w/large scroll-trimmed open wheels & pierced scrolling handles joined by a turned bar, short cylindrical base w/beaded bands & a long serpentine side panel between the wheels, England, 19th c., 6 1/2 x 11 1/2", 8 3/4" h. (ILLUS.) **$1,265**

Tin & Tole

Fine 12-Tube Cylindrical Candle Mold

Candle mold, twelve-tube, a round flat base w/flared rim supporting the slender cylindrical tubes topped by a matching round top centered by a cylindrical cap w/conical top fitted w/a small wire bail handle, 19th c., 9" d., overall 13 1/2" h. (ILLUS.)... **$575**

Three Pieces of Early Decorative Tole

Canister, cov., tole, cylindrical w/a hinged fitted cover w/small wire bail handle, dark japanned ground decorated w/stylized red, yellow & green flowers, some wear, 19th c., 4 1/2" d., 3 1/2" h. (ILLUS. center with tole document box & match holder)
.... **$288**

Early Tin Lighthouse-shape Coffeepot

Coffeepot, cov., lighthouse-style, flared tall tapering cyindricl ringed body w/a domed cover, a flattened rectangular serpentine spout, large strap handle w/hand grip, early, cover finial missing, some rust, 11 1/2" h. (ILLUS.) **$200-500**

Large Tin Cavalryman Cookie Cutter

Cookie cutter, tin, a cavalryman on horse-back aginst a solid flat back w/tiny vent hole, minor dents & rust, 19th c., 8 3/4 x 10" (ILLUS.).................................... **$489**

Large Tin Rabbit Cookie Cutter

Cookie cutter, tin, a seated rabbit on a solid sheet backing w/a small vent hole, late 19th - early 20th c., 10 1/2" l. (ILLUS.) **$201**

Early American Tole Document Box

Document box, cov., tole, rectangular w/a hinged domed cover w/a brass bail han-dle, black ground decorated around the base w/a red band w/white slashes above dark yellow leafy swags, the cover w/a border band of yellow ribbon banding around the edge & top, minor wear, hasp damaged, first half 19th c., 4 x 8", 5" h. (ILLUS.).. **$518**

Document box, cov., tole, rectangular w/a low domed cover & wire bail handle, black ground, the sides painted w/large four-arm pinwheels in dark red & yellow trimmed w/dark green dots, wear, mostly on the cover, first half 19th c., 3 3/8 x 7 3/4", 4 5/8" h. (ILLUS. bottom with tole canister & match holder)............. **$460**

Match holder, tole, hanging-type, the tall cut-out back plate w/an arched & fanned top rim & centered by a hanging hole framed by a diamond-shaped arrange-ment of dark red & yellow leaves, the squared bottom fitted w/a narrow project-ing open match holder decorated w/a smoky white band & a yellow & red fruit flanked by green leaves, slight wear, 19th c., 7 1/2" h. (ILLUS. top with tole canister & document box) **$2,128**

Fine Early American Tole Tray

Tray, tole, oblong shape w/serpentine sides w/a low rim band, center h.p. w/a scene of a three-masted sailing ship, possibly the U.S. frigate Independence, in coastal waters, surrounded by a black border band decorated w/gilt stenciled leaf & scroll bands, American, early 19th c., im-perfections, 24 x 29 5/8" (ILLUS.).......... **$1,998**

MINIATURES (Paintings)

Bust portrait of a young woman, watercolor on paper, shown facing right, her dark hair pulled up & back, wearing a white off-the-shoulder gown, second quarter 19th c., American School, in embossed brass & wood frame, 3 1/8 x 4 1/8" **$499**

Miniature of a Woman in a Brown Dress

Half-length portrait of a woman, watercolor on brown paper, standing facing left, wearing a high-waisted brown dress w/balloon sleves & a high white collar & high lacy white bonnet framing her her curly flat brown hair, unsigned, ca. 1830-40, in an early beveled rosewood veneer frame w/gilt liner, some loss to background color, 4 x 5" (ILLUS.).................... **$510**

Fine Dated Miniature of a Young Girl

Half-length portrait of a young girl, oval, painted on ivory, pretty child w/center-parted brown hair w/long sausage curls, wearing a white dress, set behind a piece of glass surrounded by an ornate gilt-brass oval framed set into a larger rectangular frame w/a black heavy mat & narrow molded brass frame, letter identifies the girl & notes the date of gift as March 13, 1860, signed by Godfred Miller, American, miniature 1 1/4 x 1 1/2", overall 3 1/2 x 4 1/4" (ILLUS.) **$1,800**

Fine Miniature of a Girl in a White Dress

Half-length portrait of a young girl, painted on ivory, oval, the young girl w/short-cropped dark brown hair seated on a red sofa facing left & wearing a high-collared white dress w/balloon-style sleeves, in a narrow oval brass frame w/hanging loop & w/a back window enclosing an oval woven hair piece, unsigned, ca. 1830, 2 x 2 1/2" (ILLUS.)................................. **$1,020**

Miniature of Girl Dressed in Red

Half-length portrait of a young girl, watercolor on paper, the girl w/short center-parted dark brown hair facing left & wearing a red dress w/small puff sleeves & a red coral necklace, antique wide flat sanded-edge frame w/gilt liner, ca. 1830, 2 3/4 x 3 1/2" (ILLUS.)............................... **$780**

Early Miniature of a Pretty Young Woman

Half-length portrait of a young woman, ivory, long oval shape, the slender standing woman posed facing left & looking at the viewer, wearing a white Empire gown, long curly brown hair, pearl drop earrings, w/a red shawl over her arm & holding a red rose, unsigned, in the original oval white-painted frame, early 19th c., 1 1/2 x 2 3/4" (ILLUS., previous page)........ **$420**

Miniature of an Elderly Gentleman

Half-length portrait of an elderly gentleman, watercolor on paper, seated in a Chippendale chair facing left, a stocky man w/short grey hair wearing a high-collared black coat, in original beveled wood frame w/worn finish, ca. 1840, 3 x 4" (ILLUS.) **$345**

Early Facing Pair of Portrait Miniatures

Half-length portraits of a man & woman, rectangular, painted on ivory, facing pair, he facing right, brown hair w/sideburns & wearing a black high-collared coat & white shirt, she facing left & wearing a balloon-sleeved black dress w/a lace collar, a large lacy bonnet at the back of her head behind tight brown curls, the ivory ground shades down to dark greenish brown, in matching molded giltwood frames, ca. 1840, some light spot foxing, each 2 3/4 x 3 3/4", facing pr. (ILLUS.) **$840**

MINIATURES (Replicas)

Blanket chest, painted & decorated poplar, rectangular hinged top w/thick molded edge opens to a deep well w/a till, the front & sides h.p. w/the original brown

Very Rare Decorated Blanket Chest

ground, a double radiating cone-shaped design in black, red, green & yellow on the front & sides, dark green & leafy borders, chip-carved base molding above a pierced & scroll-carved apron w/bracket feet, New York State, early 19th c., 9 1/2 x 15", 11" h. (ILLUS.) **$12,650**

Bucket, cov., stave construction, tapered cylindrical sides w/two brass bands & wire bail handle w/turned wood grip, old green paint, turned cover w/small finial, 19th c., 4 3/4" d., overall 6" h. **$633**

Country Victorian Tall Chest of Drawers

Chest of drawers, pine, tall country-style, a scroll-cut back crest over the rectangular top above a case w/a pair of small drawers, each w/two turned wood knobs, above three long drawers, each w/turned wood knobs, arches at bases of sides, repair to upper right corner of lowest drawer, ca. 1850, 5 1/2 x 11", 16 1/4" h. (ILLUS.)... **$288**

Miniature William IV Era Chest

Chest of drawers, satinwood, a rectangular top w/molded edges & rounded corners overhang a case w/three long graduated drawers w/tiny turned knobs, molded base on low bun feet, William IV era, England, ca. 1835, 9 1/2 x 12", 10 1/2" h. (ILLUS.).. **$1,265**

Rare Chippendale Miniature Desk

Desk, Chippendale-style pine slant-front type, a narrow rectangular to above a hinged slant lid opening to four cubbyholes, the case fitted w/a pair of small drawers above two long graduated drawers all w/butterfly brasses, molded base on simple bracket feet, apparently original brasses, probably Massachusetts, 1740-70, 11 x 18", 21 1/2" h. (ILLUS.) **$9,500**

Murphy bed, oak, designed as a tall two-door wardrobe w/a lower drawer w/ encloses the fold-down double bed, late 19th c., 3 1/2 x 8", 12" h. (ILLUS., top next column)... **$805**

Unusual Miniature Oak Murphy Bed

Rare Nantucket Scrimshaw Miniature Tea Set & Drop-leaf Table

Scrimshaw tea set & drop-leaf table, the partial service for six tea set comprising: six plates, six soup plates, five goblets, six cups, four serving bowls (three w/covers), three knives, four bowls, six napkin rings & a covered server; all of turned ivory w/red & green decoration; together w/a mahogany drop-leaf table w/the rounded-end top flanked by D-form hinged drop leaves, on an apron w/slip-out supports above the turned & tapering legs w/knob & disk feet, Nantucket Island, Massachusetts, mid-19th c., table open 11 7/8 x 15", 8 1/2" h., the complete grouping (ILLUS.)................................. **$10,755**

Rare Early English Sterling Teapot

Teapot, cov., sterling silver, Queen Anne style, footed nearly spherical body w/a short shaped spout, hinged cover & C-scroll wooden handle, English hallmarks, probably 18th c., 3 3/4" h. (ILLUS.) **$2,400**

Yarn winder, carved & turned whale pan-bone, the six turned arms attached to the upright elaborate gear mechanism, on a rectangular platform raised on three turned & canted legs, signed & dated 1876, America, 9" h. **$2,629**

MOVIE MEMORABILIA
Also see: ADVERTISING ITEMS; DOLLS; and POP CULTURE

Costumes

Elvis Presley Shirt from "G.I. Blues"

Elvis Presley, "G.I. Blues," Paramount, 1960, khaki military shirt adorned w/patches & lapel pins, interior Paramount label & Western Costume Company label, w/reprinted color image of Elvis wearing the shirt (ILLUS.) **$11,353**

Madonna Hat & Pin from "Evita"

Madonna, "Evita," Cinergi Pictures Entertainment, Inc., 1996, brown silk pleated hat w/an interior label for Iosbel 70, London & a multi-clored faux jewel brooch w/two jewels missing, worn by Madonna in the role of Evita Peron, w/reprinted color photo of Madonna wearing the hat,2 pcs. (ILLUS.) **$896**

Marlon Brando "Apocalypse Now" Prop Jacket

Marlon Brando, "Apocalypse Now," United Artists, 1979, Army khaki jacket adorned w/eight patches, not worn by Brando but used as set dressing, included w/a photo-copied script from the film (ILLUS.) **$5,378**

Three Stooges Tuxedo Jackets

Three Stooges, three tuxedo jackets worn by The Three Stooges during stage performances in the 1960s, grey or black wool, labeled for each Stooge, also a pair of oversizd trousers & three letters of authentication, the group (ILLUS.) **$4,183**

Lobby Cards

"Breakfast at Tiffany's" Lobby Card Set

"Breakfast at Tiffany's," Paramount, 1961, starring Audry Hepburn, set of eight cards, each w/a color scene from the movie, 11 x 14", the set (ILLUS., previous page).. **$1,195**

"Citizen Kane" Movie Title Lobby Card

"Citizen Kane," RKO, 1941, starring Orson Welles, title card w/a large figure of Kane against a yellow background, 11 x 14" (ILLUS.)... **$1,554**

"Creature from the Black Lagoon" Card

"Creature from the Black Lagoon," Universal, 1954, starring Richard Carlson & Julia Adams, color picture of the monster & female star w/other color scenes on a dark green ground, linen-backed, 14 x 36" (ILLUS.).................................... **$3,346**

"Not of This Earth" Lobby Card

"Not of This Earth," Allied Artists, 1957, large color portrait of a woman screaming, an alien in the foreground, 14 x 36" (ILLUS.)... **$598**

Early "Rolled Stockings" Lobby Card

"Rolled Stockings," Paramount, 1927, insert-type, close-up drawing of legs w/rolled stockings at the top, small photos of the stars along the bottom, 14 x 36" (ILLUS.)... **$1,135**

"The Eagle and The Hawk" Lobby Card

"The Eagle and The Hawk," Paramount, 1933, starring Frederic March, Cary Grant & Carole Lombard, large color scene shown, 11 x 14" (ILLUS.)............... **$179**

"White Heat" Movie Lobby Card

"White Heat," Warner Bros., 1949, starring James Cagney & Virginia Mayo, printed in red, black & shades of pink, 14 x 36" (ILLUS.)... **$896**

Posters

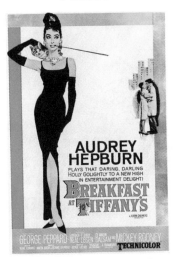

"Breakfast at Tiffany's" Movie Poster

"Breakfast at Tiffany's," Paramount, 1961, starring Audrey Hepburn, full-length portrait of Hepburn along one side, one-sheet, linen-backed, 27 x 41" (ILLUS.).... **$4,183**

Set of "The Jazz Singer" Lobby Cards

"The Jazz Singer," Warner Bros., 1927, starring Al Jolson, set of seven cards, each w/a color-tinted photo of a scene from the movie, first "talking" movie, 11 x 14", the set (ILLUS.)..................... **$13,145**

"Dancing Lady, Movie Poster

"Dancing Lady," MGM, 1933, starring Joan Crawford & Clark Gable, dramatic graphics, one-sheet, linen-backed, 27 x 41" (ILLUS.).................................. **$2,390**

"From Russia With Love" Movie Poster

"From Russia With Love," United Artists, 1963, printed in red, black & white, style B three-sheet, linen-backed, 41 x 81" (ILLUS.) **$896**

"Francis in the Haunted House" Poster

"Francis in the Haunted House," Universal, 1955, starring Mickey Rooney & Francis the Talking Mule, one-sheet (ILLUS.)
.... **$40-70**

1971 "Godzilla vs. Hedorah" Poster

"Godzilla vs. Hedorah (Smog Monster)," Toho, Japan, 1971, written in Japanese, colorful graphics, one-sheet (ILLUS.) .. **$80-120**

"Intermezzo" Movie Poster

"Intermezzo," Selnick/United Artists, 1939, starring Leslie Howard & Ingrid Bergman, color portrait of the stars in a large circle, one-sheet, linen-backed, 27 x 41" (ILLUS.) **$717**

"Lassie's Great Adventure" Poster

"Lassie's Great Adventure," 20th Century Fox, 1963, starring June Lockhart, Jon Provost & Hugh Reilly, color & two-tone photos, one-sheet (ILLUS.) **$50-100**

"Jason and The Argonauts" Poster

"Jason and The Argonauts," Columbia, 1978 re-release, bold graphics, one-sheet (ILLUS.) **$50-85**

"The Golden Voyage of Sinbad" Poster

"The Golden Voyage of Sinbad," Columbia Pictures, 1973, colorful graphics, Harrhausen special effects, one-sheet (ILLUS.) **$35-60**

"The Incredible Journey" Movie Poster

"The Incredible Journey," Disney, 1963, large color image of the animals, one-sheet (ILLUS.) **$20-35**

"The Palm Beach Story" Movie Poster

"The Palm Beach Story," Paramount, 1942, starring Claudette Colbert & Joel McCrea, one-sheet, linen-backed, 27 x 41" (ILLUS.)..................................... **$4,183**

"The Philadelphia Story," MGM, 1940, starring Cary Grant, Katharine Hepburn & James Stewart, large color bust portraits of the stars in the center, style D one-sheet, linen-backed, 27 x 41" (ILLUS., top next column) **$4,183**

"The Spoilers," Paramount, 1930, starring Gary Cooper, dramatic graphics, six-sheet, linen-backed, only known copy of this poster, 81 x 81" (ILLUS., middle next column) **$7,768**

"The Philadelphia Story" Poster

Only Known Six-sheet "The Spoilers" Poster

"Where Danger Lives" Movie Poster

"Where Danger Lives," RKO, 1950, starring Robert Mitchum, three-sheet, linen-backed, 41 x 81" (ILLUS.)...................... **$2,868**

Miscellaneous

Marilyn Monroe 1950s Alarm Clock

Alarm clock, Westclox, owned by Marilyn Monroe, used in her Beverly Hills apartment, 1950s, includes reprinted images of Monroe in her apartment showing the clock on her nightstand, 2 x 3", 4" h. (ILLUS.).... **$5,019**

Part of "Spook Stories" 1960s Card Set

Card set, "Spook Stories," Leaf Confectionery, 1963, each card w/a black & white photo of a vintage movie monster w/a funny quote, 144 card set, extremely good to near mint, the set (ILLUS. of part) **$452**

Marilyn Monroe-owned Black Silk Dress

Dress, sleeveless black silk overlaid w/floral-print black lace & adorned w/a small frontal train of extra lace, owned by Marilyn Monroe, label of Ceil Chapman, one of Monroe's favorite cocktail dress designers, w/reprinted black & white photo of Monroe wearing the dress, zipper broken, 1950s (ILLUS.) **$19,120**

Marilyn Monroe Silver Leather High-heels

High-heels, silver leather stilettos owned by Marilyn Monroe, inside label for Aliata, Italian, w/a letter from Anna Strasberg, size 7 1/2 B (ILLUS.) **$5,736**

William Bendix Movie Promotion Ad

Magazine advertisement, "Chesterfield Cigarettes," full-page, Life, 1948, features a color image of William Bendix holding a baseball bat & promoting his movie "The Babe Ruth Story" (ILLUS.) **$8**

Early "Thief of Bagdad" Movie Program

Movie program, "Thief of Bagdad," starring Douglas Fairbanks, 1924, colorful cover image, excellent condition (ILLUS.) **$228**

Cocktail Cart from "The Seven Year Itch"

Movie prop, cocktail cart, used in "The Seven Year Itch," 20th Century Fox, 1955, used in the apartment of Tom Ewell when he tries to seduce Marilyn Monroe, 18 x 25", 35" h. (ILLUS.) **$9,560**

Signed Jayne Mansfield Photograph

Photograph, black & white publicity photo of Jayne Mansfield, signed & inscribed by Mansfield, 1950s, 8 x 10" (ILLUS.)............ **$282**

Early Signed Laurel & Hardy Photograph

Photograph, sepia-toned image of Laurel & Hardy, autographed & inscribed, dated

1933, tear in top edge, large size, 11 x 14" (ILLUS.).................................... **$1,454**

South American Movie Star Postcards

Postcards, each w/a color photo of a 1950s movie star, published in Uruguay, mint condition, set of 24 (ILLUS. of part) **$304**

1970s Marilyn Monroe Thermometer

Thermometer, oversized long printed metal type w/rounded ends, a red ground w/a tall central color image of Marilyn Monroe wearing her famous white dress from "The Seven Year Itch," black wording "Some Like It Hot" evokes another Monroe film, marked by the Nostalgia Lane company, New York, New York, made as a collectible, ca. 1970s, 8" x 38" (ILLUS.).................................... **$1,554**

Early Long Carved Wood Boat Tiller

NAUTICAL ITEMS

The romantic lure of the sea, and of ships in general, has opened up a new area of collector interest. Nautical gear, especially items made of brass or with brass trim, is sought out for its decorative appeal. Virtually all items that can be associated with older ships, along with items used or made by sailors, are now considered collectible, for technological advances have rendered them obsolete. Listed below are but a few of the numerous nautical items sold in recent months.

Boat tiller, carved wood w/a tapered form w/a turned top half ending in a carved animal head w/a wide gaping mouth holding a ball w/a five-pointed star, bronze hardware, nice old dark patina, 19th c., 59" l. (ILLUS., top of page).............................. **$1,840**

Fine Inlaid Teak Seaman's Chest

Seaman's chest, inlaid teak, six-board construction, rectangular flat top inlaid w/three ornate compass stars, opening to an interior w/a lidded till, the front inlaid w/a light wood border band w/looping corners & across the center w/three large compass stars, each end w/a metal bail handle & another inlaid compass star, 19th c., 14 1/2 x 31", 16" h. (ILLUS.)...... **$1,265**

Fine English-made Cased Sextant

Sextant, brass instrument w/an ivory scale & turned wood handles, in a fitted hinged dovetailed mahogany case w/two labels & extra lenses, labels of Imorcy & Son Minories, London, England, includes a

family history of ownership, 19th c., case 11" l. (ILLUS.).. **$1,035**

PAPER COLLECTIBLES

Early Birth Record with Birds

Birth record, watercolor & pen & ink onpaper, decorated w/two large birds on leafy vines flanked by patterned outline & column-like side panels & centering a rectangular panel inscribed "Mary Hoyt Born May 6, 1807," the back signed "Henniker May 7, 1829 by Moses Connor," minor staining, unframed, 7 x 9" (ILLUS.)........ **$8,225**

Broadside, printed "List of the officers and members of the Fellowship Horse Company of Bucks County for the detection of Horse Thieves and other Villains," printed by J.S. Bryan, Doylestown, Pennsylvania, 1838, black type on yellow paper, printed vignette of men chasing a horse thief, 12 x 14" (folding w/some discoloration) **$825**

Large Calligraphic Drawing of a Lion

Calligraphic drawing, a large walking lion, ink on paper, 19th c., 22 3/4 x 28" (ILLUS., previous page) **$1,434**

Large Calligraphy Picture of an Eagle

Calligraphic picture, pen & ink, a large spread-winged eagle grasping a rattle-snake, pennants stream from the beak reading "Three things bear might sway with man - the sword, the scepter and the pen," in a fine modern ogee frame, 19th c., image 19 1/2 x 25 1/2" (ILLUS.) **$1,265**

Fine Calligraphy Picture of Napoleon

Calligraphic picture, pen & ink & watercolor, a bold image of Napoleon on a dark brown rearing horse w/a bird-decorated horse blanket & saddle, inscribed in blue ink to the left "Hll(?) with a pen by C. H. Putnam, a partial pencil sketch of buildings & trees on the reverse, 19th c., unframed, 11 x 12 1/4" (ILLUS.) **$1,000-1,500**

Magazines, "Playboy," first issue & full first year, December 1953 through December 1954, all very good condition, professionally framed (ILLUS., next column) **$4,025**

Framed Full First Year of "Playboy" Magazine

Rare Early American Drawn & Painted World Map

Map of the the World, hand-painted & decorated on paper, a red & white curtain opening to a port scene above a spread-winged eagle & the inscription "American Eagle - World" over a map of the work & the inscription "Executed by Harret (?) Monson 1820," all surroundedd by columns, smaller maps & pastoral scenes, 52 3/4 x 58 1/2" (ILLUS.)...................... **$10,755**

Delicate Lacy Snowflake Paper Cut-out

Paper cut-out, a large square of creamy brown paper, folded & cut in the center w/a large lacy six-point snowflake surrounded by a lacy border, old tape stains at corners, framed, 19th c., 42 x 43" (ILLUS.) **$115**

PAPERWEIGHTS

Two Baccarat & a Bohemian Paperweight

Baccarat Faceted Amber-Flash Horse weight, clear cut in the base w/a galloping stallion on a grassy mound decorated w/translucent golden amber, reserved on a frosted ground, the top & sides cut w/round printies, France, mid-19th c., 3" d., 1 3/4" h. (ILLUS. right with Baccarat sulphide & Bohemian flashed weight) **$1,434**

Group of Three Baccarat & St. Louis Flower Weights

Baccarat Faceted Garlanded Clematis weight, clear enclosing a clematis flower composed of two rows of overlapping ribbed white petal around a green, red & white arrowhead cane center, on a leafy green stem w/a white bud, a border garland alternating red, white & green and red & white canes, round cut top & the sides w/six round printies, sunburst-cut bottom, France, mid-19th c., 2 1/2" d., 1 1/2" h. (ILLUS. far left with other Baccarat & St. Louis flower weights)............ **$1,912**

Three Early Baccarat Flower Weights

Baccarat Faceted Garlanded Clematis weight, clear enclosing a flower w/two rows of overlapping ribbed deep coral petals around a white & red stardust center cane, growing from a curved green leafy stalk w/a red bud, a border garland of alternating white & red and red, white & green millefiori canes, surface cut at the top & around the sides w/six round panels, star-cut base, France, mid-19th c., 2 7/8" d., 1 7/8" h. (ILLUS. left with two other Baccarat flower weights) **$1,912**

Baccarat Faceted Garlanded Pompon weight, clear enclosing a flower composed of numerous rows of shaded salmon pink recessed petals w/a yellow stamen center, growing from a curved green stalk w/two green leaves, two red buds & four more leaves, a border garland alternating canes in shades of blue, red, green & white and salmon pink, green & white, cut w/six circular side printies, star-cut base, France, mid-19th c., 2 7/8" d., 1 7/8" h. (ILLUS. right with two other Baccarat flower weights) **$1,912**

Baccarat Faceted Garlanded Pompon weight, clear enclosing a flower composed of numerous rows of white recessed petals w/a yellow cane center, on a green leafy stem w/a white bud, a garland border band alternating cobalt blue, green, salmon pink & white canes and green, white & salmon pink canes, flat cut top & facet-cut sides, star-cut base, France, mid-19th c., 2 3/4" d., 2 1/8" h. (ILLUS. far right with other Baccarat & St. Louis flower weights) **$1,315**

Baccarat Faceted Sulphide weight, clear enclosing a full-length portrait sulphide of The Madonaa standing holding the Christ Child on a celestial cloud w/cherubs, set on a translucent cobalt blue ground, the top & sides cut w/geometric facets, on a narrow round foot, France, mid-19th c., 3" d., 1 5/8" h. (ILLUS. right with a Baccarat amber-flashed & Bohemian amber-flashed weight)... **$896**

Baccarat Garlanded Clematis weight, clear enclosing a white-single clematis blossom w/an arrowhead cane center, on a leafy green stem, border garland of al-

Grouping of Five American-made Paperweights

ternating millefiori canes in red, blue, green & white and red & white, star-cut base, France, mid-19th c., 2" d., 1 3/8" h. (ILLUS. second from right with other Baccarat & St. Louis flower weights) **$896**

Baccarat Garlanded Two-flower weight, clear enclosing a large white double-clematis flowers w/a yellow & red honeycomb center growing from a green leafy stem & a small red single clematis flower w/a red, white & green arrowhead cane center, a border garland alternating cobalt blue, white, green & claret and white & claret canes, star-cut base, France, mid-19th c., 3 1/8" d., 2 1/4" h. (ILLUS. center with two other Baccarat flower weights) **$4,422**

Bohemian Amber-flash Horse weight, clear w/a pale amber ground cut w/an vignette of a standing stallion by a fence, mid-19th c., 2 1/8 x 1 1/4" (ILLUS. center with two Baccarat weights) **$478**

Small Tiffany Bronze Dog Paperweight

Bronze, figural, modeled as a recumbent bulldog, signed "Tiffany Studios New York," 2" l. (ILLUS.) **$431**

Tiffany Bronze Lion Paperweight

Bronze, figural, modeled as a recumbent lion, signed "Tiffany Studios New York 932," 5" l. (ILLUS.) **$780**

New England Apple weight, model of an apple in deep rose & bright yellow, on a clear round base, base engraved "K.A. Osgood," New England Glass Co., second half 19th c., annealing cracks in surface, 3" d., 2 1/2" h. (ILLUS. second from left with four other American paperweights, top of page) **$990**

Pairpoint Rose weight, a large red rose blossom w/green leaves on a cut diamond point panel base, Bryden Pairpoint Glass Co., second half 20th c., 3 1/4" d., 2 1/4" h. (ILLUS. second from right with four other American paperweights, top of page) **$209**

Sandwich Flower weight, a flower w/ten bright blue petals w/a central cane on a deep green stem w/three leaves, dew-like airtraps, polished concave base, Boston & Sandwich Glass Co., second half 19th c., 2 3/4" d., 2" h. (ILLUS. far left with four other American paperweights, top of page) **$550**

Sandwich or New England Fruit Cluster weight, clear enclosing a cluster of five pears & leaves in yellow, red, green & rose, all on a latticinio ground, dew-like airtraps, polished concave base, Boston & Sandwich Glass Co. or New England Glass Co., second half 19th c., 2 1/4" d., 1 1/2" h. (ILLUS. third from left with four other American paperweights, top of page) **$385**

St. Louis Faceted Upright Bouquet weight, clear enclosing a floral bouquet composed of a central white clematis w/a yellow cane center & two buds in blue & dark salmon pink & three millefiori cane flowers in similar colors, all among green leaf tips within a torsade of white latticinio tubing entwined w/cobalt blue threads, encircled by mercury bands, cut w/geometric facets, France, mid-19th c., 3 1/8" d., 2 1/4" h. (ILLUS. second from left with three Baccarat flower weights) **$1,315**

Sulphide weight, clear enclosing a silvery white model of a walking dog, polished base, American, late 19th - early 20th c., overall light scratching & pitting, 2 1/8" d., 1 3/8" h. (ILLUS. far right with four other American paperweights) **$110**

Group of Four Blown & Mold-Blown Early Pungent Bottles

PERFUME, SCENT & COLOGNE BOTTLES

Decorative accessories from milady's boudoir have always been highly collectible, and in recent years there has been an especially strong surge of interest in perfume bottles. Our listings also include related containers such as pocket bottles and vials, tabletop containers & atomizers. Most readily available are examples from the 19th through the mid-20th century, but earlier examples do surface occasionally. The myriad varieties have now been documented in several recent reference books, which should further popularize this collecting specialty.

English Blue & White Cameo Scent

Cameo glass, scent-type, cylindrical form in white cut to blue w/a flower & leaf design, silver cap & base band, England, late 19th c., 2 3/4" h. (ILLUS.) **$690**

Clear blown glass, dolphin- or mermaid-shaped pungent-type, applied clear rigaree, engraved "Eliz-h Richardson" on one side & a sprig on the other, American or English, early 19th c., small rough spot on rigaree, 3" h. (ILLUS. second from left with other blown & pattern-molded pungent bottles, top of page) **$44**

Clear & white striped blown glass dolphin- or mermaid-shaped, pungent-type, scrolled shaped applied w/cobalt blue rigaree, plain lip, possibly Boston & Sandwich Glass Co., first half 19th c., some losses & roughness to rigaree, 1 3/4" h. (ILLUS. far left with three other blown and pattern-molded pungent bottles, top of page) **$77**

Sandwich Blue Mold-Blown Cologne

Cobalt blue mold-blown glass, cologne-type, tall paneled & waisted sides w/an angled shoulder to the long paneled neck w/a flattened rim, smooth base, Boston & Sandwich Glass Co., mid-19th c., 7" h. (ILLUS.) **$1,456**

Cut Glass & Sterling Tiffany & Co. Scent Bottles

Cut glass, scent-type, spherical clear bodies cut w/a band of strawberry diamond & hobstars above a panel-cut bottom & shoulder w/a flaring neck, fitted w/an ornate pointed sterling-capped stopper, silver marked by Tiffany & Co., ca. 1900, 5 1/4" h., pr. (ILLUS., previous page)..... **$1,150**

Pretty Enameled Brass Perfume Bottle

Enameled brass, lay-down perfume, tapering eight-paneled brass tube w/each panel decorated w/inlaid colored enamel forming loops & points, glass-lined w/original glass stopper under the brass cap, probably Russian, late 19th c., 3 1/2" l. (ILLUS.)..................................... **$1,438**

Rare Lalique Frosted Glass Perfume

Lalique glass, Bouchon "Fleurs de Pommier" patt., frosted clear w/blue patina, the ovoid body molded w/bands of graduated arches, the high arched & pierced long stopper molded w/a flowering tree, stopper engraved "R. Lalique - 939," matching number on the base, introduced in 1919, 5 1/2" h. (ILLUS.) **$10,755**

Medium green glass, cologne, rectangular w/two recessed label panels, sheared mouth w/applied ring, pontil scar, ca. 1840-60, 2 5/8" w., 6" h. **$616**

Teal blue pattern-molded glass, pungent-type, flattened tapering ovoid form w/24

vertical ribs, red swirl in the side, plain rim, rough pontil, American or English, first half 19th c., 2 7/8" h. (ILLUS. second from right with three other blown & pattern-molded pungent bottles) **$176**

Rare Early American Scent Bottle

Teal green mold-blown glass, scent-type, flattened ovoid shaped w/a molded feathers & fern design, inward-rolled mouth, pontil scar, possibly early Pittsburgh district, 1820-40, 2 3/8" l. (ILLUS.)............. **$2,016**

Yellowish amber pattern-molded glass, pungent-type, flattened tapering ovoid form w/26 vertical ribs, plain rim, rough pontil, American or English, tiny flake on lip, some wear, first half 19th c., 3" h. (ILLUS. far right with three other blown & pattern-molded pungent bottles, top previous page) **$165**

Solid Perfumes

Avon Goldtone Ring for Solid Perfume

Avon ring, goldtone ring w/the domed lid set w/faux pearls (ILLUS.).......................... **$25**

Corday "Le Tabouret" Footstool

Corday footstool, "Le Tabouret" creme perfume, model of a goldtone foolstool w/a faux tapetry upholstery lid, contains "Fame" fragrance (ILLUS., previous page) **$75**

Corday Horse-decorated Perfume Case

Corday horse, "Le Cheval," goldtone creme perfume case topped by a recumbent taupe composition horse (ILLUS.)............. **$125**

Estee Lauder Shopping Bag Case

Estee Lauder shopping bag, silvertone & lavender enamel decorated to resemble a marked Bergdorf Goodman shopping bag, complete w/silvertone rope handles, Estee Lauder "Pleasures" fragrance (ILLUS.) **$150**

Estee Lauder Statue of Liberty, "Liberty Lady" goldtone design in the shape of the Statue of Liberty holding aloft a tube of lipstick, enhanced w/clear crystals, the interior lid embossed w/the date 2000, Estee Lauder "Pleasures" fragrance (ILLUS., top next column) **$250**

Estee Lauder straw hat, "Sun Bonnet" goldtone design, a wide-brimmed straw hat decorated w/a red enameled ribbon trimmed w/clear crystals & enameled flowers, comes complete w/a goldtone hat stand, Estee Lauder "Pleasures" fragrance (ILLUS., middle next column).......... **$75**

Estee Lauder "Liberty Lady" Container

Estee Lauder "Sun Bonnet" Container

Max Factor Medal Perfume Holder

Max Factor medal, rare goldtone solid perfume holder in the shape of a military medal, suspended from a goldtone oval bar outlined in red, white & blue rhinestone & enclosing the word "Ace," suspending a red, white & blue ribbon that holds the rhinestone-trimmed perfume disk centered by a moveable plane propellor (ILLUS.) **$150**

PLANT WATERERS

Ceramic Frog Plant Waterer

Ceramic, model of frog sitting w/mouth agape, white w/brown & green speckles & splotches, 4 1/2" h. (ILLUS.) **$8-10**

Two-piece Frog Plant Waterer

Ceramic, model of frog w/removable head, brown, 6 1/2" h. (ILLUS.) **$15-22**
Ceramic, model of frog, yellow, in sitting position, 6 1/8" h. (ILLUS., top next column)
.... **$6-10**

Frog Plant Waterer

Brown Mushroom Plant Waterer

Ceramic, model of mushroom, brown, 3 1/2" h. (ILLUS.) **$6-8**
Ceramic, model of mushroom house w/mouse inside, ca. 1985, 4 3/4" h. **$10-15**
Ceramic, model of mushroom, light brown, 4 1/2" h. **$6-8**

Watering Can Plant Waterer

Ceramic, model of watering can, white
w/yellow rose, 4 1/4" h. (ILLUS., previous
page) **$10-18**

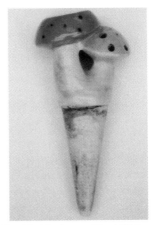

Double Mushroom Plant Waterer

Waterwheel House Plant Waterer

Ceramic, model of waterwheel house,
green, marked "God Bless This House,"
4" h. (ILLUS.) **$10-15**

Yellow Owl Plant Waterer

Ceramic, owl, stylized bird w/overall dark
yellow glaze, 4" h. (ILLUS.) **$6-8**

Windmill Plant Waterer

Ceramic, model of windmill, blue & white,
flowers around base, 6" h. (ILLUS.) **$15-20**
Ceramic, model of wishing well, brown,
sticker marked "Enesco," 5" h. **$18-25**
Ceramic, mushrooms, a larger brown-
topped one beside a shorter yellow-
topped one, both w/brown spots,
4 1/2" h. (ILLUS., top next column) **$8-12**

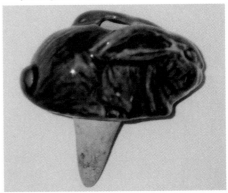

Dark Green Rabbit Plant Waterer

Ceramic, rabbit, hunched down, dark green
glaze, 3" h. (ILLUS.) **$12-18**

Ceramic, rose, yellow, 5 1/4" h. **$15-20**

Smiling Snail Plant Waterer

Ceramic, snail, dark brown shell & yellow
head w/black eyes & smiling red mouth,
4" h. (ILLUS.) **$8-10**
Ceramic, swan, all-white, 5 1/2" h. **$10-15**

Green Swan Plant Waterer

Ceramic, swan w/wings raised, dark green,
marked "INARCO, Cleve. Ohio - E-2081,"
5" h. (ILLUS.) **$12-18**
Ceramic, toadstool, Merry Mushroom,
made for Sears, 5 1/2" h. **$20-25**
Ceramic, toilet stool, yellow w/red specks,
6 1/4" h. **$6-8**

Toucan Plant Waterer

Ceramic, toucan, white body w/black head
& orange & black beak, 5" h. (ILLUS.) ... **$15-20**

POLITICAL & CAMPAIGN ITEMS

Campaign

1904 Parker-Davis Bandanna

Bandanna, 1904 campaign, Parker-Davis
Republication presidential candidates,
jugate-style design on cloth, pair of large
American flags centered by a large star
swag back above oval black & white portraits of the candidates above a red banner across the bottom reading "Good
Government For The People," very minor
staining, 22 x 23" (ILLUS.) **$187**

Rare Lincoln 1860 Campaign Parade Banner

Banner, 1860 campaign, parade-type,
Abraham Lincoln for President, two-sided silk, the white side h.p. in gold & red
lettering "Old Cambridge 1860 - Lincoln
Club - Freedom Our Cause - Lincoln Our
Man," the blue side h.p. in gold "The
Union - But Not With The Sacrifice of
Freedom," originally an 1856 Fremont
banner w/ his name replaced by Lincoln's, Boston area, some water stains
on border, fringe on three sides, framed,
45 1/2 x 52 1/2" (ILLUS.)........................ **$7,409**
Banner, 1884 campaign, Blaine-Logan Republication presidential candidates, cotton cloth printed w/blue, white & red
bands, the blue band w/white stars & the
white band printed in black w/the candidates' names, minor soiling, 27 x 40"
(ILLUS., next page) **$276**

Long 1936 Alfred Landon Campaign Banner

1884 Blaine-Logan Banner

Banner, 1936 campaign, Alfred Landon, Republican presidential candidate, long swag-style cloth printed at each end w/blue stripes w/two white stars flanking two wide bands of red & white stripes, all centered by a dark blue square printed in color w/a portrait of Landon above sunflowers & w/crossed American flags behind, printed in white "For President - Alfred M. Landon," yellow cord fringe at bottom, some light aging & fading, very small hole in bottom left corner, 36" l. (ILLUS., top of page) **$1,530**

1896 William McKinley Cane

Cane, 1896 campaign, Willian McKinley Democratic presidential candidate, hollow tin round head molded in relief w/a bust portrait of McKinley framed by "McKinley - 1896," wooden shaft, some denting & wear to head, 33" l. (ILLUS.) **$205**

Unusual 1968 Nixon Campaign Dress

Dress, 1968 campaign, Richard Nixon presidential designer dress, red satin w/a white hem w/blue applied lettering reading "Nixon For President," three applied elephants w/rhinestone eyes near the bottom printed "GOP 1968," labeled "DeZanne - New York," two felt letters missing (ILLUS.) **$213**

Two Views of Lincoln-Johnson Token

Ferrotype token, 1864 campaign, Lincoln - Johnson, round brass frame stamped w/words & stars & pierced for hanging, enclosing a small tintype of the candidates on each side, good clean portraits (ILLUS. of both sides) **$1,091**

1912 Woodrow Wilson Pennant

1872 Greeley & Brown Jugate Token

Ferrotype token, 1872 campaign, jugate tintype photo portrait of Democratic candidates Horance Greeley & his running mate, Gratz Brown, in a rectangular brass frame stamped w/flowers, photo a bit light, 3/4 x 1" (ILLUS.) **$506**

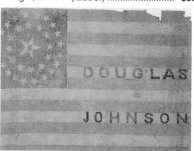

Unusual 1860 Douglas & Herschel Campaign Flag

Flag, 1860 campaign, Stephen Douglas & Herschel V. Johnson, Democratic presidential candidates, printed cloth American flag design w/the white stars arranged in rings, printed in blue w/"Douglas - Johnson," moderate fading, some damage at the top, 13 1/2 x 22" (ILLUS.) **$3,795**

Pennant, 1912 campaign, Woodrow Wilson, Democratic candidate, dark blue felt w/a printed color-tinted bust portrait of Wilson & "Our next President" in white, excellent conditioin, 23" l. (ILLUS., top of page) **$213**

1864 Shield-shaped Lincoln Photo Pin

Pin, 1864 campaign, Abraham Lincoln, silvered brass shield shape embossed w/the wording "Republican Invincibles," an oval paper photo of Lincoln in the center, original pin on back missing (ILLUS.) **$1,201**

1884 Blaine-Logan Jugate Photo Pin

Pin, 1884 campaign, jugate-type, Blaine & Logan Republication presidential candidates, brass shield & tassel frame enclosing small cardboard photos of the candidates, 1 1/8 x 1 1/4" (ILLUS.) **$248**

1904 Teddy Roosevelt Pinback Button

Pinback button, 1904 campaign, Theodore Roosevelt, colorful design of Roosevelt mounted on horseback wearing his Rough Rider outfit, American flag in the background on a hill printed in black "San Juan," black wording around the rim "Theodore Roosevelt - For President 1904," minor stain, 1 1/4" d. (ILLUS., previous page) **$743**

1908 Taft & Sherman Pinback Button

Pinback button, 1908 campaign, jugate-type, Taft & Sherman, Republican presidential candidates, large round button printed in gold, dark & light blue & centered by a portrait of the Statue of Liberty illuminating oval photos of the two candidates, some minor fading, 1 3/4" d. (ILLUS.) **$2,444**

Unusual 1864 Lincoln-Johnson Poster

Poster, 1864 campaign, Abraham Lincoln & Andrew Johnson, white ground w/a large black central oval w/black & white por-

traits of Lincoln & Johnson at the top & bottom & oval triple portraits of Union generals at each side, printed across the bottom "The Defenders of Our Union," near mint, 19 x 24" (ILLUS.)................... **$1,091**

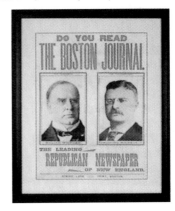

1900 McKinley-Roosevelt Poster

Poster, 1900 campaign, jugate-type for William McKinley & Theodore Roosevelt, white ground printed in red "Do You Read The Boston Journal - The Leading Republication Newspaper of New England...," large black & white photos of the candidates, some minor deterioration, 20 x 27" (ILLUS.)............................... **$991**

1920 Harding & Coolidge Poster

Poster, 1920 campaign, jugate-type, Harding & Coolidge, Republican presidential candidates, printed in black on white on heavy cardboard w/a large racing train above oval portraits of the candidates, printed in black "U.S. Special - 'Let these two Lads off at Washington, D.C.,'" very minor edge imperfections, 14 1/2 x 22" (ILLUS.).. **$463**

Nice Roosevvelt-Truman 1944 Poster

Poster, 1944 campaing, jugate-type for Franklin Roosevelt & Harry Truman, white ground printed in red "Roosevelt - Truman" w/large center sepia-tone photos of the candidates, near mint, 11 x 14 1/2" (ILLUS.) **$529**

John Kennedy 1960 Coattail Poster

Poster, 1960 campaign, coattail-type poster w/a black & white photo of John F. Kennedy & Congressional candidate Healey, red, white & blue background bands printed in white "Kennedy For President - Healey For Congress - Vote Democratic - Leadership For The 60's," 13 x 21" (ILLUS.) **$311**

Textile, 1840 campaign, William Henry Harrison, printed in dark brown & white w/an overall large floral design, the top center w/a small wreath-enclosed portrait of Harrison above a banner reading "Harrison & Reform," a scene of his Log Cabin campaign image near the bottom, matted & framed, 17 x 18" **$255**

Non-Campaign

1784 Washington Commeorative Almanac

Almanac, dated 1784 & printed & sold by Norman & White, Boston, 1783, the cover w/an engraved symbolic scene commemorating the American victory in the Revolutionary Ware, various symbolic figures standing around a small oval portrait of George Washington, cover image captioned "Washington - Victory doth thy Trumpets sound, who are with Laurels cover'd round!," 22 of 24 pp., trimmed close to right edge & bottom, original twine binding (ILLUS.) **$513**

Early 1930s Franklin Roosevelt Clock

Clock, bronzed cast metal, figural, a standing figure of Franklin Roosevelt beside a large ship's wheels enclosing a clock dial w/Arabic numerals & sweep seconds hand, "Roosevelt" molded below the wheel, the platform base printed "At the Wheel for a New Deal," excellent condition, w/original cord & plug, not running, early 1930s, 13 1/2" h. (ILLUS.) **$170**

U.S. Grant Sterling Silver Letter Opener

Letter opener, sterling silver, flat curved blade printed w/a bust portrait of Ulysses Grant titled "Gen. Grant," the flat handle cast in the shape of a Grand Army of the Republic badge, possibly 1870s or 1880s, light wear, toned patina, 4" l. (ILLUS.)..................................... **$367**

Vintage Photo Portrait of Ulysses Grant

Photograph, imperial card-sized sepia-toned portrait of U.S. Grant seated beside a table, by A. Bogardus & Co., New

York City, ca. 1880, beveled gilt edge w/only minor wear, 7 1/2 x 13" (ILLUS.).... **$493**

Washington & Warship Liverpool Pitcher

Pitcher, creamware, early Liverpool jug-style, bulbous baluster shape w/rim spout & strap handle, transfer-printed in black on one side w/a military bust portrait of George Washington & the inscription "Washington crowned with laurels by Liberty," all above a draped flag, Liberty cap & American eagle, the reverse w/a printed design of a large sailing warship flying the American flag, probably 1790s, 7 3/4" h. (ILLUS.) **$6,356**

Abraham Lincoln Woven Silk Ribbon

Ribbon, woven silk, color design of an American eagle & shield at the top above a leafy wreath enclosing a bust portrait of a beardless Abraham Lincoln, woven at the bottom "A. Lincoln - President," made in Switzerland & signed "L. Chevre," probably celebrating his inauguration in 1861, some light yellowish staining, silk brittle w/several separations, 7 3/4" l. (ILLUS.) **$253**

Textile, block-printed toile, decorated w/stripes in brown decorated w/small oval portrait medallions of U.S. Grant in white, red & black framed by white wording "Let Us Have Peace - U.S. Grant," alternating w/spread-winged reddish American eagles, narrow reddish & dark brown stripes printed vertically w/"U.S. Grant - First in Peace - First in War," ca. 1870s, framed, 12 1/4 x 14" (ILLUS. upper left with other political textiles) **$230**

Grouping of Early Printed Political Textiles

Textile, printed toile, decorated overall w/small round brown portraits of a military officer, possibly Lafayette, enclosed w/golden & red scrolling leaves & alternating w/brown spread-winged American eagles, reportedly the first printed material made in a continuous roll, framed in giltwood frame w/gold repaint, early 19th c., 6 1/4 x 7 3/4" (ILLUS. bottom right with other textiles) **$288**

Textiles, two blue-printed toile portrait panels, one printed w/a large bust portrait of George Washington w/his name in a banner under the portrait, the other w/a large bust portrait of John Adams w/his name in a banner, possibly from a series, 1780s, stains, matted & framed, 8 5/8 x 10 5/8", the set (ILLUS. upper right & lower left with other political textiles).. **$288**

Early Large Abraham Lincoln Tintype

Tintype, full-plate bust portrait of Abraham Lincoln, taken by Matthew Brady in February 1864, archivally matted & framed (ILLUS.)... **$4,235**

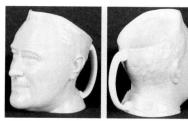

Franklin Roosevelt Ceramic Toby Mug

Toby mug, ceramic, all-white bust of Franklin D. Roosevelt, bottom marked "Franklin Roosevelt modeled by Eric Owen - produced by Mintons, England," 1930s, 6 1/2" h. (ILLUS. of front & back) **$253**

POP CULTURE COLLECTIBLES

The collecting of pop culture memorabilia is not a new phenomenon; fans have been collecting music-related items since the emergence of rock and roll in the 1950s. But it was not until the coming of age of the postwar generation that the collecting of popular culture memorabilia became a recognized movement. The most sought-after items are from the 1960s, when music, art, and society were at their most experimental. This time period is dominated by artists such as The Beatles, The Rolling Stones and Bob Dylan, to name a few. From the 1950s, Elvis Presley is the most popular. Here we offer a cross-section of popular culture collectibles ranging from the 1950s to the present day.

Rare Andy Warhol Flier

Andy Warhol flier, yellow paper w/black wording, advertising an Andy Warhol &

rock band appearance at the Fillmore, two-sided w/a Los Angeles Times review printed on the back, May 1966, 5 1/2 x 8 1/2" (ILLUS.).................... **$800-1,400**

Andy Warhol Soup Label Tee Shirt

Andy Warhol tee shirt, black & white image of a torn Campbell's soup can label, back reads "Andy Warhol at Colorado State University, Fort Collins, Colorado 1981," faded siganture on the front (ILUS.) **$75-150**

Beatles Cloth Beach Hat

Beatles (The) beach hat, black graphics on white & dark blue cloth, found in various colors, 1964, each (ILLUS.) **$75-110**

Beatles Plastic Booty Bags

Beatles (The) booty bag, translucent plastic w/cartoon graphics in color, drawstring rope handle, 1960s, each (ILLUS. of two) **$75-150**

Beatles Brunch Bag & Thermos

Beatles (The) brunch bag, upright oval blue vinyl case w/a zipper top, color images on the front, Aladdin, 1965 (ILLUS. left with thermos)............................... **$400-650**

Knock-off Beatles Cake Decoration Figures

Beatles (The) cake decorations, knock-off plastic figures in action poses, in original box titled "The Swingers," 1964 (ILLUS.) **$50-75**

Framed Torn Beatles Concern Ticket

Beatles (The) concert ticket, torn stub from Cerebral Palsy benefit, New York Parmount Theater, September 20, 1964, framed w/a photo of the group (ILLUS.) **$200-500**

Framed 1966 Concert Tour Program

Beatles (The) concert tour program book, "Beatles (U.S.A.) Ltd.," color photo of the band members, framed w/a concert ticket, 1966 (ILLUS.) **$80-150**

Tall Ceramic Beatles Cup

Beatles (The) cup, ceramics, tall slightly tapering shaped printed in black, white & blue w/pictures of the band members, made by Washington Pottery, England, 1960s, 4" h. (ILLUS.)........................... **$75-150**

One of a Set of 1964 Beatles Dolls

Beatles (The) dolls, vinyl figures of each band member w/instruments, Remco,

1964, loose in original worn box, each (ILLUS. of one)....................................... **$65-95**

1960s Plastic Beatles Guitar

Beatles (The) guitar, toy-type, "Beatles New Sound Guitar," hard plastic in white printed w/black & white portraits & red & black trim, by Selcol, England, 1964, 23" l. (ILLUS.)..................................... **$350-625**

Irish Linen with Beatles Portraits

Beatles (The) linen, large rectangular cloth printed in the center w/large portraits of the band members in brown, black, white & tan, black & white border band of musical instruments, Ulster, Ireland, 1964, 20 x 31" (ILLUS.)................................. **$75-150**

Set of Four Beatle Magazines

Beatles (The) magazine, "Beatle," set of four w/a different band member on each cover, England, 1965, each (ILLUS. of the set) **$15-30**

Beatles (The) sheet music, "Lucy in the Sky with Diamonds," 1967 .... $40-75

Beatles Talcum Powder Can

Beatles (The) talcum powder can, metal printed on the front w/full-length portraits of the group, Margo of Mayfair, 1964, 7" h. (ILLUS.) $400-800

Beatles (The) thermos, blue metal w/cup top, Aladdin, 1964 (ILLUS. right with Beatles brunch bag) $75-200

Beatles Trading Card Display Box

Beatles (The) trading cards display box, "Beatles Movie 'A Hard Day's Night,'" rectangular cardboard printed in red, black & white, Topps-Bazooka, 1964 (ILLUS.) $250-300

1964 Beatles Metal Tray

Beatles (The) tray, squared metal w/rounded corners, printed in color w/portraits of

each band member on a white ground, by Worcester, "Made in Great Britain" sticker on the back, 1964 (ILLUS.) $35-75

Glass Tumbler with Beatles Images

Beatles (The) tumbler, clear glass w/black & white starbursts w/images of each member, Dairy Queen of Canada, 1964, 4 1/2" to 5 1/2" h. (ILLUS.) $75-150

1964 Pink Vinyl Beatles Wallet

Beatles (The) wallet, pink printed vinyl w/brown photo transfer of the band, Standard Plastic, 1964 (ILLUS.) $75-160

Original Beatles Wig in Package

Beatles (The) wig, in original plastic package w/cardboard header, Lowell Toy, 1964 (ILLUS., previous page) **$75-150**

Beatles (The) Yellow Submarine cel, original production cel, 1968 .... **$250-400**

Beatles Yellow Submarine Greeting Cards

Beatles (The) Yellow Submarine greeting cards, long cards w/color images of the cartoon characters on each, Sunshine Co., 1968, boxed set (ILLUS.).............. **$75-150**

Beatles Yellow Submarine Lunch Box & Thermos

Beatles (The) Yellow Submarine lunch box, pressed steel, Thermos, 1968 (ILLUS. left with thermos)..................... **$300-650**

Beatles Yellow Submarine Switch Cover

Beatles (The) Yellow Submarine switch plate cover, color-printed cardboard, DAL Mfg., 1968, in original package, 6 x 10 1/2" (ILLUS.)................................. **$50-75**

Beatles (The) Yellow Submarine thermos, metal w/plastic cup top, Thermos, 1968 (ILLUS. right with lunch box)..... **$125-200**

Beatles Yellow Submarine Toy

Beatles (The) Yellow Submarine toy, diecast model of the submarine, sealed in original box, Corgi, 1968 (ILLUS.) **$350-550**

Early Signed Elvis Presley Publicity Photo

Elvis Presley photograph, black & white publicity shot of a young Elvis, possibly from his Sun Records days, back signed by Elvis "love ya Elvis Presley," 1950s, 8 x 10" (ILLUS. of two views) **$1,080**

Elvis Presley record & sleeve, RCA-Victor 45 rpm record of "Never Ending" on A-side & "Such a Night" on B-side, w/original photograph sleeve in red, black & white, the sleeve signed in black ballpoint ink "Thanks from - Elvis Presley," sleeve 7" sq. (ILLUS., next page)...................... **$1,195**

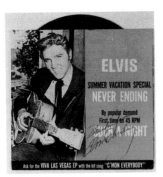

Elvis 45 rpm Record & Signed Sleeve

Elvis Presley Album Gold Record

Elvis Presley RIAA Gold Record, for album "From Elvis Presley Boulevard Memphis," presented to Taylor Harley-Davidson for the sale of more than 500,000 copies of this album, RCA Records, Inc., matted & framed, 16 x 21" (ILLUS.)..................................... **$777**

Farrah Fawcett bean bag chair, decorated w/three photos of Fawcett, Zodiac Designs, 1977, found in three sizes, each **$350-500**

Farrah Fawcett Jigsaw Puzzle

Farrah Fawcett jigsaw puzzle, box cover w/photo of Fawcett, APC, 1977, 200 pieces, complete in box (ILLUS. **$10-25**

George Harrison-signed Print

George Harrsigon autographed print, colorful romantic scenes w/black print & lower panel w/his autograph (ILLUS.) **$850-2,500**

1960s Inflatable Stop Sign Pillow

Inflatable pillow, vinyl model of a red & white Stop sign, advertising slogan on the back, Frye-Sills, Inc., 1960s, 12" sq. (ILLUS.).. **$20-45**

John Lennon autograph, depending on where it was written **$1,000-1,400**

Grouping of Mod Design Pins

Mod design pins, various stylized flower designs, enameled metal, 1960s, each (ILLUS. of a gorup, previous page) **$6-15**

1970s Mood Ring

Mood ring, "stone" changes color when worn, various styles, 1970s, each (ILLUS.) **$35-60**

P.O.W. (prisoner of war) bracelet, chrome-plated brass alloy w/black etched lettering showing the name of a P.O.W. or M.I.A. in Viet Nam & date reported missing, VIVA, 1970s **$35-75**

Paul McCartney autograph, depending on where it was written **$500-1,000**

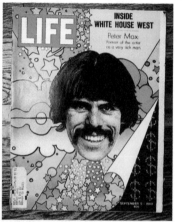

Life Magazine with Peter Max Cover

Peter Max magazine cover, "Life," September 5, 1969, face of the designer surrounded by his artwork, complete issue (ILLUS.) **$10-15**

Peter Max Signed Lithograph

Peter Max magazine lithograph, "Moon Tripping," signed, 1969, framed, 24 x 36" (ILLUS.) **$700-1,000**

Signed Peter Max Poster

Peter Max poster, "The Profile," done for Merrill Chase Galleries, Skokie, Illinois, signed "Max 71," 1971, framed (ILLUS.) **$150-300**

Peter Max tennis shoes, various designs by Max, Randy Mfg. Co., 1970s, each pair **$200-325**

Ringo Starr-autographed Drum Head

Ringo Starr authographed drum head (ILLUS.) **$350-900**

POSTERS

Early French Concert Poster

Concert, colorful images of two French ladies in costume dancing, printed in red & brown "Trianon Concert - Tous Les Soirs - Tableau de la Troupe... Spectacle Varié," marked by H. Gray, style of the 1890s, ca. 1920, laid on canvas, 36 3/4 x 51 1/8" (ILLUS.)................ **$316**

Large 1930s French Liqueur Poster

Liqueur, long colorful design of a horse race w/a central figure of a flying lady wearing a long flowing orange robe & holding aloft a bottle of the product, printed in French across the b.ottom "Premier Fils - La Vieille Marque Francaise," image by Roby, printed by L. Maboeuf, ca. 1936, framed, 51 1/4 x 79 1/2" (ILLUS.)........................ **$1,175**

Poster for French Protest Magazine

Magazine, "Le Locataire," French protest-type w/a color image of a group of poor children & their parents, title & information on a protest in black across the top, name of editor in lower left, designed by Steinler, Paris, France, ca. 1913, laid on canvas, 47 x 63" (ILLUS.) **$489**

Steamship, "Cunard Line," printed in orange & blue on a white ground w/a large image of the steamship Saxonia, reads "Cunard Line - Spend Xmas in Europe...," ca. 1885, minor wear at folds, one small internal tear, 19 x 29" (ILLUS., top next column) **$255**

Steamship, "Red Star Line," printed in German w/black wording framing an engraving of a passenger steamship, covers trans-Atlantic passages, ca. 1875, some minor loss at folds, small ares of discoloration, 25 x 38" (ILLUS., middle next column) **$230**

Early Cunard Line Steamship Poster

Red Star Line Poster Printed in German

"Born Yesterday" Theatre Poster

Theatre, "Born Yesterday," starring Judy Holliday, Henry Miller's Threatre, colorful yellow, blue & red comic design of the star being carried by a stork, 1940s, window card-type, some minor soiling, 14 x 22" (ILLUS., bottom previous page) **$1,170**

"The Charity Ball" Theatre Poster

Theatre, "The Charity Ball," printed in color on a white ground, printed across the bottom "Daniel Frohman's Lyceum Theatre Success...," ca. 1890, minor edge loss & a small tear, gold colors, 20 x 28" (ILLUS.) **$414**

Poster for "The Electric Spark" Play Lighted by Edison Light Bulbs

Theatre, "The Electric Spark - Atkinson's Follies," Alcazar Theatre, New York City, November 27, 1882, colorful images of the theatre interior & the crowd, the production featured illumination by Thomas Edison's new incandescent electric bulbs, mounted on board, loss to top & bottom borders, light uniform toning, w/an original four-page program for the play, 28 x 42" (ILLUS.) **$1,072**

Theatre, "The Squaw Man - Liebler & Co's. Production," large color image of a standing cowboy & small child w/a kneeling young woman, title across the top & image titled, Wallack's Theatre, New York City, ca. 1906, mint condition, 20 x 27" (ILLUS., top next column) **$411**

Early "The Squaw Man" Theatre Poster

World War I Liberty Bonds Poster

World War I, "Buy More Liberty Bonds," a grim color image of a young mother grasping her children, printed in the corner "Must Children Die and Mothers Plead in Vain," border tears repaired, 30 x 40" (ILLUS.)... **$76**

Rockwell "Four Freedoms" Poster Set

World War II, "The Four Freedoms," famous color images by Norman Rockwell, in original mailing envelope w/Office of War Information marking, set of 4 (ILLUS.) **$790**

Early British-Canadian Decorated Powder Horn

POWDER HORNS & FLASKS

Early Powder Horn with Name Inscribed

Horn, early horn w/a flat base plug secured w/wooden pegs, spout end turned down to a darker color w/a raised rope decoration & brass spout, scrimshaw-inscribed along the body on one side "Joseph Parmenter 1800," the back decorated w/fish, an Egyptian felucca & a three-masted sailing ship as well as an odd-looking animal, transverse across horn w/name "Joseph," crack near base plug, overall 17" l. (ILLUS.) **$1,035**

Horn, engraved scene of row of houses, trees, tulips & a vine between each tulip, raised rings around the tip, turned maple plug w/worn red-painted stripe, good patina, 19th c., 12" l. **$1,650**

Horn, engraved w/a banner held by an angel signed "Augustus Ford 1806," also engraved w/a sailing ship, The Linda of Oswego, w/a lighthouse, sun, moon & stars, eagle w/shield & several animals, pine plug missing a strap loop, good patina, 11" l. **$2,530**

Horn, engraved w/a large coat-of-arms w/lion & unicorn, scene of the city of New York w/a fort & windmill near the base, pine plug dated 1758, French & Indian War era, 15" l. **$3,575**

Horn, finely etched w/a large depiction of the British royal seal w/a human-headed lion on the left & a unicorn on the right & inscribed banner below, butt w/a wooden plug secured w/wooden pegs, base etched "HALLFAX" w/several houses & tall building w/an outline of a fort & windmill, tip decorated w/carved rings & grooves w/a small twisted wire used to secure an old crack, British-Canadian, fine yellowish brown patina, late 18th - early 19th c. (ILLUS., top of page) **$2,070**

Horn, finely etched w/various British-Napoleonic War designs, a flat pine plug w/a strap hole worked into one edge, entire edge reeded, spout end w/a very smooth raised nozzle, near plug end decorated w/a large trophy of arms w/an apparent British crest below the word "Wellington" below a spread-winged eagle holding olive branches, above this a three-masted gunboard under a fouled anchor w/British flags surrounded by laurel wreaths & the name "Nelson," right side w/a Naval officer holding a flower in one hand, opposite side w/a lady holding a flower, below the lady a set of crossed cannons w/British flags & further down the figure of Britannia holding a trident & British shield, another period woman behind her holding an olive branch & supporting a fouled anchor, toward spout end a vignette w/inscription "The. 3. Tons - by S. Cozens" surrounding three large casks, all surrounded by a laurel wreath, upper end w/a band of bunting, the lower end w/bunting & band of laurel & acanthus leaves, mellow greenish patina, overall 18" l. (ILLUS., bottom of page) **$1,840**

British Napoleonic War Era Powder Horn

Early Nicely Engraved & Dated Powder Horn

Powder Horn with Brass Accents

Horn, master size, w/large cork & brass stopper, w/decorative brass bands for holding metal loop for strap, a brass shield-shaped plaque reading "Colonia Lider Tafel F.O.R.M.N.Y. 1882," 19th c., 19" l. (ILLUS.).. **$403**

Decorated Master Powder Horn

Horn, master size, w/wood end cap, decorated w/images of heart, pinwheels, a hunter, animals & birds & signed "Dec 14, 1837 S.E.W.," made by Samuel E. Watts, Jonesboro, Maine, 18 1/2" l. (ILLUS.) **$920**

Horn, overall finely etched patterns, both geometric & arabesque w/turkeys & what resemble balloons, also crude initials "AH" & well-executed "IW - 1723/4," carved crown near spout, spout end reduced about 4" & w/a light green color & the apparent date "1821," spout worn through & wrapped w/string, base plug probably pine w/hand-forged nail in center & four wooden pegs around rim, main body fine mellow gold color, overall 16" l. (ILLUS., top of page)............................. **$3,738**

Rare Dolphin-form Scrimshaw Powder Horn

Horn, very unusual scrimshaw-decorated curving board decorated w/graduated fish scales all along the body & the top center w/a scroll inscribed "Powder - For - Us - All," the final 4" of narrow spout in black w/a small cannon mouth turning at the tip, the butt end fitted w/a very large cast-metal silver plated dolphin head, mellow greenish-yellow finish, left fin on dolphin appears to have a registration number, overall 16" l. (ILLUS.).............. **$2,875**

PURSES & BAGS

Two Fine Hermès Purses

Black leather "Kelly" purse, deep rectangular rigid tapering sides w/goldtone metal hardware & detachable strap, leather interior w/three pockets, by Hermès, boxed, mid-20th c. (ILLUS. right with Hermès bag) **$3,055**

Brown crocodile purse, deep rectangular rigid tapering sides w/goldtone metal hardware, loop handles, compartmented interior w/three pockets, by Hermès, 20th c. (ILLUS. left with other Hermès purse) **$4,113**

Fine Gold & Turquoise Mesh Bag

Gold & turquoise mesh bag, the golden mesh mounted in a long squared openwork 14k yellow gold frame decorated w/ornate leafy scrolls & set w/oval turquoise cabochons, together w/a change purse w/old European-cut diamond & demantoid garnet highlights & missing to stones, bag by Black, Starr & Frost, early 20th c. (ILLUS. of part) **$1,763**

Novelty Purses

Novelty purses put the "fun" in functional and in the years following World War II these whimsies reached their zenith of popularity. One season for this boom was the result of wartime research that led to the developement of new materials and the refinement of old. Such materials were easily adapted to a variety of peacetime uses, including fashion accessories.

Some of the new purse designs were adaptations of earlier styles: the "carryall" or compact purse was a reworking of the more upscale "minaudiere," first introduced by Van Cleef & Arpels, while beaded bags, popular since Victorian times, were now embellished with colorful plastic, wooden and oversized "caviar" beading. Tapestry and neeldepoint bags of old were also reborn, often produced from kits.

New materials and techniques were also popular with bamboo, wicker and straw bags becoming favorites, often made in shapes such as birdcages and picnic baskets. Even various commercial strawberry baskets, egg crates and cheese boxes were adapted to make purses. Of course, new types of plastics developed during the war also made improved purses that were more resistant to scuffs and water damage and could be shaped into nearly any size, shape or color. Exotic materials such as alligator, crocodile and snake skin could now be replicated in plastic to appear very "natural," complete with a head and claws.

Some new novelty purse designers specialized in applied art where a plain black canvas bag could be decorated with jewels, sequins, felt and other objects. the most famous name in this applied purse art was Enid Collins, whose "Col-

lins of Texas" linen, saddle and wood box bags featured whimiscal jeweled scenes. Other firms such as Atlas and Soure Bags had some success in this field but Collins led the way.

Another innovation was the Lucite handbag. Although they couldn't hold much, were fragile and susceptible to cracking, they were also garish and became widely popular. Major makers of Lucite purses included Charles S. Kahn; Dorset-Rex; Florida (Miami) Handbags; Gilli Originals; Gira; Llewellyn Inc. ("Lewsid Jewel"); Majestic; Maxim; Myles Originals; Nelson Originals; Patricia of Miami; Rialto; Toro; Vanity Fashions, and Wilardy Originals.

A comprehensive overview of novelty purses is included in Popular Purses: It's In The Bag! by Leslie Pina and Donald-Brian Johnson (Schiffer Publishing Ltd. 2001). Photos for this category are by Dr. Pina with text by Mr. Johnson.

Alligator Bag Complete with Head Clasp

Alligator bag, complete w/alligator head clasp (ILLUS.) **$200-250**

Bamboo Basket Bag

Bamboo basket bag, composed of sewn split strips (ILLUS.) **$70-90**

Dorset-Rex bag, woven of gilt metal strips **$100-125**

Enid Collins "Glitter Bugs" bag, linen decorated w/jeweled insects, mahogany base (ILLUS., next page) **$100-125**

Enid Collins "Night Owl" bag, a wooden box decorated w/an owl **$150-175**

Harry Rosenfeld bag, hand-tooled leather w/a daisy design **$150-175**

Jonquil Original hat & muff, multi-colored pieced velvet, New York - Paris, 1930s **$100-125**

Judith Leiber "Watermelon" bag, decorated in jewel tones **$2,000-2,250**

Enid Collins "Glitter Bugs" Bag

Leopard skin bag & belt, matching set
.... **$225-250**

Gold-threaded & Diamond Lucite Bag

Lucite bag, carpetbag shape, the sides w/an overall gold threaded design w/diamond-patterned end panels (ILLUS.)
.... **$125-150**
Lucite bag, child's, white & clear w/applied fabric flowers, silver trim...................... **$75-100**
Lucite bag, grey w/clear carved starflower lid, by Gilli.. **$100-125**
Lucite bag, horizontally-ridged base, root beer color w/a carved amber lid & handle
.... **$125-150**

Rialto Tortoiseshell Lucite Bag

Lucite bag, log-shaped, a toroiseshell pattern base & flat amber lid, by Rialto (ILLUS.) **$150-17**
Lumured beaded bag, reversible.............. **$60-75**

1960s Tubular Magazine Bag

Magazine bag, tubular form decorated w/resemble a magazine cover, made in Hong Kong, 1960s (ILLUS.) **$100-125**

Princess Charming Lady Golfer Bag

Princess Charming by Atlas bag, lady golfer design, plastic over cloth on wicker (ILLUS.)... **$100-125**
QualiCraft bag & shoe set, linen & off-white patent leather, 1960s, the set **$50-75**

Purse with Racetrack Racing Designs

Racetrack motif bag, various racing designs on a white ground, cloth appliqués under plastic (ILLUS.) **$75-100**

Soure "Ice Cream Parlor" bag, beaded design on linen under plastic.................. **$40-60**

Tally-Ho wicker bag, black w/clear plastic base, decorated w/chickens, Italy **$50-75**

"Telephone Cord" bag, multi-colored coiled plastic, 1950s............................. **$50-75**

Timmy Woods "Snow Tiger" bag, ... **$200-250**

Velvet bag, black w/silk & metal-embroidered peacock, India........................ **$100-150**

Wadsworth "Carry-All," includes a comb, change purse, mirror, etc., black & gold, 1947 .... **$100-125**

Whiting & Davis

Apron-base bag, enameled flower basket design on silver mesh **$275-325**

"Batwing" bag, red enameled flat armor mesh w/silver ring mesh border **$300-50**

Beadlite bag, w/Bakelite bead on carry chain... **$225-275**

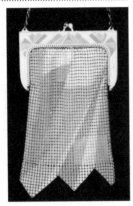

Beadlite Mesh Bag with Sunrays

Beadlite mesh, decorated w/blue & orange asymmetrical sunrays, matching enameled frame (ILLUS.)........................... **$225-275**

Egyptian Motif Beadlite Mesh Purse

Beadlite mesh (armor mesh with the appearance of a beaded bag), Egyptian motif in orange, black & gold (ILLUS.) **$225-275**

Belt, multi-color vertical & loop design on gold mesh **$15-25**

Bib, fringed gold mesh **$20-30**

Cherry pattern, on silver & grey mesh **$200-250**

Child's purse, gold mesh **$125-150**

Circular-frame bag, w/celluloid bell slide **$550-650**

Colonial couple silhouette, in black on white mesh...................................... **$450-550**

Contact lens case, gold mesh, modern **$15-30**

Dancing Woman silhouette, in black on white mesh, black & white enameled frame... **$325-375**

"Delysia Junior" (mid-size) vanity bag, blue & white enameled mesh............. **$675-775**

Double Compact Bag with Dot Stripes

Double compact bag, dot stripes in blues & reds on gold mesh (ILLUS.) **$700-800**

Double-handled bag, black & white Beadlite mesh... **$400-450**

Green dragon design, on silver mesh, jade clasp medallion **$800-900**

Jewelry box, gold mesh, large.................. **$25-35**

Jewelry box, gold mesh, small **$15-25**

Lady with Mandolin design, on off-white mesh, gold frame **$325-375**

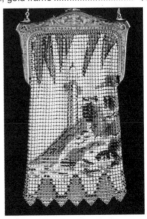

Lighthouse Design Green Mesh Purse

Lighthouse design, in shades of green mesh (ILLUS., previous page) **$350-400**

Lipstick case, gold mesh w/interior mirror, 2001 .... **$20-25**

Mandalian Manufacturing, blue butterfly design on white mesh **$275-375**

Mandalian Yellow Mesh & Panel Bag

Mandalian Manufacturing, yellow mesh w/central curtain panel, stepped base w/gold teardrops (ILLUS.) **$375-425**

Marion Davies bag, "Star Series," 1976 .... **$2,000-2,200**

Medieval tapestry design, floral motif, gold metal frame with raised jewels **$325-375**

Mickey & Minnie Mouse design, on child's purse, 1930s **$375-425**

Multicolor Modernistic Shapes Bag

Multicolor Modernistic shapes on mesh, enameled frame (ILLUS.) **$300-350**

"New Picadilly" compact bag, rose motif **$1,000-1,200**

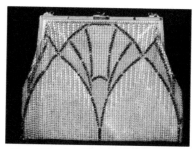

Poiret Pouch with Egyptian Palm Fan

"Poiret Pouch," Egyptian palm fan motif, Paul Poiret design (ILLUS.) **$225-250**

Red Flame Design on Ivory Mesh Bag

Red flame design, stylized flames on ivory mesh (ILLUS.).................................. **$250-300**

Renee Adoree bag, "Star Series," 1976 .... **$2,200-2,400**

Round mesh, hexagon pattern in jewel tones **$225-275**

"Shirley Temple's Bag," design of two ducks, 1936-37 .... **$275-325**

"Vandyke" base bag, red and black diamond-patterned mesh **$250-300**

RAILROADIANA

Broadside, long rectangular printed sheet titled "Map of the Arkansas Land Grant," issued by the St. Louis Iron Mountain & Southern Railway Company, double-sided, 1870s, 12 x 37" (ILLUS., next page) ... **$173**

Fine 1870s Locomotive Drawing

Early Railroad Broadside

Drawing of locomotive, pen & ink & water-color, a detailed side view of an early loco-motive, titled at the top "Elevation of En-gine No. 174 For The P&K RR," signed & dated at the bottom "Portland Company Works, July 23rd 1870," 24 1/4 x 36 7/8" (ILLUS., previous page) **$2,629**

Early Four-Lens Railroad Lantern

Lantern, enameled metal & glass, four bull's-eye lenses w/two in blue & two in amber, black body w/yellow & white shields, wire bail handle, top marked "Dressel Arlington N.J. U.S.A.," some minor rust & chipping, overall 20 1/2" h. (ILLUS.) **$127**

Early Lake Shore & Michigan Lithograph

Lithograph, printed in color w/two rectan-gular scene, the narrow upper panel titled "The Mail Carrier of 100 Years Ago," the lower panel titled "The Flight of the Fast Mail on the Lake Shore and Michigan Southern RY," ca. 1875, framed in tiger maple frame, image 21 x 28" (ILLUS.)... **$4,025**

Brass Steam Whistle Signed "Powell"

Locomotive steam whistle, brass & iron, acorn finial atop brass cylinder, long lever side handle, marked "Powell," now on a wood block base, 18" h. (ILLUS.)................ **$92**

Early Brass & Iron Locomotive Whistle

Locomotive steam whistle, brass & iron, cylindrical top w/a pull activating lever & ball & plinth finial, now on a wood base, shallow dent in side of cylinder, 21 3/4" h. (ILLUS., previous page) **$345**

Great Northern Railway Oiling Can

Oiling can, steel, cylindrical can w/side handle & very long slender spout w/curved tip, used by an engineer, stamped "G.N. RY." (Great Northern Railway), late 19th - early 20th c., 26" h. (ILLUS.).. **$92**

Union Pacific Exhibit Postcard

Postcard, real-photo type w/picture of the Big Boy engine from the Union Pacific Exhibit at the Chicago Railroad Fair, June 25 - October 2, 1949, very good condition (ILLUS.) **$5**

Electric Railroad Signal-Search Light

Signal-search light, electric w/a black metal frame around a large round light by General Electric w/sectional beveled glass lens, top handle, cloth cord, early 20th c., 15" h. (ILLUS.)............................ **$104**

RIBBON DOLLS

In the days when young girls and ladies were often judged by their handiwork, ribbon dolls were a popular art form. Sometimes also referred to as ribbon ladies or ribbon pictures, from the 1930s-50s the components were often available in kit form, complete with paper doll, ribbon supplies, instruc-tions, frame & glass. Others were made from a simple pattern sold for ten cents, while faces & bodies were homemade.

Although the majority of subjects were women, occasionally a male example will surface, often as part of a set. Women dressed in hooped skirts & carrying bouquets, baskets of flowers or parasols, brides & similar colonial-looking figures are the most often found today. While most were mounted on plain black backings some examples include exquisitely decorated backgrounds or unusual poses, including smoking a cigarette or cutting flowers in a garden. Occasionally, the artist signed & dated her work, or inscribed the back as a gift.

Woman in Lime Green Ribbon Dress

Woman, in lime green ribbon dress w/lace pantaloons, wearing floppy cap trimmed in lace, & decorated w/lace streamers & purple & yellow flowers, carrying lace encircled bouquet w/red, pink & blue streamers, 8 1/2" w. x 10 1/2" h. (ILLUS.) **$45-65**

Woman Carrying Large Lace Bouquet

Woman, in pale pink satin ribbon dress w/layers of ivory lace & matching pantaloons, carrying large lace bouquet w/red, green & pink ribbon roses & pink, white & green streamers, wearing matching pink satin & lace cap adorned w/pink & green ribbon roses, 8 3/4" w. x 10 3/4" h. (ILLUS.)........ **$45-65**

Woman in Peach Satin Dress

Woman, in peach satin dress w/beige lace shawl collar & lace pantaloons, carrying a pastel ribbon rose bouquet encircled in beige lace, w/pastel streamers, 8 3/4" w. x 10 3/4" h. (ILLUS.)................ **$45-55**

Long-haired Lady in Elegant Blue Gown

Woman Wearing Pale Green Dress

Woman, long blonde hair, standing wearing a light green satin ruffled ribbon dress & matching bonnet, lace shawl collar & pantaloons, holding a lace & ribbon bouquet, framed, 5 x 7" (ILLUS.) **$75-95**

Woman, long-haired blonde in a slightly bent pose wearing a long tiered pale blue ruffled ribbon off-the-shoulder dress w/ruffled lace front & skirt, holding a matching bouquet, framed, 9 x 11 1/2" (ILLUS., top next column) **$75-85**

Woman by Window Ribbon Doll

Woman, red hair, standing beside a window w/lacy curtains, wearing a pale pink dress w/lace on shoulders, holding a ribbon "dust cloth," ribbon pillow on the floor, black background, framed, 6 3/4 x 8 1/2" (ILLUS.)............................ **$50-60**

Woman, red hair, wearing a large ruffled peach dress & wide-brimmed hat, sitting on a gold bench, 11 1/2 x 15" **$75-95**

Woman, red hair, wearing dress made of layers of peach ribbon & beige lace, decorated w/pink ribbon roses, a pink ribbon rose in hair, 8 3/4 x 10 3/4" **$45-55**

Lady in Red Velvet Dress

Woman, red velvet dress & matching wide brimmed hat, both trimmed in black velvet & ecru lace, carrying round bouquet of red velvet, blue & yellow ribbon roses trimmed in matching lace, wearing black high-heeled shoes, 9" w. x 11" h. (ILLUS.).... **$95-125**

Woman, strawberry blonde hair, wearing a light green satin dress w/lace shoulder straps, pale pink ribbon sash, carrying a multi-colored floral bouquet surrounded by lace, lace pantaloons, 8 3/4 x 10 3/4" **$50-60**

Woman, strawberry blonde hair, wearing a moss green ribbon dress w/pink bow & streamers, carrying a coordinated floral bouquet, wearing a floppy hat, 8 3/4 x 10 3/4" **$50-60**

Demure Lady with Lacy Dress & Parasol

Woman, the demure figure w/blonde hair, standing wearing a pale pink ribbon dress w/frothy lace down the front & on the hem, carrying a lacy parasol, pink bows in her hair & on her shoes, framed, 11 x 13" (ILLUS.)................................ **$115-135**

Woman, w/black hair wearing black & white ribbon dress w/ruffled cuffs & neck band, black hat w/blue feather in hat & hand, 9 1/2" h. **$55-65**

Woman Dressed in Ivory Satin

Woman, w/brown paper hair w/full facial features, wearing an ivory satin layered dress trimmed in pink lace, w/large circle of ribbon & flowers at waist, & matching picture hat, 9" w. x 12" h. (ILLUS.) **$35-45**

Woman, wearing flaring pink ribbon skirt & matching long-brimmed pink hat, sitting on bench, 11 1/2 x 14 1/2" **$75-95**

Woman, wearing pink fabric dress w/ivory lace & gold trim, skirt hem decorated w/pink, holding pink fabric basket w/ribbon flowers, 8 x 10"................................. **$75-85**

Woman, white hair in Colonial style, wearing a dark peach satin ribbon dress, dark pink trim on top & at hem, gold lace around her shoulders & hem, velvet sash, standing on tiptoes, 11 x 13" **$90-110**

Young Girl Sitting In Chair

Young girl, long brown curls, wearing peach & lace dress w/matching hat, green printed shoes, sitting in chair, 6 3/4" w. x 8 3/4" h. (ILLUS.).................. **$35-45**

RUGS - HOOKED & OTHER
Hooked

Fine Grenfell Canada Geese Hooked Hug

Canada geese, rectangular scene of three Canada geese flying in a row w/a striped blue, pink & grey sky behind them & a tan landscape w/pale green fir trees below, wide black mottled border band w/thin white inner border band, original label from Grenfell Labrador Industries in one corner, Canada, early 20th c., 27 x 40" (ILLUS.)... **$1,955**

Rare Version of Grenfell Canada Geese Rug

Canada geese, rectangular scene of three Canada geese flying in a row w/a striped pale pink sky behind them & a landscape w/light & dark green fir trees below, wide brown border band w/thin tan inner border band, original label from Grenfell Labrador Industries on back corner, Canada, early 20th c., 26 1/4 x 39 1/4" (ILLUS.)... **$4,560**

Hooked Rug with Quaint Cottage Scene

Cottage in a landscape, rectangular, a large oval center panel w/a large quaint multi-cabled pink cottage w/dark brown thatch-like roof & a tall red & black chimney, set back on a green lawn w/meandering flower-lined path, tall leafy trees at each side, a dark gold outer border, ca. 1920s, 27 x 53" (ILLUS.)........................... **$173**

Fine Hooked Rug of a Dog in a Landscape

Dog in landscape, large recumbent animal resembling a Chocolate Labrador in dark brown w/black highlights, on a grassy mound w/a flowering shrub & reeds behind him & a rail fence in the distance, narrow black border band & narrow red inner border w/corner scrolls, burlap backing indicates it is from an E.S. Frost pattern, small section in border missing material, early 20th c., 29 1/2 x 55 1/2" (ILLUS.)... **$1,150**

Rare Room-sized Floral Hooked Rug

Floral blocks, room-sized, rectangular, the large rectangular center panel composed of fifteen squares each w/a large rounded flower blossom on a leafy stem in shades of deep pink, tan, brown & blue, wide tan border band w/a meandering grapevine in red & green & a red leafy flower in each corner, dark brown scalloped outer border, all-wool, old tag in one corner reads "Great Grandmother Abigail Voter," New Vineyard, Maine, 19th c., few small holes & some fading, overall 58 x 84" (ILLUS.) **$4,600**

Pot of Flowers Hooked Rug

Pot of flowers, square, the center w/a large cream-colored pot holding a branched plant w/cream & tan flowers on a dark greyish blue ground, large triangular corner blocks composed of numerous small squares in tans, cream & browns, one end fitted for hanging, small loss top top flower, late 19th - early 20th c., 24 x 25" (ILLUS.)... **$805**

Long Striped Hooked Rug

Stripes, long rectangular form composed of narrow multi-colored stripes in shades of brown, blue, green, yellow, orange, red & black all within a thin black border band, burlap backing, late 19th - early 20th c., 33 x 57 1/2" **$863**

Unusual Colorful United States Map Hooked Rug

United States map, colorful design of the continental United States divided into different colored states, part of Canada, Mexico & the oceans seen, blue wave border, stitched penned label on the reverse "Edith Pailes Ipswich, Mass.," early 20th c., 43 1/2 x 69" (ILLUS.)................ **$1,093**

SCRIMSHAW

Scrimshaw is a folk art byproduct of the 19th century American whaling industry. Intricately carved and engraved pieces of whalebone, whale's teeth and walrus tusks were produced by whalers during their spare time at sea. In recent years numerous fine grade hard plastic reproductions have appeared on the market, so the novice collector must use caution to distinguish these from the rare originals.

Unusual Scrimshaw Lady Doll

Doll, articulated figure of a lady w/moveable lower arms, hardwood dress & shoes, inlaid collar & necklace, first half 20th c., 7 1/4" h. (ILLUS.) **$1,673**

Rare Highly Decorated American Scrimshaw Bone

Dork, long rounded & slightly cured whale penis bone engraved w/a tall portrait of a lady, a man w/shield, military office w/sword, an anchor, flower, double head w/an eye & a man atop a flagpole flying the American flag, signed "P.P.M.," 19th c., 18" l. (ILLUS.) **$3,565**

Primitive Scrimshaw Pie Crimper

Pie crimper primitive style, a flattened oblong handle w/a long slender curved & pointed tip, mounted w/a crude notched wheel, the handle engraved w/ornate undulating scrolls, cross-hatching on the wheel, the edge w/some dot-sized decoration & "Grace Sewell," 19th c., 5 3/4" l. (ILLUS.)... **$518**

Whale tooth, engraved w/a scene of a whaling ship, large detailed ship under full sail flaying a banner engraved "Sarah," surrounded by clouds & stars, a banner across the bottom inscribed "Setauket 1854" above a whale & anchor, 7 1/4" l. (ILLUS. left with two other whale teeth).. **$3,346**

Unusual Scrimshaw Whale Tooth with an Engraved Factory Scene

Whale tooth, engraved w/an elaborate landscape w/a large factory complex behind a row of trees & a harbor in the distance, inscribed "New England Screw Co. Providence," color-tinted, mid-19th c., 7 1/8" l. (ILLUS.)................................. **$7,170**

Whale tooth, large tooth engraved w/a scene of a large urn of flowers, finely detailed, probably English, mid-19th c., 7 1/2" l. (ILLUS. right with two other whale teeth) **$1,673**

Three Nicely Decorated Scrimshaw Whale Teeth

Whale tooth, large tooth engraved w/a scene of an amorous young couple w/tinted green & red clothing, mid-19th c, 7 1/2" l. (ILLUS. center with two other whale teeth) **$1,673**

SIGNS & SIGNBOARDS

Early Apothecary Trade Sign

Apothecary, trade sign in gilded sheet metal & wrough iron, in the shape of a large gilded mortar & pestle, w/iron hanging brackets, 19th c., 19" d., 40" h. (ILLUS.) **$3,055**

Fine Dr. Russell's Bitters Sign

Bitters, "Dr. Russell's Pepsin Calisaya Bitters," color-lithographed cardboard, a large scene of a classical maiden w/a cornucopia resting in clouds above a pair of earth globes topped by an American flag wrapped around a bottle of bitters, ca. 1900, framed, excellent condition, 15 1/2 x 21 1/2" (ILLUS.) **$3,105**

Dotterweich Lager Beer Curved Sign

Beer, "Dotterweich Brewing Co. - Lager Beer - Olean, N.Y.," curved embossed tin post-mounted sign, black background printed w/gold lettering & a large spread-winged eagle atop a beer barrel, original wood hanger on the back, some professional restoration, late 19th - early 20th c., 20 1/2 x 34" (ILLUS.) **$1,495**

Two-sided Metal Bootmaker Trade Sign

Bootmaker, trade sign in painted sheet metal, rectangular form w/serpentine sides & rounded corners, gold ground painted in black & green w/corner scrolls & the name "S.S. Jackson" above two styles of boots, similar decoration on the back, signed by Booth & Co., probably American, second half 19th c., some paint wear, 18 1/2 x 22" (ILLUS.) **$2,585**

Woodward's Candy Sign

Candy, "Woodward's Peanut Butter Sticks," die-cut cardboard w/easel back, scene of a young boy in brown uniform & hat holding a box of candy & offering a piece to the young girl wearing a blue dress & white cap seated next to him, sign at bottom bordered by peanut shells & marked "Woodward's Peanut Butter Filled Stick Candy - John G. Woodward & Co. 'The Candy Men' - Council Bluffs, Iowa," wood frame, ca. 1900, 15 x 21" (ILLUS.)........................... **$1,600-2,000**

Grape-Nuts Sign

Cereal, "Grape-Nuts," embossed metal, self-framed, lithograph of young girl walking to school w/St. Bernard dog, house in background w/her mother standing at front gate, reading at the bottom "To school well fed on Grape-Nuts -

'There's a Reason'," ca. 1900, 20 x 30" (ILLUS.) **$2,200-3,000**

Kis-Me Gum Sign

Chewing gum, "Kis-Me Chewing Gum," die-cut cardboard in wood frame, scene of two young girls under a yellow umbrella, one dressed in long blue dress, the other in pink, marked at bottom "'Kis-Me' - Kis-Me Gum Co., Louisville, KY," ca. 1900, 11 x 13" (ILLUS.)...................... **$650-750**

Wrigley's Gum Trolley Sign

Chewing gum, "Wrigley's Gum," rectangular cardboard, trolley-type, yellow w/"Help Yourself! - Wrigley's" in black & red letters & "Good For You" in white letters on green arrow pointing to product displays, "On Every Dealer's Counter" in yellow letters at bottom, wood frame, ca. 1927, 12 1/4 x 22" (ILLUS.)............... **$800-900**

Wrigley's Gum Sign

Chewing gum, "Wrigley's Gum," rectangular tin w/cardboard easel-back, colorful lithograph by American Can Company shows packages of four different gum flavors on black background, marked "Wrigley's" in red letters & "Delicious Lasting Flavors" in white letters, ca. 1920s, 6 7/8 x 11" (ILLUS.)............................ **$400-500**

Unusual Chalkware Cigar Store Indian

Cigar store, figural, a tall molded polychromed chalkware figure of a standing Indian Chief wearing a feathered headdress, one arm raised to shade his eyes, the other hand holding a package of cigars, raised on a stump-form base, late 19th - early 20th c., light wear to base, 15 x 17", 57" h. (ILLUS.) **$1,725**

Colonial Club Cigar Portrait Sign

Cigars, "Colonial Club 5¢ Cigar," color lithograph showing a large half-length portrait of a lovely young lady wearing a flower-trimmed large straw hat & a low-cut green gown trimmed in lavender, dark green background w/gold lettering, late 19th - early 20th c., 11 1/2 x 22" (ILLUS.) **$900**

1920s Dentists Metal Sign

Dentist, "Ake Brothers - Painless Dentists - Formerly Dr. Leon," painted copper w/a blue ground & gold lettering w/a pointing hand at the top left, from Atlantic City, New Jersey, ca. 1920s, loss to much of the blue ground, otherwise good, 14 x 24" (ILLUS.)...................................... **$489**

Continental Fire Insurance Scenic Sign

Fire insurance, "Continental Fire Insurance Co.," color textured paper lithograph w/an expansive scene of a large group of Native Americans overlooking a group of their hunters pursuing a herd of buffalo fleeing a prairie fire, the company name in large black letters across the center of the scene, original flat oak frame, ca. 1895, two small water stains in margin, 27 1/2 x 32 1/2" (ILLUS.)........................ **$1,265**

Colt Firearms Sign

Firearms, "Colt Firearms," rectangular, lithograph of smiling girl wearing Western hat, brown skirt & belt, white blouse w/striped brown neckerchief, ammunition belt around hips & holding pistol, ca. 1900, wood frame, this version without Colt imprint cost 25¢, 39 1/2 x 37" (ILLUS., previous page) **$2,000-2,700**

Ceresota Flour Die-cut Sign

Flour, "Ceresota Flour," die-cut cardboard in wood frame, small boy wearing boots & large hat sitting on stool & slicing a loaf of bread, flour sack behind him, marked "Ceresota Flour - Prize Bread Flour of Minnesota," by Edward Deutsch & Co., Chicago, Illinois, ca. 1900, 13 x 17 1/2" (ILLUS.)....................................... **$1,500-1,800**

Clear Quill Flour Sign

Flour, "Clear Quill Flour," self-framed tin, w/cardboard back, blue w/image of white quill pen over table holding loaf of bread & slices on plate w/white flour sack at left marked w/red letters "Union Mill Company - Clear Quill - Fancy Patent - Warranted Waterloo, Iowa - 49 lbs.," red & white letters reading "Clear Quill Fancy Patent Flour - Often Buttered - Never Bettered," ca. 1890, 14 1/2 x 20 1/2" (ILLUS.)................ **$800-1,000**

Unusual Electric Mother's Flour Sign

Flour, "Mother's Best Flour," electric-type, round metal frame hanging from a metal bar, domed glass cover reverse-painted in red, white, blue, yellow & green, some wear to the plated steel frame, early 20th c., 17" d. (ILLUS.)....................................... **$578**

Dead Shot Gunpowder Sign

Gunpowder, "Dead Shot Gunpowder," rectangular paper, bird falling to the ground w/"Dead Shot" above & "American Powder Mills - Boston - Chicago - St. Louis" below, wood frame marked "Gunpowder," ca. 1910, 25 x 31" (ILLUS.)................ **$1,500-2,000**

Mission Orange Juice Sign

Juice, "Mission Orange Juice," rectangular tin, black w/yellow sun & sunrays, embossed red letters outlined in white & white letters reading "Drink Mission Orange - It's Real Juice," wood frame, ca. 1920s, 13 x 31" (ILLUS.).................... **$200-275**

Piper Lacing Button Litho with Ladies

Lacing button, "The Piper Lacing Button - Adapted for All Kinds of Lacing," colored lithographic scene of two young Victorian ladies walking outside w/their dresses pulled up to show their laced shoes, retains original top & bottom metal bands, in a narrow frame, ca. 1880s, horizontal tear in lower right, tack holes in margins, 13 1/2 x 29 1/2" (ILLUS.)......................... **$1,150**

Cetacolor Printed Fabric Sign

Laundry product, "Cetacolor," rectangular, lithographed fabric in wood frame, oval on left side depicting a woman wearing a red & white striped blouse, one side faded & flanked by black letters reading "Result Without Using Cetacolor," the other side bright w/"Result With Using Cetacolor," white & green lettering on right side reading "Not a Soap - Cetacolor - Prevents Wash Goods from Fading. - 10¢ Package.," by Acme Sign Printing Co., Dayton, Ohio, ca. 1890, 25 x 37" (ILLUS.)........ **$375-450**

Coles Nerve Tonic Sign

Nerve/blood tonic, "Coles Peruvian Bark and Wild Cherry Bitters," porcelain on metal, blue w/white letters reading "No More Malaria - Coles Peruvian Bark and Wild Cherry Bitters Will Cure You - The Best Nerve and Blood Tonic" & in upper left corner "Cure Debility " & lower right corner "Cure Dyspepsia," framed, ca. 1880, 7 1/2 x 17 1/2" (ILLUS.)......... **$750-1,000**

Early White Star Line Sign with the Olympic & Titanic

Ocean liner, "White Star Line," color lithograph showing the liner "Olympic" sailing ahead w/the "Titanic" in the distant background, originally printed in the border w/a reference to both ships but this reference overprinted or removed after the Titanic disaster, small metal tag at bottom center of the wooden frame reads "White Star Line," post-1912, excellent condition, 35 x 45" (ILLUS.)............................ **$3,840**

Nesbitt's Orange Drink Sign

Orange drink, "Nesbitt's Orange Drink," rectangular cardboard, colorful scene of girl in white bathing suit relaxing near swimming pool, orange trees in background, a table nearby w/bowl of oranges & bottle, the chair's blue tented cover marked in white & orange letters reading "Drink Nesbitt's California Orange," original Nesbitt frame, ca. 1955, 28 1/2 x 39" (ILLUS.)... **$350-450**

Overalls, "OshKosh Overalls," rectangular cardboard, top w/wide red band marked in white & yellow "OshKosh B'gosh - Union Made - The World's Best Overall," center section light background w/four men of different sizes pictured wearing overalls indicated for "Fat - or Thin - Short - or Tall," the men in middle holding yel-

OshKosh Overalls Sign

low sign marked "OshKosh B'Gosh Fits 'Em All," bottom marked "Always Buy Your Correct Size," ca. 1930, 13 1/2 x 14 1/2" (ILLUS.)................... **$300-375**

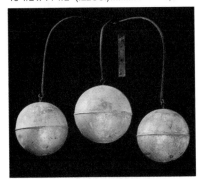

Early Victorian Pawn Broker Trade Sign

Pawn broker, trade sign in molded & gilded copper & iron, three large gilded copper balls hanging from three arched wrought-iron arms joined to a wall-mount bracket, 19th c., 28 x 42" (ILLUS.)...................... **$4,935**

Colorful Lisk's Roaster Paper Sign

Roaster pan, "Lisk's Sanitary Enameled Roaster - Seamless - Self Basting," colored lithographic scenes of a black cook kneeling by the oven & cleaning the roaster while her white mistress looks on, English brand, late 19th - early 20th c., 15 x 19 1/2" (ILLUS.)................................. **$690**

Curved Metal Dana's Sarsaparilla Sign

Sarsaparilla, "Dana's Sarsaparilla - 'The Kind That Cures - See That You Get Dana's," tall printed curved metal post sign w/an arched top, black ground w/embossed lettering printed in gold, ca. 1880s-90s, few scratches & scuffs, 9 x 13 3/4" (ILLUS.)............................... **$1,610**

Long Red Goose Shoes Sign

Shoes, "Red Goose Shoes," rectangular paper, red goose holding black high-top shoe by the laces in its beak, reads "Red Goose Shoes - The All Leather Shoe For Boys and Girls - 'They're Half the Fun of Having Feet,'" green, yellow, red & black, ca. 1910, Friedman-Shelby Shoes, 8 x 18" (ILLUS.) **$350-450**

Red Goose Shoes Sign with Crying Boy

Shoes, "Red Goose Shoes," rectangular paper, scene of mother examining shoe of crying boy, reads "Don't blame the Boy - Buy him All-Leather Shoes - Red Goose Shoes for Girls - The Friedman-Shelby 'All-Leather Shoe,'" yellow, red & green, ca. 1910, Friedman-Shelby Shoes, 8 x 18" (ILLUS., previous page) **$350-450**

Star Brand Shoes Sign

Shoes, "Star Brand Shoes," round, reverse-painted on convex glass, white background w/red & yellow letters reading "Star Brand - Shoes - Are Better," wood frame, ca. 1920s, 22" d. (ILLUS.) **$500-700**

Andrew Jergens & Co. Soap Sign

Soap, "Andrew Jergens Toilet Soap," rectangular, die-cut cardboard in wood frame, depicts two young girls in long dresses w/a large white & brown dog, marked at lower left corner "Andrew Jergens & Co. Fine Toilet Soaps - Always Pure," ca. 1880, rare, 20 x 22 1/2" (ILLUS.) **$1,600-1,900**

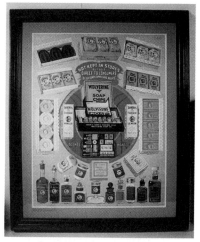

Wolverine Soap Chips Sign

Soap, "Wolverine Soap Chips," rectangular, colorful lithographed display of various products surrounding red center marked "Not Kept in Stores - But Sold - Direct to Consumers - By Our Own Canvassing Agents" & marked at bottom "Agents - Wanted," Terriff & Co., Portland, Michigan, litho by Calvert Litho Company, Detroit, Michigan, wood frame, ca. 1900, 28 1/2 x 34" (ILLUS.) **$750-1,100**

Rare Campbell's Soup Can-shaped Sign

Soup, "Campbell's Condensed Vegetable Soup," porcelain on metal design in the shape of their soup can in red, white, black & yellow, small grommet hole chip, early 20th c., 13 1/2 x 22 1/2" (ILLUS.).. **$4,255**

Round Oak Stove Doe-Wah-Jack Sign

Stoves, "Round Oak Stoves," colored heavily embossed cardboard w/the standing figure of the company logo, Doe-Wah-Jack the Native American, in an old quarter-sawn oak frame w/walnut top & base panels w/applied brass ornaments, sign w/some light soiling & scuffing, early 20th c., 8 x 22 3/4" (ILLUS.) **$288**

Interesting Iron Tavern Sign

Tavern sign, wrought iron, an upright rectangular iron bar frame w/a large arrow bar across the top w/small rings suspending an inner rectangular iron sign pierced w/two bars w/the lettering "Banbury - Way" above a lower openwork panel featuring a Colonial rider on a racing horse, on a later wood display stand, painted black w/evidence of early paint, some light bends,   overall 30 x 33 1/2" (ILLUS.)... **$1,560**

Mennen's Talcum Powder Sign

Talcum powder, "Mennen's Talcum Powder," rectangular, die-cut cardboard in wood frame, depicts young child writing in a book w/a quill pen, the page w/black letters reading "Mennen's Borated Talcum Toilet Powder - For Infants and Adults - It Cures: Prickly Heat, Nettle Rash, Chafing, Measles, Eczema, Sweaty Feet, Pimples, Etc. - Delightful After Shaving - 25¢ Per Box" & at bottom "Mennen's Sure Corn Killer," ca. 1880, rare, 19 1/2 x 22 1/2" (ILLUS.) **$1,600-1,900**

Early King Cole Tea and Coffee Sign

Tea & coffee, King Cole Tea and Coffee," porcelain on metal die-cut w/the tall oval top printed in color w/a half-length portrait of smiling King Cole, rectangular advertising panel below in black, yellow & white, a few in-painted chips at grommets w/slight bending, early 20th c., 9 x 15" (ILLUS.).. **$575**

Red Riding Hood Coats Thread Sign

Thread, "J. & P. Coats - Spool Cotton," colored lithographic scene of Little Red Riding Hood walking through the forest w/the wolf beside her, several semi-circular areas of color loss, framed, late 19th - early 20th c., 11 1/4 x 20" (ILLUS.) **$1,035**

Bagley's Smoking Tobacco Sign

Tobacco, "Bagley's Smoking Tobacco," figural wood covered w/paper, window motion display-type w/arms that move, figure of a man wearing long red trousers, long-tailed grey jacket, yellow vest & red bow tie, the black top hat marked "Bagley's Long Tom Smokin Tobacco," ca. 1890, 36" h. (ILLUS.) **$1,100-1,500**

Hickman-Ebbert Company Sign

Wagon, "Hickman-Ebbert Co.," rectangular tin, self-framed colorful lithographed scene depicting girl picking apples & a boy loading them onto a horse-drawn green wagon w/red wheels, titled "In The Shade Of The Old Apple Tree," upper left corner reads "Best at the Price - The Ebbert - Owensboro, KY - Always the Same," litho by Charles W. Shonk, frame marked "The Hickman-Ebbert Co. - Owensboro, Kentucky," ca. 1906, 25 1/2 x 37 1/2" (ILLUS.).............. **$1,600-2,100**

Molded Plaster Early Times Whiskey Sign

Whiskey, "Early Times Distillery Co. - Louisville, KY," relief-molded plaster w/a colored scene of a rustic mountain landscape w/a log cabin beside a plank road w/a horse-drawn wagon full of barrels, self-framed w/the scene title at the top "Early Times," a few plaster chips & hairlines, damage to one oxen head, late 19th - early 20th c., 35 x 44" (ILLUS.)....... **$660**

Standard Distilling Company Sign

Whiskey, "Hanover Pure Rye," round, reverse-painted convex glass front w/ornate openwork gold metal frame, image of brown horse head in center flanked by grain wreath & encircled by dark blue border w/"Standard Distilling Co. - Cincinnati, Ohio" in gold letters, further encircled by wide white border w/gold leaf letters reading "Hanover - Pure Rye," ca. 1890, 24" d. (ILLUS.) **$1,000-1,400**

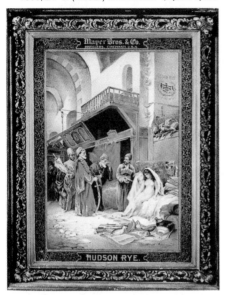

Unusual Hudson Rye Whiskey Sign

Whiskey, "Hudson Rye - Mayer Bros. & Co.," tall lithographed tin scene titled "The Slave Market," shows an Arab slave market w/men viewing a young seated nude maiden, in original ornate shadowbox frame, small surface blemishes, one nail puncture in extreme lower left corner, late 19th - early 20th c., 19 x 27 1/2" (ILLUS.) **$4,485**

Early Olco Whiskey Canvas Sign

Whiskey, "Olco Whiskey - O.B. Cook & Co., Detroit, Mich.," canvas printed in color w/a scene of four gentlemen in an early large red touring car pulling away from a rustic mountain tavern, original gilt-plaster frame, light crazing, two small punctures, late 19th - early 20th c., 23 1/2 x 35 3/4" (ILLUS.) **$2,018**

Colorful Paul Jones Whiskey Sign

Whiskey, "Paul Jones & Co. - Louisville, KY.," stone lithographed die-cut tin, self-framed w/a flaring black scalloped frame, long rectangular color scene in the center titled "The Temptation of St. Anthony," shows a black woman on the left holding a large slice of watermelon & an elderly black man on the right holding a bottle of whiskey, a young black man kneeling in the center w/a cabin in the background, creases to top & bottom left corners, a few blemishes, late 19th - early 20th c., 13 1/2 x 19 1/2" (ILLUS.) **$840**

SILHOUETTES

Bust profile portrait of a lady, hollow-cut & watercolor, woman facing right wearing a comb at the back of her pulled back hair, wearing a painted pink dress, white organdy shawl & a blue ribbon necklace & sash, unsigned but attributed to the Puffy Sleeve Artist, America, ca. 1830, in a molded giltwood frame w/rope inset, image 2 5/8 x 3 1/2" **$2,585**

Unusual Reverse-painted Silhouettes of Two Children

Full-length boy & girl, reverse-painted on glass, the girl wearing a long off-the-shoulder dress & holding one hand out, the boy wearing a cap & long coat & holding a hoop & stick, mounted against a watercolor landscape background w/a houses & trees, unsigned, framed, first half 19th c., 10 1/2 x 13 1/2" (ILLUS.) **$200-300**

Silhouettes of a Gentleman & Young Man

Full-length portrait of a gentleman, cutout, facing left & holding out letters in one hand, black & gold inked details, stamped labels in three places marked "Herve, Artist 172 Oxford St.," original bird's-eye maple frame, stains, first half 19th c., 10 3/4 x 14" (ILLUS. right with silhouette of a young man) **$805**

Full-length portrait of a young man, cutout, standing facing right, holding a top hat, wearing a vest & tailed coat, inked details in gold, white & black, oval stamped marked "Taken at the Hubard Gallery," faint penciled note on back "Bought and cleaned by C. Gavine...Glasgow 6th Nov. 1833," old rosewood frame w/split gilt liner, minor stains, 12 x 15 3/4" h. (ILLUS. left with silhouette of gentleman) **$805**

Framed Double Portrait Silhouettes of a Husband & Wife

Half-length portraits of a husband & wife, facing pair, she w/her hair pulled back w/side curls, he wearing a high-collared shirt & coat, gold inked details, glued down to cut-out pieces of card stock, attributed to E. Whittle, period giltwood frame w/replaced black & gold églomisé

mat w/flakes, first half 19th c., 10 x 12" (ILLUS.)... **$633**

Facing Silhouettes of a Woman & Man

Half-length portraits of a woman & man, hollow-cut, the lady facing right w/her hair held by a large comb, a watercolor & pen & ink dress w/a wide lacy collar & balloon sleeves, the facing man w/a watercolor & pen & ink high-collared shirt & wide-collared coat & holding a red book, red silk backing, early embossed brass & wood frames, penciled inscription on back of one frame "Dudley, Oct. - 1835," 2 1/2 x 3 1/2", pr. (ILLUS.) **$2,233**

Half-length profile portrait of a gentleman, hollow-cut, facing left, backed by black silk, wearing a white high-collared shirt w/pen & ink & watercolor detailing to his hair, vest, ruffle & collar, unsigned, ca. 1830, in stamped brass rectangular frame w/oval opening, image 3 1/4 x 3 7/8" (subtle toning) **$411**

SNOWMAN COLLECTIBLES

The new Snowman items that came onto the market during the 1990s awoke an interest in these icy fellow like never before. While the new items are easy to come by, collectors soon realized that they wanted vintage Snowmen to round out their collections. This, however, is not an easy task. These fun "Christmas" collectibles don't ever melt and are cheery guests all your long. "Frosty" is the most famous Snowman, but as these listings will show, the snowman was a popular character long before Frosty arrived on the scene.

Advertisement, "Thermo Anti-Freeze," lithograph paper snowman design **$7**

Apron, color-printed cloth decorated w/a snowman, 1950s.. **$7**

Baby rattle, plush figural snowman, made in the U.S.A., 8 1/2" l. **$10**

Bank, bisque piggy-bank style snowman **$16**

Composition Child's Snowman Bank

Bank, child's, composition, model of a snowman holding aloft a wrapped present, 1940s (ILLUS.)............................. **$24**

"Danny, The Dimpled Snowman" Book

Book, "Danny, The Dimpled Snowman," by Dorothy M. Sheppard, 1940s (ILLUS.)........ **$42**

Book, "Jolly Snowman Christmas Play - Pop-up Book"... **$15**

Book, "Merry Christmas Mr. Snowman," a Wonder Book, 1951 .... **$3**

Book, "Mr. Bingle Activity Book," early 1950s **$10**

Book, "Mr. Buttons - A Story Book with Action Puppets," A Bonnie Book, 1950s (ILLUS., top next column) **$15**

1950s "Mr. Buttons" Snowman Book

'Fuzzy-wuzzy' 1940s Snowman Book

Book, "The Snowman Who Wanted to Stay," by Sarah Derman, 'fuzzy-wuzzy' type, Whitman, 1948 (ILLUS.).................... **$27**

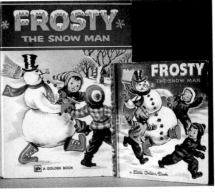

First Edition Copies of "Frosty The Snow Man"

Books, "Frosty The Snow Man," first edition copies, A Golden Book & A Little Golden Book, top condition, each (ILLUS. of both)... **$5-20**

Bowl, turned wood, painted on the interior w/a snowman scene **$25**

Candle, molded wax, by Gurley, ca. 1940s-50s **$2-5**

Candleholder, ceramic, figural snowman candle hugger, by Hold Howard, mid-20th c, ... **$7**

Candleholder, ceramic, figural snowman w/applied spaghetti-style trim, Norcrest, ca. 1950s-60s **$50**

Snowman on Box Candy Container

Candy container, composition, model of snowman torso atop the lid of a square flocked box, early 20th c. (ILLUS.) **$34**

Plastic Snowman Candy Container

Candy container, plastic, model of a white snowman w/red scarf & black top hat (ILLUS.) **$10-15**

Candy container, plastic, model of an orange snowman **$202**

Candy dispenser, plastic, PEZ, figural snowman w/no feet **$21**

Cap, child's, knitted in blue & white yarn, 1940s (ILLUS., top next column) **$15**

1940s Child's Knitted Snowman Cap

1940s Snowman "Jig Saw Christmas Card"

Christmas card, "Jig Saw Christmas Card," colorful design of a snowman cut into a jigsaw on the card, Gibson, mint in package, 1940s (ILLUS.) **$15**

Christmas card, pop-up type, snowman design, 1950s **$10**

Child's Honeycomb Christmas Card

Christmas card, "With Best Christmas Wishes," die-cut cardboard & honeycomb, a color scene of a child w/poinsettias beside a fold-out honeycomb paper snowman, dated 1948, large (ILLUS., previous page) **$15**

Old Chenille Snowman Decoration

Christmas decoration, figural snowman made of chenille, marked w/a blue "Japan" sticker, first half 20th c. (ILLUS.)......... **$10**
Christmas decoration, figure of a snowman w/an umbrella, by Rosbro **$18**
Christmas decoration, plastic figure of a snowman w/friends, Union Products, 1960s **$47**

Light-up Snowman Christmas Decoration

Christmas decoration, plastic light-up figure of a snow man holding a fir tree, w/box, by Royalite (ILLUS.)......................... **$64**
Christmas ornaments, colored-foil snowmen, 1950s, the group **$15**
Christmas tree light, figural 'bubble' light, by Royal Plastic... **$76**
Christmas tree light bulb, figural glass snowman, first half 20th c. **$12**
Christmas tree lights, string of plastic snowmen, the set...................................... **$16**

Hallmark Merry Miniature Snowman

Christmas tree ornament Merry Miniature Snowman, Hallmark, first edition (ILLUS.).... **$47**
Christmas tree ornament, papier-maché model of a snowman, Germany, early 20th c. **$15**
Christmas tree ornament The Skating Snowman, plastic, Hallmark, 1979, no box **$28**
Clock, novelty-type, Frosty the Snow Man w/blinking eyes, Germany........................... **$60**
Comic book, "Frosty The Snow Man," Dell, 1951 .... **$5**
Condiment set: salt & pepper shakers & candelabra; ceramic figural Christmas snowmen, Holt Howard, mint in box, the set **$160**
Cookie cutter, molded plastic snowman, by Hallmark... **$3-9**
Cookie jar, ceramic, model of a snowman, newer **$20**
Coolant container, "Snowman Can'd Ice," cylindrical tin printed in blue, red & white w/a snowman, ca. 1950s **$22**
Counter display sign, "Chesterfield Cigarettes," colorful snowman design, first half 20th c. **$17**
Decoration, cut-out poster board color snowman waving & carrying a shovel over one shoulder, 1950s **$5**
Decorative holiday seals, flocked snowman design, by Dennison, each.................... **$5**
Doll, snowman, by Annalee Mobilitee, 1950s **$125**

Stuffed Cloth Mr. Bingle Snowman Doll

Doll, stuffed cloth Mr. Bingle snowman, from Maison Blanche, early 1950s (ILLUS.)......... **$62**
Doorstop, cast iron, figural snowman, 7" h..... **$25**

Figurine, ceramic snowman w/spaghetti-
style trim, by Napco $17
Figurine, composition, figure of a snow la-
dy, Josef Originals, 1950s-60s $19
Handkerchief, child's, cloth printed w/a
snowman scene $14
Napkin set, hand-embroided snowman de-
signs, mid-20th c., set of 4 .... $11
Pail, child's, color-lithographed tin w/a
snowman scene, Ohio Art $341

*Colorful 1920s Snowman-decorated
Pencil Box*

Pencil box, cardboard, the long narrow cover printed in color w/a scene of children &
a snowman, ca. 1920 (ILLUS.) $20
Phonograph record, "Frosty the Snow
Man," a Peter Pan record, ca. 1950s $6

Three Older Hallmark Snowman Pins

Pins, plastic, figural snowman, various designs, by Hallmark, 1970s, each (ILLUS.
of three) $4-25

Lefton China Salt & Pepper Shakers

1880s Snowman Scene Stereoview Card

Still bank, cast iron, model of a snowman,
unmarked $72
Suitcase, hard plastic, painted w/a scene of
a snowman $43
Tablecloth, color-printed cloth w/a snow-
man design, mid-20th c. $20
Toy, battery-operated, "Abominable
Snowman," ca. 1960s, good working
condition $510
Toy, battery-operated, snowman w/glowing
eyes waves his broom, ca. 1950s-60s,
working condition $80
Toy, color-lithographed tin snowman musi-
cal roly-poly, first half 20th c. $12

Early German Snowman Pipsqueak Toy

Postcard, "A Happy New Year," a lady
dressed in red hugging a snowman, by
John Winsch, 1911 (ILLUS.) $50
Puzzle, child's tray-type, by Whitman,
1950s $12
Salt & pepper shakers, china, figure of a
snowman & snowwoman, Lefton China,
1940s, pr. (ILLUS., top next column) $40
Stereoview card, photographic scene of
Victorian children w/a snowman, dated
1888 (ILLUS., middle next column) $12

1911 New Years Snowman Postcard

Toy, pipsqueak-type, model of a snowman w/a push-down head, Germany, early 20th c. (ILLUS., previous page) **$64**

Hallmark Stuffed Cloth Snowman Toy

Toy, stuffed cloth snowman, by Hallmark, early 1970s, 6" h. (ILLUS.) **$10-15**
Toy shovel, tin color-printed w/a snowman, by Ohio Art **$37**

Early Toy Tin Tray with Snowman & Children Scene

Tray, from child's tea set, color-lithographed tin, a scene of children building a snowman, ca. 1920s (ILLUS.) **$56**

SODA FOUNTAIN & ICE CREAM COLLECTIBLES

The neighborhood ice cream parlor and drug-store fountain are pretty much a thing of the past as fast-food chains have sprung up across the country. Memories of the slower-paced lifestyle represented by the rapidly disappearing local soda fountain have spurred the interest of many collectors today. Anything relating to the soda fountains of old and the delicious concoctions they dispensed are much sought-after.

Cap, advertising beanie-type, "Icy-Frost Twins" popsicles, pictures Donald Duck, 1950s, rare **$625**

Four Roses Art Deco Advertising Clock

Clock, "Four Roses," Art Deco-style light-up electric counter-top style, the upright long vertical black glass top panel printed in red & green w/a cluster of four roses beside the white clock dial w/Arabic numerals, black hands & a red sweep seconds hand, silvered metal flanges at the sides & raised on a long low rectangular black & silver base, ca. 1931, missing narrow advertising panel on front below the dial, worn cord, 18" l., 12" h. (ILLUS.) **$144**
Comic book, "Lone Ranger Comic Book #1," advertising premium from Long Ranger Ice Cream Cones, 1939, very rare early premium, depending on condition **$4,000**

Safe-T-Cup Figural Counter Display

Counter display, "Safe-T-Cup" ice cream cones, plastic model of an ice cream cone w/a chocolate top, some versions w/a coin drop hole in the back & used as a bank, 1960s, 27" h. (ILLUS.) **$30**
Fan, advertising hand-held cardboard type, "If It's Borden's It's Got to be Good," advertising premium from Borden given away at the 1939-40 New York World's Fair, 7 1/4 x 12" **$60**

Cornet Magic Cones Metal Container

Ice cream cone container, "Cornet Magic Cones," cylindrical w/a fitted cover, printed yellow background w/red wording & central image of an ice cream cone, for O. Gauthier Company, Ltd., Montreal, Canada, 1940s, excellent condition (ILLUS.) **$75**

Ice cream container, "Bing Crosby Ice Cream," illustrated w/a photo of Bing Crosby on the top of the cardboard box, 1940s-1950s, 2 1/2 x 4", 3 1/4" h. **$55**

Ice cream container, "Hopalong Cassidy Ice Cream," cylindrical cardboard, printed w/a picture of Hopalong w/his revolvers drawn, 1940s, 6" h. **$50**

Ice cream cup lid, "Dixie Ice Cream," examples illustrated inside w/a famous cartoon character such as Howdy Doody or Disney character such as Snow White, early 1950s, 2 1/2" d., each **$60**

Ice cream cup lid, "Dixie Ice Cream," illustrated w/a picture of Western star Tom Mix on one side, the reverse w/an advertisement for his movie "Miracle Rider," 1930s **$80**

Ice cream cup lid, "Schrauth Ice Cream," illustrated inside w/a photo of actor Buster Crabb as Flash Gordon, 1930s **$60**

Royal Lace Glass & Chrome Dish

Ice cream dish or sherbet, chrome pedestal base, blue glass insert in the Royal Lace Depression glass patt., 1930s, 2 pcs. (ILLUS.) **$30-40**

Clear Royal Lace & Chrome Dish

Ice cream dish or sherbet, chrome pedestal base, clear glass insert in the Royal Lace Depression glass patt., 1930s, 2 pcs. (ILLUS.) **$5-10**

Ice cream molds, hinged pewter, in the shape of Christmas bells, early 20th c., set of 5 .... **$45**

Ice cream scoop, metal heart-shaped scoop, wooden handle, marked "J. Manos Combined Mold and Scoop," by Manos Novelty Company of Ohio, patented November 17, 1925, one of the rarest ice cream scoops, depending on condition .... **$7,000+**

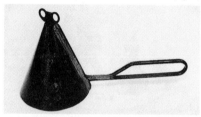

Early Cone-shaped Ice Cream Scoop

Ice cream scoop, sheet metal, cone-shaped w/twist key top & loop handle, early 20th c., some rusting, 8 1/4" l. (ILLUS.) **$40**

Ice cream scoop, turned wooden handle & chromed metal lever scoop, ca. 1920s (ILLUS. left with four plastic-handled scoops) **$85**

Group of Plastic-handled & a Wooden Handled Ice Cream Scoops

Ice cream scoops, molded plastic handle w/chromed metal lever scoop, 1930s-1940s, each (ILLUS. of four at right with one wooden-handled type, previous page) **$45-65**

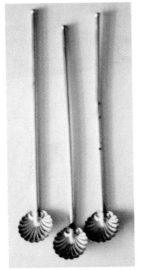

Aluminum Soda Fountain Spoons

Ice cream soda spoon, aluminum, shell-shaped bowl, the thin hollow handle served as a straw, late 1920s, 8" l., each (ILLUS. of three).. **$40**

Group of Hollywood Stars Spoons

Ice cream spoons, silver plate, premium-type, each handle featuring a portrait of a Hollywood star, including Douglas Fairbanks, Mary Pickford, Norma Shearer or Ramon Navarro, 1920s, by Oneida, 6" l., each (ILLUS. of four) **$85**

Coca-Cola Ice Cream Floats Ad

Magazine advertisement, "Coca-Cola," colorful photo of three ice cream floats made w/Coca-Cola, advertising along the bottom, June 1962, 10 1/2 x 13 1/2" (ILLUS.)... **$10**

General Equipment Sales Freezer Ad

Magazine advertisement, "General Equipment Sales, Inc., Indianapolis, Indiana," black & white illustrated ad for commercial-grade ice cream freezers, 1950s, 10 1/2 x 13 1/2" (ILLUS.).............................. **$8**

Magazine advertisement, "Seven-Up," color photo of ice cream sodas made w/Seven-Up," shows a girl & her father pouring the Seven-Up, 1950s, 10 1/2 x 13 1/2" **$10**

Magazine advertisement, "Tastee-Freez Drive-ins," color ad announcing a promotional contest w/cash prices, a small figure of a baseball player in the upper left above a large picture of a strawberry sundae, also announces All-Star Sundaes, each offered w/a small plastic figure of a baseball player as shown in the lower right, an image of a Tastee-Freez drive-in at the bottom left, May 1952, 10 1/2 x 14" (ILLUS., next page) **$10**

1952 Tastee-Freez Contest Advertisement

Paper dishes, "Sealtest Ice Cream," each printed w/advertising in a red square, 1930s-1950s, each.................................... **$3-4**

Paper wrapper, "Carvel Ice Cream Flying Saucer Bar," printed w/an image of a flying saucer, 1952, rare **$35**

Paper wrappers, for "Michigan State Ice Cream Bar," "Sure Good Ice Cream Bar," or "Cheerio Ice Cream Bar," 1940s-1950s, usually 3" l., each **$4-6**

Picture cards, "Sealtest Ice Cream," each w/a black & white photo of a Hollywood movie star such as Donald O'Connor or Audrey Hepburn, back of each reads "Compliments of Deluxe Sealtest Ice Cream," a set of 75 cards, 2 x 3", value depends on the fame of the star & the condition, each....................................... **$2 -12**

Borden's World's Fair Recipe Booklet

Recipe booklet, "108 World's Fair Recipes from Borden's," paper, colorful cover featuring Elsie the Cow, produced for the 1939-40 New York World's Fair, 6 1/2 x 9" (ILLUS.)...................................... **$50**

Good Housekeeping Ice Cream Booklet

Recipe booklet, "Good Housekeeping's Book of Ice Creams & Cool Drinks," color cover photo of various tall ice cream drinks, 1940s-1950s, 6 1/4 x 8 1/2" (ILLUS.) **$15-25**

Sifto Salt Home Made Ice Cream Booklet

Recipe booklet, "Heavenly Home Made Ice Cream - Sifto Salt - - All You Need to Know About Making Ice Cream, Sherbet and Water Ice," advertising premium, color cover photo of various ice cream treats, 1970s (ILLUS.)................................ **$10**

Breyer's Ice Cream Advertising Ruler

Ruler, wooden advertising-type for "Breyer's Ice Cream," given as a premium, 12" length w/a metal-insert top edge, late 1940s - early 1950s (ILLUS., bottom previous page)... **$10**

Frontenac Ice Cream Bricks Sign

Sign, "Frontenac Ice Cream Bricks to take Home - 25¢," enameled metal, blue & red wording on a white ground, within an arched metal bar frame raised on arched metal bar legs, edge chipping & rusting, 1940s (ILLUS.) **$125**

Silverwood's DeLuxe Ice Cream Sign

Sign, "Silverwood's DeLuxe Ice Cream," enameled metal, blue & red wording on a cream ground, raised on arched metal trestle legs, 1940s, some wear & rust (ILLUS.) **$125**
Sign, "Superior Brand Ice Cream," die-cut cardboard w/a color image of a banana split, 1940s, 11 x 15 1/4", depending on condition.. **$25-40**

Soda jerk paper hat, depending on the name of the regional dairy or of the soda fountain, 1920s-1950s, each.................. **$15-30**
Spoons, wooden, given out for Dixie Cup ice cream, value varies depending on the brand name on the spoon, each ..... **$75¢ - 1.50**

Early Horlick's Malted Milk Jar

Storage jar, "Original - Genuine - Horklick's Malted Milk," clear cylindrical glass jar w/a reverse-glass color label, back of jar embossed "Horlick's Malted Milk," ground short cylindrical neck w/a large pointed stopper, some discoloration label, late 19th - early 20th c., 9" h. (ILLUS.) **$144**

Early Green River Syrup Dispenser

Syrup dispenser, "Drink Green River," large ceramic pale yellow sphere w/knobbed cap molded w/green wording, a spigot at the bottom, resting on a tall rectangular green base, hairline across cover, old repair to cover flange, moderate overall crazing, early 20th c., 16" h. (ILLUS.).. **$575**
Syrup dispenser, "Fan-Taz," large ceramic model of a baseball on a round base, or-

ange & black wording w/a tan baseball bat, ca. 1900, 16" h. .... **$$10,000+**

Large Lipton Tea Teapot-shaped Dispenser

Tea dispenser, Lipton Tea, large ceramic model of a black teapot w/a spigot at the bottom center, raised on a tall cylindrical black glass base, early 20th c., 13 1/2" h. (ILLUS.)... **$259**

STATUARY - BRONZE, MARBLE & OTHER

Bronzes and other statuary are increasingly popular with today's collectors. Particularly appealing are works by "Les Animaliers," the 19th-century French school of sculptors who turned to animals for their subject matter. These, together with figures in the Art Deco and Art Nouveau taste, are common in a wide price range.

Bronze

Chester Beach "The Past" Faun Bronze

Beach, Chester, "The Past," squared flat base w/a rockwork design w/a dish at one side w/a young crouched faun seated on the end rim, signed "Beach - Roman Bronze Works NY," early 20th c., 4" w., 5 1/4" h. (ILLUS.).......................... **$1,610**

Debut Figure Group of Amphitrite

Debut, Jean Didier, figure group w/ the sea goddess Amphitrite standing partially nude w/two winged cupids beside her, all posed on a large scallop shell supported by two dolphins, all raised on a low round bronze molded base, bottom signed "Debut," France, late 19th c., 30" h. (ILLUS.)......... **$4,312**

Frishmuth "The Leaf" Sculpture

Frishmuth, Harriet Whitney, "The Leaf," standing nude woman w/one arm outstretched w/the other arm bent touching her shoulder, atop an angled rock on a square black marble base marked "Gorham Co. Founders 1916" & signed on the back "Harriet W. Frishmuth," early 20th c., 26 1/2" h. (ILLUS.).................... **$5,750**

Kauba, Carl, Native American Chief w/feathered headdress astride his horse & looking back over his shoulder, naturalistic ground mounted on a thick oblong tan rock slab w/a polished top & rough sides, signed "C Kauba - Geschutzt 6254," late 19th - early 20th c., 11 1/2 x 12 3/4", overall 14 3/4" h. (ILLUS., next page) **$2,875**

Kauba American Indian on Horse Bronze

Mene Bronze of "The Pointer"

Mene, Pierre Jules, "The Pointer," realistic model of a hunting dog posed in full-point, on a naturalist base raised on a molded oval plinth base, signed "PJ Mene," good brownish patina, France, late 19th c., 4 x 11", 8" h. (ILLUS.)......... **$4,025**

Rare Eskimo Hunter Bronze Group

Potter, Louis McClellan, Eskimo hunter walking holding a rifle & surrounded by four dogs, on a naturalistic base, base

signed "Louis Potter 1905 - Copyright 1905 by Gorham Mfg. Co.," 10 x 17", 18" h. (ILLUS.) **$18,400**

Small Vienna Bronze Hen Pheasant

Vienna bronze, miniature model of a hen pheasant, curved body & tail, naturalistic coloring, impressed "Austria," 3 1/2" h. (ILLUS.).. **$316**

Other

Victorian Alabaster Bust of Girl in Bonnet

Alabaster, bust portrait of a young late Victorian girl, raised on a socle base w/carved blossoms on her lace-trimmed bodice, her head turned to the right & looking down, her long curls framed by a very wide rounded upright bonnet w/a wide pierced lacy border, illegible signature, late 19th c., some chipping to edge of bonnet, overall 24" h. (ILLUS.)............. **$489**

Onyx, bust of a young girl, a domed close-fitting cap on her head w/short curly hair framing her face, wearing a simple paneled gown, scratch-carved highlights to the dress & bonnet, unsigned, late 19th - early 20th c., 10" w., 10 1/2" h. (ILLUS., next page) **$316**

Nice Onyx Bust of a Girl with Cap

French Terra Cotta Bust of a Young Woman

Terra cotta, bust portrait of a young Victorian matron w/a finger-waved coiffure & a shawl across her front, signed "E. Beuilly - 1883," Etienne Beuilly, France, 19th c., 26" h. (ILLUS.) **$460**

STEINS

Character, porcelain, Jester figural handle on tapering white cylindrical body w/a German inscription, lid inlaid w/an inverted porcelain funnel, by Schierholz, known as the Nurnberger Trichter, wear on black color, .5 L (ILLUS. right with High-wheel bicycle & Munich Child steins, next page)................................... **$604**

Character, porcelain, King Ludwig, tan-colored head of the king wearing a hunting hat, porcelain lid, by Schierholz, contemporary, .5 L (ILLUS. center with Bowling

Pin & Snowman character steins, next page).. **$335**

Character, porcelain, Munich Child, child-head inlaid lid, .5L (ILLUS. right with High-wheel bicycle & Jester-handled steins, next page)................................. **$242**

Rare Radish Woman Character Stein

Character, porcelain, Radish Woman, sad looking, purple dress & wide low-domed brown hat porcelain lid, by Schierholtz, .5 L (ILLUS.)... **$1,767**

Character, porcelain, Skull, porcelain-inlaid lid, by E. Bohne & Sohne, .5 L (ILLUS. right with Sleeping Hunter & Snake around Apple character steins)............... **$392**

Sleeping Hunter, Snake & Apple and Skull Character Steins

Character, porcelain, Sleeping Hunter, seated figure wearing a green hat & coat & dark grey pants, head from the inlaid lid, by Bauer, chip repair, .5 L (ILLUS. left with Snake & Appleand Skull steins) **$805**

Character, porcelain, Snake wrapped around Apple, tail forms the handle, lid inlay of a monkey rising out of foam, figural porcelain thumbleft of snake & apple, by E. Ohne & Sohne, pewter lid strap repaired, .5 L (ILLUS. center with Sleeping Hunter and Skull character steins)......... **$1,208**

Character, porcelain, Snowman, frowning expression, porcelain inlaid lid, by Schierholz, contemporary, .5 L (ILLUS. left with King Ludwig & Bowling Pin steins)
.... **$368**

Character, porcelain, Tyrolean Woman, smiling woman wearing regional costume & carrying a bouquet of purple flowers, shoulder & head form hinged lid, base marked "M. Pauson Munchen 1895," .5 L (ILLUS., next page)............. **$3,381**

Tyrolean Woman Character Stein

Munich Child, High-wheel Bicycle & Jester-handled Steins

Character, stoneware, high-wheel bicycle w/male rider figural pewter cover, spherical golf-ball style brown-glazed pottery body a replacement, pewter lid attachment & rear bicycle wheel repaired, .5 L (ILLUS. center with Munich Child & Jester-handled steins) **$690**

Character, stoneware, Man with Large Hat, top of hat hinged to form lid, repaired chips on the lid, 2 L, 13" h. (ILLUS. left with Man Sitting on Barrel stein) **$574**

Bowling Pin, King Ludwig & Snowman Character Steins

Character, pottery, Bowling pin, No. 1134, brown woodgrain finish w/the front molded in tan w/a child atop a large 9 among pins, inlaid lid, .5 L (ILLUS. right with King Ludwig & Snowman steins) **$197**

Large Dumler & Breiden Pottery Stein

Dumler & Breiden, pottery, the footed ovoid body molded w/a wide band decorated w/scenes from the 30 Years War, further molded shoulder & neck bands, highlighted in tan, dark green & brown, high domed pewter lid, 4 L (ILLUS.) **$242**

Man on Barrel & Man with Hat Steins

Character, pottery, Man sitting on Barrel, polychrome decoration, inlaid porcelain head lid, repair to top rim, inlay edge & handle, .5L (ILLUS. right with stoneware Man with Large Hat stein) **$483**

Fine Flower-decorated Faience Stein

Faience, white baluster-form body decorated w/a large blue rose on a leafy stem, pewter base ring & low domed cover, minor chipping on glazed handle & top rim, 7" h. (ILLUS., previous page) **$1,691**

Gerz Stein with Etched Family Scene

Gerz, No. 1326, pottery, etched colored scene of a German family in an interior, inlaid lid, 1 L (ILLUS.) **$362**

Three Steins by Girmscheid, Hauber & Reuther and Marzi & Remy

Girmscheid, No. 1262, stoneware, etched large color scene of Dwarfs drinking, inscribed base band, high domed pewter lid, artist-initialed, pewter lid strap repaired, 1 L (ILLUS.center with Hauber & Reuther and Marzi & Remy steins) **$201**

An Amber & a Green Glass Stein

Glass, amber blown cylindrical body enameled in color w/a scene of the Munich Child, domed pewter lid, .25 L (ILLUS. right with green blown glass stein) **$242**

Three Early Glass Steins

Glass, amber blown cylindrical body mounted w/a wide band of elaborate scroll-pierced pewter above the gadrooned pewter base & pedestal foot, hinged pewter-ringed lid mounted w/a carved horn figure of a stag, horn thumblift, .5 L (ILLUS. left with two other glass steins) **$386**

Glass, amber blown ovoid body enclosed by floral-cast pewter bands from the round pewter foot to the neck band, domed amber glass-inlaid lid w/dragon finisl, pewter handle, .5 L, 9" h. (ILLUS. left with two other glass steins) **$421**

Tall Amber Glass Stein with Barmaid

Glass, amber blown tall cylindrical body w/an applied ring near the base above a band of applied prunts, the front enameled in color w/a figure of a barmaid standing in front of a wide white banner, domed pewter lid w/pointed finial, 1 L (ILLUS.) **$254**

Glass, blown clear cylindrical body h.p. w/large pink roses & green leaves below crossed farm tools, pewter base ring &

domed lid, 1 L (ILLUS. center with two other glass steins) **$518**

Glass, green blown footed tall cylindrical body decorated in white enamel w/a Mary Gregory-style girl, matching glass-inlaid lid, .3 L (ILLUS. right with blown amber glass stein) **$127**

Fine Ruby-flashed & Engraved Stein

Glass, tall cylindrical blown body w/a flaring base, panel-cut & ruby-flashed & engraved around the sides w/an elaborate stag in forest scene, matching glass-inlaid lid w/dog running, ca. 1850, .5 L, 10 3/4" h. (ILLUS.) **$1,265**

Hauber & Reuther, No. 167, porcelain, etched color scene of a barmaid serving

beer, tapestry finish, domed metal lid, .5 L (ILLUS. center with two other Hauber & Reuther steins) **$182**

Three Hauber & Reuther Steins

Hauber & Reuther, No. 159, pottery, etched color scene of a German man seated drinking a stein of beer, tapestry finish, domed metal lid, .5 L (ILLUS. left with two other Hauber & Reuther steins) .. **$182**

Hauber & Reuther, No. 163, porcelain, etched color scene of a rotund man smoking & drinking a stein of beer, tapestry finish, domed metal lid, .5 L (ILLUS. right with two other Hauber & Reuther steins) **$197**

Hauber & Reuther, No. 431, pottery, etched color scene of festive dancing peasants w/large beer tuns, high domed peweter lid, 1L, hairline in rear body (ILLUS. right with Girmscheid & Marzi & Remy steins, previous page) **$362**

Marzi & Remy, No. 1518, pottery, etched w/a full-length color scene of a Germanic warrior & maiden leaving a castle, inlaid lid, 1L+ (ILLUS. right with a Girmscheid and Hauber & Reuther stein, above) **$472**

Mettlach, No. 1146, etched scene of students drinking, signed by C. Warth, inlaid lid, .5 L (ILLUS. second from right with five other character & etched Mettlach steins, bottom of page) **$397**

Six Mettlach Etched & Character Steins

Row of Five Mettlach Painted & PUG Steins

Mettlach, No. 1526, hand-painted scene of the courtyard at the Hofbrauhaus in Munich, elaborate design, high domed hinged pewter lid, 1 L (ILLUS. far left with four other Mettlach PUG steins, above) **$483**

Mettlach, No. 1909, PUG, brewery advertising w/a brewmaster at the left, advertising in black reads "Brauerei Joh Humbser Furth Bavaria imported Humbser Beer Fred'l Hollender & Company, N.Y. Sole Agents," simple domed pewter lid, discoloration on lid & near hinge & interior staining, .5 L (ILLUS. third from left with four other PUG & handpainted Mettlach steins, top of page) **$302**

Mettlach, No. 1932, etched scene of Cavaliers drinking, signed by C. Warth, inlaid lid, .5 L (ILLUS. third from right with five other character & etched Mettlach steins, bottom previous page) **$478**

Mettlach, No. 1932, etched scene of Cavaliers drinking, signed by C. Warth, inlaid lid, 1 L (ILLUS. third from left with five other character & etched Mettlach steins, bottom previous page) **$518**

Two Etched & a Cameo Mettlach Steins

Mettlach, No. 1986, etched scene of two ladies in fancy costume standing flanking a scrolling cartouche framing a panel w/"Prosit," high domed pewter lid, .5 L (ILLUS. left with an etched & cameo Mettlach stein) **$362**

Mettlach, No. 2018, Character-type, seated Pug dog, head forms the lid, inlaid lid re-

paired, .5 L (ILLUS. far right with five other etched Mettlach steins, top of page) **$417**

Fine 3L Etched No. 2095 Mettlach Stein

Mettlach, No. 2095, etched design of early Germans meeting Romans, rare version w/relief-molded flowers around the base band, inlaid hinged lid, 3 L (ILLUS.) **$2,875**

No. 2133 & 2134 Etched Mettlach Steins

Mettlach, No. 2133, etched scene of a Dwarf sitting on a branch, signed by H. Schlitt, inlaid lid & figural Dwarf thumblift, .5 L (ILLUS. left with etched Mettlach stein No. 2134, previous page) **$2,536**

Mettlach, No. 2134, etched scene of a Dwarf sitting in a bird nest, signed by H. Schlitt, inlaid lid & figural Dwarf thumblift, .3 L (ILLUS. right with etched Mettlach stein No. 2133, previous page) **$920**

Mettlach Steins No. 2324 & 2716

Mettlach, No. 2324, etched scene of a rugby match, domed pewter lid, hairline in rear of body, .5 L (ILLUS. left with Mettlach stein No. 2716) **$499**

Mettlach, No. 2652, Cameo-style, an arched central panel w/white relief figures from Gasthaus, dark blue background, Rodenstein, inlaid lid, .5 L (ILLUS. right with two etched Mettlach steins, top previous page) **$759**

Mettlach, No. 2716, etched w/a framed front tavern Gasthaus scene, signed by F. Quidenus, inlaid lid, .5 L (ILLUS. right with Mettlach stein No. 2324, above) **$592**

Rare Venus in Target Mettlach Stein

Mettlach, No. 2717, etched & glazed color scene w/a nude Venus standing in the

center of a white diamond-shaped target, perched in a leafy tree w/a continuous landscape below, inscribed upper bands, domed pewter inlaid lid, 1 L (ILLUS.)..... **$4,086**

Mettlach David & Goliath Stein

Mettlach, No. 2718, etched design of David & Goliath w/the giant wearing Medieval armor, domed pewter inlaid lid, 1 L (ILLUS.) **$2,875**

Fine Mettlach Knight Stein

Mettlach, No. 2765, etched full-length scene of a knight riding a white steed, inlaid pointed castle-form lid, signed by H. Schlitt, 1 L (ILLUS.)................................ **$2,990**

Mettlach, No. 2778, etched Carnival scene, signed by H. Schlitt, inlaid lid, .5 L (ILLUS. second from left with five other Mettlach etched & character steins, bottom of page 1058) **$2,053**

Mettlach, No. 2778, etched Carnival scene, signed by H. Schlitt, inlaid lid, 1 L (ILLUS.

Four Mettlach PUG & Etched Steins

far left with five other Mettlach etched & character steins, bottom of page 947) **$2,990**

Mettlach, No. 2800, etched Art Nouveau style design w/a large cluster of blue leafy hops against a tan & brick red ground, inlaid lid, staining on underside of lid inlay, .5 L (ILLUS. center with the Mettlach etched & cameo steins) **$252**

Mettlach, No. 3093, etched scene of a seated devil holding a large bottle, signed by H. Schlitt, inlaid lid, .5 L (ILLUS. far left with three other Mettlach PUG steins, top of page) **$2,318**

Mettlach, No. 3135, etched central design of a spread-winged American eagle framed by draped American flags, inlaid lid w/the U.S. Shield, .5 L (ILLUS. right with Mettlach St. Augustine stein) **$920**

Mettlach PUG Falstaff Stein

Mettlach, No. 1526-983, PUG (painted under glaze), color scene of Falstaff flanked by beer tuns, hinged domed pewter lid w/ball thumbrest, 3L (ILLUS.) **$604**

Mettlach, No. 1909-727, PUG, color scene of Dwarfs bowling, high domed pewter lid, signed by H. Schlitt, .5 L (ILLUS. second from right with four other PUG &

handpainted Mettlach steins, top of page) **$332**

Mettlach, No. 1909-727, PUG, scene of Dwarfs bowling, signed by H. Schlitt, domed pewter lid, .5 L (ILLUS. second from left with three other etched or PUG Mettlach steins, top of page) **$288**

Mettlach, No. 2140-952, PUG, scene of a man riding a standard safety bicycle & a boy playing w/geese & a locomotive, inlaid pewter lid, .5 L (ILLUS. far right with four other PUG & handpainted Mettlach steins, above) **$362**

Mettlach, No. 1526-1143, PUG, comical color scene of men in 18th attire drinking, domed pewter lid, signed by H. Schlitt, 1L (ILLUS. second from left with four other PUG & handpainted Mettlach steins) **$362**

Mettlach, No. 1909-1042, PUG, scene of a Victorian gentleman & lady standing on either side of a tall house key, signed by H. Schlitt, domed pewter lid, .5 L (ILLUS. far right with three other Mettlach PUG or etched steins) **$380**

Mettlach, No. 2140-1047, PUG, color scene of Dwarfs & mushrooms, domed pewter lid w/a dent, hairline in the base, .5 L (ILLUS. second from right with three other Mettlach PUG or etched steins) **$290**

Two Finely Painted Royal Vienna Steins

Porcelain, elaborate h.p. Classical scene of several women attending a central seated woman, gold rim & base bands, multicolored pattern & gold design around the rear of the body, inlaid lid w/another scene, Royal Vienna beehive mark, late 19th c., .5 L (ILLUS. right with other Royal Vienna porcelain stein & lids) **$3,019**

Porcelain, Jupitor & Calista h.p. Classical scene in a large oval reserve framed by ornate gilt leafy scrolls against a cobalt blue ground, inlaid porcelain lid w/another scene, Royal Vienna beehive mark, late 19th c., .5 L (ILLUS. left with other Royal Vienna stein & lids) **$2,530**

Two Molded Pottery German Steins

Pottery, Heidelberg color-printed central scene within a molded & enameled frame & border bands, tall domed pewter lid, music box base w/music box intact, 1L (ILLUS. left with pottery Diesinger stein)... **$217**

Large Pottery Stein with Dwarfs Scene

Pottery, PUG color scene of Dwarfss tapping a large beer barrel, domed pewter

lid, No. 1158, hairline in side & pewter repair, 3 L (ILLUS.)...................................... **$362**

Pottery, the tall ovoid body molded around the sides w/a continuous band of standing musicians, molded running goat & grass design around the wide neck w/a rim spout, highlighted overall in pale pink & black, high domed pewter lid, by Diesinger, No. 745, 2 L (ILLUS. right with Heidelberg scene pottery stein) **$389**

Three Regimental Steins with Figural Lid Finials

Regimental, porcelain, front scene of a steamer warship surrounded by a wreath, inscribed "S.M.S. Zahringen 1905-08," two side scenes & a roster list, high domed cover w/figure of a standing sailor & flag finial, Thuringen hinge attachment & eagle thumblift, .5 L, 12" h. (ILLUS. left with Regimental steins with cannon or two-soldier finials) **$1,840**

Three Regimental Steins with Varied Dates

Regimental, porcelain, large front design of a crest enclosing a large monogram & crown & "1790," flanked by long narrow roster scrolls, inscribed "2 Batt. Field Artillierie No 25 Darmstadt 1897-99," two side scenes, high domed pewter lid w/two soldier finial, lion thumblift, .5 L, 11" h. (ILLUS. left with Regimental steins dated 1908-09 and 1911-13) **$417**

Regimental, porcelain, wide colorful central band w/a military battle scene, four side scenes & roster list, inscribed "1 R. Batt. Kgl. Sachs. Field Artillery Rgt. Nr 12 Konigsbruck 1908-09," high domed pewter lid w/seated figure finial, Sachen thumblift, .5 L, 12 1/2" h. (ILLUS. center with Regimental steins dated 1897-99 & 1911-13, previous page) **$966**

Regimental, porcelain, wide colorful front scene of swags & flags flanked by military figures, four side scenes, inscribed "11 Komp. Garde Fusilier Regt. Berlin 1911-13," high domed pewter cover w/two soldiers shaking hands, eagle thumblift w/a visible Stanhope of a parade scene, brass guard star hanging from the eagle beak, .5 L, 11 3/4" h. (ILLUS. right with Regimental steins w/standing sailor and cannon finials, previous page) **$1,860**

Three Dome-lidded Regimental Steins

Regimental, porcelain, wide front color scene w/a red reserve w/a gold "18" flanked by standing military figures, four side scenes & roster list, inscribed "Kgl. Bayr 1 Infantry Regt. 8. Comp. Landau 1905-07," high domed pewter lid w/pointed finial, large figural thumblift shooting a rifle across the finial, w/a spring mechanism for shooting matching from rifle missing, lithophane bottom w/lines, .5 L, 10 1/2" h. (ILLUS. left with two other dome-lided Regimental steins) **$874**

Regimental, porcelain, wide front scene w/a shield & crossed flags flanked by standing soldiers, two side scenes, inscribed "Kgl. 16 Infantry Rgt. 4 Comp. Landschut 1902-04," domed pewter lid inlaid w/a pointed glass prism engraved w/a campfire scene, lion thumblift, .5 L, 9 1/2" h. (ILLUS. center with two other dome-lidded Regimental steins) **$529**

Regimental, pottery, a wide molded colorful front scene of a soldier standing behind a white panel w/"79," flanked by other standing figures, two side scenes & roster list, inscribed "3. Komp Infantry Reft. 3. Hannov. No 79 Hildesheim," high domed pewter lid w/seated soldier finial w/a glass Stanhope in a beer stein, .5 L, 13 1/4" h. (ILLUS. right with Regimental steins dated 1897-99 and 1908-09) **$483**

Regimental, pottery, relief-molded wide center band w/a colorful scene of a stand-

ing soldier behind crossed flags & a blue shield w/red numbers, two side scenes & roster list, inscribed "2 Reit. Battr. Field Artilllery 1 Rhein No 8 Saarbrucken 1904-07," domed pewter cover w/a figural finial of soldiers & a cannon, horse & rider thumblift, .5 L, 11" h. (ILLUS. center with Regimental steins with a standing sailor or two-soldier finial) **$845**

Rare Regimental with Large Scene

Regimental, stoneware, large color scene of a ship, soldier, cannon, flag & anchor, inscribed band reads "Seebataillon 1 Comp. Tsingtau - China 1907-10," high domed metal lid w/eagle thumblift, .5 L, 10 1/4" h. (ILLUS.) **$5,693**

Regimental, stoneware, wide front scene w/a winged shield enclosing a script "E" below a scene of a locomotive, several side scenes including early auto & locomotive, inscribed "Kgl. Bayn Eisenbahn Baon 3 Comp. Munchen 1905-07," high domed pewter lid, floral thumblift, .5 L, 10 1/4" h. (ILLUS. right with two other Regimental steins with domed lids) **$713**

Inverted Acorn-form Stoneware Stein

Stoneware, salt-glazed, footed inverted acorn-form body w/hinged pewter cover & thumbrest, swelled molded criss-cross band above the foot trimmed w/cobalt blue, wide center band molded & blue-trimmed on one side w/a scene of a man & woman at a fence, the other side w/a framed German verse, made by Whites Pottery, Utica, New York, ca. 1900, 7" h. (ILLUS., previous page) **$88**

Two Molded Stoneware Steins

Stoneware, tapering cylindrical form w/C-scroll handle & hinged domed pewter cover w/high thumbrest, Bristol glaze w/molded beaded bands around the bottom & a relief-molded "Prince of Pilsen" design of a dancing couple on one side & the framed verse "Here's to the Heart that beats for me" on the other, overall dark blue wash, excellent condition, 9 1/2" h. (ILLUS. left with other molded stoneware stein) **$176**

Stoneware, footed tapering cylindrical body w/hinged domed pewter cover w/thumbrest & C-scroll handle, Bristol glaze w/molded bands around the bottom & near the rim, relief-molded wide center design of a kitchen scene w/two hunters, a woman smoking a pipe & a reclining dog, framed German verse on the other side, highlighted w/dark blue wash, molded mark 38, excellent condition, 10" h. (ILLUS. right with other molded stoneware stein).. **$110**

SYROCOWOOD

The Syracuse Ornamental Company of Syracuse, New York ("Syroco") pioneered the concept of molded wood decorative pieces, producing near-perfect replicas of hand-carving. In the words of the company's 1942 catalog: "Syrocowood possesses the rich beauty of choice hand-carved wood designs combined with practical utility." Whether book ends or brush holders, pen sets or picture frames, Syroco's household novelty items possess a charm all their own.

Syrocowood was a product born of necessity. In 1890 Adolph Holstein found his skills as an accomplished carved in great demand. The popu-

larity of his ornately carved woodwork lead Holstein to hire additional master carvers and to found a new firm - Syroco. However, hand-carving was time consuming and only a limited number of orders could be accepted. Holstein's solution: create a master carving and a casting mold, then cast replicas of the master. Since each design required only one master carving both production and affordability were increased.

Although replicating the texture of carved wood, "Syrocowood" was actually composed of a compressed mixture of wood flour, waxes and resins. Sanding removed mold lines and each piece then received a multi-color decoration or a natural wood stain.

During Syrococ's early years the demand was primarily for decorative furniture trim, with thousands of design options shown in the company catalogs. Syroco trim adorned everything from caskets to armchairs and often took the place of hand-carved moldings in home interiors.

Due to declining interest in this type of ormamentation, Syroco was forced to explore new product avenues. By the late 1920s the company was capitalizing on the radio age, becoming a primary supplier of radio speaker grilles, tuner knobs and cabinet trim. A second marketing push lead to the products most sought after by today's collectors - wood-like novelty items that combined whimsical or heartwarming themes. Following its debut in the early 1930s, the Syroco novelty line soon included a wide range of pieces including ashtrays, bar trays, book ends, bottle openers, brush holders, clocks, coasters, coin trays, corkscrews, desk calendars, doorstops, dresser boxes, humidors, napkin rings, paperweights, pen sets, picture frames, pipe racks, plaques, statuettes, thermometers and tie racks.

Thanks to Syroco's mass productions, consumers in the 1930s and '402 found themselvess able to accessorize lavishly, yet affordably. In the words of Alexander E. Holstein, Jr., grandson of the company founder, Syroco provided "good product at a good price."

The success of Syroco soon gave rise to a host of imitators, the main competitors being: Burwood Products Co. ("Karv-Kraft") of Michigan; the Canadian firm, Durwood; Multi-Products ("Decor-A-Wood"), that specialized in licensed comic strip and Disney characters; Ornamental Arts & Crafts Co. ("Orn-A-Craft"). There was even a Syroco associate company, "Ornawood." The Syroco reputation, however, was pervasive and the term "syrocowood" became a generic, if inaccurate, term for every type of molded wood decorative object.

By the 1950s, Syrcoco had moved on to more profitable wall accessories such as sconces, shelves, plaques and mirrors often trimmed in gold or bright colors. One of the company's best sellers of that time was the multi-rayed "Sunburst Clock." The 1950s also saw a shift from the use of wood composite to an all-polymre blend. This meant pieces could be lighter, larger and sturdier. A primary example of this development is the Syr-

oco molded lawn chair, found today in nearly every chain store.

Syroco appeals to collectors on several levels. For home decorators, the coloring of Syroco items blends well with any interior while the wood tones add a dimension of luxury. For those with more than one collecting interest, Syroco pieces can be great crossover collectibles. Dog lovers like their dog figures while corkscrew collectors have a wide range of designs to choose from. For the cost-conscious, most Syrcoco products are still affordable with many pieces currently available in the $25-50 range. As the company's advertisements once stated: Syroco decorative items are "ideal for elegant living and gracious giving."

Advisor for this category, Donald-Brian Johnson, is an author and lecturer specializing in Mid-Twentieth design. Photos are by Ray Hanson.

Ashtray, "Horse Head," 8" d...................... **$25-45**

Syrocowood "Deer" Book End

Book end, "Deer," molded w/a doe & fawn backed by trees, 6 1/2" h. (ILLUS.) **$25-45**

Syrcocowood "Sailfish" Book End

Book end, "Sailfish," painted fish against woodtone water, 6 1/4" h. (ILLUS.) **$25-45**
Bottle opener, "David Copperfield" figural head top, 6 1/2" h. **$45-65**
Brush holder, "Bowling," marked w/a 'Swank' label, 8 1/2" h. **$15-25**
Brush holder, "Bulldog & Scottie," 7" h. **$25-45**
Brush holder, "PanAm Clipper," 4 3/4 x 7" **$25-45**

"Sailor" Painted Brush Holder

Brush holder, "Sailor," painted half-length figure of a sailor at the helm, the cylindrical container behind him, 6 1/4" h. (ILLUS.) **$25-45**
Brush holder, "Schooner," 4 x 5" **$25-45**
Brush holder, "Scottie & Two Westies," 5 1/2 x 7 1/2" **$45-65**
Brush holder, "Standing Airedale," 6" h. **$25-45**

"Standing Polar Bear" Brush Holder

Brush holder, "Standing Polar Bear," white bear in front of brown rail fence, 7" h. (ILLUS.) **$25-45**

Cigarette box, "Fruits & Vegetables,"
4 x 5 1/2" **$15-25**

Syroco Windmill Case with Lux Clock

Clock, "Windmill," model of a windmill w/a
moving blade atop a grassy mound, a
pointed arch front enclosing the matching
clock produced by Lux, 11" h. (ILLUS.)
.... **$150-175**
Coin tray, "Cowboy Hat," 3 x 4" **$10-15**
Corkscrew, "Monk," figural monk head top,
8" h. **$350-500**
Corkscrew, "Old Codger," figural old man
head top, 8" h. **$100-150**
Corkscrew, "Waiter," figural waiter head
top, 8" h. **$75-125**

Syrocowood "Penguin" Doorstop

Doorstop, "Penguin," painted black &
white on a narrow rectangular base,
8" h. (ILLUS.) **$85-105**

"Bear & Ball" Figural Paperweight

Paperweight, "Bear & Ball," woodtone
bear on its back holding a ball,
3 x 3 1/2" (ILLUS.) **$25-35**

Syrocowood "Hobo" Pen Set

Pen set, "Hobo," painted figure of a hobo
standing on a woodtone base w/a
stepped platform w/pen holder, 5 3/4" h.
(ILLUS.) **$25-35**
Plaque, "Four Seasons," 9 x 36" **$125-165**

"Peasant Woman" Statuette

Statuette, "Peasant Woman," painted
standing elderly woman, 7" h. (ILLUS.).. **$35-45**

Thermometer, "New York Wold's Fair," 1939-40, 5 1/2" h.................................. **$25-45**

"Top Hat" Syrocowood Tie Rack

Tie rack, "Top Hat," head of a sauve gentleman w/a long cigarette holder in his mouth, projecting wire racks, 7 x 10 1/2" (ILLUS.).. **$55-75**

TEXTILES

Coverlets

Jacquard, two-piece Biederwand-type, floral & geometric medallions in the center w/a double border of vining flowers & stars, corner block signed "Made by Jacob Long, Knox County, Ohio 1843," navy blue, red, sage green & natural, minor stains, 76 x 84" (ILLUS. of part, bottom right with Agriculture & Manufactures, leopard border & Jacob Impson coverlets)... **$1,208**

Grouping of Early Jacquard Coverlets

Jacquard, two-piece, double woven, an overall foliage center ground w/an unusual border composed of melons & flowering vines, corner blocks signed "DL West Carlisle, Ohio," navy blue & natural, ca. 1850, one in two pieces w/light stains, other w/small seam split, 80 x 86" & 82 x 88", pr. (ILLUS. of part of one in upper left with Samuel Meily, Knox County & dated 1849 coverlets).... **$1,035**

Jacquard, two-piece, double woven, center w/floral medallions, grapevine borders, corner blocks signed "Jacob Impson 1834" & "Ladys Fancy - Cortland Village," red & natural, New York, ca. 1832-45, some staining, minor wear on bound edges, 78 x 90" (ILLUS. of part, bottom left with Agriculture & Manufactures, leopard border & Jacob Long coverlets)............... **$805**

Jacquard, two-piece, double woven, center w/sunburst medallions w/tulip centers, unusual border composed of leopards & monkeys & small floral corner blocks, navy blue, maroon, tomato red & natural, possibly New York or Ohio, ca. 1830-40, damage, fring loss, two halves separated, 70 x 72" (ILLUS. of part, top right with Agriculture & Manufactures, Jacob Impson & Jacob Long coverlets)................... **$719**

Jacquard, two-piece, double woven, rose medallions in center, two borders, one w/pairs of small facing American eagles & pairs of American flags, two w/large spread-winged American eagles & domed buildings w/small monkeys along the very edge, corner block signed "Woven in Knox County, Ohio by W.K.," navy blue & natural, mid-19th c., damage, mostly along edges, some stains, 76 x 82" (ILLUS. of part, bottom left with D.L. West, Samuel Meily & dated 1849 coverlets) **$1,150**

Jacquard, two-piece Biederwand-type, the center w/rose & geometric medallions, double borders of vining flowers & stars, corner blocks signed "Samuel Meily, Mansfield, Richland, Ohio 1842," navy blue, tomato red, dark green & natural, some border & fringe loss, light stains, one end bound-over, 66 x 78" (ILLUS. of part, top right with D.L. West, Knox County & dated 1849 coverlets) **$978**

Jacquard, two-piece, double woven, center w/large floral & geometric medallions, grapevine borders w/eagles in corners, small drums & the date "1849" are in the design, possibly Indiana, navy blue, purple, salmon & natural, minor stains, some fringe loss, 72 x 82" (ILLUS. of part, bottom right with D. L. West, Samuel Meily & Knox Country coverlets).......................... **$920**

Blue & White Double-Woven Coverlet

Jacquard, double woven, two-piece, composed of rows of large oval flower & leaf medallions alternating w/rows of diamond-shaped medallions, double fern leaf border band, a thin band between the center & border woven w/the repeating word "Liberty," corner blocks signed "Lucy W. Walker, Asbury, 1848 - C. Van Nortwick Fancy Weaver," blue & white, New Jersey, 75 x 85" (ILLUS., previous page) **$500**

Four Inscribed & Dated Jacquard Coverlets

Jacquard, two-piece, double woven, floral medallions in the center, borders of buildings flanked by Masonic columns, monkeys & human figures, corner blocks marked "Agriculture & Manufactures are the Foundations of our Independence," attributed to Duchess County, New York, navy blue & natural, first half 19th c., bound edges, 80 x 85" (ILLUS. of part, top left with leopard border, Jacob Impson and Jacob Long coverlets) **$1,035**

Red & Natural Summer/Winter Coverlet

Jacquard, summer/winter, two-piece, red & natural, a central square w/a large star & surrounding fruit, wide outside border w/male & female deer in corners, turkeys & large domed state capitol building, mid-19th c., 84 x 90" **$249**

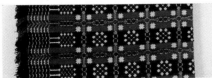

Red, White & Blue Overshot Coverlet

Overshot, two-piece, single weave, brick red, navy blue, medium blue, green & natural in a stripped & snowflake design w/a pine tree border, crisp, small areas of moth damage, mid-19th c., 74 x 93" (ILLUS. of part) **$288**

Linens & Needlework

Victorian Needlework Bell Pull

Bell pull, tapestry needlework w/colorful flowers on a tan ground, white metal end fittings, 19th c., 59" l. (ILLUS.) **$104**

Fine Chinese Silk Embroidery

Embroidery, silk, the dark blue silk ground embroidered w/a central medallion of peaches surrounded by a field of flowering lotus, in a giltwood frame, China, 19th c., 40 x 41" (ILLUS.) **$518**

Early Printed Linen & Toile Fabric

Printed fabric, linen & cotton toile w/red-printed designs on natural white including George Washington guiding a leopard-drawn chariot as well as Benjamin Franklin, Goddess of Liberty & Revolutionary soldiers, quilted, edge binding old but not original, stain, an attached typewritten paper w/hisotry, late 18th - early 19th c., 42 x 66" (ILLUS. of part).............. **$316**

Needlework Pictures

English Flags & Ship Woolwork Picture

Flags & ship, woolwork, a central circle enclossing a ship under full sail, framed by eight different flags of various countries including the United States & Britain, a crown device & red leaves on black across the top, bird's-eye maple frame, England, 19th c., 23 x 25" (ILLUS.)........ **$2,415**

Needlework Tea House Picture

Landscape, "Maggie's Tea House, Carmel, Maine," rectangular punch work paper background threaded through w/colored yarns & depicting a large three-story Colonial house w/four attached building, an undulating green road below them & above a colorful bottom border band w/a star & diamond motif, in a deep Victorian walnut shadowbox frame w/a gold liner, building became the Carmel House, mid- to late 19th c., some areas missing yarn, some water stain to backing, 15 1/2 x 21 1/4" (ILLUS.).......................... **$345**

Early Dated American Landscape Scene

Landscape with figures, a landscape w/a seated woman in late 18th c. attire under a leafy arbor to the left, reaching out to a young boy walking toward her, in silk thread in shades of tan, cream & blue on a watercolor sky background, signed "Wrought by Adaline Bradford - Aged 17 Years - Charlestown, Massachusetts School - 1813," in an old gilt-plaster frame, 22 1/4 x 24" (ILLUS.) **$6,573**

Romantic Landscape Scene with Swordsman & Woman

Landscape with figures, a romantic scene of a swordsman standing on a lakeshore gesturing to a young woman standing in a shallow boat, rocks & trees in the background, worked in silk & wool thead in shades of soft greens & earthtones, painted faces & hands, stitches on a silk & linen ground, embroidered signature "Helen Cuthbert 1816," restorations, some wear & stains, old gilt plaster frame, possibly English, 22 1/4 x 28" (ILLUS.) **$2,070**

Early Needlework Mourning Picture

Mourning picture, an exterior scene of a lady leaning against an urn-topped tomb & pointing heavenward, a weeping willow behind her, worked in silk in shades of cream, green & gold, watercolored face & hands & a watercolor background w/a church & houses in the distance, inscriptions on tomb dated 1805, 1806 & 1825, signed "Wrought by Mary Mirick - AE 14" in gold on a back reverse-painted bottom band, imperfections, in a gilt plaster frame, early 19th c., 17 x 19 1/2" (ILLUS.) **$4,994**

Needlework Portrait of Seated Lady

Portrait of a lady, seated lady in Colonial attire working outside w/a spinning wheel & a small dog reclining at her side, delicate tones of grey, white & tan against a watercolored landscape background, mounted under an black reverse-painted mat w/an oval opening trimmed in gold & accented w/four gold stars, American-made, early 19th c., 7 1/2 x 9 1/2" (ILLUS.) **$518**

Quilts

Rare Large Colorful Album Quilt

Album quilt, appliquéd top w/16 blocks in shades of orange, yellow, red & green, each block w/a different design including florals, compass wheels, a cornucopia, palm trees & a bird, a green swag & red bud border band, 19th c., 87" sq. (ILLUS.) **$2,300**

Nice Early Appliqued Flowerpots Quilt

Appliqued Flowerpots patt., a large red center pot issuing five red tulip-like blossoms on faded green leafy stems, four smaller pots w/three blossoms frame the center, a stepped cross-form pale green outer border trimmed w/red flowerheads & accented w/small pots w/three blossoms at each corner, finely quilted white background w/pinwheel flowers, checkerboard & other designs, narrow red bound edge, mid-19th c., 70 x 77" (ILLUS.) **$450**

Colorful French Rose Appliqued Quilt

Appliqued French Rose patt., composed of three rows of four four-petal blossoms in red-bordered pink & pale green leaves & red buds, scalloped red border band, hand-stitched & quilted, light discoloration & border fraying, late 19th - early 20th c., 71 x 85" (ILLUS.) **$230**

Appliqued Gladiolas patt., the white quilted ground centered by a large bouquet of colorful stylized gladiolas in shades of deep red, pink, lavender, gold & yellow on leafy pale green stems, a smaller bouquet in each corner, scalloped border, some light stains, probably 20th c., 74 x 87" (ILLUS., top next column) **$300**

Pretty Appliqued Gladiolas Quilt

Charming Heart Ring Appliqued Quilt

Appliqued Heart Ring patt., the center composed of rows of 12 rings composed of four red hearts joined by green & alternating w/small green diamonds, a scalloped green band outer border decorated w/red hearts alternating w/green diamonds, wide green outer border, some minor stains, late 19th or early 20th c., 66 x 83" (ILLUS.) **$240**

Appliqued Oak Leaf Variation Quilt

Appliqued Oak Leaf Variation patt., composed of nine leaf cluster blocks in green, dark red & gold against a white quilted ground, narrow dark red & grey border

bands, Pennsylvania, early 20th c., 82"
sq. (ILLUS.) **$201**

Early Appliqued Roses Quilt

Appliqued Roses patt., a design composed of 25 large red roses blossoms
framed by green leaves & buds arranged
in rows on the white quilted ground, half-
roses along the inner edge of the flowering vine border, all hand-stitched, some
worn spots & losses, mid-19th c. (ILLUS.)
.... **$575**

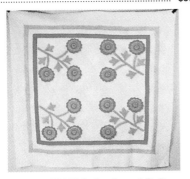

Nice Old Ohio Appliqued Quilt

Appliqued Whig Rose Variation patt.,
each corner w/a large green stem of
three large rounded blossoms in red &
green, on a white quilted ground, dark
red & pale green border bands, very
small stitches, Ohio, ca. 1860-80, 73" sq.
(ILLUS.).. **$403**

Pieced Basket patt., friendship-type, an
overall design w/twelve rows of colorful
patchwork baskets in multiple colors,
each basket w/a penned name, white
quilted background & a printed fabric
back, half-baskets around the edges,
some w/partial names, stained, some
fraying to edge, 74 1/2 x 83" (ILLUS., top
next column)... **$374**

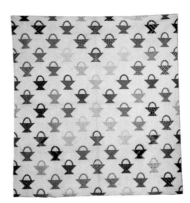

Colorful Basket Pattern Pieced Quilt

Red & White Pieced Box Pattern Quilt

Pieced Box patt., composed of groups of
red & white & red patches on a white
ground, red gingham border band,
67 x 72" (ILLUS.)...................................... **$207**

Amish Burnham Square Pattern Quilt

Pieced Burnham Square patt., composed
of dark blue, red & black patches, Amish-
made, Indiana origin, ca. 1920-30,
67 x 79" (ILLUS.)...................................... **$403**

Old Pieced Courthouse Steps Quilt

Pieced Courthouse Steps patt., composed of blocks in deep shades of red, blue, white, green, tan, brown & magenta, brown border w/machine quilting, Pennsylvania, ca. 1900, 76 1/2 x 79" (ILLUS.) **$460**

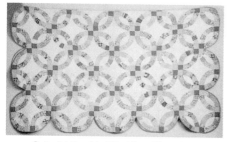

Colorful Double Wedding Ring Quilt

Pieced Double Wedding Band patt., interlocking overall rings w/each composed of small multicolored patches on a white ground, scalloped edges, 77 x 90" (ILLUS.) **$518**

Pieced Goose in the Pond Quilt

Pieced Goose in the Pond patt., composed of red, white & blue patches w/red banding & blue & white corner blocks, hand-sewn wavy line quilting, machine-sewn binding, 60 x 66" (ILLUS.) **$518**

Mennonite Lone Star Pattern Quilt

Pieced Lone Star patt., Mennonite, the large central star composed of diamond-shaped patches in shades of green, red, tan, white & yellow against a dark blue background w/a wide red border band, a blue-bordered green backing, Pennsylvania, ca 1920, 86" sq. (ILLUS.) **$240**

Streak of Lightning Pennsylvania Quilt

Pieced Streak of Lightning patt., burgundy border band w/central area of multi-colored prints & plain patches, paisley-type backing material, Pennsylvania, ca. 1900, 73 x 81 1/2" (ILLUS.)...................... **$403**

Pieced Blue & White Swastika Quilt

Pieced Swastika (Good Luck Symbol) patt., composed of blue & white patches, hand-sewn quilted ground, minor stains, 56 x 69" (ILLUS., previous page) **$230**

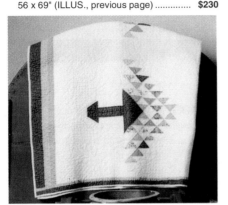

Pieced Tree Pattern Quilt

Pieced Tree patt., composed of blocks of stylized trees w/multicolored leaves & a dark brown trunk, brown & tan borders, hand-sewn good feather quilting, pencil lines intact, light stain, 66 x 78" (ILLUS.)... **$403**

Mennonite Trip Around the World Quilt

Pieced Trip Around the World patt., two-sided, the front composed of deep red & white patches, the back in pink & green, Memmonite, Pennsylvania, ca. 1900, 78 1/2" sq. (ILLUS.)................................... **$443**

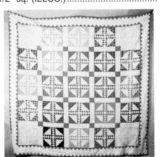

Pieced Wild Goose Chase Quilt

Pieced Wild Goose Chase patt., composed of blocks w/fabrics in soft pink, brown, blue, red & black, double blue sawtooth bands, New York State, ca. 1870-80, 102 x 104" (ILLUS.) **$316**

Samplers

Fine Signed Alphabet Sampler

Alphabets & decorative bands, rows of alphabets in various scripts each separated by a different stitched band, signed at the bottom "Bridget M. J. McCann - St. Peters School - Wilmington April 27, 1833," all within a wide undulating flower vine border, in a modern beveled mahogany frame, 15 x 16 1/4" (ILLUS.)............ **$5,060**

Alphabets & floral bands, linen ground sewn w/band of stylized flowers at the top & bottom, the center section composed of bands of alphabets in various sizes, signed "Elizabeth Gorham AE 12 March 1758," toning, fading, framed, 8 x 16 1/4" (ILLUS. right with Mary Southwick sampler) **$1,058**

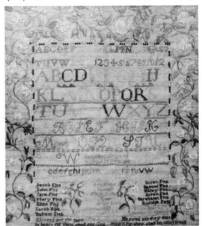

Sampler with Family Register

Alphabets, numerals & family register, worked in colorful silk threads on a loosely woven linen ground, a large central rectangular panel w/rows of alphabets &

numerals above two small lists of family names at the bottom, all enclosed on three sides w/a wide border of blue, green & white flowering leafy vines, signed Ann Fitz's Sampler Made in the year of our Lord 1828," Pennsylvania, modern frame, 21 1/2 x 24" (ILLUS.) **$3,105**

fence by a fir tree, urns of flowers & a flying angel above the house, a continuous red serpentine border band, signed "Mary Ann Otty Aged 11 y - MA Otty 1824," minor wear & stitch loss, framed, 13 1/4 x 16" (ILLUS.)................................. **$978**

Sampler with Large Landscape Scene

Alphabets, numerals & landscape, worked in silk threads in shades of pink, green, red, ivory & tan on a linen ground, upper alphabet rows above numerals & the inscription, the lower half w/a landscape w/a shepheress, dogs & her sheep by a two-story brick house w/a picket

1822 Sampler with Alphabets & Numerals

Alphabets, numerals & pious verse, two zig-zag flower vine bands at top separating the letters about bands of numerals & smaller letters all above a large pious verse at the bottom, all within a zig-zag border band, dated October 1822 & signed "Age 9 years - Jane George," in beveled mahogany veneer frame, some toning, 12" sq. (ILLUS.)............................ **$920**

Two Early Needlework Samplers

Alphabets, pious verse & floral basket, graduated rows of alphabets above panels w/the pious verse all above a large basket overflowing w/vining flowers at the bottom w/the vines encircling the central panel, dark linen background, signed "Mary N Southwick her Sampler wrought in the ninth year of her age august 22 1819," repair, few small losses, fading, framed, 14 3/4 x 17 1/2" (ILLUS. left with Elizabeth Gorham sampler) **$3,525**

Unusual Scenic Needlework Sampler

Flowers, mansion, figures & sheep, worked in silk & wool threads on a linen ground in shades of red, green, blue, yellow, white & black, depicting a large central brick mansion below large floral vases below angels w/trumpets, the mansion above a triangular lawn w/sheep flanked by a shepherd & shepherdess, inscribed at the bottom "Mery Winterbottom Work Finished May - 1842," meandering vine floral border, probably Providence, Rhode Island, 14 1/4 x 16" (ILLUS.) **$2,629**

Sampler with Verse & Landscape

Pious verse, landscape & floral clusters, worked in silk thread in gold, brown, red, blues & greens on homespun linen, the long pious verse in small letters above the signature over a landscape w/a hourse flanked by trees & a large bird on a branch, large clusters of leafy florals around the verse, a vining floral band border, signed "Sarah Bullock her work Aged 9 yrs.," stains, areas of damage,

old frame w/repaired corners, 17 1/4 x 20 1/4" h. (ILLUS.).................... **$1,495**

Tapestries

Aubusson Tapestry with Hunter Scene

Aubusson, a large central woodland scene w/a hunter in Renaissance attire w/his hunting dogs, all within a wide border of ornate flower & fruit clusters w/square pedestals & putti at the lower corners, France, probably 18th c., 5' 7" x 7' (ILLUS.).......... **$2,990**

Large Aubusson-style Woodland Landscape Tapestry

Aubusson-style, verdure-style w/a large wooded landscape w/a sherpherd & sheep beside a lake on the left, a narrow flower & leaf border band, France, late 19th c., 74 3/4 x 99 3/4" (ILLUS.)......... **$11,353**

Beauvais, from the Pastorale a Palmiers series, a scene at the bottom of a couple in 18th c. attire dancing around a maypole surrounded by courtly figures & flanked by an arcade of palm trees hung w/ribbon-tied garlands on a deep rose

18th Century French Beauvais Tapestry

ground, formerly framed, Louis XVI period, France, ca. 1775, 75 1/4 x 96 1/2"
(ILLUS.).. **$11,950**

Verdure Tapestry with Garden Landscape

Verdure-style, a large central garden landscape w/a large palace in the distance,
framed w/a bottom balustrade w/tall side
columns joined across the top w/fruiting
swags, a large bird & musical instruments in front of the balustrade, a
wrapped ribbon & flower outer border,
Europe, probably 18th c., 6' 5" x 7' 8"
(ILLUS.) **$3,680**

TOBACCIANA

*Although the smoking of cigarettes, cigars &
pipes is controversial today, the artifacts of smoking related items - pipes, cigar & tobacco humidors, and cigar & cigarette lighters - and, of
course, the huge range of advertising materials
are much sought after. Unusual examples, especially fine Victorian pieces, can bring high prices.
Here we list a cross section of Tobacciana pieces.*

*Also see: CANS & CONTAINERS and Antique
Trader Advertising Price Guide.*

Ashtrays

Early Oscar Bach Bronze Smoking Stand

Bronze, stand-type, a round openwork saucer foot cast w/grapes, leaves & vines
centered by the base of the standard
flanked by for small stylized dolphins, the
tall slender standard w/central rings & a
block supporting the rounded ashtray w/a
high arched handle from side to side &
fitted w/two rim cigar holders supported
by small stylized horses, designed by Oscar Bach w/his applied tag under the
base, ashtray insert missing, early 20th
c., overall 36" h. (ILLUS.) **$288**

Depression Era Glass Rowboat Ashtray

Glass, model of a clear glass rowboat w/ribbing in the bottom, indentations a the side rims for cigarettes, 1930s (ILLUS., previous page) **$6**

Cigar & Cigarette Cases & Holders

Fine Art Deco Cigarette Case

Cigarette case, Art Deco style, shallow rectangular shape w/rounded corners, in 18k bi-color gold w/enameled reserves depicting abstract black & red flowering branches on a green ground edged by engraved florettes, cabochon emerald thumbpiece, engine-turned sides, ca. 1930s (ILLUS.) **$1,528**

World War II Engineers Corps Lighter

Cigarette case, World War II Unit souvenir-type, silvered metal case embossed w/the insignia of the U.S. Army Engineers Corps & a map of Europe w/various German cities listed, ca. 1945, 3 1/2 x 4 1/2" (ILLUS.)............................. **$125**

Lighters

Cigarette lighter, advertising piece for Borden, decorated w/a picture of Elsie the Cow in a metal frame, 1958 .... **$175**

Cigarette lighter, advertising-type, "Goodyear Tires," engraved on the side w/the Goodyear blimp flying through clouds, also marked "Goodyear Aircraft," 1958 ..... **$550**

Cigarette lighter, Dunhill, Art Deco style table model centered by a clock dial, 1930s **$450**

Pyramidal Crystal Cigarette Lighter

Cigarette lighter, pyramidal shape in crystal glass, top pulls off to reveal a small lighter, late 1940s - early 1950s, 4 1/4" h. (ILLUS.).. **$45**

Ronson "Queen Anne" Table Lighter

Cigarette lighter, Ronson "Queen Anne" model table lighter, silver plate, 1950s, 3 1/2" l., 2 1/4" h. (ILLUS.) **$150**

Art Deco Ronson "Touch-Tip" Lighter

Cigarette lighter, Ronson "Touch-Tip" table lighter, Art Deco style, black lighter on a long octagonal chrome base, made for

Ronson by Art Metal Works, Newark, New Jersey, 1930s, 2 1/2 x 3 1/4", 4" h. (ILLUS.).. **$350**

Cigarette lighter, Ronson, "Touch-Tip" type, figural, black bartender behind a stylized bar-form case w/a brown wood-grained design & chrome trim, ca. 1936, 6" l., 7" h. **$700-1,200**

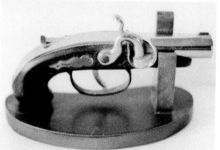

Figural Flintlock Pistol Cigarette Lighter

Cigarette lighter, table model, figural, model of a flintlock pistol in Chromium & black plastic on an oval base, marked "Japan," 1960s, 5 3/4" l., 3" h. (ILLUS.)..................... **$25**

Cigarette lighter, Zippo, commemorative, "Apollo II Crew - Moon Landing - July 20 1969" below engraved bust portraits of Collins, Armstrong & Aldrin, the reverse w/a scene of the ship on the moon, 1969 .... **$125**

Cigarette lighter, Zippo, commemorative, Elvis Presley color bust portrait on one side below his facsimile signature, the reverse w/another facsimile signature above an engraved ring inscribed "50 Years with - Elvis" around a stylized portrait of Elvis, 1987..................... **$100**

Cigarette lighter, Zippo, decorated w/Coca-Cola advertising, 1954 .... **$560**

Cigarette lighter, Zippo gift box, given to U.S. Tyre Service employees to mark 30 years of service, 1957, the set **$750**

Cigarette lighter, Zippo, sterling silver case w/a bamboo design, designed by Tiffany & Company, New York, very limited production, 1960...................................... **$4,000**

Cigarette lighter, Zippo, "The Reveler," more commonly called 'The Drunk,' shows a drunken man leaning against a street lamp, very rare, 1938 .... **$5,700**

Cigarette lighter fluid cans, metal, depending on the brand & image on the can, dozens of various designs, 1930s-1940s, each .... **$5 - 200**

Cigarette lighter & holder, advertising-type, "Hennessy Liquors," in the shape of a Hennessy bottle, top pulls up to reveal lighter & several cigarette holders, 1950s... **$250**

Miscellaneous

Many hundreds of items fall into the category of miscellaneous "Tobacciana." Prices are especially going up for cigarette cards, cigarette packs, cigarette dispensers, cigarette advertising, cigar boxes, & tobacco tags.

Unusual Horse Hoof Cigar Stand

Cigar stand, composed of a real horse hoof w/iron shoe fitted on the front w/a silvered crest, the top w/a silvered flat cap centered w/a metal upright rack w/a fluted base supporting three curved rods topped by a filigree disk framed by ring-form supports, holds a dozen cigars, probably England, 19th c., 6 1/2" h. (ILLUS.) **$316**

Arts & Crafts Style Humidor

Humidor, cov., Arts & Crafts style, brass & leaded glass, a round brass foot supporting the paneled sides composed of a geometric design in green & caramel slag glass centered by a ruby glass jewel, brass rim & low domed cover w/knob finial, ca. 1910, small dents in the cover, rusted bottom, 8 1/4" h. (ILLUS.) **$58**

Humidor, figural, carved wood model of a standing bear w/his paws raised above his head, shoulder straps support a basket at his waist holding a brass ash holder & match safe, the head hinged for the compartment, inset glass eyes, fine detail, Swiss, ca. 1890, 14 1/4" h. (ILLUS., next page) **$3,442**

Rare Carved Wood Bear Humidor

Agate & Silver European Snuff Box

Snuff box, agate & silver, the body composed of amber-colored polished agate panel sides in a hinged silver frame set w/marcasites, the overall body chased w/a checkered design, unknown maker's initials, British import marks, Europe, 19th c., 3" l. (ILLUS.) **$259**

Cast Metal Pipe Rack with Indian Chief Design

Pipe rack, cast bronzed metal, a squared upright top plate cast w/the bust profile of a Native American Chief above a long bar w/projecting cut-outs to support pipes, early 20th c., 12" l. (ILLUS.) **$125**

Unusual Iron Advertising Tobacco Cutter

Tobacco cutter, advertising-type, "Rocky Ford" brand, cast iron squared platform design w/the hinged top enclosed a color lithograph w/a scene of a crouching Native American, the flanged edges embossed "High - Grade - Havanna - Cigars," late 19th - early 20th c., overall wear, 6 1/2 x 8", 5" h. (ILLUS.) **$1,093**

Carved Wood Figural Smoking Stand

Smoking stand, carved wood, a paneled domed base carved w/pointed leaves supporting a ball & the tall draped classical figure w/hands above head supporting a round dished & leaf-carved top receptacle, late 19th c., 28 1/2" h. (ILLUS.) **$196**

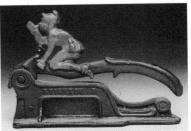

Figural Commercial Elf Tobacco Cutter

Tobacco cutter, cast iron, counter-type, "Brighton" cast into side of base, top of handle cast w/a red elf thumbing his nose, late 19th - early 20th c. (ILLUS., previous page) **$575**

Unusual Advertising Tobacco Cutter-Lamp

Tobacco cutter - lamp, advertising-type, "Cubanola" brand, cast iron & brass, an oval metal platform cutter w/gold paint, the angled top embossed "Hand Made Cubanola 5¢ Cigar" around a small center cutting hole w/a lever handle to the side, connected to a pedestal-base bulbos embossed brass kerosene font w/a lighter mechanism fitted w/a green glass chimney, late 19th - early 20th c., 5 x 8", 10" h. (ILLUS.) **$1,150**

TOY BOOKLETS & CATALOGS

Some of the best documentation of toy brands and products can be gathered from booklets that came packed with the toy or in vintage company catalogs. Results of recent on-line auctions indicate that this is a popular collecting field. Some pieces are quite affordable while others can reach very high prices.

Original Early Crandall's Advertisement

Advertisement, "Crandall's Blocks, Toys & Games for Children," full-page printed in black & white showing various toys, 1879-80 original (ILLUS.) **$35**

1918 Raleigh Dolls Advertisement

Advertisement, "Raleigh Dolls," full-page black & white ad showing various dolls, 1918 (ILLUS.) **$35**

1940s Built-Rite Toys Flyer

Advertisement, "You can have fun by the hour with these Built-Rite Toys," large fold-out flyer w/large black & white photos, 1940s (ILLUS.) **$15**

Booklet, a pattern booklet for the Chatty Cathy doll family, 1960s **$56**

Booklet, "Barbie #2," 1959 .... **$22**

Booklet, "Barbie #3," 1959-60 .... **$19**

Booklet, "Barbie #5," 1960s, in original cellophane wrap **$114**

Booklet, Betsy McCall dolls by American Character, 1958 .... **$16**

Booklet, Bild Lili (inspiration for Barbie dolls) fashions, 1950s **$60**

Booklet, "Bill Baird Puppet Marionettes," 1951 .... **$26**

Booklet, Daisy BB Gun Texas Ranger commemorative model, 1973 .... **$18**

Booklet, Dy-Dee Baby instruction booklet, 1938 .... **$22**

Booklet, Francie dolls, from the Barbie family, ca. 1970s $25
Booklet, "Gilbert Chemistry For Boys," 1920s $30
Booklet, "Hi I'm Ginny," Vogue Dolls, 1956 .... $57
Booklet, "How to Play Beat the Clock," 1950s $8

Style Booklet for Skipper, Skooter & Ricky

Booklet, "'Junior Edition' Styles for Skipper, Barbie's Little Sister, Skooter, Skipper's Friend & Ricky, Skipper's Friend - Original designs by Mattel," color drawings of each doll on the cover, late 1960s - early 1970s (ILLUS.) $12

1972 Kenner Toys Booklet

Booklet, "Kenner presents a Christmasland of toys," Snoopy toy on the cover, the Blythe doll shown inside, 1972 (ILLUS.) $21
Booklet, "Knickerbocker - Made to love. Made to last." color cover photo of little girl w/Baby Holly Hobbie doll, 1977 (ILLUS., top next column) $10
Booklet, Lego Blocks instructions $39
Booklet, "Liddle Biddle Peep" $27
Booklet, Lionel Super "O" Rudley $7
Booklet, Lionel trains, 1940 .... $23
Booklet, Lionel Trains salesman's booklet, 1954 .... $66
Booklet, "Man From UNCLE" action figure, early 1960s $27

1977 Knickerbocker Toy Co. Catalog

1950s Marcie Dolls Fold-out Booklet

Booklet, Marcie Dolls, black & white illustrated fold-out, 1950s (ILLUS.) $12

1983 Masters of the Universe Booklet

Booklet, "Masters of The Universe - Masks of Power," color images of the comic characters on the cover, 1983 (ILLUS.) $7

1983 Mattel Puppy Brite Toy Booklet

Booklet, "Puppy Brite Plush Toy," colorful photo of the puppy on the cover, Mattel, 1983 (ILLUS.).. **$5**

Star Wars Return of the Jedi Collection Booklet

Booklet, "Star Wars - Return of The Jedi Collections," large color image of Juba The Hutt, Kenner, 1984 (ILLUS.) **$9**
Booklet, "Terri Lee Fashion Parade," 1956 .... **$13**
Booklet, "The Art of Yo-Yo Playing," Cheerios cereal premium, 1950s......................... **$20**

The Littlechap Family Dolls Booklet

Booklet, "The Littlechap Family," color cover photo of the family of dolls, Remco, 1960s (ILLUS.) **$15**
Booklet, Tonka Trucks, 1960s **$14**
Booklet, Tootsietoys, 1932 .... **$28**
Booklet, "Tri-Ang Railways," second edition, 1956 .... **$108**
Booklet, Vogue dolls, 1962............................ **$15**
Booklet, "Vogue Dolls - Jill and Jan," late 1950s **$37**

Milton Bradley Games Booklet

Booklet, "Welcome to Gameland - Milton Bradley Land," color cover & parents & children entering a doorway formed to two game boxes, late 1950s - early 1960s (ILLUS.)... **$5**

G.I. Joe Booklet & Brochure

Booklet & fold-out brochure, G.I. Joe action figures, color & black & white photos, late 1960s, the group **$18**
Booklets, A.C. Gilbert Erector Sets, three early booklets, the group............................ **$73**
Booklets, "A Picture Book of Fisher Price Toys," color cover photo of a mother & her children w/a toy garage, 1962 .... **$21**
Booklets, "Barclay Manoil Soldier Molds" **$46**
Booklets, "Become a Ventriloquist with Dummy Dan," 1930s **$35**
Booklets, "Dungeons and Dragons," boxed set of 10 .... **$140**

Tammy Dolls Color Booklets

Two Strawberry Shortcake Booklets

Booklets, Tammy dolls, color covers, Ideal, 1960s, each (ILLUS. of three, previous page) $6

Booklets, "The World of Strawberry Shortcake," Kenner, ca. 1970s, each (ILLUS. of two, top of page) $9

1981 Annalee Christmas Catalog

1951 Billy & Ruth Toy Catalog

Catalog, "Annalee Christmas '81," Annalee Mobilitee Toys, 1981, color cover photo (ILLUS.).. $15

Catalog, Arcade cast-iron toys, first-half 20th c. $429

Catalog, Aurora Model kits, 1967................... $35

Catalog, Aurora model kits prehistoric scenes, 1972... $21

Catalog, "Billy and Ruth - America's Famous Toy Children - 1951 - W.T. Smith Tire Co.," colorful image of Santa Claus & Mrs. Claus getting ready for Santa to take off, small portraits of Billy & Ruth in the lower corners (ILLUS., top next column)..... $25

Catalog, "Britains Hollowcast Toy Soldiers," 1954 .... $90

Catalog, Charmin' Chatty dolls, Mattel, ca. 1960s $27

Western Auto 1940s Christmas Catalog

Catalog, "Christmas Gifts for All the Family - Western Auto," color cover photo of a family gathered around the Christmas three, late 1940s (ILLUS.)........................... $43

Catalog, Columbus Westfield Bicycles, 1930s **$40**

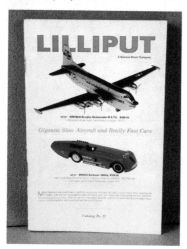

1981 Effanbee Dolls Catalog

Catalog, "Effanbee - dolls that touch your heat - 1981 Collection," heart-shaped photos showing the various dolls (ILLUS.) ... **$31**
Catalog, FAO Schwarz, 1935 .... **$95**
Catalog, FAO Schwarz Toys, 1946 .... **$43**
Catalog, Gendron Pedal Cars, 1928 .... **$805**
Catalog, Hubley Toys, 1964 .... **$39**

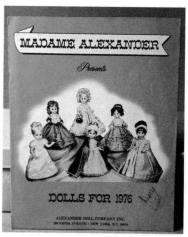

1976 Madame Alexander Dolls Catalog

Niresk 1958 Book of Gifts Catalog

Catalog, "Niresk 1958 Book of Gifts," color cover photo of the Royal Princess doll & Her Baby (ILLUS.) **$22**

Lilliput Toys 1981 Catalog

Catalog, Lilliput toys, "Gigantic Slow Aircraft and Really Fast Cars - Catalog No. 27," large color photo of a toy airplane & race-car, 1998 (ILLUS.) **$13**
Catalog, "Madame Alexander Presents - Dolls For 1976," black & white photo of various dolls against a dark green background (ILLUS., top next column) **$37**
Catalog, Marklin Model Trains, 1950s **$23**
Catalog, Matchbox vehicles, 1965 .... **$12**
Catalog, Matchbox vehicles, pocket-sized, 1962 .... **$56**
Catalog, Mattel Toys, 1971 .... **$57**
Catalog, Mattel Toys, 1973 .... **$57**
Catalog, Montgomery Wards, Christmas 1935 .... **$54**

Oklahoma Tire & Supply 1955 Christmas Catalog

Catalog, "Oklahoma Tire & Supply - Sparkling Gift Values," Christmas 1955, printed in red, white & blue w/a tree ornament reflecting a family w/various Christmas presents, including toys (ILLUS.) $22

Catalog, "The World of Annie Knickerbocker," Knickerbocker Toys, 1982 .... $20
Catalog, Tonka Toys, pocket-sized, 1960s... $108
Catalog, Transogram Toys, 1967 .... $12
Catalog, various doll shoes, 1940s $24

1915 Montgomery Ward Catalog Page

Cover of 1890s McLoughlin Bros. Reprint

Catalog, one-page from the 1915 Montgomery Ward catalog, black & white illustrations of Teddy bears & many other stuffed toys (ILLUS.) $39
Catalog, Plasticville Toys, 1952 .... $51
Catalog, Playskool Toys, 1950 .... $20
Catalog, S.A. Smith, makers of toy furniture, Brattleboro, Vermont, 1904 .... $102

Catalog reprint, McLoughlin Brothers, 1890s, cover printed in color $18

TOYS

Early Wilkins Buckboard Wagon

Buckboard wagon, cast iron, all-original wagon w/pressed steel back end in red & gold, yellow wheels, one black horse & original driver, fine paint, Wilkins, early 20th c., 12 1/2" l. (ILLUS.)....................... $863

1980s Steiff Bear Catalog

Catalog, "The Great Steiff Bear Catalog - Steiff Button in Ear - An animal from Steiff. For ever yours," color cover photo of a selection of Steiff Teddy bears, 1980s (ILLUS.)... $12

Long Arcade "Yellow Coach" Double-decker Bus

Bus, cast iron, double-decker orange bus w/black tires, top side printed "Yellow

Coach," Arcade, early 20th c., missing driver, older tires not original, 13" l. (ILLUS.) .. **$1,440**

Early Horse-drawn Cab Toy

Cab & horse, cast iron, horse-drawn small open cab w/the driver at the top rear, black w/yellow wheels, pulled by a tan horse, American-made, late 19th - early 20th c., fair original paint, 11" l. (ILLUS.)... **$575**

Rare Hubley Lady in Landau Carriage Toy

Carriage, cast iron, landau-style carriage in white w/red wheels, driven by a stylish lady wearing blue & white, pulled by a single black horse, Hubley, early 20th c., 16 1/2" l. (ILLUS.).................................. **$2,070**

Circus bandwagon, cast iron, long ornate scrolling red & gold wagon holding the band, raised on blue wheels & w/a driver dressed in red, pulled by a team of four white horses on red wheels, Hubley, formerly displayed at the Hubley offices in New York City, some paint loss, late 19th - early 20th c., 30" l. **$21,850**

Post-war Kenton Hardware Overland Circus Bandwagon

Circus bandwagon, cast-iron, "Overland Circus," large red wagon w/the band figures on the top, pulled by a pair of white horses w/riders, post-World War II version, Kenton Hardware, near mint, 16" l. (ILLUS.).. **$575**

Fine Hubley Royal Circus "Farmer's" Wagon

Circus "Farmer's" wagon, cast iron, large rectangular green & gold wagon molded on the sides w/a panel enclosing a gold rhinosceros below "Royal Circus," a large comical head of a farmer on the top, gold & read wheels & a driver dressed in red, pulled by two black horses, Hubley, formerly on display at the Hubley offices in New York City, late 19th -early 20th c., slide paint fading, repair to left rear wheel frame, one plume replaced, 16" l. (ILLUS.)....................... **$9,200**

Early Carette Automobile

Clockwork automobile, colorful lithographed tin, red & gold w/a chauffeur in black seated next to a lady passenger, Carrette, early 20th c., some corrosion to black fenders, lacking two rubber tires, 8" l. (ILLUS.)... **$2,300**

Steelcraft Restored City Dairy Delivery Truck

Delivery truck, pressed streel, open cab in green, the open bed in dark blue w/side sticker reading "City Dairy Co.," green solid metal wheels w/rubber rims, holds two-dozen milks bottles held by stakes,

Steelcraft, ca. 1930s, finely restored, 25" l. (ILLUS.) **$805**

Drum, child's, lithographed tin sides w/wooden upper & lower bands joined by string, the sides printed w/a continuous scene of American Boy Scouts involved in various activities, red, black, yellow & blue on a pale greenground, ca. 1920s, 8" d. **$210**

Drum, child's, lithographed tin sides w/wooden upper & lower bands joined by string, the sides printed w/a continuous scene of patriotic marching Victorian children, slight deterioration to drum top, ca. 1920s, 9" d. **$510**

Early Wilkins Cast-Iron Fire Chief Cart

Fire cart, cast iron, "Fire Chief Cart," a black cart stamped "F.D. Chief" & w/large red wheels, pulled by a single white horse & driven by the fire chief, Wilkins, late 19th - early 20th c., 11 1/2" l. (ILLUS.) **$2,185**

Arcade Model A Fire Chief Car

Fire chief car, cast iron, Model A Landau Sport Couple painted red, metal wheels, side marked "Chief," Arcade, early 20th c., 5" l. (ILLUS.) **$575**

Early Hubley Fire Ladder Wagon

Fire ladder wagon, cast iron, long yellow ladders atop the red wagon w/yellow wheels, eagle emblem on the side, Hubley, early 20th c., 11 1/4" l. (ILLUS.).......... **$575**

Fine Hubley Cast-Iron Fire Patrol Wagon

Fire patrol wagon, cast iron, open read wagon w/yellow wheels, figures of firemen in the back, single driver & pulled by two black & one white horse, side of wagon embossed "Fire Patrol," Hubley, early 20th c., some paint wear, 19" l. (ILLUS.) **$1,380**

Kenton Hardware Cast-iron Fire Pumper Truck

Fire pumper truck, cast iron, long red chassis w/nickel-plated boiler, driver, rear fireman, & front bumper, metal wheels, hose reel at side for missing rubber hoses, some paint wear, figures may be replacements, Kenton Hardware, early 20th c., 15" l. (ILLUS.).. **$805**

Unusual Child-sized Wood Fire Wagon

Fire wagon, child-sized, carved & painted wood, the long rectangular platform fitted w/a raised front seat w/the side supports w/large star cut-outs, a high front footboard, the back frame fitted w/a large metal-banded red barrel fitted w/a small brass bell & hose, flanked by two small ladders, large wooden-spoked rear wheels & slightly larger front wheels w/a T-post for pulling, paint in fine condition, late 19th - early 20th c., 20 x 40", overall 34" h. (ILLUS.) **$1,035**

Friction-powered Racing Motorcycle

Friction-type, lithographed tin, racing motorcycle & rider, original colorful paint, made in Japan, 1950s, 8 1/2" l. (ILLUS.) .. **$225**

"Happy Chick" Friction Toy

Friction-type, lithographed tin, rooster wearing a tuxedo while driving an antique car, marked "Happy Chick," dated 1957, w/original box (ILLUS.) **$245**

Fine Early Marklin Toy Kitchen Range

Kitchen range, enameled tin & brass, rectangular working model w/solid brass doors & claw feet, chimney & water heating tank on the back of the top, completed w/white enamelware pots & pans w/blue stripes, original alcohol/oil burner, Marklin, Germany, early 20th c., stove 9 x 13", the set (ILLUS.)........................... **$960**

Pyro Plated Dinosaur Kit

Model kit, Plated Dinosaur, Stegosaurus, 1/32 scale, Pyro, plastic kit, late 1950s - late 1960s (ILLUS.) **$20-40**

Early Blue "Eagle" Kitchen Range

Kitchen range, cast iron, high-back blue-painted design w/an oven & warming oven at one side, marked "Eagle," raised on slender legs, w/a metal pot & frying pan, hairline crack in right vertical frame, early 20th c., 8" w., 8" h. (ILLUS.) **$96**

Aurora Porthos Kit

Model kit, Porthos, of "The Three Musketeers," 1/8 scale, Aurora, 1958 (ILLUS.) **$25-75**

Model kit, Predator, 1/8 scale, limited edition of 1,000, Dark Horse, cold-cast porcelain kit **$125-175**

Halcyon Predator 2 Creature Kit

Model kit, Predator 2 Creature, Movie Classic series, plastic, painted by Joe Fex, Halcyon, 1990s (ILLUS.) **$30-45**
Model kit, Predator, soft vinyl, Billiken, 1991, 12" **$35-75**
Model kit, Prehistoric Dinosaurs, Addar, plastic kit, Super Scenes series, 1976 ... **$40-50**

Revell Roscoe the Many-footed Lion Kit

Model kit, Roscoe the Many-footed Lion, Revell, plastic kit, Dr. Seuss Series, 1959 (ILLUS.) **$100-250**
Model kit, S-Files, Flukeman, Dark Horse, cold-cast porcelain kit, 1990s **$100-150**

Aurora Saber Tooth Tiger Kit

Model kit, Saber Tooth Tiger, No. 733, 1/13 scale, yellow, painted by Evan Stuart, Aurora, 1971 (ILLUS.) **$30-40**
Model kit, Silver Knight of Augsburg - 1560, Aurora, 1956, 9" h. **$20-50**

Model kit, Sling Rave Curvette, Hawk, Weird-ohs, designed by Bill Campbell, 1964 .... **$15-40**
Model kit, Spiked Dinosaur, No. 742, 1/13 scale, tan & green, Aurora, 1971 .... **$70-85**
Model kit, Stegosaurus, 1/30 scale, Horizon, vinyl kit, 1980s-90s........................ **$35-45**
Model kit, Stegosaurus, Airfix, plastic kit, Britain/France,1979................................ **$25-35**
Model kit, Stegosaurus, Pyro reissue, Lindberg, plastic kit, 1979 .... **$10-18**
Model kit, Styracosauarus, Monogram (reissues from Aurora's Prehistoric Scenes line), 1987 .... **$30-40**
Model kit, Super Fink, Revell, plastic kit, Custom Monsters Series, designed by Ed "Big Daddy" Roth, 1964 .... **$150-350**
Model kit, Superhero series, Marx, paintable plastic figures, 1960s-70s, each......... **$4-9**
Model kit, Surfink, Revell, plastic kit, Custom Monsters Series, designed by Ed "Big Daddy" Roth, 1965 .... **$55-165**

Pressed Steel Allied Moving Van

Moving van, pressed steel, cab & long trailer marked "Allied Van Lines, Inc. - Nation-wide Moving," made by Marx in Japan, 1950s, 13" l. (ILLUS.)........................ **$200**

Early Dent Cast-iron Adirondack Steamboat

Paddle wheel steamboat, cast iron, painted white w/yellow, black,red & gold trim, the side embossed "Adirondack," by Dent, flaking to black smokestack, late 19th - early 20th c., 15" l. (ILLUS.)......... **$1,093**

Extremely Rare Vindex Green Panel Delivery Truck

Panel truck, cast iron, a closed panel-style truck painted green w/gold trim & silver metal wheels, molded on the side "Rapid Delivery," the front grille embossed "White," Vindex Toy Co., ca. 1930, overall uniform paint wear, one of two known examples, 8 3/8" l. (ILLUS.) **$19,550**

Early Bliss Painted Wood Toy Piano

Piano, wooden upright model w/working keys, painted white w/a lithographed paper panel above the keyboard showing cherubs playing musical instruments, by Bliss, early 20th c., 9" l., 8 1/2" h. (ILLUS.) **$210**

Early Buddy L Black Pickup Truck

Pickup truck, pressed steel, Model T vehicle w/black body & red-trimmed metal wheels, truck bed impressed "Moline Pressed Steel Company, East Moline, Ill." & "Buddy L" decal on rear of cab, tailgate slightly bent, very fine condition, ca. 1920s, 12" l. (ILLUS.) **$863**

Hubley Police Motorcyle & Side Car

Police motorcycle w/side car, cast iron, army-green cycle w/three tires, two policemen painted dark blue, two decals marked "Harley Davidson," also w/Hub-

ley marks, riders repainted otherwise original, ca. 1930s, 9" l. (ILLUS.) **$403**

Early Brown & White Horse Pull-Toy

Pull-toy, horse on wheeled platform base, brown & white real hide on a wooden model w/real hair mane & tail, glass eyes, leather bridle, thin platform painted cream trimmed w/brown & on four tiny metal wheels, late 19th - early 20th c., 13" l. (ILLUS.) **$540**

Early Tin Sheep on Platform Pull-toy

Pull-toy, sheep on platform, a pressed tin flattened silver sheep on a rectangular green tin platform w/small metal wheels, old sticker on bottom reads "This Sheep Made in Clinton, Conn.," early 20th c., 6" l. (ILLUS.) **$690**

Sunny Andy Street Railway Trolley

Pull-toy, "Sunny Andy Street Railway," lithographed pressed steel trolley car in dark tan, a bell rings when pulled along, Wolverine, early 20th c., 13 1/2" l. (ILLUS.) **$150**

Black Porter Carved Wood Pull-Toy

Pull-type, stylized carved wood black "Sambo" porter dressed in red & yellow & pulling a small red wagon w/blue pressed steel wheels, by Velo Walking Pulltoys, first half 20th c., 12" h. (ILLUS.) **$86**

Hubley Streamlined #5 Race Car

Race car, cast iron, streamlined boat-tailed auto w/a yellow body embossed "5," black-painted driver, silver grille, white & red solid metal wheels, overpaint on frame rails & wheels, Hubley, late 1920s - early 1930s, 9 1/4" l. (ILLUS.) **$730**

Old Rocking Horse on Red Platform

Rocking horse on platform, carved & painted wood, the white grey-dappled horse w/a removable tooled leather saddle, leather reins, string mane & tail, suspended in a metal rocking & swinging framework supported in a red-painted wooden platform, 19th c., 33" l., 27" h. (ILLUS.) **$288**

Unusual Horse Head & Seat Rocking Horse

Rocking horse on rockers, carved & painted wood, a red half-round wooden seat w/U-form crestrail over short spindles & on red arched metal side supports attached to the long green rockers w/yellow trim, a front platform mounted w/a carved flat board horse head painted white w/black & red trim, some bridle missing, probably late 19th c., 16 x 48", 16" h. (ILLUS.) **$300**

Victorian Rocking Horse on Rockers

Rocking horse on rockers, carved & painted wood, the white steed w/a worn leather saddle & bridle & carved & black-painted details, real hair tail, raised on a long blue-painted double rail rocker, original unrestored condition w/some damage, some insect damage, 19th c., 54" l., 31" h. (ILLUS.) **$863**

Early German Rocking Horse on Rockers

Rocking horse on rockers, stylized wooden horse covered in paper painted w/a grey dappled design, real hair mane & tail probably replacements, w/original saddle & stirrups, raised on long red-painted wooden rockers, Germany, late 19th - early 20th c., 42" l., 30" h. (ILLUS.) **$780**

Nice Painted Victorian Toy Sled

Sled, painted pine, the central board w/a red background & central nautical scene of a sailboat, island & water, blue & yellow trim, metal-tipped wooden runners, two front top wood sections apparently replaced, late 19th c., 14" w., 33" l. (ILLUS.) **$316**

Buddy L Restored Tanker Truck

Tanker truck, pressed steel, black open cab & dark blue tank w/"Buddy L" sticker, red closed metal wheels, finely restored, 1930s, 24" l. (ILLUS.) **$920**

Early Case Steam Tractor Toy

Tractor, die-cast metal, early open-topped steam tractor in black w/red metal wheels, complete w/driver, Case, early 20th c., some wear, 9 1/2" l. (ILLUS.) **$288**

Lionel No. 219 White Crane Car

Train car, Lionel Standard gauge No. 219 white crane, pressed steel, the crane cab w/a red roof & white sides w/a long green boom, black frame & base, some chips & scratches, some surface rust on gear housing, working, w/original box (ILLUS.) . **$403**

Very Rare Early Lionel No. 100 Electric Locomotive

Train locomotive, electric, Lional #100 2 7/8 gauge, high tin body w/a cast-iron frame, red sides & black trim, sides printed in gold "B & O - No. 5," marked, some old paint chipping, one cast-iron pin broken, ca. 1903 (ILLUS.) **$4,025**

Rare All-brass Lionel Locomotive No. 54

Train locomotive, Lionel Standard gauge brass No. 54, twin-motored model w/thick-rimmed wheels & an all-brass body, red-trimmed wheels & body, Lionel brass nameplate on cab (ILLUS.) **$3,120**

Large Lionel No. 381E Locomotive

Train locomotive, Lionel Standard gauge No. 381E, stamped metal, dark green w/light green catwalks atop a black frame, Lional label on side & marked "Bild-A-Loco," brass & copper trim, Lionel's largest electric locomotive, minor chipping (ILLUS.) **$2,933**

Lionel Standard Gauge No. 385E Locomotive & Tender

Great American Flyer President's Special Series Train Set

Train locomotive & tender car, Lionel Standard gauge No. 385E, Ives-style tender, stamped metal, rare grey color scheme w/die-cast tender, retains original flags & boxes, some discoloration, slight rust & minor chips, 2 pcs. (ILLUS., previous page) **$805**

Lionel Standard Gauge No. 392E Locomotive & Tender

Train locomotive & tender car, Lionel Standard gauge No. 392E, "Bild-A-Loco" model, black stamped metaal w/brass & copper trim, red-trimmed wheels & pilot, , brass name tag on tender, tender body restored, 2 pcs. (ILLUS.) **$719**

Train set, American Flyer Standard gauge President's Special Series, all in dark & light blue, No. 4689 locotive marked "The Commander,'" No. 4391 pullman car, No. 4393 dining car, No. 4390 club car & No. 4392 observation car, each named on a brass plate, all w/brass trim, nickel trucks, red wheels & original paper stickers, overall excellent condition, the set (ILLUS., top of page) **$7,080**

Train set: steam engine & tender, floodlight car, Sunoco tank car, operating dump car, "Pennsylvania" caboose; O-gauge, Lionel No. 1666 engine & tender, No. 2620 floodlight car, No. 2680 tank car, No. 3659 dump car, No. 2672 caboose, 1940-41, the set (ILLUS., bottom of page)... **$485**

Unusual Old Horse & Carriage Tricycle

Tricycle, carved & painted wood, composed of a red-painted seat platform w/an upholstered seat raised between to large wire-spoked wheels w/two long side rods & an iron two-pedal mechanism attached to a carved & painted articulated wooden small galloping horse in black & gold w/a bridle & bit & real hair tail & mane, front legs of horse raised on a small wire-spoked wheel, w/a black riding crop, 19th c., 46" l., 22" h. (ILLUS............. **$805**

Lionel Train Set with Tank Car

Fine Lionel No. 1 Electric Trolley Toy

Trolley, electric, Lionel #1, colorful tin body w/a green roof, yellow windows & blue lower body marked "No. 1 Electric Rapid Transit," uniform paints on lower body, roof repainted, ca. 1930s (ILLUS.) **$1,800**

Rare Lionel Trolley with No. 29 Day Coach Body

pler possibly replaced, rare, early 20th c. (ILLUS.) **$9,775**

Rare Lional #2 Closed Vestibule Trolley Car

Trolley car, electric, Lionel #2 closed vestibule car, painted tin body w/a yellow & red roof on the yellow & red body, printed below windows "#2 Electric Rapid Transit," minor chipping, discolored repair mark, ca. 1930s (ILLUS.) **$3,738**

Tootsie Toy Small Stake Truck

Truck, cast spelter, open-cab stake truck, red cab & silver stake back, black metal wheels, Tootsietoy, ca. 1930s, 3 1/4" l. (ILLUS.) **$95**

Rare Lionel No. 100 Electric Trolley Toy

Trolley, electric, Lionel #100, Standard gauge, colorful tin body w/a blue & yellow roof & body, letter board reads "#100 Electric Rapid Transit," motor mmissing a pin, steps missing at one end, some old paint flaking & chips, some touch-up, ca. 1930s (ILLUS.) **$2,013**

Extremely Rare, Early Lional #300 Electric Summer Trolley

Trolley, electric, Lionel #300 2 7/8 gauge, open tin summer car w/a converse body, overall tin body on a black cast-iron frame, yellow & maroon open sides & roof, dashboard & roof panels marked "City Hall Park - #175," metal Lionel name plate on bottom, possible touch-up onn lower roof, ca. 1903, 16" l., 8 3/4" h. (ILLUS.) **$10,120**

Trolley, electric, Lionel No. 29 Day Coach body powered on a No. 3 trolley chassis, tin body painted dark green w/yellow wording under the windows "No. 29 - N.Y.C.& H.R.R. & Co. - No. 29," some original figures inside, some chipping & flaking, small hole in middle of the roof, coupler missing on one end, other cou-

Banners Garden Truck

Truck, pressed steel, long cab & open back in green, yellow printing on sides reads "Garden Truck - Banners No. 614," ca. 1930s, 13" l. (ILLUS.) **$175**

Early Toy Maytag Washing Machine

Washing machine, cast metal, scale model of an early Maytag washer w/wringer on the top, painted grey w/polished aluminum lid & original Maytag decal, ca. 1940s, 4 x 4", 9" h. (ILLUS.)...................... **$660**

Wheelbarrow, toy-size, painted wood, flared shaped sides & frame w/wooden front wheel, original blue, red & gold painted decoration, late 19th c., overall 32" l. **$661**

Occupied Japan Wind-up Monkey Toy

Wind-up celluloid monkey playing guitar, painted celluloid monkey seated on a tin tree stump & playing his guitar, made in Occupied Japan, late 1940s - early 1950s, working, 7 1/2" h. (ILLUS.) **$58**

Schuco Wind-up Skating Monkey Toy

Wind-up cloth rollerskating monkey, felt-covered moneky wearing blue pants, red & white shirt & black boots on skates, moves forward w/a hopping action, Schuco, U.S. Zone Germany, some clothing wear, 1950s, 7 1/2" h. (ILLUS.)................. **$390**

Early Lehmann Wind-up Tin Balky Mule Toy

Wind-up tin balky mule, colorfully dressed clown w/cloth outfit rides on a cart w/large solid tin wheels printed w/clowns, a felt-covered kicking mule pulls the cart, mule missing one ear, Lehmann, Germany, working, early 20th c., 7 1/2" l. (ILLUS.) **$240**

Germany Wind-up Billiards Player

Wind-up tin billiards player, standing gentleman wearing a brown checked suit, a brown table w/a green top, working order & w/one original ball, Germany, early 20th c., 7 1/2" l. (ILLUS.)........................... **$720**

Early Marx Wind-up Tin Royal Bus Line Bus

Wind-up tin bus, long orange & dark yellow bus w/black bumpers & solid red wheels, original driver, marked along the roofline "Royal Bus Line," Marx, ca. 1930s, working, 10" l. (ILLUS.)..................................... **$748**

Marx Wind-up Tin "Busy Bridge" Toy

Wind-up tin **"Busy Bridge,"** long model of the Brooklyn Bridge complete w/walkway & tin vehicles that move back & forth, Marx, ca. 1930s, good working condition, 24" l. (ILLUS., previous page) **$431**

Early German Wind-up Fire Truck

Wind-up tin **fire ladder truck,** red open truck w/silver wheels, long yellow ladder & two firemen, marked "Continental," missing four figures & bell, Germany, early 20th c., 11" l. (ILLUS.) **$288**

Chein Clown Acrobat Windup Toy

Wind-up tin **clown acrobat,** fat clown standing on his hands, wearing a purple & green outfit, by Chein, ca, 1950s, 5" h. (ILLUS.).. **$95**

Early Wind-up Tin Dog Cart with Monkey Driver Toy

Wind-up tin **dog cart,** colorful cart w/two large rear wheels printed w/monkies, a small front wheel steered by a monkey dressed in green, a white dog pushes from behind, early 20th c., 6" l. (ILLUS.) **$920**

Rare Hey-Hey The Chicken Snatcher Toy

Wind-up tin **"Hey-Hey The Chicken Snatcher,"** caracature of a black man w/oversized feet carrying a chicken in one hand w/a small dog biting his behind, Marx, early 20th c., near mint, 8 1/2" h. (ILLUS.)... **$1,495**

Marx Windup Donkey Cart Toy

Wind-up tin **donkey cart,** farmer seated in open cart pulled by a bucking donkey, Marx, ca. 1930s, 8" l. (ILLUS.) **$225**

Hott 'N Tott Unique Art Wind-up Toy

Wind-up tin **"Hott 'N Tott,"** a black dancing banjo player standing beside a black piano player seated at an upright piano, colorful decoration, Unique Art, copyright 1921, fine working condition, 8" h. (ILLUS.) **$489**

Jack Sprat & Wife Dancing Wind-up Toy

Wind-up tin Jack Sprat & wife, hand-painted tin, a skinny Jack dancing w/his very large wife, brightly painted, Germany, early 20th c., 6 1/2" h. (ILLUS.).............. **$1,020**

Jazzbo-Jim Dancer with Original Box

Wind-up tin "Jazzbo-Jim - 'The Dancer on the Roof,'" black banjo player dances on the roof of a small cabin printed w/other black figures, w/original color-printed cardboard box, Marx, excellent conditioin, early 20th c., toy 10" h. (ILLUS.) **$1,093**

Marx Wind-up Tin "Joy Rider" Toy

Wind-up tin "Joy Rider," comical man drives a black jalopy w/a trunk in the

back, head spins & wheels hop & turn when wound, Marx, ca. 1930s, working, 7 1/4" l. (ILLUS.).. **$201**

Early Wind-up Tin Juggler Toy

Wind-up tin juggler, standing man dressed in grey w/red socks & black shoes, each arm ends in a white celluloid ball, arms swirl when wound, some paint flaking, early 20th c., 7" h. (ILLUS.)...................... **$863**

French Lady Pulling Wagon Toy

Wind-up tin lady pulling express wagon, a lady wearing a hat & dressed in red & blue w/a white apron, pulling a small cart wagon in red & blue on gold wheels, when wound her legs turn & the wagon moved forward, France, possibly R.F., slight oxidation to finish, late 19th - early 20th c., 6 1/2" l. (ILLUS.)........................... **$403**

Nice Marx Drummer Boy Wind-up Toy

Wind-up tin "Let the Drummer Boy Play," walking drummer dressed in red, white & blue pushes a large yellow & red drum on wheels, Marx, 7 1/2" h. (ILLUS.) **$403**

Early German Wind-up Limousine

Wind-up tin limousine, open auto w/a chauffeur in front & two passengers in back, red & white chassis on grey metal wheels, Germany, possibly Fischer, early 20th c., 5 3/4" l. (ILLUS.) **$633**

Windup-tin Matador & Bull Toy

Wind-up tin matador & bull, spring-type w/the matador w/sword atop one pair of wheels facing the brown attacking bull on the pair of rear wheels, moves forward & backward when wound, minor wear, early 20th c., 8 1/2" l. (ILLUS.) **$270**

Large Wind-up Tin Lincoln Transfer and Storage Moving Van

Wind-up tin moving van, large blue & yellow open cab w/driver, black metal wheels, the dark yellow enclosed back printed in black "Lincoln Transfer and Storage Co. - Movers, Packers & Shippers of Pianos & Household Goods - Gramercy 2773," American-made, ca. 1920s, front bumper missing, 13" l. (ILLUS.) **$805**

Wind-up tin moving van, stylized truck w/a red open cab & closed yellow back w/pierced holes & working "Royal Van Co.," green chassis on yellow solid metal wheels, original flat tin driver, Marx, ca. 1930s, working, 9 1/2" l. **$360**

Wind-up Tin Prussian Soldier Toy

Wind-up tin Prussian soldier, hand-painted figure of a Germany soldier lying on his stomach & firing a rifle, raised on wheels, crawls along when wound, Germany, ca. 1920s, flaking paint, 11" l. (ILLUS.) **$420**

Fine Lionel No. 43 Wind-up Speedboat

Wind-up tin speedboat, Lionel No. 43, long tin body w/a teak-colored deck, creamy white sides & bright green bottom, w/original riders, minor chipping, w/a newer display stand (ILLUS.) **$2,300**

Wind-up tin "The Great Billard (sic) Champion," color lithographed billiard player standing at one end of the table, complete w/original illustrated box & paper bag w/two original billiard balls, made for Steinfeld, Germany, late 19th - early 20th c., 6" l. (ILLUS., top next page) **$900**

German Waltzing Couple Wind-up Toy

Wind-up tin waltzing couple, a young man wearing a black tuxedo dancing w/a young blonde lady wearing a pink & white gown, hand-painted w/some flaking & minor rust bleeding, Germany, late 19th - early 20th c., 8" h. (ILLUS.) **$1,150**

Early Billiard Player Wind-up Toy

Rare German Wind-up Tin Zeppelin Toy

Wind-up tin zeppelin, complete & all-original w/a long pale yellow body mounted w/red top mounts, colorful side & rear propellers & red tail rudders, Hans Erbo, Germany, early 20th c., key missing, 16" l. (ILLUS.)... **$2,645**

Gypsy Hosiery Change Tray

TRAYS - SERVING & CHANGE

Grain Belt Beer Change Tray

Change, "Grain Belt Beer," round, metal, red & yellow logo in center below "A Barley Malt Product" w/"The Minneapolis Beer'" below, Grain Belt Brewery, Minneapolis, Minnesota, ca. 1920, 4 1/8" d. (ILLUS.) **$75-125**

Change, "Gypsy Hosiery," round, lithographed tin, center oval w/gypsy girl in red surrounded by scene of tents & horses, top marked "Gypsy Hosiery" & bottom "E.J. Schroeder, Breese, Illinois," Hargadine-McKittrick Co., litho by H.D. Beach Co., Coshocton, Ohio, ca. 1910, 6" d. (ILLUS., next column) **$100-150**

King's Pure Malt Change Tray

Change, "King's Pure Malt," oval, center w/black background & image of uniformed maid holding tray w/a glass & bottle, marked in top border "King's" & the bottom w/medals & banner reading "Panama - Pacific - Medal of Award - International Exposition," ca. 1915, 4 1/4 x 6" (ILLUS.)... **$125-200**

Change, "King's Pure Malt," oval, lithographed metal, shows bottle in center marked "Pure Malt," border marked "King's - Strengthening - Healthful - Good For Insomnia," litho by American Art

Works, Coshocton, Ohio, ca. 1910,
4 3/8 x 6" **$150-200**

Lehnert's Beer Change Tray

Change, "Lehnert's Beer," round, lithographed metal, image of stag w/large
antlers, border w/"Drink Lehnert's Beer -
Made in Catasauqua, PA," litho by American Art Works, Coshocton, Ohio, ca.
1910, 4 1/4" d. (ILLUS.) **$150-200**

Lily Beer Change Tray

Change, "Lily Beer," rectangular, metal, table set w/snack food, bottle of beer &
full glass below "Lily - A Beverage"
flanked by white calla lily, border reading "Pure As It's [sic] Name - In A Class
By Itself! - Healthful and Refreshing -
Bottled Only By Rock Island Brewing
Co. - Rock Island, Illinois," ca. 1915,
4 1/2 x 6 1/2" (ILLUS.) **$225-300**

The Davenport Co. Change Tray

Change, "The Davenport Company," round,
lithographed metal, center w/bust portrait
of lady on red background flanked by Art
Nouveau floral designs, brown border
w/yellow letters reading "Compliments of
The Davenport Co.," litho by Meek &
Co., ca. 1903, 4 1/4" d. (ILLUS.) **$100-150**

Welsbach Mantles Change Tray

Change, "Welsbach Mantles," round, lithographed tin, center w/shield form, eagle
& banner marked "Welsbach Quality"
above red scroll marked in yellow "All
mantles are not Welsbachs. See that the
mantle you buy has the Shield of Quality
on the box," yellow decorated border,
litho by Meek & Beech Co., Coshocton,
Ohio, ca. 1900, 4 1/4" d. (ILLUS.) **$125-175**

White Rock Table Water Change Tray

Change, "White Rock Table Water," round,
lithographed metal, scene w/woman
kneeling on rock over water, yellow border w/red & black lettering reads "White
Rock - The World's Best Table Water,"
litho by Charles Shonk Co., Chicago,
Illinois, ca. 1900, 4 3/8" d. (ILLUS.).... **$250-300**

West End Brewing Company Tray

Serving, "West End Brewing Co.," tin, image
of Columbia w/barrel, holding shafts of
wheat, near mint condition, some slight
chipping at rim edges, 13" d. (ILLUS.) ... **$1,380**

VENDING & GAMBLING DEVICES

Exhibit Supply Co. Photoscope Machine

Arcade, Exhibit Supply Company photoscope, steel case in blue, coin-activation turns Charlie Chaplin card reel, ca. 1929, older repaint, 8 1/2 x 14", 11" h. (ILLUS.) **$173**

Mills "Electricity Is Life" Machine

Arcade, Mills "Electricity Is Life," power-tester, battery-operated mechanism in a red-painted steel case w/yellow stenciling, 1-cent play, turning handles gives a shock, some paint wear working, 7 x 9", 12" h. (ILLUS.) **$1,093**

Peppy the Musical Clown Arcade Machine

Arcade, Williams Mfg. Co. "Peppy the Musical Clown," coin-op allow player to manipulate the clown's hands & feet w/strings, electrified, ca. 1950-56, working, 76" h. (ILLUS.)................................. **$1,380**

Rare Caille "Roulette" Slot Machine

Gambling, Caille "Roulette" counter-top slot machine, wood-finished metal & cast aluminum & nickel, roulette wheel on the top, slot panel across the top front, working, 13" sq., 16" h. (ILLUS.)................. **$33,350**

Mills "Pilot" Trade Stimulator

Gambling, Mills "Pilot" counter-type trade stimulator, cast-iron case molded w/a large sailing ship, one-reel machine w/playing card symbols, unrestored, ca. 1906, 11 1/2 x 12", 14 3/4" h. (ILLUS.) **$7,475**

Gambling, wheel of fortune, a two-sided spinning wooden wheel painted white w/black Arabic numerals, raised on a tall square post on a double-rung cross-form base, early 20th c., 67" h. (ILLUS., next page) **$345**

Wheel of Fortune on Tall Pedestal

Early "Automatic Clerk" Gum Vendor

Gypsy Fortune Teller Gumball Vendor

Large Painted Wood Wheel of Fortune

Gambling, wheel of fortune, large narrow wooden wheel painted dark yellow w/blocks painted w/card suit signs & four panels w/a racing horse, eight baluster- and ring-turned red-painted spokes around a small red & black wheels w/knob finials, late 19th - early 20th c., 42" d. (ILLUS.) **$834**

Gum machine, Mansfield's "Automatic Clerk," tall vertical glass sides w/white enamel slot panel at top reading "Winter Green - Blood Orange - 5¢," glass front etched "Automatic Clerk - Manfield's Choice Pepsin Gum," patented in 1902, missing marquee, 7" w., 12" h. (ILLUS., top next column) **$1,150**

Gumball vendor, Pierce Tool & Mfg. Co. "Gypsy Fortune Teller," 1-cent play, spinning roulette-style wheel w/gypsy designs, replaced rear door, ca. 1934, 6 x 14 1/2", 15" h. (ILLUS., middle next column) **$330**

Early Electric Popcorn Vendor

Popcorn vendor, tall square glass-enclosed top w/a metal lid, the lower cast metal case marked "Hot Popcorn - 10¢," raised on a tall trestle base, electrified, Electro-Serve Inc., Peoria, Illinois, ca. 1940s, 60" h. (ILLUS.)................................ **$360**

WATCHES

Jeweled Lady's Hunting Case Watch

Lady's hunting case watch, pendant-style, 18k gold case polished & set w/a diamond, sapphire & ruby accent, the white enameled dial w/Arabic numerals, jeweled & adjusted damascened lever escapement movement, late 19th - early 20th c. (ILLUS.) **$264**

Rare Enamel & Diamond Lady's Watch

Lady's hunting case watch, the round case decorated in green guilloche enamel centered by a rose-cut diamond starburst & bordered by tiny diamonds, suspended from a double old European- and rose-cut diamond-mounted chain & bail joined to an enameled baton & seed pearl necklace, the silvertone dial w/Arabic numerals, platinum & 18k gold mount, some enamel loss, Edwardian, England, early 20th c. (ILLUS.) **$3,878**

Lady's hunting case watch, Vacheron & Constantin, 18k gold case w/three bands of rose-cut diamonds ending in cabochon garnets, the white enamel dial w/Arabic numerals, a jeweled nickel movement, suspended from a scrolling openwork gold pink trimmed w/cabochon garnets & tiny diamonds, triple signed, fitted box, early 20th c. (ILLUS., top next column) .. **$2,585**

Rare Lady's Vacheron & Constantin Watch

Lovely Edwardian Lady's Watch

Lady's open face watch, pendant-type, enamel, platinum & diamond, the back of the platinum-topped 18k gold case in marine blue guilloché enamel centerd by a square set w/rose-cut diamonds & bordered by a narrow white enamel Greek key band, the goldtone dial w/Arabic numerals, suspended from a platinum, enamel baton & rose-cut diamond fancy link chain, Edwardian, England, early 20th c., overall 22" l. (ILLUS.) **$2,468**

Rare Mandolin-shaped Enameled Watch

Lady's verge watch, L'Epine, Paris, France, designed in the shape of a mandolin w/multicolored enamel decoration on the 18k gold ground, opens to revealed a signed gilt movement, suspended from a trace link chain, late 19th - early 20th c. (ILLUS., previous page) **$4,700**

Waltham Gold Hunting Case Watch

Man's hunting case watch, Waltham, 14k tri-color gold case engraved w/foral & leaf designs among interlocking circles, the white enamel dial w/Roman numerals & subsidiary seconds dial, jeweled adjusted nickel movement, late 19th - early 20th c. (ILLUS.) **$646**

Art Deco Open-Face Man's Watch

Man's open-face watch, Art Deco-style, 14k gold, goldtone metal dial w/Arabic numerals & subsidiary seconds dial, stepped bezel, enclosing a 17-jewel nickel lever escapement movement, w/rectangular trace link fob chain, w/Dreicer & Co. box, ca. 1930s (ILLUS of watch) **$323**

Patek Philippe Open-Face Man's Watch

Man's open-face watch, Patek Philippe, 18k yellow gold, the silvertone dial w/Arabic numerals enclosing an 18-jewel eight adjustment damascened nickel movement, the reverse w/worn monogram, 20th c., triple-signed, boxed (ILLUS.)...... **$1,880**

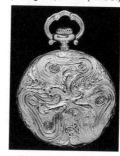

Extraordinary Tiffany Pocket Watch

Man's open-face watch, Tiffany & Co., 18k yellow gold & platinum, Art Nouveau design, gold case w/applied platinum wire in a looped clover-style design against a chased & répoussé ground w/a small bird, the gilt dial w/applied free-form Arabic numerals, curved & scrolling bi-color hands, subsidiary seconds dial, jeweled & damscened nickel lver escapment movement, ca. 1890s, triple-signed (ILLUS. of back)...................... **$35,250**

Vacheron Open-Face Man's Watch

Man's open-face watch, Vacheron, 18k gold, the white enamel dial w/Roman numerals & a subsidiary seconds dial, enclosing a jeweled lever escapement movement, early 20th c. (ILLUS.) **$646**

Wristwatches

Rare Early Cartier Lady's Wristwatch

Cartier, lady's Art Deco style, the diamond-shaped silvered dial w/Roman numerals framed by rose-cut diamonds & onyx tablets framed by more diamonds, rose-cut diamond winding stem, completed by a later strap, the platinum-topped 18k gold case enclosing a 19-jewel movement, eight-adjustment, signed by Cartier, Paris, ca. 1920 (ILLUS.)...................... **$15,275**

Fine Patek Philippe Man's Wristwatch

Patek Philippe, man's Retro style 14k gold, the square silvertone dial w/Roman & abstract numerals under a domed crystal, on a shaped end lugs attached to a pyramidal arched bracelet, an 18-jewel damascened movement, Tiffany & Co., mid-20th c., 6 1/2" l. (ILLUS.) **$1,880**

WEATHERVANES

Sheet Metal Centaur Weathervane

Centaur, sheet steel, silhouetted cut-out rearing centaur shooting a bow & arrow above a scroll-cut base, some pitting to rod & scrolls, tip of arrow detached but present, 35 1/2" l., 28 1/2" h. (ILLUS.) **$518**

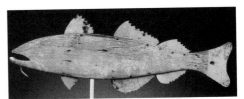

Fine Carved Wood & Metal New England Cod Fish Weathervane

Cod fish, carved wood & gilt metal, large wood body w/six gilt-metal fins & a large gilt-metal tail, open mouth w/large nail as barbel, retains 50-70% of gilding, great finish, from Kennebunkport, Maine, 19th c., piece missing from end of tail & upper slice off body, some bullet holes in metal, 49" l., 16" h. (ILLUS.) **$7,475**

Late Copper Eagle Weathervane

Eagle, copper, hollow-bodied spread-winged bird perched on a ball above a long arrow, mid-20th c., 22" w., 19" h. (ILLUS.) **$518**

Primitive Steel Locomotive Weathervane

Locomotive, steel, flat cut-out design of a primitive locomotive on four wheels, open back compartment & two looped slats to hold bar, rustry, 23 1/4" l., 13" h. (ILLUS.) **$288**

Old Copper Rooster Weathervane

Rooster, copper, molded hollow body, standing pose w/green patina, one bullet hole in one side, probably early 20th c., one foot loose at solder joint, 18 1/2"w., 22" h. (ILLUS.) **$1,495**

WITCH BALLS

Several theories exist as to the origin of these hollow balls of glass. Some believe they were originally designed to hold the then precious commodity of salt in the chimney where it would be kept dry. Eventually these blown glass spheres became associated with warding off the "evil eye" and it is known they were hung in the windows of homes of many 18th century English glassblowers. The tradition was carried to America where the balls were made from the 19th century on. They are scarce.

Nailsea, spherical, composed of eight loops of green, dark blue & red against a milk glass ground, probably American, ca. 1850-70, 3 3/4" d. **$420**

Opaque blue w/stand, the ball resting atop a matching tall slender trumpet-form vase w/ruffled rim, mid-19th c., America, overall 9 3/4" h. **$1,120**

Sapphire blue w/stand, large ball atop a tall trumpet-form vase base w/ringed stem, pontil scar, America, mid-19th c., overall 12 3/4" h. **$1,232**

WOOD SCULPTURES

American folk sculpture is an important part of the American art scene today. Skilled wood carvers turned out ships' figureheads, cigar store figures, plaques and carousel animals of stylized beauty and great appeal. The wooden shipbuilding industry, which had originally nourished this folk art, declined after the Civil War, and the talented carvers then turned to producing figures for tobacconists' shops, carousel animals and show figures for circuses. These figures and other early ornamental carvings that have survived the elements and years are eagerly sought.

Fine Carved Cigar Store Indian Princess

Cigar store Indian Princess, standing wearing a tall feathered headdress, a fringed & feathered skirt & a sash cinched at her waist, one foot resting on a plinth, one hand holding aloft a bunch of tobacco leaves, the other holding a cigar box, green-painted platform base, old repaint, wear, abrasions, second half 19th c., base 28 1/2 x 34" , overall 79" h. (ILLUS.).. **$28,200**

Rare Carved Dog Umbrella Stand

Dog umbrella stand, seated animal holding a twisted carved wood pretzel-form umbrella frame, metal drip pan below, inset glass eyes, Switzerland, ca. 1900, 21 1/4" h. (ILLUS.) **$5,405**

Large Early Pilot House Eagle

Eagle, pine, for a ship's pilot house, carved & painted as a large spread-winged bird w/neck & head extended, fierce expression, old dirty textured surface, Bellamy-style, New England, 19th c., old repair on end of beak & under the beak, small repair to a wing tip, 28" l. beak to tail, 28" w. wing tip to wing tip (ILLUS.) **$3,450**

Early Carved Figure of Evangeline

Figure of Evangeline, a standing woman w/her hands clasped in front, wearing a robe covering her head & continuing down & wrapping around her lower body, a flower-decorated inner robe, on a round gadrooned platform on a round foot, old polychrome paint & inset glass eyes, 25" h. (ILLUS.) **$575**

Figure of St. Mary, tall standing woman w/a simple long dress, removable joined arms, the hairless head set w/glass eyes, atop a beveled square base, thin old paint, 19th c., 40" h. (ILLUS., top next column) **$1,840**

19th Century Carved Figure of St. Mary

Realtistic Panther Head Carved Trophy

Panther head, a large realistically-carved trophy-style head w/open mouth w/fangs & tongue, mounted on a crossed-branch bracket w/tall brass leafy branches projecting from the top, probably Europe, late 19th c., 13" w., 17" h. (ILLUS.) **$2,703**

WOODENWARES

The patina and mellow coloring, along with the lightness and smoothness that come only with age and wear, attract collectors to old woodenwares. The earliest forms were the simplest, and the shapes of items whittled out in the late 19th century varied little in form from those turned out in the American colonies two centuries earlier. A burl is a growth, or wart, on some trees in which the grain of the wood is twisted and turned in a manner that strengthens the fibers and causes a beautiful pattern to be formed. Treenware is simply a term for utilitarian items made from "treen," another word for wood. While maple was the primary wood used for these items, they are also abundant in pine, ash, oak, walnut and other woods. "Lignum Vitae" is a species of wood from the West Indies that can always be identified by the contrasting colors of dark heartwood and light sapwood and by its heavy weight, which caused it to sink in water.

Unusual Carved Burl Basket

Basket, carved burl, one-piece type w/large natural arched handle above the shallow oblong basket, resembles bird's-eye maple, 19th c., 9 x 10", 8" h. (ILLUS.) **$690**

Nice Large Blue-Painted Wooden Bowl

Bowl, turned & painted wood, wide flaring rounded sides w/an indented rim band, natural interior & light blue-painted exterior, 18 1/2" d., 5 1/2" h. (ILLUS.) **$173**

Large Early Turned Elm Bowl

Bowl, turned elm, wide shallow rounded sides w/flat rim, good patina, 19th c., 20 1/2" d., 7" h. (ILLUS.) **$1,265**

Large Natural Turned Wood Bowl

Bowl, turned wood, deep wide rounded sides w/a molded rim band, unpainted, two eaerly zigzag staples holding a crack together runs around the diameter, 19th c., 23 3/4" d., 7" h. (ILLUS.) **$120**

Fine Large Oblong Painted Wood Bowl

Bowl, carved & painted, a flat rectangular bottom & very wide flaring sides & an oval rim, the exterior w/original old blue paint, 19th c., 14 x 25 1/4", 5 1/4" h. (ILLUS. inverted) **$1,380**

Nice Early Wood & Metal Cranberry Scoop

Cranberry scoop, wooden curved-bottom box w/a galvanized metal back & 22 long pointed wooden teeth, galvanized metal side straps, the flat top w/a rectangular wood frame enclosing a galvanized metal panel, low open top end brackets joined by front & back round grip bars, late 19th - early 20th c., 21" l., 10" h. (ILLUS.) **$200-250**

Early Dough Box on Legs

Dough box on legs, pine, a rectangular top w/breadboard ends above the deep box w/canted dovetailed sides, raised on a base w/a canted apron & four simple turned canted legs, nice old color, some minor repairs, probably late 19th c., 21 x 42", 25" h. (ILLUS.) **$489**

Early Wood & Iron Drying Rack

Drying rack, slender side posts tapering slightly w/rounded tops joined by three slender rack bars tenoned through the side posts, raised on cast-iron trestle-type feet, nice patina, first half 19th c., possibly Shaker, 28" w., 37 1/2" h. (ILLUS.)............. **$115**

Small Turned Wood Painted Jar

Jar, cov., thick round foot supporting the squatty bulbous ring-turned body w/a fitted cover w/a tall ring-turned knop finial, old mustard yellow paint, 19th c., base 3" d., 3 3/4" h. (ILLUS.) **$575**

Kraut Cutter with Heart-shaped Top

Kraut cutter, a long flat rectangular board inset w/an angled metal cutting blade, the

heart-shaped top w/a small hanging hole, well scrubbed & used surface, 7" w., 21 1/2" l. (ILLUS.)..................................... **$345**

Primitive Wooden Hanging Plate Rack

Plate rack, wall-mounted, pine frame w/flat shaped end boards w/heart-shaped tops, joined across the top w/three bars form a rack & across the botton w/two bars, fitted w/a wooden openwork rack for 18 plate slots, one end w/an attached round wire soap holder, 7 1/2 x 21 1/2", 18" h. (ILLUS.).. **$431**

Early Painted Hanging Scouring Box

Scouring box, wall-type, painted, the upright backboard w/sharply tapering curved sides w/a hanging hole at the top, a blocked projection at the center back, shaped narrow sides above the dovetailed open bottom box compartment, original old reddish brown paint, 19th c., 2 3/4 x 8 3/4", 16 3/4" h. (ILLUS.) **$900**

Fine Painted One-drawer Wall Box

Wall box, the crestboard w/scalloped sides & flat top centered by a large heart-shaped cut-out hanging hole, a wide slanted hinged lid above the slant-sided box w/raised molding around the sides & the narrow bottom drawer w/a brass knob, dovetailed construction, green old dark green ground trimmed w/light green, some paint wear, one side molding missing, 19th c., 8 x 11 1/2", 12 1/2" h. (ILLUS.)................................. **$1,438**

Early Red Wooden Wall Box

Wall box, the tall peaked backboard w/a hanging hole, the open box w/slanted sides, original dark reddish finish, 19th c., 6 x 12 3/4", 13 3/4" h. (ILLUS.) **$805**

WORLD'S FAIR COLLECTIBLES

There has been great interest in collecting items produced for the great fairs and expositions held through the years. During the 1970s, there was particular interest in items produced for the 1876 Centennial Exhibition and now interest is focusing on those items associated with the 1893 Columbian Exposition. Listed below is a random sampling of prices asked for items produced for the various fairs.

1893 Columbian Exposition

Unique 1893 Spool Display Piece

Advertising display piece, made for the American Thread Co. of Holyoke, Massa-

chusetts, a unique spool display an elaborate sphere composed of thread & spools enclosed in a large clear blown blass footed sphere w/a turned wood finial & raised on a turned wood pedestal base, paper label on the base, some spools broken, 35" h. (ILLUS.) **$1,495**

1901 Pan American Exposition

Stoneware Pan-Am Exposition Mug

Mug, Bristol-glazed stoneware, footed cylindrical body w/a molded band above the foot, one side molded in relief & trimmed in cobalt blue w/a tavern scene, the other side impressed & trimmed in cobalt blue w/a map of North & South America w/the wording "Pan-American Exposition - 1901 Buffalo - NY U.S.A.," bottom impressed "Whites Pottery - Utica, N.Y.," 5" h. (ILLUS.) **$176**

1904 St. Louis World's Fair

Match safe, brass, souvenir-type, rectangular, depicts The Electricity Building at St. Louis World's Fair in 1904, 1 1/2 x 2 5/8" **$75-150**

WRITING ACCESSORIES

Early writing accessories are popular collectibles and offer a wide variety to select from. A collection may be formed around any one segment — pens, letter openers, lap desks, inkwells, etc.—or the collection may revolve around choice specimens of all types. Material, design and age usually determine the value. Pen collectors like the large fountain pens developed in the 1920s but also look for pens and mechanical pencils that are solid gold or gold-plated. Also see: BOTTLES & FLASKS

Inkwells & Stands

Blown three mold glass well, geometric, low wide cylindrical shape w/a molded diamond point design around the sides &

top center pen hole, deep olive amber, pontiled base, Coventry, Connecticut, ca. 1815-30, 2 5/8" h. **$202**

Blown three mold glass well, geometric, low wide cylindrical shape w/a molded diamond point design around the sides & top center pen hole, deep yellowish olive, pontiled base, Keene, New Hampshire, ca. 1815-30, 2" h. **$235**

Blown three mold glass well, geometric, low wide cylindrical shape w/a molded diamond point design around the sides & top center pen hole, deep yellowish amber, pontiled base, Keene, New Hampshire, GIII-28, ca. 1815-30, 1 1/2 h. **$308**

Rare Figural Crab Tiffany Inkwell

Bronze well, figural, molded as a large crab w/a hinged shell, the large front claws framing the round well w/a shell-topped cover, chocolate brown patina, signed "Tiffany Studios New York 21149" w/Tiffany Glass and Decorating logo, inkwell section appears to be a modern replacement w/a broken hinge & minor dents to insert, early 20th c., 7 x 8" (ILLUS.) **$6,325**

Round Art Nouveau Tiffany Bronze Well

Bronze well, wide flattened round base cast w/a lappet rim band around a ring of wavy leafy vines centered by the raised well platform w/a flattened florette-cast

cap, missing insert, hinge loose, signed "Tiffany Studios New York 1039," 6 1/2" d., 2" h. (ILLUS.) **$840**

Cast-metal & glass stand, revolving-style, two matching milk glass 'bulldog head' wells w/ground lips mounted between three scrolled metal pen holder uprights above a thin rectangular cast metal base, one well w/manufacturing stress crack on mouth, ca. 1875-95, 4 3/4 x 6 5/8", 4 1/2" h. **$364**

Cast-metal & glass stand, revolving-style, two matching milk glass & cobalt blue 'snail' wells w/ground lips mounted between three scrolled metal pen holder uprights above a rectangular cast metal tray base marked "Use Congress Record Ink," blue well w/manufacturring stress chip on mouth, ca. 1875-95, 5 1/4 x 7 7/8", 4 1/4" h. **$213**

Cast-metal & glass stand, revolving-style, two matching milk glass & teal blue 'snail' wells w/ground lips mounted between three scrolled metal pen holder uprights above a rectangular cast metal tray base marked "Use Congress Record Ink," excellent condition, ca. 1875-95, 5 1/4 x 7 7/8", 4 1/4" h. **$616**

Copper Tiffany & Co. Art Nouveau Well

Copper well, Art Nouveau style, a wide flat-bottomed stepped down w/a narrow neck fitted w/a silver rim & stepped, domed cover, the body wrapped w/undulating bands of sterling silver, base marked "Tiffany & Co. 15025 Makers - 4564 Sterling Silver 925-1000 T & other Metals," early 20th c., 8 1/4" d., 6" h. (ILLUS.) **$748**

Glass well, blown glass, deep aqua, composed of three applied doughnut-shaped segments w/the top one indented to hold ink & fitted w/a Tam O'Shanter glass stopper, probably New York State, ca. 1830-60, 6 3/4" h. **$1,456**

Pottery well, figural cabin-shaped, detailed w/chimney, doors, roof & log sides, quill hole in roof, dark green & tan glazes, signed "G. E. Ohr - Biloxi," George Ohr, ca. 1880-1900, 2 1/4 x 3 3/8", 2 1/8" h. **$6,160**

Lap Desks & Writing Boxes

Fine Victorian Inlaid Lacquer Writing Box

Inlaid lacquer, rectangular w/a narrow rectangular top above a hinged slant lid decorated w/a mother-of-pearl landscape centered by a large three-storied house w/front columns & surrounded by trees w/water & a church in the background, lid opens to a fitted interior w/two crystal & silver inkwells, a pen tray & a long-lidded compartment, the lower case inlaid & h.p. w/flowers, narrow molded gilt-trimmed base band raised on flatted square feet, overall decoration of inlaid & h.p. florals, mid-19th c., 11 1/2 x 15", 5 1/4" h. (ILLUS.) **$633**

Inlaid Rosewood Lap Desk

Inlaid rosewood, rectangular w/the slanted hinged top ornately inlaid w/a mother-of-pearl floral band around the edge & centered by a floral cluster, opening to a velvet writing surface, inkpots & a pen rest, England, ca. 1880, minor separations, 8 x 11", 4" h. (ILLUS.) **$230**

Japanese Export Decorated Lacquer Writing Box

Lacquer, rectangular w/black lacquer exterior w/parcel-gilt & polychromed Oriental fan decoration around the sides, the hinged top opening to multiple paper compartments & period old rose velvet writing surface, Japanese Export, late 19th c., 12 1/2 x 18 1/2", 7 3/4" h. (ILLUS.)............. **$374**

More Exceptional
Antique and Collectibles References

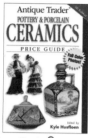

Antique Trader® Pottery and Porcelain Ceramics Price Guide
Softcover • 6 x 9 • 768 pages
3,300 color photos
Item# Z0327 • $24.99

Antiques 101
A Crash Course in Everything Antique
Softcover • 6 x 9 • 304 pages
• 350 color photos
Item# ANTQ • $19.99

Secrets to Collecting Jewelry
How to Buy More for Less
Softcover • 6 x 9 • 272 pages
400+ color photos
Item# SBCJ • $19.99

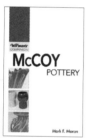

McCoy Pottery
A Warman's® Companion
Softcover • 5 x 8 • 272 pages
1,100 color photos
Item# CCMC • $17.99

Roseville Pottery
A Warman's® Companion
Softcover • 5 x 8 • 272 pages
1,100 color photos
Item# CCRV • $17.99

Fenton Glass
Warman's® Companion
Softcover • 5 x 8 • 272 pages
675+ color photos
Item# Z0332 • $17.99

Carnival Glass
Warman's® Companion
Softcover • 5 x 8 • 272 pages
650 color photos
Item# Z0331 • $17.99

Fiesta
Warman's® Companion
Softcover • 5 x 8 • 272 pages
500+ color photos
Item# Z0377 • $17.99

Antique Trader® Bottles
Identification & Price Guide
5th Edition
Softcover • 6 x 9 • 552 pages
500+ color photos
Item# BOTID5 • $19.99

Offer ACB6
krause publications
An Imprint of F+W Publications

700 East State Street • Iola, WI 54990-0001

Get your copy of these expert guides today!
Available from booksellers and other retailers
nationwide or directly from Krause Publications by
calling **800-258-0929** offer ACB6 or online at
www.krausebooks.com